MW01102694

Annals Of The Kingdom Of Ireland By The Four Masters, From The Earliest Period To The Year 1616

annala rioghachta eireann.

ANNALS

OF

THE KINGDOM OF IRELAND,

BY THE FOUR MASTERS,

FROM

THE EARLIEST PERIOD TO THE YEAR 1616.

EDITED FROM MSS. IN THE LIBRARY OF THE ROYAL IRISH ACADEMY AND OF TRINITY COLLEGE, DUBLIN, WITH A TRANSLATION, AND COPIOUS NOTES,

BY JOHN O'DONOVAN, LL.D., M. R. I. A.,

PROFESSOR OF THE CELTIC LANGUAGES, QUEEN'S COLLEGE, BELFAST.

"Olim Regibus parebant, nunc per Principes factionibus et studiis trahuntur: nec aliud adversus validissimas gentes pro nobis utilius, quam quod in commune non consulunt. Rarus duabus tribusve civitatibus ad propulsandum commune periculum conventus: ita dum singuli pugnant universi vincuntur."—TACITUS, AGRICOLA, c. 12.

VOL. VI.

DUBLIN:

HODGES AND SMITH, GRAFTON-STREET,

BOOKSELLERS TO THE UNIVERSITY.

1851.

DUBLIN:
PRINTED AT THE UNIVERSITY PRESS,
BY M. H. GILL.

ANNALA RIOGHACHTA EIREANN.

ANNALA RIOGHACHTA EIREANN.

AOIS CRIOST, 1589.

Aois Criost, míle, cúicc céd, ochtmoghat, anaoí.

MAGUIDHIR cúchonnacht mac conchonnacht (.i. an comharba), mic conchonnacht, mic briain, mic pilip mic tomais do écc 17 iun tighearna ar tiodhnacal deaccailsibh, ⁊ dollamhnaibh dámhsaibh, ⁊ danradhaibh saoí foghlamtha frioċnamhach illaidin ⁊ i ngaoidheilcc eiside. Iar nécc meguidhir cuchonnacht ro badh dóigh lá conchobhar ruadh mac conchobhair meguidhir gomadh lais tighearnas tíre ar aoí sinnsireachta. Bá sídh do ruimenrat an luchd naile gomadh é mac méguidhir (aodh) ro badh tighearna dfir a athar, co mbátar i ffrithbheart fri a roile amlaidh sin. Ro faoídh aodh techta dionnsaighidh a bhrathar domhnall mac aodha mic Maghnusa uí domhnaill (gé da rala storra ria sin) dia chuingidh fair teacht dia furtacht ⁊ dia fóirithin amhail bá ghnáthach lá a sinnsearaibh congnamh lá sliocht pilip mic tomais meguidhir. Ní baí do chenel cconaill an tan sin nech as ar mó a faoilechtain dia chabhair inás an domhnall hí sin uair bá hanglonn ⁊ ba tuaisccnigh catha eisiumh, ⁊ ní clos a drium fri a eccraitibh ittir. Nír bhó hfirsídhach ro freccradh fuighle na tteachtadh sin lá domhnall uair ro thionóil

[7] *Servants.*—The Irish anradha is the same as the Latin *calones.* They were the attendants on the gallowglasses. Sir Anthony Sentleger writes in 1543:

"Ther ys no horseman of this lande, but he hathe his horse and his two boyes and two hackeneys, or one hackeney and two chieffe horse at the leste."—See *Battle of Magh-Rath*, p. 350.

[8] *General in battle.*—This means nothing more

ANNALS OF THE KINGDOM OF IRELAND.

THE AGE OF CHRIST, 1589.

The Age of Christ, one thousand five hundred eighty-nine.

MAGUIRE (Cuconnaught, the son of Cuconnaught, namely, the Coarb, son of Cuconnaught, son of Brian, son of Philip, son of Thomas), died on the 17th of June. He was [truly] a lord in his munificence towards churches, ollaves, soldiers, and servants[y]; and a learned and studious adept in Latin and Irish. After the death of Maguire (Cuconnaught), Conor Roe, the son of Conor Maguire, thought that the lordship of the country should be his, by reason of his seniority; while the other party thought that Hugh, son of [the deceased] Maguire, should be lord after his father; so that they were thus in opposition to each other. Hugh sent messengers to his relative, Donnell, the son of Hugh, son of Manus O'Donnell (although they had previously quarrelled), to request of him to come to his aid and assistance, as it had been usual with his ancestors to aid the descendants of Philip, the son of Thomas Maguire. There was not at this time any one of the Kinel-Connell from whom he [Hugh] expected more assistance than from this Donnell, for he was a mighty champion, and a general in battle[z]; and it was never heard that he had at any time[a] turned his back on his enemies. The words of the messengers were treated with indifference by Donnell, for he immediately mustered all the forces under his command, and

than that he was wont to lead his father's forces.

[a] *At any time.*—The word ıττıր sometimes signifies "indeed," and sometimes "at all," as in this instance.

ríde ina mbaoí ina cumang fó ċédóir, ⁊ ro ḟaoíd a ṫeaċta do ridiri go haodh dia radh friss bſiṫ for a ccionn ag sgéiṫ ġabra an trainrid amail as déine conicfadh. Luidhsium gan earsnadhadh gan errfuireaċ tria ṫuaiṫ luirgc lá hor loċa herne go rainic gus an maiġin remráite. Tainic concobar ruadh co maiṫibh uaċtair fſrmanaċ an lá riaṁ gus an ionadh ccédna, ⁊ ro ḟáccaib a ionncomarba .i. lſṫass in dú sin fo dáiġ anma tiġearna do gairm de ar a barach. Do riaċt aodh gus an ionadh erdalta hisin, ⁊ fuair domnall ó domnaill ar a ċionn. Iar ffios sccel do domnall gur bó hé Conċobar ro ḟáccaib an comarba remebertmar atbert ná biadh bá desidhe, ⁊ go madh é aodh nó biadh i nionad a aṫar conadh ann sin ro gaireadh a ġairm flaṫa fó ċédoir daodh maguidhir lá domnall ua ndomnaill, ⁊ lá maiṫibh a ṫíre.

Még maṫġamhna Rossa mac airt, mic briain na moiċeirġe, mic Rémainn mic glaisne décc. Brian mac aodha óicc, mic aodha, mic Sſain buidhe tiġearna dartraiġe oirġiall, ⁊ eimſr mac conulad tiġearna fſrnmaiġe, ⁊ dearbraṫair

[b] *Precisely*, an trainrid. This phrase occurs very frequently in the sense of precisely, exactly, punctually.—See note [m], under the year 1586, p. 1856, and note [d], under 1588, p. 1866, *supra*.

[c] *Sciath-Ghabhra*.—This place is shewn on an old map in the State Papers' Office, London, under the name of Skea Castle, situated near the east side of the Upper Lough Erne, to the south-east of Enniskillen. The site of this castle is still pointed out at the little town of Lisnaskea, in the barony of Magherastephena, in Fermanagh, and about nine miles to the south-east of Enniskillen.

[d] *One slipper*, leaṫ-ass, i. e. one of a pair of slippers: "Asa .i. bróga."—*O'Clery*. When leaṫ, which literally means *half*, is thus prefixed, it signifies "one of two," such as one ear, one eye, one leg, one hand, one foot, one cheek, one horn, one shoe.

[e] *Profit*.—"Bá .i. maiṫ."—*O'Clery*.

[f] *Dartry-Oriel*, i. e. the barony of Dartry, in the west of the county of Monaghan. It is more usually called Dartry-Coininnsi, from the townland of Coninish, now divided into several subdenominations. It looks very strange that the Four Masters should have told us nothing about the fate of Hugh Roe Mac Mahon, who was the brother and heir of the Rossa mentioned in the text, and of whom local tradition remembers so much. Camden, *ad ann*. 1590, Fynes Moryson, and Cox, have given very impartial accounts of the abominable treatment which this Hugh received from the Lord Deputy, Sir William Fitz-William. The Editor is tempted to lay before the reader the following account of this horrid transaction,—which was the main cause of the frightful war which ensued,—as written by Fynes Moryson, who fairly translates Camden, adding a little of his own feelings, which are admirable, considering the murderous age in which he lived, and the virulent anti-Irish feelings of the class to which he belonged:

"About this time Mac Mahown, chieftain of Monaghan, died, who in his life-time had surrendered this his country, held by tanistry the Irish law, into her Majesty's hands, and received a re-grant thereof under the broad seal of England, to him and his heirs males, and for default of such, to his brother, Hugh Roe Mac Mahown, with other remainders. And this man dying

sent back his messengers to Hugh, to desire him to meet him precisely[b] at Sciath-Ghabhra[c] with all possible expedition. He then proceeded, without dallying or delaying, through the territory of Lurg, and along the margin of Lough Erne, until he arrived at the aforesaid place. Conor Roe and the chiefs of the upper part of Fermanagh had gone on the day before to the same place, and there left a token (namely, one slipper[d]) that the name of lord should be conferred on him on the day following. Hugh arrived at that particular place [appointed], and found Donnell O'Donnell there before him. When Donnell received intelligence that it was Conor that had left the token which we have before mentioned, he said that it should not profit[e] him, for that Hugh should be [installed] in the place of his father; upon which Hugh was immediately nominated chief by Donnell O'Donnell and the chieftains of his country.

Mac Mahon (Rossa, the son of Art, son of Brian of the Early Rising, son of Redmond, son of Glasny) died; upon which Brian, the son of Hugh Oge, son of Hugh, son of John Boy, Lord of Dartry-Oriel[f], and Ever, son of Cu-Uladh,

without heirs males, his said brother came up to the state that he might be settled in his inheritance, hoping to be countenanced and cherished as Her Majesty's Patentee; but he found (as the Irish say) that he could not be admitted till he had promised to give about six hundred cows (for such and no other are the Irish bribes). After[wards] he was imprisoned (the Irish say for failing in part of this payment) and within a few days again inlarged; with promise that the Lord Deputy himself would go settle him in his country of Monaghan, whither his Lordship took his jorney shortly after, with him in his company. At their first arrival, the gentleman was clapt in bolts, and within two days after, indicted, arraigned, and executed at his own house; all done (as the Irish said) by such officers as the Lord Deputy carried with him for that purpose. The Irish said he was found guilty by a jury of soldiers" ['gregariorum militum viliumque hominum judicio subjecit.'—*Camden*], "but no gentlemen or freeholders; and that of them four English soldiers were suffered to go and come at pleasure, but the others, being Irish kerne, were kept straight, and starved till they found him guilty. The treason for which he was condemned was because, some two years before, he, pretending a rent due unto him out of the Ferney, upon that pretence levied forces, and so marching into the Ferney in a warlike manner, made a distress for the same (which by the English law may perhaps be treason, but in that country, never before subject to law, it was thought no rare thing nor great offence). The greater part of the country was divided between four gentlemen of that name, under a yearly rent to the Queen, and (as they said) not without payment of a good fine underhand. The Marshal, Sir Henry Bagnol, had part of the country; Captain Henslowe was made seneschal of the country, and had the gentleman's chief house, with a portion of land; and to divers others smaller portions of land were assigned; and the Irish spared not to say, that these men were all the contrivers of his" [Mac Mahon's] "death, and that every one paid something" [to

an tí sin tesda .i. aoḋ ruaḋ do ḃeiṫ acc imresain ré roile fá tiġearnas na tíre.

Elinora ingen iarla desmuṁan .i. Semus mac Seain, mic tomais, mic Semuis mic geróitt bean uí ruairc, ⁊ bean meic iarla urmuṁan .i. eduard mac Semuis mic Piarais ruaiḋ mic Semais, mic emainn do écc.

Contaoisi ċonntae an cláir una ingen toirrḋealḃaiġ mic mnirċeartaiġ mic doṁnaill mic taiḋcc, mic toirrḋealḃaiġ, mic murchaiḋ na raiṫniġe, bean iarla tuaḋmuṁan .i. Conċoḃar mac donnchaiḋ, mic conċoḃair, mic toirrḋealḃaiġ mic taiḋcc uí ḃriain do écc san cclár ṁór.

Doṁnall mag congail epscop ráṫa boṫ décc 29 September.

Toirrḋealḃaċ mac taiḋcc, mic conċoḃair mic toirrḋealḃaiġ mic taiḋcc uí ḃriain ó ḃél aṫa an coṁraic décc. Ro baḋ daṁna eccaoíne an tí tesda annsin.

Taḋcc an dúnaiḋ mac donnchaiḋ mic muirċeartaiġ, mic donnchaiḋ, mic muirċeartaiġ, mic an ḃallaiġ sinnsear tuaiṫe na fearna (.i. corca baiscind), ⁊ sleaċta an ḃallaiġ décc, nír ċin i ccorp ina coiṁre a ċoṁċalma ina coṁḟoċraiḃ.

the Lord Deputy] "for his share. Hereupon the Irish of that name, besides the former allegations, exclaimed that their kinsman was treacherously executed to entitle the Queen to his land, and to extinguish the name of Mac Mahown, and that his substance was divided between the Lord Deputy and the Marshal; yea, that a pardon was offered to one of the jury for his son, being in danger of the law, upon condition that he would consent to find this his kinsman guilty.

"Great part of these exclamations were contained in a complaint exhibited against the Lord Deputy, after his return into England, to the Lords of her Majesty's Council, about the end of the year 1595, in the name of Mac Guire and Ever Mac Cooly (one of the Mac Mahowns, and chief over the Irish in the Ferney)".—Edition of 1735, vol. i. pp. 24, 25.

The guilt of Fitz-William is rendered still darker by the fact lately published from the State Papers by Mr. Shirley (*Account of Farney*, p. 88, 91, 92, 98), that in his correspondence with Burghley he expresses his anxiety for a speedy resolution of Mac Mahon's case, "That either the olde Mac Mahon *maie be pardoned* and sett at libertie, or a new one made, or that title extinguished and the territory devided." The reader will at once perceive the wickedness of Fitz-William's proposal to make a new Mac Mahon, when he considers that Hugh Roe was his brother's heir, according to the law of England, and that large bribes had been offered to the corrupt Chief-Governor to raise "one Brien Mac Hugh Oge" to the chieftainship. On the 2nd of March, 1589, Fitz-William wrote to Burghley and the Lords of the Council a long letter in which he mentions this fact as follows: "Some indede *attempted me* for him" [Brien Mac Hugh Oge] "with large offers; but as I *never* benefitted myself by the admission of him that is now in durance, so did I meane to convert his fall wholie to the proffit

Lord of Farney, and the brother of the deceased, i. e. Hugh Roe, were contending with each other about the lordship of the territory.

Elenora, the daughter of the Earl of Desmond (i. e. of James, the son of John, son of Thomas, son of James, son of Garrett), who had been the wife of O'Rourke, and [afterwards] of the son of the Earl of Desmond (i. e. of Edward, the son of James, son of Pierce Roe, son of James, son of Edmond), died.

The Countess of the county of Clare, Una, the daughter of Turlough, son of Murtough, son of Donnell, son of Teige, son of Turlough, son of Murrough na-Raithnighe, and wife of the Earl of Thomond, i. e. of Conor, son of Donough, son of Conor, son of Turlough, son of Teige O'Brien, died at Clare-more[g].

Donnell Mag Congail[h], Bishop of Raphoe, died on the 29th of September.

Turlough, the son of Teige, son of Conor, son of Turlough, son of Teige O'Brien of Bel-atha-an-chomraic[i], died; and his death was the cause of great lamentation.

Teige-an-Duna, the son of Donough, son of Murtough, son of Donough, son of Murtough, son of Ballagh, the senior [of the Mac Mahons] of Tuath-na-Fearna[k] (i. e. of Corca-Bhaiscinn[l]), and of Sliocht-an-Bhallaigh, died. There lived not in his neighbourhood in his time so brave a man.

of her Majestie and good of this state, *nothing regarding mine owne privat:* I speak it in the presence of God by whom I hope to be saved!"—*Account of Farney*, p. 89.

[g] *Clare-more*, i. e. the town of Clare (near Ennis), from which the county was named.

[h] *Donnell Mag Congail.*—He assisted at the Council of Trent in 1563, and died at Cealla Beaga, now Killybegs, in the west of the county of Donegal, in this year.—See Harris's edition of Ware's Bishops, p. 275. The name Mag Congail is now common in the county of Donegal, and anglicised Magonigle.

[i] *Bel-atha-an-chomhraic*, i. e. mouth of the ford of the confluence, now Ballycorick, a townland situated on the confines of the baronies of Clonderalaw and Islands, in the county of Clare.—See the Ordnance map of that county, sheet 50. There is a family of the O'Briens still living at this place who inherit a small estate.

[k] *Tuath-na-fearna*, i. e. the district of the alder, a district coextensive with the parish of Kildysart, in the barony of Clonderalaw, and county of Clare. The Rev. Dr. Kenny, of Kilrush, in a letter to the Editor, dated 6th April, 1847, states that "the residents never call the parish of Kildysart, in the vernacular, by any other name than ραράιρτε ṫuaıṫ na ϝeάρna."—See note [b], under the year 1575, p. 1683, *supra*, where the Editor has described Tuath-na-fearna as in the barony of Islands, by mere oversight.

[l] *Corca-Bhaiscinn.*—This should be "of East Corca-Bhaiscinn." In the Description of the County of Clare, preserved in the Library of Trinity College, Dublin, E. 2. 14, this Teige is mentioned as chief of the "Baronie of Cloynederalawe, conteyning East Carkewasken," and proprietor of the castles of "Dangen-Myburke" [i. e. Ꝺaınġean moıġe ḃuılc, now Dangan, a very large castle in ruins, in a townland of the

Corbmac mac taiḋcc mic diarmada, mic corbmaic o maiġlaiṫim décc.

Maġnus mac cuinn mic an ċalḃaiġ, mic maġnusa mic aoḋa duiḃ uí domnaill do marḃaḋ laiṁ lé finn 20 September lé sſan mac Maġnusa óig mic maġnusa, mic aoḋa duiḃ uí domnaill.

Domnall mac eoġain an loċa mec suiḃne consapal murcraiġe décc fear ro baḋ maiṫ treaḃaire, ⁊ tſg naoiḋſḋ, ⁊ rob ionmolta i ffiaḋnaisi gall ⁊ gaoiḋeal an tí tſsda ann sin.

Búrcaiġ íoċtaraċa ó ṫír aṁalgaiḋ siar do dol ar a ccoiṁed iar ndiúltaḋ bſiṫ fá brſiṫ an gobernora .i. Sir Risderd biongham. Maiġistir brún do ḋol a huċt an ġobernora co ndruing ṁóir do ṡaiġdiuiriḃ gallda ⁊ gaoiḋelċa do ṡaiġiḋ na mbúrcaċ sin tar bealaċ an diotruiḃe siar. Burcaiġ ar ttaḃairt amairs forrasoṁ, ⁊ a ttráṫ na troda do ṫſnoaḋ do ṁaiġistir brún ro sraoíneaḋ dia ṡaiġdiuiriḃ ⁊ ro díċſnoaḋ é fſin, ⁊ domnall o dálaiġ duine uasal eiriḋe aġá mbaoí cſnous coda do na saiġdiuiriḃ sin, ⁊ Remann ócc mac Remainct mic Sſain a búrc na bſinne, ⁊ soċhaiḋe ṁór do na saiġdiúiriḃ a maille friu. Ro ba móide bríġ ⁊ borrfaḋ na mbúrcaċ an brſisim sin, ⁊ ro gaḃsat for aḋannaḋ ina ndíbercc ar a haitle. Do ċóiḋ tra sliocht oiluerais mic Sſain a búrc ó ṫír aṁalgaiḋ ina ccoṁmbáiḋ, ⁊ muintir duḃda o ṫir fiaċraċ muaiḋe, clann ndoṁnaill gallócclaċ uile, Murċadh na ttuaġ mac faiḋcc, mic murchaiḋ uí flaiṫḃeartaiġ, ⁊ muintir flaiṫḃſrtaiġ ⁊ Seóḋaiġ ina foċair sium, co nár ṡan aon ro ba ion airme ó rinn iarṫaraċ iorrais co traiġ eoṫuile co maċaire luiġne, co corann, ⁊ co maċaire connaċt gan dol in aon rann i naghaiḋ an ġoḃernora. Ro gaḃsat na díbſrccaiġ sin acc

same name, in the parish of Kilchrist, or district of Tuath-ua-mBuile, in the barony of Clonderalaw, and adjoining the barony of Islands]; "Cloynetheralla" [now Clonderalaw]; "Cahercon; Ballamacollman" [now Colmanstown]; "and Derecrossan" [Derrycrossan:] "all in the territory of East Corca-Vaskin. Contemporary with this Teige-an-Duna was Turlough Mac Mahon, chief of the territory of West Corca-Vaskin, and proprietor of the castles of Carighowly" [now Carrigaholt], "Moyartha, Dunlicky, and Dunsumayne."

[m] *Magh-Laithimh*, now Molahiff, near Castlemaine, in Kerry.—See note [e], under 1581, p. 1757, *supra*.

[n] *Went on their defence*, i. e. took up arms to defend themselves.

[o] *Bealach-an-Diothruibhe*, i. e. the road or pass of the wilderness. This was undoubtedly the name of the ancient road leading from the abbey of Ballintober to Croaghpatrick, in the county of Mayo, for the position of which see map to *Genealogies, Tribes, &c. of Hy-Fiachrach.*

[p] *Came to a close fight*, literally, "at the time of the pressing of the fight by Master Brown."

[q] *John Burke of Ben*, i. e. of Benmore Castle,

Cormac, the son of Teige, son of Dermot, son of Cormac [Mac Carthy] of Magh-Laithimh[m], died.

Manus, the son of Con, son of Calvagh, son of Manus, son of Hugh Duv O'Donnell, was slain near the River Finn, on the 20th of September, by John, the son of Manus Oge, son of Manus, son of Hugh Duv O'Donnell.

Donnell, son of Owen of the Lake Mac Sweeny, Constable of Muskerry, died. The deceased was a man who had good tillage, and kept a house of hospitality, and was praiseworthy in the eyes of the English and Irish.

The Lower Burkes from Tirawly westwards, after having refused to remain under the jurisdiction of the Governor, Sir Richard Bingham, went on their defence[n]. Master Brown proceeded, by order of the Governor, at the head of a large party of English and Irish soldiers, westwards over Bealach-an-Diothruibh[o] against these Burkes. The Burkes made an attack upon them; and at the time that Master Brown came to a close fight[p], his soldiers were routed, and himself beheaded, as were also Donnell O'Daly, a gentleman who had the command of a party of the soldiers; and Redmond Oge, son of Redmond, son of John Burke of Ben[q], together with a great number of the soldiers. The vigour and fury of the Burkes were increased by this defeat; and they became more violent in their insurrection after it. The descendants of Oliver, the son of John Burke of Tirawley, went in alliance with them, as did the O'Dowdas of Tireragh of the Moy; all the Clann-Donnell Galloglagh; Murrough of the Battle-axes[r], the son of Teige, son of Murrough O'Flaherty, together with [all] the O'Flahertys and the Joyces; so that there was not one man worthy of note, from the western point of Erris to Traigh-Eothuile[s], to Machaire-Luighne[t], to Corran, and to Machaire-Chonnacht[u], who did not unite [on this occasion]

in the parish of Grange, barony of Loughrea, and county of Galway.—See note [o], under the year 1553, p. 1532, *supra*. This Redmond Burke was one of the Earl of Clanrickard's followers, who assisted Bingham on this occasion.

[r] *Murrough of the Battle-axes, &c., O'Flaherty.*—He is called Sir Morogh ne Doe by the English writers. He was very faithful to the Queen till 1586, when a party of the Governor's soldiers plundered his people.—See p. 1849, *supra*. See also *Chorographical Description of Iar-Connaught*, p. 394, *et sequent.*

[s] *Traigh-Eothuile*, a great strand at Ballysadare, in the county of Sligo.—See it already mentioned at the years 1249, 1282, 1367, 1562.

[t] *Machaire-Luighne*, i. e. the plain of Leyny, a barony in the county of Sligo.

[u] *Machaire-Chonnacht*, i. e. *Campus Connaciæ*, a great plain in the county of Roscommon already often referred to.

aiḋmilleaḋ ċoicciḋ connaċt do ló ⁊ dadhaiḋ fri ré an earraiġ. Bá isin tan sin do ċuaiḋ dias mac murchaiḋ na ttuacċ uí flaiṫbſrtaiġ .i. taḋcc ⁊ urun, ⁊ mac dearḃráṫar do Murchaḋ .i. domnall mac Ruaiḋri uí flaiṫbſrtaiġ ar iondsaiġiḋ fa leiṫimel conmaicne, ⁊ an ṁaċaire riaḃaiġ oiḋċe cascc do ṡonnraḋ. Báttar a dó nó a trí do ċédaibh diolmuineaċ ar an turus sin. Ro gaḃsat ag dénaṁ oirccne ⁊ edala iomḋa seaċnon an tíre toraċ laoí doṁnaiġ cáscc. Tánaic an tír ar gaċ taoḃ ina ttóraiġeaċt. Bá isin oiḋċe reiṁe sin tangadar banna nó ḋó do ṡaiġdiuiriḃ gan ḟios gan airiuccaḋ diomcoiméd an tíre, ⁊ ód ċualattar allġuṫ an ordanais, ⁊ caismſrta na ccolcc buiḋſn ar ná ṁaraċ do ċottar i neanaċ iomċuṁang nár ḃo hurasa diongaḃail no do ṡſcna i noirċill an tslóiġ gaoiḋealaiġ. Fuarat tartaḋcc ó flaiṫbeartaiġ dia saiġiḋ i ttoraċ an tslóiġ, ⁊ aṁuintir ina ccipe coṁḋluta ina timċell. Ro léiccriott na saiġdiuiriḋe frassa pelér fó ṫoraċ an tslóiġ gaoiḋealaiġ go ttorċair taḋcc ua flaiṫbſrtaiġ don torainn sin, ⁊ urun ua flaiṫbſrtaiġ, ⁊ taḋcc ócc mac taiḋcc uí flaiṫbeartaiġ co ndruing móir dia luċt lſnaṁna ina ttimċell do maiṫiḃ criċe seóḋaċ ⁊ cloinni donnchaiḋ, ⁊ an ṁſiḋ na ro marḃaḋ don ced frais don tslóiġ gaoiḋelaċ ro imṫiġsſt gan sccſinm gan sccaṫ, ⁊ ní ro lſnaḋ iatt seaċa sin. Ro crochaḋ dna eman mac Murchaiḋ na ttuacċ uí flaiṫbeartaiġ baoí illaiṁ i ngailliṁ fó ċſnd tri lá iar marḃaḋ taiḋcc, ⁊ muna tuititis an clann sin marchaiḋ na ttuaġ uí flaiṫbſrtaiġ for foġail ⁊ for diḃſircc in acchaiḋ prionnsa Saxan ro baḋ sccel mór a noiḋeaḋ aṁlaiḋ sin.

Diarmait ócc mac diarmata, mic denis, mic diarmata, mic concoḃair (.i. espucc luimniġ), mic murchaiḋ an dana uí ḋſdhaḋ décc, ⁊ a aḋnacal i ndisſrt tola ina baile fſin i ttriocat céd ceneoil ffſrmaic in uaċtar dál ccais.

[w] *Conmaicne*, i. e. Conmaicne-Cuile-Toladh, now the barony of Kilmaine, in the south of the county of Mayo. Machaire-riabhach is a plain in the adjoining barony of Clare, in the county of Galway.—See note [e], under the year 1469, p. 1064, *supra*.

[x] *Precisely*, do ṡonnraḋ.—This phrase might well be omitted.

[y] *Clann-Donough*.—These were a branch of the O'Flaherties, descended from Donough Aluinn O'Flaherty, the brother of Rory of Loch Cime.—See Genealogical Table in Hardiman's edition of O'Flaherty's *Chorographical Description of Iar-Connaught*, p. 362.

[z] *Conor, Bishop of Limerick*.—He succeeded in the year 1400, resigned the see in 1426, and died in 1434.—See Harris's edition of Ware's Bishops, p. 509, where this bishop is mentioned under the name of "Cornelius O'Dea."

[a] *Disert-Tola*, i. e. St. Tola's desert, or wilderness, now Dysart O'Dea, in the barony of Inchiquin, and county of Clare, where there is

against the Governor. These plunderers continued to ravage the province of Connaught, by day and night, during the spring. It was at this time that two sons of Murrough of the Battle-axes O'Flaherty, Teige and Urun, and the son of Murrough's brother, i. e. Donnell, the son of Rory O'Flaherty, went upon a predatory excursion along the borders of Conmaicne[w] and Machaire-Riabhach, precisely[x] on Easter night. They had two or three hundred horse-boys on this excursion. They proceeded to take much booty and spoils throughout the country early in the morning of Easter Sunday. The [people of the] country came from every quarter in pursuit of them. On the night before a company or two of soldiers had come, privately and unperceived, to protect the country; and these, upon hearing the loud report of the ordnance, and the clamour of the armed troops on the following day, retired to a narrow pass, which could not be easily shunned or avoided, and there lay in ambush for the Irish host. They saw Teige O'Flaherty approaching in front of the host, and his people in close ranks about him. The soldiers discharged showers of balls at the van of the Irish host, and slew by this volley Teige O'Flaherty, Urun O'Flaherty, and Teige Oge, the son of Teige O'Flaherty, together with a great number of their followers who were about them, of the chiefs of Joyce's country, and the Clann-Donough[y]. Such of the Irish host as were not killed by the first volley went away without panic or fear, and were not further pursued. Three days after the killing of Teige, Edmond, [another] son of Murrough of the Battle-axes O'Flaherty, who was in prison in Galway, was hanged; and, were it not that these sons of Murrough of the Battle-axes O'Flaherty fell in the act of plunder and insurrection against the Sovereign of England, their death after this manner would have been a great cause of lamentation.

Dermot Oge, the son of Dermot, son of Denis, son of Dermot, son of Conor, Bishop of Limerick[z], son of Murrough-an-Dana O'Dea, died, and was buried in his own town of Disert-Tola[a], in the cantred of Kinel-Fearmaic, in the upper part of Dal-Cais.

a church of considerable antiquity and architectural beauty, dedicated to St. Tola, who died in the year 732, and near it a beautiful round tower.—See Colgan's *Acta SS.*, p. 793. There was another church of this name in the parish of Kill-Uailleach, barony of Delvin, and county of Westmeath. Lanigan, in his *Ecclesiastical History of Ireland*, vol. iii. p. 171, not knowing that O'Dea's seat in Thomond was called Disert-Tola, has come to the conclusion that there was but one church of the name in Ireland, and attempts to reconcile authorities by placing Disert

AOIS CRIOST, 1590.

Aois Criost, míle, cúicc céd, nócat.

Búrcaiġ íoċtaraċa, ⁊ clann nDoṁnaill gallócclaċ do coiṁtionol ⁊ do ċruinniucchaḋ an ro ḟéḋsat do ḋaoínib (aṁail remebertmar) hi ffoġmar ⁊ i nġeiṁreaḋ na bliaḋna reiṁainn co ná baoí aon rob ionairiṁ o Ċorrṡliab na Seġsa co cenn iarṫarac Iorrais, ⁊ Uṁaill gan dol leó isin commbáiġ sin.

Sluaiccheaḋ las an ngobernoir Sir Ristserd Bingham, ⁊ lá hiarla Tuadhmuman Donnchaḋ mac Conċobair, mic Donnchaiḋ uí Ḃriain co líon a ttoiċestail an céd mí don bliaḋain si .i. mi Ianuarii do ḋol ar Ḃúrcachaiḃ co ro suiḋiġseḋ campa congaireaċ ceiṫeirnlíonṁar hi cCunga leó, ⁊ báttar Búrcaiġ hi ffoslongport ar a ccoṁair don taoiḃ ṫiar, ⁊ coinne gaċ laoí etorra go cenn coicctiḋisi co ná ro féḋaḋ a síoḋuccaḋ in airsiḋ sin. Triallaiḋ an gobernoir, ⁊ an tiarla hi ccenn na ree sin a deiċ nó a dó décc do bandaiḃ do ḋol tar beilgiḃ isteaċ do ċor cuarta i ttír Aṁalgaiḋ, ⁊ i nIorrus. Do ḋeachattar Búrcaiġ lá a ttaoḃ, ⁊ bátar acc folmaire a bfobarta acc Bearnaiġ na Gaoiṫe, ar a aoí ní ḋeirgenrat, ⁊ ro léiccseḋ an ċonair don ġobernoir, ⁊ don iarla. Bá don ċur sin do beanaḋ a ṫroiġ on alt amaċ do Ṁac Uilliam Búrc. Ro ḟill an gobernóir tar a ais go Conga, ⁊ ro ṡíoḋaiġ fein, Búrcaiġ, ⁊ clann nDoṁnaill re roile go ro ċuirsiot a mbraiġde ar laiṁ an gobernora. Do ċóiḋ an gobernoir go Baile Aṫa Luain, ⁊ ro sccaoilsiot fir Connacht dia ttiġiḃ.

Sluaiccheaḋ lánṁór las an ngobernoir hi mís Ṁarta do ḋol ar Ua Ruairc. Baoí do líonṁaire an tslóiġ sin co ro léicc an gobernoir drong dirime dá caiptínib ⁊ dá cóirniġtib co Sliab Cairpre hi ccenn muintire Heolais, ⁊ drong

Tola in the barony of Garrycastle, in the King's County, on the frontiers of Dal-Cais and Meath; but his conclusion is totally erroneous, because the two names still exist, and the memory of St. Tola is still venerated at both, though even the grave-yard of Disert Tola, in Delvin, has been effaced by the progress of cultivation. O'Dea's Castle stands in ruins a short distance to the north-west of St. Tola's church. This castle is mentioned in the Description of the County of Clare, written in 1585, and now preserved in the Manuscript Library of Trinity College, Dublin, E. 2. 14, as the residence of "Donell Moel O'Dea."

[b] *Bearna-na-gaoithe*, i. e. gap of the wind, now Windy-gap, a remarkable gap on the south-east boundary of the parish of Addergoole, barony of Tirawley, and county of Mayo.—See *Genealogies, Tribes, and Customs of Hy-Fiachrach*, p. 480, and the map to the same work.

THE AGE OF CHRIST, 1590.

The Age of Christ, one thousand five hundred ninety.

The Lower Burkes and the Clann-Donnell Galloglagh mustered and collected all the forces they were able [to command] in the summer and winter of the preceding year, as we have stated before; so that there was no one worthy of note, from the Curlieu mountains to the most western point of Erris and Umhall, who did not join them in that confederacy.

A hosting was made by the Governor, Sir Richard Bingham, and the Earl of Thomond, Donough, the son of Conor, son of Donough O'Brien; and they marched with all their forces against the Burkes in the first month of this year, i. e. January; and they pitched a camp of many troops of kerns at Cong; and the Burkes were encamped on the west side, opposite to them; and there were daily conferences held between them for a fortnight, but they could not agree on terms of peace during that time. At the expiration of this period, the Governor and the Earl proceeded, with ten or twelve companies, to go through the passes into Tirawley and Erris. The Burkes marched in a parallel line with them, and intended to attack them at Bearna-na-Gaoithe[b]; but, however, they did not do so, but the pass was ceded to the Governor and the Earl. On this occasion the son of Mac William Burke lost his foot from the ankle out. The Governor returned to Cong, and he, the Burkes, and the Clann-Donnell, were reconciled to each other; and they delivered their hostages into the hands of the Governor. The Governor then went to Athlone, and the men of Connaught dispersed for their [respective] homes.

In the month of March a very great army was mustered by the Governor against O'Rourke. This army was no numerous, that he sent a vast number of his captains and battalions to Sliabh-Cairbre[c] to oppose [the inhabitants of]

[c] *Sliabh-Cairbre*, i. e. Cairbre's mountain, now Slieve-Carbry, otherwise called the Carn Mountains, comprised principally in the parish of Killoe, barony of Granard, and county of Longford. According to the tradition in the country, with which the Tripartite Life of St. Patrick accords, this mountainous district received its name from Cairbre, the brother of Laeghaire, Monarch of Ireland in St. Patrick's time; and tradition adds that the mountain was cursed by St. Patrick, because, when he came to preach the Gospel to a place there called Aghnagon, he was presented with a hound served up in a dish for his dinner. According to the ancient Irish topographical work called Dinnsenchus (Book of Lecan, fol. 231), the conspicuous carns on this

ele duaislib a ṡlóig go droiċet Sligiġ don taoiḃ tiar do saiġid na breifne go ro ġabsat na slóig sin acc loscaḋ ⁊ acc léirscrios, ag marḃaḋ, ⁊ ag muḋuccaḋ ina mbaoí ros a ccionn is in ccriċ go coitcenn go roċtain i ccenn araile don tslóg. Ro diḃreḋ ua Ruairc don ruaṫar sin co ná fuair a ḋíon nó a ḋíden co rainicc do na tuathaiḃ i ccenn mec suiḃne na ttuaṫ .i. Eoġan ócc mac eoġain óicc, mic eoġain, mic domnaill, ⁊ baoí ina ḟoċair go crioċnuccaḋ na bliadna so, ⁊ gaċ aon naċ deachaiḋ ar ionnarbaḋ dá ḋaoínib tangattar asteaċ ar tairisheaċt i ccenn in gobernora. Baí domnall mac taiḋg mic briain uí ruairc, ⁊ aoḋ ócc mac aoḋa gallda ag congnaṁ lá gallaiḃ ua ruairc daṫċur ⁊ dionnarbaḋ. Ro ḃaí an tír etir ḟasaċ ⁊ aitiuccaḋ ar cumas an gobernora co féil micil ar ccind co ttainicc tiġearnan bán mac briain mic eoġain uí Ruairc, ⁊ brian (.i. brian ócc) na samṫaċ (Mac an í Ruairc sin do hionnarbaḋ) don tír i ttimċell na fele micil. Do ċóiḋsiot fein ⁊ fineadhaḋa na breifne ⁊ ṁuintire heolais, ⁊ na ruarcaċ baí reṁpa isin tír i naghaiḋ an gobernora, ⁊ báttar ag milleaḋ gaċ neiṫ gus a rangattar im ġallaiḃ go crioċnuccaḋ na bliaḋna so.

Daingen mór naċ derrnaḋ a ionnṡamail lé haṫaiḋ imċein do denaṁ las an ngobernoir e tir loċ cé ⁊ loċ arḃach.

Mac uí neill .i. Aoḋ gemleaċ, mac Seain ḋonnġailiġ mic cuinn ḃacaiġ mic cuinn, mic enri, mic eoġain do croċhaḋ lá hiarla tire heoġain .i. aoḋ mac

mountain were anciently called Carn Furbuidhe and Carn Maine.

[d] *Such of his people*, literally, "every one of his people that did not go into banishment."

[e] *Who remained*, literally, "who were before them," i. e. those families of the O'Rourkes who submitted to the authority of Sir Richard Bingham, and were permitted to retain their lands.

[f] *A great fort.*—On an old map of the county of Roscommon, made by L. Browne shortly after this period, this fort is shewn as situated centrally between Lough Key and Lough Arrow, which are about one Irish mile asunder. The Editor could not find any trace of this fort in the position shewn on L. Browne's map. It consisted evidently of earthen ramparts, like the fort erected soon after at the Blackwater, and those erected near Lough Foyle, and has long since been levelled. The inhabitants of Boyle shew the remains of an English fort close to that town, which they think is the one erected by Bingham; but the Editor thinks that the authority of the annalists and of a contemporaneous map is sufficient to prove its exact position.

[g] *Hugh Geimhleach*, i. e. Hugh of the Fetters. He was one of the illegitimate sons of John O'Neill, surnamed "an diomais," i. e. of the pride, or ambition. Fynes Moryson states that the Earl of Tyrone, the son of Matthew O'Kelly, who was the son of a blacksmith of Dundalk, hanged this youth, "hardly finding any, in regard of the general reverence borne to the blood of the O'Neyls, who would do the office of hangman;" and Camden, who was living at the time,

Muintir-Eolais; and another party of the chiefs of his army to the west of the Bridge of Sligo, to invade Breifny; and these troops proceeded to burn and devastate, kill and destroy, all before them in the country, until both met together again. By this excursion O'Rourke was banished from his territory; and he received neither shelter nor protection until he arrived in the Tuatha, to Mac Sweeny-na-dTuath (Owen Oge, the son of Owen, son of Owen Oge, son of Owen, son of Donnell); and with him he remained until the expiration of this year; and such of his people[d] as did not go into exile came in and submitted to the Governor. Donnell, the son of Teige, son of Brian O'Rourke, and Hugh Oge, the son of Hugh Gallda, assisted the English in expelling and banishing O'Rourke. The [whole] territory, both waste and inhabited, was under the power of the Governor until the ensuing Michaelmas, when Tiernan Bane, the son of Brian, son of Owen O'Rourke, and Brian-na-Samhthach, i. e. Brian Oge (the son of that O'Rourke who had been expelled), came into the territory. These and the tribes of Breifny, and of Muintir-Eolais, and of the other O'Rourkes who remained[e] in the country, opposed the Governor, and continued spoiling every thing belonging to the English, to which they came, until the end of this year.

A great fort[f], the like of which had not been erected for a long time before, was made by the Governor between Lough Key and Lough Arrow.

The son of O'Neill, i. e. Hugh Geimhleach[g], son of John Donnghaileach, son of Con Bacagh, son of Con, son of Henry, son of Owen, was hanged by the

states, that it was said that the Earl hanged him with his own hand; but P. O'Sullivan Beare says that he procured a Meathman who performed the office of hangman. P. O'Sullivan states, that Hugh Geimhleach offered to prove by single combat that what he had charged against the Earl was true. His words are:

"Prorex et consilium Iberniæ in Sradbaliam Vltoniæ oppidum Dubhlinna profecti Tironum in ius vocant qui crimen obiectum incunctanter negat, subdens Compedito" [Aoo Ƽeimleach] "inimico suo non esse fidem habendam, Compeditus, se singulari certamine crimen probaturum asserit: Sed ipse et Tironus ingredi prohibentur testes producturum confirmat. Die constituta, qua testes producantur, Tironus, datis vadibus dimissus Compeditum inquirendo deprehendet, et custodiæ mandat, iussusque à Prorege Dubhlinnam mittere, imperio non obediens laqua suspendat Midhiensi homine tortor: nam pietate et amore in Onellam familiam et Ioannem principem nullus tota Tironà potuit varibus vllis deduci ut Compedito mortem inferret."—*Hist. Cathol. Iber.*, fol. 124.

Camden gives the following account of the hanging of this Hugh, and of the after conduct of the Earl, in his Annals of the Reign of Queen Elizabeth, A. D. 1590:

ḟirḋorċa, mic cuinn ḃacaiġ. Ní baí ḟḟr a aera lé haċhaiḋ do ċenél eoġain mic neill ro baḋ mó eccaoine ina an taoḃ ſin.

Mac uí doṁnaill .i. doṁnall mac aoḋa mic maġnuſa, mic aoḋa duiḃ, mic aoḋa ruaiḋ mic neill ġairḃ mic toirrḋealḃaiġ an ḟiona do ḃṫiṫ aġ dol ar

"In Hibernia anno superiori Hugo Gaveloc" [Ġeiṁleaċ] "ita dictus quia in compedibus diu detentus, filius naturalis Shani O-Neal, Hugonem Comitem Tir-Oeniæ accusaverat occultos sermones conseruisse cum Hispanis quibusdam naufragio MDLXXXVIII. in Hiberniam ejectis. Comes accusationem prævertens illum ex insidiis interceptum strangulari jussit; cumque ex quadam observantia erga familiam O-Neali immanes prædones vim afferre recusarent, ipse resti ad gulam frangendam manum admovisse perhibetur. Hinc in Angliam jam vocatus, crimen supplex apud Reginam deprecatus, veniam impetravit, coramque ipsa ad Regiam Greenwichi *honorem*, ut nobiles solent, *potestatus*, sanctissime in se recepit, pacem cum Turlogho Leinigh vicinisque singulis observaturum, datis eo nomine obsidibus: nec O-Neali titulum, nec authoritatem in nobiles vicinos assumpturum; regionem Tir-Oeniam in formam Comitatus redacturum, a populo subdito pensitationes Hibernicas (*Bonaghty* vocant) non exacturum, neminem nisi ex lege morte jam inde mulctaturum, annonam præsidiariis Anglis ad Aquam Nigram, sive fluvius *More* non interclusurum, Monachos, Fratres, Moniales, et rebelles in territorium non admissurum, incolas Tir-Oeniæ ad humaniorem cultum quantum posset, adducturum; & id genus alia; ea tamen conditione interposita ut Turlogus Leinigh & finitimi Dynastæ itidem fidem ad pacem cum ipso colendam obstringerent, ne ipse quietus turbulentorum injuriis exponeretur. In Hiberniam remissus, hæc eadem se facturum coram Guil. Fitz-Williams Prorege & Regni Consiliariis, asseveranter confirmavit, & sane aliquandiu nihil omisit, quod ab obsequentissimo subdito expectari poterat, pleraque virtutis adumbrata signa præ se ferens. Corpus laborum, vigiliæ, & inediæ patiens, industria magna, animus ingens maximisque par negotiis, militiæ multa scientia, ad simulandum animi altitudo profunda, adeo ut nonnulli eum vel maximo Hiberniæ bono, vel malo natum tunc prædixerint."

Whether this Earl, Hugh, was an O'Neill or not,—and the Editor feels satisfied that Shane-an-diomais proved in England that he was not,—he was the cleverest man that ever bore that name. The O'Kellys of Bregia, of whom this Hugh must have been (if he were not of the blood of the O'Neills), were descended from Hugh Slaine, Monarch of Ireland from 599 till 605, and consequently of as royal lineage as the O'Neills themselves, if not more so, though brought low by the English at an early period. Connell Mageoghegan says that "there reigned of King Hugh Slaine's race, as monarchs of this kingdom, nine kings," and that "there were many other princes of Moy-Brey, besides the said kings of the family of O'Kelly of Brey." We may, therefore, well believe that the blood of Hugh Slaine, which was brought so low in the grandfather, found its level in the military genius and towering ambition of Hugh, Earl of Tyrone. Mr. Moore, who has formed so low an estimate of the character of the Anglo-Irish Earl of Desmond, writes of this Milesian Earl of royal lineage as follows:

"But a new claimant of political distinction had now begun to attract attention; one who was destined not only to rally round him the hearts of his fellow countrymen, but to shew *for once* to the world an instance of Irishmen conquering in their own cause.

"This remarkable man, Hugh O'Neill, was

Earl of Tyrone, Hugh, son of Ferdorcha, son of Con Bacagh. There had not been for a long time among the race of Eoghan, the son of Niall, a man more generally lamented than this Hugh.

The son of O'Donnell, i. e. Donnell, the son of Hugh, son of Manus, son of Hugh Duv, son of Hugh Roe, son of Niall Garv, son of Turlough of the Wine

the son of the late Matthew, Baron of Dungannon, and being, by the law of English descent, the immediate successor of his father, was thereby entitled to the earldom of Tyrone. In the late wars against Desmond, he had commanded a troop of horse in the queen's service; and having distinguished himself highly as a soldier, was, at the time we have reached, petitioning the Irish parliament to be allowed to assume the title, and take the possessions of the earldom of Tyrone.

"While thus affecting to look to a peerage, as the sole object of his ambition, he was already contemplating purposes of a far higher aim, nor yet had made up his mind as to which of the two paths, now opening before him, he should commit himself: whether, as a peer, he should still court distinction only through English channels; or whether, placing himself at the head of his powerful sept, he should renounce the *hollow* loyalty he had hitherto professed, and assume openly the national title of The O'Neill. Meanwhile the position he held between the two rival parties was such as to enable him, without much apparent duplicity, to turn to account the credit and influence he had acquired with both. The English authorities were proud to claim, as attached to their service, an officer known to stand so high with his own fellow countrymen; and the chieftains of Ulster, then the stronghold of Irish patriotism, forgave willingly his seeming adhesion to the cause of the enemy, as long as they saw reason to believe that his heart was wholly their's. But, however favourable to his ambitious views was this double aspect of his political character, it naturally fostered in him those habits of evasion and duplicity, which notwithstanding his great public merits, brought much discredit on his after career.

"The rank and title of the earldom of Tyrone were, without much difficulty, conceded to him; but the possessions, he was told, must depend on the pleasure of the Crown. He, therefore, resolved to appeal to the Queen; and repairing immediately to the English court, succeeded, by his address, frank manner, and well-disguised subtlety, in obtaining the object of his petition. The princely inheritance of his ancient family was restored to him, without any reservation of rent; and, among the conditions required of him, the only one that savoured at all of distrust was that which stipulated that he should claim no authority over the lords bordering on his country."—*History of Ireland*, vol. iv. pp. 99, 100.

It appears from Rot. Can. H. A. 29 Eliz. that it was provided in the grant to this Earl, that the bounds of Tyrone should be distinctly marked and defined; that two hundred and forty acres should be reserved, adjoining to the River Blackwater, for the use of a fort to be there erected; that the new Earl should challenge no authority over the neighbouring lords; that the sons of John [the Proud], and Turlough [Luineach], should be provided for; and that Turlough should be continued Chieftain of Tyrone, with a right of superiority over Maguire and O'Kane, two subordinate Lords or Urriaghs to the O'Neill. This power, ceded to Turlough Luineach, and afterwards to the Earl Hugh, cleared the way for the confiscation of Ulster.

bélaiḃ a aṫar (iar ndol dó i neneirte ⁊ in innlaicce, ⁊ iar mbeiṫ dia ṁac ele illaiṁ in áṫ cliaṫ) go ttarratt domnall ina mbaoí ó Shliaḃ anoir i ttír ċonaill fó a nert ⁊ fó a cumaċtaiḃ .i. ó bearnas go drobaoís, baoiġeallaiġ ⁊ bag-ainiġ beós. Bá saoṫ mór ⁊ bá galar meanman lá hingin tSemais mic domnaill, domnall do beiṫ for an abairt sin ar oṁan lé a roċtain i cceanndus cenel cconaill ar bélaiḃ a meic aoḋ ruaḋ baí illaiṁ in aṫ cliaṫ cecib tan nó ḋeónaiġfaḋ dia dó toċt a cuimreaċ conaḋ aire sin ro tionóileaḋ lé a mbaoí foṁámaiġṫe dia fior do ċenél cconaill .i. O doċartaiġ co na ṫionól, Mac suiḃne na ttuaṫ eoġan ócc co na soċraite, Mac suiḃne fanat co na soċraide go sochaiḋe móir dalbanchaiḃ a maille friú. Iar ffios sccel do domnall ua ḋomnaill an toiċeastal sin do beiṫ agá denaṁ cuicce, Ro tionoil side for a ccionn. Báttar iat ro eirgeattar lais Mac suiḃne bágaineaċ donnchaḋ mac maolmuire, ⁊ drong do cloinn tSuiḃne na muṁan im triar mac eoġain mic maolmuire mic donnchaiḋ mic toirrḋealḃaiġ co na soċraide, ⁊ ó baoiġill tadcc ócc mac taiḋcc mic toirrḋealḃaiġ co líon a ṫionóil. Bá hann do rala do ṁac uí domnaill beiṫ in err tíre boġaine alla niar do ġleann colaim cille, gus na maiṫiḃ sin ina foċair. Ní ro hanaḋ lás an luċt naile go rangattar an dú sin dia saighiḋ, ⁊ ro fiġeaḃ sccainnear croḋa eatorra adiú ⁊ anall, ⁊ tarlaicseat na halbanaiġ saiṫe saiġeatt a fiodḃacaiḃ fobartaċa co ro gonaḋ ⁊ co ro creċtnaigheaḋ (an .14. September) dronga diriṁe leó, ⁊ ro baḋ diḃ side Mac uí domnaill feisin co ná baí ina cuṁang eangnaṁ no urrclaiḋi do ḋénaṁ co ro marḃaḋ an dú sin ag an doire leaṫan lá taoḃ cuain teiliontt. Ba handaṁ riaṁ rias an tan sin a ḃuaiḋ agá ḃiodḃaḋaiḃ cen gur ḃó ḃiod-ḃaḋa ittir in luċt las a ttorċair (condus rala eatorra don ċur sin) ⁊ gion gur ḃó hé an domnall sin oiḋre a aṫarḋa iar ffíor níp ḃó díṁiaḋ do ṫír

[h] *Bearnas*, i. e. the Barnismore mountain, in the barony of Tirhugh.—See note [x], under the year 1522, p. 1355, *supra*.

[i] *Boylagh and Tir-Boghaine*, i. e. the inhabitants of the baronies of Boylagh and Banagh, in the west of the county of Donegal. These were the O'Boyles and the Mac Sweenys of Banagh.

[k] *Gleann Choluim Cille*, i. e. St. Columbkille's glen, or valley, now Glencolumbkille, the name of a parish and remarkable valley in the west of the barony of Tir-Boghaine, or Banagh, in the county of Donegal. The place is described as follows, in O'Donnell's Life of St. Columbkille, as translated by Colgan, *Trias Thaum.*, p. 391:

"Locus is est Tirconallensis patriæ, Occidenti proximus, in Oceanum procul excurrens, in arduos incultosque montes assurgens, in horrida demum promontoria desinens, Columbæ, a cujus asceterio celebris habetur jamdudum sacer."—lib. i. c. 15.

[l] *Doire-leathan*, i. e. the broad derry, or oak

attempted to depose his father, after he had grown weak and feeble [from age], and after his other son had been imprisoned in Dublin; so that Donnell brought under his power and jurisdiction that part of Tirconnell from the mountain westwards, i. e. from Bearnas[h] to [the River] Drowes; and also the people of Boylagh and Tir-Boghaine[i]. It was [a cause of] great anguish and sickness of mind to Ineenduv, the daughter of James Mac Donnell, that Donnell should make such an attempt, lest he might attain the chieftainship of Tirconnell in preference to her son, Hugh Roe, who was confined in Dublin, [and who she hoped would become chief], whatever time God might permit him to return from his captivity; and she, therefore, assembled all the Kinel-Connell who were obedient to her husband, namely, O'Doherty, with his forces; Mac Sweeny-na-dTuath (Owen Oge), with his forces; and Mac Sweeny Fanad, with his forces; with a great number of Scots along with them. After Donnell O'Donnell had received intelligence that this muster had been made to oppose him, he assembled [his forces] to meet them. These were they who rose up to assist him on this occasion: Mac Sweeny Banagh (Donough, the son of Mulmurry); a party of the Clann-Sweeny of Munster, under the conduct of the three sons of Owen, the son of Mulmurry, son of Donough, son of Turlough, and their forces; and O'Boyle (Teige Oge, the son of Teige, son of Turlough), with all his forces, assembled. The place where the son of O'Donnell happened to be stationed along with these chieftains was [Doire-leathan] at the extremity of Tir-Boghaine, to the west of Gleann Choluim Cille[k]. The other party did not halt until they came to them to that place; and a battle ensued between them, which was fiercely fought on both sides. The Scots discharged a shower of arrows from their elastic bows, by which they pierced and wounded great numbers, and, among the rest, the son of O'Donnell himself, who, being unable to display prowess or defend himself, was slain at Doire-leathan[l], on one side of the harbour of Telinn, on the 14th of September. Seldom before that time had his enemies triumphed over him; and the party by whom he was slain had not been by any means his enemies until they encountered on this occasion; and although this Donnell was not the rightful heir of his father[m], it would have

wood, now *anglice* Derrylahan, a townland in the parish of Glencolumbkille, barony of Banagh, and county of Donegal, bounded on the south by Teelin harbour.

[m] *Of his father*, literally, "to his patrimony or his father's territorial possessions."

conaill a oirdneaḋ fuirre dia leicctí dia ḟaighiḋ í. Torcrattar don ċaiṫ-iorgail sin i ffarraḋ doṁnaill an triar mac sin eoġain mic maolmuire mic donnchaiḋ go noíḃ céadaiḃ a maille friú i ttimcell doṁnaill.

Uater ciotaċ a búrc mac Seain mic oiluerais do écc iar rioḋucchaḋ dó le gallaiḃ.

Mag coċláin .i. Sean mac airt mic corbmaic do écc, ⁊ ní baoí fer a duiṫċe do ṡlioċt corbmaic cais ro baḋ seolta ḟeirccaire cuirte, ⁊ cairteoil, ⁊ sortaḋa saḋaile inar, ⁊ a mac Sean ócc do oirdneaḋ ina ionaḋ.

Maolruanaiḋ mac an ċalḃaiġ mic donnchaiḋ mic Seain uí cerḃaill do écc.

Mac muiris ciarraiġe .i. tomas mac emainn mic tomais, mic emainn do ecc ceannaiġe fíona, eaċ, ⁊ ealaḋan rob ferr dfior a inṁe ⁊ a aṫarḋa féin baoí illeiṫ moġa durṁór an tan sin, ⁊ Patraiccín a oiḋre do ḃeiṫ illaiṁ in aṫ cliaṫ an tan sin.

O Loċlainn uaiṫne mac maoileaċlainn, mic Ruḋraiġe mic ana décc, ⁊ a ṁac .i. Rosa, ⁊ mac a meic .i. uaiṫne do ḃeiṫ imreasnaċ ré a roile imo ionaḋ.

Soṁairle buiḋe, mac alastrainn, mic eóin caṫanaiġ ṁec domnaill do ecc.

[n] *Of his property*, i. e. a man of the same extent of territory, i. e. a lord of a single barony. Mac Coghlan, Chief of Dealbhna-Eathra, was of the race of Cormac Cas, the ancestor of the O'Briens of Thomond.—See O'Flaherty's *Ogygia*, part iii. c. 82. The castles of Streamstown, Kincora, Garrycastle, Faddan, Clononey, Esker, and Coole, were in his territory.—See note [r], under the year 1519, p. 1346, *supra*.

[o] *Thomas, the son of Edmond.*—See Lodge's Peerage by Archdall for a curious notice of this Thomas.

[p] *Sorley Boy.*—He was the first of the Mac Donnells that totally vanquished Mac Quillin, chief of the Route, in the county of Antrim, and became the founder of the Earldom of Antrim.—See note [j], under the year 1570, pp. 1641, 1642, *supra*. As this chieftain makes so conspicuous a figure in the Irish annals, the Editor is tempted to give in this place a brief outline of the history of his ancestors, and of the manner and period of their first settlement in the Glynns, and afterwards in the Route, in the present county of Antrim. Lodge traces his ancestry imperfectly; and, besides, in the account he gives of his descendants, has commited some mistakes, the chief of which consists in making Sir James the *second*, instead of the *eldest* of his sons. It may be here mentioned that there are several lines of the Mac Donnells of Scotland and Ireland given in the MS. Book of Ballymote (compiled about 1380); and many curious genealogical poems in manuscript, in the Irish language, from the sixteenth century downwards, tracing the filiations, and commemorating the privileges and achievements, of this warlike race.

I. Somhairle, Thane of Airer-Gaidheal, or Argyle [slain A.D. 1165, see *Scotochronicon*, and Chalmers' *Caledonia*], the common ancestor of Mac Dubhgaill [Mac Dougall], Mac Donnell, and Mac Rory. He married a daughter of the King of Man [See *Chron. Man.*], and had

II. Randal, fl. 1213, *q. v.* He had a son,

been no disgrace to Tirconnell to have elected him as its chief, had he been permitted to attain to that dignity. In this conflict were slain along with Donnell the three sons of Owen, son of Mulmurry, son of Donough [above mentioned], together with two hundred others, around Donnell.

Walter Kittagh Burke, the son of John, son of Oliver, died, after having concluded a peace with the English.

Mac Coghlan (John, the son of Art, son of Cormac) died. There was not a man of his property[n], of the race of Cormac Cas, who had better furnished or more commodious courts, castles, and comfortable seats, than this John. His son, John Oge, was appointed in his place.

Mulrony, the son of Calvagh, son of Donough, son of John O'Carroll, died.

Mac Maurice of Kerry, i. e. Thomas, the son of Edmond[o], son of Thomas, son of Edmond, died. He was the best purchaser of wine, horses, and literary works, of any of his wealth and patrimony, in the greater part of Leath-Mogha at that time; and Patrickin, his heir, was at this time in captivity in Dublin.

O'Loughlin (Owny, the son of Melaghlin, son of Rury, son of Ana) died; and his son, Rossa, and his grandson, Owny, were contending with each other for his place.

Sorley Boy[p], the son of Alexander, son of John Cahanagh, died.

III. Domhnall, or Donnell, the ancestor from whom the Mac Donnells have derived their surname. He had a son,

IV. Aengus, or Angus More. He is mentioned in Patent Roll, 40th of Hen. III. A. D. 1256, under the name of Aengus, filius Dovenaldi. It is doubtful whether he or his son be the "Angus of Ilay and Kintyre" of Barbour's almost contemporaneous poem on the wars and adventures of King Robert Bruce.

V. Aengus Oge. He was probably the Mac Donnell, Lord of Arygyle, slain at Dundalk in 1318, *q. v.* He married Agnes, daughter of Cumhaighe O'Cahan. There is on the Chancery Rolls, A. D. 1338, a safe conduct for Agnes, mother of John, Lord of the Isles, to go from and return to Ireland *ad libitum*. He had two sons, 1, John, Lord of the Isles, and 2, Marcus, the ancestor of the Mac Donnells of Leinster.—See note *ad an.* 1570, pp. 1691, *et seq.*

VI. John of Islay, or Eoin na h-Ile. In 1337 there is a safe conduct on the public records for him under the name of Johannes de Insulis; and there are letters patent appointing the Earl of Salisbury Royal Ambassador to him; and a letter of King Edward, beginning "Rex, nobili et potenti viro Johanni de Insulis amico suo charissimo &c." He died in 1387, according to these Annals, and this date is corroborated by a letter in Rymer's *Fœdera*, *ad an.* 1388, empowering the Bishop of Sodor to make a treaty, "Cum strenuo viro Godefredo filio Johannis de Yle, *nuper* Domini Insularum cum Donaldo filio Johanni de Yle nuper Domini Insularum cum Johanne fratre ejusdem Donaldi." By the daughter of Rory Mac Dougall, Chief of Lorne, he had, 1,

Eóġan mac an dſġanaiġ do écc.

Aoḋ Ruaḋ ua doṁnaill do ḃeiṫ hi ccuimreaċ in Áṫ cliaṫ fri ré ṫteóra mbliaḋan, ⁊ ṫeóra mís. Bá toċráḋ mór menman lais a ḃeiṫ aṁlaiḋ sin i

Ronald, ancestor of the chieftains of Clann Ronald and Glengarry; 2, Godfrey; 3, Aengus. By his subsequent marriage with Margaret, daughter of Robert II. King of Scotland, he had, 1, Domhnall, or Donnell na h-Ile, ancestor of the Earls of Ross and Lords of the Isles; 2, John Mor, ancestor of the Antrim family; 3, Alexander, the ancestor of the house of Keppoch.

VII. John Mor. He married Mary Bissett, [*rectiùsne* Margery?] the daughter [and heir] of Mac Eoin Bissett, according to Duald Mac Firbis [Lib. Geneal. 341], who states that the Bissetts are of Greek blood, and came in with William the Conqueror [*quære*, William the Lion?], and that it was by her the seven tuaths of the Glinns, to which belonged the island of Rachlainn, came to the Mac Donnells. Mac Firbis goes on to say that the Mac Donnells owned the Glinns for two hundred and thirty-seven years previous to the year 1649, in which he compiled their pedigree. On the Rolls of Scotland in 1400, there is a safe conduct "pro nobili viro Johanni de Insulis Domino de Dunwage et de *Glynns*, et pro Donaldo fratre ejus." See *State Papers*, Sir Henry Sidney, vol. i. pp. 76–79. He had a son,

VIII. Donnell Ballagh, he is mentioned on Patent Roll, 3rd of Edward IV., and he was one of the contracting parties to the celebrated treaty of Ardtornish, printed in full in Rymer's *Fœdera*. After an unsuccessful insurrection in Scotland, he fled to the Glinns in Antrim, where he was killed, and his head was sent to the King of Scotland. He married Johanna, daughter of O'Donnell, by whom he had

IX. John of Islay, who is mentioned on Patent Roll of 3 Edw. IV. He married Sabina, daughter of Felimy, son of O'Neill. His death is recorded, together with that of his son, and others his relatives, in the following words, in the Annals of Ulster, at the year 1499:

"Eoin Mor Mac Donnell, *King of the Isles*, and John Cahanagh, his son, and Randal Roe, and Donnell Ballagh [Oge], were hanged together."

This fact is mentioned in a Gaelic manuscript, the date of which is late in the seventeenth century, quoted by Sir Walter Scott, in his notes to the "Lord of the Isles," as follows:

"There happened great feuds between these families" [the Mac Ceans and Mac Donalds], "while Donald Du" [obiit at Drogheda, 1545, see *State Papers*] "was in prison; insomuch that Mac Cean of Ardnamurchan [*rectè* Mac Eoin of Ard na Murchon] destroyed the greatest part of the posterity of John Mor of the Isles and Cantyre. For John Cathanach, son of John, son of Donald Ballach, son of John Mor, son of John, son of Angus Oge" [the chief of the descendants of John Mor], "and John Mor, son of John Cathanach, and young John, son of John Cathanach, and young Donald Ballagh, son of John Cathanach, were treacherously taken by Mac Cean, in the Island of Finlagan, in Isla, and carried to Edinburgh, where he got them hanged at the Burrow Muir, and their bodies were buried in the church of St. Anthony, called the New Church. There were none left alive at that time, of the children of John Cathanach, except Alexander, son of John Cathanach and Agnes Flach" [Ilech], "who concealed themselves in the *Glens* of Ireland. Mac Cean, hearing of their hiding places, went to cut down the woods of those glens in order to destroy Alexander, and extirpate the whole race. At length Mac Cean and Alexander met, were reconciled, and a marriage alliance took place; Alexander married Mac Cean's daughter, and

Owen Mac-an-Deaganaigh[q] died.

Hugh Roe O'Donnell had [now] been in captivity in Dublin for the space of three years and three months. It was [a cause of] great distress of mind to

she brought him good children."

X. John Cahanagh, son of John of Islay. According to the Annals of Ulster, he slew, in 1494, Alexander Mac Gilespick Mac Donnell, the head of the Mac Donnells. He married Celia, daughter of Savadge, Lord of the Ardes, and had by her a son,

XI. Alexander Carragh. It appears from various documents among the printed State Papers, *temp.* Hen. VIII., that from about the year 1520, the Mac Donnells of the Isles began to form permanent settlements in the north-east of the present county of Antrim. In the list of the chieftains of Ulster in 1515, in the third part of the State Papers, p. 7, there is no mention of any Mac Donnell; but Fytz John Byssede, of the Glynnes, is mentioned as one of the "greate Englyshe rebelles of Wolster." In 1533, however, they were numerous in the Glinns, as appears from a report of the Irish Council to Cromwell, in which the following statement occurs:

"The Scotts also inhabith now buysselly a great part of Ulster, which is the Kinge's inheritaunce; and it is greatly to be fearid, oonles that in short tyme they be dryven from the same, that they bringing yn more nombre daily, woll, by lyttle and lyttle, soo far encroche in acquyring and wynnyng the possessions there, with thaidis of the Kingis disobeysant Irishe rebelles, whoo doo nowe aide theym therein after suche maner that at leyngth they will put and expell the King from his hole seignory theire." —*State Papers, Ireland*, vol. ii. p. 172.

And in a report of Alan to Cromwell in 1539, same vol. p. 136, he says:

"I moch suspect the King of Scottes, that so moch tendereth the amitie of theis men, which no King of Scottes hath been seen to doo befor. He hath also this yere twice sent for Alexander Carragh, Capteyne of the Scottes of this lande, who hath goon thider, and by his retorne it is perceyvid what busynes he had ther; but oonlie it appereth he was well enterteyned in the Courte of Scotland, though of trowthe ther was no amitie but mortalitie betwixt them; the Kinge of Scottes and antecessours having killed and put to death the said Alexander's fader, grandfader, and gretegrandfader, and exiled him owte of the Isles, whereby he was compelled to inhabite here. But I suspecte playnelie that if any busyness shalbe the said King hath interteyned this man havinge both knowlege and power with him in this land to be a chieftayne for this purpoos."

He married Catherina, daughter of Mac Eoin, Chief of Ardnamurchon, in Scotland, and had issue: 1, James; 2, Alexander Oge, who slew Shane an Diomais O'Neill; 3, Gillaspick; 4, Donnell Ballagh; 5, Angus Uaibhreach, i. e. the haughty; 6, Colla Duv-na-gCapull, i. e. Black Colla of the Horses; 7, Sorley Boy; and, according to Duald Mac Firbis, 8, Donnell Gorm. James, who was his eldest son, as appears from the State Papers most clearly, was elected Lord of the Isles on the death, at Drogheda, in 1545, of Donnell Duv, the last descendant of the last Lord of the Isles recognised by the King of Scotland. This James married the Lady Agnes Campbell, daughter of the fourth Earl of Argyle. He died of his wounds received in the battle of Glenshesk, from Shane O'Neill, in 1566; leaving issue: 1, Angus, who succeeded his father in Scotland, and is called in some Irish MSS. Mac Domhnaill na h-Alban, i.e. Mac Donnell of Scotland. He was of Duneveg, and forfeited by insur-

nḋaor ḃroitt, ⁊ nír ḃó fó a ḋaiġ ḃuḋéin aċt ar ḋáiġ ná daoírċimiḋeaċta i mbárttar a ṫír, ⁊ a ṫalaṁ, a ċairde, ⁊ a ċoiṁḟiulus in gach maigin seaċnón Ereann. Ro ḃaoí occa sccruḋaḋ ina mſnmain do gres caiḋe an tearrus eluḋa fó ġébaḋ. Nír ḃó soḋaing ḋósom an ní sin, ár dos fuccṫa i cuḃaċail ḟoirriata is in caislén gaċ noiḋċe dia iomċoiṁéd condus ficcsḃ tert ar a ḃarac. Bá imne baoí an caislén hisin ⁊ lſtanċlais lánḋoṁain lionn-uisce ina uirṫimċeall, ⁊ cláirḋroiċſt coṁḋluta fuirre fó ſrċomair ḋorais an ḋúine, ⁊ garraḋ gruamaineaċ na ngall amuiġ ⁊ hirtiġ imón dorus dia ḋúrċoiṁétt co ná diccreaḋ aon táirriḃ inunn náċ amaċ gan aṫċomarc. Ar a aoí ní ḃí friotaire ar naċ ffraġtar faill fá ḋeóiḋ. Buí Aoḋ co nḋruing dia

rection the lands of Kintire, which were granted to the Earl of Argyle, when a commission issued to the Earl of Huntly to extirpate "the barbarous people of the Isles within a year." This Angus was father of Sir James Mac Donnell of Knockinsay, whose estates descended to two daughters, co-heiresses. 2, Donnell Gorm, who, on Sept. 18, 1584, by articles, between Sir John Perrott and the rest of the Council there, and this Donnell Gorm called of the Glynnes in Ulster, "was to hold so much of the Glynnes as were the lands of Mysset, *alias* Bysset, he undertaking not to serve any foreign prince or potentate, nor "kepe any Scottes but such as be natives of Irelande without lycense." Always to serve "against Severlie Bwoy" [Sorley Boy, his own uncle], "and any other forraine Scot." This Donnell Gorm was slain by Sir Richard Bingham, at Ardnarea, in Connaught, A. D. 1586. James had also Donnell and Alexander, who were slain at Ardnarea, and two other sons who were slain by Captain Merriman in 1585. This James was also father of Ineenduv, the wife of Sir Hugh O'Donnell, and mother of the great Hugh Roe O'Donnell, of Rory, the first Earl of Tirconnell, and of Caffar O'Donnell.

XII. Sorley Boy, whom all accounts mention as the youngest son of Alexander Carragh, obtained a patent of denization of Ireland on the 14th of April, 1573, when he acknowledged the Queen's right to Ulster and the Crown of Ireland, professed obedience and swore to be a true subject, in consideration of which he was thenceforward to be considered a free denizen, "not as mere Irish, Scottish-Irish, or a stranger."—*Roll.* There are various original letters and papers relating to his affairs, and those of his brothers, preserved in the Cotton Library, Vespasian, F. 12, and Titus, B. 13, which deserve examination. The last of these is his Indenture of Submission, dated 18th June, 1586. He married Mary, the daughter of Con O'Neill, first Earl of Tyrone, and had by her, according to Duald Mac Firbis, four sons, viz., 1, Sir James; 2, Sir Randal, created Viscount Dunluce and first of the Earls of Antrim (whose genealogy may be seen in Lodge's Peerage), by James I.; 3, Donnell; 4, Aengus. Lodge adds, and correctly, another son, Alexander, who was slain by Captain Merriman in 1585.

XIII. Sir James was Lord of the Route and Glynnes. He had several children by Mary, daughter of Hugh mac Felim O'Neill of Clannaboy. But whether he was lawfully married to her was a matter of dispute after his death. His son, Alexander, who was afterwards created a baronet, rose in arms about 1614, alleging as the cause of his insurrection that he was the right heir to the lands of the Route, and not Sir Randal, his uncle.—MS. Trin. Coll. Dub-

him to be thus imprisoned; yet it was not for his own sake [that he grieved], but for the sake of his country, his land, his friends, and kinsmen, who were in bondage throughout Ireland. He was constantly revolving in his mind the manner in which he might make his escape. This was not an easy matter for him, for he was confined in a closely-secured apartment every night in the castle until sunrise[r] the next day. This castle was surrounded by a wide and very deep ditch, full of water, across which was a wooden bridge, directly opposite the door of the fortress; and within and without the door were stationed a stern party of Englishmen, closely guarding it, so that none might pass in or out without examination. There is, however, no guard[s] whose vigilance may not

lin. It is most likely that Sir James, having died during the minority of his children, their inheritance was usurped, under the colour of Tanistry, by their uncle, Sir Randal, who obtained a grant of it from King James I. in 1603; and that this insurrection took place when Sir James's heir was of age to assert his claims. The grant to his uncle from the Crown, of course, would sufficiently account for his failure. Much curious evidence could be adduced in support of this conjecture; but it would extend this note beyond all reasonable limits to adduce it.

XIV. This Sir Alexander, who was of Moyane, in the county of Antrim, in 1634 had married Evelin, daughter of Sir Arthur Magennis, first Viscount Iveagh, and had,

XV. Sir James of Ballybanagh, in the county of Antrim, second Baronet, who married Mary, daughter of Donough O'Brien, of the county of Clare. He was attainted in 1691. He had: I, Colonel Sir Alexander Mac Donnell, who is mistaken by Lodge for Colla Kittagh, who was also a Sir Alexander Mac Donnell, having been knighted by Montrose on the field, and who was slain in the battle of Knocknanos, Cnoc na n-os, i. e., Hill of the Fawns, in the county of Cork, by Inchiquin, in 1647. Colonel Alexander, the son of Sir James, married Lady Elizabeth Howard, daughter of Henry Earl of Surrey, Arundel, and Norfolk, and had issue, by her Randal, who died without issue, and who, as well as his father (who was killed in a duel, A. D. 1677), died in the life-time of Sir James, the second baronet.

XVI. The second son of Sir James was Captain Randal, who became third baronet. He commanded a ship of war in the service of Charles II., accompanied James II. to Ireland, and followed his fortunes abroad. He died about the year 1720, leaving, besides his eldest son James (who would have been fourth baronet but for the attainder, and who died unmarried, and was buried in the churchyard of St. James, Dublin, 24th May, 1728), a second son, Randall, who was commonly called Sir Randall, of Cross, county of Antrim, who commanded a regiment of the Irish Brigade in France, and died there in 1740 without issue, leaving his third brother,

XVII. John-Richard, who then succeeded to the family property.

[q] *Mac an Deaganaigh*, i. e. son of the Dean. This name is still common in Tyrone, and anglicised Mac Digany by some, and Deane by others.

[r] *Until sunrise*, condur ficcfó tert .i. go dtigeaḋ an ṁaidin, no eiriġiḋ greine. The word tert is explained "*tertia hora*" in Cormac's Glossary, and "sunrise" by O'Reilly, in his Irish Dictionary.

[s] *No guard*, literally, "however, there is no guarding of which an advantage is not got at

aos cumṫa ina ḟarraḋ i nDeiriuḋ geiṁriḋ do ṡonnraḋ i nurtosaċ oiḋċe ré riú do rata is na cubaclaiḃ foiriata i mbítis gaċ noiḋċe. Do bertsat téd réḟeaḋ ro ḟoda leó gus an ffenestter baoí for a nionchaiḃ, ⁊ dus relgsit síos fris na ruainsiṁnaiḃ go ṫarblaingsit fors an urdrocat baoí alla muiġ do dorus an dúnaiḋ. Buí id imrsiṁar iarnaiġe ar an ccoṁlaḋ fri a tarraing ċucca amaċ do neoċ an tan baḋ adlaic. Do ratsoṁ balc lán glaice do ċronn coṁḋaingsin tres an id ar na tíorda dia ttoghraim co tinnsnaċ ar an dúnaiḋ. Ro ḃaoí óccláċ do ṡainṁuintir an Aoḋa i ffroiċill a néluḋa, ⁊ do rala side dóiḃ iar ttoiḋeaċt amaċ ⁊ dá lannclaiḋiṁ láncodat lais fó a ċoim, ⁊ do bert illaiṁ an Aoḋa. Do ratt cloiḋiṁ diḃside dia roile laoċ amra do Laiġniḃ, Art Caoṁanaċ ata coṁnaic, ba háirrsiġ iorġaile ⁊ bá taoíseaċ ioṁgona eiside.

Ciḋ iat na forċoiṁeḋaiġe tra ní ro ráṫaiġsit iḋeallṁa an téluiḋ, ⁊ ciḋ an tan tucsat dia nuíḋ é, do ciṅgat fó ċéḋóir do ṡaiġiḋ ḋorais an caisteoil aṁail as déine con rangattar uair ro baḋ dóiġ leó co ttáirsittís iatt i ttraite. Iar roċtain dóiḃ gus an dorus forḟéṁiḋ forra a errlogaḋ condus tarḋsatt fri a ttoġairm ċuca an luċt do rala is na tiġiḃ batar for ionchaiḃ an dorais don taoḃ araill don trraitt. An tan tangattar side

length." The word frioṫaire is explained *vigilia* in Cormac's Glossary, and "faire no forċoiṁéd," by O'Clery.

[w] *Before they were put.*—This Irish idiom, which the Irish peasantry have introduced into their English, is not strictly correct. It could be easily corrected thus: resiu ráinic an uair a rataoí iad is na cubaclaiḃ foriatta i mbítis gaċ noiḋċe, i. e. "before the hour arrived at which they used to be put into the close cells in which they used to be every night."

[x] *Of the rope.*—This word is not in the published dictionaries; but in the Life of Hugh Roe O'Donnell, by Cucogry O'Clery, it is used to denote *a rope.* Thus, in describing the escape of which we are now treating, it is used thus: "At ragat iarttain gus an fFialtech ⁊ ruaineaṁ sioṫḟoda leo, ⁊ do releicsit síos lais an ruaineaṁ tres an ffeltiġ," "They afterwards went to the privy, having a long *rope* [ruaineaṁ] with them, and they let themselves down by the *rope* through the privy-house."—*O'Reilly's* Copy, p. 5, but it is used in the *Battle of Magh Rath*, in this sense of loop.—See p. 284, line 25.

[y] *Closed it*, literally, for one to pull it [i. e. the door] out to him when he desired it. This idiom translates very clumsily into English. It should be: "there was a strong iron chain attached to this door, by which the door was fastened on the outside when occasion required."

[z] *Awaiting their escape.*—Fynes Moryson and Sir Richard Cox seem to believe that a certain great man [the Lord Deputy William Fitz-William, who endeavoured to make profit of his office] was privy to the escape of these prisoners; and Leland, a far more honest historian than either, is of the same opinion. Leland says that they first attempted to bribe their keeper, who disclosed their offer to the

some time or other be baffled. At the very end of winter, as Hugh and a party of his companions were together, in the beginning of the night, before they were put[t] into the close cells in which they used to be every night, they took with them a very long rope to a window which was near them, and by means of the rope[x] they let themselves down, and alighted upon the bridge that was outside the door of the fortress. There was a thick iron chain fastened to this door, by which one closed it[y] when required; through this chain they drove a strong handful of a piece of timber, [and thus fastened the door on the outside], so that they could not be immediately pursued from the fortress. There was a youth of Hugh's faithful people [outside] awaiting their escape[z], and he met them on coming out, with two well-tempered swords concealed under his garments; these he gave into the hand of Hugh, who presented one of them to a certain renowned warrior of Leinster, Art Kavanagh by name[a], who was a champion in battle, and a commander in conflict.

As for the guards, they did not perceive the escape for some time; but when they took notice of it they advanced immediately to the door of the castle, for they thought that they should instantly[b] catch them. Upon coming to the gate, they could not open it; whereupon they called over to them those who happened to be in the houses on the other side of the street, opposite the door [of the castle]. When these came at the call, and took the piece of timber out of the chain, and threw open the door for the people in the castle, who [then] set out, with a great number of the citizens, in pursuit of the youths who had

Lord Deputy; that this keeper was instantly displaced by the Lord Deputy, who substituted one of his own servants in his room; "a circumstance which gave rise to a suspicion that Fitz-William himself was not unacquainted with their design, nor averse to favouring it." It is, however, quite evident from this, and the account of the escape of Hugh O'Donnell, written by Cucogry O'Clery, that the Irish did not believe that the Lord Deputy was privy to the escape. It was evidently concerted between Fitz-William and Hugh, Earl of Tyrone, who buried the secret in "altitudine profundâ animi."

[a] *Art Kavanagh by name*, "at coṁnaic, .i. ata coṁainm."—H. 3, 18, p. 529, T. C. D.—This personage is unsatisfactorily introduced here. In the Life of Hugh Roe O'Donnell, by Cucogry O'Clery, in the Library of the Royal Irish Academy, it is stated that this Art Kavanagh remained behind the fugitives, in the streets of the city, to cover the retreat: "Do rat iaraṁ sciaṫ for lorg do na hógaiḃ tré sráittiḃ ⁊ sligṫiḃ an ḃaile."—p. 4.

[b] *Instantly*, i ttraite. "Traid .i. luaṫ, no obann."—*O'Clery*. "Troid .i. obann no luaṫ í, *unde dicitur*, ticfa a traide .i. co luaṫ."—*Cormac's Glossary*. See the Editor's *Irish Grammar*, part ii. c. vi. p. 265, *Formation of Adverbs*.

fón tógairm ro ghadsat an crann baoí tres an id eirce, ⁊ do lecsit an comladh suas do lucht an caisteoill, do dheochatar co ndruing móir do lucht na cathrach illeanmhain na nócc act rulatar uadhaibh. Ní bhaoí bá do rodhain uair bátor somh alla muigh do mhúraibh an bhaile, [ria] siú ro ráthaighitt ar robttar sirloicte óbhéla doirrsi na ríoghcathrach an ionbhaidh sin for a ccionn, ⁊ Rangattar for réidh an tsléibhe baoí remhpa .i. an Sliabh Ruaidh ⁊ ní ro léicc an omhan dóibh ride arcnámh isin conair coitcinn itir. Ní ro anrat dia reimim go rangattar iar scís artair ⁊ imtheachta tarr an ruaidhshliabh rémhraite. O robdar scithigh tuirsigh tiaghaitt guran ccoilleadh cliothairdluith forcaomhnacair for a ccind, ⁊ airisit innte co madain. Do bheartsatt iarsuidhe laimh fori imdecht ar nír bo hinnill leó anmain isin ffiodhbhaidh ar omhan a ttóraigheachta, ar a aoí nír bhó tualaing aodh ar arccnámh lá a oss cumhtha, uair ro tréghdadh a throighthe to.nngeala tanaighe lá haittin an tsleibhe ar ro heitterdheligitt a nassa ffriú iar sccaoíleadh i nuamann lás an ffleachadh ná fuairreadh gó sin. Bá saeth mór lá a aos cumhtha ná ro fhedsat leó é ní bádh sírsiu, ⁊ tiomnait celeabhradh dó, ⁊ fágbhaitt bennachttoin occa. Ro fhaoídh sium a fsi muintire go aroile duine uasal do shaorclandaibh cóicidh laighen do rala hi ccaistiall ina chomhfhocraibh dus an ffoighbeadh a iomfhnadhadh nó a imdhídean occa. Felim ó tuathail a shlondadh, ⁊ bá cara do aedh ria sonn (an dasrair) uair do cóidh

[c] *Had been wide open*, i. e. happened to be open, i. e. the hour for closing them had not arrived.

[d] *Sliabh Ruadh*,—See note [m], under the year 1535, p. 1420; and note [f], under the year 1557, p. 1548, *supra*.

[e] *To know.*—" Dus .i. da fhios."—*O'Clery*.

[f] *Felim O'Toole*.—He was O'Toole of Feara Cualann, and lived at Powerscourt. He was the son of Turlough, who was son of Art, who flourished chief in 1497, son of Edmond, slain 1488, son of Theobald, son of Dermot, slain 1445, ætat. 80, son of Hugh, Lord of Imaile, slain 1376, son of David, hanged at Dublin, 1328, son of Faelan, or Felim, Lord of Hy-Murray, d. 1260, son of Gilla-Kevin, son of Walter, son of Gilla-Kevin, (whose brother, Muircheartach, chief of Hy-Muireadhaigh, was father of St. Lorcan, or Laurence O'Toole, who died in 1180, q. v.), son of Gilla-Comhghaill, who was son of Duncuan, son of Gilla-Kevin, son of Gilla-Comhghaill, son of Duncuan, son of Dunlang, who died in 1013, (whose brother Ugaire, king of Leinster, was slain at Bithlann, now Belin, near Athy, in Kildare, in the battle fought against the Danes, A. D. 976), son of Tuathal, king of Leinster, who died in 956, and from whom the surname of O'Tuathail, or O'Toole, has been derived, who was the son of Ugaire, king of Leinster, who was slain by the Danes, under the command of Sitric Mac Ivor, at the battle of Cinn fuaidh, A. D. 915, who was the son of Oilloll, son of Dunlang, son of Muireadhach, son of Bran, king of Leinster, who died in 790, who was the son of Murchadh, son of Muireadhach, from whom the tribe name of O'Muireadhaigh was derived, who was the son of Murchadh Mor, who died in 721, son of Bran Mut, king of Leinster, died 687, son of Conall, son

escaped from them; but this was fruitless, for they [the fugitives] had passed beyond the walls of the city before they were missed, for the gates of the regal city had been wide open[c] at the time; and they pursued their way across the face of the mountain which lay before them, namely, Sliabh Ruadh[d], being afraid to venture at all upon the public road, and never halted in their course until after a fatiguing journey and travelling, until they had crossed the Red mountain aforesaid. When, weary and fatigued, they entered a thick wood which lay in their way, where they remained until morning. They then attempted to depart, for they did not deem it safe to remain in the wood, from fear of being pursued; but Hugh was not able to keep pace with his companions, for his white-skinned [and] thin feet had been pierced by the furze of the mountain, for his shoes had fallen off, their seams having been loosened by the wet, which they did not till then receive. It was great grief to his companions that they could not bring him any further; and so they bade him farewell, and left him their blessing.

He sent his servant to a certain gentleman of the noble tribes of the province of Leinster, who lived in a castle in the neighbourhood, to know[e] whether he could afford them shelter or protection. His name was Felim O'Toole[f], and he was previously a friend to Hugh, as he thought, for he had gone to visit him

of Faelan, died 665, son of Colman, son of Carbry, son of Cormac, king of Leinster, died 536, son of Oilioll, king of Leinster, who was baptized by St. Patrick at Naas (whose elder brother Illann, was king of Leinster, and died in 506, and had also been baptized by St. Patrick), who was the son of Dunlang (See Tripartite Life of St. Patrick, apud Colgan, in *Trias Thaum.*, lib. iii. c. xvi., pp. 151, 152), who was son of Enna Nia, son of Breasal Belach, the common ancestor of the O'Tooles, O'Byrnes, and Mac Murroughs.

It appears from Patent Roll, 1 Jac. I., that this Felim and Brian O'Toole forfeited the whole territory of "Fercuolen," five miles in length and four in breadth, which was granted on the 27th of October, 1603, to Richard Wingfield Knight, Marshal of the King's forces.—See Erck's *Repertory of the Chancery Enrolments*, Dublin, 1846. According to a pedigree of the O'Tooles, in a manuscript in the Royal Irish Academy, this Felim had a son, Garrett, who had a son, Turlough. The Editor has not been able to trace the descendants of this Felim, to a later period. Another distinguished branch of the family resided at Castlekevin, in the district of Fir-Tire, the head of which, Art Oge O'Toole, the son of Art, son of Edmond, slain 1488, &c. received a grant of the manor of Castlekevin, and the territory of the Fertyr, from Henry VIII. He had a son, Luke, who died seised of the manor of Castlekevin in 1565, leaving a son, Barnaby, or Bernard, of Castlekevin, who rebelled with his brother-in-law, Feagh mac Hugh O'Byrne, in 1596. He died on the 17th of January, 1596, leaving a son and heir, Luke, *alias* Pheagh, aged eight[een] years. King James granted his estate to John Wakeman, Esq., who, with others, by deed dated 5th

dia fiosruġaḋ soṁ feċt naile isin ccuimreaċ i mbaoí in áṫ cliaṫ co ro naiḋmsít a ccarattraḋ diḃlíniḃ fri a roile. Luiḋ an teaċta co hairm i mbaoí felim, ⁊ atfet dó an toiscc ima ttáinicc. Bá faoíliġ sium siaṁ, ⁊ ro ṫinġeall go ndeirġenaḋ gaċ maiṫ dia ccaoṁsaḋ do aoḋ. Ar a aoí trá ní ro ḟoḋaimsíd a ċairde naċ a ċomḟuiliġe dó a ḋíclít ar uaṁan smaċt ċana

December, 1609, enfeoffed Luke, *alias* Feagh O'Toole, of all the said territory of Fertry, as fully as he possessed same; and said Luke was in possession thereof for eleven years previous to 21st April, 1636.—See Inquisition taken at Wicklow at that date. This Feagh, or Luke O'Toole, was J. P. in the county of Wicklow in 1630, and a Colonel of the Confederate Catholics in 1641. In May, 1650, he received the following commission from the Catholic Bishops, of which there is a copy authenticated by his own oath and signature in the manuscript Depositions, preserved in the Library of Trinity College, Dublin, 3555, Wicklow, vol. F. 2. 14:

"To Colonel Luke, *alias* Pheagh O'Tohill, greeting, in our Lord God everlasting.

"Sir,—The pressing calamitie of this kingdom, wherewith the holy Catholique, Apostolique, and Roman religion, his sacred Majesties Right, and the just liberties of us his loyall subjects, are like to be trode under foote by a company of prophane and mechanical Rebells (made instruments of God's wrath to punish our sinnes), together with the confidence wee have in your zeal, worth, and wisdom, to redeem those soe deare pleadges, invites us to call to your assistance, Giving you hereby full power and authoritie to levie, leade, and command a Regiment of foot, and a troope of horse, praying you to containe the said Regiment and troope as much as may be from incurring God's just anger, especially from oppressing the poore, swering, and stealing; Giving you to understand wee are hereunto authorized by his Excellency the Lord Livetenant, Marquess of Ormond, as appeareth by his letter, dated at Loughriagh the first of last April. Wee also pray you, with the consent of the gentry there, to chose among yourselves in those partes, a commander in cheefe, and that each Colonel may choose his own Officers. We will not cease to pray his divine Majestie to encouradg you to fight in his quarrell, and bless your designs. Farewell. Given at Cavan, the second of May, 1650.

"H. Ardmach.	Fr. Antonius Clunmacnosensis.
Eug. Kilmoren.	
Fr. Thomas Dublin.	Walter B. Clonfert.
Fr. Edmundus Laghlinensis.	James Dempsie, Vic. Appo. of Kildare."

"This is a true copie of the originall remayning with me.

"Luc. Toolle.

"The 7th September, 1652."

This celebrated man was imprisoned in Dublin in 1652, in his seventy-fifth year, as appears from the Depositions just referred to. He left at least four sons, namely: 1, Barnaby, who was living at Harold's Grange, near Rathfarnham, in 1641, and who is named in the list of Wicklow Rebels in the manuscript Depositions; 2, Donough, a Lieutenant-Colonel of the Confederate Catholics; 3, Christopher, a Major in the same service; and, 4, Turlough.

The Editor has not been able to trace his descendants to a later period. Two families of the O'Tooles settled in the county of Wexford, where they still inherit property. The head of the more distinguished of these families, in the last century, was Laurence O'Toole, Esq., of Buckstown and Fairfield, in the county of

on one occasion in his prison in Dublin, when they formed a mutual friendship with each other. The messenger proceeded to the place where Felim was, and stated to him the embassy on which he came. Felim was glad at his arrival, and promised that he would do all the good he could for Hugh; but his friends and kindred did not allow him to conceal him, from fear of the English govern-

Wexford. This Laurence, who was born in 1722, served in the Irish Brigade in France, and died in 1794, and was buried at Killilly, near Castle-Talbot, county of Wexford. He married, 1, a Margaret Masterson, of Castletown and Monaseed, in the county of Wexford, and had by her Colonel Count John O'Toole, of the French service, who was considered the handsomest man in Paris before the first revolution. He died at Ballinafad, near Gorey, about twenty-five years ago. This Count John O'Toole married Lady Catherine Annesley, daughter of the last Earl of Anglesea, and had by her Laurenzo O'Toole, Esq., who married a Miss Hall, of Holly-bush, Derbyshire, an heiress of very large fortune, by whom he had a son, Lorenzo O'Toole, who succeeded to his mother's property, which is worth about £20,000 per annum, and changed his name to Hall.

By his first marriage he had, 2, Luke, who was in the French service, and was guillotined at the Revolution, leaving one daughter, whose fate is unknown to the family; 3, Laurence, who settled in the Isle de Bourbon, where he married the daughter of the Governor, and died there, leaving a son now (1847) living in the island of Maida; 4, Edward, who served with Lord Rodney, but no account of him has reached his family for the last sixty years. He had also three daughters, who married, and have left issue, the third of whom, Mary, married William Talbot, Esq., of Castle Talbot, who died in 1796, by whom she had issue five sons, Matthew, William, Roger, and Laurence, and three daughters; 1, Maria Theresa, who married John, now Earl of Shrewsbury; 2, Juliana, who married Major Bishopp; and 3, Margaret, who married Colonel Bryan, of Jenkinstown.

Laurence O'Toole, Esq., the father of Count John, married, secondly, Eliza, second daughter of William Talbot, Esq., of Ballynamona, in the county of Wexford, and had by her; 1, William, who was in the Irish Brigade in France, and died, unmarried, in 1798; 2, Matthew, who was in the French service, which he left at the Revolution, and afterwards, in 1798, in Baron Hompesch's [Hessian] Hussars, and died about 1806; leaving by his wife, Frances Tighe of Warfield; 1, Matthew, Captain of 82nd regiment, now (1847) aged about forty-five; 2, Edward, now in India; and three daughters.

The third son of Laurence O'Toole, by his second marriage, was Brian O'Toole, who was a Lieutenant-Colonel in the British service, Commander of the Bath, Grand Cross of the Tower and Sword (Portugal), Cross of Merit (England), Cross of St. Louis and St. Lazare (France), Colonel of Portuguese Caçadores in the Peninsular war. He died at Fairfield, in the county of Wexford, *sine prole*, in February, 1825, and was interred at Piercestown, in the barony of Forth, where a monument was erected to his memory by his relative. John Hyacinth Talbot, Esq. of Talbot Hall, late M. P. for New Ross. 4, Andrew O'Toole, who served in the *Armée des Princes*, and died of fatigue, *sine prole*. Lawrence had also several daughters, two of whom, unmarried, are still living at Fairfield, near Wexford.

The late William Toole, Esq. of Edermine, near Enniscorthy, was the head of the second branch of the Wexford O'Tooles. He married a Miss Hatchell, and had issue: 1, Laurence

na ngall. Ro fſ iaroṁ forra a ḃfiṫrium isin coilleaḋ aṁail atruḃramar, ⁊ ro cuas leó for a iarair .i. lár an luċt atċualaiġ a ḃſiṫ isin ffiodḃaḋ, ⁊ do léiccitt co na luircc for a foilleaċt. O Rob erdalta lá feilim a faġḃáil, as í coṁairle do do róine sium ⁊ a ḃráiṫri iad badéin dia ſirġaḃáil ⁊ a ḃreiṫ do cum an tſnaḋ gus an ccaṫraiġ for ccúlaiḃ dorídisi. Do gníṫ saṁlaiḋ. O rainicc siḋe co haṫ cliaṫ, Robtar ruḃaiġe an coṁairle dia roċtain ċuca, ⁊ do rónsat neffní ⁊ bríġ mbicc don uile ġall ⁊ aittiri oile ro elaiḋſet uadaiḃ. Ro cuireaḋ isin ccarcair ċéḋna do riḋisi é ⁊ do brſta ġſimel ġlaisiarainn fóa feiḃ as cuimge conrangattar, ⁊ ro boṫ occá friṫaire ⁊ occá forċoiṁéd aṁail as deaċ ro ḟéosat. Ro clos go coitċionn fó crić nereann a elúdsoṁ saṁlaiḋ, ⁊ a ſirġaḃáil doriḋisi, ⁊ ro la soċt mór for ġaoiḋealaiḃ de siḋe.

AOIS CRIOST, 1591.

Aois Criost, mile, cuicc céd, noċatt, a haon.

O Ruairc brian (.i. brian na múrṫa) mac briain mic eoccain do ionnarbaḋ (aṁail do scriobaḋ tuas) i ttir conuill gus na tuaṫaiḃ, ⁊ baoí tuilleaḋ ar ḃliaḋain i ffoċair Mhec suiḃne eóġan ócc. Do ċóiḋ iar sin co halbain ar dáiġ caoṁna nó coṁḟurtaċta dfaġḃáil ó ríġ alban. Rugsat drong do ṁuintir na bainrioġna fair, ⁊ do bearat leó é go Saxain ⁊ co lonndain, ⁊ baí lé haṫaiḋ illaiṁ ann sin go térma na saṁna ar ccionn. Ro cuireaḋ

Toole, Esq. of Edermine, who sold Edermine to Sir John Power, Bart. of Roebuck, and died *sine prole*; 2, William Toole, Captain of the 40th Regiment, J. P., county of Wexford, now living. He possesses a small estate in the barony of Shelmaliere.

g *The English Government*, literally, "the control of the law of the English." Doctor O'Conor, in his suppressed work, *Memoirs of Charles O'Conor of Belanagare*, p. 107, says that O'Toole assured him of his protection, recommending to him, however, to lie quiet in the wood, as his giving him public protection, so near Dublin, would give umbrage to Government.

h *Great gloom*, soċt mór.—Dr. O'Conor expresses it thus:

"O'Donnell was again shut up in the Castle of Dublin, where he was loaded with irons; and his escape and the manner of his recommittal convulsed the minds of his exasperated countrymen with the alternate agitations of grief, indignation, and despair."—*Memoirs, &c.*, p. 107.

It may be here observed that it was the *after celebrity* of Hugh Roe that caused this overdrawn account of the sympathy of the Irish people with him to be written; because the senior sept of Con O'Donnell, and their adherents, would have rejoiced at seeing him cut off.

i *Brian na Murtha, son of Brian.*—Charles O'Conor of Belanagare adds, *inter lineas*, that Brian na Murtha was the son of Brian Ballagh;

ment[g]. These learned that he was in the wood, as we have said, and they (i. e. the people who had heard that he was in the wood) went in search of him, and dispersed with their troops to track him. When it was clear to Felim that he [Hugh] would be discovered, he and his kinsmen resolved to seize upon him themselves, and bring him back to the Council in the city. This was accordingly done. When he [Hugh] arrived in Dublin, the Council were rejoiced at his return to them; for they made nothing or light of all the other prisoners and hostages that had escaped from them. He was again put into the same prison, and iron fetters were put upon him as tightly as possible; and they watched and guarded him as well as they could. His escape, thus attempted, and his recapture, became known throughout the land of Ireland, at which [tidings] a great gloom[h] came over the Irish people.

THE AGE OF CHRIST, 1591.

The Age of Christ, one thousand five hundred ninety-one.

O'Rourke, i. e. Brian-na-Murtha, the son of Brian[i], son of Owen, was banished, as stated before, into the Tuatha in Tirconnell, where he remained upwards of a year with Mac Sweeny (Owen Oge). After that he passed into Scotland, in hopes of obtaining protection or assistance from the King of Scotland. A party of the Queen's people, [however], took him prisoner, and carried him into England and into London, where he remained for some time[k] in prison, [i. e.] until the ensuing November Term. The law was urged against him[l], and

and that Owen, the father of Brian Ballagh, was the son of Tiernan, son of Teige, son of Tiernan More.

[k] *For some time*, lé hachaid.—This phrase is redundant, and should be left out, i. e. it is an error of construction, not an idiomatic redundance of the language.

[l] *The law was urged against him.*—An English writer would say, he was tried according to the English law. The following account of his trial and death is given in a manuscript History of Ireland, preserved in the Library of the Royal Irish Academy, p. 452:

"Bryan O'Rourke, the Irish potentate, being thus, by the King of Scotts, sent into England, was arraigned in Westminsterhall: his indictments were, that he had stirred Alexander Mac Connell, and others; had scornfully dragged the Queen's picture att a horse-taile and disgracefully cut the same in pieces; giving the Spaniards entertainment, against a proclamation; fier'd many houses, &c. This being told him by an interpreter (for he understood noe English), he said he would not submit himself to a tryall of twelve men, nor make answer, except the Queen satt in person to judge him.

dlicceadh fair go ro daoradh dó cum báis. Ro crochadh ro dícendadh 7 do rónadh cethramhna de iaramh. Ro badh do mhóirsgélaibh gaoidheal oidheadh an Bhriain hísin, uair ní thainicc dia bhunadh freimh ó chéin mháir neach no dearsccaighfedh de de ar dearlaccadh ar dhígeineach ar dhuasaibh duanmholta ar chaithemh ar chongháir ar aobhdhacht ar foirtine ar chothuccadh cathlaithrighe ag imdhídhen a athardha ar ainffine eachtrand có a oidheadh don chur sin.

Murchadh mac Conchobhair mic Toirrdhealbhaigh, mic Taidhcc, mic Toirrdhealbhaigh, mic Briain catha an aonaigh uí Bhriain décc i ccathair Mionáin 25 Februarii, 7 a adhnacal hi cCill Fhionnabhrach.

Mairgreg ingean Domhnaill mic Conchobhair, mic Toirrdhealbhaigh, mic Taidhcc, mic Toirrdhealbhaigh mic Briain catha an aonaigh uí Bhriain, ben Toirrdhealbhaigh mic Briain mic Donnchaidh mec Mathghamhna do écc hi cCill mec Dubhain, 7 a hadhnacal i nInis Cathaigh 7 a derbhshiur ele .i. aine ben Toirrdhealbhaigh ruaidh mic Taidhcc mic Murchaidh mic Taidhcc ruaidh mec Mathghamhna do écc.

Donnchadh mac Murchaidh ruaidh, mic Briain, mic Taidhcc, mic Toirrdhealbhaigh, mic Briain catha an aonaigh do écc .8. Februarii.

The lord chief Justice made answer againe, by an interpreter, that whether he would submitt himself or not to a tryall by a jury of twelve, he should be judged by law, according to the particulars alledjed against him. Whereto he replied nothing, but 'if it must be soe, let it be soe.' Being condemned to die, he was shortly after carried unto Tyburne, to be executed as a traitor, whereat he seemed to be nothing moved, scorning the archbishop of Caishill (Miler Magrath), who was there to counsill him for his soule's health, because he had broken his vow, from a Franciscan turning Protestant."

Lord Bacon says in his Essays, that O'Rourke "gravely petitioned the Queen, that he might be hanged with a gad, or withe, after his own country fashion, which doubtless was readily granted him." And P. O'Sullevan Beare, *Hist. Cathol. Iber.*, fol. 122, says that, being asked, why he did not bow his knee to the Queen? he answered, that he was not used to bow. "How! not to images," says an English Lord. "Aye," says O'Rourke; "but there is a great difference between your Queen and the images of the saints." Walker, in his Irish Bards, gives an account of an extraordinary interview between O'Rourke and Queen Elizabeth, the truth of which Mr. Hardiman attempts to corroborate in his *Irish Minstrelsy*, vol. ii. p. 427; but it seems totally groundless, or, at least, to rest on no solid evidence. Dr. O'Conor, who was the ninth in descent from this Brian O'Rourke, has the following note on his execution in the *Memoirs of the Life and Writings of Charles O'Conor of Belanagare*, p. 112:

"The only crime which O'Rourke could be accused of was, his having received under his roof some shipwrecked Spaniards; men whom the most hardened barbarity would scarcely consider as enemies. A little before his execution Miler Magrath, appointed Archbishop of Cashel, was sent to him, to prevail on him to conform. 'No,' said O'Rorke, 'but do you remember the dignity from which you have fallen:

he was condemned to death. He was afterwards hanged, beheaded, and quartered. The death of this Brian was one of the mournful stories of the Irish, for there had not been for a long time any one of his tribe who excelled him in bounty, in hospitality, in giving rewards for panegyrical poems, in sumptuousness, in [numerous] troops, in comeliness[m], in firmness, in maintaining the field of battle to defend his patrimony against foreign adventurers, [for all which he was celebrated], until his death on this occasian.

Murrough, the son of Conor, son of Turlough, son of Teige, son of Turlough, son of Brian Chatha-an-Aenaigh O'Brien, died at Cathair-Mionain[n], on the 25th of February, and was interred at Kilfenora.

Margaret, the daughter of Donnell, son of Conor, son of Turlough, son of Teige, son of Turlough, son of Brian Chatha-an-Aenaigh O'Brien, and wife of Turlough, the son of Brian, son of Donough Mac Mahon, died at Cill-Mic-Dubhain[o], and was interred in Inis-Catha; and her sister, Aine, the wife of Turlough Roe, son of Teige, son of Murrough, son of Teige Roe Mac Mahon, died.

Donough, the son of Murrough Roe, son of Brian, son of Teige, son of Turlough, son of Brian Chatha-an-Aenaigh, died on the 8th of February.

return into the bosom of the ancient Church, and learn from my fortitude that lesson, which you ought to have been the last on earth to disavow.'" See also Lombard, *de Hib. Comment.*, p. 344; and the Abbe Mageoghegan's *Histoire d'Irelande*, tom. iii. p. 480.

The family of O'Rourke seems to have been the proudest and most inflexible of all the Irish race. On the 15th of June, 1576, Sir Brian O'Rourke, chief of the Western Breifny, and other Irish chiefs, waited, at Dublin, upon the Lord Deputy, Sir Henry Sidney, who says of O'Rourke: "And first of Owrycke, I found hym the proudest man that ever I dealt with in Ireland."—See *Letters of Sir Henry Sidney*, vol. i. p. 114. It is curious to see how this fallen Irish family has found its proud level in the present Prince O'Rourke of Russia.

[m] *Comeliness.*—Walker, in his *Irish Bards*, and Hardiman, in his *Irish Minstrelsy*, vol. ii. p. 427, assert that Queen Elizabeth was struck with the noble deportment and manly beauty of O'Rourke, had apartments assigned to him in her palace, and intimated to her Council, that she wished herself, privately, to examine him as to the affairs of Ireland; but the Editor has not been able to findany authority for this assertion.

[n] *Cathair-Mionain*, now Caherminane, a townland in the parish of Killelagh, barony of Corcomroe, and county of Clare. In the Description of the County of Clare, preserved in the Library of Trinity College, Dublin, E. 2. 14, "Cahirmenayn Castle" is mentioned as the possession of Teige Mac Murrough [O'Brien], and placed in the "Baronie of Tuogh-Morey-Conor, or Corkemroe."

[o] *Cill-Mic-Dubhain*, i. e. the church of Mac

Uilliam búrc mac Sfain, mic óiluerair, mic Sfain do marbad le duine uaral dá lucht lfnamna fin .i. lé hulartrann mac aodha buide mec domnaill.

Mac mec uilliam búrc .i. uatér na mbuillfb mac Riocaird mic Sfain an tfrmainn, mic maoílir do marbad ar ionnsaighid oidhce lá druing dia commbraithrib gaoil ⁊ gfinealaigh fin, ⁊ lá cuid do cloinn ndomnaill.

O baoighill toirrdhealbach ruadh mac neill, mic toirrdhelbaigh, aén bá dearrccaighthe tainic dia bunadh fnfim ó chfin máir port congmala dáin ⁊ deórad fir médaighthe nfimfo eccailsi ⁊ ealadan, Guaire a cheneoil ar fele ⁊ eineach, Tógbálaigh tróg ⁊ annfann do écc ina longport fin pó féil brighde, ⁊ a adhnacal co nonoir i ndun na ngall i nothairlighe a sinnsior.

AOIS CRIOST, 1592.

Aois Criost, mile, cuicc céd, nochat, a dó.

O conchobair ruadh tadcc óce mac taidcc buide, mic cathail ruaidh do chrochadh ar Session Rosa comain i mí ianuarii tria cionntaibh a chloinne bάttar for fogail ⁊ for dibfircc i nacchaidh corona saxan, ⁊ ar amlaidh baoísiom an tan sin arraidh anfann, dírадаirc ge do fuair a oidheadh amlaidh sin.

Mac diarmada maighe luircc brian mac Ruaidhri mic taidcc mic diarmada décc i mí nouember, ⁊ ro ba móide dadbar éccaoine écc an fir sin gan a chosmailfs do bfith do chloinn Maolruanaidh do ghébadh cfnnus dia eisi.

Mac conmara riabhach tighearna an taoibhe toir do cloinn cuiléin .i. domnall

---

Dubhain, now Maguane. The name is now anglicised Kilmacaduane, which is that of a church and parish in the barony of Moyarta, and county of Clare. This church is mentioned in the Life of St. Senan (published by Colgan, at 1st March, c. 44), as subject to the monastery of Inis Cathaigh, now Scattery Island, in the Shannon, near the town of Kilrush. Of the old church called Cill Mic Dubhain, the east gable and twenty-five feet of the length of the side walls still remain.

[p] *Of the Termon*, i. e. of the Termon of Balla, in the barony of Carra, and county of Mayo.—See *Genealogies, Tribes, &c., of Hy-Fiachrach*, pp. 157, 197.

[q] *Guaire.*—Guaire Aidhne was King of Connaught for thirteen years, and died in the year 662. He became the personification of generosity among the Irish poets.—See *Genealogies, Tribes, &c. of Hy-Fiachrach*, p. 391.

[r] *His own fortress.*—Besides the seats which O'Boyle had in his own territory of Boylagh, he had a castle called Baile Ui Bhaoighill, now Ballyweel, on the north side of the River Esk,

William Burke, the son of John, son of Oliver, son of John, was slain by a gentleman of his own followers, namely, by Alexander, the son of Hugh Boy Mac Donnell.

The son of Mac William Burke, namely, Walter of the Blows, the son of Rickard, son of John of the Termon[p], son of Myler, was slain, in an assault at night, by a party of his own tribe and kinsmen, and some of the Clann-Donnell.

O'Boyle (Turlough Roe, the son of Niall, son of Turlough), the most distinguished man that had come of his tribe for a long time, a sustaining pillar of the learned and the destitute, an exalter of sanctuaries, churches, and science, the Guaire[q] of his tribe in generosity and hospitality, [and] the supporter of the poor and the feeble, died at his own fortress[r], about the festival of St. Bridget, and was interred with honour at Donegal, in the burial-place of his ancestors.

THE AGE OF CHRIST, 1592.

The Age of Christ, one thousand five hundred ninety-two.

O'Conor Roe (Teige Oge, son of Teige Boy, son of Cathal Roe) was hanged at the session of Roscommon, in the month of January, for the crimes of his sons, who were [engaged] in plunder and insurrection against the crown of England; and he was at this time aged, feeble, and blind, though he suffered death[s] in this manner.

Mac Dermot of Moylurg (Brian, the son of Rory, son of Teige, son of Dermot) died in the month of November; and the death of this man was the more to be lamented, because there was no other like him of the Clann-Mulrony[t] to succeed him in the chieftainship.

Mac Namara Reagh, Lord of the western part of Clann-Cuilein, i. e. Donnell

near its mouth, opposite the monastery of Donegal. On a map of the coasts of Mayo, Sligo, and Donegal, preserved in the State Papers' Office, London, this castle is shewn in the above situation under the name of "Ba. O Boile," which is intended for Bally O'Boil, or O'Boyle's town.

[s] *Suffered death*, literally, "found or got his death in that manner."

[t] *The Clann-Mulrony.*—This was the tribe-name of the Mac Dermotts of Moylurg, in the county of Roscommon. The Mulrony from whom they descend was an O'Connor, and as the Mac Dermots asserted, the senior of all the Clann-Conor.

riabaċ mac conmſḋa, mic donnchaiḋ, mic Ruaiḋri, mic meccon ċſnnṁóir décc 11 Februarii fear caiṫmeaċ congaireaċ, dearlaicṫeċ, daonnaċtaċ eiride.

Duine uasal do ṡiol aoḋa décc isin mí ċéona .i. Sſan na nGſimleaċ mac conmara mic maṫġamna, mic aoḋa.

Mór inġſn donnchaiḋ, mic Sſain, mic maolruanaiḋ na féróicce mic taiḋcc uí cſrḃaill, bſn ṁſic uí ḃriain ara do écc, bſn ro ċaiṫ a haimsir co maiṫ, ⁊ do faccaiḃ an saoġal gan aṫais gan imḋearccaḋ.

Caitilín inġſn doṁnaill, mic fingin, mic diarmada an dúnaiḋ még carṫaiġ bſn taiḋcc mic corbmaic óicc, mic corbmaic, mic taiḋcc még carṫaig, bſn ċeillig, craibdeaċ dercaċ, deiġeiniġ do écc iar mbuaiḋ ó ḋſṁan, ó ḋoṁan, ⁊ ó daoinib.

Mac uí ṁeaċair Sſan an ġlſnda mac tomais décc.

Ḃurcaiġ Rainn mec uilliam uile co na luċt lſnaṁna ḋo ḋol ar a ccoiṁétt ⁊ iar ffios sccél don goberrnóir Sir Risderd bingam do ċóiḋ i cconntaé maiġe eó go mbáttar bailte an tire slán ⁊ ḃriste ar a ċumas .i. dún na

[u] *Maccon Ceannmhor*, i. e. Maccon of the Big Head.

[x] *Warlike.*—The adjective conġaireaċ denotes "having troops or companies." See the year 1598, where conġáir, the substantive from which this adjective is formed, is used in the sense of "troop or company of men."

[y] *Son of Hugh.*—In a manuscript, transcribed by Maurice Newby in 1715, now in the possession of Myles John O'Reilly, Esq., the pedigree of this Hugh is given as follows:

"Hugh, son of Philip, son of Cumara, son of Loughlin, son of Maccon, son of Loughlin, son of Cumeadha Mor, the stirpes of all the Sil-Aedha, son of John, son of Maccon, son of Loughlin, son of Cumeadha, son of Niall, son of Cumara, son of Donnell, son of Cumara, the progenitor from whom the Mac Namaras have derived their surname. The John na nGeimhleach in the text was the ancestor of the Mac Namaras of Moyreask, in the county of Clare. He had a son, John Reagh, who had a son Donnough, who died at Achadh-na-Croise, or Crossfield, in the county of Leitrim, on the 4th of February, 1696, in the eightieth year of his age. He had two daughters, Finola, who was married to Teige O'Rody, of Fenagh, in the county of Leitrim, and Mary, who married Murtough, son of Donnell, son of Turlough O'Brien; and three sons: 1, John, his heir, who died in the county of Clare, on the 23rd of September, 1694. 2, Donough, a most accomplished linguist, musician, and poet, who died at Moyreask, in the county of Clare, on the 16th of July, 1692, in the thirty-fifth year of his age. 3, Mahon, who had a daughter, Mary, who lived with her aunt, Finola, the wife of Teige O'Rody of Crossfield, from the year 1692, when she was eight years old, till 1701, when she was married, in her seventeenth year, to Calvagh, the son of Turlough, son of Niall Oge, son of Niall O'Melaghlin. There is a curious poem, in English, on the death of Donough, the second son of Donough above mentioned, by Teige O'Rody, in which he gives the date of his death in the following quatrain:

Reagh, the son of Cumeadha, son of Donough, son of Rory, son of Maccon Ceannmhor[u], died on the 11th of February. He was a sumptuous, warlike[x], bountiful, and humane man.

In the same month a gentleman of the Sil-Aedha died, i.e. John-na-nGeimhleach, son of Cumara, son of Mahon, son of Hugh[y] [Mac Namara].

More, the daughter of Donough, son of John, son of Mulrony-na-Feasoige, son of Teige O'Carroll, and wife of Mac-I-Brien Ara, died. She had spent a good life, and departed this world without disgrace or reproach.

Catherine, the daughter of Donnell, son of Fineen, son of Dermot-an-Duna Mac Carthy, and wife of Teige, the son of Cormac Oge, son of Cormac, son of Teige Mac Carthy, a sensible, pious, charitable, and truly hospitable woman, died, after having gained the victory over the world, the Devil, and the people.

The son of O'Meagher (John of the Glen, the son of Thomas) died.

All the Burkes, of Mac William's country, with their followers, went on their defence; and when the Governor, Sir Richard Bingham, had received intelligence of this, he proceeded into the county of Mayo, and all the castles of the country, both perfect and broken, were in his power, namely, Dun-na-mona[z],

"Thy living Vatican, poor Ireland! now is dead,
Thy records sleep in their eternal bed;
One thousand years, six hundred, ninety-two,
June the sixteenth most fatall was to you."

He also composed the following epitaph for him, which was probably inscribed on his tomb; but it is not now in the abbey of Quin:

"Donatus junior, Donati Mara Joannis,
Conditur hoc busto, pro dolor! exiguo.
Hic tenuit quicquid claris ab origine Mundi,
Mandarat fastis tristis Ierna suis.
Hispanus, Gallus, Græcus, præclarus Hibernus,
Anglus et Hebræus conditur hoc tumulo,
Musicus atque sophus logus hâc Theo conditur urna,
Scrutator Thomæ, Scoti, et Aristotelis."

To this Maurice Newby, who seems to have been acquainted with Donatus junior, appends the following memorandum:

"This said gentleman died at Mureske, in the county of Clare, on Thursday, June 16°, 1692; was buried in Quinn Abbey; was bred with Mr. Thady Roddy from a Virgilian; acquired all the above languages by his indefatigable studies and profound witt; spoke French and Spanish; read Greek and Hebrew; was most perfect in Latin, and compleat master of the Irish."

The last of this branch of the Mac Namaras was John Mac Namara, of Moyreask, Esq., who died about twenty years since. He had married a Miss De Burgh, by whom he had an only daughter, who married Daniel O'Brien, of Cratloe, Esq. His brother, Francis Mac Namara, died, s. p. in 1813.

[z] *Dun-na-mona*, now Dunamona, a townland containing the ruins of a castle, situated near the boundary of the parishes of Rosslee and Drum, in the barony of Carra. This castle belonged to a branch of the O'Kellys, who removed from Hy-Many and settled here un-

móna, cúil na ccairiol, an ġaoirícteaċ, ⁊ an cluainín. Tuccsat búrcaiġ ionnsaiġiḋ ar an ngobernóir co cúil na ccairiol, ⁊ ro baḋ ḋioġḃálaiġ iad féin ag filleaḋ dóiḃ iná an gobernóir. Ro ċuir an gobernóir iar sin féḋnaca troma do buanaḋaiḃ gallda ⁊ gaoiḋealċa diarraiḋ na mbúrcaċ sin báttar for díḃfeirc ⁊ for foġail fó ċennoḋaiḃ cnoc cennoġarḃ, ⁊ ċoillteiḃ ndorsaċ ndlúit-aiṁréiḋ. Nír ḃó cian ro ḃáttar for an iarraiḋ sin an tan ro ḟuiḋriot gur an ngobernóir go líon creaċ ⁊ gaḃál, go mbraiġdiḃ ban ⁊ fer, co mbuaiḃ, ⁊ co ccaiplíḃ iomḋaiḃ. Tangatar búrcaiġ iar sin fo ḃréiṫ an gobernora acht mac deṁain an ċorráin .i. Risderd mac Riocaird. Ro ḟealḃaiġ an gobernóir bailte an tíre ḋó féin a huġdarrás an ṗrionnsa, ⁊ ro ḟaccaiḃ Seón binggam, ⁊ bandaḋa uaḋa féin agá niomċoiṁétt.

Aoḋ ruaḋ mac aoḋa, mic maġnusa uí ḋoṁnaill baí siḋe i ccarcair, ⁊ i ccuimreaċ in áṫ cliaṫ iarr an ccéḋna héluḋ go geiṁreḋ na bliaḋna so. A mbáttar ann i nurṫosaċ oiḋċe (eirrium ⁊ a aes cumṫa .i. clann uí neill .i. Sean enri ⁊ art) fuaratar ell forr na coiṁéḋaiġiḃ riariú do rata isin bproinntiġ go ro ḃenratt a ngeimle ḋíoḃ. Do ċóttar iaroṁ gur an ffiail-teaċ, ⁊ téd réiḋ síoṫfoda leó co ro leiccit sios lar na ruainemnaiḃ triar an ffiailtiġ co riaċtattar an cclasaiġ comdoṁain baí i ttimċell an cair-

der the Lower Mac William. According to Duald Mac Firbis's genealogical work (Lord Roden's copy), p. 324, this castle was built by Henry Reagh O'Kelly, (the son of Edmond, son of David, son of John, Airchinneach, or Erenagh of Tuam, son of Melaghlin, son of William, son of Hugh, son of Donnell, son of Loughlin, son of Donnell More, son of Teige Tailltenn), head of that sept of the O'Kelly's called Clann-an-Airchinnigh, who settled in Carra in the time of Edmond-na-Feasoige Mac William Burke; and it remained in the possession of the family for four generations, that is, from the time of Henry Reagh, the first erector, down to Walter (son of David, son of Myler, son of Henry Reagh), who was the last inheritor. Henry Reagh, the builder of the castle of Dun-na-mona, had a nephew, William (son of David, son of Edmond), who also lived under the Lower Mac William Burke, in Carra, and who made the road called Bothar-na-faine. According to the tradition in the country, the O'Kellys of Dun-na-mona removed to Tiranare, in the barony of Burrishoole, where they still remain. The following inscription is to be seen on the tombstone of this family, in the abbey of Burrishoole:

"ORATE PRO ANIMA DAVIDIS OGE KELLY, QUI ME FIERI FECIT SIBI ET HEREDIBUS SUIS, ET UXORIS MABLA BARRET. A. D. 1623."

From Walter, the last inheritor of Dun-na-mona, the late Rev. Walter Kelly, O. S. A., of the convent of Ballyhaunis, in the county of Mayo, was the fifth in descent. David Oge, mentioned in the above inscription, was the son of David, and brother of Walter. He had a son, Walter Grana, who had a son, Patrick, who had a son, Walter, a priest; a daughter, Sarah, the grandmother of the Rev. Walter Kelly, who was pater-

Cuil-na-gCaisiol, Gaoisideach[a], and Cluainin[b]. The Burkes made an attack upon the Governor at Cuil-na-gCaisiol[c]; but they were more harmed on their return than the Governor. After this the Governor dispatched heavy troops of English and Irish soldiers to search for the Burkes, who were in rebellion and [engaged in] plundering, on the rugged mountain-tops, and in the bushy dense and intricate woods. They [the soldiers] had not been long in this search, when they returned to the Governor with many preys and spoils, with prisoners, [both] women and men, and with many cows and horses. After this, [all] the Burkes, except the son of Deamhan-an-Chorrain, namely, Richard, the son of Rickard[d], came and submitted to the award of the Governor; upon which the Governor, by authority of the Sovereign, took the castles of the country into his own possession, and left John Bingham and companies of his own [soldiers] to guard them.

Hugh Roe, the son of Hugh, son of Manus O'Donnell, remained in Dublin, in prison and in chains, after his first escape, to the winter of this year. One evening he and his companions, Henry and Art, the sons of O'Neill (John), before they had been brought[e] into the refection house, took an advantage of the keepers, and knocked off their fetters. They afterwards went to the privy-house, having with them a very long rope, by the loops of which they let themselves down through the privy-house, until they reached the deep trench that

nally descended from Walter, the last inheritor of the castle of Dun-na-mona. Thus: Walter, son of John, son of Patrick, son of Walter, son of David, son of Walter, the last proprietor of Dun-na-mona, son of David, son of Myler, son of Henry Reagh, the founder of this castle.

[a] *Gaoisideach*, now Gweeshadan, a castle in ruins in the parish of Drum, in the barony of Carra.—*Hy-Fiachrach*, p. 491.

[b] *Cluainin*, i. e. the little lawn or meadow, now Clooneen, a townland containing the ruins of a castle in the parish of Kilmore, in the said barony of Carra.

[c] *Cuil-na-gCaisiol*.—This name is translated *angulum murorum* by P. O'Sullevan Beare. It is now corruptly written Cloonagashel, and sometimes Cloona Castle, which is applied to a townland in the parish of Ballinrobe, barony of Kilmaine, and county of Mayo. According to the tradition in the country, Sir Richard Bingham murdered sixteen women of the Burke family in this castle.

[d] *Richard*.—Sir Henry Docwra calls him, "Riccard Bourke, *alias* the Divell's Hook's sonne." Dockwra says, that "these men uppon their submission were so pyned awaye ffor wante of ffoode, and soe ghasted with feare, within seven or eight weeks, by reason they were so roundlye ffollowed without any interim of rest, that they looked rayther like to ghosts then men."—*Relation of Services, &c. by Sir Bingham*, Mus. Brit. Harl., No. 357, fol. 235.

[e] *Before they had been brought, rectè*, "before the hour for going to dinner or supper had arrived."

teoil. Ro dringsit iaramh fris an mbruaċ alltaraċ go mbáttar for ur na clasaċ. Baoí giolla tairisi ag taṫaiġiḋe ċuca ⁊ uaḋaiḃ, ⁊ ro léicsiot a rún fris, ⁊ do rala ċuca an tan sin é co mbaoí ag dénaṁ eolais dóiḃ. Lottar

^f^ *Until.*—This construction is redundant. The probability is that they were hauled up, by means of the rope, from the trench by the trusty servant sent to conduct them. Cox had no knowledge of the recommittal of the son of O'Donnell. He writes that in December, 1590, "four considerable prisoners escaped out of the castle of Dublin, not without the privity of a great man, well bribed, as was supposed, viz.: the two sons of Shane O'Neal, O'Donell's son, and Philip O'Reilly; but the weather being very bad, and the journey tedious, Art O'Neal, one of the prisoners, dyed by the way, but the rest escaped to Ulster, where the two sons of Shane O'Neal fell into the power and possession of the Earl of Tyrone, *anno* 1594, who kept them prisoners, and would by no means enlarge them, or deliver them to the Deputy."—*Hib. Angl.*, vol. i. p. 400.

^g^ *Visiting them*, literally, "was frequenting to them and from them," i. e. he was used to bring messages to them, and to bear messages from them to their friends. According to the Life of Hugh Roe O'Donnell, by Cucogry O'Clery, this youth was named Turlough Roe O'Hogan, i. e. O'Hagan. He was Tyrone's servant of trust, employed on this occasion to bribe the Lord Deputy, Fitz-William, for allowing the prisoners to escape. Tyrone's object in procuring the liberation of these prisoners was twofold; first, to obtain the assistance of his promising brother-in-law, Hugh Roe O'Donnell, and to get Shane O'Neill's legitimate sons into his own hands, that it might not be in the power of the Government to set them up as his rivals in his premeditated rebellion. Doctor O'Conor, in his suppressed work, *Memoirs of the Life and Writings of Charles O'Conor of Belanagare*, says that one of their keepers assisted them in this escape; but his account of the manner of their escape is drawn almost wholly from his own imagination. The following account of it is given by P. O'Sullevan Beare, who also appears to have invented a few incidents, to give interest to the narrative; but it is quite evident that neither the O'Clerys, nor O'Sullevan, nor Hugh Roe himself, knew the secret practices of Hugh, Earl of Tyrone, who bribed the corrupt Lord Deputy Fitz-William, to get these prisoners into his own hands:

"Paucis post diebus ex Vltoniorum obsidibus Hugo Odonellus Ruber, Daniel Macsuinnius Cœruleus, & Huon Ogallachur, de quibus superius locuti sumus, ex arce Dubhlinnensi fugiunt. Cæterum Ruber in Felmium Otuehilem equitem Ibernum, & Reginæ ministros incidit. Felmius statuit eum inuitis regijs ministris dimittere, haud dubius se fortunarum iacturam facturum, & in discrimen venturum. Quod malum timens Rosa Nituehil Felmij soror, & Fiachi Obruinis vxor, fratri persuasit, vt suæ, atque Rubri simul saluti consuleret: idque illum facturum, si ea nocte Rubrum apud se retineret in Kehino Castello (caislean Kehin, *recte* Caislean Caoiṁġin) donec a marito suo Fiacho cum armatis veniente, quasi inuito Felmio in libertatem asseratur, nam magis fratri cauendum censuit, quam marito qui iam solitus erat rebellare, vitamque contra Protestantes, & pro eorum hostibus vouere. Quo consilio probato, Fiachus cum armata manu Rubro opitulatum contendit. Prorex quoque Dubhlinnæ certior factus cohortem mittit, quæ Rubrum vinctum trahat. Ea nocte tam copiosè pluit, vt aqua ripas inteiecti fluminis egrediente, circumiectosque campos inundante nullo modo potuerit Fiachus vada

was around the castle. They climbed the outer side, until they were[f] on the margin of the trench. A certain faithful youth, who was in the habit of visiting them[g], and to whom they had communicated their secret, came to them at this

traijcere. Interim Angli, qui flumine non prohibebantur, Rubrum Dubhlinnam deferunt. Vbi in eadem arce diligentiori custodiæ mandatur, in vincula quoque coniectus. Iterum diebus [*recte*, mensibus] aliquot transactis cum Henrico, & Arto Onellis Iohannis principis filijs, qui eodem carcere tenebantur agit, quemadmodum sese in libertatem vindicent. Quod etiam consilium cum Eduardo Eustatio puero amico suo, & cum acerrimo Protestantium hoste Fiacho communicat. Eduardus puer se illi ad fugam daturum quatuor equos pollicetur. Fiachus itineris ducem, qui illum domum suam ad Muluriam syluam ducat, & inde in Vltoniam a se incolumem mittendum promittit. Ad constitutam noctem Ruber limam comparauit, qua vinculorum clauos sibi, Henrico & Arto scidit, & sericam telam longissimam, qua se dimitterent ex arcis celsæ fastigio. Intempesta nocte superiore telæ extremitate ad latrinam ligata, Henricus primus capta tela manibus, & inter crura per latrinam descendit, nec socios spectans in Vltoniam itinere arrepto incolumis euasit. Sequitur Ruber, qui Artum spectauit. Artus, dum præceps per telam fertur, lapide ex cloaca forte cadente, malè vexatur, vixque se sustinendo est aptus. Eduardus puer, qui equos promiserat, quatuor velocissimos ephippijs instructos per tres proximos antè dies in stabulo habebat, sed illo die eo inscio peregrè ablati sunt ab amico. Itineris dux a Fiacho missus propè arcem præstolabatur, qui ea nocte, dieque sequente Rubrum, & Artum per avia, vastaque loca duxit, nè interciperentur. Tempus erat hybernum paucis diebus ante Dominici natalis festum, & loca alta niue obruta. Ob id Ruber, qui longo itinere, velocique cursu calceos consumpsit pedibus iam nudis niuis rigorem, locorumque asperitatem superans, vngues vtriusque pollicis pedum amisit niue combustos, & auulsos. Artus, etsi calceos firmiores habebat, lapidis tamen casu grauiter afflictus longum, & asperum iter ægrè metiens Rubrum tardabat. Satis fessi ad noctem perueniunt in subterraneum specum non multis milibus passuum ab ædibus Fiachi. Ibique relictis, vt constitutum erat, dux rem nunciatum ad Fiachum tetendit. Duo iuuenes, qui toto die currentes nihil cibi cæperant, fame cruciabantur, tamen itinere lassi alto somno sopiti noctem transegerunt. Iamque die secundo sol præcipitabat, & nullus a Fiacho remissus est. Tertio die inedia premente, Arte, inquit Ruber, en animantia bruta herba, & fronde pascuntur. Igitur nos etiam, qui quamuis rationis participes simus, tamen animalia quoque sumus, eadem breuem inediam toleremus, donec a fido Fiacho cibus suppeditetur. Itaque proximæ arboris frondes mandit, & deuorat, sed oblatas renuit Artus. Interim Fiachus nullum lapidem non mouebat, vt illis cibum subministraret, diu prohibitus ab illis, qui eius suspecti hominis vel leuissimos gestus, & motus notabant. Denique ad tertiam noctem, per milites quatuor cibum misit. Artus lapidis casu, longaque inedia confectus nec in os imponere cibum, nec impositum a Rubro, & militibus mandere poterat, Ruber, qui validior erat, et frondibus linquentes vires non nihil retinuit, socio efflante animam coram præ mœrore comedere recusabat: tamen Arto è conspectu remoto se cibo reficere a militibus cogitur. Postquam perturbatio, & tumultus eorum, qui Rubrum inquirebant, sedatum est, Arto inhumato Ruber pedibus æger in Fiachi domum delatus clam curatur, curatumque Fiachus per Vaterum Giraldinum Fuscum in Vltoniam ad Comitem Tironum, Tironus ad Macgui-

iaraṁ tré sraidiḃ na caṫraċ i ttrécumasc cáiċ, ⁊ ní ṫard neach dia uíḋ iad aċt aṁail gaċ naon aile uair ní ro anrat luċt an ḃaile do ṫaṫaiġiḋ an tan sin, ⁊ rortar óḃéla oslaicṫe doirrsi na caṫraċ. Rangattar iaraṁ tré gaċ niomḃoraid ⁊ tré gaċ naiṁréiḋ go ruaċtattar for rſiḋ an ruaiḋ sleiḃe triar a ndeachaiḋ aoḋ isin ċéd elúḋ. Ro ſdarsccar dorċata na hoiḋċe ⁊ tindſnus an teichiḋ (ar uaṁan a ttograma) an tí bá sine díoḃ friú .i. Enri o néill. Aoḋ ba sóaṁ díoḃ ar aoí naoirsi gion gur ḃó hé ar aoí noirbſrtais. Nír bó faoíliġ iadrom tré ſdarsccaraḋ enri friú, ar a aoi ro gaḃsat ag asccnaṁ rſmpa, ⁊ a ffſr muintire acc denaṁ eólais dóiḃ. Ḃaí an adhaiġ ag snite sneaċta gu nár bó sodaing dóiḃsiuṁ a siuḃal uair bádar gan édaċ gan ḟorḃruta iar ffágḃáil a nuaċtaireasraiḋ isin ffrailtiġ trés a ttangattar. Ḃá moa ro inſirtniġeaḋ art frir an dianastar ina aoḋ, uair bá cian foda ó ro cuimriġeadh esside, ⁊ do ċóiḋ i ttroma anḃóill tré ḟod a ċoṁnaiḋe isin ccarcair i mbaoí. Nír ḃó haṁlaiḋ sin daoḋ, ní rainicc tar aoís macdaċta, ⁊ ní ro anastair dfás no dionḟorbairt an ionbaiḋ sin, ⁊ bá huttmall ersccaiḋ a ċſmim ⁊ a imṫeaċt. O ro airiġ siuṁ Art agá enirtiucchaḋ ⁊ aidlſsce ⁊ ionmoille a ċeime ro ḟurail fair a lamh do ċor for a ġualainn badein, ⁊ an laṁ aile for gualainn an ġille. Tiaġaid ass aṁlaiḋ sin go rangattar tar an sliaḃ ruaḋ. Robdar scíṫiġ toirrsiġ iaraṁ, ⁊ ní ro ḟédsat art leó ní ba sia, ⁊ ó na ro ċumaingsiot a ḃrſiṫ leó do ronsat airisſṁ ⁊ coṁnaiḋe i ffoscaḋ allbruaiċ iomard baoí for a ccionn. Iar nanmain dóiḃ annsaiḋe ro ċuirsiot an giolla uadaiḃ lá sgélaiḃ go glſnd ṁaoílugra airm i raiḃe fiacha mac aoḋa baoí i néccrattas fri gallaibh. Glſnd daingſn dioṫoglaiġi eside, ⁊ no gnáṫaiġdís drong mór do ġiallaiḃ aṫa

rem, & Macguier ad ipsius patrem Hugonem Odonellum Tirconellæ principem mittit."—*Historiæ Catholicæ Iberniæ Compendium*, Tom. 3, lib. 2, c. iv. fol. 125.

This account of the escape of the Ulster hostages is curious, but it does not appear perfectly accurate. First, Felim O'Toole was not of Castlekevin, and Fiagh did not leave Hugh Roe O'Donnell and Art O'Neill for three days without food. But it is perfectly true that Henry O'Neill, of whom the Four Masters lose sight altogether, made his escape into Ulster, where he fell into the hands of his enemy, Hugh, Earl of Tyrone, who would neither enlarge him, nor deliver him up to the Lord Deputy.

[b] *They were grieved*, literally, "not joyous were they at the separation of Henry from them." P. O'Sullevan Beare states that Henry made his way into Ulster; and he might have added, that he was there thrown into a worse prison than that from which he had escaped, by the Earl of Tyrone, who feared that the English would set him up as a rival to him in his meditated rebellion. It appears from a letter writ-

time, and guided them. They then proceeded through the streets of the city, mixing with the people; and no one took more notice of them than of any one else, for they did not delay at that time to become acquainted with the people of the town; and the gates of the city were wide open. They afterwards proceeded by every intricate and difficult place, until they arrived upon the surface of the Red Mountain over which Hugh had passed in his former escape. The darkness of the night, and the hurry of their flight (from dread of pursuit), separated the eldest of them from the rest, namely, Henry O'Neill. Hugh was the greenest of them with respect to years, but not with respect to prowess. They were grieved[h] at the separation of Henry from them; but, however, they proceeded onwards, their servant guiding them along. That night was snowing, so that it was not easy for them to walk, for they were without [sufficient] clothes or coverings, having left their outer garments behind them in the privy-house, through which they had escaped. Art was more exhausted by this rapid journey than Hugh, for he had been a long time in captivity, and had become very corpulent from long confinement in the prison[i]. It was not so with Hugh; he had not yet passed the age of boyhood, and had not [yet] done growing and increasing at this period, and his pace and motion were quick and rapid. When he perceived Art had become feeble, and that his step was becoming inactive and slow, he requested him to place one arm upon his own shoulder, and the other upon that of the servant. In this manner they proceeded on their way, until they had crossed the Red Mountain, after which they were weary and fatigued, and unable to help Art on any further; and as they were not able to take him with them, they stopped to rest under the shelter of a high rocky precipice which lay before them. On halting here, they sent the servant to bring the news to Glenmalur, where dwelt Fiagh, the son of Hugh [O'Byrne], who was then at war with the English. This is a secure and impregnable

ten on the 19th August, 1602, by the Lord Deputy Mountjoy, to Cecil, that Henry O'Neal, the eldest son of Shane O'Neal, had then broken out of prison, and that his brother had done the like long before. And his Lordship adds: "But as things stand now, I do not see any great use to be made of them; and I fear I shall be more troubled with them than if they were still where they were. To-morrow (by the grace of God), I am again going into the field, as near as I can, utterly to waste the Country of Tyrone, &c."—See *Moryson's History of Ireland*, edition of 1735, vol. iii. p. 190.

[i] *In the prison*, literally, "in the prison in which he was," which is redundant even in Irish. P. O'Sullevan Beare states, that Art was

cliaṫ an tan do elaittís ass dol gus an ngleand ísin ar bá hinnill leó beiṫ annsaiḋe cco ttiaghdais dia ttír. O Rainic an giolla gus an maigin i mbaoí Fiaċa atféd a scéla dó, ⁊ amail ro ḟáccaiḃ na hócca ro ela ar an ccaṫraiġ, ⁊ nach bérṫaoi i mbeṫhaiḋ forra muna ṫíosta dia ccobair attraitte. Ro ḟorċongair Fiaċa fó ċédoir for drung dia aos gráḋa (doneoċ robdar tairisi lais dib) dol dia saigiḋ, ⁊ fer fó biúḋ ⁊ fear aile fó lionn ⁊ cormaim leó. Do rónaḋ saissium indsin, ⁊ rangattar bail i mbattar na fiora. Monuar nír ḃó soinmeach sadal báttarsom for a ccionn, uair ar iad robdar édġaḋa dia ccorpaiḃ aineaċtair colḃaḋa ciumaisġeala cloiċsneaċta acc reóḋ dá gaċ leṫ impa, ⁊ acc iomuaim a monar nuiréttrom, ⁊ a sreaḃannleintiḃ snáṫċaol fri a ccnesaiḃ, ⁊ a narsan imleaḃar, ⁊ a niallacrann fri a noircniḃ, ⁊ troiġtiḃ gur ḃó samalta lar na fiora dus rainic nár ḃó daoíne itir iat iar ná niompolach isin sneaċta uair ní ḟuairsiot beoġaḋ ina mballaiḃ acht amail batís mairḃ. Ro tógḃaḋ leó iad ar a liġe, ⁊ ro ḟuráilsiot forra ní don ḃiaḋ ⁊ don lionn do ṫoċaiṫem, ⁊ ní frit uaḋaiḃ idir uair gaċ deoċ nó eaḃdais nó telgdís gan ḟuireach, conaḋ ann sin atbaṫ Art fó ḋeóiḋ, ⁊ ro haḋnacht an dú sin. Dála Aoḋa ro ċongaiḃ side iar sin an ċormaim, ⁊ ro battar a ḃríoġa for forbairt iar ná hól acht a ḋí ċois namá, uair ar amlaiḋ battairside ina mballaiḃ marḃa gan moṫuccaḋ iar nat ⁊ ionḃolgaḋ ris an reóḋ ⁊ ris an sneaċta. Ro ċuirsiot na fir for iomċar eissium gus an ngliond adrubramar, ⁊ baí i ttiġ dérrit i ndiaṁair an dlúiṫfeḋa agá leiġes go ttáinicc teaċta go dícelta dia fios scél ó a ċliaṁain an tiarla ó Néill. Ro triallsom imteaċt iarsin iar mbreiṫ don teaċta sair. Bá doiliġ dósom dol isin turas sin uair ní ro fédaḋ leiġes dia troiġtiḃ gur ḃó

severely hurt by a stone, which had fallen accidentally upon him in his descent from the privy.

[j] *Instantly*, i ttraitte.—See note [s] under the year 1590, p. 1899, *supra*.

[k] *In a sequestered house.*—He was placed in this house from fear of pursuit. Dr. O'Conor ornaments the simple style of the annalists, in his account of the second escape of Hugh Roe O'Donnell, as follows, in his *Memoirs, &c.* p. 108:

"O'Donnel was carried on men's backs to the defile of Glyn Malura. Here the O'Beirnes" [O'Byrnes] "came out to meet him, and received him with shouts of exultation, mingled with expressions of the most implacable animosity to the English name: one kissed his feet, another clasped his hands, and the peasantry crowded into the castle to salute with their usual expressions of respect and veneration the young representative of the house of O'Donnel. Feasts were immediately prepared; the harpers swept the history of his illustrious family on the strings of their musical instruments, accompanied with rhapsodies of their own invention. Messengers were dispatched to the old Earl of

valley; and many prisoners who escaped from Dublin were wont to resort to that valley, for they considered themselves secure there, until they could return to their own country. When the servant came into the presence of Fiagh, he delivered his message, and how he had left the youths who had escaped from the city, and [stated] that they would not be overtaken alive unless he sent them relief instantly[j]. Fiagh immediately ordered some of his servants of trust (those in whom he had most confidence) to go to them, taking with them a man to carry food, and another to carry ale and beer. This was accordingly done, and they arrived at the place where the men were. Alas! unhappy and miserable was their condition on their arrival. Their bodies were covered over with white-bordered shrouds of hail-stones freezing around them on every side, and their light clothes and fine-threaded shirts too adhered to their skin; and their large shoes and leather thongs to their shins and feet; so that, covered as they were with the snow, it did not appear to the men who had arrived that they were human beings at all, for they found no life in their members, but just as if they were dead. They were raised by them from their bed, and they requested of them to take some of the meat and drink; but this they were not able to avail themselves of, for every drink they took they rejected again on the instant; so that Art at length died, and was buried in that place. As to Hugh, after some time, he retained the beer; and, after drinking it, his energies were restored, except the use of his two feet, for they were dead members, without feeling, swollen and blistered by the frost and snow. The men carried him to the valley which we have mentioned, and he was placed in a sequestered house[k], in a solitary part of a dense wood, where he remained under cure until a messenger came privately from his brother-in-law, the Earl O'Neill, to inquire after him. When the messenger arrived, he [Hugh] prepared to depart. It was difficult for him to undertake that journey, for his feet could

Tyrone, and soon after young O'Donnel set out for his own country.

"Mean time the Lord Deputy posted guards on all the fords of the Liffey, to prevent his escape; but Fiagh, escorted by a party of horse, galloped forward with him towards Dublin, foreseeing that the fords near the capital would not be so well guarded, since government could not suspect that he would hazard so close an approach. Here O'Donnel and he embraced each other with tears, and then, attended only by eight horsemen, he took his way through Meath, Stradbally, Sliabh Fuad, Armagh, Dungannon, to the shore of Logh Earne, where, after escaping a variety of dangers, he was joyfully received by the brave Hugh Maguire, and con-

hſiġſn dó neoċ ele a ṫurgḃáil for a eoċ, ⁊ a ġaḃáil etir a diḃ lamaiḃ do ridiri an tan no ṫarḃlaingſḋ. Ro cuir fiacha dírim marcaċ isin adaiġ lais go rainic tar aḃainn life dia imdſġail for na celccaiḃ batar fó a erċomair, uair do ċualattar goill aṫa cliaṫ go raiḃe Aodh i ngliond ṁaoílugra, conadh aire sin ro ċuirsiot luċt coiṁéda for áṫaiḃ édoiṁne na habann co ná raġadh Aodh, ⁊ na braiġde ro éla amaille fris ṫairsiḃ i ccóicceadh ulad. Bá hſiccſn do na hóccaiḃ bátar i ffarradh aoḋa gabail a bfoccus do ċaṫraiġ duiḃlinne tar aṫ ndoraid niomḋoṁain baí for aḃainn life co rangadar gan ḟorcloisteaċt do na gallaiḃ co mbáttar for faiṫċe an dúine. Ro ḃaí an luċt las ro tréccead rom feaċt riaṁ (iars an ccédna hélud .i. Felim ó tuaṫail co na ḃraṫair) i ttréċumascc an díorma agá ṫreórucċadh gus an dú sin, ⁊ ro ċſngailsiot a ccodaċ ⁊ a ccairdſs re a roile. Tiomnait celeaḃradh do, ⁊ fáccḃaid bſndaċtain occa, ⁊ sgarait fris annsin.

Dala Aoḋa uí doṁnaill ní ḃaí ina ḟoċair aċt an taon ócclaoċ do ḋeochaidh for a iarair isin ngliond oirdearc do ṁuintir Aoḋa uí neill, ⁊ nó laḃradh tſnga na ttuaṫ nſttrann, ⁊ nó ḃíodh do ġrés i ffoċair an iarla (.i. aodh o neill) an tan nó tſiġſḋ i mſscc gall gur ḃó heólaċ, ⁊ gur ḃó dána in gaċ conair baoí for a ċionn. Lotar iaraṁ for a noíḃ neaċaiḃ ána udmalla for ródaiḃ raoín ndíriġe na miḋe co rangattar for brú na bóinne ria madain ſḋ goirid ó droiċſt aṫa siar, ⁊ robtar oṁnaiġ im ġaḃail gus an ccaṫraiġ ísin conadh é ní do rónsat gaḃáil lá hur na habann go hairm i mbíodh iascaire dínniṁ dearóil, ⁊ arṫraċ bſcc occa ré hiomloccad. Do ċóid Aodh isin ccurraċ co ro ḟáccaiḃ an tiomarċorṫaiġ é forr an mbruaċ alltarach iar ttaḃairt a lán lóiġe dó. Ticc fſr muinntire aoḋa ina frisṫing, ⁊ gaḃaidh las na heocha trér an ccaṫraiġ, ⁊ do bert go haodh iad don taoḃ araill don aḃainn. Tiaġait for a neaċaiḃ, ⁊ lottar co mbádar dá ṁíle ón abainn. Ad ċiad doire doraċ dioġainn for a ccionn an ċonair ro ġaḃsat, ⁊ dúnċladh díṁór ina ṫimċell aṁail biḋ luḃgort foiriata. Ro baí dúnárus airḋirc lá hócclaċ nairſġḋa

ducted by water to his father's castle of Ballyshannon.

[1] *They were afraid.*—This artless style could be easily improved; but the Editor will allow the Four Masters their own mode of telling stories. It should be stated thus: "Tyrone's servant of trust being afraid to bring Hugh O'Donnell publicly through the streets of Drogheda, rode with him along the south bank of the Boyne, to where he knew there was a ferry, kept by a poor man, who earned his livelihood partly by fishing and partly by ferrying

not have been healed [within the time], so that another person had to raise him on his horse, and to lift him from his horse, whenever he wished to alight. Fiagh dispatched a troop of horse with him, [who accompanied him] until he crossed the River Liffey, to protect him against the snares which were laid for him; for the English of Dublin had heard that Hugh was at Glenmalure, and had therefore posted guards on the shallow fords of the river, to prevent him and the prisoners who had escaped along with him from passing into Ulster. The youths who were along with Hugh were obliged to cross a difficult deep ford on the River Liffey, near the city of Dublin; and they proceeded on their way until they came to the green of the fortress, unperceived by the English. The people by whom he had been abandoned some time before, after his first escape, namely, Felim O'Toole and his brother, were amongst the troop who escorted him to this place; and they made friendship and amity with each other. They bade him farewell, and having given him their blessing, departed from him.

As for Hugh O'Donnell, he had [now] no one along with him but the one young man who had been sent for him to the famous Glen [Glenmalure]; he was of the people of Hugh O'Neill, and spoke the language of foreign countries, and had always accompanied the Earl (i. e. Hugh O'Neill) when he went among the English; so that he was acquainted with and confident in every road by which they had to pass. They proceeded forwards on their noble, swift steeds, by the straight-lined roads of Meath, until they arrived before morning on the brink of the Boyne, a short distance to the west of Drogheda; and they were afraid[1] of going to that town, so that what they did was this, to proceed along the brink of the river to a place where a poor little fisherman used to wait with a little boat, for ferrying [people across the river]. Hugh went into this little boat, and the ferryman conveyed him to the other bank, having received a full remuneration; and his servant returned with the horses through the city [town], and brought them to Hugh on the other side of the river. They then mounted their steeds, and proceeded onwards until they were two miles from the river, when they observed a dense bushy grove, surrounded with a rampart, looking like an enclosed garden, at some distance on the way before them. On one side

people across the river. Here he conveyed Hugh across the river, and then went round with the horses through the town of Drogheda, where he was well known as Tyrone's servant."

do na gallaiḃ lá taoḃ an doire, ⁊ bá dearḃċara daoḋ ó néill eiriḋe. Iar ttoċt dóiḃ gus an dúnclaḋ scuiritt a neiċ, ⁊ tiaġaitt isteaċ isin doire baoí isin dúnċlaḋ uair ro baḋ fíréolaċ caoímteċtaiḋ aoḋa isin maiġin sin. Iar ffaġ-ḃail aoḋa hisuiḋe luiḋ siuṁ isin dúnaḋ, ⁊ fó ġeiḃ a ḟiaḋuccaḋ, fuair siuṁ airſccal dſirrit daoḋ ó ḋomnaill, ⁊ do bert lais é go ro ffſstlaḋ ⁊ co ro friotáileaḋ amail bá lainn lſis. Ro ansat hisuiḋe co ar a ḃárac daḋaigh Ro gaḃaḋ a neiċ dóiḃ i nurtosaċ oiḋċe, ⁊ lotar tar sliaḃ brſġ, ⁊ tré maċaire conaill co rangattar co traiġbaile mic buain ria madain. O Robdar ers-laicṫe doirsi an ḃaile isin madain muiċ assſḋ ro ċinnsſt gaḃail treṁit go rangatar ina rſimim for a neaċaiḃ go riaċtatar don taoḃ araill. Robtar subaiġ forffaoíliġ ar aba a ttérnuíḋ tar gaċ mbaoġal dá mbaoí rſmpa gó sin. Assſḋ do ċottar iaram gus an ffiod airm i mbaoí toirrḋealbaċ, mac enri, mic felim ruaiḋ í néill, do léiccſn a sccíri. Bá hinnill dóiḃ ann saiḋe uair bá cara ⁊ bá coiccéle dósoṁ an tí toirrḋealbaċ, ⁊ ba hionann maṫair dósiḋe, ⁊ don iarla ó neill. Airissit andsaiḋe co ar a ḃárac. Do ḋeaċattar iaram tré sliaḃ fuaitt co rangattar go hardmaċa, anait ann co dícealta in aḋhaiġ sin. Tiaġaiṫ ar a ḃárac co dún ngſnainn airm i mbaoí an tiarla aoḋ ó néill. Bá faoíliġ eissiuṁ dia ttoiḋeaċt, ⁊ ruccaḋ iad i naireccal uaigneaċ gan ḟios dá gaċ aon aċt maḋ uathaḋ dia aos tairisi

[m] *A fine mansion-house.*—According to the Life of Hugh Roe O'Donnell this mansion was at Mainistir ṁór, or abbey of Mellifont.

[n] *Conveyed him.*—The reader must bear in mind that Hugh O'Donnell could not walk at this time, as his toes had been bitten by the frost, near Glenmalure.

[o] *Sliabh Breagh*, now *anglice* Slieve Brey, a chain of hills, extending from Clogher head, in the east of the county of Louth, to Rathkenny, in the county of Meath. The part of this chain of hills lying in the county of Meath is often called Sliabh na gCearc. This mountain is called Mons Bregarum, in the Lives of St. Fanchea and St. Columbkille, and it was so called as being the only mountain in the territory of Breagh.

[p] *Tragh-Bhaile-mhic-Buain.*—This was originally the name of the strand at Dundalk, but it was afterwards applied to the town.—See it already mentioned at the years 1392, 1399, 1423, 1430, 1434, 1483, 1492, 1557.

[q] *The Fiodh*, i. e. the wood. This is still the Irish name of the Fews, in the south of the county of Armagh.

[r] *Turlough, the son of Henry.*—The name of this Turlough mac Henry O'Neill is marked on an old map in the State Papers' Office, London, as chieftain of the Fews, in the south of the county of Armagh. According to a pedigree of O'Donnell, in the possession of Count O'Donnell, of Austria, this Turlough had a daughter, Margaret, who married Hugh, son of Calvagh Roe, son of Manus, son of Con [the brother of Sir Niall Garv] O'Donnell; and she had for him a son, Carolus, or Calvagh Duv, the ancestor of the O'Donnells of Castlebar, and of the Counts

of this grove stood a fine mansion-house[m], belonging to a distinguished English youth, who was a particular friend of Hugh O'Neill. On reaching the enclosure, they unharnessed their steeds, and entered the grove which was inside the rampart, for Hugh's companion was well acquainted with the place. Having left Hugh there [in the grove], he went into the fortress, where he was kindly received. He procured a private apartment for Hugh O'Donnell, and conveyed him[n] thither, where he was attended and entertained to his satisfaction. Here they remained until the evening of the following day; their horses were got ready for them in the beginning of the night, and they proceeded across Sliabh Breagh[o], and through the territory of Machaire-Chonaill; and before morning they had arrived at Tragh-Bhaile-mhic-Buain[p]. As the gates of the town were opened in the morning early, they resolved to pass through it on their horses. [This they did, and advanced] until they were at the other side; and they were cheerful and rejoiced for having escaped every danger which lay before them thus far. They then proceeded to the Fodh[q], where dwelt Turlough, the son of Henry[r], son of Felim Roe O'Neill, to recruit themselves. They were here secure, for Turlough was his friend and companion, and he and the Earl O'Neill had [been born of] the one mother. They remained here until the next day, and then proceeded across Sliabh Fuaid[s], and arrived at Armagh, where they remained in disguise for that night. On the following day they proceeded to Dungannon, where the Earl, Hugh O'Neill, was. He was rejoiced at their arrival, and they[t] were conducted [*recte*, Hugh was conducted] into a private apartment, without the knowledge of any, except a few of his faithful people who

O'Donnell of Spain and Austria. This Turlough mac Henry O'Neill, usually called Sir Tirlagh, was transplanted from the Fews to Oldcastle, in the county of Mayo, where he got a grant of a considerable estate, which was forfeited in 1641.

[s] *Sliabh Fuaid*, i. e. the mountain of Fuad, son of Breogan, one of the chieftains who came over with the sons of Milesius, so early as A. M. 2934, according to O'Flaherty's *Ogygia*, part iii. c. 16. See also Keating's *History of Ireland*, Haliday's edition, pp. 300, 382. This mountain is shewn on an old map of Ulster in the State Papers' Office, London, under the name of Slew Bodeh, and placed between Lough Muckno [at Castle-Blayney] and Armagh. This name is still preserved and applied to the highest of the Fews mountains. It should be here remarked that Fews, the name of the territory, was formed, not from Sliaḃ Fuaıḋ, the name of this mountain, but from fıoḋ, or feaḋ, i. e. wood, which was applied to the territory before the two baronies were formed.

[t] *They.*—This is faulty. It should be: "Hugh was shewn to a private apartment," because there existed no necessity for concealing the Earl's servant, who had accompanied Hugh O'Donnell from Glenmalure to Dungannon.

batar ocá ffritáileṁ, ⁊ baoí aoḋ an dú sin ré ceṫeóra noiḋċe ag cur scísi a aisttir ⁊ a imniġ de. Do bert iaroṁ láṁ for imṫeaċt, ⁊ ceileaḃrais don iarla iar ccor dírime marcaċ lais go rainicc co hairer loċa hérne.

Ba sara dósoṁ triaṫ an tíre, ⁊ bá braṫair arrainn a maṫar .i. Aoḋ Maguiḋir uair bá hí nuala ingen Maġnusa uí domnaill a ṁaṫair. Ro ba faoíliġ Máguiḋir reṁesiuṁ. Tuccaḋ iaraṁ eṫar dia ṡaiġiḋ ⁊ téit inn. Imraiset ar iarsoḋain co rangatar gus an ccaol ccumang baoí forsan loċ co ro gabsat port an dú sin. Do cóttar drong dia ṡain muintir ina coṁḋáil annsin, ⁊ do bertsat leó é co caislén aṫa seanaiġ airm i mbáttar barda uí domnaill a aṫarsoṁ. Baí andsaiḋe co ttangattar a mbaoí ina ccoṁḟoċraiḃ isin tír dia ṡaiġiḋ dia ḟiaḋucchaḋ. Robtar faoíliġ a ṡain muintir fri daṁna na flaṫa dus rainicc, ⁊ gé ro dliġset rainset dó ar aoí a ċeneóil Ro ḃaoí daṁna nár ḃo lucċa acca dia fforḃáilte fris, uair as aṁlaiḋ baoí an tír ina ceirde creaċ etir ġallaiḃ, ⁊ gaoiḋelaiḃ gó sin. Ro ḃattar tra dá ċaiptín airḋerce .i. captin uulis ⁊ captin conaill go ndíḃ céḋaiḃ laoċ amaille friú (tangattar athaiḋ riasan tan sa a cóicceaḋ connaċt) acc ionnraḋ ⁊ acc orccain an tíre co coitċeann co mbaoí ó ṡliaḃ anoirr i ttír conuill as a ccumas cenmota caistiall aṫa seanaiġ, ⁊ caistiall dúin na ngall airm i mbaoí ó domnaill go nuathaḋ daoíne ina ḟoċair. Ar a aoí ní ro ḟédsat ní dó, ⁊ ní ḃaoí cuṁang occa gaḃáil friú im aiḋṁilleaḋ na criċe. Ba hann ro gaḃsatt na goill ísin ionataċt ⁊ aitteḃ i mainistir na mbraṫar i ndún na ngall iar ndol dia hurd ⁊ dia macaiḃ eccailsi fó ḋiaṁraiḃ, ⁊ fo ḋroiḃelaiḃ an tíre ar a nomġabáil siuṁ duaṁan a muḋaiġṫe ⁊ a mímbertha. Iar mbeiṫ athaiḋ isin mainistir dóiḃ gus an uathaḋ sluaiġ asrubramar, do

[u] *They rowed him*, i. e. the men sent by Maguire to convey him to Ballyshannon. Maguire himself did not accompany him, as we learn from the Life of Hugh Roe O'Donnell: "⁊ do ṫaod in ⁊ facḃaiḋ bennaċtain ag Maguiḋir: He went into the boat and left his blessing with Maguire."

[w] *The narrow neck.*—This is that narrow part of the Lower Lough Erne, near Belleek, called Caol na h-Eirne. It is stated in the Life of Hugh Roe O'Donnell, by Peregrine O'Clery, that Cael na h-Eirne is that part of [the lower] Lough Erne, where the River Erne escapes from it: go rangatar gus an ccael ccuarċuṁang baoi for an loċ reṁereremar, bail hi toet as an oḃ aḋḃċlosaċ iaiċ-ioṁḋa frisi raiter Eirne.

[x] *Ballyshannon.*—It is stated in the Life of Hugh Roe O'Donnell that this castle was built by Niall, the son of Turlough-an-Fhiona O'Donnell, in the year 1423.

[y] *Willis.*—Captain Willis was made sheriff of Fermanagh, despite of Maguire, who had given the Lord Deputy three hundred cows to free

attended him ; and here Hugh remained for the space of four nights, to shake off the fatigue of his journey and anxiety. He then prepared to depart, and took his leave of the Earl, who sent a troop of horse with him till he arrived at Lough Erne.

The lord of this country, namely, Hugh Maguire, was his friend and kinsman, by the mother's side; for Nuala, daughter of Manus O'Donnell, was Maguire's mother. Maguire was rejoiced at his arrival. A boat was afterwards provided for him [Hugh], into which he entered; and they rowed him[u] thence until they arrived at the narrow neck[w] of the lake, where they landed. Here a party of his faithful friends came to meet him, and they conveyed him to the castle of Ballyshannon[x], where the warders of O'Donnell, his father, were [stationed]. He remained here until all those in the neighbourhood came to him, to welcome him; and his faithful people were rejoiced at the return of the heir to the chieftainship ; and though they owed him real affection on account of his family, they had an additional cause of joy at this period ; [for, until his return] the country had been one scene of devastation between the English and the Irish. There were two famous captains, namely, Captain Willis[y] and Captain Conwell, with two hundred soldiers (who had some time before come thither from the province of Connaught), who were plundering and ravaging the country in general, so that they had [reduced] in subjection to them the entire of Tirconnell from the mountain westwards, excepting the castle of Ballyshannon, and the castle of Donegal, in which O'Donnell was [stationed] with a few men. The English, however, were not able[z] to do him any injury ; nor was he [on the other hand] able to prevent them from plundering the country. The place where the English had taken up their abode and quarters was the monastery of Donegal, the friars and ecclesiastics having fled into the wilds and recesses of the territory to avoid them, from fear of being destroyed or persecuted. After having resided in the monastery for some time, with the

his country from a sheriff. Fynes Moryson states that Captain Willis had for his guard one hundred men, and "lead about some one hundred women and boys, all which lived on the spoil of the country." Hence that Maguire, "taking his advantage, set upon them and drove them into a church, where he would have put them all to the sword, if the Earl of Tyrone had not interposed his authority."—Vol. i. p. 28. See also P. O'Sullevan Beare's *Hist. Cathol. Iber. Compendium*, fol. 126.

[z] *Were not able*, literally, "Non potuerunt isti nocere illi" [O'Donnello] "nec erat potestas illi prohibere istos a diripiendo territorium."

ḋeaċattar drong díoḃ co heoċair imliḃ an ċuain dí ṁíle cſimenn ó Ḋún na ngall siar go baile uí Ḃaoiġill óir bá hinnill leó bſiṫ isuiḋe ó ro ḃáttar braiġde na críċe for a ccumas. Nó tſiġdís ina ndeisiḃ ⁊ ina ttriaraiḃ co mbſirdís cróḋ ⁊ cſṫra, ionnmasa ⁊ edala in ro ba comḟoċraiḃ dóiḃ don tír dia saiġiḋ don ḃaile ſin. Ḃattar do ġrés acc tóċuirſḋ fuilliḋ slóiġ ⁊ soċaiḋe ċuca do ḋol tar bſrnas mór dingreim ⁊ darccain na tíre don taoḃ ṫoir do ṡliaḃ aṁail do rónsat airm imbattar.

Imṫúsa Aoḋa uí Doṁnaill iar ttogairm a ṫíre ċucca, ní ro an friú go léicc (ó ro ċuala an ṁórḃroid i mbattar cenél cconaill, milleaḋ ⁊ míḋiaċ na mainistreċ) aċt arrſḋ do róine toiḋeċt go Dún na ngall eineaċ i nionċaiḃ fris na gallaiḃ. Ní tarḋsat an tír eissioṁ i ffaill gan toċt fó a ṫogairm ina neisiḃ ⁊ ina mbuiḋniḃ aṁail as dſine conrangattar donsoċ ro ċarsat hé lásoḋain ro lásoṁ a ṫeaċta ar amus na ngall dia ráḋa riú gan iomḟuireaċ nó earnáḋhaḋ isin sglais dia haiḋmilleaḋ ní bá sire, ⁊ naċ ttoirmſccfaḋ impa teċt an ċonair baḋ lainn leó, aċt namá co ro ḟáccbaidís dia nſir ina mbaoí do ḃroid, ⁊ do ċroḋ na críċe leó. Ro ḃaoí duaṁan ⁊ dimeaccla forra soṁ co ndearnsatt indsin aṁail ro ḟorċongraiḋ forra, ⁊ roḃdar buiḋiġ do roċtain a nanmann leó, ⁊ lottar for a ccúlaiḃ dorídisi i ccóicceaḋ Connaċt. Tangattar na braiġdi iarsaṁ don ṁainistir.

Do ċuaiḋ Aoḋ ó Doṁnaill go háṫ ſnaiġ i ffriṫissi, ⁊ do bſrt lſga do lſiġſ a ċos, ⁊ ní ro ḟéḋsat lſiġſ dó co ro ḋeiliġsiot a ḋí ordain fris, ⁊ nír ḃó hóġslán go diuiḋ mbliaḋna. Baoí siuṁ aṁlaiḋ sin in oṫairliġe a ċos ó ḟél ḃriġde go mí april. O do deachaiḋ aḋuaire na haimsire sirchaiḋe for ccúla bá foda lais ro ḃoí ina oṫairliġe ⁊ ro ċuir tarcclamaḋ ⁊ tionól for a mbaoí uṁal dia aṫair alla ṫoir don tsliaḃ oirdearc .i. bſrnas mór tíre haoḋa, ⁊ ro ṫionóil ċuicce a mbaoí alla ṫiar don tsliaḃ ċéḋna .i. ó baoiġill, ⁊

[a] *Baile-Ui-Bhaoighill*, i. e. the town or residence of O'Boyle, now Ballyweel.—See note [w], under the year 1440, p. 920, *supra*. On an old map of parts of the coasts of Mayo, Sligo, Leitrim, and Donegal, preserved in the State Papers' Office, London, "Ba. O'Boile" is shewn as a castle on the north side of the "Baie of Donegale," opposite the "Monasterie of Donegalle" which is shewn on the south side of the River Eske, near its mouth.

[b] *Two and three*, literally, "in twos and threes."

[c] *Such of them as loved him.*—The reader must bear in mind that the sons of Calvagh O'Donnell, and their followers, the O'Gallaghers, O'Dohertys, and some of the Mac Sweenys, were opposed to the election of Hugh Roe as chief of Tirconnell.

[d] *Bands.*—"éis .i. buiḋean."—*O'Clery.*

small number of forces which we have mentioned, a party of them went to Baile-Ui-Bhaoighill[a], [a castle] on the borders of the harbour, about two thousand paces west of Donegal, for they considered themselves secure there, as they had the hostages of the country in their power. These were wont to go forth, in companies of two and three[b], and carry off the flocks and herds, goods and treasures, of the neighbourhood with them into this castle. They were constantly inviting additional hosts and forces to proceed across Barnesmore, to persecute and plunder the country on the east side of the mountain, as they had already treated the western portion.

As for Hugh O'Donnell, after having summoned the country to him, he did not long wait for them (when he heard of the great oppression in which the Kinel-Connell were, and of the spoiling and profanation of the monastery), but proceeded to Donegal to meet the English face to face. The [people of the] country, such of them as loved him[c], did not neglect to come at his summons; they followed him in bands[d] and in companies as expeditiously as they were able; he, thereupon, sent his messengers to the English, to tell them not to remain or abide any longer in the monastery destroying it; and, [adding] that he would not prevent them to depart in any direction they pleased, provided only they would leave behind all the prisoners and cattle of the territory they had with them[e]. They were so terrified and dismayed that they did as they were ordered; and, being thankful that they escaped with their lives, they went back again into the province of Connaught. The friars then returned to the monastery.

Hugh O'Donnell returned to Ballyshannon, and sent for physicians to cure his feet; but they were not able to effect a cure until they had cut off both his great toes[f]; and he was not perfectly well till the end of a year [afterwards]. He remained thus confined under cure of his feet from the festival of St. Bridget to April. When the cold of the spring season was over, he thought it too long he had been confined as an invalid; and he sent [persons] to assemble and muster all those who were obedient to his father to the east side of the celebrated mountain, i. e. Barnesmore, in Tirhugh; and he collected [also] all those

[e] *With them*, i. e. in their hands, or in their possession.

[f] *Both his great toes:* a ḋí oꞃḋáın .ı. ḋá óꞃḋóıꞅ a ċoıꞅe. In Irish the same word is used to express finger and toe; they are distinguished by adding láıṁe and coıꞅe.

Mac suibne ṫíre bógaine. Tánaic beós dia coṁmóraḋ ó doṁnaill a aṫair .i. aoḋ mac Maġnusa, mic aoḋa duiḃ co na commaim amaille fris .i. inġen tremais mec doṁnaill a maṫairrioṁ. Bá sé ionaḋ erdalta in ro ḋalsat na maiṫe sin re a roile hi ccill mic nénáin,⁊ bá hand nó hoirdniġṫe ua doṁnaill do ġrés i ttiġearnas for ċenel cconaill. Rainicc siuṁ gus an líon ccédna an dú sin. Tánaic ind airsir aoḋa uí doṁnaill gus an maiġin sin, Mac suibne fánat doṁnall mac toirrḋealbaiġ, mic Ruaidri, ⁊ Mac suibne na ttuaṫ eoġan ócc mac eoġain óicc mic eoġain. Ḃáttar dronga dearṁara do ċenel cconaill ná tánaicc isin ccoṁḋail sin. Ro ba diḃriḋe aoḋ mac aoḋa duiḃ mic aoḋa ruaiḋ í ḋoṁnaill,⁊ sliocht an ċalḃaiġ mic Maġnusa mic aoḋa duiḃ, ua doċartaiġ Seaan ócc mac Seaain, mic feilim mic conċobair ċarraiġ toísreaċ triocait ċétt innsi heoccain, ⁊ drong do cloinn tsuibne do ḋeachaiḋ ar a ttír, coniḋ ann ro aitreaḃsat for ur loċa feaḃail,⁊ as iad robtar toirsiġ iomġona don calḃaċ ua doṁnaill,⁊ dia ṡiol ina dsedhaiġ. Ḃáttar beós drong ṁór don ṁuintir ġallċubair gan ṫeċt ann sin tria ṁiorcais ⁊ tria ṁíorún aṁail an luċt naile.

Do ċóiḋ iaraṁ ua doṁnaill Aoḋ mac maġnusa ⁊ na maiṫe sin tangatar dia saiġiḋ do ċrúḋ a ccoṁairle, ⁊ bá sed ro cinnseḋ lá hua ndoṁnaill (ó ro airiġsetair a eirte ⁊ aiḋḃle a aoíse) a tiġernas do ṫabairt dia ṁac, ⁊ ó doṁnaill do ġairm de. Ro ṁolsat các i ccoitċinne an ċoṁairle ísin, ⁊ ro gniṫe saṁlaiḋ, uair do radaḋ ó fingil an tairċindeaċ dia saiġiḋ, ⁊ ro oirdnsetairside Aoḋ ruaḋ i ccennus na criċe lá forcongra, ⁊ lá bennaċt a aṫar, ⁊ do róine órd an anma feiḃ ro ba técta, ⁊ ro ġair ua doṁnaill de an .3. lá do mai.

Ni ro léicc ó doṁnaill aoḋ ruaḋ sccaoileaḋ don uathaḋ soċraide sin do rala ina ḟarraḋ co rainicc etir ṫroiġṫeċ ⁊ marcaċ isin ccoiccriċ i ccenél eoġain mic neill. Ní ḋeachaiḋ tra raiḃṫe, ná rsiṁrios dia saiġiḋ, ar ní ro ṡaoílsiot a eirġe siuṁ meallṁa ar in liġe ina mbaoí, ⁊ ní móa do radsat

[g] *Kilmacrenan.*—It is stated in the Life of Hugh Roe O'Donnell that Cill mic Nénain, the church in which St. Columbkille was educated, and where the O'Donnells were inaugurated, was situated on the north side of the river Leanainn, in the very centre of the Triacha ched, or cantreds of Cinel-Luighdheoch. This had been the only district over which the O'Donnells had sway until they dispossessed the O'Muldorys and O'Canannans.

[h] *Tricha-ched*, i. e. hundred, or barony, containing one hundred and twenty quarters of land.

[i] *Like the others, recte*, "great numbers of the O'Gallaghers also abstained from coming to this

to the west of the same mountain, namely, O'Boyle, and Mac Sweeny of Tir-Boghaine. There came also to join him, his father, O'Donnell, i. e. Hugh, the son of Manus, son of Hugh Duv, with his wife, the daughter of James Mac Donnell, his [Hugh Roe's] mother. The place of meeting appointed by these chieftains was Kilmacrenan[g], where the O'Donnell was usually inaugurated Lord of the Kinel-Connell. He arrived with the same number at that place. To Hugh O'Donnell's levy on this occasion came also Mac Sweeny Fanad (Donnell, the son of Turlough, son of Rory), and Mac Sweeny-na-dTuath (Owen, Oge, the son of Owen Oge, son of Owen). There were many parties of the Kinel-Connell who did not come to this assembly. Of these was Hugh, the son of Hugh Duv, son of Hugh Roe O'Donnell; and the descendants of Calvagh, the son of Manus, son of Hugh Duv; O'Doherty; John Oge, the son of John, son of Felim, son of Conor Carragh, Chieftain of the Tricha-ched[h] of Inishowen; and a party of the Clann-Sweeny, who had gone away from their [own] territory, and were dwelling at that time on the margin of Lough Foyle, and who had been leaders in battle to Calvagh O'Donnell, and his descendants after him. There was also a great number of the O'Gallaghers who did not come hither, through spite and malice, like the others[i].

O'Donnell (Hugh, the son of Manus) and these chiefs who came to meet him, then held a consultation; and the resolution which O'Donnell came to (as he felt his own feebleness and great age) was, to resign his lordship to his son, and to style him O'Donnell. This resolution was universally applauded by all, and accordingly adopted, for O'Firghil the Erenagh was sent for; and he inaugurated Hugh Roe chief of the country, by order and with the blessing of his father; and the ceremony of conferring the name was legally performed, and he styled him O'Donnell on the third day of May.

O'Donnell (Hugh Roe) did not permit those few troops he had then with him to disperse, but marched them, both horse and foot, into the neighbouring parts of [the territory of] the race of Eoghan, the son of Niall. No notice or forewarning [of this movement] had reached the others, for they did not think that he had perfectly recovered from his confinement; yet they did not intend

meeting, being, like the others, actuated by the malice and animosity which they bore to Hugh Roe, and his mother, Ineenduv, who had incited her Scottish attendants to murder Hugh, son of the Dean O'Gallagher, as has been already at full length set forth."

dia nuíd tſiċſṁ ria ccenel cconaill ó cſin ṁair. Ro creaċ loisccead in ro ba coiṁnſra doiḃ do cenel eoġain las an uathad slóiġ sin gontar airliġtear gaċ aon rob inécta ar a ruccsat. Tarṫatar an sluaġ edala iomḋa etir cſṫraiḃ ⁊ indiliḃ, ⁊ soait for ccúlaiḃ dia ccriċ buḋéin.

Bá hantt baoí dúnarus uí néill toirrdelbaiġ luiniġ ar an srat mbán in ionbaid sin, ⁊ níor ḃó gnáṫ airirioṁ uí néill riaṁ hisuiḋe gus an ttoirrḋealḃaċ ísin. Bá mór a ṁioḟolta soṁ fri cenel cconaill, ⁊ fri cliaṁain uí doṁnaill .i. an tiarla ó neill. Ro ṫarraing ua neill drong do ġallaiḃ duiblinne dia nſrtad i naċċaid cenel cconaill ⁊ an iarla uí neill .i. captin uulas, ⁊ captin fularc go ndíḃ cédaiḃ laoċ amaille friú. Bá galar mſnman lá hua ndoṁnaill ócc goill duiblinne do ṫoċt i nor a ċriċe do tairċélad a aṫarḋa, ⁊ an ċuiccid ar ċſna conad aire do róine Slóiċċead lais a ccionn treaċtmuine i ttír eoġain. Ro ṫeiċriot luċt an tíre an dala feaċt riaṁ go rangattar ciannaċta glinne gſiṁin. At cuas dósoṁ co mbuí ó neill ⁊ na goill reṁráite co líon a soċraide ina coṁḟoċraiḃ, for ḟorcongart ó doṁnaill for a ṡoċraide a nionnsaicchid airm i mbáttar. Do rónad fairsiuṁ indsin. Do ḃſrt fuabairt bioḋḃad ⁊ amus aṁnas forra hi miomſḋón laoí. Od conncatarsaiḋe cenel cconaill ċuca ní ro anrat friú act tiaġait for a niomġaḃáil co caislén baí for brú na haḃann dianid ainm Roa. Ba daingean dítoġlaiġe an caistiall ísin, ⁊ bá dún arus dua caṫáin eiside. Ro ġaḃ ua doṁnaill acc iomsuiḋe imon mbaile. Ro ḟaoíd ua caṫáin a ṫeaċta do ṡaiġid uí ḋoṁnaill, ⁊ sccríḃſnd lais ċuicce, bá hſd baoí isin litir gur ḃó dalta dósoṁ ó doṁnaill, ⁊ co ro ernaiḋm a ċaradrad rís ó ċéin, ⁊ ro ba técta ḋó fó dáiġ an ċarattrad ísin an ccreiċ táinicc for a ionchaiḃ ⁊ for a

[k] *Second occasion.*—An dala feaċt riaṁ .i. an dara feaċt roiṁe. They did not fly before him on his first irruption.

[l] *Cianachta-Glinne-Geimhin*, now the barony of Keenaght, in the county of Londonderry.—See note [o], under the year 1197, p. 107, *supra*. The River Roa, or, as it is now anglicised, Roe, flows through this barony, dividing it into two almost equal parts. The vale of this river was called Gleann-Geimhin by the Irish; and the name is still partly preserved in that of Dun Geimhin, *anglice* Dungiven, a church standing in ruins over a deep glen, through which the Roe flows.

[m] *He was informed.*—"Cuas, no ad cuas .i. do hinseadh."—*O'Clery.*

[n] *On the margin of the River Roa.*—This was probably the castle of Limavaddy, which was situated on the margin of the River Roe, in the barony of Keenaght.—See note [l], under the year 1542, p. 1472, *supra*. O'Kane had another castle at Dungiven, on the same river.

[o] *What was stated.*—The style is here very clumsy and totally devoid of art. The language

to fly before the Kinel-Connell [neither, indeed, had it been their wont to do so] from a remote period. By this small army of the Kinel-Connell the neighbouring parts of Kinel-Owen were plundered and burned; every one fit to bear arms whom they caught was put to the sword and slaughtered. The army also seized upon many spoils, both herds and flocks, and [then] returned back to their own territory.

At this time the residence of O'Neill (Turlough Luineach) was at Strabane, where, before the time of this Turlough, the O'Neill had not usually held his residence. Great was his animosity to the Kinel-Connell, and to O'Donnell's brother-in-law, namely, the Earl O'Neill. O'Neill drew a party of the English of Dublin to strengthen him against the Kinel-Connell and the Earl O'Neill, namely, Captain Willis and Captain Fullart; and they had two hundred soldiers along with them. It was anguish of mind to the young O'Donnell that the English of Dublin should have come to the confines of his territory to spy his patrimony, and the province in general; wherefore, in a week's time he made a hosting into Tyrone. The people of the country fled on this second occasion[k] before him, until they reached Cianachta-Glinne-Geimhin[l]. He [O'Donnell] was informed[m] that O'Neill and the English before mentioned were [assembled] with all their forces in the neighbourhood; and he ordered his troops to advance to the place where they were. This was accordingly done. He marched resolutely and fiercely against them in mid-day. When they perceived the Kinel-Connell approaching them, they did not wait for them, but fled, to avoid them, to a castle which was [situated] on the margin of a river called Roa[n]. This was a strong, impregnable castle, and the mansion-seat of O'Kane. O'Donnell proceeded to lay siege to the castle. O'Kane sent a messenger with a letter to him. What was stated[o] in this letter was, that O'Donnell was his foster-son; that he [O'Kane] had ratified a friendship with him long since; that by reason of this friendship, it was now lawful for him [O'Donnell] to leave to him the property

should be constructed thus: "O'Kane sent a messenger with a letter to O'Donnell, reminding him that he was his fosterfather, and that he had been at all times on terms of friendship with his father, O'Donnell, and him; that, in consequence of this friendship, O'Donnell should now spare those O'Neills who had fled to his castle with their cattle, and placed themselves under his asylum; that he had solemnly promised to protect them before he knew that it was from his own fosterson, O'Donnell, they were flying; that if O'Donnell would spare these on this occasion, he would never again admit under the shelter of his fortilace any enemies to his fosterson, O'Donnell.

ċomairce do leccaḋ ḋó an tan sin, ⁊ náċ léiccfeaḋ ċuicce doridisi dia mbeiṫ-siuṁ ina ḋiaiḋ. Do raḋ ó domhnaill an aisccid sin dó, ⁊ soais ina friṫing, ⁊ ro airis co cenn teóra noiḋċe co na laiḃ is in ccriċ ar a ndeaċattar na creaċa dia ttard comairce aga loc ⁊ accá láinṁilleaḋ. Soais tar a ais dia ṫír feisin, ⁊ ní ro airis co rainicc dún na ngall, ⁊ baí annsaiḋe fri ré dá mís aca leġes.

Ro ba fada lairsiuṁ baoí ó neill ⁊ a ġoill gan fobairt fris an ré sin, ⁊ ro ċuir tionol for a ṡloġaiḃ lotar ass iaroṁ tar bernas mór, tar finn tar moḋairn do ḋol gus an srath mbán airm i mbaoí ó neill co na ġallaiḃ, ⁊ ní ro ansat go rangattar eneaċ in ionchaiḃ friú. O neill tra ní ro ḟáccaiḃ siḋe náid a ġoill daingen an dúnaiḋ dia ffobairt sioṁ, o na fuaratar soṁ a ffreaccra im ċaiṫiorġail, bássed do ronsat teinnte ⁊ tenndala daḃannaḋ i cceiṫeóra arda an ḃaile, ⁊ ní ro scarsat fris co ros loiscsiot i mbaoí do tiġiḃ fri múraiḃ seaċtair, ⁊ ó na fuaratar na goill amaċ do ṫarraċtain na hoirecne do ċóttar dia ttiġiḃ iar ccoscar.

Imṫusa an iarla í neill ó ro ḟidir siḋe ainċriḋe a ċeneoil badéin dua ḋomhnaill (aoḋ ruaḋ) assed do róine dol do ṡaiġiḋ an iustis .i. uilliam fitz-uilliam, ⁊ protexion dfaġḃáil dua ḋomhnaill lá toċt do laṫair, ⁊ dia accallaiṁ co traiġḃaile mic buain. Fuairsiuṁ idir indsin ⁊ do ċóiḋ ar cenn í domnaill go dún na ngall, ⁊ ruc lais é co traiġ baile. Do ċóttar diblínib do ṡaiġid an iustis, ⁊ bá faoílid siuṁ friú, ⁊ ro ṁaiṫ an telúd dua domhnaill, ⁊ ro naiḋmsiot a síṫ ⁊ a ccarattrad fri roile aṁail is deaċ ro féosat, ⁊ ceileḃrait na maiṫe sin fris an iustis, ⁊ fáccbait bennaċtain occa, ⁊ soait leṫ ar leṫ dia ttiġiḃ.

Od ċualattar an drong do cenel conaill bátar i ffriṫbert fri hua ndoṁnaill sioḋuccaḋ dó fris an iustis tangattar siḋe uile fó ċóra ⁊ fó ṡíṫ dia ṡaiġiḋ. Robtar iad bá hairegda táinicc annsin Aoḋ mac aoḋa duiḃ mic

[p] *To avenge.*—"Tarraċtain .i. dioġail."—*O'Clery.*

[q] *To obtain a protection.*—This was a wise stroke of policy in the Earl O'Neill, in order to intimidate the race of Calvagh O'Donnell and their adherents, who were opposed to his brother-in-law, Hugh Roe O'Donnell. The facility with which the Chief Governor complied with this request founds a strong argument in favour of the suspicion of Fynes Moryson, who says that Fitz-William was privy to the escape of Hugh Roe O'Donnell.

[r] *Peace.*—Córa .i. siothcháin.—*O'Clery.*

[s] *Hugh, the son of Hugh Duv.*—It is stated in the Life of Hugh Roe O'Donnell, that this Hugh Duv was the senior of all the race of Dalach, the

which had come under his asylum and protection; and that he would never again admit such, should he [O'Donnell] be in pursuit of it. O'Donnell granted him this request, but, returning back, remained three days and nights in the territory whence the spoils to which he had given protection had been removed, plundering and totally devastating it. He then went back to his own country, and never halted until he had reached Donegal, where he remained two months under cure.

By this time he thought it too long that O'Neill and his English were left unattacked; wherefore, having assembled his forces, they proceeded through [the gap of] Barnesmore, and across the [Rivers] Finn and Mourne, on his way to Strabane, where O'Neill and his English were [stationed]; and they never halted until they came before them face to face. But O'Neill and his English did not come outside the donjon of the fortress to engage them; and when they were not responded to in battle, they set fires and flames to the four opposite quarters of the town, and did not depart until they had burned all the houses outside the walls; and when they could not excite the English to come forth to avenge[p] the destruction, they returned home in triumph.

As for the Earl O'Neill, when he perceived the enmity that his own tribe bore to O'Donnell (Hugh Roe), what he did was, to proceed to the Lord Justice, William Fitzwilliam, to obtain a protection[q] for O'Donnell to come before him, and confer with him, at Tragh-Bhaile-mic-Buain [Dundalk]. This he obtained at once, and went to Donegal to O'Donnell, and took him to Tragh-Bhaile-mhic-Buain, where both appeared before the Lord Justice, who was gracious to them, and he forgave O'Donnell the escape. They confirmed friendship and amity with each other as strongly as possible, and, having bid the Lord Justice farewell, and left him their blessing, they all returned to their respective homes.

When that party of the Kinel-Connell who were in opposition to O'Donnell heard that he had made peace with the Lord Justice, they all came to him in peace[r] and amity. The most distinguished of these who came there were Hugh, the son of Hugh Duv[s], son of Hugh Roe; Niall Garv[t], the son of Con,

son of Muircheartach, next after Hugh, the son of Manus, whom he expected to succeed in the government of Tirconnell. He is described as the Achilles of the Irish race, but it is added, that it was no disgrace to him to have submitted to the youth Hugh Roe, who was a man of greater eloquence, wiser counsel, loftier mind, and of greater force of character to command and enforce obedience.

[t] *Nial Garv.*—This is the Nial Garv who

aoḋa ruaiḋ. Niall garḃ mac cuinn, mic an ċalḃaiġ, mic Maġnusa mic aoḋa duiḃ co na ḃraiṫriḃ, ⁊ ó doċartaiġ Sēan ócc mac Sēain, mic feilim mic conċoḃair ċarraiġ iar na ġaḃail lairrium.

AOIS CRIOST, 1593.

Aois Criost, mile, cuicc ced, noċat, a tri.

O domnaill Aoḋ ruaḋ do ḃēiṫ i mí ianuarii na bliaḋna so ina iostaḋ aireaċais badéin illēiṫbēr for ionċaiḃ a naṁat .i. toirrdealbaċ luineaċ mac neill conallaiġ. Ro gaḃ ag imirt a eccraitti ⁊ a aincriḋe fair dia ionnarbaḋ ar a ṫiġearnas, ⁊ dia enirtiucchaḋ ar dáiġ aoḋa uí néill dóirdneaḋ ina ionaḋ. Bá fēirde dóraṁ an reiṁdeiccsi do róine uair rainicc ticcēsnas do ṡaicciḋ aoḋa uí neill, ⁊ do ratt toirrdelbaċ luineaċ aonta ⁊ uṁla dó imón ainm do ġairm de. Ro gaireaḋ iaraṁ o neill daoḋ o neill (.i. an tiarla), ⁊ leiccis toirrdealbaċ luineaċ na goill ro ḃattar lais uaḋa iar sioḋuccaḋ dó fri hua neill ⁊ fri hua ndoṁnaill. I mi Mai do ṡonraḋ do rónaḋ indsin. Ro ḃaoí dna cóicceaḋ concoḃair mic nēsa fó smaċtcáin síoḋa don dias ísin, ⁊ ro ḃadar i ngeill, ⁊ a naitire for ccumus gombtar somamaiġṫe dóiḃ.

An ċlann uilliam sin a duḃramar do ṫoċt isteaċ i ccēnd an goberrnóra fó ḟéil míċíl na bliaḋna reṁainn ro ḃoċtaidsiot na goill iatt, co nár ḟagaiḃsiot a bēg dia maoín nó dia mór maiṫēs aca ria mbeltaine na bliaḋna so ⁊ an ṁēid na ro díolaiṫriccheaḋ dia ndaoíniḃ, ⁊ ná ro ḃásaiccheaḋ ro ġaḃsat for sccaoíleaḋ ⁊ for eisrēdeḋ secnoin ereann diarraiḋ a mbēthaḋ.

Easraénta coccaiḋ ar nēirġe etir Sir Seóirsi bingam ó baile an ṁóta ⁊ brian na samṫaċ (.i. brian ócc) mac briain mic briain, mic eoġain uí ruairc fa beltaine na bliaḋna so. Bá hé aḋbar an imrēsna cuid do ċios na bainrioġna naċ sriṫ on mbrēirne ar in bféil sin. Brian ó Ruairc dia raḋa gaċ cios dá mbaoí gan díol gur ab ar an ffērann baí ina ḟásaċ ro ḃaoí, ⁊ nár

afterwards betrayed the cause of Hugh Roe to the English. It is stated in the Life of Hugh Roe O'Donnell, that this Niall Garv, who was a fierce and valiant champion, was the foster-brother and brother-in-law of Hugh Roe, but still that he submitted to him, not through love but fear.

[u] *After having taken with him.*—It is stated in the Life of Hugh Roe O'Donnell that O'Doherty and he came to meet each other with a party of twelve horse on either side; that Hugh Roe, indignant at the idea that O'Doherty alone should oppose him, took him prisoner, and kept him in irons until he rendered hostages for his future obedience.

son of Calvagh, son of Manus, son of Hugh Duv, with his kinsmen; and O'Doherty, namely, John Oge, the son of John, son of Felim, son of Conor Carragh, after having been taken prisoner by him[u] [Hugh Roe].

THE AGE OF CHRIST, 1593.

The Age of Christ, one thousand five hundred ninety-three.

O'Donnell (Hugh Roe) was during the month of January of this year at Lifford, his own lordly residence, confronting his enemy, Turlough Luineach, the son of Niall Conallagh. He proceeded to wreak his enmity and vengeance upon him, to expel him from his lordship, and weaken his power, in order that Hugh O'Neill might be inaugurated in his stead. He was the better of this precaution which he took, for the lordship came to Hugh O'Neill, and Turlough Luineach gave consent, and made his submission to him, in order that the dignity might be conferred on him. Hugh O'Neill, namely, the Earl, was then styled the O'Neill; and Turlough Luineach, after having made peace with O'Neill and O'Donnell, sent away the English whom he had with him. This was done in the month of May. The province of Conor Mac Nessa[x] was then under the peaceable government of these two; and they had the hostages and pledges of the inhabitants in their power, so that they were subject to them.

The Clann-William, whom we mentioned as having submitted to the Governor at the Michaelmas of the preceding year, were so impoverished by the English, that before the May of this year they left them not the smallest portion of their former wealth or great riches; and such of their people as had not been executed or (otherwise) destroyed were scattered and dispersed throughout Ireland, to seek for a livelihood.

A warlike dissension arose in the month of May in this year between Sir George Bingham of Ballymote and Brian-na-Samhthach, i. e. Brian Oge, the son of Brian, son of Brian, son of Owen O'Rourke. The cause of this dissension was, that a part of the Queen's rent had not been received out of Breifny on that festival, Brian O'Rourke asserting that all the rents not paid were those demanded for lands that were waste, and that he [Bingham] ought not to

[x] *The province of Conor Mac Nessa*, i. e. the province of Ulster, so called from Conor Mac Nessa, who was its king in the early part of the first century.

ḋliġ sium cíos diarraiḋ a ḟárac go mbeiṫ a suiḋiucchaḋ. Sir Seoirsi do ċur saiġdiuiriḋe is in mbreifne do ḋenaṁ creiċe i ngioll an ċíosa, ⁊ as é geall tarla ċuca bleaċtaċ briain uí ruairc badéin. Do ċóiḋ brian diarraiḋ a naisicc, ⁊ noċa nḟuair idir. Tainic sium iaroṁ dia ṫír, ⁊ ro ċuir tionol for aṁsoiḃ ⁊ for aos tuarastail i ttír eoġain, i ccenel cconaill, ⁊ i ffearaiḃ manaċ. Iar roċtain dóiḃ dia ḟaiġiḋ ní dearna airisem do ló no doiḋċe co ráinicc co baile an ṁótaiġ. An tan baoí i ccoṁfoccus an ḃaile ro léicc sccaoíleaḋ dá sceiṁeltoiḃ fá dá triuċa cloinne donnchaiḋ .i. an corann, ⁊ tír oilella. Nír ḃó mór don tír sin ná ro airgcc don aon ruaṫar sin. Ro loiscceaḋ lais ḃeós an lá sin trí ḃaile décc ar gaċ taoiḃ do ḃaile an moṫaiġ, ⁊ ro leir-creachaḋ baile an ṁótaiġ féin lais seaċ gaċ mbaile. Nír ḃó hionairiṁ a néċta cenmoṫa mac coḃṫaiġ ruaiḋ mécc saṁraḋáin ro marḃaḋ ó ḃrian, ⁊ gillibert grainne duine uasal do ṁuintir Sir seoirsi do ṁarḃaḋ on leiṫ naile. Ticc mac uí ruairc tar a ais co nairccṫiḃ, ⁊ co neḋalaiḃ ioṁḋa lais dia ṫír. An céd ṁí do saṁraḋ do ronaḋ innsin.

Sluaiccéaḋ lá máguiḋir aoḋ mac conċonnaċt diomṫnuṫ ris in slóiġ sin briain uí Ruairc. Aseḋ ro gaḃ cetus tre descert na breifne laiṁ clé lé loċ aillinne, duaċtar ua noilealla, ⁊ don ċorann do droiċeat mainistreaċ na buille go maċaire ċonnaċt. Ro léicc sccaoíleaḋ dá sceiṁeltoiḃ in urṫosaċ laoí fón tír ina ṫimċell. IS ann tarla don gobernóir .i. Sir Risderd bingam beiṫ ar cnoc i ndorus tuillsccí i mbarúntaċt Rossa commain in oiḋċe sin ag coiṁéisteaċt fris an tír ina timċeall, ⁊ do rala drong do ṁarcsloiġ an gobernora ag cuartuccaḋ na ccnoc ar gaċ taoiḃ don tulaiġ i mbaoí sium, ⁊ ní ro ráṫaiġsiot ní lá dallciaċ na maidne muiċe go ttarla iad féin, ⁊ maguiḋir co na marcsluaġ aghaiḋ in aghaiḋ. Do radsat marcsluaġ an gobernora cúl dóiḃ, ⁊ ro leanaḋ iad gan ċoigill lá maguiḋir co na ṁuintir, ⁊ ro bás agá sraoiġleaḋ, ⁊ agá síorḃualaḋ co roċtain dóiḃ gus an ccosttaḋ ⁊ gus an ccomnart airm i mbaoí an gobernóir. Ro filleaḋ doridisi ar Maguiḋir i ffriṫing na conaire céḋna, ⁊ ro bás agá leanmain go dol dó i neidirmeaḋón a ċóiriġṫeaḃ. Ot connairc an gobernóir co na baoí coiṁlíon daoíne friú ro fill

[y] *More than*, literally, "and Ballymote itself was totally plundered by him beyond every bally." The Irish preposition seaċ means *extra*, i. e. beyond, or more than, in this clause, as is evident from the context. See the Editor's Irish Grammar, part ii. chap. vii. p. 318.

[z] *Gilbert Grayne*.—Sir Henry Docwra calls him "Captain Grenn Omoley," in his Account

demand rent for waste lands until they should be inhabited. Sir George sent soldiers into Breifny to take a prey in lieu of the rent; and the soldiers seized on O'Rourkes own milch cows. Brian went to demand a restoration of them, but this he did not at all receive. He then returned home, and sent for mercenaries and hireling troops to Tyrone, Tirconnell, and Fermanagh; and after they had come to him, [he set out, and] he made no delay by day or by night until he arrived at Ballymote. On his arrival in the neighbourhood of the town, he dispersed marauding parties through the two cantreds of the Mac Donoughs, namely, Corann and Tirerrill; and there was not much of that country which he did not plunder on the excursion. He also burned on that day thirteen villages on every side of Ballymote; and he ravaged Ballymote itself more than[y] [he did] any other town. Their losses were of little account, except the son of Coffey Roe Magauran, on the side of Brian; Gilbert Grayne[z], a gentleman of Sir George's people, who was slain on the other side. The son of O'Rourke then returned back to his own territory loaded with great preys and spoils. This was done in the first month of summer.

A hosting was made by Maguire (Hugh, the son of Cuconnaught), to emulate that excursion of Brian O'Rourke. He proceeded first through the eastern part of Breifny, keeping Lough Allen to the left; then through the upper part of Tirerrill, through Corran, and across the bridge at the monastery of Boyle, into Machaire Connacht. Early in the day he dispatched marauding parties through the country around. This night the Governor, Sir Richard Bingham, happened to be on a hill near the gate of Tulsk, in the barony of Roscommon, watching the surrounding country; and a party of his cavalry went forth to scour the hills around the hill on which he was [stationed]; but they noticed nothing, in consequence of a thick fog of the early morning, until they and Maguire's cavalry met face to face. The Governor's cavalry turned their backs to them, and they were hotly pursued by Maguire and his people, who continued to lash and strike them until they arrived at the camp[a] and fortification where the Governor was. They again turned upon Maguire, and pursued him back by the same road, until he had reached the middle of his forces. When the Governor saw that he had not an equal number of men with them, he returned

of Services done by Sir Richard Bingham, already referred to.

[a] *Camp.*—Copcaö .ı. caı apcaö.—*Old Glos.*, i. e. a temporary dwelling, a camp.

tar a ais, ⁊ térna féin co na mbaoí ina ḟarradh ón ffoiréiccin sin genmotá uilliam clifart (duine uasal dearsccaiġṫe) go ccuiccear nó séisear marcaċ amaille fris do ṁarḃaḋ don ċur sin. Ro marḃaḋ don taoiḃ oile Emann mag samhradain priomaiḋ arda maċa (do rala co tesccṁaiseaċ i ffoċair méguiḋir) ⁊ an tab maguiḋir .i. caṫal mac an abbaḋ, ⁊ Macc caffraiġ feilim, ⁊ Mac a dSerḃraṫar. An 3 lá do mí iul ro marḃaitt iadsin, ar aoí tra ní ro léanaḋ Máguiḋir ó sin co hoiḋċe, ⁊ rucc creaċa, ⁊ tromairccṫe an tire, ⁊ do ċóiḋ ón ḟorlongport go a cele go coḃsaiḋ céim riġin co fearaiḃ manaċ.

Baoí Maguiḋir, ⁊ an brian ó Ruairc remráite fri ré an tsaṁraiḋ i ccaoṁaonta ċoccaiḋ ⁊ aiḋṁillte for ġallaiḃ. Baoí ḃeós brian mac aoḋa óicc mic aoḋa, mic Seain ḃuiḋe még maṫġaṁna ó ḋartraiġe oirġiall, ⁊ clann eiṁir mic conulaḋ ó ḟernmaiġ ⁊ Risderd mac uillicc a búrc .i. mac deṁain an ċorrain mar an ccédna for foġail ⁊ for díbfercc in acchaiḋ gall. Tucc-

[b] *Accidentally.*—Camden thought that the titular Primate, Mac Gauran, accompanied Maguire on this excursion designedly, to encourage him to fight against the heretics. His words are as follows:

"Ille [Mac Guyrus vir ingenii et pugnacissimi] prædabundus in vicinos agros irruit, Conacthiam ingreditur concomitante Gaurano sacrifico, qui a Papa Primas Hiberniæ designatus, jussit ut Deo fretus fortunam experiretur, certam victoriam pollicitus. Secus tamen accidit, Mac Guiro fortitudine Rich. Binghami fugato, & Primate cum pluribus occiso. Mox Mac Guyrus in apertam rebellionem prorumpit, quem Tir-Oenius Officii prosequutus, vulnus cum magna fortitudinis & fidei accipit."—*Annales Reg. Elis.*, A. D. 1593.

The account of this irruption of Maguire into Connaught, and of Archbishop Magauran's death, is given as follows by Philip O'Sullevan Beare, *Hist. Cathol. Iber.*, tom. iii. l. ii, c. 6:

"Sub hoc tempus Edmundus Macgabhranus Iberniæ Primas, Archiepiscopus Ardmachæ ex Hispania à Iaimo Flamingo Pontanensi mercatore vehitur, habens ad Ibernos Regis Hispaniæ mandata, vt Protestantibus pro Fide Catholica bellum indicant, & ab ipso quam celerrimè auxilium mittendum esse, intelligant: & ad Macguierem, qui iam bellum gerebat, profectus, cupidum bellandi virum Catholici Regis verbis & auxilij spe in incœpto facilè confirmauit. Cum Primate Macguier Brethnia Orruarki Principatu transmissa rursus Connachtam exiguis viribus ingreditur. Ea de re certior factus Richardus Binghamus Anglus eques auratus Connachtæ præfectus in illum mittit Gulielmum Guelfertum Anglum cum paruis copijs. Ad locum cui scuto miraculorum [*Skieth na bhfeart*] antiquitas nomen indidit, occurritur. Vtriusque partis equitatus peditum agmina præibat, tacitis cornibus procedens. Dies erat densissima nebula perquam obscura. Quare prius ferè vtrique alteros offenderunt, quam viderunt. Signo tuba subito dato vtrinque in pugnam proruitur. Macguier, quo erat præsentissimo semper animo, Guelfertum hasta transfodit, & interimit, eiusque equitatum fundit, & fugat. Macguierem non procul antè pedestre agmen sequebatur Primas

back, he himself and all his people having escaped scathless from that conflict, except only William Clifford, a distinguished gentleman, and five or six horsemen, who were slain on that occasion. On the other side were slain, Edmond Magauran, Primate of Armagh, who happened accidentally[b] to be along with Maguire on this occasion; the Abbot Maguire, (Cathal, son of the Abbot); Mac Caffry (Felim), and his brother's son. These were slain on the third day of July. Maguire was not pursued any more on that day[c]; and, having carried away the preys and great spoils of that country, he proceeded steadily and slowly, from one encampment to another, to Fermanagh.

The Maguire and the Brian O'Rourke before mentioned confederated during the summer to war against and plunder the English. Brian, the son of Hugh Oge[d], son of Hugh, son of John Boy Mac Mahon, from Dartry-Oriel; the sons of Ever Mac Cooley[e], from Farney; and Richard, son of Ulick Burke, i. e. the son of Deamhon-an-Charrain, were also in insurrection and rebellion against

Equo vectus et duobus tantum equitibus Felmio Maccaphrio, & Cathalo Macguiere comitatus: in quem, dum Macguier dum Guelferto dimicat, altera regij equitatus turma incidit. Primas fugiens equo corruit, & stratus humi interimitur vnà cum Felmio pugnante. Ex agmine Catholico pedites, qui Primatis vocem cognouerunt, & si illum non videbant, nebula oculorum vsum intercipiente, accurrunt, & Cathalum stricto ferro pro Primate præliantem existimantes esse ex Protestantibus multis vulneribus conficiunt, & Protestantes equorum pernicitate illæsos dimittunt. Interfecto Primate Macguier magis mæstus, quam obtenta victoria, & præda lætus domum redit. Rursus Orruarkus, & Macguier statuentes non modo Protestantibus Anglis, sed etiam ijs Catholicis Ibernis, qui illis auxiliabantur, esse officiendum in Midhia Inaliam Opheralis ditionem deprædantur. Cum quibus de præda cæpit equestri prœlio experiri Guliemus Opheral, sed in ipso equitum primo congressu Macguier pugnæ finem fecit, qua erat felicitate, & virtute, Gulielmum hasta traijciendo. Quo occiso cæteri nihil amplius institerunt, & Orruarkus, & Macguier præda potiuntur."—Fol. 127, 128.

The reader will also find a somewhat similar account of these events in Lombard, *De Hib. Com.*, p. 345; and Stuart's *Historical Memoirs of the City of Armagh*, pp. 269, 270.

[c] *On that day*, literally, "Maguire was not followed from that till night," which is not correct, because he was not followed then either.

[d] *Brian, the son of Hugh Oge.*—See his pedigree given in the *Account of the Territory or Dominion of Farney*, by E. P. Shirley, Esq., p. 150.

[e] *Ever Mac Cooley.*—He is called Farmer of the Fernie by Fynes Moryson. His pedigree is given by Mr. Shirley, *ubi supra*, and long extracts from his petitions to the Queen, and to the Lord Treasurer, are given in pp. 97–100. In a letter of recommendation of this Ever Mac Cooley, by the Lord Deputy and Council, 5th January, 1592–3, he is styled "a principall gentleman of the county of Monochan, attending the Court in England, his children civilly brought up, and have the English language."

sat na hairgialla si amus for banna saighdiuir baoí i muineacán go ro marḃaḋ leó a nurṁór conaḋ de sin tainicc proclamation do ċor in gaċ baile mór dá mbaoí in érinn dia ḟoccra na drongа sin a dubramar (co na ccoṁaontaiḃ) do beiṫ ina ttretuiriḃ.

Ro ḟoccair an iustis iarsin isin ffoghmar ar ccinn do ṁórsluaiġeaḋ na miḋe laiġen ⁊ leiṫe moġa dol i nulltoiḃ. Ro ḟóccair mar an ccéḋna gobernoir ċóicciḋ ċonnaċt sloicceaḋ ó ḟionainn go droḃaoís do ḋol ina ccoinne go herne. Dala an iustis do radraiḋe a ionaḋ féin ar an slóicceaḋ sin do ṁarasccal an iubair ⁊ diarla tíre heoġain .i. aoḋ mac firdorċa, mic cuinn ḃacaiġ. Ro imtiġsiot na slóiġ líonmara lánṁóra sin don taoḃ ṫoir do loċ erne o ċarn mór sleḃe beṫa go hes ruaiḋ. Nír ḃó laind lá hiarla tíre heoġain toċt for an tslóicceaḋ sin, ara aoí ro ḃaoí duaṁan na ngall fair gur ḃó héiccen dó a riar do ġníoṁ.

Od ċuala Aoḋ ṁáguidir toiċesteal an tslóiġ lánṁoir sin dia ḟaiġiḋ ro ċuir a ċroḋ ⁊ a ceṫra etir ḃú ⁊ innili i ccenel cconaill for a iomġaḃail. Ḃaoí féin gus an uathaḋ slóiġ tarrustair ina ḟarraḋ dia tír féin ⁊ daṁraiḃ a tíriḃ ele don taoiḃ ṫiar do loċ acc inis ceṫlionn for cionn na ngall co ná léicceaḋ tairis iatt an dú sin, ⁊ ro ġabsat iaraṁ laiṁ clí sris an loċ (aṁail reṁebertmar) go rangattar aṫ oirḋéirc fil for an eirne .i. aṫ ċúluain. An ccein báttarrsoṁ acc toċt an dú sin ro buí Maguidir co na ḟoċraitte ag coiṁimṫeaċt friú don taoiḃ tiar do loċ go rainicc gus an aṫ ċéḋna don taoiḃ araill. Ro ionnsaiġsiot iaraṁ an slóġ gall an táth, ⁊ ro ḃaoí Maguidir agá cosnaṁ friú reiḃ a ċuṁaing. Ar a aoí tra ro ḟíoraḋ an senḟocal .i. luiġiḋ iolar ar uaṫaḋ uair rob éiccen an táṫ do léiccen do na gallaiḃ, ⁊ ro sraoíneaḋ for ṁaguiḋir, ⁊ ro marḃaḋ sochaiḋe dia muintir. Ro gonaḋ iarla tíre heoġain don ċur sin.

[f] *Carn-mor*, now Carnmore, a townland in that part of the parish of Clones, which extends into the county of Fermanagh.—See Ordnance map, sheet 35. It is a part of the range of Slieve Beagh, or Slieve Baha, and contains a large carn from which it has derived its name, and which is a very conspicuous object, of which a good view can be obtained from the top of the moat at Clones. For the situation of Sliabh Beatha, *anglice* Slieve Beagh, see note [n], under the year 1501, p. 1260, *supra*.

[g] *To avoid them*, i. e. away from them.

[h] *Ath-Culuain*.—P. O'Sullevan Beare calls this "Beal au Cluoen, os vadi prati;" and it is "Bel atha cul uain," in these Annals, at the year 1597. It is still the name of a ford on the River Erne, about half a mile to the west of Belleek.—See note [u], under the year 1247, p. 341, *supra*.

the English. These people of Oriel made an attack upon a company of soldiers who were [stationed] at Monaghan, and slew the greater part of them; wherefore a proclamation was issued to every town in Ireland, declaring the aforesaid persons and their confederates to be traitors.

In the autumn following, the Lord Chief Justice commanded a great hosting of [the men of] Meath, Leinster, and Leath-Mogha, to proceed into Ulster; and the Governor of the province of Connaught ordered a hosting [of all those dwelling in the region extending] from the Shannon to the Drowes, to meet them at Lough Erne. As for the Lord Justice, he gave his own place on this hosting to the Marshal of Newry and the Earl of Tyrone (Hugh, the son of Feardorcha). These numerous and very great forces marched from Carn-mor[f] of Sliabh-Beatha to Easroe, [keeping] on the east side of Lough Erne. It was not pleasing to the Earl of Tyrone to go on this expedition; however, he had so much dread of the English that he was obliged to obey them.

When Hugh Maguire heard that this great hosting was approaching him, he sent all his property, both cows and flocks, into Tirconnell, to avoid them[g], while he himself remained at the west side of the lake, at Enniskillen, with a small army of the inhabitants of his own territory, and hired soldiers from other territories, to oppose the English, and to prevent them passing that place. The others marched with their left to the lake, as we have before stated, until they arrived at a celebrated ford on the Erne, namely, Ath-Culuain[h]. While they were advancing to that place, Maguire and his forces kept pace with them at the other side of the lake, so that he arrived at the same ford on the opposite side. The English army then proceeded to cross the ford; and Maguire attempted to defend it as well as he was able. But the proverb, "the many shall overcome the few," was verified in this instance, for Maguire was obliged to let the English pass the ford, and was defeated, with the loss of a considerable number of his people. The Earl of Tyrone[i] was wounded on this occasion.

[i] *The Earl of Tyrone.*—This is the last action in which Tyrone fought on the side of the English. The Marshal Bagnal, whose sister had been carried off by Tyrone, who married her, impeached him of divers treasons, to which he replied, offering even to appear in England and there to defend his cause, or to maintain his innocence in single combat with his adversary.—See Captain Lee's Letter to Queen Elizabeth, in the *Desiderata Curiosa Hibernica*, vol. ii. p. 91, *et sequent.*; and Leland's *History of Ireland*, book iv. c. 4. The following account of this attack upon Maguire, and the cause of Tyrone's disaffection, is given in P. O'Sullevan Beare's

Tánaicc gobernoir cóicciḋ connacht, ⁊ iarla tuadhmumhan donnchadh mac concobhair mic donnchaidh í bhriain ina ccoinne don taoibh ele don erne, ⁊ ní

Hist. Cathol. Iber. Compend., tom. iii. lib. ii. cc. 7, 10:

"Hæc dum agebantur, exercitus duo, quos in Macguierem conscribi Regina iusserat, comparati sunt. Alteri præerat Henricus Bagnal eques Auratus Iberniæ Castrametator, et Vltoniæ præfectus, qui minimé spernendas copias ex Ibernis, & Anglis præsidiarijs, Ibernisque nuper delectis ducebat. Equites habebat septingentos quorum partem maiorem, et peditum non paruam perduxit Comes Tironus, qui iussus Reginæ imperio non gerere morem, minime sibi integrum putabat. Macguier impendente periculo perculsus Odonellum, vt sibi præsidium ferat, rogat. Ex quo acceptis paucis Ibernis bipenniferis, & Scotis sagittarijs, & aliquot obæratis suis armatis longè exiguiores copias, quam hostis, habebat, quorum erant equites ferè centum. Bagnal cis Ernium flumen cum copijs omnibus constitit, inde traiecturus fluminis vadum, quod Prati nuncupatur, Macguierisque obæratos, qui eó fugerant, prædaturus. Ab altera parte Macguier consederat. Vltrò, citròque missilibus prælium inchoatur, Regij numero militum, armorum genere, natura loci prestabant. Nam, & peditatus multitudine superiores erant, equites septingentos contra centum habebant, & bombardarios contra sagittarios: neque enim sagittam tam longè iaculatur arcus, quám bombarda plumbeam pilam. Prætereà bombardarij ex sylua, quæ ad fluminis ripam pertinebat, Catholicos in planicie stantes, impunè feriebant: et sagittarij in regios arborum densitate protectos minimè poterant sagittas collineare. Ita cum pugnaretur magno Catholicorum detrimento, Comes Tironus, qui regio equitatui præerat, calcaribus additis cum omni equitatu vadum penetrat, & in Catholicos impressionem faciens omnes fundit, fusosqué insequitur non tamen longe, nam ab Iberno pedite per femur telo transfixus est, & Macguier cum equitatu suo peditibus fert subsidium. Ea pugna desiderati sunt Catholici minus ducenti, ex regijs per quam pauci. Inter Tironum, qui qui fuit graui vulnere affectus, & Bagnalem ex hac quoque victoria vetus inimicitia augetur, dum vterque sibi gloriam arrogat: Bagnal, quod ipse esset exercitus imperator, & Vltoniæ præfectus cæteros imperio regens; Tironus, quod ipse magnà equitatus partem ductitauerit, vadum cum equitibus transmiserit, Macguierianos in fugam verterit, periculum adierit, & vulnus acceperit. Ob id à Bagnale rogatus, vt litteris Reginam, & Proregem de ipsius virtute faceret certiorem, se illis coram verum dicturum respondit. Odonellus, qui cum vberiore equitatu, bombardarijs, & hastatis Macguieri suppetias ibat, ad noctem post pugnam factam peruenit, hostemque inuaderet, nisi per internuncios a Tirono clàm rogaretur, vt ipsius salutis rationem haberet, Protestantes non circumueniens, dum in eorum castris ipse esset, quæ citò foret deserturus, vt deseruit: nam timens, ne à Bagnale vinculis mandaretur, & ad Proregem vinctus traheretur (vt iussum fuisse credebatur) ea nocte e castris saucius fugit in Dunganinnam municipium suum, vbi medicamentis adhibitis breui curatur. Eodem tempore Richardus Binghamus Connachtæ præfectus Iniskellinnam magis intestina proditione, quam vi capit. Ea insula est non magna Ernio lacu cincta, in qua Macguier arcem duplici vallo cinctâ tenebat. In hanc Binghamus copijs in Connachta conscriptis ex Anglis aliquot, sed Ibernis pluribus Catholicis signa militaria pedestria quindecim, & equestria quatuor per Brethniam Orruarki ditionem tunc temporis vastam, atque direptam perduxit, vectusque pontonibus, & phasellis arcem diebus aliquot frustra oppugnat, militibus octoginta magna virtute propugnantibus: haud

The Governor of the province of Connaught and the Earl of Thomond (Donough, the son of Conor, son of Donough O'Brien) came to meet them at

dubius in cassum se vires diffundere, dato signo, propugnatores ad colloquium prouocat. Ad eum in castra prodit vnus non satis genere notus, sed cui propugnatores maximè suam salutem, & arcem credebant, quòd apud Macguierem familiaritate plurimum valebat, ab eoque donis ornabatur. Filius porcæ, vel scrophæ cognominabatur, nec incongruè: nam præterquam, quod statura erat inelegante, & facie difformi, illi etiam duo Columellares dentes ore prominebant similes suis, vel apri fulminibus. A Binghamo promissionibus, atque donis corruptus, & victus, postquam cum eo statuit, quemadmodum sit arcem proditurus, ad suos, tamquam arcem ad internecionem defensurus, rediuit. Binghamus induciarum spacio transacto more solito arcem oppugnat. Propugnatores suam quisque partem tutantur. Filius scrophæ, quasi sortiter, & animosè dimicaturus sese in exteriore vallo hostibus ostentat. Hi illum magno agmine aggrediuntur. Ille ex composito fugiens locum defensore nudum deserit, & tamquam sese recipiens, in secundum vallum celeriter confert: quò etiam sequentibus hostibus aditum permittit, arcis portam subiens, quam ingresso, miles qui ad portam in stationibus erat, venientibus hostibus portam claudere, & obserare festinat: sed illum Filius Scrophæ stricto ferro percutiendo humi sternens patefactis foribus hostes inducit, qui propugnatores omnes præter proditorem interemerunt: et senes pueros, atque fæminas, qui in arcem confugerant ex sublicio ponte, quo insula cum continente coniungebatur, præcipites dederunt. Locato in arce præsidio Binghamus, & Bagnal celeriter reuertuntur cum Tirono iam diffidentes, tum Odonellum, & Macguierem majoribus copijs refectum timentes."—*Cap.* vii.

"Hæc dum aguntur, & Odonellus Iniskellinnæ obsidionem producit, Tironus Comes magis indies Protestantibus infensus, & suspectus redditur. Principio ob victoriam apud vadum Prati de Macguiere obtentam gratiæ a Regina Bagnali relatæ sunt, Tirono verò ne actæ quidem, aut habitæ, quo nihil hic impatientius ferebat: neque tam cruciabatur, se digno prœmio fuisse fraudatum, quam eo Bagnalem ornatum, lœtantem, atque triumphantem: quippè vterque alterum inexpiabili odio persequebatur multis de causis. Bagnal Vltoniæ præfectus Tirono videbatur in prouincialium bona facere impetum, & prohibebatur. Tironus Bagnalis sororem fæminam forma conspicuam speciei pulchritudine captus rapuerat, matrimonio sibi coniunxerat, & ex Protestante conuerti ad fidem Catholicam fecerat: pactam sibi dotem à Bagnale retineri querebatur. Bagnal sæpè dixerat non tam claritate mariti sororem suam, & familiam esse decoratam, quam Papistæ rebellione, & perfidia esse breui fœdandam, & illi esse priuignos, quibus, et non sororis suæ liberis, si quos progigneret, esset hæreditas amplissima deferenda. Ob has, & alias causas vterque alterum in singulare certamen Dubhlinnæ prouocauerat, congressurique videbantur, nisi ab amicis anteuerterentur. Hinc Bagnal nullam incommodandi Tirono, & in eum accendendi Reginæ inuidiam occasionem prætermittebat. Insuper Tirono occurrebat Macmagaunus crudeli supplicio nuper affectus, & eius nomen Parlamenti decreto extinctum; alijque principes Iberni deleti in mentem veniebant. Sed Catholico viro Catholicæ Religionis libertas præcipuè ante oculos obuersabatur. Quibus & aliæ suspiciones nouè accesserunt. Iohannes Onellus Tironæ princeps cum fuisset à Scotis militibus suis per perfidiam extinctus (vt superius tradidimus) eius quoque possessiones Angliæ Reginæ fuerunt addictæ, & si frustra, nam sunt retentæ à Terentio Onello. Inter has Farnia Iberi Macmaganni municipium, reginæ etiam fuit adiudicata eo nomine, quòd ad

ḋergénsat nach ní ioir acht an gobernoir go nḟirge amach cóicciḋ Ċonnacht do ṡóaḋ go mainistir na buille ⁊ a bḟiṫ sé hathaiḋ annsin ag creachaḋ muintire heólais ⁊ iarṫair ḟḟrmanaċ. Ro sccaoilsiot sir Ċonnaċt dia ttiġiḃ ar a haiṫle. Do ḋeachaiḋ iarla tíre heoġain ⁊ an marasccál dia ttiġiḃ iar milleaḋ moráin i ffḟraiḃ manaċ. Ro ḟáccaiḃsiot bandaiġe isin tír ag congnaṁ la concoḃar ócc mac conċoḃair ruaiḋ meguiḋir baoí in eccraittḟs ré máguiḋir. Bá nḟṁsóinṁeċ ḟsaontaḋaċ ro bás ó cloċar mac ndaiṁene i ttir eoccain go ráiṫ cruaċain i cconnaċtaiḃ ⁊ ó ṫráiġ eoṫuile go breifne uí raiġilliġ an tan sin.

Mág carṫaiġ riaḃaċ .i. Eoġan mac domnaill mic finġin tiġearna cairbreaċ do écc, fḟr ceilliġ craiḃḋeċ ro ba maiṫ eneċ, ⁊ oirbḟrt eriḋe, ⁊ domnall mac corbmaic na haoíne do ġaḃail a ionaiḋ.

Maire inġean corbmaic óicc mic ċorbmaic, mic taiḋcc meg carṫaiġ bḟn uí suilleḃáin moir do écc.

Muirċḟrtaċ mac conċoḃair, mic toirrḋealḃaiġ uí ḃriain ó ḋruim laiġḟn

Iohannem pertinebat, & á Regina Comiti Essexiæ Anglo dono data. Sed tunc temporis neque adiudicatio neque donatio executioni mandata est Ibero possessiones suas obtinente. Posteà Comitis huius iam mortui filius Farniam cuidam Iohanni Talboto Angloiberno locauit, Talbotusque in Farniæ castellum, & possessionem á Reginæ iudicibus mittitur, frustra á Catholicis obiurgatus, quód minimè iustè Iberi Catholici viri possessiones ab Hæretico, qui in eas iniusta actione agebat, conduxerit. Iberi verò filij eam opportunam occasionem rati, qua gerebat Odonellus arma, amicorum manu coacta Farniam castellum noctu inuadunt. Foribus improuisó ignem admouent. Castelli inquilinus Talbotus suffocante fumo expergefactus subucula tantum indutus lecto exsilit, foresque patefacit; poné ianuam absconditus, vbi Iberi liberi cum agmine suo irruperunt, nudus egressus pedibus salutem petit, quem sua familia sequitur eiecta, & direpta. Cuius rei culpam Angli in Tironum transferebant, asserentes hoc inuito, nihil illos ausuros. Sub idem tempus Angli, qui Ardmacham Primatis Iberni sedem præsidio tenebant, templum ingredi constituunt, resistentemque æedituum, & alios sacerdotes in vincula conijcere. Ad rixam accurrens Bernardus Onellus, qui tunc forte in oppido erat, sacerdotes in libertatem asserit. Duodecim Anglos milites patibulo suspendi iubet. Reliqui præsidiarij fugiunt, cuius rei authorem fuisse Tironum Protestantes pro re certa, indubitataque confirmabant."—*Cap.* x.

Captain Thomas Lee, who wrote his memorial addressed to Queen Elizabeth in 1594, and who had commanded some troops in various posts on the frontiers of Ulster, during Fitz-William's administration, and who was well acquainted with the machinations of Bagnal, who had been planted at Newry, to effect the ruin of the O'Neills, thus writes of the trial by combat with which O'Neill offered to clear himself of Bagnal's accusations of treason :

"And then, I am persuaded, he will simply acknowledge to your Majesty how far he hath offended you ; and besides, notwithstanding his

the other side of the Erne. They effected nothing [worthy of note], except that the Governor returned with the rising-out of Connaught to the Abbey of Boyle, where he remained for some time, plundering Muintir-Eolais and the west of Fermanagh. The men of Connaught then dispersed for their homes. The Earl of Tyrone and the Marshal [also] returned to their houses, after destroying much in Fermanagh. They left companies of soldiers in the country to assist Conor Oge, the son of Conor Roe Maguire, who was at strife with the Maguire. Unhappy and disturbed was the state of [the entire extent of country] from Clogher Mac Daimhene in Tyrone to Rath-Croghan in Connaught, and from Traigh-Eothuile to Breifny O'Reilly, at this time.

Mac Carthy Reagh (Owen[k], the son of Donnell, son of Fineen), Lord of Carbery, died. He was a sensible, pious, truly hospitable, and noble-deeded man. Donnell, the son of Cormac-na-h-Aoine, took his place.

Mary, the daughter of Cormac Oge, son of Cormac, son of Teige Mac Carthy, and wife of O'Sullivan More, died.

Murtough, son of Conor, son of Turlough O'Brien, of Druim-Laighean[l], died,

protection, he will, if it so stand with your Majesty's pleasure, offer himself to the Marshal (who hath been the chiefest instrument against him), to prove with his sword that he hath most wrongfully accused him; and because it is no conquest for him to overthrow a man ever held in the world to be of most cowardly behaviour, he will in defence of his innocency allow his adversary to come armed against him naked, to encourage him the rather to accept of his challenge. I am bold to say thus much for the Earl, because I know his valour, and am persuaded he will perform it."

[k] *Owen.*—He was Sir Owen Mac Carthy Reagh, Chief of Carbery, a district in the county of Cork, now divided into four baronies.—See *Genealogies, Tribes, &c. of Hy-Fiachrach*, p. 447, in which is quoted a Chancery Record, from which it appears that Teige O'Donovan, in his replication to his brother, Donnell O'Donovan, asserts that this Sir Owen Mac Carthy was an intruder, and that Donnell Mac Carthy was entitled to be "Mac Cartie Reough, whereunto he had right by her Highnes' Patents." The Donnell mentioned in this Chancery Record is the very person referred to in the text as the successor of Owen, the son of Donnell. According to the manuscript, entitled *Carbriæ Notitia*, already often quoted, this Donnell was usually called Donnell-ni-pipy [ḋoṁnall na bpíopaiḋe] from some pipes of wine which were washed ashore during his time, which was considered an omen of good success. He married Margaret, the daughter of the Earl of Desmond, and had by her a son, Cormac, who married Eleanor, daughter of the White Knight, and had by her a son, Daniel, who married Helen, daughter of the Lord Roche, and had by her a son, Charles, who married Eleanor, daughter of Lord Muskerry, and had by her a son, Daniel Mac Carthy Reagh, who was living in the time of the writer of *Carbriæ Notitia* [1686], and married to Mary, daughter of Col. Townshend.

[l] *Druim-Laighean*, now Dromline, in a parish

décc, ⁊ a adhnacal ina ḃaile fſn .i. i nDruim laiġſn, ⁊ a ṁac concoḃar do ġaḃáil a ionaiḋ.

Muirċſrtaċ mac domnaill, mic concoḃair uí ḃriain ó ṫulċa décc.

Tadcc mac uilliam mic taidcc duiḃ uí ċeallaiġ ón ċalaḋ i ccriċ ua maine décc, ⁊ ro ba do ṁóirsccélaiḃ ó maine an tí tſsda ann sin.

O duiḃidir ċoille na manaċ .i. pilip mac uaiṫne décc, ⁊ a ṁac diarmait do ġaḃáil a ionaid.

Mairġréc ingſn uí ḃaoiġill (toirrdealḃaċ) décc.

AOIS CRIOST, 1594.

Aois Criost, mile, cúicc céd, nóċat, acſtair.

Mac maṫġaṁna .i. tiġearna corc baiscind airṫſraiġi décc .i. Tadcc mac murchaiḋ, mic taidcc ruaiḋ, mic toirrdealḃaiġ, mic taidcc, ⁊ a ṁac .i. toirrdelḃaċ ruaḋ do ġaḃáil a ionaid.

O Súillebáin béirre Eocchan, mac diarmata, mic domnaill do écc. Ar a aoí ní ḃó ó Suillebáin beirre é an tan sin gér ḃó hſḋ riaṁ, dóiġ ro ḃſn mac a dearḃraṫar an ḃliaḋain ria na écc dún baoí, ⁊ béirre de .i. domnall mac domnaill mic diarmata iar mbrſiṫ ċomairle Saxan ⁊ comairle na hereann, ⁊ ro gairſḋ ó Suillebáin béirre do domnall fſissin.

O dubda tíre fiacraċ .i. dathí, mac taidcc riaḃaiġ mic eoġain do ṁarbaḋ lá saiġdiúir do ṁuintir na bainrioġna i mbaile dia ḃailtiḃ feisin i ttír ḟiacraċ muaiḋe.

O hſidin Aoḋ buiḋe mac eoġain ṁanntaiġ, mic emainn, mic floinn do écc.

of the same name, in the barony of Bunratty, and county of Clare. In the Description of the County of Clare, in the Library of Trin. Col. Dublin, E. 2. 14, this castle is placed in "West Mac Namara's country," and the proprietor of it is set down as "Muriertagh O'Brien," who is the very person mentioned above in the text.

[m] *Tulach.*—There were two castles of this name in the county of Clare, according to the description of that county just referred to, namely, Tullagh, which gave name to the barony of Tulla, in the east of the county, and which belonged, in 1585, to "Donell Reagh Mac Nemara;" and Tullagh, in the barony of "Corkemroe," in the west of the same county, which then belonged to Sir Donell [son of Conor] O'Brien, who was the father of the Murtough above mentioned in the text. We may, therefore, safely conclude that the Tulach of the text is the castle of Tullagh, in the barony of Corcomroe.

and was interred in his own town of Druim-Laighean; and his son, Conor, took his place.

Murtough, the son of Donnell, son of Conor O'Brien of Tulach[m], died.

Teige, the son of William, son of Teige Duv O'Kelly of Caladh[n], in Hy-Many, died; and his death was among the mournful news of Hy-Many.

O'Dwyer of Coill-na-manach[o] (Philip, son of Anthony) died; and his son, Dermott, took his place.

Margaret, daughter of O'Boyle (Turlough), died.

THE AGE OF CHRIST, 1594.

The Age of Christ, one thousand five hundred ninety-four.

Mac Mahon, Lord of East Corca-Bhaiscinn[p], died, namely, Teige, the son of Murrough, son of Teige Roe, son of Turlough, son of Teige; and his son, Turlough Roe, took his place.

O'Sullivan Beare (Owen, the son of Dermot, son of Donnell) died. He was not, however, the O'Sullivan Beare at that time, though he had once been; for in the year previous to his death, his brother's son, Donnell, the son of Donnell, son of Dermot, had, by the decision of the Council of England and the Council of Ireland, deprived him of Dunbaoi [the castle of Dunboy] and Beare; and Donnell himself was nominated the O'Sullivan Beare.

O'Dowda of Tireragh (Dathi, the son of Teige Reagh, son of Owen) was slain by one of the Queen's soldiers, in one of his own castles in Tireragh on the Moy.

O'Heyne[q] (Hugh Boy, the son of Owen Mantagh, son of Edmond, son of Flan) died.

[n] *Caladh*, now Callow, in the barony of Kilconnell, and county of Galway.—See note [t], under the year 1475, p. 1097, *supra*.

[o] *Coill-na-manach*, i. e. the wood of the monks, now the barony of Kilnamanagh, in the county of Tipperary, which was O'Dwyer's country.

[p] *East Corca-Bhaiscinn*.—According to the Description of the County of Clare just referred to, "the Baronie of Cloynetherala [Clonderalaw] conteyns East Corkewasken, and Tege Mac Mahone was chiefe in the same." This Tege Mac Mahon was the father of the Murrough mentioned in the text.

[q] *O'Heyne*.—Upon the surrender of his property to the Crown, he received a re-grant of an extensive estate in the original territory, in the thirtieth year of Elizabeth.—See *Genealogies, &c. of Hy-Fiachrach*, p. 404. This is the last

Ingen ṁic uí Ḃriain ara .i. onora ingen toirrḋealḃaiġ, mic Muirċeartaiġ, mic domnaill mic taidcc ben ṗiarais mic emainn an ċalaiḋ mic piarais ruaiḋ buitilér décc.

Slóicceaḋ mór do ṫionól lár an iustis, ⁊ ráinicc gan ráṫuccaḋ tar na críochaiḃ rostar coṁfoiccsi dó gan naċ niomḟuireaċ go riaċt go hinis ceiṫ-lionn, ⁊ baoí i fforḃaisi, ⁊ i niomṡuiḋe imon dúnaiḋ, ⁊ geiḃitt an sluaġ for toġail an ṁúir lar na haiḋmiḃ bá haḋlaicc leó, ⁊ nír sccarsatt sir go ro ġaḃsat ro ḋeóiḋ, ⁊ fáccbaiḋ an iustis barda isin mbaile, ⁊ do ċuaiḋ dia ṫiġ iaraṁ.

Maguiḋir tra ó do ċuala siḋe an iustis do ṡoaḋ for cculaiḃ ro ṫionoil siḋe an líon ar lia conranaccair co mbaoí occ iomṡuiḋe an ḃaile cedna, ⁊ ro ḟaíḋ teaċta do ṡaiġiḋ uí domnaill Aoḋ ruaḋ dia cuinġiḋ fair teċt dia ḟoiriḋin. Nír ḃó héislesbaċ ro freacraḋ indsin lairsiuṁ óir do ċóiḋ dia ṡaiġiḋ co na ṡoċraiḋe, ⁊ ro ġaḃsat acc forbairi for an dún ó ṫossaċ iun go meḋon augusṫ. Ro croiṫeaḋ, ⁊ ro creachloisccead lar an soċraitte sin i mbaoí

notice of the O'Heyne family in these Annals. Duald Mac Firbis continues the pedigree of the family of Leydican for two generations more, which brings the line down to 1666, when he wrote. The Hugh Boy above mentioned in the text, had a son Hugh Boy, who had a son Owen, who seems to have been considered the head of the family in Mac Firbis's time. In 1612 O'Heyne of Leydican was Conor Crone O'Heyne, who had a son, Brian. On the 20th of February, 1612, he enfeoffed his son, Bryan O'Heyne, of and in his estates. This feoffment, the original of which is now before the Editor, runs as follows:

"To all Chresten people to whome these presents shall come, Connor Crone Oheyn of the Ledigan, in the county of Galwey, gent. send greeting in our Lord God Euerlasting. Knowe yee that I, the said Connor, for sundry good & lawfull considerations me moving, and in especiall for and in the regard and consideration both of my ffatherly care and affection, as well toward my sonne, Bryan Oheyn, as toward the establishment, continnuance, and succession of myn inheritance and living in myn owne kindred and familly, and the better ensuring and suportation of the same from ingerous challenges, suits, and vexations therevnto to be at any time pretended, wherein the impotencie of age, and state and declining yeeres, disabling me to imploy the mindfull paines and travells therevnto behoofefull, the defence and vpholding of my said Inheritance in nature and right belonging vnto my said sonne, Bryan Oheyn, haue given, graunted, enffeoffed, and confirmed, like as be these presents, I doe give, graunt, enfeoffe, and confirme, vnto the said Bryan Ohein, the third parte of a cartron of Gortenshine, the fourth parte of a cartron in the tearmon, commonly knowen by the name of Ballymollfargie and Pollantlynte and haulfe a cartron in Corroboye, being of my proper inheritance, with all and singuler the meadowes, moores, pastures, bogges, woods, vnderwoods, waters, watercourses, fishings, heats, montaines, commones, gardens, houses, land arable and land

The daughter of Mac-I-Brien Ara, Honora, daughter of Turlough, son of Murtough, son of Donnell, son of Teige, and wife of Pierce, son of Edmond an-Chaladh, son of Pierce Roe Butler, died.

A great hosting was made by the Lord Justice; and he proceeded unperceived through the adjacent territories without any delay, until he arrived at Enniskillen; and he encamped around, and laid siege to the fortress; and the army proceeded to destroy its wall with the proper engines, and they never ceased until they finally took it. And the Lord Justice left warders in the castle, and then returned to his house.

When Maguire heard that the Lord Justice had returned back, he assembled the greatest number of forces that he was able, and beleaguered the same castle, and dispatched messengers to O'Donnell (Hugh Roe), requesting him to come to his assistance. This request was promptly responded to by him [O'Donnell], for he went to join him with his forces; and they laid siege to the fortress from the beginning of June to the middle of August. [During this time] these forces plundered and laid waste all that was under the jurisdiction

pasture, vnto them or any of them belonging, or in anywise appertaining; to haue and to hould, occupie, enioy, and possess, all and euery the premisses, with their appurtenances, vnto the said Bryan Oheyn, his heires and Assignes, to his and their proper vse and vses for euer. And further knowe yee that I, the said Connor crone Oheyn, haue couenaunted and agreed that my said sonne, Bryan shall pay vnto me some reasonable rent yeerlie, during myn owne lyffe, out of the before-mentioned parcells, and after my dicease to be to the vse of him, the said Bryan, his heires and assigns, as aforesaid, for euer. And further knowe yee that I, the said Connor crone Oheyn, haue constituted, and appointed my welbeloued Teig Enurgish of the Rahine, my true and lawfull Attourney, for me and in my name, to enter into all and euery the premisses, or into any one parte thereof in name of the whole, and thereof to take full and whole possession and seizen. And for me and in my name to deliver acctuall seizen and possession vnto the said Bryan Oheyn, according the effect of this present Deede. In witness whereof, I, the said Conor Crone Oheyn, have hereunto put my hand and seale, the 20 of February, 1612.

"CONNOR CRONE OHEYNE,
is marke & seale.

"Being present when the within named Connor crone Ohein signed, sealed, and delivered this deede vnto the within named Bryen mac Connor Ohein, and as well to the within named attourney, Teig knurgish, those whose names doe follow:

"JOHN BURKE,
is marke testis.
THOMAS BURKE,
is marke testis.
THOMAS CONNOGHIN,
testis."

"Being present when the within named Teig Enurgish," &c. &c.

fo smaċt gall i cCriċ oirġiall ⁊ i mbrſifne uí Raiġilliġ co ttardsat a mbú ⁊ a ninnile a lón slóiġ dia namsoiḃ.

Baoí ó domnaill i fforlongport acc forḃairi for inis ceiṫlenn ó ṫosaċ iun co mí August aṁail atruḃramar go ttairnic a lón do caiṫſm do ḃarda an baile aċt maḋ bſcc. Rangattar teaċta do ṡaiġiḋ uí domnaill ó na halbanchaiḃ ro ṫóċuir sium ċuicce ria sin dia hairnſis dó co ttangattar co doire, ⁊ robtar iatt tangattar an dú sin domnall gorm mac domnaill ⁊ mac leóid na hara. Do ṫaod iaraṁ ua domnaill dia niomḟorttaḋ co nuathaḋ dia ṡlóġ amaille fris, ⁊ ro ḟáccaiḃ drong ṁór ele díḃ ag Mághuiḋir do ċongnaṁ lais, ⁊ ro ḟuráil forra airisioṁ acc iomsuiḋe an ḃaile.

Iar ffios scel don iustis (.i. Sir uilliam fitzuilliam) co mbadar barda innsi ceiṫlenn ind earbaiḋ lóin ⁊ bíḋ ro ḟorċongair ar droing ṁóir dḟearaiḃ miḋe, ⁊ ar uaislib raġailleaċ ⁊ biongamaċ coicciġ connaċt (.i. im sſoirsi ócc mbiongam) toċt do brſiṫ lóin go hinis ceṫlenn. Do cotar na maiṫe sin iaraṁ a ccſnd a cele a ccoinne an lóin co caḃán baile uí raiġilliġ, ⁊ ro gaḃaḋ leó laiṁ dſs lé loċ Eirne tre ḟſraiḃ manaċ go rangattar fó ṫuairim cſiṫre mile don ḃaile.

Od ċualaiḋ Maguiḋir aoḋ dáil an tslóiġ sin do bſiṫ gus an mbaile (las na lóintiḃ remraite) do ċoiḋsiḋe co na soċraiḋe buḋéin, ⁊ gus an soċraiḋe ro ḟaccaiḃ o domnaill lais, ⁊ im ċorbmac mac an ḃarúin .i. dearbraṫair an iarla uí néill go ro gabsat airisſm i nſnaċ erḋalta iomċumang in ro ba dóiġ leó a roċtain sium dia saiġiḋ. Ro ba torḃa an ſdarnaiġe ísin, uair rangattar gan ráṫuccaḋ dóiḃ badéin i ccſnd muintire meguiḋir ag bél aṫa sainrſdhaigh. Ro fiġſḋ iorġal aiġṫiḋe ainttrennda, ⁊ sccaindſr croḋa comnart ſtorra atti ú ⁊ anall, co ro sraoíneaḋ fó deóiḋ tria nſrt iombualta lá Maguiḋir co na ṡoċraiḋe for an luċt naile co ro fáccbaḋ ár ccſnd lais, ⁊ ro boí occ lſnṁain an maḋma co cian ar an maiġſn sin. Bá díriṁ a ttorcratar do ṡaorċlandaiḃ ⁊ daorċlandaiḃ is in iomaireacc sin. Ro fáccḃaḋ eiċ, arm, ⁊ édala iomḋa an dú sin lá taoḃ na neaċ ⁊ na ccapall bátar fo a neireḋaiḃ lóin do roċtain co hinis ceṫlenn. Térnatar sceolanga uaiṫe

[r] *Ara*, now Arran, an island lying to the east of Cantire in Scotland. General Stewart in his curious map of the antient Highland districts, in his Sketches, &c., of the Highlanders of Scotland, does not place Mac Leod on this island, but writes the name across the Isle of Skye, Glenelg, and other places.

[s] *At the mouth of a certain ford*, ag bél aṫa sainrſdhaiġ.—See note [m], under the year 1586, p. 1856; and note [d], under the year 1588,

of the English in the territory of Oriel, and in Breifny O'Reilly; and they gave their cows and flocks as provision stores to their soldiers.

O'Donnell, as we have stated, was encamped, laying siege to Enniskillen, from the middle of June to the month of August, until the warders of the castle had consumed almost all their provisions. Messengers came to O'Donnell from the Scots, whom he had before invited over, to inform him that they had arrived at Derry. And those who had come thither were Donnell Gorm Mac Donnell, and Mac Leod of Ara[r]. O'Donnell then set out with a small number of his forces to hire them; and he left another large party of them with Maguire to assist him, and he ordered them to remain blockading the castle.

When the Lord Justice, Sir William Fitzwilliam, had received intelligence that the warders of Enniskillen were in want of stores and provisions, he ordered a great number of the men of Meath, and of the gentlemen of the Reillys and the Binghams of Connaught, under the conduct of George Oge Bingham, to convey provisions to Enniskillen. These chieftains, having afterwards met together, went to Cavan, O'Reilly's town, for provisions; and they proceeded through Fermanagh, keeping Lough Erne on the right, until they arrived within about four miles of the town.

When Maguire (Hugh) received intelligence that these forces were marching towards the town with the aforesaid provisions, he set out with his own forces and the forces left him by O'Donnell, together with Cormac, the son of the Baron, i. e. the brother of the Earl O'Neill; and they halted at a certain narrow pass, to which they thought they [the enemy] would come to them. The ambuscade was successful, for they came on, without noticing any thing, until they fell in with Maguire's people at the mouth of a certain ford[s]. A fierce and vehement conflict, and a spirited and hard-contested battle, was fought between both parties, till at length Maguire and his forces routed the others by dint of fighting, and a strages of heads was left to him; and the rout was followed up a great way from that place. A countless number of nobles and plebeians fell in this conflict. Many steeds, weapons, and other spoils, were left behind in that place [by the defeated], besides the steeds and horses that were loaded with provisions, on their way to Enniskillen. A few fugitives of Meath and of

p. 1866, *supra*. It was first written bel aṫa na mḟirleaċ do ḟorraḋ; but the four last words are cancelled, and raimṗḃaiġ interlined in the handwriting of Michael O'Clery.

dfearaibh Midhe ⁊ do raghailleachaibh ar an ccaithiorghail sin, ⁊ ní ro hanadh leó side go rangattar go Breifne Uí Raighilligh. Bá sí conair do dheachaidh Seoirsi óce bionngam gus an uathadh at rula lais ar an láthair sin tria Lsrccain cloinne Cobhthaigh Még Samhradháin, tria Breifne Uí Ruairc, ⁊ assidhe go Sliccech. Ro claochlaídhsiot ainm for an áth agá ttuccadh an mór maidhm sin .i. bel áth na mbriosccadh do ghairm de fó dháigh an ro fáccbhadh do bhriosccaibh, ⁊ do bsccbhairgsnaibh oca an lá sin.

Ot chualattar aos coimhéda an bhaile sraoíneadh for an slóigh do beartsat an caislén do Mhaguidhir, ⁊ do beart som maithsimh nanacail dóibh.

[t] *Reillys.*—The chief of the Reillys, or O'Reillys, at this time was Sir John, the son of Hugh Conallagh O'Reilly. He died on the first of June, 1596, when his brother, Philip O'Reilly, was set up by O'Neill as the O'Reilly, though not without strong opposition from Maelmora Breagh, the son and heir of Sir John, who was supported by the English.

[u] *The Largan*, a district in the barony of Tullyhaw, and county of Cavan.—See *Chorographical Description of Iar-Connaught*, p. 347.

[w] *Bel-atha-na-mBriosgadh*, i. e. Mouth of the Ford of the Biscuits. It is translated: *Os vadi biscoctorum panum*, by P. O'Sullevan Beare.—*Hist. Cathol.*, fol. 135. The site of this battle is still traditionally remembered, but the name is obsolete. The ford is on the River Arney, in the barony of Clanawley, under Drumane bridge, about five miles to the south of Enniskillen.

[x] *Defeat.*—Cox says that news was brought to Dublin on the 11th of August, 1594, "that Cormock Mac Baron (Tyrone's brother), who besieged Iniskelling, had defeated the English, being 46 horse and 600 foot, under the conduct of Sir Edward Herbert and Sir Henry Duke." Philip O'Sullevan Beare gives the following circumstantial account of this rencounter in his *Hist. Cathol. Iber. Compend.*, tom. 3, lib. 2, c. xi. fol. 133, 134, 135:

"In hoc rerum statu Iniskellinnæ arcis præsidium ab Odonello circumsessum fame premebatur. Ac filius quidem scrophæ arcis proditor, qui in ea ab Anglis erat relictus, sus vorax esuriente ventre afflictus cum commilitonibus quinquè noctu per lacum lintre missus, quòd regionum, et itinerum expertus erat, nunciatum, quanto in discriminé versaretur arx, & à Catholicis interceptus vna cum socijs multis vulneribus interficitur. Nihilominus Angli angustiarum arcis minimé nescij suppetias ire festinant. Carnes salsæ, caseus, magna copia biscocti panis parantur. Præsidiarij milites euocantur: Ibernorum delectus habetur; ex omnibus nuper conscriptis Ibernis, & Anglis præsidiarijs duo millia, & quingenti coguntur, quorum erant equites quadringenti. His imperator præficitur Henricus Dukus Anglus eques auratus Iphaliæ principatus præfectus, & castrametator Fool etiam Anglus, de quorum consilio certior factus Odonellus, legatos ad Tironum mittit, Protestantes Iniskellinnæ subsidio venire: id se vsque ad internecionem prohibiturum: quanto in periculo res sit sita, manifestum esse, & ita Tironum à se pro hoste habendum nisi ipsi in tanto discrimine posito ferat auxilium. Qua legatione audita diuersis curis anxius Tironus distrahebatur, cum animo suo reputans Odonellum incerta spe Hispani auxilij gerere bellum, antequam Hispana signa in Ibernia videat ac ita rem Catholicorum in summo discrimine esse sitam, etiam si ipse ferat opem; sin minus Catholicis opituletur, Protes-

the Reillys[t] escaped from this conflict, and never stopped until they arrived in Breifny O'Reilly. The route taken by George Oge Bingham and the few who escaped with him from the field was through the Largan[u], [the territory] of the Clann-Coffey Magauran, through Breifny O'Rourke, and from thence to Sligo. The name of the ford at which this great victory was gained was changed to Bel-atha-na-mBriosgadh[w], from the number of biscuits and small cakes left there to the victors on that day.

When the warders of the castle heard of the defeat[x] of the army, they surrendered the castle to Maguire; and he gave them pardon and protection[y].

tantibus tamen se esse suspectum, & ita vtrisquè fore hostem iudicatum. Aduentante vero Reginæ exercitu Cormakus Onellus Tironi frater cum equitibus centum, & bombardariis velitibus trecentis ed Odonellum in castra venit, missusne á Tirono, an suo ductu, minimè satis omnibus constabat. Macguier, & Cormakus cum peditibus mille ex Odonelli castris hosti obuiam eunt, vt illum incursionibus prohibeant, somnoquè, & quiete priuent, quominus strenué cum Odonello posteà prælietur. Interim Dukus non longius tribus milibus passuum sub vesperum consistit á Farnij fluminis vado. Vbi tenebris primis à Macguiere, & Cormako missis Sclopistis densissima plumbearum pilularum vi improuisó obruitur: quos contra Dukus quoque bombardarios suos mittit. Ita vtraque parte per noctem totam è minus præliante, regij periculo, & bombardarum sonitu somno priuantur. Postero die post lucis exortum Dukus ex vniverso exercitu agmina tria instruens equitum, & sclopetariorum alis munita, quód impedimenta magna habebat, iumentorum quæ commeatum baiulabant, asinariorum, calonum, atque meretricum, ea in duas partes diuidit, alteram inter primam, & secundam aciem, & inter hanc, & vltimam alteram collocat. Quomodo instructus milites præteritæ noctis vigilia semisomnes è castris mouens à Catholicis continuò tela iacientibus gressum comprimere sæpé compellitur, eosdem vicissim longius remouens. Ad horam diei vndecimam non longius bombardæ iactu à Farnio vado venit. Vbi equites ad pedes descendere iubet, quód erat locus equestri prælio minus idoneus. Hic Macguier, et Cormakus cum peditibus mille totis viribus dimicant. Eorum bombardarij agmini primo fortius reluctantur, & vltimo non modo bombardarij, sed etiam hastati insistunt. Cæterum primum agmen ferro viam aperiens, & hinc inde Catholicos arcens vadum aggreditur. Interim Catholici bombardarij, qui vltimum agmen impugnabant, Protestantium scloperariorum alas in agmen compellunt, illudque plumbeis glandibus continenter carpendo faciunt trepidare: ordinibusque iam laxatis incompositum Catholici hastati irruendo penitus disturbant, & cum altera parte impedimentorum primum confundunt: deinde ad medium agmen compellunt. Hic medium agmen duplex certamen inibat, alterum componendo vltimum agmen, alterum Catholicis resistendo: sed vtrumqué Catholici vrgendo confundunt, & per alteram partem impedimentorum pellentes agmini primo miscent. Ita totus exercitus turbato, confusoque tumultu penetrat vadum, relicto commeatu, & omni impedimento, equis tantum seruatus, qui præcipuæ curæ equitibus erant. Mox quid agendum sit, Dukus consultat. Georgius Binghamus Iunior redeundum esse censet, ne post amissum commeatum omnes inedia vincantur pari fato cum Iniskellinnæ propugnatoribus, quibus opitulari non poterant. Contra castrametator Fool, quod

Tanaicc iustis nua i nErinn i mí iul na bliaḋna so. Sir uilliam Russel a ainm fein. Arsead ro cinnsḋ lais gaċ baile dá mbaoí isseilḃ na bainrioghna i nerinn lón ⁊ lán storús do ċor ind daimḋeóin i mbaoí ina aghaiḋ. Ro fóccrad lais dfreaaiḃ miḋe, laiġsn, muṁan, ⁊ connaċt toiḋeċt go líonṁar léirṫionoilte ina ḋoċom co baile áṫa luain an seisead lá décc do ṁí September. In ecmaing na ree sin tánaicc an iustís aṁail ro ṫingeall go háṫ luain, ⁊ ro ascna assaiḋe co ros ċomáin.

AOIS CRIOST, 1595.

Aois Criost, mile, cúicc céd, noċat, a cúicc.

Ard iustis na hérenn .i. Sir uilliam Russel do ṫoċt for tarraing druinge do coṁarsanaiḃ, ⁊ do ċoiḃnesaiḃ ḟiachaċ mic aoḋa, for ḟiachaiḋ

nomen stultum significat, stultè reclamat, & obtestatur, vt arci Reginæ succurrant. Locus, in quo Protestans constiterat, humiditate impeditus erat, vbi equi in vliginem hausti vsui esse non poterant. Ideo à Catholicis magis impunè missilibus sauciatur. Ob hoc Fool alam sclopetariorum contra Catholicos producit, vt eos remoueat, dum rursus exercitus per ordines componatur. Cæterum cito cæpto destitit tragula traiectus, & occisus. Quo totus Protestantium exercitus consternatus desertis etiam equis vllo sinè ordine, & imperio ad vadum quod ante paulò traiecerat, reuertitur. Quo prohibetur à Catholicis fulminatoribus, qui partim impedimenta diripiebant, partim vadum obsidebant. Vnde dubius, quid potissimum consilij caperet, ad aliud angustibus vadum, quod supra in flumine intra sagittæ missum conspicatur, concitato cursu sese confert, & in illud præcipitat prius, quam fuit á Catholicis occupatum. Qua verò celeritate, & trepidatione penetrabat, & vadum erat altitudine, centum circiter milites subruuntur, quorum super corpora cæteri transeunt. Protestantem ex Ibernis pauci sequuntur, quorum ille paucitatem spernens consistit parumper, dum Dukus Anglici exercitus imperator cum alijs cohortium ducibus armis, & vestibus præter subuculam exuitur. Quibus tamen exutis non satis leuatus, nec aptus currendo inter quatuor Ibernos milites ex suis trahitur. Fugientes & pauidos Catholici ex manibus dimiserunt, diripiendis impedimentis animum intendentes. Nam pauci qui vltra vadum fuerunt secuti, statim rediuerunt. Ob quod ex Protestantibus Anglis, & Catholicis Ibernis, qui cum illis stipendium merebant, pauci supra quadringentos flumine, ferroqué perierunt. Equi, magna strues armorum, commeatus, & omnia impedimenta capta sunt. Inter quæ vis biscoctorum panum ingens in ipso vado strata loco nouum nomen indidit. Exercitus regij fusi, & fugati diuulgato nuncio Iniskellinna arx ab Odonello circumsessa in deditionem venit, propugnatoribus ex pacto dimissis, & Macguier est in integrum restitutus.

"Macsuinnius Tuethius vnus ex authoribus belli, qui obsidioni interfuit, breui post receptam arcem naturæ cedens triste sui desiderium Catholicis reliquit: in cuius locum suffectus est Melmurius Macsuinnius Mauri Lenti filius antecessori constantia minimè par, vt inferius apparebit. Obsidione soluta Odonellus memor

A new Lord Justice came to Ireland in the month of July of this year. Sir William Russell[x] was his name. He formed a resolution that provisions and stores should be put into every town in the Queen's possession in Ireland, in despite of all those who were opposed to him. He issued a proclamation to the inhabitants of Meath, Leinster, Munster, and Connaught, ordering them to meet him at Athlone, with all their forces assembled, on the 16th of September. The Lord Justice accordingly went to Athlone at that time, and proceeded from thence to Roscommon.

THE AGE OF CHRIST, 1595.

The Age of Christ, one thousand five hundred ninety-five.

The Chief Justiciary of Ireland, Sir William Russell, marched to Baile-na-Cuirre[a] in the month of January, against Fiagh, the son of Hugh [O'Byrne], at

truculentiæ, qua fœminas, senes, & infantes ex Iniskellinnæ ponte Angli præcipitauerant, cum omnibus copiis Connachtam, quam Richardus Binghamus hæretica tyrranide oppressam tenebat, inuadit: incursionibus longè, latèque factis Anglos colonos, & inquilinos diripit, fugat, occidit, viro nulli à decimo quinto anno vsque ad sexagesimum nato, qui Ibernicè loqui nesciebat, parcens. In Inalia Lomphortum pagum, quem opherali ademptum Brunus Anglus Hæreticus possidebat, accendit. Protestantium præda Onustus in Tirconellam redit. Ea inuasione in Connachta nullus agricola, nullus inquilinus, nullus omninò Anglus mansit præter eos, qui arcium, & munitorum oppidorum mænibus defendebantur. Nam qui igne, & ferro consumpti non sunt, bonis spoliati in Angliam secesserunt, illos, per quos in Iberniam deducti sunt, diris obsecrationibus prosequentes."—*Cap.* xi.

[y] *Pardon and protection.*—O'Sullevan seems to have been misinformed on this subject. On his authority Leland asserts that the garrison were butchered by the Irish; and he adds:

"In all the barbarous triumph of incensed conquerors they pierced into Connaught, and committed the most afflicting outrages in all the well-affected quarters; besieged the English fort of Belleek; cut off a detachment sent to its relief; and practised their usual barbarity on the garrison, when famine had compelled them to surrender. To complete his triumph, O'Donnel was enabled to establish one of the degenerate De Burghos, his associate, chieftain of the district, by the name of the Mac William: while Bingham, the Queen's Lord President of Connaught, was totally destitute of such a military force as might enable him to exert his usual vigor against such outrages."—Book iv. c. 4.

[x] *Sir William Russell.*—He was the youngest son of Francis, Earl of Bedford. He landed at Howth on the 31st of January, 1594, and went the next day to Dublin, but refused to accept of the sword till the Council had first given him in writing, under their hand, an account of the disturbed state of the kingdom; which being done, he was sworn on Sunday, the 11th of August, with great solemnity.—See Cox's *Hibernia Anglicana*, vol. i. p. 403.

[a] *Baile-na-Cuirre*, now Ballinacor, in Glenmalure, in the barony of South Ballinacor, and

buḋéin co baile na cuirre hi mí Ianuarii do sonraḋ. Iar ndol dóiḃ i ccomhfoccus don ḃaile ria siú rainicc leó dol tar dorus an dúnclaiḋ baoí ina timċell ro clos co teccṁaiseaċ fuaim droma ó na saiġdiúiriḃ acc dol do ṡaiccíḋ an ḃaile. Ḃfóccair fiacha co na muintir, ⁊ at raġat co hobann, ⁊ ro ċuir drong dia ṁuintir diomċosnaṁ an dorais co ro ċuir a ṁuintir uile fſraiḃ, macaiḃ, mnáiḃ tré ḋoirsiḃ élaiḋ an ḃaile amaċ, ⁊ do ḋeachaiḋ fſin ina lſnṁain co rucc lais ina niomláine iatt fo ḋiaṁraiḃ, ⁊ fo ḋroiḃelaiḃ sa maiġin ros innill lais.

Iar mbeiṫ dfiachaiḋ for a iomġaḃáil tainic ina cſnd uáter riaḃaċ mac ġearailt mic tomais do ġearaltaċaiḃ ċille dara. Dála an iustis baí siḋe co cſnd deiċ lá i mbaile na cuirre iar ná ḟáccḃáil dfiachaiḋ, ⁊ ro ḟaġaiḃ barda nó ḋó do saiġdiuiriḃ agá iomċoiṁétt ⁊ ticc fſin tar a ais co háṫ cliaṫ.

Do ċóiḋ dna uatér riaḃaċ ⁊ araill do ċloinn fiachaċ mic aoḋa ar ionnsaiġiḋ oiḋċe (in ionam codalta) fó cſnd cóicc lá ndécc iar sin co cruimġlinn i ndoras aṫa cliath. Ro loiscceaḋ ⁊ ro léirscriosaḋ an baile sin leó, ⁊ ruccsat ina mbaoí ina ccumang diomċar don ċſnd luaiḋe boí for tſmpall an ḃaile, ⁊ gér ḃó soilléir soḟaiccsiona luisne ⁊ lassaċa an ḃaile agá losccaḋ do sráidiḃ áṫa cliaṫ do ċóiḋ uater as gan ḟuiliuccaḋ gan foirḋſrccaḋ fair.

A ccionn mís iar sin tucc uater ammas for baile duine uasail dia ſsccairdiḃ baí ina coṁfoċraiḃ, ⁊ gid é an duine uasal baoí siḋe co fſiṫmeaċ fuireaċair i ffoiċill a ionnsaiġṫe dia earccairdiḃ. An tan do ċuaiḋ uáter co na ṁuintir fon mbaile ro ionnsaiġ an duine uasal co cróḋa cailcc nſiṁneaċ i ccoinne uatéir co ro ṫuairccsiot a ċele co hainṁín ſsccairdſṁail co ro treċtnaiġſḋ uater ina ċois don ċur sin. Ruccsat a ṁuintir leó hé gus an sliaḃ bá coiṁnſsa dóiḃ, ⁊ ro ċuirsiot dia lſiġſs é hi ffoṫoll talṁan ar nár ḃeólaċ aon triar idir. Nír ḟáccaiḃsiot ina foċair acṫ aon ḃuaċaill lſga dia ḟíor ṫanusiḃ buḋéin nó ṫſigſḋ siḋe gaċ ré lá do ṫionól luiḃſnd fó na coilltiḃ bá coiṁnſsa ḋó. Do rala iomacallaṁ ós ísiol etir é ⁊ drong dſsccairdiḃ uateir go ro naiḋmsiot re roile, ⁊ ro ṫarraing siḋe líon cſngail

county of Wicklow. In the *Leabhar Branach*, or Book of the O'Byrnes, in the Library of Trinity College, Dublin, H. 1. 15, the name is written baile na corru, which means, town of the weir or dam.

b *Through the postern-doors*, literally, "the escaping doors."

c *Cruimghlinn*, i. e. the crooked glen or valley,

the instance of Fiagh's neighbours and acquaintances. Upon their arrival in the neighbourhood of the castle, but before they had passed through the gate of the rampart that surrounded it, the sound of a drum was accidentally heard from the soldiers who were going to the castle. Fiagh, with his people, took the alarm; and he rose up suddenly, and sent a party of his people to defend the gate; and he sent all his people, men, boys, and women, out through the postern-doors[b] of the castle, and he himself followed them, and conveyed them all in safety to the wilds and recesses, where he considered them secure.

While Fiagh was [thus] avoiding [his enemies], Walter Reagh, the son of Gerald, son of Thomas, one of the Geraldines of Kildare, came to join him. As for the Lord Justice, he remained for ten days at Ballinacor, after it had been deserted by Fiagh; and, having left one or two companies of soldiers to defend it, he himself returned to Dublin.

Fifteen days after this, Walter Reagh and some of the sons of Fiagh, the son of Hugh, set out upon a nocturnal excursion (in sleeping time) to Cruimghlinn[c], near the gate of Dublin. They burned and totally plundered that town [bally], and took away as much as they were able to carry of the leaden roof of the church of the town; and though the blaze and flames of the burning town were plainly visible in the streets of Dublin, Walter escaped without wound or bloodshed.

In a month after this, Walter made an attack on a neighbouring castle, belonging to a gentleman of his enemies. But the gentleman was wary and vigilant, in readiness against any attack of his enemies. When Walter and his people attacked the castle, the gentleman came to a bold and fierce combat with Walter; and they struck at each other furiously and inimically, and Walter was wounded in the leg. His people carried him off to the nearest mountain, and they placed him under cure in a subterranean cave, with the situation of which no three persons were acquainted. They left with him only one young physician of his own faithful people, who was wont to go every second day to the nearest woods to gather herbs. A conversation privately occurred between this man and a party of Walter's enemies; and he, having leagued with them,

now Crumlin, or Cromlin, near Dolphin's Barn. It is at least two Irish miles from St. James's Gate, which was then the outermost of the gates of Dublin.

uatſir ina ċſnd. Rugaḋ uatér iaraṁ go haṫ cliaṫ, ro crochaḋ tra, ⁊ do ronaḋ cſṫramna ḋe.

Cóicceaḋ ulaḋ uile déirġe in aon rann, ⁊ in aon aonta in aghaiḋ gall an bliaḋain si.

Slóicċeaḋ lá clandaiḃ néill hi mí feḃra i ndutchaiġ barúin sláine co nár ḟágḃattar aṫṁaoín dia nſir is na tíriḃ sin darḃar nó dáitiuccaḋ dindiliḃ nó dáirnſir.

Sluaicċeaḋ ele lá clandaiḃ néill co cſnandus co ro milleaḋ, ⁊ co ro mór-aircſḋ an tír ina nuirṫimċell leó.

Slóicċeaḋ lá Máguidir aoḋ mac conċonnaċt mic conċonnaċt ⁊ lá Mag-maṫġaṁna brian mac aoḋa óicc, mic aoḋa, mic sſain buiḋe co breifne uí Raiġilliġ. Ro hindraḋ, ⁊ ro hairccſḋ an tír co tinnearnaċ leó, ⁊ dna ḃeós ní ro ḟáccaiḃsiot boṫ nat i ndionfaiḋe diar nó triúr don ċaḃan uile gan forlosccaḋ cenmoṫa mainistir an ċaḃáin ina mbattar goill an tan sin.

[d] *Hanged and quartered.*—The following account of the adventures and fate of this Walter is given by P. O'Sullevan Beare, in his *Hist. Cathol. Ibern. Compend.*, tom. 3, lib. 2, c. ix. fol. 131:

"Rursus Lageniorum parui tumultus renouantur, quibus ansam præbuit Petrus Giraldinus Hæreticus. Is ob inhumanam crudelitatem iustitiæ minister ab Anglis creatus non modò viros, sed etiam fœminas, & infantes (ea erat truculentia) morte plectebat. Præcipua quadam libidine Vateri Giraldini Fusci sanguinem appetebat. Eius pagum Gloranem cum sicariorum manipulo repente inuasit, sed frustra, nam tum Fuscus aberat, & eius vxor, quæ intererat, fuga salutem petiuit. Haud diu post Fuscus cum Terentio, Felmio, & Raymundo Obruinibus Fiachi filijs affinibus suis, equitibus duodecim, & peditibus ferè centum Petri castellum improuisò aggreditur. Foribus primum, inde reliquo castello igne iniecto illum cum familia comburit. Interim Angli accolæ cum equitum turma, & peditibus aliquot Fuscum circumueniunt, in quos ille faciens impetum paucos vulneribus afficit, omnes in fugam vertit. Hinc Fuscus, & cum filijs Fiachus hostes indicati diligenter, & acriter ab Anglis impetuntur. Fuscus in municipio suo Glorane à Protestantibus, & Ibernis auxiliaribus, maximè Buttleris improuisò circumdatus sese cum paucis armatis in paruum munimentum, quod repentinos casus timens, vallo, fossaque obduxerat, recepit. Istud hostes oppugnant ; ille propugnare conatur. Hostium multitudine vndiq : aggrediente Fusci frater Giraldus fortissimé prælians plumbea glande confoditur: Cæteri plerumque vulneribus afficiuntur. Fuscus, quod, & munimentum diutius tueri nequiuit, & commeatu carebat, per medios confertissimos hostes erumpens cum paucis euasit. Tempore minimé longo transacto cum vespertino crepusculo per pagos milites distribueret, ipse cum comitibus duobus domum á cæteris dissitam ingressus hostium milites sexdecim offendit. Strictis vtrinque gladijs regij quinque grauiter vulnerantur; alter ex duobus Fusci militibus occiditur: ipse mallei ictu fracto pene femore sternitur. Ducem humi iacentem alter comes, qui Georgius Omorra vocabatur

[betrayed Walter], and led a party to where he was, who bound him. Walter was afterwards taken to Dublin, where he was hanged and quartered[d].

The entire province of Ulster rose up in one alliance and one union against the English this year.

An army was led by the O'Neills, in the month of February in this year, into the country of the Baron of Slane, and left no property after them in those districts, of corn, dwellings, flocks, or herds.

Another army was led by the O'Neills to Kells, and they spoiled and totally ravaged the whole country around.

An army was led by Maguire (Hugh, the son of Cuconnaught, son of Cuconnaught, son of Cuconnaught), and by Mac Mahon (Brian, the son of Hugh Oge, son of John Boy), into Breifny O'Reilly, and they quickly plundered and ravaged that country; and they left not a cabin in which two or three might be sheltered in all Cavan which they did not burn, except the monastery of Cavan, in which English [soldiers] were[e] at that time.

tollens, humeris impositus hostium manibum eripere molitur fugiendo ad comilitones qui in proximo pago diuersabantur. Quoties insectantium cursu superabatur, toties Fuscum humi relinquens stricto ferro cum quatuor, aut quinque certabat, quibus in fugam versis, illum iterum sublatum, quam concitatissimo poterat cursu portabat, donec socij auxilio accurrerint. A quibus Fuscus absconditus cum curaretur, à custode suo ab Anglis deprehenso capitis timore proditur, & Dubhlinnam delatus ferreo veru longo, & acutissimo infixus perimitur. Post Fusci necem Fiachus cum regijs copijs quater signa prosperé contulisse. Sub quam victoriarum prosperitatem fortuna minimé diu Catholicis secunda vertit alteram paginam, Terentius Obruin trium filiorum, Fiachi natu simul, & virtute maximus, quod Anglis patrem prodere constituerit, insimulatur. Fiachus id eò facilius credidit, quòd monitus fertur à Rosa Nituehile vxore sua Terentij nouerca quæ Dubhlinnæ ab Anglis custodia tenebatur, nimium ne mariti vitæ timente, an Protestantium arte, & fallacia decepta, incertum. Ergo Terentio deprehenso, quia paternus, inquit Fiachus, amor me non sinit digna pæna perfidiam tuam vlcisci, his te tradam, quibus tu me eras proditurus, vt sicut paternam pietatem es expertus, ita hostilis humanitatis facias periculum. Terentius Dubhlinnam vinctus delatus non modò se falso crimine purgauit, sed totam familiam longè honorificentissima morte cohonestauit: nam sæpe ab Anglis rogatus, & præmijs inuitatus, vt regiæ sectæ subscriberet, maluit Catholicam Christi Iesu legem confitens acerbo supplicio mori, quam negans viuere, patri præcipuè triste sui desiderium relinquens, qui breui quoque quodam, quem fidissimum habebat, prodente, & hostes ducente cum paucis familiaribus regiorum multitudine circumuentus capite truncatur. Nec ob id tamen eius filij Felmius, & Raymundus arma à mora omiserunt."

[e] *In which English were.*—Ina mbáttar goill. This should be: ina mbattar barda o ġallaiḃ, "in which an English garrison was then stationed."

Maccon mac concoiccriche mic diarmata mic taidg caimm ui cleirigh ollamh uí domhnaill hi sſnchas, Saoí foirccthe, ſrgna, ealadanta hi sſnchas, ⁊ i ndán, soerlaḃraiḋ soingṫe co mbuaiḋ ninnsgni, naiṫſirg ⁊ nſrlaḃra, fſr craiḃdeach caondutrachtach diada deſſrcaċ do écc i lſitir maolain i ttuadmumain.

Sir Seón nórais generál coccaiḋ na bainrioghna do ṫeċt i nErinn oċt ccéd décc saigdiúir i ndeireaḋ mi febru do corcc coccaḋ ulltaċ, ⁊ ċonnaċtaċ.

Slóiccead lá hua ndomnaill Aoḋ ruaḋ do ḋol i cconnaċtoiḃ. Arsſḋ do luiḋ cetus tar eirne (an trſs lá don marta do ṡonraḋ) laiṁ ḋeas fri loċ melge mic coḃṫaiġ, go bealaċ uí michiḋein, ⁊ airisis hisuiḋe in aḋaiġ sin tres an mbreirne go braidsliaḃ, ⁊ do roine coṁnaiḋe an adhaiġ sin annsaiḋe. Nír ḃó soḋaing doroṁ ell nó baoġal dracċḃáil for ċoicceaḋ olnéccmaċt an ionḃaiḋ sin, ar ro battar goill ind ionattaċt, ⁊ in aittreḃaiḃ isin ccriċ co coitċionn, ⁊ go ronraḋaċ ina sortaiḃ airſċais, ⁊ ina dúnarusaiḃ diotoġlaiġiḃ. Ḃaí cetus Sir Risderd bingam goḃernóir ċoicciḋ connaċt i Ross comáin, drong ṁór ele do ġallaiḃ i mainistir manaċ fil for bru buille, drong ele hi ttuillsce in eittirmſḋon maiġe hai fri ráiṫ cruachan anoir ttuaiṫ. Drong isin bport nua (dún ro ċlaiḋriot na goill badéin) etir loċ cé, ⁊ loċ narḃaċ. Drong i mbaile an ṁótaiġ, ⁊ drong ṁór ele hi slicceach. Ráinicc fios Sccel gus an ngobernóir co ros ċomáin go mbaoí ó domnaill acc triall don tír, ⁊ ní ro hanaḋ laissiḋe co riaċt go mainistir na búille, ⁊ ro for-ċongraḋ lais for a mbaoí do ġallaiḃ is na bailtiḃ reṁraite teaċt dia saiċċiḋ an dú sin, uair bá dóiġ lais coniḋ ísin conair no ċingfeaḋ ó domnaill co na sloġaiḃ.

Acc dol dua domnaill go coilltiḃ conċoḃair ro foráil for a soċraiḋe airisſṁ fri a ninneall ⁊ fri a ttaisbénaḋ. Do rónaḋ fair sium sin, ⁊ nír bó hadḃal an líon baí hisuiḋe uair noca raiḃe aċt cſiṫre ċéd nama fri

[f] *Erudite.*—"Foirgṫi .i. teagaisgṫe."—*O'Clery.*

[g] *Leitir-Maelain,* now Lettermoylan, a subdivision of the townland of Glangee, in the parish of Dysart-O'Dea, barony of Inchiquin, and county of Clare.

[h] *The lake of Melge, the son of Cobhthach,* now *Anglice* Lough Melvin.—See note [e], under the year 1455, p. 994, *supra.* This lake is said to have derived its name from Melge Molbhthach, the son of Cobhthach, Monarch of Ireland, A. M. 3696.—See O'Flaherty's *Ogygia,* part iii. c. 39.

[i] *Ballaghmeehin.*—This is the name of a Roman Catholic parish forming the eastern portion of the parish of Rossinver, barony of Rossclogher, and county of Leitrim.—See this place already

Maccon, the son of Cucogry, son of Dermot, son of Teige Cam O'Clery, Ollav to O'Donnell in history, an erudite[f] and ingenious man, professed in history and poetry; a fluent orator, with the gift of elocution, address, and eloquence; a pious, devout, religious, and charitable man, died at Leitir-Maelain[g], in Thomond.

At the end of the month of February Sir John Norris, the Queen's general, came to Ireland with a force of eighteen hundred soldiers, to suppress the war in Ulster and Connaught.

A hosting was made by O'Donnell (Hugh Roe), to march into Connaught. He first crossed the Erne, on the third day of March, and moved on, keeping the lake of Melge, the son of Cobhthach[h], on his right, until he arrived at Ballaghmeehin[i], where he stopped that night. He then proceeded on through Breifny, until he came to Braid-Shliabh[k], where he stopped for one night. It was difficult for him at that time to get an advantage of or surprise the province of Olnegmacht[l], because the English held their abode and residence throughout the country in general, and especially in its chief towns and impregnable fortresses. In the first place, Sir Richard Bingham, the Governor of the province of Connaught, was [stationed] at Roscommon; another large party of the English [was stationed] in a monastery which is [situated] on the bank of the Boyle; another in Tulsk, in the very centre of Moy-Ai, to the north-east of Rathcroghan; another in the fort, a fortress erected by the English themselves between Lough Key and Lough Arrow; another at Ballymote; and a great party at Sligo. News having reached the Governor at Roscommon, that O'Donnell was on his march into the country, he made no delay until he arrived at the monastery of Boyle, and ordered all the English of the towns above mentioned to come to him at that place, for he thought that it should be by that way that O'Donnell would pass with his forces.

O'Donnell, on his way to Coillte-Chonchobhair[m], ordered his troops to halt, to be drawn out in array, and reviewed. This they accordingly did, and the number he had there was not great, being only four hundred men fit for valour

referred to at the years 1439 and 1480.

[k] *Braid-Shliabh*, now Braulieve.—See note [r], under the year 1586, p. 1581, *supra*.

[l] *Olnegmacht*.—This is the most ancient name of the province of Connaught, and the Nagnatæ of Ptolemy is probably an attempt at writing it.

[m] *Coillte-Chonchobhair*, a woody district in the north-east of the barony of Boyle, and county

hſngnaṁ ⁊ fri hurrsclaigi dóig ní deacatar slóig ele ina ṫóiċſstal an tan sin inge cenel cconaill, acṫmad uathad do ċóicceaḋ olnecmaċt bátar acc tairsċélaḋ, ⁊ acc séducċaḋ conaire dó, im concobar ócc mac diarmada, ⁊ im ċonn mac an dubaltaiġ, mic tuaṫail uí conċobair. Tiaġait an slóġ iaraṁ iar na ttairsbénadh go rangattar don ḃúill, ⁊ tiaġait ṫairsi acc droiċſt cnuic an biocara i nurṫorac oiḋċe, arsaiḋe dóiḃ tré moiġ luircc, ⁊ tre moiġ naoí co riaċtattar lá doḃarsoillsi na maidne co ráiṫ cruaċan. Ro léicceaḋ sccaoíleaḋ ⁊ sccarraḋ dá sccemeltaċaiḃ aṁail ro ṫſccairscc siumh dóiḃ ré ttoċt an dú sin. Ḃá fairsing foirlſtan ro lſṫsat na laoċ ḃuiḋne ó raile, ar do ċuaiḋ drong díoḃ do ḋuthaiġ uí conċoḃair ruaiḋ ⁊ uí ainliġi, cuid ele go droiċet ḃeóil aṫa moḋa for suca, ⁊ dream ele ḃeós tar an ccaislén riabaċ siar. Ro baḋ lór do ḋiclſiṫ an tslóiġ ſsin an dluiṁċeó diaḋ ⁊ dſthaiġe ro lſṫ o na forloiscctiḃ in gaċ airm ro gabsat an slócch dá gaċ leṫ i nuirtimċeall raṫa cruaċan. Tangatar an luċt do ċóiḋ go haṫ moḋa, ⁊ an ḟoirſnd ele do ċuaiḋ go hairteaċ ⁊ go cloinn cſiṫearnaiġ ria miḋmſḋón laoí go ráiṫ cruaċan, gér ḃó díċuṁaing doibh toiḋeaċt inellṁa lá haiḋble a ccreaċ, ⁊ a nedala, ⁊ fó ġébdaís ní baḋ mó dia mbſiṫ ina ccuṁang a ngluasaċt nó a niomáin ittir. Do ċóiḋ iaraṁ ó doṁnaill, ⁊ an luċt sin co na ccreachaiḃ go hailfinn, ⁊ baí athaiḋ annsaiḋe acc furnaiḋe an sccemelta do ċuaiḋ uaḋa go duthaiġ uí conċobair ruaiḋ ⁊ uí ainliġi. Ro arccná iaraṁ a hailfind laiṁḋſs lé haṫ slisſn co huíḃ briúin. Airisis ann an aḋhaiġ sin co ro ṫionóilsiot a ṁuintir uile ina ḋocom co na ccreaċaiḃ leó. Ní ro tionoileaḋ lá haoínneaċ do ġaoiḋealaiḃ ré ré ċian daimsir saṁail ina mbaoí do ċroḋ (dairccttiḃ aen laoí) an dú sin.

Ro ḟorċongair ua doṁnaill ar a ḃarac ar a ṁuintir a ccreaċa do ċor tar sionainn, ⁊ ro ḟaoiḋ a ġlaslaiṫ, ⁊ gaċ aon nár ḃó tualaing arm dimbirt

of Roscommon.—See note [d], under the year 1471, p. 1071, *supra*.

[n] *Cnoc-an-Bhiocara*, i. e. hill of the vicar, now Knockvicar Bridge, on the River Boyle, about five miles to the north-east of the town of Boyle, in the parish of Ardcarne, barony of Boyle, and county of Roscommon.—See the Ordnance map of that county, sheet 6.

[o] *Bel-atha-Mogha*, i. e. mouth of the ford of Mogha, now *anglice* Ballimoe, the name of a ford, bridge, and village on the River Suck, on the borders of the counties of Roscommon and Galway.

[p] *Caislen-riabhach*, now Castlerea, a small town in the west of the county of Roscommon.—See note [o], under the year 1489, p. 1168, *supra*.

[q] *Airteach*.—This is still the name of a dis-

and action; for no other forces joined his muster besides the Kinel-Connell, except a few from the province of Olnegmacht, who acted as spies and guides in pointing out the way to him, under the conduct of Conor Oge Mac Dermot, and Con, the son of Dubhaltach, son of Tuathal O'Conor. This host, after having been reviewed, marched on until they arrived at the River Boyle, and crossed it at the bridge of Cnoc-an-Bhiocara[n] early in the evening. From thence they proceeded through Moylurg and Moy-Nai, and next morning, by break of day, arrived at Rathcroghan. Here, as he [O'Donnell] had instructed them before they arrived at that place, marauding parties were detached and sent forth; far and wide did these heroic bands disperse from each other, for one party of them proceeded to the country of O'Conor Roe and O'Hanly, another to the bridge of Bel-atha-Mogha[o], on the River Suck, and a third party westwards, beyond Caislen-riabhach[p]. The dense cloud of vapour and smoke which spread in every place where these forces passed, all around Rathcroghan, was enough to conceal their numbers. The party that had gone to Ath-Mogha [Ballimoe], and those who had gone to Airteach[q] and Clann-Keherny[r], returned to Rathcroghan before mid-day, though it was difficult for them to return in regular order, by reason of the immensity of their preys and spoils; and they could have procured more, if they had been but able to carry or drive them. O'Donnell and these went on with their preys to Elphin, and remained there for some time, awaiting the party who had gone to the country of O'Conor Roe and O'Hanly. He afterwards proceeded on from Elphin, keeping Ath-sliseau[s] on the right, until he arrived in Hy-Briuin, where he remained that night, until all his people had come to him with their spoils. None of the Irish had for a long time before collected (by one day's plundering) so much booty as he had there.

On the next day O'Donnell ordered his people to convey their preys across the Shannon; and he sent his recruits, and all those unfit to wield arms, with

trict in the modern barony of Frenchpark, in the county of Roscommon.—See its exact limits pointed out in note [s], under the year 1297, pp. 468, 469, *supra*.

[r] *Clann-Keherny*.—This is still the name of a district in the modern barony of Castlerea, in the west of the county of Roscommon.—See O'Flaherty's *Ogygia*, part iii. c. 46. It is chiefly comprised in the parish of Kilkeevin.

[s] *Ath-Sliseau*, now Bellaslishen Bridge, on the road leading from Elphin to Strokestown, in the county of Roscommon, and about a mile to the south of the former.—See note [i], under the year 1288, p. 446, *supra*.

las na creaċaiḃ ⁊ las na hédalaiḃ co muintir eólais. An tan báttar deireaḋ an tslóiġ acc teċt tar an áṫ ċédna ar ann do riaċtattar glasláiṫ ⁊ aos diuḃraicṫi na ngall, ⁊ do ḃſratt deaḃaiḋ dia roile co ro creċtnaiġitt ⁊ go ro gonaitt dronga sttorra. Ar a aoí do deaċattar cenel cconaill tars an aḃainn, ⁊ do ċóttar dia ttiġiḃ co na nédálaiḃ iar mbuaiḋ ⁊ cosgar.

Slóiccheaḋ ele lá hua nDoṁnaill (aoḋ ruaḋ) i cconnaċtaiḃ an toċtmaḋ lá décc do ṁí april. Ḃassſḋ a ccédna huiḋe tar eirne laṁ ḋſs lé loċ melge co mbattar in adhaiġ sin i Ros inbir. Tiaġait ar a ḃaraċ co cill fearga, ⁊ airisitt annsaiḋe fri deireaḋ a ṡlóiġ do brſiṫ forra, ⁊ iar roċtain dóiḃ lotar iaraṁ trés an mbreirne co braidsliaḃ assaiḋe co maċaire ċonnaċt, ⁊ a ndeachaiḋ uaḋ gan creachaḋ ar an sluaiccéaḋ roiṁe ro tſcclamaḋ a ccreaċa ċuicce go haon maiġin don ċur sin. Do ċóiḃ iaraṁ gus na hairecc-ṫibh ⁊ gus na hédalaiḃ sin lais go liaṫdruim muintire heolais an aḋaiġ sin.

An tan bá dóiġ lá a easccairdiḃ eiriom do ṡoaḋ tar a ais i nultaiḃ ní hſḋ sin do róine itir, acht ro ṗaiḋ teaċta go hinclſiṫe do saiġiḋ méguidir Aoḋa co ttiosaḋ ina ḋoċom don angaile, ⁊ ro lá luċt tairceltа roiṁe for an ccriċ, ⁊ ro forcongair forra co ttíostais ina ḋoċom i mionad erḋalta. Ro asscena fſirrin iaraṁ co taoí táiṫſnaċ co rainicc co na slóġaiḃ an dá angaile isin moiċdeaḋóil (duthaiġ an dá ua ḟſrgail inorin ciḋ ria riú ro ḃátar goill acc fortaṁluccáḋ forra) ⁊ ro ḃaoí aon do na gallaiḃ faḋſin hi bport aisſċais uí fſrġail .i. críostóir brún a ċoṁainm. Rangattar sirte sássluaiġ uí ḋoṁnaill ⁊ meguiḋir ó ṡliaḃ cairpre co hſiṫne co ro ċuirriot gaċ ní gus a rangattar do na tíriḃ sin fó troimnell teineaḋ, ⁊ fo smuit ċeó ḋoḃarḋa duiḃċiaċ. Ro gabaḋ leó an longport, uair ro ċuirriot tene gaċa slſsa ⁊ gaċa hairċinn de gur ab lá téitt résſḋ tuccsat crioſtóir brún co na ċliaṁain, ⁊ co na mnaiḃ araon amaċ. Ro loisccead dna cúicc fir décc do braiġdiḃ an tíre (ḃáttar illaiṁ acc an ccrioſtóir réṁraite) ná ro cuimgſḋ danacal nó do ṫſrarccain la trſtan, ⁊ lá tſndáldaċt na teineaḋ.

[t] *Ros-inbhir*, now Rossinver, a townland and parish in the barony of Dartry, and county of Leitrim.

[u] *Cill-Fhearga*, i. e. the church of St. Fearga, now Killarga, a parish in the barony of Dromahaire, and county of Leitrim.

[w] *Sliabh-Cairbre*, now *anglice* Slieve Carbry, a mountainous district in the ancient territory of Cairbre Gabhra, now the barony of Granard, in the north of the county of Longford.—See note [c],

the preys and spoils, into Muintir-Eolais. When the rear of the army was crossing the ford, they were overtaken by the recruits and musketeers of the English ; and a battle ensued, in which many were hurt and mortally wounded on both sides. The Kinel-Connell, however, crossed the river, and carried off their spoils, after triumph.

Another hosting was made by O'Donnell (Hugh Roe) into Connaught, on the eighteenth day of the month of April. He first crossed the Erne, and marched on, keeping Lough Melvin on the right, until he arrived at Ros-inbhir[t], where he stopped for that night. From thence he went to Cill-Fhearga[u], where he waited for the coming up of the rear of his army. Upon their arrival they proceeded through Breifny to Braid-Shliabh, and from thence into Machaire-Chonnacht ; and such part of it as had escaped being plundered on the former expedition was plundered now ; and they collected the preys together to him. After this he proceeded onward with these preys and spoils, and arrived the same night in Leitrim in Muintir-Eolais.

Now his enemies thought that he would return into Ulster ; this, however, he did not do, but privately dispatched messengers to Maguire (Hugh), [requesting] that he would come to him in Annaly ; and he sent spies before him through the country, and ordered them to meet him at a certain place. He himself then marched onwards, secretly and expeditiously, and arrived with his troops at the dawn of day in the two Annalys (these were the countries of the two O'Farrells, though the English had some time before obtained sway over them) ; and one of the English, Christopher Browne by name, was then [dwelling] in the chief mansion-seat of O'Farrell. The brave troops of O'Donnell and Maguire marched from Sliabh-Cairbre[w] to the River Inny, and set every place to which they came in these districts in a blaze of fire, and [wrapped it] in a black, heavy cloud of smoke. They took the Longford[x], for they had set fire to every side and corner of it, so that it was [only] by the help of a rope that they conveyed Christopher Browne and his brother-in-law, and both their wives, out of it. Fifteen men of the hostages of that country (who had been in the custody of the aforesaid Christopher Browne) were burned [to death], who could not be saved, in consequence of the fury and violence that prevailed.

under the year 1590, p. 1885, *supra.*

[x] *The Longford*, i. e. the fortress. This is more usually called Longphort-Ui-Fhearghail, i. e. O'Farrell's fortress, and from it the town

Ro gaḃaitt ḃeós teóra caistialla ele lá hua nDoṁnaill isin ló cédna. Ro marḃaitt, ⁊ ro mudhaiġit daoíne iomḋa don ċur sin, ⁊ ro baḋ dia saor ċlandaiḃ hobſrd, mac feargura, mic briain ro marḃaḋ lá Maguiḋir tré iomraiṫne. Ro herġaḃaḋ mac an priora uí raiġilliġ lá druing naile don tslóiġ. Ro léirṫeacclamaḋ, ⁊ ro láintionóileaḋ in ro ba lainn leó do croḋ na criċe ar gaċ aird dia saicchiḋ. Lottar iaram co na ccreachaiḃ ⁊ co na nédálaiḃ co ro ġaḃsat longport i tteallaċ dúnchaḋa in adhaiġ sin. Ro lſiccitt scceiṁealta uaṫa ar ná ḃaraċ co mainistir an caḃáin dus an bfuiġbittís baoġal for na gallaiḃ báttar i fforḃairsi ann, ⁊ o ná fuairsiot i ffécmais an ḃaile iatt do beartsat leó gaċ ní gus a rangattar dia nedalaiḃ. Tangattar iaram an adhaiġ sin co tellaċ eaċḋaċ alla ṫiar do ḃél aṫa conaill. Ticcitt iaram dia ttiġiḃ iar mbuaiḋ neċtra don ċur sin.

O ro ba dſrḃ lá gallaiḃ an tiarla ó neill do eirġe i ccommbáidh uí ḋoṁnaill is in ccoccaḋ ro ċuir an iustis ⁊ an ċoṁairle dſiċ ccéd laoċ go hiobar ċinn traġa do ḟorbairsi for ċenel neoġain, ⁊ ro ġeall an iustis co na ṡloġaiḃ toċt ina lſnṁain dorccain ⁊ do ṁilleaḋ an tíre.

Ro ḟaiḋ ua neill a teacta hi ccſnd uí doṁnaill dia ċuingiḋ fair teaċt dia ċoṁḟurtaċt in aghaiḋ an anfforlainn ro ḋail dia ṡaigiḋ. Nir bó hſirlſḃaċ ro hſirtſḃ sin la hua nDoṁnaill uair ro tionoileaḋ a sloġa lais, ⁊ ráinicc tré ṫír eoccain go hairm i mbaoí ó néill, ⁊ do ċóttar ar aon co foċard muirṫſṁne hi mí Mart do ṡonraḋ. Od ċualaiḋ an iustis a mbſiṫ ina oirċill diḃlínib an dú sin ro airis in aṫ cliaṫ don ċur sin.

Seoirsi ócc bingam baoí i slicceaċ ó goḃernóir ċóicciḋ ċonnaċt Sir Rirderd bingam do ċuaiḋ an Seoirsi hisin long co na foirinn laṁ dſr fri hérinn

of Longford has taken its name.—See note [r], under the year 1448, p. 957, *supra*.

[y] *The son of the Prior*.—He was Maelmora, or Myles, the illegitimate son of Philip O'Reilly, who was commonly called the Prior, though he was not an ecclesiastic.—See note [d], under the year 1583, p. 1809, *supra*.

[z] *Teallach-Dunchadha*, now the barony of Tullyhunco, in the west of the county of Cavan.—See note [l], under the year 1282, p. 437, *supra*.

[a] *To which they came*.—This phrase, which is very common in this Annals, sounds awkwardly enough in English. The phrase "which they could finger," so often used by Cox, would be better English.

[b] *Teallach-Eachdhach*, now *anglice* Tullaghagh, or Tullyhaw, a barony forming the north-west portion of the county of Cavan.—See note [r], under the year 1258, p. 371, *supra*.

[c] *Bel-atha-Chonaill*, now *anglice* Ballyconnell, a small town in the barony of Tullyhaw. See it already mentioned under the years 1470, 1475.

Three other castles were also taken by O'Donnell on the same day; and on those occasions many persons were slain and destroyed, of whom one of the freeborn was Hubert, the son of Fergus, son of Brian [O'Farrell], who was accidentally slain by Maguire. The son of the Prior[y] O'Reilly was taken prisoner by others of the army. As much of the property of the country as they wished to have was collected and gathered, [and brought] to them from every quarter. They then proceeded with their preys and spoils, and pitched their camp that night in Teallach-Dunchadha[z]. On the next day they sent marauding parties to the monastery of Cavan, to see whether they could get an advantage of the English who were quartered in it; but as they did not find any of the English about the town, they carried off every thing of value belonging to them to which they came[a]. They marched that night to Teallach-Eachdhach[b], west of Bel-atha-Chonaill[c]; and from thence they returned home, after the victory of expedition on that occasion.

When the English felt satisfied that the Earl O'Neill had risen up in alliance with O'Donnell in the war, the Lord Justice and Council sent a thousand warriors to Iubhar-Chinn-tragha[d], to make war on the Kinel-Owen; and the Lord Justice promised to follow them, and plunder and ravage the country.

O'Neill sent his messengers to O'Donnell, requesting him to come to his assistance against the overwhelming forces that had come to oppose him. O'Donnell did not listen inattentively to them, for he assembled his forces, and proceeded through Tyrone, to the place where O'Neill was; upon which both went to Fochard-Muirtheimhne[e]. This was in the month of May. When the Lord Justice heard that they were both in readiness there to meet him, he remained in Dublin for that time.

George Oge Bingham, who was [stationed] at Sligo under Sir Richard Bingham, the Governor of Connaught, went[f] with a ship and its crew north-eastwards,

[d] *Iubhar-Chinn-tragha*, i. e. the yew of the head of the strand, now Newry.—See it already mentioned at the years 1526, 1593.

[e] *Fochard-Muirtheimhne*, now Faughard, a celebrated hill, on which stand the ruins of a church, about two miles to the north of Dundalk, in the plain of Muirtheimhne, now the county of Louth. This place is much celebrated in Irish history as being the birth-place of St. Bridget, and the site of the battle in which Edward Bruce was slain in 1318.—See Colgan's *Trias Thaum.*, p. 566, note 13; Ussher's *Primordia*, pp. 627, 705, 706, 884; and note [r], under the year 1318, p. 520, *supra*.

[f] *Went.*—An English writer would say "sailed."

soirttuaiḋ do denaṁ fogla hi ccenel cconaill, co ro ġabsatt hi ccuan na súiliġe. Fuarattar faill forr an tír an tan sin, co ro innirsit mainistir ṁuire baoí for ur na traġa, ⁊ ruccsat a cculaḋaċa oiffrinn ⁊ a cailíri leó co néḋalaiḃ oile. Arraiḋe do ḋeaċattar iaraṁ co toraiġ (oilén in ro bſndaċ colum cille an naoíṁérlaṁ eiside). Ro creaċsat ⁊ ro oirccsiot i mbaoí isin oilén, ⁊ rangattar iaraṁ tar a nais co sligeaċ.

Ad cuas dua ḋoṁnaill aiḋṁilleaḋ a criċe dia éis (la heaċtrannċoiḃ) ticcsiḋe a tír eoġain dia tarraċtain, ⁊ nír ḃó cian an ernaiḋe ḋó i ttír ċonaill an tan rangattar teaċta uí neill dia saiġiḋ, dia aisnſis dó an iustís co na slóġ do ṫoċt i ttír eoġain. Soais ina ḟrithing doridisi co ráinic airm i mbaoí ó néill. Bá faoiliḋ sium friss. Bá haḋḃal an tsoċraiḋe tanaicc an iustis .i. Sir uilliam russell, uair boí general coccaiḋ na bainrioġna i nerinn a maille fris .i. Sir Seon Norris, ⁊ iarla tuaḋṁuman donnchaḋ mac conċoḃair uí ḃriain iadsaiḋe uile co na soċraiḋe. Ní ro hanaḋ leó siḋe co rangattar co hiuḃar ċinntraġa, arraiḋe co hard maċa. Bá hſḋ ro ċinnsiot hisuiḋe gan airisioṁ go roċtain dóiḃ go haḃainn ṁóir hi ccſirtmſḋon tíre heoccaín. Acc artcnaṁ i réiḋ dirġe na conaire dóiḃ etir ardmaċa ⁊ aḃann ṁór at connatar an longport lán ndaingſn, ⁊ an cipe coṁnart caṫa i mbátar cenel cconaill ⁊ eoġain imon iarla ua neill ⁊ im ua ndoṁnaill, ⁊ iar ná airiuccaḋ sin don tsluaġ gall airisitt isin maiġin sin co ar a ḃaraċ. Do ċottar iaraṁ tar anais co hardmaċa. Do ḋeaċattar na gaoiḋil ina lſnṁain co ro ġabsat longport in aṫḟoccus dóiḃ. Báttar frí ré ċóicc lá ndécc aghaiḋ in aghaiḋ aṁlaiḋ sin gan saiġiḋ do neaċtar aca for aroile, uair ro ḃaoí an iustis co na ṡlóġ i ndaingniġṫiḃ ardamaċa acc toccḃáil tor ⁊ acc doiṁniuccaḋ díocc i ttimċeall an ḃaile. Ro faccaiḃ an iustis a ccionn na ree sin trí ḃanna saiġdiuir ag iomċoiṁett ardamaċa, ⁊ tſid fſin tar a ais don iuḃar, ⁊ báttar gaoiḋil ina lſnmain co dorus an iuḃair. Do ṫaod an

[g] *Mary's Abbey.*—This was the Carmelite abbey of Rathmullan.—See note [n], under the year 1516, p. 1334, *supra.*

[h] *Torach*, now Tory Island, off the north coast of the barony of Kilmacrenan, and county of Donegal.—See note [x], under the year 1202, p. 132, *supra.*

[i] *Revenge.*—"Tarraċtain .i. dioġail."—*O'Clery.*

[k] *The Abhainn-Mhor*, i. e. the great river, now the River Blackwater, which flows for several miles between the counties of Tyrone and Armagh.—See note [z], under the year 1483, p. 1125, *supra.* By Tír Eoġain the Four Masters, at this period, meant the entire territory possessed by the O'Neills, and the other fami-

to commit depredations in Tirconnell; [and they sailed round], keeping Ireland to the right, until they put into the harbour of Swilly. They obtained an advantage of the country at this time, so that they plundered Mary's Abbey[g], which was [situated] on the brink of the Strand, and carried off the Mass vestments, chalices, and other valuable articles. They then sailed to Torach[h] (an island consecrated by St. Columbkille, the holy patron), and preyed and plundered every thing they found on the island, and then returned back to Sligo.

O'Donnell having been informed of the spoliation of his territory, in his absence, by strangers, he returned from Tyrone to revenge[i] it; but his stay had not been long in Tirconnell when O'Neill's messengers came to him to inform him that the Lord Justice had arrived with an army in Tyrone. He, thereupon, went back to the place where O'Neill was, who rejoiced at his arrival. The army brought by the Lord Justice (i. e. Sir William Russell) was very immense, for he had with him Sir John Norris, the Queen's general in Ireland, and the Earl of Thomond (Donough, son of Conor O'Brien), with all their forces. These never halted until they arrived at Newry, from whence they proceeded to Armagh. Here they resolved not to delay, until they should reach the Abhainn-mhor[k], in the very middle of Tyrone. On their march over the direct road from Armagh to this river, they beheld the fortified camp, and the strong battle-array of the Kinel-Owen and Kinel-Connell, under the Earl O'Neill and O'Donnell; and when the English army perceived this, they remained where they were[l] until the next morning, when they returned back to Armagh. The Irish went in pursuit of them, and pitched their camp near them. They remained thus face to face for the space of fifteen days, without any attack from either side[m]; for the Lord Justice and his army were within the fortifications of Armagh, [engaged in] erecting towers, and deepening the trenches around the town. At the expiration of this time the Lord Justice left three companies of soldiers to defend Armagh, and he himself returned to Newry; and the Irish went in pursuit to the gate of Newry. In a week afterwards the Lord Justice set out

lies of the race of Eoghan. At an earlier period the River Abhainn-mhor, which was originally called the Dabhall, would be described, not as in the middle of Tir-Eoghain, but as flowing between Tir-Eoghain and Oirghialla; for the latter territory comprised the counties of Armagh and Monaghan, and, more recently, those of Louth and Fermanagh.

[l] *Where they were*, literally, "in that place," which is rather clumsy.

[m] *From either side*, literally, "without either of them attacking the other."

iustis fo ċenn seachtmaine iarttain lé lón go Muineaċan. Do ċóiḋ assiḋe co na ṡlóġ co hAṫ cliaṫ.

Ní ro laṁsat goill aon tslóicceaḋ do ḃreiṫ co hUlltoiḃ go cenn athaiḋ iar sin, acht aon tsluaicceaḋ amáin do rónaḋ lá Sir seon norais, ⁊ lá Sir tomas oris a ḋearḃraṫair .i. presidens da ċuiccidh Muṁan, go neirġe amaċ muiṁneaċ ⁊ miḋeaċ do ḋol in Ulltoiḃ. Do ċuas leó co hiuḃar ċinn traġa, ⁊ ro triallsat assiḋe co hArdmaċa. Iar ndol i ngar do leiṫ na conaire dóiḃ is ann do ralatar na gaoiḋil for a ccionn, ⁊ ro ġabsat accá ccailcc, ⁊ accá ccaiṫeṁ accá ttollaḋ, ⁊ accá ttersgaḋ co nár leiccsiot codladh nó longaḋ socracht no saḋaile dóiḃ fri ré ceiṫeora nuair ffiċet. Ní ro léicceaḋ dna aon troicch seaċa sin ar a naghaiḋ iatt, ⁊ robtar buiḋiġ a maiṫe do roċtain a nanmann leó tar a nais gus an iuḃar, iar ffaccḃáil daoíne, eaċ, airm, ⁊ edala co hiolarḋa dóiḃ. Ro gonaḋ an general Sir Seón noris, ⁊ Sir tomas a ḋearḃraṫair don cur sin. Nír ḃó ḃeann baoġal doiḃsiḋe dol isin ccóicceaḋ iar sin.

Iar soaḋ don treoirsi reṁraite co slicceaċ iar norccain mainistre

[n] *Towards Armagh*.—This should evidently be "towards Monaghan;" for we are informed by P. O'Sullevan Beare, who seems to have had the account of the rencounter between the Earl of Tyrone and Segrave from living witnesses, that this conflict took place at Cluain-tibrat, near Monaghan. The following is O'Sullevan's account of this conflict, but it rests on his testimony alone, for no older or contemporaneous writer has handed down any account of it, and all subsequent writers have merely copied him:

"Norris dux tantus cum exercitu suo Auriliam Macmagannorum ditionem ingressus non procul à Munichano in campum, qui Pratum Fontis dicitur, peruenit: vbi copias suas hosti spectandas præbet. Onellus imperator nihil imperitior, sed viribus longè impar occurrit. Ibi duarum bellicosisimarum insularum duo longé clarissimi duces primum signa conferunt. Erat ille locus planicies aperta, & patens sed humiditate parum impedita. Ex circumiectis vliginibus aquæ confluentes vadum faciebant, per quod erat Anglis commodius transeundum. Illud vadum Onellus obsidet; adire tentat Norris; eum remouere Onellus conatur. Equestris simul pugna, & bombardariorum velitatio circum vadum incipit. Equites regij armorum munimine, Iberni hominum dexteritate præstabant. Iberni fulminatores collineandi scientia longè antecedebant. Quod commodum sæpius commune partis vtriusque erat: nam in regio exercitu sæpè plures erant Iberni, quam Angli. Regij bombardarij bis à Catholicis confutati sunt, reclamante Norrise, qui vltimus omnium pugna excedebat. Ac sub eo quidem equus plumbea glande confossus cadit. Omnes partis vtriusque equites Macguieri non iniuria primas concesserunt. Cum Norris ægrius ferret suos bis reiectos locum non sustinuisse, Iaimus Sedgreius eques Ibernus Midhiensis corporis, & animi robore excellens ipsum, & Bagnalem ita alloquitur. Mittite mecum equitum turmam, & ego polliceor vobis, Onellum esse mihi ex ephippijs saltem detrahendum. Consistebat Onellus ab altera

with provisions, to [victual] Monaghan, and from thence he proceeded with his army to Dublin.

For some time after this the English did not dare to bring any army into Ulster, except one hosting which was made by Sir John Norris and his brother, Sir Thomas Norris, the President of the two provinces of Munster, with the forces of Munster and Meath, to proceed into Ulster. They marched to Newry, and passed from thence towards Armagh[n]. When they had proceeded near halfway, they were met by the Irish, who proceeded to annoy, shoot, pierce, and spear them, so that they did not suffer them either to sleep or rest quietly for the space of twenty-four hours. They were not permitted to advance forward one foot further; and their chiefs were glad to escape with their lives to Newry, leaving behind them many men, horses, arms, and valuable things. The General, Sir John Norris, and his brother, Sir Thomas, were wounded on this occasion. It was no [ordinary] gap of danger for them to go into the province after this.

The aforesaid George [Bingham] returned to Sligo, after having plundered

parte vadi quadraginta equitibus, & bombardarijs paucis stipatus, inde prælium contemplans, & imperia dans. Tertio equites, & bombardarij pugnam redintegrant. Et Sedgreius quidem comitatus turma electissimorum equitum Ibernorum, et Anglorum vadum aggreditur. In ipso vado pauci equites cadunt à scloperarijs corporis Onelli custodibus icti. Nihilominus Sedgreius in Onellum irruit: vterque in alterius lorica hastam frangit. Mox Sedgreius Onellum collo deprehensum ex equo deturbat; Onellus inuicem Sedgreium ex equo detrahit: ambo in certamen validæ luctæ manus conserunt: Onellus prosternitur, qui tamen animo tanto fuit, vt iacens Sedgreium sub lorica inter femina per genitalia stricto pugione confossum interfecerit. Circum Sedgreium octodecim equites splendidi regij succumbunt, & signum capitur: cæteri fuga salutem petunt: vnà quoque omnes regiæ copiæ pedem referre coguntur, septingentis plus minus desideratis Catholici pauci sunt vulneribus affecti: eorum nullus memorabilis numerus occisus. Postero die redeuntem Norrisem, & nitrato puluere non satis abundantem Onellus secutus ad viam Finnuis infestius occurrit: vbi Ohanlonus summus exercitus regij signifer crure vulneratur, & alij glandibus plumbeis confossi cadunt. Munichanum arcem, quam tribus peditum cohortibus, & equitum turma Hinchus Anglus tenebat, inedia coactus dedidit, ipse ex pacto incolumis dimittitur."—*Hist. Cathol. Iber.*, tom. 3, lib. 3, c. ii.

The name here written Sedgreius by O'Sullevan, is written Segrave by the Abbé Ma-Geoghegan. The descendants of this gigantic warrior are still extant in the county of Wicklow, and the present head of the family is six feet eight inches in height. Lombard states, in his Commentaries, p. 345, that Sir John Norris bore high testimony to the valour, discipline, and military skill of O'Neill and his native Irish soldiers on this occasion, and that he expressed a wish that he had had their assistance in his services abroad.

[o] *No gap of danger.*—This should be Oıṗ ba beaṗn baoġaıl, &c.

naoṁ muire hi ráiṫ ṁaolain, ⁊ eccailsi ċolaim cille i ttoraiġ, nír bó foda an ré ro léicc dia ḋó gan a naiṫe fair, uair boí duine uasal do ḃurcaċaiḃ ina caoíṁteaċt co ndíḃ laoċaiḃ décc i maille fris .i. uillecc a búrc mac rémainn na sccuab. Do radaḋ dimiccin ⁊ tarcaisne dorisiḋe feċt nan lá Sſoirsi ⁊ las na gallaiḃ ar ċſna. Ro ba fearcc ⁊ ro ba londus laissiom indsin, ⁊ ro baoí ina ṁſnmain aiṫe a ḋíṁiaḋa ar Sheoirsi dia ccaoṁsaḋ ⁊ toċt iaroṁ i muinteaṙus uí doṁnaill ar bá dearḃ lais gur ḃó hinnill dó ḃſiṫ ina ḟoċair. Fuair siom iaraṁ baoġal an treóirsi réṁraite lá naén dia mbaoí i nairſccal i.nuathaḋ sochaiḋe Ráinic siom dia ḟaiccsiḋ, ⁊ ro ċuir ina aċċaiḋ a aindliccheaḋ ⁊ a eccóir fair, ⁊ ní ffuair freaġra ba lainn lais o ná fuair tairrngiḋ a cloiḋeaṁ, ⁊ imris fair co ro ḃſn a ċſnd dia ċúil ṁſiḋe. Geiḃiḋ an baile iaraṁ, ⁊ ro ḟaiḋ a ṫeaċta co háṫ sſnaiġ ḃail i mbáttar muintir uí ḋoṁnaill. Cuiridsiḋe teaċta co tír eoġain airm i mbaoí ó doṁnaill feissin. At fiadat a scéla ḋó, ⁊ at ċuaiḋ siuṁ don iarla ua néill iarttain. Robtar failiḋ diḃlinib don ṁarḃaḋ ísin. Celeḃraiḋ ua doṁnaill don iarla ar a ḃarac, ⁊ ní ro airis aċt a noiḋċiḃ co na sluaġ lais go ráinicc co slicceaċ fó ġeiḃ fáilte ⁊ do ratt uillſcc a búrc an baile ḋó, ⁊ bá sáiṁ lais a ṁſnma. I mí iún do rónaḋ indsin.

An tan at ċualattar i mbáttar for dſbſircc do ċoicceaḋ ċonnaċt (.i. búrcaiġ ioċtarac, clann ndoṁnaill, Siol cconċoḃair, Ruarcaiġ, ⁊ clann maolruanaiḋ, ⁊ ní hiad aṁáin aċt a mbáttar ar fóccra ⁊ ar faoinnel iar ná naṫċur ⁊ iar ná nionnarbaḋ lá bionġamaċaiḃ i nulltoiḃ ⁊ i nionadaiḃ ele)

[p] *Rath-Maelain*, now Rathmullan.—See note [g], p. 1968, *supra*.

[q] *Redmond-na-Scuab*, i. e. Redmond of the Sweeping Excursions. The word sccuab, which is cognate with the Latin *scopæ*, literally denotes a broom or besom.

[r] *Was offered iusult.*—P. O'Sullevan Beare states, that Ulick Burke was vexed because the Irish soldiers, who had accompanied George Bingham into Tirconnell, had not received a fair dividend of the booty carried off from that country:

"In Connachta Georgius Binghamus Iunior Sligacham arcem cum peditibus ducentis, quorum pars erant Iberni, tenebat. In qua præsidij causa relicto Vlligo Burko Raymundi filio nobili Iberno cum parte militum, ipse cum cæteris in Vltoniam duobus phasellis vectus Rathmelanem municipium Macsuinnij Fanidi, qui tunc aberat, inuadens monasterium Carmelitarum diripit, religiosis in arcem fugatis. Onustus præda Sligacham reuertitur. Cum divideretur præda, milites Iberni iure suo fraudati Vlligo videntur: qui cum iisdem agit, quemadmodum Binghami & Anglorum iniurias vlciscantur. Diem qua castellum illis adimat, constituit. Ea cum venisset, Iberni Anglos aggrediuntur. Binghamus ab Vlligo pugione confossus, & cæteri, vel occisi,

the monastery of the Blessed Virgin at Rath-Maelain[p], and the church of St. Columbkille on Torach; but God did not permit him to remain for a long time without revenging them upon him, for there was in his company a gentleman of the Burkes, who had twelve warriors along with him, namely, Ulick Burke, the son of Redmond-na-Scuab[q]. Upon one occasion he was offered insult[r] and indignity by George and the English in general, at which he felt hurt and angry; and he resolved in his mind to revenge the insult on George, if he could, and afterwards to get into the friendship of O'Donnell, for he felt certain of being secure with him. He afterwards got an advantage of the aforesaid George, one day as he was in an apartment with few attendants; he went up to him, and upbraided him with his lawlessness and injustice towards him, and as he did not receive a satisfactory answer, he drew his sword, and struck at him till he severed his head from his neck. He then took the castle, and sent messengers to Ballyshannon, where O'Donnell's people then were; and these dispatched messengers to Tyrone, where O'Donnell himself was. They relate the news to him, and he then went to the Earl O'Neill; and both were much rejoiced at that killing. On the following day O'Donnell bade the Earl farewell, and, setting out with his army, did not halt, except by night, until he arrived at Sligo. He was welcomed; and Ulick Burke delivered up the town to him, which made him very happy in his mind. This happened in the month of June.

When intelligence of the death of George Bingham, and the taking of Sligo, came to the hearing of those of the province of Connaught who were in insurrection, namely, the Lower Burkes, the Clann-Donnell, the Sil-Conor[s], the Rourkes, and the Clann-Mulrony[t], and not these alone, but also those who had been proclaimed, and roving after having been expelled and banished into Ulster

vel fuga salutem petentes deuastatæ religiosæ domus Carmelitarum pœnas sacrilegi luerunt. Arx Odonello traditur, qui in ea Vlligum præsidio præfecit. Sub idem quoque tempus Baleanmotam castellum Georgio Binghamo Maiori Tumultachus, & Cathalus Macdonachæ eripiunt."—*Hist. Cathol. Iber. Compend.*, tom. 3, lib. 3, c. iii. fol. 139.

[s] *Sil-Conor.*—These were the O'Conors of Sligo. The O'Conors of Machaire-Chonnacht, in the county of Roscommon, were, at this period, loyal to the English sovereign.—See *Memoirs of the Life and Writings of Charles O'Conor of Belanagare*, p. 112.

[t] *The Clann-Mulrony.*—This was the tribe-name of the Mac Dermots of Moylurg, in the county of Roscommon, and of the Mac Donoughs of Tirerrill and Corran, in the county of Sligo.

marbaḋ Seóirsi, ⁊ gabáil slicciġ tangattar do ṡaiġiḋ uí ḋomnaill go sliccech, ⁊ do ċóiḋ gach aon aca iaram do ṡaiġiḋ a aṫarḋa dilsi badéin, ⁊ gach aitt-reabṫaiġ dar ċuirsit goill ina ffſrandaiḃ (ina airſt báttar fſin ar foccra) ro gaḃsat leó mar lucht lſnamna ón uair sin amach. Báttar iaram ermór a raiḃe o rinn iarṫaraicc iorrais, ⁊ umaill co droḃaoís daon rann, ⁊ daon aonta lá hua ndomnaill fó ċſnd aon ṁiosa. Nír bó hiomḋa caislén nó coṁ-daingſn is na tíriḃ sin nách baoí slán nó brisde for a ċumas fris an ré cédna.

Tánaicc ó domnaill iaram co dún na ngall, ⁊ baí i hisuiḋe go meaḋon augusc. Ro hairnſiḋeaḋ do siḋe tarscar albanach do ṫeacht i ttír illoch febail .i. Mac leoid na hara, do ṫaéd siḋe ċuca dia ffostaḋ. Sé céd rob-dar iad a líon, ⁊ iar mbſiṫ athaiḋ isin tír iar lſiccſn a sciṫ, ⁊ a mſirtin, ⁊ iar na ffostaḋ lais, ro tſcclamait a ṡlóġa co na amsaiḃ lais, ⁊ lotar tar eirne, tar droḃaoís, tar duiḃ tars an sliccicch, tar ſr ndara, tar sliaḃ ngaṁ, go luiġne arsaiḋe co rainicc go goirdealḃachaiḃ. Baí ionattacht ⁊ aittreaḃad ag gallaiḃ hi ccaislén ṁór ṁec goirdealḃaiġ an tan sin, ⁊ ro ġaḃ ua domnaill co na ṡlóġaiḃ acc iomsuiḋe an baile gur bó hſiccſn don ḃarda an baile do ṫaḃairt uaṫa fó ḋeoiḋ. Do ṫaod iaram go rainicc dún mór mec feorais. Ro sccaoílsiot a sceiṁelta go conmaicne, go muintir mur-chaḋa, go lſiṫimel an maċaire riaḃaiġ, ⁊ go tuaim dá ġualann. Ro gaḃaḋ leó turlach mocháin, ⁊ sochaiḋe ṁór do ṁaithiḃ an tíre im Risderd mac mec feorais. Ro creachaḋ ⁊ ro lérindreaḋ an tír ina nuirtimċeall leó co rucc-sat a croḋ, ⁊ a cſtra a hionnmasa, ⁊ a heḋala doneoch gus a rangattar, ⁊ soait for ccúlaiḃ.

Ot ċualaiḋ goberṅóir ċóiccid ċonnacht .i. Sir Risderd bingam ó domnaill do ḋol ṫairis siar hí cconnachtaiḃ ro ṫionóil siḋe cóicc ḃanna décc do ṡaiġ-

[u] *The Sligeach*, i. e. the river of Sligo, now called the Gity.

[w] *Castlemore-Mac-Costello*, i. e. Mac Costello's great castle.—See note [s], under the year 1284, p. 441, *supra*.

[x] *Dunmore-Mic-Feorais*, i. e. the great dun or fort of Mac Feorais, or Bermingham, now Dunmore, eight miles to the north of Tuam-daghualann, or Tuam, in the county of Galway.—See note [s], under the year 1284, p. 441, *supra*.

[y] *Conmaicne.*—The barony of Kilmaine, in the county of Mayo, was called Conmaicne Cuile Toladh, and the barony of Dunmore, in the county of Galway, was called Conmaicne Cineil Dubhain.—See map to *Tribes and Customs of Hy-Many*.

[z] *Muintir-Murchadha*, a district comprising at this period about the northern half of the ba-

and other places, by the Binghams, they came to O'Donnell to Sligo; and each of them went afterwards to his own patrimonial inheritance; and every inhabitant whom the English had established in their lands during the period of their proscription adhered to them as followers from that hour forth. In the course of one month the greater part of the inhabitants of the district, from the western point of Erris and Umhall to the Drowes, had unanimously confederated with O'Donnell; and there were not many castles or fortresses in those places, whether injured or perfect, that were not under his control.

O'Donnell then went to Donegal, and remained there till the middle of August. He was informed that a number of Scots had landed at Lough Foyle, with their chief, Mac Leod of Ara; he went thither to hire them. They were six hundred in number. After being hired by him, and after remaining some time to rest and recruit themselves, he assembled his forces and hirelings, and they marched across the Erne, the Drowes, the Duff, the Sligeach[u], and Eas-dara, across Sliabh-Gamh, into Leyny, and from thence into Costello. The English held at that time abode and residence in Castlemore-Mac-Costello[w]. O'Donnell with his forces laid siege to this castle; and the warders were finally obliged to surrender it. He then proceeded to Dunmore-Mic-Feorais[x], and dispatched marauding parties into Conmaicne[y], Muintir-Murchadha[z], to the borders of Machaire-Riabhach[a], and to Tuam-da-ghualann. They took Turlach-Mochain[b], and a great number of the chiefs of the country, together with Richard, the son of Mac Feorais. They plundered and totally ravaged the country all around them, and carried off its flocks and herds, its wealth and riches, from all those they had met on their route, and [then] returned back.

When the Governor of the province of Connaught, namely, Sir Richard Bingham, heard that O'Donnell had passed by him westwards into Connaught, he assembled fifteen companies of soldiers, both horse and foot, and marched

rony of Clare, and county of Galway. It appears from an Inquisition taken at Athenry in 1584, that the Earl of Clanrickard had a chief rent of twenty marks per annum, out of the territory or cantred called Moyntermoroghow, in which the abbey of Rosserill is situated.—See *Chorographical Description of Iar-Connaught*, p. 368.

[a] *Machaire-Riabhach.*—See note [c], under the year 1469, p. 1064, *supra*.

[b] *Turlach-Mochain*, i. e. Mochan's dried lough, now Turlough-vohan, near Tuam, barony of Dunmore, and county of Galway. In the Life of Hugh Roe O'Donnell, Turlach Mochain is called a castle in the country of Mac Feorais: "Turlaċ Moċán caisteall siḋe fil i nduṫaiġ ṁeic ḟeorais."

diúiriḃ etir marcaċa ⁊ troiġṫeaċa co ráinicc go muinċinct coirrsleiḃe ar ḋáiġ ammais do ṫaḃairt for ua ndoṁnaill acc tionntuḋ dia eaċtra. Iar na ḟios sin dua doṁnaill ro fillsiḋe tar a ais biucc co na airccṫiḃ ⁊ co na éḋalaiḃ on ccampa go ċele go goirdealḃchaiḃ, go luiġne dioċtar ó nailella trés na triḃ droiċſdaiḃ .i. droiċſt ċuile maoíle, droiċſt baile ſsa dara, ⁊ droiċſt sliġiġe. Ḃáttar tra goill accá iarṁoirecht aṁail as déine con- rangattar is na conairiḃ sin. Ro ſioirḋeiliġſstair ua doṁnaill dirim marcsluaiġ, ⁊ ro forċongair forra airisſiṁ i ndſireaḋ a ṡlóiġ ar naċ fag- ḃaittis urtosaċ an tsloiġ gall giollanraḋ, nó aos diairm dia ṁuintir riuṁ i mbaoġal. Rainicc riuṁ iaraṁ co na chreachaiḃ lais gan naċ frioṫorccain co riaċt i ccoṁfoċraiḃ gleanda dalláin. Tánaicc an goberrnóir for a lorcc co ro gaḃ longport i mainistir ṡliccigh dforḃairi for ḃardaiḃ uí doṁnaill báttar isin ccaislén. Ro ṗaíḋ ua doṁnaill ar a ḃaraċ buiḋſn marcslóiġ do ṫaiscélaḋ forr na gallaiḃ, ⁊ dfios sccél an dúnaiḋ ⁊ na nócc báttar ann co rangattar go himeal bord na haḃann gus an ccnoc dia ngarar Ráiṫ dá ḃriotócc, ⁊ at ciad na goill páncán seaċnón an ḃaile.

Ro ḃaí ócclaoċ uallaċ borrfaḋaċ i ffarraḋ Sir Risderd an tan sin ro ba mac sſtar dó buḋḋſin captin martin a ainm. As esside bá toíseaċ marcslóiġ ḋó. Ní ro ḟulaing side deccsan a namatt i ccoṁfoccus dó gan a ffuabairt, ⁊ tainicc co na ḋiorma tar droiċſt sligiġi anall. Od ċiad muintir uí doṁnaill iad dia saiġiḋ soait for ccúla (o naċ raḃattar coiṁlíon friu) aṁail as déine conrangattar. Tiaġait na goill ina ndiúiḋ, ⁊ nís tár- rattar idir soait iaraṁ for ccula. Ro airnſiḋriot muintir uí domnaill a sccéla, ⁊ aṁail ro bás occa ttogsaim, ⁊ aṁail do érnairiot lá luas a nſċ. Iar ccloisteċt an sccéoil sin lá hua ndoṁnaill bá sé airſcc ar rainicc lais celcc do indell for cionn na nallmuireaċ isin cconair ccédna. Ro ṫſglaim

[c] *Top.*—"Muinċinn .i. uaċtar."—*O'Clery, in Leabhar Gabhala*, p. 3.

[d] *Cul-maoile.*—This was the old name of the place now called Cul-Mhuine, *anglice* Colooney. According to the tradition in the country the castle of Cul-Maoile was some distance from the present village of Colooney; but if we can rely on the maps of Connaught made about this period, the castle of Collounie, opposite which was the bridge, stood on the south side of the River Owenmore, close to where it receives a stream from Loughdargan. This is the exact situation of the present village of Colooney, which is certainly the Cul-Maoile referred to above in the text by the Four Masters.

[e] *Gleann-Dallain*, a remarkable valley, situated partly in the county of Sligo, and partly in Leitrim. The church of Cill-Osnata, now Kil-

to the top[c] of the Coirrshliabh [Curlieu hills], with the intention of making an attack upon O'Donnell, on his return from his expedition. When O'Donnell received intelligence of this, he soon returned back, with his preys and spoils, from one encampment to the other, through Costello, Leyny, the lower part of Tirerrill, and over the three bridges, namely, the bridge of Cul-maoile[d], the bridge of Ballysadere, and the bridge of Sligo. Through these passages the English went in pursuit of him as quickly as they could. O'Donnell detached a troop of cavalry, and ordered them to fall to the rear of his army, to prevent the van of the English army from coming into collision with the attendants or unarmed portion of his people. He afterwards moved on with his preys, till he reached the neighbourhood of Gleann-Dallain[e], without any opposition.

The Governor followed in his track, and took up his quarters in the monastery of Sligo, to besiege O'Donnell's warders who were in the castle. On the next day O'Donnell sent a party of cavalry to reconnoitre the English, and learn the state of the fortress, and of the men[f] who were in it; and they advanced to the banks of the river, to the hill which is called Rath-Dabhritog[g], from which they espied the English moving up and down[h] throughout the town.

There was at this time along with Sir Richard his own sister's son, a proud and haughty youth, Captain Martin by name, who was the commander of his cavalry. He could not bear to see his enemies so near him without attacking them, and proceeded with his squadron across the bridge of Sligo. When O'Donnell's people perceived them advancing, they returned back as speedily as they were able, as they were not equal to them in number. The English pursued them; but not overtaking them, they returned back. O'Donnell's people then related how they had been pursued, and how they had escaped by means of the swiftness of their horses. When O'Donnell heard this story, the resolution he came to was, to lay a snare for the foreigners on the same passage.

asnet, in the barony of Dartry, or Rossclogher, in the county of Leitrim, is in it.—See Colgan's *Acta Sanctorum*, p. 337.

[f] *Of the men*, literally, "of the youths."

[g] *Rath-Dabhritog*, i. e. Dabhritog's rath, or fort, now Rath hill, in the townland of Rathquarter, in the parish of Calry, barony of Carbury, Sligo. In the deed of partition of the Sligo estate, dated 21st July, 1687, this townland is called Raghtabretoke, Rathavritoge, *alias* Rath. The fort on this hill commands the entire town of Sligo. It is a square fort, evidently constructed from the materials of the original one during the civil wars of 1641, or 1688.

[h] *Up and down.*—" Sáncán .ı. anonn ⁊ anall."—*O'Clery.*

iaraṁ an céd marcaċ ro ba deaċ dia sluaġ co ttriḃ céadaiḃ troiġteaċ co na ttrealṁaiḃ diuḃraicṫi .i. fioḋbaca co na saiġet bolccaiḃ. Ro ḟorconġair forra celcc do inneall fá ṁile do ṡlicceaċ, ⁊ dírim ḃecc marcṡluaiġ dfaoídeaḋ uaṫa co himel ḃord na haḃann do ḃréccaḋ an tṡlóiġ gall, ⁊ dia ttíorta ina llenmain gan aiririom fri hiomairecc co roċtain dóiḃ tar an maiġin in ro hindleaḋ an ċelcc. Do rónaḋ fairrium sin uile. Ot ċonnairc captin martin an tuathaḋ marcṡlóiġ for ur na haḃann do ċóiḋ co ndírim móir marcṡlóiġ a maille fris dia ttéttarraċtain lotar roṁ remhpa co hionmall ainésccaiḋ an ccédna feaċt, nír ḃó cian do na hóccaiḃ iaraṁ gur ḃó héiccen dóiḃ ḃeiṫ acc eaċlorccaḋ a neaċ lá a ḋéine ⁊ lá a ḋiogaire ro báttar goill ina ndeaḋhaiḋ. Ro cuireaḋ deireaḋ for aon díoḃriḋe .i. feilim riaḃaċ mac daueid, dia aiṁḋeóin lá hionmaille a eiċ co nár ḃó tualaing freṡtal a muintire, ⁊ go mbó héiccen dó aiririom fri a naiṁdiḃ, ⁊ teaċt tar forċongra a tiġearna .i. toċar do fris na gallaiḃ. O rob erḋalta lais a ṁarḃaḋ fó ċédóir. Soais a ġhaiḋ fris an tí bá nesaṁ ḋó don luċt batar ina llenmain, ⁊ rob eiriḋe captin martin, ⁊ acc tóccḃáil a láiṁe dósiḋe in oirċill a airm dimirt for an tí do rala in eccoṁlann for a ċionn do raḋ feilim a ṁéur hi suaineṁ an ṡoġa baí occa i nerlaiṁe dia ḋiuḃraccaḋ co ro amais captin martin i ndeirc a occsaille ceċ ndíreaċ gur treġdastair a ċriḋe ina ċliaḃ. Ḃá heidiġṫi sium tra cenmotá an tionaḋ sin triar ro gaotta. Iompaíd na goill for ccúla iar nguin a ttreinḟir ⁊ a ttoísiġ iomġona, ⁊ do berad leó hé for iomċar faon fotarsna i ffanntairiḃ écca co rangattar an baile, ⁊ fuair bás in aḋhaiġ sin. Od ċonnairc ó domnaill na goill do ṡoaḋ for

[1] *Bank of the river.*—P. O'Sullevan Beare says that Rothericus, the brother of O'Donnell, and Felimy Mac Davet, crossed the river; but his account of this transaction seems anything but correct. His words are as follows:

"Sequente autumno, sub quod tempus Norris cum Onello minus prospero marte contendit, Richardus Binghamus ad Sligacham recuperandam, & occisi consanguinei pœnas de Vlligo sumendas facit expeditionem. Vlligum Sligachæ obsidione cinctum oppugnat. Vlligus cum propugnatoribus egressus pro munitionibus quotidie certat. Odonellus obsidionem soluturus cum mille, & sexcentis militibus auxilia venire festinat. Apud Duraranem in hostis conspectu tentoria pandit. Duobus primis diebus interlabens flumen vtriusque partis equitatus adequitans iaculis leuiter vltrocitroque velitatur. Tertio die Rothericus Odonelli frater cum Felmio Macdaveto, & alio equite fluuium traiectus castra contemplatur. In illum Martin Anglus, qui in Binghami exercitu præstantissimus eques habebatur, procurrit, turma sua, cuius dux erat, stipatus. Rothericus admisso equo ad suos adcurrit. Martin sequens suorum primus vadum traijiciebat. Quem Felmius conuersus

He then selected one hundred of the best horsemen of his army, and three hundred infantry with their shooting implements, namely, bows with their arrow-quivers; he ordered them to lie in ambush within a mile of Sligo, and to send a small squadron of horse to the banks of the river, to decoy the English army; and should they [the foreigners] pursue them, not to wait for an engagement, until they should have come beyond the place where the ambuscade was laid. This was accordingly done. When Captain Martin perceived the small squadron of cavalry on the bank of the river[i], he advanced directly with a numerous body of cavalry, to wreak his vengeance upon them. The others at first moved slowly and leisurely before them, but these young heroes were soon obliged to incite their horses forward, the English having pursued them with such speed and vehemence. One of them, namely, Felim Reagh Mac Devit[k], was [however] compelled to remain behind, in consequence of the slowness of his horse; and, being unable to accompany his own people, he was obliged to disobey the orders of his lord, that is, to fight the English [before he had passed the ambuscade]. As he was certain of being immediately slain, he turned his face to the nearest of his pursuers, who was Captain Martin; and, as he [Captain Martin] raised his arm to strike his antagonist with his weapon, Felim placed his finger on the string of the javelin, which he had in readiness to discharge, so that he struck Captain Martin directly in the arm-pit, and pierced his heart in his breast. He was covered with mail, except in the spot where he was wounded. The English, seeing their champion and commander mortally wounded, returned back, carrying him, in his weakly condition, and in the agonies of death, in a recumbent posture, to the town, where he died on that night. When O'Donnell saw that the English had retreated, he was enraged, until the decoying party

hasta traiectum, & interfectum in ipso flumine equo deturbat, & ipse cum Rotherico, & alio commilitone incolumis euasit. Postero die obsidionis quarto, Binghamus, obsidio relicto domum redit, quem Odonellus secutus missilibus carpit."—*Hist. Cathol. Iber. Compend.*, tom. 3, lib. 3, c. iii. fol. 140.

[k] *Felim Reagh Mac Devit.*—He is still vividly remembered in the traditions of the barony of Inishowen, in the county of Donegal. He was the head of the Mac Devits of Inishowen, who are, according to Cucogry O'Clery, a branch of the O'Dohertys, and the very man who afterwards burned the town of Derry, from which circumstance the Mac Devits are even to this day called "Burnderrys" by their Presbyterian neighbours. They are at present a very numerous sept in the neighbourhood of Londonderry, and throughout the barony of Inishowen, in the county of Donegal.

ccúlaiḃ ro lonnaiġeaḋ eissiḋe co ro ṫoingsiot luċt na fássuabarta tar ċenn Feilim co ná baoí ní dia imḋeaġail gan a ṁarḃaḋ lá captin martin aċt maḋ an taén ḟorccom sin. Ro tlaṫaiġestair a ṁenma iaram ó ran-gattar scéla ċuicce ar a ḃarać co ro écc an captin.

Dala an goberнora ro líon side dfercc 7 do lonnas iar marḃaḋ a ḃraṫar, 7 ro ḟorċongair for a ṡlóġ aidme togla an ċaisteoil do ḋénaṁ leó dus an ccaéṁsaittís a erġaḃail for ṁuintir uí doṁnaill bátar ann. Do rónaḋ leó soṁ indsin do ċranncaingel 7 do ċuḃaċlaiḃ na ccéileḋ ndé, 7 dá gaċ aidme rangatar a lis baí isin mainistir. Do raḋṫa iaram seisceaḃa bó 7 daṁ for na haidmiḃ sin dia neacctair. Ro fuccṫa ḃeós roṫaḋa faoí dia ḟóg-luasaċt gus an dúnaiḋ. Ro líonta iaram do laoċraiḋ, 7 do láṫaiḃ gaile, 7 do ṡaorraiḃ i ffoiṁdin togla an ḃaile. Ro tréntairrngset léo an lúiṫeać sin lá dorcatta urṫossaiġ na hoiḋċe co ro suiḋiġṫe hé fri huillinn an ċais-teóil, 7 gaḃait for scaoíleaḋ an ṁúir iarttáin báttar dinid saoir isin mbaile, 7 ro ġaḃsat acc bloḋaḋ an ḃalla fo a nesċomair do diuḃraccaḋ a

[l] *Bore testimony*, ro ṫoingsiot.—In the Life of Hugh Roe O'Donnell the reading is:

"Dus riccset rianlaċ na fassuaḃarta hi ffreacnarcus na flaṫa (gér ḃa doiliġ dóiḃ itir ar aiḋḃle a ḟuarna) 7 att ríaḋat aṁail do rála dóiḃ, 7 ro toingset uile dar ċenn an ċuraiḋ ro gon captin martín na buí ní nom beraḋ ass muna tarddaḋ an taon ḟorgomh sin genmoṫá cuṁaċta an ċoiṁdeaḋ. The soldiers of the ambuscade came in the presence of the chief (though it was difficult for them to do so, on account of the intensity of his anger), and they related how it happened with them; and they all testified, in behalf of the champion who had" [mortally] "wounded Captain Martin, that nothing could have saved him except that one thrust, except the power of the Lord."

Here it will be observed that the language of the apology for Mac Devit is defective; for the cause of O'Donnell's anger was, not because Felim Reagh had saved himself by killing Captain Martin, but because he had remained behind the decoying party, and thus prevented O'Donnell's ambuscade from cutting off the English pursuers. The apology should be thus worded: "And they all bore testimony, in behalf of Felim, that his horse was lame, and that he could not by any exertion have prevented himself from being overtaken by the enemy in the manner in which he was, and they shewed that this was demonstrated by the imminent danger to which he was brought, for that no human calculation could have anticipated that he alone could have killed a warrior cased in armed mail, at the head of a fierce troop of cavalry, or even, if he could, that this would have caused so select a body of cavalry to run away from a single Irish horseman, leaving their captain's mortal wound unrevenged. O'Donnell, on considering that the laming of Mac Devit's horse was accidental, and that it could not have been prevented by any precaution, suppressed his anger; and his mind was much consoled on hearing of the death of the haughty young Englishman."

[m] *Crannchaingel*, i. e. the latticed partition dividing the chancel from the nave, in the abbey

bore testimony[l] in behalf of Felim, [that his horse was lame, which prevented him from keeping up with his party, and] that there was nothing to have saved him from being slain by Captain Martin, excepting the one [chance] thrust; but his anger afterwards subsided when news reached him on the next day that the Captain had died.

As for the Governor, he was filled with anger and fury after the killing of his kinsman; and he ordered his army to construct engines for demolishing the castle, to see whether they could take it from O'Donnell's people who were in it. This they constructed of the crannchaingel[m], and of the bed-chambers of the Culdees[n], and of other implements which they found befitting for the purpose in the monastery. They covered these engines on the outside with the hides of cows and oxen, and wheels were put under them to remove them to the fortress. They were afterwards filled with heroes, warriors, and artisans, for the purpose of razing the castle. This mighty train[o] was drawn by them in the beginning of the night to the corner of the castle; and they immediately proceeded to destroy the wall. At this time some artisans who were within the castle began to pull down the opposite wall, in order that the youths within

church. "Cꞃannċaingel .ı. cꞃannċlıaċ ıeıꞃ laeċaıƀ ⁊ cleıꞃċıƀ."—*Cormac's Glossary.*

[n] *Culdees.*—Here the term céıle ꝺé is used to denote monks, or friars.

[o] *Mighty train.*—The engines constructed by Bingham on this occasion were called *sows*. Sir George Carew, in his *Pacata Hibernia*, vol. i. p. 124 (Dub. ed.), thus speaks of one of them:

"The castle, therefore, they besiege, and placed an Engine, well known in this country, called a sovv, to the walls thereof, to supp the same. But the Defendants did so well acquit themselves in a sally, as they tare the sovv in peeces, made her *caste her pigs*, and slevv tvventy-seven of them dead in the place."

P. O'Sullevan Beare calls this machine, "muchum Bellicum," and describes this siege of the castle of Sligo briefly, but clearly and elegantly, in the following words:

"Neque Binghamus quidem dormit. Tomoniæ, & Clanrickardæ Comites Ibernos euocat: Connactæ delectum habet: Midhienses præsidiarios, et equites Angloibernos recipit. Cum signis militaribus viginti quatuor Sligacham obsidione vallatam oppugnat. Vlligus Burkus cum propugnatoribus egressus cum munitionibus acriter dimicat. Tandem ab oppugnatorum multitudine in arcem compulsus, ex turribus, pinnis, fenestris, et reliquis munitionibus missilia iaculando hostes arcet. Regij *muchum bellicum*" [muc ċoꝫaıḋ] "machinamentum militibus subter agentibus arcis muro admouent, murumque forare, & subruere incipiunt, Vlligus magnæ molis trabe funibus ligata ex arcis fastigio nunc dimissa, nunc in altum sublata *muchum*, & milites, qui sub eo latebant, conterit. Odonellus obsessis auxilio veniens appropinquat. Binghamus fugit. In oppugnatione regij sexcenti milites obierunt. Arcem vero quòd erat tam laboriosum, defendere, Odonellus demolitur."—*Hist. Cathol. Iber. Compend.*, tom. 3, lib. 3, c. iv. fol. 140, 141.

mbioḋḃaḋ do na hóccaiḃ báttar istiġ. Do ċódar araill ele don ḃarda for taiḃliḃ an dúnaiḋ, ⁊ ro ġaḃsat for tealccaḋ táiṫleac ttuinigṫe, ⁊ carracc ccsnoġarḃ forra anuas gomtar miona mionḃrúite gaċ ní fris a ccomraicctis. Tiaġaid tra drong ele do luċt an ḃaile for fenestribh ⁊ for forléraiḃ an caisteoil, ⁊ gaḃait for diúḃraccadh a nuḃaill ṁealluaiḋe, ⁊ a ttrom ċaor tteinntiḋe forra go ro foirrgitt an fiallaċ baí isna cuṁdaiġṫiḃ cláraiġ don ċloiċṫreas, ⁊ don dian ndiubraccaḋ sin. Ní ro fuilngit las na gallaiḃ a ccrécctnuccaḋ ní baḋ mó, ⁊ ó ná ro ḟédsat ní don dúnadh ro ḟaġaiḃsiot a ttesġdairi toġalta múir, ⁊ soait ina ffrithing ós iat beóġonta, ⁊ robtar buiḋiġ do roċtain a nanmantt leó. Bá cráḋ criḋe las an ngoberrnoir Sir Risderd bingam ná caeṁnaccair a aincriḋe dimirt for ḃardaiḃ an dunaiḋ, ná for naċ naon do ṁuintir í domnaill, ⁊ impóidis for a ais tar corrsliaḃ, tar maġ naoi co rainicc Rosscommain. Do ḋeaċaidh ó domnaill iaraṁ tar éirne, ⁊ ro léicc a albanaiġ uaḋa iar ttaḃairt a ttuarustail dóiḃ. Téid tar a ais co sliccеaċ co ro brissiot las an caislén duaman gall dia aittreaḃaḋ.

Teroitt a búrc mac uatéir ċiotaiġ, mic seain, mic oiluerais mic Seain do ġaḃáil forbairi for ḃél leice, baile sin i mbarúntaċt tíre haṁalgaiḋ hi cconntae maiġeó, ⁊ bá hiad barda an goberrnora báttar ann. Iar roċtain na scél sin gus an ngoberrnóir, ro ḟorail for a dearḃraṫair .i. captin Iohn bingam, ar captin foal, ar captin mennri ⁊ ar a mac uilliam buide diúid co ndruing móir do ḋaoiniḃ uaisle ele a maille friú dol dfurtaċt an ḃaile co lón ⁊ co narmáil dia saiġiḋ, ⁊ riasiú ráinicc leó an barda dfóirithin fuair teróitt a búrc an baile. Tiaġaidsium tar a nais fó aiṫmela, ⁊ ro gaḃ teróitt acca ttoraiġeaċt, accá ttrésġdaḋ, ⁊ acca ttimċeallaḋ agá mbuaiḋreaḋ, ⁊ accá mbásuccaḋ tar an ċaoṁlaoí co ro ḟáccaiḃsiot daoíne, arm, ⁊ éideaḋ iomḋa. Ro marḃaḋ las an lá sin captin foal, captin mennri, ⁊ mac oiḋreaċta uilliam diúid, ⁊ soċaiḋe ele do ṡaorċlandaiḃ, ⁊ do ḋaor-

[p] *It preyed*, literally, "It was anguish of heart to the Governor."

[q] *Bel-leice*, i. e. Mouth of the Ford of the Flag, translated *os rupis*, by P. O'Sullevan Beare in *Hist. Cathol. Iber.*, *&c.*, fol. 136, now Belleek, a rocky ford on the River Moy, about a mile to the north of the town of Ballina, in the parish of Kilmore-Moy, barony of Tirawley, and county of Mayo.—See *Genealogies, Tribes, and Customs of Hy-Fiachrach*, p. 480, and the map to the same work. In an old map of parts of the coasts of Mayo, Sligo, and Donegal, preserved in the State Papers' Office, London, this castle is shewn under the name of "Ca: Bellecke," as on the

might hurl the stones down on their enemies. Some of the warders also ascended to the battlements of the castle, and proceeded to cast down massy flags and ponderous, rough rocks, which broke and shattered to pieces every thing on which they fell. Others within the castle went to the windows and loopholes, and commenced discharging leaden bullets and showers of fire upon them; so that the soldiers who were in the wooden engines were bruised by that dropping of the stones, and by the incessant firing. The English did not remain to be wounded further; and, finding that they could effect nothing against the castle, they abandoned their wall-destroying domicile, and returned home, severely wounded, and glad to escape with their lives. It preyed[p] upon the heart of the Governor, Sir Richard Bingham, that he was not able to wreak his vengeance upon the warders of the fortress, or on any of O'Donnell's people. He returned back [homeward] across the Curlieus, and over Moy-Nai, [never halting] until he arrived at Roscommon; and O'Donnell [also] returned [homeward] across the Erne, and discharged the Scots, having paid them their wages. He went back to Sligo, and demolished the castle, lest the English should inhabit it.

Theobald Burke, the son of Walter Kittagh, son of John, son of Oliver, son of John, laid siege to Bel-leice[q], a castle in the barony of Tirawley, in the county of Mayo, and it was then defended by the Governor's warders. When the Governor received intelligence of this, he ordered his brother, Captain John Bingham, Captain Foal[r], Captain Mensi, the son of William Boy Tuite, with many other gentlemen, to go to the relief of the castle with provisions and arms; but, before they could relieve the warders, Theobald had obtained possession of the castle. They then returned home in sorrow; and Theobald went in pursuit of them, piercing, surrounding, disturbing, and slaying them throughout that fair day, so that they lost many men, [and much] arms and armour. On this day he slew Captain Foal, Captain Mensi, and the son and heir of William Tuite, with many others, both of the gentlemen and common people, not enu-

west side of the River Moy, a short distance to the north of the point where it receives the River Brosnagh.

[r] *Foal.*—P. O'Sullevan Beare calls him Foollurtus, and states that he was accompanied by Dudus, i.e. Tuite, an Anglo-Irishman; by Hugh and William Mosten, the sons of an Englishman, by an Irish mother; George Bingham, junior, and Minche, who were Englishmen.—See *Hist. Cathol. Iber. Compend.*, tom. 3, lib. 2, c. xii.

ċlanḋaiḃ náċ áiriṁṫear. ba do ṫoraḋ ſingnaṁa, eirriomail, ⁊ aiṫearraiġ eolais ro imṫiġ gaċ a nḋeachaiḋ ar ḋíḃ an lá sin.

O Neill toirrḋealbaċ luineaċ mac néill ċonallaiġ, mic airt, mic cuinn mic enrí, mic eoġain do écc. Bá heriḋe aen ar mó ro ḋearlaic ḋionnṁaraiḃ ⁊ ḋeḋalaiḃ ḋéiccriḃ, ⁊ ḋollaṁnaiḃ, ⁊ do luċt cuinġſḃa neich do tiġearnaḋaiḃ Ereann ina coiṁre, uair ro herḟuaccraḋ uaiḋriḋe co minic ro erinn ḋá gaċ aen baí la hiarraiḋ nſiṫ toiḋeaċt ina ḋoċom i ffeiliḃ geine an ċoiṁḋe do ḟonnraḋ, ⁊ iar na ttarraċtain ní ṫſiġſḋ aen ró ḋiomḃa uaḋa gan riar; tiġſrna agá mbíḋir soċaiḋe ile for a tuillṁe ⁊ for a tuarustol, tiġſrna ro ba soċonáiġ fri síḋ, ⁊ ro ba coṁnart fri coccaḋ condus sala aoſs, ⁊ einirte dó, ⁊ ro hordaiġſḋ oiḋre ina ionaḋ deiċ mbliaḋna ria na ḃás ar an bparlimenṫ ro congṁaḋ in áṫ cliaṫ i nainm na bainrioġna elisabeth .i. Aoḋ mac an ḟirḋorca (.i. an barun), mic cuinn mic cuinn, mic enri, mic eoġain dia ro gairſḋ iarla ar an bparliminṫ sin. Bá hand atbaṫ ua neill isin srat mbán, ⁊ a aḋnacal in ard sraṫa.

Mag aénġusa aoḋ mac aoḋa, mic doṁnaill óicc fſr a aṫarḋa ro baḋ mó ainm ⁊ erdearcus i ffiaḋnaisi gall ⁊ gaoiḋel ereann décc go ṗeaċtnaċ.

Toirrḋealbaċ mac briain mic donnchaiḋ, mic donnchaiḋ ḃacaiġ tiġearna corca baiscinn iartarṫaiġe, fſr ro ba mór tſirt ⁊ tuarusccḃáil ar fud ereann do réir a aṫarḋa (uair ní bai occa aċt triuċa ċéd namá) do écc ⁊ a ṁac taḋcc caoċ do gaḃail a ionaid.

Remann na sccuab mac uillicc na ccſnd, mic Riocaird mic uillicc cnuic tuaġ do écc.

[s] *Superior knowledge*, aiṫearraiġ eolais.—The word aiṫearraċ, which is spelled aiṫioraċ in O'Reilly's Dictionary, signifies craft, science, or skill.

[t] *An heir*.—This is not exactly correct, for the Parliament held at Dublin in 1585 only conceded to his rival, Hugh, the rank and title of the Earldom of Tyrone, leaving the possessions to be annexed thereunto, to the pleasure of her Majesty. In 1587 the Queen granted to Hugh, by letters patent, under the great seal of England, the Earldom of Tyrone, and the inheritance annexed to it, without any reservation of rent; but it was provided that the sons of the late Shane O'Neill should have sufficient provisions allotted to them, and that Turlough [Luineach] should be continued Irish chieftain of Tyrone, with a right of superiority over Maguire and O'Cahan. It appears from a patent, 20th Elizabeth, that the Queen had intended to create Turlough Luineach Earl of Clanoneill and Baron of Clogher; but it is quite clear that this patent was never perfected, as his son, Arthur, who makes so conspicuous a figure in the great rebellion, was simply knight. There are still extant several Irish poems, addressed to Tur-

merated; and all who escaped did so by virtue of their prowess, valour, and superior knowledge[s].

O'Neill (Turlough Luineach, the son of Niall Conallagh, son of Art, son of Con, son of Henry, son of Owen) died. He had bestowed most wealth and riches upon the learned, the Ollavs, and all those who sought gifts of [any of] the lords of Ireland in his time; for he had often issued a proclamation throughout Ireland to all those who sought gifts, [inviting them] to come to him on the festivals of the nativity of our Lord; and when they came, not one departed dissatisfied, or without being supplied. He was a lord who had many soldiers in his service for pay and wages,—a lord prosperous in peace, and powerful in war, until age and infirmity came upon him; and an heir[t] had been appointed in his place, ten years before his death, at the parliament held in Dublin in the name of Queen Elizabeth, namely, Hugh (the son of Ferdorcha the Baron, son of Con, son of Con, son of Henry, son of Owen), who had been styled Earl at this parliament. O'Neill died at Strabane, and was interred at Ardstraw.

Magennis (Hugh, the son of Hugh, son of Donnell Oge), a man, of his patrimony[u], of greatest name and renown among the English and Irish of Ireland, died penitently.

Turlough, the son of Brian, son of Donough, son of Donough Bacagh [Mac Mahon], Lord of West Corca-Bhaiscinn[w], a man of great fame and character throughout Ireland, considering his patrimony, for he had but one cantred[x], died; and his son, Teige Caech, took his place.

Redmond-na-Scuab, son of Ulick-na-gCeann, son of Rickard, son of Ulick [Burke] of Cnoc-Tuagh, died.

lough Luineach, inciting him to shake off the English yoke, and become monarch of Ireland like his ancestors, Niall Frasach, Niall of the Nine Hostages, Con of the Hundred Battles, and Tuathal Teachtmhar, whose lineal heir he is stated to be, and whose example he is encouraged to follow. But he was so old when he was made O'Neill, that he seems to have then retained little military ardour to tread in the wake of his ancestors; and he was so much in dread of the sons of Shane the Proud and of Hugh Earl of Tyrone, that he continued obedient to the Queen of England.

[u] *Of his patrimony*, i. e. a man who was more famed and renowned than any other chieftain of equal territorial possessions in Ireland. This Irish idiom translates very awkwardly into English.

[w] *West Corca-Bhaiscinn*, now the barony of Moyarta, forming the south-west portion of the county of Clare.

[x] *Cantred*, ṫrıoċa céd signifies a cantred, hundred, or barony, containing one hundred and twenty quarters of land.

O Gallċubair Sir Eóin mac Tuaṫail, fer ro baḋ mór ainm ⁊ oirdercus ag gallaiḃ, ⁊ ag gaoiḋelaiḃ an tansin do écc .25. April.

Mainistir ṁuineaċáin i noirġiallaiḃ do beiṫ ag gallaiḃ an bliaḋainsi, ⁊ banna saiġdiuir agá hiomċoiṁéd do ġnaṫ. Rainic sgéla uaṫa co háṫ cliaṫ co mbáttar i tterce lóin. Iar ná cloisteċt sin don iustis Sir uilliam Russel, ⁊ do Sir seon norris ro ḟurailset sé ḃanna fiċet saiġdíuiriḋe do Shaxanċoiḃ ⁊ deirennċoiḃ co ndaoíniḃ uaisle iomḋa a maille friú do ċor lá lón ⁊ lá gaċ naiḋilcce rangattar ales go muineaċan, ⁊ rangattar rompa gan ráṫuccaḋ gan friṫbeart gus an mbaile, ⁊ iar mbeiṫ in aḋhaiġ sin i muineaċan dóiḃ ro triallsat imṫeaċt ar a ḃaraċ do ḋol don iuḃar. An tan tra rangattar feḋ becc ó muineaċan soir do rala muintir uí neill dóiḃ for a ccionn. Bá hainmín sceccairdeṁail an fiaḋuccaḋ fuairsiot annsin uair ro gaḃaḋ aga ccaiṫeaṁ ⁊ agá ccoṁḟuabairt agá marḃaḋ, ⁊ agá muḋucchaḋ on cceṫeora huair ria meḋón laí co fuineḋ nell nóna co nár ḃó hurusa ríoṁ nó áireṁ in ró fáccbaḋ do ṁuintir an iustis etir ṡaor ⁊ daor, ⁊ in ro fáccbaḋ ḃeós deaċaiḃ, ⁊ déiḋeḃ dainnaiḃ, ⁊ dioḟaobraiḃ, dearraḋ, ⁊ déḋaċ uasal, do caiplib, ⁊ do ċliaḃaiḃ lóin in gaċ conair ro imtiġsiot an lá sin. Ro gaḃaḋ forlongport leó in iomḟoċraiḃ an iuḃair, ⁊ tangatar bardai ina ccoinne ón iuḃar ar maidin ar ná ṁaraċ, ⁊ rob serbaḋaċ uirbernaċ ro ḃattar acc dol gus an mbaile sin, ⁊ ní ro ṡaoilset ag fágḃail aṫa cliaṫ go ffuigbedís a hionnaṁail sin diomarġoil in ulltoiḃ. A mí mai do ṡonraḋ do feraḋ an trescomarc sin.

Captin Felli duine uasal do ṁuintir na bainriogna agá mboí urlaṁus ⁊ iomċoiṁéd a ḟearann ón ngobernoir do marḃaḋ i ccaislén in airċín i ffiull la a muintir féin.

O domnaill do ṫionol a ṡlóiġ i mí december do ḋol i ccóicceaḋ connaċt. As í conair do luiḋ do ṡlicceaċ go tráiġ neóṫuile, co tír ḟiaċrach, ⁊ tars

[y] *Sir John.*—In Ware's Annals of Ireland, and in Moryson's History of Ireland, he is called Sir Owen Mac Toole, which is tolerable; but Cox calls him Sir Owen O'Toole, which is totally incorrect, though copied by all modern compilers. He was detained in prison for some years by the bribe-accepting Sir William Fitz-William, Lord Deputy of Ireland.

[z] *A message*, literally, "news or tidings."

[a] *For Newry.*—P. O'Sullevan Beare gives a brief account of an engagement which took place about this period (but he does not give the exact date), at the church of Kilclooney, eight miles from Newry, where six hundred of the English party, and two hundred of the Irish, were slain.

O'Gallagher (Sir John', the son of Tuathal), a man of great name and renown among the English and Irish of this time, died on the 25th of April.

The monastery of Monaghan in Oriel was this year in the possession of the English, and a company of soldiers constantly guarding it. A message[a] from them reached Dublin that they were in want of provisions. When the Lord Justice, Sir William Russell, and Sir John Norris, heard this, they ordered that twenty-six bands of English and Irish soldiers, together with many gentlemen, should be sent with provisions and all other necessaries to Monaghan. And these marched onward to the town without being noticed or opposed; and, having remained that night in Monaghan, they prepared the next morning to set out for Newry[a]. When, however, they had gone a short distance from Monaghan eastward, they were met by O'Neill's people; and ungentle and unfriendly was the salute they received there, for they [O'Neill's people] proceeded to shoot, strike, kill, and destroy them, [and the engagement lasted] from the fourth hour before noon until the dusk of the evening; so that it would not be easy to reckon or enumerate all those of the people of the Lord Justice, both gentle and plebeian, who were lost, or the number of steeds, of coats of mail, of arms, of various weapons, of wares, of rich raiment, of horses, and hampers of provisions, that were left on every road over which they passed on that day. They [i. e. the survivors] pitched a camp near Newry, and companies [of soldiers] came for them the next morning; and deficient and broken[b] were they in going to that town. Little had they thought, when leaving Dublin, that they should receive such an attack in Ulster. This conflict took place in the month of May.

Captain Felli, a gentleman of the Queen's people, who had the superintendence and care of the lands of the Governor [of Connaught], was treacherously slain in the castle of Aircin[c] by his own people.

In the month of December O'Donnell mustered an army to march into Connaught. The route he took was to Sligo, Traigh-Eothuile, Tireragh, and across

[b] *Deficient and broken were they*, ꞃob ꞅꞃbaḋaċ uıꞃbꞅꞃnaċ ꞃo baꞇꞇaꞃ. This should be, "deficient and broken were the companies."

[c] *Aircin.*—This castle stood at the village of Killeany, on the Great Island of Aran, in the bay of Galway. In 1585, on the composition then effected, all the patents of West Connaught were granted to be held as of "the Queen's manor, or Castle of Arkyne." In Cromwell's time it was pulled down, and a large fort erected on its site.—See *Chorographical Description of Iar-Connaught*, p. 78.

an muaiḋ co tír naṁalgaḋa. Batar clann uilliam búrc i ffriṫḃeart fri a roile im tiġearnas an tíre, uair an dar lá gach fír díḃ bá dó báḋéin ro baḋ dír. Tangattar roṁ uile fo toġairm uí doṁnaill iar ttoiḋeċt dó don tír ro ḃaoí ríoṁ agá sccrúdaḋ fri a coṁairlſchaiḃ cia dioḃraiḋe dia ngoirfeaḋ ticcſrna. Conaḋ fair do ċinnsiot fa ḋeóiḋ tiġearna do ġairm do ṫepóitt a búrc mac uateir ċiotaiġ, mic Sſain mic oiluerais, ar ḋáiġ as é do ḋeachaiḋ ċuicce sium cetus iar ná ionnarbaḋ do ġallaiḃ as a ḋuthaiġ, ⁊ ro ṫinġeall roṁ dó co ndiongnaḋ a ċobair dia ccaoṁsaḋ, ⁊ ro ḃaoí ḃeós i ttuile a aoise fri foiṁdin imniġ ⁊ ettualaing an ċoccaiḋ i mbaoí sium. Ro gaireaḋ iaraṁ a gairm flaṫa de i ffiaḋnaisi na slóġ a ccoitċinne gé ro ḃattar araill dia ċenel ro ba sine, ⁊ ba moa ar aoí ngarma inás. Do raḋaḋ geill ⁊ aittire ó na búrcaċaiḃ oile baoí i frithḃeart friss for laiṁ ṫepóitt iar na oirdneaḋ. Ro airis ó doṁnaill hi rann mec uilliam fó nodlaicc mór na bliaḋna so i mbarúntaċt ċille mſḋóin, ⁊ is na briġiḃ hi ccloinn muiris.

Bai ard iustis na hereann .i. Sir uilliam Russel i ngaillim in ionbaiḋ sin. Ro luaiḋſḋ sioṫċáin go cſnd dá ṁíos gan urraḋa gan árach etir ua ndoṁnaill ⁊ connaċtaiġ do lſiṫ, ⁊ an iustís don lſiṫ ele acc fáccḃáil na gaillṁe ḋó. Ni ḃaoí aon ċonntae hi cconnaċtaiḃ cenmotá conntae an ċláir namá ná bátar uile no dronga dirime as gach conntae díḃ daon rann ⁊ daon lſiṫ lá hua ndoṁnaill don ċur sin ó droḃaoís co conmaicne mara, ⁊ ó muaiḋ co sionainn. Battar ann dna síol cceallaiġ cenmotá conċoḃar mac donnchaiḋ riaḃaiġ, mic taiḋcc duiḃ uí ċeallaiġ uair ro gaḃaḋ lais siḋe an calaḋ ar ḟſrdorċa mac ceallaiġ mic doṁnaill, mic aeḋa na ccailleaċ uí ċeallaiġ. Do ċóiḋ tra feardorċa gus an líon baí hi ccſnd uí doṁnaill, ⁊ ro gair ó doṁnaill tiġearna de. Ro eirġſttar síol madagain isin ccoccaḋ ccéḋna aċt ó madagáin aṁáin .i. doṁnall mac seaain, ⁊ a ṁac Anmċaḋ. Lottar clann Remainn

[d] *He.*—In the original the verb is in the third person plural, which destroys the unity of the sentence.

[e] *Walter Kittagh*, i. e. Walter the left-handed.

[f] *Cill Meadhoin*, i. e. the middle church, now the barony of Kilmaine, in the south of the county of Mayo.

[g] *Brees*, a castle in the parish of Mayo, in the barony of Clanmaurice.—See *Genealogies, Tribes, and Customs of Hy-Fiachrach*, p. 482.

[h] *Conmaicne-mara*, now Connamara.

[i] *The Callow*, a castle in the barony of Kilconnell, and county of Galway.

[k] *Hugh na gCailleach*, i. e. Hugh of the nuns, or hags.

[l] *Except the O'Madden.*—It would appear from the Journal of Sir William Russell, Lord Deputy of Ireland, preserved in the British Museum,

the Moy into Tirawley. The Clann-William Burke were at variance with each other concerning the lordship of the territory, each man of them [i. e. of the candidates] thinking that he himself was entitled to it. They all came at the summons of O'Donnell, on his arrival in the country; and he consulted with his advisers as to which of them he would nominate lord; he[d] finally decided upon nominating as lord Theobald Burke, son of Walter Kittagh[e], son of John, son of Oliver, because he had been the first to come over to him after his expulsion from his country by the English; and he [O'Donnell] had promised to assist him, if in his power. Moreover, this Walter was in the bloom of youth, and able to endure the hardships and toils of the war in which they were engaged. His title of chief was conferred on him in the presence of the forces in general, although there were others of his tribe older and greater in point of dignity than he. Hostages and pledges were delivered into the hands of Theobald by the other Burkes who were in opposition, after his election. O'Donnell remained with Mac William in the barony of Cill Meadhoin[f], and at Brees[g] in Clanmaurice, during the Christmas of this year.

At this time Sir William Russell, the Chief Justiciary of Ireland, was at Galway; and, on his leaving Galway, a peace of two months was proclaimed, but without pledges or hostages, between O'Donnell and the Connacians, on the one side, and the Lord Justice, on the other. There was not at this time any county in Connaught, excepting the county of Clare only, in which the inhabitants, or great numbers of them, had not joined and united with O'Donnell, from the Drowes to Conmaicne-mara[h], and from the Moy to the Shannon. Among them were the O'Kellys, excepting Conor, the son of Donough Reagh, son of Teige Duv O'Kelly; for he had (forcibly) taken the Callow[i] from Ferdorcha, the son of Kellagh, son of Donnell, son of Hugh na gCailleach[k] O'Kelly; upon which Ferdorcha, with all his number [followers], went over to O'Donnell, who appointed him lord [of Hy-Many]. The O'Maddens rose up in the same war, except the O'Madden[l] alone, namely, Donnell, the son of John, and his son,

manuscript add. 4728, fol. 61, *b*, that the Lord Deputy believed that O'Madden himself had joined this rebellion, for his secretary writes:

"O'Madden himself being gone out in action of Rebellion, and had left a ward of his principle men in his castle" [of Cloghan], whoe assoone as they perceaved my Lord to approach neare, they sett three of their houses on fire, which were adjoyninge to the Castle, and made shott at vs out of the Castle, which hurt two of our souldiers and a boye. And being sent to by my Lord to yeild vpp the Castle to the Queene,

na scuar mic uillicc a búrc, ⁊ an lucht adrubramar go ro gabhadh ⁊ co ro brisfedh, mísliuc uí madaccáin, Tír atháin, ⁊ urmhór bailtedh na tíre leó cenmotá an longport. Ro lomadh ⁊ ro léirscriosadh cluain fearta brénainn ⁊ ro gabhadh espucc an baile leó. Baí annsidhe eoghan dubh mac maoileachlainn bailbh uí madagain ó thuaith lusmaighi hi ccuma cáich. Do cuas leó iaramh tar sionainn i ndealbhna i ffearaibh ceall, ⁊ acc sóadh dóibh tar a nais co brú sionna do tairrngeadh dá banna saighdiúiridhe baí ar órda isin midhe ina niarmhoireacht, ⁊ ní riacht rabhadh nó rathuccadh remhpa go riachtadar gan fios gan airiuccadh co ro iadhsat imon mbaile i mbáttar na foghladha co ro marbhadh dronga díbhsidhe im anmchaidh mac maoileaclainn modardha mic maoileachlainn mic breasail, ⁊ im cobhthach óg mac cobhthaigh uí madagain. Térnatar clann Remainn a búrc ón mbrisiomh sin co nurmhór a muintire amaille friú.

Ro briseadh lá hua ndomhnaill don chuairt sin trí caisléin décc do chaislénaibh connacht. Iar ttocht dua domhnaill tar muaidh co tír fiachrach ro ghairrsidhe ua dubhda do thadhcc mac taidhcc riabhaigh mic eoghain, ⁊ ó hEghra riabhach il-luighne. * * * ⁊ Mac donnchaidh tíre hoilella do Mhuirgheas caoch mac taidhcc an triubhais, ⁊ mac donnchaidh an chorainn do Rudhraighe mac aedha, ⁊ mac diarmada maighe luircc do chonchobhar mac taidhcc mic diarmada. Do bert lais iaramh braighde gach tíre gur a rainicc i ngioll lé comhall, ⁊ soais tar a ais go ráinic tar éirne iar ccriochnuccadh a thurais.

Braighde connacht uile (durmhór) batar illáimh i ngaillimh on ngobernoir Sir Risderd biongam. Feacht ann dia mbáttar mesgtha mesaighthe iar nól

their answere was to Capten Thomas Lea, that if all that came in his Lordship's companie were Deputies, they would not yeild, but said they would trust to the strenght of their castle, and hoped by to-morrowe that time that the Deputy and his companie should stand in as great feare as they then were in; expecting, as it should seeme, some aid to relieve them."—See this famous reply of O'Madden's people referred to in Brewer's *Beauties of Ireland*, vol. ii. p. 152; and *Tribes and Customs of Hy-Many*, pp. 149, 189; where the whole account of the siege is printed from Sir William Russell's Journal.

[m] *Meelick-I-Madden*, now Meelick, on the brink of the Shannon, in the barony of Longford, and county of Galway.—See it already mentioned at the years 1479 and 1557.

[n] *Tir-athain*, now *anglice* Tiran, a district in the parish of Killimor-Bulloge, in the barony of Longford. The district so called is now divided into several townlands.

[o] *Longphort*, now Longford, a castle of considerable strength lying in ruins in the parish of Tirinescragh, in the barony of Longford, to which it has given name. This was O'Madden's chief castle.—See *Tribes and Customs of Hy-Many*, p. 151.

[p] *The bishop.*—The bishop of Clonfert at this period was Stephen Kerovan, a native of the town of Galway. He succeeded in 1582, and

Anmchadh. The sons of Redmond na-Scuab, son of Ulick Burke, and those we have mentioned, went and took and destroyed Meelick-I-Madden[m], Tir-athain[n], and all the castles of the country, except Longphort[o]. They plundered and totally devastated Clonfert-Brendan, and took the bishop[p] of that town prisoner. Among the rest, on this occasion, was Owen Duv, the son of Melaghlin Balbh O'Madden, from the district of Lusmagh[q]. They afterwards proceeded across the Shannon, into Delvin and Fircall; and, upon their return to the banks of the Shannon, two companies of soldiers, who had been billeted in Meath, were drawn in pursuit of them[r]. These soldiers advanced unnoticed, until they had surrounded the castle [of Cloghan], in which the plunderers were, when they slew many of them, and, among the rest, Anmchadh[s], son of Melaghlin Moder, son of Melaghlin, son of Breasal [O'Madden]; and Coffagh[t] Oge, the son of Coffagh O'Madden. The sons of Redmond Burke, with the greater part of their people along with them, escaped from conflict.

On this occasion thirteen of the castles of Connaught were broken down by O'Donnell. After crossing the Moy into Tireragh, he conferred the title of O'Dowda upon Teige, the son of Teige Reagh, son of Owen, the O'Dowda; in Leyny he nominated * * * the O'Hara Reagh; and he appointed Maurice Caech, the son of Teige-an-Triubhais[u], the Mac Donough of Tirerrill; Rory, the son of Hugh, the Mac Donough of Corran; and Conor, the son of Teige, the Mac Dermot of Moylurg. He took away hostages from every territory into which he had come, as a security for their fealty; and he [then] returned home across the Erne, having terminated his expedition.

The hostages of the greater part of the province of Connaught, who had been imprisoned in Galway by the Governor, Sir Richard Bingham, being in-

died in 1602.—See Harris's edition of Ware's Bishops, p. 642.

[q] *Lusmagh*, now Lusma, a parish in the south of the King's County, adjoining the county of Tipperary, and bounded on the west by the River Shannon. This was a part of O'Madden's country of Sil-Anamchy, and still belongs to the diocese of Clonfert.

[r] *Drawn in pursuit of them.*—These were induced to come into Fircall by some of Teige O'Molloy's people who were aiding the English.

[s] *Anmchadh.*—In Sir William Russell's Journal he is called "Ambrose Mac Molaghline Mottere O'Madden, of Clare-Madden, Gentleman."

[t] *Coffagh.*—In Sir William Russell's Journal he is called "Coheghe O'Madden of Clare-Madden." For a list of the chief men who were slain or taken on this occasion, see *Tribes and Customs of Hy-Many*, pp. 150, 151.

[u] *Teige-an-Triubhais*, i. e. Thaddæus or Timothy of the Trowse, or pantaloons.

ḟiona isin ccéd mí dḟoġmar na bliadna so co ro iompáidsiot etorra féin élúdh as in bpriosún i rabatar, ⁊ imṫeacht dáis nó déiccean. Iar ccinnead na coṁairle sin dóiḃ do ċuirsiot a nglais ⁊ a ngeimle díoḃ, ⁊ bátar doirrsi an ḃaile esslaicṫe an tan sin, ⁊ bá hionam proinnigṫe do ċách i ccoitċinne uair bá hurṫorach oidċe ann do ċóidsiot tarr an dorus siar don ḃaile. Ro gaḃad an droichet forra gur ḃó héiccin dóiḃ an aḃann aggarḃ dionnsaiccid fo a nurċoṁair, ⁊ bá anaoinḟeacht battar saide ag fágḃáil na haḃann ⁊ aos óccbaid an ḃaile iar ndol tar droichet an ḃaile ina ccoṁairrcis. Ro marḃad cuid do laṫair, ⁊ ro hiompaídsed an ċuid ele díoḃ gus an bpriosún ós imṫigsedar. Iar ndol do na scélaiḃ sin gus an ngobernóir, Ro ċuir side sgriḃenn go gaillimh dia forċongra gach aon ro aontaiġ elúdh don ċur sin a ċrochad gan ḟuireach. Ro crochad ar furailem an gobernora Mac mec uilliam búrc .i. Emann mac Risderd an iarainn, Mac uí concoḃair ruaidh * * * mic taidcc óicc mic taidcc ḃuiḋe, mic caṫail ruaidh Mac ṁec dauid hoberd mac hoiberd buiḋe, mic uilliam, mic tomais Murchad ócc mac murchaid na ttuaġ mic taidcc uí ḟlaiṫbeartaiġ Domnall mac Ruaidri mic taidcc uí ḟlaiṫbeartaiġ, ⁊ maoílir mac tEpoit, mic uáteir ḟada.

AOIS CRIOST, 1596.

Aois criost, mile, cúicc céd, nocat, a sé.

Mag carṫaiġ mór décc .i. Domnall, mac domnaill, mic corbmaic ladraiġ mic taidcc, ⁊ gér ḃó Mág carṫaiġ mór do gairṫi de ro hoirdneadh co honórach ina iarla riar an tan sin hé ar forċongra prionnsa saxan. Ní baoí oidre

[w] *Created Earl.*—He was created Earl of Clancare [Clann Cárṫaiġ], and Baron of Valencia, on the 4th of June, 1565.—See Cox's *Hibernia Anglicana*, vol. i. p. 320. Hooker says that when John or Shane O'Neill [Prince of Ulster, as he styled himself] heard that Mac Carthy More had surrendered himself and his possessions to the Queen of England, that he had been graciously received, his lands restored to him, to be held of English tenure, and that he himself was created a lord of Parliament by the name of the Earl of Clancare, he said to some English commissioners sent to treat with him: "I keep a lacquay as noble as he. But let him enjoy his honour; it is not worthy of O'Neale. I have indeed made peace with the Queen at her desire; but I have not forgotten the royal dignity of my ancestors. Ulster was theirs, and shall be mine. With the sword they won it; with the sword I will maintain it."

It should be remarked, however, that Hooker is not to be depended upon in his report of what Shane O'Neill said on this occasion; for it appears from Shane's evidence in England

toxicated and excited after drinking wine, plotted together in the month of August in this year to make their escape from the prison in which they were, by stratagem or force. This resolution being adopted by them, they knocked off their chains and fetters. This was in the early part of the night, while the gates of the town were still open; and it was the time at which all in general were dining, for it was the beginning of the night, when they passed out through the gate of the town westward. The bridge was gained upon them, so that they were obliged to face the rough river which lay before them; but, at the same time that they were leaving the river, the soldiers of the town, who had crossed the bridge, were ready to meet them. Some of them were slain on the spot, and others were turned back to the prison from which they had fled. When the news of this reached the Governor, he sent a writ to Galway, ordering that all those who had consented to escape on this occasion should be hanged without delay; and there were hanged by order of the Governor, namely, the son of Mac William Burke (Edmond, the son of Richard-an-Iarainn); the son of O'Conor Roe, i. e. * * *; the son of Teige Oge, son of Teige Boy, son of Cathal Roe; the son of Mac David (Hubert, the son of Hubert Boy, son of William, son of Thomas); Murrough Oge, the son of Murrough of the Battle-axes, son of Teige O'Flaherty; Donnell, the son of Rory, son of Teige O'Flaherty; and Myler, the son of Theobald, son of Walter Fada [Burke].

THE AGE OF CHRIST, 1596.

The Age of Christ, one thousand five hundred ninety-six.

Mac Carthy More died, namely, Donnell, the son of Donnell, son of Cormac Ladhrach, son of Teige; and although he was usually styled Mac Carthy More, he had been honourably created Earl[w] by order of the Sovereign of England.

that he was a man of astute mind; and it is quite certain that he would not, when in boasting mood, have condescended to compare himself to the Earl of Clancare, who had but a few years previously emerged from slavery, for it was not till the year 1565, that he was emancipated from the yoke of the Earls of Desmond, whose vassals his ancestors had been for many centuries, to whom they had rendered the most servile tributes in Earl's beeves, and in "the damn'd exaction of coyn and liverie." There is a very curious list of the rents and services rendered to the Earls (of Desmond) by the Mac Carthys and others, preserved in the Carew Collection of Manuscripts at Lambeth Palace, No. 617, p. 212. That this Earl of Clancare possessed but little of

ferḋa dia éis nó hoirrnfiḋe ina ionaḋ cenmoṫa aen ingen do rala na mnaoí ag mac meg carṫaiġ riaḃaiġ .i. acc fingin, ⁊ ro ba dóiġ lá cáċ gur ḃó hesiḋe ro baḋ oiḋre ar an még carṫaiġ sin atbaṫ .i. domnall.

Mac suiḃne na ttuaṫ eoġan ócc mac eoccáin óicc mic eoccáin mic domnaill fir toṫaċtaċ toirbertaċ, na ro ṫuill táinsium, nó tarcaisne or o gaḃ

the heroism of his ancestor is quite evident from all that we know of his history; and one can hardly avoid concluding that he was a craven coward, from his submission to Sir Henry Sidney, beginning, "The most humble submission of the unworthy and most unnatural Earl of Clancahir, otherwise called Mac Carthy More, unto the Right Honourable Sir Henry Sidney, Knight," preserved on Patent Roll, 13 Elizabeth, and printed by Mr. Hardiman in his Ancient Irish Deeds (*Transactions R. I. A.*, vol. xv. Antiquities, pp. 73, 74). But it should be borne in mind that since the death of the Red Earl of Ulster, in 1333, O'Neill's ancestors were not only free from all Anglo-Irish exactions, but that they compelled the English of the Pale to pay them "black rent." The comparison between O'Neill and Mac Carthy is, therefore, a mere stupid joke of Hooker. It is, however, repeated by Leland, who has given many Anglo-Irish fables as true history.

[x] *Who could be installed.*—Donnell, Earl of Clancare, had one natural son, Donnell, who usurped the name and title of Mac Carthy More; but Fineen, or Florence, the youngest son of Donough Mac Carthy Reagh, who was married to Ellen, the only daughter of the Earl of Clann-Cartha, claimed the name and title of Mac Carthy More, and by the influence of the Earl of Tyrone he was established in that dignity. The writer of *Carbriæ Notitia*, already often referred to, after giving the pedigree of Mac Carthy More, has the following remarks upon the disputes between the different families of the Mac Carthys, about their respective rights to the headship in 1686, when this writer flourished:

"By this pedigree it appears that Mac Carthy Reagh, in the person of O Donnell Gud, became a separate branch of this noble family in the time of Donnell More in Curragh, who probably gave them Carbry for their portion and inheritance; and that Mac Donough did the like some time after and received their Estate in Duhallow, from their father, Cormock Fune; and that the Lords of Muskry more lately, in the person of Dermond More Muskry, became a distinct branch of this family, and were seated in Muskry by their father, Cormock mac Donell Oge.

"It is likewise manifest that Donell, Earle of Clancar, dying without issue male, his daughter and heir was married to Florence Mac Donough Mac Carthy Reagh, whose pedigree shall follow more at large. By virtue of which marriage Florence claimed the name and title of Mac Carthy more, which Donell, naturall son of the deceased Earle of Clancar, had usurp'd; and by the help of Tyrone, who was then come into Munster, he was establisht in that name and dignity, and his grandson and heir, Charles, is at this day ownd and stild Mac Carthymore. Nevertheless the followers of these great men doe often dispute which branch of this family is the principall, or chief of the Clancarthyes. Mac Carthymore alleages that he, having the title and name, and being likewise, by his grandmother, heir to the last Earle of Clancar, ought to be acknowledged chief without dispute.

"To this the others Answere, that by the father's side (which is chiefly regarded in Ireland), he is younger son of Mac Carty Reagh, and ought not to exalt himselfe above the Chief of his house. That an Irish title and name must

There was no male heir who could be installed[x] in his place, [or any heir], except one daughter [Ellen], who was the wife of the son of Mac Carthy Reagh, i. e. Fineen; and all thought that he was the heir of the deceased Mac Carthy, i. e. Donnell.

Mac Sweeny-na-dTuath (Owen Oge, the son of Owen Oge, son of Owen, son of Donnell), an influential and generous man, who had never incurred

be governe'd by the Irish Law of Tanistry, which, like the royal Law Salique in France, will not admit women to inherit estates and principalities,—suitable to the Law of Entailes in England, which excludes this very Mac Cartymore from being Earle of Clancar, tho' he be his heire at Common Lawe; neither had Tyrone any legall power in Munster to conferr the title of Mac Cartymore on any body that had not just right to it.

"Mac Carty Reagh alleages that he is the eldest branch of this noble family, which, by the Law of Tanistry, ought to be preferred; that he is a degree nearer of kin to the common ancestor, Donell More in Curragh, King of Cork" [*recte*, Desmond] "than any of the pretenders; that Carbry is an antienter principality than either Muskry or Duhallow; and that Mac Cartymore is a younger brother of his house.

"But the lords of Muskry say that because Mac Carty Reagh is the Eldest branch of this family, that is, the first that separated from the common stock, he is therefore excluded from the inheritance till all the later branches are lopt of by death; for the Tanistry respects the age and meritt, yet designs only impotent age; and, therefore, a man's vncle thatt be Tanist, but not his great grand vncle if alive; and soe by the Law of England, a brother shall be preferred before an unckle, and an unckle before a great unckle; soe that by both Laws the nearest of kin to him that was last seizd shall be his heir, and the Lords of Muskry are the undoubted heirs male to Cormock Mac Daniell Oge, Prince of Desmond, and to all his ancestors, even to Donell More in Curragh, from whom Mac Carty Reagh descends; and they deny any difference in their degrees of kindred to the said Donell More; and if there were it matters not, since a man's grandson and heir ought to be preferred before his second son. As for the antiquity of Carbry, it prooves nothing in this dispute; and as for the relation between Mac Cartymore and Mac Carty Reagh, whatsoever it may argue amongst themselves, tis nothing to a third person; and, therefore, they conclude the Crown of England has done them justice in giving, or rather restoring, to them the stile and title of Earle of Clancarthy.

"But, be this as it will, my province leads me to the particular pedigree of Mac Carty Reagh, who were lords of this great territory of Carbry, and had the greatest chief rents out of it that was paid out of any seigniory in Ireland, insoe much that the Mac Cartyes have been stiled Princes of Carbry, as well in many antient historys and records, as in his severall letters Pattents from the Kings of England. I begin with Donnell Gud, because I have already shewn his pedigree upward to Calahane of Cashell, King of Munster." He then gives Mac Carthy Reagh's pedigree down to his own time, 1686.

There is a very curious tract, on the subject of this dispute between the Mac Carthys, preserved in the Carew Collection of Manuscripts at Lambeth, No. 601, p. 241, entitled: "Florence Mac Cartie's Reasons to prove that the

ceandus a ċríċe co ló a eitsioċta ḟir caiṫmeaċ congaireaċ deaslaicṫeaċ daonnaċtaċ comnart fri coṫuccaḋ agus fri hionnsaiġiḋ co mbuaiḋ ccéille ⁊ ccomairle fri síḋ, ⁊ fri ṡococcaḋ do ecc 26. Ianuarii, ⁊ mac a ḋerbḃraṫar .i. Maolmuire mac murchaiḋ ṁaill do ġaḃail a ionaiḋ.

O Raiġilliġ .i. Seaan ruaḋ mac aoḋa conallaiġ mic maoilmorḋa mic Seaain do écc, ⁊ gé do hordaiġeḋ maille lé composision a hucht na bainríoġan aṫhaiḋ siar an tan sin ticcfedar a ḋuiṫċe féin do beiṫ ag gaċ aon do ṡlioċt ṁaoilṁórḋa uí Raiġilliġ ro gair ua néill aoḋ mac firdorċa o raiġilliġ do ṗilip mac aoḋa conallaiġ for an mbreifne uile, ⁊ níor ḃó cianṡaoġlaċ soṁ iar ngairm tiġearna de uair ro marḃaḋ ria ccionn leiṫ raiṫe go tecmaiseaċ la muintir uí neill (lás ro hoirdneaḋ eisium) ⁊ ro gaireaḋ ó raiġilliġ demann mac ṁaoilṁórḋa sinnsear an dá tiġearna reṁráite.

Mac iarla deasmuṁan décc .i. tomas mac Séamais, mic Seaain mic tomáis droiċit aṫa.

Tepoit mac Piarais mic emainn buitelér tiġearna caṫrać dúin iarscaiġ, ⁊ treana cluana meala do écc. Fear deaslaicteach duasṁór ro ba mó duanaire dfionngallaiḃ ereann durṁór eiriḋe ⁊ a ṁac tomas do ġaḃáil a ionaiḋ.

Mag eoċaccáin .i. niall mac Rossa mic connla décc.

Remann mac gearailt tiġearna tuaiṫe broṫaill do ḃásuccaḋ i ccorcaiġ tré ċiontaiḃ a ḋibeircce in aghaiḋ gall.

An tan tra ro ḟioir an iustis, ⁊ comairle na hEreann calmacht ⁊ comnart na ngaoiḋeal ina naghaiḋ, ⁊ gaċ aén do raḋsatt go somamaiġṫe dóiḃ badéin siar an tan sin ag dol daoín leiṫ fris na gaoiḋelaiḃ reṁraite ina naghaiḋ, bá sí comairle arriċt leó teċta do ċor do ṡaiġiḋ uí néill, ⁊ uí domnaill do cuingiḋ ṡioḋa ⁊ ċaoncomraic forra. Bá siad ro toġaḋ fri hiom-

Earl of Clancare's land ought to descend to Ellen, his [Florence's] wife."

[y] *John Roe.*—This was Sir John O'Reilly.—See note [b], under the year 1583, p. 1804, *supra.*

[z] *Descendants of Maelmora.*—See note [d], under the year 1583, p. 1809, *supra.*

[a] *Edmond, the son of Maelmora.*—See note [c], under the year 1583, p. 1806.

[b] *Thomas of Drogheda,* i. e. who was executed at Drogheda.—See note [w], under the year 1468, p. 1050, *supra.*

[c] *Cathair-Duna-Iascaigh,* now Cahir, a well-known town in the county of Tipperary.—See note [p], under the year 1559, p. 1570, *supra.*

[d] *Trian-Chluana-meala,* i. e. Clonmel-third. This was the name of the barony of Iffa and Offa East, in the south-east of the county of Tipperary.—See note [o], under the year 1559, p. 1570, *supra.*

[e] *Tuath-Brothaill,* i. e. the district of Broghill. This is still the name of a manor, with a castle, near Charleville, in the north of the county of

reproach or censure from the time that he assumed the chieftainship of his territory to the day of his death; a sumptuous, warlike, humane, and bounteous man; puissant to sustain, and brave to make the attack; with the gift of good sense and counsel in peace and war; died on the 26th of January; and his brother's son, Mulmurry, the son of Murrough Mall, took his place.

O'Reilly, i. e. John Roe[y], the son of Hugh Conallagh, son of Maelmora, son of John, died. And though, by a composition made some time anterior to this period, by the Queen's authority, it was ordained that each of the descendants of Maelmora[z] O'Reilly should [exclusively] possess the lordship of his own territory, yet O'Neill (Hugh, the son of Ferdorcha) nominated Philip, son of Hugh, the O'Reilly over all Breifny; but he did not live long after being styled Lord, for he was accidentally slain by O'Neill's people (by whom he had been inaugurated); and [then] Edmond, the son of Maelmora[a], who was senior to the other two lords, was styled the O'Reilly.

The son of the Earl of Desmond died, namely, Thomas, the son of James, son of John, son of Thomas of Drogheda[b].

Theobald, the son of Pierce, son of Edmond Butler, Lord of Cathair-Duna-Iascaigh[c] and Trian-Chluana-meala[d], died. He was a liberal and bounteous man, and had the largest collection of poetical compositions of almost all the old English of Ireland; and his son, Thomas, took his place.

Mageoghegan, i. e. Niall, the son of Rossa, son of Conla, died.

Redmond Fitzgerald, Lord of Tuath-Brothaill[e], was executed at Cork, for his crimes of insurrection against the English.

When the Lord Justice and the Council of Ireland saw the bravery and power of the Irish against them, and that all those who had previously been obedient to themselves were now joining the aforesaid Irish against them, they came to the resolution of sending ambassadors to O'Neill and O'Donnell, to request[f] peace and tranquillity from them. The persons selected for negociating

Cork.—See Smith's *Natural and Civil History of Cork*, book ii. c. 6. Roger Boyle, the third son of Richard, Earl of Cork, took the title of Baron from this place.—3 Car. I.

[f] *To request.*—Leland says, book iv. c. 4, that "the Queen, now principally attentive to the affairs of France, and the progress of the Spanish arms in this country, was well pleased at any prospect of composing the vexatious broils of Ireland." And he adds that O'Neill, "having discovered the real weakness of his enemy, determined to recommence hostilities without the slightest regard to promises or treaties, which he considered as mere temporary expedients."

luaḋ naiṫirecc ſtorra .i. tomas buitiléir iarla urmuman, ⁊ airdeaspocc caisil maolmuire magraiṫ. Rainicc iarla urmuman go traiġ ḃaile, ⁊ airisis annsin, ⁊ ro ḟaiḋ a ṫeaċta go hua neill dia aisnéis dó na tosca imá ttáinicc. Faoiḋiḋ ua neill na sccéla céḋna dionnsaiġiḋ uí domnaill. Do ċóiḋ ua domnaill díṙim marcṡlóiġ go hairm i mbaoí ua neill, tiaġait díblínib co foċairḋ muirṫemne. Tánaic an tiarla, ⁊ an tairdespocc dia saiġiḋ. At fétsat do na flaiṫiḃ in toisc ima ttangattar .i. gur ab do ċuinġiḋ síoḋa do ḋeaċattar, ⁊ at fétsat na comaḋa ro ṫinġeall an iustis .i. dilsiucchaḋ cóicciḋ conċobair dóiḃ ríoṁ génmota an mbloiḋ tíre fil ó dún dealgan co bóinn in ro aittreaḃsat goill ó ċéin máir siar an tan sin, ⁊ ro ġeallsat fris sin ná tiostais goill forra tar tórainn cenmotát na goill báttar hi ccarraicc fergusa hi ccáirlinn, ⁊ i niuḃar cinntraġa do léicceḋ fri creic ⁊ conraḋh do ṡíor, ⁊ ná léiccfiḋe maoír nó luċt toḃaiġ cíosa nó cana dia saicciḋ act an cíos do ratta for a sinnsearaiḃ (reaċt riaṁ) do ioḋnacal dóiḃ-riuṁ co hát cliaṫ, ⁊ ná cuinġiḋfe geill nó eittire orra act maḋ sin, ⁊ do bérṫa an ccéḋna do na gaoiḋelaiḃ attract hi ccommbáiḋ uí domnaill hi ccóicceaḋ connaċt. Do ċóiḋ tra ó neill, ⁊ ó domnaill, ⁊ i mbatar ina ffarraḋ do maiṫiḃ an ċóicciḋ do sccrúdaḋ a ccomairle im na haiṫeascaiḃ sin do breaṫa cuca, ⁊ iar mbeiṫ athaiḋ foda dóiḃ-riḃe ⁊ do na maiṫiḃ arċeana acc foraiṫmeat an ro togaeṫa lá gallaiḃ ó do riaċtatar érinn lá bréccṫingealltoiḃ ná ro comailleaḋ dóiḃ idir, ⁊ an líon do ḋeaċatar doiḋeḃaiḃ anairce dia naireaċaiḃ dia nuaislib, ⁊ do ṡaorċlandaiḃ soiċenélċoiḃ cén náċ tuccait itir, act do gaitt a naṫarḋa foraiḃ, Ro imeccláiġsiot co mór co ná comaillfe friú an ro tinġeallaḋ

[g] *Mulmurry Magrath.*—He wrote his own name "Milerus Magrath." He was of the Magraths of Termon-Magrath, on the borders of the counties of Donegal and Fermanagh. He was a Franciscan friar, and had been appointed Bishop of Down by Pope Pius V.; but afterwards, embracing the Protestant religion, he was, in 1570, promoted to the bishopric of Clogher, and soon afterwards elevated to the archbishopric of Cashel, which he governed for forty-two years.—See Harris's edition of Ware's Bishops, pp. 206, 483.

[h] *Faughard-Muirtheimne*, now Faughard, near Dundalk, in the county of Louth.—See note [e], under the year 1595, p. 1967, *supra*.

[i] *To request a peace.*—"A mean solicitation on the part of government to Tyrone."—*Leland.*

[k] *The province of Conchobhar*, i. e. of Ulster, which in Conchobhar Mac Nessa's time extended to the Boyne.

[l] *Stewards*, i. e. sheriffs.

[m] *They feared.*—This fear on the part of the Irish arose from the practises of the Marshal Bagnal, who was doing all in his power to ruin O'Neill and the Irish chieftains of Ulster. When O'Neill saw that it was impossible to remove

between them were Thomas Butler, Earl of Ormond, and Mulmurry Magrath[g], Archbishop of Cashel. The Earl of Ormond repaired to Traigh-Bhaile [Dundalk], and there halted; and he sent his messengers to O'Neill, to inform him of the purport of his coming; upon which O'Neill sent the same intelligence to O'Donnell; and O'Donnell came to the place where O'Neill was, with a body of cavalry, [and] both set out for Faughard-Muirtheimne[h]. Here the Earl and the Archbishop came to meet them. They stated to the chiefs the object of their embassy, namely, to request a peace[i]; and they stated the rewards promised by the Lord Justice, namely, the appropriation to them of the province of Conchobhar[k], except the tract of country extending from Dundalk to the River Boyne, in which the English had dwelt long before that time. They promised, moreover, that the English should not encroach upon them beyond the boundary, excepting those who were in Carrickfergus, Carlingford, and Newry, who were at all times permitted to deal and traffic; that no stewards[l] or collectors of rents or tributes should be sent among them, but that the rents which had been some time before upon their ancestors should be forwarded by them to Dublin; that beyond this no hostages or pledges would be required; and that the Irish in the province of Connaught, who had risen up in alliance with O'Donnell, should have privileges similar to these. O'Neill, O'Donnell, and all the chiefs of the province who were then along with them, went into council upon those conditions which were brought to them; and, having reflected for a long time upon the many that had been ruined by the English, since their arrival in Ireland, by specious promises, which they had not performed, and the numbers of the Irish high-born princes, gentlemen, and chieftains, who came to premature deaths without any reason at all, except to rob them of their patrimonies, they feared[m] very much that what was [then] promised would not be fulfilled to them;

the Marshal, or to enjoy peace, or do any service by which he could distinguish himself whilst Bagnal was Marshal of Ulster, he refused to meet her Majesty's Commissioners, stating by letter, that "he could not attend the Commissioners with safety or with honour; that he had little hope of any performance of articles, as he had been already deceived by confiding in the Queen's officers; that the intentions of the Lord General were ever just and honorable, but had been fatally counteracted by the Deputy: and as Sir John Norris was speedily to be removed from his command, and the grievances of the Northerns to be submitted to a new Chief Governor, whose principles and character were entirely unknown, he had the less reason to expect an equitable conclusion."—Leland's *History of Ireland*, book iv. c. 4.

dóiḃ coniḋ fair deiriḋ leó fó ḋeóiḋ an tríḋ do éimġſḃ. Ro aisnſiḋsiot iaraṁ in aiṫſscc don iarla, ⁊ do ċóiḋ siḋe co háṫ cliaṫ do ṡaiġiḋ an iustís ⁊ na coṁairle, ⁊ at féṫ dóiḃ a ḋiúltaḋ imón síṫ, ⁊ a frſcra ó na gaoiḋelaiḃ. Ro ċuir an iustis ⁊ an coṁairle teaċta go Saxaiḃ do ṡaiġiḋ na bainrioġan dairnſis a scél diriḋe coniḋ and fo cſrd si iolar ndaoíne go hErinn co na naiḋmiḃ teċta leó co nár ḃó luġa oldáṫt fiċe mſle a líon daor tuarustail, ⁊ daṁsoiḃ ro ḃattar in urḟaiċill coccaiḋ do ġaoiḋealaiḃ. Ro tſcclamaḋ iaraṁ sloiċċeaḋ lán ṁór la generál coccaiḋ na bainrioġan in Erinn .i. Sir Iohn noris do ḋol i ccoicceaḋ connaċt ar daiġ in ro éirigh i ccoṁbaidh coccaiḋ na ngaoiḋel díoḃ do cſnnsucchaḋ. Tainicc iarla ċloinne riocaird .i. Uillecc mac Riocaird Shaccsanaiġ, mic uillicc na ccenn co lion a ṡoċraitte ina ttionol. Tánaicc tra iarla tuaḋmuṁan .i. donnchaḋ mac conċoḃair, mic donnchaiḋ uí ḃriain co na ṡoċraitte on modh ccedna. Tangattar tra dronga dírime nach airiṁtear cenmoṫatsaiḋe. Aċt cſna atberat aroile na ro tionoileaḋ fri ré cian daimsir in erinn for seilḃ an ṗrionnsa saṁail don tsluaiġeaḋ isin ar lionmaire a lerṫionoil, ar allmurḋaċt ⁊ ar iongġnaiṫe a ninnill, ⁊ a neccoiscc. Iar ttorraċtain doiḃ féin uile go haon ḃaile .i. go haṫ luain do ṡaiġiḋ an generala lottar iaraṁ co Roscomáin, ⁊ í ccoṁḟoċraiḃ mainistre na búille iarttain ⁊ o na fuairsiot connaċtaiġ for a ccionn ann sin aṁail ro ṡaoílsiot, iompaíd tar a nais siar hi rann Mheic uilliam go cionnlaċa, ⁊ go maiġin go ro ġaḃsat campa coṁḟairsing la taoḃ abann Roḋba.

An tan ro batar an tsoċraitte lan ṁór acc tómaiṫſm toċt an dú sin, Ro ṡaíḋ Mac uilliam burc tesóitt, a ṫeċta go hUa ndoṁnaill dia ċuinġidh fair toiḋeċt dia ḟoiriṫin, nír bó failliġtech ro ḟreccraḋ indsin la hua ndoṁnaill uair rob erlaṁ eiriḋe do ṫeċt i ccoicceaḋ mſḋba riariu rangattar na teaċta dia ṡaiġiḋ. Scriobtar litre, ⁊ scriḃſnna uaḋa go gaoiḋelaiḃ coicciḋ olneccmaċt dia ḟorcongra forra toiḋeċt ina ḋoċom go hionad erdálta baí forr an cconair do saiġiḋ longport an generala Sir Iohn noris, ⁊ do ḋeachaiḋ buḋſin hi ccſnn tsſba co na sloġ lais tar eirne, tar Slicceċ, laṁ ḋſs fri

[n] *His having been refused the peace.*—An English writer would say: "he informed the Lord Deputy and the Council of the answer given by the Irish, and how they had rejected his proposals for a peace."

[o] *Ceann-lacha*, i. e. the Head of the Lake, now Kinlough, a townland in the parish of Shrule, in the barony of Kilmaine, and county of Mayo. It is so called from its situation at the head or extremity of Lough Corrib.

so that they finally resolved upon rejecting the peace. They communicated their decision to the Earl, who proceeded to Dublin to the Lord Justice and the Council, and related to them his having been refused the peace[n], and the answer he had received from the Irish. The Lord Justice and Council sent messengers to England to the Queen, to tell her the news; so that she then sent a great number of men to Ireland, with the necessary arms. Their number was no less than twenty thousand; and they were composed of mercenaries and [native] soldiers. A great hosting was mustered by the Queen's general of war in Ireland, namely, Sir John Norris, to proceed into the province of Connaught, in order to reduce all those who had risen up in the confederation of the Irish in the war. The Earl of Clanrickard, i. e. Ulick, the son of Rickard Saxonagh, son of Ulick na gCeann, came to join his levy with all his forces. The Earl of Thomond, i. e. Donough, the son of Conor, son of Donough O'Brien, came likewise with his forces; and also many others besides them, not enumerated, came to join him. In short, some say that no army like this had for a long time before been mustered in that part of Ireland possessed by the Sovereign [of England], in the numbers of the muster, the exotic and strange character of their equipment and appearance. When all these had come together at Athlone to meet the General, they then proceeded to Roscommon, and afterwards to the vicinity of the monastery of Boyle; but, not finding the Connacians there before them, as they had expected, they returned back, and marched towards the territory of Mac William, to Ceann-lacha[o], and to Maighin[p], and pitched a spacious camp on the brink of the River Robe.

When this great army was threatening to come to this place, Mac William Burke (Theobald) sent his messengers to O'Donnell, requesting of him to come to his relief. Not negligently did O'Donnell respond to this [request], for he had been prepared to proceed into the province of Meave [Connaught] before the messengers arrived. He sent letters and writings to the Irish of the province of Olnegmacht [Connaught], to request of them to meet him at a certain place on the road, leading to the camp of the General, Sir John Norris; and he himself set out on his journey with his army across the Erne and the Sligo,

[p] *Maighin*, now Moyne, a townland containing the ruins of a church and castle, in the parish of Shrule, barony of Kilmaine, and county of Mayo.—See *Genealogies, Tribes, and Customs of Hy-Fiachrach*, p. 494, and the map to the same work.

sruiḃ sleiḃe gaṁ tre luighne, ⁊ tre crich gailſng. Tangatar trá gaoidil an ċoicciḋ gan iompuireaċ fon toġairm isin. Tanaicc ann cetus Brian óg (.i. o ruairc) mac briain mic briain mic Eogain uí ruairc. Tánaic ann ó con-coḃair ruaḋ, ó ceallaigh, Mac diarmata maiġe luirg. Tangatar ann an dá ṁac donnchaiḋ, an dá Ua ſghra, ⁊ ua duḃda. Iar ttorrachtain na ngaoideal sin co háit naén ḃaile, ní ro hanaḋ leó go ro gaḃsat longport for ionchaiḃ Sir Iohn noris don taoḃ araill don Roḋba ceḋna.

Ro bai iomaiṫiġidh ſtorra anonn ⁊ anall aṁail biḋ fri sioh ⁊ fri cair-dine, ⁊ nír bó hſḋ ón iar ffír, aċt bá do ḃraṫ ⁊ taiscélaḋ ⁊ do ṫabairt bréicce imo roile dia ccaoṁsattaís. Airisitt athaiḋ aṁlaiḋ sin aghaiḋ i naghaiḋ co ttairnic a lóinte do na gallaiḃ conaḋ é ní ro chinnsiot déirġe an ṗuirt i mbáttar ó ná ro ċuṁaingsiot ní do na gaoiḋealaiḃ. Do ġníatt saṁlaiḋ ⁊ do ċóiḋ an generál go gaillim, assiḋe go baile áṫa luain, ⁊ ro ḟáccaiḃ saiġdiúiri hi ccunga, ⁊ mar an cceḋna i ngaillim, i mbaile ath an rioġ, isin mullach mór ua maine, hi ccill ċonaill i mbél aṫa na sluaiġeaḋ i Ross comáin, hi ttuillsgi, ⁊ i mainistir na búille.

Ua conċoḃair sligiġ do ṫeċt in erinn co ngallaiḃ iomḋa lais hi ffoġmar na bliaḋna so.

Do cuirſḋ Sir Risderd biongam co na braiṫriḃ a cuṁachtaiḃ cóicciḋ ċon-naċt, ⁊ ruccaḋ iaḋsiḋe co haṫ cliaṫ, ⁊ do cuirit assaiḋe go Saxoiḃ ⁊ ro cuireaḋ neach ele ba fſrr inás ina ionad i ngobernoracht ċoiccid connaċt .i. Sir Conerr clifort a coṁainm. Bá fſr tioḋnaicṫe séd ⁊ maoíne do ġal-laiḃ ⁊ do gaoiḋelaiḃ eisiḋe, ⁊ ní ṫainicc do ġallaiḃ i nErinn is na dſiḋſncoiḃ nech ba fſrr inás. Iar ttoċt do co haṫ cliaṫ ro baí ag coṁcruinniuccaḋ daoíne ⁊ acc uirtriall armála do ḋul hi cconnachtaiḃ. Do ċoiḋ iaraṁ co líon slóiġ, ⁊ soċaiḋe co baile aṫa luain, ⁊ do sccaoil a ḃanḋaḋa i ccampa ⁊ hi ffoslongport ar ḃailtiḃ ó maine, ⁊ cloinne Riocaird .i. gaillim, baile áṫa an rioġ, an mullaċ mór, conga, ⁊ an lſiṫinnsi. Do ċottar drong mór do ṁaiṫiḃ cóicciḋ connaċt do ṡaiġiḋ an gobernora, ⁊ do ġabsat lais fo dáiġ a allaḋ ⁊ a árd tuarusccḃala. Ro ba diḃsiḋe ó concoḃair ruaḋ .i. Aoḋ mac toirrḋealḃaiġ ruaiḋ, ⁊ mac diarmata .i. concoḃar, ⁊ ro naiḋmsiot a ccaratt-raḋ fris.

[q] *Brian Oge.*—Charles O'Conor adds in the margin that this Brian Oge was the son of Brian-na-Murtha.

[r] *Mullaghmore-Hy-Many*, now Mullaghmore, near Mount-Bellew. This castle is now a heap of ruins.—See *Tribes and Customs of Hy-Many*,

keeping the stream of Sliabh-Gamh on the right, through Leyny and the territory of Gaileanga. The Irish of the province came at the summons to meet him; and, first of all, O'Rourke (Brian Oge[q], the son of Brian, son of Brian, son of Owen); thither came O'Conor Roe, O'Kelly, Mac Dermot of Moylurg; thither came the two Mac Donoughs, the two O'Haras, and O'Dowda. When these Irish came together at one place, they made no delay until they pitched their camp, confronting Sir John Norris, on the opposite side of the same River Robe.

There was a communication between them on both sides, as if through peace and friendship; but this, in truth, was not so, but to spy, circumvent, and decoy each other, if they could. Thus they remained, face to face, until the English had exhausted their provisions; and the resolution they came to was, to leave the camp in which they were, as they could not do any service upon the Irish. They [accordingly] did so; and the General proceeded to Galway, and from thence to Athlone; having left soldiers in Cong, Galway, Athenry, Mullaghmore-Hy-Many[r], Kilconnell, Ballinasloe, Roscommon, Tulsk, and the monastery of Boyle.

In the autumn of this year O'Conor Sligo returned to Ireland with a great number of Englishmen.

Sir Richard Bingham and his relatives were deprived of their power in the province of Connaught; and they were brought to Dublin, and sent off from thence to England; and a far better man than he was appointed in his place to the governorship of Connaught, by name Sir Conyers Clifford. He was a distributor of wealth and jewels upon the English and Irish; and there came not of the English into Ireland, in latter times, a better man than he. On his arrival in Dublin, he proceeded to muster men and arms, to proceed into Connaught. He afterwards marched, with the entire of his troops and forces, to Athlone, and distributed his companies in camps and fortresses among the towns of Hy-Many and Clanrickard, namely, Galway, Athenry, Mullaghmore, Cong, and Lehinch[s]. A great number of the chiefs of the province of Connaught repaired to the Governor, and adhered to him, on account of his fame and high renown. Among these were O'Conor Roe, i. e. Hugh, the son of Turlough Roe, and Mac Dermot, i. e. Conor, who formed a league of friendship with him.

note [d], p. 18.

[s] *Lehinch*, a castle in the parish of Kilcommon, barony of Kilmaine, and county of Mayo.—See note [h], under the year 1412, p. 811, *supra*.

O concoḃair Sligiġ tra iar ttoċt dó a Saxoiḃ co hErinn ro ġaiḃriḋe ag cēndsuccaḋ Connacht aṁail ar dēch ro ḟēd a hucht gall, ⁊ ro ġaḃsat clann ndonnchaiḋ cuile muine lais. Ḃaí ḃeos baile an ṁótaiġ ar a ċumas. Ro ġaḃsat mar an ccédna muintir Airt lais, uair ba hiadsiḋe roptar tairisi dfior a ionaid do ġres, ⁊ roptar ḟaoiliġ dia roċtain dia saiġiḋ, ⁊ ro lionsat duaill, ⁊ do ḋíomas, ⁊ ro ġaḃsatt acc baiġ ⁊ acc bagar ar ċenel cconaill.

O domnaill dna óṫ cualaiġ siḋe forccaḋ an sccéoil sin, ⁊ a ndolsoṁ i ccombáiḋ gall ina aġaiḋ, ní ro airis fri tecclamaḋ slóiġ cenmotá aṁsaiġ ⁊ aés tuarustail ⁊ do taéd iaraṁ tar Slicceach siar go Ross oirce an roptar tairisi la hUa cconcoḃair in gach dú i mbáttar i ndiaṁraiḃ, ⁊ i ndroiḃelaiḃ daingne an tire co ná ro ḟaccaiḃ mil ninnile leó, ⁊ ní ro creach acht iadsoṁ namá, ge ro ċoiccill doiḃ co minic rēime ar a ndínnime ⁊ ar a ndēroile go ros brost a mbriaṫra diúmsaċa, ⁊ a naincriḋe na ro ḟedsat do ḋicleiṫ Ua domnaill dia norgain an tan sin.

Conċoḃar, mac taidg, mic concoḃair ui ḃriain o bél aṫa an ċomhraic do ḋol for diḃēircc ⁊ for foġail, uair baísiḋe, ⁊ drong do ċloind trichigh amaille fris ar ionnarbaḋh o na naṫarḋa araon la gaoiḋealaiḃ an tuarsceirt, ⁊ tainic ina lēnmain roċtain dia ttír, ⁊ asseaḋ loctar do ċloinn Riocaird, do Shleḃ eċtge, ⁊ dioċtar cloinne cuilein. Ro bás ina lēnmain o gach tír do ṫír co ro gaḃaḋ Concoḃar fa deoidh ar in ccoill móir, ⁊ ruccaḋ é hi ccēnd an presidens isin ccéd mí dfoghmar do ḟonnraḋ, ⁊ ro básaigeaḋ he i ccorcaiġ ar terma na Saṁna.

Taḋcc, mac toirrḋealḃaiġ, mic donnchaiḋ, mic concoḃair uí briain (iar mbēiṫ ré ḟoda for foġail) do ġaḃail i mbuitilerachaiḃ, ⁊ a ḃásuccaḋ tre coṁairle iarla urṁuṁan.

[t] *Cul-muine.*—This is the present Irish name of Collooney, in the barony of Tirerrill, and county of Sligo; but it is more usually called Cul-Maoile, or Cuil-Maoile, in these Annals.—See the years 1291, 1526, 1586, 1601.

[u] *The O'Harts.*—These were seated in the north of the barony of Carbury, in the county of Sligo, between Grange and Bunduff, and opposite the island of Inishmurry.

[v] *Bel-atha-an-chomhraic,* now Ballycorick, near the town of Clare, in the county of Clare.—See note [l], under the year 1589, p. 1879, *supra.*

[w] *Sliabh-Echtghe,* now Slieve Aughty, a large mountainous district on the confines of the counties of Clare and Galway. See it already mentioned at the years 1263, 1570, 1572, 1578.

[x] *The lower part.*—This phraseology of the Four Masters is different from the present local use of the word ioċtar, lower, which means that part of the county next the Lower Shannon.

[y] *Coill-mhor.*—There are several places of this name in Munster; but as Conor O'Brien was

O'Conor Sligo, after his return from England, proceeded, on behalf of the English, to reduce Connaught; and he was joined by the Clann-Donough of Cul-muine[t], and he had also Ballymote in his power. The O'Harts[u] also adhered to him, for they had always been faithful to the man who held his place; and they rejoiced at his arrival, and were filled with pride and arrogance, and began to defy and threaten the Kinel-Connell.

When O'Donnell heard this fact rumoured, and that these people had joined the English against him, he did not wait to muster an army, except his soldiers and mercenaries, and proceeded westward across the [River] Sligo, and plundered all those who paid obedience to O'Conor, wherever they were, [even those] in the wilds and fast recesses of the country; so that he did not leave a single head of cattle among them. He plundered but these only; and though he had often spared them on former occasions, on account of their littleness and insignificance, yet their own haughty words and animosity, which they were unable to repress, provoked O'Donnell to plunder them on this occasion.

Conor, the son of Teige, son of Conor O'Brien, of Bel-atha-an-chomhraic[v], went into insurrection, and began to plunder; for he, together with a party of the Clann-Sheehy, having been expelled from their patrimonies, were along with the Irish of the north. It came into their minds to return to their own territory; and they passed through Clanrickard, by Sliabh-Echtghe[w] and the lower part[x] of Clann-Cuilein. They were pursued from territory to territory, until Conor was at last taken in the Wood of Coill-mhor[y], and brought before the President in the first month of autumn; and he was hanged at Cork in the [ensuing] November[z] Term.

Teige, the son of Turlough[a], son of Donough[b], son of Conor O'Brien, after having been a long time engaged in plundering, was taken in the country of the Butlers, and executed by advice of the Earl of Ormond.

executed at Cork, it looks very likely that he was taken at Coill-mhor, a celebrated haunt of insurgents, near Charleville, in the north of the county of Cork.—See it already mentioned at the years 1579, 1580, 1581, 1582.

[z] *November Term*, i. e. Michaelmas Term, as it is called by the lawyers.

[a] *Turlough*.—He was the brother of Conor O'Brien, third Earl of Thomond, and was hanged in 1581.

[b] *Donough*.—He was the second Earl of Thomond. This Earl Donough left three sons, viz., Conor, his successor; Turlough, who was hanged in 1581; and Teige, who, according to Duald Mac Firbis, had three celebrated sons, viz., 1, Col. Dermot, surnamed the good; 2,

Uaitne, mac Ruḋraiġe óicc, mic Ruḋraiġe caoíċ, mic conuill uí morḋa do bſith ina duine uasal hi ccſrdaiḃ coccaiḋ an tan sa, ⁊ laoiġis do lſirsccrios lais etir ioṫ, arḃar, ⁊ áitiuccaḋ co ná baoí énní isin tír o ġlas gſta no bádúin amaċ nach baoí for a ċumas. Ro marḃaḋ dna lais duine uasal do Shaxancoiḃ bai hi ssrádbaile laoiġisi aga raiḃe blaḋ mór don tír a huġdarrás an ṗrionnsa .i. Corbi mac maiġistir Frauus a ainm.

Clann emainn an ċalaiḋ, mic Semais, mic Piarais ruaiḋ mic Semuis, mic émainn mic Risdſird buitilér do ḋol for foġail beós tre iomtnuṫ le hiarla urmuṁan, ⁊ a naṫair emann an ċalaiḋ do ġabail tre na ccionntaiḃsiḋe.

Emann, mac Risdſird, mic Piarais ruaiḋ do gabail mar an cceḋna.

Fiacha mac Aoḋa, mic Sſain o ġlionn maoílugra do bſiṫ ag milleaḋ laiġſn ⁊ miḋe an tan sa.

AOIS CRIOST, 1597.

Aois Criost, mile, cuicc céd, nochat, a seacht.

Ua domnaill Aoḋ ruaḋ, mac Aoḋa, mic Maġnasa do bſiṫ i ffoslongport i mbreifne ċonnaċt fri sliaḃ dá én anoir on tan ro hoirccſḋ sainṁuintir

Turlough, who attended the Parliament held at Dublin in 1585; and 3, Col. Murtough O'Brien, who was living in 1664. The Editor is of opinion that this Col. Murtough was the father of Donnell Spaineach, the ancestor of Terence O'Brien of Glencolumbkille, notwithstanding the evidence of the manuscript pedigree already quoted at p. 1834, A. D. 1585.

[c] *A gentleman of the English.*—This was Alexander, third son of Francis Cosby. Francis, Alexander's eldest son, was also slain on this occasion.—See note [d], under the year 1580, p. 1739, *supra*. Mr. Hardiman has given the following account of the conflict between Oweny O'More and the Cosbies, from an original MS. which belonged to the late Admiral Cosby:

"In the year 1596, Owny Mac Rory O'More," [ex-] "Chieftain of Leix, demanded a passage for his men over Stradbally bridge, and the request, being considered as a formal challenge to fight, was refused. On the 19th of May, Cosby, hearing that the O'Mores were on the march, headed his kerne, and proceeded to defend the bridge, taking with him his eldest son, Francis, who was married a year before to Helena Harpole, of Shrule, by whom he had a son, William, born but nine weeks before this fatal battle of the bridge. Dorcas Sydney (for she would never allow herself to be called Cosby), and her daughter-in-law, placed themselves at a window of the abbey, to see the fight, and for some time beheld their husbands bravely maintaining their ground. At length Alexander Cosby, as he was pressing forward, was shot, and dropped down dead. Upon this his kerne, with melancholy and mournful outcries, began to give way; and Francis Cosby, the son, apprehensive of being abandoned, endeavoured to save himself by leaping over the bridge, but the moment he cleared the battlements he was also shot, and fell dead

Owny, son of Rury Oge, son of Rury Caech, son of Connell O'More, was at this time a gentleman [skilled] in the arts of war; and Leix was totally ravaged by him, both its crops, corn, and dwellings, so that there was nothing in the territory outside the lock of a gate or a bawn which was not in his power. He slew a gentleman of the English[c], who was [seated] at Stradbally-Leix, who possessed a large portion[d] of the territory by authority of the Sovereign, namely, [Alexander] Cosby, the son of Master Frauus[e].

The sons of Edmond of Caladh, son of James, son of Pierce Roe, son of James, son of Edmond, son of Richard Butler, also turned out to plunder, in consequence of their animosity towards the Earl of Ormond; and their father, Edmond of Caladh, was taken prisoner for their crimes.

Edmond, the son of Richard, son of Pierce Roe [Butler], was also taken prisoner.

At this time Fiagh, the son of Hugh, son of John [O'Byrne], from Glenmalure, was plundering Leinster and Meath[f].

THE AGE OF CHRIST, 1597.

The Age of Christ, one thousand five hundred ninety-seven.

O'Donnell (Hugh Roe, the son of Hugh, son of Manus) encamped in Breifny of Connaught[g], to the east of Sliabh-da-en, after having plundered, as we have

into the river, &c. &c. The feuds between the O'Mores and Cosbies still raged with violence. The infant" [William] "having died, Richard Cosby succeeded to the estate, and became leader of the kerne. Eager to revenge the deaths of his father and brother, he challenged the O'Mores to fight a pitched battle. They met in 1606, in the glen of Aghnahely, under the rock of Dunamase, and the engagement was the most bloody ever fought between these rivals. After a long and doubtful conflict, fortune declared in favour of Cosby. The O'Mores were defeated, with considerable loss, and seventeen of the principal of the clan lay dead on the field. The revolutions of the seventeenth century completed the destruction of the O'Mores, but confirmed the Cosby family in its possessions."—*Irish Minstrelsy*, vol. ii. p. 165.

[d] *A large portion.*—The Cosby Manuscript, quoted by Mr. Hardiman, states that the Cosbys at one time possessed half the Queen's County, and a township over.

[e] *Master Frauus*, Maiġistir Frauṡ.—This is a mere error of transcription, for "Maiġistir Francis."

[f] *Meath.*—P. O'Sullevan Beare gives an account of several engagements which took place about this period between O'Neill and the English, in the neighbourhood of Armagh, but without any minute chronology.

[g] *Breifny of Connaught*, i. e. Breifny O'Rourke, or the present county of Leitrim, so called to

uí concobaiṙ laiꞅ aṁail ꞃeṁebeꞃtmaꞃ. Ro ḃaíꞅiḋe ag eꞃnaiġe a ṗoċꞃaitte, ⁊ a ṫoicheꞅtal do bꞃſiṫ ꝼaiꞃ aꞅ gaċ aiꞃm i mbáttaꞃ ⁊ iaꞃ ttecclamaḋ doiḃ dia ṗaiġiḋ i noſiꞃeaḋ lanuaꞃꝫ aꞅꞅeaḋ lottaꞃ i ttꞃioċa ċéd ua noilella, aꞅꞅaiḋe don ċoꞃann, tꞃe ṁaċaiꞃe connaċt, hi ccloinn conmaigh hi ccꞃich maine. Iaꞃ ttoċt do i nſidiꞃmſdon Ua maine ꞃo lſicc ꞅcceiṁelta ꞅcꞃiobluaṫa uaḋ ꝼa ṫuaiṫ an ċalaiḋ, ⁊ ꝼa uaċtaꞃ na tiꞃe, ⁊ do beꞃtꞅat bó ṫainte iomḋa, ⁊ cꞃſċa coṁaiḋble leo hi ccoinne uí doṁnaill go baile áṫa an ꞃioġ, ⁊ ge ꞃo ṗóbaiꞃꞅiot an ḃaꞃda an baile do ḃaꞃdaċt níꞃ bó toꞃḃa doiḃ an tinnꞅccſtal uaiꞃ ꞃo cuiꞃꞅiot muintiꞃ uí ḋoṁnaill teinnte ⁊ tſndála ꝼꞃi doiꞃꞅiḃ daingſn ndúnta an ḃaile, ⁊ tuccꞅat oꞃſimiꞃſḋa dioṁóꞃa dia ꞅaiċċiḋ, ⁊ ꞃo ċuiꞃꞅiot ꝼꞃiꞅ na muꞃaiḃ iad go nuſchꞃat ꝼoꞃ taiḃliḃ an ṁúiꞃ. Ro lingꞅiot iaꞃaṁ do na taiḃliḃ go mbataꞃ ꝼoꞃ ꞅꞅaidibh an ḃaile, ⁊ ꞃo eꞅꞅlaicꞅiot na doiꞃꞅi don luċt bataꞃ imuiġ. Ġabaitt iaꞃaṁ ꝼoꞃ toġail na ttiġſḋ ttaiꞅccſḋa, ⁊ na tteġdaꞅ ꝼꝼoiꞃiata co ꞃuccꞅat eiꞅtiḃ ina mbaoí indiḃ dionnmaꞅaiḃ, ⁊ dédalaiḃ. Aiꞃiꞅit in adhaiġ ꞅin iꞅin mbaile hi ꞅin. Níꞃ bó ꞅoḋaing ꞃíoṁ nó aiꞃſṁ ina ꞃuccaḋ duṁa, ⁊ diaꞃann dedach ⁊ duꞃadh aꞅ in mbaile ꞅin aꞃ na maꞃach. Ḃa haꞅ an mbaile cedna ꞅin ꞃo lſicc ꞅccſiṁealta uaḋ daꞃccain cloinne ꞃiocaiꞃd aꞃ gach taoḃ daḃainn. Ro leiꞃcꞃeachaḋ, ⁊ ꞃo laimndꞃeaḋ laꞅ na ꞅceṁeltoibh ꞅin o lſthꞃáiṫ go maġ ꞅſnċoṁlaḋ. Ro loiꞅcceaḋ, ⁊ ꞃo lomaiꞃcceaḋ laꞅ an ccuid eile díḃ ó ḃaile [áṫa] an ꞃíoġ ⁊ ó ꞃaiṫ ġoiꞃꞅgín ꞅiaꞃ go ꞃinn mil, go mſḋꞃaiḋe, ⁊ go doꞃuꞅ na gaillṁe. Ro loiꞅcceaḋ leo tſgh bꞃighde i ndoꞃuꞅ ꞅꞃaiꞃꞃi na gaillṁe. Do ꞃonaḋ ꞅoꞅaḋ, ⁊ ꞅáꞃlongꞃoꞃt la hua ndoṁnaill co na ꞅloġaiḃ in adhaiġ ꞅin etiꞃ uaꞃán móꞃ ⁊ gaillim ag cloich an línꞅigh do

distinguish it from Breifny O'Reilly, or the present county of Cavan, which was at this period a part of Ulster.

[h] *Caladh*, now Callow, a district comprised principally in the barony of Kilconnell, in the county of Galway.—See map to *Tribes and Customs of Hy-Many.*

[i] *Leathrath*, now Laragh, a townland containing the ruins of a castle in the parish of Kilimor-Daly, and about six miles north-east of the town of Athenry, in the county of Galway.

[k] *Magh-Seanchomhladh*, i. e. the Plain of the old Gate. This name is now obsolete.

[l] *Rath-Goirrgin*, i. e. the Rath of Goirrgin, one of the chiefs of the Firbolgs, who flourished here in the first century. It was anciently called Aileach Goirrgin. The name Rath Goirrginn is still retained, and is anglicised Rathgorgon, which is applied to a townland in the parish of Kilconerin, barony of Athenry, and county of Galway. It contains a moat, which was originally surrounded with a fosse, and the ruins of a castle of considerable extent.

[m] *Rinn-Mil*, i. e. the point or promontory of Mil, one of the Firbolgic tribe called Clann-Uathmoir. The name is now pronounced in

said before, the faithful people of O'Conor. He was awaiting [the arrival of] his forces and muster from every quarter where they were; and when they had all assembled, which was at the end of the month of January, they marched into the territory of Tirerrill, from thence into Corran, through Machaire-Chonnacht, and into Clann-Conway and Hy-Many. Having reached the very centre of Hy-Many, he sent forth swift-moving marauding parties through the district of Caladh[h], and the upper part of the territory; and they carried off many herds of cows and other preys to O'Donnell, to the town of Athenry; and though the warders of the town attempted to defend it, the effort was of no avail to them, for O'Donnell's people applied fires and flames to the strongly-closed gates of the town, and carried to them great ladders, and, placing them against the walls, they [*recté*, some of them] ascended to the parapets of the wall. They then leaped from the parapets, and gained the streets of the town, and opened the gates for those who were outside. They [all] then proceeded to demolish the storehouses and the strong habitations; and they carried away all the goods and valuables that were in them. They remained that night in the town. It was not easy to enumerate or reckon the quantities of copper, iron, clothes, and habiliments, which they carried away from the town on the following day. From the same town he sent forth marauding parties to plunder Clanrickard, on both sides of the river; and these marauders totally plundered and ravaged [the tract of country] from Leathrath[i] to Magh-Seanchomhladh[k]. The remaining part of his army burned and ravaged [the territory], from the town of Athenry and Rath-Goirrgin[l] westwards to Rinn-Mil[m] and Meadhraige[n], and to the gates of Galway, and burned Teagh-Brighde[o], at the military gate of Galway. O'Donnell pitched his camp for that night between Uaran-mor[p] and Galway,

Irish Rinn míl, and anglicised Rinvile. It is a townland in the parish of Oranmore, not far from the town of Galway; and there is a castle in ruins in the western part of this townland, said to have belonged to the family of Athy.

[n] *Meadhraighe*, now *anglice* Maaree, a peninsula extending about five miles into the bay of Galway, to the south of the town. It is exactly coextensive with the parish of Ballynacourty.—See map to *Tribes and Customs of Hy-Many*, and *Chorographical Description of Iar-Connaught*, p. 42.

[o] *Teagh-Brighde*, i.e. St. Bridget's house. This, which was otherwise called St. Bridget's Hospital, was situated on the east side of the town of Galway. It was built by the Corporation in 1542.—See *Chorographical Description of Iar-Connaught*, p. 40.

[p] *Uaran-mor*, i.e. the great well, or cold spring, now Oranmore, a considerable village, situated at the head of one of the arms into which the upper end of the bay of Galway

ḟonnraḋ. Do ċaiḋ ó domhnaill ar na ṁarach go mainistir an ċnuic i ndorus na gaillme, ⁊ ro baí iomaiṫigiḋ uaḋ go luċt an ḃaile ag cuingiḋ cricé ⁊ ceannaigheċta a nerraḋ neccsamail, ⁊ a nédgaḋ nuasal for araill do na creachaiḃ. Arsseaḋ ro chinn iaram sóḋ tar a ais, ⁊ munbaḋ troma na ttionol creach, iomat na nairccneaḋ, ⁊ aidble na hédala ro baḋ doiġ na hansaḋ don ruim sin go gort innsi guaire hi ccenel aoḋa na heċtge. Luiḋ ua domhnaill co na ṡlogaiḃ ⁊ co na ccreaċaiḃ leó tre ceastlar ċoicciḋ connaċt hi ffrithing na conaire céḋna, ⁊ ní ro airis go ro ġaḃ longport hi ccalraiġe fri Slicceach anoir, ⁊ ro ḟaoiḋ a ġiollanraiḋ, ⁊ a aés díairin lá araill dia ċreachaiḃ tar Samaoir baḋ ṫuaiḋ.

Dala uí concoḃair ṡliccig (donnchaḋ mac caṫail óicc) ro teacclamaḋ slog lán mór lais do ġallaiḃ ⁊ do ġaoidelaiḃ gan beacc iar bfeil briġde do ṫoċt go Slicceach.

O domhnaill tra baísiḋe hi ccalraiġe (amhail remebertmar) hi ffoiċill forra ⁊ do beart ammus for slog uí ċonċoḃair ria siú rangatar go Slicceach. Ní ro hanaḋ frissiḋe idir, acht maḋ uaṫaḋ tarrtar do deireaḋ an tsloiġ ag traiġ neoṫuile, gontar, báitter iadsaiḋe. Ro marḃaḋ ann mac meic uilliam burc .i. mac Risdeird mac oiluerais, mic Seain, ⁊ drong oile naċ airiṁtear cenmoṫasom. Do ċaiḋ ua concobair for ccúla, ⁊ nir bó slán lais a ṁeanma im ṫoideċt an turas sin. Tánaic trá Ua domhnaill dia ṫigh, ⁊ ro leicc sccaoileaḋ dia ṡloiġaibh do léccaḋ a sccísi daiṫle a nairtir imchein. ⁊ ro ḟaccaiḃ a amsa ⁊ a aés tuarustail i ccóicceaḋ connacht i nurḟaiċill ċoccaid uí ċoncoḃair ⁊ na ngall battar lais, ⁊ niall garḃ mac cuinn, mic an ċalḃaiġ uí domhnaill i ttoísigeċt forra. Ro ġabsat fein for indreaḋ ⁊ aidhmilleaḋ na ngaoideltuaṫ ro sirseattar i ccommbaiḋ uí concoḃair ⁊ na ngall go ttarodsat for ccúla do ridisi drong mór diḃ im Mhac diarmata Conċoḃar toisech maiġe luirec, ⁊ ruccaḋ eisiḋe do ṡaigiḋ uí domhnaill go ndearna a ṁuintearus fris an dara feċt, ⁊ co ttarat a riar dó. Do rónsat

branches. On the shore of the bay are the ruins of Oranmore castle, erected by the Earls of Clanrickard, now attached to the residence of Mr. Blake.

[q] *Cloch-an-Lingsigh*, i. e. Lynch's stone, or stone house, or castle. This name is now obsolete.

[r] *Mainistir-an-chnuic*, i. e. the Monastery of the Hill, or Knock Abbey.

[s] *Gort-insi-Guaire*, i. e. the town of Gort, in the territory of Kinelea-of-Slieve Aughtee, or O'Shaughnessy's country.—See it already mentioned at the years 1571, 1573.

[t] *Calry*, a parish in the barony of Carbury, lying between Glencar and Lough Gill, to the

precisely at Cloch-an-Lingsigh[q]. On the following day O'Donnell proceeded to Mainistir-an-chnuic[r], at the gate of Galway, and communicated with the inhabitants of the town, requesting traffic and sale of their various wares and rich raiment for some of the preys. He then resolved upon returning back; and were it not for the burden of the collected preys, the multiplicity of the plunders, and the vastness of the spoil, it is certain that he would have not stopped on that route until he had gone to Gortinnsi-Guaire[s] in Kinel-Aedha-na-hEchtge. O'Donnell, with his forces and their preys, returned by the same road, through the very middle of the province of Connaught, and never halted until he pitched his camp in Calry[t], to the east of Sligo; and he sent his calones and the unarmed part of his people to convey some of the preys northward, across the River Samhaoir[u].

As for O'Conor Sligo (Donough, the son of Cathal Oge), he mustered a numerous army of English and Irish troops, a short time after the festival of St. Bridget[w], to march to Sligo.

O'Donnell, as we have already mentioned, was in Calry, in readiness to meet them; and he made an attack upon the army of O'Conor before they could reach Sligo. None of O'Conor's army waited to resist him, excepting a few in the rear, who were overtaken at Traigh-Eothaile. These were wounded or drowned; and the son of Mac William Burke, namely, the son of Richard, son of Oliver, son of John, and many others not enumerated, were slain. O'Conor returned back; and he was not happy in his mind for having gone on that expedition. O'Donnell also returned home, and dismissed his tribes, that they might rest themselves after their long expedition; and he left his soldiers and hirelings in Connaught, under the command of Niall Garv, the son of Con, son of Calvagh O'Donnell, to carry on war against O'Conor and the English people who were along with him. These proceeded to plunder and destroy the Irish tribes who had risen up in confederacy with O'Conor and the English; so that they won over a great number of them [to the Irish side] again, and, among others, Mac Dermot (Conor), Chief of Moylurg, who was brought before O'Donnell, and formed a league of friendship with him a second time, and gave

east of the town of Sligo. This district was anciently called Calraighe Laithim.—See map to *Genealogies, Tribes, &c., of Hy-Fiachrach.*

[u] *Samhaoir*, an old name of the River Erne.—See Keating's *Hist. of Ireland*, Haliday's edition, p. 168; and O'Flaherty's *Ogygia*, part iii. c. 3.

[w] *The festival of St. Bridget.*—This falls on the 1st of February.

toísiġ na ttuaṫ bádar frí Coirrsliaḃ a tuaiḋ an ccedna, ⁊ do rattsat a ngeill, ⁊ a naittire dUa Domhnaill.

Ceiṫre bairille, ⁊ secht fficit bairille púdair do ṫeċt on mbainrioġain go hAṫ cliaṫ hi mí márta do ṡaiġiḋ a muinntire. Iar ccor an ṗúdair hi ttír ro tairrngeaḋ é co sráid an ḟíona co mbaoí uile in aen ionadh ar gaċ taeḃ don tsraid, ⁊ do ḋeachaiḋ aoiḃel teineaḋ isin bpúdar. Ní fes trá an do niṁ, fá a talmain tainic an Splangc hísin, aċt cena ro ṁeaḃaiḋ na bairilleḋa ina naén breó lassaċ ⁊ luaṁainteineaḋ an 13 do ṁárta do ṡonnradh, co ro toccḃaḋ cúirte cloċ, ⁊ cuṁdaiġṫe croinn na sráitte da ffoṫaiḃ fulaing, ⁊ da bforsadhaiḃ congmala isin aér ḟoarḃuas co mbíoḋ an trail ṗíoṫfoda, ⁊ an ċloċ cian tuimiġte, ⁊ an duine ina éccoscc ċorrarḋa for foluaṁain isin aer ós cenn an ḃaile la tuinnsiuṁ an tren ṗúdair conaċ eidir ríoṁ, airem, nó airnes an ro milleaḋ do ḋaoíniḃ onórċa, daér gacha ceirde, do ṁnaiḃ, do ṁaiġdenaiḃ, do clannaiḃ daoíne uasal ticceaḋ ar gach aird deirinn do denam foġlama don ċaṫraiġ. Nir bó daṁna eccaoine an ro milleaḋ dór, nó dairgeatt, nó do ṡoṁaoine saoġalta in aiṫṡecchaḋ in ro milleaḋ ⁊ in ro muḋaigheaḋ do daoiniḃ las an torainnċles sin. Nír bo hí an tsráid sin aṁain ro dioṫaiccheaḋ don cur sin, aċt an ceṫraiṁe fa nesa di don ċaṫraigh ċedna.

Ua Concobair Donnchaḋ mac Caṫail óicc do cengal ċairdesa, ⁊ carattradh etir a ċliaṁain (mac mec Uilliam burc) .i. Tepoitt na long mac Risdeird an iarainn, mic Dáuid, mic Emainn, ⁊ goberndir ċoicciḋ Connaċt .i. Sir Conerr Clifort. Iar ndenaṁ a ccodaiġ re roile doiḃ do ṫarrainġ Tepoitt an goberndir ⁊ bannaḋa ċoicciḋ Connaċt i ttír Aṁalgaḋa, ⁊ hi rann ṁeic Uilliam go ro haṫcuirseḋh, ⁊ go ro hionnarbaḋ leo Mac Uilliam (Tepóitt mac Uaiteir Ciotaiġ mic Seain, mic Oiluerais) ass a aṫarḋa hi ccenn uí Ḋoṁnaill. Ro lomaḋ ⁊ ro leirsccriosaḋ leó gaċ aén frisa mbaoí a rann ⁊ a ċarattradh isin tír dia éis. Ro ġaḃ an tír don cur sin la Tepoitt na long ⁊ las an

[x] *Wine-street*, now Winetavern-street. Harris notices the ignition of this powder, under the year 1596, thus:

"A. D. 1596. A great quantity of gunpowder being landed at the Wood-quay, to be conveyed to the Castle of Dublin, by accident took fire on the 11th of March, and did great damage to the city."—*History of the City of Dublin*, p. 321.

[y] *Placed on both sides of the street*, literally, "After the putting of the powder to land, it was drawn to the street of the wine, so that it was all in one place on both sides of the street."

[z] *To O'Donnell*.—This is a strange idiom. The meaning is that they expelled him from his ter-

him due submission. The chiefs of the territories bordering on the Curlieu Mountains did the same, and delivered up their hostages and securities to O'Donnell.

One hundred and forty-four barrels of powder were sent by the Queen to Dublin, to her people, in the month of March. When the powder was landed, it was drawn to Wine-street[x], and placed on both sides of the street[y], and a spark of fire got into the powder; but from whence that spark proceeded, whether from the heavens or from the earth beneath, is not known; howbeit, the barrels burst into one blazing flame and rapid conflagration (on the 13th of March), which raised into the air, from their solid foundations and supporting posts, the stone mansions and wooden houses of the street, so that the long beam, the enormous stone, and the man in his corporal shape, were sent whirling into the air over the town by the explosion of this powerful powder; and it is impossible to enumerate, reckon, or describe the number of honourable persons, of tradesmen of every class, of women and maidens, and of the sons of gentlemen, who had come from all parts of Ireland to be educated in the city, that were destroyed. The quantity of gold, silver, or worldly property, that was destroyed, was no cause of lamentation, compared to the number of people who were injured and killed by that explosion. It was not Wine-street alone that was destroyed on this occasion, but the next quarter of the town to it.

O'Conor (Donough, the son of Cathal Oge) established friendship and concord between his brother-in-law (the son of Mac William Burke), i. e. Theobald-na-Long, the son of Richard-an-Iarainn, son of David, son of Edmond, and the Governor of the province of Connaught, i. e. Sir Conyers Clifford. After their reconciliation Theobald drew the Governor and the companies of the province of Connaught into Tirawley, and into Mac William's country, and expelled and banished Mac William (Theobald, the son of Walter Kittagh, son of John, son of Oliver) from his patrimony, to O'Donnell[z]; they despoiled and totally plundered all those who remained in confederation and friendship with him in the territory. The country [generally], on this occasion, adhered to[a] Theobald-na-

ritory, leaving it optional with him to go wherever he wished; but that he fled to his friend O'Donnell, as the person most likely to shelter him, and assist him to recover his patrimony.

[a] *Adhered to.*—Ro ġaḃ an tír, &c., la tepoitt, literally, "the country on this occasion took with Theobald of the Ships, and with the Governor." This idiom is still in common use, as:

ngobernóir. Iompair an gobernoir iar sin go baile aṫa luain, ⁊ ro sccaoilsiot na bandaiġi ar a ngairisionaiḃ. Ba doairnſir a ruccsat dairccniḃ ⁊ dédalaiḃ a rann ṁeic uilliam an tan sin.

Dala ṁeic uilliam iar ttoċt dosoṁ co hairm i mboí ó doṁnaill dacaoine a imniḋ fris ro airis ina ḟochair co mí mſḋóin saṁraiḋ. Do ġní O doṁnaill iaraṁ slóicċeaḋ hi ccóicceaḋ connaċt do congnaṁ la Mac uilliam, ⁊ rainic tar muaiḋ ua naṁalgada gan naċ ndoġraing. Ní ċuṁgatar (no caeṁnaccatar) an tír friṫbeart fris go ro gaḃ a ngialla, ⁊ a naittire, ⁊ do beart soṁ na braiġde isin do Mhac uilliam, ⁊ fáccḃais an crioċ fa uṁla dó. ⁊ forráccaiḃ Ruḋraiġe Ua doṁnaill a ḋſrḃraṫair buḋſisin tanairi ceneoil cconaill ina ḟarraḋ dia nſrtaḋ i naġaiḋ a naṁatt go slóġ mor dia ṁilſḋaiḃ troiġṫeaċ, ⁊ dia aṁsoiḃ amaille friss. Iompaiḋis Ua doṁnaill ina ḟriṫing dia ṫír.

Ro ṫionoil Ua concoḃair ⁊ teroitt na long sloġ mór do ġallaiḃ, ⁊ do ġaoiḋelaiḃ iar ffaccbáil na tíre dUa doṁnaill do ḋioġail a naincriḋe for Mhac uilliam ⁊ ro ionnarbsat Mac uilliam an dara feaċt, ⁊ Ruḋraiġe don ċur sin as in tír ar ni raḃatarsiḋe coiṁlion daoine friú. Bá sí coṁairle airriċt la Ruḋraiġe ⁊ la Mac uilliam ina mbaoi ina ccoṁḟocraiḃ do ċroḋ ⁊ dinnile an tire co na naittreabtachaiḃ, ⁊ co na muinntſraiḃ do ċor rſmpa tar muaiḋ ua naṁalgaḋa, ⁊ tré ṫír ḟiaċraċ ṁuaiḋe do ṫoċt fo ṁámur uí doṁnaill go rangattar sliaḃ gaṁ ria nadhaiġ, ⁊ gaḃaitt acc arccnaṁ triar an sliabh fod na hoidhche.

Imṫúra an ġoibernóra ó ro ċuir sium ua conċoḃair, ⁊ tſróitt na long co na sloġaiḃ do ḋioċur meic uilliam as an tír, Ro ṫſglaimsiḋe lion a ṡoċraitte for cind Meic uilliam ⁊ Ruḋraiġe isin conair na ro ċuṁaingsiot do ṡeachna no diomġabail. Roptar iad bátar do ṡaorclandaiḃ i ffarraḋ an ġoibernora an tan sin .i. Uillſcc mac Riocaird Shaccsanaiġ, mic uillicc na ccſnd, iarla ċloinne Riocaird co na ṁac Riocard barún dúine coillín eisiḋe, Donnchaḋ mac concoḃair, mic donnchaiḋ ui ḃriain iarla tuaḋmuṁan, ⁊ Murchaḋ mac Murchaiḋ mic diarmata uí ḃriain barún innsi uí cuinn go

"cuir uait do lſnán ⁊ gaḃ le d' ċéad ṁnaoí: Put away thy concubine, and *take with* thy first wife."—See the Editor's *Irish Grammar*, part ii. c. viii. p. 310.

[b] *Equal to their's*, i. e. Mac William and Rury O'Donnell had not forces sufficient to contend with those of Theobald of the Ships and the Governor.

Long and the Governor. The Governor then returned to Athlone, and the companies of soldiers were distributed among the garrisons. The preys and spoils taken from Mac William's people on this occasion were indescribable.

As for Mac William, when he went to O'Donnell to complain to him of his sufferings, he remained with him until the middle month of summer. O'Donnell then made a hosting into the province of Connaught to assist Mac William, and he crossed the Moy into Tirawley without meeting any danger; and the country was not able to oppose him, so that he seized their hostages and pledges; and he delivered up these hostages, and left the country in obedience to him; and he left Rury O'Donnell, his own brother, Tanist of Tirconnell, with him, to strengthen him against his enemies, a great number of foot-soldiers, and other troops. O'Donnell [then] returned back to his own country.

When O'Donnell left the country, O'Conor and Theobald-na-Long mustered a great army of English and Irish, in order to wreak their vengeance on Mac William; and they banished him a second time, and Rury along with him, on that occasion, from the territory, for they had not a number of men equal to their's[b]. The resolution then adopted by Rury and Mac William was to send all the property and cattle of the territory in their vicinity, together with the inhabitants and families, before them, across the Moy of Tirawley, and through Tireragh of the Moy, to come under the jurisdiction of O'Donnell. [This they did], and they arrived before nightfall at Sliabh-Gamh, and during the whole night they continued crossing the mountain.

As for the Governor, as soon as he had sent O'Conor and Theobald-na-Long to banish Mac William from the territory, he mustered all his forces, to meet Mac William and Rury on a road which they could not shun or avoid. The noblemen who attended the Governor on this expedition were these: Ulick, the son of Rickard Saxonagh, son of Ulick-na-gCeann, Earl of Clanrickard, with his son, Rickard, Baron of Dun-Coillin[c]; Donough, the son of Conor, son of Donough O'Brien, Earl of Thomond; Murrough, the son of Murrough, son of Dermot, Baron of Inchiquin; and many other distinguished

[c] *Dun-Coillin*, now Dunkellin, in the parish of Killeely, which gave name to the barony of Dunkellin, in the county of Galway. Not far from this castle is a hill with a rude stone seat, or chair, called Clanrickard's chair, which is believed to be the place where the Mac William Oughter was inaugurated, before he became Earl of Clanrickard.

sochaiḋiḃ oile do ḋaġdaoiniḃ cenmoṫáṫ. Ba hann do rala don goibernoir bſiṫ an adhaiġ sin hi ccaislen ċuile maoíle fil for aḃainn móir fri sliaḃ gaṁ aniar [*recte* anoir], ⁊ fri sliaḃ dá én anoir [*recte* aniar] co ccoicc céd décc laoċ do gleire ġaisccſḋach ina ḟoċair ann. Ba conair ċoitcſnn nar bo soḋ-aing do seachna an ṁaiġſn i mbaoi sium. At cuas do Ruḋraiġe ua doṁnaill ⁊ do mac uilliam an gobernoir da bſiṫ rſmpa for an cconoir na ro ḟedsat do ṡeċna. Ar fair ro chinnsiot ó rangatar ria maidin i ngarfoccus don ċaislen, a ccſṫra, a ninnile, a ngiollanraiḋ, ⁊ a naés diairm do légaḋ uaṫa i sliġiḋ ba hinnille inás an conair in ro baḋ mſnmarc leo buḋſin do ġabail, ſḃ imchian on ċaislen, ⁊ iad buḋſisin do ḋul tar an aḃainn gan raṫuccaḋ hi ccoṁfocraiḃ an caisteóill ó naċ raḃsat coiṁlíon sloiġ fri a mbiodḃadaiḃ. Do codar soṁ tra gan airiuccaḋ gan forcloisteċt tar an aḃainn go mbatar don taoḃ araill. Andar leo soṁ ċſna do riġensat anacal ⁊ imoſgail dia ccſthraiḃ ⁊ dia ngiollanraiḋ, Nir bo haṁlaiḋ tarla doiḃsiḋe itir uair ro clos búireaḋ ḃéiceaḋ na mbó ṫainteaḋ, ⁊ na nanmann neicciallaiḋ, ⁊ foġurnuall aosa a niomána isin muiċdeḋoil. Do lſiccſt marcsloiġ an ġoiḃernora ina ndronġaiḃ ⁊ ina ndíormaiḃ fo ċoṁġáir na ccſṫra dus an ttairsittis iad. Ruccsatt din for inḋiliḃ iomḋaiḃ, ⁊ do ḋeachaiḋ in ro baḋ móo uaḋaiḃ dioḃ. Ro marḃaḋ drong ṁór do na gilliḃ ⁊ daos na hiomána. Ba don ċur sin do marḃaḋ Maolmuire mac Conulaḋ meic an baird saoí firḋana ro ḃaí ar ṁaiṫiḃ a ċeneoil buḋſin. Ní ro ḟédsat a muinntir buḋſisin anacal do taḃairt doiḃsiḋe la hiomat an tsloiġ do rala for a nionċaiḃ. Ba méla mór lais an ngobernoir a ndol seaċa seriú tarraiḋ grſim forra. Tiaġait na gaoiḋil ass aṁlaiḋ co rangatar tars an eirne buḋ tuaiḋ. Sóais an gobernoir ina ḟriṫing, ⁊ nír bó slán lais a ṁſnma ó do srnáirſt a naiṁde uaḋa iar na ffaġbail in uathaḋ aṁlaiḋ sin.

Fiacha mac Aoḋa mic Sſain o ġlſnd Mhaoilugra do ṫuitim iar ttar-

[d] *Abhainn-mhor*, i. e. the Great River, now *anglice* Avonmore, a river which rises in Templehouse lake, and joins the Coolany river between Collooney and Ballysadare.

[e] *Sliabh Gamh and Sliabh-da-en.*—These are mountains in the county of Sligo. The gap between them, in which the little town of Collooney stands, was anciently called Bearnas-mor Tire hOilella, i. e. the great gap of Tirerrill.—See map to *Genealogies, &c., of Hy-Fiachrach.*

[f] *This was not the case*, literally, "Not thus it happened to them indeed."

[g] *Of the irrational animals*, na nanmann néicciallaiḋ. This would be written na n-ainmiḋe n-éġcialla, according to the modern system of orthography. The prefix é, when negative,

men besides them. The Governor lay on the first night in the castle of Cul-Maoile [Collooney], which is situated on the Abhainn-mhor[d], to the east of Sliabh Gamh[e], and to the west of Sliabh dá-én, having fifteen hundred select warriors along with him there. This place where he remained was a general passage, and it was not easy to avoid it. Rury O'Donnell and Mac William were informed that the Governor was before them upon a road by which they could not avoid [passing]. And when before morning they had arrived at a place very near the castle, they resolved on sending off their herds and flocks, their calones, and the unarmed portion of their forces, by a way at a great distance from the castle, and more secure than that by which they themselves intended to proceed, whilst they themselves should cross the river without being noticed, at a short distance from the castle, as they had not a force equal to that of the enemy. They crossed the river [accordingly] unnoticed and unheard, and landed in safety at the other side; and they thought that they had ensured the safety and protection of their cattle and attendants; but this was not the case[f], for the loud lowing of the herds of kine and irrational animals[g], and the shouts of their drivers, were heard early in the morning from the castle; and the Governor's cavalry set out in troops and squadrons in the direction of the lowing of the cattle, to see if they could take them. They seized upon a great number of cattle, but the greater part of them escaped from them. A great number of the servants and drivers were killed. It was on this occasion also that Mulmurry, the son of Cu-Uladh Mac Ward, a learned poet, and one of the most distinguished men of his own tribe, was killed. Their own people were not able to protect them, in consequence of the great numbers that were opposed to them. It was great annoyance to the Governor that they should have passed him by before he could lay hold of them. The Irish thus made their way northwards across the Erne. The Governor returned back; and he was much dejected because his enemies had thus escaped from him.

Fiagh, son of Hugh[h], son of John [O'Byrne] from Glenmalure, was slain

eclispes the consonant to which it is prefixed.

[h] *Fiagh, son of Hugh.*—He was chief of that sept of the O'Byrnes called Gaval-Rannall, and had his residence at Ballinacor, in Glenmalure, in the county of Wicklow. Though not the chief of the O'Byrnes he was by far the most warlike and powerful man of his name since the death of Dunlang, the son of Edmond, who was the last inaugurated O'Byrne.—See note [t], under the year 1580, p. 1746, *supra*. There are several poems on his battles and victories preserved in the *Leabhar Branach*, or Book of the O'Byrnes,

raing ceilcce da combraṫair fair ar furáilṁ ard iustís na hEreann Sir uilliam Russel isin céd mí do ṡamrad na bliadna so.

preserved in the Library of Trinity College, Dublin, H. 1. 14, from one of which it would appear that all the O'Byrnes acknowledged him as their leader, if not chief; but it is quite evident that some of the senior branches of the O'Byrnes were very jealous of his greatness, and that this led to his betrayal and death is but too evident from these poems, and all contemporaneous authorities. P. O'Sullevan Beare briefly alludes to his betrayal in his *Hist. Cathol. Iber.*, tom. 3, lib. 3, c. x. fol. 145:

"Iam me Lageniorum res vocant, qui tametsi paruis viribus, magna tamen constantia, & virtute pro Catholica religione manum conseruerunt. Postquam Fiachus Obruin vir strenuus, & Hæreticorum hostis acerrimus fuit per proditionem extinctus, eius filij Felmius, & Raymundus arma a patre mota non omiserunt. Dum Raymundus in Lagenia tumultus in Hæreticum excitatos ducit, Felmius in Vltoniam ad Onellum contendit auxilium petitum."

There is a curious poem in the *Leabhar Branach*, fol. 110, *p. a.*, on the death of Fiagh, in which the writer states that he saw his body quartered and his head spiked on a tower in Dublin,—a sight which pierced his heart with anguish.

I. Fiagh O'Byrne left three sons, namely: 1, Felim, who was M. P. for the county of Wicklow in 1613, and who was living in 1629. 2, Redmond, or Raymond, of Killaveny, J. P. in the county of Wicklow in 1625, the ruins of whose castle are still to be seen, and are shewn on the Ordnance map as "Raymond's Castle." This Redmond had three sons: Felim of Killaveny; Feagh of Kilcloghran, proclaimed a rebel, and a price set on his head, 8th February, 1641; and John. 3, Turlough. And one daughter, who was married to Walter Reagh Fitzgerald, of whose fate some account is given under the year 1595.

II. Felim, son of Fiagh. He married Una, or Winifred Ni Toole. He was living in 1629, a prisoner in Dublin Castle. In his complaint to the Privy Council of his unjust trial and condemnation at Wicklow in 1628, he says that his wife, the mother of his five sons, who was in previous good health, died within two days after his condemnation: "her hart stringes broke."—MS., F. 3. 17, T. C. D. He had eight sons: 1, Brian, who, with his brother Turlough, was committed to Dublin Castle in 1625, and was living in 1629; 2, Hugh, Lieutenant-Colonel of the Confederate Catholics in 1641, and who was proclaimed a rebel by Parsons and Borlase, Lords Justices, 8th February, 1641; 3, Gerald, living in 1604, and seems to have died young, at least before 1628; 4, James, living in 1603; 5, Turlough, living in 1628; 6, Feagh, *alias* Luke; 7, Cahir, living in 1629; 8, Colla; and a daughter, who married John Wolverton, Esq. J. P. of the county of Wicklow in 1625. Seven of these sons are named in the above order in the remainders of Phelim mac Pheagh's grant of lands from King James I., dated 28th March, 1604. Colla, who was born after that period, is mentioned in Phelim mac Pheagh's suit in 1628-9, when he was a close prisoner in Dublin Castle with his five sons. Duald Mac Firbis mentions only three of his sons, namely, Hugh, Colla, and Brian. Cahir, his seventh son, had a son, Hugh, who had a son, Cahir, the last generation of this family given in the *Leabhar Branach.*

III. Brian, the son of Felim. He had a son, Shane mac Brian mac Phelim of Ballinacor, who was Colonel of the Confederate Catholics in 1641, after which period this family of Ballinacor disappear from history. The accusations against

in the first month of summer in this year, having been treacherously betrayed by his relative, at the bidding of the Chief Justiciary of Ireland, Sir William Russell.

these sons of Felim, on which their estates were confiscated, affords an appalling picture of human depravity and perfidy in those murderous times; but as the substance of them, and the manner in which the whole trial was conducted, has been already given by the late Matthew O'Conor, Esq. of Mount Druid, in his *History of the Irish Catholics*, the Editor shall rest content with laying before the reader the following extracts from Felim's complaint to the Privy Council, of his unjust trial and condemnation at Wicklow in 1628, as preserved in a manuscript in the Library of Trinity College, Dublin, F. 3. 17:

"Lord Esdmond tried to induce Owen Byrne, a prisoner in Dublin Castle, to accuse Bryan and Tirlagh (Phelim's sons), and racked him in vain for that purpose. Then Lord Esmond sent Cahir mac Hugh Duffe, a neare cousin of said Owen, and Morogh mac Hugh mac Owen, brother in law to said Owen, to use their influence to make him depose against Tirlagh and Phelim.

"This Cahir mac Hugh Duffe, and the said Morogh, are doeing, theise 29 years at least, what they could against Phelim and his sonnes, both in helping to take theire landes from them and inventing many false matters against them to procure their death, as is well known; for said Cahir mac Hugh Duffe and the aforesaid Morogh, and his son, Morrish, came to the Lord Chichester, then Deputy, and informed his Lordship that Phelim and Bryan releeved one Torlogh O'Toole, which his Lordship well knew was but meere malice.

"Garrald mac Ferdoragh being a prisoner for some criminal fact, which he acknwledged had no means to save his life but by accusing men, was procured by William Græme and others, to accuse Phelim and his sonnes. This Garret's father was committed to Wicklow by Phelim's son in law, John Wolverston, for stealing cows, and was executed for that fact. Gerald himself was committed for suspicion of felony by Phelim, but acquitted.

"This Garret's brother in law, Shane Bane mac Teige mac Hugh, being in rebellion, was taken by Hugh mac Phelim, and brought to Wicklow by the Lord Chief Justice, where he was executed, which said Garret bore in mynde to revenge it when he could.

"Shane O'Toole, Patricke O'Toole," [were] "prisoners in the castle of Dublin about 1621. Shane O'Toole was executed by martial law, and at his death left betweene him and God, that he was executed for not agreeing with said Garret mac Ferdoragh, and his confederates, in accusing Brian mac Felim, Tirlagh mac Phelim, and Cahir mac Phelim.

"Patrick O'Toole was pardoned for his accusations.

"Art O'Neale and Brian More, son in lawe to Art O'Neale, being in company with Donagh mac Shane, committing of a robbery, were taken by one of Phelim's sons, and the robbery found in their hands, were sent here to his Majestie's castle of Dublin, and seeing no other means to save their lives but to accuse others, as they were demanded, the said Arte O'Neale and Bryan More offered to make an escape at once with Dermot O'Toole, and to rob the porter's coffer.

"Shane Duffe mac Teige Moyle and Mortagh mac Teige Moyle, several times sollicited to accuse Phelim and his sons, and when they did not, they were two or three dayes bound, ready to be executed by martial lawe.

"Lord Esmond had, in his prison at Limerick" [near Gorey, county of Wexford], "one Laughlin More mac Teige, which Laughlin his

Iustis nua do ṫocht i nEirinn i ttosach mís Iun co narmail ⁊ co saighdiuiribh iomdaibh lais .i. Lord Burough, tomás a comhainm. Iar nglacadh an ċloidhimh dóiside on iustis baí ann fri ré trí mbliadhan go sin .i. Sir uilliam Russel, Ro benadh lais an oiffice do bí ag Sir Iohn norus ó na prionnsa de .i. generaltacht an ċoccaidh, ⁊ ro gabh féin an oiffice sin fri a ais. Tucc iaramh fóccra dfearaibh laighen, ⁊ midhe, ⁊ don mhéid baí umhal don bainrioghain o ċomar trí nuisce go dún dealgan toċt ina doċom (co líonmhar ler tionoilte an ficheatmhadh lá do mí iul) go droicheat aṫa. Ro freccradh na fóccarta sin la hiarla cille dara, la gallaibh midhe, ⁊ laighen. Tánaicc tra an Iustis gus an lion as lia ro ḟéd gus an maighin cceadna, ⁊ iar roċtain i ccenn a roile do na slóghaibh do arccnatar go tír eoghain co rangattar gan toirmeasc gan tairisiumh go habhainn móir, ⁊ an ní dob annamh la hUa neill frith faill iomcoimhétta

Lordship knows to be one that hated Felim and his sonnes. He was a foster-brother of Shane Bane mac Teige, which Hugh mac Phelim brought to Wicklow to execution.

"Phelim mac Pheagh took two of those that were concerned in Pont's murder.

"The Sheriff that impanelled the grand jury which found several bills against Phelim and his sonnes, is married to Lord Esmond's niece, and tenant to Sir William Parsons, and the Lord Esmond procured this, his nephew, to be made Sheriffe of sett purpose to conclude his owne, and the rest of said Phelim's adversaries, their pretended and long-continued unjust hosting, and therefore said Sheriff elected Sir James Fitz Pierce to be forman of the grand jurie, a known open enemy to Phelim and his sons; first, because he sett upon said Phelim at his going to Rathcuile, to the late Earl of Ormond; secondly, because Phelim was at the killing of said Sir James, his father; and thirdly, because the said Sir James did, for proofe of his continuall malice, prefer a peticion to the Lord Grandison, alledging the said Phelim and his predecessors to be all bastards for ten or eleven degrees. Moreover, said Sir James had no freehold in the county of Wicklow.

"Finally, said Brien and Turlogh are most miserably kept in close restraint here in his Majestie's Castle of Dublin, without getting their dyett from his Majestie, or leave for any of theire friends to come to them with their owne meanes to releeve them in presence of the constable and his son. Their accusers, on the contrary, are kept at his Majesties charges, and besides, Bryan and Turlogh have irons upon them, and the most part of their condemned accusers are without irons.

"(Signed), BRYNE BYRNE.
TIRLAGH BEARNE.

"*Copia vera.*"

The Editor has not been able to trace the history of this family to a later period, and believes that the race of Fiagh mac Hugh O'Byrne, chief of Gaval-Rannall, have long since become extinct. According to the tradition in the country, the late Garrett Byrne, Esq. of Ballymanus, was not of his descendants, but of a branch of the Gaval-Rannall who became spies and informers to ruin the great O'Byrnes of Ballinacor, a tradition which clearly points to Cahir mac Hugh Duffe and his confederates above referred to, who were for twenty-nine years inventing many false matters against Phelim and his sons.

A new Lord Justice, Lord Borough[i], Thomas by name, arrived in Ireland in the beginning of the month of June, with much arms and many soldiers. After receiving the sword from Sir William Russell, who had been Lord Justice for three years before, he deprived Sir John Norris of the office which he held from his Sovereign, namely, the generalship of the war, and took that office to himself. After this he issued a proclamation to the men of Leinster and Meath, and to all those who were obedient to the Queen, from the Meeting of the three Waters to Dundalk, to meet him with all their forces, fully mustered, at Drogheda, on the twentieth day of the month of July. These orders were responded to by the Earl of Kildare, and by the English of Meath and Leinster. The Lord Justice came to the same place with as many men as he had been able to muster. After these forces had met together, they marched to Tyrone, and arrived at Abhainn-mhor without opposition or delay; and, what was seldom

See note [n], under the year 1585, p. 1840, *supra*. The Ballymanus family, too, are either extinct or reduced to poverty and obscurity.

The Lord Esmond who ruined the illustrious family of Ballinacor, was Sir Laurence Esmond, the son of William Esmond, Esq., of Little Limerick, near Gorey, in the county of Wexford. He married a Miss Ellice Butler, by whom he had no issue, and the peerage ceased at his death; but it appears that he had a natural son, Thomas Esmond, by a Miss O'Flaherty, to whom his estates passed by will. This Thomas Esmond, who was educated a Roman Catholic by his mother, is the ancestor of the present Sir Thomas Esmond of Ballynatrasna, in the county of Wexford, who inherits none of the wickedness or treachery of the Lord Esmond his progenitor.

William Parsons was a very poor man, in humble station, who came to Ireland towards the close of the reign of Elizabeth. He proved a very useful discoverer of forfeited estates in the capacity of Surveyor-General. He was appointed Lord Justice, with Sir John Borlase, in 1640, and continued in the Government till 1643, when he was removed, charged with treason, and committed to prison, with Sir Adam Loftus and others. His descendants became extinct in the male line in 1764. The present Earl of Ross, so illustrious for his scientific attainments, descends from his brother, Laurence Parsons.

[i] *Lord Borough*.—Thomas Baron Borough, a man almost wholly ignorant of the art military, was appointed Lord Deputy, and arrived in Dublin on the 15th of May, and received the sword in St. Patrick's Church on Sunday, the 22nd of the same month. He had supreme authority in martial as well as civil causes, and immediately ordered to his presidency of Munster General Norris, who is described by Camden as "Vir sanè magnus, & ìnter maximos nostræ gentis hoc ævo duces celebrandus; which affront (together with the disappointment of the chief government, which he knew he merited, and earnestly expected), and the many baffles Tyrone had put upon him, broke his heart."—See Cox's *Hibernia Anglicana*, vol. i. p. 413. P. O'Sullevan Beare states that it was believed that Norris had sold himself to the devil, who carried him off unexpectedly; and he gravely concludes from this, that O'Neill had often defeated, not only

fair co rainicc an lustis tar an aḃainn gan taċar, gan toirmeascc go mbaí don taoḃ araill di. Ro muraḋ ⁊ ro morclaiḋeaḋ las an lustis an port iomcoiṁeta baí acc ua neill for ur na haḃainn, ⁊ ro toccaiḃ fein port nua dó buḋein isin mbruaċ alltarach don aḃainn ċeona. ⁊ ge ro fríṫ an uain sin ar Ua neill tre eolus ⁊ tre ṫionċoscc ṫoirrdelbaiġ, mic Enri, mic Feilim ruaidh uí neill ní ro laṁ an lustis, na aen dia ṡloġaiḃ dol fó aén mile tairis sin i ttir eoġain, ⁊ ní mó ro leicceaḋ suan no saḃaile, codlaḋ, no cuṁsanaḋ doiḃ acht deaḃaiḋ ⁊ diuḃraccaḋ forra ó ṁuinntir Uí néill do ló ⁊ doiḋce. Ḃá dirím doairneaḋsis an ro marḃaḋ, ⁊ in ro muḋaiġeaḋ do daoiniḃ an lustis, ⁊ an ro bearnaḋ deaċaiḃ, ⁊ dedalaiḃ dioḃ.

Do ḋeachaiḋ an lustis in aroile lo for cnoc bai i ccoṁfoċraiḃ don campa do ṁiḋeaṁain ⁊ do ṁoirḋeċain an tire ina uirṫimcell, ⁊ ba ferr dó na tíosaḋ ioir, uair do marḃaḋ drong ṁor dia deaġdaoiniḃ la hUa neill co

General Norris, "peritissimum Anglorum imperatorum omni pugnandi apparatu superiorem, *sed ipsum etiam diabolum*, qui illi ex pacto fuisse opitulatus creditur vicerit."—*Hist. Cathol. Iber. Compend.*, tom. iii. l. 3, c. x.

[j] *An advantage was got.*—An English writer would say: "And O'Neill having, contrary to his wont, neglected to guard the pass, the Lord Justice crossed the river without any difficulty."

[k] *Further:* literally, "beyond that."

[l] *A hill.*—P. O'Sullevan Beare calls this hill *Droum fliuca*, which he translates *Collis madidus*, in his *Hist. Cathol. Ibern. Compend.*, tom. iii. l. 3, c. xi. where he gives the following curious account of this conflict:

"Annus ab ortu Domini millesimus quingentesimus nonagesimus septimus cum verteretur, Thomas Burughi Baro vir animo elatus, manu largus, belli præceptis imbutus, comitate gratus in Iberniam Prorex missus aduentu primo suo, qua erat vrbanitate, & affabilitate, aliquot Lageniorum, & aliorum Ibernorum animos in se conuertit. Cum Onello, Odonello, & alijs vnum mensem inducias componit. Per quas cum de pacis conditionibus minimé conuenisset, maiorem belli molem in Onellum vertit. Illi copiosus erat exercitus, qui anteà sub Rusello, & Norrise meruerant, & nouè ex Anglia missi; quibus cum in Vltoniam proficiscitur. Sequuntur Midhienses Angloiberni cum iustis copijs duce Barnabale Balisimiledæ Barone. Quo procedente Balarriecham peruenerat Richardus Tirellus cum quadringentis peditibus ab Onello missus, vt motus, vel in Lagenia augeret, vel in Midhia moueret. Is Tirellus Angloibernus erat, sed Catholicus, sicut cæteri, & iniurijs Anglorum prouocatus é carcere ad Onellum fugerat. Ei cum tam exiguas vires esse Barnabal comperisset, in illum mittit filium suum peditibus mille stipatum, haud dubius, quin adolescens dignum aliquod facinus faceret, quo Proregem magno merito sibi deuinciret, Tirellus miles veteranus prælio expertus Midhienses fundit, & fugat, atque multis occisis Barnabalis filium captum ad Onellum defert, á quo fuit posteà pretio commutatus.

"Burughus Ardmacham, & Portmorem, quas Onellus deseruit, occupat. Progredi frustra tentat ab Onello prohibitus, qui duobus castris vias occludit: in alteris erant Macmagaunus, & fratres Onelli Cormakus, & Artus in Colle madido castrametati intra duos iactus bombardæ

the case with O'Neill, an advantage was got[j] of his vigilance, having, contrary to his wont, neglected to guard the pass, and the Lord Justice crossed the river without [receiving] battle or opposition, and landed [safely] at the other side of it. He then razed and demolished a watching-fort which O'Neill had on the bank of the river, and erected a new fort for himself on the opposite bank of the same river. But though this advantage was taken of O'Neill, through the guidance and instruction of Turlough, the son of Henry, son of Felim Roe O'Neill, neither the Lord Justice nor any of his forces dared to advance the distance of one mile further[k] into Tyrone; for they were not allowed rest or ease, sleep or quiet, but a succession of skirmishes and firing was kept up on them, both by day and night. It would be impossible to calculate or describe the number of the Lord Justice's men who were killed and disabled, and the number of horses and [other] spoils that were taken from them, on this occasion.

On a certain day the Justice went upon a hill[l] which was near the camp, to reconnoitre and survey the country around; but it would have been better for him that he had not gone thither, for a great number of his chief men

ad hostem, in via, quæ ducit ad Pinnam superbam: in alteris Onellus ipse cum Iaimo Macdonello Glinniæ principe tentoria pandit ad Fontem Masanum. Prorex itinere prohibitus Norrisium munimentum, quod Onellus diruerat, reædificare cœpit, Onellus opus impedire: interdiu, & noctu ab equitibus, & peditibus maximé iaculatoribus cominus, & eminus leuia prælia committuntur. Onello venit auxilio Odonellus, cuius equitatus, cum hostis equitibus, & Terentio Onello Henrici filio Onelli fratre vterino, qui Reginæ partes sequebatur egregiè manum conseruit. Nocte, qua Catholici in regiorum castra impetum fecerunt, fama tenet, Prorogem fuisse vulneratum, quæ veranè sit, ad me periculum non recipio. Constat illum ex castris reuersum Killdario comiti imperium relinquentem intra paucos dies è vita discessisse.

"Kildarius imperio lætus, & glorians, quod Prorex efficere non potuit, præstare conatur, vlterius progredi. Per syluam, & vias occultas cum nobilioribus equitibus & magis strenuis militibus procedens, postquam itineris maximam difficultatem superauit, nuncio allato Catholici occurrentes prælium committunt: quo sunt occisi sexaginta equites regij, & inter eos Turner exercitus regij Tesserarius Maximus, Franciscus VVaghan Proregis leuir, Thomas VValenus Angli. Comes Killdarius hastarum ictibus equo turbatus, rursus in equum impositus à duobus fratribus Ohikijs Ibernis suæ nutricis filijs malè concussus, & vulneratus fugit, & paucis etiam post diebus moritur. Ohikij dum herum in equum imponunt, ipsi circumuenti interficiuntur. Multi regij fuerunt vulneribus affecti: quotquot eo in loco à castris aberant, fusi, & fugati in castra compulsi sunt. Citò regius exercitus domum redit, postquam inter Portmorem, & Pinnam suberbam à fine veris per menses circiter quatuor cum Catholico dimicauit, & præsidio Portmore sub Thoma Villiamse Anglo, & Ardmachæ relicto. Mox quoque Iberni, quos Burughus Reginæ consiliauerat, rebellarunt.

na muinntir. Ro baḋ diḃside dearbraṫair mna an lustís, ⁊ ardmaor a ṡluaiġ co sochaiḋe moir do ċaiptinib ⁊ do daoinib uaisle cenmoṫát. Ro marḃaḋ ann din araill do muinntir iarla ċille dara, ⁊ munbuḋ goire an ċampa don lustis ní raghaḋ ass an iomairscc sin an lion do érna ḋíoḃ. Do rala diarla cille dara (.i. henrí mac ġḟroitt tre biṫin gona, no ḟiaḃrasa cecib díoḃ) gur bó hḟiccḟn dó triall tar a ais do ṡaiġiḋ a aṫarda, ⁊ iar roċtain dó go droicḟt áṫa fuair bás isin mbaile sin. Ruccaḋ a corp go cill dara ⁊ ro haḋnaicḟoh co nonoir ⁊ co nairmittin i noṫairliġe a ṡinnsear he. Ro hoirdneaḋ a ḋḟrbraṫair .i. Uilliam ina ionad.

Iar ccríochnuccaḋ an ṗuirt nuí sin las an lustis ar brú aḃann moire, ⁊ iar ttaḃairt da uíḋ a ḋioṫ daoine, ⁊ ná ro léicceaḋ dó dol tairis sin isteach isin tír do ċuir biaḋ ⁊ bárda isin mbaile, ⁊ ro triall fḟin toċt tar a ais. Do ċóiḋ cétus don iuḃar, ⁊ assaiḋe co haṫ cliaṫ, ⁊ ro sccaoilsiot a ṡluaġ dia ttiġibh.

An tan tra ro triall an lustis gus an sloiġḟḋ céona i ttír eóġain, Ro cuir sgríbḟnn go gobernoir ċoicciḋ connaċt dia ḟorċongra fair dol gus an lion sluaigh as lia no biaḋ ina ċumang isin ccḟnn ṫiar do coicceaḋ ulaḋ for Ua ndomnaill an ccḟin no biaḋ soṁ i ttír eoġain. Nir bo hḟislisea ċ ro frecsraḋ an ḟorcongra sin las in ngobernóir, uair ro ċuir toġairm for iarla tuaḋmuṁan donnchaḋ mac concobair, ⁊ for ḃarun innsi uí chuinn Murċaḋ mac Murchaiḋ, for iarla cloinne riocaird uillecc mac Riocaird Shaxanaiġ, ⁊ for a ṁac Riocard mac uillicc barún dúine coillin. Ro ċuir ḃḟos toġairm ⁊ tionól for uaislib ċonntae maiġe eó, ⁊ Rossa commain co na sochraite. Do ṗorail for na maiṫiḃ uile toċt ina ḋocom go mainistir na buille an cḟṫramaḋ lá fiċḟt do mí Iul do ṡonraḋ, ⁊ go mbiaḋ fḟin co na ḃandaḋaiḃ for a ccind an dú sin. Tangatar side uile gus in maiġin remraite isin ló cḟttna. Ba he lion a ttionoil iar roċtain i ccenn aroile doiḃ da bratṫaiġ ar ḟiċit do ṫroiġṫeċaiḃ, ⁊ deiċ mbratacha marcṡloiġ. Ro ascnatar airiḋe go Slicceaċ, ⁊ iaraṁ go heirne go ro ġabsat longport lionṁar lainṁḟnmnaċ

[m] *The brother.*—This was Sir Francis Vaughan. Sir Richard Cox, who passes over this battle very lightly, says, "that after the Lord Deputy had taken the fort of Blackwater, and garrisoned it with English, returned thanks to God for this victory, but that they were called from prayers to arms upon the appearance of the Irish forces, with whom they skirmished successfully; yet so as that the Deputy's brother-in-law (Vaughan) and several others were slain,

were slain by O'Neill and his people. Among these were the brother[m] of the Lord Justice's wife, and the chief officer of his army, together with a great number of captains and other gentlemen besides. Some of the Earl of Kildare's people were also slain there; and had not the camp of the Lord Justice been so near at hand, the number that escaped would have survived this engagement. The Earl of Kildare (Henry, the son of Garret), in consequence either of a wound or a fever, was obliged to set out on his return home; but when he had gone as far as Drogheda he died in that town. His body was carried to Kildare, and interred with great honour and reverence in the burial-place of his ancestors. His brother, William, was installed in his place.

The Lord Justice, after having finished the new fort[n] on the bank of the Abhainn-mhor, and having observed his loss of men, and that he was not permitted to penetrate further into the country, he placed provisions and warders in this fort, and then set out to return back. He went first to Newry, and from thence to Dublin, and his army dispersed for their [several] homes.

At the time that the Lord Justice was engaged in the foregoing expedition, he sent a written dispatch to the Governor of Connaught, ordering him to proceed, with all the forces he could possibly muster, to the western extremity of Ulster, against O'Donnell, while he himself should remain in Tyrone. This order was promptly[o] responded to by the Governor; for he sent for the Earl of Thomond (Donough, the son of Conor), for the Baron of Inchiquin (Murrough, the son of Murrough), for the Earl of Clanrickard (Ulick, the son of Rickard Saxonagh), and his son, Rickard, Baron of Dunkellin; and also dispatched orders to the gentlemen of the counties of Mayo and Roscommon, requiring them to collect and muster their forces. He ordered all the chieftains to meet him at the monastery of Boyle, on the twenty-fourth day of the month of July, precisely when he himself, with all his bands [of soldiers], would be at that place. They all [accordingly] came on that day to the aforesaid place. When assembled, they amounted to twenty-two standards of foot, and ten standards of cavalry. They marched from thence to Sligo, and from thence to the Erne, and pitched

and particularly two foster-brothers of Henry, Earl of Kildare, for grief whereof the Earl soon after dyed."—*Hibernia Anglicana*, vol. i. p. 413.

[n] *The new fort*.—Moryson says that this English fort "was only a deep trench or wall of earth, to lodge some one hundred soldiers in."—Vol. i. p. 58.

[o] *Promptly*: literally, "not negligently."

for ur Samhaoire fríoḃglaisi. Ro baí do ṁenmnaiġe an tslóiġ hisin andar leó co na baí cumang i ffreastail nó a ffrioṫolma i ccoicceaḋ ulaḋ uile.

Do eirġestar slóġ an ġobernora isin muichḃeḋoil ar a barach do ḋul tar an aḃainn. Bai din iomċoiṁéd o ua ndoṁnaill for gach náṫ for an éirne. Acht ċena fuaratar soṁ baoġal for áṫ niomḃoraiḋ buí fuirre .i. áth cúil uain, ⁊ ro chingsiot go diocra dúrcroidheach do saiġiḋ an áṫa hísin. Ro ġaḃsat na forcoiṁedaiġe occa ndiubraccaḋ gan dichell, ⁊ acc iomċosnaṁ an áṫa friú aṁail ar deach ro ḟedsat. Acht chena ní ro chumaingsiot a ċianċosnaṁ fris in líon sloiġ ⁊ soċaiḋe batar ina naghaiḋ go riacht an gobernoir co na sloġaiḃ tairis co mbattar don taeḃ araill. Ar a aoí tra do rónaḋ echt aḋḃal an lá sin .i. Murchaḋ mac Murchaḋa mic diarmata, mic Murchaḋa uí briain barún innsi uí chuinn. Baí side allamuiġ do na saiġdiuiriḃ for a eoċ eattorra, ⁊ a niomḃoṁain occa nimdeaġail for ḃaṫaḋ, ⁊ acca mbrosdaḋ tairis. Ba sedh ro chedaiġ an chinnemhain dó a amus co hinnelldírech la haon do ṁuintir uí doṁnaill durchor pilér i scaoileaḋ a éideḋ plata i ndeirc a occraille co ndechaiḋ tremitt isin deirc araill. Ní ro cuimgeḋ a anacal go ro sgarccar fri a eoch i fuḋoṁain an tsrota go ro baideḋ é fo ċedóir. Ba hecht mór eidir gallaib, ⁊ gaoiḋelaibh an tí torċair annsin, ar airde a inme, ⁊ ar uaisle a ḟola ger bo hócc ar aoí naoisi eiside, ⁊ gemaḋ toccbail a ċuirp ⁊ a aḋnacal co honórach ro dlecht do ḋenaṁ, ni ro hanaḋ frisiḋe las an slóġ acht roċtain gan oirisiuṁ go mainistir easra ruaiḋ. An 31 do mí iul do riachtattar an dú sin, ⁊ dia Saṫairn ar aoi laiṫe sechtmaine. Ro ġabsat longport ar gach taoḃ don ṁainistir i muiġ, ⁊ istiġ. Batar hisuiḋe on tan tangatar tar eirne ria mednón laí dia Saṫairn co madain dia luain. Ba isin doṁnach sin batar isin mainistir tangatar an loingeas ro ġeall ina ndiaiḋ o ġaillim i mbaoí a nordanas, ⁊ a ngonnaḋa mora co na stoirus archena ar ḋaiġ a niompulaing an ceein no beitis isin ccoiccrich.

[p] *Samhaoir:* i. e. the River Erne.

[q] *Ath Cul-Uain.*—See this ford already mentioned at the years 1247 and 1593.

[r] *And he fell:* literally, "he could not be protected until he was separated from his horse in the depth of the stream," which would sound very strangely in English.

P. O'Sullevan Beare observes that the Baron of Inchiquin and O'Conor Sligo vied with each other in valour in crossing the ford on this occasion:

"In ipso vado, vt alias, Oconchur, & Maurus Baro de virtute certabant, & dum vterque alterum præcedere conatur, Maurum suus equus in alveum lapsus discutit, & Maurus armorum pondere grauis in imum flumen haustus amplius

their extensive camp on the banks of the limpid Samhaoir[p]. The high spirit of this army was such, that they thought that all Ulster would be incapable of coping with them in battle.

On the following morning, by break of day, the Governor's army rose up to cross the river; [but] O'Donnell had posted guards upon all the fords of the Erne. However, they got an advantage at one difficult ford, namely, Ath-Cul-Uain[q], and to this they vigorously and resolutely advanced. The guards of the ford proceeded to shoot at them without mercy, and to defend the ford against them as well as they were able; but they were not able to defend it long against the numerous force and army opposed to them; so that the Governor and his army crossed it, and gained the other side. On this day, however, a lamentable death took place, namely, [that of] Murrough, the son of Murrough, son of Dermot, son of Murrough O'Brien, Baron of Inchiquin, as he was on horseback, in the depth of the river, outside the soldiers, saving them from drowning, and encouraging them to get across past him. But destiny permitted that he was aimed at by one of O'Donnell's people with a ball exactly in the arm-pit, in an opening of his plate armour, so that it passed through him, and out at the opposite arm-pit. No assistance could be given him; and he fell[r] from his horse into the depth of the current, in which he was immediately drowned. The person who there perished was much lamented by the English and Irish, on account of the greatness of his wealth, and the nobility of his blood, though young as to age; and although it would have been meet that his body should have been taken up, and honourably interred, the army did not stop to do so, but proceeded directly to the monastery of Assaroe[s], which they reached the 31st of July, the day of the week being Saturday. They encamped around the monastery, and also within it, and thus remained from the forenoon of Saturday, when they crossed the Erne, until Monday morning. On the Sunday on which they were in the monastery the ships arrived which were promised to be sent after them from Galway, with ordnance and great guns, and other stores for their support, whilst they should

non extitit. Cliffordus vadum trajectus frustra repugnantibus paucis ab Odonello dispositis arcem quatuor tormentis oppugnat."—Fol. 161.

[s] *Assaroe.*—Some of the walls of this abbey are still to be seen about a mile to the west of Ballyshannon, and its burial ground is very extensive, and contains some interesting tomb-stones.—See note [l], under 1184, p. 64, *supra.*

Ro ġabsat an loingſs sin cuan acc inis Saiṁer i nucht earra ruaiḋ, ⁊ ro ċuirsiot a ttórus isin inis go líon a iomċoimſtta maille fris. Do rattaḋ dna an tordanas i ttír dia luain, ⁊ ro suiḋiġſḋ é ro ercoṁair ċaisléin Ḃeoil áṫa sſnaiġ. Ruccsat a slóġ on mainistir go mullaċ Síṫe Aoḋa ar aghaiḋ an dúnaiḋ, ⁊ i ttimceall an ordanáis. Ro ġabsat dia luain, dia mairt, ⁊ dia céḋaoín acc diubraccaḋ an baile do ċaeraiḃ tromaiḃ, torannṁóraiḃ teinntiḋi, a gonnaḋaiḃ guṫárḋaiḃ gránoiḃleaċaiḃ an ordanais iomṫruim aḋbail ṁoir hi sin ro ṡuiḋiġsiot for ionċaiḃ an dúnaiḋ, go cclos a ffuamanna ⁊ a ffoġarṫormán i ccléiṫiḃ aeoir, a ffod, ⁊ in imċſin uaḋaiḃ. Ro lasat dronga diomóra do roiġniḃ a laoċ fó ḃun an baile co trealmaiḃ toġalta múr leó, co nſioſḃ nimpſmar niomdaingſn niarnaiġe imá ccorpaiḃ, co ccaṫ-barraiḃ caéṁṗolurtaiḃ ima cſnḋaiḃ co léiḃſnḋ lainḋſrḋa do ċruinnsicciaṫaiḃ coiṁlſtna cruaiḋ iarainn ina nuirṫimċeall dia nimḋſġail for diubraicṫiḃ a namat. Nir bó torḃa doiḃrium ón an daġḟuabairt do bſrtsat for an dúnaiḋ, ⁊ ba fſrr dóiḃ na tiastair an turas do ḋeaċatar dia ṡaiġiḋ, uair ro dáilte ar an ccaislen forra froissċſta caer ttaiḋliġ tteinntiḋe a gonn-aḋaiḃ foraiġṫe fírḋírġe, ⁊ a musccaéḋiḃ morċortais, ⁊ araile do ċairrgiḃ cſnngarḃaiḃ ⁊ do tromclocaiḃ tuiniġṫe, do ṡailgiḃ, do ṡonnaiḃ baí for tailḃliḃ an dúnaiḋ ro ercoṁair a ndiubraicṫe, co nar bo dion no daingſn do luċt na toġla na cumdaiġṫe battar forra go ro muḋaiġſḋ dronga dſrṁára diḃriḋe, ⁊ co ro scioṫaiġſḋ araill báttar bſoġonta co nar anrat re a nairleach ní baḋ síri, ⁊ do bertsat a ndromanna fri a naimdiḃ co raeiṁeaḋ forra gus an ccampa. Ḃatar luċt an dúnaiḋ acca ndiuḃraccaḋ ina ndeaḋhaiḋ co ro marḃaḋ cinnteċ ar eccinnteċ dioḃ.

[t] *Inis-Saimher*, now called in Irish Inis Saṁaoir, and sometimes Fish Island, from a fish-house which was built on it by the late Dr. Sheil of Ballyshannon. It is situated immediately under the great cataract at Ballyshannon.

[u] *The ordnance.*—P. O'Sullevan Beare states that they planted four cannon against the castle of Ballyshannon, which was then defended by Hugh Craphurd [Crawford], a Scotchman, with eighty soldiers, of whom some were Spaniards and the rest Irish. They left three of these cannon behind.—*Hist. Cathol. Iber.*, tom 3, lib. 5, c. viii. fol. 160, 161.

[w] *The castle of Ballyshannon.*—The site of this castle is pointed out in a field on the east side of the town of Ballyshannon, called the Castle Park, but the walls are level with the ground and scarcely traceable.

[x] *Mullach-Sithe-Aedha*: i. e. the hill or summit of Aedh's tumulus, so called from Aedh Ruadh mac Badhairn, king of Ireland, who was drowned in the River Erne or Samhaoir, A. M. 3603, according to O'Flaherty's Chronology,

remain in this strange territory. This fleet put in at Inis-Saimer[t], close to Assaroe, and landed their stores on the island, leaving a sufficient number to guard them. On Monday the ordnance[u] were landed and planted against the castle of Bally-shannon[w]. The troops were then removed from the monastery to Mullach-Sithe-Aedha[x], opposite the fortress, and about the ordnance. On Monday, Tuesday, and Wednesday, they continued to fire on the castle[y] with heavy balls, emitted with loud report and flashing flames from the loud-sounding, red, shot-vomiting guns of that heavy and immense ordnance which they had planted opposite the fortress, so that their reports and loud thundering in the regions of the air were heard far and distant from them. They sent large parties of their choicest soldiers to the base of the castle with wall-razing engines, and with thick and strong iron armour about their bodies, and bright-shining helmets on their heads, and with a bright testudo of round, broad, hard iron shields around them, to protect them from the shots of their enemies. The resolute attack they made upon the fortress, however, was of no avail to them; and it had been better for them that they had not come upon this journey against it; for from the castle were poured down upon them showers of brilliant fire from well-planted, straight [aimed] guns, and from costly muskets, and some rough-headed rocks and massive solid stones, and beams and blocks of timber, which were [kept] on the battlements of the fortress, in readiness to be hurled down [when occasion required]; so that the coverings of the razing party were of no shelter or protection to them, and great numbers of them were destroyed, and others who were severely wounded became so exhausted that they delayed not to be further slaughtered, and, turning their backs to their enemies, they were routed to the camp. The people of the fortress kept up a constant fire on them, and killed an unascertained number of them.

and buried at this place.—See note [n], under the year 1194, p. 99, *supra*. This hill is now called Mullaghnashee, and the parish church of Bally-shannon stands upon it. According to the tradition at Ballyshannon, an ancient earthen fort, and the mound of Aedh Ruadh, or Red Hugh, were destroyed in 1798, to form a modern English star-fort which now crowns the summit of Mullaghnashee.

[y] *They continued to fire on the castle.*—The original could not bear to be literally translated into English. The closest that could be understood is the following: "They proceeded on Monday, Tuesday, and Wednesday, shooting at the bally with heavy, loud-sounding, fiery balls from the loud-roaring, shot-vomiting guns of that heavy and immensely great ordnance which they planted opposite the fortress." The word

Do ḃertsat drong do marcṡloiġ Ui domnaill saiġin iomruaicṫi for marc-sloiġ na ngall, ⁊ nír tá i ffforaiṫmet no i ccuiṁne in ro gonaḋ etorra cen-moṫa Ua concobair Sligiġ donnchaḋ mac caṫail oig ro gaetta eiside don ċur sin, uair baí side ⁊ o concobair ruaḋ Aoḋ mac toirrdealbaiġ ruaiḋ ⁊ teroitt na long co líon a soċraitte i ffarraḋ an ġobernora an tan sin.

O domnaill dna bairiḋe i tteirce sloiġ, ⁊ in uathaḋ soċaiḋe an Saṫarn tanaicc an Gobernoir gur an ttromḋáiṁ sin don tír. Ro ḃatar a ḋaoíne ⁊ a ṡoċraitte acc tecclaim ⁊ acc tionol as gaċ aird ina ḋoċom, go riaċta-tar a nurṁor ria miḋmeḋon dia luain. Tánaic din Máguiḋir Aoḋ mac con connaċt mic conconnaċt ⁊ o Ruairc Brian ócc, mac Briain, mic Briain ḃallaiġ co na ttionól ina ḋoċom, ⁊ iar roċtain do na maiṫiḃ sin i ccenn a roile, nír ḃó suaiṁneċ sáḋal ro leiccriot don gobernóir co na sloġaiḃ, uair ro bai deaḃaiḋ, ⁊ diuḃraccaḋ, iomairecc ⁊ iombualaḋ, ⁊ iomruaccaḋ uaṫa for an ccampa gaċ laoí fri ré na trí lá ro ḃatar som ag buanċaiṫem an baile. No ċuirdís slóġ uí domnaill ciomṡa an ċampa ċonnaċtaiġ ina ċertmeḋon, ⁊ a lar ina leiṫimel co ná leiccdís ingeltraḋ dia neċaiḃ nó dia nairnéis tar colḃa an ċampa amach ⁊ ní mó ro leiccriot fén, nó arḃar dia saiġiḋ anonn. Ro bai tra an gobernoir co na sloġ i tteennta ⁊ in iomċuṁga móir deriḋe, uair gemaḋ sóaḋ ro baḋ lainn leó ní bai ina ccuṁang aén áṫ coitċenn for an Eirne do ṡaiġiḋ ó ċaoluisce co haṫ senaiġ. Nír ḃó slán las ná maiṫiḃ a menma (gerḃo hiolarḋa a soċraitte) ar a tteccmail i nedarḃaoġal amlaiḋ sin aga naiṁdiḃ. An tan imorro do ḃert an gobernoir, na hiarlaḋa, ⁊ na maiṫe archena dia nuíḋ an guassaċt ro ṁór irrabatar ro ġaḃsat ag cruḋ a ccoṁairle o túr oiḋche dia céḋaoin go dorḃsolus na maidne dia dardaín .i. an 15 dAugust. Coniḋ fair derid leo fo deóiḋ isin moiċḋeadoil ceimniuccaḋ ar a ccertaghaiḋ on maiġin i mbattar hi Síṫh Aoḋa gur an leic ainṁín, aggairḃ, ḟuarrsothaiġ, ḟuḋoṁain os ur earsa

caor, or caer, means a mass of iron, a fire-brand, a thunderbolt, but is here applied to a cannon ball. It will be observed that Ordunais is in the genitive case singular, governed by gonnaḋaiḃ, from which it is clear that they took ordnance to be a generic term.

[z] *Cael-Uisge*, i. e. narrow water, now Cael-na-h-Eirne, where the Lower River Erne escapes from the lake.

[a] *Ath-Seanaigh*, i. e. Seanach's Ford. This was the name of a ford on the River Erne at the town of Ballyshannon, which has taken its name from it.

[b] *Rocky ford*, leic.—The word leic is the oblique form of leac, a flag-stone, or flat surface, such as exists in many places at the bottom of

A party of O'Donnell's cavalry made a routing attack upon the English cavalry; and there is no record or remembrance of the numbers that were [mortally] wounded between them; but, among the rest, O'Conor Sligo (Donough, the son of Cathal Oge) was severely wounded, for he and O'Conor Roe (Hugh, son of Turlough Roe) and Theobald-na-Long, with all their forces, were along with the Lord Justice at this time.

O'Donnell, however, had been in want of forces, and had only a small number on the Saturday on which the Lord Justice came into the country with this powerful force; but his people and forces were assembling and flocking to him from every direction, so that the most of them had reached him before the noon of Monday. On this occasion Maguire (Hugh, the son of Cuconnaught, son of Cuconnaught) and O'Rourke (Brian Oge, the son of Brian, son of Brian Ballagh) came to join him, with their forces; and after these chiefs had assembled together, they allowed the Lord Justice and his army neither ease nor rest, for they carried on skirmishing and firing, conflict, assault, and onslaught, on the camp, every day during the three days that they continued battering the castle. O'Donnell's army frequently drove those who were on the outskirts of the Connaught camp into the very centre of it, and those who were in the centre to the outskirts; and they did not permit their horses or other cattle to go forth outside the boundary camp to graze, nor did they permit hay or corn [to be carried] in to them. The Governor and his army were thus reduced to great distress and extremities; for, though they should wish to depart, they could not approach any common ford on the Erne from Cael-Uisge[a] to Ath-Seanaigh[a]. The chiefs, though numerous were their forces, were much dispirited on finding themselves placed in such peril by their enemies. When, therefore, the Governor, the Earls, and the chiefs in general, had perceived the great danger in which they were, they held a consultation from the beginning of night on Tuesday, to the morning twilight of Wednesday, the 15th of August; and the resolution they finally came to at the day-break was, to advance forward at once from the place where they were at Sith-Aedha to the rough, turbulent, cold-streamed, rocky ford[b] over the brink of Assaroe, called

the River Erne. In the Life of Hugh Roe O'Donnell the reading is as follows:

"Do berṫsat iarom a n-uċtḃruinne for an sliġe n-aġairḃ n-ainmeinic sin, ⁊ ro baoi do ṫreisi ⁊ do ṫrennsic hi sruṫ na Sinaḃann (aṁail ro ba bés di), ⁊ dainstairgniḋe na druim

ruaiḋ dianid ainm cassan na ccuraḋ, go ro ċingset gan airiuccaḋ gan forċloistecht do ṡluagh Uí Ḋomhnaill ina ndrongaiḃ, ⁊ ina ndíormaiḃ gus an cconair nanaiṫnid nainmnic sin. Ro baí do treisi an tsrota ⁊ deinirte druinge don tslogh ⁊ a neachraiḋ iar ngabáil a mbíḋ forra, go ndeachaiḋ líon dírime da mnaiḃ da ffearaiḃ, da naés anbfann anárrachta, da neachaiḃ, da ccaiplíḃ, ⁊ da gach nearnail baí leó archeana la sruṫ Easa ruaiḋ siar co muir. Ro ḟáccaibsiot a nordanás, ⁊ a cconḃaiḃ bíḋ ⁊ diġe ar cumas Conallach don chur sin. Ar a aí ċeana do ḋeachatar airiġ, ⁊ uaisle an tsloigh, ⁊ an ro ba comhnart diob tar Eirne iar ngábaiḋ ⁊ iar nguasacht mór. Ro ḃatar barda an ḃaile acca ndiuḃraccaḋ amail as déine conrangatar, ⁊ ro ġabsat acca niarmhoracht go hur na haḃann ar ḋáiġ ḃásaiġthe a mbioḋbaḋ, ⁊ sccél do roċtain go hua nDomhnaill co na ṡlóġ. Ot cualaiḋ o Domhnaill foġur an diuḃraicte atrácht co na ṡlóġ fo ċettóir, tiaġait ina ttrealmaiḃ troda go tinnearnach, ⁊ ro ċeimniġsiot gus an aḃainn amail as déine ro ḟeorat. Iar nglanaḋ do ṡlóġ an ġobernora os ur na haḃann do ċoiḋsiot i ninnell, ⁊ i nordúccaḋ. Ro ċuirsiot a mna, a ngiollanraiḋ, ⁊ a naés díairm, a ffir ġonta, ⁊ ina mbaí leó do ċaipliḃ carairte etorra ⁊ muir. Ro ċuirsiot a nanraiḋ, ⁊ a naés ursclaiġi ina ndiuiḋ, ⁊ don taoḃ araill a leiṫ fri tír ar ba dearḃ leo fo ġebdais a ttogsaim o na sloġaiḃ battar ina niarmóracht. Lotar muintir uí Domhnaill ina leanmain tar an aḃainn gan díċċioll, ⁊ ni ro anrat a nearmór fri a néдgaḋ nach fri a fforḃruta ar a ṫinnesnaiġe leo tárrachtain an tsloiġ lotar for éluḋ uaṫa. Ro ġabsat aga ttimcellaḋ ⁊ ag taiġeraḋ troda friú co mbattar ag caiṫeaṁ ⁊ ag comfuabairt a ċele ó Eirne co magh cceдne hi ccoirpre droma cliab. Fearṫar glés fleachaḋ ann an tan sin go mbo hionggnaṫ a méd, co nár cuṁaingsiot na sloiġ adiú

leice duiḃsleiṁne mar conair coitċinn do ṫromṡlóġ, ⁊ dan d'eneirte ⁊ do aḋlaiġe na nGall d'esbaiḋ airḃearta bíḋ gur ro báiḋit ile dia ffearaiḃ, dia mnaiḃ, dia neaċaiḃ, ⁊ dia ccaiplíḃ, go rucc tréan an tsroṫa i fuḋoṁain earra ruaiḋ iatt."

"They afterwards gave their breasts to the rough, unfrequented passage; but from the strength and vehemence of the stream (as was usual with it), from the difficulty of the black and slippery surface of the flag, as the common passage of the great host, and moreover from the feebleness of the English, from the want of their proper ration of food, many of their men, women, steeds, and horses, were drowned and carried by the impetuosity of the stream into the gulph of Assaroe."

[e] *Casan-na-gCuradh*, i. e. the path of the heroes, translated *Semita Heroum* by P. O'Sullevan Beare:

"Regij maiores Catholicorum vires timentes, ab Odonello acrius indies pugnis quassi, & de-

Casan-na-gCuradh[c], and they advanced to that [to them] unknown and seldom-crossed trajectus, in troops and squadrons, without being noticed or heard by O'Donnell. In consequence of the strength of the current, and the debility of some of the army and the horses, from having been deprived of food, a countless number of their women, and men of their inferior, unwarlike people, of their steeds and horses, and of other things they had with them, were swept out westwards into the sea by the current of Assaroe. They left their ordnance and their vessels of meat and drink in the power of the Kinel-Connell on this occasion. The chiefs and gentlemen of the army, however, and such of them as were strong, crossed the Erne after great danger and peril. The warders of the castle continued firing on them as rapidly as they were able, and pursued them to the brink of the river, in order to exterminate their enemies; and intelligence [of their movements] reached O'Donnell and his army. When O'Donnell heard the report of the firing, he immediately rose up with his forces, and, having quickly accoutred themselves in their fighting habiliments, they advanced to the river as speedily as they could. When the Governor's army had cleared the opposite bank of the river they went into order and battle array. They placed their women, their calones, their unarmed people, their wounded men, and such of their horses of burden as they had, between them and the sea. They placed their warriors and fighting men behind them, and on the other side towards the country, for they were certain of receiving an attack by those forces who had pursued them. O'Donnell's people went in pursuit of them across the river without delay; and they were so eager to wreak their vengeance on the army that fled from them that they did not wait to put on their armour or outer garments. They began to surround them and sharpen the conflict against them, and both parties continued shooting and attacking each other from the Erne to Magh-gCedne in Carbury-Drumcliff[d]. At this time there fell a shower of rain in such torrents that the

fessi, obsidione soluta, tribus tormentis relictis, quartoque vix in nauim, qua fuit vectum, imposito, summo mane flumen per quod venerant, traijcientes, in vadum cui nomen est Semita Heroum, sese tam incompositè præcipitant vt nonnulli obruantur. Fugientes sequitur Odonellus interimens nonnullos. Flumine & ferro eo die regij trecenti perierunt."—Fol. 161.

The name is still remembered, and the ford pointed out, immediately above the great cataract of Assaroe.

[d] *Magh-gCedne, &c.*—This should be: "From the Erne through Magh-gCedne, and until they arrived in Carbury of Drumcliff."

naċ anall a nairm diomluaḋ, no dimirt, go ro fliuchaḋ a bpócoide púdair, ⁊ glesa a nglan ġonnaḋ. Acht ba moa ro lá for muintir Uí domhnaill na fforsa fſrtana hiṡin, inár for ṡlóg an ġobernora ar ro ḟáccaiḃsiot a ffosbruta amail remhebertmar. Nir bó samlaiḋ tra don luċt naile badar eidiġṫe iadsuiḋe os cſnn a nerraḋ dia nectair.

Do ċoiḋ an gobernoir co na slóġaiḃ go Sligeċ in adhaiġ sin, ar na ṁarach go mainistir na búille, ⁊ an trear lá go tuaiṫ áṫa liacc. Ro sccaoilsiot maiṫe connaċt dia ttiriḃ ⁊ dia ttiġiḃ, ⁊ an gobernoir go baile aṫa luain.

Rortar subaiġ soiṁſnmnaiġ gaoiḋil coicciḋ ulaḋ iar soaḋ an lustís a tír eóġain gan umhla, gan aittidin, ⁊ an gobernóra a tír conaill in aén mí amail ro sccriobamar.

Iar ffaccḃail tire heoġain don lustís amail ro remhráiḋsiomar, ⁊ iar ffaccḃáil bíḋ, ⁊ bárda isin bport nua sin do ṫoccaiḃ se fſin ar brú aḃann moire dó ḋechaiḋ go haṫ cliaṫ. Dala Uí neill co na muintir ní anaḋ siḋe co lſicc do ló ⁊ doiḋche, gan bſiṫ do gres acc téttarraccain baoġail gabála, no gona for an bport sin, no for an mbárda báttar ann.. In aroile laiṫe ro ionnsaiġ sium an baile hiṡin, ⁊ ro marḃaḋ dſichnebur ar ḟicit dia daoiniḃ, ⁊ ní ro ċumaing ní don baile. O ro ḟidir an lustir a ḃárda do ḃſiṫ ag a mſsccbuaiḋreaḋ amlaiḋ sin, ⁊ a mbſiṫ i ttſirce lóin ro ṫionóil slóġ lánṁor do ṫoċt do ċor bíḋ ⁊ gaċ naḋailcce arċſna isin mbaile. Ar ttoċt don lustír co na slóġ co hardmacha ro gluaisside co marcsloiġ an tsluaiġ ina uirṫim-cell isin cconair ccoitċinn ſḋ ria na ṡaiġdiuiriḃ ⁊ ria na cóiriġtiḃ ar daiġ go ffuicchḃeaḋ drong eiccín do muintir Uí néill i nſdarḃaoġal. An tan rainicc i ccoṁfoċraiḃ aḃann moire ar ann do rala moġal marcsloíġ, ⁊ sruitléġaḋ saiġdiuiriḋe do ṁuintir uí neill dó. Ro fſraḋ iomairecc aṁnas ⁊ iomrua-ccaḋ earsccairdſṁail ſtorra. Ro marḃaḋ daoine ⁊ ro fáccḃaḋ eiċ on lustir isin ngleo troid sin. O rangatar a ṡaiġdiuiri do ṡaiġiḋ an lustir do ċóiḋ

[e] *The apparatus of their fine guns*, glesa a nglan ġonnaḋ.—These were match-locks.

[f] *Thirty of his men were slain.*—From the notices of this fort given in the Life of Hugh Roe O'Donnell, it would appear that this fort was one of very considerable strength. P. O'Sullevan Beare gives the following account of O'Neill's attempt at taking it in his *Hist. Cathol. Iber. Compend.*, tom. 3, lib. 4, c. iii.:

"O'Nellus quandoquidem frustra conatus est Ardmachæ præsidium commeatu intercludere, Portmorem saltem munimentum cibi inopia in suam potestatem redigere molitur. Quod obsidenti Odonellus, qui venit auxilio, persuasit, vt expugnare tentaret. Eius altitudinem coniectura dimensi, scalas, quæ quinos homines ampli-

forces on either side could not use or wield their arms, so drenched with wet were their powder-pouches and the apparatus of their fine guns[e]. These showers of rain did more injury to O'Donnell's people than to the Governor's army; for they [the former] had left their outer garments behind, as we have said before; but not so the others, they wore coverings over their battle dresses.

The Governor proceeded with his forces to Sligo that night; from thence on the next day to the abbey of Boyle, and on the third day to the district of Athleague. The chiefs of Connaught, then dispersed from their territories and houses, and the Governor went to Athlone.

The Irish of the province of Ulster were joyful and in high spirits after the Lord Justice had returned from Tyrone without receiving submission or respect, and the Governor [of Connaught] from Tirconnell, in the same month, as we have just mentioned.

When the Lord Justice had left Tyrone, as we have before stated, after having placed provisions and warders in the new fort, which he himself had erected on the bank of the River Abhainn-Mhor, he went to Dublin. As for O'Neill and his people, he rested neither day nor night, but watched every opportunity of taking this fort by stratagem or assault, or wreaking his vengeance on the garrison. On a certain day he attacked the fort; but thirty of his men were slain[f], and he effected nothing against the fort. When the Lord Justice received intelligence that his warders were harassed in this manner, and that they were in want of provisions, he mustered a numerous army to place provisions and all other necessaries in the fort. When the Lord Justice, with his army, had arrived at Armagh, he went with the cavalry of the army about him along the public road, some distance before his foot-soldiers and companies, with the expectation of meeting some of O'Neill's people in an unprotected position. When he came near the Abhainn-Mor he fell in with a troop of horse and a body of infantry of O'Neill's people. A fierce conflict and spiteful engagement ensued between them, [and] many men and horses were lost by the Lord Justice in that sharp battle. When the foot soldiers had come up with the Lord Justice, he advanced to the fort, and some say that he was never well

tudine capiebant, faciunt, perfectasque munimento incipiunt admouere. Eos propugnatores primum crebris tormentorum ictibus arcere festinant, & appropinquantes bombardicis pilulis impugnant, ab iis vicissim impugnati. Arci scalæ applicantur. Cæterum propugnatores qui didi-

don ṗurt, ⁊ atbertsat araile nar bó slán soṁ on ló sin alle. Ro faccaibsiot biaḋ, ⁊ bárda isin mbaile ar na maraċ. Ro triallsat toċt tar anais, ⁊ ni ḋeaċatar tar Ardmaċa in adhaiġ sin. Ro baḋ i ccarrat, no in árach ro iomċairsiot a muintir (no a ṫairisiġ ⁊ a aes grada) an lustis gan fios durṁor a ṡloiġ an lá sin. Ro baí caiṫeṁ, ⁊ coiṁdeaḃaiḋ ar ċampa an lustis ó Ua neill an adhaiġ sin dia ro marḃaḋ árd ṁaor an tsluaiġ ⁊ soċaiḋe ele cenmotasoṁ. Ro ascnátar assein co hiuḃar ċinntraġa. Fuair an lustis bas isin mbaile sin fo ḃiṫin na ngon do radad fair acc toċt a hArdmaċa gus an bport nua. Tuccaḋ coiṁéitt cloiḋiṁ an righ don tresurer, ⁊ do lustis beinnsi an righ .i. Sir Robert gardiner go toċt do lustis nua o Saxoiḃ.

O domnaill dna ba doiliġ laissiḋe an gobernoir ⁊ na hiarlaḋa do ṫernúḋ aṁail do érnatar, ⁊ ar a aí ní ro ionnsaiġ cétar nae diob araile go diúḋ foġmair. Ba foda la hUa ndoṁnaill báttar goill connaċt gan ammus forra, ⁊ fors an luċt ro eiriġ ina ccombaiġ, ⁊ do roine a muintearus frissium feċtsiaṁ. Ba diḃsiḋe ó concobair ruaḋ Aoḋ mac toirrḋealḃaiġ ruaidh, baí sium aga scrúdaḋ cionnas no creaċfaḋ a ċrioċ. Ba dodaing dosomh ón indsin, ar ba hinnill aiṁreiḋ an tionaḋ i mbaoí, ⁊ ba foccus dó an tionaḋ ina ccuirfeaḋ a innili ⁊ a ṁaoíne arċena ar iomġabáil a ḃiodḃaḋ muna ṫiosta gan raṫuccaḋ fair. Ro geall o Ruairc dosoṁ naċ léiccfeaḋ ó domnaill gan fios dia ṡaiġiḋ gan raḃaḋ do ċor cuicce. Ro ṫionoil O domnaill a ṡloġ, ⁊ do ċóid i cconnaċtaiḃ go ro airis fri gleann dallain a maroéir, gabais longport hisuiḋe. Iar ffios scél dó co mbaí an caradrad sin etir Ua ruairc ⁊ ó concoḃair, ba sí cealcc do rad im ua ruairc, a ṫeċta do ċor dia ṡaiġiḋ dia tóċuireaḋ gus an longport i mboí sium. Ro ġeall Ua ruairc [teaċt] cuccae ar a ḃarach, ⁊ ní ro ṡaoil go ffúicfeḋ Ua domnaill an longport go ttiosaḋ soṁ ina ḋocom Nír bo hed sin do roine Ua doṁnaill, acht iar ccor a ṫeċta go hUa ruairc ro ḟáccaiḃ a longport iar meḋon laí, ⁊ ro léicc dar Sliccech buḋḋéas, ⁊ ní ro airis co rainic go coirrsliaḃ. Do ġní iomsuireaċ becc ann sin co ro ṫoċaiṫsiot a ṁuintir ní dia lóintiḃ, ⁊ co ro léiccsiot

cerant, scalas in se ædificari, fossam, quæ munimentum circumdabat, excauando profundiorem effecerant. Ob quod scalæ pleræquè ad cacumen arcis non pertingebant. Ita qui ad summos scalarum gradus peruenerant, altius ascendere non valentes, deficientibus scalis, cum propugnatoribus frustra præliantur. Quæ veró scalæ ad arcis summitatem pertinebant, tam paucæ fuerunt, vt facilé primi ascensores occisi sint, antequam a commilitonibus fuerint adiuti. Centum viginti Catholici interierunt, &c."—Fol. 149.

[6] *The Chancellor*.—He was Adam Loftus,

from that day forth. On the next day they left provisions and warders in the fort, and then prepared to return back, but went no further than Armagh that night. It was in a carriage or in a litter that his people (or his faithful friends and servants of trust) carried the Lord Justice on that day, without the knowledge of the greater part of his army. O'Neill kept up a constant fire and attack upon the Lord Justice's camp during the night, by which the chief leader of the army and several others besides were slain. From thence they proceeded to Newry, and he died of the wounds which he had received between Armagh and the new fort. The keeping of the sword of state was then intrusted to the Chancellor[g] and the [Chief] Justice of the King's [Queen's] Bench, Sir Robert Gardiner, until a new Lord Justice should come from England.

O'Donnell was greatly chagrined that the Governor and the Earls should have escaped as they did. There was, however, no attack[h] from either side until the end of Autumn. O'Donnell thought it too long that he had left unattacked the English of Connaught and those Irish who had risen in alliance with them, and who had previously made friendship with himself. Among these was O'Conor Roe (Hugh, the son of Turlough Roe); and he [O'Donnell] was meditating how he could plunder his territory. This was very difficult for him to do; because the position he occupied was secure and intricate, and he had near him a fastness into which he could send his cattle and other possessions, beyond the reach of his enemies, unless they should come upon him unawares; [and] O'Rourke had promised him that he would not permit O'Donnell to march towards him without sending him notice. O'Donnell assembled his forces, and proceeding into Connaught, halted south-west of Gleann-Dallain[i], where he pitched his camp. When he received intelligence that a friendship subsisted between O'Rourke and O'Conor, he deceived O'Rourke by sending messengers to him to invite him, to his camp where he was. O'Rourke promised to go to him on the following day; for he thought that O'Donnell would not leave the camp until he should arrive there; but O'Donnell did not act so; for, after he had sent his messengers to O'Rourke, he left the camp at noon, and, proceeding southwards across the Sligo, never stopped until he arrived at the Curlieu Mountain. Here he made a short stay, while his troops were

Archbishop of Dublin.

[h] *No attack:* literally, "Howbeit neither of them attack the other till the end of Autumn."

[i] *Gleann-Dallain*, now Glencar, near Sligo.

a scís, ⁊ dna nír bo háil laiss dol tar sliaḃ buḋḋesin la soillsi an lai idir. Iar ttoċt urṫosaiġ na hoidhċe dia saiġiḋ lodar tar an sliaḃ buḋḋesin, ⁊ tar búill go rangatar tria maġ luircc an daġda, ⁊ tria muinchinn machaire connaċt ria madain. Ro léicsiot a sceimelta uaṫa i nurṫosaċ laí fo diaṁraiḃ ⁊ fo diṫreḃaiḃ na criċe ina nuirṫimċell co na ro fáccaiḃsiot míol ninnili o ách Slisen co baḋgna, ⁊ ro crechloisccead leo ina mbaoi storra siḋe. Iompaidit iaram ina fFrithing co na mbóṫaintiḃ, ⁊ co néḋalaiḃ iomḋa leó. Ba haḋnár la hUa ruairc an tír do ċreachaḋ gan airiuccaḋ dó, nír bo luġa ba méla lás an ngobernóir Sir conérs clifort creachlosccaḋ an tire baí fo a ṁámus, ⁊ fo a ċuṁaċtaiḃ.

Slóiċceaḋ la Máguidir Aoḋ, mac conconnacht, mic conconnaċt, ⁊ lá corbmac mac firdorċa, mic cuinn ḃacaiġ uí néill (ar tarraing ṡíl fFergail) go muilenn cerr na miḋe go ro ċreachrat an tír ina ttimcell, ⁊ ro léir sciorsaḋ leó an Muilend cerr fein, co nár ḟaccaiḃsiot aṫṁaoín dór, nó dairgett, duṁa, na diarann, deḋeḋ na derraḋaiḃ allmurḋa, ná daoín ní buḋ éidir diomċar no do ṫiomáin isin mbaile gan a ṫaḃairt leo, ⁊ acc toċt doiḃ tar a nais do ċuirsiot an baile tre doiġir donnruaiḋ ḋercclassaċ, ⁊ tiaġait iaram slán dia ttiġibh.

Oilen buitiler inġen iarla urmuṁan .i. Piarus ruaḋ, mac Semais, mic emainn, mic Risderd ben an dara hiarla do hoirdneaḋ ar ṫuaḋmuṁain .i. donnchaḋ, mac concobair mic toirrḋealḃaiġ uí briain décc.

Muircertaċ ulltaċ mac Seain décc i ndruim na loiste 10 feb. iars an noṁaḋ bliaḋain ochtmoġat a aoisi.

Sir Iohn norus baí na ġeneral ar coccaḋ na bainrioġan isin fFraingc, ⁊ i nerinn do ḋol don ṁuṁain iar mbuain a oiffici ḋe las an lustís nua ro tainicc i nerinn fo ḋeoiḋ. Baí siḋe hi fFarraḋ a derḃraṫar Sir tomas norus baí na ṗresidens uaḋaroṁ isin muṁain fri ré da bliaḋan décc roiṁe sin. Ro ġaḃ galar Sir Iohn go ro écc in oibne i fFoġmar na bliaḋna

[j] *Magh-Luirg-an-Daghda*, i. e. the plain of the tracts of Daghda, who was king of the Tuatha De Dananns, *anglice* Moylurg, now the plains of Boyle, in the county of Roscommon.

[k] *Upper part.*—Muinċinn .i. uaċtar, O'Clery in *Leabhar Gabhala*, p. 3.

[l] *Ath-Sliseau*, now Beal Atha-Sliseau, on the River Uair, near Elphin.—See it already mentioned at the years 1288, 1309, 1342, 1595.

[m] *Baghna*, now Slieve Baune, a well-known mountain in the east of the county Roscommon.

[n] *Second Earl of Thomond*, literally, "the second Earl who was inaugurated over Thomond," is not correct phraseology, according to

taking some refreshments and resting themselves, because he did not at all wish to pass southwards over the mountain by daylight. When the beginning of night came on them they proceeded southwards over the mountain and across the River Boyle; and before morning they had passed through Magh-Luirg-an-Daghda[j], and the upper part[k] of Machaire-Chonnacht. Early in the day they sent marauding parties into the wilds and recesses of the country in every direction; and these left not a single head of cattle from Ath-Slisean[l] to Baghna[m], and they plundered and burned all that lay between these limits. They then returned back with their herds of kine and many other spoils. O'Rourke was ashamed that the country should have been plundered without his knowledge; and the Governor, Sir Conyers Clifford, was not less grieved that a country, which was under his rule and jurisdiction, should have been [thus] plundered and burned.

An army was led by Maguire (Hugh, the son of Cuconnaught, son of Cuconnaught), and Cormac, the son of Ferdorcha, son of Con Bacagh O'Neill, at the instance of the O'Farrells, to Mullingar, in Meath, and they preyed the country around them, and totally pillaged Mullingar itself, in which they did not leave in the town any property of gold, silver, copper, iron armour, or foreign wares, or any other thing that could be carried or driven from the town, which they did not take away with them. Upon their return back they set the town in a dark, red blaze and conflagration; and they afterwards returned safe to their homes.

Ellen Butler, the daughter of the Earl of Ormond (Pierce Roe, the son of James, son of Edmond, son of Richard), and wife of the second Earl of Thomond[n] (Donough, the son of Conor, son of Turlough O'Brien), died.

Murtough Ultach [Donlevy], the son of John, died at Druim-na-loiste[o], on the 10th of February, after [having passed] the eighty-ninth year of his age.

Sir John Norris, who had been the General of the Queen's army in France and Ireland, was deprived of his office by the new Lord Justice, who had last arrived in Ireland, and went to Munster, where he remained with his brother, Sir Thomas Norris, who had been previously President under him of Munster for the period of twelve years. John was seized with a disease and died sud-

the English law of succession.

[o] *Druim-na-loiste*, now Drumnalust, a townland in the parish of Inver, barony of Banagh, and county of Donegal.

so. ⁊ ba he Sir tomás rob oidhre ar a ḟoṁaoinib. An Sir tómas sin do ġnóuġad na hoiffici céona sin baí aicce féin roiṁe sin .i. bfiṫ na ṗresidenc iar nécc a dearbraṫar;

Emann, mac uillicc na ccend, mic Riocaird, mic uillicc cnuic tuaġ o baile hiliġi décc hi Saṁrad na bliadna so.

An duḃáltaċ mac tuaṫail uí concobair decc.

Conn, ⁊ diarmaitt da ṁac an duḃaltaiġ sin, ⁊ mac ṁec diarmata maiġe luircc .i. Maolruanaid, mac briain, mic Ruaidri, mic taidg do dol fa baile Mhec dáuid .i. glinnscci go ro ġabsat gaḃala. Acc filleadh doiḃ co na ccreiċ on mbaile rucc mac meic dáuid orra i lúib na Sucae go rasímead forra, marbṫar lais conn o concoḃair in aen láṁ ṁarcaiġ as luga rob olc i cconnaċtaiḃ, ⁊ an Maolruanaid sin mac ṁec diarmata, ⁊ drong mór do ḋaoiniḃ uaisle cenmoṫát. Do ṫaéd mac Mheic dauid dia tigh iar mbuaid ccoscair;

Mac uilliam do ṫoċt dia tír fo ṡaṁain na bliadna so .i. teboitt mac uáteir ċiotaigh, ⁊ a bfith athaid i ndaingnigtib a duithce daiṁdeóin a earccarat. Na huṁaill do ċreachad lais an tan sin, ⁊ a dearbraṫair Tomás do ṁarbad i ccloinn ṁuiris na mbriġ don ċur ċeona.

Sean óg mac Riocaird mic Seain an tsesmainn do ṁarbad ar ionnsaiġid oidċe la cuid do ċloinn ndoṁnaill ar oilén na nenuigséd ar fionnloċ ceara.

Iar ffáccbail baruin innsi uí chuinn i ttír ċonaill aṁail a dubramar, tarla fearann ina ṡeilḃ an tan sin, ⁊ i seilḃ a ṡinnsear reiṁe ar brú na Sionna don taoiḃ tall, Port croisi a coṁainm. An tan at ċualatar burcaigh ḃruaicch na Sionna, ⁊ clann uilliam aér tri maiġi bás an ḃaruin, asseadh ro chinnsiot a huġdarrás seancairte a sinnsear toirmesc do ċor ar ṡoi-

[p] *Died suddenly.*—P. O'Sullevan Beare tells a strange story about Sir John Norris and the Devil, which would do credit to the writer of the Life of Dr. Faustus.—See it already referred to at p. 2021, *supra*.

[q] *Edmond of Baile-Hilighi*, i. e. Edmond Burke of Balleely, in the barony of Loughrea, and county of Galway.

[r] *Died.*—Charles O'Conor adds that he died at Breaccluin, now Bracklon, near Strokestown, in the county of Roscommon.

[s] *Mac David.*—He was the head of a sept of the Burkes who were seated at Glinske, near the River Suck, in the east of the county of Galway.

[t] *The Owles*, i. e. the baronies of Murresk and Burrishoole, in the west of the county of Mayo.

[u] *Clann-Muiris-na-mBrigh*, i. e. Clanmaurice of Brees, now the barony of Clanmorris, in the county of Mayo. The ruins of the Castle of Brees, from which this territory received the

denly[p] in the autumn of this year; and Sir Thomas was the heir to his property. Sir Thomas continued in the same office after the death of his brother.

Edmond (the son of Ulick-na-gCeann, son of Richard, son of Ulick of Cnoc-Tuagh), of Baile-Hilighi[q], died in the summer of this year.

Dubhaltach, the son of Tuathal O'Conor, died[r].

Con and Dermot, the two sons of this Dubhaltach, and the son of Mac Dermot of Moylurg (Mulrony, the son of Brian, was son of Rory, son of Teige), made an irruption into Glinske, the castle of Mac David[s], and took preys. On their return from the castle with their booty, the son of Mac David came up with them at a sinuous winding of the Suck, and defeated them, and slew Con O'Conor, by no means one of the least expert horsemen in Connaught, Mulrony Mac Dermot, already named, and many other gentlemen. The son of Mac David then returned home in triumph.

Mac William (Theobald, the son of Walter Kittagh) returned to his territory at Allhallowtide this year, and remained in the fastnesses of his country in despite of his enemies. During this time he plundered the Owles[t]. His brother, Thomas, was slain in Clann-Muiris-na-mBrigh[u], on the same occasion.

John Oge, the son of Rickard, son of John of the Termon, was slain in a nocturnal assault by a party of the Clann-Donnell, on an island of Annies[w] in Finnloch-Ceara[x].

At the time when the Baron of Inchiquin was lost in Tirconnell, as we have stated, he had in his possession, as his ancestors had before him, lands on the farther brink of the Shannon, called Port-croisi[y]. When the Burkes of the Shannon side, the Clann-William of Aes-tri-Maighe[z], had heard of the death of the Baron, they resolved, on the authority of an old charter of their ancestors,

distinguished adjunct of na-mBrigh, are still to be seen in the parish of Mayo in this barony.

[w] *Annies*, in the parish of Robeen, barony of Kilmaine, county of Mayo.—See *Genealogies, Tribes, and Customs of Hy-Fiachrach*, p. 490.

[x] *Finnloch-Ceara*, now Lough Carra, near Ballinrobe, in the county of Mayo.—See *Genealogies, &c., of Hy-Fiachrach*, p. 491.

[y] *Port Croisi*, now Portcrush, a townland on the south side of the Shannon, in the parish of Castleconnell, and county of Limerick. See note [d], under the year 1506, p. 1287, *suprà*.

[z] *Aes-tri Maighe*: i. e. the people of the three plains, now the barony of Clanwilliam, in the north-east of the county of Limerick. According to O'Heerin's topographical poem, this territory had belonged to the Irish family of O'Conaing. They were dispossessed, shortly after the English Invasion, by the Clann-William Burke, who fixed their chief residence at Caislean-Ui-Chonaing, i. e. O'Conaing's Castle, now corruptly anglicised Castleconnell.

ġníoṁaiḃ muinntire an ḃarúin, ⁊ a maṫar (.i. mairgrecc ingſn tómair ciosocc) isin ffſronn sin. Do ċodar drong do ċenél fſrmaic (.i. dúṫaiġ an ḃarúin) i ccionn Mhairgréige do congnaṁ, ⁊ do ċuidiuccaḋ fria. Do ċuaiḋ dna Mairgreg, ⁊ an luċt sin dionnsaiġiḋ a mſiṫle ⁊ a muinntire co port croisi. O Ro ḟidirsiot na búrcaigh remráitte an ní sin .i. Tomás, mac teróitt, mic uilliam, mic emainn, ⁊ uillſcc mac uilliam, mic emainn ro tionoilsiot an lion as lia ro fedsat ⁊ ro ionnsaiġsiot Mairgrecc ⁊ muinntir an ḃarúin. Feaċar sccainnſr cróḋa ſtorra ⁊ ger bo huathaḋ do ṁuinntir an ḃarúin ro ġabsat go cróḋa agá nimdſgail budſin. Ro marḃaḋ daġdaoíne ſtorra ar gach taeḃ. Ro fáccbaḋ do lſith burcach uillecc mac Uilliam burc, mic Emainn, ⁊ triúr nó cſṫrar do ḋaġḋaoinib ele. Torċair dna ḃſos don taeḃ araill Aoḋ o hóccáin, an taén ṁac duine oirecta as luġa rob olc maiṫ, ⁊ inṁe baí i cconntae an ċláir, ⁊ daġduine ele .i. Murchaḋ, mac donnchaiḋ, mic murchaiḋ ruaiḋ, mic briain, ⁊ mac an ċrúirigh .i. tómas mac Criostora.

Captin tirial, Captin nungent, caéṁánaiġ, Síol cconċobair failġiġ Síol mórḋa, ⁊ gaḃal raġnaill do ḃſiṫ, acc denaṁ coccaiḋ, fogla, ⁊ díbſirge moire illaiġnib, ⁊ i mbuitilercoiḃ ó ḟel Muire go nodlaicc móir na bliaḋna so, ⁊ as eiṁilt a sccriobaḋ an ro loitsiot, ⁊ in ro millsiot is na tirib sin fris an ré sin. Ro marḃaḋ leo dna da ḃanna Puirt laoiġisi an seċtmaḋ la do december.

Goberndóir ċairrge fſrgusa ⁊ trí ḃanna ṡaiġdiúir amaille fris do ṁar-

[a] *Their mother.*—Murrough O'Brien, fourth Baron of Inchiquin, who was drowned in the River Erne in 1597, was married to Margaret, the daughter of Sir Thomas Cusack, Lord Chancellor of Ireland, and had by her Dermot, fifth Baron of Inchiquin, and other children. The baron's own mother was Mable, eldest daughter of Christopher Nugent, Baron of Delvin.

[b] *Kinel-Fearmaic.*—This was originally the tribe name of the O'Deas, but it was at this period applied to a territory co-extensive with the present barony of Inchiquin, in the county of Clare.

[c] *Reapers.*—The word meiṫel, which makes meiṫle in the genitive singular, is still used in the south-east of Munster to denote "*a party of reapers*," which is unquestionably the meaning of the word in the text, for the baron was drowned in July, and this rencounter between the Burkes of Castleconnell and his wife Margaret took place soon after. The word meṫel is explained in Cormac's Glossary thus:

"Meṫel, *quasi* meṫal, *ab eo quod est meto.*"

[d] *Gavall-Rannall.*—This was the tribe name of the O'Byrnes of Ranelagh, in the present county of Wicklow, of whom Felim, the son of Fiagh O'Byrne, was chief at this period.

[e] *To Christmas:* literally "from the festival of Mary to the Big Christmas of this year."

[f] *Port-Leix.*—This is still the Irish name of the town of Maryborough, in the Queen's County.

[g] *The Governor of Carrickfergus.*—He was Sir

to prevent the Baron's family and their mother[a] (i. e. Margaret, the daughter of Thomas Cusack) from working on those lands. A party of the people of Kinel-Fearmaic[b], the Baron's territory, went to aid and assist Margaret, and she set out with them to her reapers[c] and people to Port-croisi. When the aforesaid Burkes, namely, Thomas, the son of Theobald, son of William, son of Edmond, and Ulick, the son of William, son of Edmond, had learned this, they assembled as large a number as they were able, and attacked Margaret and the Baron's people. A fierce battle was fought between them; and though the Baron's people were few in number, they proceeded valiantly to defend themselves. Several gentlemen were slain between them on both sides. On the side of the Burkes fell Ulick, the son of William, son of Edmond Burke, and three or four other gentlemen. On the other side also there fell Hugh O'Hogan, by no means the least distinguished son of a chieftain, for goodness and wealth, in the county of Clare, with another gentleman, namely, Murrough, the son of Donough, the son of Murrough Roe, son of Brian [O'Brien], and the son of Cruise, namely, Thomas, the son of Christopher.

Captain Tyrrell, Captain Nugent, the Kavanaghs, the O'Conors Faly, the O'Mores, and the Gavall-Ranall[d], were making great war, plunder, and insurrection in Leinster, and in the country of the Butlers, from the festival of the Virgin Mary to the Christmas[e] this year; and it would be tedious to write of all they plundered and destroyed in these territories during this period. On the 7th day of December they slew two bands of soldiers that were stationed in Port-Leix[f].

About Allhallowtide this year the Governor of Carrickfergus[g] and three

John Chichester, the brother of Sir Arthur, the founder of the Donegal family. P. O'Sullevan Beare gives the following account of this rencounter, in his *Hist. Cathol. Ibern. &c.*, tom 3, lib. 4, c. ii. fol. 149.

"Hyeme sequente Ioannes Chichester Anglus eques Auratus, qui Rupem Fargusiam arcem firmo præsidio tenebat, cum peditibus quingentis, & equitum turma prædatum egreditur. Cui fit obuius ad Alfracham tumulum, & vadum Iaimus Macdonellus Glinniæ princeps peditibus quadringentis, & equitibus sexaginta stipatus. Bombardarij bombardarios aggrediuntur: á Catholicis regij propulsantur. Iohannes cum equitatu veniens auxilio bombardarios suos restituit in pugnam, & Catholicos recedere cogit. Iaimus quoque equitatum in pugnam ducens bombardarijs suis confirmatis in Iohannem proruit, & tribus hastæ ictibus percussus, lorica tamen defenditur. Iohannes occisus equo labat, cuiius etiam equitatus, & peditatus terga vertit. Sequitur Iaimus per tria circiter millia vsque ad arcem, per quod interuallum, regijs, vt quisque à Catholicis cursu superabatur, occisis, vix cladis nuncij effuge-

ḃaḋ la Sémus mac Soṁairle buiḋe mec Doṁnaill hi ccloinn Aoḋa buiḋe ro Shamhain na bliaḋna so.

Clann tsíṫigh .i. Murchaḋ baclaṁach mac Murchaiḋ bailḃ, mic Maġnusa méc Siṫhiġ co na ḋerbraṫair Ruaiḋri, & Emann, mac Murchaiḋ bacaiġ, mic Emainn mic Maġnusa ṁec Sitigh do ḃaruccaḋ la gallaiḃ a los a ccoccaiḋ, & a ndíbfercce.

Iar nécc an Iustis .i. Tómas lord burough isin iuḃar do ḃiṫin a ġon, & iar ttaḃairt ċoiṁéda cloiḋiṁ an ríġ i nErinn don troinrisler, & do Sir Robfrd gardiner Iustis bfinnsi an ríġ aṁail do raiḋsmar, ba hé neach dia ro hordaicceaḋ generalaċt coccaiḋ, & rioṫcana na hErenn diarla Urmuṁan .i. tómas, mac Semus, mic Piarais ruaiḋ, coniḋ aire sin do gaḃaḋ ossaḋ etir an iarla sin & maiṫe ċoicciḋ ulaḋ. Nír bó cian iar sin go ndeachaiḋ an general .i. an tiarla Urmuṁan sin, & iarla Tuaḋmuṁan .i. Donnchaḋ mac Concoḃair i ccoicceaḋ ulaḋ i mí december gar ria nodlaic, & ro battar féin, O néill, & O Doṁnaill fri ré tsóra noiḋce in aén maiġin & iomluaḋ rioḋa etir na hiarlaḋaiḃ sin a huċt na bainrioġan fri gaoiḋelaiḃ leiṫe cuinn, & rob é criochnuccaḋ a ndala, siṫ do ḋenaṁ etir galloiḃ & gaoiḋelaiḃ fá móid na niarlaḋ sin go beltaine ar ccind. Teċta & sccriḃenna na ngaoiḋel rémraitte, sior na nairtsccal & na ccoingell ar a ngeḃdais siṫ doiḃ féin, & da ccoṁrann coccaiḋ in gach airm i mbáttar do ċor do ṡaiġiḋ na bainrioġna go Saxoiḃ la hiarla Tuaḋmuṁan, & gibe sccela do ṫiucfaḋ anoir i mbeltaine imirt a ḃus dia réir.

O Concoḃair Sliccigh Donnchaḋ mac Caṫail óicc, do ḋol i Saxoiḃ go becc ria nodlaic na bliaḋna so.

runt. Barnabal Baro cum Midhiensibus copijs Angloibernis, & aliquot Anglis cohortibus Auriliam deuastans á Macmagauno Aurilliæ principe funditur, & fugatur."

Lodge, however, says that Mac Donnell had laid an ambuscade for Chichester.

[h] *Murrough Baclamhach:* i. e. Murrough or Morgan of the Lame Hand.

[i] *The Lord Borough.*—Mr. Moore, in his *History of Ireland*, vol. iv. p. 108, has the following remark on the chief Governor:

"The only circumstance at all memorable, that connects itself with this Lord's name is the doubt that exists as to the manner of spelling it; some writing Burke, while Camden makes it Borough, and the owner of the name himself wrote Bourgh."

Camden calls him "Thomas Baro *Borough*, vir acer, et animi plenus, sed nullis fere castrorum rudimentis."—*Ann. Reg. Eliz.*, A. D. 1597.

[k] *And therefore.*—This should be: "and the result of this appointment of Ormond was, that a cessation ['Cessationem armorum vocant Hibernici.'—*Camd.*] of two months took place between

companies of soldiers were slain in Clannaboy by James, the son of Sorley Boy Mac Donnell.

The Mac Sheehys, namely, Murrough Baclamhach[h], the son of Murrough Balbh, son of Manus Mac Sheehy, with his brother, Rory, and Edmond, the son of Murrough Bacagh, son of Edmond, son of Manus Mac Sheehy, were executed by the English for their war and insurrection.

After the Lord Justice, Thomas Lord Borough[i], had died of the effects of his wounds at Newry, and the keeping of the regal sword had been given to the Lord Chancellor and to Sir Robert Gardiner, Justice of the King's [Queen's] Bench, as we have stated, the person who was appointed to the generalship of war and peace in Ireland was the Earl of Ormond (Thomas, the son of James, son of Pierce Roe), and therefore[k] an armistice was concluded between this Earl and the chiefs of the province of Ulster. Not long after this [namely], in the month of December, and shortly before Christmas, this Earl of Ormond and the Earl of Thomond (Donough, the son of Conor), went into the province of Ulster, where they and O'Neill and O'Donnell passed three nights together at one place; and a treaty concerning a peace was carried on by those Earls, on behalf of the Queen, with the Irish of Leath-Chuinn; and the issue of their meeting was, that a peace was made between the English and the Irish, on the oath of these Earls, until the May following. The proposals and writings of the Irish aforesaid, and an account of the articles and conditions on which they would accept of peace for themselves and their confederates in the war, in every place where they were seated, were dispatched to the Queen to England by the Earl of Thomond[l]; and whatever news[m] should arrive from England in May should be acted upon here.

O'Conor Sligo (Donough, the son of Cathal Oge) went to England a short time before the Christmas of this year.

him and the chiefs of Ulster."—See *Carte's Ormond*, Introd., p. 59. Fynes Moryson says that this conference took place at Dundalk, on the 22nd of December, 1597.—See folio edition, p. 22; Dublin edition of 1735, vol. i. pp. 51, 52, 53; and Cox, vol. i. p. 414.

[l] *By the Earl of Thomond.*—This may be an error of the transcriber for "la hiapla upmuman," i. e. by the Earl of Ormond.

[m] *News*, Scela.—This is a bad word, and the Four Masters could have found technical words in abundance in their own language to express this idea more distinctly. The word ꞅꞃeaꝣꞃaꝺ would be better, if they did not wish to introduce the technicalties of the old Irish laws. An English writer would say: "And both

An barun insin uí ċuinn tar a ttangamar, Ro guineaḋ, ⁊ ro báiḋeaḋ ag toċt don goḃſrnoir, ⁊ do na hiarlaḋhaiḃ remraite co na sloġaiḃ tar éirne, Ro tóccbaḋ a ċorp lá corbmac ua ccléiriġ Manaċ do manchaiḃ Mainistreċ Essa ruaiḋ, ⁊ ro haḋnaiceaḋ an corp co nonóir aṁail ro ba teċta lais isin mainestir. Ro eiriġ ſraonta ⁊ imreasain eittir braiṫriḃ dúin na ngall ⁊ na manaiġ deriḋe, ⁊ ro fuiġillsit na braiṫre gur ḃó ina mainistir féin ro dleaċt an corp do aḋnacal, ar bá i mainestir S. Proinseis ina ṫír baḋéin no haḋnaicṫi sinnsir an ḃarúin fri ré foda riasan tan sin. Ro ḃáttar na manaiġ accá ḟosttaḋ aca baḋéin co ndeaċsat na braiṫri ⁊ na manaiġ do láṫair uí doṁnaill, ⁊ na deisi epscop báttar isin tír Rémann o gallċuḃair epscop doire, ⁊ niall o baoiġill epscop Raṫaboṫ gur ro brſiṫhaiġsiot na maiṫe sin an barún Murchaḋ, mac murchaiḋ, uí ḃriain do aḋnacal i Mainestir S. Proinseis i ndun na ngall. Do rónaḋ aṁlaiḋ sin, ar ro tóccbaḋ an corp i ccſn ráiṫe iar na aḋnacal i mainistir Essa Ruaiḋ gur ro aḋnaicsſt na braiṫre aca baḋéin é co nonóir ⁊ go nairṁittin aṁail ro ba díor.

O concoḃair donn Aodh mac diarmatta mic cairpre baoí illáiṁ ag Ua ndoṁnaill fri ré ḟoda do légaḋ (an 4 do december) a gſiṁel la hua ndoṁnaill iar ttaḃairt a oiġrere dó, ⁊ ro naiḋm árach ⁊ rátha fair buḋ dſin im rſir uí doṁnaill do ḋénaṁ tria biṫe fo ṡlanaiḃ, ⁊ fo ṁionnaiḃ dé ⁊ na heccailsi, ⁊ do ratt frisin braighde dó fri coṁall .i. a ḋias mac budſin, Mac oiḋrechta uí ḃſirn, céd mac uí Ainliḋe, ⁊ oiḋhre uí ḟloinn ⁊c̄a.

AOIS CRIOST, 1598.

Aois Criost, mile, cúicc céd, noċat, a hocht.

An tab caoch .i. Uilliam, mac dáuid, mic Emainn, mic uillicc a búrc dia ro ġair ḟſin Mac uilliam iar nécc an Mhſic uilliam baí na ṫiġearna roiṁe .i. Risderd mac oiluerais, mic Sſain. Nir bó soinṁeċ fuairsiuṁ an ġairm

parties agreed that such decision as should be sent from England should be adhered to in Ireland."

[n] *Already spoken.*—See p. 2027, *supra*.

[o] *Redmond O'Gallagher, &c.*—These were the Roman Catholic bishops of these dioceses. George Mountgomery held the sees of Derry and Raphoe, in conjunction with that of Clogher, by letters patent, dated the 13th of June, 1595, but it would appear that he never exercised any episcopal jurisdiction in these northern dioceses, in which the Reformation had at this time made so

As for the Baron of Inchiquin, of whom we have already spoken[n] as having been wounded and drowned when the Governor and the aforesaid Earls were crossing the Erne with their forces, his body was taken up by Cormac O'Clery, one of the monks of the monastery of Assaroe, and the body was buried by him, with due honour, in the monastery. In consequence of this a dispute and contention arose between the friars of Donegal and the monks of Assaroe; the friars maintaining that the body should be of right buried in their own monastery, because the ancestors of the Baron had been for a long period before that time buried in the Franciscan monastery in his own country, and the monks insisting that it should remain with themselves; so that the friars and the monks went before O'Donnell, and the two Bishops who were then in the country, namely, Redmond O'Gallagher[o], Bishop of Derry, and Niall O'Boyle, Bishop of Raphoe, and these chiefs, decided upon having the Baron, Murrough, the son of Murrough O'Brien, buried in the monastery of St. Francis at Donegal. This was accordingly done, for the body was taken up at the end of three months after its interment in the monastery of Assaroe, and the friars reburied it in their own monastery[p] with reverence and honour, as was meet.

O'Conor Don (Hugh, the son of Dermot, son of Carbry), who had been for a long time imprisoned by O'Donnell, was set at liberty by him on the 4th of December, after he [O'Conor] had given him his full demand; and he solemnly bound himself to be for ever obedient to O'Donnell, by guarantees and oaths of God and the Church; and he also delivered up to him, as hostages for the fulfilment of this, namely, his own two sons, the heir of O'Beirne, the eldest son of O'Hanly, and the heir of O'Flynn, &c.

THE AGE OF CHRIST, 1598.

The Age of Christ, one thousand five hundred ninety-eight.

The Blind Abbot (i. e. William, the son of David, son of Edmond, son of Ulick Burke), who had styled himself Mac William after the death of the last lord, namely, Richard, the son of Oliver, son of John, did not happily enjoy his

little progress. See *Harris's edition of Ware's Bishops*, p. 275.

[p] *In their own monastery*: literally, "with themselves," which would not be well understood in English. It is strange that the Cistercian monks of Assaroe, and the Franciscans of

ṫighearna sin uair ro hionnarbaḋ é ar a aṫarḋa la Sir Risderd bingam go mbaí ina ionnarbṫach ó ṫír do ṫír go ro écc hi cclоinn cuilein hi mí september, ⁊ ro hadnaicedh é hi ccuimnche irróiṁ adnacail síl aoḋa. Ar e Mac uilliam bai ann an sin teboitt mac uateir ciotaigh, mic Seain, mic Oiluerais dia ro ġair ó doṁnaill Mac uilliam aṁail ro sccriobamar reṁainn.

O caṫain Ruaiḋri, mac magnusa, mic donnchaiḋ, mic Seain, mic aiḃne decc an ceṫraṁaḋ la decc do mí april, ⁊ a ṁac doṁnall ballaċ doirdneaḋ ina ionaḋ.

Riocard, mac Seain, mic tomáis, mic Riocaird óicc a búrc ó ḋoire mic laċtna decc hi mí August.

Siuḃan ċam ingean iarla dearmuṁan .i. Semus, mac Seain, mic tomáis droicit áṫa décc i ngeimreaḋ na bliaḋna so, iar ccaiṫeaṁ mór mbliaḋan i mbaintreḃṫaċas iar ndíṫ a deirḃḟine ⁊ na ndeiġḟear ndiongmala lár ro hearnaiḋmeaḋ í diaidh indiaidh.

Mac donnchaiḋ tíre hoilellae .i. Muirgheas caoċ mac taiḋcc an triuḃair do ṁarḃaḋ i mbreifne uí ruairc i ttimcell ḟuadáin creiche, ⁊ Mac donnchaiḋ do ġairm do ċoncoḃar ócc mac maoileċlainn ó ḃaile an dúin.

Occán, mac Seain, mic [Maoileaċlainn Uí] occáin ó ard croine decc in earraċ na bliaḋna so.

Donegal, should have thus contended for the body of a Protestant baron.

[q] *Sil-Aodha:* "i. e. semen, progenies seu, genus Aidi, seu Hugonis." This was one of the tribe names of the Mac Namaras of Thomond, who were otherwise called Ui-Caisin and Clann-Coileain. — See note [y], under the year 1592, p. 1910, *supra.*

[r] *Doire-mic-Lachtna:* i. e. *Roboretum filii Lachtnai,* now Derrymaclaughny, a townland containing the ruins of a castle, situated a short distance to the north-east of the hill of Cnoc-tuagh, or Knockdoe, in the barony of Clare, and county of Galway.—See map to *Tribes, &c. of Hy-Many,* on which the situation of this castle is shewn.

[s] *Baile-an-duin,* now Ballindoon, near Ballinafad, in the barony of Tirerrill, and county of Sligo. See it already mentioned at the years 1352 and 1468. The family of Mac Donough, who are an offset of the Mac Dermots of Moylurg, retained some property in the county of Sligo till very recently. In 1688, Terence Mac Donough, Esq., of Creevagh, was M. P. for the town of Sligo; he died in 1713.—See *Memoir of O'Conor,* p. 141. He was the only Catholic counsel that was admitted to the Irish bar after the violation of the Conditions of Limerick. This Terence, who is traditionally called in the country, "the great Counsellor Mac Donough," was the lawyer who saved to Donough Liath O'Conor, of Belanagare, a small tract of property from confiscation. A bill of discovery had been filed against this Donough by Mr. French, of French Park, under the Statute 1 Anne, chap. 32, but

title of lord, for he was expelled from his patrimony by Sir Richard Bingham; after which he went about wandering as an exile from territory to territory, until he died in Clann-Cuilein [in Thomond], in the month of September; and he was buried in the abbey of Quin, in the burial-place of the Sil-Aedha[q]. The Mac William who was lord at that time was Theobald (the son of Walter Kittagh, son of John, son of Oliver), whom O'Donnell had nominated Mac William, as we have written before.

O'Kane (Rory, the son of Manus, son of Donough, son of John, son of Aibhne) died on the fourteenth day of the month of April; and his son, Donnell Ballagh, was installed in his place.

Rickard, the son of John, son of Thomas, son of Rickard Oge Burke, from Doire-mic-Lachtna[r], died in the month of August.

Joan Cam, the daughter of the Earl of Desmond, namely, of James, the son of John, son of Thomas of Drogheda, died in the winter of this year, having spent many years in [a state of] widowhood, after the destruction of her tribe, and of the worthy men to whom she had been successively espoused.

Mac Donough of Tirerrill (Maurice Caech, the son of Teige-an-Triubhis) was slain in Breifny-O'Rourke, as he was carrying off a prey from thence; upon which Conor Oge, son of Melaghlin, from Baile-an-duin[s], was appointed the Mac Donough.

Ogan[t], the son of John, son of [Melaghlin O'h-]Ogain of Ard-Croine, died in the spring of this year.

Mac Donough managed the reply so ably, and being supported by the interests of Lord Kingsland and Lord Taaffe, finally succeeded in restoring Donough O'Conor to about seven hundred acres of land, which descended to his son, Charles O'Conor, of Belanagare, the historian. The family of Mac Donough have now scarcely any property remaining, and the race have latterly fallen into obscurity.

It will be seen, from reference to the statement under the year 1468 (*ante*, p. 1053), that the then Lord of Tirerrill was also Lord of Baile-an-duin.

[t] *Ogan, son of John.*—This passage is left imperfect by the transcriber, who omitted the words in brackets, which are supplied from Duald Mac Firbis. The O'Hogans were seated at Ardcrony, four miles to the north of the town of Nenagh, in the county of Tipperary. The Ogan mentioned in the text had four brothers: Conor, of Ardcrony; John, Prior of Lorha; Gillapatrick, Erenagh of Lorha; and William. Their line of pedigree is given by Duald Mac Firbis as follows, p. 403:—Ogan, son of John, son of Melaghlin, son of John, son of Thomas, son of Siacus, son of Conor, Bishop of Killaloe, son of Teige, son of Donough, son of Donnell, son of Dermot, son of Rory, &c. A considerable portion of O'Hogan's castle is still to be seen at Ardcrony.

Muirchertach cam mac Concobhair, mic Mathghamhna, mic Tomáis o Chnoc an lacha i ttrioca céd Corco Baiscind airthearaighi decc hi mí Marta.

Baothghalach, mac Aodha, mic Baothghalaigh, mic Muirchertaigh Méc Flannchadha on Cnoc fionn hi cconntae an Cláir decc hi mí April. Fear eisidhe co sulbaire indsce illaidin, i ngaoidilcc, ⁊ i mbérla.

Diarmait, mac Emainn, mic Ruaidhri í Dheadhaidh o Tulaigh uí Dheadhaidh do mharbhadh la dibhfeargachaibh conntae an Cláir a mí Iul.

Iarla Tuadhmumhan do dhol i Saxoibh i ttós mís Ianuarii. Techta ⁊ sccribhenn na nGaoidhel ar chena, ⁊ Riocard, mac uilliucc, mic Riocaird Shaxanaigh mic uilliucc na cceann barún dúine cuillin do dhol beós hi Saxoibh isin earrach do sonnradh.

Iar ndénamh na síodha remebertmar ó nodlaic mór go beltaine etir gaoidhelaibh leithe cuinn ⁊ an generál iarla urmumhan, Ro fhorailsiot gaoidil an tuaisceirt for a mbaoí do dhíbhfeargachaibh illaighnibh ⁊ isin midhe (.i. caomhánaigh, Siol cconcobhair, Siol mórdha, gabhal raghnaill, Tuathalaigh, Tirialaigh, ⁊ Uinnsionnaigh) sccur go lfecc dia ffoghail, ⁊ dia ndíbhfeircc. Do ronsat som innsin for congra a naireach. Ro chsaigh an Generál Iarla urmumhan dóibh iomaithighidh laighfn, midhe, ⁊ oirthir mumhan, ⁊ a mbiadh ⁊ a ndeogh do thochaithfm go ttíosadh sgéla síodha nó coccaidh chuca fo beltaine a Saxoibh. Ro battar som trá lár an ccomhairleccadh sin acc tairsel ⁊ tathaighe gach tire ina ttimcell ó chill manntáin i mioctar laighfn go Siúir ⁊ o loch garman go Sionainn. Nír bó sodhaing do na tiribh sin fulang a naimbrfth an airfett sin.

Semus (.i. dearbhrathair iarla urmumhan) mac Eduaird, mic Semais, mic Piarais ruaidh buitiler, ⁊ Mac még Piaruis Sirriam conntae tiopprat árann (go ndaoinibh uaisle iomdha a maille fris) do dhol fo chaiscc

[u] *Cnoc-an-lacha:* i. e. hill of the lough or lake, now Knockalough, a townland containing the ruins of a castle in the parish of Kilmihil, barony of Clonderalaw, and county of Clare.

[v] *Cnoc-finn:* i. e. the White fair Hill, now Knockfin, in the barony of Corcomroe, and county of Clare. According to the Description of the County of Clare, preserved in T. C. D., E. 2. 14, the castles of Knockefyne and Tuomolyn belonged to Conogher Maglainehy. The Boethius MacClancy above mentioned was sheriff of Clare, and a member of the Parliament of 1585. According to the tradition in the country, he murdered some shipwrecked Spaniards in 1588.

[w] *Tully O'Dea:* i. e. O'Dea's hill, now Tully, near Dysart-O'Dea, in the barony of Inchiquin, and county of Clare. About the year 1584, when the Description of the County of Clare, preserved in the Library of Trin. Coll., Dublin, E. 2. 14, was written, the only places marked as belonging to the O'Deas are, "Beallnalyke" [near Ruane], and Moghowny, belonging to Ma-

Murtough Cam, the son of Conor, son of Mahon, son of Thomas [Mac Mahon] of Cnoc-an-lacha[u], in the territory of East Corca-Baiscinn, died in the month of March.

Boethius, the son of Hugh, son of Boethius, son of Murtough Mac Clancy, from Cnoc-Finn[v], in the county of Clare, died in the month of April. He was a man fluent in the Latin, Irish, and English languages.

Dermot, the son of Edmond, son of Rory O'Dea of Tully-O'Dee[w], was killed in the month of July by the insurgents of the county of Clare.

The Earl of Thomond went to England in the beginning of the month of January. The proposals and letters of the Irish in general were also sent to England; and Rickard, the son of Ulick, son of Rickard Saxonagh, son of Ulick-na-gCeann, Baron of Dunkellin, also went to England in the spring.

After the concluding of the peace which we have already mentioned, from Christmas to May, between the Irish of Leath-Chuinn and the General, the Earl of Ormond, the Irish of the North issued orders to all the insurgents of Leinster and Meath, namely, the Kavanaghs, O'Conors, O'Mores, the Gaval-Rannall[x], the Tooles, Tyrrells, and Nugents, to desist for a short time from their acts of plunder and rebellion; and they did so, at the bidding of their chiefs. The General, the Earl of Ormond, permitted them to frequent Leinster, Meath, and the east of Munster, and to eat and drink [with the inhabitants], until news should come from England, in May, respecting peace or war. By this instruction they continued traversing and frequenting every territory around them, from Cill-Mantain[y], in the lower part of Leinster, to the Suir; and from Loch-Garman[z] to the Shannon. It was not easy for [the inhabitants of] these territories to bear their inordinate demands during this period.

James (i. e. the brother of the Earl of Ormond), the son of Edward, son of James, son of Pierce Roe Butler, and the son of Mac Pierce, sheriff of the county of Tipperary[aa], and many other gentlemen, proceeded precisely at Easter

howne O'Dea, and Desert, belonging to Donell Moel O'Dea."

[x] *Gaval-Ranall*, i. e. the O'Byrnes of Ranelagh, in the south-west of the now county of Wicklow.

[y] *Cill-Mantain*, i. e. the town of Wicklow.—See note [y], under the year 1454, p. 991, *supra*.

[z] *Loch Garman*, i. e. the town of Wexford.

[aa] *Of Tipperary*, Ƭiopραc άραnn.—This name signifies the well of Ara, the name of an ancient territory. This well, which gave name to the town of Tipperary, is now closed up. It was situated near the north bank of the River Ara, at the rear of Mr. O'Leary's house, the front of which is in the main street of Tipperary.

do ṡonnraḋ ar ionnsaiġiḋ ar ḃrian riaḃaċ ó mórḋa duine uasal don ḟſḋain ġaoiḋelaiġ baí acc denaṁ na cárcc i nuiḃ cairin ⁊ ro baḋ do luċt na hionnsaiġṫe a ḋomaoín ⁊ a doḃarṫan uair ro ḟáccḃaḋ drong mór dia ndaoiniḃ uaisle, dia noireċt, ⁊ dia saiġdiuiriḃ, ⁊ ro gaḃaḋ ann Sémus mac eduaird buitileir, ⁊ do raḋ brian riaḃaċ é diarla urmuṁan ro ċſnn seċtmuine iar sin ar dáiġ na síoṫċana a duḃramar, ⁊ ar na ḋſrḃaḋ naċ do ċſo an generala (.i. an iarla) tuccaḋ an ionnsaiġiḋ sin.

Ua ruairc brian óg, mac briain, mic briain ballaiġ, mic eoġain, bá fearccaċ riḋe fri hUa ndoṁnaill Aoḋ ruaḋ mac Aoḋa mic maġnusa ro ḋaiġ oirccne Uí concoḃair ruaiḋ ṫairis aṁail ro sccrioḃamar reṁainn, ⁊ araill ele nír bó rioḋach etir é, ⁊ a ḋſrḃraṫair buḋéin .i. taḋg o ruairc mac briain mic briain ḃallaiġ im ċoṁroinn a ccriċe ⁊ a ffſrainn fri a roile. Conaḋ aire sin ro ernaiḋm Ua ruairc a ċor ⁊ a ċarattraḋ fris an ngobernóir Sir conerś clisort. Nír bó sáiliġ Ua doṁnaill do cloisteċt an sccéoil sin, uair bádar cáirde ruarcaiġ dia cenel o ċſin máir, ⁊ ba braṫair dó eissiuṁ buḋéin, ⁊ nír bó lainn lais ammus rair no indraḋ a criċe aṁail cáċ ele i cconnaċtaiḃ, ⁊ ba dſrḃ lais gomaḋ éiccin dó a hionnraḋ muna ttíoraḋ i ccombáiḋ na ngaoiḋel doriḋisi, uair nír bó síoḋaċ soṁ fris naċ aén no biaḋ i cclſiṫ gall. Nó ḃioḋ feċt ann aga ḟoarġuiḋe co hinċlſiṫe im ṡóḋ ina ṡriṫing, ⁊ feċt ele ag baiġ ⁊ acc baccar indraḋ a ṫire muna ttíoraḋ sor ccúlaiḃ. Ro baí Ua ruairc acc coisteċt fris an ttreċtaireċt sin ó urṫoraċ earraiġ co beltaine ar ccind, ⁊ do ċoiḋ an tan sin co haṫ luain, ⁊ do raḋ a braiġde don ġobernoir, ⁊ do bertsat a moide ⁊ a ngeallaṁ im ċoṁall dia roile, ⁊ gér bó tairisi an tingeallaḋ nír bó cian ro coṁailleaḋ.

Tainicc ffſccra a Saxoiḃ ar sccriḃſnnaiḃ í neill, í doṁnaill, ⁊ na ngaoiḋel badar i naén rann friú, ⁊ ní ro ṡaoṁ an ḃainrioġain ná an ċoṁairle na nſiṫe ro iarrsat do ṫabairt doiḃ, ⁊ o na ro faomaḋ tuccsat na gaoíḋil a ccaon-

[a] *Befell the assailants*, i. e. the disasters which they had intended for Brian Reagh O'More fell upon themselves.

[b] *League of friendship.*—This friendship was of very short duration indeed, and Clifford met his death soon after in attempting to force the pass of the Curlieus, which was defended by O'Rourke and O'Donnell.

[c] *He was not at peace.*—Hugh Roe O'Donnell's intense hatred to the English seems to have principally arisen from his having been so long detained in prison without any ostensible reason, for the English writers themselves acknowledge that he was captured treacherously, and loaded with irons after his recommittal, though there were strong reasons for believing that the Vice-

on an incursion against Brian Reagh O'More, a gentleman of the Irish party, who was passing Easter in Ikerrin; but disaster and misfortune befell the assailants[a], for many of their gentlemen, of their followers, and of their soldiers, were slain; and James, the son of Edward Butler, was taken prisoner, but Brian Reagh delivered him up, in a week afterwards, to the Earl of Ormond, on account of the peace we have mentioned, and after it had been ascertained that it was not by the permission of the General (i. e. the Earl) this attack had been made.

O'Rourke (Brian Oge, the son of Brian, son of Brian Ballagh, son of Owen) was angry with O'Donnell (Hugh Roe, the son of Hugh, son of Manus), because of his having plundered O'Conor Roe against his wish, as we have written before; and, moreover, he was not at all on terms of peace with his own brother, i. e. Teige O'Rourke, the son of Brian, son of Brian Ballagh, [in consequence of a disagreement] about the partition of their territory and land. Wherefore, O'Rourke confederated and formed a league of friendship[b] with the Governor, Sir Conyers Clifford. O'Donnell was not pleased at hearing this news, for the O'Rourkes had from a remote period been the friends of his tribe, and he [the present O'Rourke] was his own kinsman, and he did not wish to make an incursion against him, or plunder his territory, as he would treat all others in Connaught; but he felt certain that he must needs plunder him unless he should return to the confederacy of the Irish, for he [O'Donnell] was not at peace[c] with any one who was under the tutelage of the English. For a certain time he privately solicited him to return, and at another time he menaced and threatened to plunder his territory unless he should come back. O'Rourke continued to listen to these messages from the beginning of spring to the May following, at which time he went to Athlone, and delivered up his hostages to the Governor; and they made [mutual] vows and promises to be faithful to each other; but though the engagement was sincere [at the time], it was not long kept.

An answer arrived from England to the letters of O'Neill, O'Donnell, and the other Irish chiefs who were in alliance with them. The Queen and the Council did not consent to grant them the conditions they demanded; and,

roy was privy to his escape. This, and the loss of his two great toes, raised his open hatred to the English name to a pitch of sublimity which disqualified him from being a great statesman like Tyrone, though, according to Cucugry O'Clery, "a Cæsar in command."

coṁrac ar ċoccaḋ, a cceannsa ar ċeannairrce, ⁊ a síṫ ar sraonta co ro ḃeaṫhaiḋ-sioc beóġnís a seanġoṁ doriḋisi a ttús saṁraiḋ na bliaḋna so.

Iar ndeiliuccaḋ re roile don ġobernoir ⁊ dUa Ruairc fo ṡíṫ ⁊ fo caírdine fo Bealtaine i mbaile áṫa luain, ⁊ ot connairc ua Ruairc nár bó síoḋaċ goill, ⁊ gaoiḋil fri roile, ⁊ nar bo tréisi do ġallaiḃ olḋás do ġaoiḋelaiḃ don ċur sin ro imecclaiġ síḋe indreaḋ a tíre dUa Domhnaill conid eḋ do roine toċt fo a ṫoġairm, ⁊ an ro aṫaiġ fris do dénaṁ ar coṁairle a ṁuinntire, uair rob usa leó an gobernoir do ḃeiṫ fo a ccoṁair ina díoġaltas Uí Ḋomhnaill ina ndeaḋhaiḋ dia nandaoís hi ccléiṫ an ġobernora.

Iar naiḋm a ċarattraḋ don chur sin dUa Ruairc fris Ua nDomhnaill do ċoiḋ Ua Ruairc co na ṡoċraitte ar tarraing uí ḟearġail ḃáin (.i. Ross, mac uilliam, mic domhnaill) isin miḋe, ⁊ ro creachaḋ leo an Muileann cearr, ⁊ on Muileann cearr go baile mór loċa seimhdiġe.

Sloicceaḋ ele la hUa Ruairc is in ccéid mí dfoġmar, ⁊ ní ro airis go rainicc bealach an tirialaiġ, ⁊ co bealac ċille briġde i ffearaiḃ tulach. Do roine creacha ⁊ marḃta i mbealaċ an tirialaiġ, ⁊ ro ḟill tar a ais dia ṫir gan guin gan gabhaḋh.

Iar ndol na síoḋa remraite for ccul tainicc Remann a burc mac Seaain na Seamar mic Riocaird Shaxanaiġ, mic uillicc na cceann co ndruing da ḃraiṫriḃ ócca maille fris do ċéd daoiniḃ i cceann Uí neill da éccaoine fris gur bó hí sseccra ḋearḃraṫar a aṫar fair .i. Iarla cloinne Riocaird uilleacc a burc, da mbeiṫ an Remann sin reiḋ ar leiṫeacc aon ḟallainge dia duṫċas, no dia aṫarḋa o ṡruṫair go haḃainn da loilġech na tiuḃraḋ an oirecc sin fein do

[d] *Ballymore-Lough Sewdy.*—See note [r], under the year 1450, p. 970, *supra.*

[e] *Tyrrell's-Pass*, a neat little town near the hill of Croghan, in the barony of Fertullagh, in the south of the county of Westmeath.

[f] *Pass of Kilbride*, a well-known place near Tyrrell's-Pass.

[g] *Sruthair*, now Shrule, a village on the boundary of the barony of Clare, in the county of Galway, and the barony of Kilmaine, in the county of Mayo. A stream anciently called Sruthair, flowing by this village, was the north-west boundary of Clanrickard.

[h] *Abhainn-da-Loilgheach*, i. e. the River of the two Milch Cows, now Owendalulagh, a mountain stream which rises in the townland of Derrybrien, and parish of Killeenadeema, in the mountain of Sliabh Echtghe, now Slieve Aughty, to the south of the town of Loughrea, in the county of Galway, and which, flowing westwards, falls into Lough Cutra, near the town of Gort. This formed a portion of the southern boundary of Clanrickard.—See map to *Tribes and Customs of Hy-Many*, on which the position of this stream is marked. The name of this stream is accounted for by a legend in the Dinnsenchus,

because they did not, the Irish exchanged their peace for war, their quietness for turmoil, and their tranquillity for dissention; so that they rekindled the ancient flame of hatred in the beginning of the summer of this year.

After the Governor and O'Rourke had parted from each other in peace and friendship, in May, at the town of Athlone, and when O'Rourke saw that the English and Irish were not at peace with each other, and that the English were not at this time more powerful than the Irish, he was afraid that O'Donnell would plunder his territory; and therefore he came at the [first] summons of O'Donnell, and did whatever he requested him. This he [O'Rourke] did by advice of his people, for they felt it safer to have the Governor in opposition, than to be pursued by O'Donnell's vengeance for remaining under the protection of the Governor.

O'Rourke, after having confirmed his friendship with O'Donnell on this occasion, proceeded with his forces, at the instance of O'Farrell Bane (i. e. Ross, the son of William, son of Donnell), into Meath; and they plundered Mullingar, and [the country] from Mullingar to Ballymore-Lough Sewdy[d].

Another hosting was made by O'Rourke in the first month of autumn; and he did not halt until he arrived at Tyrrell's-Pass[e], and the Pass of Kilbride[f] in Fertullagh. He seized a prey, and slew some persons at Tyrrell's-Pass, and (then) returned home to his country without wound or danger.

After the peace before mentioned had been set aside, Redmond Burke, the son of John of the Shamrocks, son of James, son of Rickard Saxonagh, son of Ulick-na-gCeann, with a party of his young kinsmen, [all] of the first distinction, came to O'Neill to complain to him of the answer he had received from his father's brother, namely, the Earl of Clanrickard, Ulick Burke: that "if Redmond would be satisfied with one mantle's breadth of his inheritance or patrimony, from Sruthair[g] to Abhainn-da-Loilgheach[h], he" [the Earl] "would

which states that Sliabh Echtghe, the mountain in which it rises, derived its name from Echtghe Uathach, the daughter of Ursothach, son of Tinde, one of the Tuatha De Danann colony. She married Fergus Lusca mac Ruidi, who held this mountain in right of his office of cup-bearer to the King of Olnegmacht. He had no stock, but she had, and she came to him with her cows, according to the law entitled, *Slabhradh fuithir fosadh*, and he gave up the mountain to her. On this occasion, according to the legend, two cows were brought hither, of remarkable lactiferousness and equally fruitful; but, on their removal hither, it turned out that one of them, which was placed to graze on the north side of the mountain, did not yield one-third as much

ċomaiḋ ċoccaiḋ nó síoḋa ḋó. Ro ġaḃ ó néill an ċossaoíct sin Rémainn, ⁊ ro ġeall a ċoḃair dia ttíoraḋ de ⁊ tucc uaċtaránṫaċt dó ar nuimir airiḋe do ċédaiḃ saighdiuiriḋe ⁊ ro ċſdaiġ dó gaċ aén ḃall dſirinn aga mbſiṫ buain no báidh le Saxancoiḃ dargain ⁊ daḋbalscrios. Iar ffaccḃáil uí néill do Remann a burc ⁊ dia braiṫriḃ do ċuattar i ccommbaiḋ gaoíḋel laiġſn co mbattar ina ffarraḋ re hſḋ an tramraiḋ sin.

Sé céd saiġdiúir do ṫoċt o Shaxoiḃ don taoiḃ buḋ dſs dſirinn do ċuiḋiuccaḋ i nacchaiḋ earccarat an prionnsa. Iar ttoċt doiḃ go dún ngarḃáin arsaḋ ro chinnsiot dol hi ccſnn an genérala .i. Iarla urmuṁan, ⁊ ag gaḃáil doiḃ tre lſiṫimel laiġſn do rala drong do ġaoiḋelaiḃ an ċſnntair sin doiḃ. Fechair iomairſcc ſtorra co ro marḃaḋ dſiċnebar ⁊ ceiṫre ċétt dioḃ isin maiġin sin.

Sluaiccéaḋ la hiarla urmuṁan do ḋol illaoiġis a mí lún. Rob é líon a sloigh cſiṫre banna ḟicſt dia ccois, ⁊ da ċéd marcaċ. Do roine an tiarla coṁnaiḋe im tráṫ nóna ar cnoc árd baí i nimel an tíre. Ro hairnſiḋeaḋ don Iarla in aḋhaiġ sin na baoí aċt uathaḋ dia haes iomcoiṁſtta isin tír. Ro ḟorċongair ar a ḃarac ar ṁac a dſrbraṫar .i. Sémus mac Eduaird mic Semuis buitilér dol go ré, nó a seaċt do ḃandaḋaiḃ amaille fris tar beilġiḃ isteaċ isin cſnn ba nſsa dó don tír dus an ffuigbeaḋ ect, nó aiṫſs re a ḋénaṁ, ⁊ ger ḃó doiliġ la Sémus dol an turus sin a muċa na maidne dia doṁnaiġ do ċóiḋ ann ar forcongra an Iarla. An céd ḃealaċ i ndeachaiḋ as aṁlaiḋ fuair é ar na ṫſsccaḋ, ⁊ ar na ṫrſinġſrraḋ, ⁊ brian riaḃaċ ó mórḋa, go ccéd go lſiṫ saiġdiúir iar ttoċt dia iomċornaṁ isin ló céona. Ba haiġtiḋe aḋuaṫmar an tairbenad tucc brian co na ḟoċraite do Shemus ⁊ dia ṡaiġdiúiriḃ, ⁊ nó ḃíod rſmpo ⁊ ina ndeaḋhaiḋ ga ttacmaing, ⁊ ga ttimċeallaḋ, ga ttrſsgdaḋ, gá ttaoḃ ammus, go ro ḟáccbaḋ cuirp creċtnaiġte cnſstollta re hſḋ naṫġairitt sſchnóin an ḃealaiġ lairs. Ro marbaḋ ecc mór ann sin .i. Sémus mac eduaird mic Semais, mic Piarais, fſr a aesa as ar

milk as the one placed on the south side. This river forms the boundary between the fertile and barren regions of Sliabh Echtghe, alluded to in this legend.

[i] *Hearkened to*, literally, received this complaint.

[j] *Six hundred soldiers*.—The Editor has not been able to find any account of this conflict in any other authority. Peter Lombard, in his work, *De Regno Hiberniæ Commentarius*, published in 1632, p. 406, records that, in the year 1598, Sir Samuel Bagnal was dispatched from England with two thousand foot and one hundred horse, and that he landed with these forces

not give him so much, as a reward for war or peace." O'Neill hearkened to[i] this complaint of Redmond, and promised to assist him, if in his power; and he gave him the command of some hundreds of soldiers, with permission to plunder and devastate any part of Ireland which had any connexion or alliance with the English. When Redmond Burke and his kinsmen left O'Neill, they went into the confederation of the Irish of Leinster, and remained with them during this summer.

Six hundred soldiers[j] arrived from England in the south of Ireland, to assist in opposing the enemies of the Sovereign. On their arrival at Dungarvan[k], they resolved to proceed [directly] to join the General, i. e. the Earl of Ormond; and as they passed along the borders of Leinster, a party of the Irish of that district met them; and a battle was fought between them, in which four hundred and ten of the soldiers were slain.

A hosting was made by the Earl of Ormond in the month of June, to proceed into Leix. His forces amounted to twenty-four companies of foot, and two hundred horse. In the evening he encamped on a high hill on the borders of the territory. The Earl was informed that night that there were only a few to guard the territory, [and] on the morning following he ordered his brother's son, i. e. James, the son of Edward, son of James Butler, to go with six or seven companies through the passes into the nearest part[l] of the territory, to see whether he could perform any exploit or achievement; and although James was loth to go on that expedition early on Sunday morning, yet he set out at the command of the Earl. The first road he went by he found it cut down and deeply furrowed, Brian Reagh O'More having come with one hundred and fifty soldiers to defend it on the same day. Fierce and terrific was the salute which Brian and his forces here gave James and his soldiers. They were attacked in the front and in the rear, hemmed in and surrounded, speared and shot; so that in a short time bodies were left [stretched] mangled and pierced along the pass. A lamentable death occurred here, namely, James, the son of Edward, son of Pierce, son of Pierce, a man of whom greater expectations had

at Wexford, whence he marched for Dublin, but was attacked by the Irish Catholics, who slew great numbers of them.

[k] *Dungarvan*, a sea-port town in the south of the county of Waterford.—See note [o], under the year 1574, p. 1676, *supra*.

[l] *Nearest part*, literally, "the nearest head of the territory."

mó dóig daoine da raibhe beó do buitilerchoibh an tan sin, ⁊ an méd ná ro mudhaigheadh dia muinntir isin maighin sin do deochatar tar a nais ina sccéolangaibh sciathbhriste do ṡaighidh an iarla ⁊ an ċampa. Ro gonadh brian riabhach ua mordha ffírin ⁊ nír bo cian iar sin go ffuair bás do ġaibh cró na ngon do radadh fair don chur sin. Ba isin lo sin fén i ndiaidh na troda remráite tainicc Uaitne mac Ruḋraiġe óicc uí mordha, ⁊ Remann mac Seáin na sémar, ⁊ Captin tirial, ⁊ ro ġabhsat forslongport i nurcomhair ċampa an iarla. Ria meadhon laoí dia luain ar na ṁarach an tan do saoileadh an tiarla do dol isteach isin tír ba hedh do roine sóadh tar a ais co cill cainnigh ⁊ a ṡaighdiuiri do ċor ina ngarasunaibh.

An port nua sin isa sccela ro sccriobhamar remainn, baísidhe aga iomcoiméd le linn triodha ⁊ coccaidh acc muintir na bainriogna. An tan tra na ro ḟiodhaighsiot goill, ⁊ gaoidil fri roile i nurḟorac samhraidh, Ro ċuir Ua néill iomcoiméd for an mbaile go mbattar an bárda i ttéirce bídh isin mí deidhenach don tsamhradh. Iar ndol do na sccelaibh sin co hath cliath, ba hí

[m] *Brian Reagh O'More.*—P. O'Sullevan Beare calls him "Bernardus Fuscus O'Morra."—See *Hist. Cathol. Iber.*, tom. 3, lib. 3, c. x. He gives the following account of the resistance made against the Earl of Ormond by the O'Mores and adherents in tom. 3, lib. 4, c. iv.:

"Vtrumquè periculum, & Lageniensis motus, & Portmor arx commeatus inopia laborans præter cætera Elizabetham Angliæ Reginam angebat, quæ sedulò suis, vt vtrique damno eant obuiam, & Lageniorum tumultum pacent, & Portmori munimento subsidium ferant, imperat. Ad id ex Anglia tyrones mittuntur: præsidiarij euocantur: Ibernorum prouincialium delectus habetur: equitum, & peditum omnis generis millia circiter octo coguntur. Ex ijs, qui vel senio confecti, vel ætate immaturi præliando minus idonei videantur, dimittuntur. Angli tyrones nuper acciti in præsidijs collocantur. Ex cæterorum numero Iberni, & Angli pedites quater mille, & quingenti, & equites quingenti robore, reique militaris peritia electi ad opitulandum Portmori destinantur. Ex auxiliaribus Ibernis, paucisque militibus legionarijs Ibernis, & Anglis millia duo, quorum erant equites pauci, ad Lagenienses motus supprimendos Vrmonio Comiti attribuuntur. Quibus haud dubitabat Vrmonius, quin subigeret Lisiam, & omnes Lageniæ motus pacaret. Lisiam, in qua plus esse negocij videbatur, primum aggreditur. Bernardus Omorra, qui pedites tantum trecentos habebat, in summis rerum angustijs Vrmonium auso prohibere minimè cunctatur, itinerum angustias obsidens. In illum Vrmonius mittit pedites mille Ibernos, & Anglos Duce Iaimo Buttlero nepote suo ex fratre Eduardo. Bernardus loci natura fretus præliari non dubitat. Iaimus copijs in duas partes diuisis illum adit. Vnde Bernardus commoditatem loci deserere coactus, cum altera parte, in qua Iaimus erat, in plano missilibus, maximè bombardicis pilulis dimicat, & pilulem iactu vulneratus magis animo accensus, quàm fractus, suos cohortatus acrius pugnat. Iaimus duplici plumbea glande triectus vir religione Catholicus, & genere clarus pro Hæreticis prælians miserrimé periuit. Quo

been formed than of any other of his age of the Butlers living at that time. And such of his people as had not been cut off at that place returned as broken-shielded fugitives to the Earl and the camp. Brian Reagh O'More[m] himself was wounded; and it was not long after[n] till he died of the virulence of the wounds which he received on this occasion. On this very day, after the battle aforesaid, Owny, the son of Rury Oge O'More; Redmond, the son of John of the Shamrocks [Burke]; and Captain Tyrrell, came and pitched their camp opposite the Earl's camp. Before the noon of the next day, Monday, when it was thought that the Earl would march into the territory, he returned to Kilkenny, and sent his soldiers into their garrisons.

The New Fort, of which we have before written an account, was defended during the time of peace and war by the Queen's people; but when the English and Irish did not make peace [as had been expected] in the beginning of summer, O'Neill laid siege to the fort, so that the warders were in want of provisions in the last month of summer. After this news arrived in Dublin, the

interfecto cæteri terga vertunt. Et alteraquoque copiarum pars auxilio veniens funditur. Fugientes Bernardus secutus stragem multorum edidit, maioremque fecisset, nisi Vrmonius, subueniens pauidos recepisset: qui re infecta à Lisia discessit. Bernardus intra quatriduum vulnere moritur. Cuius obitu tota Lagenia non magno negocio fuisset forsitan pacanda, nisi Huonis Omorræ peroportunus aduentos conspiratos confirmasset. Quo tempore Huon ab Onello petebat auxilium, apud illum erat, Raymundus Burkus Lietrimæ Baro possessionibus orbus. Quemadmodum enim superius demonstrauimus, Iohannes Burkus Lietrimæ Baro ab Vlligo fratre suo Anglorum permissu fuerat occisus Raymundo filio impubere relicto, & Baronatus administratio Reginæ abiudicata eo nomine, quòd Anglorum instituto penes reges solet esse tutela nobilium ætate minorum. Baronatus autem administrationem Regina dono dedit Phintoni Anglo Iberniæ consilij secretario, à quo illam pecunia emit Vlligus Clanrichardæ comes Raymundi patruus, & ita in possessionem missus Raymundo, qui iam per ætatem tutela exierat, Baronatum restituere differebat. Raymundus intenta lite illum Anglorum, & Reginæ iudicio superauit. Cæterum, quia sub hoc tempus bellum exardebat, priusquam Raymundus fuit possessione potitus, omiserunt Angli sententiam suam executioni mandare, ne Comitis viri potentis iram tam periculoso tempore lacesserent. Idcirco Raymundus Onelli opem implorabat ad paternam hæreditatem recuperandam. Onellus Tironæ defendendæ intentus, quia differebat auxilium, spem tantum præbens, Raymundus vnà cum Huone in Lageniam proficiscitur, ac etiam Dermytius Oconchur vir nobilis ex Connachta, quos omnes Connachti, qui finibus pulsi apud Onellum agebant, sequuntur. Richardus etiam Tirellus, cuius mentionem fecimus, ab Huone conducitur, quibus cum Huon in Lisiam venit eodem die, quo Bernardus cum hostibus pugnauit, sed nec pugnam integram, nec Vrmonium à Lisia discedentem potuit assequi."

[n] *It was not long after.*—An English writer would say: "he died soon after of his wounds."

airle ro ċinnsiot an coṁairle an ro ba disle, ⁊ as mo ro dsrḃaḋ isin cCoccaḋ do ṡaiġdiuiriḃ na bainrioġna i nErinn hi ccoṁḟocraiḃ Aṫa cliaṫ, ⁊ Ḃaile aṫa luain do ṫionol go haoin ionadh, ⁊ iar na roċtain co haon Ḃaile ro tscclamaḋ eistiḃ ceithre míle saiġdiúir dia ccois ⁊ se ċéd marcaċ, ⁊ ro cuireaḋ iad-side le lón gus an bport nua. Ro cuireaḋ leó side an ro ba lor leó do biúḋ, do ḋiġ do ṁarcaiġeċt, do luaiḋe, do ṗúdar, ⁊ da gaċ naiḋilcc ar ċsna. Lottar iaraṁ co droichsct áṫa, assiḋe go traiġ baile, ⁊ don iuḃar, ⁊ go hArdmaċa, airissit in Ardmaċa in adhaiġ sin. Sir hanry Ḃeging marusgál an Iuḃair as é ba general dóiḃ.

Iar ffios dUa neill an tsoċraitte adbal mor sin do bsiṫ acc tionol dia ṡaiġiḋ Ro ċuir a ṫeċta do ṫoċuireaḋ Uí domnaill, ⁊ dia cuingiḋ fair teċt dia foiriḋin ar an anfforlann ecctrann báttar ag toċt dia ṫír. Do ċoiḋ din O domnaill fo ċédóir co lsr ṫionol a laoċraiḋe etir troiġṫeaċ, ⁊ marcaċ, ⁊ drong mór do ċóicceaḋ ċonnaċt amaille friss do ċoḃair a ċoiccele for an ffoirlion ro ḋalsat ċuicce. Tangatar Ḃsor gaoiḋil coicciḋ ulaḋ uile is in tsoċraitte ceona go mbáttar inellma for cionn na ngall riasiú rangatar go hArdmaċa. Ro toċlaḋ leo dna domaindíocca talṁan for cionn na ngall forsan cconair ccoitchinn in ro baḋ doigh leo a roċtain dia saiġiḋ.

Imṫusa na ngall iar mbsiṫ adhaiġ in Ardmaċa ro sirgsttar a mocha do lo ar na ḃaraċ, ⁊ asseaḋ ro chinnsiott a mbiaḋ, a ndeoċ, a mná, ⁊ a mion-daoine, a ccapaill, a ccarairde a ngiollanraiḋ, a ndaorsccarsluaġ dfaccḃáil isin mbaile sin Ardamaċa. Ro ḟoccairsiot dá gaċ aén baí infsoma aca etir marcaċ ⁊ troiġṫeaċ dol in gaċ airm nó ḟurailfeaḋ an marusccal ⁊ cuingsḋa an tsloiġ ar ċsna forra arccnaṁ i naghaiḋ a namat. Do ċottar iaraṁ i ninnell ⁊ i nordduccaḋ aṁail as dsċ ro ḟédsat. Ro ċsimmiġsiot iaraṁ tre rsiḋ ḋirge gaċa róid bai rsmpa ina ttuinntiḃ tiuġa toirtsmla, ⁊ ina ndoirsḋaiḃ dluiṫe dosccaoilte go rangatar gus an ccnoc os cionn Ḃeóil an áṫa buiḋe. Iar roċtain dóiḃ hisuiḋe att conncattar Ua neill, ⁊ Ua dom-

[o] *Beging.*—This should be Bagnall.

[p] *Marshal of Newry*, *recte*, Marshal of Ulster.

[q] *Squadrons:* literally, "in dense and impenetrable derrys or oak woods," which is not a very correct figure to apply to an army on their march.

[r] *Béal-an-atha-buidhe*, i. e. Mouth of the Yellow Ford. The site of this battle is shewn on an old "Map of the Country lying between Lough Erne and Dundalk," preserved in the State Papers Office, London, as on the banks of the River Callen, to the north-east of the city of Armagh. The place is called Ballymackilloune, and the following words are written across the spot: "Here

Council resolved to assemble together the most loyal and best tried in war of the Queen's soldiers in Ireland, [who were those] in the neighbourhood of Dublin and Athlone; and when these [soldiers] were assembled together, four thousand foot and six hundred horse were selected from among them, and these were sent to convey provisions to the New Fort. A sufficient supply of meat and drink, beef, lead, powder, and all other necessaries, were sent with them. They marched to Drogheda, from thence to Dundalk, from thence to Newry, and from thence to Armagh, where they remained at night. Sir Henry Beging[o], Marshal of Newry[p], was their General.

When O'Neill had received intelligence that this great army was approaching him, he sent his messengers to O'Donnell, requesting of him to come to his assistance against this overwhelming force of foreigners who were coming to his country. O'Donnell proceeded immediately, with all his warriors, both infantry and cavalry, and a strong body of forces from Connaught, to assist his ally against those who were marching upon him. The Irish of all the province of Ulster also joined the same army, so that they were all prepared to meet the English before they arrived at Armagh. They then dug deep trenches against the English in the common road, by which they thought they [the English] would come to them.

As for the English, after remaining a night at Armagh, they rose next morning early; and the resolution they adopted was, to leave their victuals, drink, their women and young persons, their horses, baggage, servants, and rabble, in that town of Armagh. Orders were then given that every one able to bear arms, both horse and foot, should proceed wherever the Marshal and other officers of the army should order them to march against their enemies. They then formed into order and array, as well as they were able, and proceeded straightforward through each rood before them, in close and solid bodies, and in compact, impenetrable squadrons[q], till they came to the hill which overlooks the ford of Beal-an-atha-bhuidhe[r]. After arriving there they perceived O'Neill

Sir H. Bagnall, Marshal of Newry, was slaine." The name Béal-an-atha-buidhe, *anglicè*, Bellanaboy, is now applied to a small marsh or cut out bog, situated in the townland of Cabragh, about one mile and three-quarters to the north of the city of Armagh. A short distance to the north of this bog stands a white-thorn bush, locally called the "Great Man's Thorn," which is said to have been planted near the grave of Marshal Bagnall. Captain Tucker, R. E., who surveyed this part of Ireland for the Ordnance Survey, has marked the site of this battle on the Ordnance

na ll, Uí eachdhach uladh ⁊ airghialla, toísigh ⁊ tighernaill, láthgaile ⁊ gaisccidh an tuaisceirt amaille friú ina naén bhroin aighthighe for a ccionn iar na

map by two swords in saltier, and the date 1598.—See the Ordnance map, Armagh, sheet 12.

Accounts of this battle have been given by Camden, Fynes Moryson, Philip O'Sullevan Beare, and Peter Lombard, and from them by Mageoghegan, Taaffe, O'Conor, and a host of modern writers of no authority. Philip O'Sullevan Beare gives by far the most circumstantial account of it, and the Editor is tempted, on account of the extreme rarity of his work, to give the whole of it in this place:

"In Lagenia dum hæc aguntur, Henricus Bagnal Anglus eques Auratus Iberniæ castrametator, & Vltoniæ præfectus in oppidum Jurem in Vltoniæ finibus situm, & valido Hæreticorum præsidio munitum non longius á Portmore munimento millibus passuum vndeviginti maiorem regium exercitum ad opitulandum Portmori ducens peruenit. Inde tertijs castris substitit in vrbe Ardmacha. Erat Bagnal millitaris artis peritus, & quod raró in imperatore inuenies, consilio simul, & animi magnitudine præstans, in rebus secundis cautus; in aduersis animosus, in victos, & dedititios minus contumeliosus Anglis plerisque: qui nunquam conuitijs parcunt. Itaque gentis suæ Ducum audeo paucos illi conferre, anteponere pauciores. Erat Onello non solum publica causa Religionis, & Reginæ, sed etiam priuatis inimicitijs infensissimus. Ducebat quatuor millia, & quingentos pedites sub signis quadraginta, & totidem cohortium ducibus, optionibus, signiferis, & tesserarijs, & equites quingentos sub signis octo, quorum magister erat Monteguus Anglus. In vniuerso numero pauló plures Iberni, quam Angli stipendium faciebant, veterani omnes, Angli superstites eorum, qui vel duce Iohanne Norrise in Gallia belligerauerant, vel à præsidijs Belgicis fuerant acciti, vel ab huius belli principio rei militaris regulas in Ibernia perceperant: Iberni quoque qui sub bellicæ disciplinæ præceptis contenti in legionibus Reginæ stipendium merentes suæ virtutis documenta sæpè præbuerant. Erant ibi nonnulli iuuenes Iberni genere clari, præsertim Melmorrus Orelli principis filius ab raram staturæ elegantiam, & miram faciei venustatem cognomento Pulcher, & Christophorus Sanlaurentius Baronis Hotæ filius. Ibi nullus tyro, nullus militiæ rudis. Omnes omni genere armorum instructissimi: pedites, & equites cataphractarij: Bombardarij alij grauibus, alij leuibus sclopis ad pugnam parati, gladio, & pugione accincti, galeis capita munientibus. Totus exercitus plumeis apicibus, sericis baltheis, cæterisque militaribus insignibus fulgebat. Ænea machinamento rotis vehebantur, trahentibus equis. Sulphurei pulueris, globorum ferreorum, atque plumbeorum vis magna suppetebat. Caballi, bouesque biscocti panis, falsæ carnis, casei, butyri, seruitiæ sat & exercitui in vinctum, & arci Portmori in commeatum portabant. Impedimenta muliones comitabantur, lixarum, pabulatoremqué numerus magnus sequebatur.

"Distabat á Bagnale Portmor arx tribus millibus passuum Ibernicis ab Onello obsessa, & inedia laborans. Qui cum de Bagnalis aduentu intellexisset, contra illum castra mota mille passibus vltra munimentum, & intra duo millia passuum ad Armacham collocat, relictis paucis, qui Portmoris propugnatores eruptionibus prohibeant. Eo die Catholici recensuerant peditum quatuor millia, & quingentos, & equites circiter sexcentos. Interfuit Odonellus, qui Connachtos duce Maculliamo Burko stipendiatos circiter mille, & Tirconnellos suos, vtrosque ad numerum duorum millium duxit. Cæteri Onellum, eius fratres, & consanguineos, & magnates cum eo veteri iure coniunctos sequebantur. Ac planè eó conuenerat omnis ferè Vltoniæ nobilis iu-

and O'Donnell, the Ui Eathach Uladh, and the Oirghialla, having, together with the chieftains, warriors, heroes, and champions of the North, drawn up one

uentus, atque multi Connachti iuuenes ortu minime obscuri. Erant tamen armis longè inferiores, namque tum equitatus, tum peditatus erat leuis armaturæ præter paucos bombardarios grauium scloporum. Ob id Onellus de hostis apparatu præliandi, militis robore, ducis animo deliberato certior factus, dubium erat, quin vir cautus locum desereret, uisi Farfasius Oclerius Ibernicorum vatum interpres confirmasset Diui Vltani vaticinio fuisse prædictum eo in loco Hæreticum fuisse profligandum, & præsensionem Ibernico metro prolatam in libro diuinationum sancti ostendisset. Qua confirmatus Onellus ad pugnam suos hac oratione cohortatur.

"Quod á Deo optimo maximo (viri Christianissimi, atque fortissimi) summis precibus sæpe petiuimus, atque contendimus, id, & amplius etiam hodie diuino quodam munere sumus assecuti. Vt pares aliquando cum Protestantibus dimicaremus, Deum, atque cœlites, semper exoramus. Huc orationes nostras, huc vota intendimus. Iam verò non modo pares, sed etiam plures numero sumus. Igitur qui pauciores agmina Hæretica fudistis, eisdem plures obstabitis. Ego quidem non in exanimi cataphracta, non in tormentorum inani sonitu, sed in viuis, & intrepidis animis constituo victoriam. Mementote, quoties nobiliores duces, maiores copias, & ipsum etiam Bagnalem minus parati, & instructi superaueritis. Angli nec animo, nec virtute, nec præliandi constantia fuerunt vnquam cum Ibernis conferendi. Qui veró Iberni contra vos dimicaturi sunt, Catholicæ fidei oppugnatæ, sui sceleris, atque schysmatis conscientia consternabuntur: eadem Catholica fide vobis vires augente hic Christianam religionem, patriam, liberos, vxores defendendum. Hic Bagnal Hæreticorum omnium acerrimus vester hostis, qui in bona vestra impetum facit, qui vestrum sanguinem sitit, qui meum honorem oppugnat, debito supplicio afficiendus. Hic vlciscendum dedecus illud, quod, ego apud Tumulum Album accepi à Bagnale parte castrorum eiectus. Hic mors commilitonum vestrorum, quos in Portmoris oppugnatione amisimus, vindicanda, & arx ipsa, quam diu obsidetis, dum eam commeatu intercluditis, expugnanda. Hic obtinenda victoria, quam vobis Dominus Diui Vltani prædictione pollicetur. Ergo Deo, cælicolisque iuutibus rem fæliciter gerite. Contra Bagnal ita suos alloquitur.

"Fortitudine vestra, commilitones invictissimi, fretus, vos mihi socios elegi, rudes, atque ignaros in præsidijs constituens, & fæces omnium, homines imbecillos Vrmonio Comiti relinquens, quorum ignauia æquo illum rem fædè gesturum putaui, ac mihi promisi gloriosam victoriam opera vestra reportandam. Id namque vestræ magnanimitatis, atque virtutis periculum semper feci, vt non possim non concipere hodiernæ victoriæ spem indubitatam, atque certissimam. Neque credo, quin fatali quadam fælicitate tot casus aduersos, tot discrimina, incolumes euaseritis, vt hodie faustè vincendo totam vitam decoretis, commilitonumque vestrorum á rebellibus, atque perfidis aduersa fortuna Norrisis, & Burughi peremptorem mortem vlciscamini. Quid? Audebunt ne insani corpore nudo cum armatis, cum viris coporis, & animi robore præstantissimis congredi. Demens ego sim, si conspectum vestrum sustinuerint, & nisi hodie totam Vltoniam sub iugum mittatis, totamque Iberniam Reginæ subigatis, ipsique ingente præda potiamini. Mementote vestræ virtutis, qui me duce Ardmachæ opem tulistis, Onello non minima parte castrorum ad Tumulum Album exuto. Ad vesperum, qui mihi Onelli, vel Odonelli caput dono dederit, huic mille auri libras polliceor, & singulis recipio pro meritis

suidiuccadh, ⁊ iar na sámhucchadh for na hsnaighibh erdalta an ro badh dóigh leó iadsomh do rochtain dia saighidh.

gratias quam accumulatissimas, & á Regina, & a me esse referendas Eamus, properemus, ne victoriam nostram differamus.

"Concione absoluta Bagnal ante solis exortum Ardmacha castra mouet decimo quinto circiter die, quam Comes Vrmonius fuit à Bernardo Omorra repulsus. Hastati in agmina tria erant digesti, quæ præibant & sequebantur equitum, & fulminatorum alæ. Sereno, & grato die vexillis explicatis, tubarum clangore, tibiarum concentu, tympanorum militarium sonitu homines, & equi ad pugnam accensi per lætam planiciem nemine prohibente procedunt. Mox excipiebat iter angustius iuniperis, sed humilibus, atque rarissimis consitum. Hoc Bagnal ingressus hora circiter septima á quingentis imberbibus adolescentibus, bombardarijs velitibus ab Onello missus densissima globulorum grandine per totum arboretum continuata obruitur. Velites ponè iuniperos stantes, & inter arbores cursitantes equites; atque pedites éminus iactu sternunt, & eó tutius, quod & equites regij propter iuniperos esse non poterant, vel suis adiumento, vel Catholicis impedimento, & præoccupantibus velitibus locus erat æquior, quam venientibus regijs. Ab his augustijs magna difficultate Bagnal denique copias expediuit non parum vexatas acri velitatione, & tristes ob impunè receptum damnum à velitibus, qui puerile, atque ridiculum hominum genus videbantur. Lata planicies vsque ad Catholicorum castra succedebat. In hanc egresso Bagnale regius equitatus in Catholicos velites quam celerrimo gradu currit. Cæterum per primam planiciei partem in ipso maximé itinere, sed & circum illud Onellus crebras foueas, atque fossas excauauit stratis super virgulis, & fæno sparso dissimulatas. In quas cataphractarij equites incauti cadunt, casuque crebro equorum simul, & assessorum crura franguntur, qui, vt à socijs leuarentur, haud absque contentione Catholici velites sinunt. Strata gemmate regius exercitus non nihil animo fractus equitibus, atque peditibus aliquot desideratis, & sauciatis in minus impeditum planum peruenit. Hic Onelli velitibus defessis vegetes, & integri succedunt, à Bagnale quoque velites, & grauis armaturæ bombardarij mittuntur èminus vtrinque acerrimè dimicatur. Regij quoque equites cataphractarij in certamen prodeunt. His occurrunt Catholici equites ferentarij, vel leuis armaturæ. Cataphractarij cataphractarum munimine tutiores locum obtinebant. Ferentarij dexteritate, & velocitate præstantes, & iterum, atque iterum circumactis equis in pugnam redeuntes vulnera plura inferunt, loco tamen cedentes. Cataphractarij hastis sex circiter cubita longis dextero femini innixis cominus pugnant. Ferentarij armati hastis longioribus, quas medias manu tenentes super dexterum humerum gerunt, raró nisi ex commodo feriunt, interim tela ligneo hastili quatuor ferè cubitorum ferrea cuspide infixa iaculantes. Ita Bagnal procedens sæpe ab Onelli leui armatura subsistere coactus, sæpè etiam eandem repellens haud procul á Catholicorum castris substitit hora diei ferè vndecima. Hic planicies illa duplici uligine hinc, inde coarctabatur, et inter utramque uliginem humile, et tenue vallum altitudine quatuor pedum, profundiorem vero fossam interius per quartam milliarii partem Onellus duxit, magis, ut esset hosti impedimento, quam sibi adiumento. Inter medium vallum, & regium exercitum exsiliebant turbidi coloris latices ex uliginibus coeuntes. Unde forsan locus multis dicitur vadum pallidum (*Beal atha bui*, os vadi pallidi) & si aliis placeat vadum Sancti Buiani vocari. Pro vallo, et utroque exercitu equitum, & fulminatorum pugna vehementius instauratur. In æstu pugnæ scloperarius Anglus, qui nitratum puluerem inter pugnandum consumpsit,

terrible mass before them, placed and arranged on the particular passages where they thought the others would march on them.

sulphur sumpturus in Lagenam in quâ erat, fortè iniecit manum, quâ bombardicum funem ignitum tenebat. Iniecto igne accensa Lagena, et duæ proximæ nitri plenæ nonnullos combustos in ærem tollunt. Interim Bagnal contra Catholicorum vallum, et agmina disponit ænea machinamenta, quorum unum sulphure, et Globis onustum, dum exploditur, vehementia pulueris in varia frusta diruptum interficit circumstantes nonnullos. Cæteris Bagnal vallum discutit, et hastatorum Catholicorum agmina tormentis nuda verberat, eorum equitibus, et bombardarijs, qui pro vallo continenter certant, minimè obstantibus: aliquot partes valli solo æquat, et ab eo arcet agmina: in quorum locum irrumpunt duo prima regia agmina, alterum adversus Onellum, alterum aduersus Odonellum læuum cornu tenentum, et aliquot agminum ordines vallum transgrediuntur, in quorum subsidium agmen ultimum Bagnal ducit. Eodem tempore equitatum et bombardarios Catholicorum intra vallum pulsos regius equitatus, et bombardarii sequuntur, et æquo jam loco utrique strenuè præliantur, et utrique mixti viri viros amplexi equis detrahunt. Hic hastati Catholici, qui tormentorum ictibus à vallo fuerunt remoti, videntes tormenta non esse iam hosti usui, sese in agmina regia conuertunt nondum tamen manum conserunt. Eodem temporis momento Bagnal qui munitus erat cataphracta, et casside ex calybe factis grauis sclopi iactum sustinentibus ratus se iam vicisse, ut liberius lætam prælij faciem videret et facilius respiraret, armaturæ gravis pondere fatigatus, cassidis conspicilium aperit, et tollit, nec prius demisit, et clausit, quam iacuit humi exanimis plumbea glande fronte confossus. Cuius morte tertium, agmen in quo erat, magna trepidatis inuasit. Agmina duo ad quæ ducis extincti nuncius nondum fuit perlatus, rem fortiter gerunt. Catholici quoque nihil segniter prælium committunt. Odonellus bombardariorum virtute sese tuetur. Onelli agmen magis periclitari videtur. In hoc ancipiti rerum statu Onellus, qui iuxta suum agmen equo insidebat cum equitibus quadraginta, et totidem Bombardarijs, bombardarios, jubet, ut regium agmen glandibus carpant. Obedientes imperio bombardarij non parum molestant, et ordines cogunt laxare agmen fulminatorum ope nudum. Perculsis Onellus addit terrorem cum quadraginta equitibus in medium agmen laxatis habenis irrumpendo. Onellum sequens suum hastatorum agmen clamore sublato regium in fugam vertit hora ferè prima pomeridiana. Id conspicati ij quoque qui cum Odonello certant, agmine turbato terga vertunt. Monteguus etiam cum equitatu pedem refert. Bombardariorum alæ sese fugæ mandant. Onellus, Odonellus, et Macguier, qui præerat equitatui, fugientium tergis hærent. Fossa, vallumque regiis erat magis impedimento tunc fugientibus, quam anteà aggredientibus, qui cadentes alij super alios fossam implent, & iacentes ungulis equorum pedibusque pedibus obteruntur. Ultimum agmen, in quo Bagnal erat, duce mortuo mæstum et trepidum turbatis aliis auxilio non erat. Tamen Melmorrus Orellus cognomento Pulcher trepidos iubet adesse animo et secum hosti resistere, speciosius esse interfici præliantes, et ultos, quam fugientes impunè occidi, et adhuc fieri posse, ut hostis impetum sustineant, ipsumque repellant. Pulchri cohortatione nonnulli confirmati, maximè iuvenes Iberni cum eo consanguinitate coniuncti redintegrant prælium. Quibus pugnantibus Pulcher sese in omnes partes vertit, ut magis laborantibus, et periclitantibus opem ferat. Cæterum illi pauci, qui cum eo manserunt, & a regijs deserti et à Catholicis circumuenti multis vulneribus affecti cadunt et Pulcher ipse solus relictus pugnans fortissimè sternitur. Et omnes

An tan do bfretsat airiġ an tuaisceirt dia nuíḋ an guasaċt ro ṁór ro baí for cinḋ ḋoiḃ, Ro gaḃsat for grfsaċtlaoíḋheaḋ a muinntire im ċalma

regij effusa fuga salutem pedibus quærentes per planiciem, quà venerant, et arboretum, inde Ardmacham usque dissipati, et palantes occiduntur. In Ardmachæ templa sese receperunt equites, & circiter mille, & quingenti pedites. Perierunt prælio regiorum plus duo millia, & quingenti, et inter eos Bagnal exercitus imperator, cohortium duces viginti tres, multi optiones, signiferi, et tesserarii. Capta sunt signa militaria triginta quatuor omnia militaria tympana, tormenta bellica, magna vis armorum, et totus commeatus. Neque victoribus quidem pugna fuit incruenta, et si enim minus ducenti fuerunt desiderati, tamen plus sexcenti fuerunt vulnerati. In Ardmachæ templa, quæ regiorum præsidio tenebantur, qui sese abdiderunt, á victoribus obsidentur. Monteguus cum equitatu noctu tenebrarum auxilio fugit. Eum sine ordine, et effusa fuga fugientem ex Onelli castris secutus Terentius Ohanlonus cum parte equitatus impedimenta, et equos ducentos capit, duces tres interficit: Romlius etiam Anglus dux cum die sequente iuxta iter Tabacci herbæ fumum fistula sorberet, deprehensus occiditur. Pedites ex pacto inermes dimittuntur, Ardmacha, & Portmore Onello traditis."—*Hist. Cathol. Iber. Compend.*, fol. 150–155.

Camden, who knew the names and movements of the English party better than O'Sullevan, gives the following brief but valuable account of this battle in his *Annal. Reg. Eliz.*, A. D. 1598:

"Toto hoc anno rebellio Hibernica admodum exarsit. Tir-Oenius enim, etsi veniam, quam simulate imploraverat ab Ormundio Locumtenente, sub magno Sigillo Hiberniæ impetraverat, ex improviso munimentum ad *Blackwater* obsidione incinxit. Ad eam solvendam Locum-tenens exercitus Generalis (nullus enim adhuc Prorex substitutus) selectissimas submisit turmas scilicet xiii vexillationes sub Henrico Bagnallo Marescallo, acerbissimo Tir-Oenii adversario. Die xiv. Augusti a castris prope Armacham triplici acie moverunt: primam duxerunt Marescallus & Percius; mediam Cosbius, & Thomas Maria Wingfeldius; postremam Cuinus & Billingus. Equitum turmis præfuerunt Calisthenes Brookus, Carolus Montacutus, & Flemingus. Vix mille passus confecerant, nimio plus inter se disparati per colles leviter surgentes, inter uliginosam hinc planiciem, inde sylvas, cum in primam aciem Tir-Oenius, acrioribus odii in Marescallum stimulis excitatus, omnibus viribus involaret: statimque eo inter confertissimos hostes occiso, primam illam aciem a cæteris longius subsequentibus & ex objectu collis ne conspectam, dum ordines laxarat, multitudine facile oppressit: eodemque momento pulvis tormentarius fortuito in media acie igne concepto multos sustulit, & plures mutilavit; Cosbiusque, qui missus ut primæ aciei recolligeret, magna clade affectus. Montacutus tamen non sine magno periculo reduxit; Wingfeldus cum postrema acie, pulvere tormentario deficiente, Armacham rediit. Ita Tir-Oenius perjucundum de adversario triumphum, & de Anglis victoriam insignem, reportavit. Nec sane, ex quo in Hibernia pedem firmarunt, major clades accepta, xiii strenuis ordinum ductoribus desideratis; & mille quingentis e gregariis, qui fœda fuga dissipati, totis campis palantes cæsi victique. Superstites non suam ignaviam, sed ducum imperitiam, quod jam in morem cessit probrose culparunt. Nec sine culpa videbantur, qui adeo disparati præter militarem disciplinam incesserunt contra barbaros, qui semper in unum conferti impetu magis quam consilio pugnant.

"Paulo post munimenti ad Blackwater subsequuta est deditio, cum præsidiarii, fide & armis ad extremam famem retentis, spem omnem subsidii evanuisse viderent.

When the chiefs of the North observed the very great danger that now threatened them, they began to harangue and incite their people to acts of

"Hæc victoria rebellibus gloriosa, & imprimis usui; hinc enim arma & commeatum nacti & Tir-Oenius per Hiberniam magna fama, tanquam libertatis auctor, ubique celebratus, ferocia & superbia supra modum intumuit."

Fynes Moryson, in his *History of Ireland*, edition of 1735, vol. i. p. 58, 59, also confesses that the English received a great overthrow on this occasion. The following are his words:

"Because the English fort of Blackwater was a great Eye-sore to him" [Tyrone], "lying on the chief passage into his country, he assembled all his forces and assaulted the same; but Captain Thomas Williams, with his company under him, so valiantly repelled the great multitudes of the assailants, with slaughter of many, and the most hardy attempting to scale the Fort (which was only a deep trench or wall of earth to lodge some one" [*recte*, three] "hundred soldiers), as they utterly discouraged from assailing it, resolved to besiege it afar off, and knowing they wanted victualls, presumed to get it by famine.

"This Captain, and his few Warders, did with no less courage suffer hunger, and having eaten the few horses they had, lived upon herbs growing in the ditches and walls, suffering all Extremities till the Lord Lieutenant, in the month of August, sent Sir Henry Bagnol Marshal of Ireland, with the most choice companies of foot and horse troops of the English Army, to victual this fort, and to raise the Rebels siege. When the English entered the pace and thick woods beyond Armagh, on the east side, Tyrone (with all the Rebels Forces assembled to him) pricked forward with rage of Envy and settled Rancour against the Marshal, assailed the English, and, turning his full force against the Marshal's person, had the success to kill him, valiantly fighting among the thickest of the Rebels. Whereupon the English being dismayed with his death, the Rebels obtained a great victory against them. I term it great, since the English from their first arrival in that kingdom never had received so great an overthrow as this, commonly called, the defeat of Blackwater; thirteen valiant Captains and fifteen hundred common soldiers, (whereof many were of the old companies which had served in Britanny under General Norris) were slain in the field. The yielding of the fort of Blackwater followed this Disaster, when the assaulted Guard saw no Hope of Relief; but especially upon Messages sent to Captain Williams from our broken Forces retired to Armagh, professing that all their safety depended upon his yielding the Fort into the Hands of Tyrone, without which Danger Captain Williams professed that no Want or Misery should have induced him thereunto.

"Shortly after Sir Richard Bingham, late Governor of Connaught, and unworthily disgraced, was sent over to succeed Sir Henry Bagnol in the Mastership of that kingdom.

"By this victory the Rebels got plenty of Arms and Victuals; Tyrone was among the Irish celebrated as the Deliverer of his Country from Thraldom, and the combined Traitors on all sides were puffed up with intolerable pride. All Ulster was in Arms; all Connaught revolted, and the Rebels of Leinster swarmed in the English Pale, while the English lay in their Garrisons, so far from assailing the Rebels, as they rather lived in continual fear to be surprised by them."

It is difficult to believe that Moryson's account of the fort, called Portmore, or Portnua, by the Irish, is correct. Cucogry O'Clery, in his Life of Hugh Roe O'Donnell, states that it was a strong earthen fort, having "fighting towers," with windows and loop-holes to fire through, and that the English garrisoned it with three hun-

do ḋénaṁ. ⁊ atbertsat friú munbuḋ leó coscar an la sin na biaḋ a naṫ-maoín da éis, aċt a marḃaḋ, ⁊ a muḋuccaḋ gan ċoiccill ⁊ no bérṫa araill

dred select warriors to check the Kinel-Owen. This writer gives a much better account of this battle than that abstracted by the Four Masters. He says that very few of the Irish were dressed in armour like the English, in comparison with whom they were "naked;" but that they had a sufficient quantity of spears and broad lances with strong handles of ash; of straight, keen-edged swords, and thin polished battle-axes; but devoid of the flesca and ecclanna, which distinguished the axes of the English. They had also javelins, bows and arrows, and guns with match-locks.—*O'Reilly's copy*, p. 53.

The most curious part of Cucogry O'Clery's account of this battle is the speech of O'Neill to the Irish, and the prophecy read to them by Fearfeasa O'Clery. As the speech of O'Neill, given by P. O'Sullevan Beare, was composed by O'Sullivan himself, in imitation of Sallust, Livy, and Tacitus, the Editor is tempted to lay before the reader the very words of Cucogry O'Clery, which are evidently more authentic than those of O'Sullevan Beare:

"Ro ġaḃ O Neill ⁊ O Doṁnaill ag gréssaċt laoiḋeaḋ na ngalgat ⁊ ag maoiḋeaṁ na mileaḋ, ⁊ ag tionċosg na ttréinḟear, ⁊ asseaḋ atbeartsat friu:

"A ḋeaġṁuinter, ar siad, na huaiṁniġḟesi siḃ, ⁊ na gaḃaiḋ gráin rias na gallaiḃ ar allṁurdaċt a ninnill, ⁊ ar ionggnaiṫechiu a n-eittiġ ⁊ a narm, ⁊ la torainnbeice a ttrompa, a ttábúr ⁊ a ccairmeartta caṫa, ⁊ ar a n-iomat lionṁaireaċt féisin ar ar dearḃ deiṁin comaḋ forra bus roen isin lo baġa sa aniu. Ar deatta linn ón, ar atáiṫísi for fíor ⁊ atát an luċt oile for goí, ogaḃar ccuimriuch i ccaircriḃ, ⁊ ogaḃar ndiċísndaḋ do ġaitt bar n-aṫarda ndilis foraiḃ. Atá dna lanḟaoileaċtaim linn co n-eitirglesi an lá sa aniu eitir fír ⁊ goi feḃ atbert Morann mac Maein an sinarusc airdearc: 'ní friṫ, ní fuiġbiṫer breitem bus fíriu caṫrae,' amail at clos lind ó ár ffileadaiḃ, ⁊ do ro ionċoirccriut dúinn ó ċéin ṁáir. Araill ann dna ar usa daoiḃ bar n-aṫarda féisin do ċosnaṁ fri hainfine eaċtairċeineoil oldas aṫarda neich oile do ṫionġaire iar na bar ttosann as bur ttír ndilis fil in bar seilḃ ó ré 3500 bliadan d'aois domain gus an laiṫisiu aniuṁ.

"Atbeartsat na huasail ⁊ na hairiġ cor bo fíor do na flaiṫiḃ ar fuiġeallsat. Ro ġaḃ greim doiḃriuṁ an dúirġréssaċt do ronsat for na deiġḟearaiḃ, uair raċtatar mísnmanna na mileaḋ ⁊ aiccennta na n-annraḋ go ro lion bruṫ ⁊ briġ ⁊ ailġís imbearta arm Conaill, Eoġain, airġiallaiġ ⁊ Ui Eaṫaċ Ulaḋ la h-aiṫearsga a fflath, ⁊ a ff'or ċodnaċ ⁊ ro ṫingeallsat dóiḃ na tiuḃratais troiġ for ccúla ⁊ no foḋemdais a n-aiḋeaḋ for aon laṫair ria siu ro baḋ raon forra.

"Fáṫ oile dna ima ro eiriġ aicceanta na n-óg. At coadatar doiḃ co ro tiorchan naoiṁ Bearchán fáiḋ Dé co ttiuḃarṫa caṫ in du sin for gallaiḃ Duiḃlinne la h-Oeḋ O néill ⁊ las an ccóigeaḋ ar ċéna, uair ro ṫingeall co ttiucfatais ina ṫoiriṫin ⁊ cenel Conaill sainreaḋ.

"Ro ċreitsít na curaiḋ na h-ereraḋ an fáiḋ naoṁ soa. Ar é ro foillsiġ dóiḃ cétus reméṫsrcanta an naoiṁ aroili fili oirdeirc do ṡainṁuinter uí doṁnaill do rala ina ṡaraḋ for an sluaiġeaḋ fri h-aireag tuile dó. Fearfeasa O Cléiriġ a ċoṁainm. Ro iomċoṁairc siḋe cia h-ainm baoí for an maiġin sin. Ro hairnéiḋeaḋ dó. At beart soṁ gur ro ṫairngir naoiṁ bearchan sraoineaḋ for ġallaiḃ an du sin ria Oeḋ Ua Neill amuil at rubromor, ⁊ gur bo meaḃair lais fri ré ḟoda an tairċeardal do roine an fír naoṁ, ⁊ ro ġaḃ occ gréssaċt ⁊ occ laoiḋeaḋ na laoċraiḋe amail

valour, saying that unless the victory was their's on that day, no prospect remained for them after it but that of being [some] killed and slaughtered without

ro ba du dia inegramail, co ndebair inso.

"A ccath an Atha buidhe
Ar lair tuitfe na danair
Iar ndithiughadh Allmhuireach
Bidh faoilidh fir ó Thóraigh."

"O'Neill and O'Donnell proceeded to incite and harangue the heroes, and to exhort the soldiers, and to instruct the mighty men, and they said:

"'Brave people,' said they, 'be not dismayed or frightened at the English on account of the foreign appearance of their array, and the strangeness of their armour and arms, the sound of their trumpets, and tabours, and warlike instruments, or of their great numbers, for it is absolutely certain that they shall be defeated in the battle of this day. Of this we are, indeed, convinced, for ye are on the side of truth, and they are on the lie, fettering you in prisons, and beheading you, in order to rob you of your patrimonies. We have, indeed, a high expectation that this very day will distinguish between truth, as Morann, the son of Maen, said in the celebrated proverb: *There has not been found, there never will be found, a more veritable judge than a battle-field,*' [This is not unlike the notion about the wager of battle among the English], 'as we have heard from our poets, who have instructed us from a remote period. Moreover, it is easier for you' [now] 'to defend your own patrimony against a race of strangers, than to seek another's patrimony, after being expulsed from your own native country, which has been in your possession from the year of the World three thousand five hundred, to this very day.'

"The gentleman and the chieftains said that what the princes had uttered was true. The spirited exhortation of the chiefs made the desired impression, for the minds of the heroes, and the courage of the common soldiers, were raised; and the Kinel-Connell, Kinel-Owen, Airghialla, and Ui-Eathach-Uladh were filled with fury, vigour, and a desire of plying their arms, by the harangues of their princes and true leaders, and they promised to them that they would not yield a foot, and that they would suffer death on that field sooner than be defeated.

"There was another cause also for the exaltation of the minds of the youthful soldiers. It was told to them that St. Bearchan, the prophet of God, had prophesied that a battle would be fought at that place against the Galls of Duibhlinn" [Dublin] "by an Oedh O'Neill" [Hugh, descendant of Niall] "and by the province in general; for he had promised that they" [the inhabitants of the province of Ulster] "would come to his relief, and the Kinel-Connell in particular. The heroes believed that the prophet of God would not tell a lie. The person who had first exhibited this prophecy was a certain famous poet of the faithful people of O'Donnell, who accompanied him" [O'Donnell] "on this expedition, to excite and encourage him. His name was Fearfeasa O'Clery. He asked what was the name of that place, and, being told it, he said that St. Bearchan had predicted a defeat of foreigners at that place by an Oedh Ua Neill" [Aidus, nepos Nigelli], "as we have said; and that he had, for a long time, a recollection of the prophecy which the true saint had delivered; and he proceeded to harangue the heroes, as was proper for one like him, and he said" [reciting the words of St. Bearchan]:

"In the battle of the Yellow ford,
By him the Danars" [barbarians] "shall be slain;
After cutting off the foreigners
The men from Tory shall rejoice."

The Editor has been much puzzled what to

diḃ hi ccarcraiḃ, ⁊ hi ccuimrigṫiḃ feiḃ do raḋṫa gaoiḋil go minic feċt riam, ⁊ an do ernaisfeḋh ar in ccaiṫġleo sin, no haṫcuirfiḋe ⁊ no hionnarbfaiḋe hi ccriochaiḃ ciana comaigṫiḃ. Atbertsat friú beós gur bó hura doiḃ cosnaṁ a naṫarḋa frisin ainfine neaċtairċeneoil sin oldas duthaiġ neich ele do ġaḃail ar eiccin iar na nionnarbaḋ soṁ ar a ttír ndílis buḋéin. Ro gaḃ greim tra an ghearrfaċt laoiḋeaḋ sin do bertsat na maiṫe for a muinntir, ⁊ ro ġeallsat na hócca gomdís eallma dfulang a noiḋeḃa riariú nó ḟoḋeṁdais an ros oman leo soṁ do ṫeccmail doibh.

make of this prophecy, that is, whether it was a pure extempore invention of O'Clery's to excite the common soldiers, by convincing them of the certainty of victory, or an application of an older prophecy to the present occasion; but he has been for some years convinced, from the word *Danair* introduced in the second line, that the quatrain above given was taken by O'Clery from a prophecy relating to the period of the Danes in Ireland, and that O'Clery ingeniously transferred it (as the Cromwellians did quotations from the Old Testament in the next century) to the present occasion. A similar prophecy was circulated on the Protestant side, by the Earl of Thomond, before the battle of Kinsale, the details of which were so strikingly fulfilled, that the incredulous Sir George Carew, Governor of Munster, or his secretary, felt it his duty to put it on record in the following words:

"Although no man is lesse credulous than myselfe is of idle Prophesies, the most whereof are coyned after things are done; yet I make bold to relate this which succeeds, for a long time before the thing I speak of was brought to light, myself was an eye witness when it was reported; in concealing it I should wrong the trueth, which makes me bold to remember it: Many times I did heare the Earl of *Thomond* tell the Lord President, that in an old Booke of Irish prophesies which hee had seene, it was reported, that towards the latter dayes there should be a battell fought betweene the English and the Irish, in a place which the Booke nameth, neere unto Kinsale. The Earle of *Thomond* comming out of England, and landing first at Castlehaven, and after at Kinsale, as aforesaid: in the time of the siege, myself and divers others heard him again report the Prophesie to the President, and named the place where (according to the Prophesie) the field should be fought. The day whereupon the victorie was obtained, the Lord President and the Earle rode out to see the dead bodies of the vanquished, and the President asked some that were there present by what name that ground was called; they, not knowing to what end he did demand it, told him the true name thereof, which was the same which the Earle so often before had reported to the President. I beseech the reader to believe mee, for I deliver nothing but trueth: but, as one Swallow makes no Summer, so shall not this one true Prophesie increase my credulitie in old Predictions of that kinde."—*Pacata Hibernia*, book ii. c. 21. For some account of other prophecies of this nature, see note [l], under the year 1583, pp. 1796, 1797, *supra*.

Dr. Leland asserts, without any authority whatever, that "the superstitious Irish were driven, even to phrenzy, by their priests, who assured them, from old prophecies, that this day would prove fatal to heresy."—Book iv. chap. 4. But it is quite clear, from the words of Cucogry O'Clery, that this prophecy was

mercy, and others cast into prisons and wrapped in chains, as the Irish had been often before, and that such as should escape from that battle would be expelled and banished into distant foreign countries: and they told them, moreover, that it was easier for them to defend their patrimony against this foreign people [now] than to take the patrimony of others by force[s], after having been expelled from their own native country. This exciting exhortation of the chiefs made [the desired] impression upon their people; and the soldiers declared that they were ready to suffer death sooner than submit to what they feared would happen[t] to them.

not read by a priest; nor was it ascribed to St. Ultan, as O'Sullevan Beare asserts, but to St. Bearchan of Cloonsast, in Fidh-gaibhle [Figile], in Offaly.

In an Irish poem by Duffy O'Duigenan, written this year, on the History of the O'Neills, and preserved in Trinity College, Dublin, H. 1, 14, fol. 140, it is stated that this battle was fought on the festival of St. Bartholomew, and that seventeen hundred English soldiers, and twenty-three captains, were slain, among whom was a knight of great distinction, and the Marshal of Ireland, and the son of O'Reilly, who had joined the English.

Cox, who passes over this victory as lightly as possible, grumbles that the Irish got so much reputation by it, that the "English could act only on the defensive part, and not that itself without continual fear and danger."—Vol. i. p. 415. By foreign nations Tyrone was hailed as the deliverer of Ireland, and he received from the Pope (through the hands of the Spanish envoys, Martin de la Cerva, and Matthæo Oviedo, the Pope's Archbishop of Dublin) a number of indulgences, and, still more precious, "a crown of phœnix feathers!"—See Camden's *Annal. Reg. Eliz.*, A. D. 1599, p. 744, and Moryson's *History of Ireland*, edition of 1735, vol. i, p. 102. And it may be remarked that, from this time to the defeat at Kinsale, O'Neill was as much monarch of all Ireland, and more universally talked of throughout Europe, than any of his ancestors since the time of Niall of the Nine Hostages.

[s] *To take the patrimony of others by force.*—This alludes to the custom among the Irish, since the English invasion, of settling by force in other territories, after having been driven from their own by the English. Thus Mac Carthy More had settled in Kerry after being expelled by the English from the plains of Cashel; the O'Donovans and O'Sullevans acquired new settlements in the country of the O'Driscolls, after their expulsion from the plains of Limerick and Clonmel; the O'Flahertys settled in the mountains of Connamara, after being expelled by the Burkes from Magh Seola, on the east side of Lough Corrib; the O'Byrnes and O'Tooles acquired new settlements in the mountains of the present county of Wicklow, after being expelled from the plains of Moy-Liffey and Moy-Alvy by Meyler Fitz-Henry and the Baron Walter de Reddlesford, &c., &c. It is curious to observe that the Irish chieftains, in their speeches, did not think of reminding their followers that it might be probable that, on losing this battle, they might be reduced to utter helplessness, incapable of acquiring any new settlements.

[t] *Would happen:* i. e. the soldiers declared that they would rather be slain in this battle than survive it, in case the English were the victors, under whose iron hand they dreaded to become enslaved.

Dala an Mharusccail co na ġallaiḃ iar ffaicsin na ngaoiḋeal for a ccionn ni ro tairbſinsiot nach nairrḋe nuireccla ioir, acht ro cſimniġsiot co comhnart for a ccſstacchaiḋ co ro lingsiot tarr an cceḋna lſtan clair lán ndomhain do rala for a ccionn, ⁊ torchrattar araill diobh innte side acc toċta tairrsi dóiḃ. Ro doirtsiot iaram an slóġ gaoiḋelach go dioġair darac-tach, ⁊ go hainmin aggarḃ ina ccſnd, ⁊ ro ġairsiot rſmpa ⁊ ina ndeadhaiḋ, ⁊ dá gach lſiṫ diobh. Rob siccſn dia ttorach anmhain re hiomġuin ⁊ airisiumh re hiombualadh, ⁊ coṫuccaḋ re caiṫſm co ro tanaiġſḋ a ttiuġ, co ro huirbſr-naiġ a nuarail, ⁊ co ro traoṫaḋ a ttrſóin. Acht ċſna asseaḋ a ċumair ro marbaḋ an general .i. Marusccal an iubair, ⁊ amhail nach gnaṫ caṫlaṫair do ċosnamh las an lucht fris a nſdarsccarṫar a ccuingiḋ caṫa, ⁊ a ccſnd cos-taḋa ⁊ comhairle ro sraoineaḋ for muintir an generála ro dſóiḋ tre nſrt iomġona, ⁊ iombualta darr na foṫollaiḃ talmhan ⁊ tarr an lſtanclair lán ndomhain tarr a ttuḋcatar. Ro bás acca nairleċ ⁊ acca naṫċuma, aga ccumaċ, ⁊ aga ccnaimhġsrraḋ go lſiḋmheaċ lámhtaraiḋ las an lucht battar ina lſnmain.

Ba hann sin do ḋeonaiḋ dia, ⁊ do cſdaiġ an coimḋe daén do ṡaiġdiuiriḃ na bainrioġna go ro ċaith i mbaoí do ṗudar ina uirṫimċell la lionṁuire a lámhaiġ, ⁊ do ċóiḋ gus an mbairille púdair ba coimhnſsa dó do ṁerlionaḋ a ṁiosúr ⁊ a ṗócóide co ro sceinn driṫle ó a ṁairsde isin brúdar baí isin mbairille go ro ḃlosccustair side in áirde isin aér sdarbuas ⁊ gach bairille ro ba coimhnſsa dó diaiḋ a ndiaiḋ, ⁊ bſós an gonna mór do rala aca. Ro tócc-ḃaḋ dna on muḋ ccéḋna anáirde drong mór do na daoíniḃ bátar in uirṫimcell an pudair hisin. Ro baí dna an tulaiġ ina nuirṫimceall ina haén meall doḃarḋa dorċa duiḃ ciach co cſnn athaiḋ do ló iar sin. An do érnatar do ṁuintir na bainrioġna gan marḃaḋ gan muḋuccaḋ, gan doġ, gan dianoiḋeaḋ ro ṫriallsat tar a nais co hardmaċa. Nir bo hiomcomhairceċ ro bás ina lſnmain ga ttraoṫaḋ, ga ttimċeallaḋ, gá naiḋeaḋ, ga nairlech, na ndſiriḃ na ttriaraiḃ, na fficṫiḃ, na ttrioċtaiḃ, go rangatar tar na múraiḃ isteach in Ardmacha.

[u] *Close lines*, literally, "so that their thick was thinned."

[v] *They were being slaughtered.*—It is almost impossible to translate this sentence into English, without transposing the words, and changing the passive into the active voice.

[w] *The Lord.*—The word coimḋe occurs very frequently in the *Leabhar Breac*, and other ancient manuscripts, in the sense of "*the Lord*," and is always applied to Christ, in a religious

As for the Marshal and his English [forces], when they saw the Irish awaiting them, they did not shew any symptom whatever of fear, but advanced vigorously forwards, until they sallied across the first broad [and] deep trench that lay in their way; and some of them were killed in crossing it. The Irish army then poured upon them vehemently and boldly, furiously and impetuously, shouting in the rear and in the van, and on either side of them. The van was obliged to await the onset, bide the brunt of the conflict, and withstand the firing, so that their close lines[u] were thinned, their gentlemen gapped, and their heroes subdued. But, to sum up in brief, the General, i.e. the Marshal of Newry, was slain; and as an army, deprived of its leader and adviser, does not usually maintain the battle-field, the General's people were finally routed, by dint of conflict and fighting, across the earthen pits, and broad, deep trenches, over which they had [previously] passed. They were being slaughtered[v], mangled, mutilated, and cut to pieces by those who pursued them bravely and vigorously.

At this time God allowed, and the Lord[w] permitted, that one of the Queen's soldiers, who had exhausted all the powder he had about him, by the great number of shots[x] he had discharged, should go to the nearest barrel of powder to quickly replenish his measure and his pouch; and [when he began to fill it] a spark fell from his match into the powder in the barrel, which exploded aloft overhead into the air, as did every barrel nearest, and also a great gun which they had with them. A great number of the men who were around the powder were blown up in like manner. The surrounding hilly ground was enveloped in a dense, black, gloomy mass of smoke for a considerable part of the day afterwards. That part of the Queen's army which escaped from being slaughtered [by the Irish], or burned or destroyed [by the explosion], went back to Armagh, and were eagerly pursued[y] [by the Irish, who] continued to subdue, surround, slay, and slaughter them, by pairs, threes, scores, and thirties, until they passed inside the walls of Armagh.

sense, not to the Holy Trinity, as O'Brien and O'Reilly have most erroneously asserted. It is also applied to a temporal lord.

[x] *By the great number of shots*: literally, "from the multiplicity of his shooting."

[y] *Eagerly pursued.*—It is stated in the Life of Hugh Roe O'Donnell, that the recruits and *calones* of the Irish army returned to strip the slain, and to behead those who lay severely wounded on the field:

"Impaiſſt a nglaſlaiṫ, ⁊ a ngiollanraiḋ, ro ġabſat ag fodbaḋ an ḟianlaiġ at roch-airſt iſin caṫ, ⁊ occ diċennaḋ na druinge robtar beoġaoite ann."

Ro ġabsat Gaoíḋil acc iomḟuiḋe an ḃaile in gaċ aird ina iomṫacmong, ⁊ battar ag caiṫeṁ ⁊ ag coiṁdiuḃraccaḋ a ċele co cenn trí lá, ⁊ teora noiḋce co ro sccíṫigit goill ro ḋeóiḋ. Ro ċuirsiot teċta hi ccenn na ree hisin do saiġiḋ na nGaoiḋel dia raḋ friú co ffúicfitís an purt dia lleiccṫí don ḃarda báttar ann toċt gan guin gan gaḃaiḋ dia saiġiḋ gus in mbaile sin Ardamaċa, ⁊ iar roċtain doiḃ hisuiḋe (dia ttardṫa eineaċ ⁊ maiṫeṁ nanacail dóiḃ, ⁊ a ttiodhlacaḋ slán as an tír go roċtain dóiḃ hi ccriċ innill) go ffúicfidís Ardmaċa buḋéin. O ro haisnéiḋeaḋ na haiṫesca sin do na Gaoiḋelaiḃ do ċóttar na maiṫe do ċrúḋ a ccoṁairle dus cioḋ do ġendaís imon ccaingin sin. Ro bátar drong díoḃ aga ráḋa nar bo cóir na goill do léccaḋ as an iomċumang i mbatar co ro marḃṫa iad idir, no go neiblidís a naenar do ġorta. Ar a aí ba fair deiriḋ leó ro ḋeóiḋh a léccaḋ uaḋaiḃ as na maigniḃ i mbatar, acht namá na berdaís leo biaḋ no deoch, éideaḋ, arm, na ordanas, púdar na luaiḋe as in bfort gionmoṫá a ṫronc ⁊ a arm do léccaḋ las in ccaptín baí ann. Ro aéntaiġhsiot dá gach leiṫ anmain ar na coinġellaiḃ sin, ⁊ ro ċuirsiot drong dia ndaoiniḃ uaisle ar gaċ taeḃ daccallaiṁ an ḃarda gus an bfurt, ⁊ iar naisnéis sccel doiḃsiḋe ro ḟáccaiḃsiot an baile acc Ua néill aṁail ro forcongraḋ forra. Tánaicc an captín, ⁊ an barda go hArdmaċa hi ccenn an ro ṁair dia ṁuinntir, ⁊ ro cuireaḋ ioḋlacaḋ leó uile ó Ardmaċa gus an iuḃar, ⁊ on iuḃar go rangattar hi ffine gall. Iar ffáccḃáil tíre heóccain doiḃsiḋe, Ro forcongair Ua néill for ḋaoiniḃ sainreḋaċa, uaisle, ⁊ anuaisle an árṁaig dáireṁ ⁊ daḋnacal ⁊ ba seḋh a líon iar na náireṁ go leir, dá míle go leiṫ imon ngenerál, go noċt ccaiptíniḃ décc, ⁊ drong mór do ḋaoiniḃ uaisle naċ ttaḃairṫer a nanmanna for aird.

Roptar meirtniġ, míṁenmnaiġ muinntir na bainríoġna ⁊ roptar súḃaiġ soforḃfaoiliġ Gaoiḋil don caiṫġleó sin. An ochtmaḋ lá do mí August do ferad an iomarġail sin áṫa buiḋe. Do ċódar maiṫe ulaḋ dia ttiġiḃ iar niolach coscair, ⁊ coṁmaiḋme ge ro ḟáccbaḋ daoine iomḋa uaḋaiḃ.

Baile an Móṫaigh baí ag muinntir na bainrioġna fri re trí mbliaḋan ndecc gus an tan sa do ġabáil la a ḋuṫċasaċaiḃ féin (hi saṁraḋ na bliaḋna

¹ *Unmolested,* literally, "without wounding or danger."

² *Were dispirited,* Roptar meirtniġ, mimenmnaiġ.—This is a very old construction, which would not be at all understood at the present day in any part of Ireland. The above sentence would be constructed in modern Irish as follows:

The Irish then proceeded to besiege the town, and surrounded it on every side; and they [of both parties] continued to shoot and fire at each other for three days and three nights, at the expiration of which time the English ceased, and sent messengers to the Irish to tell them that they would surrender the fort [at the Blackwater], if the warders who were [stationed] in it were suffered to come to them unmolested[a] to Armagh, and [to add] that, on arriving there, they would leave Armagh itself, if they should be granted quarter and protection, and escorted in safety out of that country into a secure territory. When these messages were communicated to the Irish, their chiefs held a council, to consider what they should do respecting this treaty. Some of them said that the English should not be permitted to come out of their straitened position until they should all be killed or starved together; but they finally agreed to give them liberty to pass out of the places in which they were, on condition, however, that they should not carry out of the fort meat or drink, armour, arms, or ordnance, powder or lead [or, in fine, any thing], excepting only the captain's trunk and arms, which he was at liberty to take with him. They consented on both sides to abide by those conditions; and they sent some of their gentlemen of both sides to the fort, to converse with the warders; and when these were told how the case stood, they surrendered the fort to O'Neill, as they were ordered. The Captain and the warders came to Armagh, to join that part of his people who had survived. They were all then escorted from Armagh to Newry, and from thence to the English territory. After their departure from Tyrone, O'Neill gave orders to certain persons to reckon and bury the gentlemen and common people slain. After they had been reckoned, there were found to be two thousand five hundred slain, among whom was the General, with eighteen captains, and a great number of gentlemen whose names are not given.

The Queen's people were dispirited[a] and depressed, and the Irish joyous and exulting, after this conflict. This battle of Athbuidhe was fought on the 10th day of August. The chiefs of Ulster returned to their respective homes in joyous triumph[b] and exultation, although they had lost many men.

Ballymote, which had been in the possession of the Queen's people for the space of thirteen years before this time, was taken in the summer of this year

"ba meirtneaċ mí-ṁeanmnaċ muintir na bainríoġna, ⁊ ba subaċ so-ḟorḃḟaoileaċ Gaoidil do'n ċaiṫġleo sin."

[b] *Joyous triumph*, iolaċ coscair. The word

ṡo) .i. la cloinn nDonnchaiḋ an ċorainn (.i. tomaltaċ ⁊ caṫal duḃ). Ḃai an gobernoir Sir conerr clifort, ⁊ O Domnaill Aoḋ ruaḋ acc daoraḋ an ḃaile for aroile, ⁊ acc tairccsin ceannaigh da chionn do ċloinn nDonnchaiḋ. Rob é crioċnuccaḋ an dála clann nDonnchaiḋ do tabairt an ḃaile dUa Domnaill do ḋruim ceannaiġ, ⁊ ċonnarta i mí meḋóin ḟoġmair na bliaḋna so. Ceiṫre ced punt, ⁊ tri ced bó do raḋ Ua Domnaill do ċloinn nDonnchaiḋ ar an mbaile.

Slóicceaḋ adbal la hiarla urmuṁan do ċur lóin hi bport laoiġisi, ⁊ iar narccnaṁ isin sliġiḋ doiḃ do rala for a ccionn isin cconair do ḋeaċatar Uaitne mac Ruḋraiġe óicc, mic Ruḋraiġe caoić uí mórḋa, ⁊ Remann mac Seaain na Seasmar mic Riocaird Shaxanaiġ, ⁊ captin tirial .i. Rirdeard mac tomáir óicc tirial. Ro baḋ moo ina luaċ an lóin do caill iarla urmuṁan don turus sin do ḋaoínib deaġhaiḃ, ⁊ darm, ⁊ as ar eiccin terna an tiarla fein iar na ġuin.

Ro ċuir Ua neill sccribheann illaiġnib isin ccéid mí dfoġmair na bliaḋna so dia furailem ar Remann a burc, ar Uaitne ua morḋa, ⁊ ar captín tirial, coimeitt laiġneaċ dfaccbail for an ccuid ele dia ccompann coccaid ⁊ iad fein do ḋol do denaṁ gaḃaltais, ⁊ do ṫaḃairt araill do na tirib báttar ina nacchaiḋ isteach dáir nó deiccean. ⁊ ro forcongair forra do ṡonraḋ dol don muṁain ro ṫoġairm ċloinne tómáis ruaiḋ, mic Semuis, mic Seaain mic an Iarla. Iar léghaḋ na sccribeann do na huaislib a dubramar do ċottar siḋe gus an lion, ⁊ gus an ccongaib as lia ro ḟeḋsat i norrsaiġib. Tangattar an tir sin dia saiġiḋ ar a ttoil fein gionmoṫa Mac giollapatraicc fíngin, mac briain mic fíngin. Lottar ar a haiṫle gus an ccionn tuaiḋ do ṡliab blaḋma ar dáiġ gaoidel oirṫir muṁan, ⁊ iarṫair miḋe do chur daén rann friú .i. ó Maolmuaiḋ, ⁊ conall mac caṫaoír, ⁊ Mág coċláin .i. Seaan óg, mac Seaain, mic airt, mic corbmaic, ⁊ O cearbaill an calbaċ, mac uilliam uidir, mic firganainm, mic maolruanaiḋ. Ge ro bátar na maiṫe sin le haṫhaiḋ ag seasaṁ a huċt a bprionnsa ro baḋ buiḋe leó an óccbaiḋ anaiṫniḋ sin ro

iolaċ is explained "subaċas no luṫġáir, i. e. joy, or enthusiastic exultation," by O'Clery.

[c] *Auctioning:* literally, "were making the castle dear upon each other," i.e. bidding against each other, or outbidding each other's price, as at an auction.

[d] *Fineen, the son of Brian.*—He was Florence, the son of Brian, or Bernard Fitzpatrick, the first Baron of Upper Ossory, who slew Rury Oge O'More in 1578, from which period the heads of the Fitzpatrick family continued remarkably faithful to Queen Elizabeth,

by its rightful inheritors, the Clann-Donough of Corran, namely, Tomaltagh and Cathal Duv. The Governor, Sir Conyers Clifford, and O'Donnell (Hugh Roe) were auctioning[c] the castle against each other, in offering to purchase it from the Clann-Donough. The close of the bargain was, that the Clann-Donough gave up the castle to O'Donnell, for a purchase and contract, in the middle month of the autumn of this year. Four hundred pounds [in money] and three hundred cows was the price which O'Donnell gave the Clann-Donough for the castle.

A great hosting was made by the Earl of Ormond, to place provisions in Port-Leix [Maryborough]. When they had advanced a certain distance on their way, they were met by Owny, the son of Rury Oge, son of Rury Caech O'More; by Redmond, the son of John, son of John of the Shamrocks, son of Rickard Saxonagh [Burke]; and by Captain Tyrrell, namely, Richard, the son of Thomas Oge Tyrrell. On this expedition the Earl of Ormond lost more than the value of the provisions in men, horses, and arms; and it was with difficulty the Earl himself escaped, after being wounded.

In the first month of the autumn of this year O'Neill sent letters to Leinster, requesting Redmond Burke, Owny O'More, and Captain Tyrrell, to intrust the guarding of Leinster to some of their allies in the war, and to proceed themselves to make conquests, and to bring some of the adverse territories over to their cause, by solicitation or force; and he particularly requested them to go into Munster, at the invitation of the sons of Thomas Roe, son of James, son of John, son of the Earl [of Desmond]. The gentlemen whom we have mentioned, after reading the letters, proceeded with the greatest force and arms they could command into Ossory. The people of that territory spontaneously came to [join] them, except Mac Gillapatrick (Fineen, the son of Brian[d], son of Fineen). They afterwards went to the northern extremity of Slieve Bloom, in order to induce the Irish of East Munster and Westmeath to join them, namely, O'Molloy, and Connell, the son of Cahir [O'Molloy]; Mac Coghlan (John Oge, the son of John, son of Art, son of Cormac), and O'Carroll (Calvagh, the son of William Odhar, son of Ferganainm, son of Mulrony). Although these chieftains had for some time stood by their Sovereign, they were glad to obtain

and strenuous opponents of the Irish insurgents, which saved their property from confiscation.—See Cox's *Hibernia Anglicana*, vol. i. p. 354.

baí acc taistel gacha tíre daontuccadh síothchána uadhaibh ⁊ o ro siodhaighsiot iadsein tuccsat a naccahaidh ar an dá urmumhain ⁊ nír bo síoh no caratradh ro iarrsat forra, acht a ccreachadh fo cédóir tré na nescairdes fri hiarla urmumhan, ⁊ ro gabhadh cúicc caisléin do bhailtibh urmumhan leó, Ro badh dibhsidhe druim aidhneach ar brú na Sionna. Ro chongaibh Rémann a burc aicce fein fo chomhair coccaidh cloinne riocaird do fhrestal ⁊ do fhriothailem ass. Batar dan a dó nó a trí do sheachtmuinibh co campamhail ina ccomhnaidhe isin tír sin, ⁊ cresca airir Siúiri, ⁊ cloinne huilliam acca ttabairt dia saighidh do chum a ffoslongport, ⁊ a ccomharsain gaoidel acc tocht dia naccallaimh, ⁊ acc dol i naénrann friú. Ro badh dibhsidhe ó duibhidir choille na manach .i. diarmait, mac uaitne, mic Pilip, ⁊ clann Mheic briain ó ccuanach .i. clann Muirchertaigh, mic toirrdhealbhaigh, mic muirchertaigh, ⁊ Rianaigh im chonchobhar na mainge mac uilliam chaoich, mic diarmata uí mhaoilriain, ⁊ siol mbriain ócc dhuithche ara.

Iar ndol do na gaoidhelaibh sin i ccommbáidh ⁊ hi ccaradradh muinntire Uí neill, ⁊ ar ccor gach tíre gus a rangatar daén rann friú, Ro triallsat (go neirghe amach na noirer sin) i ngerraltachaibh ar tarraing cloinne tomais ruaidh mic an iarla. Asseadh lottar cédamus hi cconntaé luimnigh. Ba hann boí an Presidens .i. Sir tomás norus an tan sin hi ccill mocheallocc. Iar na tuiccsin dó na baoí intrebhtha fris an ngarraidh ngaoidhelaigh do chuaidh ar a niomghabhail go corcaigh. Do chódarsomh dna tar máigh siar i cconallchaibh i ccomfhochraibh slebhe luachra, ⁊ glinne corbraighe. Táinicc Sémus mac tomáis ruaidh ina cceann hi cconallchoibh don chur sin, ⁊ bai an dara mac (.i. Seaan) do cloinn tomáis ruaidh ina ffochair fein ar na himtheachtaibh sin aga ttarraing don tír. Do bheirthi an ghamhnach no in bhó inlaogha ar shé pinginnibh ⁊ an láir ghroighe ar thrí pinginnibh, ⁊ gach muc dá febhus ar phinginn ⁊ na connartha sin aga ffoccra, ⁊ acca ffurail in gach campa i mbídis.

Ot cualaigh iarla urmumhan caithreim na ccathbhuidhean sin tainicc co na

[e] *Druim-Aidhneach*, now *anglice*, Druminagh, a townland containing the ruins of a castle, situated on the margin of Lough Derg, which is an expansion of the Shannon between Killaloe and Portumna, in the parish of Derryglass, barony of Lower Ormond, and county of Tipperary. It has lately received the modern name of Castle Biggs from the present proprietor. According to the tradition in the country this castle was erected by O'Madden in despite of the O'Kennedys.

[f] *The borders of Sliabh-Luachra and Gleann Corbraighe.*—These places are far asunder, the Sliabh Luachra mountains being near Castle

terms of peace from those strange warriors, who were traversing every territory. After agreeing upon terms of peace with these, they turned their faces towards the two Ormonds; and from them they sought neither peace nor friendship, but proceeded to plunder them at once, on account of their enmity towards the Earl of Ormond. They took five of the castles of Ormond, one of which, Druim-Aidhneach[e], on the margin of the Shannon, Redmond Burke kept to himself, for waging and maintaining war on Clanrickard out of it. They remained for two or three weeks encamped in that country; and the spoils of the region bordering on the Suir, and those of Clann-William, were carried to their camp; and their Irish neighbours came to converse and join in the same confederation with them. Among those who joined them were O'Dwyer of Kilnamanagh, i e. Dermot, the son of Owny, son of Philip; the sons of Mac Brian O'gCuanach, namely, the sons of Murtough, son of Turlough, son of Murtough; the Ryans about Conor-na-Mainge, the son of William Caech, son of Dermot O'Mulryan; and the race of Brian Oge of Duharra.

After these Irish [septs] had formed a confederacy and friendship with O'Neill's people, and after having induced [the people of] every territory into which they came to join them, they marched with the rising-out [i. e. forces] of these districts, at the instance of the sons of Thomas Roe, son of the Earl [of Desmond], into the country of the Geraldines. They first went to the county of Limerick. The President, Sir Thomas Norris, was at this time at Kilmallock; and when he perceived that he was not able to contend with the Irish party, he went to Cork, to avoid [meeting] them. They [the Irish] then proceeded westwards, across the River Maigue, into Connello, and to the borders of Sliabh-Luachra and Gleann-Corbraighe[f]. James, the son of Thomas Roe [Fitzgerald], came to join them in Connello on this occasion; and James, the second son of Thomas Roe, was already along with them upon these expeditions, for he had come to draw them into the country. At this time they offered and sold at their camp a stripper, or cow in calf, for sixpence, a brood mare for threepence, and the best hog for a penny; and these bargains were offered and proclaimed in every camp in which they were.

When the Earl of Ormond heard of the progress of these warlike troops, he

Island, in Kerry, and Gleann-Corbraighe in the north-west extremity of the county of Limerick. It is the glinn or valley from which the Knight of Glinn takes his titular title.

ṁarcṡluaġ co na coiriġtiḃ fo na ttuairim go conntae Luimniġ, ⁊ ro ċuir sccela go Corcaiġ dá ḟurail ar in bPresidens tecct ina coinne go Cill Mocel-lócc. O ro ḟidirsiot an sluaġ gaoidelaċ batar i niarṫar Conallaċ an ní sin, ro ceimniġsiot aniar i niomfocraiḃ Ċille Mocellócc ⁊ tuccsat a ttaisbenaḋ féin don dá tiġearna sin tarla aga ttóraiḋecht. Do ḋecatar na tiġearnaiġe sin (ar iomġaḃail esccmála friusom do ċed a ċele) go Maiġ Eala[g]. Tiaġaitt sium ina ndeaḋhaiḋ go dorus Maiġe Heala, ⁊ ro gabsat aga ngresnuccaḋ, ⁊ aga ngriosaḋ, ⁊ aga raḋ friú na fuiġbittís díol fiaċ ina ffoltanas bad fenn, ina iadsom dionnsaiġiḋ an tan battar i naén ṁaiġin. Ar a aoí sin arsead ro chinnsiot na daoíne mora hiṡin an Presidens do ḋol go Corcaiġ, ⁊ an tiarla dfilleaḋ tar a ais i mbuitileraċaiḃ.

O ro ḟáccbaḋ an tír don chur sin ar cumas an tsloiġ gaoidelaiġ do gairsiot Iarla Desmuman a huġdarras Uí Neill[h] do Shémus, mac Tomáis ruaiḋ, mic Sémuis, mic Seain mic an Iarla, ⁊ an tír sin (.i. gGeraltaiġ ó Ḋun-ccaoín go Siuir) baí tilte teċtaiġhṫe acc Saxanchoiḃ[i], lán dáitiuccaḋ, ⁊ diolṁaoínib, ní ro faccbattar som (fo cenn ḟecht lá ndécc) én ṁac Saxanaiġ

[g] *Magh Ealla:* i. e. the plain of the River Ealla, now Allo. From this name it is evident that the name Ealla was anciently applied to that part of the Blackwater lying between Kanturk, where the modern River Ealla ends, and the town of Magh Ealla, now *anglice* Mallow. P. O'Sullevan Beare calls this place *Moala.* It was a manor belonging to the Earl of Desmond, and upon his attainder it was granted, by Queen Elizabeth, to Sir John Norris, a most distinguished general, who settled the crown of Portugal on the royal house of Braganza, and was then Lord President of Munster.—See Smith's *Natural and Civil History of Cork*, vol. i. p. 331.

[h] *By the authority of O'Neill.*—This clearly shews that since O'Neill had received the consecrated crown of "phœnix feathers" from the Pope, he was regarded as the lawful monarch of Ireland. The English writers, however, made so light of this regal power, arrogated to himself by the ex-Earl of Tyrone, that they continued to style his vassal "the *Sugane* Earl."—*Moryson*, ed. 1735, vol. i. p. 61. Cox (vol. i. p. 415), states that this Sugane Earl was "the handsomest man of his time;" and Camden calls him "hominem obscœnissimam!"

[i] *The Saxons.*—These were the English Undertakers who settled in Munster after the ruin of the Geraldines. Fynes Moryson gives the following account of the doings of O'More, and the other allies of O'Neill in Munster on this occasion: "After the defeat of the *Blackwater*, Tyrone sent *Ony mac Rory O'More*, and one Captain Tyrel (of *English* race, but a bold and unnatural enemy to his country and the English), to trouble the Province of Munster, against whom Sir *Thomas Norris*, Lord President, opposed himself; but as soon as he, upon necessary Occasions, had withdrawn his forces to *Cork*, many of the Munster men now, first about *October*, 1598, broke into rebellion, and joined themselves with *Tyrone's* said Forces, spoiled the Country, burnt the Villages, and pull'd down the Houses and Castles of the *English*, against

set out with all his cavalry and infantry for the county of Limerick, to meet them, and sent a message to Cork, requesting the President to come to meet him at Kilmallock. When the Irish army, who were encamped in the west of Connello, heard of this, they marched eastwards towards Kilmallock, and shewed themselves to these two lords, who were in pursuit of them. Upon seeing them, the lords (i. e. the Earl and the President) agreed to avoid meeting them, and turned off towards Magh-Ealla[g]. The Irish pursued them to the gate of Magh-Ealla, and proceeded to defy, provoke, and dare them [to battle], saying that they could never wreak their vengeance upon them better than now, when they were [all] together in one place. Notwithstanding this, what the two great men determined upon was, that the President should repair to Cork, and that the Earl should return to the territory of the Butlers.

As the country was left in the power of the Irish on this occasion, they conferred the title of Earl of Desmond, by the authority of O'Neill[h], upon James, the son of Thomas Roe, son of James, son of John, son of the Earl; and in the course of seventeen days they left not within the length or breadth of the country of the Geraldines, [extending] from Dunqueen to the Suir, which the Saxons[i] had well cultivated and filled with habitations and various wealth, a

whom (especially the female Sex) they committed all abominable Outrages. And now they raised *James Fitzthomas*, a *Geraldine*, to be Earl of *Desmond* (which Title had, since the Wars of *Desmond*, been suppressed), with Condition that (forsooth) he should be Vassal to O'Neal. The Munster Rebellion broke out like a Lightning, for in one Month's Space almost all the Irish were in rebellious Arms, and the *English* were murthered, or stript and banished. Thus having inflamed *Munster* with the Fire of Rebellion, and leaving this Sedition to be cherished and encreased by this new Earl of *Desmond*, and other Rebels of that Province, the Ulster forces returned back to Tyrone. The Infection which *Munster* Men have drawn from the corrupted Parts in Rebellion did more and more spread itself, so as the old practices, long held by the Arch-traitor *Tyrone* to induce them to a revolt, now fully attained their wished Effect; to the working whereof, in the Hearts of the Seditious, there wanted not many strong Motives, as the hatred which those *Geraldines* bear to those Undertakers (of whom I formerly spoke in *Desmond's* War) which possessed their Ancestor's Lands; also the Encouragement they received by the good Success of the Rebells, and no less the hope of pardon upon the worst Event."—Vol. i. p. 61.

P. O'Sullevan Beare says that Pierce Lacy was instrumental in drawing O'More, and others of O'Neill's allies, into Munster on this occasion. He describes this outbreak of the rebellion in Munster as follows, in his *Hist. Cathol. Iber. Compend.* tom. 3, lib. 5, c. ii.

"In hoc statu rerum Petrus Lessius nobilis eques Momonius vir animi plenus, nec eloquentiæ inanis Anglos, in quos aliquod crimen commiserat, fugiens, in Lageniam Huonem Omorram adit, eique persuadet, vt in Momonias faciat ex-

ar a fad, nó ar a fírlſiṫſcc gan marḃaḋ, nó gan ionnarbaḋ eiste. ⁊ ní mo ro ḟáccaiḃsiot ar fſḋ na ree céona cſnnáit, na caislén, ná én ḟód do ḋúṫaiġ gſraltaċ gan cur i seilḃ iarla ḋſsmuṁan, aċt namá caislén na mainge hi cconntae ċiarraiġe, ⁊ Earr geiḃtine i nuiḃ conuill gaḃra, ⁊ Maġ eala i cconntae corcaiġe. Iar ccriocnuccaḋ an ṁórsaoṫair sin le bſcc naimsire do na sſirḃíseachaiḃ sin Uí neill ro gaḃattar cſd, ⁊ ceilebraḋ ag an Iarla ḋſsmuṁan sin do óirdnſdar fſin. Do ċoiḋ Uaitne ó morḋa (⁊ an mſid baí acc frſccra dó do na fſḋnaċaiḃ sin) illaoiġisr. Do ḋeachaiḋ Remann a burc (gus an luċt baoí for a ḟosttaḋ, ⁊ forr mbaoí a ċuṁaċta don ċongáir ceona) go hurmuṁain. Do ṫaéd eirġe amaċ na nullṫaċ báttar ar aon las na huaislib sin dia ttirib, ⁊ dia ttiġib gan easbaiḋ ionṁais no éḋala do ṫarḃa tusais na huaire sin. Ro an Captin tirial i ffarrad Iarla ḋſsmuṁan, ⁊ baí an tiarla ag caiṫſṁ, ⁊ acc cuarṫuccaḋ na muṁan, ⁊ acc dol i ndaoínib diaiḋ i ndiaiḋ re hſḋ an dá mísr baí rſiṁe do ḋſireaḋ na bliadna so.

Ticcſrna Mhóta gairſtt .i. Emann, mac Risdird, mic piarais builter do dol i muinterarus ui neill i ffoġmar na bliadna so.

Ticċſrna ṫrſna cluana meala, ⁊ caṫrach ḋúini iasccaiġ .i. tomás mac teróid mic Piarais, mic Emainn, ⁊ barún luaċmaiġi, ⁊ drong ṁór do ġillib ócca buitilerach do eirġe i ccoṁmbáiḋ coccaiḋ na ngaoiḋel.

peditionem: id plerosque Momonios summopere exoptare: rebellandi cupidos esse: omnes Giraldinos Iaimum Giraldinum creaturos Desmoniæ Comitem, & Ducem secuturos: Maccarrhas Desmoniæ aliquem sibi principem electuros. Quod Huon consilium probans, Onello consentiente, in hanc opinionem amicos suos, qui in Lagenia bellum administrabant, mouet. Hi erant Raymundus Burkus Lietrimæ Baro cum Gulielmo fratre, Dermysius Oconchur cum duobus fratribus Carbrio, & Quinto, Richardus Tirellus. Huon ducens pedites octingentos, & equites circiter triginta celerius omnium opinione in Momonias ire contendit, Lisiæ custodia Edmundo fratri demandata. Comes Vrmonius regij exercitus imperator, illi obuiam iturus videbatur, sed non iuit, vel Huonis celeritate anteuersus, vel prælio experiri non ausus. Thomas Norris Anglus Momoniarum præfectus suæ provinciæ non ignarus esse à prouincia hostem arcere, præsidiarios milites, Momoniarum delectum, Momonios optimates, quam maximas breuitate temporis vires potuit comparare, Moalam conuocat, præseferens ibi velle cum Huone confligere. Illi Huon appropinquans magnificas litteras scribit, quibus ab eo petit, vt acie dimicet. Quam conditionem Norris recusans Moalæ constituto præsidio Corcacham refugit. Huon sequitur, & eius velites cum Norrisis vltimo agmine leuiter missilibus pugnant. Sine mora multi præter opinionem Momonij ab Anglis deficiunt, Patritius Giraldinus, qui Macmoris, & Lacsnaæ Baro dicitur, Gulielmus Giraldinus eques Auratus Kierrius Rasinnanæ dominus, Edmundus Giraldinus eques Auratus vallis, Edmundus Giraldinus eques Auratus Albus & omnes fere nominis

single son of a Saxon whom they did not either kill or expel. Nor did they leave, within this time, a single head residence, castle, or one sod of Geraldine territory, which they did not put into the possession of the Earl of Desmond, excepting only Castlemaine, in the county of Kerry; Askeaton, in Hy-Connell-Gaura; and Magh-Ealla [Mallow], in the county of Cork. When these agents of O'Neill had [thus], in a short time, accomplished this great labour, they took their leave of and bade farewell to this Earl of Desmond, whom they themselves had appointed. Owny O'More, and such part of the forces as adhered to him, set out for Leix; Redmond Burke and that part of the same hosting which he had employed, and over which he had command, proceeded to Ormond; and the Ulster troops who were along with these gentlemen proceeded to their territories and homes, not without wealth or booty acquired[j] on this expedition. Captain Tyrrell remained with the Earl of Desmond; and the Earl continued spending and subjugating Munster, and gaining more and more[k] people over to his side, during the remaining two months of this year.

The Lord of Mountgarrett[l], namely, Edmond, the son of Richard, son of Pierce Butler, concluded a friendship with O'Neill in the autumn of this year.

The Lord of Clonmel-Third and Cahir, namely, Thomas, the son of Theobald, son of Pierce, son of Edmond, and the Baron of Luachmhagh[n], with many others of the young Butlers, joined in this war of the Irish.

Giraldini Momonij, quorum plerique Iaimum Giraldinum Desmoniæ Comitem renunciarunt, quo nomine à nobis etiam hinc erit appellandus. Conspirarunt etiam Dermysius, & Donatus Maccarrhæ Allæ principatus competitores, Daniel Maccarrhæ Magni filius, Patritius Condon, Odonnochuus Onachtæ, Odonnochus vallis. Desciuerunt quoque alij viri clarissimi, Rocheus Faramniæ Vicecomes, Richardus Buttlerus Montis Gerarti Vicecomes, qui Onelli filiam vxorem habuit, Thomas Buttlerus Catharæ Baro, & alij: sed plures in Reginæ amicitia manserunt, non solum ciuitates omnes, & magistratus, sed principes, vel optimates. Illicò ex Connachta confluunt multi, qui depopulata patria inedia laborabant, & à Momonijs armantur, ducibus Dermysio Oconchure, Gulielmo Burko, Richardo Tirello, Bernardo Okealla, & alijs. Momonij quoque milites conscribuntur, & duces creantur. Ita in Momonijs bello accenso, Huon in Lageniam reuertitur."—Fol. 157.

[j] *Acquired:* literally, "without want of wealth or booty of the benefit of the expedition of this time."

[k] *Gaining more and more:* literally, "going into people gradually," i.e. "becoming more populous, or more numerously followed."

[l] *Mountgarrett.*—A castle situated on the east side of the River Barrow, and a short distance to the north of the town of New Ross, in the county of Wexford. The keep of Lord Mountgarrett's castle still remains in tolerable preservation.

[n] *Luachmhagh*, now Loughmoe, a church giving

O Doṁnaill (.i. Aoḋ ruaḋ) do ċor ṡlóiġ, ⁊ ṡoċraitte a tír ċonaill la Mac Uilliam (.i. teboitt, mac uatéir ċiotaiġ, mic Sſain, mic oiluerair) hi rann ṁeic uilliam i ffoġmar na bliaḋna ro. Ro ċuir din Ua doċartaiġ lair (go roċaiḋe móir amaille fris) .i. Sſan ócc, mac Sſain, mic feilim, mic con-coḃair ċarraiġ. Ba ruaill má ro hairiġeaḋ iad in aén tír dar ġaḃrat, nó triara ttudcatar go rangatar na huṁaill gan ráṫuċċaḋ, ⁊ ba hinntiḃriḋe battar urṁór cruiḋ, ⁊ cſṫra, innile, ⁊ airnſiri rainn ṁeic uilliam uile. Ro lſir ṫionóileaḋ leó ina mbaoí do croḋh for tír ó oilenaiḃ bſcca amach, ⁊ ger ṁór an tecclamaḋ, ⁊ an cruinniuccaḋ creach do rónsat ní ḟuarattar roiṁ duaḋ no doċar ina ttimċeall, acht ualaċ a nairttriġhṫe ⁊ a niomána aṁáin go rangatar slán tar a nair dia ttiriḃ .i. Mac uilliam go tír aṁalgaiḋ, ⁊ Ua docartaiġ go hinir eoghain.

AN tan tra do ċóidh ó doṁnaill i reilḃ ḃaile an Mhótaiġ i mí mſdóin faġmair na bliaḋna ro aṁail reṁebſrtmar, ro ċuirriot conallaiġ a ccaor-aiġeaċta hi cconntaé ṡliġiġ, ⁊ baí Ua doṁnaill fſin ina coṁnaiġe i mbaile an Mótaigh ó aimsir a faġbala go diuid nodlacc móir. Ro ċuir Ua Doṁnaill tionol for a ṡloġaiḃ in gach airm i mbatar. Tangatar ina ḋoċom cétur cenel cconaill go lion a ttionoil. Tánaicc dna Mac uilliam burc teboid mac Uatéir ciotaiġ co na mbaoí fo a ṁámur, ⁊ iar roċtain doiḃriḋe go haon maiġin do ṡaiġiḋ uí ḋoṁnaill go baile an motaigh i ndeireaḋ mír december do ṡonraḋ ar fair dſiriḋ lair dol hi ccloinn Riocaird ge ro ḃattar luċt an tire i ffaitċſr ⁊ i ffuirſċrur ⁊ ge ro baí a uaṁan, ⁊ a uirea-ccla forra. Luiḋ rium co na ṡloġaiḃ gan raḃaḋ, gan ráṫucchaḋ go rainicc go taí táitſnach go dorur cille colgan hi ccrepurccail na maidne muiċe. Rolſicc iaraṁ sccaoileaḋ da sccciṁeltoiḃ in gaċ aird don tír ina uirtimceall, ⁊ fo urlár cloinne Riocaird do ṡonnraḋ. Do riacht drong díoḃ i niomfocraiḃ doireċt rémainn, ⁊ rainicc drong ele go dún guaire hi ccoill ua ffiaċrach.

name to a parish and village in the barony of Eliogarty, county of Tipperary, and about five miles to the north-east of Thurles. Near this village are still to be seen the magnificent ruins of the ancient castle, and more modern mansion house, of Purcell, titular Baron of Loughmoe.

[m] *The small islands:* i.e. the islands in Clew Bay.

[n] *Caused.*—The language is here too abrupt. The literal translation is: "O'Donnell put a gathering on his hosts in every place in which they were."

[o] *Kilcolgan,* Cill ċolgain: i.e. St. Colgan's Church, now Kilcolgan, near Clarinbridge, in the county of Galway.—See Colgan's *Acta Sanctorum,* p. 350, where this place is referred to

In the autumn of this year O'Donnell (i. e. Hugh Roe) sent a body of forces from Tirconnell with Mac William (Theobald, the son of Walter Kittagh, son of John, son of Oliver) into Mac William's territory. He sent with him on this occasion O'Doherty (John Oge, the son of John, son of Felim, son of Conor Carragh) with a great force. They were scarcely noticed in any country by which they marched, or through which they passed, until they arrived in the Owles; and it was in these [territories] the greater part of the herds and flocks of cattle of all Mac William's country then were. They collected all the cattle that were on the main land outside the small islands[m]; and though great was the gathering and collection of preys they made, they encountered no danger or difficulty on account of them, save only the trouble of removing and driving them off. And they returned safe to their territories, i. e. Mac William to Tirawly, and O'Doherty to Inishowen.

When O'Donnell had obtained possession of Ballymote, [which was] in the middle of autumn, as we have before mentioned, the Kinel-Connel sent their creaghts into the county of Sligo; and O'Donnell himself resided at Ballymote from the time it was given up to him until after Christmas. O'Donnell [at this time] caused[n] his forces to be mustered in every place where they were: first, the Kinel-Connell, with all their forces, came to him; and next, Mac William Burke (Theobald, the son of Walter Kittagh), with all those who were under his jurisdiction: and when these had come together to O'Donnell, to Ballymote, [which was] precisely in the end of the month of December, the resolution he adopted was, to proceed into Clanrickard, although the inhabitants of that territory were on the alert and on their guard, such was their fear and dread of him. He marched silently and quietly with his forces, and arrived unnoticed and unobserved at the gate of Kilcolgan[o] by break of day. He then sent marauding parties in every direction around him, through the level part of Clanrickard. One party went to the borders of Oireacht-Redmond[p], and ano-

as near Athcliath Meadhruidhe.

[p] *Oireacht-Redmond*: i. e. the tribe of Redmond, *anglice* Eraght Redmond, which was a tribe name assumed by a sept of the Burkes of Clanrickard. It appears, from an Inquisition taken at Galway in 1608, that the barony of Kiltartan, in the county of Galway, comprised three territories, viz.: Kinelea, otherwise called O'Shaghnes's country, comprising one hundred and five quarters of land; Eraght-Redmond, fifty-eight and a half quarters; and Killovyeragh, otherwise O'Heyne's country, forty-five quarters. These districts are still well known in the barony of Kiltartan.

Do rónaḋ éċta móra lár an luċt sin do ċoiḋ go coill ua fFiaċrach .i. da ṁac Rossa mic Uaitne mic maoileċlainn uí loċlainn, toirrḋelḃaċ buiḋe, ⁊ brian do ṁarḃaḋ. Ro marḃaḋ dna duine uasal do ċloinn nDoṁnaill gallócc-laċ baí i fFarraḋ Mhic uilliam ar an sluaiġeḋ sin .i. Aoḋ buiḋe ócc, mac Aoḋa buiḋe, mic maolmuire mec doṁnaill la toirrḋelḃaċ buiḋe, mac Rossa don ċur sin ria na marḃaḋ buḋéin. Ro marḃoḋ beós la druing ele do muinntir Uí doṁnaill, dá ṁac uilliam mic Seáin ó rinn ṁíl, ⁊ mac tSeoitt mic dabóg ó ḋoire uí doṁnaill, ⁊ mac a ṁeic. Ro gabaḋ dna la Magnus, mac Aoḋa mic magnusa la dearḃrataír uí doṁnaill Mac hobeird ó disert cellaiġ .i. uilliam, mac uillicc ruaiḋ mic uillicc óicc. Gerbtar iomḋa iolarḋa buannaḋa on iarla ar ordа hi cCloinn Riocaird Rainicc la hUa nDoṁnaill a ruccaḋ cuicce do ċreaċaiḃ coṁaiḋble, do ṫáintiḃ troma, dairccṫiḃ ⁊ dédalaiḃ do breith lais ar an tír gan troid, gan taċar go rainicc iomlán tar a aiss go baile an Mhotaigh.

Ro baí imreasain ⁊ easaonta etir druing do daoiniḃ uaisle tuaḋṁuṁan im coṁroinn, ⁊ im ċoṁaiġtes a ccríċe, ⁊ a fFearainn, a mbailteaḋ, ⁊ a mbuan caislen ro baḋ eiṁilt do sccríoḃaḋ no daisnéis.

O ro haisnéiḋeaḋ do ḃainríoġain Shaxan ⁊ don ċoṁairle go ro ringeattar Eireannaigh na haghaiḋ aṁail ro haisnéidheaḋ ceana, ⁊ an líon dearmáir dia daoiniḃ torcratar an bliaḋainsi, Asseaḋ ro ċhinn an prionnsa ⁊ an coṁairle Sir Rirdeird bionġam do léiccean anoir go noċt míle do saiġdiuiriḃh amaille friss do ċruaḋuccaḋ ⁊ do coṫuġaḋ an ċoccaiḋ aḃus go ttíosaḋ Iarla os erex dia ro horḋaiġeaḋ an tan sin toċt in erinn ó ṗélbrigde amach i ccúlaḋ, i ccostus, ⁊ in armail na ro tionnscnaḋ a hionnsaṁail do cor go hérinn riaṁ ó ro ġaḃsat Saxoin do laiṁ a gaḃail gus an tan sin. An Sir Rirderd remraite Ridire onorach eirriḋe do muintir na bainrioġna, roḃ

[q] *Dun-Guaire*, now Dungorey, a townland containing the ruins of a castle near the town of Kinvarra, said to occupy the site of the palace of Guaire Aidhne, King of Connaught, in the seventh century, ancestor of the family of O'Heyne, by whom this castle was erected.—See *Genealogies, &c., of Hy-Fiachrach*, p. 67.

[r] *Rinn-Mhil*, now Rinvile, near Oranmore, on the shore of the bay of Galway.

[s] *Doire-Ui-Dhomhnaill:* i. e. O'Donnell's Derry, or Oak Grove, now Derrydonnell, in the parish of Athenry, and about three miles to the east of Oranmore. For the origin of this name see the year 1213, p. 179, *supra*, and note [d], *ibid.*

[t] *Mac Hubert of Disert-Ceallaigh.*—This was an Irish name assumed by the head of a sept of the Burkes seated at Isertkelly, a castle in a parish of the same name, situated to the south-

ther to Dun-Guaire[q], in Coill-Ua-bhFiachrach. This part who went to Coill-Ua-bhFiachrach committed lamentable deeds, namely, they slew the two sons of Ross, the son of Owny, son of Melaghlin O'Loughlin, i. e. Turlough Boy and Brian. But a gentleman of the Clann-Donnell Galloglagh, who was along with Mac William on that expedition, namely, Hugh Boy Oge, the son of Hugh Boy, son of Mulmurry Mac Donnell, had been slain on this occasion by Turlough Boy, the son, before he himself fell. By another party of O'Donnell's people were slain the two sons of William, son of John [Burke] of Rinn-Mhil[r], and the son of Theobald, son of Dabuck, from Doire-Ui-Dhomhnaill[s], with his brother's son. Mac Hubert of Disert-Ceallaigh[t], namely, William, the son of Ulick Roe, son of Ulick Oge, was taken prisoner by O'Donnell's brother, Manus, son of Hugh, son of Manus. Although the Earl had great numbers of hired soldiers quartered in Clanrickard, O'Donnell happened to carry off out of the territory all the immense spoils, heavy herds, and other booty and property, which had been collected for him, without battle or conflict, until he arrived safe at Ballymote.

There existed strife and dissensions among some of the gentlemen of Thomond, concerning the division and joint-tenure[u] of their territory lands, towns, and strong castles, which it would be tedious to write or describe.

When it was told to the Queen of England and the Council that the Irish had risen up against her in the manner already described, and the vast numbers of her people who had been slain in this year, the resolution adopted by the Sovereign and the Council was, to send over Sir Richard Bingham with eight thousand soldiers, to sustain and carry on the war here, until the Earl of Essex should [be prepared] to come, who was then ordered to go to Ireland after the festival of St. Bridget with attire and expense, and an army, such as had not been attempted to be sent to Ireland, since the English had first undertaken to invade it, till that time. This Richard aforesaid was an honourable knight[w] of

west of the town of Loughrea, in the county of Galway.

[u] *Joint tenure.*—"Comaiteċeaр .i. comhap."—*O'Clery.*

[w] *Honourable knight.*—By this the Four Masters mean a man on whom honours had been heaped by his Sovereign. On account of certain complaints which had been lodged against this honourable knight, of *illibata fides*, by the chieftains of Connaught, he was removed and incarcerated by the Queen, who felt convinced that he had killed too many of the Burkes in cold blood; but when she heard of the defeat of her Field-marshal, Sir Henry Bagnal, she was per-

eolach i nErinn eiriḋe, ⁊ baí na gobernóir i cCóicceaḋ Connacht seal do bliaḋnaiḃ roiṁe sin. An tiarla of Essex sin a duḃramar beós, neach é baí hi cCion, ⁊ hi cCrisdeṁain, ⁊ i nonóir ag an mBainrioġain, neach é do nioḋ foġail ⁊ forġaḃáil for prouinnsiḃ iarṫair Eorpa a hucht na bainríoġna céḋna, ⁊ ba léssiḋe ro gaḃaḋ caṫair ḋaingen diotoġlaiġi hi rioġacht na Spainne gar béis riar an tan sin. Calis ainm na cathrach isin.

Iarla Tuaḋmuṁan do ḃeiṫ hi Saxoiḃ on callainn go céle an bliaḋain si.

Iarla Cille dara .i. Uilliam, mac Gearoitt, mic Gearoitt do ḋol hi Saxoiḃ isin earrach.

O Concoḃair Sliccigh Donnchaḋ mac Caṫail óicc do ṫocht a Saxoiḃ isin nGeiṁreaḋ.

As do na daoiniḃ uaisle do Ṫuaḋmuṁain batar i nimresain frisa roile amail a duḃramar Taḋcc mac Concoḃair mic Donnchaiḋ uí Briain ler gabaḋ droiċet Puirt croissi, ⁊ gion gur bo heriḋe céttus ro ṫionnsgain a gaḃail for Mairgreig ciorócc ar ċuicce do ṫuit fo ḋeóiḋ. Ro gabaḋ lais caislen Cluaine i nuibh Caisin, ⁊ caislen na Sccairbe i noirṫir ó mBloid ar ṫurnaé ṁeic epscoip na Miḋe. Ro baḋ diob beós Concoḃar mac Domnaill mic Maṫgamna, mic Briain uí Briain do ġaḃail baile an ċaisléin i cCloinn Ċuiléin uachtaraiġ ar Mhac Conmara Fionn, Sean, mac Taiḋg, mic Conmeḋa. Ba diob dna Toirrdealbach mac Maṫgamna, mic Toirrdealbaiġ, mic Maṫgamna ó Ċoill ó fFlannchaḋa

suaded that Bingham had acted with that severity due to such obdurate rebels, and accordingly set him at liberty, and appointed him as successor to Marshal Bagnal. Camden mentions these facts briefly as follows, in his *Annal. Reg. Eliz.*, A. D. 1598:

"Ad hujus insolentiam" [O-Neali] "comprimendam imprimis habilis visus est Richardus Binghamus, contra rebelles in Hibernia fortis & fœlix si quis alius. Ille igitur qui jampridem Connacthiæ Præfectura, provincialibus de severitate quiritantibus, amotus, in Angliam vocatus, & in custodiam datus, nunc remittitur cum honore & authoritate Marescalli Hiberniæ & Lageniæ Generalis. Verum statim atque appulit Dubliniæ diem obiit. Vir genere claro & antiquo in agro Dorsettensi, sed veteranæ militiæ gloria clarior. Ad S. Quintini enim Conquestum in Armonica ad Leitham in Hebridibus, Scotia, Creta Insula, ad Chrium contra Turcas, in Gallia & Belgio militavit, & quæ dixi, in Hibernia gessit."

[x] *Calis.*—This is a mere error of the transcriber of Cadis, i. e. Cadiz.

[y] *Portcroisi*, now Portcrush, on the Shannon, not far from O'Brien's Bridge.—See it already mentioned under the years 1506, 1510, 1597.

[z] *Cluain*, now Cloone, near the village of Tulla, on the east of the county of Clare.

[a] *Sgairbh*, now Scarriff, a small town in the parish of Tomgraney, in the north-east of the county of Clare.—See it already mentioned under the year 1564.

[b] *Hy-mBloid.*—This was the name of a sept of

the Queen's people, and was acquainted with Ireland; for he had been Govenor of the province of Connaught for some years before. The Earl of Essex, whom we have also mentioned, was one who was in favour, esteem, and honour with the Queen, and one who had made plunders and descents upon the provinces of the west of Europe for the same Queen. It was he who, a short time before, had taken a strong and well-fortified city in the kingdom of Spain, named Calis[x].

The Earl of Thomond remained in England the entire of this year, from one calend to the other.

The Earl of Kildare (William, the son of Garret, son of Garret), went to England in the spring.

O'Conor Sligo (Donough, the son of Cathal Oge) returned from England in the winter.

Among those gentlemen of Thomond, of whom we have spoken as being at strife with each other, was Teige, the son of Conor, son of Donough O'Brien, by whom the bridge of Portcroisi[y] was taken; and although he was not the first who had attempted to take it [by force] from Margaret Cusack, it was to him it finally fell. He also took the castle of Cluain[z] in Hy-Caisin, and the castle of Sgairbh[a], in the east of Hy-Bloid[b], from the attorney of the Bishop of Meath's son[c]. Among these was also Conor, son of Donnell, son of Mahon, son of Brian O'Brien, who took Baile-an-chaislein[d], in Upper Clann-Cuilein, from Mac Namara Finn (John, the son of Teige, son of Cumeadha). Among them was Turlough, son of Mahon, from Coill O'Flannchadha[e], who took from

the Dal-Cais, of whom the O'Kennedys, O'Shanahans, O'Duracks, and O'Kearneys, were the most distinguished families. These families were dispossessed in 1318, by Turlough na Caithreime O'Brien, aided by the Mac Namaras, who, shortly after this period, took possession of the whole region lying between the River Fergus and the Shannon. The name Ui mBloid is still retained in the ecclesiastical division, and is now applied to a deanery in the east of the county of Clare.

[c] *The Bishop of Meath's son*: i. e. the son of Hugh Brady, Bishop of Meath, who succeeded in 1563, and died in 1583. How the son of that Bishop came to have property in Clare, the Editor has not been able to discover. The Bradys of Tomgraney, who suppose that their real name is O'Grady, still possess property in the neighbourhood of Scarriff. The present Lord Chancellor of Ireland is descended from this Bishop, according to the tradition in the family.

[d] *Baile-an-chaislein*, now Castletown, in the parish of Dury, a short distance to the east of Ennis, in the county of Clare.

[e] *Coill-O'bhFlannchadha*: i. e. O'Flannchada's

lér gabaḋ Doire Eoġain ar Sheóirsi ciosócc, diar ḃó duṫċasaigh cedus clann amlaoiḃ, mic céin Uí Sheachnasaigh, ⁊ do ċeangail Maṫgaṁain, mac Toirrdheal-ḃaiġ buicc uí briain le coill o fFlannchaḋa. Ba do na daoiniḃ uaisle céona Toirrdhealḃaċ mac Murchaiḋ mic Concoḃair uí briain ó Ċaṫair ṁionain, co na braṫair Diarmait ruaḋ do ḋol i ccombáiḋ ċoccaiḋ na nGaoiḋeal. Ro bad díoḃ trá Taḋg caoċ, mac Toirrdhealḃaiġ, mic Briain, mic Donnchaiḋ, mec Maṫ-gaṁna do ġabail luinge Saxanaiġe fa nodlaicc mór iar mbeiṫ di for seċrán athaid fada siar an tan sin. Aseaḋ do rala di go ro gaḃ port i cCorca Bais-cinn iarṫaraiġe i ccoṁfoċraiḃ Ċairrge an Coḃlaiġ, Ro bean Taḋg an long co na somaoín dia foirinn. Nir bó cian iar sin gur ḃettrom a tarḃa do Thadcc, ⁊ gur ḃó trom a tóraiġeċt fair. An Taḋg ceona do ġabail an Dúin ḃicc baile dia ḃailtiḃ féin baí ag ceannaighe ó Luimneach a ngioll le fiaċaiḃ.

wood. This was a woody district in the parish of Kilkeedy, barony of Inchiquin, and county of Clare, and on the borders of the county of Galway. The old inhabitants of this district informed the Editor, in the year 1839, that they had seen considerable remnants of Coill O'bhFlannchadha, in the townlands of Bun-a-chiopain and Ait-tighe-doighte, in the parish of Kilkeedy. They also told him that the castles of Doire-Eoghain, or Derryowen, and Cluain-Dhubhain, were always considered as in the district of Coill O'bhFlannchadha.

[f] *Cathair-Minain*, now Caherminane, in the parish of Kilelagh, barony of Corcomroe, and county of Clare.—See note [n], under the year 1591, p. 1907, *supra*.

[g] *Carraig-an-Chobhlaigh:* i. e. the Rock of the Fleet, now corruptly pronounced in the Irish language Carraig a' ċoḃalṫaiġ, now anglicised Carrigaholt, a village in the barony of Moyarta, in the south-west of the county of Clare. It is situated on a bay to which it gives name, and near the Moyarta River, which falls into the Lower Shannon. Near the village, on a rocky cliff overhanging the bay, are the ruins of the castle of Carraig-an-Chobhlaigh, built by Mac Mahon, chief of Western Corca-Vaskin.

[h] *Of debt.*—The chieftain mortgaged this castle to a Limerick merchant, and, taking advantage of the troubles, ousted the merchant without paying the debt.

Under this year Camden records the death of three learned Englishmen, of whom one was the poet Edmund Spenser,—who lived for about nineteen years in Ireland, which he described as being "as beautiful and sweet a country as any under heaven,"—of whom he gives the following notice:

"Tertius, Ed. Spenserus patria Londinensis, Cantabragiensis etiam Academiæ alumnus, Musis adeo arridentibus natus, ut omnes Anglicos superioris ævi Poëtas, ne Chaucero quidem concive excepto, superaret. Sed peculiari Poetis fato semper cum paupertate conflictatus, etsi Greio Hiberniæ proregi fuerit ab epistolis. Vix enim ibi secessum & scribendi otium nactus, cum a rebellibus è laribus ejectus & bonis spoliatus, in Angliam inops reversus statim expiravit. Westmonasterii prope Chaucerum impensis Comitis Essexiæ inhumatus, Poetis funus ducentibus, flebilibusque carminibus & calamis in tumulum conjectis."—*Annal. Reg. Elis.*, A. D. 1598.

Ware, however, states, in the Preface to his

George Cusack Derryowen, at first the patrimony of the sons of Auliffe, the son of Cian O'Shaughnessy. Mahon, the son of Turlough Boy, obtained Coill O'Flannchadha. Among the same gentlemen was Turlough, the son of Murrough, son of Conor O'Brien, from Cathair Mionain[f], and his kinsman, Dermot Roe, who joined in the war of the Irish. Among them, moreover, was Teige Caech, the son of Turlough, son of Brian, son of Donough Mac Mahon, who, about Christmas in this year, captured an English ship that had been going astray for a long time before. It happened to put in at a harbour in Western Corca-Bhaiscinn, in the neighbourhood of Carraig-an-Chobhlaigh[g]. Teige took away this ship from the crew, and all the valuable things it contained. It was not long after till Teige found the profit very trivial, and the punishment severe. The same Teige took Dunbeg, one of his own castles, from a Limerick merchant, who had it in his possession, in lieu of debt[h].

Edition of Spenser's *View of the State of Ireland*, that he died in the year 1599, though others have it wrongly 1598. Spenser came to Ireland in 1580, as Secretary to the Lord Grey, and got a grant, in 1585, of 3000 acres of the lands of the county of Cork, forfeited by the rebellion of the Earl of Desmond and his confederates, and resided in the castle of Kilcolman, two miles north-west of Doneraile, where he wrote his *View of the State of Ireland*, in the year 1596, and finished his celebrated poem, "*The Faery Queen.*"—See Smith's *County Cork*, book ii. c. vii. Ware says that it were to be wished that some passages in his *View of the State of Ireland* "had been tempered with more moderation;" and Walter Harris, who was a man of great research and honesty, though deeply imbued with prejudices against the Irish Catholics, has added the following words in brackets to Ware, giving his opinion of Spenser's *View of the State of Ireland*:

"This Book lay in MS. in Archbishop Usher's Library, and was from thence published by Sir *James Ware*, the year aforesaid" [1633] "and dedicated to the Lord *Wentworth*, then Lord Deputy of *Ireland*. The Scope and Intention of the Book was to forward the Reformation of the Abuses and evil Customs of *Ireland;* and some things in it are very well written, particularly as to the Political main design of reducing *Ireland* to the due Obedience of the Crown of *England*. But in the History and Antiquities of the Country he is often miserably mistaken, and seems rather to have indulged the Fancy and Licence of a Poet, than the Judgment and Fidelity requisite for an Historian. Add to this his want of Moderation, in which, it must be confessed, he was exceedingly defective."—*Irish Writers*, p. 327.

It is very much to be regretted that Thierry and other writers, being deceived by the celebrity of his name, have helped to perpetuate some of his fictions; but truth will finally triumph; and the Editor, who intends to publish a review of Spenser's *View of the State of Ireland*, in which he will give him full credit for his discernment of abuses, and expose all his intentional figments, shall take no further notice of this divine bard-hunter, except that we learn from Ben Jonson's letter to Drummond of Hawthornden, that he died in London, in 1599, *for lack of bread!*

AOIS CRIOST, 1599.

Aois criost, mile, cúicc céd, noċaṫ, anaoí.

An tiarla chille dara sin a dubramar do ḋol hi Saxoiḃ isin mbliaḋain reṁainn .i. Uilliam, mac geroitt, mic geróitt, Ro triall toċt in erinn i nſrrach na bliaḋna so. Iar ndol do hilluing co noċt ffſraibh décc do ṁaiṫiḃ na miḋe, ⁊ ḟine gall maille fris, o ro ṡeolsat ſḋ fairccriona isin ffairrgi ní confacus bſó aéin neich dioḃ orin alle ⁊ ro baḋ a tiriḃ oile fo cſnn da ṁíos iar sin tainicc dſiṁin a mbáis go Saxoiḃ ⁊ go hErinn. Ni ro ḟaccaiḃ-sium mac, na dſrbraṫair ina ḋſóiḋ do gébaḋ a ċoṁorbus, aċt ro hoirdneaḋ coiṁmbraṫair dó (.i. gearóitt, mac eduaird mic geróitt, mic tómais, mic Sſain ċaim) las an mbainrioġain ⁊ la coṁairle Shaxan. Nſch eisiḋe baí na ċaptin for ṡaiġdiuiriḃ ag dénaṁ sſirḃísi don ḃainríoġain go ro lſicc dia an inṁe sin dia ṡaiġiḋ gan caṫ, gan coccad, gan gáḃaiḋ, gan guassaċt.

O maolmuaiḋ .i. Conall mac caṫaoir decc i nearraċ na bliaḋna so, ⁊ a mac .i. an calbaċ do ġaḃail a ionaid a huċt na bainrioġna. Araill do ḋaoiniḃ uaisle a ċiniḋ acc fóccra ⁊ acc fuaidreaḋ fair (do rſir gnaṫaighte gaoiḋeal) a ndiaiḋ an anma sin.

Fſrgus, mac briain, mic briain, mic Ruḋraiġe, mic caṫail uí ḟſrgail décc i mí márta, ⁊ ro baḋ adbar eccaoine ina ṫir fſin eisidhe.

Domnall, mac neill ṁſirgiġ, mic maolmuire, mic Aoḋa, mic neill do ṁarḃaḋ la Maolmuire mac briain óicc, ⁊ la hAoḋ mbuiḋe, mic firḟſḋa ṁec suiḃne ⁊ iadsiде (do crochaḋ) do loscaḋ la hUa ndoṁnaill Aoḋ ruaḋ ar mullaċ siṫe Aoḋa hi ccionaidh a migniomh, ⁊ tre ċoll a reachta.

Semus, mac toirrḋealḃaiġ, mic tuaṫail uí gallcuḃair do crochaḋ la hUa ndoṁnaill ar mullaċ na Siṫe ós ſss ruaiḋ an cſṫraṁaḋ lá do ṁárta iar na ḋſrḃaḋ fair co mbaoí ag braṫh ⁊ ag taiscelaḋ Uí ḋoṁnaill, ⁊ acc tarraing gall dia ṫír.

[i] *According to the custom of the Irish.*—Do réir gnáṫaiġṫe Gaoiḋeal: i. e. *secundum consuetudines Gadeliorum.* Calvagh O'Molloy succeeded as the eldest son of his father, according to the laws of England; but others of his tribe, who would be preferred to him according to the Irish law of tanistic succession, attempted to depose him.

[j] *Mullach-Sithe-Aedha,* now Mullaghnashee, or Mulnashee, the hill on which the church of Ballyshannon stands.

[k] *Violating his law,* Tre ċoll ar reaċta.—The

THE AGE OF CHRIST, 1599.

The Age of Christ, one thousand five hundred ninety-nine.

The Earl of Kildare, whom we have spoken of in the last year as having gone to England, namely, William, the son of Garrett, son of Garrett, prepared to return to Ireland in the spring of this year. He went into a ship with eighteen of the chiefs of Meath and Fingall; [and] after they had sailed till out of sight at sea, none of them was alive ever since; and it was from other countries, in two months afterwards, that an account of the certainty of their deaths arrived in England and Ireland. He [the Earl] left neither son nor brother behind him to succeed to his title; but his kinsman, Garrett, the son of Edward, son of Garrett, son of Thomas, son of John Cam, was appointed by the Queen and Council of England. He had been [only] a captain over soldiers in the Queen's service, until God permitted this property to devolve to him, without battle or war, peril or danger.

O'Molloy (Connell, the son of Cahir) died in the spring of this year; and his son, Calvagh, took his place, being appointed by the Queen. Some of the gentlemen of his tribe vied and contended with him (according to the custom of the Irish[i]) for that name.

Fergus, the son of Brian, son of Brian, son of Rury, son of Cathal O'Farrell, died in the month of March; and [his death] was the cause of lamentation in his own territory.

Donnell, the son of Niall Meirgeach, son of Mulmurry, son of Hugh, son of Niall [Mac Sweeny], was slain by Mulmurry, the son of Brian Oge, and Hugh Boy, the son of Ferfheadha Mac Sweeny. Both of these [i. e. the slayers] were hanged [and] burned by O'Donnell (Hugh Roe), on Mullach-Sithe-Aedha[j], for this crime, and for violating his law[k].

James, the son of Turlough, son of Tuathal O'Gallagher, was hanged by O'Donnell on Mullach-na-Sithe, over Assaroe, on the fourth day of March, it having been proved against him that he was spying and betraying O'Donnell, and drawing the English into his country.

word coll is nearly synonymous with ráruġaḋ, and denotes to break or violate. In O'Clery's Glossary it is explained by the modern word milleaḋ.

Seoirsi ciosocc, mac tomáis do marḃaḋ i mí iuil la toirrḋelḃaċ, mac maṫġaṁna mic toirrḋealḃaiġ mic maṫġaṁna, mic an espuicc uí briain isin ḋúṫhaiġ a aṫar, uair do rad Sir Risderd bionġam dúṫhaiġ ṁaṫġaṁna uí briain (iar na ċur cum báis lais) don treoirsi remraite, ⁊ bairium a noiaid a aṫarḋa co ro marḃaḋ Seoirsi lais don chur sin, ⁊ ro haḋnaiceḋ eisiḋe i mainistir innsi.

Mac uí concoḃair ċiarraiġe .i. donnchaḋ maol, mac concoḃair, mic concoḃair, mic Seain do marḃaḋ i mí August la druing damsaiḃ iarla desmuṁan .i. la cloinn Maġnusa óicc, mic maġnusa, mic emainn mec sitħiġ, ⁊ ro bad diṫ mór las an iarla an marḃaḋ sin, ar ba dia ċompann coccaiḋ ó concobair baḋéin .i. Sean, ⁊ a derbraṫair an donnchaḋ sin co na mbaoí ina ttír uile.

Sean mac an ġiolla duiḃ, mic Semuis uí ċinnéittiġ ó ḃaile an ġarrḋa ċnuic síthe úna i nurmumain do marḃaḋ la hAoḋ, mac murchaiḋ uí cinneittiġ ó ḃaile uí ċuirc.

Prioir loṫra i nurṁumain .i. Sean, mac Seain, mic giollapattraicc uí óccáin do ṁarḃaḋ la druing do ṡiol ccinneittiġ i mí iul do ṡonnraḋ.

Mór ingen domnaill mic concoḃair, mic toirrḋealḃaiġ uí briain décc i mí ianuarii ben sin rob ionmolta i moḋaiḃ mna.

Iarla tuaḋmuṁan .i. donnchaḋ mac concoḃair ui briain do toiḋeċt a Saxoiḃ hi mí Ianuarii, ⁊ anmain do hi ffarrad Iarla urṁuman i mbuitilerachaiḃ co cend athaid iaraṁ.

Mac do cloinn uí neill .i. Conn, mac Aoḋa, mic firdorċa, mic cuinn ḃacaiġ do ṫoċt i mí Ianuarii do ḋénaṁ cuarta ag cáirdiḃ ⁊ ag coṁpann coccaiḋ a aṫar illaiġniḃ, ⁊ isin muṁain, dia fios cia díoḃ ro baí i mbun a ccarattrad ⁊ a ttinġeallta dua neill, ⁊ do ġaoiḋelaiḃ. Ro an urṁór an earraiġ is na tíriḃ sin, ag faġbáil bíḋ dia aṁsaiḃ, ⁊ aga nertad isin ccoccad i mbáttar.

[l] *Misfortune*, diṫ: literally, "loss."

[m] *Baile-an-Gharrdha-Chnuic-Sithe-Una*, now Ballingarry, a townland giving name to a parish in the barony of Lower Ormond, about half a mile from the conspicuous hill of Cnoc-Sith-Una, now *anglice* Knocksheegowna, and about four miles to the south-east of Burrisokeane.

[n] *Ballyquirk*, a townland, with a castle in good preservation, in the parish of Lorha, barony of Lower Ormond, and county of Tipperary.—See note [w], under the year 1561, p. 1584, *supra.*

[o] *Lothra*, now Lorha, a small village with the ruins of several churches and abbey walls, in a parish of the same name, barony of Lower Ormond, and county of Tipperary. The pedigree of John O'Hogan, Prior of Lothra, who was the

George Cusack, the son of Thomas, was slain in the month of July by Turlough, the son of Mahon, son of Turlough, son of Mahon, son of the Bishop O'Brien, on account of his father's territory. For Sir Richard Bingham, after he had put Mahon O'Brien to death, had given up his [Mahon's] territory to the aforesaid George; and he [Turlough] persevered in his endeavours to recover his patrimony, until he slew George on this occasion. And he [George] was buried in the monastery of Ennis.

The son of O'Conor Kerry (Donough Mael, the son of Conor, son of Conor, son of John), was slain in the month of August, by a party of the soldiers of the Earl of Desmond, namely, by the sons of Manus Oge, son of Manus, son of Edmond Mac Sheehy; and that slaying was deemed a great misfortune[l] by the Earl; for O'Conor himself (John) was his ally in war, as was his brother, this Donough [who was slain], and all who were in their terrritory.

John, the son of Gilla-Duv, son of James O'Kennedy, from Baile-an-Gharrdha-Chnuic-Sithe Una[m], in Ormond, was slain by Hugh, the son of Murrough O'Kennedy, from Ballyquirk[n].

The Prior of Lothra[o] in Ormond (John, the son of John, son of Gillapatrick O'Hogan), was slain by a party of the O'Kennedys in the month of July.

More, the daughter of Donnell, son of Conor, son of Turlough O'Brien, died in the month of January. She was a woman praiseworthy in the ways of woman.

The Earl of Thomond (Donough, the son of Conor O'Brien), returned from England in the month of January, and remained for some time afterwards with the Earl of Ormond, in the country of the Butlers.

One of O'Neill's sons, namely, Con, the son of Hugh, son of Ferdorcha, son of Con Bacagh, went, in the month of January, on a visit among the friends and warlike confederates of his father in Leinster and Munster, to ascertain who they were that were firm in their friendship and promises to O'Neill and the Irish. He remained in those territories during the greater part of the Spring, obtaining provisions for his soldiers, and confirming them in the war

brother of Hogan O'Hogan, of the castle of Ardcrony, near Nenagh, is given differently by Duald Mac Firbis, as follows: "John, son of John, son of Melaghlin, son of John, son of Thomas, son of Siacus, son of Conor, Bishop of Killaloe." It is probable that Mac Firbis has omitted a generation i. e. Gilla-Patrick, between John and Melaghlin.

ḃaí iomaṫaiġi coinne, ⁊ carattraḋ etir an mac sin uí néill ⁊ Mac iarla tuadmuman .i. tadg mac concobair uí briain ar gaċ taeḃ do Shionainn.

Toirrḋealḃaċ, mac domnaill, mic concoḃair uí ḃriain dfostaḋ óccḃaiḋ ⁊ aésa tuarastail i ffriorṫosaċ na bliaḋna so do ċongnaṁ lás an mbainrioġain i naghaiḋ a hſsccarat. Dſrbraṫair ócc iarla tuaḋmuman .i. domnall, mac concoḃair, mic donnchaiḋ do bſith i ccſnous, ⁊ hi ccoḋnaċus muintire iarla tuaḋmuman ag congnaṁ bſós lás an mbainrioġain.

Iar ngaḃail na luinge Saxanaiġe sin tar a ttangamar ṫuas do taḋg caoċ, mac toirrḋealḃaiġ, mic maṫġaṁna ro ḟás moṫuccaḋ míoṁuinntſrais, ⁊ airrḋe sſraonta etir é ⁊ an mac sin an iarla .i. domnall. Do ċuaiḋ an taḋg sin i ccſnn iarla uſrmuman, ⁊ do róine a ṁuinntſrus mar gaċ rann ele dar ċſngail a ccor ffriss. Iar ttoċt do ṫaḋg iarttain tar Sionainn tucc ionnsaighiḋ oiḋche ar an ócc macaéṁ ar ḋomnall ua briain an seaċtṁaḋ la décc do mí febru go cill Muire ó mbracáin. Do gaḃaḋ ⁊ do gonaḋ domnall lais, ⁊ ro marbaḋ drong da ḋaoíniḃ diolmuine. Ruccaḋ é fſin don ḋún bſcc dia iomċoiṁſtt co na baoí aċt seaċtmain illáiṁ an tan do lſicceaḋ amach é gan urraḋa, gan árach.

Ua domnaill .i. Aoḋ ruaḋ, mac Aoḋa, mic maġnusa, baí siḋe na coṁnaiḋe i mbaile an ṁóṫaiġ i cconntaé sligiġ ó ro sraoínte caṫ in Aṫa buiḋe i nurṫosach August go féil briġde na bliaḋna so. Bá fada laissium gan dol isin ccoiccrich ris an ré sin ⁊ ni fidir caiḋe an tionad erḋalta irraġaḋ uair ní ro ḟáccaiḃ áird, nó aircionn, diaṁair na droiḃél i ccoicceaḋ connaċt na ro innrestair, nó na tard geill, ⁊ eidire uaḋaiḃ, genmoṫá tuaḋmuma an tsainrid. Ro ḟóccraḋ imorro sloiġſḋ lais do ṫoċt i ttuaḋmuṁain in ecmaing na ree remraite. Tangatar tra cenel cconaill céttus ina tionól. Ro baḋ diḃsiḋe Aoḋ ócc, mac Aoḋa duiḃ mic Aoḋa ruaiḋ, mic néill gairḃ uí domnaill, Niall garḃ, mac cuinn, mic an ċalbaiġ, mic maġnusa, mic Aoḋa duib, O doċartaiġ Sſan ócc, mac Sſain, mic Felim mic concoḃair ċarraiġ, O baoiġill Taḋg ócc, mac taiḋcc, mic toirrdealbaiġ, mic neill, Mac suiḃne

[p] *Teige, the son of Conor.*—This Teige was the brother of Donough, fourth Earl of Thomond, who was very loyal to the Queen and her government. Teige seems to have been disaffected, but very little of his history is known, except that he had three illustrious sons, Colonel Dermot, surnamed the Good, Colonel Murtough, who figured during Cromwell's usurpation, and Turlough.

[q] *Kilmurry-Ibrickane.*—This is the name of a

in which they were [engaged]. There was a communication and friendly correspondence carried on between this son of O'Neill and the son of the [late] Earl of Thomond (Teige, the son of Conor[p] O'Brien), on both sides of the Shannon.

Turlough, the son of Donnell, son of Conor O'Brien, hired soldiers and mercenaries in the very beginning of this year, to assist the Queen against her enemies. The young brother of the Earl of Thomond, also Donnell, the son of Conor, son of Donough, had the leading command of the Earl of Thomond's people in assisting the Queen.

After the taking of the English ship, of which we have above treated, by Teige Caech, the son of Turlough Mac Mahon, an appearance of enmity and an indication of contention arose between him and this son of the Earl, i. e. Donnell. Teige repaired to the Earl of Desmond and made his friendship with him, like every other party who had ratified their treaty with him. After Teige had returned across the Shannon, he made a nocturnal assault upon young Donnell at Kilmurry-Ibrickane[q], on the seventeenth day of the month of February. He wounded and made a prisoner of Donnell, and slew many of his faithful people; and he conveyed him to Dunbeg to be confined, but he was only a week confined there, when he was set at liberty without securities or conditions.

O'Donnell Hugh: i. e. Roe, the son of Hugh, son of Manus, had resided at Ballymote, in the county of Sligo, from the gaining of the battle of Ath-Buidhe, in the beginning of August, to the festival of St. Bridget in this year. He felt it long to have remained during this time without going into some enemy's territory, but he knew not to what particular place he should go; for he had not left a quarter, limit, wilderness, or recess, in the whole province of Connaught [the inhabitants of] which he had not plundered, or from which he had not taken pledges and hostages, save Thomond alone. Wherefore, at the time aforesaid, he ordered an army to be mustered in order to proceed into Thomond. First of all assembled the Kinel-Connel, among whom were Hugh Oge, the son of Hugh Duv, son of Hugh Roe, son of Niall Garv O'Donnell; and Niall Garv[r], the son of Con, son of Calvagh, son of Manus, son of Hugh Duv; O'Doherty (John Oge, the son of Felim, son of Conor Carragh); O'Boyle (Teige Oge, the

church and parish in the barony of Ibrickan, in the county of Clare.

[r] *Niall Garv*.—This is the Niall who afterwards betrayed Hugh Roe O'Donnell to the English.

ránacc doṁnall, mac toirrḋealḃaiġ, mic maolmuire, Mac suiḃne báġaineaċ donnchaḋ, mac maolmuire ṁeirgiġ, mic maolmuire, mic neill, iadsiḋe uile co na soċraittibh. Tánaicc isin toirċeastal céona Máguiḋir Aoḋ mac conċonnacht mic conconnacht, mic conconnacht, mic briain, mic Pilip, mic Tómair, ⁊ Mac uí ruairc .i. tadcc mac briain, mic briain ballaiġ, mic eoġain, ⁊ an Mac Uilliam do hoirdneaḋ la hUa ndoṁnaill féin riar an tan sin .i. teróitt mac uatéir ċiotaiġ mic Seáin, mic oiluerair.

Iar ttocht do na maiṫiḃ sin uile co na soċraitte do ṡaiġiḋ Uí doṁnaill go baile an Mhótaiġ. Ro baí daidble, ⁊ diomat an tsluaiġ go ro léicc sluaġ isriann Mhéic uilliam dioḃ an ccéin no ḃiaḋ soṁ i ttuaḋmuṁain ⁊ ba siad na hairiġ sortar coḋnaiġ sorrairiḋe .i. Mac Uilliam ⁊ niall garḃ mac cuinn uí doṁnaill. Ro sirséḋ ⁊ ro sairimtiġséḋ lar an luċt sin on ccéinn ṫoir do ġoirdealbaċaiḃ go huṁall cloinne giobúin[s]. Ro gaḃaḋ leo don ċur sin oilen Léthardáin[t], ⁊ ro marḃaḋ oċt ffir décc do ṁaithiḃ cloinne giobúin, gionmotá soċaide ele do ḋaoiniḃ a maille friú. Ruccsat créċa, airccte, ⁊ éḋala iomḋa leo ag soaḋ doiḃ ón rann.

Dala Uí doṁnaill co na ṡloġaiḃ ro arccnáttar do ḋol i ttuaḋmuṁain ⁊ ní ro hairireaḋ leo go rangatar gan raṫuccaḋ go mbátar don taeḃ istiġ dabainn hi ccloinn Riocaird. Ro gaḃaḋ longport léthan laoċarmaċ leo im tráṫ nóna do ló ar an ruaiḋḃéiṫigh[u] etir ċill colgan ⁊ ard raiṫin[w]. Bátar hi suiḋe ag cinnéḋ a ccoṁairle dur cionnus nó ḟoibérdais an ccríċ naimiúil gur a ttuḋcatar, ⁊ go ro ċaitést ní dia lóintiḃ, ⁊ go ro ċuilriot a suan toirrchim ria ndol hi ccéinn ṁórartair, ⁊ ṁórṡaoṫair doiḃ cen mo tát an luċt friotaire báttar leó. Bádar samlaiḋ go meḋon oiḋce. Ro forċongraḋ forra iaraṁ la hUa ndoṁnaill eirġe gan ḟuirech darccnáṁ isin ccoicríoch ria siú ro baḋ solus lá doiḃ. Atraiġriot iaraṁ ro céḋóir. Lottar réṁpa iaraṁ i réiḋ ḋíorġa gaċa róid gach nóirech go rangattar a moichdedoil na maidne isin

[s] *Umhall of Clann-Gibbon:* i. e. Upper Umhall or Murresk, in which the Mac Gibbons, now Gibbons, were seated.

[t] *Leath Ardan*, now Lahardaun, a lough in the townland of Ballyballinaun, parish of Aghagower, barony of Burrishoole, and county of Mayo.—Ordnance Map, sheet 88.

[u] *Ruaidh-Bheitheach:* i. e. the red birch, now *anglice*, Roevehagh, a townland containing a small village in the parish of Killeely, barony of Dunkellin, and county of Galway.—See this place referred to at the years 1116 and 1143, in the earlier portion of these Annals, as published by Dr. O'Conor. See also the map to *Tribes and Customs of Hy-Many*.

[w] *Between Kilcolgan and Ardrahin.*—The ham-

son of Teige, son of Turlough, son of Niall); Mac Sweeny Fanad (Donnell, the son of Turlough, son of Mulmurry); and Mac Sweeny Banagh (Donough, the son of Mulmurry Meirgeach, son of Mulmurry, son of Niall): all these with their forces. Into the same rendezvous came Maguire (Hugh, the son of Cuconnaught, son of Cuconnaught, son of Cuconnaught, son of Brian, son of Philip, son of Thomas); the son of O'Rourke (Thomas, the son of Brian, son of Brian Ballagh, son of Owen); and the Mac William, whom O'Donnell himself had some time before nominated, namely, Theobald, son of Walter Kittagh, son of John, son of Oliver.

When all these chieftains had come with their forces to Ballymote, to O'Donnell, they formed so numerous and vast an army that he sent a force into the territory of Mac William, while he himself should be in Thomond; and the chieftains who were [appointed] leaders of this force were Mac William and Niall Garv, the son of Con O'Donnell. This force searched and mightily overran [the country] from the eastern extremity of Costello to Umhall of Clann-Gibbon[s], and during that excursion took the island of Leath Ardan[t], and slew eighteen of the chief men of the Clann-Gibbon, besides many other persons. They carried off great preys, plunders, and spoils, on their return from the territory.

As for O'Donnell and his forces, they marched forward to proceed into Thomond, and made no delay until they arrived, without being observed, inside the river in Clanrickard; and in the evening they pitched an extensive camp of armed heroes at Ruaidh-Bheitheach[u], between Kilcolgan and Ardrahin[w]. Here they remained to consult with each other as to how they should attack the strange territory towards which they had come; and, having eaten some of their provisions[x], they [all] went to take a sleep, except the sentinels, before they should undertake their great journey and toil. Thus they remained until midnight, when O'Donnell commanded them to rise up without delay, to march into the neighbouring territory before the day should break upon them. They rose up forthwith, and proceeded straight onwards by each direct road, until,

let of Roevehagh is nearly due east of Kilcolgan, and not exactly between it and Ardrahin.

[x] *Eaten some of their provisions.*—All this is much better told in the Life of Hugh Roe O'Donnell, by Cucogry O'Clery, which states, "that after having pitched their camp and lighted fires, they sat down to take refreshments and to drink to each other in ale and Spanish

ccſnn ṫoir do ċoill ó fflannchada, do tríoċa céd ceneoil ffſrmaic i ttuadmuṁain. Ro rannsat a scſiṁelta an dú sin. Ro lſiccset drong diob don taob budh tuaidh isteċ i mboirinn im tadg ua ruairc, ⁊ im Mac suibne mbaġainech, ⁊ drong ele tſr isteaċ go baile uí occáin na coilleadh moire, go tulaiġ uí deadhaid, go dorus baile uí ġriobṫa. Do ḋeachaidh maguidir go ndruing moir do sloġ amaille fris [co h-inis Ui Chuinn]. Do taéd tra Ua domnaill go ttoċacht ⁊ go ttiuġ a ṡloiġ amaille fris durlar ċoille ó fflannchada, do ḃealaċ an ḟiodḟail go cill ingine baoiṫ i nuaċtar dalccais ria midmſdon laoí. Sóait an lucht do choidh budſin, tar a nais budh tuaid, do ḋruim fionnglaisi, do ċorad ḟinn, ⁊ go cill ingine baoith i ccomdáil í domnaill. Tuccad dia saiċċidh an dú sin creaċa ċeneoil ffſrmaic uile on dísſrt, go glſnd coluim ċille, ⁊ go tolaiġ ċumann, ⁊ ó cluain sailċſrnaiġ go lſim an eich.

Ní riaċt la Mac uí ruairc na la Mac suibne teċt na ċſnd la creaċaib bóirne in adhaiġ sin. Ni rainicc bſós la Máguidir teċt don lſiṫ aile, ar ro gabsatar side longport in gaċ airm irrucc adhaiġ forra.

Iar mbſiṫ hi ffosslongport dUa domnaill in adhaiġ sin hi ccill ingine baoiṫ ro ḟaccaib an baile ar a ḃárach ria mſdón laí, ⁊ asseadh do ḋeaċaidh i ttrioċait

wine, without fear or dread, in the territory of their enemy."—*O'Reilly's copy*, p. 61.

[y] *Coill-ObhFhlannchadha:* i. e. the wood of the Ui-Flancy, a woody district in the parish of Kilkeedy, in the north-east of the barony of Inchiquin, and county of Clare.

[z] *Baile-Ui-Ogain:* i. e. O'Hogan's town, now Ballyhogan, a townland in the parish of Dysart, barony of Inchiquin, and county of Clare. Coill mhor, i. e. the great wood, was the name of a woody district comprising the lands of Ballyhogan and several of the adjoining townlands.

[a] *Tully-O'Dea*, a townland in the same parish, about three miles to the north of the church of Dysart.

[b] *Baile-Ui-Ghriobhtha:* i. e. the town of O'Griffy, now Ballygriffy, a townland containing the ruins of a castle in the same parish. In a *Description of the County of Clare*, written about the year 1584, this castle is called Ballygriffie, and mentioned as belonging to O'Griffie.

[c] *Inchiquin.*—The Four Masters have left the sense imperfect here, and four blank lines. It is stated in the Life of Hugh Roe O'Donnell, that Maguire, with his part of the army, set out to scour the lands near Kilnaboy, where he met Conor O'Brien, whom he wounded, and took prisoner, and carried to his (O'Brien's) own castle of Inchiquin, which he took, and in which he remained till the next day.

[d] *Bealach-an-Fhiodfail.*—The position of this road is still pointed out by the old natives of the parish of Kilkeedy, as extending from Rockforest to Kilnaboy. Fhiodhfail was the name of a wood now called Coill an ḟioḋḟail, comprised in the townland of Rockforest (which is but an attempt at translating it from fiodh, *a forest*, and fail or ail, *a stone or rock*), in the parish of Kilkeedy, about five miles eastward from Corofin.

[e] *Cill-Inghine Bhaoith*, now Kilnaboy, near Corofin.—See it mentioned before under 1573.

[f] *Druim-Finnghlaisi.*—This name is now ob-

by morning twilight, they arrived in the eastern extremity of Coill-O'bhFlannchadha[y], in the cantred of Kinel-Fearmaic, in Thomond. Here they formed marauding parties, and sent one of them northwards into Burren, under the command of Teige O'Rourke and Mac Sweeny Banagh; and another party southwards into Baile-Ui-Ogain[z] of Coill-mhor, to Tully-O'Dea[a], and to the gate of Baile-Ui-Ghriobhtha[b]. Maguire, with a strong body of his forces, went forth [towards Inchiquin[c]]. O'Donnell [himself] proceeded, with the flower and main body of the army, through the middle of Coill-O'bhFlannchadha, Bealach-an-Fhiodhfail[d], and, before mid-day, arrived at Cill-Inghine-Bhaoith[e], in the upper part of Dal-gCais. Those who had gone to the south returned to the north by Druim-Finnghlaisi[f] and Corofin, and joined O'Donnell at Cill-Inghine-Bhaoith. Thither the spoils of all Kinel-Fearmaic, from Diseart[g] to Glencolumbkille[h], and to Tulach-Chumann[i], and from Cluain-Sailchearnaigh[k] to Leim-an-eich[l], were brought to O'Donnell.

The son of O'Rourke and Mac Sweeny were not able to return to him on that night with the spoils of Burren; nor was Maguire able to return from the other direction, for they had pitched their camps wherever the night overtook them.

O'Donnell remained that night encamped at Cill-Inghine-Bhaoith, and left it before noon on the following day; and he then proceeded to Kilfenora, in

solete, but the situation of the place is certain, as it is shewn on the engraved map from the Down Survey, under the anglicised form of Drumfinglass, as lying due south of Corofin, and between it and Dysart.

[g] *Disert*, now Dysart.

[h] *Glencolumbkille*, ᵹlinn coluim cille: i.e. St. Columbkille's Glen. This is a wild and beautiful valley in the east of the parish of Carron, barony of Burren, and county of Clare, and close to the verge of the county of Galway. There is in this valley a small church dedicated to St. Columbkille, and near it is the residence of Terence O'Brien, Esq., now the senior representative of Donnell Spaineach, the son of Col. Murtough O'Brien, who capitulated with General Waller.

[i] *Tulach Chumann*, now Tullycummon, a townland in the parish of Kilnaboy, adjoining Castletown in the barony of Burren.

[k] *Cluain-sailchearnaigh*, now Cloonselherny, a townland containing the ruins of a castle, in the east of the parish of Kilkeedy, barony of Inchiquin, and county of Clare, and close to the boundary of the county of Galway.

[l] *Leim-an-eich*, i.e. *Saltus Equi*, now Lemaneh, a townland containing the ruins of a large castle in the parish of Kilnaboy, in the barony of Inchiquin, close to the boundary of that of Burren. This castle was erected by the ancestors of Sir Lucius O'Brien of Dromoland. From the situation of the places here mentioned, it is quite evident that Kinel-Fearmaic comprised the entire of the present barony of Inchiquin.

ċéd corcumruadh go cill ḟionnabrach. Ro sgaoilit sceimhealta eirte sidhe budh dheas go hEidhnigh, gur an mBrentir Ffearmacaigh, ⁊ cCorcamaigh [cCormacaigh] go dorus innsi Díomain, go cill easpuicc Lonáin, go baile Paidín, ⁊ tar a nais soir go cill ḟionnabrach co na ccreachaibh, ⁊ co na nédalaibh i ccoinne Uí Domhnaill. Anais hi suidhe go horbarach co ruccsat a sloigh fair ar gach aird i mbáttar. Tánaicc din Mac uí Ruairc, ⁊ Mac Suibhne bághaineach go ccreachaibh boirne dia saighidh. Tánaicc dna Mághuidhir go ccreachaibh ⁊ go nairccnibh iomdha dia ionnsaighidh don leith aile. An tan at connairc Ua Domhnaill na cnuic aga líonadh, ⁊ aga ndubhadh ina uirthimchell do ṫaintibh do ṫromalmhaibh gacha tíre tresa ttudcatar a ṡlóigh. Ro triall róadh tar a ais do dhromchladh na bóirne bfinngairbhe a moich néll na maidne dar boirinn go ros gabh roimhe don nuachongbail don turlach, go mainistir chorcumruadh, do chartair na ccléireach ⁊ do roine airisemh na hoidhce sin isin Ruba i niarthar ua Ffiachrach aidne. Do ṫaéd ar a bharach tre uachtar cloinne Riocaird, lá dorus baile átha an rióg. Ní haithristear a imthechta iaramh o tá sin go baile an Mhotaigh, Acht ro baí Mac uilliam ⁊ Niall garbh ua Domhnaill for a cionn illeithimel Ua maine go nairccnibh, ⁊ go nedalaibh iomdha leó a rann Mheic uilliam.

Ro ionntramhlaigh an traoí sinchaidh ⁊ fir dána Mac bruaideadha Maoilín óg gur bo i ndiogail diosccaoilte grianáin oiligh la Muircertach mór mac

[m] *Eidhneach*, now Inagh, the name of a river and of a Roman Catholic parish near Milltown Malbay, in the west of the county of Clare.

[n] *Brentir of the Fearmacaigh and Cormacaigh:* i. e. the fetid district of the Kinel-Fearmaic and Ui-Cormaic, so called from its situation on the frontiers of the territories of these tribes. Brenter, or, as it is now locally called, Bréintre, is a district comprising seven townlands, lying north-east of Sliabh Callain, or Mount Callan, in the west of the county of Clare. A family of the O'Connells were transplanted hither, from Kerry, in Cromwell's time; but the whole district is now the property of the Marquis of Thomond, under whom Charles O'Connell, Esq., of Ennis, rents two townlands of this district.

[o] *Inis-Dimain:* i. e. Diman's holm or island, now Ennistimon, a small town in the west of the county of Clare.

[p] *Cill-Easbuig-Lonain.*—This is a mistake of the transcriber for cill easpoig ḟlannáin: i. e. the church of Bishop Flannan, now Killaspuglonane, a townland containing an extensive burial ground, in the barony of Corcomroe, and county of Clare.

[q] *Baile-Phaidin*, now Ballyphaudeen, a townland in the parish of Kilmacreehy, in the barony of Corcomroe.

[r] *Nuachongbhail*, now *anglice* Noughaval, an old church, giving name to a townland and parish in the barony of Burren and county of Clare, and adjoining the parishes of Kilnaboy and Kilfenora.

[s] *Turlach*, i. e. dried lough. There are many places of this name in the northern part of the county of Clare; but the Turlach here referred

the cantred of Corcomroe. From thence he dispatched marauding parties southwards to Eidneach[m], to Brentir of the Fearmacaigh[n], to Cormacaigh, to the gate of Inis-Dimain[o], to Cill-Easbuig-Lonain[p], and to Baile-Phaidin[q], who returned to him to Kilfenora, in an easterly direction, loaded with spoils and booty. O'Donnell remained here until the following day, when his troops came up with him from every quarter in which they had been dispersed. The son of O'Rourke and Mac Sweeny Banagh came up with the spoils of Burren; and Maguire came up from another direction with much booty. When O'Donnell saw the surrounding hills covered and darkened with the herds and numerous cattle of the territories through which his troops had passed, he proceeded on his way homewards, over the chain of rugged-topped mountains of Burren; and, passing by Nuachongbhail[r], Turlach[s], the monastery of Corcomroe, and Carcair-na-gCleireach[t], arrived at Rubha[u], in the west of Hy-Fiachrach-Aidhne, where he stopped for the night. On the morrow he passed through the upper part of Clanrickard, and by the gate of Athenry. His adventures from this forward are not related, until he arrived at Ballymote, except that he was met by Mac William and Niall Garv O'Donnell at the frontiers of Hy-Many, with many preys, and spoils, and booty, which they had carried off from Mac William's country.

The learned historian and poet, Mac Brody (Maoilin Oge), represented that it was in revenge of the demolition of Grianan Oiligh[w], formerly, by Murtough

to is Turlach-na-gcoilean, an old castle to the right of the road as you go from Corofin to the New Quay, in the barony of Burren, and county of Clare. It is very near the old church of Termon Cronan.

[t] *Carcair-na-gCleireach*, i. e. the Narrow Pass of the Clerics or Priests. This name is still well-known (as the Editor has good reason to remember), and is applied to a steep pass over a rocky hill in Burren, in the townland of Rossalia, parish of Abbey-Corcomroe, barony of Burren, and county of Clare. It is called in English "the Corker road."

[u] *Rubha*, now Roo, or Rue, a townland near the little town of Kinvarra, in the barony of Kiltartan, and county of Galway, and on the boundary of the barony of Burren, in the county of Clare. A castle called Coradh-an-Rubha, *anglice* Corranrue, which belonged to O'Heyne, stood at this place till the year 1755, when it fell at the very moment that the earthquake happened at Lisbon.

[w] *Grianan-Oiligh*, now Greenan-Ely. The ruins of this fortress of the Kings of the northern Hy-Niall race, are still to be seen on Green-Hill, in the barony of Inishowen, and county of Donegal, about six miles to the north-west of Derry.—See the Ordnance Memoir of the parish of Templemore. This fortress was demolished, and many of its stones carried off as a trophy, by Murtough More O'Brien, in the year 1101.

toirrḋealḃaiġ [mic taiḋg] mic briain ḃoroiṁe feċt riaṁ Ro ċſdaiġ dia (tria eſccaine ċolaim cille for síol mbriain) léirscreachaḋ ⁊ láimnoreaḋ tuaḋ-muṁan la hua ndoṁnaill don ċur sin, ⁊ tainicc an Maoílin ócc céona i ccſnn Uí doṁnaill do chuinġidh airicc a ċruiḋ táraṫatar drong do na sloġaiḃ hi-sin. ⁊ do raḋaḋ dó in óiġe conaḋ ann do roine Maoilin an rann

Do baí i ndán i ndioġail oiliġ,
a Aoḋ ruaiḋ do rſc an faiḋ
toċt ḃar sluaiġ go hiaṫ ṁaġ naḋair,
a tuaiḋ iarṫar caḃair caiġ.

IS an ccſid ṡeaċtmain do Márta tánaicc goberrnoir cóicciḋ connaċt .i. Sir conerr clifort go gaillim go sloġ mór do daġdaoínib uaisle ⁊ go saiġ-diuiribh iomḋa amaille friú. Iar mbſiṫ dó i ngar do ṡeċtmain i ngaillimh ro ċuir a ṡeaċt, nó a hoċt do bandaḋaiḃ gallda ⁊ gaoiḋelċa go conntaé an cláir dia ḟios cia dob uṁal, no dob ſsuṁal don ḃainrioġain innte do órdaiġ teroitt díolmain ⁊ captin lſstair, ⁊ Sirriam ċonntaé an clair fſin .i. Risſrd sgorlócc hi ccſnnus forra go roċtain doiḃ co hairm i mbaoí toirrdealḃaċ

[x] *The curse of Columbkille.*—The reader will bear in mind that the Earl of Thomond was at this time a Protestant, and exercising the "bitterness of marshall law" against the Irish poets. In the Life of Hugh Roe O'Donnell, by Cucogry O'Clery, the words in which St. Columbkille is said to have delivered this prophesy are quoted, but they are decidedly modern, and fabricated for the occasion.—See the year 1572, p. 1657, *supra.*

[y] *Land of Magh-Adhair:* i. e. Thomond, so called poetically from Magh Adhair, the place where the O'Briens were inaugurated. This place, now called in English Moyry Park, is situated in the townland of Toonagh, parish of Clooney, barony of Upper Bunratty, and county of Clare, and about three miles and a half west from Tulla. The mound on which the O'Briens were inaugurated is still to be seen at this place. It is of an irregular form, and measures 102 feet in length, and 82 feet in breadth. According to all the ancient Irish accounts of the Fir Bolgs, this place received its name from Adhar, son of Umor (the brother of Aengus, who built the stone fort of Dun-Aengusa, on the Great Island of Aran), who was chief of this plain in the first century, long before the race of Heber and Oilioll Olum had obtained dominion in Thomond. For some account of the inauguration of chiefs of the O'Briens, at this place, see the *Caithreim Thoirdhealbhaigh*, at the years 1242, 1267, 1277, and 1311. See also *Circuit of Muircheartach Mac Neill*, p. 47, printed for the Irish Archæological Society, where the situation of this mound was pointed out for the first time since the invention of printing.

[z] *From the North.*—This line is very artfully contrived by Mac Brody, who intended that O'Donnell and Teige, the brother of the Earl of Thomond, should understand by it, that the Irish of the south expected that their deliverer would come from the north; and, on the other

More, son of Turlough [son of Teige], son of Brian Boroimhe, that God, in consequence of the curse of Columbkille[x] upon the O'Briens, had permitted Thomond to be totally plundered and devastated on this occasion by O'Donnell. This Maoilin Oge came to O'Donnell, to request of him the restoration of his cattle, which a party of the troops had carried off; and they were all given back to him; upon which Maoilin composed the following quatrain:

It was destined that, in revenge of Oileach,
O Hugh Roe! the Prophet announced,
Thy troops should come to the land of Magh-Adhair[y];
From the North[z] the aid of all is sought.

In the first week of March the Governor of the province of Connaught, Sir Conyers Clifford, went to Galway with a great army of distinguished gentlemen and soldiers. After having been nearly a week in Galway, he sent seven or eight companies of English and Irish soldiers to the county of Clare, to know who were loyal or disobedient to the Queen there. He appointed Theobald Dillon, Captain Lester, and Richard Scurlock[a], the sheriff of the county of Clare, as commanders over them, until they should arrive at the place where Turlough

hand, if, in case he should be persecuted for it by his own lord and master, the Earl of Thomond, he could shew that it should be punctuated thus:

"Do bai i ndán i ndíoġail Oilġ,
A Aoḋ ruaiḋ, do rís an fáiḋ,
Toċt bar sluaiġ go hiaṫ ṁaiġe n-Aḋair
A tuaiḋ. Iarṫar cabair ċáiġ."

"It was in destiny in revenge of Oileach,
O, Hugh Roe, the prophet announced
The coming of your host to the land of Magh Adhair
From the North. Let the help of all be sought."

By understanding the quatrain in this way, the last three words would mean nothing more than, "The Lord help us all;" and it would convey no direct insult to the Earl of Thomond (Donough O'Brien, fourth Earl), who firmly believed that it had been prophesied that he himself was predestined to be the instrument in subduing the northern rebels.—See *Pacata Hibernia*, book 2, c. xxi. That St. Columbkille had predicted that the northern Hy-Niall would one day plunder Thomond in revenge for the demolition of the northern palace of Oileach, was not too hard for this Earl's belief, and that it was fulfilled on this occasion, when his territory was overrun with fire and sword by Hugh Roe O'Donnell, was a harmless inference by Mac Brody, who may have appeared to regret it before the Earl; but the last line, if read, "A tuaiḋ iarṫar cabair ċaiġ, from the North the aid or relief of all is sought," would cause the Earl to exercise the "bitterness of Marshall law" against him, as recommended by the *divine* poet Spenser.

[a] *Scurlock.*—This name is now more usually written Sherlock.

ó briain dia ttuccaḋ mar an ccéona ugdarrás uairtiḃ. Ḃádair an ċéd adhaiġ hi ccill caeídi i noirṫer o ffermaic iar roċtain doiḃ don tír.

Ot cualatar i mbaoí do ḋaoíniḃ diolmuine for muintersus Taidhcc mic concobair uí briain roċtain doiḃside don tír bádar ina noirchill, ⁊ acc dol tre ḃealaċ an ḟiodḟáil o ċill caoídi riar do muinntir na bainrioghna ar na ḃaraċ ro ionnsaiġsiot muintir taidhg iad go ro marḃaḋ daoíne iomḋa etorra da gaċ leth. Ger bo mó ro marḃaḋ do ṁuintir na bainrioghna, ni hinnister eċt oirdearc dioḃ do ṫuitim. Ro marḃaḋ do leiṫ na ngaoidel duine uasal do ṡíol mbriain .i. diarmaitt ruaḋ, mac murchaiḋ, mic concobair. Tar a nesrnaḋ ann do léicceaḋ an tslighe do muintir na bainrioghna go ro ġabsat airisem ⁊ coṁnaiġe hi ccill inġine baoíṫ i ndeireaḋ laoí.

Asseaḋ ro chinn taḋg mac concobair uí briain iar sin sídiuccaḋ fris an mbainrioġain, ⁊ diultaḋ dia aṁsaiḃ, ⁊ go sonnradhaċ do luċt tabairte an tachair remraite. Ro ċuir a ṫeċta do ṡaiġiḋ tepóitt diolṁuin go cill inġine baoíṫ, ⁊ gus an ngobernóir don ġaillim.

Ro ḟáccaiḃ tepóitt diolmuin ⁊ muinntir na bainrioghna cill inġine baoiṫ ar a ḃarach, ⁊ do ċóidsiot go hairm i mbaoí toirrdelḃaċ mac domnaill uí briain baí ina ċleiṫ ḟosccaiḋ, ⁊ ina ṫulaiġ toirlenga ag gach aén le buḋ áil do ṁuinntir na bainríoghna. O rangattar soṁ ⁊ toirrdealbaċ hi ccenn a ċele ro ġabsat iomḟuiḋe im ċaṫair mionain i mbaruntacht Chorcmodruaḋ baile eisiḋe baí ina uaiṁ lattronn, ⁊ ina ṁuine meirle gur a tticcedh slad, ⁊ sáruccaḋ an tíre ina ṫimcell a los toirrdelḃaiġ, mic murchaiḋ, mic concoḃair ui briain duine uasal eisiḋe baí hi rann gaoiḋel an tan sin. Rob éiccen an baile sin do ṫaḃairt ar láiṁ muinntire na bainrioghna.

Ro faccaiḃ Toirrdealḃaċ ⁊ tepóitt co na ṁuinntir caṫair mionain, ⁊ do coidsiott hi ccorcḃaiscind iarṫaraiġ do ḋénaṁ síoḋa le taḋg caoċ mac maṫġaṁna ⁊ ó na ro ḟedsat a síoḋuccaḋ ruccsat creacha ⁊ édala iomḋa as an tír. Lotar soir ar a haiṫle do ċorcoḃaiscind airtheraiġ, ⁊ iaraṁ go

[b] *Cill-Caeidi:* the church of St. Caeidi, now Kilkeedy, an old church giving name to a parish in the east of the barony of Inchiquin, and county of Clare. The Ui-Fearmaic, otherwise Cinel-Fearmaic, were the O'Deas and their correlatives, whose territory comprised all this barony.

[c] *Teige, the son of Conor O'Brien.*—He was the Earl of Thomond's brother.

[d] *Bealach-an-Fhiodhfail,* now the Rockforest road, extending from Kilkeedy to Kilnaboy, in the barony of Inchiquin.

[e] *Cathair-Mionain,* now *anglice* Caherminane, a castle in the parish of Killelagh, barony of Corcomroe.—See note [n], under the year 1591,

O'Brien was, to whom authority over them was likewise given. On their arrival in the territory, they remained the first night at Cill-Caeidi[b], in the east of Hy-Fearmaic.

When the faithful friends of Teige, the son of Conor O'Brien[c], had heard of their arrival in this country, they lay in ambush, and, as the Queen's people were on the following day marching westwards from Cill-Caeidi, through Bealach-an-Fhiodhfail[d], Teige's people attacked them, and many persons were slain between them on both sides; but although there were more of the Queen's people slain, the death of no distinguished man of them is recorded. [But] on the side of the Irish was slain a gentleman of the O'Briens, namely, Dermot Roe, the son of Murrough, son of Conor. Besides what was done there, the pass was ceded to the Queen's people, who at the close of the day halted and rested at Cill-Inghine-Bhaoith [Kilnaboy].

The resolution which Teige, the son of Conor O'Brien, adopted after this was, to make peace with the Queen, and to dismiss his hirelings, and especially those who had made the aforesaid attack. He sent his messengers to Theobald Dillon, to Cill-Inghine-Bhaoith, and to the Governor, to Galway.

On the following day Theobald Dillon and the Queen's party left Cill-Inghine-Bhaoith, and proceeded to the residence of Turlough, the son of Donnell O'Brien, who was a sheltering fence and alighting hill to any of the Queen's people that wished to go to him. When they and Turlough met together, they laid siege to Cathair-Mionain[e], in the barony of Corcomroe, a castle which was then a den of robbers and a cover for plunderers, into which the plunder and spoil of the surrounding country were wont to be carried to Turlough, the son of Murrough, son of Conor O'Brien, a gentleman who was in alliance with the Irish at that time. The castle was obliged to be surrendered to the Queen's people.

Turlough and Theobald, with their people, then left Cathair-Mionain, and proceeded to West Corca-Bhaiscinn[f], to make their peace with Teige Caech Mac Mahon; but, as they could not come on terms of peace with him, they carried off many preys and spoils from the territory. Then, after this, they passed eastwards into East Corca-Bhaiscinn[g], and afterwards to Ennis, where

p. 1907, *supra*.

[f] *West Corca-Bhaiscinn:* i. e. the barony of Moyarta, in the south-west of the county of Clare.

[g] *East Corca-Bhaiscinn:* i. e. the barony of

hInis, go mbaoí Seission cúicc lá décc aca i nInis, ⁊ daoine uaisle an tíre ⁊ na Conntaé uile acca ffrisccra. A ccionn na ree sin do deachaidh tepoitt diolmuin ⁊ captin lestair ar an tír iar ffaccbáil ceiṫre mbanna saighdiuiridhe, Shirriam, ⁊ Shuibṡirriam (amaille le hadhṁail ar ċíos na bainrioghna do ḋiol) innte.

Tánaicc dna iarla tuadhmuman hi ccionn trecṫmaine iar sin don tír ar mbeiṫ dó a ngar do raiṫe i mbuitilerachaibh. O do riacht go tuadhmumain, assead ro triall gan codladh da oidhce i nen ḃaile go ndechaidh do dioghail easonora ⁊ ionnraighṫe a dearbhrathar ar tadhg caoċ, mac matġamhna. Ro ṫionoil urṁor an tire ina ḋocom do ḋol hi ccorcbaiscinn iarṫaraiġ, ⁊ ro ṡuidh re haghaidh ċairrge an coḃlaiġ an luan ria ccaisc hi mí april do ṡonnradh. Tuccadh crodh ⁊ ceṫra an tire uile o ċnoc doire, go leim concullainn dia saiġidh gus an ffoslongport sin. Fuair an tiarla an baile fo ċenn ceiṫre lá ar a haiṫle, ⁊ ar ndiṫreabh saoire na caisc ro ṫarraing an tiarla ordanas o luimneaċ do ḋol re hacchaidh an dúin ḃicc, ⁊ iar suidhiuccadh an ordanáis for ionċaibh an ḃaile ní ro anrat an ḃarda fri haon urcor do ċaiṫemh friú an tan ro foccradh uaṫa an baile don iarla, ⁊ ní ḟuairsiot do ṁaiṫemh nanacail acht an seal badar agá mbreiṫ go garmain na croiċe in ro crochadh ina ccúpladaibh iatt aghaidh i naghaidh. Fuair an tiarla dún mor ṁeic an fferṁacaiġ on modh ccédna. Iar ngaḃail na mbailtead mbaiscneaċ sin don iarla ro léicc an tordanás mór uadha go luimneaċ, ⁊ do ċuaidh fein tar sliaḃ soir go hurlár tuadhmuman. Tucc sé da duṫċaraċaibh fein gach baile dár gabadh

Clonderalaw, in the south of the county of Clare, adjoining West Corca-Bhaiscinn.

[h] *For the dishonour*, literally, "for revenging of the dishonour and attack of his brother on Teige Caech Mac Mahon."

[i] *Carraig-an-Chobhlaigh*, i. e. the Rock of the Fleet, now called corruptly, in Irish, carraig a coḃaltaiġ, and anglicised Carrigaholt, a village in the parish and barony of Moyarta, in the south-west of the county of Clare, about a mile and a half to the north of Kilcredane point. Near the village, on a rocky cliff overlooking the bay, to which it gives name, stands the castle of Carraig an Chobhlaigh, which was built by Mac Mahon, chief of West Corca-Vaskin, or the barony of Moyarta. It is in good repair, and occasionally dwelt in by Mr. Burton, to whose family it has belonged since the confiscation of the property of Lord Viscount Clare in 1690.

[k] *Cnoc-Doire*, now Knockerra, a hill situated close to the boundary of the baronies of Moyarta and Clonderalaw, and about four miles to the east of the town of Kilrush, in the county of Clare.

[l] *Leim-Chonchulainn:* i. e. Cuchullainn's Leap, now corruptly Loophead [for Leap-head], a headland in the north-western extremity of the

they held a session for fifteen days; and the gentlemen of the county in general attended them. At the end of this period Theobald Dillon and Captain Lester departed from the territory [of Thomond], leaving in it four companies of soldiers, a sheriff, and a sub-sheriff, and after having received a promise that the Queen's rent should be paid in it.

About a week after this, the Earl of Thomond came into the country, after having been nearly a quarter of a year in the country of the Butlers. Upon arriving in Thomond, he proceeded, without sleeping two nights in any one town, until he went to take vengeance on Teige Caech Mac Mahon for the dishonour[h] which he had shewn to his brother, and the attack which he had made against him. The greater part [of the forces] of the country collected to him, and, marching into West Corca-Bhaiscinn, encamped before Carraig-an-Chobhlaigh[i] on the Monday before Easter, in the month of April. The property and cattle of the entire country, extending from Cnoc-Doire[k] to Leim-Chonchulainn[l], were carried to him to that camp. In four days afterwards the Earl obtained possession of the town; and when the Easter holidays were over, he carried ordnance from Limerick for the purpose of assaulting Dunbeg[m]; and when the ordnance was planted against the castle, the warders did not await the discharge of one shot, when they surrendered the castle to the Earl; and the protection they obtained lasted only while they were led to the gallows-tree, from which they were hanged in couples, face to face. In the same manner the Earl obtained possession of Dun-mor-mhic-an-Fhearmacaigh[n]. After having taken these castles of Corca-Bhaiscinn, the Earl sent the great ordnance [back] to Limerick, and proceeded himself eastwards across the mountain to the plain of Thomond. He restored to the lawful inheritors every castle that had been

county of Clare. This head is now always called Ceann léime, i. e. "Head of the Leap" in Irish. Mr. Brannan, in his Irish poem describing the Shannon, says that Loop-head is a corrupt translation of Ceann léime, or Leap-head, and asks, if the Irish language were lost what philologer could ever discover that Loop-head was a translation of Ceann léime. A still greater corruption of the same name has taken place in Connamara, where Ceann léime has been anglicised Sline-head, and Slime-head, for Leam-head.

[m] *Dunbeg.*—See its situation already pointed out under the year 1598.

[n] *Dun-mor-mhic-an-Fhearmacaigh:* i. e. the great *dun*, or fort of the son of Fearmacach, now Dunmore, a ruined castle within less than a mile of Dunbeg, in the parish of Killard.—See it already referred to under the year 1598.

maille le honoir don ḃainríoġain. Ro baḋ díḃsein doire eoġain, dá ḃaile caisléin cluaine. ⁊ lios Aoḋa finn.

Iarla os essex (.i. Roibert) do ṫeacht i nErinn fo ḃealtaine na bliaḋna so amail do tinġeallaḋ go niomat nionnmais, ⁊ narmála, ⁊ muinission, Pudair, luaiḋe, bíoh, ⁊ dighe, ⁊ atbeirdís luċt a ffairsccsiona na tangatar a hionnṡamail sin darmáil go herinn riaṁ gus an tan sin ó do ruaċt Iarla strangboe ⁊ Roibert mac stiaṁna le diarmait mac murchaḋa la riġ laiġen feċt riaṁ. Iar ttoċt diarla os essex go baile atha cliaṫ ro herfuaccraḋ neiṫe iomḋa lais, ⁊ ro ba diḃriḋe cétus gaċ aon do ġaoiḋelaiḃ la baḋ aiṫreċ dol in acchaid na bainrioġna go ffuicċeaḋ maiṫeamnas ⁊ pardún in gaċ coir da nderna gó sin. Ba dona foccartaiḃ céadna gaċ aén dearennchoiḃ a dérаḋ, go ro bearnaḋ a ḃaile, no a ḋuthaiġ ḋe la Saxanachaiḃ a los anbforlainn, nó ḟoiréiccne go ffuicċeaḋ aiseacc ina indligeadh foġar ⁊ eisteċt don chur sin. Ar a aí nír bó mór do clannaiḃ gáoiḋel do ċoiḋ san toġairm sin. Ro cuireaḋ lás an iarla sin gararsuin saiġdiúiriḋe maille le gaċ ní rangatar aleas go carraicc fergura, go hiuḃar ċinn trága go tráiġ ḃaile duine dealgan, go droiċet átha, go cill manntáin go nás laiġen, ⁊ go araile bailte gen mo ṫát. Ro teccla maḋ dan laissiḋe seaċt mile saiġdiuir don armáil as ferr fuair, ⁊ do ċuaiḋ a háth cliaṫ siar gaċ ndíreaċ, uair ro hairneadh dó na baí i nerinn do luċt fogla na bainrioġna orra ro baḋ usa dó dionnsaicchiḋ ináid gseraltaiġ feiḃ ro ḃádar don ċur sin. Ni ro hanaḋ las an iarla co na ṡloġaiḃ go rangatar i cceartmeadhón ċoiccid laiġen, ⁊ nír bó saiġid carat i cceann dó gaoiḋil laiġen dionnsaiġid don ċur sin. Rortar iadsiḋe dan Domnall spainneaċ mac donnchaiḋ, mic caṫaoir ċarraiġ ċaoṁánaiġ, ⁊ Uaitne, mac Ruḋraiġe óicc, mic Ruḋraiġe uí morḋa, Siol cconco-

[o] *Doire-Eoghain*, now Derryowen, a castle in the parish of Kilkeedy, barony of Inchiquin, and county of Clare.

[p] *Cluain*, now Cloone.—See it already referred to under the year 1598, *supra*. In 1584 the castle of Cloone, or Cloyne, in the country of West Mac Namara, belonged to Donogh O'Grady.—MSS. T. C. D., E. 2. 14.

[q] *Lis-Aedha-finn*, i. e. the Fort of Hugh the Fair, now Lissofinn, a townland containing the ruins of a castle situated to the south-west of the village of Tulla, in the parish of Tulla, barony of Upper Tulla, and county of Clare. This place took its name from Aodh Finn, the ancestor of Mac Namara Finn.

[r] *About May*.—He landed on the 15th of April this year, and was sworn in Dublin on the same day. He was invested with larger powers and furnished with more splendid allowances than had ever before been conferred on

taken, to the dishonour of the Queen. Of these were Doire-Eoghain[o], the two castle-towns of Cluain[p] and Lis-Aedha-finn[q].

The Earl of Essex (Robert) came to Ireland, as had been promised, about May[r] this year, with much wealth, arms, munition, powder, lead, food, and drink; and the beholders said that so great an army had never till that time come to Ireland since the Earl Strongbow[s] and Robert Fitz-Stephen came in former times with Dermot Mac Murrough, King of Leinster. When the Earl had arrived in Dublin, he published many proclamations, among which the first was [to the effect], that every one of the Irish, who was sorry[t] for having opposed the Queen, should receive forgiveness and pardon in every crime they had till then committed. Among the same proclamations was this, that every one of the Irish who would assert [and prove] that they had been deprived by the Englishmen of their mansions or patrimonies, by force or violence, should be heard and attended to, and obtain a restoration of such property as he was unlawfully deprived of. Not many of the Irish, however, responded to these proclamations.

Garrisons of soldiers, with all necessaries, were sent by this Earl to Carrick-fergus, to Newry, to Dundalk, to Drogheda, to Kilmantan [Wicklow], to Naas of Leinster, and to other towns besides. He then selected seven thousand soldiers of the best of his army, and marched [them] from directly [south] westwards; for he had been informed that there were not of the plunderers of the Queen in Ireland a tribe that could be more easily invaded than the Geraldines, as they were then [circumstanced]. The Earl and his troops never halted until they arrived in the middle of the province of Leinster; and [surely] his approach to the Irish of Leinster was not the visit to friends from afar! These were Donnell Spaineach, the son of Donough, son of Cahir Carragh Kavanagh; Owny, the son of Rury Oge, son of Rury O'More; the

any Lord Deputy, and provided with an army the largest that Ireland had ever seen landed on her shores, consisting of 20.000 foot and 2,000 horse. His instructions were to prosecute the Ulster rebels, and to plant garrisons at Lough Foyle and Ballyshannon; all which he neglected, but wasted his time in doing little service.—See Camden's *Annal. Reg. Elis.*, A. D. 1599; P. O'Sullevan Beare's *Hist. Cathol. Iber. Compend.*, tom. 3, lib. 5, c. ix.; and Cox's *Hibernia Anglicana*, vol. i. p. 416.

[s] *Since the Earl Strongbow.*—The Four Masters should have added that the Earl Strongbow did not bring so great an army into Ireland as Essex had on this occasion.

[t] *Sorry.*—The language is here defective. It

bair Failgiġ, Gabal Raġnaill, ⁊ soċaiḋe do daoinib uaisle ele naċ airiṁṫer. Tuccatar din an luċt sin amais aiġṁeile, easscairdeṁla, ⁊ debṫa doilġe doiḟḟrestail dó in snaiġiḃ aiṁreiḋiḃ, ⁊ i mbeilġiḃ bélcuṁġaiḃ i ttocraitter re a roile go ro dioṫaiġeaḋ morán do ṁuinntir an iarla leó. Ar a aoí tar gaċ nettualang da ffuair ráinicc fadeoiḋ i mbuitilerachaibh. Ticc Iarla Urmuṁan maille le honoir, ⁊ le hairmittin ina ċhenn. Tánaicc din ticcearna

should be: "that such of the Irish as were sorry for having joined in the rebellion should, on returning to their allegiance, receive pardon and forgiveness."

[u] *Gaval-Ranall:* i. e. the O'Byrnes of Ranelagh, in the present county of Wicklow, who were at this time the most powerful sept of the O'Byrnes of Wicklow.

[w] *Narrow passes.*—The English writers make no mention of this attack by O'More; but O'Sullevan Beare says that five hundred of Essex's army were killed by Huon (i.e. Uaithne, a name now sometimes anglicised Anthony) O'More, in a defile called Bearna na gCleti, i. e. the Gap of the Feathers. This name is now obsolete, nor has any evidence been yet discovered to prove the exact situation of the place.

P. O'Sullevan Beare gives the following account of Essex's progress on this occasion in his *Hist. Cathol. Iber. Compend.*, tom. 3, lib. 5, c. ix.:

"Tandiu per tot regios imperatores, & exercitus re infœliciter gesta, statuunt Angli summis viribus Catholicos extinguere. In quam rem Robertus Essexiæ Comes, qui tunc temporis omnium Anglorum primus fama rerum gestarum habebatur, authoritate nulli secundus Iberniæ Prorex, & exercitus regij Imperator creatur. Qui Londino profectus sub finem Martij mensis anno millessimo quingentesimo nonagesimo nono (vt docet Camdenus) Dubhlinnam appulit. Vbi ex ijs, qui nuper ex Anglia venerant, & in Ibernia fuerant, comparato, quam maximo potuit, exercitu, in Onellum facturus expeditionem videbatur, & ita in illum Onellus sese parabat, & etiam Odonellus Onello laturus opem. At ille præter omnium spem in Momonias ire contendit septem millia peditum, & equites nongentos ductitans. Cui in Lagenia per iter angustum exercitum ducenti factus obuius Huon Omorra cum quingentis peditibus vltimum agmen fundit, aliquot milites, atque duces occidit, spolia, & inter cætera multos plumeos apices capit. Vnde locus hodie dicitur Transitus plumarum In Momonias Essexius cum peruenisset, statim obsidet Catharam arcem Thomæ Buttleri Baronis, in qua tantum septem, vel octo bombardarij custodiæ causa erant relicti. Arci auxilio veniunt Comes Desmonius, Raymundus Baro, & eius frater Gulielmus ducentes mille tantum pedites, & equites paucos, copias regijs minimè conferendas (neque enim se parauerant quod existimabant in se Essexium tam citó signa non fuisse laturum.) Ad arcem aditus erat per pontem, quem Vinkel Anglus tribunus militum non inualida manu tenebat. Secundo die obsidionis Gulielmus Burkus cum peditibus quingentis, & ducentis equitibus arci opitulatum profectus Vinkelem ex ponte eijcit nonnullis regijs interemptis, & Iaimo Thomæ Baronis fratre cum quinquaginta peditibus in arce præsidio collocato incolumis revertitur. Tamen arx continuè tormentis quassata diruitur, Desmonio non obstante, qui nullum pugnandi tempus intermittendo, conabatur oppugnationem prohibere. Decima nocte oppugnationis Iaimus cum militibus prostratam arcem relinquens ad suos fugit. Essexius in arce relicto præsidio Lomnacham adit, Catholicis

O'Conors Faly, the Gavall-Ranall[u], and many other gentlemen not enumerated. These people made fierce and desperate assaults, and furious, irresistible onsets on him, in intricate ways and narrow passes[w], in which both parties came in collision with each other, so that great numbers of the Earl's people were cut off by them. The Earl, however, in despite of all the difficulties which he met, at last arrived in the country of the Butlers. The Earl of Ormond came to receive him with honour and respect; as did also the Lord of Mountgar-

non ausis occurrere. Inde Asketiniam petit, præsidium firmaturus. Iam Daniel Maccarrha, Comesque Desmonius duo millia, & quingentos milites coegerant, cum quibus itineris angustias obsident. Primo ad hostem versus venientem fuit constitutus Gulielmus, secundo Dermysius Oconchur in locis planis, & expeditis: Vltimo Vaterus Tirellus, & Thomas Plunketus in ipsis itinerum angustissimis faucibus cum quingentis, & octoginta militibus sunt collocati. Inter quos si medius hostis circumueniretur (vt sperabatur) impunè delendus videbatur. Ac ita illud fuisse imperium datum à Petro Lessio tesserario maximo, vt illum Vaterus & Thomas primum, deinde Dermysius, & Gulielmus à tergo adorirentur, multi confirmant, sed vaterus, & Thomas contrarium afferebant. Itaque die Saturni Essexius copias in quatuor agmina distinctas ad angustias ducit, iamque Tomoniæ, & Clanrichardæ Comites, & Macpieris Baro primum agmen ex Ibernis militibus habentes Gulielmum, & Dermysium prætereunt nemine repugnante, vt erat iussum. Deinde Vaterum, & Thomam prætereuntes ex angustijs in planum sese conferebant. Quod cum Dermysius vidisset ratus per perfidiam á Vatero, & Thoma hostem dimitti, in æquo loco, vbi erat, cœpit præliari, & á multitudine hostium cedere loco coactus ad Gulielmum sese recipit. Ambo rursus prælium redintegrantes tres horas hostes secuti acriter dimicant, sed parum damni inferentes, quia fuit hostis angustijs dimissus, in quibus Vaterus, & Thomas totis viribus resistere debebant. Cæterum hi causabantur, sibi imperatum fuisse, ne præliarentur, donec alij pugnam inchoarent, sed contrarium multi affirmant, & dicunt illos pactos fuisse cum Essexio per quendam Tirellum, ne ipsi obessent. Vt secundum crimen punirentur Daniel Maccarrha censuit, non tamen comes militum secessionem timens. Postea rixa orta Thomas fuit á Petro Lessio interfectus. Vt redeamus ad rem Essexius Asketiniam peruenit, in cuius castra Catholici noctu faciunt impetum. Asketinia firmiore præsidio munita Essexius vlterius progredi non ausus die Lunæ sequente rediuit per aliud iter. Vbi ex arboreto iuxta Finiteri pagum Catholici erumpentes primum, vltimum, & media agmina simul inuadunt. Henricus Norris eques Auratus Anglus Iohannis, & Thomæ frater in Catholicos equo vectus firmo bombardariorum agmine vallatus plumbea glande confossus equo corruit. Alij ex regijs multi, & ex Catholicis nonnulli desiderantur: nam ab hora nona ante meridiem, vsque ad quintam pomeridianam fuit pugnatum, donec Essexius Cruomuiæ consederit. Vnde rursus Desiam vsque Desmonius sequitur per sex dies noctu, & interdiu prælians, & eius exercitum extenuans. Post Essexij reditum Dubhlinnam arx Cathara à Iaimo Buttlero Baronis fratre præsidiarijs Anglis occisis, breui recuperatur.

"Secundum expeditionem rursus Essexius facit in Oconchures Iphalios, & Omorras, cum quibus parum prosperè pugnans exercitum indies minuit. Quare in Onellum profecturus ex Anglia subsidium petit."

ṁóta gairētt .i. Emann, mac Risderd, mic piarais buitiler baí hi muinntearus uí néill athaiḋ riar an tan sin. O do ruaċtatar buitileraiġ hi ccēnn an iarla lottar go líon a soċraitte hi ttrian cluana meala, ⁊ ro ġabsat acc iomsuiḋe im ċaṫair dúine hiasccaiġ. Tomás, mac tepoitt, mic piarais buitileir ro baḋ tiġċērna for an mbaile hiṡin, ⁊ baí siḋe hi ccombáiḋ uí néill ⁊ iarla dēsmuṁan athaiḋ riar an tan sin. Nír bó torba don iarla co na sloġaiḃ an iomsuiḋe i mbatar go ro tairrngēḋ ordanas mór leó ó ṗort láircce dia saiġiḋ, ⁊ go ro lēccaḋ an lēṫ fa nēsa doiḃ don ḃaile, conaḋ iar sin rob éiccēn doiḃ an baile do taḃairt diarla os erex ⁊ don bainríoġain;

Is na laiṫiḃ in ro ṡuiḋ iarla os erex re haghaiḋ ċaṫraiġ dúine hiasccaiġ tanaicc presidens dá ċóicciḋ muṁan .i. Sir tomás norris ó ċorcaiġ go cill mocellócc do ṫoċt do laṫair an iarla ria riú diccsēḋ go luimneaċ. Baiside i ngar do ċoicṫiḋes ina ċoṁnaiḋe isin mbaile sin ag iomḟuireaċ fris an iarla do ṫecht tar Siúir, ⁊ no ġnaṫaiġeaḋ gach re lá cuairt do ċur im ċnocaiḃ ċonntae luimniġ dus an ffuiġḃeaḋ baoġal gona no gaḃála ar druing éiccin do ḃioḋḃaḋaiḃ na bainrioġna. In araile ló dia ndeachaiḋ is in ccēnn ṫoir don ċonntae do rala dó (⁊ gan neaċ aca acc iarraiḋ araile) Tomás a burc, mac teboitt, mic uilliam, mic Emainn ó ċaislén uí conaing. Ni baí aén neach for eoch i ffochair ṫomáis gionmoṫaroṁ buḋdēin. Batar dna a ngar do ċéd raighdiúir ġaoiḋelaċ ina ṗarrad. Iar na ffaicsin don presidens tucc siḋe ranntaċ solaṁaiġ dia ṡaiġiḋ go ro díolaiṫriccheaḋ a ffoccus drisic do muinntir tomáis don ċur sin, ⁊ do dingentaí ní baḋ mó munbaḋ a ṫúrcc ro gonaḋ an presidens uair do rala forccoṁ fēġ fíoraṁnus do ṗíce do hi ccompac ċorráin a ġeill ⁊ uaċtair a ḃraġat. Ot conncatar a ṁuintir eissiuṁ ar na crecṫnuccaḋ aṁlaiḋ sin ro iaḋsat ina uirṫimcell go ruccsat

[x] *Lord of Mountgarrett.*—Moryson says that "in the county of Kilkenny the Viscount of Mountgarret, a Butler of the Earl of Ormond's family, was son-in-law to Tyrone, and that he was, at this period, in rebellion with his brethren, and with some of his sons, and with his followers, being in number one hundred and thirty foot, and twenty horse; that he held the castles of Ballyragget and Colekil, but that the rest of the castles, and the whole county, were held by the Earl of Ormond for the Queen."—Vol. i. p. 72.

[y] *Cathair-Duine-Iascaigh*, now Cahir, in the county of Tipperary. There is a view of this castle, as it stood at this period, in the *Pacata Hibernia*.—See Dublin edition of 1810, p. 76.

[z] *To fall in with*: literally, "*offendit illi.*" P. O'Sullevan Beare, states that he met Thomas

rett[x] (Edmond, the son of Richard, son of Pierce Butler), who had been in alliance with O'Neill some time before. As soon as the Butlers had joined the Earl, they proceeded with all their forces to Trian-Chluana-Meala, and laid siege to Cathair-Duine-Iasgaigh[y]. Thomas, the son of Theobald, son of Pierce Butler, was lord of that town; he was in alliance with O'Neill, and the Earl of Desmond, for a period previous to that time. The siege carried on by the Earl and his forces was of no avail to them until they drew great ordnance from Waterford to it, by which was thrown down the nearest side of the fortress, after which the fortress was forced to surrender to the Earl of Essex and the Queen.

In the days that the Earl of Essex was storming Cathair-Duine-Iasgaigh, the President of the two provinces of Munster, i. e. Sir Thomas Norris, came from Cork to Kilmallock to wait on the Earl before he should go to Limerick. He was nearly a fortnight residing in the town, awaiting the coming of the Earl across the Suir, and was in the practice of scouring the hills of the county of Limerick every other day, to see whether he could kill or capture any of the Queen's enemies. On a certain day that he went to the eastern extremity of the county he happened to fall in with[z] Thomas Burke, the son of Theobald, son of William, son of Edmond of Castleconnell, neither being in search of the other. Thomas alone[a], of all his people, was on horseback; he had nearly one hundred Irish soldiers along with him. When the President saw him he made a determined and dexterous attack upon him, and about twenty of Thomas's people were cut off on the occasion; and more would have been slain, were it not that the President was so soon mortally wounded; for he received a violent and venomous thrust of a pike where the jaw-bone joins the upper part of the neck. When his people saw him thus wounded, they collected around him and carried him back to Kilmallock[b], where he remained

Burke at Killthilia, now Kilteele, a small village in the barony of Coonagh, in the east of the county of Limerick, and about two miles to the south of Pallasgreen.

[a] *Thomas alone.*—The original is *incorrect Irish*, and, if literally translated, would stand in English thus: "There was no one on a horse along with Thomas *except himself*." This is nearly as bad as Milton's

"——— God and his son except,
Created thing nought valued he nor shunned."
—*Paradise Lost*, book ii. lines 679, 680.

[b] *Kilmallock.*—P. O'Sullevan Beare says that he returned to Maola, now Mallow, where he died in fifteen days after his arrival, and this is probably the truth.

leó e tar a ais go cill Moċellocc, ⁊ baí sé seaċtmuine ina oṫairliġe fo lamhaibh lêġ go fFuair bás iaramh i mí iul sainrid.

O ro gabadh Caṫair dúine hiarsccaiġ la hiarla os esex, tanaicc féin ⁊ iarla urmumhan, ⁊ maite an tsloiġ go luimneaċ, ⁊ ro fáccaibh a ċampa don taoibh amuiġ do luimneaċ. Tánaicc ina ċinn don baile ceDna gobernóir coicciḋ connaċt .i. Sir Conerr Clifort ⁊ iarla cloinne riocaird .i. Uillicc mac Riocaird Shaxanaiġ, ⁊ iarla tuadhmumhan Donnchadh mac Concobair uí briain. O ro ċrioċnaiġsiot na huaisle sin a ccomhairle hi fFoċair aroile ro ḟill an gobernóir ⁊ iarla cloinne riocaird tar a nais hi cconDachtoibh. Ro triall iarla os essex, iarla urmumhan, ⁊ iarla tuadmumhan dol i muimhneaċaibh dus ann fFuiġbittís ell ngabala for ġallcaċaibh.

An ċéd oidhce ro ḟáccaibsiot luimneaċ i mí iun ro ġabsat campa for ur abann áṫa dara. Ag gabail doibh ar a baraċ dia saṫairn sian seaċ móin robair ro ṫairbḟinsiot amsaiġ ⁊ óccbaidh iarla dḟsmumhan, ⁊ an gasraidh Gearaltach a ngnúisi dóibh. Ba sraoċda forgranna an siaduccadh, ⁊ an sailtiuġadh tuccatar drior ionaid a bprionnsa ar a ċéd ċuairt dia saiġidh, óir ro lḟiccsiot dé, ⁊ detaċ a ndubh púdair, ⁊ saite peiler a gonnadaibh gér radarcaċaibh fo a súilibh. Ro clos lais beós glaéidbḟicḟbaċ, gáir ⁊ gridhan a ngalgat, ⁊ a ngiollanraide i nionad na humla, ⁊ na honóra, ⁊ na mbriaṫar sḟimh somblasta ro badh cubaidh do ċantain frisr. Act ċena rob e iomsccaradh na hiorgaile sin, iliomat daoine do díolaiṫriuccadh o iarla os essex, ⁊ gan arsstar badh ionáirmhe do lḟiccḟn dó an lá sin go ro gabh longport ḟó bḟcc ó earr geibtine soir. Dia domhnaiġ ar a baraċ arsseadh ro chinn iarla os essex, iarla urmumhan, ⁊ iarla tuadhmumhan marcsluaġ do ċor le muinirrion

[c] *Under the care*, literally, "under the hands of physicians."

[d] *In the month of July.*—The English writers make no mention of the manner of Sir Thomas Norris's death. P. O'Sullevan Beare gives some curious particulars of his battle with the Munster chiefs, totally omitted by the Four Masters. He mentions his death before the expedition of Sir Conyers Clifford against O'Donnell, at Ballyshannon, when Murrough O'Brien, Baron of Inchiquin, was drowned (1597). O'Sullevan is probably right, for he appears to have been better acquainted with the affairs of Munster at this period than the Four Masters. Sir Richard Cox says that "there is little credit to be given to that author, and yet, that some things that he says must be allowed to be true." O'Sullevan's words are as follows:

"Aliquot inde mensibus Thomas Burkus Castelconelli Baronis frater, qui ab Anglis desciuit receptis à Raymundo Barone, & eius fratre Guilielmo militibus in Muscria Kurkia castella non satis munita expugnabat. Quæ circa loca Norris qui cum exercitu erat, cum equitibus am-

six weeks on his sick bed under the care[c] of physicians, when he died in the month of July[d] precisely.

When the Earl of Essex had taken Cathair-Duine-Iasgaigh, he and the Earl of Ormond, with the chiefs of the army, proceeded with their army to Limerick, and pitched his camp outside Limerick. To this town the Governor of the province of Connaught, i. e. Sir Conyers, the Earl of Clanrickard, i. e. Ulick, son of Richard Saxonagh, and the Earl of Thomond (Donough, the son of Conor O'Brien), came to meet him. When these nobles had finished their consultation, the Governor and the Earl of Clanrickard returned back to Connaught; [and] the Earl of Essex, the Earl of Ormond, and the Earl of Thomond, proceeded into Munster, to see whether they could get an opportunity of invading the Geraldines.

On the first night after they had left Limerick, in the month of June, they encamped upon the banks of the river of Adare[e]; [and] as they advanced westwards on the next day, Saturday, through the bog of Robhar[f], the soldiers and warriors of the Earl of Desmond and the Geraldine host shewed them their faces. Fierce and morose was the salute and welcome which they gave to the representative of their Sovereign on his first visit to them [and to his army]; for they discharged into their eyes the fire and smoke of their black powder, and showers of balls from straightly-aimed guns; and he heard the uproar, clamour, and exulting shouts of their champions and common soldiers, instead of the submission, honour [that should have been shewn him], and of the mild and courteous words that should have been spoken to him. Howbeit, the result of this conflict was that great numbers of the Earl of Essex's men were cut off, and that he was not suffered to make any remarkable progress on that day; so that he pitched his camp a short distance to the east of Askeaton. On the next day, Sunday, he and the Earls of Ormond and Thomond resolved to send a body of cavalry to lay up ammunition in

plius ducentis, & peditibus mille in Thomam ire contendit, illumque cum equitatu, & bombardarijs ad Killthiliam nanciscitur. Thomas, qui ducentos tantum pedites tunc habuit, loco cedere putauit. Ea re non contentus Norris in eius vltimos ordines cum equitatu proruit: in cuius impetum Thomas sese conuertit, & Iohannes Burkus Nobilis Connachtus Norrisem hasta per Galeam ferit in capite ferream hastæ cuspidem relinquens. Norris vulnere afflictus Moalam redit vbi intra quindecim dies moritur."—*Hist. Cathol. Iber. &c.*, tom. 3, lib. 5, c. vi.

[e] *The river of Adare:* i. e. the River Maigue.

[f] *Robhar*, now *anglice* Rower, a townland on the west side of the River Maigue, in the parish of Adare, county of Limerick. It is now divided

go hſs geiḃtine, ⁊ gan iad fſin do dol ní baḋ sia siar is in mumain don chur sin. Acc filleaḋ doiḃ soir ar a ḃárac dia luain la taeḃ baile an eleteraiġ fuaratar troid tſnn, ṫalcair, ⁊ gleo gonac gáiḃṫeac o ġſsaltacaiḃ, ⁊ ro marḃaḋ drong dírim do muinntir Iarla of essex an lá sin im Ridire oirḋſirc ro baḋ mór ainm ⁊ onoir .i. Sir hanrg norris. Do chuaiḋ Iarla of essex iar sin go cill Moċellócc, ⁊ iar mbſiṫ tri hoiḋce dó isin mbaile sin tucc a acchaiḋ buḋḋſs ar chſnn feaḃrat sleḃe caoín mic dſirccdualaiġ do ḋol i ccrioċaiḃ roisteċ, ⁊ an tan do saoíleaḋ gaḃáil dó go corcaiġ ba sí conair i ndeachaiḋ dar áṫ mainistreċ ḟſrmaiġe, hi cconaċail, hi maiġ ſle, ⁊ do lios mór moċuda. Báttar din ġſsaltaiġ ag caiṫſṁ, ag coiṁlſnmain, ag toccraim, acc tóraiġecht, acc fuiliuccaḋ, acc foirḋſrccaḋ forra an airſtt sin. O rainicc Iarla of essex do na dſiriḃ ro ḟillriot Gſsaltaiġ go mſrrdacht, ⁊ go móir ṁſnmain dá ttíriḃ, ⁊ dá ttiġiḃ. O ráinicc an tiarla ceona go dún ngarḃáin so air Iarla tuadmuṁan uaḋ laiṁ le fairrge go heoċoill, go corcaiġ, ⁊ iaraṁ go luimneaċ. Do ṫaéd Iarla of essex o ḋún garḃáin go port láirge, assiḋe i mbuitileraċaiḃ, ⁊ illaiġniḃ. Nír bó sóinṁeċ ro ascnátar tre gaċ conair triasa ttuḋcattar ó tá port lairge go haṫ cliaṫ, uair ro báttar gaoiḋil laiġſn aga ttograim, ⁊ acca niarmóireċt, aga ttacmang ⁊ acc ttimcellaḋ go ro marḃait, ⁊ go ro mudhaiġit drecta dſrmara dioḃ in gaċ séd, ⁊ in gaċ sliġe in ro ġaḃsat. Ba sſḋ atḃſrdſs gaoiḋil Ereann gur bó fſrr dó na tiasaḋ an turus sin ó aṫcliaṫ go huiḃ conaill gaḃra, ⁊ tilleaḋ dó tar a ais lár an céd ċoinnsgleo ro coṫaiccheaḋ na aghaiḋ gan uṁla gan

into two parts, of which the greater is called Rowermore, and the smaller Rowerbeg.

[g] *Baile-an-Eleteraigh*, now Finneterstown, in the parish of Adare, about nine miles from the city of Limerick. This name was originally baile an ḟeiriteeraiġ, i. e. Ferriter's town, of which the form given by the Four Masters, and the present local Irish and anglicised forms of the name, are corruptions. There is another place of the name in the parish of Drehidstrasna, in the barony of Connello, where formerly dwelt a branch of the Fitzgeralds descended from John More na Sursainge [of the surcingle], natural son of the celebrated John of Callan.

[h] *Ceann-Feabhrat.*—See note [b], under the year 1579, p. 1721, *supra.*

[i] *Mountain of Caoin, &c.*, now Slieve Reagh, in the south of the county of Limerick.—See note [d], under the year 1560, p. 1580, *supra.*

[j] *Roche's country:* i. e. the barony of Fermoy, in the county of Cork.

[k] *The monastery of Fermoy*, a small town in the barony of Clangibbon, in the county of Cork, where, on the bank of the Blackwater, an abbey for Cistercian monks was founded in the year 1270, by Sir Richard de Rupella, who was Lord Justice of Ireland in the year 1261. The barony of Clangibbon, in which this monastery

Askeaton, and not to proceed any further westwards into Munster themselves on this occasion. On their return eastwards the next day, Monday, [when they arrived] near Baile-an-Eleteraigh[g], they received a stout and resolute conflict, and a furious and formidable battle, from the Geraldines; and many of the Earl of Essex's people were slain on that day, and, among the rest, a noble knight of great name and honour, i. e. Sir Henry Norris. The Earl of Essex then proceeded to Kilmallock; and, having remained three nights in that town, he directed his course southwards, towards Ceann-Feabhrat[h], [a part] of the mountain of Caoin[i], the son of Dearg-dualach, with the intention of passing into Roche's country[j]; and, instead of proceeding to Cork, as it was thought he would have done, he directed his course across the ford at the monastery of Fermoy[k], and from thence [he marched with his forces] to Conachail[l], Magh-Ile[m], and Lismore-Mochuda[n]. During all this time the Geraldines continued to follow, pursue, and press upon them, to shoot at, wound, and slaughter them. When the Earl had arrived in the Desies, the Geraldines returned in exultation and high spirits to their territories and houses. On the arrival of the same Earl in Dungarvan, the Earl of Thomond parted from him there, [and proceeded] along the seaside to Youghall, and from thence to Cork, and afterwards to Limerick. The Earl of Essex proceeded from Dungarvan to Waterford, thence into the country of the Butlers, and into Leinster. They marched not by a prosperous progress by the roads along which they passed from Waterford to Dublin, for the Irish of Leinster were following and pursuing, surrounding and environing them, so that they slew and slaughtered great numbers of them in every road and way by which they passed. The Gaels of Ireland were wont to say that it would have been better for him that he had not gone on this expedition from Dublin to Hy-Connell-Gaura, as he returned back after the first conflict that was maintained against him, without [having received] submission or re-

is situated, is a part of the ancient Irish territory of Feara Muigh-Feine, the name of which is still preserved in that of the barony of Fermoy, which is much smaller than the ancient territory.—See Smith's *Natural and Civil History of Cork*, book ii. c. vii.

[l] *Conachuil*, now Conna, a village near which are the ruins of a castle, in the barony of Kinatalloon, in the east of the county of Cork.

[m] *Magh-Ille*, now Moygeely, a townland containing the ruins of an abbey in the valley of the River Bride, in the same barony, and close to the boundary of the county of Waterford.

[n] *Lismore-Mochuda:* i. e. the town of Lismore, on the River Blackwater, in the county of Waterford, where St. Carthach, or Mochuda,

aiḋiḋe ó geraltaċaiḃ, ⁊ gan aéin cem baḋ ionmaoiḋim re a ḟagbail ina im-ṫeċtoiḃ, aċt aṁain gaḃail caṫraċ duine hiarccaiġ.

Baí ó concobair sligiġ donnchaḋ mac caṫail óig ar aon la hiarla os essex ar in sluaiġeaḋ sin go soaḋh dóiḃ on muṁain aṁail ro airneiḋsemar, ⁊ acc tilleaḋ doiḃ soir ó ċonallcoiḃ go conntae luimniġ ba hannsaiḋe ro sccar Ua concoḃair friú, ⁊ do chuaiḋ hi cconnachtoiḃ hi ccenn an ġobernora Sir conerr clifort. Ni baí eiṁ aén ḃaile dia ḃailtiḃ ar cumas uí concoḃair hi cconntae ṡliccig an tan sin cenmotá aén ċaistiall namá do ḃailtiḃ cloinne donnchaiḋ tire hoilella, ⁊ ba hann baísiḋe for eochairimliḃ aḃann móire, Cul maoile a ainmsiḋe. O ro baí ua concobair athaiḋ mbicc hi ffarraḋ an ġobernora ro arccná do ló ⁊ daḋaiġ go rainicc gus an mbaile hi mí Iul do ṡonnraḋ. O do ruaċt ua concoḃair go cúl maoile tuccaḋ araill do ceṫraiḃ muinntire Ui doṁnaill (batar an tan sin secnóin an tíre, gan airiuccaḋ da muinntir féin) go hUa cconcoḃair gus an mbaile.

Ot cuas dua doṁnaill an ní sin ro ba lainn lais Ua concoḃair do ṫoċt don tír, ⁊ ba só lais an do roine dus an ttairrseḃ lais a ndeirgsene riar an tan sin do aiṫe fair. Ro ḟorcongair Ua doṁnaill for a marcsloiġ gan anaḋ fri a ṁileḋaiḃ troiġṫeaċa co roistís an caislen co ná roichedh la hUa cconcoḃair fácċḃáil an ḃaile ria riú riostair an sloġ. Do rónaḋ fairsiuṁ innsin, ar ní laṁṫa urṫuarachṫ a ḃreiṫre ioir. Lotar iaroṁ an marcsloiġ feiḃ as dein ro nuccsat co rangatar an baile, ⁊ tangattar iaraṁ an sluaġ ina lenmain co ndeirnsat ciorcaill ḃodba dioḃ i niomṫacmang an dúnaiḋ. Ba dangen dioṫoġlaiġi an caistiall hi sin, ⁊ nír bó soḋaing forċoiṁétt forr an tí las buḋ lainn a ḟaccḃail, ar ba gar foccus do droiḃelaiḃ doiṁteċta an tionaḋ i ttarrustair é. Gaḃair Ua doṁnaill longport ar belaiḃ an ḟeḋa baí don taoḃ araill don aḃainn baí la hur an ḃaile. Ro hordaiġeḋ luċt feiṫme ⁊ foraire lais in oiḋċiḃ ⁊ hi láiḃ forr an dúnaiḋ da gaċ leṫ, ⁊ no bídis drong diormanna mora dia ṁarcsloiġ for a neaċaiḃ isin ffrioṫaire ó ṫuineḋ nell nóna co hadmaḋain, ná ro elaiḋeḋh Ua concoḃair uaḋaiḃ. Ro leth tra na sccela sin fo erinn .i. Ua concoḃair sliccig do ḃeiṫ isin iomcuimge sin ag Ua ndoṁnaill hi ccúil maoile, ⁊ o ro clos la hiarla os essex in ní sin ro raiḋ

formed a religious establishment about the year 663.—See Lanigan's *Ecclesiastical History of Ireland*, vol. ii. pp. 353, 355.

° *The Clann-Donough:* i. e. the Mac Donoughs of Tirerrill, who were at this time tributary to O'Conor Sligo.

spect from the Geraldines, and without having achieved in his progress any exploit worth boasting of, excepting only the taking of Cathair-Duine-Iasgaigh.

O'Conor Sligo (Donough, the son of Cathal Oge) was along with the Earl of Essex on this hosting until their return from Munster, as we have related. It was on their return from Connello eastwards, through the county of Limerick, that O'Conor parted from them; and he then went to Connaught, to the Governor, Sir Conyers Clifford. O'Conor had none of all his castles in the county of Sligo in his possession at this time, except only one castle, belonging to the Clann-Donough[o] of Tirerrill, which was situated on the banks of Abhainn-mhor; Culmaoile[p] was its name. O'Conor, after remaining a short time with the Governor, proceeded onwards, both by day and night, until he reached this castle, [which he did] in the month of July. On O'Conor's arrival at Culmaoile, some of the cattle of O'Donnell's people that were then throughout the country were brought to him to the castle, without being noticed by their owners.

When O'Donnell was informed of this, he was glad that O'Conor had come into the country, and he was pleased at what he had done, that he might try if he could take vengeance on him for his former doings. O'Donnell then ordered his cavalry not to wait for his foot-soldiers, but to proceed to the castle before O'Conor could have time to leave it. This was done at his bidding, for his word durst not be disobeyed[q]. The cavalry proceeded as quickly as they were able, until they arrived at the castle; the army followed them, and formed themselves into extensive circles around the fortress. This castle was an impregnable stronghold, and it was not easy to watch a person determined to leave it, for the place in which it was situated was close to impervious fastnesses. O'Donnell pitched his camp before a wood that lay on the other side of the river, in front of the castle. He appointed parties to reconnoitre and watch by day and night on every side of the fortress; and strong squadrons of his cavalry were mounted on their horses on guard from the dusk of the evening to day-break, in order that O'Conor might not escape from them. The news spread throughout Ireland that O'Conor Sligo was thus blockaded by O'Donnell at Culmaoile, and when the Earl of Essex heard it, he dispatched mes-

[p] *Culmaoile*, now Colooney.

[q] *Durst not be disobeyed.*—Cucogry O'Clery states, in his life of this Hugh Roe O'Donnell, that "he was a *Cæsar* in command."

teċta do ṡaiġiḋ gobernóra coicciḋ connaċt, ⁊ ro aṫain de toċt ina ċoinne lá dáiriḋe go ffearaiḃ ceall. Fuair an gobernóir mór ffórlainn ⁊ ffoireiccne ag gabáil tre ffearaiḃ cell ag dol i ndáil in iarla ar ro marḃaḋ soċaiḋe mór do daescarṡluaiġ ⁊ do ḋaġdaoiniḃ uaḋa. Ro baḋ diḃḟiḋe Risderd, mac uilliam, mic Risderd, mic oiluerais a burc, duine uasal do burcaċaiḃ tíre haṁalgaiḋ, ⁊ do cuireaḋ guais a ḟágḃala ar an ngobernoir féin. Ar a aoí rainicc hi ccenn an Iarla, ⁊ báttar fri ré dá lá co na noiḋċiḃ i ffarraḋ aroile acc sgrudaḋ a ccoṁairle. In eacmaing na ree sin ro léicc an tiarla fuilleaḋ sloiġ, ⁊ saiġdiuiriḋe lár an ngobernoir, ⁊ ro ḟorcongair fair iar roċtain baile áṫa luain dó a ḟurail ar teróitt na long, mac Risderd an iarainn, mic emainn, mic uillicc, ar Murchaḋ na maor[r], mac doṁnaill an ċoccaiḋ[s], mic an ġiolla duiḃ uí ḟlaiṫḃeartaiġ, ⁊ ar éirġe amaċ na gaillme an sdorus bíḋ ⁊ diġe, ⁊ a naiḋme dénma cairteóil tánaicc ó Shaxoiḃ go gaillim, do ḃreiṫ timcell ḃuḋ tuaiḋ tar ceannaiḃ cuan, ⁊ calaḋport go cuan Sliccig, ⁊ an gobernoir féisin co na uile ṡoċraitte do toċht do tír tré reiḋ dírge gacha roid go roicheaḋ go cuil maoile, ⁊ Ua concoḃair sliccig dfurtaċt, ⁊ dfoiriṫin ar an airc, ⁊ ar an eiccendail i mbaoí ag Ua doṁnaill. Ro forcongair an tiarla beós ar an ngobernóir gan sód tar a ais for cculaiḃ co ro cuṁdaiġte caislen daingean díoṫoglaiġi hi Sliceach lais nó ġeḃaḋ fri hullṫoiḃ do ġrés.

O ro ġaḃ an gobernóir do laiṁ innsin uile ceileḃrais don iarla ⁊ do taéd go baile aṫa luain ⁊ ro smacht for ṫeróitt na long, for Murchaḋ na maor, ⁊ for muinntir na gaillme go ttíosttais hi loingeas fri hor nérenn gaċ nóireċ aniar[t] go Sliceach. Ni ro léicceadh soṁ i neirlis innsin uair do ruaċtatar gan anaḋ, gan oirisiuṁ go ro ṡeolsat a ccoḃlaċ laiṁ deas fri tír go ro gaḃsat isin ccuan fri Sliceach aniar. Anaitt annsaiḋe feiḃ ro hearbaḋ friú go ffeastaois sgéla an tsloiġ. Do taéd din an gobernóir buḋéin go sorr comain, ⁊ ro tesclamaḋ lais ina mbaoí ina cumang do ġallaiḃ ⁊ ġaoiḋealaiḃ báttar foṁámaiġte don ḃainrioġain ina coṁfoċraiḃ. Ro baḋ

[r] *Murrough-na-Maer*: i. e. Murrough of the Stewards.

[s] *Donnell-an-chogaidh*: i. e. Donnel, or Daniel, of the War.

[t] *Directly from the west to Sligo*.—This language is not to the point, for the people of Galway should first sail due west for more than twenty miles, and next due north for more than seventy miles, before they could turn from the west towards the Bay of Sligo. Therefore the phrase go nóireċ aniar is useless. It should be, "should proceed in ships from Galway

sengers to the Governor of the province of Connaught, commanding him to come to meet him on a certain day in Fircall. The Governor encountered great toils and difficulties in passing through Fircall on his way to meet the Earl; for great numbers of his common soldiers and chieftains were slain, among whom was Richard, the son of William, son of Richard, son of Oliver Burke, a gentleman of the Burkes of Tirawly; and the Governor himself was in danger of being lost. Howbeit, he made his way to the Earl, and they remained for a period of two days and nights together in consultation. At the expiration of this time the Earl sent additional forces and soldiers with the Governor, and he ordered him, when he should reach Athlone, to command Theobald-na-Long, the son of Richard-an-Iarainn, son of Edmond, son of Ulick [Burke], Murrough-na-Maer[r], son of Donnell-an-chogaidh[s], son of Gilla-Duv O'Flaherty, and the rising out of Galway, to convey [in ships] northwards around the headlands and harbours to the harbour of Sligo, the store of viands and drink, and the engines for constructing castles, which had arrived from England in Galway; while the Governor himself was to proceed by land, by the most direct roads, until he should arrive at Cul-Maoile, to relieve and release O'Conor Sligo from the constraint and jeopardy in which he was placed by O'Donnell. The Earl, moreover, ordered the Governor not to return back until he should have erected a strong, impregnable castle in Sligo, as a constant defence against the Ulstermen.

The Governor having undertaken to execute all these commands, he took his leave of the Earl, and proceeded to the town of Athlone; and he commanded Theobald-na-Long, Murrough-na-Maer, and the people of Galway, that they should proceed in ships along the coast of Ireland [to Erris head, and then] directly from the west to Sligo[t]. These did not neglect his orders, for they got ready, without waiting or delaying, and sailed with their fleet, keeping the land on their right, until they put in at the harbour to the west of Sligo. Here they remained[u], as they had been ordered, until they should receive information concerning the army. The Governor himself repaired, in the mean time, to Roscommon, and assembled all those under his control, of the English and Irish who were obedient to the Queen in its neighbourhood.

around to Sligo."

[u] *Here they remained:* literally, "they remained here, as was ordered to them, until they should know the news of the army."

diḃféin clann iarla cloinne riocaird .i. barún duine coillin Riocard ⁊ tomás, ó concobair donn .i. Aodh, mac diarmata, mic cairbre, Teboid díolmuin ⁊ Mac suibne na ttuath Maolmuire mac murchaidh moill, mic Eóghain óig baoí for fogail, ⁊ sraon ó Ua ndomhnaill i ffarradh an gobernóra an tan sin. Do ċeaċatar iaram ó Rosscomáin co tuillsce, ḃátar dna ocht mbrataċa fichet saighdiúiridhe acc facbáil an ḃaile sin doiḃ isin domnaċ ria lughnasadh do ṡonradh. Rainicc an gobernoir co na ṡlógh ria midhon laoí an lá sin go mainistir na builli ⁊ ro ḃuí hisuidhe acc faiċill an uirtriallta do róine so ḋeoidh.

Dála Uí domhnaill ó ṫairnic lais an iomsuidhe do ḋrud ⁊ do ḋlúṫucchadh fris in dúnaidh i mbaoí ó concoḃair amhail ro ba data lais co ná léicthe neach innonn, no ille isin mbaile, Ro ḟaccaiḃ Niall garḃ ó domhnaill i ttoísighecht aésa an iomċoimétta, ⁊ ro ṫionoilsce dó gach ní bá dís do ghniomh. Luidh feisin co na ṡluagh co coirrṡliaḃ na seghsa, ⁊ gaḃais longport hisuidhe ar na tíosadh an sluagh eachtrann tairis gan rathuccadh, uair ón ccéidfecht ro clos lais uirthriall an gobernóra dia saicchidh for forcongra iarla os essex baoí ina foiṁdin ⁊ ina foiċill fri ré dá ṁíos go cóicc decc August i naircionn an ḃealaigh buidhe fri coirrṡliaḃ a tuaidh. Acht ċena ro ḃattar a sloġa for sccaoileadh ⁊ for eissreidheadh uadha i nionadaiḃ eccsamla .i. drong dioḃ i niomsuidhe forsan ccaisttiall i mbaoí O concoḃair ⁊ araill fri hucht bruinne teboitt na long, ⁊ an coḃlaigh remráitte Araile dioḃ ag coimétt forsna conairiḃ ó tá loċ cé fri seghais anoir, go loch techet fri Seghais aniar. Atbertsat a ṫoísigh, ⁊ a comhairligh lá hUa ndomhnaill nat boí congaiḃ caṫa occa amhail ro badh techta i naghaidh gall uair na battar a slóigh in aen maighin leo. Do radsom for dáil mbicc ⁊ for ndímhni fuigle na nuasal

[v] *For.*—The style is here left very imperfect. The uair should be omitted, and the two sentences remodelled thus: "As for O'Donnell, having, to his satisfaction, succeeded in blockading the castle of Collooney upon O'Conor, so as not to suffer himself, or any of his people, to pass in or out, he left his relative, Niall Garv O'Donnell, with a sufficient number of men, to carry on the siege; for he had heard that Sir Conyers Clifford, Governor of Connaught, was approaching, by order of the Earl of Essex, to raise the siege, and, as soon as he was convinced that this was the fact, he proceeded, with the main body of his forces, to the extremity of the pass of Bealach Buidhe, to the north of Coirrshliabh, and there pitched his camp, to intercept the progress of this army of the strangers, and remained in readiness to attack them for a period of two months, that is, from the 15th of June to the 15th of August."

Of these were the sons of the Earl of Clanrickard, namely, Rickard, Baron of Dunkellin, and Thomas; O'Conor Don, i. e. Hugh, the son of Dermot, son of Carbry; Theobald Dillon; and Mac Sweeny-na-dTuath (Mulmurry, the son of Murrough Mall, son of Owen Oge), who was this time plundering, and in revolt from O'Donnell, along with the Governor. They afterwards proceeded from Roscommon to Tulsk, and on leaving that town, [which was] precisely on the Sunday before Lammas, they had twenty-eight standards of soldiers. The Governor arrived with his army at the abbey of Boyle before the noon of that day; and he remained there to prepare for his final march.

As for O'Donnell, after having to his satisfaction succeeded in closing and strengthening the siege of the fortress in which O'Conor was, so as not to suffer any one to pass into or out of the castle, he left Niall Garv O'Donnell in command of the besiegers, instructing him in everything that was proper to be done, [and] proceeded himself with [the main body of] his army to Coirrshliabh-na-Seaghsa [the Curlieu hills], and there pitched his camp to prevent the army of the strangers from passing that way unnoticed. For[v], from the first time he heard that the Governor was approaching him by order of the Earl of Essex, he was in wait and in readiness for him for a period of two months (until the 15th of August), at the extremity of Bealach-Buidhe[w], to the north of Coirrshliabh. At this time his forces were dispersed, and away from him in various places: one division of them besieging the castle upon O'Conor, another watching the motions[x] of Theobald-na-Long and the fleet before-mentioned, and others of them placed to guard the passes which are situated from Lough Key at the east of [the mountain of] Seaghais to Lough Techet[y] to the west of Seaghais. The chief of his army and his advisers remarked to O'Donnell, that they had not battle engines fit to oppose the English [and that they should not risk an engagement], because they had not their forces together. But he made little or no account of the words of those gentle-

[w] *Bealach-Buidhe:* i. e. the yellow road or pass, now Bellaghboy, near Ballinafad, in the barony of Tirerrill, and county of Sligo.—See note [x], under the year 1497, p. 1232, *supra*.

[x] *Watching the motions:* "fronting or breasting." A party of O'Donnell's forces marched along the coast, keeping the fleet in view, so as to prevent them from landing, or, at least, from going to the relief of Collooney. Theobald Burke arrived in the bay, but was prevented, by O'Donnell's people, from landing.

[y] *Lough Techet*, now Lough Gara, situated to the west of the town of Boyle.—See note [k], under the year 1256, p. 357, *supra*.

⁊ atbſrt nar bó la líon ócc bristear caṫ, aċt cecib nſch tairisniġſs i niort an coimdeaḋ ⁊ ḃíos for fír, as é as coscrach, ⁊ bſirſ buaiḋ for a bioḋbadhaiḃ.

Baí Ua domnaill samlaiḋ gus an ccuicc décc dAugust amaíl a dubramar ⁊ ba heisiḋe comainm an laoí in ro ḟaoíḋ Muire a spiorat, ⁊ ro aoín sium trſḋan i nonóir na hí naem muire amail ro baḋ bés dó, ⁊ ro ceileabraiḋ oiffrionn dósom, ⁊ don tslóg arcſna, ⁊ ro ṫócaiṫ corp crſost iar ttabairt a ċoibſion ⁊ iar naitricche dioċra ina ṗſctoiḃ, ⁊ ro ḟorail for a ṡloġaiḃ ernaiġte dioċra go dia im ṡláinte a nanmann céttus, ⁊ imá snáḋaḋ on éiccſndáil móir ro baí for cind dóiḃ ó ġalloiḃ.

An gobernóir trá in airſtt baíſiḋe hi ffors i mainistir na búille, no bíoḋ ag báigh ⁊ ag baccar, ag taṫaoír, ⁊ acc tarcusal for an tuaisceart gaċ laoí ⁊ agá ġeallaḋ go rachaḋ da naiṁḋſóin tars an sleiḃ buḋ tuaiḋ, ⁊ ro triall an lá hisin, in ní sin ro ṫinġeall do ċomallnaḋ.

O ro ḟidir O domnaill an ní sin ro ḟorcongair for a sloġaiḃ toċt go haonmaiġin dia ttairealḃaḋ ⁊ dia nordúccaḋ, ⁊ iar na ttairelḃaḋ cisinnus ro rannaḋ lais a ṁuinntir a ndé ar a haiṫle. Ro lá a ġille diana dſinmnſḋaċa, ⁊ a occḃaiḋ utmall anbraidh, ⁊ a aés diuḃraicṫe for lſiṫ co na ngonnaḋaibh guṫárda gérradarcaċa, co na ffiodḃacaiḃ tailce toinnmíne, ⁊ co na ffoġaḋaiḃ fuilteċa foibriġte, co na nuile aiḋmiḃ imṫeilccṫe arcſna. Ro ordaiġ taoíseaċ troda ⁊ tuir congmala caṫa mar aén rú go ffossmacht uaṫa fors na hócca dia nurud, ⁊ dinge, ⁊ dluṫuccaḋ i ccſnn an caṫa dursccláiġi ⁊ diomġuin dar a nſire tan báḋ ullaṁ a naiḋme diubraicte aca. Do raḋ a uaisle, a airiġ, ⁊ a ḟosus occlaoiġ isin dara lſiṫ go cclaiḋmiḃ daingniḃ déḟaoḃraċa, ⁊ go mbiailiḃ blathsnaoighte bél tana, go manaoísiḃ moirleaḃra muirneċa fri tairisium troda ⁊ tachair. Do róine éiṁ troiġtiġ dia ṁarcſluaġ hi mſscc a ṁíleaḋ ar ḋoḋainge na conaire ro baí for a ccionn. Iar roinn a muinntire aṁlaiḋ sin dUa domnaill ro ḟorail for an aos diuḃraicte co reiṁtiastair an luċt naile gus an slog neċtrann ria riú tiostais

[a] *Promising:* i. e. boasting.

[a] *Shooting parties:* i. e. his musketeers and archers. The verb diubraic signifies, simply, to shoot, or discharge, and may be applied to the pelting of stones, as well as the discharging of musketry, arrows, or javelins.

[b] *To hew down and wound,* dursccláiġi ⁊ diomġuin.—In the Life of Hugh Roe O'Donnell the reading is:

"D'ursclaiġe ⁊ d'iomġuin tar a n-éire tan ba hanfuiriṫe a n-aiḋme diuḃraicṫe."

[c] *Veteran soldiers,* forasóglaċ .i. óglaċ aosda,

men, and said that it was not by numbers of men that a battle is gained, but that whoever trusts in the power of the Lord, and is on the side of justice, is always triumphant, and gains the victory over his enemies.

Thus O'Donnell remained until the 15th day of August, as we have stated, which was the anniversary of the day on which the Virgin Mary yielded her spirit; and he observed the fast, in honour of the Blessed Virgin, as was his wont; and mass was celebrated for him and the army in general; and he received the body of Christ, after making his confession and doing rigid penance for his sins. And he ordered his forces to pray fervently to God, first for the health of their souls, and [next] to save them from the great peril which hung over them from the English.

While the Governor was at the abbey of Boyle, he was daily in the habit of menacing and threatening, reviling and reproaching, the northerns, and promising[z] that he would pass northwards across the mountain in despite of them; and on this day [i. e. the 15th of August] he undertook to perform what he had promised.

When O'Donnell received intelligence of this, he ordered his forces to be assembled together, to be reviewed and marshalled; and after they had been reviewed, he then divided them into two parts. In one division he placed his swift and energetic youths, and his nimble and athletic men, and his shooting parties[a], with their high-sounding, straight-shooting guns, with their strong, smooth-surfaced bows, and with their bloody, venomous javelins, and other missile weapons. Over these soldiers he appointed a fight-directing leader, and a battle-sustaining champion, with command to press, urge, and close them to the battle, and to hew down and wound[b] after them, when they should have their missile weapons ready. In the second division he placed his nobles, chiefs, and veteran soldiers[c], with strong, keen-edged swords, with polished, thin-edged battle-axes, and with large-headed lances, to maintain the fight and battle. He then converted his cavalry into pedestrians among his infantry, in consequence of the difficulty of the way that lay before them. When O'Donnell had thus arranged his people, he commanded his shooting party[d] to advance before the other division, to meet and engage the foreign army before they

an aged soldier.—*O'Clery*.

[d] *Shooting party*.—This sounds awkward in English, but neither "musketeers, nor archers" would express the idea.

tar iomḋoraiḋ an tsléiḃe do ṫoċar friú, ⁊ dia ndiuḃraccaḋ idir, ⁊ go mbeit-siuṁ gus an druing aile i nercoṁair caṫa doiḃ ḃail in ro baḋ dearḃ lais a ngaḃail uair ba huraide sraoineaḋ forra fo deoiḋ diamdaoís crechtnaiġte uadaibhsium a ttosaċ.

No bioḋ eiccin forċoiméḋaiġe ó Ua nDoṁnaill gaċ laoí imaseach for inn an tsléiḃe ar ná tíosaḋ an slóġ eaċtrann ṫairisin gan ráṫuccaḋ. Do rala drong dioḃ an lá sin ann, ⁊ báttar acc fairccsi na mainistreċ uadaiḃ, ⁊ na foirne ro baí innte. An tan bátar acc an ffaircsi, at ciad an slog ag gaḃáil a narm, acc tuccbail a meirgeadh, ag seinm a ttrompaḋ ⁊ a ccairmeist caṫa ar chena Ro lásat sccéla go deinmneaċ do ṡaiġiḋ Uí Doṁnaill. Iar na cloisteċt sin dósoṁ atbert frisin bfoirinn ro ordaiġ i reiṁṫús na conaire co ndianarccnaidís reiṁiḃ do ḋeaḃaiḋ fris na gallaiḃ riasiú tíostais tar moithriḃ an maiġ sleiḃe. Lottar iaraṁ aṁail ro hearbaḋ friú co nairde aiccniḋ, ⁊ co meanmain miliḋ lá gaċ naoinḟer aca go rangatar inn an tsléiḃe go tinnesnaċ rias na gallaiḃ. Léiccis O Doṁnaill ina ndeaḋaiḋ go coḃsaiḋ céimniġin gus an ffianlaċ ffossaiḋ ⁊ gus na trenfearaiḃ tairisme ro ṫogurtair ina ṫimcell go mbatar isin ionad erḋalta in ro baḋ deiṁin leó na goill do ġabail. Airisit annsein for a ccionn.

[e] *Summit*, " inn .i. caċ bárr."—*Cormac's Glossary*.

[f] *Awaited their coming up.*—O'Sullevan says that O'Donnell felled trees to render the passes of the mountain more difficult.

" O'Donnellus in ea montis parte quæ dicitur Iter Pallidum (*Bealach Bui*), arbores hinc inde cædi et in viâ sterni jubet ut venientibus impedimento, et resistenti sibi munimento sint: nam in eo loco statuit dimicare, citra quem duobus fere millibus passuum castra collocaverat." —*Hist. Cathol.*, fol. 165.

Dr. O'Conor, in the *Memoirs of the Life and Writings of Charles O'Conor of Belanagare*, pp. 117, 118, has preserved a great part of the speech delivered by O'Donnell to his army on this occasion; he has translated it from an Irish copy of the same, in the handwriting of his grandfather. It runs thus:

" O'Donnell, impatient for the moment which, he was certain, would be decisive of the fate of his country, harangued his men in their native language; he shewed them that the advantage of their situation, alone, gave them a decided superiority over their opponents. Moreover," added he, " were we even deprived of those advantages I have enumerated, we should trust to the great dispenser of eternal justice, to the dreadful avenger of iniquity and oppression, the success of our just and righteous cause; he has already doomed to destruction those assassins who have butchered our wives and our children, plundered us of our properties, set fire to our habitations, demolished our churches and monasteries, and changed the face of Ireland into a wild, uncultivated desert. On this day, more particularly, I trust to heaven for protection; a day dedicated to the greatest of all

should pass the difficult part of the mountain, and [he told them] that he himself and the other division would come in contact with them at a place where he was sure of vanquishing them, for [he knew] that they could be more easily defeated in the end, should they be first wounded by them [his first division].

O'Donnell had kept watchmen every successive day on the summit[e] of the mountain, that the army of the foreigners might not cross it unnoticed. On this day the party of them who were there began to reconnoitre the monastery, and the troops that were in it. While they were thus reconnoitring, they perceived the army taking their weapons, raising their standards, and sounding their trumpet and other martial instruments. They sent the news speedily to O'Donnell. When he heard it, he commanded the troops whom he had appointed to take the van in the pass to march rapidly, to engage the English before they could pass the rugged parts of the flat mountain. They marched as they were commanded, each with the magnanimity and high spirit of a hero; and they quickly reached the summit of the mountain, before the English. O'Donnell set out after them, steadily and with a slow pace, with the steady troops and faithful heroes whom he had selected to accompany him; [and they marched] until they arrived at the place by which they were certain the English would pass; and there they awaited their coming up[f].

saints, whom these enemies, contrary to all religion, endeavour to vilify; a day on which we have purified our consciences to defend honestly the cause of justice against men whose hands are reeking with blood, and who, not content with driving us from our native plains, come to hunt us, like wild beasts, into the mountains of Dunaveeragh. But what! I see you have not patience to hear a word more! Brave Irishmen! you burn for revenge. Scorning the advantage of this impregnable situation, let us rush down and shew the world, that, guided by the lord of life and death, we exterminated those oppressors of the human race; he who falls will fall gloriously, fighting for justice, for liberty, and for his country; his name will be remembered while there is an Irishman on the face of the earth; and he who survives will be pointed at as the companion of O'Donnell, and the defender of his country. The congregations shall make way for him at the altar, saying, 'that hero fought at the battle of Dunaveeragh.'"

The speech put into the mouth of O'Donnell, by P. O'Sullevan, is far inferior to this, and it is to be suspected that Dr. O'Conor has improved upon the original. O'Sullevan has these words in his *Hist. Cathol. Iber. Compend.*, tom. 3, lib 5, c. x.:

"Mariæ Deiparæ Virginis sacrosanctæ ope hostem Hæreticum cum anteà semper vicimus, tum hodiè potissimum profligabimus Virginis nomine heri ieiunauimus, & hodiernum festum celebramus. Ergo eodem nomine fortiter, & animose cum Virginis hostibus pugnemus, & victoriam obtinebimus."—Fol. 165, 166.

According to Cucogry O'Clery, O'Donnell spoke much better to the purpose than either

Dala an tsloiġ remeṫeċtaiḋ ro hordaiġeaḋ isin torach, gaḃaitt acc airccnaṁ na conaire hi ccoṁdáil na ccaṫ neaċtrann go mbattar ucht fri huċt. O ro ċoṁfoiccsiġsiot dia roile, do reilccitt na gaoidil frossa fuileaċa foṫaiḃ dfoġadaiḃ altċaéma uinnsionn ⁊ saiṫe saiġſtt sruiḃger a fiodḃacaiḃ foda fſiodmnſretmara, ⁊ cassairċſta caor ccróiḋſicc, ⁊ ubaillmeall laindſrcc luaiḋe a gonnadaiḃ cſirt díriġe caolradairc. Ro freccraḋ na froissdiubraicṫe sin la hóccḃaiḋ Saxan go cclos a ffumanna, ⁊ a ffreaccarṫa, ⁊ a ffoġartorann i ffoiṫriḃ, i ffiodḃadaiḃ, i ccairtiallaiḃ, ⁊ i ccuṁdaiġtiḃ cloċ na ccríoċ ccoṁfoccus. Ba maċtnaḋ mór na diccridís aér uirṁſta ⁊ arada for dreimne ⁊ dársaċt la coisteċt friss na cairmſrtaiḃ caṫa, fri mac alla, ⁊ fri tormán an trendiuḃraiccte. Ro treċtnaiġſiot curaiḋ, ⁊ ro loitſiot laoċraiḋ aniú ⁊ anall ſtorra. At bſrtrat a ttoisiġ troda ⁊ a nairiġ iomġona fri muinntir uí ḋomnaill gan airisiumh for ioncaiḃ na nallmurach, aċt a ttacmang, ⁊ a ttimcellaḋ ima ccuairt. Larodain ro iaḋsat iompa da gaċ lſiṫ feiḃ at ruḃraḋ friú, ⁊ gaḃait aga ndiuḃraccaḋ go dian, dſinmnſdaċ, díċoinnircill go ro láisiot a nſitſda caṫa inntiḃ ar mſdón la dlús ⁊ dſine na deaḃṫa. Ciḋ fil ann trá, aċt ro ḋílsiġsiot na goill ro ḋeóiḋ a ndromanna do ṫreinfſraibh an tuaiscirt, ⁊ ro sraoínſiot lár an uathaḋ forr na hilċédaiḃ. Ba haiṁiarmartaċ ro toirneaḋ goill tar a nais do ṡaiġiḋ an ionaiḋ innill o ttudċattar. Ro baí do ṫinnſnus teichiḋ forra co na ro ṡill neach uadaiḃ tar a ais for caéṁ nó for ċaraitt, ⁊ co na fſdattar an beó fa an marḃ ro baí aén dia ro faccaibsiot ina ndiúiḋ iar ttabairt cúil doiḃ dia mbiodḃadaiḃ. Ní ṫernáisſiot dna ciḋ sgeolanga dioḃ munbaḋ uaite a naéra airliġ batar ina lſnmain, ar ní ro ċuṁaingsiot airleaċ an neiċ no ḟédfaittís la lſroacht ⁊ la líonmaire na soċaiḋe batar

of these writers have told us. He addressed his people in a loud and majestic voice; he exhorted them to put their trust in the Trinity, as they were on the side of truth and justice, while the English were on the side of falsehood and injustice, robbing them of their patrimonies and their means of support. "Fight bravely now, while you have your bodies at liberty and your weapons in your hands, for if you lose this day's battle, you shall be deprived of your arms, and your bodies shall be confined in dungeons and bound with hempen cords."

Fynes Moryson, who passes over this battle very lightly, says that the English lost only some 120 men, among whom was the Governor of Connaught, Sir Conyers Clifford, and a worthy captain, Sir Alexander Radcliff. But P. O'Sullevan Beare asserts (*ubi suprà*), that 1,400 of the royalists, or Queen's forces, perished.

"Perierunt ex regijs cum Cliffordo præfecto, & Henrico Ratcliffo alio nobili Anglo, mille, & quadringenti, qui feré Angli, & Midhienses An-

As for the advanced division, which was commanded to take the van, they proceeded on their way towards the battalions of the foreigners until they met them breast to breast. As they approached each other the Irish discharged at them [the enemy] terrible showers of beautiful ash-handled javelins, and swarms of sharp arrows, [discharged] from long and strong elastic bows, and volleys of red flashing flames, and of hot leaden balls, from perfectly straight and straight-shooting guns. These volleys were responded to by the soldiers of England, so that their reports, responses, and thundering noise were heard throughout the woods, the forests, the castles, and the stone buildings of the neighbouring territories. It was a great wonder that the timid and the servants did not run panic-stricken[g] and mad by listening to the blasts of the martial music, the loud report of the mighty firing, and the responses of the echoes. Champions were wounded and heroes were hacked between them on the one side and the other. Their battle leaders and captains commanded O'Donnell's people not to stand fronting the foreigners, but to surround and encircle them round about. Upon which they closed around them on every side, as they were commanded, and they proceeded to fire on them vehemently, rapidly, and unsparingly; so that they drove the wings of their army into their centre by the pressure and vehemence of the conflict. Howbeit, the English at last turned their backs to the mighty men of the north, and the few routed the many! The English were furiously driven back to the fortified place from which they had set out; and such was the precipitateness of their flight, after they had once turned their backs to their enemies, that no one of them looked behind for relative or friend, and that they did not know whether any of those left behind were living or dead. Not one of the fugitives could have escaped, were it not that their pursuers and slayers were so few in number, for they were not able to cut down those in their power, so numerous and vast was the number of them who were flying before them. They did not, however,

gloibeni erant: nam Connachti propter locorum peritiam facilius sunt elapsi. Ex Catholicis centum quadraginta fuerant vulnerati & desiderati. Capta sunt regiorum omnia ferè arma, signa, & tympana militaria, impedimenta, & multæ vestes. Onellus, qui Odonello auxilio veniebat, duorum dierum itinere aberat. Cliffordi nece diuulgata Navalis classe Galueam reuehitur. Oconchur sese Odonelli arbitrio permittens ab eo in integrum Sligachæ principatum restituitur alijs donis cumulatus, & sacramento rogatus ipsi deinceps in Protestante fore auxilio."

[g] *Panic stricken.*—See *Battle of Magh Rath*, p. 231, line 22.

i raen reampa. Ar a aoí ní ro anrat dia ttograim co rangatar ionn tar muraiḃ na mainistreċ ara ttuḋcattar ria sin.

Do rala O Ruairc an tan sin alla noir don ċoirrsliaḃ illongport for leiṫ. Tingeallaḋ side dUa doṁnaill beiṫ i noirċill na ngall dia ffuabairt a ccuma ċáiċ cecib tan bad adailcc. Ot ċualaig side buirseḋ beiceḋ na ttrompaḋ, ⁊ na ttápur, thromṫorann, ⁊ talaṁcuṁscughaḋ an treinduiḃraicṫe atraċt ar a longport co na laoċraiḋ lais, ⁊ tuargaiḃsiot a niodhna caṫa forra, ⁊ ní ro anrat dia reimim go rangatar gur an maigin i mbátar muinntir Uí doṁnaill ag gnioṁ an iomairicc. Gaḃaittriuṁ ag cloidmeḋ, ⁊ acc diuḃraccaḋ na ccuraḋ a ccuma cáiċ, go ro fáccḃaḋ iolar cenn ⁊ fodḃ lar na feinnedaiḃ. Ro marbaḋ an gobernoir Sir coners clifort go lion dírime uime do Shaxanchaiḃ, ⁊ deireannchaiḃ ⁊ ro baḋ i nurtosaċ na hiorgaile ro farccḃaḋ faén ina liġe forr an sleiḃ, ⁊ é beó ġaoite, ⁊ ba hainffios do na hóccaiḃ cia ro ġon céttus, aċt namá ba peiler do ċoid treimit, ⁊ ni tardsat an óicc aiṫne fair go ttorrachṫ ó Ruairc fo deóid gur in airm i mbaoi ⁊ do ḃert aiṫne fair gur bó hé an gobernóir baí ann, ⁊ ro forcongair a dícennaḋ. Do rónad iaraṁ gur bó taṁan tescc ġerrṫa iar mbein a chinn de.

Ba mór an teċt an tí torċair annsin, ba doiliġ míniaċ dimirt fair. Nír bó sáiṁ la gaoidelaiḃ ċoicciḋ meḋba a eccsoṁ, uair ba fer tiodhnaicṫe séd, ⁊ maoine doiḃ é, ⁊ ní eiḃreoh gaoí friú. Ní daoín leich do gaḃaḋ las an ngobernoir ar in ngleótroid sin, uair ruccaḋ a ċorp da adnacal go hoilén na trinóitte for loch cé i mbarúntaċt maige luircc hi cconntae Rossa comain, ⁊ ruccaḋ a ċenn iaraṁ go cul maoile i mbaruntacht tíre hoilella hi cconntae sliccigh.

Iar ttearnaṁ daér an maḋma gur in mainistir iompaíd muinntir Uí doṁnaill ina ffriṫing go ccennaiḃ, ⁊ go ffoḋbaiḃ a mbíoḋbaḋ leó ⁊ tiacchaitt dia sccoraiḃ go ffaoilte moir, ⁊ go suḃaiġe, ⁊ tuccsat altuccaḋ buide a ccoscair don ċoimde, ⁊ don ní naeṁ muire. Ba seoh aon ġlor na soċaide, naċ a niort iomġona ro sraoineaḋ for na gallaiḃ, aċt tria ṁiorḃuiliḃ an

[h] *To fire on them,* literally, "to sword and to shoot the champions like all."

[i] *Stretched on the mountain.*—The spot where Clifford was killed is still pointed out near the old road called Bealach-Buidhe, in the townland of Garroo, on the slope of the Coirrshliabh mountain. A small octagonal tower was built to mark the spot by the King [Lorton] family, but this is now nearly destroyed.

[j] *A ball.*—According to P. O'Sullevan Beare, and the account of this battle in note [l], p. 2134, *infra,* Sir Conyers Clifford was pierced through

desist from pursuing them until they [the English] got inside the walls of the monastery from which they had previously set out.

O'Rourke was at this time in a separate camp on the eastern side of Coirr-shliabh. He had promised O'Donnell that he would be ready to attack the English like the rest, whenever it would be necessary; [and] when he heard the sound of the trumpets and tabors, and the loud and earth-shaking reports of the mighty firing, he rose up from his camp with his heroes, who put on their arms; and they made no delay, till they arrived at the place where O'Donnell's people were engaged in the conflict. They proceeded, like the others, to cut down champions with their swords, and fire on them[h] [with their guns, arrows, and javelins], until the soldiers left behind many heads and weapons. The Governor, Sir Conyers Clifford, was slain, together with a countless number of English and Irish about him. He was left feebly stretched on the mountain[i], mortally wounded in the commencement of the conflict. It was not known to the soldiers who first wounded him (nothing was known about his death, except only that it was a ball[j] that passed through him), and the soldiers did not recognise him, until O'Rourke at last came up to the place where he was, and recognised that it was the Governor that was there. He ordered him to be beheaded, which being done, his body was left a mutilated trunk. The death of the person here slain was much lamented. It was grievous that he came to this tragic end. The Irish of the province of Meave [Connaught] were not pleased at his death; for he had been a bestower of jewels and riches upon them; and he had never told them a falsehood. The Governor passed not in one direction from this battle; for his body was conveyed to be interred in the Island of the Blessed Trinity in Lough Key, in the barony of Moylurg[k], in the county of Roscommon, and his head was carried to Cul-Maoile, in the barony of Tirerrill, in the county of Sligo.

When the routed party had escaped into the monastery, O'Donnell's people returned back with the heads and arms of their enemies, and proceeded to their tents with great exultation and gladness; and they returned thanks to God and the Blessed [Virgin] Mary for their victory. The unanimous voice of the troops was, that it was not by force of arms they had defeated the Eng-

the body with a pike.

[k] *Barony of Moylurg*, now the barony of Boyle, in the north-west of the county of Roscommon.

coimdeaḋ, ⁊ tre ſdarġuiḋe uí domnaill co na ſloġ, iar ttócaitſin glanfuine cuirp críoſt ⁊ a fola do i nurtoraċ an laoí hiſin indeadhaiḋ an troiſccṫe ro aoín do naeṁ muire an la riaṁ.

Imṫúsa na nġall iar ffilleaḋ uaḋaiḃ do ṁuinntir Uí domnaill ro lſiccſet hi ccſnd tréda go tinneſnaċ an ṁſid ro mair díoḃ go rangattar dia ttiġiḃ fo ṁela, ⁊ méḃail.

[1] *Sorrow and disgrace.*—The accounts given of this battle by Camden and Moryson are very unsatisfactory, and the prejudiced historian Cox, and even Leland, have made very light of it. These writers do not appear to have known that any of O'Donnell's forces were in this engagement. The best Irish account of this battle is that given in the Life of Hugh O'Donnell, by Cucogry O'Clery, of which the account in the text is an abstract. The most minute and satisfactory English account of it was written by John Dymmok, who was in Ireland at the time, and who wrote this account as he "hard it related." This, which was edited for the Irish Archæological Society, in 1843, by the Rev. Richard Butler, is as follows:

"*A brief Relation of the Defeat in the Corleus, the* 15 *of August*, 1599.

"Sr. Conyers Clifford, governor of Connaght, going to the releefe of O'Connor Sligo, with 1900 men, vnder 25 ensignes, and about 200 English and Irish horse, came to the entrance of the Corleus, the moste dangerous passage in Connaught the 15 of August, about 4 a clocke in the afternoone, being then highe tyme to lodge his men after a paynefull jorney, where understanding that the rebells had not possessed that passage, he resolved to march thorow the same night; whereupon putting his troops in order, the vanguard was conducted by Sr. Alexander Ratcliff; the Lord of Dunkellin sonne to the erle of Clanricchard followed with the battell; and Sr. Arthure Savadg brought up the reare guarde. The horse (where also the baggage was left,) had directions to stand betweene the abbey of Boyle, and the entrance into the passage, under the commaund of Sr. Griffin Markham, until the same should be freed by the foote about a quarter of a myle from the mowth of the passage, had the rebells traversed the same with a barri[ca]do with doble flancks, in which and in other places of advantage thereabouts were lodged about 400 of them, contrary to that which was advertised to the governor. They which possessed the barricadoes, at the approach of our vantguard, delivered a small volly of shott upon them, abandoninge the same allmoste without any force, which the governor possessing, made yt passable by openyng the midst, and placed guardes upon the same, appoyntinge to the angle of the sinister flancke Rogers, lieutenant to Sr. Hen. Carye, to the angle of ye Dexter flancke, Rafe Constable (a gentleman very esteemed to the governor for his vertu) and not much distant from him upon the same flancke, Capt. Water Fludd, and Capt. Windsore gevinge to them 40 men a piece, with comaundement that they should not abandon their places untill they heard further from himself. Thinges being thus ordered, the vantguard, followed by the batle and rearguard, advanced in short tyme by a narrow waye betwixt 2 large boggs to the side of a woode half a myle broade, through which lyeth a highe waye so broade as yt geveth liberty for 12 men to march in front, the same rysinge equally and gently untill yt have passed the woode where yt is caryed upon the syde of a high hill, which yt leaveth on the left hand and ye hill and grownde adjoyninge being

lish, but through the miracles of the Lord, at the intercession of O'Donnell and his army, after having received the pure mystery of the body and blood of Christ in the morning, and after the fast which he had kept in honour of the Blessed [Virgin] Mary on the day before.

As for the English, after O'Donnell's people had departed, they took to the road expeditiously, such of them as survived, and arrived at their homes in sorrow and disgrace[l].

a mayne bogg, vpon the right hand lyeth a thicke woode not more than muskett shott from the same, in either of which places, although the rebell from their contynuall practiz, have exceeding advantage of our men, yet have they more advantage upon the bogge, which they well knowinge made at this tyme choice thereof, and even thither were followed by S[r] Alex. Ratcliff, who although he were in the beginninge of the skirmish shott in the face, yet he ever contynewed to spend all his powder upon them; and no supply coming unto him, prepared to charge them with a small number of such choice pikes as would either voluntarylie follow him or were by him called forth by name from the body of the vantguard; but before he could come to joyne with them, he had the use of a legg taken from him with the stroake of a bullet, by which ill fortune he was forced to retyre, susteyned upon the armes of 2 gentlemen, one of which receivinge the lyke hurte, died in the place, as did also himselfe, soone after, being shott throughe the boddy with a bullet. There was with Sir Alex: Ratcliff in the head of the vantguard Capt. Henry Cozbye, whome at his goinge to chardge he invited to accompany him; and perceivynge him slacke, 'well, Cozsby,' said he, 'I see I must leave thee to thy basenes, but I must tell the before my departure, that yt were much better for the to dye in my company by the hands of thy countrymen, then at my returne to perish by my sworde;' but Cosby, which is the generall disposition of all tru cowards, yeelding to have the terme of his lyfe a while deferred upon any condition, stood fyrme with at least a third parte of the vantguard, untill he see the adversyty of this noble knight, when by example of his turninge heade the vanguarde fled in such route, that yt discomfited the batle, with y[e] sight of which (not abiding any impression), was broken the rearguard, the whole forces being almost without any enemyes force in a moment put all in confusion, which disorder the governor endeavouringe (but in vaine) to reforme, whilest he had any strength left in him, was after much fruitless travell, susteyned breathless upon the armes of S[r] John mac Swine and Capt. Olyver Burke's lieutenant, who perceivinge the disordered flight of the whole army (disparing to save their lyves by other meanes) perswaded him to retyre himselfe with them; when he reproovinge the baseness of his men, replyed Romane lyke, that he would not overlyve that daies ignomynye. But that affection which moved S[r] John Mc. Swyne to vse intreatyes, perswaded him now to practiz force, by which they caryed him from the pursewing rebells some few paces, where enraged with a consideration of the vildeness of his men which he often repeated, brake from them in a fury, and turning head alone, alone made head to the whole troopes of pursewers, in the midst of whome, after he was stroake through the body with a pyke, he dyed fighting, consecrating by an admyrable resolucion, the memory of his name to imortallitye, and leaving the example of his vertu to be in-

Forraiġitt muinntir Uí Ḋomhnaill ina bpuirliḃ in aghaiḋ sin, ⁊ ro aḋnaicsiot an meid ro marbaḋ uaḋaiḃ, ⁊ ot cualattar sóaḋ do na gallaiḃ for ccúlaiḃ tiagait go caislén cúla maoile airm i ffarccaiḃsiot an iomṡuiḋe for Ua cConcoḃair. Ot cualaiġ ó concoḃair an caṫraéineḋ sin coirrsleiḃe for Sir conerс clifort ⁊ a ṫuitim ann, fa dícreidmeach lais innsin go ro taiselḃaḋ cenn an goḃernóra dó. Ot connairc sium an cend ro ḃen ceill dia ċomfurtaċt ar an capcair i mbaoí, ⁊ asseḋ do rinne teċt for eineach Uí Domnaill ⁊ a óighriar do ṫabairt dó. Ba daġaisle dósom ón, óir do raḋ ó Domnaill eiriuṁ i fforlaṁus ⁊ hi ccendus a ċriche, ⁊ do ríoḋnaċt asccaḋa ioṁḋa deoċaiḃ, dinnliḃ, ⁊ da gaċ naḋailcce arċena dó go ros aittreaḃ a ṫír iar sin.

Teroitt na long dna ot cuas dósiḋe sraoíneaḋ for na gallaibh, ⁊ tuitim an ġoḃernora, ⁊ o concoḃa r do taḃairt ar in caistiall amail ro airneidsiom, ba sed ro chinnsiuṁ occa gan friṫḃert fri hUa nDoṁnaill ni ba siri, ⁊ ro naiḋm a carattraḋ ris iartain, ⁊ ro ċedaigh Ua Doṁnaill don loinges reimraite iompúḋh for a ccúlaiḃ gus an ngaillimh doridhise.

Daoine uaisle do ṁaṫġaṁnachaiḃ a hoirġialloiḃ go ccéd do saiġdiuiriḃ amaille friú do ḃeiṫ ar fosttaḋ ag Ua cCerḃaill .i. ag an cCalḃaċ, mac uilliam uiḋir m'c ḟirġanainm, i nearraċ na bliaḋna so, ⁊ a nionam a ttuarustail do eirneḋ doiḃ do ḋeachaiḋ ó cerḃaill co na muinntir isin oiḋċe dia

tytuled by all honorable posterities. There died lykewyse Godred Tirwhit, brother to Mr. Robert Tyrwhit of Ketleby, in Lyconshire, fighting by the syde of Sr Alex. Ratcliff, of whome cannot be sayde lesse, then that he hath left behinde him an eternall testemony of the noblenes of spiritt, which he deryved from an honorable famylye. But these went not alone, for they were accompanied to the gates of death by dyvers worthy, both lieutenants and ensignes, who were followed, (for that they were not followed by them to fight) by 200 base and cowardlye raskalls. The rest which els had all perished were saved by the vertu of Sr Griffin Markham, who chardginge the pursewers in the head of my Lo: Southamptons troope gave securitie to this ignominious flight having in his chardge the smaller bone of his right arme broken with the stroake of a bullett, and that which addeth moste to the commendation of his chardge is, that it was presented upon the narrow waye between the two boggs before mencioned, and forced with the losse of some both men and horses into the bogg vpon the right hand, where the rebells followed eagerly the execution of our men, untill the feare they apprehended vpon the sight of our horses, caused them to stay their pursuite and to thinke upon their owne safetye.

"This defeat was geven by O'Rvrke, and mac Dermon O'Donnell being there, but came not to fight, to whome the governors head was sent that night for a present; his bodye was conveyed to a monastery not far from thence, as

O'Donnell's people remained that night in their tents, and interred all those that were slain of their people; and when they heard that the English had returned home, they proceeded to the castle of Cul-Maoile, in which they had left O'Conor blockaded. When O'Conor had heard of the victory of the Curlieus, gained over Sir Conyers Clifford, and of his fall there, he did not believe it until the Governor's head was exhibited to him. When he saw the head he gave up the hope of being released from the prison in which he was, and what he did was to come forth on the mercy of O'Donnell, and to make full submission to him. This was a good resolution for him; for O'Donnell placed him in the full power and chieftainship of his territory, and made him many presents of horses, cattle, and all other necessaries; so that O'Conor then settled in his territory.

When Theobald-na-Long was informed that the English had been defeated and the Governor slain, and that O'Conor had been let out of the castle, as we have related, the resolution he came to was, not to oppose O'Donnell any longer. He afterwards confirmed his friendship with him; and O'Donnell permitted the aforesaid fleet to go [sail] back again to Galway.

Some gentlemen of the Mac Mahons of Oriel, with one hundred soldiers, were hired by O'Carroll (Calvagh, the son of William Odhar, son of Fergananim), in the spring of this year; and at the time that their wages should be given them, O'Carroll with his people went to them by night and slew them

appeareth by mac Dermons letter to the constable of Boyle, which is censured by S^r. John Harrington (from whom I received a coppy of yt) to be barbarous for the Latyn but cyvill for the sence. For confirmacion of whose judgment the letter yt selfe is contented by my hand for justyfication of his barbarisme to appeare before as many as will vouchsafe to read yt.

"'Conestabulario de Boyle salutem: Scias quod ego traduxi corpus gubernatoris ad monasteriū Sanctæ Trinitatis propter ejus dilectionem, et alia de causa, si velitis mihi redire meos captiuos ex prædicto corpore, quod paratus sum ad conferendum vobis ipsum; alias, sepultus erit honeste in prædicto monasterio et sic vale, scriptū apud Gaywash 15 Aug. 1599: interim pone bonum linteamen ad predictum corpus, et si velitis sepelire omnes alios nobiles, non impediam vas erga eos.

"'Mac Dermon.'

"By this lettre is too truly interpreted a troublesome dreame of the governors, which he had about a yeare before this defeat, when, being wakened by his wife out of an unquiet sleepe, he recounted unto her that he thought himselfe to have beene taken prisoner by O'Donell, and that certen religious men (of compassion) conveied him into their monastery where they concealed him and so indeed as he dreamed or rather prophesied the monastery hath his boddye, the worlde his fame, and his frends the want of his vertu."

saiġiḋ go ro marḃaḋ lais iad ar a ndérġaḋaiḃ codalta, ⁊ ina ttiġiḃ órda. Ro crochaḋ cioḋ araill ḋiobh is na crannaiḃ ba coiṁnesa ḋó, aċ nama tesna luċt baile ḋioḃ ass ḋaiṁḋeoin ui ċerḃaill.

Iar marḃaḋ Presidenṫ ḋa ċoicceaḋ Muṁan, ⁊ goḃernora coicciḋ Connaċt aṁail ro airnesiḋriom ina nionaḋaiḃ coṁaḋais, do ḋeachaiḋ Iarla os Essex, ⁊ O Neill .i. Aoḋ mac Firḋorċa, mic Cuinn Ḃacaiġ hi ccoinne ⁊ hi ccoṁḋáil re roile is na ceḋlaiṫiḃ do mís September, ⁊ ba he crioċ a ccoinne síṫ do naiḋm eterra go cenn ḋa ṁíos, ⁊ a rann fein do ġallaiḃ, ⁊ do ġaoiḋelaiḃ do ḃeiṫ ag gach aon aca in airett sin. O Ro ḟioḋaigh Iarla oss Essex fri hUa Neill an tuċt sin do ċuaiḋ go baile Aṫa cliaṫ, ⁊ nir bo cian ro airis ann an tan do ḋeachaiḋ go Saxoiḃ iar Staṫá rioġda ro ṫairḃein aṁail as onóraiġi ro ṫairrfein Saxanaċ riaṁ in Erinn. Ro ḟáccaiḃ Ere gan síth gan suaimhnes, gan lustis, gan goḃernóir, gan Presidens, aċt aṁáin iomchoiṁett

[m] *A conference.*—Camden, Dymmok, and Moryson have given a curious account of this conference, which took place at Ballyclinch, now Anaghclart Bridge, on the River Lagan, between the counties of Louth and Monaghan, near the chief town of the county of Louth. These writers assert that Tyrone made humble submission to the Lord Deputy on this occasion. But this statement cannot be true, for O'Neill's demands, on this occasion, were not those of a submissive suppliant, but of a powerful chief; for among the demands which he required to be transmitted to the Queen were, that the Catholic worship should be tolerated; that the principal officers of state and the judges should be natives of Ireland; that O'Neill, O'Donnell, Desmond [i. e. the Desmond created by the Prince of Ulster!], should enjoy the lands possessed by their ancestors for the last two hundred years, and that one-half of the army in Ireland should consist of natives.

Camden's account of the meeting between these two grandees of towering ambition is exceedingly interesting, and sufficiently minute for all historical purposes. It runs as follows:

"Interim in Anglia supplementum, quod Prorex petiit, conscribitur, & mittitur; verum pauculis interjectis diebus, aliis literis edocuit, se nihil aliud hoc anno amplius præstare posse, quam cum MCCC peditibus & CCC equitibus Vltoniæ limites adire. Quo cum pervenisset, Tir-Oenius se cum suis in collibus è longinquo uno & altero die ostendit, demumque per Haganum" [O'Hagan ejus ministrum], "colloquium cum Prorege orat. Ille abnuit: sin Tir-Oenius hoc vellet, die crastino ante principia in acie colloqui posse, respondet. Quo die levi facta velitatione, eques è Tir-Oenii turmis alta voce exclamat, Comitem pugnare nolle, sed cum Prorege colloqui velle, at nullo modo inter acies.

"Die insequente Proregi agminatim pergenti Haganus obvius nuntiat, Tir-Oenium misericordiam Reginæ & pacem exposcere, &, ut tantisper exaudiatur, obsecrare; quod si concederet, illum cum omni observantia ad vicini fluminis vadum (*Balla Clinch* vocant) expectaturum, haud procul a Loutho primario Comitatur oppido. Eo Prorex quosdam præmisit qui locum explorarent: illi Tir-Oenium ad vadum offendunt: qui docet quamvis flumen intumuis-

on their beds, and in their lodging houses. He hanged some of them from the nearest trees. The party of one village, however, made their escape in despite of O'Carroll.

After the killing of the President of the two provinces of Munster, and of the Governor of Connaught, as we have related in their proper places, the Earl of Essex and O'Neill (Hugh, the son of Ferdorcha, son of Con Bacagh) came to a conference[m] in the first days of the month of September, and the end of their conference was, that a peace was ratified between them till the end of two months, during which time each of them was to have his own part of the English and Irish. When the Earl of Essex had concluded a peace with O'Neill at this time, he proceeded to Dublin, and he remained not long there when he went to England, after having displayed a regal pomp the most splendid that any Englishman had ever exhibited in Ireland. He left Ireland without peace or tranquillity, without Lord Justice, Governor, or President,

set, facile utrinque exaudiri posse. Hinc Prorex, turma equitum in proximo colle disposita, solus descendit; Tir-Oenius equo ventre tenus in aquas immisso Proregem in ripa magna observantia salutat, et multis ultro citroque verbis, *sine arbitris habitis*, fere hora est consumpta. Post unam & alteram horam Conus filius Tir-Oenii nothus Proregem subsequutus, patris nomine obsecrat ut alterum haberetur colloquium ad quod primarii aliquot viri utrinque admitterentur. Assensit Prorex, modo non sint plures quam sex. Die præstituto Tir-Oenius, cum Cormaco fratre, Mac-Gennyso, Mac-Guiro, Evero Mac-Cowley" [Mac-Mahon], " Henrico Ovingtono, & O-Quino, ad vadum se ostendit. Ad eos Prorex cum Comite Southamptoniæ, Georgio Bourchiero, Warhamo S. Legero, Henrico Danversio, Edwardo Wingfeldo, & Gulielmo Constablo, Equitibus Auratis, descendit. Quos singulos magno comitate Comes, & verbis non multis collatis, placuit, ut quidam Delegati die insequente de pace agerent. Inter quos convenit ut induciæ ab ipso die in singulas sex septimanas, usque ad Calend. Maii haberentur ita tamen ut utrinque liberum sit, post præmonitionem quatuordecim ante dies factam, bellum renovare. Quod si quis Comiti confœderatus assensum non præbuerit, illum Proregi prosequendum relinqueret."—*Annal. Reg. Elis.*, A. D. 1599.

Of Essex's journey to the north, on this occasion, two minute accounts have been printed. The first, which was sent by Essex himself, with a private letter, to the Queen, was printed in the *Nugæ Antiquæ*. The second was written by John Dymmok, supposed to have been in attendance upon Essex, and was printed in the second volume of Tracts relating to Ireland, for the Irish Archæological Society.—See Shirley's *Account of the Territory or Dominion of Farney*, pp. 107, 109, where large extracts from Essex's own account of it are printed.

The conference between O'Neill and Essex has been made the subject of a vignette design, by H. K. Browne, which has been engraved to illustrate the frontispiece to the fourth volume of Moore's History of Ireland. The subject has been also painted by I. E. Doyle.

cloidiṁ an rig ag an chancellour, ⁊ ag Sir Roberd Gardiner. Ní fes tra daon dfirennchoib an do ṫeċt tar a air do ridiri, no an danaṁain ċoir do ċóid an tiarla a herinn an tan sin.

Mac ṁec suiḃne ḃaġainiġ .i. doṁnall mac neill mfirgiġ do ṁarḃad le Maolmuire, mac briain óicc, ⁊ le hAodh mbuidhe mac firfeda ṁec suiḃne ⁊ iadsidhe ina ndís do lorccadh a ccionaidh a míġníoṁa la hUa ndoṁnaill for mullach síṫe Aodha hi ffiadhnaisi cáiċ i ccoitċinne tre ċoll a peaċta.

O cinnéidiġ fionn Uaitne mac donnchaidh óicc mic Aodha mic aṁlaoiḃ o ḃaile uí eachdhaċ i nurṁuṁain ioċtair i cconntae ṫhiopprat árann do écc i mí nouember ⁊ ó cinneittiġ do ġairm don ġiolla duḃ ua ċinneidiġ.

Maiġistir [O] niallain Semus, mac doṁnaill, mic aṁlaoiḃ, mic donnchaidh uí niallain, fer tighe naoídheadh coitchinn, ⁊ saoí i nealadhnaiḃ do écc i mí october i mbaile uí aille i mbarúntaċt chuinnche hi cconntae an cláir.

Caislen na mainge do ġaḃail la hiarla dfesmuṁan fa ṡaṁain na bliadna so ar ṁuinntir na bainríoġna, tria aidilge airbfrta bit do bfit for an mbárda.

Loch gair beos do ġaḃail las an iarla cédna for ṁuinntir na bain-ríoġna.

Ua concoḃair Sliccigh donnchadh mac caṫail óicc do bfit i muinntearus, ⁊ hi ccarattradh Ui ḋoṁnaill on aimsir in ro marḃadh an goberneoir go diuid na ro. Ba haiṫfrradh ar glan, ⁊ ba coimm ria cciot dórom toċt isin ccarattradh sin ó na fuaisttingealltoiḃ imrigne ettarḃaċa, no geallta dó ó ḃliadain co bliadain go sin. O ro ba riarac Ua concoḃair dUa doṁnaill, do radsidhe dua ċonċoḃair dírime do ḃuaiḃ, do ċaiplib, ⁊ dá gaċ nfrnail cfṫra ⁊ innile, darḃar bfos, ⁊ da gach naidhilge oile rainicc a lfs do aitreḃ ⁊ do

[n] *For violating his law.*—This is a repetition, nearly word for word, of an entry already given, p. 2092.

[o] *Baile-Ui-Eachdhach:* i. e. O'Haugh's town, now Ballyhough, a townland in the parish of Aglishcloghane, about four miles to the north-east of Burrisokeane, in the barony of Lower Ormond, and county of Tipperary. An old castle stood in this townland till the 6th of January, 1839, when it was blown down by a storm.

[p] *Baile-Ui-Aille,* now Ballyally, a townland in the parish of Templemaley, barony of Upper Bunratty, and county of Clare.—See note [s], under the year 1559, p. 1571, *supra.*

[q] *Loch-Gair,* near the town of Bruff, in the county of Limerick.—See it already mentioned under the years 1516 and 1579. The strength of this place is described by Sir George Carew, about this period, as follows:

"The four and twentieth" [of May, 1600], "the Armie encamped at the Brough" [Bruff],

excepting only that he delivered up the regal sword to the Lord Chancellor and to Sir Robert Gardiner. It was not known to any of the Irish at this time whether the Earl had gone to England to remain there or return back again.

Mac Sweeny Banagh, i. e. Donnell, the son of Niall Meirgeach, was slain by Mulmurry, the son of Brian Oge, and Hugh Boy, the son of Ferfeadha Mac Sweeny; and both these were hanged by O'Donnell, in the presence of all in general, on Mullach-Sithe-Aedha, for violating his law[n].

O'Kennedy Finn (Owny, the son of Donough Oge, son of Hugh, son of Auliffe), of Baile-Ui-Eachdhach[o], in Lower Ormond, in the county of Tipperary, died in the month of November, and Gilla-Duv O'Kennedy was then styled the O'Kennedy [Finn].

Master O'Nialain (James, the son of Donnell, son of Auliffe, son of Donough O'Niallain), a man who kept an open house of hospitality, died in the month of October at Baile-Ui-Aille[p], in the barony of Quin, in the county of Clare.

About the 1st of November this year Castlemaine was taken by the Earl of Desmond from the Queen's people, in consequence of the warders wanting the necessary food.

Loch-Gair[q] was also taken by the same Earl from the Queen's people.

O'Conor Sligo (Donough, the son of Cathal Oge) continued in friendship and amity with O'Donnell from the time that the Governor was slain to the end of this year. It was a change for the better, and a shelter for him, to come over to this friendship from the cold, slow, and unprofitable promises made him [by the English] from year to year. When O'Conor became obedient to O'Donnell, he gave O'Conor a countless deal of cows, horses, and every other description of herds and flocks, as also of corn and of other necessaries, to

"where the President left a Warde, partly to offend the Rebels of Loghguire, three miles distant from thence, and partly to open the way betwixt Kilmallocke and Limerick, which, for two yeares space, had been impassible for any subject. The five and twentieth, the army passing neere Loghguire, which was as yet held by the Rebels, the President, attended with a Troope of Horse, rode to take a particular view of the strength thereof, as also by what way he might most conveniently bring the Cannon to annoy the same. Hee found it to bee a place of exceeding strength, by reason that it was an Iland, encompassed with a deep Lough, the breadth thereof being, in the narrowest place, a caliever's shot over; upon one side thereof standeth a very strong Castle, which, at this time, was manned with a good Garrison, for there was within the Iland *Iohn Fitz-Thomas*, with two hundred men at the least, which shewed themselves prepared to defend the place."—*Pacata Hibernia*, book i. c. vi.

áitiuccaḋ a thíre, iar na bfeith ina fasach gan ionatacht gan aitiúcchaḋ fri hathaiḋ imchéin go sin.

Ua Domhnaill do ḋul do ríoḋucchaḋ eitir cloinn uilliam ina nesaonta .i. eitir Mac uilliam, teboitt mac uatéir ciotaig, ⁊ teboitt na long mac Risderd an iarainn i mís december. Iar ndenaṁ a sioḋa dó, Ro triall do dol hi ccloinn Riocaird, Ar a aoí ní deachaiḋ tar uarán mór isteċ don chur sin. Baí teóra haiḋce hi ccampa i niomḟoccus an ṁachaire riaḃaiġ, ⁊ na gaillṁe. Do radaḋ crech cuicce o Spairre an ḃaile ṁóir ⁊ ge do ḃaí a oṁan, ⁊ a imeccla hi ccoitcinne airriḋe co léim concculainn ní dernġene nach ní acht soaḋ tar a ais don cur soin i nultaiḃ.

Coicceaḋ ulaḋ ina linn lain, ina ṫopar ṫecht ⁊ ina ṫuinn teccle isin mbliaḋain si gan guais caṫa na creiċe, gona, na gaḃála forra a hentaoiḃ derinn ⁊ a neccla soṁ for gaċ ein tír ioir.

AOIS CRIOS[T], 1600.

Aois Criost, mile, Se céd.

An tiarla of essex (.i. Robeird) a duḃramar do ṫoċt i nerinn i mbeltaine na bliaḋna so do cuaiḋ torainn, ⁊ do ḋol hi Saxaiḃ fo ṡaṁain na bliaḋna ceona. Ba haṫċoranaċ, imḋeacċtaċ, fiomach, forġruamḋa an fiaḋuccaḋ fuair ó ċoṁairle Shaxan iar ttoċt dó dia saiġiḋ. Ro tuḃaḋ fris céttus tláiṫe, ⁊ time a ḟoġnaṁa don ḃainrioġain an ccéin baí i nerinn, ⁊ na baí aiḋilcce neiṫ fair ro ḃaḋ lainn lais do cum ċoccaiḋ ⁊ caṫaiġte. Araill ele dna ro tuḃaḋ friss, a ḋol gan cead gan ceileḃraḋ don coṁairle ṫoir no aḃus go Saxoiḃ don chur sin. Iar na raḋ sin friss, ⁊ iar ccor dál iomḋa na leiṫ dóiḃ, ro forconġaḋ fair deiliuġaḋ re gach dignite, re gaċ gairm, ⁊ re gach onóir baoí occa on mbainríoġain, ⁊ ro furailseḋ for a aos iomcoiṁeta giall, ⁊ eiḋire na cúirte, a conġḃáil aca buḋéin go ro ḟíoṫlaiḋeḋ fecc an prionnsa

[r] *Gate.*—The Spairre is now pronounced sparra, and still applied to a military gate, at Athenry, Galway, and Limerick, as the Editor has ascertained by inquiry among the old Irish people dwelling in and near those towns.

[s] *Taking his leave of.*—This should be: "without the permission of the English or Irish Privy Council, or without taking his leave of the latter."

[t] *The sovereign's anger.*—In Harington's *Nugæ Antiquæ* (printed in 1804), vol. i. p. 302, *et seq.*, there is a very curious account of Essex's insane conspiracy. Harington says, that as he knelt at her feet, and sought to excuse his

replant and inhabit his territory, after it had been a wilderness, without habitation or abode, for a long time till then.

In the month of December O'Donnell went to make peace between the Mac Williams, i. e. between the Mac William (Theobald, the son of Walter Kittagh) and Theobald-na-Long, son of Richard-an-Iarainn. After having made peace between them, he set out to go into Clanrickard; but, however, he did not proceed beyond Oranmore on that occasion. He remained three nights encamped in the neighbourhood of Machaire-riabhach, and of Galway; and a prey was brought to him from the very gate[r] of the great town; and although a fear and dread of him was spread from thence to Leim-Chonchulainn, he achieved nothing further on this occasion, but returned into Ulster.

In this year the province of Ulster was a still pool, a gentle spring, and a reposing wave, without the fear of battle or incursion, injury or attack, from any other part of Ireland; while every other territory was in awe of them (i.e. of the people of Ulster).

THE AGE OF CHRIST, 1600.

The Age of Christ, one thousand six hundred.

The Earl of Essex (i. e. Robert), of whom we have spoken in the preceding year as having arrived in Ireland in the month of May, and as having gone to England about the first of November, met with a repulsive, reproachful, sharp, and sullen reception from the Council of England, when he appeared before them. It was objected to him that his service for the Queen, while in Ireland, had been feeble and dastardly, while he wanted nothing which he deemed necessary for war or battle. Another thing objected to him was, his having come to England on that occasion without the permission of, or taking his leave of,[s] the English or Irish Council. After these were stated to him, and many other accusations were laid to his charge, he was commanded to relinquish every dignity, title, and honour, which he held from the Queen; and the keepers of the hostages and pledges of the court were ordered to detain him in their custody until the Sovereign's anger[t] against him should be appeased.

unfortunate master, she catched at his girdle and swore "by God's son, I am no Queen: that man is above me." Then she demanded of Harington a journal which he had been ordered to keep of the transactions in Ireland; and on reading it, she said fiercely: "By God's son ye

fris. Iar sin tra ro cinnfedh leo aithfhrach oifficeach, ⁊ armála do leiccen i nErinn .i. Sir Serlus Blunt Lord Mountiogh ina lustis, uair ni baí lustis i nErinn fri ré da bliadhain gus an tan sin, ⁊ Sir Seoirsi Carú ina Presidens os cenn da cóicceadh Mumhan. Ro hullmaigheadh coblach i mbátar lion badh lia oldás se míle fer narmach co na ccongaibh techta do thocht ar aon lás na hoifficceachaibh sin go hErinn ⁊ iadsidhe uile do thocht do mhuir, ⁊ do tír go coicceadh Uladh an tsainrit. Ba im féil Pattraicc dna do ronadh na cinnte sin la comhairle Shaxan.

Duine uasal do thigh uí Concobhair Duinn .i. Diarmait, mac an Dubhaltaigh, mic Tuathail, baí sidhe hi ccenndus ar dhruing moir do shaighdiuiribh Gaoidhealacha batar i namhsaine acc iarla Desmumhan, isin Mumhain fri ré na bliadhna so anall. Do chaedh Diarmait i ndeireadh na bliadhna céona a ttosach mis December for cuairt i ccenn Uí Neill, ⁊ fuair failte occa. Iar ccriochnuccadh a cheilidhe dó amhail ro badh lainn lais, ro cheadaigh Ua Neill sóadh ina frithing a ttosach mis Ianuarii na bliadhna so, ⁊ dol isin Mumhain. Ro fhoráil Ua Neill fair a aisnéis is na tíribh i raghadh go mbaoí fein co na shlóghaibh ina dhiúidh d'fhios Midhe, Laighen, Mumhan, ⁊ an taoibhe ba dhes d'Erinn, dus cia diobh baí hi ccairdine no hi ffrithbheirt fris. Iar roctain do Dhiarmait co na dhrongbhuidhin go haentaidh Ghaoidhelaigh airther Mumhan, Ro triall i naithghiorra gacha conaire do dhol go hiarla Desmumhan, ⁊ do bhert a aghaidh ar Uaithnibh, ⁊ ar Cloinn Uilliam bhruaich na Sionna.

Ot cualaidh barún chaislein uí Chonaing Risderd, mac Tepoitt, mic Uilliam, mic Emainn a Burc, Diarmait do thocht an dú sin, Ro chruinnigh sidhe ⁊ a

are all idle knaves and the Lord Deputy worse." During this foolish conspiracy was executed Captain Thomas Lee, who wrote, in the year 1594, "A brief Declaration of the Government of Ireland, opening many Corruptions in the same, discovering the Discontentments of the Irishry, and the Causes moving those expected Troubles."—See p. 1696, *supra*. Camden gives the following account of his conduct and death in his *Annal. Reg. Elis.*, A. D. 1601 :

" Die Februarii duodecimo Thom. Leæus, Henrici Leæi Georgiani ordinis equitis præclari agnatus, notissimæ audaciæ, militum in Hiberniæ ductor Tir-Oenio intimus, & Essexio devotus, qui eadem nocte, qua Essexius Consiliarios adire recusaraverat, operam suam ad Essexium intercipiendum aut perimendum obtulerat, Roberto Crosso ductori classiario, gloriosum esse, innuit, si sex viri animosi Reginam simul adirent, eamque vi adigerent, ut Essexium, Southamptonium & reliquos, custodia emitteret. Hæc mox Consialiariis Crossus detulit, Leæusque quæsitus, primis tenebris juxta ostium sanctioris cubiculi Regii deprehensus est, cogitabundus pallens, sudore diffluens, & sæpius percunctans, an Regina jam cœnatura, an consiliarii

After this they came to the resolution of sending a different officer to Ireland, with an army, namely, Sir Charles Blunt; Lord Mountjoy[u], as Lord Justice (for there had not been a Lord Justice in it for two years before that time); and Sir George Cary [Carew], as President over the two provinces of Munster. There was a fleet fitted out, in which there was sent a force of upwards of six thousand armed men, with befitting warlike engines, to accompany these officers to Ireland; and all these were to proceed by sea to the province of Ulster in particular. These resolutions were made by the English Council about Patrick's Day.

A gentleman of the house of O'Conor Don (Dermot, the son of Dubhaltach, son of Tuathal) was in command over a large party of Irish soldiers who were in the service of the Earl of Desmond, in Munster, during the last year. This Dermot went, towards the end of the same year, in the beginning of the month of December, on a visit to O'Neill, and received welcome from him. Having finished his visit to his satisfaction, he asked permission of O'Neill to return back in the beginning of January in this year, and proceeded into Munster. O'Neill desired him to mention it in the territories through which he should pass, that he [O'Neill] himself, with his forces, was marching after him to visit Meath, Leinster, Munster, and the southern side of Ireland, to know which of them were in friendship and which in opposition to him. When Dermot arrived with his force among the Irish confederates of the east of Munster, [and told them that O'Neill was on his march to visit them], he proceeded by the shortest ways to go to the Earl of Desmond; and he directed his course by Uaithne[w] and Clanwilliam[x], on the borders of the Shannon.

When the Baron of Castleconnell (Richard, the son of Theobald, son of William, son of Edmond Burke) heard of Dermot's arrival there, he and his

adessent: inter hæc captus & examinatus, postero die in judicium raptus, ex testimonio Crossi & sua confessione damnatus, ad furcas Tiburnas trahitur: ubi confessus, se hominem fuisse nocentissimum, in hac autem causa innocentem: & nihil contra Reginam vel cogitasse protestatus, supplicio afficitur. Et pro temporum ratione salutaris hæc visa est severitas."

[u] *Lord Mountjoy, &c.*—They landed at the hill of Howth on the 24th of February, 1599 (1600). Sir George Carew staid at Dublin for some time to get his commission and instructions, and to learn the state of the kingdom, and on the 7th of April, 1600, went to his province.—See *Pacata Hibernia*, book i. chap. 1.

[w] *Uaithne*, now Owny, forming two baronies, one in the county of Limerick, and the other in that of Tipperary.—See note [n], p. 979, *supra*.

[x] *Clanwilliam*, a barony in the north-east of the county of Limerick.

ḋerbraṫair Comás an líon ar lia ro ḟeḋsat do ṁarcaċaiḃ ⁊ troiġṫeaċaiḃ dia muinntir féin, ⁊ do ṁuinntir na bainrioġna, ⁊ ro gabsat acc diuḃraccaḋ Diarmata co na ṁuinntir ó ṫa mainistir Uaitne go droiċet bunḃriste hi cconntae Luimniġ go ro díoṫaiġeaḋ morán dá ḋaġḋaoinib, ⁊ da ḋaorccarṡluaiġ in airect sin. Aġ dol do Diarmait co na ṁuintir tar an droiċet remraite ba hann ro bedgsat an dá mac sin tepoitt a burc .i. an barún, ⁊ Comás la huaḃar, ⁊ andárachte a hucht a muintire féin, i ccrioslach ḋromġbuiḋne Diarmada. Ni rainicc leosom sóaḋ slan tar a naiss an tan ro hiaḋaḋ impa, ⁊ ro trasccrait, ⁊ ro claiḋmit gan ċoigill la a mbioḋbaḋaiḃ. Ba damna eccaoíne a ndearnaḋ la Diarmait co na muinntir don ċur sin .i. marḃaḋ an ḃarúin ⁊ Comáis, ger bo hócc ar aoí naoise iadsiḋe sortar ferrḋa ar aoí nanma, ⁊ noirḃertaiss.

Sloicceaḋ la hua neill .i. Aoḋ mac firdorcha, mic cuinn ḃacaiġ, a mí Ianuary na bliaḋna so do ḋol ar in taoiḃ bu ḋes desinn do ċengal a ċaratt-raḋ le a coṁpann coccaiḋ, ⁊ daiṫe a anfolaḋ ar a easccairdiḃ. Iar ffaccḃáil ċoicciḋ ulaḋ dUa neill assiḋ do luiḋ hi ccoiccriċh miḋe, ⁊ breifne ⁊ do ḋealḃna móir go ndesna diogbala mora ar fud an tíre, go ttarat barún delbna .i. Crioftoir, mac Risdird, mic crioftora a riar fein dUa neill. Ro lainṁilleaḋ lais maċaire cuircne, ⁊ gaċ ní dar ḃen le tepoitt diolmuin mar an ccédna. Do ṫaéd iaraṁ o néill go dorus ḃaile aṫa luain don taoiḃ ṫes do cloinn ċolmáin, do ċenel ḟiachach hi ffearaiḃ ceall. Baí siḋe naoí noiḋce hi longport isin tir hísin, ⁊ do báttar fir ċeall, uaċtair laiġen, ⁊ iarṫair miḋe dia oiġreir, ⁊ acc naiḋm a ccarattraḋ friss.

Acc ḟáccḃail na tíre sin dUa néill assiḋ luiḋ tar muinchinn sleḃe blaḋma siar, ⁊ ro leicc tri sceimelta i naén ló so ḋuthaiġ Ele ar ḋáiġ a ḃioḋbanais re hUa cceḃaill tiġearna éle .i. an Calḃaċ mac uilliam uiḋir, mic fir gan ainm a ndioġail an duinemarḃṫa daorċlanda, ⁊ na dersccmarsra díoḟulaing ro

[y] *Uaithne*, now Abbington, a townland in a parish of the same name, in the barony of Owneybeg, in the north-east of the county of Limerick.

[z] *Bun-briste*, now Bunbristy bridge, near Grange, about eight miles to the south of the city of Limerick.

[a] *Delvin-More*: i. e. the barony of Delvin, in the county of Westmeath.

[b] *Machaire-Cuircne*, now the barony of Kilkenny west, in the county of Westmeath.

[c] *Clann-Colman*, now the barony of Clonlonan, in the county of Westmeath.

[d] *Kinel-Fiachach*, now the barony of Moycashel, in Westmeath.

[e] *Fircall*, a territory comprising the baronies

brother, Thomas, mustered all the forces they were able, both horse and foot, of his own and the Queen's people; and they continued to fire on Dermot and his people [while they were passing] from the monastery of Uaiṫbne[y] to the bridge of Bun-briste[z], in the county of Limerick; and many of his officers and common soldiers were slain during this time. As Dermot and his people were crossing the aforesaid bridge, these two sons of Theobald Burke, i. e. the Baron and Thomas, advanced with pride and boldness in front of their own forces, and towards the borders of Dermot's party. But they were not able to return back safe, for they were surrounded, prostrated, and unsparingly put to the sword by their enemies. What Dermot and his people committed on this occasion was the cause of lamentation, namely, the killing of the Baron and Thomas; for, though they were young in age, they were manly in renown and noble deeds.

A hosting was made by O'Neill (Hugh, the son of Ferdorcha, son of Con Bacagh) in the month of January in this year, and he proceeded to the south of Ireland, to confirm his friendship with his allies in the war, and to wreak his vengeance upon his enemies. When O'Neill left the province of Ulster, he passed along the borders of Meath and Breifny, and through Delvin-More[a], and did great injuries throughout the territory, [and continued to waste it], until the Baron of Delvin (Christopher, the son of Richard, son of Christopher) came and submitted to O'Neill on his terms. He [also] totally spoiled Machaire-Cuircne[b], and all the possessions of Theobald Dillon. O'Neill afterwards marched to the gates of Athlone, and along the southern side of Clann-Colman[c], and through Kinel-Fiachach[d], into Fircall[e]. In this country he remained encamped nine nights; and the people of Fircall, of Upper Leinster, and Westmeath, made full submission to him, and formed a league of friendship with him.

On leaving this country, O'Neill passed over the upper part[f] of Slieve Bloom westwards, and sent forth three parties in one day to ravage Ely, because of the enmity he bore O'Carroll, Lord of Ely, i. e. Calvagh, the son of William Odhar, son of Ferganainm, and in revenge of the base murder and intolerable massacre which he had committed upon the gentlemen of the Mac Mahons of

of Ballycowan, Ballyboy, and Eglish or Fircall, in the King's County.

[f] *Upper part*, muınnċınn .ı. uaċċaṗ.—*O'Clery*, in *Leabhar Gabhala*, p. 3.

imir ré ar na daoiniḃ uaisle doirġiallaiḃ még maṫġaṁna bátar ar a ionċaiḃ, ⁊ ar a fordaḋ aṁail ro airnſiḋmar isin mbliaḋain reṁainn. Ro bſn droċḋiaċ an ṁiġníoṁa ísin do ḋuṫaiġ Ele don chur sin, uair ruccaḋ eiste a huile ṡealḃa soġluaiste a maoine, ⁊ a mór ṁaiṫſs co nár fáccḃaḋ innte aċt luaiṫreaḋ i nionad a harba ⁊ aoiḃle i nionaḋ a háitiġhte. Do raḋaḋ i noṫairliġe écca, ⁊ oiḋſḃa dronga dſrmára da ffſraiḃ, da mnaiḃ, da macaiḃ, ⁊ da ninġſnaiḃ. Ro fáccḃaḋ bſos daoine uaisle da ḟine fſin, ⁊ da fialus i ffrſsabra friss ó ccſrḃaill isin tír.

Do ṫaéd iaraṁ Ua neill reṁe go bruaiċimliḃ ḃealaiġ móir ṁaiġe dala, do Ross cré, do uiḃ cairín, do ċorco ṫſinſḋ on ffoslongport go a ċéle dó aṁlaiḋ sin go rainicc go dorus mainistre na croiche naoiṁ. Nír bo cian doiḃ hi suiḋe an tan tuccaḋ an croċ naoṁ ċuca dia ccoṁḋa ⁊ dia ccomairce, ⁊ do bſrtsat na gaoiḋil toirbearta troma, almsana, ⁊ offrála ioṁḋa da maoraiḃ, ⁊ da manċoiḃ i nonóir in coimde na ndúla. Tuccsat tra tſrmonn, ⁊ tairisecht don mainistir co na muraiḃ, ⁊ co na fearonnaiḃ foġnaṁa, ⁊ dna dia huile aittreaḃtachaiḃ ar cſna.

Airisiḋ din Ua néill athaiḋ do mí ḟebru haimsire ro in imliḃ Ele dſs-ceartaiġe, iarṫair buitilérach, ċoirr Siuire, ⁊ coille na manach.

Baí Iarla urmuṁan .i. tomás mac Semus, mic Piarais buitiler, Iarla ċille dara .i. gearoitt, mac eduaird, mic gearóitt, ⁊ barún delḃna .i. Crios-tóir, mac Risdeird mic criostora co na mbaoí a ffoġnaṁ ⁊ i nuṁla ag an mbainrioġain ó tá sin go baile áṫa cliaṫ ag baccar ammass ⁊ ionnsaiġiḋ do ṫabairt ar Ua neill gaċ noiḋċe, ⁊ ge ro ċoccairsiot in ní sin, ní ro crioċ-naiġeaḋ leo hé.

Do ḋeachaiḋ O neill iar sin go dorus Caisil. Tainic dia ṡaiġiḋ gus an maiġin sin, an tiarla dſsmuṁan ro hoirdneaḋ fos a ṡorcongrasoṁ ⁊ ar a uġdarrás buḋſin in aghaiḋ statuite an prionnsa roiṁe sin .i. Sémus mac tomais ruaiḋ, mic Semais, mic Sſain, ⁊ batar faoiliḋ cach dioḃ fri a roile. Ro arccnátar rſmpa iaraṁ tar Siúir siar, do ċnámhcoill do ṡleiḃ muice,

[g] *Bealach-mor-Muighe-dala*, now Ballaghmore, near Borris-in-Ossory.—See note [e], 1750, *supra*.

[h] *Corca-Teineadh.*—This was the ancient name of the parish of Templemore, in the north-east of the county of Tipperary.—See note [a], under the year 1580, p. 1749, *supra*.

[i] *From one encampment:* i. e. pitching his camp wherever he stopped.

[k] *Its houses.*—The abbey church of the Holy Cross still remains in good preservation, as do some of the *murs*, or houses, but particularly the abbot's *mur*, or stone house.

Oriel, whom he had under his protection and in his service, as we have related, in the preceding year. The evil destiny deserved by that wicked deed befel the territory of Ely on this occasion, for all its moveable possessions, wealth, and riches were carried away, and nothing left in it but ashes instead of its corn, and embers in place of its mansions. Great numbers of their men, women, sons, and daughters were left in a dying and expiring state; and some gentlemen of his own tribe and kindred were left in opposition to O'Carroll in the territory.

After this O'Neill moved onwards to the borders of Bealach-mor-Muighe-dala[g], to Roscrea, to Ikerrin, and to Corco-Teineadh[h], from one encampment[i] to another, until he arrived at the gate of the monastery of the Holy Cross. They had not been long here when the Holy Cross was brought out to shelter and protect them; and the Irish presented great gifts, alms, and many offerings, to its keepers and the monks, in honour of the Lord of the Elements. They gave protection to the monastery and steward in respect to its houses[k] and glebe-lands, and to all its inhabitants.

O'Neill remained for some time in the month of February on the borders of Southern Ely[l], [also] in the west of the country of the Butlers, in Cois-Siuire[m], and in Kilnamanagh[n].

The Earl of Ormond, i. e. Thomas, the son of James, son of Pierce Butler; the Earl of Kildare, i. e. Garret, the son of Edward, son of Garret; and the Baron of Delvin, i. e. Christopher, the son of Richard, son of Christopher, with all those who were in the service of, or in obedience to the Queen, from thence to Dublin, threatened every night to attack and assault O'Neill; but, though they meditated doing so, they did not accomplish it.

O'Neill afterwards proceeded to the gates of Cashel, and there came to him to that place the Earl of Desmond, who had been previously appointed by his own command, and on his authority, contrary to the statute of the Sovereign, James the son of Thomas Roe, son of James, son of John, and they were rejoiced to see each other. They afterwards proceeded westwards, across the

[l] *Southern Ely*: i.e. Eile-Ui-Thogartaigh, now Eliogarty.

[m] *Cois-Siuire*, a district belonging to a sept of the Burkes, situated on the west side of the River Suir, to the west of Cashel, in the county of Tipperary.

[n] *Kilnamanagh*, the country of the O'Dwyers, a barony in the county of Tipperary.

doirṫear Ṡléiḃe Cláire, don ḃearnaiġ ḋeircc, do ċloinn Ġiobúin, do crich Róisteċ, ⁊ do ḋúthaiġ an ḃarraiġ móir. Ni ro loitsedh ⁊ ní ro lainmilleadh la hUa Néill ní is na tíribh i ttaidhlsedh gen mo tá an luċt no frioth tairisedh fris i mbiodhḃanus bunaidh do ġrés. Do ḋeaċaidh iaraṁ go dúthaiġ an ḃarraiġ uair bá daoin leċ las an mbainrioġain no bioḋ do ḃunaḋ. Asé ra barrach ann an tan sin, Dauid, mac Semuir, mic Risdird, mic tomais mic emainn. Airisidh Ua neill isin tír co ro crsċhloiscceadh, ⁊ go ro cuarttaiġsedh lais hí ó ċúil go cuil etir maġ, ⁊ moṫar, etir mín, ⁊ ainmin co ná baoí súil na saoilechtain aon duine fri a haitiuccadh, no fri a haittreaḃadh go haimsir imchein.

Do ċoidh tra ó néill tar corcaiġ, ⁊ tar laoí (.i. aḃann) ba deas go ro suidhighsedh longport lais etir laoi, ⁊ bannDain (.i. aḃann) i ttórann murscraiġe

[o] *Cnamhchoill*, now Cneamhchoill, a short distance to the east of the town of Tipperary.—See the exact situation of this place already pointed out and proved in note [y], under the year 1560, p. 1578, *supra*.

[p] *Sliabh-Muice*, now Sliabh-na-muice, and *anglice* Slievenamuck, a low mountain on the north side of the glen of Aharlagh, in the barony of Clanwilliam, and about four miles to the south of the town of Tipperary. It extends from Bansha to Corderry, within a mile of the village of Galbally.

[q] *Sliabh-Claire*, a considerable hill, on which stands a remarkable cromlech, the tomb of Oilioll Olum, King of Munster in the third century, situated a short distance to the east of the church of Duntryleague, in the barony of Coshlea, and county of Limerick, and about three miles to the north-west of the village of Galbally.

[r] *Bearna-dhearg:* i. e. the Red Gap or Chasm, a celebrated gap in the mountain of Sliabh Caoin, now Slieve Reagh, about one mile to the south of Kilflin church, on the borders of the counties of Limerick and Cork. This gap is well known to the readers of ancient Irish history, as the place where Mahon, the brother of Brian Borumha, King of Munster, was murdered in cold blood by the ancestors of the O'Mahonys and O'Donovans, in the year 976. It lies between the hills of Kilcruaig and Bearnadhearg, *anglice* Red Chair, the former on its east, and the latter on its west side.

[s] *Loyal to the Queen.*—The Lord Barry, although he had been an accomplice in Desmond's rebellion, had now become a staunch partisan of the Queen. In a letter, which O'Neill addressed to him, he says:

"You are the cause why all the nobility of the south, with each of whom you are linked, either in affinity or consanguinity, have not joined together to shake off the yoke of heresy and tyranny, with which our souls and bodies are opprest."

In answer to this letter Lord Barry declares, "that her Highness had never distrained him for matters of religion;" and adds: "though ye, by some overweening imaginations, have declined from your dutiful allegiance unto her Highness, yet I have settled myself never to forsake her."—*Pacata Hibernia*, book i. c. 1.

[t] *Extremity:* literally, "from corner to corner."

[u] *Lee.*—This river has its source in Iveleary, in the mountain range which separates the counties of Cork and Kerry, and issuing from

Suir, by the route of Cnamhchoill[o], Sliabh-Muice[p], by the east of Sliabh-Claire[q], and Bearna-dhearg[r], through Clann-Gibbon, through the country of the Roches, and through the territory of Barry More. O'Neill did not injure or waste any in these territories through which he passed, excepting those whom he found always opposed to him in inveterate enmity. He afterwards marched into the country of Barry More, who was always on the side of the Queen. The Barry at this time was David, the son of James, son of Richard, son of Thomas, son of Edmond; and, as he was loyal to the Queen[s], O'Neill remained in the territory until he traversed, plundered, and burned it, from one extremity[t] to the other, both plain and wood, both level and rugged, so that no one hoped or expected that it could be inhabited for a long time afterwards.

O'Neill then proceeded southward, across the River Lee, and pitched his camp between the Rivers Lee[u] and Bandon[w], on the confines of Muskerry and Carbery. To this camp all the Mac Carthys, both southern and northern, came

the romantic lake of Gougane Barra, after a course of about forty miles, divides itself into two unequal branches, one mile above the city of Cork, and again meeting after a separation of nearly two miles, discharges itself into the ocean below Cove.

[w] *Bandon*, a river flowing through the towns of Bandon, or Bandonbridge, and Inishannon, and discharging itself into the harbour of Kinsale, in the county of Cork.—See it already mentioned under the year 1560. It appears from a letter to Donough Moyle Mac Carthy, dated March 2nd, 1599, signed by Florence Mac Carthy, Owen Mac Egan, and Donnell O'Donovan, and published in the *Pacata Hibernia*, book ii. ch. 6, that O'Neill was encamped at this time at Iniscare [Inishcarra]. This letter runs as follows:

"Cousin Donogh, wee haue us commended to your selfe, and to your brother Florence: I haue (I assure you) taken the paines to come hither to Tyrone, not so much for any danger of my owne, as to saue the countrey of Carberry from danger and destruction, which, if it bee once destroyed, your living" [i. e. food] "(in my opinion) will growe very scarce. These two Gentlemen, your Brother" [in law], "Odonevan, and Owen Mac Eggan, are verie careful with mee of your good. Therefore, if ever you will bee ruled by us, or tender the wealth of your selfe and your Countrey, wee are heereby earnestly to request you to come and meete us to morrowe at Cloudghe; and so requesting you not to fayle heereof in any wise, to God's keeping I commit you.

"Your very loving Friends,

"FLORENCE MAC CARTIE.
OWEN MAC EGGAN.
DONNELL ODONEVAN.

"*O'Neale's Campe at Iniscare,*
Martij 2, 1599."

This Donnell O'Donovan was chief of his name, and the eldest legitimate son of Donnell-na-gCroiceann O'Donovan, son of Teige, son of Dermot.—See note [r], under the year 1581, p. 1762, *supra*.

John Collins of Myross, in his pedigree of the late General Richard O'Donovan, of Bawnlahan, who was the lineal descendant of this Donnell O'Donovan, asserts that O'Donovan was never

⁊ cairbreach. Tangatar síol ccárthaigh uile thes ⁊ tuaidh do thigh í néill ar in ffoslongport sin. Tánaicc ann din diar baí i nSraonta, ⁊ i ffrithbhsrt

implicated in the rebellion of the Earl of Desmond, or in that of O'Neill. But this is not true; for, that Donnell-na-gcroiceann, the O'Donovan who died in 1584, was implicated in the rebellion of the Earl of Desmond, is quite evident from P. O'Sullevan Beare's *Hist. Cathol. Iber.*, tom. 3, lib. 1, c. i. p. 115, where "Odonnobhanus" is set down among the "*Veteres Iberni, qui pro fide Catholica pugnaverunt*;" and that his eldest legitimate son, this Donnell O'Donovan, who succeeded as chief of his name in 1584, and who submitted to O'Neill on this occasion, had been a rebel so early as 1585, when he burned to the ground the house of the Lord Bishop of Ross, which had been a short time before built by William Lyon, Bishop of Cloyne, is quite obvious from the manuscript entitled *Carbriæ Notitia*, and Harris's edition of Ware's Bishops, p. 565, where Harris quotes a Visitation Book of 1613, stating "that William Lyon built a House at Ross [in 1582], which cost him at least three hundred pounds, which, in little more than three years after, was burnt down by *the Rebel* O'Donovan."

It also appears, from the *Pacata Hibernia*, book 2, c. vii. that of the twelve thousand pounds divided among the rebels of Munster by Dr. Owen Mac Egan, the Pope's Bishop of Ross, this O'Donovan obtained £200. P. O'Sullevan Beare also states that O'Donovan joined O'Driscoll More and two knights of the Mac Carthy family, to assist the Spanish Admiral Zubiaur, when he landed at Castlehaven.

"Adfuit etiam Odriscol Magnus cum Cornelio filio, et aliis, Odonnobhanus & equites Maccarrhæ. Quorum aduentu Anglus territus se nauibus continet, & Zubiaur lœtus, & confirmatus tormentis ex nauibus expositis Anglicam classem biduum acerrimè oppugnat."—*Hist. Cathol. &c.*, tom. 3, lib. 6, c. viii.

But we learn from a letter of the Lord Deputy and Council, written on the 20th of March, the last day of the year 1601, to the Lords in England, that Sir Florence O'Driscoll, O'Donovan, and the two sons of Sir Owen Mac Carthy, who were O'Donovan's brothers-in-law, had joined the English. His Lordship writes:

"As for Sir Finnin Odrischall, Odonnevan, and the two Sonnes of Sir Owen Mac Cartie, they and their Followers, *since their comming in*, are growne very odious to the Rebels of those parts, and are so well divided in factions amongst themselves, as they are fallen to preying and killing one another, which we conceiue will much availe to the quieting of these parts."—*Pacata Hibernia*, book 2, c. xxx.

This explains the words of P. O'Sullevan Beare, tom. 3, lib. 7, c. i., where he says:

"Osulleuanus Gulielmo Burko, Richardo Tirello, & aliis conductis, obæratorum delectu conscripto & sociorum auxiliis milliá militum circiter duo iuuentutis electæ comparat. Quibus ea hyeme Torrentirupem (Carraig an neasaig) arcem quam solam in Beantria tenebat Eugenius Osulleuanus semper Reginæ partes secutus, partem aggere, turribus, vineis, musculis, pluteis oppugnatam, partim æneis tormentis quassatam in suam potestatem redegit. Odonnobhanum ad Anglos reuersum, & alios Anglorum auxiliares deprædatur. Regias copias, quæ in Momonijs erant, terrore perculsas in oppida munita, & arces compellit."

Again, it appears from the following passage in the instructions given to the Earl of Thomond, on the 9th of March, 1601, that O'Donovan, and his Irish neighbours, were under protection:

"The service you are to perform is, to doe all your endeavours to burne the rebels Corne in Carbery, Beare, and Bantry, take their Cowes,

into the house of O'Neill in this camp [i. e. submitted to him]. Thither repaired two who were at strife with each other concerning the Lordship of Desmond,

and to use all hostile prosecution upon the persons of the people, as in such cases of rebellion is accustomed.

"Those that are in subjection, or lately protected (as Odrischall, Odonevan, and Sir Owen Mac Cartie's sonnes), to afford them all kind and mild vsage."—*Pacata Hibernia*, book 3, c. ii.

By these authorities the Editor is satisfied that Collins is wrong in asserting that this family never joined in either of the great rebellions of Desmond or O'Neill.

According to a pedigree of O'Donovan of Carbery, preserved in a manuscript at Lambeth Palace, Carew Collection, No. 635, fol. 151, this Donnell O'Donovan, who submitted to O'Neill at Inishcarra, and afterwards relapsed to the English who pardoned and protected him, married the daughter of Sir Owen Mac Carthy Reagh. He had eleven sons, two of whom, Donnell and Conogher, are given in this document by name, but the others are marked, "*nine sons more, all children*," which shews that this pedigree was penned during the life-time of this Donnell O'Donovan, who lived to a great age. It appears by a Chancery record, signed by Adam Loftus, Lord Chancellor of Ireland, in February, 1592, that this Donnell O'Donovan became chief of his name on the death of his father, in 1584, and that he had married, some time before 1592, the daughter of the "great and potent" Sir Owen Mac Carthy Reagh. But there remains sufficient evidence to shew that he had been previously married to Helena Barry, daughter of William Barry, of Lislee, in the barony of Barryroe, the son of James fitz Richard Barry, Viscount Buttevant, and that she was the mother of his son and heir, Daniel O'Donovan, and probably of three others of his sons. This appears from an ode addressed to his eldest son on his succession to the chieftainship of Clancahill in 1639, by Muldowny O'Morrison. Of his eleven sons the names of only eight have been ascertained from contemporaneous documents, viz.:

1. Donell or Daniel O'Donovan, Chief of Clancahill. He accompanied Lord Castlehaven at the taking of Mallow, Doneraile, Milton, Connagh, and Rostellan, but he submitted to the peace of Ormond, in 1648, and afterwards raised, at his own expense, two companies of foot to serve His Majesty, by commission from the Duke of Ormond. It appears, from the King's letter in his favour, that, in 1649, he was reduced to great extremities by Cromwell's forces, "who seized upon all his estate, burning, killing, and destroying all that came in their way; and blew up with powder two of his, the said Donnell's, castles."

It further appears, from the family papers at Bawnlahan and Montpellier, that this O'Donovan surrendered his castles to the Commonwealth, Colonel Robert Phaier (Governor of Cork for the Parliament in 1649 and till 1660), having engaged to him "some satisfaction." This Daniel had four sons, the eldest of whom was the Right Honourable Daniel O'Donovan, M. P. for Baltimore, and a colonel of thirteen companies of foot, in the service of James II., and who was put on his trial for high treason at the Cork assizes of 1684. This appears from various documents, and particularly from his petition to James II. in 1689, in which he states that "his father raised two companies of foote, commanded by Petitioner's uncles, who were both slain in his late Majesty's service. That, by his late Majesty's letter, Petitioner was to be restored to an ancient estate, worth about £2000 per annum, but, by the partiality of the late Government, was deprived of it. That Petitioner suffered long imprisonment by the op-

re roile im tigearnur dSrmuman .i. mac még cárthaiġ riaḃaiġ fíngin, mac donnchaiḋ, mic doṁnaill, mic fingin, ⁊ mac még cárthaiġ móir .i. doṁnaill,

pression of the late Earl of Orrerie, and was tried for his life before Lord Chief Justice Keating and Sir Richard Reynalls, upon account of the late pretended plot. That Petitioner, by Commission, raised, about Christmas, a Regiment of foot, and ever since kept them without any subsistence from your Majestie, whereby Petitioner is exposed to censure, &c., &c. That Petitioner's habitation and estate are exposed to the sea, and pirates frequently annoying the inhabitants, so that it is requisite to have still men in arms thereabouts."

The descendants of this Colonel Daniel, the eldest son of the O'Donovan who submitted to O'Neill, became extinct, in the senior line, in the late General Richard O'Donovan, of Bawnlahan (the son of Daniel, son of Richard, son of Colonel Daniel O'Donovan, M.P.), in the year 1829, and in the next and only surviving line, in 1841, in Captain Cornelius O'Donovan, who died without issue at Dingle in that year.

2. The second son of the O'Donovan who submitted to O'Neill was Teige, who died in 1639, and who is now represented by O'Donovan of Montpellier, near Cork, who is the present chief of the O'Donovans, according to the English law of primogeniture, which has been observed by this family since the year 1584, but scarcely ever before that year; for it appears from a Chancery record, already quoted, that, previously to that year, "the best and worthiest of the blood of the O'Donovans" was elected to be chief, according to the law of tanistic succession. On the nature of this succession the celebrated Jesuit, Edmund Campion, wrote the following remark, in 1571, in his *Historie of Ireland*, cap. vi.:

"The inheritance descendeth not to the sonne, but to the brother, nephew, or cousin-germaine, eldest and most valiant: for the Childe being oftentimes left in nonage, or otherwise young and unskillfull, were never able to defend his patrimonie, being his no longer than he can hold it by force of armes. But by that time he grow to a competent age, and have buryed an Uncle or two, he also taketh his turne, and leaveth it, in like order, to his posterity. This custome breedeth among them continuall Warres and treasons."

3. The third son of the O'Donovan who submitted to O'Neill was Captain Morogh O'Donovan, who had command of one of his brother's companies of foot, and was killed in His Majesty's service, at Rathmines, during the siege of Dublin, in 1649. This Morogh had one daughter, Joan, who was living in 1629, as appears by her grandfather's will, made in that year, but no son of his is anywhere mentioned.

4. The fourth son of the O'Donovan who submitted to O'Neill was Donough or Denis O'Donovan, who was his son by Joan, or Juanna Mac Carthy, as appears from an Irish poem addressed to him in his mother's lifetime. This Donough had a son, Captain Daniel O'Donovan, who took Castletownshend on the 9th of March, 1688-9, and who is the ancestor of the present James O'Donovan, of Cooldurragha, who is believed, among the peasantry of Carbery, to be *the O'Donovan*, since the death of Captain Cornelius O'Donovan, of Dingle, in 1841.

5. The fifth son of the O'Donovan who submitted to O'Neill was Dermot, or Jeremias, who was wounded at Prague in 1648, where he was highly commended for his dexterity and bravery, as appears from Carve's *Lyra*, pp. 332, 333, in which the following notice of him is given:

"Ferdinandus Tertius Romanorum Imperator cum Pontificia dispensatione Mariam Leopoldinam *Lincii* sibi copulavit. 26 Mensis Quintilis

namely, the son of Mac Carthy Reagh, i. e. Fineen, the son of Donough, son of Donnell, son of Fineen, and Mac Carthy More, i. e. Donnell, son of Donnell,

Konigsmarchius arcem Pragensem cum parva parte ex improviso per stratagema occupavit, ubi præter ingentem thesaurum, & spolia Cardinalem ab Harach, cum variis Regni proceribus intercepit: nihilominùs novâ & antiquâ civitate potiri non potuit, quare postmodum Carolus Pfaltzgravius Suecorum Supremus Bellidux cum nonnullis copiis illuc advenit, ubi sine intermissione ambas civitates tormentis bellicis quatere cæpit: tamen à Cæsarianis strenuè resistentibus, perditis aliquot millibus, repulsus fuit. Inter hos quidem Hiberni fortiter dimicarunt, quorum duces Jeremias *Donovan*, & Joannes *Murrian* [Mulrian?] è quibus Donovan in Læva globulo trajectus fuit, unde ob suam dexteritatem, ac magnanimitatem à supremis Ducibus Civitatis apud suam Cæsaream Majestatem plurimùm recommendatus fuit."

6. The sixth son of this O'Donovan, was Captain Richard, who, as stated in the King's letter already quoted, "had command of one of his brother's companies of foote, and retired himselfe and company into forraigne partes, and there was also killed in our service, when he had first, as Captaine of the other foote company in Collonell O'Driscoll's Regiment, contributed his best endeavours for the furtherance of our service, till the late usurped power became prevalent in our said kingdome of Ireland." This Richard had a son, Richard, who was educated in the University of Toulouse, where he obtained the degree of Doctor of both Laws, and afterwards studied the Canon Law in England, and was appointed Judge of the High Court of Admiralty in Ireland by James II. This Dr. Richard O'Donovan was elected Member of Parliament for Baltimore in April, 1689, but he resigned to Jeremie O'Donovan, head of the sept of Clanloughlin. This Dr. Richard O'Donovan left four sons, and some of his race, many of whom served in the English navy, are still extant, but the Editor has not been able to learn where they are.

7. The seventh son of the O'Donovan who submitted to O'Neill was Keadagh O'Donovan, who is mentioned, in his father's will, as a boy in 1629, and who was living in 1689, when he is referred to as one of the burgesses of Baltimore. He had two sons: 1. Daniel, the ancestor of Richard Donovan, Esq., of Lisheens House, Ballincollig; and 2. Richard, the ancestor of Timothy O'Donovan, Esq., of Ardahill, near Bantry, who is married to a niece of the late Daniel O'Connell, Esq., M. P.

No reference to the Conogher mentioned in the Lambeth pedigree, or to the other three sons, who were children when that pedigree was written (circ. 1610), has been found in the family documents at Bawnlahan or Montpellier. They probably died young or left their native territory. According to the vivid tradition among that sept of the O'Donovans to which the Editor belongs, his ancestor, whose name was Edmond O'Donovan, removed from Bawnlahan, in the county of Cork, to Gaulstown, in the south of the county of Kilkenny, some time previously to 1643; and the Editor has been long of opinion that he was one of the sons of this O'Donovan, who succeeded in 1584, by his first wife, Helena Barry.

The Editor has carefully examined all the tombstones, parish registries, and old persons of the race of this Edmond recently, and had questioned others, now many years dead, on the exact nature of this tradition, and found that the tradition is simply as follows: Edmond, the son of O'Donovan of Bawnlahan, in the county of Cork, killed the eldest son of O'Sullivan Beare [*quære* Dermot, son of Sir Owen, ætatis 20, A. D. 1616?] in a dispute about the boundary between

mac Domhnaill, mic Domhnaill mic Corbmaic Ladhraigh. Tangatar ann meic Ríogh Ealla. Tangattar ann uí Donnchudha, uí Donnabháin, ⁊ uí Mathghamhna.

their estates, which adjoined each other, and, fearing the vengeance of the O'Sullivans, fled to the county of Kilkenny, where he took shelter with William, son of Walter Bourke, commonly called "the Gaul Bourke," whose daughter, Catherine, he married. His father having discovered where he was, came to Gaulstown, accompanied by several gentlemen, to bring him home. The fugitive, Edmond, apprehensive that his father, who dreaded the English Government, might wish to coax him home to have him put on his trial, according to the English laws, for the killing of O'Sullivan's son, hesitated, for some time, before he would make his appearance; but at length, by advice of the Gaul, he consented to come to an interview with his father, but with such a guard as to prevent him and his attendants from seizing his person. They parleyed near the gate of the castle of Gaulstown. The father earnestly entreated him to return home, saying that it was the belief among the septs of Carbery that the death of O'Sullivan's son was accidental, and that no enmity then existed between the two families on account of it, and that both wished the fugitive to return home. Edmond replied, that he had no wish to return home; that he was married, and dwelt at a place called Ballinlaw; that his posterity might return to Bawnlahan; but for himself, if he got the whole of Carbery, he would not think his life safe, and would not live there. His father returned home in anger, and Edmond was soon after slain, together with his father-in-law, the Gaul Bourke, at Ballinvegga (March 18, 1642-3), where a spirited battle was fought between General Preston and the Duke of Ormond, in which a great slaughter was made of the county of Kilkenny gentlemen. The descendants of this Edmond, as carefully traced by the Editor, were as follows:

I. Edmond left two infant sons, viz.: Richard, who grew up a fierce freebooter, and lived at Ballinlaw, one of Gaul Bourke's castles, out of which, according to tradition, he shot many persons; but he was finally shot himself, at Snow Hill, on the brink of the River Suir. He had led a party of men across the Suir, who seized on a prey of cattle in Gaultier, in the county of Waterford, but, being overtaken by a strong force, he was deprived of the booty, and obliged to cross the river by swimming. The Gaultier men pursued him in boats, and shot him dead, with his own gun, on the opposite strand, near Snowhill. This is said to have been the last *creach*, or prey, attempted in this part of Ireland. This Richard left one daughter, but no son.

II. Conchobhar, or Cornelius, the second son of Edmond, who lived with his mother at Ballymountain, near Gaulstown, where the ruins of his house were shewn when the Editor was a child. He lived an honest man, and married Rose Kavanagh, of the family of Ballyleigh, in the county of Carlow, the aunt of the "renowned warrior," Brian-na-Stroicė Kavanagh, who fought with great bravery at the Boyne and Aughrim, in the service of James II. He had by her three sons, viz.: John Donovan of Ballynearl, William of Drumdowney, the Editor's great grandfather, and Edmond, who went to France. John of Ballynearl, who was usually called Shane-*na-gcrann*, i. e. John of the Trees, from the number of trees which he planted, and Shane *a' phudair*, from powdering his wig, was a very respectable gentleman. He was born in 1672, and died in 1735, aged sixty-three years, as appears from his tombstone in the churchyard of Dunkitt. He lived at Ballynearl, near Kilmacow, in the barony of Iverk, and county of Kilkenny, where

son of Donnell, son of Cormac Ladhrach. Thither repaired the sons of the chiefs of Allow. Thither repaired the O'Donohoes, O'Donovans, and O'Mahonys,

he acquired a considerable property by marriage and otherwise. His hatred of the Cromwellian settlers amounted almost to insanity, and, in one of his angry moods, he let drop words about the glaring injustice of the Act of Settlement, on account of which he was committed for Treason, on the evidence of one of those settlers. He was tried at Kilkenny; but his neighbour, John Bishopp, Esq., of Bishopp's Hall, *alias* Gaulskill, made the most strenuous exertions to defeat his accuser, and succeeded, amid the rage of party feelings, in procuring an acquittal. His relatives, the Fitzpatricks of Upper Ossory, and the Kavanaghs of the mountains of Carlow, are said to have flocked into the town of Kilkenny on the day of his trial, determined to rescue him in case of his being condemned, and twenty-four beardless youths entered the court-house, dressed in their sisters' clothes, having swords concealed under their mantles! No riot, however, took place, for, on John's acquittal, they left the town quietly, very grateful to Mr. Bishopp for the high testimony he bore to their cousin's character. This John had many sons, of whom three went to France, but the Editor has not been able to learn their names. Four of his sons remained in Ireland, of whom three were buried in the churchyard of Dunkitt, as appears from a large tombstone near the south wall of the old church, viz.: the Rev. Edmond Donovan, P. P. of Kilmacow; Dominick Donovan of the Ferrybank, Waterford; and William Donovan, a youth of gigantic size and strength, who died of the small-pox in the twentieth year of his age. He had another son, Cornelius Donovan of Graigoving (Ʒráiʒ O'ꝼꝼinn), whose only son, Thomas, died at Illud, a few years since, without issue. The race of this John are now extinct in Ireland.

Edmond, the third son of Cornelius, went into the French service. The last account ever heard of him by his family was his having been taken prisoner at Waterford in 1739, whither he had come over to enlist men, *alias* "Wild Geese," for the French service. The Editor's grandfather saw him in the hands of the authorities, and conveyed to the old gaol of Waterford, but was not able to get in to speak to him; but, in about a week afterwards, the prisoner sent a messenger from the village of Passage, to his brother William, who was then living at Aughmore (a part of Drumdowney), stating that he had been set at liberty, and that he was ready to set sail for France. His family never afterwards heard from or of him. He had gone into the French service with several of his relatives, the Kavanaghs of the county of Carlow, who were all killed in the wars except Morgan More, who was considered to be the largest man in Europe in his time, and who returned to Ireland, after various romantic adventures, and died at an advanced age at Graiguenamanagh about the year 1780.

III. William Kavanagh O'Donovan, the second son of Cornelius of Ballymountain, son of Edmond of Bawnlahan. The old people who remembered him, when the Editor was young, were wont to describe him as immoderately vain of his descent from the Kavanaghs of Ballyleigh and the Burkes of Gaulstown, who stated in their family epitaph, that they were descended from Sir William de Burgo, who was "Vice-chamberlaine to Kinge Edward the Third." He always asserted that his grandfather, Edmond, was the *eldest* son of O'Donovan of Bawnlahan, in the county of Cork (an assertion which the Editor has not been yet able either to substantiate, or entirely to refute), but he knew little or nothing of the history of his paternal ancestors beyond a vague idea of their being descended from the

Tangatap ann upmop gall, ⁊ gaoidel da cóiccid mumhan (ina mbaoí o baile móp amac) go numla ⁊ gonuppaim dUa neill, ⁊ an tí láp ná piacht pochtain

kings of Munster, and possessed of very extensive estates till deprived of the greater part of them by Cromwell and William III. Though proud, almost to lunacy, of his Irish and Anglo-Norman lineage, and imbued with irremoveable prejudices against the Cromwellian settlers,—to whom he was wont to say, without reserve, that they were descended from "English pick-pockets,"—he was induced to marry the daughter of one of those settlers, namely, Mary, the daughter of Richard Oberlin or Hoberlin, who came over with his father, Richard Hoberlin, in Cromwell's army, in 1649. This woman, who had been brought up in all the puritanical prejudices of her time, fell in love with William, though she detested his race and his religion! Laws, and even religious prejudices, sometimes prove but insignificant barriers against the propensities of humanity, and the powerful affection of the sexes. In this instance a plebeian Puritanical heiress married a proud but poor Papist; thereby so horrified her grandmother that she returned to England; and in course of time, being far removed from puritanical preachers, gradually submitted to all the ceremonies of the Church of Rome; permitted all her children to go to Mass, who, strange to say, learned to hate and despise the Cromwellian settlers. By Mary Hoberlin, William had five sons and eight daughters, whose progeny have since contributed largely to the population of Newfoundland, Canada, and the United States of America; but the Editor has not been able to trace their exact localities. The sons were: 1. Richard, born in 1718; he was a man of powerful strength of body, but of a ferocious and murderous disposition, inheriting the pride, vanity, and folly of his father, and the iron constitution, stature, and recklessness of his Cromwellian grandfather. After he had grown up to man's estate, perceiving the power which the laws allowed him to obtain over his father, he quarrelled with him about certain lands which were obtained in right of his mother, but the father not acceding to his demands, he conformed to the established religion of the State with a view to dispossess his father and mother; but not succeeding at all to his satisfaction, he left his father, and the last account heard of him was his having committed suicide on board an English man-of-war. The second son was Edmond, the Editor's grandfather; 3. Cornelius of Ballyfasy; 4. John of Rochestown; and 5. William of Attateemore. When this William, the fifth son of William, was a child, there was no Roman Catholic school in the barony of Ida, and he remained illiterate till he was about thirty-five years old, when, fired with the love of learning, he went to school along with his own children, and, amidst the ridicule of his neighbours, learned to read and write! It is painful to allude to the laws which, at this period, brought the enthusiastic people of Ireland to this level. The descendants of the proud and improvident ancient Irish chieftains multiplied, about this period (from 1704 to 1789), in obscurity and poverty, as if destined, in future ages, to send forth swarms to people the back woods of America.

William, No. III., held the lands of Drumdowney on lease, and he possessed, in fee, the townlands of Ballyvrougham, Ballybrahy, and Knockbrack, in the barony of Ida, and county of Kilkenny; and, with a view to carry on trade as a merchant, he built a store-house at the Ferry-bank, Waterford, which was burned to the ground, about the year 1748, by an accidental fire, which involved him in such difficulties and anxieties as hastened his death, which took place in the year 1749, as appears from his tombstone.

and the greater number of the English and Irish of the two provinces of Munster (except those in the great towns), to submit and pay their homage

IV. Edmond, son of William. He was born in the year 1720, and married, in 1750, Mary Archdeacon, daughter of John, son of Patrick, son of Pierce Archdeacon, of Ercke, in the county of Kilkenny, who was commonly called "Sir Pierce Mac Oda."—See note ', under the year 1544, p. 1488, *supra*; and who was also descended from Edmond Denn the Tory (who was believed to be the representative of William Denn, Lord Justice of Ireland in 1260), from whom Sliabh-Ua-gCruinn, in the south of the county of Kilkenny, was called Tory Hill.

This Edmond took the lands of Attateemore, *alias* Putney's Part, in the parish of Kilcolumb, barony of Ida, and county of Kilkenny, from Colonel Dyas of Melville, in 1763, where he settled, with his wife and family. He had five sons: 1. William (born in 1752, died in 1802), whose descendants have settled in various parts of the United States of America; 2. Patrick, born in 1754. This Patrick was a good scholar, and travelled much in his youth, and, after varieties of strange and romantic adventures by sea and land, he returned to Ireland about the year 1784. He was a very sensible man, of strong powers of intellect, good memory, and much experience. He was the living repertory of the traditions of the counties of Kilkenny, Carlow, and Wexford. The Editor spent much of his time with him in the years 1821, 1822, and 1823, and from him he first caught that love for ancient Irish and Anglo-Irish history and traditions which have since afforded him so much amusement. He died in November, 1831, and was interred at Dunkitt, leaving several sons who are still living. 3. John, born in 1758, died in 1837, leaving three sons still, or lately, living near Waterford; 4. Edmond, the Editor's father, of whom presently; 5. Michael, still living in the eighty-fourth year of his age, who has several sons living; and 6. Cornelius, who died young. This Edmond, son of William, died on the 26th December, 1798, aged seventy-eight. After his death Nicholas the *Keener*, the local dirge-composer, the last of his profession in this part of Ireland, came to the Editor's father, offering to sing the pedigree of the deceased, and praise all his relations, widely diffused throughout the region extending from Mount Leinster to Waterford, and from Waterford to Carrick-on-Suir; but the latter would not allow him to proceed, as he knew that Nicholas would sing much hollow flattery about the glories of the Kavanaghs, &c.; he turned the *Keener* out of his house, which was considered a daring violation of ancient custom; and the traditions remained unsung ever since. But a few years before, on the death of his nephew, John, son of William, son of William, son of Cornelius, son of Edmond of Bawnlahan, the traditions were, for the last time, sung in the most sincere and enthusiastic strain of natural eloquence by his nurse, Bridget Dwyer, who repeated his pedigree and recounted many members of the Kavanaghs, his relatives, and various other families whom the Editor has not been able to identify.

V. Edmond Oge, son of Sean-Edmond. He was born, in the year 1760, at Kilcolumb, in the barony of Ida, and county of Kilkenny, but removed to Attateemore, *alias* Putney's Part, in 1763, with his father, mother, and grandmother. His elder brothers, William, Patrick, and John, did not remain with their father after they had grown up, but went to seek their fortunes to different parts of the world. The Editor's father, Edmond, alone remained in Ireland, and took a lease, in his own name, of the lands of Attateemore some time about the year 1791, and, being an industrious man, he was pretty

ina ḋocom díoḃ, ráinic comarḋa umla, ⁊ seóid uaḋa dia ṡaiġiḋ cenmoṫá an barraċ mór rémraite, ⁊ ticcſrna murccraiġe .i. Corbmac mac diarmata, ⁊ ó Suilleḃáin bſirre .i. doṁnall, mac doṁnall, mic diarmata. Tarraiḋ O néill oċt mbraiġde décc do ṁaiṫiḃ muṁan ar in fforlongport sin, ⁊ baí fri ré ḟiċſt lá ag crúḋ cſrt, ⁊ caingſn fſr muṁan, ⁊ accá síoḋucchaḋ fſin fri aroile ina nſsaonta.

Maguidir .i. Aoḋ mac conconnaċt bairiḋe i ffarraḋ í neill an tan sin. Laiṫe naén (a mís marta na bliaḋna so, gar bſcc ria ffeil Patraicc) dia ndeachaiḋ siḋe díorma marcslóiġ, ⁊ araill do ṫroiġṫeċoiḃ do ċor cuarta na noirſr i nimeċtair an longpuirt, ⁊ ni ro hairireaḋ lais go ráinicc go dorus chinn tráile, ⁊ assiḋe go rinn Chorráin .i. baile an ḃarraiġ óicc hi ccenel Aoḋa. Soaid iaraṁ co naircenib ⁊ co nédalaiḃ, co lion ffaob ⁊ ffeolmaiġ. O rordar sccitigh diúdlaoí iar ccian artar la haiḋble a naircene ⁊ a nédala, ba sſḋ do ronsat muinntſr ṁéguidir airisſṁ isin maiġin ba coiṁnſsa doiḃ do ċoṁda a ccreach ⁊ a nedala, ⁊ Ro triall Máguidir gan anaḋ gan airisioṁ do ḋenaṁ go roċtain dó go longport uí néill. An tan ro fáccaiḃ Máguidir an forlongport torac an laoí sin fſin do ḋeachaiḋ sgéla go Corcaiġ do ṡaiġiḋ Sir Uáram salender (fſr ionaid Presidens dá ċoiccid muṁan) dia airnſis dó Maguidir do ḋol ar an longport i nuachaḋ sloiġ aṁail do ċoiḋ, ⁊ an lſth i ndeachaiḋ. Ni ṫard Sir Uaram i ffaill in ní sin, aċt ro tſcclamaḋ lais gasraiḋ do ṁarcsloiġ mſrḋa fo ċedóir, atiad armḋa eidiġte, ⁊ ro gluais a Corcaiġ amach do ṡaiġiḋ ſnaiġ iomċuṁaing in rob erḋálta lais Máguidir do roċtain dia ṡaiġiḋ acc sóaḋ dó tar a ais. Cian,

affluent during Napoleon's wars. He was married on the 6th of October, 1788, to Eleanor Hoberlin, of Rochestown, by the Rev. Dr. Stephen Louer, Vicar-General and Protonotary Apostolic of the see of Ossory. He had by her, Michael, who died in May, 1840, leaving one son, Edmond, now living; 2. Patrick, who died young; 3. William, still living in America; 4. John, the Editor of these Annals, who was baptized by the Rev. John Fitzpatrick, P. P. of Slieveroe, on the 26th of July, 1809, "Edmundo Wall & Eleanorâ Neill sponsoribus."—*Regist. Par. Slieveroe:* and 5. Patrick, still living. This Edmond, who was a man of great strength, courage, and *illibata fides*, died on the 29th of July, 1817, desiring his eldest son, who sat by his bedside till he expired, to remember his descent, which he repeated to him emphatically several times over, in the Editor's hearing, and not to allow his children to disperse, if possible! He requested that his body should be buried "along with the good men at Dunkitt, but not under the large tombstone." This was complied with, and the Editor, in twenty-four years afterwards, remembering his dying request, caused the following epitaph to be inscribed to the memory of him and his ancestors:

to O'Neill; and such of them as were not able to come to him sent him tokens of submission and presents, except Barry, before mentioned, and the Lord of Muskerry, i. e. Cormac, the son of Dermot [Mac Carthy], and O'Sullivan Beare, i. e. Donnell, the son of Donnell, son of Dermot. O'Neill obtained eighteen hostages of the chieftains of Munster at that camp; and he remained twenty days examining the disputes and covenants of the men of Munster, and reconciling them to each other in their contentions.

Maguire, i. e. Hugh, the son of Cuconnaught, was along with O'Neill at this time. One day in the month of March of this year, a short time before the festival of St. Patrick, he sent out a troop of cavalry, and another of infantry, to scour the districts in the neighbourhood of the camp; and he did not halt till he arrived at the gates of Kinsale, and from thence [he went] to Rinn-Corrain[x], the castle of Barry Oge, in Cinel-Aedha[y]. He afterwards returned back with preys and spoils, with a deal of accoutrements and flesh meat. As Maguire's people were fatigued at the end of the day, after a long journey, on account of the vastness of their plunders and spoils, they halted and encamped at the nearest [convenient] place, to protect their preys and spoils; but Maguire set out, [resolved] to make no stay or delay until he should arrive at O'Neill's camp. When Maguire had left the camp in the morning of that day, a message was sent to Cork to Sir Warham Salender[z], deputy of the Governor of the two provinces of Munster, acquainting him that Maguire had gone forth from the camp with a small force, as indeed he had, and [mentioning] the direction in which he had passed. Sir Warham did not neglect this thing, but immediately assembled a body of vigorous, well-armed, mail-clad horsemen, and marched with them from Cork to a narrow defile, by which he was sure Maguire would pass on his return back. He had not been long in this ambush[a] when he saw

"POSTERIS EDMUNDI O'DONOVAN
DE GAULSTOWN, GALLI DE BURGO GENERI,
VIRIS VERE HONESTIS AC PIIS,
MENTIS CORPORISQUE VI POLLENTIBUS,
QUORUM CORPORA HIC JACENT SEPULTA;
AC PRÆSERTIM PATRI EDMUNDO,
DE ATA-TEMORIA,
QUI OBIIT 29[a] DIE JULII A. D. 1817,
ET AVUNCULIS GULIELMO ET PATRICIO,
JOANNES O'DONOVAN
HOC MONUMENTUM POSUIT."

[x] *Rinn-chorrain*, translated *cuspis falcis* by P. O'Sullevan Beare, and anglicised Rincorran.—See *Pacata Hibernia*, book 2, c. xiii.

[y] *Cinel-Aedha*, now Kinelea, a barony in the south of the county of Cork.

[z] *Salender:* i. e. St. Leger, now pronounced, in Ireland, Salenger. P. O'Sullevan Beare writes it Salincher.

[a] *In this ambush.*—A very different account of this transaction is given in the *Pacata Hibernia*,

gairit, baoisiuṁ isin ſoarnaiḋe hisin at chí Máguiḋir cucca co na uathaḋ marcsloiġ, ⁊ iar ffairccsin a roile doiḃ nír bó cſim ar ccúlaiḃ, ⁊ nir bo rún iomgaḃala, na mſnma tſichme ro ba gnésac lár an tí do riaċt hisuiḋe, aċt a aiccneaḋ darduccaḋ ⁊ arccnaṁ for a aghaiḋ do ḃáruccaḋ a ḃioḋḃaḋ aṁail do roine don chur sin, uair ro ionnsaiġ sium ⁊ Sir Uaram a ċéle go haṁnas aindiarraiḋ, ⁊ go dána durcroiḋeaċ go ro ġon ceċtarnae dioḃ aroile. Aċt cſna torċair Uáram fo céḋoir lá Maguiḋir. Do roċratar beós coiccſr don ṁarcsloiġ baí hi ffarraḋ Sir Uáram lá Máguiḋir mar an ccéḋna. Ar a aoí tra ro gonaḋ ⁊ ro gertreaġdaḋ eisium buḋſin isin iorġail sin co nár bó hinḟſḋma fri fſrstal anfforlainn don chur sin. Coniḋ ſoh do roine dol trſmpa gan airisiuṁ fri hiomġuin ní báḋ sisi, ⁊ nir bo cian do ċoiḋ a hionad an iomairecc an tan dus fairic anbfainne écca ċucca gur bo hſiccſn dó dſḋail fri a eoch co nerbail gan ḟuirec ar a haitle. Do ċóiḋ an

book 1, c. ii., in which it is stated, that "Sir Warham St. Leger and Sir Henry Power riding out of the Citie for recreation to take the aire, accompanied with sundry Captaines and gentlemen, with a few horse for their Guard, not dreaming of an enemie neere at hand, carelesly riding, every one as he thought good; within a mile of the Town, or a little more, Sir Warham St. Leger, and one of his servants, a little straggling from his companie, was, in a narrow way, suddenly charged by Mac Guire, who, with some horse (likewise dispersed), had spread a good circuit of ground, in hope either to get some bootie, or to have the killing of some Subjects: they charged each other. Sir Warham discharged his Pistoll and shot the Traytor, and he was strucken with the other Horseman's staff in the head, of which woundes either of them dyed, but none else, on either side, was slaine."

[b] *On perceiving each other*, iar ffaircсsin aroile doiḃ. This phrase is incorrect language. It should be constructed thus: "iar ḃ-fairsin a ḃioḋḃaḋ nír ḃo céim ar g-cúlaiḃ do róine, ⁊ nír ḃo rún iomġaḃála na meanma teichṁe ro tairelḃ, aċt (mar ba gnésaċ), a aiccneaḋ d'árduġaḋ, ⁊ arccnaṁ for a aghaiḋ do ḃaruc-ċaḋ a ḃioḋḃaḋ."

[c] *Five of the horsemen.*—It is stated in the *Pacata Hibernia*, book 1, c. ii., that Sir Warham St. Leger and Maguire were mutually slain by each other, but that "none else, on either side, were slaine," and it is to be suspected that the Four Masters are wrong. P. O'Sullevan Beare gives the following account of this rencounter, and of O'Neill's expedition to the South of Ireland, in his *Hist. Cathol. Iber. Compend.*, tom. 3, lib. 5, c. xii.:

"Paucis inde diebus in Vltoniam venerunt Frater Mathæus Ouetensis Hispanus Dubhlinnæ Archiepiscopus, & Martinus Gerda nobilis eques Hispanus deferentes à Summo Pontifice omnibus, qui pro fide in Anglos arma caperent, indulgentias, et peccatorum veniam, et Onello Phœnicis pennam, & á Rege Catholico Philippo Tertio (nam secundus obierat diem) viginti duo millia aureorum numorum in militum stipendium. Hispanis legatis reuersis, Onellus relictis in Tirona validis præsidijs ipse cum nonnullis belli socijs non spernendas copias ducens, & visum frustulum sacrosanctæ Crucis, quod in

Maguire coming on with a small party of cavalry; and after perceiving each other[b], the person who had arrived thither did not retreat back, or exhibit a desire to shun, or an inclination to fly; but, rousing up his courage, as was his wont, he advanced forwards to kill his enemies, as he did on this occasion, for he and Sir Warham attacked each other fiercely and angrily, boldly and resolutely, and mutually wounded each other severely. But, however, Sir Warham was immediately slain by Maguire, and five of the horsemen[c] who were along with Sir Warham were also slain by Maguire; but he was himself so deeply and severely wounded in that conflict, that he was not able to contend with an overwhelming force on that occasion, so that he passed through them without waiting for further contest; but he had not passed far from the scene of battle when he was overtaken by the languor of death, so that he was obliged to alight from his horse, and he expired immediately after. The death of Maguire

monasterio Sanctæ Crucis fuisse fertur, & exploratum Ibernorum animos, & an hostis auderet occurrere, in Momonias hyeme media procedens in agro Corcachano tentoria collocat. Vbi Macguier è castris digressus ab Edmundo Maccaphrio signifero suo, Nello Odurnino, & vno sacerdote comitatus incidit in VVarhamum Salincherum Anglum equitem Auratum Momoniarum præfectum equitibus sexaginta stipatum. Inter eos præter publicas inimicitiarum causas ea etiam priuata æmulatio erat: quòd Macguieri Iberni, VVarhamo Angli præter omnes partis vtriusque equites fortitudine, & dexteritate palmam, & principem locum deferebant. Macguier conspecta hostilis equitatus multitudine, nec fugere, nec sese dedere ex sua dignitate esse putauit. Sed additis equo calcaribus in medios hostes proruit. Illum hasta vibrantem plumbea glande ex bombardula VVarhamus ferit. Nihilominus Macguier VVarhamum hasta appetit & ictum euitare cupientem capitis declinatione per cassidem transfigit, & hastam á capite pendentem relinquens stricto gladio per medios hostes euadit, duobus equitibus etiam saucijs, & sacerdote sequentibus: rursusquè circumacto equo proruens omnes fundit, & fugat, nec longè secutus priusquam in castra venit ad Onellum, equo descendens à sacerdote expiatus ex vulnere animam efflat. Cuius equus posteà cibo spontè abstinuisse fertur, donec inedia perierit. VVarhamus quoque ex vulnere ad insaniam redactus intra dies quindecim è vita discessit. Onellus secum deferens Donatum Maccarrham Allæ competitorem, ne in Anglorum gratiam rediret, in Vltoniam reuertitur, Vrmonio Comite, qui videbatur prælio dimicaturus, nihil obstante. Vertebatur annus millesimus sexcentesimus, cum Carolus Bluntus Montis læti Baro cum proregio imperio mense Februario in Iberniam mittitur. Qui profectus in Vltoniam omnium antecessorum minimé progressus Fachartam tantum peruenit. Vbi tribus amplius mensibus castrametatus, & ab Onello quotidianis prælijs, & vallo fossaque ductis in itinere interclusus aditu ad Ardmacham, & Iurem infecta re Dubhlinnam redit. Onellus nihil memorabile damni fecit præterquám, quôd Petrum Lessium Momonium strenuum equitem, cuius superius mentionem fecimus, bombardæ iactu in capite vulneratum desiderauit."

bás sin Mhéguidhir i nuetmaille menman ⁊ i nimirte aiccnidh dUa neill, ⁊ do ṁaiṫiḃ gaoidel arċena. Nír bó maċtnaḋ son ar bá heiside rinn ágha, ⁊ iomġona, sciaṫ imḋeġla, ⁊ anacail tuir foṫaighte, ⁊ fulaing, uaitne einiġ, ⁊ engnaṁa na noirġiall ina reiṁes, ⁊ urṁoir ġaoidel archena.

Atbeartat araile na roiseaḋ O neill ar an muṁain go beltaine ar ccinn munbaḋ oidheaḋ Mhéguidhir amlaiḋ sin. Coniḋ eḋ do roine gaḃail don taoibh buḋeas soir do Chorcaiġ, do ḋúṫaiġ an ḃarraiġ móir, do ċríċ Roisteċ, ⁊ do ċloinn ġiobúin. Ceileaḃrais do Mhuiṁneachaiḃ iar sin, ⁊ ro ġeall dia ccaoṁraḋ ón ccoccaḋ baí fair acc Saxanchoiḃ toċt do riḋiri dfioirġleóḋ a nimreasain ⁊ do ċrúḋ a ccaingean, ⁊ dia ríoḋuccaḋ fri a roile. Rucc dna drong dia raétclannaiḃ i ngeillsine, ⁊ i ngeiṁliḃ lais go riaċt go tír eoġain. Ro ḟáccaiḃ araill ele dioḃ i norláiṁ Iarla dearmuṁan, ⁊ Rémainn mic Seaain a burc. Do raḋ a uġdarrás féin, ⁊ barántas ar ḃuannacht da míle fear do diarmait ó ċoncoḃair, ⁊ do cloinn tSeain a burc i ngeallṫacaiḃ ar daiġ a cconganta, ⁊ a ffollamnaiġṫe do bheiṫ acc iarla dearmuṁan. Luiḋ Ua neill iarttain a reiḋ dírġe gaċa róid do cliaiḋ Máil mic Uġaine, do Shiúir, laiṁḋeas le Caiseal, gé ro baoí an lustis, ⁊ an Presidens go narmáil iomḋa do ṁuir, ⁊ do tír iar ttecht go haṫ cliaṫ is na céd laiṫiḃ do Márta ⁊ gé ro baí Iarla tuaḋmuṁan ⁊ Iarla urmuṁan hi luimneaċ i noirchill ar a ġaḃailsiuṁ a ndeas do ċoiḋ siuṁ tarra hi ffrioṫroscc, ⁊ a ffriṫing gaċa conaire in ro ġaḃ ag dol don muṁain go roċtain dó tar a ais i ttír eoġain gan turbaiḋ gan tesccṁáil, gan amus bealaiġ, ná bearnaḋ, gan eċt, baḋ ionmaoiḋiṁ dfaġḃáil uaḋa, aċt Máguiḋir a aénar aṁail remebertmar.

Iarla urmuṁan, ⁊ Iarla tuaḋmuṁan do ḋol o luimneaċ i ccoir Siuire i niarmóireacht Uí néill, ⁊ ar ndol dó tairrsiḃ gan tacar, gan tesccmail, ro loisccead arḃar ⁊ foirgnem hi ccloinn ġiobúin i ndutaiġ in Ridire finn lá hiarla tuaḋmuṁan. Do ċoidhriot an da Iarla sin i mbuitilerachaiḃ, ⁊ go cill ċainnigh coniḋ innteriḋe do rorsat an ċaiscc, ⁊ lottar iar saoire na cáscc co háṫ cliaṫ dfiaḋuccaḋ, ⁊ donoruccaḋ na noiffiçceaċ nua sin tangatar i nerinn .i. Lord mountioy an lustis, ⁊ Sir Seoirsi Carew Presidens

[d] *Valour and prowess.*—P. O'Sullevan Beare agrees pretty well with this character of Maguire, and Sir John Davis acknowledges that he was "a valiant rebel."

[e] *Cliadh-Mail-mhic-Ugaine*, a district lying between the hill of Knockany and the mountain of Slieve Reagh, in the barony of Coshlea, and county of Limerick.—See note [d], under the

caused a giddiness of spirits, and depression of mind, in O'Neill and the Irish chiefs in general; and this was no wonder, for he was the bulwark of valour and prowess[d], the shield of protection and shelter, the tower of support and defence, and the pillar of the hospitality and achievements of the Oirghialla, and of almost all the Irish of his time.

Some assert that O'Neill would not have returned from Munster until the May following, had it not been for the death of Maguire. He proceeded to the south-east of Cork, and through the country of Barry More, Roche's country, and Clann-Gibbon. He then took his leave of the Munstermen, promising them that, if he could seize an opportunity during this war waged upon him by the English, he would return again to settle their disputes, confirm their covenants, and establish peace among them. He took with him to Tyrone some of their chieftains, as hostages and prisoners, and left others of them in the hands of the Earl of Desmond, and of Redmond, the son of John Burke. He transferred his own authority, and gave a warranty for the hiring of two thousand men, to Dermot O'Conor and the sons of John Burke, in the country of the Geraldines, in order that the Earl of Desmond might have their assistance. O'Neill then passed on through the direct roads by Cliadh-Mail-mhic-Ugaine[e], and by the Suir, keeping Cashel to the right; and although the Lord Justice and the President had a great army, by land and sea, having landed in Dublin in the first days of March, and the Earls of Thomond and Ormond were at Limerick, awaiting his return from the south, he passed by them on his return by the same roads through which he had gone to Munster, until he got back to Tyrone, without receiving battle, opposition, or attack, upon any road or pass, and without losing any person of note, except Maguire alone, as we have before stated.

The Earl of Ormond and the Earl of Thomond set out from Limerick along the Suir, in pursuit of O'Neill; but he having passed them without receiving battle or rencounter, the Earl of Thomond burned corn and dwellings in Clann-Gibbon, the country of the White Knight. These two Earls [then] proceeded to the country of the Butlers, and to Kilkenny, where they passed Easter; and after the Easter holidays, they repaired to Dublin, to welcome and pay their respects to the new officers who had come to Ireland, namely, Lord Mountjoy,

year 1560; note [t], under 1570; and a passage under 1579, p. 1719, *supra*, in which Athneasy, a ford on the Morning Star River, is referred to as in the very centre of this territory.

da ċóiccidh muṁan. Iar ndenaṁ a ccuarta do na hiarladaiḃ sin i nÁth cliath, sóait tar a nais gan fuireċ, ⁊ an Presidens maraén rú go rangatar go cill cainniġ.

Nír bó cian iar sin go ro gaḃadh lá coinne etir Iarla urmuṁan ⁊ Uaitne mac Rudhraiġe óicc uí ṁordha go ccoiṁlíon daoíne, airm, ⁊ éidigh la ceaċtarnae isin iomaccallaiṁ isin. Rucc Iarla urmuṁan an Presidenc ⁊ Iarla tuadh-muṁan dia lfith féin isin ccoinne sin. An tan rangatar do díb lfitib gur an tulaiġ iomaccalṁa ro toġadh ſtorra a ccoṁfocraib ḃeóil áṫa ragat. Bátar ag cearrnuccadh a ccaingſn, ⁊ ag aiġnſs ima naccarṫaiḃ for a roile

[f] *Carey*.—He wrote it Carew himself, as appears from the State Papers; but his contemporary, Sir Henry Docwra, writes it Carey. The name is now called in Irish Cappún, Carroon, in the south of Ireland. For a full account of his appointment to the Presidency of Munster the reader is referred to the *Pacata Hibernia*, book 1, c. i. ii. and iii.

[g] *Bel-atha-Raghat*, now Ballyragget, a small town situated on the left bank of the River Nore, in the barony of Fassadinin, and county of Kilkenny, and not far from the boundary of the Queen's County. The ruins of the castle of Ballyragget are of considerable extent. They are situated in the demesne of Ballyragget Lodge, which belongs to Kavanagh of Borris-Idrone. In the *Pacata Hibernia*, book 1, c. iii., is given a minute account of the manner in which the Earl of Ormond was taken, in a joint letter from the Lord President of Munster and the Earl of Thomond to the Lords of the Council. In this letter it is stated, that this conference was held at a place called Corronneduffe, eight long miles from Kilkenny. There are two drawings of the taking of the Earl of Ormond which belong to two distinct points of time; one in the *Pacata Hibernia* (*ubi suprà*), which refers to the moment of meeting, when both parties were ranged opposite each other, and the parley beginning; and a sketch in Trinity College, Dublin, which has been engraved for Ledwich's Antiquities of Ireland (see second Edition, p. 276), which shews the taking of the Earl after the conference.

Leland says, book 4, c. v., "that the rebels of all quarters were considerably elated at this event, while the friends of Government, in this time of danger and jealousy, easily entertained suspicions that a leader, who had usually acted with due circumspection, could not have ran so blindly into danger unless he had formed a clandestine scheme of delivering himself into the hands of the rebels." The loyalty of Ormond, however, was not suspected by Carew or Thomond, or even by his enemy, Sir Charles O'Carroll, who, in a letter to the Lord Deputy Mountjoy at this period, acknowledges the Earl's loyalty, but observes, that "he hath no heyre male of his body to inherit his title," and that his next heirs were not over loyal to Her Majesty. This wily Irishman then writes:

"If the Erle of Tyrone (as his fact well deserveth) were cutt off, who were then so mightie in Ireland as the Erle's kindred, who, degeneratinge from his Lordship, yf they were once invested with that honnor, I will not say they would, but may well feare least they would follow their old bias, and become as undutyfull as they haue bene. And perhapps it boath is, and willbe nedfull for her Majestie to have a duteful subiect nere them that may be a meanes to crosse their actions. I know not to what

as Lord Justice, and Sir George Carey[f], the President of the two provinces of Munster. After having paid this visit to Dublin, the Earls returned back without delay, accompanied by the President, until they arrived at Kilkenny.

It was not long after this when a day of meeting was appointed between the Earl of Ormond and Owny, the son of Rury Oge O'Moreach, to have an equal number of men in arms and armour, to hold a conference; and the Earl of Ormond brought the President and the Earl of Thomond to be present, at his own side, at that conference. When they arrived at the appointed place, which was in the neighbourhood of Bel-atha-Raghat[g], they began to state their [mutual] covenants, and to argue their claims on each other, until a gentleman[h]

end the plott is laid, and followed with such heat by his Lordshipp, to cut me off uppon so slight an occasion. Yet, consideringe with myself my own loialtie (in which I hoappe, by God's Grace, boathe I and myne shall contynue) and the occasion of suspition heretofore gyven by those who are lick to inheritt after his Lordshipp, it gyves me occasion to suspect that which I feare may follow."

Leland remarks that Mountjoy, who possibly was not dissatisfied at the removal of a man who rivalled him in authority, and conceived that this event might induce the Queen to send him reinforcements from England, affected to treat it with indifference. Ormond remained in O'More's hands from the 10th of April till the 12th of June, when he was set at liberty upon delivering sixteen hostages for the payment of £3000.—See the *Pacata Hibernia*, book 1, c. vii.

[h] *A gentleman.*—His name was Melaghlin O'More.—See Ledwich's *Antiquities*, p. 275. Peter Lombard, Comment., pp. 436, 437, 438. It looks strange that the Four Masters should have known nothing about the real cause of the taking of the Earl. Sir George Carew writes, that the Earl of Ormond, "after an hower, or more, was idly spent, and nothing concluded, &c., was desirous to see that infamous Iesuit, Archer, did cause him to bee sent for; assoone as he came, the Earle and hee fell into an Argument, wherein hee called Archer Traytor, and reproved him for sending, under pretext of Religion, her Majesties subjects into Rebellion."

The most curious account of this conference is given by P. O'Sullevan Beare in his *Hist. Cathol. Iber. Compend.*, tom. 3, lib. 5, c. viii., which runs as follows:

"Interim in Lagenia Huon Omorra Portum Lisiæ arcem commeatu intercludendo in magnas angustias deducit. Comes Vrmonius regij exercitus imperator arci laturus opem cum amplius quatuor millibus equitatus, & peditatus Dubhlinna profectus ad riuulum nomine vadum Nigrum pervenit. Vbi Huon circiter mille, & quadringentos milites ducens illum in aperta planicie aggreditur. Acriter, & contentiosè dimicatur. Huon hostis alas ad agmina sæpè compellit, itidem hostis multitudine repulsus. Vrmonius eo die milites sexcentos amisit, quorum corpora ædibus accensis combusit, ne intelligeretur tantum sibi damni fuisse illatum. Nam mos est Anglis occisos suos occulendi, hostes verò in publicis locis spectandos collocandi. Catholici sexaginta succubuerunt: circiter octoginta sunt vulneribus affecti. Vrmonius multitudine militum iter sustinens in arcem commeatum intulit. Cathirius, Mauritius, & Iohannes Oconchures Iphalij equites

go ro cuir duine uasal do ṁuinntir Uaitne a láiṁ i nésiḃ, ⁊ i naradnaċaiḃ eich Iarla urmuṁan, go ro ḟodaim an tiarla a ġabáil fo ḋeóid. Ot connairc an Presidenṫ ⁊ Iarla tuadmuṁan in ní sin sóait a neich for cculaiḃ, ⁊ ní ro anrat go rangatar go cill chainnigh. Acht chena ro gonad Iarla tuad-muṁan isin teccmail sin. Rucc Uaitne mac Rudraiġe Iarla urmuṁan leis ar daingniġṫiḃ a ḋuiṫce. Ro bad sccel iongnad seaċnón ereann Iarla urmu-ṁan do ḃeiṫ illáiṁ an ionnar sin. Do ḋeachaid tra an Presidenṫ, ⁊ Iarla tuadmuṁan isin tseċtmain iar ngabail Iarla urmuṁan o ċill ċainniġ go Portlairge, aissiḋe go heochoill, ⁊ o eochoill go corcaigh. Ot ċualaiġ Iarla desmuṁan ⁊ fínġin mac donnchaid még cárṫaiġ a ttoċt an dú sin, tangatar go lion a ttionoil go ro ġabsat longport fairsing fianḃoṫaiġ go mbáttar ina cciorcaill bodba ar gach taoiḃ do Chorcaiġ ṫes ⁊ tuaid. Ḃátar sri ré coicthidhesi comlaine amlaid sin go ro gabad ossad miosa etir Ḟínġin Mág cárṫaiġ, ⁊ an Presidens, ⁊ iar naidm an ossaidh etorra do deachaid Iarla desmuṁan ar fud an tíre do ċuinġid bíd dia ḃuandadaibh. O ro ḟidir an Presidenṫ, ⁊ Iarla tuadmuṁan go ro sccaoilsiot an luċt battar ina naghaid o aroile, ⁊ go mbaoí an ċonair ó ċorcaiġ go luimneaċ soimṫeċta aca, Ro arccnátar a dó nó a trí do ċédaiḃ marcaċ go mile nó dó saiġdiúir ó ċorcaiġ go maiġ eala, ó ṁaiġ eala go cill moċellócc, ⁊ o ċill

cum centum peditibus improuisò scalis altissimis admotis Cruochanum castellum, quod in Iphalia principatu Thomas Morus eques Auratus, & Siffirdus Angli præsidio tenebant, ascendunt, & propugnatoribus occisis expugnant. Rursus Comes Vrmonius regij exercitus imperator, & Huon Omorra vterque in alterius conspectum copias perducit. Erat tunc apud Huonem Pater Iacobus Archerus è Societate Iesu Ibernus vir Catholicæ Religionis amplificandæ studiosissimus, perindeque Hæresis hostis accerimus, & ob id ab Anglis odio inexpiabili habitus; quippè qui primum Onello, deinde Huoni, tandem Osulleuano, & alijs Catholicis praua dogmata oppugnantibus, suo studio, consilio, suaque opera, & industria minimè defuit, ac sua etiam authoritate Catholicorum agmen cogens cum Hæreticis signa sæpènumerò contulit. Hic religiosus motus spe reducendi Vrmonium ad sanam mentem petit, vt liceat colloqui. Colloquendi facultatem Vrmonius non negat. Itaque ex altera parte Vrmonius Dionysius Obrien Tomoniæ Comes, Lomnachæqué princeps, & Georgius Caruus Anglus Momoniarum præfectus equis vecti; ex altera verò religiosus Archerus pedes tribus Ibernis militibus comitatus in vtriusque exercitus conspectu ad colloquium conueniunt, nulla incolumitatis fide interposita. Ibi Archerus, qui linguam Anglicam optimè callebat propter Caruum Ibernicum idioma non intelligentem, Anglico sermone pié, sanctèquè suo more incipit facere verba. Eum Vrmonius interrumpit futile quoddam argumentum in Summi Pontificis sanctitatem objiciendo. Qua re subiratus Archerus cum pristinum oris habitum aliquantum mutasset, & simul baculum,

of Owny's people placed his hand on the reins of the bridle of the Earl of Ormond's horse, and finally determined to take him prisoner. When the President and the Earl of Thomond perceived this, they turned their horses back, and did not halt until they arrived at Kilkenny. The Earl of Thomond, however, was wounded in that rencounter. Owny, the son of Rury, [then] took the Earl of Ormond with him into the fastnesses of his territory; [and] it was a wonderful news all over Ireland that the Earl of Ormond should be detained in that manner.

The week after the taking of the Earl, the President and the Earl of Thomond went from Kilkenny to Waterford, from thence to Youghal, and from Youghal to Cork. When the Earl of Desmond and Fineen, the son of Donough Mac Carthy, heard of their arrival at that place, they set out with all their forces; and, pitching an extensive camp of tents, they formed a wide circle on every side of Cork, north and south Thus they remained for a whole fortnight, when Fineen Mac Carthy and the President concluded an armistice for a month. The armistice being agreed on, the Earl of Desmond went forth through the country to procure provisions for his retained soldiers. When the President and the Earl of Thomond learned that their adversaries had parted from each other, and that the road from Cork to Limerick was left open to them, they went forth with two or three hundred horsemen, and with one or two thousand soldiers, from Cork to Magh-Ealla[i], from thence to Kilmallock, and from thence

seu stipitem, quo seniles artus sustinebat, dextera fortè tolleret, tres Iberni pedites, qui eum comitabantur, Anglici sermonis ignari, velle religiosum stipite cum Vrmonio congredi, existimarunt. Quamobrem periculum, quòd inermi religioso ab armato impendere putabant, anteuertere cupientes duo Urmonium aggressi equo deturbant, tertius quoque ferrum stringit: in quorum auxilium pluribus accurrentibus ex Catholico exercitu, multitudinem veriti Comes Tomonius, & Caruus se fugæ mandant. In Archerum regij magna turba proruunt: Quibus Cornelius Orellus ab Huone missus occurrit. Vtrinque equestri pugna & bombardariorum velitatione dimicatur, donec nox prælium diremerit. Postero die pars vtraqué ab eo loco discessit. Vrmonius ab Huone custodiæ mandatus ad fidem Catholicam ab Archero conuertitur. Sed Onelli iussu veterum amicitiarum memoris incolumis dimissus iterum ad pristinum Hæresis vomitum rediuit, de Archero verò silentio inuoluendum non est, eum Hæreticis non modò terrori, sed etiam adeó vel admirationi, vel stupori fuisse, vt per maria siccis pedibus incedere, per aerem volare, aliaque supra hominum vires assecutum esse crediderint, inde non Archerum, sed Archidiabolum rectius appellandum esse confirmantes."

[i] *Magh-Ealla:* i. e. the Plain of the River Ealla, or Allo, now the town of Mallow, in the county of Cork.—See note [g], under the year 1598, p. 2080. *suprà.*

moċellócc go luimneċ. Tainicc dna iarla dfsmuṁan hi cconallchoiḃ go soċraite ḋfrṁáir dfiṫfṁ 7 dfoirċoiṁfcc ar an bpresidens 7 ar Iarla tuaḋmuṁan.

Ba isin tan sa do rala accallaiṁ inclfiṫe etir an Presidens, 7 Iarla tuaḋmuṁan do ṫaoiḃ, 7 Diarmait mac an duḃaltaiġ uí concoḃair don taoiḃ araill. Neaċ eiside baí ag crfic a aṁsaine la hiarla dfsmuṁan tar cfnn tuillṁe, 7 tuarusdail, séd, 7 somaoine sri ré mbliadna riar an tan sa 7 batar aṁsa iomḋa iolarḋa fó a smaċt, 7 fó a ċuṁaċta an tan sin. Asseaḋ airfcc ro ṫionċoiscc a ainsén do ḋiarmait, Iarla dfsmuṁan do ṫairbert[k] don Presidens, 7 dIarla tuaḋmuṁan dar cfnn ionnmais, 7 edala, 7 ar ṡaoirsi, 7 ar ṡoċar dúthaiġe do fḟin, 7 dá gaċ aon no geḃaḋ lais, 7 ro ḟaoíḋ

[k] *To deliver up.*—P. O'Sullevan Beare tells this story somewhat better; but he and the Four Masters were ignorant of the machinery set at work by Carew to effect this dishonourable capture of the Sugane Earl. But Carew himself, who appears to pride himself on his powers of cunning, subtlety, and treachery, has thought proper to transmit a detailed account of it to posterity in the *Pacata Hibernia*, from which the Editor is tempted to present the reader with the following abstract of it.

The two most powerful leaders of the rebels in Munster were James Fitzgerald, commonly called the Sugane, or Straw-rope Earl, and Dermot O'Conor Donn, who commanded fourteen hundred bonnaghtmen, or mercenary soldiers, consisting of Ulstermen and Connaughtmen, employed in the Earl of Desmond's country, by commission from O'Neill, the Pope's King of Ireland. This Dermot O'Conor was married to the Lady Margaret, the daughter of the late unfortunate Gerald Earl of Desmond, and sister to the present heir to that title, who was detained a prisoner in the Tower of London while his dignity and estates were usurped by the Sugane Earl. In this complicated state of affairs Sir George Carew "resolved to try the uttermost of his witt and cunning" to turn it to advantage. In a very secret manner he provided and sent a fit agent to sound the inclination of the Lady Margaret, and, finding her fit to be wrought upon, it was propounded that if her husband would take the Sugane Earl prisoner, and deliver him into the hands of the President, he should receive one thousand pounds sterling, and that he should have a company of men in pay from the Queen, and other conditions of satisfaction to herself and her brother. The Lady Margaret, who, by an English education, contracted an affection for English government, and was particularly solicitous for the interests of her brother, naturally hated the man who had usurped his dignity by Irish law, on O'Neill's authority, and prevailed upon her husband to form a scheme for delivering the Straw-rope Earl into the hands of the Lord President.

The President's secretary and historian gives, as matter of triumph, some very vile details of the little and paltry wiles to which the Lord President had recourse on this occasion. In that age of cold-blooded murders and dishonourable dealings, such details were read with amusement, while, to us of the nineteenth century, they sound worse than the history of the Red Indian or the Bushmen of Africa! One

to Limerick. The Earl of Desmond then went into the Connelloes with numerous forces, to reconnoitre and watch the President and the Earl of Thomond.

At this time it was that a private interview had taken place between the President and the Earl of Thomond, on the one side, and Dermot, the son of Dubhaltach O'Conor, on the other. He was one who had been for a year before in the military service of the Earl of Desmond, for hire and wages, jewels and riches, and he had many hireling soldiers under his jurisdiction and command at this time. The resolution which his misfortune suggested to Dermot was, to deliver up[k] the Earl of Desmond to the President and the Earl of Thomond, in consideration of receiving wealth and property, and the freedom and profits of an estate, for himself and every one who should adhere to him. He sent mes-

Nugent, who had been a servant to Sir Thomas Norris, had turned over to the rebels after the death of his good master, and by the efficiency of his services acquired their esteem and confidence; but, imagining that he could get on better under the wings of the President, he came to submit to him, and to desire pardon for his faults committed. Answer was made, that "for so much as his crimes and offences had been extraordinary, he could not hope to be reconciled unto the State except he would deserve it by extraordinary service, which, saith the President, if you shall perform, you may deserve, not only pardon for your faults committed heretofore, but also some stores of crowns to releeve your wants hereafter." He promised to destroy either the Sugane Earl or his brother John. As a plot was already laid against the Sugane Earl by Dermot O'Conor, and as his death could only serve to raise up new competitors for his title, Nugent was instructed to murder John. He seized his opportunity and attempted to despatch him, but, as his pistol was just levelled, he was seized upon and condemned to die. At his execution he confessed his design, declaring that the Lord President had many others hired and sworn to effect what he intended.

The plot of Dermot O'Conor for seizing the Sugane Earl remained still to be executed, and to promote its success all the ingenuity of the wily Lord was exerted. At a period when his officers expected some manly and honourable warfare in the field, he suddenly dispersed his forces into different garrisons, in order to inspire the rebels with confidence, and to induce the leaders to make the like disposition of their troops. He next forged a letter (of which a copy is ostentatiously printed in the *Pacata Hibernia*), as if addressed by the Lord President to James Fitz-Thomas, acknowledging many obligations for his secret services to the State, and exhorting him to deliver up Dermot O'Conor alive or dead. Dermot, furnished with this letter, which it was to be supposed he had intercepted, sought an interview with the Sugane Earl, took occasion to quarrel with him, and took him prisoner, as a traitor, in the name of O'Neill! produced his letter, which was in Carew's own handwriting, as a proof of this his guilt, and conveyed him, and some of his companions, to Castlelishin, of which he held the command, informing the Lord President of his success, and eagerly expecting his reward. But before Carew could arrive to receive his prisoner, John Fitz-Thomas, and the spirited rebel, Pierce Lacy, who had suspected the real pur-

teċta go hincleiṫe fris na torccaiḃ sin do ṡaighiḋ an ṗresident, ⁊ an Iarla, ⁊ ro naidhmsiot a ccura diḃlínibh amhlaidh sin. Ní ro léicc trá Diarmait hi ffaill an ní fo ttarat laimh uair ro gabaḋ lais (in a roile laiṫe a ttosaċ mis Iuill na bliadhna so) Iarla Desmumhan ina oireċtas féin i cceṫraimṫeóin a tíre, ⁊ a ṫalman ar rob adbal cumhachta Diarmata, ⁊ rortar iolarda a daóine isin tír ísin. ⁊ iar ngabail an Iarla lais ar e ionad in ro lá dia iomċoimhéd é i mbaile do bailtiḃ an Iarla féin .i. Caislén an lisín[1] i nglémeódón gearaltach. Ro ċuir líon a imdidin, ⁊ barndacta an baile do ċeiṫirn ċonnaċtaigh i ccaoimhteċt an Iarla dia iomċoimhéd isin mbaile ísin. Do ċóid féin hi ccenn aile don tír go ro ḟaóid a teċta i ccenn an President ⁊ Iarla tuadhmhumhan dairnéis sgel doiḃ, ⁊ do ċuingid gaċ neich ro geallaḋ dó dar cenn an Iarla.

Ot cualatar gearaltaiġ gabail an Iarla ⁊ a beiṫ isin eiccendáil israibe ro ṫionoilsiot sliocht Muiris mic Gearailt ar gaċ airm i mbátar i na roile laiṫe i ccomfoċraib ċaislein an lisin. Tánaicc ann din Mac muiris ciarraiġe .i. Pattraicín, mac tomais, mic emainn ⁊ an Ridire ciarraiġeċ .i. Uilliam, mac Seain, mic Uilliam, Ridire an ġlenna Emann, mac tomáis, mic Emainn, mic tomáis, An Ridire Fionn .i. Emann, mac Seain ⁊ derbraṫair don Iarla budéin .i. Sean, mac tomáis ruaidh, ⁊ duine uasal do búrcaċaiḃ diar bo hainm uilliam, mac Seain na ssinar mic riocaird ṡaxanaiġ baoí ar fosdaḋ i ffoċair an Iarla ó ro hoirdneaḋ é ina Iarla go nuicce sin. Iar ttoċt doiḃside uile hi ccenn a roile nír bó cian ro bátar i niomaccallaimh an tan ro chinnsiot iad féin do roinn ar ċeṫramhnaiḃ an baile, ⁊ dol da ṡobairt fo ċédóir, ⁊ gan dergain do ġráḋ a ccorp, nó a ccaomhanmann go mbendaís an tiarla ar dáis no deiccen. Ro ċeimniġset ar a haiṫle for a ccetraghaiḋ go rangatar go múraiḃ an baile, ⁊ ní ró ráchaiġsiot éiccen, no anfforlann da ffuairsiot, ⁊ do rorratt bris mbicc dia ro marbaḋ, ⁊ dia ro mudhaiġeḋ dia muinntir go ro gabaḋ an baile for an mbárda leo fo deóid, ⁊ go ttarsat an tiarla ass daimdeóin gan fuasclad uadaiḃ dia

pose of O'Conor, mustered four thousand men of their followers and rescued the Sugane Earl. The career of Dermot O'Conor was afterwards brief and inglorious, and his fate tragical, as he richly merited by his base treachery.

[1] *Caislen-an-lisin:* i. e. the Castle of the Little Fort, translated Castellum Castri by P. O'Sullevan Beare, *Hist. Cathol. Ibern.*, fol. 169. This castle is described in the *Pacata Hibernia* as near the great fastness of Connilloe. Its ruins

sengers privately with these conditions to the President and the Earl, and they mutually ratified these covenants. Dermot did not neglect what he had taken in hand, for he took the Earl of Desmond prisoner, one day in the beginning of the January of this year, at a meeting of his own people, in the very middle of his own territory and land; for Dermot's power was great, and his men were numerous, in that territory. And, after having taken the Earl prisoner, he sent him to be incarcerated in one of the Earl's own castles, namely, in Caislen-an-Lisin[l], in the very heart of the country of the Fitzgeralds. He left a sufficient number of guards, consisting of Connaught kerns, to defend and guard the castle, along with the Earl, and to keep him there. He himself repaired to another part of the territory, and sent his messengers to the President and the Earl of Thomond, to tell them the news, and to demand what had been promised him for [securing] the Earl.

As soon as the Geraldines heard of the capture of the Earl, and the perilous position in which he was placed, the descendants of Maurice Fitzgerald collected from every quarter, on a certain day, to the neighbourhood of Caislen-an-Lisin. Thither repaired Mac Maurice of Kerry, i. e. Patrickin, the son of Thomas, son of Edmond; the Knight of Kerry, i. e. William, the son of John, son of William; the Knight of Glin, i. e. Edmond, the son of John, son of Thomas; the White Knight, i. e. Edmond, the son of John; and the brother of the Earl himself, i. e. John, the son of Thomas Roe; and a gentleman of the Burkes, whose name was William, the son of John of the Shamrocks, son of Richard Saxonagh, who had been retained in the service of the Earl since he had been appointed Earl until then. All these having met together, they were not long in consultation when they came to the resolution to divide themselves in four divisions for the four quarters of the castle, and proceed forthwith to attack it, and not to look to the love of body or precious life, until they should rescue the Earl by consent or violence. They then advanced straight forward until they arrived at the walls of the castle; and they felt not the resistance or opposition they received, and they made little account of the numbers of their men who were killed and destroyed, until at last they took the castle from the warders, and rescued the Earl out, in despite of them, without,

are still visible in the townland of Castle-Ishin, parish of Knocktemple, in the county of Cork, not far from the borders of the county of Limerick.

ċionn, gan fuiliuccaḋ, gan foirrḋearccaḋ fair féin. Do raḋsat maiṫem nanacail don ḃárda.

Do ċóidh ṫra an gaḃáil sin iarla dfesmuman a míṁes, ⁊ a míonóir do ḋiarmait o ċoncoḃair seachnón ereann, ⁊ iar ndol don iarla i mesc a muinntire tucc foccra do diarmait, ⁊ dá gaċ Connaċtaċ baí ina ḟoċair, ⁊ da ccéiṫearnaiḃ an tír dfáccḃáil. Do ronsat iaraṁ fo ċédóir innsin, ⁊ lotar a ngeraltachaiḃ go niomat nionnmara ⁊ nédala, nimirsfeḋ, ⁊ nairnfesi co nár ḃurusa ariom a ruccsat connaċtaiġ dilċenel gaċa hédala riaṁ ⁊ iaraṁ a ngeraltaċaibh fri hféh a nseaonta féin fri roile gó sin.

A ttorac mís Iul ar a haiṫle do ġluais an Presidens, ⁊ Iarla tuaḋmuman go ttionol ttaidbreaċ do ṡaiġdiuiriḃ ó Luimneaċ don taoḃ ba tuaid do Shionainn siar tré ċonntae an ċláir go rangatar baile még colmáin i ttrioċa céd ċorcoḃaiscinn airṫersaiġi. Do ċóidsiot annsin i niniloctaḋ tar Sionainn go cloiċ glenna baile eiriḋe sil for bruaċ na Sionna don taoiḃ ṫes, ⁊ ro baḋ do ḃailtiḃ Ridire an ġlenna é, ⁊ bá on nglenn sin ina bfuil an baile .i. glenn corbraiġe ro hainmniġeaḋ an Ridire, ⁊ an ċloċsoin gur ar ċruinnigh an congáir mór dia saiġiḋ. Tánaicc ordanás mór ó Luimneaċ i nairṫraiġiḃ i ccoinne an Presidens, ⁊ iarla tuaḋmuman don baile ceona. Ar suiḋe do.ḃ re na aghaiḋ do ċuaiḋ aca ar in mbaile fo ċenn dá lá, ⁊ do brisettar blaḋ de las an ordanás mór. Ro lingsiot é da gaċ taoiḃ ar a haiṫle, ⁊ ro marḃsat fiċe, nó dó do ṡaorċlannoiḃ, ⁊ daorċlannoiḃ do ṁuinntir an Ridire bátar ag bardaċt an ḃaile go soċaiḋe do ṁnaiḃ ⁊ do ṁiondaoiniḃ. Ro marḃaḋ bes dren do ṁuinntir an ṗresidens, ⁊ an Iarla lás an mbárda, ⁊ nír bo soḋaing an baile sin do ġaḃáil munḃaḋ sccaoileaḋ a ṁuinntire siar an tan sin ó iarla dfesmuman.

Ot ċualaiġ O Conċoḃair ciarraiġe .i. Sean mac Concobair uí ċonċobair armáil an tíre ar ttanuccaḋ, ⁊ cloch glenna ar na gaḃail gan guin, gan guaraċt do ċoiḋ i ccenn an presidens ⁊ an Iarla, ⁊ do ġeall a ḃeiṫ daoin leiṫ

[m] *Baile-Mic-Colmain*, now Colmanstown, a townland in the parish of Killofin, barony of East Corca-Vaskin Clonderalaw, and county of Clare.—See note [q], under 1581, p. 1760, *supra*.

[n] *Cloch-Gleanna*. This was the name of the castle of Glin, in the north-west of the county of Limerick. It is translated Vallirupes by P. O'Sullevan Beare in his *Hist. Cathol. Iber.*, fol. 170: "Quibus domesticis perturbationibus dum Catholici fluctuant et conficiuntur, Caruus Vallirupem (*Cloch-Gleanna*) equitis Aurati Vallis arcem tormentis quassam in suam potestatem redigit." This castle was 102 feet in length and 92 in breadth. A plan of it, as then be-

indeed, paying the price of his ransom, and he himself without being wounded or losing a drop of blood. They extended mercy and protection to the warders.

This capture of the Earl of Desmond had spread abroad to disrespect and dishonour of Dermot O'Conor; and when the Earl went among his people he gave warning to Dermot, and to every Connaughtman who was with him, and to their kerns, to quit the country. This they immediately did; and they carried with them from the country of the Geraldines much wealth, moveable property, and cattle; and it would be difficult to enumerate all the different kinds of spoils which the Connaughtmen carried off from the Geraldines before and after their contentions with each other on this occasion.

In the beginning of July following, the President and the Earl of Thomond set out from Limerick with a fine muster of soldiers, and marched westwards along the northern side of the Shannon, through the county of Clare, until they arrived at Baile-Mic-Colmain[m], in the cantred of East Corca-Bhaiscinn; [and] from this they ferried themselves across the Shannon to Cloch-Gleanna[n], a castle on the southern bank of the Shannon.

The castle at which this great host had gathered was one of the castles of the Knight of Glin; it is situated in Gleann-Corbraighe, from which it received the name of Cloch-Gleanna, and the Knight the appellation of Ridire-an-Ghleanna[o]. Heavy ordnance were brought in vessels from Limerick to meet the Earl and the President here. Having sat before the castle, they reduced it in two days, and made a breach in it with the heavy ordnance. They then rushed into it from every side, and slew a score or two of gentlemen and plebeians of the Knight's people, who were guarding the castle, together with some women and children. Some of the President's and Earl's men were also slain by the warders; and it would not have been easy to take the castle were it not that the Earl of Desmond's people had previously dispersed from him.

As soon as O'Conor Kerry, i. e. John, the son of Conor, heard that the forces of the country had been thinned, and that the castle of Glin had been taken without difficulty or danger, he repaired to the President and the Earl, and promised thenceforward to be on the side of his Sovereign. He gave up his

sieged, is given in the *Pacata Hibernia*, Dublin edition of 1810, p. 112.

[o] *Ridire-an-Ghleanna:* i. e. the Knight of Glin, or the Valley, so called from Glin, anciently Glencorbry, in the north-west of the county of Limerick.

lá a ṗprionnsa ó sin amach. Do rad a ḃaile .i. carraicc an ṗuill do ḋruim ċoingill, ⁊ connarṫa don pPresidens, ⁊ don Iarla. O ro clos a ccoitcinne hi cCiarraiġe ⁊ hi cCloinn Muiris muinntir na bainrioghna d'faġbháil an áiṫesra sin ar a nesccairdibh do ġabsat acc brisedh a mbailteadh, ⁊ acc faccḃáil a náitiġṫe, ⁊ a ndúnárus óḃéla oslaicṫe, Ruccsat a mna ⁊ a muinntera ar cúlaibh a cCnoc Cenn Garḃ, ⁊ a ccoillteadh cluṫairdiaṁra a cCois Mainge, ⁊ i cComhfoċraibh Desmumhan.

An tan din ro fidir an pPresident, ⁊ an tIarla (.i. Tuadhmuṁan) go ro ṫeichsiot an tír uile dursṁor ar gach taeḃ d'Féil, ⁊ do Ċasán do ċuirsiot saiġdiuiri go Leic snaṁa i nGarsún. Longport Mheic Muiris eiside, ionnas go mbaoí garasún uáṫa i Licc ṡnáṁa, i cCarraicc an ṗuill hi cCloiċ Glenda, i nEas Geiḃtine, i fFianaind, i tTráigh lí, i nArdfearta, i lLios Caṫain, ⁊ i mbailtiḃ Cloinne Muiris ar ċena cenmoṫá Lios Tuaṫail. Ro fill an Presidens, ⁊ Iarla Tuadhmuṁan go Luimneaċ iar mbreiṫ buadha for an turus sin, ⁊ tainicc dia saiġidh urṁor Ċonallaċ conntae Luimniġ ⁊ Caonraiġe ar nesirġe doiḃ i naghaidh Iarla Desmuṁan go mbátar daoinleiṫ la a bprionnsa.

Mac Muiris Ciarraiġe .i. Patraiccín, mac Tomáis, mic Emainn, mic Tomáis do écc hi meadhón a aoísi, ⁊ a aimsire iar mbeiṫ dó i naéntaidh Iarla Desmuṁan isin ccoccadh reṁraite. Rob adbar eccaoine fer a ċroṫa, a ṗola, ⁊ a ḟialċaire décc inellṁa aṁlaidh sin. A ṁac Tomás do ġabáil a ionaid.

An Róisdeach .i. Muiris, mac Dauid, mic Muiris, mic Dauid do écc a mí Iún na bliadhna so, macaeṁ soiṫim, soidhealbda, foġlamṫa illaidin, i nGaoidhilcc, ⁊ i mbérla eiside. A ṁac .i. Dauid do ġabail a ionaid.

[p] *Carraic-an-phoill*, now Carrigafoyle, on the Shannon, in the barony of Iraghticonor, and county of Kerry.—See note [w], under the year 1580, p. 1730, *supra*.

[q] *Kerry*.—By Kerry is here meant Iraghticonor, or O'Conor Kerry's country.

[r] *Fial*, now *anglice* the Feale, a river rising in the barony of Duhallow, near the borders of the counties of Cork, Kerry, and Limerick, and, flowing in a north-westerly direction, passes by Abbeyfeale and Listowel, and meets the River Brick, to the north of Rattoo, from which point their united waters form what is now called the Casan or Cashen River. The name *Casan*, or Casán Ciarraiġe, i. e. the path of Kerry, it being, as it were, the high road into the country, was originally applied to this river as far as it is navigable for a currach or ancient Irish leather boat; and the church of Disert Triallaigh, near Listowel, is referred to in an ancient Irish manuscript, quoted by Duald Mac Firbis, as on the margin of the Casán Ciarraiġe.—See *Genealogies, Tribes, &c., of Hy-Fiachrach*, p. 38, note [j].

[s] *Askeaton*. There is a view of the castle and monastery of Askeaton, as taken on this occa-

castle, i. e. Carraic-an-phuill[p], upon certain covenants and conditions, to the President and the Earl.

As soon as it was generally heard through Kerry[q] and Clanmaurice that the Queen's people had gained this triumph over their enemies, they [the inhabitants] proceeded to demolish their castles; and, leaving their mansions and residences wide open, they brought their women and families to the rear of their rough-headed hills, and their shady and solitary woods along the River Mang, and in the vicinity of Desmond.

When the President and the Earl (i. e. of Thomond) learned that the greater number of the inhabitants of the country, on each side of the Fial[r] and the Casan, had fled from their habitations, they placed garrisons in the castle of Lixnaw, the residence of Mac Maurice, as also in Carraic-an-phuill, the Rock of Glin, Askeaton[s], Fianaind[t], Tralee, Ardfert, and Lis-Cathain[u], and throughout all the castles of Clanmaurice, excepting Lis-Tuathail[w]. The President and the Earl of Thomond returned to Limerick, having gained the victory on that expedition; and the greater part of the inhabitants of Connello, in the county of Limerick, and of Kerry, came to them, having turned against the Earl of Desmond, and joined their Sovereign.

Mac Maurice of Kerry, i. e. Patrickin, the son of Thomas, son of Edmond, son of Thomas, died in the prime of his life, after having joined the Earl of Desmond in the aforesaid war. It was a cause of lamentation that a man of his personal form, blood, and hospitality, should thus die in his youth. His son, Thomas, assumed his place.

The Roche, i. e. Maurice, the son of David, son of Maurice, son of David, died in the month of June of this year. He was a mild and comely man, learned in the Latin, Irish, and English languages. His son, i. e. David, took his place.

sion, given in the *Pacata Hibernia*, book 1, c. vii. —See Dublin edition of 1810, p. 94.

[t] *Fianaind*, now Fianait, and *anglice* Fenet, a townland with the ruins of a church and castle, on a point of land extending into Tralee Bay, in the barony of Troughanacmy, county of Kerry.

[u] *Lis-Cathain*, now Liscahan, a castle in the parish of Ardfert, barony of Clanmaurice, and county of Kerry.—See the *Pacata Hibernia*, book 1, c. x., where there is a long account given of Florence Mac Carthy's attempt to get possession of this castle, which is not half a mile distant from Ardfert.

[w] *Lis-Tuathail*, now Listowel, a small town on the bank of the River Feale, in the barony of Iraghticonor, and county of Kerry. A plan of this castle is given in the *Pacata Hibernia*, book 1, c. x., Dublin edition of 1810, p. 120.

O cCearḃaill .i. an calbach mac uilliam uiḋir, mic firganainm, miċ maol-ruanaiḋ do marḃaḋ a mí Iúl le foḋaoínib uaisle do ṡiol cCearḃaill, ⁊ do ṡiol mEaċair. Fear colgḋa, cosantach an calḃaċ sin, uille ċruaiḋ la a ċoṁarsanaiḃ gall, ⁊ gaoiḋel, Ridire dainm ⁊ donóir a huġdarrás an ṗrionnsa.

Iomat cangleac, ⁊ congal, deaccmarta, ⁊ dortaḋ fola in ro diotaiġitt drongḃuiḋne dearíṁe do ṫaḃairt etir Saxanċaiḃ ⁊ gaoiḋil laiġean isin samradh so.

Uaitne o morḋa do leiccean Iarla urmuman amaċ a mí Iún ⁊ se braiġde décc do ġaḃail dó ass do ċéḋmacaiḃ, ⁊ doiḋreaḃaiḃ na saérclann rob onóraiġe bátar foṁamaiġṫe don Iarla a ngioll le coṁall gaċ coingell, ⁊ gaċ airteaccal dar hiomnaisccead air ina ḟuasclaḋ.

An tuaitne ceḋna mac Ruḋraiġe óicc mic Ruḋraiġe caoiċ uí morḋa, ro ba duine uasal oirdeirc, aḋbclosach, iomraiteach re hathaiḋ, do ṁarḃaḋ la muinntir na bainrioġna i nanfforlann iomairicc ettualaing ro fearaḋ eatorra diḃlínib a ccoṁfoċraiḃ laoiġisi a mí August na bliaḋna so. Ba mór tra ro ċuir an marḃaḋ sin do ġail do ġaisccead, ⁊ do ġérraittecht gaoiḋel laiġean ⁊ Ereann uile for ccúlaiḃ. Duine eiside baí ina aén oiḋhre o ċeart ar a ḋuthaiġ, ⁊ do ḃean urlaṁas a aṫarḋa a los a laṁa, ⁊ a cruas a croiḋe a dornaiḃ danar, ⁊ deóraḋ ag a mbaoí a reṁdísle ag dol i ruḋracus re hathaiḋ roiṁe sin go ttarḋsoṁ í fó a smaċt, ⁊ fo a ċumaċtoibh buḋéin, ro breiṫ a maor, ⁊ a ḃuannaḋh do réir gnaṫaiġṫe gaoiḋeal co na baoí aon baile dia aṫarḋa ina ḟéccmais ó or go hor gen mo ṫá Port laoiġisi na má.

[x] *Calvagh.*—He was the Sir Charles O'Carroll who wrote the letter to the Lord Deputy above quoted, p. 2166.

[y] *Was slain.*—P. O'Sullevan Beare states, that Owny O'More, having incautiously separated from his people, was shot through the body by a musket-ball. Fynes Moryson gives a curious account of the Lord Deputy's expedition into Leix, on which he slew this celebrated Irish chieftain; and the Editor is tempted to present the reader with Moryson's own words, as they are exceedingly important in shewing the high state of cultivation to which Owny O'More had brought the territory of Leix at this period:

"But the best service at that time done was the killing of Owney mac Rory, a bloody and bold young man, who lately had taken the Earl of Ormond prisoner, and had made great stirs in Munster. He was the chief of the O'More's sept in Leax, and by his Death (17th of August, 1600) they were so discouraged that they never after held up their Heads. Also a bold, bloody Rebel, Callogh mac Walter, was at the same Time killed; besides that, his Lordships staying in Leax till the 23rd of August, did many other Ways weaken them; for during that time he fought almost every Day with them, and as often did beat them. Our Captains, and, by

O'Carroll, i. e. Calvagh[x], the son of William Odhar, son of Ferganainm, son of Mulrony, was killed, in the month of July, by some petty gentlemen of the O'Carrolls and O'Meaghers. This Calvagh was a fierce and protecting man, a strong arm against his English and Irish neighbours, and a knight in title and honour by authority of the Sovereign.

In this summer many conflicts, battles, sanguinary massacres, and bloodsheds, in which countless troops were cut off, took place between the English and Irish of Leinster.

Owny O'More set the Earl of Ormond at liberty in the month of June, having received in his place sixteen hostages, consisting of the eldest sons and heirs of the most honourable gentlemen who were subject to the Earl, as pledges for the fulfilment of every condition and article agreed upon for his liberation.

The same Owny, son of Rury Oge, son of Rury Caech O'More, who had been for some time an illustrious, renowned, and celebrated gentleman, was slain[y] by the Queen's people in an overwhelming and fierce battle which was fought between them on the borders of Leix, in the month of August of this year. His death was a great check to the valour, prowess, and heroism of the Irish of Leinster and of all Ireland. He was, by right, the sole heir to his territory [of Leix], and had wrested the government of his patrimony, by the prowess of his hand and the resoluteness of his heart, from the hands of foreigners and adventurers, who had its fee-simple possession passing into a prescribed right for some time before, and until he brought it under his own sway and jurisdiction, and under the government of his stewards and bonnaghts, according to the Irish usage; so that there was not one village, from one extremity of his patrimony to the other, which he had not in his possession, except Port-Leix [Maryborough] alone.

their Example (for it was otherwise painful), the common Soldiers, did cut down with their Swords all the Rebels Corn, to the Value of £10,000 and upwards, the only Means by which they were to live, and to keep their Bonnaghts (or hired Soldiers). It seemed incredible that by so barbarous Inhabitants the Ground should be so manured, the fields so orderly fenced, the Towns so frequently inhabited, and the Highways and Paths so well beaten, as the Lord Deputy here found them. The reason whereof was, that the Queen's Forces, during these wars, never till then came amongst them."

Then it is quite clear that civilization and agriculture would have advanced in this country if the Queen's forces had never come into it. By this observation Moryson shews who the barbarous people really were, for, certainly, the

Iar sgaoileaḋ dá dibeꞃccaċaiḃ eaċtarċeneóil ó iarla desmuṁan do ċóiḋ gus an uathaḋ slóg do rala ina ḟoċair go caislen na mainge. Ní baí eiṁ do ḋagḋaoiniḃ gearaltaċ daon aonta friss, no ag congnaṁ lais aċt mac an Mheic muiris sin sa hécc ro airneiḋriom .i. tomás, mac Patraicin ⁊ Ridire an ġlenda, ⁊ Piarus ócc doles.

Sgriḃenn do ṫeaċt a Saxoiḃ don muṁain i mí Iúil no bliaḋna so, ⁊ ba he a toṫacht, Mac ócc Iarla desmuṁan .i. Semus mac Geroid, mic Seain, baí i ngiallnus ag an mbainrioġain (a ccionaiḋ a aṫar, ⁊ derbraṫar a aṫar do ḋol hi ccoccaḋ fuirre) do leigen ar a ċimiḋeċt las an mbainrioġain iar ndol fá na grasaiḃ dó, iar mbeiṫ bliaḋain ar ḟichit i ccuimrech lé. Baoí beós isin sgriḃenn sin a erḟuaccra hi ccoṁḋálaiḃ ⁊ i mbailtiḃ mora muṁan go raiḃe an tócc mac sin .i. Sémus mac Gearoitt ag teaċt anoir ina Iarla onórach a huġdarrás an prionnsa, ⁊ go ffuiccéaḋ gach aon dia ḋuthaiġ baí

people who manured the fields so well, and fenced them so orderly, in the absence of the soldiers of the invaders, who destroyed all tillage, should not be called barbarians.

[z] *Pierce Oge De Lacy.*—See note under the year 1186, p. 75, *supra.* He is called Petrus Lessius by P. O'Sullevan Beare, and Pierce Lacy in the *Pacata Hibernia.*

[a] *A letter.*—This letter, which exhibits deep political craft and wisdom, was written, in the Queen's name, by the Chief Secretary, Cecil, to Sir George Carew, Governor of Munster, on the 1st of October, 1600, and has been published in the *Pacata Hibernia,* book 1, c. xiv.

[b] *Gone under her mercy.*—This phrase is incorrect, or at least has no meaning, because he had been under her mercy for twenty-one years. It should be: "after he had promised to be faithful and active in suppressing the rebellion and the Pope's religion in Ireland."

[c] *An honourable Earl.*—He was but provisionally restored, for Carew was directed either to deliver or retain his patent according to the expediency of affairs, and the services he might be able to perform. It appears that this youth had been carefully educated, from his childhood, as a Protestant, in the Tower of London, by order of the Queen, who wished to preserve him for State purposes. He was sent over under the conduct of a Captain Price, a sober and discreet gentleman, and an old commander in the wars, who landed with his charge at Youghal, on the 14th day of October, and proceeded thence to Mallow, where he presented to Sir George Carew the heir of the great rebel, and Her Majesty's letter, signed by Cecil, and her letters patent, under the great seal of England, for his restoration in blood and honour. Carew, to make trial of the disposition and affection of the new Earl's kindred and followers, consented that he might make a journey from Mallow into the county of Limerick, accompanied by Meyler Magrath, Archbishop of Cashel, and Master Boyle, Clerk of the Council (afterwards the great Earl of Cork). They came to Kilmallock, one of the strongholds of his ancestors, towards the evening, where he was at first received with the warmest and most enthusiastic welcome by the people, and almost immediately after viewed with feelings of loathing and abhorrence. But this strange vicissitude will be best narrated in the words of Carew himself, or of his secretary,

After his strange insurgents had dispersed from the Earl of Desmond, he repaired with his few remaining forces to Castlemaine. None of the Geraldine chieftains [now] sided with or assisted him, except the son of that Mac Maurice whose death we have recorded, namely, Thomas, the son of Patrickin, the Knight of Glin, and Pierce Oge De Lacy[z].

A letter[a] came from England to Munster in the month of July [*recte* October] of this year, the purport of which was, that the young son of the Earl of Desmond, i. e. James, the son of Garrett, son of James, son of John, who was detained by the Queen as a hostage, in revenge of his father and father's brothers having rebelled against her, had been released from his captivity by the Queen, after he had gone under her mercy[b], and after he had been kept by her twenty-one years in captivity. It was, moreover, [ordered] in this letter that it should be proclaimed throughout the assemblies and great towns of Munster that this young son, i. e. James, the son of Garrett, was going over as an honourable Earl[c], by the authority of the Sovereign; and that every one in his country who

Stafford, as printed in the *Pacata Hibernia*, book 1, c. xiv.:

"And to Master Boyle his Lordship gave secret charge, as well to observe the Earle's waies and cariage, as what men of quality, or others, made their addresse unto him, and with what respects and behaviour they caried themselves towards the Earle, who came to Kilmallock upon a Saturday, in the Evening; and by the way, and at their entry into the Towne, there was a mightie concourse of people, insomuch as all the Streets, Doores, and Windowes, yea, the very Gutters and tops of the Houses, were so filled with them, as if they came to see him whom God had sent to bee that Comfort and Delight their soules and hearts most desired; and they welcomed him with all the expressions and signs of Ioy, every one throwing upon him Wheat and Salt (an ancient Ceremony vsed in that Province, upon the Election of their new Majors and Officers, as a Prediction of future peace and plenty). That night the Earle was invited to Supper to Sir George Thornton's, who then kept his House in the Towne of Kilmallock; and although the Earle had a Guard of Souldiers, which made a Lane from his lodgings to Sir George Thornton's House, yet the confluence of people that flockt thither to see him was so great, as in halfe an houre he could not make his passage thorough the crowd, and after Supper he had the like encounters at his returne to his lodging. The next day, being Sunday, the Earle went to Church to heare divine service, and all the way his countrey people vsed loud and rude dehortations to keep him from Church, unto which he lent a deaf ear; but, after Service and the Sermon was ended, the Earle comming forth of the Church was railed at & spat upon by those that, before his going to Church, were so desirous to see and salute him: Insomuch as, after that publike expression of his Religion, the town was cleered of that multitude of strangers, and the Earle, from thenceforward, might walke as quietly and freely in the towne, as little in effect followed or regarded as any

hi ccoccadh gó sin aisecc a fola ⁊ a onóra, ⁊ nemhchuimhne ar a choiribh, ⁊ pillsidh tar a ais do shaighidh an phrionnsa, ⁊ an iarla óicc si. Ba he trath fa ttainicc an tiarla ócc rémhraite go herinn go narmáil moir amaille fris ón mbainrioghain a mí october do shonradh. Ar ttecht dó go Corcaigh do choidh an Presidens, ⁊ Iarla tuadhmumhan ina chenn dia fiadhuccadh. Tangatar iaramh diblinibh go maigh eala go cill mocheallocc ⁊ go luimneach, Tánaicc gus an Iarla ócc gach duine daittreibhtachaibh gearaltach ar ffaicsin na fírfhine bunaidh doibh, ⁊ an dream aga raibhe iomchoimhett caislen na mainge o Shemus, mac tomáis tuccsat side an baile don iarla ócc .i. do Shemus mac gearóitt, ⁊ do rad an tiarla a shealbh don presidens. Ni baí din aén bhaile i norláimh Mhic muiris .i. tómas acht lios tuathail amhain amhail a dubhramar, ⁊ gidh eiside ro gabadh é lá gobernóir Ciarraighe .i. Sir seorlus Uolment a mí nouember na bliadhna so.

Ingen Iarla tuadhmumhan onóra ingen choncobhair mic donnchaidh uí briain, bean an mhic muiris sin a dubhramar do thocht ar teicheamh fogla, ⁊ dibheirge a fir dia duthaigh ar protexion an Presidens ⁊ Iarla tuadhmumhan ⁊ a hécc iar sin i ndaingen meic mathghamhna, ⁊ a hadhnacal i mainistir innsi.

Ard chonsapal gearaltach .i. Ruaidhri, mac maghnusa, mic emainn, mec sithigh décc.

other private Gentleman. This true relation I the rather make, that all men may observe how hatefull our Religion, and the Professors thereof, are to the ruder and ignorant sort of people in that Kingdome. For, from thenceforward, none of his father's followers (except some few of the meaner sort of Freeholders) resorted vnto him; and the other great Lords in Munster, who had evermore beene overshadowed by the greatnesse of Desmond, did rather feare then wish the advancement of the young Lord. But the truth is, his Religion, being a Protestant, was the only cause that had bred this coyness in them all; for, if he had been a Romish Catholike, the hearts and knees of all degrees in the Province would have bowed unto him. Besides, his comming was not well liked by the vndertakers, who were in some jealousie that, in after times, he might be restored to his Father's inheritances, and thereby become their Lord, and their Rents (now paid to the Crown) would, in time, be conferred upon him. These considerations assured the President that his personal being in Munster would produce small effects, but onely to make tryal of what power he had."

The only service that this young Earl was able to perform, was the recovery of Castlemain for the Crown, by his negotiations with Thomas Oge Fitzgerald, the Constable. Having obtained the surrender of this fort, which was strongly opposed by Florence Mac Carthy and the Sugane Earl, young Desmond returned to the English Court, where, it being understood that he was no longer worth feeding, he suddenly disappeared. Mr. Moore thinks he was poisoned, but he quotes no authority.

[d] *Pardon*, literally forgetfulness or oblivion.

was in rebellion would now, upon their return to the Sovereign and this young Earl, obtain a restoration of their blood and honours, and a pardon[d] of their crimes. This young Earl arrived in Ireland, accompanied by a great force, in the month of October following. Upon his arrival in Cork[e], the President and the Earl of Thomond repaired thither to welcome him. They all afterwards came to Mallow, Kilmallock, and to Limerick. All the inhabitants of the country of the Geraldines, upon beholding the true representative of the family, came to this young Earl; and the people who had the keeping of Castlemaine for James, the son of Thomas, gave it up to the young Earl, i. e. to James, the son of Garrett; and the Earl gave the possession of it to the President. There was then no town in the possession of Mac Maurice, i. e. Thomas, except Listowel alone, as we have said; and even this was taken in the month of November by Sir Charles Volment[f], the Governor of Kerry.

The daughter of the Earl of Thomond, Honora, the daughter of Conor, son of Donough O'Brien, and wife of the Mac Maurice we have mentioned, fled from the plundering and insurrection of her husband, and came to her native territory under the protection of the President and the Earl of Thomond, and afterwards died at Dangan-Mac-Mahon[g], and was buried in the monastery of Ennis.

The Chief Constable of the Geraldines, i. e. Rory, the son of Manus, son of Edmond Mac Sheehy[h], died.

[e] *In Cork.*—This is incorrect, for, as we have already seen from the Lord President's own account of it, Captain Price, a trusty and discreet person, who was appointed by the Queen to deliver this young Earl into the President's hands, landed, with his charge, at Youghal, on the 14th of October, and from thence brought him to Mallow to the President, where they arrived on the 18th of the same month.

[f] *Volment.*—He wrote the name Wilmot himself. There is a most minute and interesting account of the taking of this castle by Sir Charles Wilmot, given in the *Pacata Hibernia*, book 1, chap. xvi.

[g] *Dangan-Mac Mahon*, now Dangan, a very large castle in ruins, in a townland of the same name in the district of Tuath-Ua-mBuilc, parish of Kilchrist, barony of Clonderalaw, and county of Clare. It is stated in the *Pacata Hibernia*, book 1, c. xiii., that this Lady Honore ny Brien procured the murder of Maurice Stack, a very brave servant of the Lord President; and that her brother, the Earl of Thomond, upon hearing of it, was infinitely grieved; and that for it he held his sister in such detestation that, from that day forward to the day of her death, which occurred not many months afterwards, he never did see her, nor could abide the memory of her name.

[h] *Mac Sheehy.*—The first of this family who came to Munster settled in the county of Limerick as leader of gallowglasses to the Earl of

Ar ffaccḃáil gearaltach do Ḋiarmait mac an duḃaltaiġ, mic tuathail uí Chonchobair iar ngaḃail iarla desmuṁan Shemais, mic tomais aṁail a duḃramar, ⁊ a ḃein de go haiṁḋeonaċ doridiri, tánaicc an diarmait sin go duthaiġ uí concobair ruaiḋ do na cluaintiḃ. Fuair protexion ón lustís (baoi acc denaṁ seirḃísi, ⁊ acc foġnaṁ don ḃainrioġain illaiġniḃ ⁊ i nulltoiḃ i ffoġmar na bliaḋna so) no go ttainicc an tiarla ócc desmuṁan so tar a ttangamar go herinn .i. Sémus mac gearóitt. Ar ttecht dósuiḋe do chuir toġairm ar diarmait, uair ro rós diarmait derbriúr don iarla sin ar a ċuairt ċoccaiḋ i ngearaltaċaiḃ an bliaḋain roiṁe sin ⁊ atbearatt aroile gur ab di tainicc gaḃail Sémais, mic tomáis ar ḋaiġ gomaḋ usaide a derḃraṫair féin dfaġbail ón eisiuṁ do ṫairḃirt dia chionn. O do ruaċt sgríḃenn an iarla go diarmait ro triall toċt so na ṫoġairm maille le ceḋ ⁊ le protexion an lustis ⁊ Presidens da ċóicceaḋ muṁan. Ag gaḃail dó siar tuaiḋ tre ċoicceaḋ connaċt do ḋol tar Sionainn go luimneaċ Ro lean teroitt na long mac Risdird an iarainn, ⁊ daviḋ mac uillicc an timchill é tre ḃioḋbanus, ⁊ ruccsat fair i nuathaḋ buiḋne i ccoṁfoċraiḃ guirt innsi guaire, ⁊ ro dícennaḋ diarmait leó, iar na faġbáil ar ḃecc mbuiḋne ⁊ ge ro frit é aṁlaiḋ sin ba gar uair siar an tan soin nár bó doiġ don luċt sin a ionnsaiġiḋ, ar ba coḋnaċ soṁ for ċóicc céd decc fer, ⁊ ba hanġlonn é buḋéin, aċt namá na cuṁaing neaċ iomġaḃail écca cecib tan dus ficc tiuġlaiṫe neich.

Ticcerna sléḃe árdachaiḋ décc i ngeiṁreaḋ na bliaḋna so .i. Sémus, mac Piaruis mic Semuis buitiler.

Desmond, in the year 1420. He built the castle of Lisnacullia, Lios na coille, i.e. Woodfort, in the parish of Cloonagh, barony of Lower Connello, and county of Limerick, and about five miles to the north of the town of Newcastle. The ruins of this castle, which was a fortress of considerable strength, still remain in good preservation.

[i] *Until.*—This sentence is left unfinished by the Four Masters. It should be constructed as follows: "When Dermot O'Conor left the Geraldines," &c., &c., "he first procured a protection from the Lord Deputy, and then proceeded to the Cloonties, in O'Conor Roe's country, where he remained until the young Earl of Desmond sent for him," &c., &c.

[k] *Through enmity.*—Carew, or his secretary, states: "Theobald sent to the Earle of Clanrickard for a protection, pretending that what he did was done in revenge of his Cousen, the Lord Burke's, death. But the Earle, misliking the Action, instead of a protection, returned him this letter insuing."

He then gives Ulick Clanrickard's letter, expressing the Earl's indignation at his conduct.

[l] *Gort-innse-Guaire*, now the town of Gort, in the barony of Kiltartan, and county of Galway. There is a detailed account of this killing of Dermot O'Conor given in the *Pacata Hibernia*, book 1, c. xvii., where it is stated that "Theobald

Dermot, the son of Dubhaltach, son of Tuathal O'Conor, on leaving the Geraldines, after the Earl of Desmond (James, the son of Thomas), whom he had taken prisoner, had been forcibly rescued from him, proceeded to Cluainte, in the country of O'Conor Roe. He had obtained a protection from the Lord Justice (who was doing the Queen's service in Leinster and Ulster in the autumn of this year), until[l] this young Earl of Desmond, i. e. James, the son of Garrett, of whom we have treated, had arrived in Ireland. On his arrival he sent for Dermot, for Dermot had married a sister of this Earl while on his military sojourn in the country of the Geraldines the year before; and it is said by some that it was through her the capture of James, the son of Thomas, was effected, in order that she might the more easily obtain her own brother, by delivering the other in his stead. As soon as the Earl's letter reached Dermot, he prepared to go, at his invitation, by the permission and protection of the Lord Justice and the President of the two provinces of Munster. But, as he was passing in a north-west direction through the province of Connaught, to cross the Shannon to Limerick, he was pursued by Theobald-na-Long, the son of Richard-an-Iarainn, and by David, the son of Ulick-na-Timchill, through enmity[k]; and they overtook him in the vicinity of Gort-innse-Guaire[l], and, finding Dermot attended only by a small number of troops, they beheaded him. Though he was found in this condition, these people would not have dared to attack him thus a short time before, for he was a leader of fifteen hundred men, and he himself was a stout champion. But no man can escape death when his last day has arrived.

The Lord of Sliabh-Ardacha[m], i. e. James, the son of Pierce, son of James Butler, died in the winter of this year.

ne Long Burke, who had a company of an hundred Foot in her Majesties pay (notwithstanding all Dermot's Safe guards) assaulted him, who, for his safetie, retired into an olde Church, burnt it over his head, and in comming foorth of the same hee killed about fortie of his men, and tooke him prisoner, and the morning following cut off his head." Carew adds: "Her Majestie's honour was blemished, and the service hindred, by this malitious and hatefull murther; who, considering of the fact, besides sharpe rebukes and reprehensions, the Lord Deputie was commanded presently to casheere and discharge him both of his Command and Entertainment."

[m] *Sliabh Ardacha*, now Slieveardagh, or Slewardagh, a barony in the east of the county of Tipperary. According to O'Heerin's topographical poem, this was originally the country of a family of O'Deas.

Remann a burc mac Seaain na ssmar, mic Riocaird ṡaxanaiġ, do bḟiṫ ina ḋuine uasal, oirdearc, iompáiteach do réir gnaṫaiġṫe gaoídel an tan so. Baoí sidhe co na ḋeirbḃraiṫribh (Seaan óg, uilliam, ⁊ tomás) isin dá urmumain ⁊ i néle i samhradh, i ffoghmar, ⁊ i ngeimhreadh na bliadhna so. Baoí do lesdhacht ⁊ do lionmhairecht sloiġ, ⁊ socaidhe ag an cclainn sin tSeaain a búrc gur fáraiccheadh, ⁊ gur folmhaiġeadh na tíre, ⁊ na ceinntair fa coimhnesa doibh leó. Ro gabhadh dona bailte caislén iomdha i néle, ⁊ in urmhumhain leó don cur sin. Ba dibhsidhe Suidhe an Róin, bel aṫa dúin gair, ⁊ cúil o ndubháin i nEilibh, ⁊ port a tolchain i nurmhumhain.

Iar ttuitim Uaithne mic Rudhraiġe óicc uí mordha (amhail ro airnedhsiom) do lingeadh laoiġis la Saxanchoibh go ro ġabsat acc aṫnuadhucchadh a naitreabh aolcloch, ⁊ acc suidhe hi sein áitibh slechta conuill ċernaiġ diar bó doṁgnas duthaiġe laoiġis, doiġ ni raibhe a diol doidhre badh hionnsamhail dUaithne agá himdhídhen orra.

Siol cconcobhair failġe .i. Sliocht briain mic caṫaoir mic cuinn mic an ċalbhaiġ do bhiṫh hi ccoimhbáidh gaoidhel fri ré a trí no a ceaṫair do bliadhnaibh gus an tansa. Ro briseadh, ⁊ ro gabhadh leó an airecht sin urmhor caislén Ua ffailge, acht namá an daingean, ⁊ beccán ele a maille friss. Tánaicc dona ardaiustis na hÉreann dia saiġidh fá lughnasadh na bliadhna so go niomat cliaṫh ⁊ sráccadh, go niomat sseal, ⁊ corrán, go ttucc sgrios ⁊ sgotbuain ar barraibh airche, ⁊ anairche an tíre, ⁊ tánicc deiridh a haittreabhaiġ do dol ar toronn, ar teicheadh, ⁊ ar ionnarbadh i nullcoibh ⁊ i ttíribh oile go diuidh na bliadhna so.

[n] *Suidhe-an-roin*, now Shinrone, a small town in the barony of Clonlisk, in the King's County.—See Ordnance Map, sheet 42. See note [e], under the year 1533, p. 1416, *supra*.

[o] *Bel-atha-Duin-Gair*: i. e. Mouth of the Ford of Dungar, now called simply Dungar, an old castle in ruins in the parish of Corbally, barony of Ballybritt, and King's County, and close to the boundary of the county of Tipperary.—See the Ordnance Map, sheet 43.

[p] *Cuil-O-nDubhain*: i. e. the corner or angle of the O'Duanes, now Coolonuane, and sometimes anglicised Cullenwaine, a townland giving name to a parish in the barony of Clonlisk, in the south of the King's County, adjoining the county of Tipperary.—See the Ordnance Map, sheet 46.

[q] *Port-a-Tolchain*, called Portolohane in the Down Survey, and now shortened to Portland, a townland in the parish of Lorha, barony of Lower Ormond, and county of Tipperary.—See note [k], under the year 1442, p. 925, *supra*. No part of this castle, which was erected by O'Madden, is now standing. It is not to be confounded with the castle of Coillte-Ruadha, which belonged to Mac Egan, and which is still in good preservation.

[r] *Conall Cearnach*.—He was the chief of the

Redmond Burke, the son of John of the Shamrocks, son of James, son of Richard Saxonagh, was at this time an illustrious and celebrated gentleman, according to the usages of the Irish. He and his brothers, John Oge, William, and Thomas, remained in the two Ormonds, and in Ely, during the summer, autumn, and winter, of this year; and so great and numerous were the troops and forces of these sons of John Burke, that they ravaged and desolated all the adjacent territories and cantreds. They took many castles on this occasion in Ely and Ormond, among which were Suidhe-an-roin[n], Bel-atha-Dun-Gair[o], and Cuil-O'nDubhain[p], in Ely; and Port-a-Tolchain[q], in Ormond.

After the fall of Owny, the son of Rury Oge O'More, as we have related, Leix was seized by the English; and they proceeded to repair their mansions of lime and stone, and to settle in the old seats of the race of Conall Cearnach[r], to whom Leix was the hereditary principality, for there was no heir worthy of it like Owny, to defend it against them.

The O'Conors Faly, namely, the descendants of Brian, the son of Cahir, son of Con, son of Calvagh, were for three or four years in the Irish confederation, up to this time. During this period they took and destroyed the most[s] of the castles of Offaly, [and, indeed, all], except Dangan[t] and a few others. About Lammas this year the Lord Justice came into their country with many harrows and pracas[u], with many scythes and sickles, and destroyed and reaped[w] the ripe and unripe crops of the territory; and the consequence of this was, that the inhabitants fled, and remained in exile and banishment in Ulster and other territories until the end of this year.

Heroes of the Red Branch in Ulster, early in the first century, and the ancestor of O'More and the seven septs of Leix.

[s] *The most*, urṁor.—This phrase is incorrect, and should be struck out, as incumbering the sentence.

[t] *Dangan*, now Philipstown.—See note [*], under the year 1546, p. 1498, *supra*.

[u] *Praca*.—This term is applied in Munster, to a harrow with very long pins, still used for the purpose of opening, or ripping up the soil around the giuṁar, or grass-corn, when the winter winds have rendered it too hard and stubborn. The Lord Deputy, who was a great student in botany and natural philosophy, used the *praca*, on this occasion, for the purpose of tearing up the corn after it had shot into ear, thus rendering it useless; as corn, after arriving at that stage of maturity, will not, if disturbed at the root, grow any more. This was a grand preparation for the awful famine which soon after ensued in Ireland, to the great destruction of the Milesian race.

[w] *Destroyed and reaped*.—This is possibly a mistake for sgrios no sgoṫbuain, "destroyed or reaped," for Mountjoy was too wise a man to

Doṁnall spáineaċ, mac donnchaiḋ, mic caṫaoir carraiġ ċaonṁánaiġ do sioḋughaḋ ris an lustis isin foġmar do ṡonraḋ. Clann Ḟiachaċ, mic Aoḋa, mic Sſain do ṡioḋucchaḋ ris mar an ccéḋna.

An coḃlach Saxanach ro hordaiccéaḋ lás an mbainríoġain, ⁊ la coṁairle Shaxan do ċor go herinn do ṡaiġiḋ ċoicciḋ ulaḋ. An tan ro hordaiccéaḋ Lord mountioy ina lustis ós erinn im ḟeil patraicc do ṡonnradh aṁail a duḃramar, ro bás gan fuireaċ, gan eassnaḋaḋ ag fúr, ⁊ acc ullmuġaḋ an ċoḃlaiġ ísin in gaċ congaiḃ rainicc a lſs aṁail as déine ⁊ as dſinmneaḋaiġe forcaéṁnacair hi Saxoiḃ don chur sin, uair ba tocráḋ mor mſnman la bainrioġain Saxan, ⁊ lás an ccoṁairle ṫoir, ⁊ aḃus an cosnaṁ ⁊ an coṫuccaḋ doronsat cenél cconaill, ⁊ Eoġain go nulltoiḃ arcſna ⁊ i mbaoí daon rann friú ina naghaiḋ do ġrés, ⁊ dna ba cuiṁneaċ leo ḃeos ⁊ ro bai na ġalar inclſiṫe ina ccriḋe in ro marbaḋ, ⁊ in ro mudhaiġſḋ dia muintir, ⁊ in ro ṫoċaithriot dia narccat, ⁊ dia nionnṁus la coccaḋ na hérenn go sin. Conaḋ é airſcc ar rangatar an coḃlaċ remraite do ċor go herinn go ro ġaḃsat cuan i nách cliaṫ a mí April na bliaḋna so. Ro faoiḋitt assiḋe i nurṫosaċ saṁraiḋ

destroy such part of the corn as was ripe, when he had an army to carry it away.

[x] *Donnell Spaineach.*—He was so called because he was in Spain for four years. "Daniel Keuanus cognomento Hispaniensis, quod in Hispania annos circiter quatuor fuerit commoratus."—*Hist. Cathol. Iber. Compend.*, tom. 3, lib. 4, c. vi.

[y] *Harbour of Dublin.*—This account, which the annalists had from common bruit only, is far from being accurate. Sir Henry Docwra himself informs us, in his curious and valuable little work, *Narration of his Services at Lough Foyle*, written in the summer of 1614, and never yet printed, that the fleet put in first at Knockfergus, now Carrickfergus. His account of the preparation and arrival of this fleet is very curious, and the Editor deems it his duty to lay it here before the reader, that he may compare the English and Irish accounts of the same important event. After detailing the causes which moved him to write this Narration, which were urgent and honourable, he proceeds as follows:

"I had lying by mee some memoriall noates and a greate Number of letters, that if they were well searched ouer, togeather with the helpe of myne owne memorie, were able to bring to light the truth of that which otherwise was like to perish and Consume in Darkenes. I spent a little time to pervse them, & these are the effectes the doing thereof hath produced.

"The Army, consisting in List of 4000 foote & 200 horse, whereof 3000 of the foote, & all the horse, were levied in England, the other 1000 foote were taken of the old Companys about Dublin, & all assigned to meete att Knockfergus, the first of May: That part levyed in England was shipt at Helbree, neere vnto westchester, on the 24th of Aprill, 1600. And of these a Regiament of 1000 ffoote and 50 horse, were to be taken out imediatelie vpon our landing, & assigned to S[r] Mathew Morgan, to make a plantation with att Ballishannon.

"The Provisions wee carried with vs at first

Donnell Spaineach[x], the son of Donough, son of Cahir Carragh Kavanagh, made peace with the Lord Justice in autumn. The sons of Fiagh, son of Hugh, son of John [O'Byrne], likewise made peace with him.

The English fleet, which had been ordered by the Queen and Council of England to be sent, by Patrick's Day, against the province of Ulster, at the time that Lord Mountjoy was appointed Lord Justice over Ireland, as we have said, was being prepared and equipped, without delay or neglect, with all the necessary engines, in England; for it was a great annoyance of mind to the Queen and the Councils there and here that the Kinel-Owen, the Kinel-Connell, and Ulstermen in general, and those who were in alliance with them, had made so long a defence and stand against them; and they also called to mind, and it preyed like a latent disease upon their hearts, all of their people that had been slain and destroyed, and of their wealth that they had expended, in carrying on the Irish war till then, so that they resolved to send this fleet to Ireland; and it arrived in the harbour of Dublin[y] in the month of April of this year. From thence they set out in the very beginning of summer (by advice of the

were a quantetie of deale Boards & Sparrs of ffirr timber, a 100 flock bedds, with other necessaries to furnish an Hospitall withall; one Peece of Demy Cannon of Brass, two Culverins of Iron, a master Gunner, two master masons, & two master Carpenters, allowed in pay, with a greate number of Tooles & other vtensiles, and with all victuell & munition requisite.

"Soe, with those men from England, and with these Provisions aforesaide, on the xxv. day of Aprill wee sett saile, and on the 28th, in the Euening, put in att Knockfergus, where wee staide the space of 8 dayes before the Companyes from Dublin came all vnto vs.

"The last of them coming in by the 6th of May, on the 7th wee sett saile againe, and the windes often fayling, sometimes full against vs, it was the 14th before wee could putt in to the mouth of the Bay at Loughfoyle; & noe sooner were wee entred, but wee fell on ground, & soe stucke till the next day; then, at a full tide, wee waighed our Anchors, sayled a little way, and rune on ground againe.

"On the 16th, in the morning, wee gott loose, & about 10 of the Clocke (100 men lying on shoare, & giuing vs a volie of shott, & soe retyring) wee landed att Culmore, & with the first of our horse & foote that wee could vnshipp, made vp towards a troupe of horse and foote that wee sawe standing before vs on the topp of a hill, but, by ignorance of the wayes, our horses were presentlie boggt, & soe, at that day, wee made none other vse but onelie to land our men. The next day, the place seaming to my Judgement fitt to build, wee beganne about the Butt end of the old broken Castle, to cast vp a fforte, such as might be capable to lodge 200 men in.

"Sixe days wee spent in labour about it, in which meane space, makeing vpp into the countrie with some troupes (onely with intent to discouer), wee came to Ellogh, a castle of O'Dogharteys, which he had newlie abandoned, & begunne to pull downe; but seeing it yett

(tria coṁairle iarla ċloinne riocaird ⁊ iarla tuaḋmuṁan) ⁊ ro forcongraḋ forra toċt go loċ feḃail mic lodain. Seolaitt iaraṁ laimh clí fri hErinn

Tenentable, & of good vse to be held, I put Captaine Ellis Floudd into it, & his Companie of 150 men.

"On the 22nd of May wee put the Army in order to marche, & leauing Captaine Lancellott Atford at Culmore, with 600 men, to make vp the workes, wee went to the Derry, 4 myles of, vpon the River side, a place in manner of an Iland, Comprehending within it 40 acres of Ground, wherein were the Ruines of a old Abbay, of a Bishopps house, of two Churches, &, at one of the ends of it, of an old castle; the Riuer, called Loughfoyle, encompassing it all on one side, & a bogg, most comonlie wett, and not easilie passable except in two or three places, dividing it from the maine land.

"This peece of Ground wee possest ourselves of without Resistaunce, & iudging it a fitt place to make our maine plantation in, being somewhat hie, & therefore dry, & healthie to dwell vpon; att that end where the old Castle stood, being Close to the water side, I presentlie resolved to raise a fforte to keepe our stoore of Munition & victuells in, & in the other, a little aboue, where the walls of an old Cathedrall church were yet standing, to erect annother for our future safetie and retreate vnto vpon all occasions.

"Soe then I vnloaded & discharged the Shipping that brought vs, all but those reserued for Sr Math: Morgan, & two Men of Warre vnder Comaund of Captaine George Thornton & Captaine Thomas Fleminge, which were purposlie assigned to attend vs all that Sommer; & the first bussines I setled myselfe vnto was to lay out the forme of the said two intended ffortes, & to assigne to every Companye his seuerall taske, how and where to worke.

"I know there were some that presentlie beganne to censure mee for not sturring abroade, & makeing iourneyes vp into the Countrye, alleadging wee were stronge enough & able to doe it; I deny not but wee were, but that was not the scope and drift of our coming; wee were to sitt it out all winter; Prayes would not be sett without many hazards & a greate Consumption of our men, the Countrie was yet vnknowne vnto vs, & those wee had to deale with were, as I was sure, would Chuse or Refuse to feight with vs, as they sawe theire owne advantage. These Considerations moued mee to resolue to hould an other Course, & before I attempted any thinge els, to setle & make sure the footing wee had gayned.

"The two shipps of warre, therefore (the Countrie all about vs being wast & burned), I sent with souldiers in them to coast all alonge the shoare for the space of 20 or 30 myles, & willed wheresoeuer they found any howses, they should bring a way the Timber & other materialls to build withall, such as they could. And O'Cane hauing a woode lying right ouer against vs (on the other side of the River) wherein was plentie of old growne Birch, I daylie sent workemen with a Guard of souldiers to cutt it downe, & there was not a sticke of it brought home, but was first well fought for. A Quarrie of stone & slatt wee found hard at hand. Cockle shells to make Lyme, wee discouered infinite plentie of in a little Iland in the mouth of the Harbour as wee came in, and with those helpes, togeather with the Provisions wee brought, & the stones and rubbidge of the old Buildings wee found, wee sett our selues wholie, & with all the dilligence wee could possible to fortefying & framing & setting vpp of howses such as wee might be able to liue in, & defend ourselves when winter should Come, & our men be decayed, as it was apparant it would be. And whether this was the right Course to

Earl of Clanrickard and of the Earl of Thomond); and they were ordered to put into the harbour of the Lake of Feabhal, son of Lodan[a]. They then sailed,

take or noe, let them that sawe the after Euents be the Judges of.

"My lord Deputie att the time wee should land (to make our discent the more easie) was drawne downe to the Blackwater & gaue out that hee would enter the Countrey that way; wherevpon Tyrone & O Donell had assembled theire cheifest strength to oppose against him: But his lordship now knowing wee were safe on shore, & possest of the ground wee went to inhabite, withdrewe his Campe & retourned to Dublin, & then being deliuered of that feare, those forces they had brought togeather for that purpose, being now encreased by the addition of more, & estimated (by Comon fame) to be about 5000 in all, they came downe with vpon vs, & placing themselves in the night within litle more then a mile from where wee lay, earelie in the morning at the Breaking vpp of the watch, gaue on vpon our Corps de Gaurd of horse, chased them home to our foote Sentynells, & made a Countennunce as if they came to make but that one dayes worke of it; but the Alarume taken, & our men in Armes, they contented themselves to attempe noe further, but seeking to drawe vs forth into the Countrey where they hoped to take vs at some aduantages, & finding wee stoode vpon our defensiue onelie, after the greatest parte of the day spent in skrimish a litle without our Campe, they departed towards the Eueninge, whither did wee not thinke it fitt to pursue them.

"An now did S[r] Mathew Morgan demaund his Regiament of 1000 foote, & 50 horse, which at first (as I saide before) were designed him for a Plantation att Ballyshannon, but vpon Consultation held how hee should proceed, & with what Probabilitie he might be able to effect that intended bussines, there appeared soe many wants & difficulties vnthought on, or vnprouided for before, that it was euident those forces should be exposed to manifest Ruine, if at that time, & in the state as thinges then stoode, hee should goe forward; the truth whereof being certified both by himselfe & mee to the lords of the Councell in England, as alsoe to the lord Deputie & Councell of Ireland, wee received present directions from them both to suspend the proceeding in that action till annother time, & soe I discharged the Rest of the shipping reserued for that iourney, & not long after the Companys growing weake, & the list of the foote reduced to the number of 3000, that Regiament was wholie dissolued & made as a parte onelie of our army.

"On the first of June, s[r] Arthur O Neale, sonne to old Tirlogh Lenogh that had beene O Neale, came in vnto mee with some 30 horse & foote, a Man I had directions from the state, to labour to drawe to our side, & to promise to be made Earle of Tyroane, if the other that mainteyned the Rebellion could be dispossessed of the Countrey. By his advice within fewe dayes after I sent s[r] John Chamberlaine, with 700 men, into O Canes Countrie, to enter into it by Boate from O Doghertyes side, because at the hither end, lying right ouer against vs, was a Continuall watch kepte, soe as wee could not stirre but wee were sure to be presentlie discouered. These men, marching all night, put ouer at Greencastle, & by breake of day, on the 10th of June, fell in the middest of theire Creagtes vnexpected, Ceazed a greate Pray, & brought it to the Waterside. But for want of meanes to bring it all away, they hackt & mangled as many as they could, & with some 100 Cowes, which they put abord theire Boats, besids what the Souldiers brought away kild, they retourned."

[a] *The lake of Feabhal, son of Lodan,* now Lough

co ro ġaiḃsiot port isin maiġin sin ro hérbadh friú. Iar roċtain doiḃ i ttir ro toccḃadh leo ar gaċ taeḃ don ċuan trí puirt do trinsiḋiḃ talṁan aṁail ro hordaiġeaḋ doiḃ i Saxoiḃ, port diḃsiḋe ar chuitt Uí neill don tír i niomḟocraiḃ oireachta uí catháin .i. dun na long, ⁊ dá port i nduthaiġ uí doṁnaill, port diobh isin chúil móir i ndúṫhaiġ uí ḋoċartaiġ hi ttrioċa ċéd innsi heoġain, ⁊ port oile don taoḃ ṫiarṫes de sin i ndoire choluim ċille. Ro gaḃsat na goill fo cedoir acc doiṁniuccaḋ díocc ina ttimcell, ⁊ acc denaṁ daingen ṁúr criaḋ, ⁊ dúnclaḋ ndíomor co mbatar ionċosnaiṁ fri bioḋbaḋaiḃ. Rostar daingne ⁊ rostar innille olttáit na cúirte cloċ aolta ⁊ na caṫracha sin i ccaitti ré ḟoda ⁊ saoṫar dermáir occa ndenaṁ. Ar a haiṫle sin ro bloḋsat an ṁainistir, ⁊ an daṁliacc, ⁊ ro haiḋmilleaḋ leo ina mbaoí dobair ecclastacḋa isin mbaile co neadrnsat tiġe ⁊ cuḃachla diobh. henry docura ainm an generala baoí leó. Ridire erdearc eside co ngaois ⁊ co nglioccas, ⁊ ro baḋ rinn áġa, ⁊ ersġaile din. Sé mile ba sé lion tangatar an dú sin. Iar ttocht co doire doiḃsiḋe do ronsat briġh mbicc don ċuil móir ⁊ do ḋún na long. Batar na goill ré foda na ro leicc in oṁan, nó an imeccla doiḃ toċt tar na muraiḃ sechtair, acht ed mbecc, ⁊ no ḃidís drong mór dioḃ hi ccaṫair gach noiḋche, ar na tardṫa ammus forra, go ro líonaitt do ṡaoṫ ⁊ do ġalar la hiomcuimgi an ionaid i mbátar, ⁊ la tes na síne samrata. At baṫsat iolḃuiḋne dioḃ don teidhm isin.

Iomṫúsa Uí Doṁnaill o ro airiġsiḋe a nemṫaṫaiġe ar a sccoraiḃ sechtair la faitċes ⁊ oṁan, ba sed do roine nemhni do ḋenam dioḃ, ⁊ ro teclamaitt a sloigh lais do ḋol i ndeiscert ċóicciḋ connaċt dionnraḋ na ttuaṫ bádar ar gaċ taeḃ do sleiḃ echtge, ⁊ tuaḋmuṁain do ṡonraḋ. Deiṫbir ón ar báttar iad na hiarlaḋa .i. Iarla cloinne riocaird ⁊ Iarla tuaḋmuṁan ro ḟurail for an lustir, ⁊ for an ccoṁairle an tarccar tromsloiġ sin do chur cuicce sium

Foyle, situated between the counties of Londonderry and Donegal.—See note [f], under the year 1248, p. 331, *supra*.

[a] *Dun-na-long*, i.e. the Fort of the Ships, now Dunnalong, on the east side of the River Foyle, in the barony of Tirkeeran, and county of Londonderry.

[b] *Oireacht-Ui-Chathain*, i.e. O'Kane's country. Dunnalong was in the territory of O'Gormly, which was tributary to O'Neill.

[c] *Cuil-mor*, i.e. the Great Corner or Angle, now Culmore, a fort on a point of land over Lough Foyle, about five miles to the north of Londonderry, in the barony of Inishowen, and county of Donegal.

[d] *Of them*, i.e. of the materials obtained from them.

[e] *Six thousand men*.—This is not correct, nor

keeping their left to Ireland, until they put into the harbour of that place, as they had been directed. After landing, they erected on both sides of the harbour three forts, with trenches sunk in the earth, as they had been ordered in England. One of these forts, i. e. Dun-na-long[a], was erected on O'Neill's part of the country, in the neighbourhood of Oireacht-Ui-Chathain[b]; and two in O'Donnell's country, one at Cuil-mor[c], in O'Doherty's country, in the cantred of Inishowen, and the other to the south-west of that, at Derry-Columbkille. The English immediately commenced sinking ditches around themselves, and raising a strong mound of earth and a large rampart, so that they were in a state to hold out against enemies. These were stronger and more secure than courts of lime and stone, or stone forts, in the erection of which much time and great labour might be spent. After this they tore down the monastery and cathedral, and destroyed all the ecclesiastical edifices in the town, and erected houses and apartments of them[d]. Henry Docwra was the name of the general who was over them. He was an illustrious Knight, of wisdom and prudence, a pillar of battle and conflict. Their number was six thousand men[e]. When these arrived at Derry they made little account of Culmore or Dun-na-long. The English were a long time prevented, by fear and dread, from going outside the fortifications, except to a short distance; and a great number of them were on the watch every night, that they might not be attacked [unawares]; so that they were seized with distemper and disease, on account of the narrowness of the place in which they were, and the heat of the summer season. Great numbers of them died of this sickness.

As for O'Donnell, when he perceived that they were not in the habit of going outside their encampments, through fear and dread, he made no account of them, and assembled his forces, to proceed into the south of Connaught, to plunder the countries that lay on both sides of Sliabh-Echtge[f], and especially Thomond. He had good reason for this, indeed, for it was these Earls, namely, the Earl of Clanrickard and the Earl of Thomond, who had requested the Lord Justice and the Council to send over this great army, to keep him[g] in his [own]

is it a matter of surprise that the Four Masters should not have known the exact number. Sir Henry Docwra himself states that he had only four thousand foot and two hundred horse.

[f] *On both sides of Sliabh-Echtge*, i. e. Clanrickard and Thomond.

[g] *To keep him*, i. e. to give him something to do at home, and prevent him from overrunning

dia ḟosdaḋ ina ṫír ina neccmais ar a mſince leo nó tſiġſḋ som dia ttír ḟſissin. O ro chinn for an ccoṁairle sin ro ḟaccaib ó dochartaiġ taoíseaċ innsi heoġain .i. Sſan óg, mac Sſain, mic felim uí doċartaiġ hi ffoichill forr na hallmurchoiḃ ar na tiostais dionnsaḋ a ċriche. Ro ḟáccaibh dna Niall garḃ ó doṁnaill, ⁊ arail dia ṡluaġ i niomḟuiḋe forra alla niar, ſtorra, ⁊ trioċa ċéd énda mic néill. Ro tionoileaḋ a ṡloiġ lais iar sin co ndiccsſḋ tar eirne siar. Do bſrt lais céttus gaċ aén baoí fo a ṁamus i nullτoiḃ ar in slóiġeaḋ sin. Bátar tra connaċtaiġ ó Suca go drobaoís, ⁊ o iarṫar tíre haṁalgaiḋ go breifne uí raicchilliġ acc ḟſiṫſṁ, ⁊ acc furnaiḋe ar a ḋolsoṁ dia saiġiḋ go baile an mótaiġ iar na ttocht fo a ṫoġairm sium. Ba do na connachtoiḃ baí hisuidhe acca ernaiḋe sium O ruairc Brian óg mac briain, mic briain ḃallaiġ mic eoġain, O concoḃair Sliġiġ Donnchaḋ, mac caṫail óicc, mic taiḋg, mic caṫail óicc gus na tuathaiḃ filſt fri coirrsliaḃ a tuaiḋ co muir, O concoḃair ruaḋ Aoḋ mac toirrḋealḃaiġ ruaiḋ mic taiḋcc buiḋe, mic caṫail ruaiḋ go lion a ṫionoil, Mac diarmata maiġe luirc .i. concoḃar, mac taiḋg, mic eogain, mic taiḋg co na muinntir, ⁊ Mac uilliam búrc .i. tepóitt mac uatéir ciotaiġ, mic Sſain, mic oiluerais co na ṫoiċſstal.

Ar ndol dUa doṁnaill co na soċraitte a hulltoib i ndáil na cconnaċtaċ sin go baile an Mótaiġ ro arccna don ċorann, tre lár maiġe haí an ḟind-ḃſndaiġ, do cloinn connmaiġ, do ċríċ maine mic eaċḋaċ, ⁊ durlár cloinne Riocaird gan caṫ gan coinnsgle gan guin duine uaḋ, ná lais co ro ġaḃ sosaḋ ⁊ longport i niarṫar cloinne riocaird i noireaċt rémainn im tráṫnona dia saṫairn ⁊ an ḟeil eoin ar an mairt ar ccind. Rangattar raibte roiṁe i ttuaḋmuṁain an tan sin, ⁊ ro baḋ doiġ leó na gluaisfeaḋ as an ionad i ttárrustair oidche doṁnaiġ go sorcha maidne dia luain. Nír ḃo hſḋ sin

Clanrickard and Thomond. If O'Donnell had remained at home to guard his own Tirconnell, instead of making forays into Clanrickard and Thomond, Docwra's forces would have been rendered completely powerless; and had Niall Garv remained faithful to Hugh Roe, he could have easily annihilated Docwra's men.

[h] *The cantred of Enda, son of Niall:* i. e. Tir-Enda, i. e. the territory of Enda, son of Niall of the Nine Hostages. According to Teige, the son of Tibot Mac Linshy, who had been steward to the celebrated Hugh Roe O'Donnell, and who was living in 1620, this territory contained thirty quarters of land. It was the name of the north-east part of the barony of Raphoe, adjoining the Lagan, which is still well known, and comprising, according to Mac Linshy, forty-six quarters of land.—See note [d], under the year

territory, away from them, for they deemed it [too] often that he had gone into their territories. Having adopted this resolution, he left O'Doherty, chieftain of Inishowen, i. e. John Oge, the son of John, son of Felim O'Doherty, to watch the foreigners, that they might not come to plunder his territory. He also left Niall Garv O'Donnell, and some of his army, encamped against them on the west side, between them and the cantred of Enda, son of Niall[h]. He then mustered his forces, to proceed westwards across the River Erne. He took with him on this hosting, in the first place, all those who were under his jurisdiction in Ulster; and the Connacians, from the River Suck to the Drowes, and from the west of Tirawly to Breifny O'Reilly, were expecting and awaiting his arrival at Ballymote, whither they were gone at his summons. Among the Connaughtmen who awaited him there were O'Rourke (Brian Oge, the son of Brian, son of Brian Ballagh, son of Owen); O'Conor Sligo (Donough, the son of Cathal Oge, son of Teige, son of Cathal Oge), together with the people of the districts which lie from Coirrshliabh northwards to the sea; O'Conor Roe (Hugh, the son of Turlough Roe, son of Teige Boy, son of Cathal Roe), with all his muster; Mac Dermot of Moylurg, i. e. Conor, son of Teige, son of Owen, son of Teige, with his people; and Mac William Burke, i. e. Theobald, the son of Walter Kittagh, son of John, son of Oliver, with his muster.

When O'Donnell and his forces out of Ulster had joined these Connaughtmen at Ballymote, he marched through Corran, through the middle of Magh-Ai-an-Fhinnbheannaigh[i], through Clann-Conway, and through the territory of Maine, son of Eochaidh[j], and the level part of Clanrickard, without giving battle or skirmish, and without killing or losing a man; and he halted and pitched his camp in the west of Clanrickard, in the Oireacht-Redmond[k], on the evening of Saturday, the Tuesday following being the festival of St. John. On this occasion, notice [of his approach] was sent into Thomond before him [by spies]; and they thought that he would not move from the place where he was stopping on Saturday night till daylight on Monday morning. But this is not what he

1175, p. 19, *supra*.

[i] *Magh-Ai-an Fhinnbheannaigh*, now Machaire Chonnacht, in the county of Roscommon. For its exact situation see note [h], under the year 1189, p. 87, *supra*.

[j] *The territory of Maine, son of Eochaidh:* i. e. Ui-Maine, or Hy-Many, O'Kelly's country.—See *Tribes and Customs of Hy-Many*, pp. 4, 25.

[k] *Oireacht-Redmond*.—A district in the barony of Kiltartan, in the county of Galway, belonging to a sept of the Burkes.—See note under the year 1599.

do róine sium, aċt eirġe a moiċdeḋoil na maidne dia domhnaigh co ro ṫairm-ċimnigh ar a aghaidh doireċt rémainn, do ċenél Aoḋa, do ċenél dúnġaile, ⁊ do cloinn cuiléin uaċtair go rainicc tar forġus siar iar narccain urṁoir na noirsir sin ria miḋmsdon an laoí sin. Gaḃais Ua domhnaill longport in adhaiġ sin for brú an forġair fri cluain ráṁata aniar ar loscadh innsi uile cenmothá an mainistir. Ro léicc sccaoileaḋ da sccеiṁealtaiḃ do arccain na noirsir ina ṫimċell. Ba fairsing foirlsṫan an tsirréiḋeaḋ o a roile do sonsat na sccеiṁelta sin, uair ro cuartaiġeaḋ, ⁊ ro creaċloisccеaḋ, ro hinnraḋ, ⁊ ro hoirccеaḋ leó (on ionam céDna do ló go hoiḋċe) ó ċraicc uí ċiordubain i niocṫar na coiccriche hi ttrioċait céd na noilén, co caṫair murchaḋa hi ccorcabaiscind iarṫaraiġ go dorus cille muire, ⁊ Caṫrach Ruiss, ⁊ in ṁagha i nuiḃ bracáin go dorus ḃaile Eoin goḃann i ccorcamod-ruaḋ, ⁊ boithe neill hi ccenel fsrmaic. Rob ioṁḋa dna daoṫhain dsġduine uasail no tiġearna tire ag cuideċta csṫhrair nó cúiccir do ṁuintir ui doṁ-naill ar sccáth muine, ⁊ i lúib tuimm hi ttuaḋmuṁain in oidhche sin.

Ro éiriġ Ua domhnaill ar a ḃaraċ isin maḋain dia luain go foraiḋ ionmall, gan tosraim, gan tinnesnas co na sloġaiḃ ar a bpupallḃoṫaiḃ belscálánca ⁊ gaḃait occ ascnaṁ na conaire fiarṫarsna tuaḋmuṁan sairtuaiḋ gach ndíreaċ doirṫsr ó ccorbmaic, dorlár ċeneoil ffsrmaic, ⁊ do ḃoirinn go rangatar ria nadhaiġ go mainistir ċorcomodruaḋ, ⁊ go carcair na ccléireaċ co na ccreaċaiḃ, ⁊ co na ngaḃalaiḃh leó. Bátar na slóiġ ag túr ⁊ acc

[l] *Cinel-Aedha*, *anglice* Kinelea, was O'Shaughnessy's country, in the south-east of the barony of Kiltartan.

[m] *Cinel-Donghaile.*—This is the tribe name of the O'Gradys, and it became, as usual in Ireland, that of their territory also. In latter ages this territory comprised the parishes of Tomgraney, Mayno, Inishcaltra, and Clonrush, of which the two latter parishes are now included in the county of Galway, but both belong to the deanery of O mBloid and diocese of Killaloe.

[n] *Craig-Ui-Chiardubhain:* i. e. O'Kirwan's rock, now Craggykerrivane, a townland in the parish of Cloondagad, barony of Clonderalaw, and county of Clare.

[o] *Cantred of the Islands*, now the barony of Islands in the same county.

[p] *Cathair-Murchadha:* i. e. Murrough's Stone Fort, now Cahermurphy, a townland containing the ruins of a caher or Cyclopean stone fort, in the parish of Kilmurry Mac Mahon, barony of Clonderalaw, or East Corca-Bhaiscinn, in the same county.

[q] *Kilmurry:* i. e. Kilmurry, in the barony of Ibrickan.

[r] *Cathair-Ruis*, now Caherross, a townland containing the ruins of a castle in the parish of Kilmurry Ibrickan.—See note [s], under the year 1573, p. 1672, *supra*.

[s] *Baile-Eoin-Gabhann*, now Ballingowan, or

did, but rose up at day-break on Sunday morning, and marched forward through Oireacht-Redmond, through Cinel-Aedha[l], through Cinel-Donghaile[m], and through Upper Clann-Cuilein, and before the middle of that day had passed westwards across the River Fergus, after having plundered the greater part of these districts. On that night O'Donnell pitched his camp on the banks of the Fergus, to the west of Clonroad, after having plundered the entire of Ennis, except the monastery. He sent forth marauding parties, to plunder the surrounding districts; and far and wide did these parties spread themselves about the country; for from that time of the day till night they traversed, burned, plundered, and ravaged [the region extending] from Craig-Ui-Chiardhubhain[n], in the lower part of the frontiers of the Cantred of the Islands[o], to Cathair-Murchadha[p] in West [*recte* East] Corca-Bhaiscinn, to the gates of Kilmurry[q] of Cathair-Ruis[r], and of Magh in Hy-Bracain to the gate of Baile-Eoin-Gabhann[s] in Corcomroe, and of Both-Neill[t] in Kinel-Fearmaic. Many a feast, fit for a goodly gentleman, or for the lord of a territory, was enjoyed throughout Thomond this night by parties of four or five men, under the shelter of a shrubbery, or at the side of a bush.

On the following morning, Monday, O'Donnell set out with his forces from their tents and pavilions, steadily and slowly, without pursuit or hurry; and they proceeded on their way diagonally across Thomond, exactly in a north-easterly direction, through the east of Hy-Cormaic[u] and the level of Kinel-Fearmaic, and through Burren, and arrived before night, with their preys and spoils, at the monastery of Corcomroe, and at Carcair-na-gCleireach[w]. The troops continued scouring and traversing the country around them while day-

Ballygowan, *alias* Smithstown, a townland in which are the ruins of a castle in good preservation, in the parish of Kilshanny, barony of Corcomroe, and county of Clare.—See note [y], under the year 1573, p. 1670, *supra*.

[t] *Both-Neill:* i. e. Niall's booth, hut, or tent, now *anglice* Bohneill, and in Irish *Cuirt Bhoithe Neill*, a castle situated in a townland of the same name, in the parish of Rath, barony of Inchiquin, and county of Clare. In a list of the castles of the county of Clare preserved in a manuscript in the Library of Trinity College, Dublin, E. 2. 14, this castle is set down as belonging to "Teige mac Morogh O'Brien."

[u] *Hy-Cormaic*, a district in the barony of Islands, and county of Clare, now supposed to be co-extensive with the parish of Kilmaley, but it was anciently much larger, as has been already proved.—See note [p], under the year 1573, p. 1668, *supra*.

[w] *Carcair-na-gCleireach:* i. e. the Narrow Road of the Clerics. This name is still preserved, and is applied to a narrow and steep road extending from the abbey of Corcomroe towards Corranrue, in the barony of Burren, and county of Clare. It is usually called the Corker road in English.

taistel na tíre ina ttimcell tar an caemh laiṫe co nár ḟáccaibset aittreabh, no árus badh ionáirimh gan loscadh gan léir sccrios. Ro badh smúittċeó diadh ⁊ deathaiġe in tír uile dia néar só a bfairsccriona da gaċ leiṫ iompa imaccuairt, ⁊ ro badh lór dia ccor for fordal conaire aidble na dobairċiach deathaiġe baoí uaistiḃ eattarbuas in gach ionadh a ttabhratais i naghaidh isin ló céttna.

Atraġatt na sloigh im Ua nDomhnaill ar a ḃárach dia mairt, ⁊ lotar tar beilgiḃ beannchairrgiḋe na bán Ḃóirne, ⁊ tar an ccarcair ccumhaing ccaolródaiġ gan troid, gan taċar, gan tóraiġeċt, gan tograim go rangatar go meandata maiġreaiḋe Meadhraiḋe. Airisitt an adhaiġ sin ar cnoc an gearráin báin eitir chill Ċolgan ⁊ gaillimh. Ro eidirdeiliġsiot a ccreaċa ⁊ a ngabála fri aroile, ar a barach an dú sin, ⁊ ro baí gaċ drong diob iarttain ag dírġeadh ⁊ acc dlúiṫiomáin a ṡealba saindírle budeisin hi séd ṡliġtiḃ caomċoiġidh Con-naċt. Nir bo foda an uiḋe ruccsat an ló sin eiccin, ar robtar scíthiġ tuirsiġ, ⁊ ní ro ċuilsiot a samhċodladh an adhaiġ riamh ar uamhan a fobarta ó a mbiodhḃadhaiḃ iar nindreadh a ttíre tárra. Do ġniatt longport i ccom-foċraib dóiḃ an adhaiġ sin ó ro laiseat in imeccla díoḃ. Ro gabsat a ngille, ⁊ a naradha acc urgnamh a bproinne go ro ṫóchaiṫsiot iaramh a mbiúdh gomtar sáithiġ, contuilsiot hi sáimhe gó ar a ḃarach. Atraċtatar an slóġ ar a suan ⁊ tiaġait hi cceann tréda. Ro chéadaiġ Ua domhnaill do Mhac uilliam, ⁊ don luċt dus rangatar a hiarṫar connaċt soadh dia ttiġiḃ. Luidh fein soir gaċ ndíreaċ is na conairiḃ coitċeanna go ráinicc dfoidh laoí go conmaicne cúile tola i nedirmeadhón an ċoiccidh. Airisit ann an adhaiġ sin.

Ro forċongair Ua domhnaill ar a ḃaraċ for a muinntir a ninnile criċe arċeana, ⁊ a néadala do leiccean uadhaiḃ dia ttiġiḃ, a ngiollanraidh, a naés diairm, ⁊ gonta do leiccean leó. Ro badh don druing rortar aṫgaoite dia maiṫiḃ an tan sin. Tadhcc ócc, mac neill, mic neill ruaidh, mic néill, mic toirrdhealḃaiġ óicc, mic toirrdhealḃaiġ ḃearnaiġ uí ḃaoiġill, ⁊ duiḃgionn, mac ṁeccon, mic con-

[x] *Set them astray.*—The word fordal is explained by O'Clery, "do-eól .i. seaċrán, i. e. want of knowledge, i. e. going astray."

[y] *Carcair:* i. e. of Carcair-na-gCleireach.

[z] *Meadhraighe.*—This is latinized *Medrigia* by O'Flaherty in his *Ogygia*. The name is still preserved (pronounced *Maaree*) and is applied to a peninsula extending into the bay of Galway, and comprising the whole of the parish of Ballynacourty, about five miles to the south of the town of Galway.

[a] *Cnoc-an-ghearrain-bhain:* i. e. the Hill of the White Garron or Horse, now Knockagarranbaun, a hill on which a fair is held yearly,

light remained; so that they left no habitation or mansion worthy of note which they did not burn and totally destroy. All the country behind them, as far as they could see around on every side, was [enveloped in] one dark cloud of vapour and smoke; and, during the entire of that day, the vastness of the dark clouds of smoke that rose over them aloft in every place to which they directed their course, was enough to set them astray[x] on their route.

On the following day, Tuesday, O'Donnell and his forces rose up and proceeded through the rocky passes of White Burren, and through the close and narrow road of Carcair[y], without receiving battle or skirmish, and without being followed or pursued, until they reached the mansions on the smooth plain of Meadhraighe[z]. They remained that night on the hill of Cnoc-an-ghearrain-bhain[a], between Kilcolgan and Galway. On the following day they divided the spoils and booty among one another at that place; and each party of them were then guiding and closely driving their own lawful portions of the property along the roads of the fair province of Connaught. The journey which they performed on that day was not a long one, for they were weary and fatigued, not having been able to sleep on the night before, through fear of being attacked by the enemies whose country they had plundered. Having now altogether laid aside their apprehensions, they made an encampment for the night before they had gone far. Their servants and attendants proceeded to prepare their dinner, and, having taken food till they were satisfied, they retired to rest until morning, when the army, rising from their slumber, proceeded on their journey. O'Donnell permitted MacWilliam and those who had come from Iar-Connaught to return to their homes. He set out himself in a directly eastern direction, along the common roads, until he arrived, at the end of the day, in Conmaicne-Cuile-Tolaigh[b], in the very centre of the province, where he remained for that night.

On the next day O'Donnell ordered his people to send away all their cattle-spoils and plunders home to their houses, and to let their servants and the unarmed and wounded go along with them. Among those of their chiefs who were mortally wounded at this time were Teige Oge, the son of Niall, son of Niall Roe, son of Turlough Bearnach O'Boyle; and Duigin, the son of Maccon,

situated about a mile to the north of the village of Clarinbridge.

[b] *Conmaicne-Cuile-Tolaigh*, now the barony of Kilmaine, in the south of the county of Mayo.

coiccriche uí Cléirigh, ⁊ ba hann ro gonadh iadside, aráon la druing ele do ṁuinntir Uí Domhnaill ro báttar ag ionnsaighidh an cláir móir for Iarla Tuadh-mumhan. As ón cclár sin ainmnighthear conntae an cláir. Atbathsat an diar remraite for an cconair ag sóadh doibh, ⁊ ro iomchuirett araon dia ttíribh co ro hadhnaicitt i nDún na nGall.

Ro léicc trá Ua Domhnaill drong mór dia mílidhaibh ⁊ dia amsaibh las na creachaibh, ⁊ las an lucht remraite do ṡeóduccadh conaire doibh. Ro comhairléicc d'Ua Ruairc, ⁊ dia muinntir toidhecht dia ttighibh, ⁊ do Chonnachtaibh archena. Forthais trá Ua Domhnaill cóicc céd laoch do roighnibh a ṁíleadh ina ḟochair co seascat marcach dia ṡainṁuintir badhéin a maille friú. Airisit isin longport i mbátar in adhaigh riamh go hiar medhón laí. Lottar iaramh tres an ccoicceadh soirdheas go mbáttar acc Loch Riach i ccrepuscul na maidne ar a bárach. Ba heiside port aireachais Iarla Cloinne Riocaird. Ro léiccriot a sccéimelta ar gach leith díobh d'indreadh na criche, co ro ṫionoilsiot ina mbaoí do crodh, ⁊ d'innili in gach aird ina niomfochraibh, ⁊ do ratsat leo go haon maighin. Tiaghait co na ccreachaibh leo tres an ccoicceadh soir gur gabsat longport i nimel an tíre fri Suca i ndeas, adhaigh an domhnaigh do ṡonradh, airisit hisuidhe co madain an luain. Lottar ar a bárach tar Ath Liacc Ffionn for an Suca, ⁊ tre Magh naoí mic Allguba go rangatar gus an Seghais im thráth nóna, gabhait longport fris an abhainn a tuaidh in adhaigh sin. Tiaghait ar a barach tar Coirrṡliabh na Seghsa, ⁊ tre criochaibh an Chorainn ⁊ co baile an Mhótaigh. Scaoilit na sloigh dia ttighibh iaramh, co nédálaibh ⁊ co nionnmhasaibh.

Mac uí Neill .i. Sir Art, mac Toirrdhealbhaigh Luinigh, mic Neill Conallaigh, mic Airt mic Cuinn, do dhol hi ccenn na nGall (ro gabh port i nDún na long) do chocadh ar Ua Neill, ⁊ an tan céona sa dfághail báis i ffarradh na nGall rémraite.

Imthúsa Uí Domhnaill, baí co na ṡloghaibh gan fogluasacht o do ruacht a Tuadh-mumhain iarsan turus remraite go September ar ccinn. Iar léccadh a

[c] *The county of Clare is named.*—This is a mere note, which very much incumbers the narrative; but it is very correct, and refutes the idea that the county of Clare has derived its name from Sir Thomas de Clare.

[d] *Seaghais.*—This was the old name of Coirr-shliabh, or the Curlieu range of hills, on the borders of the counties of Roscommon and Sligo.

[e] *Died among the English.*—He joined Docwra with thirty horse and thirty foot on the 1st of June, and died on the 28th of October following. The Queen intended creating him Earl of Tyrone.—See Docwra's *Narration*; and Moryson's *History of Ireland*, book i. c. 2.

son of Cucogry O'Clery; who were both [accidentally] wounded by another party of O'Donnell's people, as they were attacking Clar-mor upon the Earl of Thomond. From this Clar the county of Clare is named[c]. The two aforesaid died on the road, returning home; and they were both carried to their territories, and were buried at Donegal.

O'Donnell sent a large party of his warriors and soldiers with the preys and people aforesaid, to clear the way for them; and he advised O'Rourke and his people, and the other Connaughtmen in general, to return home. O'Donnell retained five hundred heroes of his choice soldiers, and sixty horsemen, of his own faithful people. They remained in the camp in which they had been the night before until after mid-day. They then proceeded through the province in a south-easterly direction, and arrived, by the twilight of the following morning, at Loughrea. This was the chief residence of the Earl of Clanrickard. They sent out marauding parties in every direction to plunder the country; and these collected all the cattle and herds in their neighbourhood in every direction, and brought them to one place. They came with their preys eastwards across the province, and on Sunday pitched their camp with them near the borders of the province, to the south of the Suck, where they remained until Monday morning. On this day (Monday) they proceeded across Athleague, and through the plain of Nai, son of Allgubha [i. e. Machaire-Chonnacht], and in the evening arrived at Seaghais[d], where they encamped northwards of the river for that night. On the next day they crossed Coirrshliabh-na-Seaghsa, and proceeded through the territory of Corran to Ballymote. The forces then dispersed for their homes with spoils and riches.

The son of O'Neill, namely, Sir Art, the son of Turlough Luineach, son of Niall Conallagh, son of Art, son of Con, went over to assist the English, who were fortified at Dun-na-long, in order to wage war against O'Neill. This Art died among the English[e].

As for O'Donnell, he remained with his troops, without making any excursion [out of Tirconnell], from the time that he returned from the aforesaid expedition in Thomond to the September following[f]. After his soldiers and

[f] *September following.*—This appears to have been copied from the Life of Hugh Roe O'Donnell. It is not true that O'Donnell remained inactive in his own territory till September; for, according to Docwra, O'Donnell made the attack described in the text on the 29th of July.

sccísi dia amhsaibh, ⁊ dia aos tuarastail an airsfett sin, Ro thochuir sium iaddsidhe chucca dus an ffuicchbhedh baoghal for na Gallaibh. Ro hairnfidhedh dó

Docwra gives a most curious and minute account of the attack made on him by the Irish, and the coming over to his side of Sir Arthur O'Neill and Niall Garv O'Donnell, with their followers, without whose intelligence and guidance little or nothing could have been effected by Docwra, who candidly acknowledges the fact, and remarks: "Although it is true withall they had theire owne ends in it, which were always for private revenge, and wee ours, to make use of them for the furtherance of the publique service." His journal of the transactions that took place in the neighbourhood of Derry and Lifford, from this period to the first of November, is as follows:

"On the 28th of June came some men of o'Doghertyes, & lay in ambush before Ellogh; the Garrison discouering them, fell out & skirmisht; a litle of from the Castle wee perceived them, from the Derry, to be in feight. I tooke 40 horse & 500 ffoote, & made towards them; when they Sawe vs coming they left the skirmish & drewe away: wee followed vp as fast as wee could, &, coming to the foote of a mountaine, which they were to pass ouer in theire retreate, wee might see them all march before vs, though but slowlie, yet with as much speede as they were able to make, being, to our grieffe, about 400 foote & 60 horse, & wee makeing as much hast on our partes to ouertake them. By that time the last of them had obtained the topp of the hill: S[r] John Chamberlaine & I, with some 10 horse more, were come vpp close on theire heeles, all our foote, & the rest of our horse, coming after vs as fast as they could, but all out of breath & exceedinglie tired. Hauing thus gained the very topp of the hill, & seeing but fewe about me, I stayed and badd a stand to be made till more Company might come vpp; and withall, casting my head about, to see how our men followed, I seeing the foote farr behinde, & our horse but slowlie Clyming vpp; turning about againe I might see S[r] John Chamberlaine unhorsed, lying on the ground, a stones cast before mee, & at least a Dozen hewing at him with theire Swords. I presentlie gaue forward to haue rescued him, & my horse was shott in two places & fell deade vnder mee, yet they forsooke him vpon it, & wee recouered his bodie, but wounded with 16 woundes, & instantlie giving vp the Ghost, wherevpon wee made a stand in the place, & staying till more Companie came vp, wee brought him off, & sufferred them to march away without further pursuite.

"On the second of July I put 800 men into Boates, and landed them att Dunalong, Tyrone (as wee were tould) lying in Campe within two myles of the Place, where I presentlie fell to raiseing a Forte. His men came downe & skirmisht with vs all that day, but perceiuing the next wee were tilted, & out of hope to be able to remoue us, they rise vp & left vs quietlie to doe what we would, where, after I had made it reasonablie defensible, I left S[r] John Bowles in Garrison with 6 Companyes of Foote, & afterwards sent him 50 horse.

"On the 14th of July came O'Donnell with a troupe of 60 horse, &, earely in the Morninge, as our watch was ready to be discharged, fell vpon a Corpes de Guard of some 20 of our horse, but they defended themselues without loss, & orderlie retyred to the Quarter, only Captaine John Sidney was hurte in the shoulder with the blowe of a staffe.

"On the 29th of July he came againe with 600 Foote & 60 horse, and lay close in ambush in a valley within a quarter of a myle of our outmost horse sentinells; & Moyle Morrogh mac Swyndoe (a man purposelie sent with mee by the state, and soe well esteemed of as the

hirelings had within this period rested themselves, he summoned them to him, to see whether he could get any advantage of the English. He was informed

queene had giuen a Pention of vi[s] a day vnto during his life, & the present Comaund of 100 English souldiers) having intelligence with him, caused some of his men to goe, a litle before Breake of Day, & driue forth our horses (that were vsually euery night brought into the Iland to Graze) directlie towards him, In soe much as, vpon the sodaine, before any thinge could be done to preuent it, he gott to the number of 60 into his power, & presentlie made hast to be gone. But with the alarum I rise vp from my Bedd, tooke some 20 horses, and such foote as were readie, Bidd the rest follow, & soe made after them. At fower myles end wee ouertooke them, theire owne horses kept in the reare, flanked with foote, marching by the edge of a Bogge, & those horse they had gott from vs sent away before with the foremost of theire foote. When they sawe vs cominge, they turned heade & made readie to receiue vs; wee charged them, & at the first encounter I was stricken with a horseman's stafe in the Foreheade, in soe much as I fell for deade, & was a goode while deprived of my sences; Butt the Captaines & Gentlemen that were about me (whereof the cheife that I Remember were Captaine Anthony Erington, Captaine John Sidney, Captaine John Kingsmyll, & Mathew Wroth, a Corporall of my horse Companie) gaue beyond my Bodie & enforced them to giue ground a good way, by meanes whereof I recouered myselfe, was sett vp on my horse, & soe safelie brought of, & Conducted home, & they sufferred, with the prey they had gott, to departe without further pursuite.

"I kepte my Bedd of this wound by the space of a fortneth, my chamber a weeke after, & then I came abroade; & the first thinge I did, I tooke a viewe & particuler muster of all the Companyes. How weake I found them, euen beyonnd expectation (though I had seene them decay very fast before), is scarselie credible; &, I thinke, noe man will denye but it was euen then a strange Companie, that, of 150 in list, could bring to doe service 25 or 30 able, at the most.

"Then did I alsoe manifestlie discouer the Trechery of the said Moyle Morrogh Mac Swynedo" [Mulmurry Mac Sweeny Doe], "hauing intercepted the Messenger that he employed to O'Donnell in all his Bussines, out of whose mouth I gott a full Confession of all his Practices, & especiallie, that it was hee that caused his men of purpose to driue forth our horses, which he was so manifestlie convinced of as hee had not the face to denie it, wherevpon I deliuered him to Captaine Flemminge, who was then going to Dublin, to carry to my lord Deputie, there to receiue his tryall; who, putting him vnder hatches in his shipp, & himselfe coming to shoore with his Boate, the hatch being opened to sett Beere, he stept vp vpon the Decke, & threwe himselfe into the Riuer, & soe Swamme away to O'Canes side, which was hard by; they in the shipp, amazed with the soddayneness of the fact, & doing nothing that tooke effect, to prevent it.

"On the 24th of August came Roorey, brother to O Cane (hauing before made his agreement with mee, to serue vnder S[r] Arthur O Neale), & brought with him 12 horse, 30 foote, & 60 fatt Beeues,—a Present welcome at that time, for besides that fresh meate was then rare to be had, our provisions in stoore were very neere spent. I gaue him thereof a Recompence for them in money, & allowed him a small parte of souldiers to goe forth againe, whoe returned the next day, & brought 40 more. Annother small Pray hee sett againe within fewe dayes after, & then, thinking hee

gur ḃo gnáṫ deachraiḋ na ngall toċt for inġeltraḋ do ḟaiġidh ḟerġuirt fásaigh baoí for ioncaiḃ an ḃaile .i. doire, ⁊ drong do ṁarcṡluaġ na ngall aga

had gayned himselfe Credite enough, hee came & demaunded 800 men to doe an enterprise withall, that should be (as he tould a very faire & probable tale for) of farr greater importance & seruice to the Queen. I had onelie the persuation of Sr Arthur O Neile (who I verylie thinke was a faithful & honnest Man), granted him some men, though not halfe the Number he askt, because, in truth, I had them not. But before the time came they should sett forth, Sr Arthur had changed his opinion, & bad mee bewarre of him. I stayed my hand therefore, & refused him the men. He apprehended I did it out of distrust, & with many oathes & Protestations indeuored to perswade mee of his truth & fidelitie; But finding all would not prevaile, he desired I would suffer him to goe alone with such men of his owne as he had, & he would retourne with such a testimonie of his honnestie, as I should neuer after haue Cause to be doubtefull of him more. I was content, soe hee left mee Pledges for his retourne; hee offered mee two that accepted of theire owne accords to engage theire liues for it, & himselfe besids promised it with a solemn oath taken vpon the Bible, soe I lett him goe. The next day he came backe to the waterside, right ouer against the towne, with 300 Men in his Companye, and, hauing the River betweene him & vs, called to the souldiers on our side, & bad them tell mee he was there returned, according to promise, But ment noe Longer to serue against his owne Brother; & if for his Pledges I would accepte of a Ransome of Cowes, he would send mee in what reasonable Number I should demaund; But threatned, If I tooke away theire lives, there should not an English man escape that euer came within his danger. This being presentlie brought vnto mee, & approued to be true by Repetition in myne owne sight & hearing, I caused a Gibbett to be straight sett vp, brought them forth, & hanged them before his face; & it did afterwards manifestlie appeare this man was, of purpose, sent in, from the very begining, to betraye vs, & at this time he had laid soe faire a Plott, all was done by directions of Tyrone, who lay in Ambush to receiue vs.

"And now the winter beganne to be feirce vpon vs; our men wasted with continuall laboures, the Iland scattered with Cabbins full of sicke men, our Biskitt all spent, our other prouisions of nothing but Meale, Butter, & a litle Wine, & that, by Computation, to hould out but 6 dayes longer. Tyrone & O'Donell, to weaken vs the more, Proclaming free passage & releife through theire Countrie, to send them away, to as many as would leaue vs and departe for England. Our two fortes, notwithstanding all the dilligence wee had beene able to vse, farre from the state of being defensible. O'Donell, well obseruing the opportunitie of this time, if his skill and Resolution had beene as good to prosecute it to the full, on the 16 of September came, with 2000 Men, about midnight, vndiscouered, to the very edge of the Bogge that divides the Iland from the mayne Lande (for our horses were soe weake & soe fewe that wee were not able to hould watch any further out), & there, being more then a good muskett shott of, they discharged theire peeces, whereby wee had warning enough (if neede had beene) to put our selues in Armes at leysure. But there was not a Night, in many before, wherein both myselfe & the Captaines satt not vp in expectation of this attempt, and Captaine Thomas White, having some 20 horse readie in Armes for all occasions, came presentlie, & brauelie charged vpon the first that were now past ouer the Bogg & gott into the Iland, kild about 14

that the horses of the English were sent out every day, under the charge of a party of English cavalry, to graze upon a grassy field that was opposite the

or 15, whose bodies wee saw lying there the next day, & the rest, takeing a fright, confusedly retyred as fast as they could; yet, to make it seene they departed not in feare, they kept thereabouts till the morning, & then, assoone as it was broad day Light, they made a faire Parade of themselues vpon the side of a hill, full in our sight, & soe marched away.

"The very next day came in a supplie of victuells, very shortlie after 50 newe horse, & shortelie after that againe 600 foote, & withall, because the lords had beene aduertized the stoore howses wee erected at first, of Deale boardes onelie, were many wayes insufficient, & vnable to preserue the munitions and victuells in, they sent vs, about this time, two frames of Timber for howses, with most thinges necessarie to make them vp withal, which they ordayned to supplie that defect with; & now alsoe, where before the souldiers were enioyned to worke, without other allowance than theire ordinarie pays, Theire lordships, vpon advertisment of the inconueniencie thereof (which in truth was such as, doe what wee could, the workes went but exceeding slowlie forward, & with very much difficulty), I then receiued orders to give them an addition to their wages (when they wrought vpon the fortifications) of 4[ds] a day; & soe wee were then, in all things, fullie & sufficientlie releeued.

"On the third of October came in Neile Garvie O Donell, with 40 horse & 60 Foote; a man I was also directed by the state to winne to the Queene's seruice, & one of equall estimation in Tyrconnell, that Sir Arthur O Neale was of in Tyrone. The secreet message that had past betweene him & mee, hee found were discouered to O Donnell, and therefore somewhat sooner then otherwise he intended, & with less assuraunce & hope of many Conditions, that hee stood vpon. Yet, it is true, I promised him, in the behalfe of the Queene, the whole Countrey of Tirconnell to him & his heires; & my lord Deputie & Councell at Dublin did afterwards confirme it vnto him vnder theire hands; & his Coming in was very acceptable att that time, & such as we made many vses of, & could ill haue spared.

"The next day after hee came, wee drewe forth our forces, & made a journey to the Ile of Inche, where, by his information, wee had learned there was a good Prey of Cattell to be gott; but the tides falling out extraordinarie high, wee were not able to pass them to gett in, so as wee were forced to turne our Course & goe downe into O-Dogherties Countrie, though to litle purpose, for, knowing of our coming, hee draue away all before vs, onelie some stacks of Corne wee found, which wee sett on fire.

"The 8th of October I assigned vnto the said Neale Garvie 500 foote & 30 horse, vnder the leading of S[r] John Bowles, to goe to take the Liffer, where 30 of O Donnells men lay in Garrison in a Forte in one of the Corneres of the towne; & most of them, being abroad when they came, were surpriced & slaine, & the place taken; yet soe as one of them had first putt fire into the Forte, which consumed all the Buildings in it; but the rest of the Howses scattered abroade in the towne (which were about 20) were preserued & stood vs afterwards in singuler good steade.

"O-Donell having heard of the takeing of this Place, came on the xi[th] of October, with 700 foote & 100 horse, & encamped himselfe about 3 myles off at Castle Fyn. The next day he came & shewed himselfe before the Towne, our Garrison made out, had a skirmish with him of an houre longe, wherein Neale Garuie behaved himselfe Brauelie; Capten Augusten

fforcoiṁett gach laoí. Ot cualaiġ siuṁ innsin ro ġaḃ aga sccrúdadh cionnus no ḃeradh amus for an eachradh ísin, conadh é ní do róine drong mór dia ṁiledaiḃ, ⁊ dírim marcach (nar bo luġa oldát sé céd a líon etir troiġteach, ⁊ marcach) do bhreith lais go dícelta i ndorchata na hoidhce go huct allḃruaich iomdomain ro baí isin maiġsliaḃ tarla for aghaidh doire a tuaidh, ḃail in ro ba réil doiḃ muintir an baile, ⁊ nar bó sofaiccsiona doiḃsidhe iarsoṁ. Ro ċuir uathadh becc da ṁarsloġ i nionadaiḃ ionfoilġidhe a ffoccus don baile hi cceilg forr na heoċa, ⁊ for a naés coiṁetta co na hiompaídis a nechrada for a ccúlaiḃ dorídisi cecib tan ro badh lainn leo. Báttar din an tuctt sin ar na ninnell go hurtosaċ an laoí. At ciat an echra ċuca dars an urdrochat (co na luċt forcoimetta) aṁail ro ġnathaiġsiot. Ro eirgsttar marcsluaġ uí doṁnaill dóiḃ dar a néisi, ⁊ do radratt ammus for luchd an forcoiṁetta, marḃaitt drong dioḃ, ⁊ terna a roile la luas a neachradh ⁊ a nérma. Ġaḃaitt muinntir Uí doṁnaill acc iomáin eaċraide na ngall ro a ccumang. Ticc a sloġ buddéin dia ccoṁfurtacht for na galloiḃ, ⁊ ro ċuirsiot na heich reṁpa. Ro ḟoráil Ua doṁnaill for druing dia ṁarcsloġ dol lás na heocha, ⁊ gan anṁain ffrisiuṁ idir co riostaís co hionad innill. Do ronadh aṁlaidh. Anais o doṁnaill ro deóidh ⁊ an líon ro ṫoġ dia ṁarcsloġ ina ḟarradh co na ṁíledaiḃ troiġteċ.

Ot ciad na goill deiliuccadh a neoċ friú éirgitt fo céddoir, ⁊ gaḃaitt a narma, ⁊ do leiccet i ndeadhaidh uí doṁnaill. Do deaċaidh an generál Sir henry docura co na ṁarcsloġ for a neoċaiḃ (doneoċ ro fortt a neoċa i nionadaiḃ innilli dioḃ, ⁊ na ro sccar friú don ċur sin), ⁊ tiaġait isin toghraim aṁail as déine ro ḟedsat. Ot connairc ó doṁnaill marcsluaġ na ngall for dianimrim ina ḋeadhaidh anuas i ndeóidh a ṁilead troiġteaċ co na diorma marcsloġ ina ḟoċair co rucsat marcsloġ na ngall fair. Do beratt

Heath tooke a light hurte in his hand, & some 10 or 12 Men on ech side were slaine.

"On the 24th he came againe, & laide himselfe in ambush a myle from the towne, watching to intercept our men Fetching in of turfe, which, before our Coming, the Irish had made for their owne Provision. The Alarme taken, the Garrison made forth againe, & Neale Garvie behaued himselfe brauelie as before, charged home vpon them, killed one, hurt one or two more with his owne hands, & had his horse slaine vnder him. Captaine Heath took a shott in the thigh, whereof he shortelie after died, & some 20 more there were hurte & slaine.

"On the 28th of October dyed S[r] Arthur O'Neale of a fevour, in whose place came presentlie after one Cormocke, a brother of his, that clamed to succeed him as the next of his kinne, & had, in that name, good entertainments from the Queene. But shortelie after came his

town, i. e. Derry; when he heard this, he began to meditate how he could make a descent upon those horses; and this is what he did: he took privately, in the darkness of the night, a large party of his soldiers, and a squadron of cavalry (amounting to no less than six hundred, between horse and foot), to the brink of a steep rocky valley, which was on the flat mountain to the north of Derry, from whence they could plainly see the people of the town, who could not easily see them. He placed a small party of his cavalry in ambush for the horses and their keepers, at concealed places not far from the town, so as to prevent them from returning to the town when they should wish to do so. They remained thus in ambush until the break of day, when they perceived the horses with their keepers coming across the bridge as usual. O'Donnell's cavalry set out after them, and attacked and slew some of the keepers; but others made their escape by means of the fleetness and swiftness of their horses. O'Donnell's people then commenced driving off as many of the English horses as had been left behind in their power. The main body of their own force coming up to assist them against the English, they sent the horses before them. O'Donnell ordered a party of his cavalry to go off with the horses to a secure place, and not to wait for himself at all until they should reach a secure place. This was accordingly done; [and] O'Donnell remained behind, with a body of his cavalry which he selected and with his foot soldiers.

When the English perceived that their horses had been taken away from them, they immediately arose, and, taking their arms, set out in pursuit of O'Donnell. The General, Sir Henry Docwra, with his horsemen mounted on their horses (i. e. such of them as retained their horses in secure places, and had not lost them on that occasion), joined in the pursuit as rapidly as they were able. When O'Donnell saw the cavalry of the English in full speed after him, he remained behind his infantry with his troop of cavalry, until the Eng-

owne sonne, Tirlogh, that was, indeed, his true & imediate heire, whome the state accepted of, & admitted to inherite all the fortune & hopes of his father. Hee had not attained to the full age of a man, &, therefore, the service he was able to doe was not greate, but some vse wee had of him, & I thinke his disposition was faithfull & honest.

"All this while, after Liffer had beene taken, O'Donell kept vp & downe in those parts, watching still to take our men vpon some advantage, but finding none, & hearing two Spanish shipps that were come into Calebegg with Munition, Armes, & Money, on the 20th of November he departed towards them, & betweene Tirone & him intending to make a dividend of it."

side amus calma for Ua ndoṁnaill dar cſnn a ccrſiche, ⁊ a nſiniġ. Fors-aighis o doṁnaill frissin deaḃaiḋ go déola dúrċroiḋech, ⁊ fſrṫar iomairſcc aṁnus ſtorra cſċtar na dá lſiṫe. Teilccis aroile commbratair dua doṁnaill .i. Aoḋ mac Aoḋa duiḃ mic Aoḋa ruaiḋ uí doṁnaill, foġa foġaḃlaiġi ar amus an ġeneral Sir henry docura co ttarla i ttul a édain gan iomroll go ros gon go haiċſr aṁnus. Soais an ġeneral for ccúlaiḃ iar na ṫreaġdaḋ saṁlaiḋ, ⁊ sóaitt na goill arċſna iar nguin a ccodnaiġ, a ccſnn coṁairle, ⁊ a ttrſinḟir fo ṁéla, ⁊ aṫais, ⁊ ní ro lſnsat a nſchra ní ba sirí. Tiaccait muintir Uí ḋoṁnaill dia sccoraiḃ, ⁊ ro ríṁeaḋ leo a neaċra dus fuccsat, fuillſḋ for díḃ cédaiḃ each bá sſḋ a líon. Rannais Ua doṁnaill na heoċa as a haiṫle fors na huaisliḃ iar na ccoṁraṁaiḃ.

Baí imorro Ua doṁnaill i fforḃaissi fors na gallaiḃ gan foġluaschṫ as a ṫír go dſirſḋ october. Ro ṫionnsccain annside dol go tuaḋṁuṁain do riḋiri dia hindreaḋ. Ro ṫſcclamaḋ a sloġ lais iar ccinnſḋ for an ccoṁairle sin, ⁊ ní ro airis co rainicc tar Slicceach siar, ⁊ co baile an ṁótaigh. Ro ḟáccaiḃ Niall garḃ, mac cuinn, mic an ċalḃaiġ, mic Maġnasa Uí doṁnaill dar a éisi isin ccrích dia hiomcoiṁſtt fors na gallaiḃ ar na tiostaís dia hindreaḋ.

Gabaitt na goill ag áil ⁊ acc atach Neill gairḃ uí doṁnáill go hinċlſiṫe, ⁊ acc eráil ríġi an tire fair diamaḋ iad baḋ coscraċ. Ro ṫinġeallsat asccaḋa ioṁḋa, ⁊ maoine mára dó frissin dia ttíosaḋ ina ccommbáiġ. Baí siuṁ ag coisteċt fris na coṁtaiḃ athaiḋ ḟoda co ro ḋeónaiġ a ainḟén dó fo ḋeóidh dul dia saiġiḋ la míairle an aésa fſiġ for uallaiġ bátar imaraen friss, ⁊ ros aiṫreaċ dó cioḋ iar ttrioll. Do ḋeaċatar a ṫriar dſrḃraiṫreaċ lais isin coiṁſirġe sin .i. Aoḋ buiḋe, Doṁnall, ⁊ Conn. Ro ba fſirde ón do ġalloiḃ a ndolsoṁ dia nionnsaiġiḋ, uair rortar scíṫiġ, mſirtniġ gan coḋlaḋ

[8] *Hugh, son of Hugh Duv.*—He is described, in the Life of Hugh Roe O'Donnell, by Peregrine O'Clery, as "the Achilles of the Irish race." Sir Henry Docwra little knew who it was that struck him when he wrote: "At the first encounter I was stricken with a horseman's staffe in the forehead, in soe much as I fell for dead, and was a good while deprived of my senses," &c., &c. The weapon cast at Docwra was a javelin, not a mere stick or staff; and P. O'Sullevan Beare says that Docwra's helmet was pierced by it.

"Secundo die, quàm in terram exsiluerunt, Odonellus occurrens centum sexaginta octo equos eis adimit, et rursus equos iuxta oppidum pascentes Catholici rapiunt, quos sequuntur Angli. Equestre prœlium fit. Hugo Odonellus cognomento Junior Docrium telo per Galeam fixo fracto cranio vulnerat."—*Hist. Cathol. Iber.*, tom. 3, lib. 6, cap. v. fol. 171.

lish came up with him. They made a courageous attack upon O'Donnell for [the recovery of] their spoils, and of what was under their protection. O'Donnell sustained the onset valiantly and resolutely; and a fierce battle was fought them. One of O'Donnell's kinsmen, namely, Hugh, the son of Hugh Duv[g], son of Hugh Roe, made a well-aimed cast of a javelin at the General, Sir Henry Docwra, and, striking him directly in the forehead, wounded him very severely. When the General was thus pierced, he returned back; and the English, seeing their chief, their adviser, and their mighty man, wounded, returned home in sorrow and disgrace, and pursued their horses no further. O'Donnell's people proceeded to their tents, and, on reckoning the horses which they had carried off, they found them to exceed two hundred[h] in number. O'Donnell afterwards divided the horses among his gentlemen, according to their deserts.

O'Donnell remained besieging the English, without moving from his territory, until the end of October, when he began to make preparations to go again into Thomond, to plunder it. After having come to this resolution, he assembled his forces, and made no delay until he came westwards across the Sligo, and to Ballymote. He left Niall Garv, the son of Con, son of Calvagh, son of Manus O'Donnell, behind him in the territory, to defend it against the English, and prevent them from plundering it.

The English [now] began privately to entreat and implore Niall Garv O'Donnell [to join them], offering to confer the chieftainship of the territory upon him, should they prove victorious. They promised him, moreover, many rewards and much wealth, if he would come over to their alliance. He listened for a long time to their offers; and his misfortune at length permitted him to go over to them[i], by the evil counsel of envious and proud people who were along with him; but for this he was afterwards sorry. His three brothers, namely, Hugh Boy, Donnell, and Con, joined him in this revolt. The English were, no doubt, the better of their going over to them; for they were weary

[h] *Two hundred.*—Docwra says that the number was sixty, but the probability is, that this is a mistake of his transcriber (for we have not his own autograph), for 160. P. O'Sullevan Beare makes the number 168.

[i] *To go over to them.*—P. O'Sullevan Beare states that Niall Garv was deserted by his wife for his treachery towards her brother on this occasion. "Asper eam occasionem opportunam ratus, ad Anglos se confert (ob id a Nolla coniuge sua Odonelli sorore desertus), quibus Leffiriam, quam ipse custodiæ causæ tenebat tradit. In ea Angli decem cohortes collocant."—*Hist. Cathol. &c.*, tom. 3, lib. 6, c. v. fol. 171.

gan cuṁsanaḋ gaċ noiḋċe la hoṁan Uí Ḋoṁnaill, ⁊ soscar saéthaiġ, gallsaiġ la hiomcuiṁge an ionaid i mbátar, las na biaḋaiḃ sḟnnda, ⁊ las an ffeoil saillte sḟsḃgoirt, ⁊ la hḟsḃaiḋ úirḟeola, ⁊ gaċ tuara ba toich doiḃ. Ros airchis Niall ó Doṁnaill im gaċ ní ba tḟsḃaiḋ forra, ⁊ ro ḟuasccail doib as in ccarcair ccuṁaing i mbátar. Ḃḟris deich ccéd laoċ go Lḟiṫbear lais, baile eiriḋe for ur an loċa cedna, ⁊ ba dúnárus oirdeirc dUa Doṁnaill eiriḋe, ⁊ ba hédaingḟn an ionḃaiḋ sin, uair ni raiḃe dúnaiḋ diogainn, na caistiall claċ aolta ann fri re ḟoda, iar na bloḋaḋ feċt riaṁ, aċt maḋ dúnclaḋ dínniṁ ar na imḋénaṁ do ċriaiḋ ⁊ dfódaiḃ an talṁan, ⁊ caol ċlais édoṁain uisccidhe ina timcell ag iomḟuireċ la haiṫġin an dúin bai ann roiṁe do ṫusccḃáil doridhise.

Ro ḟaccaibhriot an taér coiṁḟtta an port sin fár la huaṁan ⁊ imeccla ó ro ráthaiġsiot na goill ċuca, ⁊ gan ó Doṁnaill do bḟiṫ ina ffoccus. Laroḋain tangattar na goill don port, ⁊ ro ṫoccaiḃsiot múir moraiḋble ⁊ duṁaḋa criaḋ, ⁊ cloċ for a sccaṫ gur bo daingḟn fri caṫuccaḋ eistiḃ i nacchaiḋ a naṁat.

Luiḋ araile fḟr do ṁainṁuinntir Uí Ḋoṁnaill ina ḋeadhaiḋ go ffior sccél an tíre, ⁊ atféd dó ina nḋḟsnaḋ innte dia éisi. Ba hiongnaḋ mór, ⁊ ba maċtnaḋ mḟnman la hUa nDomhnaill a ḃraṫair, ⁊ a ċliaṁain diomsúḋ fair, uair ba sí dḟirḃsiur Uí Ḋomhnaill nuala, ro ba bainséitiġ don tí niall. Impáis Ua Doṁnaill a coicceaḋ connaċt, ar ní rainicc tar baile an mótaiġ siar an tan ruccsat sgela fair, ⁊ iompaíd a slóġ aṁail as dḟine ro ḟéosat. Aċt cḟna ni ruaċt la a ṁílḟḋaiḃ O Doṁnaill do ḟsḟtal, aċt maḋ uaṫaḋ dia ṁarcsloġ go rainicc hi ccoṁfoċraiḃ don Lḟiṫḃḟr réṁráite. Ní ṫairnic las na gallaiḃ crḟcha, na airccne do ḋénaṁ reriú ráinicc O Doṁnaill for ccúlaiḃ, aċt a bḟiṫ ag daingniuccaḋ a longport, ⁊ ag claiḋe múr, ⁊ ot ċualattar ó Doṁnaill do ṫoiḋeċt, ní ro lḟicc a eccla doiḃ an port i mbáttar dfáccḃáil for cḟnn aoin nḟiṫ dia mbaoí derḃaiḋ forra.

Aiririḋ Ua Doṁnaill i nionaḋ nar ḃó hḟidirċian o na gallaiḃ co ruccsat

[k] *For want of*, literally, "without sleep, without rest every night, for fear of O'Donnell."

[l] *Of their situation*, literally, "of the place in which they were."

[m] *The same lough*: i. e. the same lough on which Derry is situated. The reader is to bear in mind that the Irish called all the extent of water from Lifford to the sea by the name of Lough Foyle. What modern map-makers call the River Foyle, the ancient Irish considered as

and fatigued for want of[k] sleep and rest every night, through fear of O'Donnell; and they were diseased and distempered in consequence of the narrowness of their situation[l], and the old victuals, the salt and bitter flesh-meat they used, and from the want of fresh meat, and other necessaries to which they had been accustomed. Niall O'Donnell provided them with every thing they stood in need of, and relieved them from the narrow prison in which they were confined. He took ten hundred warriors with him to Lifford, a town upon the banks of the same lough[m], and a celebrated residence of O'Donnell; but at this time the place was not fortified; for there had not been any strong fortress or castle of lime and stone there for a long time before (the one there last having been destroyed), or any thing but a small rampart of earth and sods, surrounded by a narrow, shallow ditch of water, as preparations for the erection of a fortress similar to the one which had been there before.

The guards, as soon as they perceived the English approaching, vacated this fort through dread and fear, because O'Donnell was not near [to assist] them. The English thereupon entered the fort and raised large mounds and ramparts of earth and stone to shelter them; so that they were sufficiently fortified to hold out against their enemies.

One of O'Donnell's faithful people followed after him with information concerning the state of the country, and told him what had happened in his absence. O'Donnell was much surprised and amazed that his kinsman and brother-in-law had thus turned against him, for Nuala, the sister of O'Donnell, was the wife of Niall. O'Donnell returned from the province of Connaught; for he had not passed westwards beyond Ballymote when the news overtook him, and his forces as quickly as they were able; but [no part of] his soldiers were able to keep pace with him, except a few of his cavalry, and he arrived in the neighbourhood of Lifford aforesaid. The English had not been able to make preys or depredations before O'Donnell returned back, but were [employed] strengthening their fortress, and erecting ramparts; and when they heard that O'Donnell had arrived, they were afraid[n] to come out of their fort for anything they wanted.

O'Donnell remained at a place not far from the English, until some of his

a part of the lough.

[n] *They were afraid*, literally, "fear did not permit them to leave the fort in which they were for any thing they were in need of."

uaṫaḋ dia ṁilsḋaiḃ troiġṫeach fair. Ba foda la hUa nDomhnaill batar na goill gan fuabairt, ⁊ ní ro airis fris an slóġ ní ba sia co ros tairbhsin an tuaṫaḋ ro baí do na gallaiḃ for taeḃ Cruacháin Lighsen alla noir fris an aḃainn atuaiḋ. Ot ciatt na goill eiside do riaċtattar a ḋoċom, ⁊ niall garḃ ó Domhnaill co na ḃráiṫriḃ remhpa a ttoirisheacht na troda. Do ḃeraṫ raiġin nuġra for aroile gan naċ ndánatur deaḃṫa an la sin cetus, acht a ḃeiṫ i nurfaiċill for a ċele, uair ní ro ḟaoilsiot na goill ó Dómhnaill do ḃeiṫ i ttesirce slóiġ amhail ro baí ⁊ báttar imecclaiġ im ċeilcc do ṫabairt impa, co nar bo háil dóiḃ dol i nimċéine on mbaile ar a aoíḋi. Bá son ccuma ccéḋna do muinntir Uí Domhnaill ba hecconnda doiḃrein dol i meisce a namat i niompoiccsi an puirt lar an uathaḋ slóiġ ro báttar. Ro siodhḃeiliġsiot fri aroile ce nib fó ċóra, ⁊ caoncompaic ro sccarsat. Ro gonaḋ araill uaḋaiḃ do siú, ⁊ anall lá diuḃraicctiḃ sleġ, ⁊ saiġett, ⁊ uḃaillṁell luaiḋe. Acht namá ba mó ro creċtnaiġit do ṁuinntir Uí Ḋomhnaill ar a nuaiti isin iomairecc. Tiaġaitt na goill dia ttiġiḃ iarttain, ⁊ do ṫaétt Ua Domhnaill co na ṁuintir dia sccoraiḃ, ⁊ ba go ffuarnaḋ, ⁊ go ffeirg luinne luiḋ Ua Domhnaill ainnriḋe ar ba mela lais gan a ṡloġ do ṫoċt ċuicce an lá sin, uair ba ḋeimin lais dia mbeittis occa an ionbaiḋ sin na digsitis goill uada feiḃ do ḋeachatar. Ro dlúṫaiġestair Ua Domhnaill ar a haiṫle a niomḟuiḋe fors na gallaiḃ iar mbreiṫ dia ṁilsḋaiḃ fair co Leicc, ⁊ gabais longport fo dí mile ceimenn don Leiṫḃeir atrubramar for sċáṫ a ersa trebṫa go ro erlaṁaiġtís na harḃanna batar i niompoiccsi do na galloiḃ. Nó laaḋsom aés braiṫ, ⁊ taisccélta fors an mbaile gaċ noiḋċe ar na ro leiccelḋ neach anonn nach alle mura roistis dars an aḃainn buḋearr ⁊ dna ní ro ḟaccaiḃ conair na earrsus éluḋa fo mile ceimeinn don ḃaile ar na ro lá forairedha, ⁊ edarnaiḋe forra do coiṁét, ⁊ do ḟriothaire fors na gallaiḃ na tíostais tairsiḃ gan ráṫuccaḋ, ⁊ for ċloinn ċuinn Uí Ḋomhnaill sainriḋh, ⁊ for a ṁuintir, ar

° *Cruachan-Lighean*, now Croaghan, a remarkable hill giving name to a townland in the parish of Clonleigh, barony of Raphoe, and county of Donegal. The summit of this hill is about two miles north and by west of the bridge of Lifford.

According to the Ulster Inquisitions this townland belonged to the monastery of Clonleigh.—See also the Life of St. Cairneach in Colgan's *Acta Sanctorum* at 28th March, p. 782, where Cruachan-Ligean is described as situated "ad occidentalem ripam freti siue sinus vulgo Loch-febhuil nuncupati, iuxta Lefferiam oppidum."—See the references to Druim Lighean, which was an alias name of this place, under the years 1522, 1524, and 1583.

foot-soldiers had come up with him. O'Donnell thought it too long the English remained without being attacked, and he did not wait for the coming up of [the main body of] his army, but exhibited before the English the small number he had, on the south side of Cruachan-Lighean°, to the north of the river. When the English perceived him they marched out to meet him, with Niall Garv O'Donnell and his brothers in the van, as leaders of the battle. They skirmished with each other, but there was no obstinate conflict on that first day, though they continued in readiness for each other; for the English thought that O'Donnell was in want of forces[p], as he [really] was; and fearing that an ambush might be laid for them, so that they did not wish to go far from the town for that reason. It was the same case with O'Donnell's people. It would be unwise in them to come in collision with the enemy so near their fort, with the small force of which they consisted. They [at length] separated from each other, though not in peace or friendship. Some were wounded on both sides by the discharging of javelins, arrows, and leaden balls; but more of[q] O'Donnell's people were wounded in this skirmish on account of the fewness of their number.

The English then proceeded to their houses, and O'Donnell and his people went to their tents; and it was with anger and indignation that O'Donnell returned thither; for it grieved him that his army had not come up with him on that day; for he was certain that, if he had had them with him at that time, the English would not have escaped from him as they had. O'Donnell afterwards, when his army had come up with him, laid a close siege to the English, and pitched his camp within two thousand paces of Lifford above-mentioned, in order to protect his husbandmen, so that they might save the corn crops in the neighbourhood of the English. He sent out spies and scouts every night to reconnoitre the town, and not to permit any one to pass in or out, unless they should pass southwards across the river; and he left no road or passage within one thousand paces of the town upon which he did not post guards and ambuscades, to watch and spy the English, and hinder them from passing out unnoticed, but especially the sons of Con O'Donnell and their people, for these he consi-

[p] *In want of forces*, literally, "in dearth or scarcity of forces."

[q] *More of.*—This idea is not very correct. It should be expressed thus: "But O'Donnell's suffered more in this skirmish than the enemy, on account of the fewness of their number."

ar forra ba duilġe laissium a ċoimſtt, ⁊ ar iad ro dera dósom iliomat na nſdarnaiġe, ⁊ in aéra frioṫaire.

Baoi sium fri ré triochat laiṫe an dú sin co ttairnic la lucht na criche a narḃanna dullṁuġaḋ go ro cuirsiot é a minċliabaibh ⁊ a mſnḃolccaib dia ttarrúḋ, ⁊ imḟſḋain for eachaiḃ, ⁊ cairliḃ dia ḃrſiṫ nionadaiḃ daingniḃ ḃail na rístaís a naṁaitt ċucca.

In araile aimsir dUa domnaill ria siú ro ḟáccaiḃ an longport hisin co ndeachaid for ammus na ngall dus an ccaoṁsaḋ a ccealgaḋ ar na múraiḃ amach forr an maiġrſiḋ. O do ḋeaċatar muintir uí domnaill for ionchaiḃ an ḃaile, ro batar na goill acca ffaircsi, ⁊ ní ro ḟaiġsſtt forra uair at genrat gur bó do chuingiḋ uġra, ⁊ deabṫa do dſchattar. Iompaidsitt muintir Uí domnaill tar a nais doridire ó na fuairsiot an ní for a ttarosat iarraiḋ. Do ġniatt airisſiṁ for ur na haḃann alla tuaiḋ dianiḋ ainm an daol ſḋ goiritt on mbaile. Tiaġait dronga móra díoḃ dia sccoraiḃ, ⁊ fri aroile torccaḋ, ar ní ro ḟaoilsſtt na goill dia lſnṁain an la hísin. Ot ċonairc Niall garḃ ó domnaill, muintir uí domnaill co hſsraoíte anfúirite atbert friss na gallaiḃ gur ḃó cóir dóiḃ ammus do ṫabairt forra. Gabaitt na goill occá nſiosḋ for a eráilsium co taoi taoiṫſnach in ſitirnisḋón a múr ar na baḋ foḋſrc dia naiṁdiḃ comtair armṫa éidiġṫe. O robtar erlaṁa iaraṁ dus ficcſtt darr na múraiḃ seaċtair i nurd caṫa. Lasoḋain do lſiccſt for amus muintire Uí domnaill fon reim sin ⁊ an tí Niall i remṫús co na ḃraiṫriḃ, ⁊ co na muintir i maille friss.

At chí o domnaill chucca iatt, ⁊ ba fó lais a ffaiccsin dia ṡaiġiḋ, ⁊ ro ṡuidiġſstair a ṁilsḋa ina nionaḋaiḃ erḋalta fo a nſrċomair co na ṁoḋna áiġ ⁊ nír relcc a ndiubraccaḋ co mbátar forr an mbruaċ alltarach don aḃainn. Ima comrainicc dóiḃ iarttáin co mbátar mſscc ar ṁſscc, ⁊ fſrṫar gleo ainmín éccrattach storra díḃlinib. Scuchait a marrcloiġ do ċum aroile co mbátar acc tuinnseaṁaḋ a ċele do ṁanaoísiḃ móirleaḃra, ⁊ do ċraoiseachaiḃ cſnnġlassa. Do ratt Niall ó domnaill tuinnseaṁ don tslſiġ sſimniġ siothfoda ro ioctar a slinnéin for ḋſrḃraṫair uí ḋomnaill for Maġnus go ro clannastair an ccraoisiġ inn go ro ṫrſġdastair a inmſḋoncha triar an éideaḋ do rala uime. Ot connairc Ruḋraiġe ó domnaill

[r] *Beyond the reach*, literally, "where their enemies would not reach them."

[s] *Dael*, now Deel, or, as it is called by the descendants of the Scotch settlers, Dale-burn, a

dered were difficult to be watched, and it was on account of them that his sentinels and ambuscades were so numerous.

He remained here for the period of thirty days, during which time the people of the country were enabled to save their corn and carry it away in small baskets and sacks, on steeds and horses, into the fastnesses of the country beyond the reach[r] of their enemies.

On one occasion O'Donnell, before he left this camp, went towards the English, to see if he could induce them to come outside the fortifications on the level plain. When O'Donnell's people had arrived opposite the town, the English began to reconnoitre them; but they did not sally out against them, for they perceived it was to offer defiance and challenge for battle they had come. O'Donnell's people then returned back when they did not obtain what they wanted, and they halted for some time on the brink of a river called Dael[s], a short distance to the north of the town. Large parties of them went to their tents, and about other business, for they did not think that the English would follow them on that day. When Niall Garv O'Donnell perceived O'Donnell's people scattered and unprepared for action, he told the English that they ought now to attack them. The English at his bidding armed themselves quietly and silently in the centre of their fortifications, in order that their enemies could not see them until they were armed and accoutred. When they were ready they sallied out from their fortifications in battle array, and then, with Niall and his brothers and people in the van, advanced against O'Donnell's people.

O'Donnell saw them advancing, and rejoiced at seeing them coming; and he placed his soldiers in their proper stations fronting them, with their warlike weapons; and he did not permit to shoot at them until they had arrived at the opposite bank of the river. They afterwards met together hand to hand, and a sharp and furious battle was fought between both parties. The two hosts of cavalry rushed to the charge, and began to fight with large spears and greenheaded lances. Niall O'Donnell gave Manus, brother of O'Donnell, a thrust of a sharp, long lance under the shoulder-blade, and, piercing the armour with which he was clad, he buried it in his body, and wounded his internal

river which flows through the barony of Raphoe, and discharges itself into the Foyle a short distance to the north of the town of Lifford.—See note [e], under the year 1557, p. 1557, *supra*.

(ríoġdamhna Ceneoil cConaill) a ḋerbráthair do ġuin do ḃert ammus calma forr an tí Niall, go ttard forgoṁ amnas aichser do ġae mór fo serċomair a ochta fair. Tuarccaiḃ Niall torraċ an eiċ airdéṗmaiġh allmardha do rala foa sdorra, go ro ḃernartair an forgaṁ hi ttul a édain don eoch go rainicc an inchinn. Ro blaḋartair cró ionnsma na craoisiġe icca ssersgaḋ tarrainng for a hais don tí Ruḋraiġe co bfarcaiḃ a hiarn isin eoch co ná baoí laissiomh act maḋ an díċealtair ina ḋurn. Ro thaṫamair an teach deiside fo ḋéiḋ. Mo nuar aṁ náċ daéin lér ro ḟersat an laochraiḋ sin Ceneóil cConaill a mbarainn fri a mbioḋḃaḋaiḃ ⁊ nách hi ccóra bátar uair ní ro cuṁsccaiġte an ccein báttar saṁlaiḋ, ⁊ ni ro hionnarbta, ⁊ ní ro toirnitt as a ffoirb noilis amail do rónta ciḋ iarttain.

Dala na nGall ind airsett bátar an marcṡlóġ occ iompuḃaḋ aroile do radsatt a naiġthe i naoinfeaċt for traiġhteachaiḃ uí Domhnaill go ro sóaitt remhpa biucc, act namá ní ro gonta uaḋaiḃ, actmadh uaite, uair ní ro lensat na goill tarr an ccaṫlaṫair reacttair, ⁊ ba sed fo dersa doiḃ gan a lenmain, uair ro gonad a ttaoíseaċ isin tachar ⁊ rob eiccen doiḃ iompoḋ leis go letbér go ffuair bás iarttain. Ro lensat drong mór do ṁuinntir Uí Domhnaill iad sed cian, ⁊ gabaitt aga ndiuḃraccaḋ, ⁊ acca ccloiḋmeḋ go ro marbaḋ, ⁊ go ro gonaḋ soċaiḋe díoḃ. Ro baḋ doiġ la haos na tograma go sraoinfiḋe forra dia lenaḋ an sloġ iad ni ba sia. Act namá ní ro léicc an aitmeile don luċt forr ro sraoíneaḋ cedamus a lenmain dorídisi.

Iompaidis O Domhnaill do na sccoraiḃ iar nimṫeċt do na gallaiḃ. Ba triamain toirrseaċ ro bás isin longport ind adhaiġ sin fo daiġh ṁeic a fflaṫa, ⁊ a ríoġḋamhna (dia maraḋ deis a ḃraiṫreaċ) do beith fri hiomgno

[1] *The steed.*—The Four Masters should have omitted this short sentence, which so much incumbers their narrative. P. O'Sullevan Beare, who had wooed the historic Muse with more success than any of the Four Masters, describes this battle much more elegantly, as follows, in his *Hist. Cathol. Iber. Compend.*, tom. 3, lib. 6, c. v.:

"Erat Asper vir animo magno, & audaci, & rei militaris scientia præditus, atque multos a sua parte Tirconellos habebat, quorum opera, & virtute fretus in plano cum Catholicis manum conserere non recusabat: Fidem tamen Catholicam semper retinuit Hæreticorum ceremonias auersatus, sicut & Artus [Onellus] qui citò e vita discessit. Circum Leffiriam verò, & Lucum a regijs & Catholicis acriter & sæpe dimicatum est. Memorabilis est equestris pugna, qua regijs fugatis Magnus Odonelli frater Asperum loco cedentem hasta transfossurus fuisset, nisi eius ictum remoueret Eugenius Ogallachur cognomento Iunior ipsius Magni Comes pietate & amore in Onellam suorum dominorum familiam motus. In quam familiam dispari animo fuit Cornelius Ogallachur, qui Aspero persuasisse

parts. When Rury O'Donnell, Roydamna of Kinel-Connell, perceived his brother wounded, he made a brave attack upon Niall, and aimed a forcible and furious thrust of a large javelin at Niall's breast; but Niall raised up the front of the high-rearing foreign steed which he rode, so that the spear struck the steed in the forehead, and penetrated to his brain. Rury broke the socket of the javelin in drawing it back by the thong, and left the iron blade buried in the horse; so that he held but the handle of it in his hand. The steed[t] finally died of this. Wo is me that these heroes of Kinel-Connell were not united in fight on one side against their enemies, and that they were not at peace; for, while they remained so, they were not banished or driven from their native territories, as they afterwards were!

As for the English, while the cavalry were battling with each other, they faced O'Donnell's infantry in a body, and drove them a short distance before them; but, however, only a few of them were wounded; for the English did not pursue them from the field of contest, because their leader[u] had been wounded in the conflict; and they were obliged to return with him to Lifford, where he afterwards died. A great number of O'Donnell's people pursued them for a long distance, and continued to shoot at and cut them down with the sword, so that numbers of them were slain and wounded. The pursuers thought that they should have defeated them [the enemy] if the main host pursued them further; but fear did not permit those who had been repulsed in the beginning to pursue them again.

When the English went away O'Donnell returned to his tents. And dispirited and melancholy were they that night in the camp, on account of the son of their chief[v], and their Roydamna (if he should survive his brothers),

fertur, vt ad Anglos faceret transitionem, & Magnum vulnerauit apud Moninem iuxta Leffiriam, vbi equitatus vtrinque incompositè concurrit, & Magnus equo vectus interquinque equites Ibernos regios ab Aspero in dextero latere hasta percutitur, & circumuentus a Cornelio sub humero icitur. Hastarum cuspides licet loricam non penetrauerint tamen Magno in corpus infixerunt. Rothericus fratri auxilio veniens Asperi pectus hasta appetit: Asper loris tractis equi caput tollens eius fronte excipit Rotherici ictum, quo equus fixus exanimis cum aspero corruit. Sed Asper a suis leuatus Leffiriam reuertitur, Odonello cum peditibus appropinquante. Magnus ex vulneribus egit animam intra decimum quintum diem, & breui Cornelius ab Odonello deprehensus laqueo strangulatur."—Fol. 171, 172.

[u] *Their leader.*—This was Captain Heath. "He tooke a shott in the thigh whereof he shortlie after died."—*Docwra.*

[v] *The son of their chief.*—His father, Hugh,

mbais. O ráinicc O Domhnaill don longṗort ro ḟorail árach ríonnċaolaiġ do ḋenaṁ do Mhaġnus ó Domhnaill dia iomċar tar an mbſrnnus. Do ġníṫe ón amail ro hſrbadh. Tiaġait dronga mora lais dia aés ionṁaine, ⁊ ṡain ṁuinntir co riaċtattar co Dún na nGall. Ro dérgaḋ iomdaiġ oṫrais dosom annsaiḋe. Do raḋaḋ lſġa Uí Domhnaill ċuicce dia lſiġſs, ⁊ ní ro ḟedsat lſiġſs dó. Atbſrtsat gur bo marḃ. Ro baí mainistir hi ccomḟoċraiḃ don dúnaḋ i mbáttar mſic bſthaḋ dord .S. Fronséis, ⁊ no ṫiccſḋ an luċt ba hſccnaiḋe dioḃ dia ṡaiġidsiuṁ do eisteċt a coiḃsion do ṗroċſpt dó, ⁊ dſrnaiḋm a ċairdſsa fſrisin cCoimdeaḋ. Do ġnísiom a faoísiḋe gan nach ndiċioll Ro ċaiestair a ṗeacta fri Dia, ⁊ ba haiṫreaċ lais a ṁiaḋmſnman ⁊ a ionnoccḃáil an ccſin ro ṁair. Ro ṁaiṫ bſós a ġuin don tí ros gon ⁊ atbſrt gur bo hé fſirin fodſra, uair as é ro ṡaiġ fair céttus. Bairiuṁ amlaiḋ sin fri ré seċtṁaine ag foichill écc gach aon laithe, ⁊ aṫair toċċaiḋe don ord remráite ina ṡarraḋ do ġres dia iomcoiṁſt for innelſdaiḃ diaḃail. Ro ṫoċaiṫ corp an Coimdeaḋ iarttain, ⁊ fuair bás ar a haiṫle (22 October) iar mbuaiḋuccaḋ for dſṁon, ⁊ doman. Ro haḋnacht iaraṁ i noṫairliġe a ṡinnsear isin mainistir remráite.

Ro baí a athairsiuṁ .i. Aoḋ mac Maġnusa, mic Aoḋa duiḃ ina ṡeandataiḋ aga ġoire a ffoccus don mainistir. At cuas doséin a ṁac do eiplt ro lá fair go mór go mbaí hi riuscc athaiḋ iarsin. Battar trá a anmcairde aga ṫioncoscrom im lſs a anma do ġrés.

An taoḋh so mac Maghnasa, mic Aoḋa óicc, mic Aoḋa ruaiḋ, mic neill ġairḃ do écc an ⁊ do december. Tiġearna ċenél cConaill innsi hEoghain, ⁊ ioċtair ċonnacht fri ré sé mbliaḋan fichſt go ro hſinirtniġſḋ lá gallaiḃ go ttárd a ṫiġearnas co na ḃſnnachtain dia ṁac do Aoḋ ruadh iar na éluḋ ó ġallaiḃ, fſr fuair tiġearnas gan ḟeill, ġan fionġail, gan coccaḋ, gan comfuaċaḋ an tAodh mac maghnusa hisin iar nſcc a ḋſrḃraṫar an Calḃach. Fſr aghmar ionnsaiġṫeaċ go mbuaiḋ ccroda, ⁊ tacair i ttiġſrnas, ⁊ ria ttiġſrnass, Indriġṫſoir, ⁊ aircceṫſoir na ccoiccrioch ⁊ na ccomarsan dias bó

was still living, but was not the chief ruler of Tirconnell at the time, for he had resigned to his eldest son, Hugh Roe, as early as the year 1592, when it is stated by the Four Masters that he was old and feeble.—See p. 1929, *supra*.

[w] *Sons of life:* i. e. religious persons. It is the antithesis of meic báis, i. e. sons or children of death, which means malefactors, or wicked or irreligious persons.

[x] *Confessors.*—Anmċairde is the plural of anmċara or anamċara, which is translated "confessarius" by Colgan in his *Trias Thaum.*,

being in a dying state. As soon as O'Donnell arrived at the camp he ordered a litter of fair wattles to be made for Manus O'Donnell, [on which] to carry him over Barnis. This was according to orders. Many of his dear friends and faithful people accompanied him to Donegal, where a sick man's couch was prepared for him, and O'Donnell's physicians were brought to cure him; but they could effect no cure for him. They gave him up for death. There was a monastery in the neighbourhood of the fortress in which were sons of life[w], of the order of St. Francis; and the wisest of these were wont to visit him, to hear his confession, to preach to him, and to confirm his friendship with the Lord. He made his confession without concealment, wept for his sins against God, repented his evil thoughts and pride during life, and forgave him who had wounded him, declaring that he himself was the cause, as he had made the first attack. Thus he remained for a week, prepared for death every day, and a select father of the aforesaid order constantly attending him, to fortify him against the snares of the devil. He received then the body of the Lord, and afterwards died on the 22nd of October, having gained the victory over the devil and the world. He was interred in the burial-place of his ancestors, in the aforenamed monastery.

His father, i. e. Hugh, the son of Manus, son of Hugh Duv, was at this time a very old man, living in a state of dotage near the monastery. He was informed of the death of his son; he was greatly affected; and he was in a decline for some time afterwards. His confessors[x] were always instructing him respecting the welfare of his soul.

This Hugh, the son of Manus, son of Hugh Oge, son of Hugh Roe, son of Niall Garv, died on the 7th of December. He had been Lord of Tirconnell, Inishowen, and Lower Connaught, for twenty-six years, until he was weakened by the English, and bestowed his lordship, with his blessing, on his son, Hugh Roe, after he had escaped from the English. This Hugh, the son of Manus, had attained the lordship after the death of his brother Calvagh, without treachery or fratricide, war or disturbance. He was a valiant and warlike man, and victorious in his fights and battles before and during his chieftainship, and the preyer and plunderer of the territories far and near that were bound

p. 294, and "synedrus seu confessarius" at p. 298. The term literally signifies "friend of the soul," and is used in ancient Irish writings in the sense of spiritual director or father confessor.

dú a riaruccaḋ occ saiġiḋ cert a ċeneoil forra go mbattar foṁamaiġthe dó, fer ro lá sníoṁ, ⁊ dfeiċitte an tsaoġail de iar ttairbirt a ṫiġearnais dia ṁac, ⁊ ro baḋ deġairiltniḋ a leiṫ fria dia acc ttuillem focraicce dia anmain fri re oċt mbliaḋan go ro écc don ċur so, ⁊ ro haḋnacht co nonóir, ⁊ co nairmidin (aṁail ro baḋ dior) i mainistir S Fronséis i ndún na ngall i noṫairliġe na ttiġearnaḋ tangatar roiṁe diaiḋ i ndiaiḋ.

Imthusa Uí ḋoṁnaill iar ffosbaḋ dó an triocait laiṫe sin hi ffosḃaisi for na gallaiḃ, Ro triall an longport i mboí frisin an ré sin dfáccḃail ⁊ dol go hionad ele nar bó heissinnille ro baḋ sia biucc o na gallaiḃ for ur na finne alla ṫiar, estorra, ⁊ bernas, uair ros uaṁan lais uacht na gairḃsine geiṁriota dia ḟeinnedaiḃ ag friothaire ⁊ ag forcoiṁett for na ġallaiḃ gaċ oidhċe dóiġ ba i nionam na saṁna an tan sin, ⁊ ba mithid lais a sloġ do breiṫ i nionadh cumsanta iar na mór ṡaoṫar, uair ní ro ċuilsiot a suiṁe fri haṫaiḋ foda. Loctar na sloiġ gus an maiġin remraite. Gaḃait longport hi suiḋe i ffosccaḋ na fioḋḃaiḋe i niomḟoċraiḃ na haḃann. Do níad fianboṫa ⁊ foirccneṁa ar a haiṫle, ⁊ gaḃaitt acc tescaḋ an ḟeda ina nuirtimceall co ndernsat daingen airḃe estorra ⁊ a naṁaitt co nar bó rodaing a saiġiḋ treimit. Ro ṫócaiṫ samlaiḋ co rangattar sccéla dia ṡaighiḋ dí luing do ṫeaċt on Spáinn dionnsaighiḋ na ngaoidel báttar isin ccoccaḋ i mbaoí argatt ⁊ arm, púdar ⁊ luaiḋe. Ba hann ro gaḃsiot side port hi ccuan i ninḃir ṁóir hi cconnaċtaiḃ. Ro ḟaoídsiom na sccéla céḋna co hua néill, ⁊ do ċóiḋ badéin go connaċtaiḃ i mí december do ronnaḋ ⁊ fáccḃaiḋ a dearḃraṫair Ruḋraiġe ua domnaill go nurṁór a ṡlóiġ isin longport atrubramar dia éis acc iomċornaṁ na criċe. Iar roċtain dóroṁ go tír ḟiaċraċ muaiḋe ro lá a ṫecta gus an luingeis réiṁeberṫmar dia oráil forra teaċt go cuan na cceall mbecc, ⁊ ro airis feisin i ndún néill ar bá féil geine an ċoimḋeaḋ ann an tan sin, ⁊ do róine na céd laiṫe don tsollamain dairmitniuccaḋ aṁail ro baḋ dír. Rangattar sccéla ċuicceriom co ttainicc ó neill ina diaiḋ don tír, ⁊ ní ro airisiom ní baḋ síre aċt triall a ccomḋáil í neill conus ralattar dia roile tul hi ttul for an cconair. Tiagaitt gan

[y] *Of Invermore*, inḃir mór, *Portus magnus*, now Broad Haven, in the north of the barony of Erris, and county of Mayo. Docwra says that these ships put in at Calebeg, now Killybegs.

[z] *Killybegs*.—See this place already referred to under the years 1513, 1516, 1550.

[a] *Dun-Neill*: i. e. the Dun or Fort of Niall, now Dunneill, *alias* Castlequarter, a townland in the parish of Kilmacshalgan, barony of Tire-

to obey him, asserting the right of his tribe from them until he made them obedient to him; a man who had laid aside the cares and anxieties of the world after having given up his lordship to his son, and who was a good earner in the sight of God, meriting rewards for his soul for a period of eight years until he died at this period. He was interred with due honour and veneration in the monastery of St. Francis at Donegal, in the burial-place of the lords who had successively preceded him.

As for O'Donnell, at the expiration of the thirty days during which he continued besieging the English, he prepared to leave the place in which he had been during that period, and to go to another place not less secure, a little further from the English, on the west brink of the River Finn, between them and Barnis; for he was afraid [of the effects] of the cold, rough, wintry season on his soldiers, who were watching and guarding every night against the English; for it was then Allhallowtide; and he thought it time to bring his army to a place of rest after their great labour, for they had not slept at ease for a long time. The forces proceeded to the aforesaid place. They pitched a camp under the shelter of the wood that was in the vicinity of the river. They erected military tents and habitations, and proceeded to cut down the trees around them, and raised a strong rampart between themselves and their enemies, so that it was difficult to get across it to attack them. Here he passed the time until news reached him that two ships had arrived from Spain to the Irish who were engaged in the war, with money and arms, powder and lead. These ships put in at the harbour of Invermore[y] in Connaught. He sent the same news to O'Neill, and went himself to Connaught in the month of December; leaving after him his brother, Rury O'Donnell, with the greater part of his forces, in the camp which we have mentioned, to defend the country. On his arrival in Tireragh of the Moy, he sent messengers to the above-mentioned ships, to request them to come into the harbour of Killybegs[z]. He remained himself at Dun-Neill[a]; for it was the festival of the Nativity of the Lord, and he solemnized the first days of the festival with due veneration. News came to him that O'Neill had come after him into the country; and he delayed no longer, but set out to meet O'Neill. They met soon after on the road, face to

ragh, and county of Sligo.—See *Genealogies, Tribes, &c., of Hy-Fiachrach*, pp. 134, 135, 171, 175, 262, 305, 306, and the map to the same work.

airisiomh go rangattar go dún na ngall. Tangadar dna maiṫe lſiṫe cuinn ina ndocum gus an maiġin sin.

Tanaig trá an loingſs a dubramar go cuan teilionn lá taoḃ na cceall mbſg. Do radaḋ i mbaoí inntiḃ dargatt, ⁊ dá gaċ naḋailcce (ro faoíḋheaḋ gus na haireachaiḃ) dia saiġiḋ go dún na ngall, ⁊ ro rannaḋ a ndó .i. lſṫ dua néill, ⁊ dia compann coccaiḋ, ⁊ an lſṫ naill dua ndomhnaill, ⁊ dia mbaoí for a raint.

Siubhan ingſn Mhéguiḋir cúconnaċt (dia ngoirṫi an comharba) mac conċonnaċt, mic briain, mic Pilip, mic tomais bſn an ḃaruin uí néill .i. fſrdorċa, mac cuinn, mic cuinn, mic enrí, mic eoġain, ⁊ bá hisiḋe maṫair í neill .i. Aodh, ⁊ ċormaic a dearbraṫar, ⁊ iar marḃadh an ḃarúin ro pósaḋ isiḋe le hénrí mac feilim ruaiḋ mic airt mic aoḋa mic eoġain, mic neill óicc, ⁊ rucc mac soinſmail dó .i. toirrḋealḃaċ. Bean ro baḋ port coṫaiġṫe ⁊ congḃala truag ⁊ trén, dámh ⁊ deórad, feḋb ⁊ dilleaċt, eccailsi ⁊ ealaḋan, boċt ⁊ aiḋilcc-neaċ, bean ro ba cſnn áṫcomhairc, ⁊ comhairle duaislib, ⁊ doireaċaiḃ ċóicciḋ conċoḃair mic neasa, bſn bíṫe bannda diaḋa, ḋéarcaċ ċſnnsa, ċoimnircleaċ go ccaondúṫraċt, ⁊ co sſirc ndé ⁊ coiḃnſssam do écc i maċaire na croisi 22. Iunii, ⁊ a haḋnacal i mainistir duin na ngall iar ccaiṫſm cuirp criost ⁊ a ḟola, iar nongaḋ, ⁊ iar naiṫriġe iar ttioḋnacal almsan niomḋa durdaiḃ eccailsi dé, ⁊ go sonraḋaċ dord .S. Franceis ar dáiġ a héccnairce do ġaḃail etir marḃaiḃ.

Slóicceaḋ lá hard lustis na hereann Lord mountiog a mí September do ḋol i ttír eoccain. Do cuas lais cetus co droiċſt aṫa, assaiḋe go dún dealgan, ⁊ go bealaċ an maiġre. Tainicc ó neill isin ccſnn oile don ḃealaċ. O Ro ḟidir an iustís ó neill do ṫeaċt an dú sin bá sſḋ do róine campa do ṡuiḋiuccaḋ don taoḃ a ttarla é badéin don ḃealaċ go mbaoí an ċonair sin gan aṫaiġe, gan iomaḋall sſtorra athaiḋ ḟada. O ro ba cian las an iustis

[b] *Harbour of Teilionn*, now Teelin, a small harbour about a mile and a half long, but very narrow, situated about seven miles westwards of Killybegs, in the barony of Banagh, and county of Donegal.

[c] *Province of Conor Mac Nessa:* i. e. Ulster.

[d] *Machaire-na-Croise:* i. e. the Plain of the Cross, now Magheracross, a townland in a parish of the same name, barony of Tirkennedy, county of Fermanagh.—See note [l], under the year 1509, p. 1301, *supra*.

[e] *Bealach-an-mhaighre*, now Bothar-a-mhaighre, *anglice*, the Moyry Pass, an old road extending across the townland of Carrickbroad, parish of Killeavy, barony of Orior, and county of Armagh, about three hundred paces from the

face, and went forthwith to Donegal. Thither the chiefs of the North went to meet them.

The ships aforementioned put in at the harbour of Teilionn[b], near Killybegs. All the money and other necessaries that were in them [which were sent to the Irish chiefs] were brought to them to Donegal, and divided into two parts, of which O'Neill and his confederates in the war received one, and O'Donnell and his allies the other.

Joan, the daughter of Maguire (Cuconnaught, usually styled the Coarb, son of Cuconnaught, son of Brian, son of Philip, son of Thomas), and the wife of the Baron O'Neill, i. e. Ferdoragh, the son of Con, son of Con, son of Henry, son of Owen, [died]. She was the mother of O'Neill (Hugh), and of his brother, Cormac. After the killing of the Baron, she was married to Henry, the son of Felim Roe, son of Art, son of Hugh, son of Owen, son of Niall Oge [O'Neill], for whom she bore a prosperous son, namely, Turlough; a woman who was the pillar of support and maintenance of the indigent and the mighty, of the poets and exiled, of widows and orphans, of the clergy and men of science, of the poor and the needy; a woman who was the head of counsel and advice to the gentlemen and chiefs of the province of Conor Mac Nessa[c]; a demure, womanly, devout, charitable, meek, benignant woman, with pure piety, and the love of God and her neighbours. She died at Machaire-na-croise[d] on the 22nd of June, and was interred in the monastery of Donegal, after receiving the body and blood of Christ, after unction and penance, after having made many donations to the orders of the Church of God, and more especially to the monastery of Donegal, that she might be prayed for there among the dead.

A hosting was made by the Lord Justice of Ireland, Lord of Mountjoy, in the month of September, to proceed into Tyrone. He marched first to Drogheda, thence to Dundalk and Bealach-an-mhaighre[e]. O'Neill came to the other end of the pass. When the Lord Justice learned that O'Neill had arrived at that place, he pitched a camp at his own end of the pass; so that the pass was not travelled or frequented for a long time between them. The Lord

boundary of the counties of Louth and Armagh. The ruins of a small castle are still to be seen here, on the north of the pass. Fynes Moryson, who gives a minute account of this expedition of Mountjoy into Ulster, calls this place Ballinemoyree, and describes it as "between Dundalk and the Newry."—See his *History of Ireland*, Dublin edition of 1735, vol. i. p. 79.

baoí an bealaċ agá ġabáil friſ do ṡionnſcain aon do ló toċt treiṁit daiṁ-ḋeóin uí néill. An tan ro airiġ ó néill an ní sin ro léicc saiṫſḃa seoilnſiṁ-nſċa saiġdiúiriḋe dá saiġiḋ (fó cosṁailſs foiċſḃ fírḃeaċ a ḃruinniḃ bſċ-lann) a boṫaiḃ ⁊ a bélscáṫaiḃ an forlongpuirt. Gabaitt agá nguin, ⁊ agá ngérteſġdaḋ, gá ccailcc, ⁊ gá ccoṁtollaḋ gur ḃó héiccſn dóiḃ filleaḋ a ffrithing na conaire ceḋna gur an ccampa iar marḃaḋ lín díriṁe dá nuaisliḃ, dá naireachaiḃ, da nglaslaiṫ, da ngiollanraiḋ. Ro ḟáccaiḃsiot ḃeós ile dá gaċ ſrnail éḋala do ċaiplib, ⁊ dſchaiḃ dfaiḋḃ airm, ⁊ éitteaḋ isin iomairſcc sin.

Fuair an iustis a ccſnn trill iar sin ell ⁊ elang a ffoscoimett uí neill ar an mbealaċ go ndeachaiḋ trſiṁit gan troit, gan taċar, a mí october do ṡonraḋ. An tan ro ráthaiġ ó neill an ní sin do ṫaot for an sligſḋ siar an lustis co mbáttar in dá campa eineaċ i nionchaiḃ fri aroile go diúiḋ na míosa ceḋna. Ní ro léicceaḋ tra an iustis seaċa sin i ttír eoġain don ċur sin, gur ḃó héiccſn dó filleaḋ don taoḃ ṫoir do ḃealaċ an maiġre do lſiṫimel na noirṫear. Do ṫaod iaram i nartraiġiḃ a cuan cairlinne co fine gall, ⁊ arraiḋe co háṫ cliaṫ. Ní ro triall dna an lustis dol tar bealaċ an maiġre arteaċ go cſnn athaiḋ iar sin.

Sir Sſón chemberlin coirnel do ġallaiḃ doire do ḋol sloġ mor for ua ndoċartaiġ dia indreaḋ ⁊ dia orccain, do rala ua doċartaiġ (go nuaṫad slóiġ ina ḟarraḋ) fris na gallaiḃ. Ro fiġſḋ erġal aṁnas ſtorra go ro sraoíneaḋ for na gallaiḃ go ro marḃaḋ an coirnel lá hua ndoċartaiġ go ndruing ele a maille fris.

Niall garḃ ó domnaill trá, baí side co na ḃraiṫriḃ, ⁊ co na ġallaiḃ a maille fris hi lſiṫḃear aṁail ro airnſiḋſinar, ⁊ do rónaḋ slóicceaḋ leó go hoirſċt uí ċaṫáin do ċuingiḋ creaċ oirene, ⁊ ní ro hanad leó go rangadar go dianait. Do ralattar drecta déarṁara do muinntir ⁊ nell dóiḃ. Fſċar iomairſcc ſtorra go ro gonaḋ soċaiḋe uadaiḃ adiú ⁊ anall go ro ṁeaḃaḋ

[f] *Sir John Chamberlain.*—This entry is evidently misplaced by the Four Masters, for we learn from Docwra's *Narration*, that "Sir John Chamberlaine was mortally wounded with 16 wounds, on the 28th of June."

[g] *A hosting.*—Sir Henry Docwra does not detail these forays in his *Narration*, but he makes a general allusion to them, which is exceedingly valuable to the historian, in the following words:

"After hee" [O'Donnell] "was gone, the Garrison, both heere and at Dunalong, sett divers preyes of catle, and did many other services all the Winter longe, which I stand not upon to make particular mention of, &, I must

Justice, thinking it too long that the pass had been blocked upon him, he attempted to force it one day, in despite of O'Neill. When O'Neill perceived this thing, he sent forth from the tents and booths of the camp fierce and energetic bands of soldiers against him, like unto swarms of bees issuing from the hollows of bee-hives. They proceeded to wound, pierce, hew, and hack them, so that they were compelled to return back by the same road to the camp, after the killing of countless numbers of their gentlemen, officers, recruits, and attendants. They also left behind much booty of every description, as horses, steeds, accoutrements, arms, and armour, in this conflict.

Some time after this the Lord Justice got an advantage and opportunity of O'Neill's watch on this pass, and proceeded through it in the middle of October without battle or opposition. When O'Neill perceived this, he got before the Lord Justice on the way; and both remained encamped face to face until the end of the same month. The Lord Justice was not permitted to advance beyond this place into Tyrone on this occasion, but was compelled to return by a route east of Bealach-an-Mhaighre, along the borders of the Oriors. He afterwards proceeded in vessels from the harbour of Carlingford into Fingal, and from thence to Dublin. The Lord Justice did not attempt to go beyond Bealach-an-Mhaighre for some time after this.

Sir John Chamberlain[f], a colonel of the English of Derry, marched with a numerous force against O'Doherty, to plunder and prey him. O'Doherty, with a small party, met the English; and a fierce battle was fought between them, in which the English were defeated, and the colonel and others were slain by O'Doherty.

Niall Garv O'Donnell remained with his brothers, and with his English, at Lifford, as we have already stated; and they made a hosting[g] into Oireacht-Ui-Chathain, in quest of prey and booty; and they did not halt until they arrived at the Dianait[h], where a great number of O'Neill's people met them. A battle was fought, in which many were slain on both sides, and O'Neill's people were

confess a truth, all by the helpe & advise of Neale Garvie & his Followers, and the other Irish that came in with Sir Arthur O'Neale, without whose intelligence & guidance little or nothing could have been done of ourselves, although it is true withall, they had theire owne ends in it, which were alwayes for private Revenge, and wee ours, to make use of them for the furtherance of the Publique service."

[h] *Dianait*, now the Burn Dennet, a stream flowing through the parish of Donaghedy, barony of Strabane, and county of Tyrone.

for ṁuintir í Neill. Imraoi Niall co na ġallaiḃ go néḋálaiḃ iomḋaiḃ, ⁊ go ccosccar dia ttiġiḃ go leiṫḃer do ridhisi.

Fecht naile iar sin do ċoidh Niall co na braiṫriḃ, ⁊ co na ġallaibh i ttir eoghain go ro crechaḋ glenn aichle go leir leo.

Brisemaiḋm ele leo ar ċloinn an ḟirdoirche mic Eoin mec Domnaill ag cnoc buidb la taoḃ an tsraṫa báin, ⁊ daoine do ṁarḃaḋ leo. Tóirrḋealḃaċ óg ó coinne go ndruing ele do ġaḃail, ⁊ trí ficit marcc do ḃein dfuasccladh ass.

An baile nua hi ttír Eoġain, ⁊ caislen na deircce do ġaḃáil lá niall, ⁊ la gallaibh, ⁊ a mbein dioḃ doridisi gar becc iar sin.

Ruḋraiġe mac Eiccnecháin, mic Eiccnechain, mic neċtain, mic toirrḋealḃaiġ an ḟiona í domnaill décc.

AOIS CRIOST, 1601.

Aois Criost, mile, se céd, a haon.

Clann tSeáin na Semar, mic Riocaird Shaxanaiġ tar a ttangamar a ttrasta tarla doiḃriḋe beiṫ i ccampa i nDuthaiġ í Ṁeachair i nuiḃ Cairín is na céḋlaiṫiḃ do mí Ianuari. Tánaicc braṫ, ⁊ tairscelaḋ ó Buitilerchaiḃ orra isin maiġin sin iar na ċur amaċ do ḋruing da ndaoínibh uaisle co ffuiġṫi uain, ⁊ searḃaoġal ar an ionnsaiġiḋ isin ionaḋ sin i mbáttar. Conaḋ aire sin tainicc Sir uáter, mac Seáin, mic Sémais buitiler, ⁊ Mág Piarais .i. Sémus, mac Emainn, mic Semais, ⁊ drong do ḋaoiniḃ uaisle an dá ċonntae .i. Conntae ṫiobrat árann ⁊ Conntae cille cainnigh hi ccoinne, ⁊ hi ccoṁḋáil, oidhce dáiriġe, go háit naontadhaiḋ naonḃaile. Ba he crioċ ar ċansatt ina niomaccallaiṁ, ⁊ ba hair ro ansat ionnsaighiḋ do ṫaḃairt ar in ccampa ċonnaċtach san moiċḋeíḃail ar na ṁarach.

Tarla ní neṁġnaṫaċ, ⁊ célṁuine ċinneṁnaċ don ḟoslongport ḃúrcach sin .i. faill dfaġḃail ina niomċoimett go rangatar a nescaraitt ina ninmeḋon. Ro fáġḃaitt iad ina ffaoinliġe ḟoḋḃṫa ḟeoilġerrta, ⁊ ina ccollaiḃ corcarda crosḃuailte seċnón a mboth, ⁊ a mbelsgálan. Ro marḃaḋ don ċur sin.

[i] *Gleann-Aichle*, now Glenelly, a remarkable valley in which the old church of Badoney, near Strabane, in Tyrone, is situated.—See Colgan's *Trias Thaum.*, p. 181, n. 171.

[j] *Cnoc-Buidhbh*, now Knockavoe.—See note [a], under the year 1522, p. 1356, *supra.*

[k] *Baile-Nua:* i. e. Newtown, now Newtown-Stewart, in the barony of Strabane, and county

defeated. Niall, with his English, then returned to their houses in Lifford, with many spoils and in triumph.

On another occasion after this, Niall, with his brethren and with his English, went into Tyrone, and the entire of Gleann-Aichle[i] was plundered by them.

They gave another defeat to the sons of Ferdorcha, the son of John, son of Donnell, at Cnoc-Buidhbh[j], near Strabane, where they slew many persons. Turlough Oge, O'Coinne, and some others, were taken prisoners; and they afterwards exacted sixty marks for his [Turlough's] ransom.

Baile-Nua[k] in Tyrone, and Castlederg, were taken by Niall and the English; but they were recovered from them shortly afterwards.

Rury, the son of Egneaghan, son of Egneaghan, son of Naghtan, son of Turlough-an-Fhina O'Donnell, died.

THE AGE OF CHRIST, 1601.

The Age of Christ, one thousand six hundred one.

The sons of John of the Shamrocks, the son of Rickard Saxonagh, of whom we have already treated, happened to be encamped during the first days of the month of January in O'Meagher's country, in Ikerrin. Spies and scouts came upon them in that place from the Butlers, after it had been reported by some of their gentlemen that an advantage and opportunity could be had by attacking them in the place where they [then] were. For this purpose Sir Walter, the son of John, son of James Butler, and Mac Pierce, i. e. James, the son of Edmond, son of James, with some of the gentlemen of the two countries, i. e. of the county of Tipperary and of the county of Kilkenny, came to a conference and meeting on a certain night, at an appointed place. The result of their conference, and the resolution to which they agreed, was, to attack the Connaught camp at day-break next morning.

An unusual accident and a sad fatality occurred to the camp of the Bourkes, namely, an advantage was taken of their [want of] watching, so that their enemies came into the midst of them. They left them lying mangled and slaughtered, pierced and blood-stained corpses, throughout their tents and booths.

of Tyrone. Docwra, who stormed this castle on the 24th of May, describes it as "a pile of stone, strong and well built, 6 myles distant from the Liffer on the way to Dungannon."

O Seachnasaigh .i. Seaan mac an ġiolla duibh, mic diarmata, mic uilliam boí for ionnarbaḋ o na aṫarḋa aṁail gach foghlaiḋ ele hi ffarraḋ ċloinne Seaain a búrc. Do gabaḋ ann Seaan ócc mac Seaain a búrc, ⁊ ruccaḋ é da iomcoiṁétt go cill ċainnigh. Terna Rémann a burc, ⁊ Uilliam as in iomairecc sin go ndruing dá ndaoinibh a maille friu. Lottar arrídhe i neilibh, ⁊ nir bó cian a ccoṁnaiḋe isin ccriċ sin an tan do arccnatar i nulltoibh iar ffágbail na mbailtedh bai leo dairther muṁan conuicce sin ar bhecc inomċoiṁétta. Ar ndol dóibh i ccenn ġaoidel an tuaisceirt .i. O neill, ⁊ ó domhnaill ro ġab Rémann a búrc acc fortaḋ aṁra do ḋol i ccloinn Riocairtt ⁊ o ro forttad lais iadsiḋe tainicc is na ceolaiṫibh desrach tar Eirne. Ro gab tre leiṫimel breifne Uí ruairc, do ċonntae Shliccigh, do ċonntae Rossa comáin, ⁊ tar Shuca isteach i ccloinn connmaigh. Gabtar lais tiġearna na tire sin .i. Mac dauid, Fiacha, mac hobeird buiḋe, mic uilliam mic tomais. Tánaicc Remann iar sin go tuaiṫ an ċalaiḋ i nuaċtar ua maine hi cconntaé na gaillṁe. An tan at ċualaigh iarla ċloinne Riocaird .i. Uilleacc a burc an ní sin. Do ċuaiḋ sidhe isin ccenn ṫoir da ṫír dfriṫeaṁ, ⁊ dforċoiṁétt ar Rémann. Tar gaċ coiṁétt da ndearna, do coiḋ Remann an tres oidhce décc do ṁís marta gan airiuccaḋ, gan forċloisteċt don iarla, nó da forairiḃ ṫarra hi ccloinn Riocaird go rainicc go tuaiṫ ċenel feiċín don taoib ṫes do barúntacht liaṫdroma hi cconntae na gaillme. Do leicc Remann ar adhmadain na hoiḋce sin a cuid sgeiṁelta fo coṁair gaċ en baile don tuaiṫ ó maigh glas go crannoig még cnaiṁin, ⁊ on ċoill bric go sliabh. Baoí urṁor roṁaoine na tuaiṫe co na

[l] *John, the son of Gilla Duv.*—He was the son of Sir Roger O'Shaughnessy by the Lady Honora, daughter of Murrough O'Brien, Earl of Thomond, but he had been born four or five years before their marriage, for which reason he was disturbed in his possession by his paternal uncle, and, after his death, by his brother Dermot, who was legitimate according to the laws of England.—See *Genealogies, &c., of Hy-Fiachrach*, pp. 376, 377, 378.

[m] *Tuath-an-Chalaidh:* i. e. the tuagh or district of the Callow or Strath. This is now principally comprised in the present barony of Kilconnell, in the county of Galway.—See *Tribes and Customs of Hy-Many*, p. 74, note [j].

[n] *Hy-Many* is here used to denote O'Kelly's country at this period, not what it was originally, for the territory of Caladh is not in the upper or southern part of the ancient Hy-Many, which extended to the frontiers of Thomond.

[o] *The district of Kinel-Feichin:* i. e. of the tribe or race of Feichin, the son of Feradhach, chief of Hy-Many, a district extending into the parishes of Ballynakill and Tynagh, in the barony of Leitrim, and county of Galway.—See *Tribes and Customs of Hy-Many*, p. 15, and the map to the same work.

[p] *Magh-glass:* i. e. green plain, now Moyglass,

On this occasion was slain O'Shaughnessy, i. e. John, the son of Gilla-Duv[l], son of Dermot, son of William, who had been banished from his patrimony, as indeed had been all those plunderers who were along with the sons of John Burke. John Oge, the son of John Burke, was taken prisoner, and conveyed to Kilkenny, to be confined. Redmond Burke, and William, together with a party of their people, escaped from this affray; [and] they went from thence into Ely, but they did not remain long in that territory, when they proceeded into Ulster, leaving the castles which until then they had possessed in East Munster under slender guard. On their arrival among the Irish of the North, namely, O'Neill and O'Donnell, Redmond proceeded to hire soldiers, to march into Clanrickard; and, as soon as he had mustered [a sufficient number of] these, he led them, during the first days of spring, across the Erne, and passed along the borders of Breifny O'Rourke, through the counties of Sligo and Roscommon, and across the River Suck, into Clann-Conway. He made a prisoner of the lord of this territory, namely, Mac David (Fiach, son of Hubert Boy, son of William, son of Thomas); and he afterwards proceeded to Tuath-an-Chalaidh[m], in the upper part of Hy-Many[n], in the county of Galway. When the Earl of Clanrickard, i. e. Ulick Burke, heard of this thing, he went to the eastern extremity of his country, to await and watch Redmond; but, notwithstanding all his vigilance, Redmond, on the thirteenth night of the month of March, without being heard or noticed by the Earl or his sentinels, passed by them into Clanrickard, until he arrived in the district of Kinel-Feichin[o], in the south of the barony of Leitrim, in the county of Galway. Towards the end of that night, and by the dawning of day, Redmond sent forth his marauding parties through every town of that district, from Magh-glass[p] to Crannog-Meg-Cnaimhin[q], and from Coill-bhreac[r] to the mountain[s]; and before the noon of that day Redmond

a townland lying to the north-west of Woodford, in the parish of Ballynakill, barony of Leitrim, and county of Galway.—See the Ordnance Map, of that county, sheet 125.

[q] *Crannog-Meg-Cnaimhin:* i. e. the Crannoge, or wooden house of Mac Nevin, now Crannoge-Macnevin, a townland in the parish of Tynagh, barony of Leitrim, and county of Galway.—See *Tribes and Customs of Hy-Many*, p. 68, note [v], and the map to the same work, on which the position of this place is shewn.

[r] *Coill-bhreac:* i. e. the Speckled Wood, now Kylebrack, a townland in the parish and barony of Leitrim, in the same county.—Ordnance Map, sheet 116.

[s] *The mountain:* i. e. the mountain of Slieve Aughty, now sometimes corruptly called Sliebaughta.

huile maiṫſſ roġluaiste ar cumas Remainn ria mſḋón laoí an laiṫe sin. Do ṫaéḋ iaram do ḋenaṁ comnaiḋe go coilltiḃ ḃairr na tuaiṫe, ⁊ baoiſiḋe a cſṫair, no a cúicc do laiṫiḃ ar an luaġaill sin, ag tarrainġ ċuicce o na coṁarranaiḃ ⁊ acc daingniuccaḋ ina ṫimcell co ttainicc Iarla cloinne Riocaird gus an armáil as mó da ḟfuair daér na tuaiṫe a maille ris gur ṡuiḋiġ campa ag mainistir ċenél ḟeiċin. Battar a cſṫair, no a cúicc do laiṫibh fon ionnad sin, ⁊ marbṫa nſṁoirḋſrica dá nḋénaṁ ſtorra go ttainicc Taḋg, mac briain na murṫa, mic briain ḃallaiġ, mic eoġain uí ruairc drong dáraċtaċa dóccḃaiḋ airmnſiṁniġ do ċongnaṁ la Remann. O do ruccsat an dá ḟſḋain i naoínfeċt ar an Iarla ro éirigh on ffoslongport irraiḃe, ⁊ do cuaiḋ tar beilġiḃ isteach i ccloinn Riocaird, Lſnaitt sium é co baile locha riach, ⁊ ó do ḋeachaiḋ an tiarla co na muinntir uaḋaiḃ don ċur sin, ro cuartaiġeaḋ, ⁊ ro crſchloirsceaḋ leosoṁ ó liaṫdruim go hard maolldubáin, ⁊ co dorus an ḟſḋáin i niarṫar ċeneoil aoḋa. Ba isin tan sin do marḃaḋ uaṫa tiġearna tire do ṁuiṁneaċaiḃ .i. Mág donnchaiḋ, donnchaḋ mac corbmaic óicc, mic corbmaic. Ba sſḋ foḋſra dó tſccmáil ar an turas sin ó néill dia ḃrſiṫ i mbraiġdſnas ar in mumain i nerraċ na bliaḋna ro do ċuaiḋ ṫorainn, ⁊ a bſiṫ i nulltoiḃ osin alle go ro gluais lár an ccloinn sin tSſain a búrc, ⁊ gur tuit i ccoccaḋ cloinne huilliam aṁlaiḋ sin.

Iar roċtain do Remann ⁊ da scceiṁeltoiḃ i ttórann tuaḋṁuṁan ro suiḋiġſḋ campa leó don taoḃ ṫiar do loċ cúṫra. Tainicc ina ċſnn annsin duine ócc uasal do dál ccais .i. Taḋg, mac toirrḋealḃaiġ, mic doṁnaill, mic concobair uí ḃriain, tria coṁairle ⁊ aslaċ anndaoíne ecciallaiġ gan aṫcoṁarc, gan ḟiarfaiġiḋ dá aṫair, nó diarla ċloinne riocaird fris a mbaoí

[t] *Kinel-Fheichin*, pronounced Kinel-éghin. This is the monastery called Kinalekin by Archdall (*Monast. Hib.*, p. 293), who erroneously places it in O'Flaherty's country. It is more correctly called Kinaleghin in an Inquisition dated 22nd April, 1636, which places it in Clanrickard. The ruins of this abbey, which are of considerable extent, are situated in the parish of Ballynakill, barony of Leitrim, and county of Galway, about three miles and a half to the north-east of the village of Woodford. The abbey church, which is now very much shattered, measures one hundred and twenty-four feet in length. There are within it many curious monuments and epitaphs to different members of the family of Burke.—See the map to *Tribes and Customs of Hy-Many*, on which the exact situation of this monastery is shewn under the name "Mainistir ċineil ḟeiċin."

[u] *Leitrim:* i. e. the castle of Leitrim, in the parish and barony of the same name, in the south of the county of Galway.

[w] *Ard-Maeldubhain*, now Ardmealuane, a castle in ruins, in the parish of Beagh, barony of

had in his power the greater part of the property, and all the moveable effects, of that territory. He afterwards went to take up his abode in the woods situated in the upper part of that district, and continued for four or five days moving about in this manner, plundering his neighbours, and strengthening [the ramparts] around himself, until the Earl of Clanrickard, accompanied by all the troops he had been able to muster in the district, arrived, and pitched his camp at the monastery of Kinel-Fheichin[t]. Thus they remained for four or five days, during which time some persons not illustrious were slain between them, until Teige, the son of Brian-na-Murtha, son of Brian Ballagh, son of Owen O'Rourke, arrived with bold companies of sharp-armed soldiers to assist Redmond. When these two parties combined overtook the Earl, he left the camp in which he was, and proceeded through the passes into Clanrickard. The others pursued him to Loughrea; and, the Earl and his people escaping from them on this occasion, they traversed, plundered, and burned the country from Leitrim[u] to Ard-Mael-dubhain[w], and as far as the gate of Feadán[x], in the west of Kinelea. At this time they lost a Munster lord of a territory, i. e. Mac Donough[y], i. e. Donough, the son of Cormac Oge, son of Cormac. What brought him on this expedition was this, he had been carried off as a hostage by O'Neill in the spring of the preceding year, and had remained in Ulster until [having regained his liberty] he set out with those sons of John Burke, and so fell in this war of the Clann-William.

When Redmond arrived with his marauders on the confines of Thomond, they pitched a camp on the western side of Loch-Cutra[z]. Here he was joined by a young gentleman of the Dal-Cais, namely, Teige, the son of Turlough, son of Donnell, son of Conor O'Brien, [who had been induced to join him] through the advice and solicitation of bad and foolish men, and without consulting or taking counsel of his father or the Earl of Clanrickard, to whom he was related

Kiltartan, and county of Galway.—See the Ordnance Map of that county, sheet 128, and note [w], under the year 1579, p. 1713, *supra*.

[x] *Feadan*, now Fiddaun or Fiddane, a townland containing the ruins of a castle built by O'Shaughnessy, chief of Kinelea, in the parish of Beagh, barony of Kiltartan, and county of Galway.—See the Ordnance Map, sheet 128, the map to *Tribes and Customs of Hy-Many*, and *Genealogies, &c., of Hy-Fiachrach*, p. 381.

[y] *Mac Donough.*—He was the head of a powerful sept of the Mac Carthys, and called, by the Irish, Lord of Duhallow, now a barony in the north-west of the county of Cork.

[z] *Lough Cutra*, now Lough Cooter, a beautiful and celebrated lake in the parish of Beagh, barony of Kiltartan, and county of Galway.—See O'Flaherty's *Ogygia*, part iii. c. 11.

a coṁġaol, ⁊ a ċarattraḋ. O ro naiḋm clann tSeain a burc, ⁊ Taḋg ó briain a ccoṁaonta ċoccaiḋ re a roile, ro iarr tadg a cceann trí lá iar sin cuideaċta lais, do ċor ċuarta hi ccúil eiccin do Ṫuaḋmuṁain. Ní ro héraḋ eisiuṁ imon aiscciḋ sin, uair tangattar drong do daoinib uaisle an ḟorslongpuirt co na cceiṫeirnaib lais. Ro baḋ dibhréin Uilliam mac Seain a burc, ⁊ mac meic Uilliam burc .i. Uatér mac uilliam mic dauiḋ, mic emainn, mic uillicc. Ar ffáccbáil an ḟorlongpuirt doib do ġabsat do ċoiccrích ċeneóil aoḋa, ⁊ na heċtge, ⁊ do ċenel dúnġaile. Sgaoilit a sgeiṁealta ar gaċ taoib dforġar, fa ioċtar o ffearmaic, ⁊ fa uaċtar ċloinne cuiléin. Do cuaiḋ cuid díob go baile uí aille[a], ⁊ a ffoccus do ċluain raṁḟoda. Sóaid tar a nais co na nedálaib go cill reaċtais[b] hi ccloinn ċuiléin uaċtair in adhaiġ sin. Ag faccbáil an baile sin dóib ar na ṁáraċ rucc orra eirge amaċ an dá cloinn cuiléin co na ndaoínib uaisle. Ruccsatt orra bfós bannaḋa iarla tuaḋmuman. Ġabaitt an tóir Ṫuaḋmuiṁneaċ sin acc diubraccaḋ na ndibeirceaċ go ro marbsat drong da ndaoínib ó tá sin go míliuc uí ġrádaiġ[c] i noirṫear ċenél dúngaile. Impaídid an tóir, ⁊ ruccsat an luċt naile an ccreaich gus an ccampa iar ffaccbail druinge dá ndaoinib uaisli, ⁊ daosccarsluaġ. Ro baḋ dibside an mac sin meic uilliam a dubramar .i. Uater mac uilliam burc. Ro gonaḋ dna isin ló céḋna Taḋg mac toirrḋealbaiġ uí briain durċor peileir gur bó heiccean dó ar ndol don campa daiṁḋeóin a aiccniḋ aiṁriaraiġ, ⁊ a ṁeanmanraḋ ṁearḋána anmain i noċtairleabaiḋ, ⁊ dol fa láṁaib leagh.

Tangatar daoine dearmara a hionadaib eccsaṁla do ṁuintir na bainríoġna hi ffurtaċt iarla cloinne riocaird. Ro bad dibside a hoċt, nó a naoí do braataċaib saiġdiúiride ó ṗresidens dá cóicciḋ muṁan. Tánaicc ann mac an iarla féin baí re hathaiḋ riar an tan sin hi ffoċair an lustís drong buiḋéin dóccbaid anaitniḋ. Tánaic din fear ionaid gobernóra ċoicciḋ connaċt, ⁊ tangatar bfós congnaṁ sloiġ on ngaillim. Iar ccloisteaċt an ċruinniġte

[a] *Baile-Ui-Aille*, now Ballyally, near Ennis.—See it already referred to under the years 1559 and 1599.

[b] *Cill-Reachtais*, now Kilraghtis, an old church giving name to a parish situated about four miles to the north of the town of Ennis, in the barony of Upper Bunratty, and county of Clare. According to the tradition in the country, the poets Teige and Maelin Oge Mac Brody were born near this church.

[c] *Miliuc-Ui-Ghrada:* i. e. O'Grady's Meelick, now Meelick, a townland in the parish of Clonrush, barony of Leitrim, and county of Galway. This townland, and the whole of the parishes of Inishcaltra and Clonrush, once belonged to O'Grady, as a part of his territory of Cinel

and friendly. When the sons of John Burke and Teige O'Brien had entered into a confederacy with each other, Teige requested, in three days afterwards, that he should get a company to go on an incursion into some angle of Thomond. He was not refused this request, for some of the gentlemen of the camp went along with him, with their kerns. Among these were William, the son of John Burke, and the son of Mac William Burke, i. e. Walter, the son of William, son of David, son of Edmond, son of Ulick. On leaving the camp, they passed along the borders of Kinelea, and Echtghe, and Kinel-Dunghaile. They sent off marauding parties along both banks of the Fergus, into the lower part of Hy-Fearmaic, and the upper part of Clann-Cuilein. Some of them proceeded to Baile-Ui-Aille[a], and near Clonroad; and they returned that night with their spoils to Cill-Reachtais[b], in Upper Clann-Cuilein. On their leaving this town, on the following morning, they were overtaken by the rising-out of the two Clann-Cuileins, with their gentlemen. They were also overtaken by the companies of the Earl of Thomond. These pursuing forces of Thomond proceeded to shoot at the insurgents, and killed many of their men, from thence to Miliuc-Ui-Ghrada[c], in the east of Cenel-Donghaile. The pursuers [then] returned, and the others carried off the prey to their camp, after having lost some of their gentlemen and common people. Among these was that son of Mac William whom we have already mentioned, namely, Walter, the son of William Burke. Teige, the son of Turlough O'Brien, was wounded on the same day by the shot of a ball; so that on his arrival at the camp he was obliged, in despite of his unbending mind and his impetuous spirit, to betake himself to the bed of sickness, and go under[d] the hands of physicians.

A great number of the Queen's people came from various places to assist the Earl of Clanrickard. Of these were eight or nine standards of soldiers, [sent] from the President of the two provinces of Munster. Thither came the Earl's own son, who had been for some time before along with the Lord Justice, with a band of foreign soldiers; thither also came the Deputy of the Governor of the province of Connaught, and there came also an auxiliary force from Galway.

Donghaile, in Thomond, and are still in the deanery of O-mBloid, in the diocese of Killaloe.—See the map to *Tribes and Customs of Hy-Many*, on which the exact position of this place is shewn.

[d] *Go under.*—An English writer would say: "And place himself in the hands of physicians."

sin do cloinn tSeáin a búrc, ro aṫraiġsiot tar a nais soir leiṫ le sliaḃ ar daingniġtiḃ tuaiṫe Ċenél Feiċin, ⁊ airisit is na sléiḃ ḃoṫaiḃ issaḃattar roiṁe sin. Nír bó cian doiḃ isuiḋe an tan tangattar clann an iarla .i. barún Dúine cuillin, ⁊ Sir tomás a burc, ⁊ gach neach baoí insema dá cloinn i reiṁtúr na soċaiḋe go slóġaiḃ líonmara a maille friú don tuaiṫ ina ttóraiġeacht, ⁊ Ro gabaḋ longport taiḋbreaċ teandalaċ leo ar urlár na tuaiṫe. Ní raiḃe Iarla ċloinne Riocaird féin isin ffoslongport sin, uair do rala teiḋm tinnesa, ⁊ gaḃaḋ ger earrláinte dó isin treaċtmain roiṁe sin, co nár bo hiontsluaiġiḋ an tan sin hé.

Iar ffios sgél dFior ionaid gobernora ċóicciḋ connaċt ⁊ do ḃarún Dúine cuillin Tadg o briain do ḃeiṫ bfógonta isin ffoslongport sin Remainn a burc, ro ċuirsiot prótexion a huċt na bainríoġna cuicce, ⁊ tainicc siuṁ dia saiġiḋ. Ro ċuir an barún ioḋlacaḋ lais go baile do ḃailtiḃ an iarla .i. liaṫ druim ⁊ nír bó cian a ṡaoġalsoṁ isuiḋe uair atbaṫ gan ḟuireċ, ⁊ ro haḋnaiceaḋ é i mbaile Loċa riach, ⁊ i mbaile áṫa an rioġ diaiḋ i ndiaiḋ in aoin treċtmain. Ba mairicc tír o ttesda an tócc plannda ro écc ann sin, uair ba coimdes ar gaċ trealaṁ troda, ⁊ ar gaċ aiḋmiḃ ergaile ba gnaṫ etir eirennchoiḃ diomluaḋ i ngurt gaisccidh. Ba lán do ṁire, do ṁeanmain, do lúṫ, do láṁaċ, do ṁíne do ṁacaoṁdaċt, diomraḋ, ⁊ deinech eisiḋe.

Dála an ċampa sin tuaiṫe ċeneil Feichin battar uċt re huċt gaċ aon lá ag coiméett ar a ċéile o ḟeil Patraicc co dereaḋ mís april co ndeachaiḋ teirce ⁊ traothaḋ illóintiḃ ⁊ hi ffeólmach ċloinne Seain a burc, conaḋ aire sin ro ṫriallsat an tír dfágḃail ⁊ iar ffaccbáil an tíre doiḃ tarla creach uí ṁadagain ċuca .i. doṁnall mac Seáin, mic breasail. Do ċódar araiḋe tar Suca. Báttar clann an iarla ina lenmain in airett sin, ⁊ ro marḃaḋ daoine iomḋa etorra diblinib don ċur sin. Clann tSeáin a búrc do ḋol i ttír conaill iar sin i ccenn uí ḋoṁnaill, ⁊ clann an iarla dfilleaḋ dia ttír, ⁊ dia ttiġiḃ. Iar ffilleaḋ doiḃ dia ndúṫaiġ ar aṁlaiḋ fuaratar a naṫair is na déiḋencoiḃ iar ndenaṁ a ṫiomna, iar cceilebraḋ da ċairdiḃ collnaiḋe, ⁊ iar ccríoċnuccaḋ a ḋál ndoṁanda don iarla .i. Uillecc mac Riocaird, mic Uillecc na

[e] *The mountain:* i. e. Slieve Aughty, now corruptly Sliebaughta.

[f] *Kinel-Fheichin*, Cenél Feiċin: i. e. the tribe or race of Feichin, the son of Feradhach, son of Lughaidh, chief of Hy-Many. It was the name of a district in the south of the county of Galway, comprising a considerable portion of the barony of Leitrim. The name is now applied

When the sons of John Burke heard of this muster, they removed back eastwards, along the mountain[e], into the fastnesses of the district of Kinel-Fheichin[f], and remained in the ready huts in which they had been before. They had not been long here when the sons of the Earl, namely, the Baron of Dunkellin and Sir Thomas Burke, with every one of his sons that was capable of bearing arms, arrived in the district in pursuit of them, at the head of very numerous forces, and pitched a splendid and well-furnished camp in the very middle of the district. The Earl of Clanrickard himself was not in this camp, for he had been attacked by a fit of sickness, and a severe, sharp disease, the week before, so that he was not able to undertake an expedition at this time.

When the Deputy of the Governor of Connaught and the Baron of Dunkellin received intelligence that Teige O'Brien was lying severely wounded in that camp of Redmond Burke, they sent him a protection in behalf of the Queen, upon which he repaired to them. The Baron sent an escort with him to Leitrim, one of the Earl's castles. But he did not live long there, for he died shortly afterwards[g]; and he was buried successively at Loughrea and Athenry in one week. Alas to the country that lost this young scion! He was expert at every warlike weapon and military engine used by the Irish on the field of battle. He was full of energy and animation, [and distinguished for] agility, expertness, mildness, comeliness, renown, and hospitality.

As for the camps in the district of Kinel-Fheichin, they were front to front, guarding against each other daily, from the festival of St. Patrick to the end of the month of April, when the provisions and stores of flesh meat of the sons of John Burke began to grow scant and to fail; and they, therefore, proceeded to quit the territory; and after their departure they carried off a prey from O'Madden, i. e. Donnell, the son of John, son of Breasal, and then proceeded across the Suck. The sons of the Earl, in the mean time, continued to pursue them; and many persons were slain between them on this occasion. The sons of John Burke then went to Tirconnell, to O'Donnell; and the sons of the Earl returned to their own country and their houses. Upon their return to their patrimony, they found their father, i. e. Ulick, the son of Rickard, son of Ulick-na-gCeann, in his last moments, after making his will, and bidding farewell to

to the monastery only.—See note [t], p. 2230, *sup.* —See *Tribes and Customs of Hy-Many*, p. 15.

[g] *Shortly afterwards:* literally, "and his life was not long there, for he died without delay."

ccſnd ro écc a mí May i mbaile loċa riaċ, ⁊ ro haḋnacht i mbaile áṫa an riogh co nairmidin moir. Ro badh do ṁoirrſcélaiḃ a aimsire etir erennchoiḃ an tí tſsda ann sin, Tiġearna forraiḋ fírḃrſṫach, go ngnuis aghaiḋ ċaoín ionḟlaṫa, no ḃíoḋ uis re a agallaiṁ, tais re a ṫiorṫaċaiḃ, colġḋa re a ċoṁarsain, ⁊ coṁtrom a ccoiccſrtaibh, fſr nar fionnaḋ a ṁaoiṫe na a ṁſirtniġe i ngurt gáḃaiḋ o ro gaḃ gairsceaḋ gur an lo at baṫ. A ṁac .i. Riocard do oirdneaḋ[h] ina ionadh. Conaḋ do ḃliaḋnaiḃ báis an Iarla at rubraḋ.

Se céd décc is bliaḋain ḃairr,
o ṫáinicc crioſt i ccolainn,
lia ar ccás gaċ terma da ttícc,
go bás an Iarla Uillicc.

O dochartaiġ Sſon óсс, mac Sſain, mic Feilim, mic concobair carraiġ decc, 27. Ianuarÿ tiġſrna triocait céd[i] innsi heóġain eiriḋe, ní baí eiṁ tiġearna ṫríoċait céd do ġaoiḋelaibh ba fſrr láṁ ⁊ einеċ, ⁊ ro ba croḋa coṁairle inás. O doṁnaill do ġairm í dochartaiġ dFeilim óсс .i. dearbraṫair Shſain. Clann Ailin,[k] ⁊ clann ndaibſitt[l] do breiṫ caṫaoir mic Sſain oicc hi ccſnn gall go doire, ⁊ an generál Sir henrÿ docura do ġairm í doċartaiġ[m] ḋe ar ulca la hua ndoṁnaill.

[h] *Was appointed*, do oirdneaḋ.—This phrase is incorrect, because no election had taken place, but Rickard succeeded to his father according to the laws of England.

[i] *Triocha-ched:* a cantred, hundred, or barony, containing one hundred and twenty quarters of land.

[k] *The Clann-Ailin:* i. e. the Mac Allens, or Allens. They are really Campbells.

[l] *The Clann-Devitt:* i. e. the Mac Devitts, of whom the celebrated Felim Reagh, who slew Captain Martin at Sligo in the year 1595, and who afterwards burned Derry, was the chief at this period.

[m] *Styled him O'Doherty.*—Sir Henry Docwra himself has written the following account of the death of Sir John O'Doherty; of the manner in which he obtained the young Cahir O'Doherty from O'Donnell; and of his attempt to make O'Doherty independent of Niall Garv O'Donnell, after the latter had aspired to the O'Donnellship:

"And nowe came a practice of O Donell's to open a discouverie, which had long beene mannaged in secret, & as he thought Carried Close within the Compass of his owne & his associats knowledge; Captaine Alford, that had the keeping of Culmore, fell into priuate familiaritie with Hugh Boy and Phelim Reogh (of the Septs of the mac Dauids), two Principall men about O Doghertie, & of as good Credite & estimation with O Donell. These men requested to haue leaue to buy Aquavitæ, Cloath, & such other Comodities as that place afforded, which the Captaine & I, hauing our ends in it, as well as they theires, gaue them free libertie to doe, & with more free access then any other. They measuring theire hopes by theire good enter-

his earthly friends, and settling his worldly affairs. The Earl died, in the month of May, in the town of Loughrea; and he was interred at Athenry with great solemnity. The person who died here was [the subject of] one of the mournful news of the time among the Irish. He was a sedate and justly-judging lord; of a mild, august, chief-becoming countenance; affable in conversation, gentle towards the people of his territory, fierce to his neighbours, and impartial in all his decisions; a man who had never been known to act a feeble or imbecile part on the field of danger, from the day he had first taken up arms to the day of his death. His son, Rickard, was appointed[h] in his place. To commemorate the year of the Earl's death, the following was composed:

Sixteen hundred years and one besides,
From the time that Christ came into a body,
The advocate of our causes at every term,
To the death of the Earl Ulick.

O'Doherty (John Oge, the son of John, son of Felim, son of Conor Carragh) died on the 27th of January. He was Lord of the triocha-ched[i] of Inishowen; and there was not among all the Irish of his time a lord of a triocha-ched of better hand or hospitality, or of firmer counsel, than he. O'Donnell nominated Felim Oge, i. e. the brother of [the deceased] John, the O'Doherty; but the Clann-Ailin[k] and the Clann-Devitt[l] took Cahir, the son of John Oge, to the English, to Derry; and the General, Sir Henry Docwra, styled him O'Doherty[m], to spite O'Donnell.

tainement, of all presentlie aboard him, to knowe if hee would sell the Foarte. Hee seamed not vnwilling, soe he might be assured of some good & reall reward in hand. Many Meetinges & Consultations they had about it, & all with my knowledge. In the end it was resolued his Reward should be a Chaine of Gould in hand, which the Kinge of Spaine had formerlie giuen to O Donell, & was worth aboute 8 scoore poundes, a 1000[li] in money the first day the Treason should be effected, & 3000[li] a yeare pention during his life from the Kinge of Spaine, & for this he should onelie deliuer vpp the Foarte, with Neale Garvie in it, whome he should purposlie invite that Night to Supper. The time was sett & all thinges prepared. The Chaine, as a reall achiument of theire designe, I had deliuered into my handes. But when the day came, they tooke a distast, &, without aduenture of future loss, were contented to giue ouer theire bargaine. And about Christenmas this yeare dyed S[r] John O Doghertie in Tirconnell, being fledd from his owne Countrey, with his goods & people; a man that in shewe seamed wonderfull desireous to yeald his obedience to the Queene; but soe as his actions did euer argue he was otherwise minded. But it is true O Donell had at our first coming Ceazed his

Remann o Gallcoḃair epscop doire do ṁarḃaḋ la gallaiḃ i noirecht uí catháin 15 marta.

Sémus mac Soṁairle buiḋe mic Alastrainn mic eóin ċaṫanaiġ, aon

sonne, afterwards called Sr Cahir O Doghertie, into his hands, & kepte him as a Pledge vpon him, which might iustly serue for some colour of excuse, that he was not at libertie to vse the freedome of his owne will. Being nowe Deade, O Donell set vp in his place one Phelim Oge, a brother of his, neglecting the sonne, who had bene bredd & fostred by the said Hugh Boye & Phelim Reaugh. These men tooke it as the highest iniurie" [that] "could be done vnto them, that theire Foster Child should be depriued of that which they thought was his cleere & vndoubtible right, & therevpon seriouslie addressed themselues vnto Mee, and made offer, that in case I would maintaine the sonne against the vncle, & procure he might hold the Countrey, according to the same Lettres Pattents his father had it before him, they would worke the meanes to free him out of O Donell's hands; to bring home the People & Catle that were fledd, & with them, togeather with themselues, yeald obedience & seruice to the state. Many messages & meetinges wee had about it, & none but, to my knowledge, O Donell was still made acquainted with, yea, & with the very truth of every particuler speach that past amongst vs; yet soe was he deluded (being himselfe a Crafte Master at that arte) that in the end a Conclusion was made between vs, theire demaunds were graunted by mee, & confirmed by my lord Deputie & Councell, hee perswaded to sett the young man at libertie, & when he had done, the people with theire goods retourned into the Countrie, tooke theire Leaves of him, & declared themselues for our side, & from that day forward wee had many faithfull & singuler goode seruices from them; theire Churles & Garrans assistinge vs with Carriages, theire Catle, with plentie of fishe, meate, & Hugh Boye & Phelime Reaugh with many intelligences & other helpes; without all which, I must freelie confess a truth, it had beene vtterlie impossible wee could haue made that sure & speedie Progress in the Warres that afterwardes wee did.

"But therevpon begune Neale Garvie's discontentment, for presentlie he directed some men of his to be cessed vpon this Country. O Doghertie & Hugh Boy, with greate indignation, refused to accept them. Complainte came before mee; I asked him wherevpon it was that hee challenged this power ouer annother man's land; he tould mee the land was his owne, for the Queene had given him all Tyrconnell, & this was parte of it. I aunswered it was true. I know well the whole Countrey of Tyrconnell was promised him in as large and ample manner as the O Donnells had beene accustomed to hould it; But I tooke it there were many others in that Countrey that had lands of their owne as well as they, whose intrest I neuer conceiued was intended to be giuen to him. Hee replied, not onelie the Countrey of Tyrconnell, but into Tyrone, Farmanaght, yea, & Connaught, wheresoeuer any of the O Donnells had, at that time, extended theire Power, hee made Accompte all was his; hee acknowledged noe other kinde of right or intrest in any man else; yea, the very persons of the People he challenged to be his; & said he had wronge, if any one foote of all that land, or any one of the Persons of the People, were exempted from him. I saide againe these Demaunds were, in my Judgement, very vnreasonable, but hee should receive noe wronge by Mee; Let him haue patience till wee might heare from my lord Deputie, & whatsoever his

Redmond O'Gallagher, Bishop of Derry, was killed by the English in Oireacht-Ui-Chathain, on the 15th of March.

James, the son of Sorley Boy[n], son of Alexander, son of John Cahanagh,

Judgement was, I must & would obay. Wounderfull impatient he was of any delay, but necessitie enforceing him, & the case sent to my lord, he returned this aunswere, with the aduise of the Councell: That the vttermost could be challenged vpon the O Dohertyes was but a cheife Rent, sometimes paide to O Neale, sometimes to O Donnell, but that whatsoeuer it were, they were of opinion was extinct euer since they held immediatelie from the Crowne; if Neale Garvie thought otherwise his reasons should be heard with fauour when time should serue, & noe parte of that was promised him but should be made good; In the mean while he must be Contented, O Doughertye must & should be exempted from him: which hee tooke with a greate deale more indignation & furie, then became a man that was to raise his fortune onelie by the fauour of annother.

"But the Springe coming now on, & hauing the helpe of this Countrey for Carriages, towards the latter end of March I drewe Forth & made a iourney vpon mac Swyne Fanaght, whose Countrie lyes diuided from o Doghertyes by a Bay of the sea. I came vpon him vnawarrs, & surprised & gott into my possession about 1000 of his Cowes, before hee had Leasure to driue them away. Himselfe came vnto Mee vpon it, & desired his submission to the Queene might be accepted of, & vsed the mediation of O Doghertye & Hugh Boy, that I would restore him the Prey. Much entreatie & importunitie I was prest withall, & thinking with myselfe it might be a goode Example to such others as I should afterwards haue occasion to deale with, that I Sought not their goods soe much as theire obedience (reseruing a parte onelie for reward of the souldiers labour), I was contented & gave him backe the rest, taking his oath for his future fidelitie, & six pledges, such as I was aduised to choose, & was borne in hand, were very sufficient to binde him, & whereof his owne sonne was one; & to have a tye on him besids, I left Captaine Ralph Bingley, with his Companye of 150 Men, in Garrison in his Countrey, att the Abbay of Ramullan. It is true, for all that, not long after, with out Compulsion, he made his Reconciliation with O Donnell vnder hand, promised to betray the Garrison that lay vpon him, & secreetlie wrought to gett his Pledges out of my hand; But fayling in both, & yet resolued to goe on his Course, he draue away all his Catle & goods, & openlie declared himselfe an Enymy against vs. In reuenge whereof I presentlie hunge vpp his Pledges, & in September following made annother iourney vpon him, burnt & destroyed his houses & Corne; wherevpon, Winter approching, insued the death of most of his People; & in December after, at the earnest entreatie of Neale Garuie, I tooke his Submission againe, & sixe more Pledges, & from that forward he continewed in good subiection."

P. O'Sullevan Beare has the following short notice of the same defection of the Mac Devitts from O'Donnell, *Hist. Cathol. Iber.*, &c., tom. 3, lib. 6, c. v.:

"Odocharta diem obit (vulnus Odonello magnum) Cathirium filium puerum relinquens, qui quòd rebus gerendis ineptus erat, Felmius Odocharta Inisonæ princeps ab Odonello creatur. Qua re infensus Hugo Cathirii nutritius, & cætera factio ab Odonello desciscentes Beartam" [Burt] "arcem Inisonæ principatus caput Anglis tradit."—Fol. 172.

[n] *James, the son of Sorley Boy.*—He was Sir

ḃarr áiġ cloinne doṁnaill ina ré ciḋ fri síḋ, cíoḋ fri coccaḋ do écc luan cásg.

Mac uí bRiain ara décc a mí febru .i. toirrḋealḃaċ mac muirċſrtaiġ mic doṁnaill mic taiḋcc. Ní baí a ċoṁaorta do ṫiccſrna tíre i nerinn in oiḋhce atbath. Duine erccaiḋ, ionnsaiġṫeaċ, do ḃſireaḋ a lorcc iomlán lais ar gaċ tír i ttſiġſḋ, ⁊ rob annaṁ aonḃuiḋſn ag dol uaḋ san iomlaine i ttiaġdais dia ṫír, nſċ do ċosain an ſng iaṫġarḃ, echrſiḋ, baí occa co ro écc, ⁊ a aḋnacul ina longport fſin i mbaile an ċaisleín.

O Raġailliġ décc a mí april .i. Emann, mac maoilṁorda, mic Sſain, mic

James Mac Donnell, Lord of the Route and Glynnes, in the north of the present county of Antrim.—See note [p], under the year 1590, pp. 1892, 1896, *supra*.

[o] *Baile-an-chaislen:* i. e. town of the castle, now Castletown, a townland verging on Lough Derg, containing the ruins of a castle and church in the territory or barony of Arra or Duharra, in the county of Tipperary.

[p] *Edmond, the son of John.*—He was usually called Edmond O'Reilly of Kilnacrott.—See note [c], under the year 1583, p. 1806, *supra*. The O'Reillys, formerly of the Heath House, in the Queen's County, those of Thomastown Castle, in the county of Louth, the Counts O'Reilly of Spain, and the Reillys of Scarva, in the county of Down, are all descended from this Edmond. His present senior representative is Myles John O'Reilly, Esq., late of the Heath House, in the Queen's County, and now living in France. His pedigree runs as follows, as made out by the late Chevalier O'Gorman for Count Alexander O'Reilly, and as tested by the Editor with various original documents, now before him:

I. Edmond O'Reilly of Kilnacrott, near Ballyjamesduff, in the barony of Castlerahin, and county of Cavan, was chief of East Breifny, and member of the Parliament of 1585.—See note [s], under that year, p. 1830, *supra*. The pedigree of Count Alexander O'Reilly, compiled by the Chevalier O'Gorman, gives this Edmond but one wife, namely, Bridget, daughter of Richard Nugent, the eighth Baron of Delvin; but it is stated in an old pedigree on paper of the Reillys of Scarva, of which the Editor has obtained a copy from James Myles Reilly, Esq., Barrister-at-law, of Scarva, in the county of Down, that he was married twice: first, to Mary Plunkett, by whom he had three sons, Cahir, whose descendants are extinct or unknown, John, and Terence Neirinn, ancestor of the Reillys of Scarva; and, secondly, to Elizabeth Nugent, by whom he had three sons, Myles, Farrell, and Charles. This accords with the Genealogy of Lord Dunsany's family, in which it is stated that Robert, the fifth Baron Dunsany, had nine daughters, one of whom married Edmund O'Reilly of Kilnacrott.

II. John O'Reilly. He was evidently the second son of Edmond of Kilnacrott by his first marriage, though O'Gorman makes him his third son by Bridget Nugent. He married Catherine, daughter of Sir James Butler, and had by her one son.

III. Brian O'Reilly, who died in 1631, leaving by his wife, Mary, daughter of the Baron of Dunsany, four sons, namely, Maelmora, or Myles, No. IV., of whom presently; 2. Cathal; 3. Owen; 4. Hugh.

IV. Maelmora O'Reilly. He was a very able military leader during the civil wars of 1641, and is still vividly remembered in the

the most distinguished of the Clann-Donnell, either in peace or war, died on Easter Monday.

Mac-I-Brien Ara, namely, Turlough, the son of Murtough, son of Donnell, son of Teige, died in the month of February. There was no [other] lord of a territory in Ireland so old as he on the night that he died. He was an active, warlike man, who had led his followers in safety from every territory into which he had gone, and seldom had any troop who had entered his territory returned from him scathless; a man who had defended the rugged and hilly district which he possessed until his death. He was interred in his own fortified residence of Baile-an-chaislen[o].

O'Reilly, i. e. Edmond, the son of Maelmora, son of John[p], son of Cathal, died

traditions of the country under the name of "Myles the Slasher." He shewed prodigies of valour during the years 1641, 1642, and 1643; but in 1644 being encamped at Granard, in the county of Longford, with Lord Castlehaven, commander of the army of the Confederate Catholics, who ordered him to proceed with a chosen detachment of horse to defend the bridge of Finea against the Scots, then bearing down on the main army with a very superior force, Maelmora was slain at the head of his troops, fighting bravely on the middle of the bridge. His body was discovered on the following day, and conveyed to the monastery of Cavan, and there interred in the tomb of his ancestors. He married Catherine, daughter of Charles O'Reilly of Leitrim, colonel of infantry during the civil wars. He had by her three sons, namely, 1. Colonel John; 2. Edmond; 3. Philip.

V. Colonel John Reilly. He seems to have been the first of this family who dropped the prefix O. He was formerly of Clonlyn and Garryrocock, in the county of Cavan; but is mentioned in 1713, as of Ballymacadd, in the county of Meath. He was elected knight of the shire for the county of Cavan, in the Parliament held in Dublin on the 7th of May, 1689. He raised a regiment of dragoons at his own expense, for the service of James II., and assisted at the siege of Londonderry in 1689. He had two engagements with Colonel Wolsley, the commander of the garrison of Belturbet, whom he signally defeated. He fought at the battles of the Boyne and Aughrim, and was included in the articles of Capitulation of Limerick, whereby he preserved his property, and was allowed to carry arms. According to *An alphabetical List of the Names of such Persons of the Popish Religion, within the Kingdom of Ireland, who have Licenses to carry Arms*, printed by Andrew Croke, printer to the Queen's most excellent Majesty, in Copper Alley, Dublin, 1713, it appears that Lieutenant-Colonel John Ryley, late of Clonlyn, in the county of Cavan, now of Ballymacadd, in the county of Meath, and Garryrocock, in the county of Cavan, had license to carry "1 sword, 1 case of pistols, and 1 gunn." He married Margaret, daughter of Owen O'Reilly, Esq., by whom he had five sons and two daughters. The sons were, 1. Captain Conor, who died without issue in May, 1723; 2. Myles Reilly, of the city of Dublin, merchant; 3. Brian Reilly; 4. Luke Reilly; 5. Conor Reilly; all of whom died without issue, except Myles and Brian.

Colonel John Reilly, on the intermarriage of

Caṫail fſr arsaidh, arachliaṫ, cuiṁnech cianaosta, baoí esccaiḋ iomluaġ-aillec daiġneaḋ, ⁊ dinntinn ina aosdiḋ, ⁊ a aḋnacul is an ccaḃan i mainistir

his eldest son and heir, Captain Conor Reilly, with Mary, daughter of Luke O'Reilly, Esq., of Tonogh, in the county of Cavan, on the second day of May, 1692, executed articles to limit his estates by proper deeds to the uses of the said marriage; and upon the payment of the marriage portion of Conor, he, on the 23rd of March, 1702–3, perfected a settlement, limiting the estate therein set forth to himself for life; remainder to his eldest son, Conor, for life; remainder to the issue of Conor in tail; remainder to his second son, Myles Reilly, for life; remainder to John Reilly, eldest son of said Myles, &c.; with a remainder to Brian, Owen, and Thomas, the younger sons of said Colonel John Reilly. He died on the 17th day of February, 1717. He made his last will on the 17th day of September, 1716, of which the following is a faithful copy:

"In the Name of God, Amen. I, John Reilly, of Ranepark, and late of Ballymacad, in the County of Meath, Gent., being in perfect sense and memory, I thank God, Do Recommend my Soul to God, and my body to be buried in whatever place my friends shall think fitt or Convenient, and in as Decent a manner as the sd. friends shall think fitt. Imprimis, I leave to my Grandson, John Reilly, Son to my son, Miles Reilly, Mercht. in Dublin, the Fifty pounds I am Intitled to at my Death, to Charge my Estate with. I leave to my son, Miles Reilly, the Mercht. in Dublin, the Remainder of the lease of Dromloman, if any there be at my Death. I leave to my Son, Owen Reilly, During his Naturall life, the Lease of Derrysherridan; the Lease of Dulerstowne, Feremore, and Baterstowne, together with the whole Lease of Scurlogstowne; and if any the said Leases be unexpired at his Decease, that the Reversion and Remainder of them may come to the proper use of James Reilly and George Reilly, sons to the said Owen Reilly. I leave to my son, Bryan Reilly, the Lease of Ranally, together with what of the Lands of Dunganny lyes by the Boyne Side to the Road that Leads from Killcool to Navan, on which lands are the Ganders Mill, and the great white thorn bush that is on the Park, next the Bective. I leave to my son, Thomas Reilly, the other parte of Dunganny, on which the two Farmers Houses are that lived there formerly, with Sherlock and Sherridan; together with the Peice of Rannally, on which James Ginole lived, each of my said sons, Bryan and Tho. Reilly, paying the rents reserved by the said Leases to the Landlords, as my Exrs. shall order, or their Survivors. And it is my will that if either of the said Leases to my said sons, Bryan and Thomas, be unexpired at their Decease, the Remainder and Reversion thereof may come to the eldest sons of each of them. I leave also to my son, Thomas, the lease of Carrigach. I likewise leave to my son, Bryan Reilly, aforsd. the reversion of the lease of Laythendroanagh and Carnan, and part of Cornecreach; and it is my will that if any of the said leases be undetermined at the Death of the said Bryan, the Rem[r]. Reverc̄on, and profitts of them may come to his son, Miles Reilly. I leave to my wife 100[li], Ster. out of my personall Estate, together with six Milch Cows, and my riding Grey Nagg, together with what She pleases to have of the Houshold Stuff, except what is hereafter excepted; as also it is my will to leave her the silver Cup that I now have, and six Silver spoons. I leave to my sisters, Honora and Rose Reilly, sixteen pounds, Ster., to be Equally Divided amongst them. I leave to my dau[rs] Katharine Nugent and Mary Connor, to be Equally Divided between them, the Sume of Eighty pounds, Ster. I leave to my Brother,

in the month of April. He was an aged, grey-headed, long-memoried man, and who had been quick and vivacious in his mind and intellect in his youth. He

Phillip Reilly, the Sum of ten pounds, Ster. I leave to my brother, Edmd. Reilly, to Divide as he thinks fitt among some Orphans Entayled upon him, the Sum of Fifteen pounds, Ster. I leave to my Nephews, Miles, Caheir, & Thomas Reilly, the Sume of Twelve pounds, Ster., to be Equally Divided between them. I leave to my son, Conor Reilly, my watch and one pistole to buy a ring. I leave twelve pounds, Ster. to be Divided amongst the poor widows of Killeagh, Killbride, Crosserlogh, Castlerahan, Monterconaght, and Lorgan, as my Exs. Shall Think fitt. I order to be putt into the hands of my wife the Sum of Eight pounds, Ster., to be disposed of for Good works that I have ordered her to get done. I leave all my stock and personal effects, after Deducting all the aforesd. Legacies, &c., Equally to be Divided between my four sons, viz., Miles, Bryan, Owen, and Thomas Reilly; and it is my will that Miles and Owen Reilly, my sons, be my Exs. in Chief in Executing this will. And to this I putt my hand & Seal this Seventeenth day of September, one Thousand seven hundred and Sixteen.

"JOHN REILLY (loc. sigil.).

"Witness present at the signing & sealing hereof.

"EDM. REILLY.
HENRY SHERLOCK.
JOHN PLUNKETT."

This Colonel John Reilly was buried in the old church of Kill, in the parish of Crosserlogh, barony of Castlerahan, and county of Cavan, where his tomb exhibits the family arms: two lions supporting a dexter hand proper; the crest, an oak tree on a mount with a snake descending its trunk proper; motto, FORTITUDINE ET PRUDENTIA; and the following epitaph:

"HERE LIETH INTOMBED THE BODY OF COLLONEL JOHN REILLY, WHO WAS ELECTED KNIGHT OF THE SHIRE FOR THE COUNTY OF CAVAN, IN THE YEAR 1689, AND DEPARTED THIS LIFE THE 17TH DAY OF FEBRUARY, $16\frac{16}{17}$, AND LEFT FIVE SONS AND TWO DAUGHTERS.

"THIS TOMB WAS ERECTED BY CONOR, MILES, BRYAN, OWEN, AND THOMAS REILLY, GENTLEMEN, TO COMMEMORATE THEIR FATHER, COLONEL JOHN REILLY, WHO DIED FEBRUARY 17TH, $17\frac{16}{17}$, AGED 70 YEARS."

VI. MYLES REILLY, of the city of Dublin, merchant. Upon the decease of his eldest brother, Captain Conor Reilly, without issue, in the year 1723, he succeeded to the estates of Colonel John Reilly (by virtue of the settlement of his father); and, being a successful merchant in Dublin, he added to them considerably by purchases of his own, made in the names of Protestant friends. He died in Dublin in June, 1731. He married, in August, 1698, Mary Barnewall, by whom he had issue three sons, viz.: 1. John Reilly, born on the 17th of June, 1702; 2. Dominick Reilly; 3. Francis Reilly, who all died without issue.

VII. JOHN REILLY, of the Middle Temple, Esq., Barrister at Law. On the death of his father, Myles Reilly, of Dublin, he succeeded, as tenant for life, to the entailed estate of his grandfather, Colonel John Reilly, and to his own paternal inheritance. He studied the English laws, and became a pleader of some eminence. In the year 1731 he was deputed, by the Roman Catholics of Ireland, to solicit the English ministry for some alleviation of the Penal Laws, under which their industry was paralyzed; and he repaired to London, where, it is said, he ruined his fortune to support the dignity of his embassy. He levied a fine and suffered a recovery to bar the remainder-men,

8. Ffonrfeir ⁊ mac a dfhbrathar .i. Eoghan mac Aodha conallaigh doirdnead ina ionad.

and in 1765 sold his estate to his cousin, James Reilly, son of Thomas Reilly, who was the youngest son of Colonel John Reilly, and last in remainder in the settlement of his grandfather. After this sale he returned to London, where he died, without issue, in the year 1767. This John was considered chief of his name in Ireland, though he never used the prefix O, even under his arms, which he had elaborately engraved for his book plates. Let us now return to

VI. Brian Reilly of Ballinrink, the third son of Colonel John Reilly. He served as a captain in his father's regiment of dragoons in 1689, 1690, 1691, and was included in the Capitulation of Limerick. He married Margaret, daughter of Luke Mac Dowell, Esq., of Mointeach, now Mantua, in the county of Roscommon. He had by her six sons, viz.: 1. Myles Reilly of Tullistown, of whom presently; 2. Alexander Reilly, whose issue is extinct; 3. Matthew Reilly, who died *s. p.* in London in 1780; 4. Luke Reilly, who died *s. p.*; 5. Conor Reilly, who died *s. p.*; and Edmond Reilly, who died at the age of 16 in 1732. This Brian died on the 6th of September, 1748, aged seventy-two years, as appears from his epitaph in the church of Kill, in the county of Cavan.

VII. Myles Reilly, Esq., of Tullistown, in the county of Cavan. He married Sarah, daughter of William Fitzsimons, Esq., of Garadice, in the county of Meath, and had by her three sons, namely: 1. John Alexander O'Reilly (who restored the prefix O'), colonel of infantry in the regiment of Hibernia in Spain, and who lived some years in England, where he died, without issue, in 1800, in the fifty-fourth year of his age. Of this John Alexander O'Reilly, his kinsman, Lieut.-Colonel Don Antonio O'Reilly, of Cadiz, speaks as follows in a letter to Myles John O'Reilly, Esq., dated June 30th, 1812: "By the small pedigree that you enclosed I see you are nephew to John Alexander O'Reylly, cousin-german to my father, who, in the year 1767, entered the Spanish service, a cadet in Hibernia's regiment, and, in the year 1772, bought a company in Ireland's regiment, retiring from service in 1787, being then captain of grenadiers, with the degree of lieutenant-colonel, and married Miss Mary Lalor. He was very much esteemed both by my father and my uncles, and even by all of us, &c. &c. His nice education and good breeding foretold" [i. e. indicated] "his origin; and his capacity, bravery, and learning, were worthy of higher employments and better protection than he met with here. I was entirely ignorant of his death until I was noticed of it by your brother."—See the *Gazeta de Madrid*, Del Viernes, 5 De Abril, De 1793. 2. Dowell O'Reilly, of whom presently; 3. Mathew O'Reilly, the father of the late William O'Reilly, Esq., of Thomastown Castle, Member of Parliament for Dundalk, and of Dowell O'Reilly, Esq., Attorney-General of Jamaica, and grandfather of Myles O'Reilly, Esq., of Thomastown Castle, who is the head of the second senior branch of this family. This Myles Reilly, of Tullistown, died in Dublin on the 4th of February, 1775, aged sixty-seven years and nine months, and was buried in the family vault at Kill, in the county of Cavan.

VIII. Dowell O'Reilly, Esq., of the Heath House, Queen's County. He was married twice; first, in 1775, to Margaret, daughter of John O'Conor Faly, of the city of Dublin; and secondly, in 1780, to Elizabeth, daughter of James Knox, Esq., of Moyne, in the county of Mayo, by whom he had four sons, viz.: 1. Myles John O'Reilly, of whom presently; 2. James Fitzsimon O'Reilly, a captain in the British army, and lieut.-col. in the Spanish service, stationed at Ma-

was buried in the monastery of St. Francis at Cavan; and his brother's son, namely, Owen, the son of Hugh Conallagh[q], was elected in his place.

jorca on the 2nd of April, 1812; 3. Alexander O'Reilly, who died young; 4. Dowell O'Reilly, a captain in the British navy, and first lieutenant of La Durvallante of thirty-eight guns, who had one son, Lieut. Dowell O'Reilly, who died a few years since without issue.

IX. Myles John O'Reilly, Esq., late of the Heath House in the Queen's County, and now living in France, in the sixty-seventh year of his age. He was married, on the 16th of January, 1829, to Elizabeth Anne Beresford, eldest daughter of the Honourable and Reverend George de la Poer Beresford, at the church of Fenagh, in the county of Leitrim, by the Rev. George Beresford, Junior; and he had by her three sons, now living, viz.: Myles George O'Reilly, born October 30th, 1829; 2. George Beresford O'Reilly, born March 31st, 1832; 3. Henry Tristram O'Reilly, born November 29th, 1836; and two daughters, Susanna Rachel and Elizabeth Ellen.

This Myles John O'Reilly is the present senior representative of Edmond O'Reilly of Kilnacrott; and if the race of Hugh Conallagh be extinct, he is the senior of all the O'Reillys. Let us now return to

VI. Thomas Reilly of Baltrasny, the youngest son of Colonel John Reilly, Knight of the Shire for the county of Cavan in 1689. He was lieutenant in his father's regiment, and served in all the campaigns of 1689, 1690, and 1691; he was at the siege of Limerick, and had benefit of the Articles of Capitulation of that city, A. D. 1691. He married Rose Mac Dowell, daughter of Colonel Luke Mac Dowell of Mointeach, now Mantua, in the county of Roscommon, and had by her many children, of whom James O'Reilly Esq., of Baltrasny, who was born in 1718, the ancestor of O'Reilly of Baltrasny, was the eldest, and Alexander Count O'Reilly, of Spain, the youngest.

VII. Alexander Count O'Reilly. He was born at Baltrasny, near Oldcastle, in the county of Meath, in the year 1722. He was generalissimo of His Catholic Majesty's forces, and inspector-general of the infantry, grand commander of the Order of Calatrava, captain-general of Andalusia, and civil and military governor of Cadiz, and the great favourite of Charles III. of Spain. This is the General Count O'Reilly referred to by Lord Byron as having attempted to take Algiers.

In the year 1786 he employed the Chevalier Thomas O'Gorman to compile for him a genealogical history of the House of O'Reilly, a work undertaken for the purpose of proving the nobility of blood of his family, preparatory to the marriage of his eldest son with the Countess Buenavista. This genealogy, duly authenticated by the Ulster King at Arms, splendidly emblazoned and engrossed on full-sized vellum, in the Latin language, and richly bound in red morocco, together with a translation in English on smaller folio vellum and similarly bound, were transmitted to Count O'Reilly in Spain by the late Dowell O'Reilly, Esq., of the Heath House. The larger copy was deposited in the archives of Spain, and the translation in the Count's private library. The sum of 1000 guineas, or £1137 10*s.*, was paid to the Chevalier O'Gorman as the expense of this work, and of the various books, documents, and attestations therewith transmitted; the original receipt for which, with several originals of the correspondence connected therewith, the property of Myles John O'Reilly, Esq., are now in the possession of the Editor. This receipt, which is in the Chevalier O'Gorman's own handwriting, is worded as follows:

"Rece[d] from His Excellency, General Count O'Reilly, by Col. J. A. O'Reilly, five Hundred

Ar ndol don cloinn sin tSeain a búrc i ccenn uí doṁnaill (aṁail ro airnéidriomm) ro ġaḃsat acc ingréim, ⁊ ag foġail for ṁuintir na bain-riogna in gach airm a ttiaġdaír i naoinfecht la hUa ndoṁnaill. Conaḋ aire

& seventy-six pounds nineteen shillings & seven pence, & by Dowell O'Reilly, Esq., Five Hundred & sixty pounds ten shillings & five pence sterling, making in all the sum of one thousand Guineas, being in full of all accounts for compiling the History of the family of the said General Count O'Reilly. Witness my hand this 28th day of October, 1790, ninety.

"Le Chevr O'Gorman."

A copy of the English translation, duly attested by the Ulster King at Arms, is deposited in the Office of Arms in Birmingham Tower, Dublin Castle, from which a transcript in quarto, made by the late Edward O'Reilly, author of the Irish Dictionary, with some curious addenda by that industrious compiler, is now in the possession of the Editor.

This General Count Alexander O'Reilly married Donna Rosa Las Casas, by whom he had four sons, viz.: 1. Don Conor O'Reilly, a lieutenant in the regiment of Hibernia, who died in 1751; 2. Don Dominic O'Reilly, lieutenant-general, who died in 1796; 3. Peter Paul, who succeeded as Count O'Reilly, of whom presently; 4. Don Nicholas O'Reilly, a brigadier-general and Governor of Mon Juich, who died in Barcelona, in the year 1797, leaving by his wife, Anne Mary Tichbourn, Don Antonio O'Reilly, lieutenant-colonel, living at la Plaza de Cadiz, on the 30th of June, 1812, when he wrote a long and interesting letter to Myles John O'Reilly, Esq., of the Heath House, giving an account of the members of the O'Reilly family then existing in Spain.

VIII. Peter Paul Count O'Reilly, living at Havanna, the capital of Cuba, in 1812, as appears from a letter written at Majorca on the 1st of June that year, by Lieutenant-Colonel James O'Reilly, to his brother, Myles John O'Reilly, Esq. This Count O'Reilly married the Countess Buenavista, by whom he had several children, still or lately living in the Island of Cuba, where their property principally lies.

We will now return to Toirdhealbhach-an-iarainn, i. e. Turlough, or Terence of the Iron, who was the third son of Edmond of Kilnacrott, and the founder of the family of Scarva, in the county of Down, whose descendants became very respectable. O'Gorman does not mention this Turlough; but it appears from a genealogy of the O'Reillys, preserved in a manuscript in the Library of Trinity College, Dublin, H. 1. 15, that Edmond of Kilnacrott had two sons of the name Turlough, one called Turlough Gallda, or the Anglicised, and the other, Turlough-an-iarainn, or of the Iron.

II. Terence-an-iarainn O'Reilly.

III. Brian O'Reilly.

IV. John Reilly of Belfast.

V. Myles Reilly of Lurgan.

VI. John Reilly, Esq. He married Lucy Savadge, by whom he had James Reilly, who died *s. p.*, and

VII. John Reilly, Esq., of Scarva, M.P. for Blessington, and who was High Sheriff of the county of Down in 1776, and High Sheriff of Armagh in 1783. He married Jane Lushington, by whom he had: 1. John Lushington Reilly, of whom presently; 2. William Edmond, High Sheriff of Down in 1815, M. P. for Hilsborough, who left one son, John Reilly; 3. James Myles Reilly, Esq., Barrister-at-law, who married Emily Montgomery, by whom he has six sons, John, James, Myles, Francis Savadge, William Edmond Moyse, and Hugh, and three daughters, Emily, Jane Hester, and Theodosia.

VIII. John Lushington Reilly. He was High Sheriff of the county of Down, and col-

After the sons of John Burke had gone to O'Donnell, as we have already stated, they continued, whithersoever they went, in company with O'Donnell, to harass and plunder the Queen's people; for which reason the Lord Justice of

lector of the port of Galway. He married, in the year 1807, Louisa Temple, by whom he had five sons, viz.: 1. John Temple Reilly, Esq., the present head of the Scarva family; 2. Gustavus; 3. Robert; 4. William Charles; 5. James Myles; and six daughters: 1. Isabella; 2. Jane; 3. Louisa; 4. Mary; 5. Charlotte; 6. Gertrude.

[q] *Owen, the son of Hugh Conallagh.*—This Owen, who died this year without issue, was the third son of Hugh Conallagh. After his death, Maelmora, or Myles, the fourth son of Hugh Conallagh, succeeded as Chief of East Breifny, and enjoyed this dignity till the Plantation of Ulster in 1609. He died in 1635, and with him ended the succession of the chiefs of East Breifny. The descendants of Sir John O'Reilly, however, and several other branches, were restored to considerable tracts of land. The following persons of the name of O'Reilly are mentioned in Pynnar's *Survey of Ulster*, as in Harris's *Hibernica*, pp. 144-153:

"1. Shane Mc Phillip O-Rellie, nine hundred acres in the precinct of Castlerahin; 2. Mullmorie Mc Phillip O-Reyley, a thousand acres called Iterry-Outra, in the precinct of Tullaghgarvy. 3. Captain Reley, a thousand acres, called Liscannor, in the precinct of Tullaghgarvy; all his Tenants do Plough by the Tail. 4. Mulmorie Oge O-Relie, three thousand acres, &c., in the same. His tenants do all plough by the Tail. 5. Mullmory Mc Hugh O-Reley, 2000 acres, called Commet, in the precinct of Clonemahown. 6. Phillip Mc Tirlagh, 300 acres, called Wateragh, in the same."

The descendants of some of these persons became very distinguished military leaders during the civil wars. Philip, the son of Hugh, son of Sir John, son of Hugh Conallagh O'Reilly, raised a brigade of twelve hundred men, composed chiefly of his own name and family, and served with distinction as Lieutenant-General in the service of the Confederate Catholics of Ireland during the civil wars of 1641. After the reduction of Ireland by Cromwell, A. D. 1652, he retired with his brigade into the Spanish service in the Netherlands, where he died, and was buried in the Monastery of St. Dominic, at Louvain. His only son, Hugh Roe O'Reilly, by his wife, Rose O'Neill, was slain by the Cromwellians, in the county of Cavan, in the year 1651, leaving by his wife, Margaret, daughter of Conor O'Brien, Lord Viscount Clare, an infant son, Hugh Junior O'Reilly, who was drowned on his passage from Spain. After his death the next branch of the descendants of Sir John O'Reilly, namely, Edmond Boy, the son of Maelmora, son of Hugh, son of Sir John, was considered the O'Reilly. He went to France in his youth, and served in the King's lifeguards; but returned to Ireland in 1688, with James II., by whom he was appointed governor of the county of Cavan. After the capitulation of Limerick in 1691, he followed King James into France, where he died in the year 1693, leaving issue by his wife, Joan, the daughter of Brian O'Farrell of Moat, an only son, Owen, who married the daughter of Colonel Felix O'Neill, by whom he had a son, Edmond O'Reilly, who at the beginning of the revolution in France, was living at Paris, with the rank of Lieutenant-Colonel of Dillon's regiment, and knight of the order of St. Louis. This is the last of the race of Sir John O'Reilly that the Editor ever heard of. Andrew Count O'Reilly, general of cavalry in the Austrian service, who died in 1832, was the second son of James O'Reilly, Esq., of Ballinlough, county of Westmeath.

sin ro ḟoráil Ard Iustis na hEreann for Iarla Urmuṁan, dearbhraṫair na cloinne sin .i. Sean óg a búrc (a duḃramar do ġaḃail la druing do daoiniḃ uaisle buitilerach i ndúthaiġ uí Ṁeachair i nuiḃ cairin isin ccéd seachtmain don bliadain si) do básuccaḋ. Do rónaḋ ind sin a mí Iún do sonnradh.

Concoḃar mac muircheartaiġ gairḃ, mic briain, mic taiḋg uí ḃriain do ecc fa beltaine hi ccraicc ċorcráin, ⁊ a aḋnacal i mainistir innsi.

Maire ingen cuinn í domhnaill bean í baoighill taidcc óicc, mac taidcc mic toirrdhealbhaiġ decc 6. nouember ⁊ a hadhnacal i ndún na ngall.

O concoḃair Slicciġh donnchaḋ mac caṫail oicc do ġabháil lá hua ndoṁnaill Aoḋ ruaḋ mac aoḋa mic Maġnusa. Bá hé foċann na gaḃala isin .i. Ua doṁnaill ar fFaġḃail a ḟear co mbaoí ua conċoḃair dia ḃraṫ, ⁊ dia tairccélaḋ don Iustis ⁊ do ġallaiḃ duiḃlinne ar ro ṫingeall an Iustis achaiḋ riasp an tan sin co ffuiccbeaḋ a ṫír buḋéin dua conċoḃair on mbainrioġain, ⁊ co léiccsiḋe iarla ócc deasmuṁan .i. Semus mac gearóitt (baoí i laiṁ hi londain) do ḟaicciḋ a aṫarḋa ar bá hí maṫair an Iarla óicc hísin bá bain-ḟéiciġ dua ċonċobair. O ro ba forréil, ⁊ o ro bá dearḃ lá hua ndoṁnaill innsin, Ro herġaḃaḋ ua conċoḃair lais, ⁊ rob éiccean baile an ṁótaiġ do raḋ roṁ dua ċonċoḃair riasp an tan sin, ⁊ cúl ṁaoíle do ṫaḃairt dua doṁnaill doriḋise ⁊ ro cuireaḋ ua conċoḃair dia ioṁcoiṁétt go hoilén loċa hiasccaiġ hi ttír ċonaill.

An tiarla ócc ro ċloinne riocaird ro airnsioṡmar dóirdneaḋ i nionatt a aṫar .i. Riocard a búrc. Ro ḟorcongair Iustis na hEreann .i. Lord mountiog fairrsiḋe toċt go líon slóicch ⁊ sochaiḋe co mainistir na buille, ⁊ arrsiḋe co Slicceé maḋ dia ttíosaḋ díoḃ. Tangattar ar forailseṁ an Iustis do ḟaicchiḋ an Iarla drong díríṁe do na gallaiḃ báttar hi fforbairi ón mbainrioġain hi mbailtiḃ móra na muṁan .i. Luimneaċ, cill mo ceallócc, Ear geibtine, et cetera. Tangattar dna isin toiċeartal cedna sochaiḋe do saiġdiuiriḃ na gaillṁe ⁊ baile aṫa luain. Ar ttoċt dóiḃsiḋe uile go haon ḃaile do ḟaicciḋ an iarla bá hedh a ninnitioṁ uile dol co mainistir na

[r] *Their brother John:* literally, "the brother of these sons, i. e. John Oge Burke."

[s] *Craig-Chorcrain,* now Cahercorcrane, in the parish of Rath, barony of Inchiquin, and county of Clare.—See note [s], under 1584, p. 1822, *supra.*

[t] *Loch-Eascaigh,* now Lough Esk, situated about three miles to the north-east of the town of Donegal. On a map of parts of the coasts of the counties of Mayo, Sligo, and Donegal, preserved in the State Papers Office, London, a castle is shewn on an island in this lake, opposite which is written "Lo: Eske, where Sir

Ireland ordered the Earl of Ormond to put to death their brother, John[r] Oge Burke, whom we have mentioned as having been taken prisoner in the first week of this year, in O'Meagher's country of Ikerrin, by some of the gentlemen of the Butlers. This was accordingly done in the month of June.

Conor, the son of Murtough Garv, son of Brien, son of Teige O'Brian, died about May-day, at Craig-Chorcrain[s], and was buried in the monastery of Ennis.

Mary, daughter of Con O'Donnell, and wife of O'Boyle (Teige Oge, son of Teige, son of Turlough), died on the 6th of November, and was buried at Donegal.

O'Conor Sligo (Donough, the son of Cathal Oge) was taken prisoner by O'Donnell (Hugh Roe, the son of Hugh, son of Manus). The cause of this capture was this: O'Donnell had received intelligence that O'Conor was spying upon and betraying him to the Lord Justice and the English of Dublin; for the Lord Justice had promised some time before that he would obtain his own territory again for O'Conor from the Queen, and that the young Earl of Desmond (whose mother was the wife of O'Conor), namely, James, the son of Garrett, who was in custody in London, would be let home to his patrimony. When this fact was clear and certain to O'Donnell, he took O'Conor prisoner; and Ballymote, which he had previously given to O'Conor, and Cul-Maoile [Collooney], were obliged to be again surrendered up to O'Donnell; and O'Conor was then sent into imprisonment in an island on Loch-Eascaigh[t] in Tirconnell.

The young Earl of Clanrickard, whom we have mentioned as having been appointed in the place of his father, was ordered by the Lord Justice of Ireland, i. e. Lord Mountjoy, to march with all his host and forces to the monastery of Boyle, and from thence, if he could, to Sligo. At the command of the Lord Justice, countless numbers of the English, who were in garrison for the Queen in the towns of Munster, namely, in Limerick, Kilmallock, Askeaton, &c., came to join the Earl; [and] numbers of the soldiers of Galway and Athlone came to join the same hosting. When all these had collected together to the Earl,

Neale Garve chieflie resided." On a small islet near the southern shore of this lough are still to be seen the crumbled ruins of this castle. This lough is now adorned, on its western shore, by a considerable extent of wood, and partly embosomed by the wild craggy hills which here form the commencement of the great mountain district of Barnismore.

buille ⁊ co sliccſc, ⁊ ar ndol dóiḃ tar suca, assſḋ ro ċinnsſtt arccnáṁ soir gaċ ndíreaċ a ródaiḃ raoíndírġe maċaire ċonnaċt go rangattar co hailfinn a ccoicceriċ maiġe luirecc, ⁊ ua mbriúin na sinna cloinne caṫail, ⁊ Moiġe haoí an finnbſndaiġ.

O Ro clos la hua ndoṁnaill an tóiċſstal slóiġ lánṁóir sin do ṫoċt gus an maiġin reṁeberttmar ro tarcclamaḋ a ṡlóiġ dia ṡaiġiḋ, ⁊ ní ro airissiḋe co rainicc tar coirrsliaḃ ⁊ tar buill i maiġ luirecc co ro ṡuiḋiġ a longport eineaċ a nionċaiḃ friú. Báttar athaiḋ aṁlaiḋ sin tul a ttul acc fſiṫſṁ ⁊ acc forċoiṁéd aroile. Robtar ioṁḋa a ndeaḃṫa ⁊ a ndunoirccne, a niomarubaḋ, ⁊ a nimſroreccain in airſtt báttar a ffoiċill for a roile co ro sgiṫiġit an sluaġ gall, ⁊ go ro ṡairsſtt fo aiṫṁéla dia ttiġiḃ.

Rangattar iarttain sccéla go hua ndoṁnaill Niall garḃ mac cuinn, mic an ċalḃaiġ co na ġallaiḃ, ⁊ co na ġaoiḋelaiḃ do ṫoċt anoir tar bſrnas go ro gaḃ longport i ndun na ngall i nuirṫſr ṫíre haoḋa. Iar ffios sccél dUa doṁnaill goill do ṫoċt an dú sin bá doiliġ mór lais míḋiaċ na mainistre, ⁊ goill do bſiṫ accá hionattaċt, ⁊ agá haitreaḃaḋ inon na mac mbſthaḋ ⁊ na ccéileḋ ndé diar bó ruiḋlſs í có sin, ⁊ ní ro daṁar dó gan dol dia ffurtaċt maḋ dia ttíosad ḋe. Ba hſḋ do róine sium bruġaḋa, ⁊ biattaiġ ċenél cconaill co na ccſṫraiḃ ⁊ co na ninnilib ofágḃail sſcnóin ioċtair connaċt, ⁊ araill dia aṁsaiḃ accá nioṁċoiṁétt ar ċuanaiḃ, ⁊ cſiṫearnaiḃ, ⁊ eaċtarċenélaiḃ. Luiḋ feisin go nurṁór a ṡlóiġ lais dar Slicceaċ dar duiḃ, tar droḃaoís ⁊ tars an eirne ba tuaiḋ go ro gaḃ longport i nionad innill acc an ccarraicc do ṡonnraḋ bá moa oldatt dí ṁíle cſimeann ó ḋún na ngall bail a mbaoí niall garḃ ua domnaill co na ġallaiḃ. Imṫusa uí ḋoṁnaill ro ḟorcongraiḋ siḋe for uréċtaiḃ dearṁara dia ṡloġaiḃ imársſc beiṫ occ ioṁsuiḋe na mainistre do ló ⁊ daḋhaiġ ar ná tíostais goill sſctair a múraiḃ daiḋṁilleaḋ naċ nſiṫ isin tír. Nír ḃó sóinṁſc airſrḋa ro ċaiṫſiot an dí ṡoċraitte [a naimsir] ar ro ḃaí marḃaḋ, ⁊ muḋucchaḋ deaḃaiḋ, ⁊ diuḃraccaḋ acc cſċtarnae díoḃ for aroile. Battar na goill a ccuiṁge, ⁊ a ttſnnta ṁóir las an

[u] *Hy-Briuin-na-Sinna:* i. e. the race of Brian of the Shannon. This was the tribe-name of the O'Monahans, who were seated in the county of Roscommon, between Elphin and Jamestown; but at this period the O'Beirnes were the chiefs of this territory.

[v] *Clann-Cathail.*—This was the tribe-name of the O'Flanagans, who were seated in the district lying between Belanagare and Elphin, in the county of Roscommon.

[w] *Magh-Aoi-an-Fhinnbheannaigh.*—This was another name of Machaire-Chonnacht, i. e. *Cam-*

they determined to march to the monastery of Boyle and to Sligo; and after having crossed the Suck they agreed to march directly eastwards along the straight roads of Machaire-Chonnacht until they arrived at Elphin of Moylurg, Hy-Briuin-na-Sinna[u], Clann-Chathail[v], and Magh-Aoi-an-Fhinnbheannaigh[w].

As soon as O'Donnell heard of the arrival of this numerous army at the place which we have before mentioned, he assembled his forces, and did not halt until he crossed the Curlieus, and the [River] Boyle, into Moylurg; and pitched his camp directly opposite them [his enemies]. They remained thus for some time face to face, spying and watching each other. Many were the conflicts, manslaughters, and affrays which took place between them while they remained thus in readiness for each other, until [at length] the English army became wearied, and returned in sorrow to their houses.

After this, news reached O'Donnell, that Niall Garv, the son of Con, son of Calvagh, with his [O'Donnell's] English and Irish, had come from the east [of Tirconnell], across Bearnas, and encamped at Donegal, in the east of Tirhugh. When O'Donnell received the news that the English had arrived at that place he felt grieved for the misfortune of the monastery, and that the English should occupy and inhabit it instead of the Sons of Life and the Culdees, whose rightful property it was till then; and he could not forbear from going to try if he could relieve them. What he did was this: he left the farmers and betaghs of Tirconnell, with their herds and flocks throughout Lower Connaught, with some of his soldiers to protect them against [invaders from] the harbours, kerns, and foreign tribes, [and] he himself proceeded with the greater part of his army, across the [rivers] Sligo, Duff, Drowes, and Erne, northwards, and pitched his camp in strong position exactly at Carraig, which is upwards of two thousand paces from Donegal, where Niall Garv O'Donnell and his English were [stationed]. As for O'Donnell he ordered great numbers of his forces alternately to blockade the monastery by day and night, so as to prevent the English from coming outside its walls to destroy anything in the country. Neither of the armies did by any means pass their time happily or pleasantly, for killing and destroying, conflict and shooting, were carried on by each party against the other. The English were reduced to great straits and

pus Connaciæ, now popularly called the Maghery, and applied to an extensive plain lying between Strokestown and Castlerea, in the county of Roscommon.

caiṫis ċianfoda in ro ċungaibset muintior í doṁnaill iatt, ⁊ nó elaidis araill díḃ ina ndeisiḃ, ⁊ ina ttriaraiḃ go longport i doṁnaill lás in adailcce ⁊ las an ccuiṁge a raḃattar dſ·ḃaiḋ airbísrta biṫ. Ro ṫoċaiṫsiot saṁlaiḋ go diúid September go ro ḋeónaiġ dia a ḋíoġail ⁊ a aiṫbe for na gallaiḃ an mídiaċ ⁊ an míimirt do berttrat for reiccléraiḃ ⁊ ċuḃaċlaiḃ na sruiṫsḋ sráilincsttlaiġ .i. Mainistir dúin na ngall, ⁊ mainistir na maċaire bicce[w] i mbattar na goill attrubramar a fforbais ⁊ a fforlongport inntiḃ, ⁊ araill ele hi ccaislén dúin na ngall. Ḃasseaḋ díoġal[x] do bfrit dia foraiḃ cecib cruṫ ac rala .i. tene do dol isin púdar baoí leó (fri foiṁdin an ċoccaiḋ) i mainistir dúin na ngall co ro loiscceaḋ cuḃaċla clársuaiġte, ⁊ cuṁdaiġte cloċ ⁊ clarad na mainistre arċéna. O ro airiġsiott an luċt foraire ⁊ forċoiṁétta baoí ó ua ndoṁnaill ar na gallaiḃ an doiġear ḋonnruaiḋh deargslassaċ, ⁊ an Smúit ċeó diaḋ, ⁊ dísthaiġe ro meabaiḋ uas an mainistir ro ġabsatt ag diúḃraccaḋ a nuḃaillṁioll luaiḋe, ⁊ a ccaor ttsinntiġe ar ḋáiġ go ttíosaḋ ua doṁnaill dia saiġid a ttraitte do fuabairt na ngall, ar bá cian leó airisioṁ fri teaċtaiḃ do ċor ina ḋoċom. Nír ḃo héis·leḋaċ ro freccraḋ an

[w] *Machaire-beg:* i. e. the Little Plain, now Magherabeg, a townland verging on the bay, about a quarter of a mile to the south of the town of Donegal. Some of the ruins of this nunnery are still to be seen.

[x] *The vengeance.*—P. O'Sullevan Beare thus notices the burning of the monastery of Donegal on this occasion, in his *Hist. Cathol. Iber.* tom. 3, lib. 6, c. 5, fol. 173: "Ac regii quidem violati monasterij pænas luerunt: namque noctu sulphur, vel opera alicuius ab Odonello adhibiti, vel casu, vel diuinitus accensum monasterium subitò comburit, partim per ærem tollens. Propugnatores partim igne consumuntur, partim tecto, & pariete labante obruuntur."

Sir Henry Docwra given the following account of these transactions in his *Narration*:

"Now had O Donnell, O Caine, Cormocke mac Baron, & all the Cheifes of the Countrie thereabout, made all the forces they were able, to attend the issue of this intended Meeting of my lord & Mee, and had drawne themselues togeather about Cormocke mac Barron's country, where they might be readie to fall vpon either of vs as they should see theire best advantage; &, conferring with Neale Garuie, I then found, by O'Donnell's absence, the countrie behinde him was left without guard, the Abbay of Dunnagall was kepte onelie by a fewe fryers, the situation of it close to the Sea, & very Convenient for many seruices, especiallie for a stepp to take Ballyshannon with, which was a worke, the manifould attempts & chargeable Preparations the Queene had beene att to accomplish, & my lord himselfe had soe latelie aymed att, & valued equall to this other of meeting him at Blackwater, did argue would be of speciall importance & good acceptation, I concluded, therefore, & sent him away (the said Neale Garvie), with 500 English souldiers, to put themselues into this place, which they did on the second of August.

"On the 6th August I receiued a supplie of 200 Bundells of Match from Sir Arthur Chi-

distress by the long siege in which they were kept by O'Donnell's people; and some of them used to desert to O'Donnell's camp in twos and threes, in consequence of the distress and straits in which they were from the want of a proper ration of food. Thus they passed the time until the end of September, when God willed to take revenge and satisfaction of the English for the profanation and abuse which they had offered to the churches and apartments of the psalm-singing ecclesiastics, namely, of the monastery of Donegal, and the monastery of Machaire-beg[w], in which the English whom we have mentioned were quartered and encamped, and others of them who were in the castle of Donegal. The vengeance[x] which God wreaked upon them was this, however it came to pass, viz., fire fell among the powder which they had in the monastery of Donegal for carrying on the war; so that the boarded apartments, and all the stone and wooden buildings of the entire monastery, were burned. As soon as the spies and sentinels, whom O'Donnell had posted to spy and watch the English, perceived the brown-red mass of flames, and the dense cloud of vapour and smoke that rose up over the monastery, they began to discharge their leaden bullets and their fiery flashes, in order that O'Donnell might [hear them, and] immediately come to them, to attack the English, for they thought it would occasion too long a delay to send him messengers. This signal was not slowly responded

chester, from Knockfergus, & my lord, hauing shortlie after performed at Blackwater what his intentions were, according to the opportunitie of that time, withdrewe his Army, And then O Donnell, with those forces he had, returned & laide seige to these men, which Continewed at least a moneth; &, in the meane time, on the 19th of September, the Abbay tooke fire, by accident or of purpose, I could neuer learne, but burnt it was, all save one Corner, into which our men made Retreate, & through the middest of the fire were forced to remoue theire Provisions of victuell, & the very barrells of Powder they had in store. Captaine Lewis Oriell comanded in chiefe. The face of this nights worke (for the fire beganne in the Eueninge) is easilie to imagination to behould; O Donnell's men assayling, & ours defendinge, the one with as much hope, the other with as good a resolution, as the accident on the one side, & the necessitie on the other gaue occasion for. The next day, when the fflame was spent, & that it appeared our men had gott a Corner of the house which nowe stood by it selfe, & out of Danger to be further annoyed by the fire, O Donnell sent Messengers of sumons vnto them, offered them faire Conditions to departe, terrified them with his strength, & their impossibilitie to be releeued, but all in vaine; theire passage to the sea was still theire owne, by land they sent mee word of their estate, & violentlie repelled his Messenger. Heere againe I must confess Neale Garuy behaued himselfe deseruinglie, for though I had, at that time, many informations against him that could not but breed some iealousies of his fidelitie, yet wee sawe hee Continewed to

urḟóccra sin lá hua ndoṁnaill co na ṡlóġ ar ro ċingsiott go dian deinmneasttaċ aṁail as déine ro ḟéodsat ina ndrongaiḃ, ⁊ ina ndíormaiḃ go hairm abáttar a muinntir gus an mainistir. Ba fuiliḋ foirniata an ḟuabairt do ḃeartsat for na gallaiḃ ⁊ for a ccairdiḃ, ⁊ for a ccoṁḟuiliḋiḃ ro ḃaoí tan. Bá duiliġ díċuṁaing do ṁuinntir í ḋoṁnaill frestal diuḃraicṫe na nócc báttar isin mainistir hi ccaistiall dúin na ngall, ⁊ isin luing baí for an ccuan for a moncaiḃ. Acht ċena robtar iatt muintir í ḋoṁnaill báttar foirtille gé ro díoṫaigitt soċaiḋe díoḃ. Bá do na huaisliḃ do roċair ó ua ndoṁnaill hisuiḋe taḋcc mac caṫail ócc mec diarmatta, caiptin oirdearc do ṡíol ṁaoilruanaiḋ eisiḋe. Do roċair don leiṫ ele conn ócc, mac cuinn dearbraṫair neill uí doṁnaill co ttriḃ céDaiḃ araon ris isin orccain sin. O ro airiġ niall garḃ o doṁnaill an eiccendáil a mbáttar a ṁuintir ⁊ na goill do ḋeachaiḋ gan airiuccaḋ siar lá hor an ċuain gus an maċaire mbecc go hairm hi mbáttar drong ṁór do na gallaiḃ, ⁊ do beirt lais iatt is in cconair ccétna dfuritaċt na ngall ele báttar i ttennta ag ua ndoṁnaill co na muinntir, ⁊ ro ġaḃsat foirenn na luinge ag deaḃaiḋ, ⁊ ag diuḃraccaḋ tar a cceann go roċtain dóiḃ tar na múraiḃ meadónchaiḃ isteaċ isin mainistir.

An tan do rat ua doṁnaill dia uíd daingen innille an ionaitt ina mbáttar, ⁊ an forlíon slóiġ do riaċtattar i ttóiritin na ngall ro ḟorċongair for a ṁileaḋaiḃ déirġe na deaḃṫa, ⁊ sóaḋ for ccúlaiḃ ar nír ḃó miaḋ lais a muḋuccaḋ i neccoṁlann. Do rónaḋ fó ċédóir fairsioṁ innsin, ⁊ do beirt a longport ní bá goire biucc don ṁainistir ⁊ ro ċuir araill dia muinntir isin maċaire mbecc airm i mbáttar na goill rucc niall garḃ lais dfurtaċt a ṁuintire. Lá feile micil do ṡonraḋ ro loiscceaḋ an ṁainistir, ⁊ do rónaḋ innsin.

Baoí ó doṁnaill samlaiḋ isin iomsuiḋe sin for ġallaiḃ, ⁊ accá ttaḃairt a ttennta, ⁊ a niomcuiṁge ó ḋeireaḋ september go diúid october gan náċ ngníoṁ noirdearc do ḋénaṁ stoppa in airett sin go riaċt fios scél ċuca an coḃlaċ Spainneaċ do nangattar don taoiḃ badeas déirinn dfurtaċt na ngaoiḋeal báttar isin ccoccaḋ.

the last, tooke such parte as our men did, had many of his men slaine at this seige, & amongst the rest a brother of his owne."

[y] *Con Oge, the son of Con.*—He is the ancestor of Manus O'Donnell, Esq., of Castlebar, and also of the Counts O'Donnell of Spain and Austria, as shall be shewn in the Appendix.

[z] *A Spanish fleet.*—Docwra has the following notice of the same event:

"But now came the Newes of the Spanyards

to by O'Donnell and his army, for they vehemently and rapidly advanced with their utmost speed, in troops and squadrons, to where their people were at the monastery. Bloody and furious was the attack which they made upon the English and their own friends and kinsmen who were there. It was difficult and [almost] impossible for O'Donnell's people to withstand the fire of the soldiers who were in the monastery and the castle of Donegal, and in a ship which was in the harbour opposite them; yet, however, O'Donnell's people had the better of it, although many of them were cut off. Among the gentlemen who fell here on the side of O'Donnell was Teige, the son of Cathal Oge Mac Dermot, a distinguished captain of the Sil-Mulrony. On the other side fell Con Oge, the son of Con[y], the brother of Niall Garv O'Donnell, with three hundred others, in that slaughter.

As soon as Niall Garv O'Donnell perceived the great jeopardy in which his people and the English were, he passed unnoticed westwards, along the margin of the harbour, to Machaire-beg, where a great number of the English were [stationed]; and he took them with him to the relief of the other party of English, who were reduced to distress by O'Donnell and his people; and the crew of the ship proceeded to fight, and kept up a fire in defence of them, until they had passed inside the central walls of the monastery.

When O'Donnell observed the great strength of the place in which they were, and the great force that had come to the relief of the English, he ordered his soldiers to withdraw from the conflict and to return back; for he did not deem it meet that they should be cut off in an unequal contest. This was done at his bidding; and he removed his camp nearer to the monastery, and sent some of his people to Machaire-beg, where the English whom Niall Garv had brought with him to assist his people were [stationed]. The burning of the monastery, and this occurrence, happened precisely on Michaelmas-day.

O'Donnell remained thus blockading the English, and reducing them to great straits and exigencies, from the end of September to the end of October, without any deed of note being achieved between them during that time, until news [at length] reached them that a Spanish fleet[z] had arrived in the south of Ireland, to assist the Irish who were at war.

arrivall at Kinsaile, whereupon O Donnell broke upp the seige to march towards them. Tyrone made hast the same way, and soe alsoe did my Lord Deputie; and it is true the Countrey was

Sluaiccheaḋ la hard lustis na hEreann Lord mountjoy hi mí Iun do ḋul i nUlltoiḃ. Ní haiṫristear a imṫeċta co rainic co bealaċ an Ṁaighre. No ḃioḋ cosnaṁ ⁊ coimheacc do ġnaṫ o Ua neill an dú sin. Ro maċtaitt ⁊ ro mudhaiġit daoine iomḋa, ⁊ ro ḟáccbaḋ soċaiḋe, déctoiḃ gall ⁊ gaoiḋel i ttimċell an ḃealaiġ sin etir Ua néill, ⁊ goill go minic go ffuair an lustís faill ⁊ elang na huaire sin fair (an ní rob annaṁ lais) go mtaoí ciuṁsa ⁊ cestlár an ḃealaiġ for a ċumas don chur sin. Ro gaḃ campa isin ionad ba haḋailcc lais don ċonair isin. Do ronaḋ caislen cennsraolta i nsiach erḋalta baí for an cconair sin lais. Iar ccrioċnuccaḋ an caisléin dó a ccionn mís ro ḟáccaiḃ dá ced saiġdiúir ina ḃardacht. Do dechaiḋ fein roiṁe iar sin go Sliaḃ fuaid, go hArdmaċa, ⁊ tar abhainn móir isteach do ḋol gus an bport mór do tóccbaḋ la hard lustis na hEreann Lord burough ceitre bliaḋna riar an tan sin, ⁊ ro bad ag cur lóin isin bport sin hi cceann trill iar na toccbail tánaicc timdiḃe saoġail an lustis sin budhein la hua neill. Ro ḃean bfós Ua néill an port céona (fo ceann mbliaḋna iar mbás an iustís) do muintir na bainrioġna iar ttaḃairt áir fear ⁊ feindeaḋ forra aga ḃein díoḃ, ⁊ bai an baile acc Ua neill ó sin anall gus an tan so a ttáinicc an lustís nua so dia ṡaiġiḋ. Iar ndol dó i ccoṁfoccus don port sin ro ḟáccaiḃsiot muintir Uí neill an baile óbél oslaicṫe for cionn a námat ⁊ a neascarat amail rob ainminic leó gó sin.

Is na céulaiṫibh iar ngabáil ċampa don lustis isin bport sin do ḋeachaiḋ do ṁiosṁain, ⁊ do ṁoirḋeċain, ⁊ do breiṫ radairc ar an tír ina timċell. Ar ndol dó ar brú na beinne buirbe do rala dó for brú ḃealaiġ do ḃeilgiḃ an tíre, araill do ceiṫirn uí néill go niata naiṁdiḋe, go gruamḋa, gnúisdorrḋa, ⁊ ro fearaḋ iomairecc uaṫmar aingiḋ eatorra anall ⁊ anall go ro marbaitt soċaiḋe ile an dú sin. Acṫ namá ro baḋ mó do marbaḋ do ṁuintir an lustis oldas dócċbaiḋ uí néill.

Ro ṡuí an lustis daiṁdeóin gaċ anforlainn da ffuair gus in ccampa

nowe left voide, and noe powerful enymy to encounter withall, more than the Rivers and the difficulties of the passage of the ways."

[a] *Bealach-an-Mhaighre.* — This is called by Fynes Moryson "the pace of the Moyry," and on an old map of Ulster, preserved in the State Papers Office, London, the fortifications erected by Lord Mountjoy on this occasion are marked under the name of "The Castle and Forte of the Moierie Pace," and a part of the road "The causie of Moierie." The castle was standing in good preservation in 1834, when the Editor examined this locality with great care. The road is now called Bothar a Mhaighre, and is still

A hosting was made by the Lord Justice of Ireland, Lord Mountjoy, in the month of June, to proceed into Ulster. Nothing is related of his progress until he arrived at Bealach-an-Mhaighre[a]. This place was defended and watched by O'Neill's guards. Many men and troops of the English and Irish had been often lamentably slain and slaughtered about that pass between O'Neill and the English. But the Lord Justice got an opportunity and advantage of him [O'Neill] at this time, a thing which seldom had happened [previously]; so that the borders and very centre of the pass were in his power on this occasion. He then pitched his camp on the spot which he thought proper on that road, [and] erected a castle of lime and stone upon a certain part of that road. Having finished this castle in the course of a month, he left two hundred soldiers to guard it, [and] proceeded forward, with the remainder of his forces to Sliabh Fuaid, to Armagh, and across the Abhainn-mor[b], he went to Portmore, a fortress which had been built four years before by the Lord Justice Borogh, who, shortly after its erection, while attempting to lay up provisions in it, came to a premature death by O'Neill. Moreover, O'Neill had taken the same fort from the Queen's people (about a year after the death of the Lord Justice); having in taking it from them made a slaughter of their men and heroes; and the fort had remained in O'Neill's possession thenceforward until this time that this new Justice came to it. When he came near this fort, O'Neill's people left it wide open to their foes and enemies, a thing that was unusual with them till then.

On the first days after the Lord Justice had encamped in this fortress, he set out to view, reconnoitre, and explore the country around. On arriving at the borders of Benburb[c], he was encountered near one of the passes of the country by some of O'Neill's kerns, in a heroic and hostile manner, with fierce and grim visages, and a frightful fierce battle was fought between them, in which many were slain on both sides, at that place; but, however, there were more of the Lord Justice's slain than of O'Neill's soldiers.

The Lord Justice returned back to the camp, in despite of all the over-

traceable at Jonesborough, near the boundary between the counties of Louth and Armagh.

[b] *Abhainn-mhor:* i. e. the Great River, always called the Blackwater River by English writers.

[c] *Beann-borb:* i. e. the bold ben or cliff, or, as it is translated by P. O'Sullevan Beare, *Pinna superba;* now Benburb, a castle standing in ruins on a remarkable cliff over the Blackwater river, on the borders of the counties of Tyrone and Armagh.

ina ffriṫing, ⁊ an tuairim miosa go leiṫ baí isin bport sin ní ḋeachaidh aon dia ṡlóghaiḃ eaḋ aoín ṁíle ṫairis sin isteaċ i ttír Eoghain, co ro ḟill tar a aiss hi ffini ghall, ⁊ go baile aṫa cliaṫ a mí August, iar ffáccbail ghararún san port mór, i nArdmaċa, i maċaire na crannċa, i mbealach an ṁaighre, i ccarraicc ḟerghusa, isin iubhar hi ccáirlinn, isin tsráidbhaile, i ndroichet aṫa et cetera. Ro baḋ méduccaḋ anma ⁊ onóra don lustis a ḟod, ⁊ a imthechte do ḋeachaiḋ i ttír eóghain don chur sin, aṁail na ro ċumaing fer a ionaid dol le ré a trí, nó a ceṫair do bliadhnaiḃ gus an tan sin.

Iarla os essex fer foirtill, feidhmláidir, aghmar, aiṫearaċ a huċt prionnsa Saxan, fer nó gnáṫaigcceadh beiṫ ina reṁtoiseaċ fogla ⁊ gabaltais acc feraiḃ Saxan i naile criochaiḃ, ḃaisseḋ dna leiṫ bliadain ina ainm, ⁊ in ionad an prionnsa i nerinn aṁail reṁebertmar. Ro triallsiḋe isin ccedmí don bliadhainsi tár ⁊ tarcaisne do ṫabairt don prionnsa ⁊ aiṫerrach cuir do ċor don ċoróin. O Ro hairiġeḋ an ṁeabal sin la feraiḃ lonndan, Ro eirghettar go haṫlaṁ urlaṁ i naghaidh in iarla go ro toirneaḋ, ⁊ go ro togramsed é ó gaċ ionad dia roile tré sráidiḃ an baile, ⁊ dna tar an mbaile amaċ gur bo heiccen dó dol go teagh essex dia imdídean. Nír bó cian dó an dú sin an tan ro forcongradh fair ar éiccen é fein dfóccra ⁊ dfurailem ina ḋaoírċimiḋ díairm do ṁuinntir na bainriogna. Ro cuireadh eriḋe iaraṁ dia ċoṁda go trétúrḃa don tor, ⁊ gaċ aon aga mbaoí cuid no coṁairle, buain, no báiḋ rir an ffeilghníoṁ sin ro malartnaigheadh iad ina ccetramhnaiḃ comroinnte ar gearadhaiḃ, ⁊ ar doirsiḃ an baile. Ro dícennaḋ an tiarla isin ochtmaḋ lá

[d] *Name and renown.*—Mountjoy had certainly affected more for the Queen by this expedition than either Bagnal, Norris, or Essex, who were thought to be more able generals. For a minute account of Mountjoy's expedition into Ulster this year, the reader is referred to Moryson's *History of Ireland*, book ii. c. 1. It is astonishing to see how little the Four Masters knew about the private political intrigues of Mountjoy on this occasion. He proclaimed Tyrone twice, and offered £2000 to any one who should bring him in alive, and £1000 to any one who should bring in his head. The English historians of the time remark, with some anger at the fact, "that, so much revered was O Neale in the North, that none could be induced to betray him."

Mr. Moore, who had access to the State papers, which, however, he very sparingly and cautiously quotes, has the following account of an attempt made by an Englishman to assassinate the Arch-rebel, in his *History of Ireland*, vol. iv. p. 129:

"The large reward held out by the Queen for Tyrone's head had hitherto failed, in spite of the medly mob of adventurers he had around him, to induce a single desperate arm to aim at the chieftain's life. He was far more in danger, however, from another and more civilized quar-

whelming opposition which he met; but, during the period of about a month and a half that he remained in that fortress, not one of his forces advanced the distance of one mile beyond that place into Tyrone; so that he returned to Fingal and to Dublin in the month of August, having left garrisons at Portmore, Armagh, Machaire-na-Cranncha [Magheracranagh], Bealach-an-Mhaighre, Carrickfergus, Newry, Carlingford, Dundalk, Drogheda, &c. It was an exaltation of the name and renown[d] of the Lord Justice to have gone that length and distance into Tyrone on this occasion, such as his predecessors had not been able to do for the three or four years before.

The Earl of Essex, a brave, energetic, warlike, and victorious man, in the service of the Sovereign of England; a man who had been appointed chief leader of plundering and invasion by the men of England in other countries, and who had been in the name and place of the Sovereign in Ireland for half a year, as we have said before, began, in the first month of this year, to offer insult and indignity to the Sovereign, and [to exert himself] to transfer the crown. As soon as this treachery was perceived by the men of London, they quickly and actively rose up against the Earl, and chased and pursued him from one place to another, through the streets of the town, and also outside the town, so that he was compelled to go into Essex-house to defend himself. He had not been long there when he was summoned and compelled to deliver and surrender himself up an unarmed prisoner to the Queen's people. He was afterwards sent to be confined, as a traitor, to the Tower; and all those who had any share, counsel, participation, or alliance, in this act of treachery[e], were quartered, and [their members] placed on the gates and portals of the town. The Earl

ter. In the month of August this year, an Englishman, whose name is not mentioned, went and offered to Sir Charles Davers, the new Governor of Armagh, to take the life of Tyrone. He gave this officer no intimation as to the manner in which he intended to effect his purpose, nor required from him any assistance; and the only help he appears to have received was the leave given him, at his own request, by the Governor, to pass by the English sentries when going at night into Tyrone's camp. When brought, afterwards, before the Lord Deputy, at Knockfergus, he acknowledged having once drawn his sword to kill the chief, and was pronounced to be of unsound mind, 'though,' as the Lord Deputy gravely added, 'not the less fit, on that account, for such a purpose.'"

[e] *Act of treachery.*—An English writer would say, "act of treason" or "high treason." For a full account of the trial and execution of Essex the reader is referred to Camden's *Annal. Reg. Elis.*, A. D. 1601: "Deo gratias egit, quod nunquam fuit Atheus aut Papista, sed spem totam in Christi meritis defixerat."

deg do mí febru. Ro básaiġeaḋ mar an ccédna isin ccoir remráite Captin lee duine uasal eiside baí ag forcongra for an Iarla, ag cuidiuccaḋ ⁊ acc comairliuccaḋ an gníoṁ hisin do ḋenamh.

Semus, mac tómais ruaiḋ, mic Semuis, mic Seain, mic an Iarla (dia ro gairsoh Iarla Desmumhan a hucht gaoidel amhail remebertmar) do chor a derbrathar Sean, mac tomáis ruaiḋ, ⁊ Meic muiris ciarraiġe, tomás mac patraiccín, mic tomáis, mic emainn, mic tómais, ⁊ piarusa do lés go hulltoiḃ iar ndol i neimirt, ⁊ i nionnlaicce dó isin ccleith coccaiḋ i mbaí fri galloiḃ, diarraiḋ caḃra ⁊ congantra for gaoiḋelaiḃ an tuaisceirt ⁊ ro anrom buḋéin co nuathaḋ buidhne a maille fris aga díclet, ⁊ aga ḋuaithniuccaḋ etir a fiorchaitroibh i nuarḃotaiḃ uaiccneacha, ⁊ i nuamhtollaiḃ talman. Baísiumh athaid amlaiḋ sin go ffuair an Ridire fionn feacht ann (.i. Emann mac Seain) brath ar Shémus do ḃeith i nuamhaiḋ fainrseaig hi ccomfochraiḃ a tíre, conad é ní do róine a bhratair gaoil ⁊ genelaiġ ⁊ a thiccerna i ttrétuireachd seal do bliadnaiḃ resime sin do fasuccaḋ imon mbloid mbicc tíre i mbaí, uair

[f] *Was beheaded.*—"Caput tertio ictu erat amputatum, primus autem sensum etmotum abstulit."—*Camden.*

[g] *Captain Lee.*—He was the intimate friend of Hugh O'Neill, Earl of Tyrone, and the author of a memorial addressed to Queen Elizabeth, entitled, "A Brief Declaration of the Government of Ireland," &c.—See p. 1697, and also note [t], under the year 1600, p. 2144, *supra.*

[h] *And he resolved,* literally, "so that the thing he did was."

[i] *His relation by kindred:* i. e. his blood relation.

[k] *For the small portion of land.*—This is an ironical mode of expressing the White Knight's petty motive for taking the Sugane Earl. It appears, however, from the *Pacata Hibernia*, book ii. c. iii., that the White Knight had a weightier reason than this for seizing on the pseudo Earl of Desmond. After sending his brother John and Pierce Lacy to the north of Ireland, the Sugane Earl attempted to elude his pursuers by taking refuge among the glens and fastnesses of Eatharlach, in the south-west of the county of Tipperary, where he could change, as occasion required, from one lurking-place to another; and a poor harper, named Dermot O'Dugan, was now the only one, of all his followers, who ventured to afford him shelter. It was under this harper's humble roof, at a place called Garryduff, that a party of soldiers, one night, nearly surprised him as he was about sitting down to supper; and his mantle, which he left behind when taking flight, discovered to them that he had been of the party, and followed in chase of him. The harper, and two other companions, conveyed the Sugane Earl into the thickest part of the fastness, and then discovered themselves to the soldiers, and left the wood, "with the lapwing's policie," that the soldiers might pursue them, and leave the other secure within his fastness. This stratagem was successful, for the soldiers, supposing that the Sugane Earl was one of the three, pursued them till evening, by which time they had arrived in the White Knight's country, where, losing sight of their game, they returned to

was beheaded[f] on the 18th of February. Captain Lee[g], a gentleman who had incited the Earl, and who was aiding and advising in him this [traitorous] act, was likewise executed in a similar manner for the aforesaid crime.

James, the son of Thomas Roe, son of James, son of John, son of the Earl (who had been styled Earl of Desmond by the Irish, as we have said before), having become weak and powerless in the *cliath* of war in which he was engaged against the English, he sent his brother, John, the son of Thomas Roe, and Mac Maurice of Kerry (Thomas, the son of Patrickin, son of Thomas, son of Edmond, son of Thomas), and Pierce De Lacy, to Ulster, to request aid and assistance from the Irish of the North, and remained himself with a small party, concealing and hiding himself among his true friends in sequestered huts and caverns underground. He remained thus for some time, until, upon a certain occasion, the White Knight (Edmond, the son of John) was informed that James was in a certain cave on the borders of his (the Knight's) country; and he resolved[h] to lay violent hands on his relative by kindred[i] and pedigree, and his lord in treason for some years before, for the small portion of land[k]

Barry's Court, and informed the Lord Barry of all that had occurred. On the next morning, the Lord Barry, right glad to have so plausible a cause of complaint against the White Knight, whom he detested, proceeded forthwith to the Lord President, to whom he related all the particulars of the pursuit of the great rebel; remarking, that if the White Knight's people had assisted the soldiers, he could not possibly have escaped them. The Lord President immediately sent for the White Knight, who, being rebuked by his Lordship with sharp words and bitter reprehensions for his negligence in so important a business, and menaced that, as he had undertaken to be responsible for the loyalty of his whole tribe, he was answerable, both with life and lands, for any default made by any of them. The White Knight, taking these threatenings to heart, humbly entreated the President to suspend his judgment for a few days, promising that if the said Sugane Desmond was now in his territory, or should hereafter repair thither, he would give the President a good account of him, alive or dead; that otherwise he was satisfied that both his lands and goods should remain at the Queen's mercy. With these protestations he departed; and having, at length, received intimation that the Sugane Earl had taken shelter in a cave in the mountain of Slieve Grot [Sliaḃ ᵹ-Cꞃoꞇ], over the glen of Aherlow, and was there lurking, with a small party, the White Knight proceeded, in company with Redmond Burke, of Muscraighe Chuirc, to perform his task. Coming to the mouth of the cavern he called upon the Earl, in a loud voice, to come out and surrender himself. The Sugane Earl, however, "presuming on the greatness of his quality," came forward to the mouth of the cavern, assumed command over the whole party, and boldly ordered that the White Knight should be seized and secured. Instead, however, of attending to his command, they instantly disarmed and secured himself and his foster-brother, and con-

ni raiḃe ina ṡeilḃ don ṁumain acht an uaiṁ sin ina ttarla don chur soin. Ro láṁaiġeadh Sémus las an Ridire impiriḋe go ro gaḃadh lais é ⁊ do ḃſrt iaraṁ go corcaiġ hi ccſnd an ṗresidens gan pardún, gan protexion diarraidh dó. O do ruacht Sémus for laiṁ an ṗresidens, fuair a iomcoiṁſt gan eislis go mí Iúl do sonradh. Ba isin mí cedna tainicc Fínġin mac donnchaidh még cárṫaiġ (ar a ttuccṫaoí Mág carṫaiġ mór an tan sin) hi ccſnn an ṗresidens go corcaiġ, ⁊ aṁail as dſine ráinicc don ḃaile ro gaḃadh é ina ḃraġaitt don ḃainrioġain ⁊ ro ġaḃ Fínġin acca ḟoccra os aird gan dſclſiṫ, gur bó ar breiṫhir ⁊ ar protexion na bainriogna ro bás aga ġaḃail. Nír ḃó torba dósoṁ innsin, ar ro cuireadh soṁ, ⁊ Sémus mac tomáis go Saxoiḃ a mí Augusṫ do sonradh. O do ruachtatar i ffiadhnaisi coṁairle Saxan ro forcongradh an tor do ṫaisenadh mar ṫeġdais caiṫme, ⁊ codulta doiḃ o sin amach go crích a mbáis, nó a mbſthaidh do rſir toile dé, ⁊ a bprionnsa.

Ionadh gobernora do ḃſiṫ acc Iarla tuadhmuman (donnchadh mac Concoḃair uí ḃriain) hi cconntaé an cláir ó ló marbṫa gobernora coiccidh connacht (Sir coners clifort) la hUa ndoṁnaill ar in ccoirrsliaḃ. Ro congṁadh Session cóicc lá ndécc lais i mainistir innsi im feil briġde na bliadna so go ro crochadh se fir décc ar in session sin lais. An tiarla céDna do ḋol hi Saxoibh hi mís márta co na ḋſrbraṫair doṁnall a maille friss, ⁊ doṁnall do ṫeacht anoir im Luġnasadh, ⁊ an tiarla danṁain dia éisi go lſicc.

An tiarla ócc dſsmuman so a duḃramar do ṫocht a Saxoiḃ ina Iarla hi ffoġmar na bliadna so do ċuaidh torainn .i. Sémus mac Gearóitt mic Semuis mic Sſain, do ċuaidh side hi Saxoiḃ i nearraċ na bliadna so, ⁊ ro baí ṫoir gur

ducted them to the White Knight's castle. For this capture the White Knight, who was once the intimate friend and most zealous adherent to the cause of the Sugane Desmond, received a reward of 1000 pounds. The subsequent history of the Sugane Earl is painful. Carew, after he had read his own very humble and degrading narration (in which he attempts to exculpate himself by accusing his brother John, and expresses a hope that, as the saving of his life is more beneficial to Her Majesty than his death, it may please Her Majesty to be gracious unto him), discovered that, in addition to other acts of treason, he had written letters to the King of Spain in the year 1599, assuring him that Nero, in his time, "was far inferior to the Queen of England in cruelty," and imploring aid "in money and munition" to enable the Irish to crush her power. Being indicted for treason at Cork, he was convicted, and condemned to be executed. But a motive of policy, which he himself, with considerable astuteness, suggested to the Government, was the means of preserving his life. He reminded them that, as long as he lived, his brother John could not succeed to the title, and as this appeared, of the two, the lesser danger, he was permitted to

which he then had; for he possessed not of Munster at that time but that cave in which he then was! For this [cave] he seized upon James, and made him a prisoner, and afterwards took him to Cork to the President, without asking pardon or protection for him. When James was delivered up into the hands of the President, he was carefully kept in confinement until the month of July. It was in the same month that Fineen, son of Donough Mac Carthy (who was at this time called Mac Carthy More), went before the President at Cork; but as soon as he had arrived in the town he was made a prisoner for the Queen; but Fineen began to declare aloud, and without reserve, that he had been taken against the word and protection. This was of no avail to him; for he and James, the son of Thomas, were sent to England in the month of August, precisely; and on their appearance before the English council, it was ordered that they be shewn the Tower as their house of eating and sleeping from that forward to the time of their deaths, or end of their lives, according to the will of God[l] and of their Sovereign. The office of Governor in the county of Clare was held by the Earl of Thomond (Donough, the son of Conor O'Brien) from the day on which the Governor of the Province of Connaught, Sir Conyers Clifford, was slain by O'Donnell on Coirrshliabh. About the festival of St. Bridget of this year, he held a session for fifteen days, in the monastery of Ennis, and he hanged sixteen men at that session. The same Earl went to England in the month of March, accompanied by his brother Donnell; and Donnell returned home about the following Lammas, and the Earl still remained there after him.

The young Earl of Desmond, namely, James, the son of Garret, son of James, son of John, whom we have made mention of as having come from England as an Earl in the autumn of the past year, went over to England in the

live. This reason, however, was of little moment, for, by the same power which King O'Neill exercised in making him Earl, while the true heir, James fitz Garrett, was living a State prisoner in the Tower of London, he could now appoint his brother John prince of the Geraldines, by inauguration, without any regard to the English laws of primogeniture, which would compel this warlike race to submit to a cripple, a coward, or a lunatic, as their Earl!

[l] *According to the will of God.*—This sentence was written for Farrell O'Gara, who was very loyal to his Sovereign, Charles I.; but the Four Masters could not have been sincere in saying that the will of God and the pleasure of Elizabeth were concurrent, unless they were fatalists, and believed that "whatever is is right." Or else that they believed that heretical princes,

an ccéid mí do ġeiṁreaḋ go ro écc an ionḃaiḋ sin, ⁊ munbaḋ tuitim a aṫar i naghaiḋ na ba.nrioġna, ⁊ aṁail ro díoṫaiġit a daoíne, ⁊ a dſġluċt lſnaṁna la galloiḃ, nó ḃiaḋ dá ċúicceaḋ muṁan ina hen tuinn bróin, ⁊ barġaire, dogra, ⁊ doġailsi i ndeadhaid in óicc mſic hisin, aoín aoibel beo na freiṁe fíor dúṫċasa, gérsca diarsma glainċinid an ġréicc ċeineóil ġſralṫaiġ, ⁊ as móide rob adbar imsníoṁa a oiḋeaḋ, gan oiḋre mſic, no braṫar uadh fſin, nó dia ḟialus re a oirdneaḋ ina ionad, aċt maḋ uaṫaḋ ⁊ an tuaṫaḋ sin fſin codarsna do reċt an prionnsa.

Captin tirial Risderd mac tomais mic Risdſrd do ḃſiṫ i ffarraḋ uí néill re hſḋ na bliaḋna so anall. An Captín sin do ṫoċt fa luġnasaḋ na bliaḋna so co ccſiṫſrnaiḃ congmála ó Ua neill lais hi ccoicceaḋ laiġſn. Ní roiċ ríoṁ, airnſis, nó áirſṁ ina ndſrna an captin sin do crſċaiḃ do ṁarḃṫaiḃ, do ġaḃáil ḃailtſḃ, ⁊ daoíne, dairccniḃ, ⁊ dedalaiḃ hi cconntaé cſiṫſrlach, hi cconntae chille dara, hi cconntae ua ffailġe ⁊ hi cconntaé tiopprat árann ó luġnasaḋ gus an ccſid mí do ġſiṁreaḋ ar ccionn.

Burcaigh ioċtaracha .i. Mac uilliam burc teróitt mac Uaṫéir ċiotaiġ baoí hi ccſſiṫ uí ḋomnaill, ⁊ dia ro ġoir tiġſrna fecṫriaṁ, ⁊ teroitt na

excommunicated by the Pope, as well as anointed Catholic sovereigns, "were God's Ministers and Agents upon earth," and that what they do "is beyond the limits of subjects to looke into."

[m] *Grecian*, *recte* Trojan.

[n] *Those few.*—James Fitzthomas, the Sugane Earl of Desmond, in his Relation to Sir George Carew, written immediately before the death of this young Earl (*Pacata Hibernia*, book ii. c. 3), states that there were then living three others of his sept and race, "one in England, my Vncle Garrets Sonne, James, set at liberty by Her Majestie, and in hope to obtain Her Majesties favour; my brother" [John] "in Vlster; and my cosen, Maurice fits Iohn, in Spaine." In his letter to the King of Spaine, dated 14th March, 1599, the same James, *alias* the Sugane Earl, tells His Majesty that he was the rightful heir to the Earldom of Desmond:

"I referre the consideration hereof to your Majesties high judgement; for that Nero, in his time, was farre inferior to that Queene in cruelty. Wherefore, and for the respects thereof, high, mighty Potentate, my selfe, with my Followers and Retainers, And being also requested by the Bishops, Prelates, and religious men of my countrey, have drawen my sword, and proclaimed warres against them for the recovery, first of Christ's Catholike religion, and next for the maintenance of my own right, which, of long time, hath beene wrongfully detained from mee and my father, who, by right succession, was lawfull Heire to the Earldome of Desmond, for hee was eldest sonne to Iames, my grandfather, who was Earle of Desmond; and for that Vncle Gerald (being the younger brother) tooke part with the wicked proceedings of the Queene of England, to farther the unlawfull claime of supremacie, vsurped the name of Earle of Desmond in my father's true title; yet, notwithstanding, hee had not long enjoyed his name of Earle, when the wicked English annoyed him,

spring of this year, and remained there until the first month of winter, when he died. Had it not been that his father fell [in his war] against the Queen, and that his people and faithful followers were cut off by the English, the two provinces of Munster would have been one scene of sorrow, lamentation, grief, and affliction after [i. e. for the loss of] this youth. He was the only living heir of the genuine stock; the last [in a direct line] of the remnant of that illustrious Grecian[m] tribe, the Geraldines; and his death was the more to be lamented, because there was no heir of either son or brother of his own, or of his family, to be appointed in his place, except a few, and those few[n] opposed to the law of the Sovereign.

Captain Tyrrell (Richard, the son of Thomas, son of Richard) had remained with O'Neill during the preceding part of this year. This captain came about the Lammas of this year, with some retained kerns [which he obtained] from O'Neill, into Leinster. It would be impossible to reckon, describe, or enumerate the preys he made[o], the deaths he caused, the castles he took, the men he made prisoners, or the plunders and spoils he obtained throughout the county of Carlow, in the county of Kildare, [and] in the county of Offaly and Tipperary, from Lammas to the first month of the following winter.

The Lower Burkes, namely, Mac William Burke (Theobald, the son of Walter Kittagh), who was confederated with O'Donnell, and who had been

and prosecuted wars, that hee, with the most part of those that held of his side, was slaine, and his country thereby planted with Englishmen."

Carew, or his secretary, remarks, on this letter, that James Fitz Thomas was "the Impe of a borne Bastard," who had no portion or inheritance in any part of Desmond; and yet he acknowledges that "hee was, within one year before his apprehension, the most mightie and potent Geraldine that had been of any of the Earles of Desmond, his predecessors. For it is certainly reported that he had eight thousand men, well-armed, under his command at one time, all which he imployed against his lawfull Soveraigne."

As to the Sugane Earl being styled "the Impe of a borne Bastard," by Carew, bastardy was a taunt so commonly bandied about at this time, to serve political purposes and law fictions, that it is hard to believe it on the authority of a bitter enemy, without very clear evidence. The Irish firmly believed that Queen Elizabeth herself was an excommunicated bastard, and therefore should not be submitted to as Sovereign of England; while, on the other hand, her English subjects, who believed that her sister Mary was a bastard and an incestuous offspring, were convinced, we are told, that Elizabeth was "the most virtuous prince, the meekest and mildest that ever reigned; whose beautie" [ætatis 69!] "adornes the world."—*Pacata Hibernia*, book iii. c. xiii.

[o] *Enumerate the preys he made.*—The original could not be literally translated into English, because there is only one verb used. The

long mac Risdſird an iarainn, baí ag imirt do ġrés a huċt na bainrioġna, bádar síoḋaċ socarṫanaċ fri aroile (ciḋ ón tan ro naidm o domnaill codaċ 7 carattraḋ ſtorra) gus an ccſid mí dſrraċ na bliaḋna so. Ro éiriġ comḟuaċaḋ coccaiḋ, 7 aṫcuimmiuccaḋ aincriḋe ſtorra, 7 ba he teróitt na long ro ba ḟoċa re dúsccaḋ na diomḃaiḋ, 7 re faḋóḋ na fſrḟſirge 7 re ḟoraiṫmſt na fala ro haccraḋ ſtorra, go ndſrnsat sliocht uillicc a búrc aénbáiḋ i naghaiḋ Mhſic uilliam teróitt mac uatéir go ro aṫcuirsiot 7 go ro ionnarbsat as a aṫarḋa é, gur bo hſiccſn dó dol do ḟaiġiḋ uí domnaill. Ro hoirdneaḋ Mac uilliam ele hi ccſnnas an tíre dia éiri la sliocht uillicc, 7 la tſsoitt na long .i. Risdſrd mac Riocaird (.i. dſman an corráin) 7 ar frisrium aṫbſirṫi mac dſmain an ċorráin.

O do ḋeachaiḋ tra Mac uilliam teróitt mac uatéir hi ccſnn uí domnaill ro acaſin a imnſḋ 7 a éttualang frisr, 7 amail ro toirneaḋ as a ṫír. Ba saéth la hUa ndomnaill an ní sin, ar a aoí ní ro ḟéd a ḟóiriḋhin i ttratte, uair baí féin co na ṡloġaiḃ, 7 co na ṡoċraitte hi ffoiṁdin 7 hi ffoiċill na ngall do nangatar dia tír, co ná caéṁnacair dul i neċtairċríċh dfurtaċt ċaeiṁ, na coiccele lár an anfforlann baí fair ina tír buḋſin. Baí Mac uilliam ina ḟarraḋ ón ccéid mí dſrraċ go féil Michil ar ccind. Ro ḟaoidh ó domnaill an tan sin an líon as lia ro féd do ṡoċraitte lais do ḋol dfior a aṫarḋa hi rann Mhſic uilliam. Iar ndol dó co na ṫóiċſstal i nſidirmſḋón an tíre do rala an Mac uilliam sin ro hoirdneaḋ la sliocht uillicc a burc, 7 lá teróitt mac Risdſird an iarainn do riġe 7 do frſsaḃra frisrium for a chionn an ċonair do ḋeachaiḋ. Ro fiġſoh iomairſcc aintteſnnta ſtorra cſċtarnae, 7 ro ġaḃ cáċ dioḃ ag foraiṫmſt a sſnġoṁ 7 a nuaḟalaḋ dia roile, go ro sraoíneaḋ fo dſóidh for Risdſrd mac Riocaird a burc go ro marḃaḋ é buḋſin isin mbreisim sin. Conaḋ amlaiḋ sin do ċóiḋ críoch a ḟlaiṫſsa.

Cobhlach Spáinneach do ṫeċt don taeḃ badſs dſirinn. Don Iohn de

nearest that could be understood in English is as follows:

"There is no reckoning, narrating, or enumerating of what that Captain effected of preys, of killings, of town-and-people-taking, of plunders, and of spoils, in the county of Carlow," &c., &c.

[p] *Combined*, literally, "made one alliance against Mac William."

[q] *The son of Deamhan-an-chorrain:* i. e. the Demon of the Reaping-hook, called by Sir Henry Docwra, "the Devill's Hook Son;" and by P. O'Sullevan Beare (*Hist. Cathol. Iber.*, fol. 180), "Richardus Burkus Dæmonis Falcati filius."

styled Lord by him some time before, and Theobald-na-Long, the son of Richard-an-Iarainn, who had always acted on behalf of the Queen, remained peaceable and amicable towards each other from the time that O'Donnell established friendship and amity between them, to the first month of the spring of this year, when commotion of war and revival of animosity arose between them; and Theobald-na-Long was the cause of the resuscitation of the enmity, and the rekindling of the strife, and the revival of the hatred, that [now] arose between them. The descendants of Ulick Burke combined[p] against Mac William (Theobald, the son of Walter), and expelled and banished him from his patrimony; so that he was compelled to go to O'Donnell. Another Mac William was appointed after him for the government of the territory by the descendants of Ulick and by Theobald-na-Long, namely, Richard, the son of Rickard, usually called the son of Deamhan-an-Chorrain[q].

When Mac William (Theobald, the son of Walter) came to O'Donnell, he complained to him of his sufferings and difficulties, and [told him] how he had been banished from his country. This circumstance was grievous to Donnell; but, however, he was not able to relieve him immediately; for he was engaged, with his troops and forces, watching and restraining the movements of the English, who had arrived in his territory; so that he was not able to move into any external territory to relieve friend or ally, by reason of the overwhelming force that oppressed him in his own territory. Mac William remained with him from the first month of spring to the Michaelmas following, at which time O'Donnell sent with him, to visit his patrimony in Mac William's country, as many men as he could [spare]. On his arrival with his muster in the very middle of the territory, he was met on the road through which he was marching by the other Mac William, who had been set up against him as his rival and opponent, by the descendants of Ulick Burke, and by Theobald, the son of Rickard-an-Iarainn; and a fierce battle was fought between them, in which they were mutually mindful of their ancient grudges and recent enmities, until at length Richard, son of Rickard Burke, was defeated, and he himself killed in the conflict, and thus came the end of this chieftainship.

A Spanish fleet[r] arrived in the south of Ireland. Don Juan de Aguila was

[r] *A Spanish fleet.*—For a list of the names of commanders and captains that came in this fleet, the reader is referred to the *Pacata Hibernia*, book 2, c. x. P. O'Sullivan Beare gives the

Agola ainm an toisiġ ro baḋ generál doiḃ. Ba he ionad in ro ġabsat port hi ccuan chinn tsáile ag bun glaislinne banndan hi ccoiccrich ċríche cúrsach do ṫaoḃ, ⁊ ċineoil aoḋa .i. dúṫaiġ an ḃarraiġ óicc don taoiḃ ar aill. Ar ttecht doiḃsium go cCinn tsáile ro ṫóccaiḃsiot daingen, ⁊ díden, cosnaṁ, ⁊ coṫuccaḋ an ḃaile ċuca féin o na haittreaḃtachaiḃ báttar acca ionatacht

following account of the arrival of this fleet in his *Hist. Cathol. Iber. Compend.*, tom. 3, lib. 6, c. vii. :

"Hæc in Ibernia dum geruntur, Philippo III. Regi Catholico curæ fuit Ibernis ferre opem, qui iustum exercitum comparari fecit, quemadmodum Onellus, & Odonellus petierant. Is exercitus cum in Iberniam traijciendus fuisse sperabatur, regia classis mittitur in Terceras insulas, vt, & Anglorum classi, quæ eó adijsse ferebatur, obuiam iret, & nauibus Indicum aurum, & argentum asportantibus præsidio esset. Qua mora efficitur, vt exercitus Ibernia designatus maiori parte sit dissipatus, militibus morientibus, & fugientibus. Reliquo præficitur Imperator Iohannes Aquila eques Hispanus rei militaris peritus, qui in Gallia Armorica contra Gallos, & Anglos magna virtute præstitit. Didacus Brocherus splendidus eques Hispanus ex Religione Diui Iohannis artibus rei bellicæ terra, marique clarus ex Terceris reuersus regia classe, cui præerat, Aquilam accipiens in Iberniam soluit, qui in altum cum fuisset prouectus, orta tempestate classis in duas partes diuiditur. Altera pars septem nauium Petri Zubiauris Proprætoris nauim sequens, & pelago diu errans in Gronium Galletiæ oppidum ventorum vi defertur. Altera pars, quæ maior erat, Prætoriam nauem secuta anno millesimo sexcentesimo primo mense Septembri in Keansaliam appulit Momoniarum oppidum, quod hæret portui magno, & tutissimo meridiem spectanti. Cui etiam imminent duo castella hinc, inde, exstructa, quibus, si tormentis firmata teneantur, inuitis, haud facilis est aditus in portum. Ab altera parte tumulus surgit, vnde machinamentis dispositis oppidum potest commodius vel oppugnari, vel propugnari. Ab occidente flumen abluit importando subsidio idoneum. Oppidani animo libentissimo, & obuijs (vt aiunt manibus) Aquilam Hispanum imperatorem, & eius exercitum (duo millia & quingenti pedites erant) expulso Anglorum præsidio, in oppidum intulerunt. In quo Aquila se diu non mansurum putans, in Rincarrano altero ex duobus castellis, quæ portui imminent, cohortem vnam præsidij causa ponit: bellicum machinamentum vnum é nauibus exponit, causatus illis nauibus, quas Zabiaur ducebat, machinamenta sibi decreta portari Inter illum, & cohortium duces, Mathæumque Ouetensem Dubhlinnæ Archiepiscopum simultates, & dissensiones oriuntur. Daniel Osulleuanus Bearræ, & Beantriæ princeps Aquilæ nunciatum mittit, sibi, & amicis suis milites mille armatos esse, & totidem inermes conscribendos, modo ille suppeditet arma, quibus instruantur, eoque numero se Proregi iter occlusurum, & obsidionem prohibiturum, donec Onellus, & Odonellus auxilio veniant. Aquila respondit (vt Osulleuanus mihi retulit) armorum copiam sibi non esse, quód à Zubiaure ferebantur, & aliorum etiam Momoniorum animos minimè solicitat, Onelli, & Odonelli consilium expectans.

"Bluntus Iberniæ Prorex erat tunc temporis Anthloniæ, quò copias suas accersiuerat, non ignarus Hispanos in Iberniam expeditionem facturos fuisse, vt exploratores Angli monuerunt. Vnde Keansaliam petens cum Comite Clanrichardæ, Angloibernis, Iberniæ consilio regio, regijsque copijs omnibus, quæ hominum septem millia continebant, Aquilam obsidione

the name of the chief who was general over them. The place at which they put in was the harbour of Kinsale, at the mouth of the green river of Bandon, on the confines of Courcy's country[s] on the one side, and Kinalea, the country of Barry Oge, on the other. On their arrival at Kinsale they took to themselves the fortifications, shelter, defence, and maintenance of the town from the inhabitants[t] who occupied them till then. They quartered their gentle-

vallat. Rincarranum haud magno negocio expugnat. Keansaliam dispositis in tumulo tormentis acriter oppugnat. Illi Comes Tomonius, qui tunc temporis in Anglia erat, cum octo millibus tyronum Anglorum auxilio mittitur. Altera parte Reginæ classis portum occupans oppidum tormentorum ictibus discutit. Hispani nihil animis consternati properant oppidum propugnare, eo tormento, quod ipsi è nauibus exposuerunt, & duobus, quæ erant in oppido, hinc anglicas naues oppugnatione remouere, inde hostium castra infestare, & tabernacula diruere interdiu pro muro fortiter, & animosè dimicare, noctu facere crebras eruptiones, excubitores, & circitores interficere, tormentis clauos infigere, quo modo maiore Anglorum, quam Hispanorum clade dimicatur: nam in conserenda manu est Hispani peditatus nota firmitas. Carolus Maccarrha Ibernæ cohortis, quæ ex Hispania profecta erat, dux contra Anglos fortiter prælians cecidit occisis prius duobus Anglis ducibus, & clauis tormento infixis. Principio obsidionis Osulleuanus Bearræ princeps á Prorege euocatus imperio non paruit, causatus oportere se domi spectare, vt fines suos à finitimis hostibus defendat, cum quibusdam familiaribus suis fictum, atque simulatum bellum gerere incipiens."

[s] *Courcy's country*, now the barony of Courcies, in the south of the county of Cork, where a branch of the family of De Courcy settled early in the thirteenth century.—See note [n], under the year 1204, p. 140, *supra*. It is stated in a manuscript at Lambeth (Carew collection, No. 635, fol. 139), that "the Baron Courcie, of Pobble Courcies, in the county of Cork, is descended from a second brother to Courcye, Earle of Ulster," and that, "by the marriage of the daughter and heir of Cogan, he was of great possessions in Munster." It may be here remarked that this notice of the descent of the De Courcys was written before the claim to the privilege of being covered in the royal presence had been set up by the Barons of Kinsale, a privilege claimed by this family on the grounds that they are the heirs and descendants, in the direct line, from the great Sir John De Courcy, Earl of Ulster; but they are not his descendants, nor had he aught to which they could succeed as heirs at the time of his death, except his high-mindedness and inflexible valour.

[t] *From the inhabitants.*—"The Spaniards being close at the Haven's mouth, the wind suddainely scanted, whereupon they tacked about and made for Kinsale. Within the Towne Captaine William Saxey's Company lay then in garison; but because the town was of small strength, unable to withstand so powerfull an Enemy, order was given to Sir Charles Wilmot that they should quit the same, and retraite to Corke. Vpon the three and twentieth of this instant" [September] "the Enemy landed their forces in the haven of Kinsale, and marched, with five and twentie colours, towards the Towne; upon their approach, the Townsmen, not being able to make resistance (if they had been willing thereunto), set open their Gates, and permitted them, without impeachment or contradiction, to enter the Towne; the Soveraigne, with his White rod in his hand,

gó sin. Ro pannsat a ndaoine uaisle, ⁊ a ccaiptini, ⁊ a naér conganta ar gach obair cloinn ⁊ cloiche baoí isin mbaile. Ro tairrngeadh leó don baile ar a loingis a bpróuision bídh ⁊ dighe, ordanáis, pudair, luaidhe, ⁊ gach nadailcce archena baí leó. Ro cuirsiot a loingis uatha tar a nais dia ttírib. Ro suidhighsiot a ngonnadha móra, ⁊ a naidhme caithme ⁊ cosanta in gach ionad in ro badh doigh leó a nesccairde dia nionnsaighidh. Ro órdaighsiot beos lucht faire, ⁊ forcoimhétta uadaibh imareach ina nuairib tectha amhail ro ba gnaithbés doibh re ttocht an dú sin, uair ba derbh deimhin leo go ttiucfadh an lustís go narmáil na bainrioghna dia ffuabairt an tan ro roisedh a sccela dia saighidh.

Baí imorra baile ele don taoibh thoir do chuan chinn tSáile diar bo hainm rinn corrain i ndúthaigh an bharraigh óicc hi ccenel Aodha do fonnradh. Ro cuirsiot na Spainnigh drong da ndaghdaoinibh isin mbaile sin dia bhárdacht mar an ccédna.

Iar cclos na sccel sin do lustis na hereann, ní ro airis go riacht go cenn tSaile gus an lion as lia ro féd doneoch baí umhal don bainrioghain i nerinn. Do riacht ann president dá coicced mumhan go sochraitte na mumhan a maille fris. Do riacht iarla cloinne riocaird, ⁊ gach cenn sloigh, ⁊ sochaidhe baí umhal daithe an lustís hi gconnachtoibh co na ttoicestal amaille fris gus in maighin ccédna. Tángatar beós laighnigh, ⁊ midhigh feib ro forcongradh forra ón lustis on modh remraite.

Iar roctain doibh go haoín ionadh ro suidhighedh ⁊ ro rámhaighsedh campa leó le haghaidh chinn tSáile. Do radsat aghaidh ar rinn corráin arrsidhe, ⁊ ní ro leicesiot ciúnas, na comhnaidhe, tathamh, no tionnabhradh dóibh le hathaidh foda, acht deabhtha diana, ⁊ ammais feroda aga ttabairt doibh dia roile gur bó héiccen do na bárdaibh iar gach nécceendáil da ffuairsiot tocht diaidm for

going to billet and cease them in severall houses more ready then if they had been the Queen's forces."—*Pacata Hibernia*, b. 2, c. x.

[u] *Before their arrival at that place:* that is, as they had always done at home in Spain, and in the Low Countries, where Don Juan de Aguila had fought for some time.

[w] *With the forces of Munster along with him.*—An English writer would say: "Thither arrived the President of Munster, accompanied by the forces of that province."

[x] *To come out unarmed.*—Moryson states that the Spanish captain, who defended Rincorran, had his leg broken, and that the Alfiero offered to surrender, if he himself alone were permitted to hold his arms; that, this being refused, he resolutely resolved "to bury himself in the castle, but that his company, seeing him desperately

men, captains, and auxiliaries, throughout the habitations of wood and stone, which were in the town. They conveyed from their ships into the town their stores of viands and drink, [their] ordnance, powder, lead, and all the other necessaries which they had; and then they sent their ships back again to their [own] country. They planted their great guns, and their other projectile and defensive engines, at every point on which they thought the enemy would approach them. They also appointed guards and sentinels, who should be relieved at regular hours, as had been their constant custom before their arrival at that place[u], for they were very sure that the Lord Justice would come to attack them with the Queen's army, as soon as the news [of their arrival] should reach him.

There was another castle, on the east side of the harbour of Kinsale, called Rinn-Corrain, situate in Kinelea, the territory of Barry Oge; in this town the Spaniards placed a garrison of some of their distinguished men, to guard it in like manner.

When the Lord Justice of Ireland heard these news, he did not delay until he arrived at Kinsale, with all the forces he was able to muster of those who were obedient to the Queen in Ireland. Thither arrived the President of the two provinces of Munster, with the forces of Munster along with him[w]. The Earl of Clanrickard, and every head of a host and troop that was obedient to the command of the Lord Justice in Connaught, together with their forces, arrived at the same place. Thither in manner aforesaid came the Leinstermen and Meathmen, as they had been commanded by the Lord Justice.

After they had come together at one place, they pitched and arranged a camp before Kinsale, and from this they faced Rinn-Corrain; and they allowed them [the garrison there] neither quiet, rest, sleep, nor repose, for a long time; and they gave each other violent conflicts and manly onsets, until the warders, after all the hardships they encountered, were forced to come out unarmed[x],

bent not to yield, did threaten to cast him out of the breach, so as they might be received to mercy; that he consented, at length, to yield; that all his people should be disarmed in the castle, and that he himself should wear his sword till he came to the Lord President, to whom he should render it up." The Spaniards, who thus yielded, were eighty-six in number, and four women, besides a great multitude of Irish churls, women, and children, but no swordsmen. About thirty Spaniards were slain in the defence of this castle, those in Kinsale not making one shot at the besiegers, but standing as men amazed! P. O'Sullevan Beare asserts that the

fasraṁ an Iustís iar ffaccḃáil a munisioin, ⁊ a nordanáis. Ro rann an Iustis iadsiḋe ar ḃailtiḃ móra na Muṁan go ffesaḋ cionnas no ḃiaḋ a eidirġléoḋ etir an luċt naile ḋioḃ battar hi ccenn tráile. Bá don chur sin ro marḃaḋ Cairbre óg, mac Cairbre mic Aeḋaccáin baí na ḟer brataiġe ag mac Iarla Urmuṁan.

An Iustis tra baíssiḋe co na ṡloġaiḃ, ⁊ Spainnigh chinn traile ag caiṫeṁ ⁊ acc coiṁḋiuḃraccaḋ aroile isin ced mí do ġeiṁreaḋ go ro coṁairléicc an ḃainrioghain ⁊ an ċoṁairle dIarla Tuaḋmuṁan toċt go niomat long ⁊ laoiḋeng, go ndaoiniḃ, ⁊ go ndeġarmáil, ⁊ go lón lais do caḃair ⁊ do coṁḟurtaċt muintire an prionnsa i nErinn. Iar ttocht don Iarla ⁊ don coḃlaċ go cuan chinn traile tangattar i ttír do ṫaoḃ muintire an Iustis don ċaladport. Ceiṫre mile fer ba sé an líon boí fo ṁámus Iarla Tuaḋmuṁan don armail sin. Atḃerat a roile munbuḋ med na menmanraiġe ⁊ na meirniġe ro ġaḃ an Iustís ria nIarla Tuaḋmuṁan, ⁊ riar an soċraitte sin go ffúicfeaḋ an forlongport fár folaṁ, ⁊ go sccaoílfeḋ goill ar a mbailtiḃ mora ar a haiṫle. Ro ġaḃ Iarla Tuaḋmuṁan campa ar leiṫ leis fein isin uillinn ba goire do chionn tráile do ċampa an Iustís.

Do ḃertsat Spainnigh an tan sin ionnsaiġiḋ oiḋhche ar ċeṫhraṁain do ċampa an Iustís go ro marḃaḋ soċaiḋe leó, ⁊ do ḃertsat clocha ⁊ geinnte

English took Rincorran without much trouble; but Fynes Moryson, who was present, states that they had much to do in taking it.—See his *History of Ireland*, book ii. c. 2, edition of 1735, vol. i. pp. 345, 349.

[y] *Advised*, ro ċoṁairléicc.—This is a very strange verb to use. It should be ro ḟorcongair, or ro ḟorail, requested or ordered.

[z] *Many ships.*—The Earl of Thomond sailed from England with thirteen ships, in which he transported one thousand foot and one hundred horse.—See the *Pacata Hibernia*, b. ii. c. 15 and 16, and Moryson's *History of Ireland*, book ii. c. 2, edition of 1735, p. 362.

[a] *Four thousand men.*—It would appear from the English authorities that this number is exaggerated; but it is highly probable that it was reported by spies among the Irish, with a view to terrify them, that the Earl of Thomond had four thousand men under his command.

[b] *Taken by.*—An English writer would say, "were it not for the great courage and high spirits with which the Lord Deputy was inspired, at the arrival of the Earl of Thomond with these forces," &c.

[c] *Wedges.*—P. O'Sullevan Beare expresses it better, though more briefly, thus: "Noctu facere crebras eruptiones, excubitores, et circitores interficere, tormentis clauos infigere," &c.; and Fynes Moryson, who gives a very minute account of the siege of Kinsale in his *History of Ireland*, book ii. c. 2, has the following reference to this irruption, in which the Spaniards attempted to cloy the cannon of the English:

"This Night the Trenches where the Cannon was planted, on the East side of the Town, were

and surrender at the mercy of the Lord Justice, leaving their ordnance and their ammunition behind them. The Lord Justice billeted these throughout the towns of Munster, until he should see what would be the result of his contest with the other party who were at Kinsale. It was on this occasion that Carbry Oge, the son of Carbry Mac Egan, who was ensign to the son of the Earl of Ormond, was slain.

The Lord Justice, and his forces, and the Spaniards at Kinsale, continued to shoot and fire at each other during the first month of winter, until the Queen and Council advised[y] the Earl of Thomond to go with many ships[z] and vessels, with men, good arms, and stores, to relieve and succour the Sovereign's people in Ireland. On the Earl's arrival with the fleet in the harbour of Kinsale, they landed on that side of the harbour at which the Lord Justice's people were. Four thousand men[a] was the number under the Earl of Thomond's command, of this army. Some say that, were it not for the great spirit and courage taken by[b] the Lord Justice at the arrival of the Earl of Thomond and this force, he would have left the camp void and empty, and afterwards would have distributed the English [forces] among the great towns of Munster. The Earl of Thomond pitched a camp apart to himself, at that angle of the Lord Justice's camp which was nearest to Kinsale.

At this time the Spaniards made an assault by night upon a quarter of the Lord Justice's camp, and slew many men; and they thrust stones and wedges[c]

manned with the Lord Deputy's Guard (commanded by Captain James Blount), with Sir Thomas Bourk's Company, and Sir Benjamin Berry's Company (both commanded by their Lieutenants), by Capt. Rotheram's Company (commanded by himself), by Capt. Hobby's Company (commanded by himself), Capt. Nuse's (commanded by his Lieutenant), and by Capt. Roger Harvey his Company (himself commanding in chief as Captain of the Watch there at Night, for as every Colonel watched each third Night, so every Captain watched, in one Place or other, each second Night). Also, this Night, the Fort on the West side near the Town, between the two Camps, which was cast up the Day before, was manned by Capt. Flower (commanding in chief) and his Company, by Capt. Spencer and his Company, by Capt. Dillon and his Company, and by the Companies of Sir Arthur Savage, Sir John Dowdal, Captain Masterson, and Sir William Warren (commanded by their Lieutenants), together with certain Squadrons out of the Earl of Thomond's Quarter in our second Camp, which stood in Guard without the Trenches. Now, within an Hour after night, and some two Hours before the Moon rose, it being very dark and rainy, the Spaniards, impatient of the Forts building [on a Rath on the west side of the town, to guard the Artillery], the day before so close to the Towne's West-gate, and resolving to attempt bravely on our Ordnance, planted on the East-side, made a

i ngonna mór dordanár na bainrioghna ar daigh go ro ṫoirmiscedís imo mbiodhḃaḋaiḃ a ndiuḃraccaḋ ass, ⁊ no muirfitís ní ba mó munbad Iarla cloinne Riocaird uair ba heiriḋe gur an lucht tarla ina ṫimċell ro ḟill na Spáinnigh tar anais go cenn tráile. Ní baí eiṁ orraḋ aén uaire do ló, no doiḋche etir an dá ċampa sin gan fuil aga dortaḋ eturra on céd ló ro ṡuiḋigh an lustís a ċampa re haghaiḋ chinn tráile go sccarsat re roile amhail atfiaḃar síosana.

O ro clos sccela an ċoḃlaigh Spainnigh sin la hUa neill la hUa ndoṁnaill ⁊ lá gaoiḋealaiḃ leithe cuinn archena, ba sed ro chinnsiot (gion go ndeachsat a nairigh ⁊ a nuaisle i naoin ionad dforḃaoh a niomaccallma ⁊ do ċriochnuccaḋ a ccoṁairle) daon aiccenḋ, ⁊ daén ṁenmain, gach tighearna tíre aca dfaccḃáil iomchoiṁeta, ⁊ imdeghla for a ċrich, ⁊ for a caoíṁḟesonn, ⁊ dol doiḃ co na rann, ⁊ co na soċraitte gan anaḋ, gan airisiuṁ do caḃair ⁊ do ċoṁfurtaċt na Spáinneach tangatar for a ttoghairm ⁊ for a ttarraing, uair bá cráḋ criḋe, ⁊ ba mesccḃuaidreaḋ menman leo a mbeith isin airc ⁊ isin eiccenḋáil i mbáttar aga mbioḋbaḋaiḃ, gan a ccoṁfurtaċt dia ccaoṁraitís.

Ua Doṁnaill dna ba heiriḋe cétus do rionnsccain tocht an turus sin. O ro ḟáccaiḃ siḋe lucht coiṁeta for a ċaoraigheċt, ⁊ for a muintir uile hi cconntaé Shliccigh ro arccná i nurṫosaċ geimriḋ a baile an mótaigh. Báttar iad dronga do na maiṫiḃ báttar ina ḟarraḋ O ruairc Brian óg, mac briain, Clann tSeáin a búrc, Mac diarmata maighe luirg, Siol cconcuḃair ruaiḋ, O ceallaigh, ⁊ na maiṫe battar for ionnarbaḋ ina ḟoċairsiuṁ a muṁain frisan mbliaḋain sin anall .i. Mac muiris ciarraighe tómas mac patraiccin,

brave sally with some 2000 Men, and first gave slightly towards the Trenches on the West-side; but presently, with a Gross, and their chief Strength, fell upon the Trenches in which the Artillery lay, on the east side, continuing their Resolution to force it with exceeding fury, having brought with them Tools of divers Sorts to pull down the Gabbions and the Trenches, as also spikes to cloy the ordnance."—See edition of 1735, vol. ii. p. 20.

Again: "The Enemy sallying on our Fort, guarding our Cannon, cloyed a Demi-Culverin of ours, which, being a little crased, was left without the Fort, but the next morning it was made serviceable again. Some of them were killed upon the Cannon and upon the powder, and the Trenches about the Cannon were, in some places, filled with dead Bodies; for, in that particular Attempt, they left 72 Bodies dead in the Place, and those of their best Men, whereof some were found having spikes and Hammers to cloy the Cannon. And, in general, among the bodies, many were found to have spells, Characters, and hallowed Medals, which

into a great gun of the Queen's ordnance, in order that they might prevent their enemies from firing on them out of it; and they would have slain more, were it not for the Earl of Clanrickard[d], for it was he and those around him that drove the Spaniards back to Kinsale. There was not one hour's cessation, by day or night, between these two camps, without blood being shed between them, from the first day on which the Lord Justice sat before Kinsale until they [ultimately] separated, as shall be related in the sequel.

When O'Neill, O'Donnell, and the Irish of Leath-Chuinn in general, heard the news of [the arrival of] this Spanish fleet, the resolution they came to, with one mind and one intention (although their chieftains and gentlemen did not assemble together to hold their consultation or conclude their counsel), was, that each lord of a territory among them should leave a guard and protection over his territory and fair land, and proceed, without dallying or delaying, to aid and assist the Spaniards, who had come at their call and instance; for it was distress of heart and disturbance of mind to them that they should be in such strait and jeopardy as they were placed in by their enemies, without relieving them, if they could.

O'Donnell was the first who prepared to go on this expedition. Having left guards over his creaghts and all his people in the county of Sligo, he set out from Ballymote in the very beginning of winter. The following were some of the chiefs who were along with him: O'Rourke (Brian Oge, the son of Brian); the sons of John Burke; Mac Dermot of Moylurg; the sept of O'Conor Roe; O'Kelly[e]; and the chiefs who had been banished from Munster, and were with him during the preceding part of this year, namely, Mac Maurice of Kerry (Thomas, the son of Patrickin); the Knight of Glin (Edmond, the son of Tho-

they wore as Preservations against Death; and most of them, when they were stripped, were seen to have scars of Venus Warfare."—*Id.* p. 22.

[d] *The Earl of Clanrickard.*—This perfectly agrees with Moryson, who writes: "Then his Lordship" [The Earl of Clanrickard] "and the rest charged the Enemy's Gross, being without the Fort, and break them, and did Execution upon them, falling towards the Town, and so returning thence, entered the West Fort again, with little Resistance, for the Enemy abandoned it. This Fort his Lordship and his Company made good, till he was relieved from" [by] "the Lord Deputy," &c., &c.

[e] *O'Kelly.*—He was O'Kelly of Aughrim. The head of the O'Kellys of Screen, now represented by Denis Henry Kelly, Esq. of Castlekelly, in the county of Galway, served as captain of foot under Richard Earl of Clanrickard, and fought against the disaffected Irish and Spaniards at Kinsale.—See *Tribes and Customs of Hy-Many*, p. 114.

Ridire an ġlſnda Emann mac tómais, Taḋg caoċ mac toirrḋealḃaiġ mic maṫġaṁna, ⁊ diarmait mael mac donnchaiḋ még cárrtaigh. Loccar na sloiġ sin tria conntae Rossa comáin, doirtſr ċonntaé na gaillṁe, tria Shíol nanmchaḋa, ⁊ go Sionainn. Ro tairmioṁċuirsoh i nách cróch iadsiḋe tar Sionainn, assiḋe doiḃ do delbhna még cochláin, go fſraiḃ ceall, go muinchinn sleḃe blaḋma, ⁊ go huíḃ cairín.

Ro an O doṁnaill a ngar dfichit lá ar cnoc dróma saileaċ in uíḃ cairín acc iomḟuireċ la hUa neill baí acc tocoṁlad co hionmall ina ḋeadhaiḋ. No ḃíoḋ muintir Uí doṁnaill ag creaċloscaḋ, ⁊ acc indreaḋ an tíre ina ttimċeall in airſcc battar hi ffoss in ḋú sin, co na baoí tſsḃaiḋ nſiṫ sob aḋailcc do ṡloġ ina longsortroṁ cian gairitt battar hi suiḋe.

Oc cualaiġ Ard Iustis na hereann O doṁnaill do bſiṫ ag ascnáṁ dia nionnsaiġiḋ ro ċuir presidenṫ da ċoicciḋ muṁan .i. Sir Seoirsi Carr go ccſiṫre miliḃ saiġdiúir a maille fris, i nairſs dá la ror a ċionn ar ḋáiġ ṫoirmſsccta in uirtrialla baoí ror mſnmain dó, ⁊ do ġaḃail na conaire coitċinne rair. O ro ḟidir o doṁnaill an presidens co na morṡlóġ do ṫeaċt hi ccoṁḟoċraiḃ Chairil ro ascná side co na soċraitte ó uíḃ cairín siar

[f] *Ath-Croch*.—This was the name of a ford on the Shannon, near the place now called Shannon Harbour.—See *Tribes and Customs of Hy-Many*, note [g], p. 5; also note [j], under the year 1547, p. 1500, *supra*.

[g] *Druim-Saileach*: i. e. *dorsum salicum*.—This is mentioned in O'Heerin's Topographical poem as on the confines of Corca-Thine, now the parish of Templemore, in the county of Tipperary. It is now called Moydrum, and is a conspicuous ridge, or long hill, in the barony of Ikerrin, in the north of the county of Tipperary, and about five miles to the south of the town of Roscrea. The following account of O'Donnell's movements is given in the *Pacata Hibernia*, book ii. c. xiv:

"O'Donnell fearing our forces, &c., &c., durst not enter farther into the countrey, because hee could not avoyd us, and, at that time, hee had no other way to passe, for the mountaine of Slewphelim (which, in Summer time, is good ground to passe over) was, by reason of great raines, so wett and boggye, as that no Carriage or Horse could passe it.

"This mountaine is in the county of Tipperarie, towards the Shenan, and from thence to come into the county of Limerick, the passage is through a straight, neere to the Abbey of Ownhy, which Abbey, from the place where O'Donnell incamped, in Omagher's countrey, is, at the least, twentie Irish miles. Having (as wee thought, by lodging where wee did) prevented his passage, there hapned a great frost, the like whereof hath been seldome seene in Ireland, and the enemy being desirous to avoid us, taking the advantage of the time, rose in the night and marched over the Mountaine aforesaid; whereof, as soone as wee were advertised, wee likewise rose from Cassell, whither wee were drawen (mistrusting that they would take the advantage of the frost), fower howers before day, in hope to crosse him before he should passe the Abbey of Ownhy, supposing that it had not been possible

mas); Teige Caech, the son of Turlough Mac Mahon; and Dermot Mael, the son of Donough Mac Carthy. These forces marched through the county of Roscommon, through the east of the county of Galway, and through Sil-Anmchadha, and to the Shannon. They were ferried over the Shannon at Ath-Croch[f]; and they proceeded from thence into Delvin-Mac-Coghlan, into Fircall, as far as the upper part of Slieve-Bloom, and into Ikerrin.

O'Donnell remained near twenty days on the hill of Druim-Saileach[g], in Ikerrin, awaiting O'Neill, who was marching slowly after him; and, while stationed at that place, O'Donnell's people continued plundering, burning, and ravaging the country around them, so that there was no want of anything necessary for an army in his camp, for any period, short or long.

As soon as the Lord Justice of Ireland heard that O'Donnell was marching towards him, he sent the President of the two provinces of Munster, namely, Sir George Carew, with four thousand soldiers[h], to meet him, in order to prevent him from making the journey on which his mind was bent, by blocking up the common road against him. When O'Donnell discovered that the President had arrived with his great host in the vicinity of Cashel, he proceeded with his

for him to have marched farther (with his cariage) without resting. The next morning, by eleaven of the clock, wee were hard by the Abbey, but then wee understood that O'Donnell made no stay there, but hastned to a house of the Countesse of Kildares, called Crome, twelve miles from the Abbey of Ownhy, so as his march from Omagher's countrey to Crome (by the way which hee tooke), without any rest, was above two and thirtie Irish miles, the greatest march, with cariage (whereof he left much upon the way), that hath beene heard of. To overtake him we marched, the same day, from Cashell to Kilmallock, more than twentie Irish miles, but our labour was lost. The morning following, Odonnell, with all his forces, rose from Crome, and lodged that night in the straight of Conneloghe, where hee rested a few days to rest his tired and surbated Troopes. The president, seeing that this lightfooted Generall could not be overtaken, thought it meete to hasten to the campe at Kinsale to prevent his coming thither," &c., &c.

Moryson remarks on the same subject: "This day (Nov. 23) the Lord President advertised that O'Donnell, by advantage of a frost (so great as seldom had been seen in Ireland), had passed a mountain, and so had stolen by him into Munster."—*Hist. of Irel.* book ii. c. ii. vol. ii. p. 14.

[h] *Four thousand soldiers.*—Philip O'Sullevan Beare's account fairly enough agrees with the Four Masters, where he writes:

"His Caruus Anglus Momoniarum præfectus peditum quatuor millia & equites quingentos, ex Proregis castris ductitans in Vrmoniæ Comitatum obviam tetendit: vbi calles, & viarum angustias intereluadit."—*Hist. Cathol.*, tom. 3, lib. 6, c. ix.

But it is quite clear that the Irish had this number from flying report only, for we learn from the *Pacata Hibernia*, book 2, c. xiv., that Carew had not half this number of forces.

duaċtar urmuṁan do mainistir uaiṫne, do cloinn uilliam bruaiċ na sionna go dorus luimniġ, ⁊ siar baḋēr co rainicc gan anaḋ gan airisioṁ a ló nó in adhaiġ tar máiġ isteaċ i nuiḃ conaill gaḃra. O ro raṫhaiġ an Presidens ó domnaill do ḋol tairis i ndaingniġṫiḃ an tíre, ⁊ an ro baḋ mēnmarc lais do ḋol for neṁní, soais co na ṡlóġ tar a ais hi ccēnnt an lustis. Ro léicceaḋ mac muiris don ċur sin lá hua ndomnaill go ndruing don tslóccċ amaille fris dfiossruccaḋ, ⁊ dféccaḋ cloinne muiris. Acc sirēḋ na tíre dóiḃriḋe fuarattar cuid do ḃailtiḃ na críċe in ēoarbaoġal go ro gaḃaitt leó. Robtar iat a nanmanna lēc ṡnáṁa, caisslén gērr arda fērta, ⁊ baile í ċaola. Ro ċuirsiot bardaḋa uaṫaiḃ is na bailtiḃ ísin. Bá don ċur ċédna do gaḃaḋ lá hua cconċobair ciarraiġe (Sēan mac conċoḃair uí conċoḃair) a ḃaile fēin .i. carracc an ṗuill baoí ag gallaiḃ tuillēḋ ar bliaḋain riar an tan sin ⁊ do ċóiḋ féin co na ḃaile i ccommaiḋ uí domnaill.

Baoí tra ó domnaill a ngar do ṡēcṁain is na hoirēraiḃ sin ó cconaill gaḃra ag creachaḋ ⁊ ac coṁlomaḋ, ag indraḋ, ⁊ acc orccain tíre gaċ aoin baoí ina coṁfoċraiḃ agá mbaoí buain no báiḋ lé gallaiḃ. Do ċuaiḋ dna ua domnaill iar sin tar muinċinn sleiḃe luaċra do cloinn Aṁlaoíbh do múscraiġe, ⁊ co banndain hi ccairbreachaiḃ. Tangattar imorro gaoidil muṁan uile dia ṡaiġiḋ an dú sin cen moṫá Mag carṫaiġ riabaċ .i. domnall mac corbmaic na haoíne, ⁊ corbmac mac diarmada, mic taidcc tiġearna múscraiġe. Ro ġeallsat na gaoidil sin uile bēiṫ daon rann ⁊ daon aonta lais ó ṡin amaċ.

Imṫusa í neill .i. aoḋ mac firḋorċa mic cuinn ḃacaiġ ro ṗágaiḃ siḋe (sēcṁuin iar ramain) tír eoġain do ḋol do ċaḃair na Spáinneaċ reṁráite. Iar ndol dó tar bóinn ro gaḃ ag crēċlosccaḋ críċe breaġ ⁊ miḋe. Luiḋ iar sin diarṫar miḋe, ⁊ doirṫear muṁan tar siúir siar ⁊ noċa naiṫristear a imṫeaċta go roċtain dó go banndain airm i mbaoí ó domnaill. Baoí ḃeós Sēan mac tomais ruaiḋ mic an Iarla i ffoċair uí neill ar an turus sin.

[i] *The Maigue:* a river flowing by Adare in the county of Limerick.—See it already mentioned at the years 1464, 1581, and 1600.

[k] *That his intention:* literally, "that what was intended by him came to nothing;" i. e. that he could not intercept or overtake O'Donnell, who performed on this occasion "the greatest march, with the encumbrance of carriage, of which there exists any record."

[l] *Ballykealy:* a castle in ruins in the parish of Kilmoyly, barony of Clanmaurice, and county of Kerry.—See note [p], under the year 1582, p. 1781, *supra.*

[m] *Clann-Auliffe:* a district in the barony of

forces from Ikerrin westwards, through the upper part of Ormond, by the monastery of Owny, through Clanwilliam, on the borders of the Shannon, to the gates of Limerick, and south-westwards, without halting or delaying by day or night, until he crossed the Maigue[i], into Hy-Connell-Gaura. As soon as the President perceived that O'Donnell had passed him by into the fastnesses of the country, and that his intention[k] was frustrated, he returned back with his force to the Lord Justice. On this occasion Mac Maurice was permitted by O'Donnell to go with a part of the army to visit and see Clanmaurice. As they were traversing the country, they got an advantage of some of the castles of the territory, and took them. These were their names: Lixnaw, the Short-castle of Ardfert, and Ballykealy[l]. In these they placed warders of their own. It was on the same occasion that O'Conor Kerry (John, the son of Conor) took his own castle, namely, Carraic-an-phuill, which had been upwards of a year before that time in the possession of the English, and that he himself, with the people of his castle, joined in alliance with O'Donnell.

O'Donnell remained nearly a week in these districts of Hy-Connell-Gaura, plundering, devastating, ravaging, and destroying the territories of every person in his neighbourhood who had any connexion or alliance with the English. After this O'Donnell proceeded over the upper part of Sliabh-Luachra, through Clann-Auliffe[m], through Muskerry, and to the Bandon in the Carberys. All the Irish of Munster came to him there, except Mac Carthy Reagh (Donnell, the son of Cormac-na-h-Aaoine) and Cormac, the son of Dermot, son of Teige, Lord of Muskerry. All these Irishmen promised to be in alliance and in unison with him from thenceforward.

As for O'Neill, i. e. Hugh, the son of Ferdorcha, son of Con Bacagh, he left Tyrone a week after Allhallowtide, to go to assist the aforesaid Spaniards. After he had crossed the Boyne he proceeded to plunder and burn the territories of Bregia and Meath. He afterwards marched through the west of Meath, and through the east of Munster, westwards across the Suir; but his adventures are not related until he arrived at the [River] Bandon, where O'Donnell was. John, son of Thomas Roe, son of the Earl [of Desmond], was along with O'Neill on this expedition.

Duhallow, in the north-west of the county of Cork. It was the country of the Mac Auliffes, who were at this period tributary to Mac Donough Mac Carthy, Chief of Duhallow.

O do ruachtattar maithe gaoidel co na sochraide go haon bhaile ro gabhsatt longport don taobh ba thuaidh biucc do longport an lustis i mbél guala hi ccenel aodha. Ro badh iomdha din cenn slóigh ⁊ sochaide, tighearna tíre, ⁊ taoiseach tuaithe hi ffarradh uí néill, ⁊ uí domhnaill isin maighin sin. Ro badh mór tra menma ⁊ meisneach, gérraitteacht ⁊ gaisccedh an lochta báttar an dú sin co ná baoí ard no airchenn hi ccóicc coicedhaibh ereann for nár lásatt side nó drong eigin díobh a nadhuath ⁊ a nurgrain, a nuamhan, ⁊ a nimsccla do ghallaibh, ⁊ do ghaoidelaibh báttar hi ffrithbhert friú gus an tan sin. Robtar mince iomda a ccatha, a ccomhramha, a ccreacha, a ccomhruathair, a nechta, a naidhbhena for a mbiodhbhadhaibh i naile criochaibh go halt na huaire ísin. Ní thapla friú dna tren tar na tiostais, ná forlíon ar nárbhad fortail an ccenn baoí an coimde, ⁊ an conach ag congnamh friú, ⁊ in airsett do rónsatt tol a ttighearna dia ⁊ ro chomhaillsiot a aithenta, ⁊ a thiomna. Ro badh daighlíon tabharta tachair ⁊ cloiche catha dia neccraittibh cidh arail do na fóirnibh báttar isin ffoslongport sin cen co mbittís féin uile ag congnamh fri aroile, dia ndeonaicchedh dia dóibh cathucchadh co séitreach síor chalma daoín menmain, ⁊ daon aonta tar cenn a nirsi, ⁊ a nathardha isin dhídhenndáil thenntea i tecomnac-cair a mbiodhbhadha aca don chur sin.

Do rattsat tra gaoidil iomchumhga mór for ghallaibh óir nír léiccsiot fér, arbhar, nó uiscce, tuighe, no teine do fhaighidh champa an lustis. Báttar athaidh amhlaidh sin ag iomchoimhett for aroile go ro fhaoídh don Iohn generál na spáinneach scribeann co hincleithe do fhaighidh gaoideal dia aslach forra arail do champa an lustis dionnsaicchidh aon doidhchibh, ⁊ go soichfeadh féin an cuid ele dhe isin oidhche chédna uair báttar féin i niomchumhga móir ag gallaibh feibh ro bhattar na goill a ndiochumhang ag gaoidealaibh.

Ro ghabhsat airigh chenél cconaill, ⁊ eoccain acc sgrúdadh a ccomhairle imon ccaingin sin ⁊ báttar sfaontadhaigh fri ré im chinnedh ar aon comhairle uair bá sí airle uí neill gan a ionnsaicchidh ettir fó cedóir acht gabháil forra

[n] *Bel-Guala*, now Belgooly, a village in the townlands of Lybe and Ballindeenisk, in the parish of Kilmonoge, barony of Kinelea, and county of Cork.

[o] *The tribes*, or the hosts. This seems to have been copied nearly word for word from the Life of Hugh Roe O'Donnell, by Cucogry O'Clery.

[p] *Not to attack.*—Had O'Neill been permitted to fight the English after his own fashion, on this occasion, he would, most undoubtedly, have gained such another victory as he had already acheived at Ath-buidhe, in Ulster. But the impatience of the insolent and inefficient Spanish commander at Kinsale, the self-suffi-

When the Irish chiefs and their forces met together at one place, they encamped a short distance to the north of the camp of the Lord Justice at Bel-Guala[n], in Kinelea. Many a host and troop, and lord of a territory, and chief of a cantred, were along with O'Neill and O'Donnell at this place. Great were the spirit, courage, prowess, and valour, of the people who were there. There was not a spot or quarter in the five provinces of Ireland where these, or some party of them, had not impressed a horror and hatred, awe and dread of themselves among the English and Irish who were in opposition to them, till that time. Frequent and numerous had been their battles, their exploits, their depredations, their conflicts, their deeds, their achievements over enemies in other territories, up to this very hour. They met no mighty man whom they did not subdue, and no force over which they did not prevail, so long as the Lord and fortune favoured, that is, so long as they did the will of their Lord God, and kept his commandments and his will. Efficient for giving the onset, and gaining the battle over their enemies, were the tribes[o] who were in this camp (although some of them did not assist one another), had God permitted them to fight stoutly with one mind and one accord, in defence of their religion and their patrimony, in the strait difficulty in which they had the enemy on this occasion.

The Irish reduced the English to great straits, for they did not permit hay, corn, or water, straw or fuel, to be taken into the Lord Justice's camp. They remained thus for some time watching each other, until Don Juan, the General of the Spaniards, sent a letter privately to the Irish, requesting them to attack a part of the Lord Justice's camp on a certain night, and [adding] that he himself would attack the other part of it on the same night; for they [the Spaniards] were reduced to great straits by the English, as the English were distressed by the Irish.

The chiefs of the Kinel-Connell and Kinel-Owen began to deliberate in council on this suggestion; and they were for some time dissentient on adopting this resolution, for it was O'Neill's advice not to attack[p] them immediately by

ciency of the Spaniards, and the impetuous ardour of young O'Donnell, all united to overrule the counsels of the wary O'Neill. The two passages following, from the *Pacata Hibernia* and Fynes Moryson, will shew that O'Neill could have defeated the English without much fighting on this occasion :

"Our Artillery still played upon the Towne

isin tſnnta i mbáttar go neiblidís lá gorta, ⁊ dearbaiḋ gaċ aiḋilcce ro baḋ tſrḃaiḋ doiḃ aṁail atbaṫ araill dia ndaoiniḃ, ⁊ dia neoċaiḃ arċſna gó sin. Ua domhnaill dna bá craḋ criḋe, ⁊ bá haḋnár laissiḋe coisteaċt fri coraoíd ⁊ fri hſiccſndáil na sráinneaċ gan a ffurtaċt ar a nettualang i mbáttar diamaḋ a écc, nó a oiḋeaḋ, nó díṫ a ḋaoíne tíoraḋ ḋe, conaḋ fair deiriḋ leó fó ḋeóiḋ campa an lustir do ḟuabairt aṁail ro hſrbaḋ friu.

An tan ro ċoṁfoiccsiġ an oiḋċe erḋalta in ro ċinnsiot an indsaiġiḋ sin gaḃaitt gaoiḋil a nſrraḋa áiġ ⁊ imairecc go fſrrḋa forffaoíliġ go mbáttar erlaṁ inimṫeaċta. Báttar imrſsnaiġ a nairiġ fri araile ag iomċosnaṁ ṫossaiġ ionnsaiġṫe na hoiḋċe sin do bſiṫ ag gaċ droing díoḃ. Conaḋ aṁlaiḋ ro ċéimniġsiot ina ttríḃ cóiriġtiḃ coṁnarta caṫa, ⁊ ina ttríḃ lorccḃuiḋniḃ lſrḋa, líonṁara gualainn fri gualainn, ⁊ uillinn fri huillinn dar imealḃord a longport amaċ, Ua neill go ccenél eoccain gur an líon tarrurtair ina ḟarraḋ do airġiallaiḃ, ⁊ do uiḃ eaċḋach ulaḋ ina ccipe coṁnart for lſiṫ. Ua domnaill co ccenél cconaill, ⁊ co na urraḋaiḃ, ⁊ co cconnaċtaibh arċſna isin ccipe araill. Ina mbaoí duaislib muṁan, laiġſn, ⁊ fear miḋe co na soċraiḋe (doneoċ ro éiriġ i ccommbáiḋ ċoccaiḋ gaoiḋel díoḃ, ⁊ ro ḃaoí for ionnarbaḋ i nulltoiḃ fris an mbliaḋainsi anall) báttar siḋe isin tſrſ cipe go coḃsaiġ céimniġin gan cumasc fór slóġ naile.

Iar narccnáṁ dóiḃ dar an longport seaċtair aṁlaiḋ sin, do rala fordal conaire ⁊ Sſċrán sliccíḋ do na sloccaiḃ lá dobar ḋorċa na hoiḋċe co nár urmaisſttar a neolaiġ saiġiḋ gur an ionaḋ ċinnte baoí for ionchaiḃ campa an lustir go soillsi laoí ar aḃarac. Atbearat araile go ro ċuir neaċ sainriṫ do ġaoiḋelaiḃ raḃaḋ ⁊ rémairneis gur an lustir go mbáttar gaoiḋil ⁊

(as it had done all that while) that they might see wee went on with our businesse, as if we cared not for Tyrone's comming; but it was withall carried on in such a fashion, as wee had no meaning to make a breach, because we thought it not fit to offer to enter, and so put all in hazard untill wee might better discover what Tyrone meant to do, whose strength was assured to be very great, and wee found, by letters of Don Iohn's (which wee had newly intercepted), that hee had advised Tyrone to set upon our Campes, telling him that it could not bee chosen, but our men were much decayed by the Winter's siege, and so that wee could hardly be able to maintaine so much ground (as wee had taken) when our strength was greater, if we were well put to on the one side by them, and on the other side by him, which he would not faile for his part to doe soundly."—*Pacata Hibernia*, book ii. c. xx.

"If Tyrone had laine still, and not suffered himself to be drawn to the plaine Ground by the Spaniards Importunity, all our Horse must needs have been sent away or starved."—Mory-

any means, but to keep them still in the strait in which they were, until they should perish of famine, and the want of all the necessaries of which they stood in need, as some of their men and horses had already perished. O'Donnell, however, was oppressed at heart and ashamed to hear the complaint and distress of the Spaniards without relieving[q] them from the difficulty in which they were, even if his death or destruction, or the loss of his people, should result from it; so that the resolution they finally agreed to was, to attack the Lord Justice's camp, as they had been ordered.

When the particular night upon which it was agreed they should make this attack arrived, the Irish cheerfully and manfully put on their dresses of battle and conflict, and were prepared for marching. Their chiefs were at variance, each of them contending that he himself should go foremost in the night's attack; so that the manner in which they set out from the borders of their camp was in three strong battalions, three extensive and numerous hosts, shoulder to shoulder, and elbow to elbow. O'Neill, with the Kinel-Owen, and such of the people of Oriel and Iveagh-of-Uladh as adhered to him, were in a strong battalion apart; O'Donnell, with the Kinel-Connell, his sub-chieftains, and the Connaughtmen in general, formed the second battalion; [and] those gentlemen of Munster, Leinster, and Meath, with their forces, who had risen up in the confederacy of the Irish war, and who had been in banishment in Ulster during the preceding part of this year, were in the third battalion, [and marched] steadily and slowly, without mixing with any other host.

After they had marched outside their camp in this manner, the forces mistook their road and lost their way, in consequence of the great darkness of the night, so that their guides were not able to make their way to the appointed place, opposite the camp of the Lord Justice, until clear daylight next morning. Some assert that a certain Irishman[r] had sent word and information to the Lord

son's *History of Ireland*, book ii. c. ii.

[q] *Without relieving.*—The construction of the original is here clumsy. It should be: "O'Donnell was grieved at heart on hearing of the distress of the Spaniards, and replied boldly to O'Neill, at the council, that it was shameful to listen so long to the complaints and reproaches of the Spaniards without going to their relief; and added, that it was his opinion, that they were bound in honour to accede to the proposal of the Spanish general, even if they foresaw a certainty of losing their own lives, and of the annihilation of their forces."

[r] *A certain Irishman.*—It is stated in the *Pacata Hibernia*, book ii. c. xxi., that this information was sent to the Lord President of Mun-

Spáinniġ ag tabairt aṁais fair an adhaiġ ṡin conaḋ aire sin baoí an Iustis ⁊ armail na bainrioġna ar a mbḟrnaḋaiḃ baoġail, ⁊ ar a nḟaiġiḃ erḋalta do cosnaṁ an ċampa fri a mbiodhḃaḋaiḃ. O do ḋeachaiḋ dorċata na hoiḋċe for cculaiḃ, ⁊ ó ro baḋ foreil soillsi an laoí do ċáċ i ccoitcinne bá-hann tſccoṁnaccair do ṁuintir uí neill toċt i ccoṁfocraiḃ muinntire an Iustis gan ráṫuccaḋ do na gaoiḋealaiḃ ittir, ⁊ o robtar anffuiriṫe do beartsat taoḃ friú acc airisiuṁ frí a nordluccaḋ, ⁊ fri a ninnell, ⁊ danmain fria ua nDoṁnaill ⁊ fris an luċt naile do rala for fordal aṁail reṁebert-inar.

Od connairc an Iustis an ní sin ro léicc diormaḋa diana dſinmnſoaċa dia nionnsaiċċiḋ go ro mſsccsatt for muinntir uí néill go mbádar agá marḃaḋ, ⁊ agá muḋuccaḋ acá ttraothaḋ, ⁊ acca ttanuccaḋ go ro bſnaḋ a cúicc nó a sé do ḃratachaiḃ dioḃ ⁊ go ro marḃaḋ daoíne ioṁḋa uaḋhaiḃ.

ster by Brian Mac Hugh Oge Mac Mahon, a principal commander in the Irish army. The statement is as follows, as printed by Stafford, who was present at the time:

"Tuesday the two and twentieth of December, Brian Mac Hugh Oge Mac Mahon, a principall Commander in the Irish Army, whose eldest sonne, Brian, had many yeares before been a Page in England, with the Lord President, sent a Boy unto Captaine William Taaffe, praying him to speake unto the Lord President to bestow upon him a bottle of *Aquavitæ*, which the President for old acquaintance sent unto him. The next night, being the three and twentieth, by the same Messenger, hee sent him a Letter, praying him to recommend his Loue vnto the President, thanks for his *Aquavitæ*, and to wish him the next night following to stand well upon his Guard, for himselfe was at the Councell, wherein it was resolved that on the night aforesaid (towards the break of day), the Lord Deputie's Campe would be assaulted both by Tyrone's Armie (which lay at their backes), and by the Spanyards from the Towne, who, upon the first Allarme, would bee in readiness to sally."

The same fact, and the straying of the Irish forces, are mentioned by Fynes Moryson, book ii. c. ii., in the following words:

"This evening one of the chief Commanders in Tyrone's Army, having some Obligations to the Lord President, sent a Messenger to him for a Bottle of Usquebaugh; and by a letter wished him that the English Army should that Night be well upon their Guard, for Tyrone meant to give upon one Camp, and the Spaniards upon the other; meaning to spare no man's life, but the Lord Deputy's and his. Don Jean del Aguila after confessed to the Lord President, that, notwithstanding our Sentinels, he and Tyrone the night following had three Messengers the one from the other. All the Night was clear with Lightning (as in the former Nights were great Lightnings with Thunder) to the Astonishment of Many, in respect of the Season of the year. And I have heard by many Horsemen of good credit, and, namely, by Captain Pikeman, Coronet to the Lord Deputy's Troop, a Gentleman of good estimation in the Army, that this Night our Horsemen set to watch, to their seeming, did see Lamps burn at the points of their staves or spears, in the midst of these Lightning Flashes. Tyrone's Guides missed

Justice, that the Irish and Spaniards were to attack him that night, and that, therefore, the Lord Justice and the Queen's army stationed themselves in the gaps of danger, and certain other passes, to defend the camp against their enemies. When the darkness of the night had disappeared, and the light of the day was clear[s] to all in general, it happened that O'Neill's people, without being aware of it, had advanced near the Lord Justice's people; but, as they were not prepared, they turned aside from them to be drawn up in battle array and order, and to wait for O'Donnell and the other party, who had lost their way, as we have before stated.

As soon as the Lord Justice perceived this thing, he sent forth vehement and vigorous troops to engage them, so that they fell upon O'Neill's people, and proceeded to kill, slaughter, subdue, and thin them, until five or six ensigns[t] were taken from them, and many of their men were slain.

the way, so as he came not up to our Camp by Night, as the Spaniards ready in Arms hourly expected, but early about the Break of next day."

[s] *The light of the day was clear.*—"Cum clare illuxisset admirans Onellus Aquilam non irrumpere, nec pugnæ signum dare," &c.—*O'Sullevan.*

[t] *Five or six ensigns.*—Moryson writes: "The Irish Rebels left 1200 bodies dead on the field, besides those there killed in 2 miles chase; we took nine of their Ensigns, all their Drums and Powder, and got more than 2000 Arms. And had not our men been greedy of the Spaniard's Spoil, being very rich; had not our Foot been tired with continual watchings long before in this hard Winter's Siege; had not our Horse especially been spent by ill keeping and Want of all Meat for many Days before (by Reason of Tyrone's Nearness, so as the Day before this Battle it had been resolved in Council to send the Horse from the Camp for Want of Means to feed them; and if Tyrone had lain still, and not suffered himself to be drawn to the plain Ground by the Spaniards' Importunity, all our Horse must needs have been sent away, or starved); had not these Impediments been, we had then cut the Throats of all the Rebels there assembled, for they never made Head against them that followed the Execution, nor scarce ever looked behind them, but every Man shifted for himself, casting of his Arms, and running for Life, insomuch as Tyrone after confessed himself to be overthrown by a sixth Part of his Number, which he ascribed (as we must and do) to God's great Work, beyond Man's capacity, and withal acknowledged that he lost above 1000 in the Field, besides some 800 hurt. This we understood by the faithful Report of one who came from him some few days after, and told the Lord Deputy moreover, that he tormented himself exceedingly for this his overthrow.

"After the Battle the Lord Deputy, in the midst of the dead bodies, caused Thanks to be given to God for this victory; and there presently knighted the Earl of Clanrickard in the Field, who had many fair Escapes, his garments being often pierced with shot and other Weapons, and with his own Hand killed about 20 Irish Kerne, and cried out to spare no rebel. The Captiue Spanish Commander, Alonzo del Campo, avowed that the Rebels were 6000 Foot and 500

Ua doṁnaill dna do riaċt siḋe do lsttaoiḃ muinntire uí neill iar ffraoin-eaḋ forra, ⁊ ro ġaḃsiḋe for arlaċ iompuiriġ for luċt an teichiḋ ag nsreaḋ

Horse; whereas the Lord Deputy had but some 1200 Foot and less than 400 Horse. So before Noon his Lordship returned to the Camp, where commanding Vollies of Shot for joy of the Victory, the Spaniards, perhaps mistaking the Cause, and dreaming of the Rebels' Approach, presently sallied out, but were soon beaten into the Town, especially when they saw our Triumph, and perceived our Horsemen from the Hill on the West-side to wave the Colours we had taken in the Battle, and among the rest especially the Spanish Colours (for such most of them were, the Rebels in woods not using that martial Bravery). The same day an old written Book was shewed to the Lord Deputy, wherein was a Prophesy naming the Ford and Hill where this Battle was given, and foretelling a great Overthrow to befal the Irish in that place."—Book ii. c. ii.

P. O'Sullevan Beare gives the following brief account of the defeat of the Irish at Kinsale, *Hist. Cathol. Iber.*, tom. 3, lib. 6, c. iv:

"Odonellus, & eius socij Orruarkus, Macdiarmuda, Macsuinnius Tuethius, Okealla, Raymundus Baro, Rothericus, & Capharius fratres, Daniel Ochonchuris Sligachi frater, Gulielmus Burkus Raymundi Baronis frater tria militum millia, quorum equites quandringenti erant, mouent, vt Aquilæ ferant opem. His Caruus Anglus Momoniarum præfectus peditum quatuor millia, & quingentos, & equites quingentos ex Proregis castris ductitans in Vrmoniæ Comitatum obuiam tetendit: vbi calles, & viarum angustias intercludit. Odonellus magnis ignibus accensis, vt castrorum speciem ostenderet, præter Caruum exercitum noctu incolumem duxit & diuersis in locis Onellum quadraginta dies spectat. Caruus voti minimè compos copias suas ad Proregem ad Keansaliam reducit. Onellus occasionem nactus Midhiam inuadit, vbi Anglos, & Angloibernos longé, latéque deprædatus domum spolijs onustus reuertitur, occiso Darsio Platinæ domino, qui secutus ad prælium lacessebat. Inde Keansaliam media hyeme petit. Eum comitabantur Macmagaunus, Macguier occisi in Corcachano agro frater nomine Cuconnachtus, Raynaldus Macdonellus Glinniæ princeps, Macmoris Lacsnaæ Baro, Richardus Tirellus, & alij ex sua familia, qui omnes duo millia, sexcentosque pedites, & equites quadringentos expeditos ductitabant. Cum quibus Onellus in Oriria Barria Odonellum assequitur. Vnde ambo in ea Carbriæ parte, quæ Kenealmeka dicitur, castra collocant. Eò venit Osulleuanus Bearrus ducens copias suas, cum quibus Portucastelli fuit, & Hispanos trecentos à Zubiaure acceptos duce Alfonso Ocampo. Osulleuanum secuti sunt Oconchur Kierrius, Daniel Osulleuani Magni filius, Magnus, & Daniel Macsuinnij, & alii equites. Hinc omnes profecti apud Culcarrinnam syluam mille passibus ab hoste locata castra vallo circummuniunt. Vbi inter se, & Hispanos Anglos medios magnis difficultatibus continent, prohibentes, ne ad eos ex oppidis, & ciuitatibus, aut vlla parte frumentum, commeatusué supportetur, & intercipientes eos, qui castris pabulandi causa exibant. Quamobrem Angli non longo spacio progressi, vt habeant celerem receptum, in angustijs minus liberè, & audacter pabulantur, & accepto modico detrimento, vel hoste procul viso sarcinas proijcientes fugiunt: inde dies omittentes noctu pabulantur: postremò nullo modò pabulatum castris eggredi audent: & quidquid antea commeatus habuerunt, totum penè consumunt. Ita eos primum inedia, mox fames, tandem pestilentia inuasit. Ibernorum exercitus copia rerum abundabat. Hispani quoque in plures dies victu minimè carent, quem, vel ipsi ex Hispania vexerant, vel oppidum præbet, ab hostium irrup-

O'Donnell advanced to the side of O'Neill's people after they were discomfitted, and proceeded to call out to those who were flying, to stand their ground,

tionibus tuti, & sua virtute, & munitionibus, quas fecerant. Optimates Momonij, qui eòvsque neutram partem iuuabant, se Catholicæ religioni, patriæque defendendæ non defuturos, auxilio quam celerrimè venturos pollicentur. Iberni milites legionarij, & auxiliares, quorum virtute fretus Anglus locum tenebat, Onello per internuncios promittunt ad eum ante triduum se transituros, fidemque cœperunt implere, bini, terni, & deni Anglum deserentes. Quod si omnium transitio spectaretur, iam de Anglo fuisset actum: nam ex quindecim millibus militum, quos habebat obsidionis initio, octo millia, ferro, fame, frigore, morbo occubuerunt, quorum pars maior erant ex Anglia nuper auxilio missi tyrones inertes, periculi, & laboris impatientes. Reliquorum vix duo millia erant Angli, cæteri Iberni, & Angloiberni. Quibus periculis Prorex perculsus statuit obsidio excedere, Corcacham se recipere, & dumtaxat mœnia defendere, quo modo sine conflictu, & vulnere Catholici victoriam possent obtinere. Cui rei peccata nostra obstiterunt. Imprimis Aquila missis crebrò litteris iterum, atque iterum vehementer contendit, vt Onellus se cum ipso coniungat. Onellus, Osulleuanus, & alij ne rem eo discriminis deducant, sentiunt, sed potius Ibernorum transitionem, & hostis fugam spectent. Odonellus, & alij plures contrarium censent. Itaque vicit maior pars prudentiorem. Dies constituitur, qua Onellus sub matutinum crepusculum iuxta hostium castra consistat, vt Aquila faciens ex altera parte eruptionem se cum illo coniungat. Qua de re Aquilæ litteræ ad Onellum datæ á Prorege intercipiuntur. Onellus triplici acie instructa in eum locum ire contendit. Angli, qui Catholicorum consilium minimè ignorabant, adhuc noctu eo in loco, in quem Onellus venire constituit, tympanorum militarium strepitu, tubarum clangore, bombardarum sonitu falsam, fictamque pugnam ineunt. Aquilæ exploratores missi simulatam speciem pugnæ fuisse retulisse traduntur. Odonellus cum acie sua totam noctem imperitia ducum itineris errans procul aberat. Onelli, & Osulleuani acies pugnæ classicum audientes, & arbitratæ Aquilam esse egressum in destinatum locum celeri cursu noctu perueniunt. Vnde hostibus in munimenta regressis, cum in quiete summa, & silentio castra vidissent, stratagemma intellexerunt: & paululum sub armis moratæ cælo iam albente vltra præfixum sibi locum paulò pergunt, & primi ordines Osulleuani aciei, quæ prima erat, non longé à vallo subsistunt, non tamen ab hoste visi humili tumulo conspectum prohibente. Cum claré illuxisset, admirans Onellus Aquilam nec erumpere, nec pugnæ signum dare, cum Osulleuano, Hispanis cohortium ductoribus, & paucis alijs in tumuli cacumen ascendit. Vnde hostis castra intentissima meditatione contemplatur. Ea vallo, fossa, turribus, tormentis erant munitissima, milites in armis, equi frænati. Ibernos etiam numero seperabant: nam multi ex castris, præcipuè Momonij pabulatum, & frumentatum, pridiè illius diei profecti aberant. Odonellus cum acie tertia non peruenerat. Quamobrem Onellus ex ducum sententia rem in alium diem differens, agmina pedem referre iubet. Quæ quingentos passus reuersa Odonellum offenderunt, & eodem momento temporis Proregis equitatus adfuit, quem vadum proximi fluminis traiectum Odonellus cum equitatu suo adcurrens per idem vadum repulsum in fugam vertit. Rursus Proregis equitatus reuersus vadum traijcere tentat. Odonellus ratus illum inter se, & vadum facilè opprimi posse, loco sensim cedit, quod dum facit pars ipsius equitatus vel casu, vel alicuius dolo, & perfidia agmen ipsius Odonelli auersis equis ingressa pedites cogit ordines laxare. In-

na hiorgaile for a ṁuinntir badéin go ro ṁeabaid for a ġlór, ⁊ for a ġuṫ lá haidble na haccallma ⁊ na harḋgarma baoi occa for ċáċ a ccoitċinne ag cuinġid for a saorċlannaiḃ airirium ina ḟoċair acc iombualad fri a mbioḋḃadaiḃ. Atbeiread friú dna gur ḃó nár, ⁊ meaḃal dóiḃ an ní nſṁġnáṫ ro triallsat .i. a ndromanna do ṫabairt fri a naiṁdiḃ aṁail nár ḃó bés dia mbunad ḟréiṁ riaṁ gó sin. Acht ċſna níor ḃó torḃa dóroṁ i ndſrgſine uair ó ro ṁeaḃaid don ċécna buidin ro ṁeaḃaid dá gaċ drung ele diaid a ndiaid. Acht namá gé ro sraoínead forra nír ḃó hadḃal an líon ro marḃad dioḃ ar uaite loċta a ttograma in aiṫḟéccad ina mbaoi reampa.

Bá follus diomḃa dé ⁊ a nainḟén for gaoidelaiḃ glan ḟódla don ċur sa, óir ro bad mſince raon madma ria nuaṫad dſḃride for ilċédaiḃ do ġallaiḃ inár a nduruim do ṫaḃairt fri a naiṁdiḃ i ngort gliad, ⁊ i mbſirn ḃaoġail (in gaċ airm a ccompaictís) gus an laite hísin. Bá hádḃal, ⁊ bá dírim in ro fáccḃad isin maigin sin gér ḃó deḋbal an líon do roċrattar ann, uair ro fáccḃad gérraideaċt ⁊ gaisccead, ⁊ raṫ ⁊ roconaċ, uaisle ⁊ ionnraiccid, aireaċas ⁊ airbeart, eineaċ, ⁊ eangnaṁ, cródaċt ⁊ cosnaṁ, cráḃad ⁊ caoín isin insi gaoideal isin iomairſcc sin.

Tangattar an gaoidealsloġ im ua néill, ⁊ im ua ndoṁnaill tar a nais siar co hinis eoccanáin an adhaiġ sin. Monuar tra ní haṁail ro ṡaoilsiot toċt on turus sin ḃáttar in adhaiġ sin ar rob iomḋa aiṫḃſr iom aiṫḃſr, Mairgnſċ ⁊ mſirtſn, duḃa, ⁊ dogailsi ro ḃaoí seaċnón a longport in gaċ aird, ⁊ ní ro ċuilsiot a saiṁe, ⁊ ní mór má ro froinnigsiot. Bá hucctmall anbsaid aimiarmaircaċ a ccoṁairle ar roċtain i ccſnn aroile dóiḃ conad ſḋ ro ċinnsiot fó deoid O neill ⁊ Ruḋraiġe dſrbraṫair uí doṁnaill co na nurradhaiḃ, ⁊ maiṫe lſiṫe cuinn arċſna do ṡoad tar a nais dia ttíriḃ dimdſgail a ccriċe, ⁊ a ffſrainnt ar eaċtair ċenelaiḃ, O doṁnaill aod ruad, Remann

compositi pedites sese fugæ mandant. Idem facit Onelli agmen, & etiam Osulleuani hostibus minimé cogentibus, & principibus frustra reclamantibus. Ita panico terrore omnes perculsi sunt, vel potius diuina vindicta fugati. Fugientibus regius equitatus nihil audaciter hæret, putans in insidias se trahi. Multi equites Iberni, qui ab Anglorum parte stabant, Catholicos frustra confirmant, suadentes, vt in prælium redeant, seque illis fore auxilio. Onellus, & Odonellus eos in pugnam reducere non potuerunt Osulleuanus Tirellus Hispani duces cum paucis reuersi hostis impetum partim sustinuerunt. Hoc die succubuerunt ex Onelli exercitu pedites ducenti. Ex Anglis tres viri nobiles. Comes Clanrichardus ob virtutem equitis Aurati nomine à Prorege donatur."

[u] *Generosity.*—The word eangnaṁ has two

and to rouse his own people to battle [and so continued], until his voice and speech were strained by the vehemence and loudness of the language in which he addressed all in general, requesting his nobles to stand by him to fight their enemies. He said to them, that this unusual thing which they were about to do, was a shame and a guile, namely: to turn their backs to their enemies, as was not the wont of their race ever till then. But, however, all he did was of no avail to him, for, as the first battalion was defeated, so were the others also in succession. But, although they were routed, the number slain was not very great, on account of the fewness of the pursuers, in comparison with those [flying] before them.

Manifest was the displeasure of God, and misfortune to the Irish of fine Fodhla, on this occasion; for, previous to this day, a small number of them had more frequently routed many hundreds of the English, than they had fled from them, in the field of battle, in the gap of danger (in every place they had encountered), up to this day. Immense and countless was the loss in that place, although the number slain was trifling; for the prowess and valour, prosperity and affluence, nobleness and chivalry, dignity and renown, hospitality and generosity[u], bravery and protection, devotion and pure religion, of the Island, were lost in this engagement.

The Irish forces returned that night, with O'Neill and O'Donnell, to Inis-Eoghanain[w]. Alas! the condition in which they were that night was not as they had expected to return from that expedition, for there prevailed much reproach on reproach, moaning and dejection, melancholy and anguish, in every quarter throughout the camp. They slept not soundly, and scarcely did they take any refreshment. When they met together their counsel was hasty, unsteady, and precipitate, so that what they at length resolved upon was, that O'Neill and Rury, the brother of O'Donnell, with sub-chieftains, and the chiefs of Leath-Chuinn in general, should return back to their countries, to defend their territories and lands against foreign tribes; [and] that O'Donnell (Hugh

meanings, prowess and bounty; and as it is here used as a synonime with eineać, hospitality, it is quite clear that it is intended to be used in the latter sense, although it has been hitherto almost invariably used in the sense of prowess.

[w] *Inis-Eoghanain:* i. e. Eoghanan's Island (Eoghanan, a diminutive of Eoghan, being a man's name common amongst the ancient Irish), now Inishannon, a small town near Bandon, in the county of Cork.—See note [l], under the year 1560, p. 1581, *supra*.

mac Sſain a búrc, Captin aoḋ mus mac Roibſrd do ḋol don Spainte dac-caoíne a nimniġ, ⁊ a necculaing lá ríġ na Spáinne.

Ro ḟáccaibſiott na maiṫe sin drong dia ranntaiḃ coiccriċe isin muṁain agá haiḋmilleaḋ dia néis .i. Captin tiriel, ⁊ an ċuid ele do cloinn tSſain a búrc, ⁊ araill do ḋaoíniḃ uaisle cen mo ṫát. Ro ordaiġsiott na hard gaoiḋil sin .i. Ua néill, ⁊ ua domnaill a ccſnnas, ⁊ a nuaċtaranaċt sin dua Suilleḃán beirre .i. do ḋomnall mac domnaill mic diarmatta ar bá heiriḋe cſnnḟort cſnnais bá ḟſrr dia rannsom isin muṁain, ar ċeill ⁊ ar croḋaċt an tan sin.

An tſr lá do ṁí Ianuarii ro mſḃaiḋ an maiḋm sin for ġaoiḋealaiḃ.

AOIS CRIOST, 1602.

Aois Criost, Mile, Se céd, a dó.

Iar sraoinſḃ maḋma cinn tsáile lá gallaiḃ for gaoiḋealaiḃ (aṁail ro scrioḃaḋ ċſna) an tſr lá do ṁí Ianuarii, ⁊ for an uaṫaḋ Spáinnſċ do muintir ríġ na Spainne do rala a maille friú an tan sin, Ro ġaḃ dſinmne, ⁊ dásacht, ⁊ utmoille mór mſnman Ua domnaill (Aoḋ ruaḋ) co ná ro ċuil ⁊ ná ro loing hi saiṁe fri ré tri lá ⁊ teóra noiḋċe iaraṁ go ro bſn ceill dia ċaḃair i nerinn conaḋ í airle ro ċinn i nſcṁaing na ree sin (tre coṁairle uí néill gion gur ḃó lainn lairsiḋe a coṁairléċċaḋ dó) Ere dfaccḃáil, ⁊ dol don Spainn dionnsaiġiḋ an riġ an 3. Pilip do ċuinġiḋ fuilleaḋ soċraitte, ⁊ coṁḟurtaċta uaḋaiḃ, uair ro baḋ dóiġ lairsioṁ gur ḃó hé rí na Spainne aon ro baḋ mó conicfeaḋ a ḟóirithin, ⁊ lás ar lainne congnaṁ lás an ccáċ nó ċaṫaiġfeaḋ dar cſnn an ċſidiṁ catolice Róṁanaiġ do gres ⁊ araill ele tria na ḃáiḋ fri gaoiḋealaiḃ ar a ttoċt céttus do ġaḃáil Ereann as in Spainn aṁail as follas isin leaḃar dianiḋ ainm in leaḃar gaḃala.

O ro sgrúd soṁ an ċoṁairle ísin báttar iatt do raeġa soṁ ina ċaoímṫeaċt do ḋol for an ſctra sin, Remann a búrc mac Sſain, Captin aoḋ murr mac Robſrd, ⁊ flaiṫrí mac fiṫil uí ṁaoilċonaire aṫair togaiḋe

[x] *Hugh Mus.*—This is a mistake of the transcriber for Hugh Mustian or Mostyn.—See the *Pacata Hibernia*, book ii. c. xxii.

[y] *On the third day of the month of January.*—The Irish were defeated at Kinsale on the 24th of December, 1601, according to the old style then observed by the English, but on the 3rd of January, 1602, according to the Irish and

Roe), Redmond, the son of John Burke, and Captain Hugh Mus[x], the son of Robert, should go to Spain to complain of their distresses and difficulties to the King of Spain.

These chiefs left some of their neighbouring confederates in Munster, to plunder it in their absence, namely: Captain Tyrrell, the other sons of John Burke, and other gentlemen besides them. These high Irishmen, namely, O'Neill and O'Donnell, ordered that the chief command and leadership of these should be given to O'Sullevan Beare, i. e. Donnell, the son of Donnell, son of Dermot; for he was, at this time, the best commander among their allies in Munster, for wisdom and valour.

On the third day of the month of January[y] [1602] this overthrow was given to the Irish.

THE AGE OF CHRIST, 1602.

The Age of Christ, one thousand six hundred two.

After this defeat of Kinsale had been given by the English (as has been already written), on the third day of the month of January, to the Irish and the few Spaniards of the King of Spain's people who happened to be along with them at that time, O'Donnell (Hugh Roe) was seized with great fury, rage, and anxiety of mind; so that he did not sleep or rest soundly for the space of three days and three nights afterwards; so that he despaired of getting succour in Ireland. At the expiration of that time, the resolution he came to (by the advice of O'Neill, who, however, gave him this advice with reluctance), was, to leave Ireland, and go to Spain to King Philip III., to request more forces and succour from him; for he thought that the King of Spain was the person who could render him most relief, and who was the most willing to assist those who always fought in defence of the Roman Catholic religion; and, moreover, on account of his [Philip's] attachment to the Gaels, from their having first come out of Spain to invade Ireland, as is manifest from the Book of Invasions.

Having come to this resolution, the persons he selected to accompany him on this journey were: Redmond Burke, the son of John; Captain Hugh Mus [Mustian], son of Robert; and Flaithri, the son of Fithil O'Mulconry[z], a

Spaniards.

[z] *Flaithri, the son of Fithil O'Mulconry.*—He was a Franciscan friar, and, at this time, the Pope's Archbishop of Tuam. He was a very learned

durd .S. Fronses rob anmċara dósom, ⁊ araill dia ṡainṁuintir buḋéin cen mo ṫác. Iar ccloisteaċt na comairle sin lá cáċ a ccoitċinne ro baḋ lór do truaiġe ⁊ do neiṁéle an laṁċomairt anffoill, ⁊ an ġolṁairccneaċ dfsṁair, ⁊ an nuallġuḃa ardaccaointeach do rónaḋ seaċnóin lonġṗuirt uí doṁnaill an tan sin. Ro baḋ dfiṫḃir dóiḃsiom innsin (dia ffeasdaoís é an tan sin) uair ní ḟacattar a ccoḃnaċ náċ a ccoimsiġ talmanda an tan sin i ninis Eireann acc follaṁnuccaḋ flaiṫsa uairtiḃ ó sin alle.

Do ḋeachaiḋ imorra ua doṁnaill co na fiallaċ[a] i luing hi ccuan an ċaisléin[b] an 6. lá do ṁí Ianuarii, ⁊ ros iomluaiḋ tinfeḋ na céd ġaoiṫe dus fainicc tsiar an ffairrcce ffraoċ aiġṁéil go ro ġaḃsat cuan an 14. la don mis ceḋna i ccomḟoċraiḃ don ċruinne, baile oirdearc eiside hi ríoġaċt na galise isin spainn ⁊ bá hannsiḋe baoí tor breoġain frisa raiti brigantia ro cuṁdaċt feaċt riaṁ lá breoġan mac bráṫa, ⁊ bá hassaiḋe tangattar clann miliḋ Espáinne mic bile mic breoġain do céd gaḃail Eireann for ṫuathaiḃ de ḋanann. O do ruacht ua doṁnaill i ttír isin ccruinne ro gaḃ for tairtel an baile, ⁊ do ċóiḋ do ḋéġain tuir breoġain. Ḃá faoiliġ riom dia roċtain i ttír an dú sin ar ro baḋ dóiġ lais gur ḃó célṁaine ṁór maiṫsḃ dó a ṫoċar gus an maiġin as ar ġaḃsat a ṡinsir nert ⁊ cuṁaċta for Erinn feaċt riaṁ.

theologian; and, at his solicitation, Philip III. of Spain, founded in 1616 the College of St. Anthony of Padua, at Louvain, for Irish Franciscans.—See Harris's edition of Ware's *Irish Writers*, p. 110, and O'Reilly's *Descriptive Catalogue of Irish Writers*, p. 182.

[a] *Heroes.*—"fiallaċ .i. fianlaoċ no fuireann laoċ no ġaisgeadaċ."—*O'Clery.*

[b] *Cuan-an-chaislein:* i. e. the Haven or Harbour of the Castle, now Castlehaven harbour, near Castletownshend, in the south of the county of Cork. The editor of the *Pacata Hibernia* gives the following account of the reception of O'Donnell in Spain, from a letter found in the Castle of Dunboy, which was written on the 4th of February, 1602, new style, by Patrick Sinnot, an Irish priest remaining at the Groyne with the Earl of Caraçena, to Dominic Collins, a Jesuit.

"Sundry other things he related of Odonnel's landing in the Asturias, who, with the Generall Pedro de Zubiare, embarqued at Castlehaven the * * Ianuary; the next day after he came to the Groyne, where he was nobly received by the Earl of Caraçena, who invited Odonnell to lodge in his house; but hee, being Sea-sicke, in good manner refused his curtesie, wherefore, the Earle lodged him in a very faire house, not farre from his. But, when his sea-sicknesse was past, he lodged in the Earle's house; and upon the twenty-seventh of Ianuary Odonnell departed from the Groyne, accompanied by the Earle and many Captaines and Gentlemen of qualitie, who evermore gave Odonnell the right hand, which, within his government, he would not have done to the greatest Duke in Spaine; And, at his departure, he presented Odonnell with one thousand duckets, and that night hee

chosen father of the Franciscan order, who was his confessor; with others of his own faithful people besides them. When this resolution was heard by all in general, it was pitiful and mournful to hear the loud clapping of hands, the intense tearful moaning, and the loud-wailing lamentation, that prevailed throughout O'Donnell's camp at that time. They had reason for this, if they knew it at the time, for never afterwards did they behold, as ruler over them, him who was then their leader and earthly prince in the island of Erin.

On the sixth day of the month of January, O'Donnell, with his heroes[a], took shipping at Cuan-an-chaislein[b]; and, the breath of the first wind that rose wafting them over the boisterous ocean, they landed on the 14th of the same month in the harbour near Corunna[c], a celebrated city in the kingdom of Gallicia in Spain. And it was here stood the tower of Breogan[d], usually called Braganza, which had been erected in ancient times by Breogan, the son of Bratha, and from which the sons of Milesius, of Spain, the son of Bile, son of Breogan, had set out in their first invasion of Ireland, against the Tuatha-De-Dananns. When O'Donnell landed at Corunna, he walked through the town, and went to view Breogan's Tower. He was rejoiced to have landed at that place, for he deemed it to be an omen of good success that he had arrived at the place from whence his ancestor had formerly obtained power and sway over Ireland. After having

lay at Santa Lucia, the Earle of Caraçena being returned; the next day hee went to Saint James of Compostella, where he was received with magnificence by the Prelates, Citizens, and religious persons, and his lodging was made ready for him at Saint Martins, but before hee saw it hee visited the Archbishop, who instantly prayed him to lodge in his house, but Odonnell excused it; the nine and twentieth, the Archbishop saying Masse with pontificall solemnity, did minister the Sacrament to Odonnell, which done, he feasted him at dinner in his house, and at his departure hee gave him one thousand duckets. The King, understanding of Odonnell's arrival, wrote unto the Earle of Caraçena concerning the reception of him, and the affaires of Ireland, which was one of the most gracious Letters that ever King directed, for by it, it plainely appeared that hee would endanger his kingdome to succour the Catholikes of Ireland to their content, and not faile therein, for the perfecting whereof great preparations were in hand. Odonnell carried with him to the Court, Redmond Burke, Father Florence, Captaine Mostian, and nine Gentlemen more, where they were nobly received."—Book ii. c. xxvi.

[c] *Corunna*, a sea-port town of Gallicia, in Spain, at the mouth of the Groyne, about twenty miles south-west of Ferrol, and thirty-five north by east of Compostella.

[d] *Tower of Breogan.*—The rock on which this tower stood is now occupied by a pharos or lighthouse, parts of the interior of which are, according to Dr. Wilde, very ancient. For the account of the migration of the Scoti or Milesians from Breogan's Tower, or Braganza, in Gallicia, as

Iar mbs̃iṫ athaiḋ mbicc acc léccaḋ a sccísi isin ccruinne do ċóiḋ go hairm i mbaoi an rí isin Castilla uair ba hann do rala ḋó bs̃iṫ an tan sin (Iar niomṫoiċell a flaiṫs̃ra) isin ccaṫraig dianiḋ ainm Samora, ⁊ ó do deachaiḋ ó domnaill hi ffiaḋnaise in ríġ ro léicc for a ġluiniḃ é ina ḟrs̃cnairc, ⁊ do roine uṁla, ⁊ aiḋiḋe ḋó aṁail ro bá dú dia ṁiaḋuṁlaċt ⁊ ní ro ḟaoṁ eirġe co ro ṫingeall an ríġ a ṫeóra hitċe dó. Bá s̃ḋ an céḋna diḃsiḋe, Armail do ċor lais dionnsaiġiḋ Ereann co na ccongaiḃ comaḋais, ⁊ co na naiḋmiḃ teaċta cecip tan robdar erlaṁa. An dara, gan ns̃ċ do ṡaorclandaiḃ duaisle a ḟola do ċor in niort náċ hi ccuṁaċta uassa ná uas fior a ionait do ġrés dia ngaḃaḋ morḋaċt an ríġ ns̃rt ⁊ cuṁaċta for Erinn. An tres̃s ittċe gan ces̃rt a ṡinns̃r do laġduġaḋ, ná duirḃs̃rnaḋ fair fein nó for ḟior a ionaiḋ tre biṫe in gaċ maiġin i mbaoí ns̃rt, ⁊ cuṁaċta aga ṡinns̃raiḃ i nErinn riaṡ an tan sin.

Ro geallaitt innsin uile lás an Ríġ dósoṁ, ⁊ fuair airṁiḋin ṁór uaḋa naċ dóiġ go ffuair gaoiḋeal riaṁ i ndeireaḋ aimsire a coṁmór donóir ó náċ ríġ naile.

Iar ndénaṁ a ṫoscca aṁlaiḋ sin dua domnaill fris in ríġ, Ro ċuinniġ an rí fair soaḋ tar a ais don ċruinne ⁊ airisioṁ annsiḋe com bó fúiriṫe dó toċt ina frithing. Do róine sioṁ inn sin, ⁊ baoí hi ffoss go léicc go mí august ar ccionn. Bá cráḋ criḋe, ⁊ bá saoṫ ms̃nman lá hua ndomnaill a ḟod ro ḃáttar gaoiḋil gan furtaċt gan fóiriḋin uaḋa ⁊ rob imċian lais baoí an armáil ro geallaḋ ḋó gan roċtain go haon ṁaiġin, Ro triall dorisiḋisi do ḋol do laṫair an ríġ dia fios créd an ts̃ssnáḋaḋ nó an tiomḟuireaċ baoí for an soċraiḋe ro geallaḋ lais, ⁊ ó do ruaċt soṁ don ḃaile dianiḋ ainm Simancas (dá léicce o uallaḋolíḋ do ċuirt an ríġ) bá s̃ḋ do ḋeónuiġ dia, ⁊ do cs̃ḋaiġ a hainḟén ⁊ a hécconaċ, a missccaiṫ, ⁊ a mallaċt dinis éireṁóin, ⁊ do ġaoiḋelaiḃ glanḃanḃa arċs̃na go ro gaḃ galar a écca, ⁊ easláinte a

believed in Hugh Roe O'Donnell's time, the reader is referred to the *Leabhar Gabhala* of the O'Clerys, and Keating's *History of Ireland*, Haliday's edition, p. 261.

[e] *Samora:* i. e. Zamora, in the province of Castile. In the Life of Hugh Roe O'Donnell the reading is as follows:

"Do ċoiḋh co hairm a mbaoi an Riġ isin Caistilla, ar ba hann do rála do a beith an tan sin (iar ttimċeallaḋ a ḟlaiṫiusa)."

[f] *Had power and sway.*—The King of Spain could have hardly understood what Hugh Roe O'Donnell meant by this. Niall Garv O'Donnell shortly afterwards explained it fully to Sir Henry Docwra, who has written the following account of Niall's demands after he had got

rested himself for a short time at Corunna, he proceeded to the place where the King was, in [the province of] Castile, for it was there he happened to be at this time (after making a visitation of his kingdom), in the city which is called Samora[e]. And as soon as O'Donnell arrived in the presence of the King, he knelt down before him; and he made submission and obeisance unto him, as was due to his dignity, and did not consent to rise until the King promised [to grant] him his three requests. The first of these was, to send an army with him to Ireland, with suitable engines and necessary arms, whatever time they should be prepared. The second, that, should the King's Majesty obtain power and sway over Ireland, he would never place any of the nobles of his blood in power or authority over him or his successors. The third request was, not to lessen or diminish on himself or his successors for ever the right of his ancestors, in any place where his ancestors had power and sway[f] before that time in Ireland.

All these were promised him [to be complied with] by the King; and he received respect from him; and it is not probable that any Gael ever received in latter times so great an honour from any other king.

When O'Donnell had thus finished his business with the King, he was desired by the King to return back to Corunna, and remain there until every thing should be in readiness for his return [to Ireland]. This he did; and he remained there until the month of August following. It was anguish of heart and sickness of mind to O'Donnell that the Irish should remain so long without being aided or relieved by him; and, deeming it too long that the army which had been promised him had been without coming together to one place, he prepared to go again before the King, to know what it was that caused the retarding or delay [in the raising] of the army which he had promised; and when he arrived at the town which is called Simancas, two leagues from Valladolid, the King's Court, God permitted, and the misfortune, ill fate, wretchedness, and curse attending the Island of Heremon[g], and the Irish of fair Banba in general,

himself inaugurated at Kilmacrenan:

"Hee replied, that not onelie the Countrie of Tyrconnell, but Tyrone, Farmanagh, yea, and Connaught, wheresoever any of the O'Donnells had, at that time, extended their power, hee made accompte all was his; he acknowledged noe other kinde of right or interest in any man else, yea, the very persons of the people he challenged to be his."

[g] *The Island of Heremon.*—This is one of the many arbitrary bardic names for Ireland, and given it from Heremon, son of Milesius of Spain,

oiḋeḋa Ua Domhnaill, ⁊ baoí fri ré seacht la nDécc ina lighe co nerbail fó ḋeóiḋ ineacmaing na ree sin an 10. lá do September do ronnradh isin tigh baoí ag righ na Spáinne badhéin isin mbaile sin (Simancas) iar ccaoí a ċionadh, ⁊ a ṫargabhál, iar naitrighe dioċra ina peacċaibh ⁊ ḋoailcibh, iar ndenamh a ċoibsion gan dioloċt fri a anmċairdibh sprioradalltaibh iar ccaiṫeamh cuirp Ċriost, ⁊ a ḟola, ⁊ iar ná ongadh amhail ro badh teċta a lamhaibh a anmċarat, ⁊ a sruiṫeḋ sccalartaċḋa budhéin an tatair flaiṫri ua maolċonaire (confessóir, ⁊ comhairleaċ spiratalta ui ḋomhnaill, ⁊ rob airdespuc tuama iarttain cidh ar a los) ⁊ an taṫair muiris ullteaċ mac donnchaidh braṫair boċt durd S. Ffronseis a conueint mainistre duin na ngall, bá do longportaibh í ḋomhnaill eiside.

Ruccadh dna a ċorp go Ualladolíd (go cúirt an righ) hi cceiṫirriadh cumhdaċta go ndrongaibh dírimhe do Stata, do ċomhairle ⁊ do ġarda an righ ina uirṫimċeall go locrannaibh laramhnaibh, go rudrallaibh solusṫaibh do ċéir caomhalainn ar comhlaradh dá gaċ leiṫ de. Ro hadhnacht iaramh i mainistir S. Ffronseis isin ccapittil do ronnradh co miadhaċ mór onoraċ ionnas ar airmhidnighe ro hadhnacht aoin neach do ġaoidhelaibh riamh. Ro ceilebradh oifrinn ⁊ hymna iomdha, clairseċtail, ⁊ cantaice ceoilbinne do ráiṫ a anma, ⁊ ro gabhadh a écenairc amhail ro badh dir.

Mo nuar tra ro badh liaċ do soċhaidibh muiceṙċra an tí testa annsin ar bá heside cenne coinne ⁊ comhairle áṫcomhairc, ⁊ iomagallmha ermhóir gaoidhel ereann cidh fri síḋ cidh fri coccadh. Tigearna toṫaċtaċ toirbeartaċ go fforrmalta flaṫa, ⁊ co ndluṫuccadh reaċta, leó ar neart, ⁊ cumhaċta go ttomhaiṫem ⁊ co fforrprraic i ngníomh, hi mbreitir, co ná lamhṫa a urtuaraċt itir, ar bá hescen cecib ní nó forċongradh do denamh rair fó ċedóir amhail adbeiread a beoil. Colum ar ċennsa, ⁊ ar ailgine fri ndimhed, eccalsa, ⁊ ealadhan, ⁊ fri gaċ naon ná friṫ tairisedh frirr ⁊ ro badh riaraċ dó. Fer ro ding a ómhan ⁊ a imeccla ar ċách a ccéin ⁊ a fforcus, ⁊ for nár lá náċ aon imeccla itir. Tighearna dioċuirṫe díbearccaċ, mudhaighṫe meirleaċ, mórṫa mac mbethadh ⁊

the first sole monarch of Ireland of the Scotic or Milesian race.

[h] *Seventeen days.*—The original is here redundant and very clumsy, and the Editor has been obliged to deviate a little from the original construction.

[i] *Requiem.*—"Eagnairc .i. impiḋe."—H. 3. 18, p. 539. "Ecenairc .i. guiḋe Dé."—*O'Clery.* The text is copied almost word for word from Cucogry O'Clery's Life of Hugh Roe O'Donnell.

would have it, that O'Donnell should take the disease of his death and the sickness of his dissolution; and, after lying seventeen days[h] on the bed, he died, on the 10th of September, in the house which the King of Spain himself had at that town (Simancas), after lamenting his crimes and transgressions, after a rigid penance for his sins and iniquities, after making his confession without reserve to his confessors, and receiving the body and blood of Christ, and after being duly anointed by the hands of his own confessors and ecclesiastical attendants: Father Flaithri O'Mulconry (then confessor and spiritual adviser to O'Donnell, and afterwards Archbishop of Tuam on that account), and Father Maurice Ultach [Donlevy], the son of Donough, a poor friar of the order of St. Francis, from the convent of the monastery of [the town of] Donegal, which was one of O'Donnell's fortresses.

His body was conveyed to the King's palace at Valladolid in a four-wheeled hearse, surrounded by countless numbers of the King's state officers, Council, and guards, with luminous torches and bright flambeaux of beautiful wax-light burning on each side of him. He was afterwards interred in the monastery of St. Francis, in the Chapter precisely, with veneration and honour, and in the most solemn manner that any of the Gaels had been ever interred in before. Masses, and many hymns, chaunts, and melodious canticles, were celebrated for the welfare of his soul; and his requiem[i] was sung with becoming solemnity.

Alas! the early eclipse[k] of him who died here was mournful to many; for he was the head of the conference and counsel, of advice and consultation, of the greater number of the Irish, as well in peace as in war. He was a mighty and bounteous lord, with the authority of a prince to enforce the law; a lion in strength and force, with determination and force of character in deed and word[l], so that he durst not at all be disobeyed, for whatever he ordered to be done should be immediately executed, accordingly as he directed by his words; a dove in meekness and gentleness towards the Nemeds, the clergy, and the literati, and towards every one who had not incurred his displeasure, and who submitted to his authority; a man who had impressed the dread and terror of himself upon all persons, far and near, and whom no man could terrify; a lord, the expeller of rebels, the destroyer of robbers, the exalter of the sons of life,

[k] *Eclipse.*—"Erċra .ı. *eclipsis.*"—*Cormac's Glossary.*

[l] *In deed and word.*—Cucogry O'Clery states that Hugh Roe was "a Cæsar in command."

riaġṫa ṁac mbáis, neaċ ná ro léicc a ḟairbriġ, ná a iomarcraiḋ a ḋiúbairt na a ḋimiaḋ gan a aiṫe ⁊ gan a ḋioġail gan ḟuireaċ. Imeaċtraiḋ aindiuid aṁnas, andána na noirſir, Airccṫeoir coġṫaċ creaċaċ, coinġlſcaċ na ccoiccríoċ, diosgaoilteaċ, dian, dſinmnſtach dúr doċoiscc gall, ⁊ gaoiḋel báttar ina acchaiḋ, aon ná ro léicc ḋe gan dénaṁ gaċ ní ro baḋ toisccide do ḟlaiṫ an ccſin ro ṁair. Buaḃall bionnglorac go mbuaiḋ ninnscne ⁊ nurlaḃra, ceille, ⁊ coṁairle, go ttaidḃrſḋ seirce ina ḋreiċ attar lá gaċ aen at as cíoḋ, tairrngeartaċ tingealltaċ ro ḟiortiorcanaḋ lá ḟáidiḃ ré ċian ria na ġein, ⁊ co sainrſḃach las an naoiṁ éplaṁ Colaim cille mac ḟeilim dia nébairt

Ticfa ḟſr an énga aird,
do béra golmairec in gaċ tír,
buḋ é sin an donn diaḋa,
is biaḋ .x. mbliaḋna na ríġ.

Bá tróġ tra ro bás ag gaoiḋealaiḃ ereann iar nécc uí doṁnaill, doiġ ro ċlaoċlaisiot a nairrḋe ⁊ a naigſnta, oir do rattsat a milſttaċt ar mioḋlaċar, móirṁſnma ar ṁſirtniġe, ⁊ uallċa ar insle. Ro sgaiṫ a ngráin, a ngaiscceaḋ, a ngal, a ngérraiteaċt, a ccosgar, ⁊ a ccaṫḃuaiḋ iar ná oiḋeaḋ, Tallsatt céill dia ccaḃair gur bó hſigſn dia nurṁór dol for ioċt eccrat, ⁊ ainffine, ⁊ araill ele for eisrſiḋeaḋ ⁊ for sgaoileaḋ, ní nama ar ḟud Ereann, act seaċnóin na ccſnnaḋaċ go coitċſnd ina naittreabṫaċaiḃ boċta dinnime dearoile, ⁊ drong ele ag creic a naṁsaine lá hſċtar ċenelaiḃ go ro marḃaitt, ⁊ go ro muḋhaiġitt drecta dearṁara do ṡaorclandaiḃ soiċenelċoibh ḟſr nereann i naile crioċaiḃ cianiḃ coṁaiġṫiḃ, ⁊ ro baḋ áḋḃa aineoil ⁊ ſccalsa andúċcasa robtar Róṁa adnaicṫe dóiḃ, ar aba écca an aoín ḟir sin do érna uaḋaiḃ. Act ċſna ro baḋ eiṁilt, ⁊ ro baḋ dioċuṁaing ríoṁ nó airnéis do na mór olcaiḃ ro ḟíolaiḋh, ⁊ ro ḟíorclandaiġ i ninis Ereann a los écca aoḋa ruaiḋ uí doṁnaill an tan sin.

Iar Sccaoileaḋ do ġaoiḋelaiḃ iar maiḋm chinn tSaile aṁail reṁebertmar ro ċuir an Iustis an Presidens, Iarla tuadmuṁan, ⁊ Iarla cloinne riocaird

[m] *Dispersed.*—See Moryson's *History of Ireland*, book ii. c. ii., edition of 1735, pp. 62, 68. Don Juan vehemently exclaimed against the cowardice and barbarity of the Irish on this occasion; and in his first conference with Sir William Godolphin, he pronounced them to be "not only weak and barbarous, but, as he feared, perfidious friends." But whoever will examine the history of this General will find that he was totally unfit and insufficient for the enterprise

the executioner of the sons of death; a man who never suffered any injury or injustice, contempt or insult, offered him, to remain unrevenged or unatoned for, but took vengeance without delay; a determined, fierce, and bold invader of districts; a warlike, predatory, and pugnacious plunderer of distant territories; the vehement, vigorous, stern, and irresistible destroyer of his English and Irish opposers; one who never in his life neglected to do whatever was desirable for a prince; a sweet-sounding trumpet; endowed with the gift of eloquence and address, of sense and counsel, and with the look of amiability in his countenance, which captivated every one who beheld him; a promised and prophesied one, who had been truly predicted by prophets a long time before his birth, and particularly by the holy patron, Columbkille, the son of Felim, who said of him:

> A noble, pure, exalted man shall come,
> Who shall cause mournful weeping in every territory.
> He will be the pious Don,
> And will be ten years King.

Pitiable, indeed, was the state of the Gaels of Ireland after the death of O'Donnell; for their characteristics and dispositions were changed; for they exchanged their bravery for cowardice, their magnanimity for weakness, their pride for servility; their success, valour, prowess, heroism, exultation, and military glory, vanished after his death. They despaired of relief, so that the most of them were obliged to seek aid and refuge from enemies and strangers, while others were scattered and dispersed, not only throughout Ireland, but throughout foreign countries, as poor, indigent, helpless paupers; and others were offering themselves for hire as soldiers to foreigners; so that countless numbers of the freeborn nobles of Ireland were slain in distant foreign countries, and were buried in strange places and unhereditary churches, in consequence of the death of this one man who departed from them. In a word, it would be tedious and impossible to enumerate or describe the great evils which sprang and took permanent root at that time in Ireland from the death of Hugh Roe O'Donnell.

When the Irish had dispersed[m], after the defeat at Kinsale, as we have before mentioned, the Lord Justice, the President, the Earl of Thomond, and

he had undertaken. He had previously commanded a Spanish force in Bretagne (A. D. 1594), and is charged, by the historian Davila, with having allowed the French and English to cap-

go maithiḃ an tslóiġ gall airċēna rēmpa, cēnntsaile dionnsaiġiḋ ⁊ dol trias na doirsiḃ dogaḃala ⁊ trias na beilgiḃ bernbristte do rónaḋ las an ordanas nallmurḋa naḋḃal ṁór baoí leó acc caiṫēm, ⁊ ag comḋiuḃraccaḋ an ḃaile ón céd ló ro ṡuiḋiġsiot campa for a ionċaiḃ gus an laiṫe sin. Do ċualaiġ donn Iohn an ní sin, ⁊ ó ro ḟioir na gaoiḋil gus a riaċt, ⁊ ro baḋ dóiġ lais dia ċaḃair do comṡgaoíleaḋ uaḋ ⁊ a fagḃáil isin ionaḋ iomċuṁang, ⁊ isin ccarcair comḋluta i mbaoí, ⁊ ná baoí for cumas dó sóaḋ for ccúlaiḃ go a ċairdiḃ, na ḋola ar a aghaiḋ for a sēccairttiḃ ar a naiḋḃle, ⁊ ar a niolarḋaċt, ⁊ ar feaḃus a nimdēgla, ⁊ a niomċoiṁéda do ló ⁊ daḋhaiġ, arí comairle ro ċinn teaċta do ċor uaḋa hi ccēnn an Iustis, an Presidens, Iarla cloinne riocaird, ⁊ Iarla tuaḋṁuman go maithiḃ an tslóiġ dia ráḋa riú go ttiocfaḋ for ionċaiḃ an Iustis ⁊ na ttiġearnaḋ sin, act namá an baile do léccaḋ da ṁuinntir go féil Patraicc ar ccionn, cēd dola ⁊ teaċta isteaċ ⁊

ture Morlaix and Quimper, without making any able effort to relieve them; and the same writer states, that at Crodon, a fort which defended the mouth of Brest harbour, after exposing a brave garrison to destruction, through cowardice and incompetence, he yielded that most important position which he had ample means to defend. The late Mathew O'Conor, in his *Military Memoirs of the Irish Nation*, censures Don Juan for landing an army in the south to assist in a war whose principal seat was in the north; and this charge is well-founded, if we can rely on the documents published in the *Pacata Hibernia*, book iii. c. xxv., for it appears from the examination of Richard Owen, who had been servant to O'Neill, and who afterwards went out of Ireland with Sir William Stanley, that O'Neill and O'Donnell sent letters to King Philip III., the contents of which were "to pray Aides to subsist the warre, according to the promise made by the old King; that if the Aides were sent for Vlster, then Tyrone required but fower or five thousand men; if the King did purpose to send an Army into Mounster, then he should send strongly, because neither Tyrone nor Odonnell could come to help them."

Before Don Juan embarked for Spain, a kind of affectionate friendship appears to have grown up between him and Carew, President of Munster, arising principally from the contempt which both entertained for the Irish. After Don Juan's arrival in Spain he sent Carew a present in "wines of Ripadavia, Limmons, and Oranges," accompanied by a most friendly letter, which the cautious President forwarded to the Lords of the Council in England, who authorized him both to write to Don Juan, and to send him a present in return, if he were so disposed. Carew wrote him a polite letter, and a present of an "ambling hackney." The concluding part of this letter runs as follows:

"And whensoever your Lordship shall have occasion to send any of yours into these parts, hee shall bee vsed with the like courtesie. I haue received profit by the booke of fortification which your Lordship left me at your departure, and hold it as a Relique in memory of you; and, as a good Scholler, I haue put some things in practise, whereof your Lordship, at your returne hither againe (which I hope in God will be never), may be a witnesse whether I have committed any error in the art or no.

the Earl of Clanrickard, with the chiefs of the English army in general, resolved to attack Kinsale, and to force their way through the fast gates, and through the shattered breaches which they had made by the great foreign ordnance which they had with them, firing and playing upon the town from the time they had pitched their camp before it to that day. As soon as Don Juan heard of this thing, and when he learned that the Irish, to whom he had come, and who, he thought, would have relieved him, were dispersed from him, and that he was left in the narrow place and blockaded prison in which he was, and that it was not in his power to return back to his friends or to go forth against his enemies, on account of their vastness and numerousness, and on account of the goodness of their defence and watching by day and night, the resolution he came to was, to send messengers to the Lord Justice, the President, and the Earl of Clanrickard, and the Earl of Thomond, and the [other] chiefs of the army, to state to them that he would surrender to the Lord Justice and these lords, if only they would allow his people to remain in the town until Patrick's Day following, and to give liberty to his people and to the people of the Queen

My greatest defect hath beene the want of the helpe of so great a Master as your Lordship is, of whom I am desirous to learne, not onely that art, but in all else concerning the military profession, in which I doe give your Lordship the preheminence. To conclude, I rest in all I may (my dutie reserved to the Queene, my mistress,) affectionately ready at your Lordship's service, and so, kissing your hands, I beseech God to preserve you many happy yeares."

This present and letter he sent, under a cautious disguise, in a small barque, laden with Irish commodities, by Walter Edney, lieutenant to Captain Harvey, and who had a son living in Spain. The following account of his adventure, and of the treatment of Don Juan shortly after his return to Spain, as printed in the *Pacata Hibernia* (*ubi supra*), shews that the King of Spain was not satisfied with the services he had performed in Ireland.

"Although Queene Elizabeth, of happy memory, was dead before Lieutenant Edney returned, yet I hold it not impertinent, in this place, to recount his successes. When he was landed at the Groyne, hee understood that Don Iuan de Aguila, by the accusation of the Irish fugitives, was in disgrace, confined to his house, where (of grief) shortly after he dyed. His [Edney's] Letters and Pasports were taken from him by the Earle of Carazena, and sent to the Court, and himselfe stayed untill the King's pleasure was knowen. The Irish Traytors inveighed much against him, saying, that under pretext of Trade, and bringing of presents, hee came as a spie. Neverthelesse, he was well intreated, and had the libertie of the Towne, and to weare his sword, with allowance from the King of a Ducat per diem, for his dyet. His goods were sold for the best advantage, and his Barque returned into Ireland; but the President's present to Don Iuan the Earle of Carazena detayned to his owne use, and after nine moneths restraint, Edney was enlarged, and returned into England in Iuly, 1603."—*Edition of* 1810, book iii. c. xii. p. 625.

amaċ aga muintir féin, ⁊ ag muintir na bainrioghna i ccumascc araile, ⁊ dna cétt malarta a nairgitt ⁊ a nérraḋ, ⁊ gaċ néiṫ rangattar alés. Dia tticceaḋ furtaċt no caḃair o ríġ na Spainne dia saiġiḋ in aisṫe sin, driachaiḃ ar an Iustis donn Iohn do léiccén iomlán i mesce a ṁuinntire, ⁊ muna tticceaḋ, an Iustis ⁊ na tiġearnada sin dia iodlacaḋ tar a ais don Spainn, ⁊ donn Iohn do iodlacaḋ an loingis do raċaḋ lais ina niomláine go hErinn do riḋise.

Ro héistéḋ aitésce na tteaċtaḋ las an Iustis ⁊ las na maiṫiḃ arċeana ⁊ ro haontaiġéḋ dóiḃ aṁail ro cuinniġsiot. Iar naiḋm ⁊ iar narsccaḋ a ccoingeall dóiḃ diḃlinib tánaicc donn Ion hi ccénn an Iustis, ⁊ ro fiadaiġeaḋ go honoraċ é lás an Iustis, ⁊ las na maiṫiḃ báttar ina ḟarraḋ. Do ṫaod an Iustis an Presidens, ⁊ donn Iohn go Corcaiġ, ⁊ do sgaoílsiot caċ dia ttiġiḃ ar a haiṫle.

Imṫusa Iarla Tuadhmuman tanaic siḋe dia tir iar mbéiṫ aṫaiḋ ḟoda ina héccṁais hi Saxoiḃ, ⁊ hi ccampa Ċinntsaile, ⁊ níor bó cian ro ḃaoí hi ffos iar roċtain dó dia duthaiġ an tan ro ionnsaiġ na daoíne uaisle ro baoi ag aiḋmilléḋ, ⁊ ac lot a tíre, o ro clos leó donn Ion do toċt i nÉrinn gus an uair sin. Ro baḋ diobsiḋe Toirrḋealḃaċ, mac Maṫġaṁna, mic Toirrḋealḃaiġ, mic Maṫġaṁna Uí Briain, ⁊ Conċoḃar mac Doṁnaill mic Maṫġaṁna mic Briain Uí Ḃriain. Bá heigin ḋoiḃsiḋe na bailte baoi ina norlaiṁ gus a ttairrngeḋis cuid aittreabṫaċ, ⁊ aesa anffainn an tire dia saiġiḋ (.i. Doire Eoġain ⁊ Baile an Ċaisléin) da ċor in orlaiṁ ḋaoíne ccoṁṫrom lás nár lainn lot tíre inntiḃ no eistiḃ. Do rattaḋ focal, ⁊ cairde caictiḋisi ón Iarla ḋoiḃsiom le ceileaḃraḋ dá ccairttiḃ, ⁊ leis an tir dfagḃáil, ⁊ gan soaḋ tar a nais dorisi gan céd an Iustis ⁊ na coṁairle.

Dála na ndaoine uasal riasiu ro ċaiṫsiot disréḋ a ffocail ro triallsat

[a] *Among his people.*—This is a mistake. The Lord Deputy Mountjoy consented to no such condition, nor did Don Juan seek it. The Articles of Composition made on this occasion, between the Lord Deputy and Council and Don Juan De Aguila, are printed in the *Pacata Hibernia*, book ii. c. xxiii. The first article was: "That the said Don Iuan de Aquila should quit the places which he holds in this Kingdome, as well of the Towne of Kinsale as those which are held by the Souldiers under his command in Castlehaven, Baltimore, and the Castle of Beere-haven, and other parts, to the said Lord Deputie, or to whom he shall appoynt, giving him safe transportation (and sufficient) for the said people, of ships and victualls, with the which the said Don Iuan with them may go for Spaine, if he can at one time, if not, in two shippings."

The second article was: "That the Souldiers, at this present, being under the command of

to pass in and out, and mingle with each other; and also liberty to exchange money and wares for anything they required; that if relief or assistance should in the mean time come to him from the King of Spain, the Lord Justice should be bound to let Don Juan at large among his people[n]; that if no relief should arrive, that the Lord Justice and these lords should convey him and his people to Spain: Don Juan engaging to return back safe to Ireland the fleet that should be sent with him.

The proposals of the envoys were hearkened to by the Lord Justice and chiefs in general, and their requests were acceded to; and when their conditions were ratified and confirmed by both [parties], Don Juan came to the Lord Justice, and was honourably received by him and the other chiefs who were along with him. The Lord Justice, the President, and Don Juan, went to Cork, and all afterwards dispersed for their respective homes.

As for the Earl of Thomond, he returned to his territory after having been a long time away from it in England and in the camp at Kinsale; and he was not long at rest after arriving in his patrimony when he attacked the gentlemen who had been plundering and destroying his territory since they had heard of the arrival of Don Juan till that hour. Among these were Turlough, the son of Mahon, son of Turlough, son of Mahon O'Brien, and Conor, the son of Donnell, son of Mahon, son of Brian O'Brien. These were compelled to deliver up the castles which they had in their possession, and into which they had carried to them the property of the inhabitants and helpless people of the territory, namely, Derryowen and Baile-an-Chaislein[o], into the custody of just men, who did not wish to plunder the country by means of them[p]. A fortnight's parole and respite was given them by the Earl, that they might bid farewell to their friends [and prepare] to quit the country, to which they were not to return without the permission of the Lord Justice and the Council.

As for the gentlemen, before the expiration of their parole, they prepared

Don Iuan, in this Kingdome, shall not beare Armes against her Majestie, the Queene of England, wheresoever supplyes shall come from Spaine, till the said Souldiers be unshipped in some of the ports of Spaine, being dispatched (as soone as may be) by the Lord Deputy, as he promiseth upon his Faith and Honour."—See also Moryson, book ii. c. ii. vol. ii. p. 62.

[o] *Baile-an-Chaislein*, now Castletown, in a townland of the same name, in the parish of Dury, not far from the town of Ennis, in the county of Clare.

[p] *By means of them*, literally, "into them, or out of them."

an tír dfaġbáil, ⁊ lottar tré cloinn Cuiléin go rangadar Cill Da lua, assaiḋe tar Sionainn go hara, ⁊ ro triallsat airisioṁ na hoiḋċe sin do denaṁ i nDúṫaiġ ara. Ot ċualattar clann Toirrḋealbaiġ Carraiġ mic Toirrḋealbaiġ, mic Muirċeartaiġ mic Domhnaill, mic Taidcc uí Ḃriain .i. Donnchaḋ ⁊ Domhnall báttar acc iomsút a huċt na bainrioġna) iadsoṁ do ṫoċt don tír amail tangattar, iar ndeiliuccaḋ ré focal an Iarla, ⁊ gan focal an ṗrionnsa, nó aoín nfiċ eile aca, Ro ionnsaiġsiott iatt in gaċ maiġin i mbáttar go ro herġabaitt leó, cen mo tá Toirrḋealbaċ mac Maṫġaṁna uí Ḃriain do ċóiḋ iar ttoċaiṫeṁ a sroinne fó ċoilltiḃ clutair diaṁra, ⁊ fó ċnocaiḃ cenngarḃa dia imḋídean for a easccairdiḃ. Atiad na maiṫe ro gabaḋ annsiḋe, Concobar mac Domhnaill, mic Maṫġaṁna uí Ḃriain, Ḃrian ballaċ mac Maṫġaṁna ⁊ Tadcc ulltaċ mac Maṫġaṁna uí Ḃriain gus an líon do rala ina ffoċair, ⁊ iar na ngaḃáil tuccaḋ hi ccuimreaċ iad tar a nais hi ccenn an Iarla go Cill dá lua, ⁊ ro crochaḋ iatt ina ccúpladaiḃ is na crannaiḃ bá coiṁnesa dóiḃ aġaiḋ i naghaiḋ.

Iar sccaoileaḋ ⁊ iar mbásuccaḋ na ndaoíne uasal, ⁊ na ffoġlaḋ sin lás an Iarla do ċóiḋ go Luimneaċ, ⁊ assiḋe go Corcaiġ hi ccenn an Iustis. Ro foṙċongair an Iustis for an Iarla dol go Béirre go ttriḃ míliḃ saiġdiúir a maille fris, dus an ccaoṁsaḋ ammus do ṫabairt ar Ua Suillebáin mBeirre, ⁊ ar na daoiniḃ uaisle báttar ina farradh .i. drong do ṡíol cCarṫaiġ, Captin tirial, Mac Muiris Ciarraiġe O Concobair, ⁊ Ridire an Ġlenna. Ni ṫard an tIarla i neislis an forċongra sin, aċt luiḋ reiṁe gan anaḋ gan airisioṁ go rainicc mainistir Ḃendtraiġe i nDúṫaiġ cloinne Eoġain uí Ṡuillebáin. Báttar clann Eoccáin ag congnaṁ las an Iarla i naġaiḋ uí Suillebáin dóiġ do ḃeith Ó Suillebáin Dún Baoí ⁊ Berre dia naṫairrioṁ do ḃrisiṫ na coṁairle toir ⁊ a bus, ⁊ baoí aga rádha gur bó dó ro baḋ dleaċt cíos dfaġbáil i mBendtraiġe.

Bá sé ionad a raibe o Suillebán co na ṡlóġ an tan sin ag cenn an ġabair

[q] *Nearest trees*, literally, "the nearest trees to them."

[r] *Three thousand soldiers.*—This number is exaggerated, and the Irish had it from common report only.—See the *Pacata Hibernia*, book iii, c. ii., where the true number is given.

"To make tryall whether the Rebels in the Countrey of Carbery would submit themselves upon the sight of an Army, having beene lately wasted and spoyled by the Garrissons at Baltimore, Castlehaven, and Bantry, upon the ninth of March (which was the day the Lord Deputy departed from Corke) the President directed the Earle of Thomond, with two thousand and five hundred Foote in List (which were, by the Pole, but twelve hundred Foote and fiftie Horse)

to quit the country, and proceeded through Clann-Cuilein until they arrived at Killaloe; from thence across the Shannon into Ara; and they prepared to make a stay for that night in Duhara. When the sons of Turlough Carragh, son of Turlough, son of Murtough, son of Donnell, son of Teige O'Brien, namely, Donough and Donnell, who were acting in behalf of the Queen, heard that they had arrived in that manner in the territory, after the expiration of the period of the word of the Earl, and not having the word of the Sovereign or any one else, they attacked them in every place where they were, and made prisoners of them [all], except Turlough, the son of Mahon O'Brien, who, after he had taken his dinner, had betaken himself to the shady, solitary woods, and the rough-headed hills, to shelter himself from his enemies. These were the chieftains who were there taken: Conor, the son of Donnell, son of Mahon O'Brien, Brian Ballagh, the son of Mahon, and Teige Ultagh, the son of Mahon O'Brien, with the number [of forces] that happened to be along with them. And when taken they were sent back in fetters to the Earl to Killaloe, and they were hanged in pairs, face to face, from the nearest trees[q].

After the dispersion and execution of these gentlemen and plunderers by the Earl, he went to Limerick, and from thence to Cork, to the Lord Justice. The Lord Justice ordered the Earl to proceed to Beare, with three thousand soldiers[r], to see if he could [advantageously] make an attack upon O'Sullivan Beare and the gentlemen who were with him, namely, a party of the Mac Carthys, Captain Tyrrell, Mac Maurice of Kerry, O'Conor [Kerry], and the Knight of Glin. The Earl did not neglect this order; and[s] he passed forward, without halting or delaying, until he arrived at the monastery of Bantry, in the territory of the sons of Owen O'Sullivan. The sons of Owen were assisting the Earl against O'Sullivan, because the O'Sullivan had taken Dun-Baoi and Beare from their father by the decision of the Council beyond and here[t], and was accustomed to say that he should by right receive the rents of Bantry.

The place at which O'Sullivan and his forces were at this time [stationed]

to march into Carbery, and from thence into Beare, there to view in what manner the Castle of Donboy was fortified, of the incredible strength whereof much was noysed."

[s] *And:* literally, "but," which is not correct language.

[t] *Beyond and here:* i.e. the English and Irish councils.

etir an armáil don taoiḃ sin, ⁊ dol isteaċ go Bérre. Ionaḋ eisiḋe baoí ina ċonair ċoitċinn do ḋol isin tír, ⁊ baoí aiṁréiḋ iomċuṁang lé gaḃáil triṫe darmail ṁóir na bainrioġna, gion go mbſiṫ gſrrṫa coilleaḋ, ⁊ talṁan, daoíne, ordanás, ⁊ armáil suiḋiġṫe for a ccionn aṁail ro ḃaoí an tan sin do gaḃáil na conaire forra. Ḃaoí an tiarla i ngar do ṡſcṫṁain i mainistir Ḃſndtraiġe, ⁊ coinne etir é féin ⁊ o Suilleḃáin, ⁊ ó náċ rangattar i ngar dia roile, ⁊ nár bursa don iarla ná don armáil in tslige iomċuṁang sin damas nó dionnsaiġiḋ, do ḟágaiḃ an tiarla gararún saiġdiúiriḋ i noilén Faoít ré haghaiḋ uí Suilleḃáin, ⁊ do ċóiḋ fſin tar a ais go Corcaiġ hi ccſnn an lustis.

Taḋcc caoċ mac Toirrḋealḃaiġ mic Briain, mic Donnchaiḋ mec Maṫġaṁna do ṁarḃaḋ go tſccṁaiseaċ durċor peileir lá a ṁac fſin i mBérre a mí Maii na bliaḋna so. Ḃá hamlaiḋ do rónaḋ an marḃaḋ sin. An Presidenτ, ⁊ iarla Tuaḋmuṁan, ⁊ an gobernóir ciarraiġeaċ .i. Sir Serlus uelment ⁊ tiġearnaiḋe na Muṁan doneoċ ḃaoí ḋíoḃ ag congnaṁ lás an bprionnsa do ṫaḃairt a naiġṫe uile ar Ḃérre, ⁊ ar Ua Suilleḃáin. Tarla do Ṫaḋcc caoċ gur ḃſn ré long cſndaiġe amaċ ar an ffairrge siar an tan sin. Ro iarr ó Suilleḃáin iaraċt na luinge sin ar Ṫaḋġ dia cur don Spainn do ċuingiḋ caḃra ar ríġ na

[u] *Ceim-an-ghabhair:* i. e. the Goat's Pass, now Keamagower, *alias* Cromwell's Bridge, in the parish of Kilcaskin, over which was the common passage into the barony of Beare, in the west of the county of Cork. According to the tradition in the country, O'Donovan was at strife with O'Sullevan Beare on this occasion, and had some fighting with him at this place. This tradition is confirmed by the following account of O'Sullevan's movements after the defeat of the Irish at Kinsale, given by P. O'Sullevan Beare, in his *Hist. Cathol. Iber. Compend.*, tom. 3, lib. 7, c. i.:

"Post fœdus Aquilæ Osulleuanus in Hispaniam mittit Dermysium Odriscolem probatæ fidei, & prudentiæ virum celerem opem rogatum, & Danielem filium suum natu maximum paternæ fidei pignus, & obsidem. Quibus cum vnâ ego, quoque puer, & alij iuuenes nobiles venientes á Carazenæ Comite Galletiæ præfecto viro vetusta nobilitate claro, & in Ibernicam gentem maximè pio honorificentissimè sumus excepti. Vbi ego Patritio Sinoto populari meo Grammatico, & Rhetorico polito, & limato latinæ linguæ, Rotherico Vendanna Hispano ingenij acutissimi Philosophiæ, sed alijs aliarum doctrinarum præceptoribus sum vsus. Interim Osulleuanus omni ratione, & studio conandum putauit, vt vsque ad Hispani auxilij aduentum se, & eos, quos ad Hispanorum partes sequendas mouerat, ab hostis impetu defenderet. Ei auxilium ferunt Daniel Maccarrha Clancarrhæ principis filius, Daniel Osulleuani Magni filius, Cornelius, & Dermysius Odriscolis Magni filij, Dermysius Osulleuanus pater meus, Dermysius, duo Dionysij, & Florentius Maccarrhæ Fusci, equites Macsuinnij, Dionysius Odriscol cum suis fratribus. Ad eum confugiunt Oconchur Kierrius, Macmoris Lacsnaæ Baro, eques Auratus Kierrius, eques Auratus vallis, Iohannes Giraldinus Comitis frater, Iaimus Buttlerus Baronis Catharæ frater superiore bello suis possessionibus

was at Ceim-an-ghabhair[u], between the army on that side and the entrance into Beare. This place was the common pass into the territory, and it was intricate and narrow to be passed through by this large army of the Queen, even should there be no trees felled, or trenches sunk in the earth, or no men, ordnance, or army planted there against them, as indeed there was at that time to defend the pass against them. The Earl remained nearly a week in the monastery of Bantry, a conference being [expected] between him and O'Sullivan; but as they did not come near each other, because it was not easy for the Earl, or the army, to attack or force this narrow pass, he left a garrison of soldiers in Oilen-Faoit[w], to oppose O'Sullivan, and went back himself to Cork to the Lord Justice.

Teige Caech, the son of Turlough, son of Brian, son of Donough Mac Mahon, was accidentally killed with the shot of a ball by his own son, in Beare, in the month of May of this year. This death occurred in the following manner: the President, the Earl of Thomond, the Governor of Kerry, i. e. Sir Charles Wilmot, and such of the lords of Munster as were aiding the Sovereign, turned their faces against Beare and O'Sullivan. Before this time Teige Caech happened to have captured a merchant's ship at sea; [and] O'Sullivan asked him for a loan of that ship, to send it to Spain, to ask assistance from the

eiecti. Osulleuanus Gulielmo Burko, Richardo Tirello, & alijs conductis, obæratorum delectu conscripto & sociorum auxilijs millia militum circiter duo iuuentutis electæ comparat. Quibus ea hyeme Torrentirupem arcem, quam solam in Beantria tenebat Eugenius O'Sulleuanus semper Reginæ partes secutus, partim aggere, turribus, vineis, musculis, pluteis oppugnatam, partim æneis tormentis quassatam in suam potestatem redegit. Odonnobhanum" [O'Ꝺonnaḃáın, nunc *anglice* O'Donovan], "ad Anglos reuersum, & alios Anglorum auxiliares deprædatur. Regias copias, quæ in Momonijs erant, terrore perculsas in oppida munita, & arces compellit."

[w] *Oilen-Faoit:* called *Fuidia insula* by Philip O'Sullevan Beare—(*Hist. Cathol. Iber.*, fol. 182). It is now called Whiddy Island, and is situated in the east side of Bantry Bay, about three miles west of the town of Bantry. It is a beautiful island belonging to the parish of Kilmacommoge and barony of Bantry. The following notice of this event is given in the *Pacata Hibernia:*

"Heerupon the Earle lefte with Captaine George Flower, besides his owne Company, the Companies of Sir John Dowdall, the Lord Barry, Captain Francis Kingsmill, Captain Bustock, and Captaine Bradbury, which were seven hundred men in List, in the Whiddy (an Iland lying within the Bay of Bantrie), very convenient for the Service, and himself with the rest of his Forces returned to Corke, where, having made a relation of the particulars of his journey, it was found necessary that the President, without any protractions or delay, should draw all the Forces in the Province to a head against them," &c., book iii. c. 2.

Spainne riariú nó ċingfeaḋ arṁáil na bainríoġna fair. Ro ráiḋ taḋg ná tiuḃraḋ an long ḋó, ar ní ḃaoí do ḋaingſin ⁊ do ċosnaṁ aicce air fein, acht an long, ⁊ iar na ráḋ sin ḋó ro ċuir a ṁac féin go mbarḋaiḃ ele amaille friſ do ċoſnaṁ na luinge. Do ċóiḋ ó Suillebáin i mbád do ḃuain na luinge amaċ go haiṁḋeónaċ ⁊ do rala taḋcc amaille friſ isin mbád an tan sin. Ro ḟuagair taḋcc dia ṁac toirrḋealbaċ, ⁊ don ḃarda ó Suilleḃain co na ṁuinntir do ḋiúḃraccaḋ. Do rónaḋ leósoṁ innsin, ⁊ tar gaċ ndiuḃraccaḋ do tarlaicſiḋ ſtorra ro amais toirrḋealḃaċ taḋcc durċor do ṗeilér i nuaċtar a ċléiḃ go ffuair bás isin ocht maḋ la iar sin. Ba hé an taḋcc sin tiġearna corca baiscinn iarṫaraiġi co ro haṫċuireaḋ ⁊ go ro hionnarbadh ar a aṫarḋa lá hiarla tuaḋmuṁan tri bliaḋna riaſ an tan so go ttorċair aṁail a duḃramar. Ní ḃaoí aon trioċa ċéd déṙinn na baoí a ḋiongṁála do ṫiġearna is an taḋcc sin, ar láiṁ, ar ṫíoḋlacadh ar ċſnnaċ fíona, eaċ, ⁊ ealaḋan, ⁊ dá mbſiṫ duthaiġ, nó oiḋrſċt aicce as é an tí sin lás a ttorċair roḃ oiḋre diongṁala dia ſiſi.

Imṫura iarla tuaḋmuṁan iar ndol ḋóiḋe go corcaiġ hi ccſnn an lustis as í comairle ro ċinn an lustis, an tiarla do ṫionntúḋ do riḋisi go slóġaiḃ lais gus an oilén in ro ṗáccaiḃ siuṁ gararún ria sin .i. oilén faoíſt, ⁊ coblaċ co nordanás do ċor timċeall ar muir go rangattar hi ccoṁfoċraiḃ dúin baoí go ro ġabſat calaḋport, ⁊ gaḃaitt oilén dianiḋ ainm baoí ḃerre, ⁊ ro marbaḋ leó a ḃarda (im a ccaiptín Risdſrd mac Rosa mic connla meg eoċaccain).

ˣ *Among the shots:* literally, "beyond every shooting."

ʸ *Aimed,* ro amair.—This verb is incorrectly applied here, as it is stated in the beginning that the father's death was accidental. Ro amair denotes intention on the part of Turlough, and the Four Masters should have added, "ḋ'urchar n-imroill, by a mistaking, or random shot."

ᶻ *West Corca-Bhaiscinn,* now called the barony of Moyarta, and comprising the south-western angle of the county of Clare. It is stated in the *Pacata Hibernia,* book iii. c. 6, that, on the third of June, "Teg Keugh Mac Maghon, a principall Rebell (in an Iland adjoyning to the Dorseys) was casually shot through the body by his owne sonne, whereof he dyed the third day following."

ᵃ *Which arrived:* literally, "until they arrived," which is inelegant.

ᵇ *Dun-Baoi:* i. e. the fort of Baoi. This is called Dunboy by English writers. There is a plan of it, as it was besieged on this occasion, given in the *Pacata Hibernia.*—See Dublin edition of 1810, p. 526. There is no vestige of it remaining at present.

ᶜ *Conla Mageoghegan.*—See note ᵒ, under the year 1580, p. 1726, *supra,* and also the Miscellany of the Irish Archæological Society, p. 182. There is a most circumstantial account of this stubborn siege of the castle of Dunboy ["and so

King of Spain before the Queen's army should advance upon him. Teige said that he would not give him the ship, because he had no means of protecting or defending himself but the ship; and, upon saying this, he sent his own son, together with other guards, to defend the ship. O'Sullivan went into a boat, to wrest the ship by force; and Teige happened to be along with him in the same boat. Teige called out to his son, Turlough, and the guards, to fire on O'Sullivan and his people. They did so; and, among the shots[x] discharged between them, Turlough aimed[y] Teige with the shot of a ball in the upper part of his breast; so that he died on the eighth day after that. This Teige had been Lord of West Corca-Bhaiscinn[z], until he was expelled or banished from his patrimony by the Earl of Thomond three years before that time when he was as we have stated. There was no triocha-chead [barony] in Ireland of which this Teige was not worthy to have been Lord, for [dexterity of] hand, for bounteousness, for purchase of wine, horses, and literary works; and if he had a territory or inheritance the person by whom he fell would have been the rightful heir to succeed him.

As for the Earl of Thomond, after he had gone to Cork to the Lord Justice, the resolution to which the Lord Justice came was, that the Earl should again return with forces to the island on which he had previously left a garrison, namely, Oilen-Faoit; and he sent a fleet with ordnance round by sea, which arrived[a] in the vicinity of Dun-Baoi[b], and, having put to land, they took an island called Baoi-Bheirre, and slew its guards, together with their captain, Richard, the son of Ross, son of Conla Mageoghegan[c]. The [crews of the]

obstinate and resolved a defence had not bin seen in this kingdome"] printed in the *Pacata Hibernia*, book iii. chapters vi. vii. and viii. The Editor of the *Pacata* says that, on the 5th of June, Richard Mac Goghagan, the constable of Dunboy, parleyed with the Earl of Thomond, who requested him to render the castle unto the Queen; but that "all the Eloquence and artifice which the Earle could use avayled nothing, for Mac Goghagan was resolved to persevere in his wayes; and, in the great love which he pretended to beare unto the Earle, hee advised him not to hazard his life in landing upon the Mayne, for I know (sayd hee) you must land at yonder Sandy Bay, where, before your comming, the place will be so trenched and gabioned, as you must runne upon assured death."

This castle, which O'Sullevan Beare had taken from the Spaniards, as appears from his letter to the Earl of Caraçena, and which he refused to surrender to the English in conformity with Don Juan's articles of capitulation, was besieged and stormed by Carew, Lord President of Munster, with the most unrelenting perseverance, and defended by Mageoghegan and the warders, con-

Tucsat an coḃlaċ, a narm, ⁊ a nordanás hi ttír ag dún baoí go ro gaḃsat, ⁊ ro toċlaḋ leó díocc ḋaingsin díṫoglaiġi do ṫreinnsi trén láidir ar ḋaiġ an

sisting of one hundred and forty-three select fighting men, with a stubborn bravery unparalleled in modern history. At length, when the castle was nearly shattered to pieces, Mageoghegan retired into a vault, determined to blow up, with powder, what remained of the castle, unless the surviving part of the garrison should have promise of life. This was refused them by the Lord President, and the last fate of Mageoghegan is described by the Editor of the *Pacata Hibernia*, book iii. c. viii., as follows:

"His Lordship gaue direction for a new battery upon the Vault, intending to bury them in the ruines thereof, and after a few times discharged, and the bullets entering amongst them into the Celler, the rest that were with Taylor" [an Englishman's son, appointed chief after the disabling of Mageoghegan] "partly by intercession, but chiefly by compulsion (threatening to deliver him up if hee were obstinate), about ten of the Clock in the morning of the same day" [18th of June] "constrained him to render simply, who, with eight and fortie more, being ready to come forth; and Sir George Thornton, the Sergeant Major, Captaine Roger Harvie, Captaine Power, and others, entering the Vault to receive them, Captaine Power found the said Richard Mac Goghegan lying there mortally wounded, and, perceiving Taylor and the rest ready to render themselues, raised himselfe from the ground, snatching a lighted Candle and staggering therewith to a barrell of powder (which for that purpose was unheaded), offering to cast it into the same, Captaine Power took him and held him in his armes, with intent to make him prisoner, untill he was, by our men (who perceived his intent) instantly killed, and then Taylor and the rest were brought prisoners to the Camp."

It is stated in the same work that, on the same day, fifty-eight of them were executed by the President, who deemed it prudent that Taylor, and one Tirlagh Roe Mac Swiny, and twelve others, should be reserved alive, "to trie whether he could draw them to doe some more acceptable service than their lives were worth."

P. O'Sullevan Beare gives a curious list of the Irish who opposed O'Sullevan Beare on this occasion, as will appear by the following extract from his *Cathol. Iber. Compend.*, tom. 3, lib. 7:

"His motibus Angli vehementer soliciti & auxii quam maximam possunt belli molem in Osullevanum constituunt vertere. Georgius Caruus Momoniarum præfectus Corcacham regias copias convocat. Auxilia Ibernorum accersit. Illi præsto fuerunt, aliquot Angloiberni, & hi Momoniæ magnates, sine quibus Angli parum negocii possent Osullevano facessere, Dionysius O'Brien, Lomnachæ princeps quondam et Tomoniæ Comes, Macarrha Fuscus Carbriæ princeps, Carolus Macarrha Muscriæ princeps, Barrius Magnus Botevanti Vicecomes, Odonnobhanus, eques Auratus Albus, Eugenius Osullevanus Osullevani quidem patruelis, hostis tamen infestissimus, Dermysius Osullevani Magni frater, Dionysius et Florentius Maccarrhæ fratres qui Osullevanum deseruerunt. Urmoniæ comitatus delectus, & auxiliares ab aliis missi. Totus exercitus continebat plus quatuor millibus militum quorum vix quingenti erant Angli. Cæteri erant Iberni et Angloiberni, qui desperatis rebus a Reginâ descissere minimé sibi tutum et integrum existimabant," &c. &c.—Cap. ii. fol. 182, b.

The taking of this castle of Dunbaoi is thus described by the same writer (*ubi supra*, lib. 7, c. iii. fol. 183):

"Iterum Caruus auctis copiis supra quinque millia hominum omnes Osullevani vires statuit contundere, in Beantriam perueniens in Agello

fleet landed with arms and ordnance at Dun-baoi, where they formed a strong and impregnable ditch, and a stout and firm trench, from which to play upon

Rubro, (Gurtin Rua), patente planicie castrametatur, inde in Bearram penetrare cogitans, Dumbeam castellum (*anglice* Birhauen) et cæteras Osulleuani arces oppugnatum. Osulleuanus iter occupans quingentos ab hoste passus tentoria figit militum numero longè inferior, sed virtute et loci commoditate fretus hostem incursionibus prohibet, et commeatu intercludit. Caruus se vallo, fossaque muniens menses duos castrorum finibus milites continet, donec proximè ad maritimam oram applicent naues octodecim rostratæ, & tectæ & aliæ minores Manapia, Corcacha, & ex Anglia missæ, in quas exercitum impositum iuxta Dumbeam exponit arcem obsidens. Illam tenebant centum vigenti pedites ab Osulleuano constituti duce Richardo Macgochegano viro nobili: qui munitiones egressi pro muro cum hoste fortiter dimicant, illum arcis oppugnatione diu prohibentes: & intra munimenta compulsi ex pinnis fenestris atque turribus sese firmiter tuentur. Caruus aperta vi tormenta in arcem agere tentans cum à propugnatoribus prohiberetur, & eruptionem facientibus & missilia ex munitionibus iaculantibus fossam homine cubitos duos altiorem in arcem dirigit, et rursus transuersum aggerem obducit magna propugnatorum contentione pro viribus opus interrumpentium: et in fossam cum è castelli turribus non esset prospectus, per eam trahit tormenta quinque, quibus in transversa fossa dispositis arx continuè quatitur. Interim propugnatores frequenter erumpunt hostem ex oppugnatione dimovere conantes, levia prælia cominus committendo, & eminus ex munitionibus ignitos globos bombardis tormentisque iaciendo. Iam vero crebris tormentis laxata lapidum, mœniumque compage arx difficiebat. Magna pars concidit, pars alia consequens procumbebat. Per ruinam regius exercitus in arcem impetum facit. Utrinque magna cæde facta propugnatores impetum sustinent. Regii rursus pergunt eminus arcem tormentis, consumere, & bombardis propugnatores ex muro, turribusque dimouere. Ingente fragore frusta munimenti ruunt, trahentia milites secum, saxaque collisa armatos obruunt. Regii per ruinam irrumpunt, quos propugnatores globulis & lapidibus consternunt, hastis transfigunt, gladiis iugulant, admotis clypeis, saxisque revolutis deorsum per ruinam præcipitant, totaque repellunt. Adhuc regii munimentum tormentis eminus oppugnant, & machinis tutò convellentibus, munitionibus affatim corruentibus, propugnatore passim cadente non datur libera facultas ruinæ defendendæ: per eam oppugnatores irruunt, & in aulam, ad quam usque Castellum erat collapsum, cohortes tres signa inferentes dimidiam occupant. Ibi propugnatoribus occurrentibus manus cruenter conseritur: multis utrinque vulneribus inflictis, multis viris interemptis, regii terga vertere coguntur, aulam et ruinam totam deserentes. Qui sauciis receptis iterum irruptionem faciunt recente, vegetoque milite cum defesso, & vulnerato, & magna multitudine cum paucis confligentes. Primum de ruinâ dimicatur: unde propugnatoribus expulsis cohortes septem in aulam aquilas conferunt eò sibi iniquam, quod in eâ se non poterant explicare. Ibi in longam moram pugna protrahitur: multi mutuis vulneribus succumbunt: magna corporum atque armorum strages iacet. Aula tota sanguinis rivulis fluit. Propugnatorum pars longè maxima cadit, præsertim Dux Richardus, cuius animi magnitudo cum generis claritate de principatu contendebat, maximé strenuè prælians inter cadavera semianimis procumbit atque lethalibus vulneribus affectus. Reliquorum etiam nemo non vulneribus affligitur. Superstites aulam relinquentes in inferiora tabulata se recipere compelluntur. Vnde acerrimé pug-

ḃaile do ċaiṫſṁ lá hordanas. Ḃáttar agá ċaiṫſṁ athaidh samhlaidh go ro lſccadh, ⁊ co ro láinḃrirſḋ an baile leó go talṁuin ⁊ go ro marbadh an ḃarda, ⁊ an drong ná ro marḃadh díoḃ ro crochadh iatt ina ccupladhaiḃ lá hiarla tuadhmuṁan.

O Suilleḃáin imorro iar mbſin an ḃaile sin de, do ċuaidh co na buar, ⁊ co na ḃóṫáintiḃ, co na ṁuinnteraiḃ, ⁊ co na imirgiḃ ar cúlaiḃ a ċnoc cſnngarḃ i ndiaṁraiḃ, ⁊ i ndroiḃélaiḃ a ṫíre. Ḃaoí an tiarla co na ṡlóccaiḃ, ⁊ o Suilleḃáin co na socraide ag caiṫſṁ, ⁊ ag coṁḟuabairt aroile go haimsir na nodlacc. Do rónsatt an dá ṡluaġ sin forḃais ⁊ forslongport aghaidh ar aġaidh isin ngl ſnn garḃ ⁊ bá do dicſnn daingin uí Suilleḃáin an glſnd sin. Ḃáttar a ḋaoíne ag ſdarrccaradh go hinclſiṫe gan aṫcoṁarc lá hua suilleḃáin. Ro imṫiġ uadh cettur captin tirial, ⁊ rob ſiccſn dóroṁ badéin imṫſċt gan ḟios, gan airiuccadh don iarla ar saoire na nodlacc. Ḃá sſḋ a cceadna huide ar an ngl ſnn garḃ go baile Muirne, an dara hoidċe i ccoiccriċ duiṫċe uí ċaoíṁ ⁊ ṁég aṁlaoiḃ. An trſs oidċe i nard patrraicc. An cſṫraṁadh oidċe ag sulċóid, an cúicceadh oidċe, ⁊ an sſirſḋ oidċe i mbel na coilleadh, an

nantes tantum cum virtute, tum desperatione, quæ ad honesté moriendum sæpè magnum incitamentum est, valuerunt, ut hostem primum, aula deinde arce tota exuerint. Illicò nox dirimit pugnam. Postero die regij rem per legationes conficere ducunt. Propugnatores deiecta, labefactaque maiori arcis parte, amisso duce, vulneribus fatigati, multis malis defessi pacti, ut incolumes dimitterentur, castellum dedunt mense Septembri decimo quinto die obsidionis. Postquam Regij sunt castellum ingressi, Richardus nondum exanimis cum Anglicum sonum audijsset linquentem animum reuocat, & sulphureo pulueri, cujus non exigua facultas erat in castello ignem pergit applicare hostes proculdubio combusturus, nisi antequam rem perficeret, spiritu destitueretur. Pactum, & fides Anglica religione dedititiis seruatur: nam viri & fœminæ laqueo strangulantur.

[d] *Attacking each other.*—It is stated in the *Pacata Hibernia*, book iii. c. xvii., that the English "attacked the fastness where the rebels, with their cattle, were lodged in Glengarrem [Glengarrew], whereupon ensued a bitter fight, which was maintained, without intermission, for six hours, during which many were slain on both sides; but the greatest losse fell upon the Traytors: there were taken from them, in that dayes service, 2000 Cowes, 4000 sheep, and 1000 Garrans."

On the next morning after O'Sullevan's departure, being the 4th of January, 1602, Sir Charles Wilmot came to seek the enemy in their camp, where he found nothing but hurt and sick men, "whose paines and lives, by the Souldiers, were both determined"!! *Quære,* whether was this murdering or slaying?

[e] *Gleann-garbh,* translated *Vallis Aspera,* by P. O'Sullevan Beare, now *anglice* Glengarriff, a singularly picturesque valley near Bantry Bay.—See a description of it in the Dublin Penny Journal, vol. i. pp. 117, 118, and in Windele's *Description of Cork and its Vicinity.*

[f] *Baile-Muirne,* now Ballyvourney, a small

the castle with ordnance. They thus continued the firing until the castle was razed and levelled with the ground, and the warders were [for the most part] killed; and such of them as were not killed were hanged in pairs by the Earl of Thomond.

O'Sullivan, after being deprived of this castle, went with his cows, herds, and people, and all his moveables, behind his rugged-topped hills, into the wilds and recesses of his country. The Earl [of Thomond] and his army, and O'Sullivan and his forces, continued shooting and attacking[d] each other until the Christmas times. The two armies were entrenched and encamped face to face in Gleann-garbh[e], which glen was one of O'Sullivan's most impregnable retreats. His people now began to separate from O'Sullivan secretly without asking his leave. First of all Captain Tyrrell went away from him, and he was obliged himself to depart in the Christmas holidays, without the knowledge of, and unperceived by the Earl. In the first day's march he went from Gleann-garbh to Baile-Muirne[f]; on the second night he arrived on the borders of the territories of O'Keeffe[g] and Mac Auliffe; on the third night [he arrived] at Ardpatrick[h]; on the fourth night, at Sulchoid[i]; on the fifth and

village in the barony of Muskerry, in the county of Cork, where there are some ruins of a church dedicated to St. Gobnait. P. O'Sullevan Beare says that O'Sullevan Beare, his kinsman, with his forces, encamped, the first night, at a place called Acharas, and that, on the next day, being the first of January, 1603, they arrived at Ballyvourney, before noon, where they left gifts, and prayed to St. Gubeneta that they might have a prosperous journey. The same writer, and also the Editor of the *Pacata Hibernia*, state that, as they passed along the skirts of Muskerry, they were skirmished with by the sons of Teige, the son of Owen Mac Carthy, where they lost some of their men and most of their carriage.

[g] *O'Keefe and Mac Auliffe*.—These families were seated in the present barony of Duhallow, in the north-west of the county of Cork.

P. O'Sullevan states that the inhabitants of these territories were hostile to O'Sullivan: "Quos accolæ noctem totam eiaculando magis molestia, quam vulnere afficiunt."—Fol. 189.

[h] *Ardpatrick*, a village in the barony of Coshlea, and county of Limerick. It is stated in the *Pacata Hibernia*, that, in passing by Liscarroll, John Barry, brother to the Viscount, with eight horsemen and forty foot, charged their rear at the ford of Bellaghan, where he slew and hurt many of them. P. O'Sullevan Beare says that they fought for an hour at this ford, where O'Sullevan lost four men, and the Queen's adherents lost more than four. The Editor of the *Pacata*, however, does not acknowledge the loss of more than one on Barry's side.

[i] *Sulchoid:* i. e. *Salicetum*, the Sallow Wood. —*Cor. Glos.*, *in voce*. This place retains its name to the present day, and is now anglicised Solloghod or Sallowhead. It is situated on the confines of the counties of Limerick and Tipperary, but in the barony of Clanwilliam, in the latter county, and four miles to the west of the town of Tipperary.

seachtmaḋ oiḋċe hi lLeaṫarach, an toċtmaḋ oiḋċe i mbaile achaiḋ ċaoín. Ní ḃaoí sioṁ lá, ná aḋhaiġ in airsect sin gan deaḃaiḋ, ⁊ diantograim dioġaltaċ fair, ⁊ ro fuilngseḋ, ⁊ ro freagraḋ go feardha fír ḃeóḋa lais sioṁ innsin. Iar ndol dó in naoṁaḋ oiḋċe gus an ccoill dianiḋ ainm coill ḟinne, do rónsat airisioṁ fri ré dá oiḋċe an dú sin. Ḃaoi donnchaḋ mac cairpri ṁec aeḋagáin ina ccoṁḟocraiḃ, ⁊ baoí side acc dénaṁ dánachta deaḃṫa, ⁊ diubraicṫe ar ua Suilleḃáin co na muinntir gur ḃó héiccen a ṁarḃaḋ ro ḋeóiḋ ar ní ḟaoṁ corcc for coṁairle uí Suilleḃáin. O ná fuarattar coitseba, ináitt artraiġe ele ineallṁa ro marbaiḋ leó a neaċraiḋ ar dáiġ a ffeola diṫe, ⁊ diomċar, ⁊ a ccaḋal croicenn do ċor im ḟiotslataiḃ slimriġne do ḋénaṁ curaċ dioḃ dia nimċor tar an Sionainḋ sriobuaine (.i. ag aṫ coilleaḋ ruaiḋ)

[k] *Baile-na-coille:* i.e. the town of the wood, now Ballynakill, a village in the parish of Tome, barony of Kilnamanagh, and county of Tipperary.

[l] *Leatharach*, now Latteragh, in the barony of Upper Ormond, and county of Tipperary, and about eight miles south of the town of Nenagh. In the *Feilire Aenguis*, at p. 27, the scholiast calls this place Letracha Odhrain, and places it in Muscraighe Thire.—See also Colgan's *Acta Sanctorum*, pp. 151, 461.

[m] *Baile-achaid-caoin.*—This place is still called Balloughkeen by the old natives, but it is usually shortened to Loughkeen in the anglicised form. It is the name of a townland and parish in the barony of Lower Ormond.

[n] *Coill-fhine.*—This was the name of a wood adjoining Port-a-tulchain, now Portland, in the parish of Lorha, in the barony of Lower Ormond. P. O'Sullevan Beare calls this wood Brosnacha, from its situation near the river now called the Little Brosnach.

[o] *Donough, the son of Carbry Mac Egan.*—It is stated in the *Pacata Hibernia*, book iii. c. 17, that "the sherife of the county of Typperarie fell upon their reare and slew many of them." But the author of this work did not think it necessary to add, that O'Sullivan's people retorted upon him, and slew and wounded many of his people. This, however, was the case, if we can believe P. O'Sullevan Beare, who gives a most minute and interesting account of the journey performed by his kinsman, Daniel, his father, Dermot, and their surviving followers and adherents, after their flight from Glengarriff through Munster and Connaught, until he arrived in O'Rourke's country. The following is his account of the manner in which they crossed the Shannon at Port-a-tulchain.—*Hist. Cathol. Iber.*, tom. 3, lib. 7, c. ix. fol. 190, 191.

"Hic in summum discrimen Osulleuanus videbatur deductus, quód Sininnum amnem amplum, & nauigabilem non poterat transmittere, phasellis, atque nauigijs ab hoste remotis, & cauto pœnis acerbissimis, ne illum vllus portitor transportaret. Propter inediam etiam milites viribus destituuntur. Ob id animos omnium iugens desperatio subit. In hoc ancipiti statu rerum pater meus Dermysius Osulleuanus se nauim breui confecturum, & famem militum extincturum profitetur.

"Postero die qui septimus erat Ianuarij mensis, Dermysij consilio in Brosnacham densissimam, atque tutissimam syluam sese abdentes, & coesis arboribus in valli speciem compositis, fossaque leuiter facta circumuallantes,

sixth nights [he remained] at Baile-na-Coille[k]; on the seventh night at Leatharach[l]; and on the eighth at Baile-Achaidh-caoin[m]. He was not a day or night during this period without a battle, or being vehemently and vindictively pursued, all which he sustained and responded to with manliness and vigour. Having arrived on the ninth night at a wood called Coill-fhinne[n], where they remained for two nights, Donough, the son of Carbry Mac Egan[o], who lived in their vicinity, began boldly to attack and fire upon O'Sullivan and his people, so that at length he was obliged to be slain, as he would not desist [from his attacks], by the advice of O'Sullivan. Not finding cots or boats in readiness, they killed their horses, in order to eat and carry with them their flesh, and to place their hides on [frame-works of] pliant and elastic osiers, to make curraghs[p] for conveying themselves across the green-streamed Shannon, [which they crossed] at Ath-

biduum duas naues ex viminibus, & arboribus condunt, equis duodecim occisis, quorum corijs nauigia integuntur, & carnibus omnes vescuntur præter Osulleuanum, Dermysium, & Dermysium Ohuallachanum. Nauis, cuius Dermysius fuit architectus hunc in modum conficitur. Vimina crassiore parte terræ infixa, & ad medium inuicem reflexa, restibusque reuincta corpus nauis constituebant: cui è solida tabula statumina, transtraque interius adduntur. Exterius corijs vndecim equorum cooperitur, remis, atque scalmis coaptatis. Carina, & materiei necessitate, & saxa, cautesque vitandi causa erat plana: longitudo pedum viginti sex, latitudo sex, & altitudo quinque, præterquam quod ad fluctus propellendos prora magis aliquantum eminebat. Altera nauis, cuius construendæ equites Omallæ magistri erant, viminibus sine iugis contexta habens carinam circularis formæ instar parmæ, & latera longe altiora, quam carina exigebat, contenta fuit vno equi corio, quo carina est obducta. Hæ naues ad Sininni Oram nomine Portulachanum militum humeris noctu portantur, quibus Osulleuanus suos clam traijcere cœpit. Omallæ milites decem suam nauim conscendunt. Cæterum nauis, cum parua, tum ineptæ structuræ pondere pressa in medio flumine cum hominibus obruitur. Dermysij nauis, quæ triginta simul armatos capiebat, alios incolumes transtulit, equos nantes à puppi loris trahens.

"Oriente die post milites transmissos Donatus Makeoganus, qui Syluas Rubras castellum prope tenebat, armata manu impedimenta circumueniens, cœpit sarcinas diripere, calonum, cruore solum spargere, fœminas incusso pauore in flumen inijcere. Thomas Burkus cum hastatis circiter viginti, totidemque fulminatoribus in excubijs, & insidijs ab Osulleuano dispositus, vt commodius cæteri flumen traducerentur, suos in pugnam cohortatus Donatum improuiso adortus cum comitibus quindecim interficit: reliquos vulneribus ferè affectos in fugam vertit. Catapultarum sonitu excitati accolæ ad vtramque ripam fluminis confluunt. Quare Thomas cum excubitoribus, fæminæ, calonesque trepidatione tanta, & tumultu nauiculam imflendo submergunt, ita tamen proximè ad oram, vt nemo perierit, & nauis iterum aquis subducta excubitores traiecerit. Calones alij nando flumen penetrant: alij non facta per accurrentes accolas transmittendi potestate in varias partes dissipati sese occultant. Nauim, ne sit hostibus vsui, Osulleuanus iubet dilacerari."

[p] *Curraghs*.—The Editor of the *Pacata Hi-*

go rangattar gan gabaiḋ gan guasaċt tairsi go mbattar don taoiḃ araill i síol nanmċaḋa Lottar aissiḋe go mbáttar an taonṁaḋ oiḋċe décc acc sċórium ó maine. Iar ttoraċtain dóiḃ isuiḋe ro cruinniġsiot na hiaṫa ⁊ na haicmſḋa rortar coiṁnſs dóiḃ rſmpa ⁊ na nosḃaiḋ go ro gairsiot dá gaċ taoiḃ ina timċeall. Bá do na huaislib rucc forra don ċur sin mac Iarla cloinne riocaird tomas mac uillicc, mic Riocaird saxanaiġ, ⁊ Mág coċlain Sſan óсс, mac Sſain mic airt, ⁊ ó madaccain .i. Domnall mac Sſain, mic brſsail, ⁊ a mac anmchaiḋ, ⁊ drong dſglaṁḋa do ṡíol cceallaiġ, ⁊ sochaiḋe ele naċ airiṁtear co na soċraitte uile amaille friu.

Rob éiccſn dua suillebáin, dua ċoncobair ciarraiġe, ⁊ duilliam búrc mac Sſain na sſmar co na mbſcc buiḋin (uair ní rabattar siḋe uile, aċt earbaiḋ ar tri céd) anṁain acc sċhórum ó maine le hiomġuin, ⁊ ré hiombualaḋ, coṫugaḋ lé caṫlaṫair, ⁊ fromaḋ a ffíorgaiscceaḋ fris na hilcéḋaiḃ báttar

bernia calls the kind of boats they constructed *Nevogs.*

q *Ath Coille-ruaidhe:* i. e. the Ford of Redwood. This ford was opposite Donough Mac Egan's Castle of Kiltaroe, or Redwood, in the parish of Lorha, barony of Lower Ormond, and county of Tipperary. P. O'Sullevan Beare says that they crossed the Shannon at Port-a-tolchain (now Portland, in the same parish); but that author has committed some very glaring topographical errors in his Description of the rout of O'Sullevan Beare through the County of Tipperary, from which it is quite clear that he was writing from memory, or imperfect notes taken from the dictation of his father or cousin, and that he had no accurate map of Munster before him.

r *The many hundreds.*—The editor of the *Pacata Hibernia* agrees with this, book iii. c. 17:

"Being in Connaught, they passed safely through the county of Galway, until they came into the Kellies' Countrey, where they were fought withall by Sir Thomas Burke, the Earle of Clanrickard's brother, and Captaine Henry Malby, who were more in number then the Rebels. Neverthelesse, when they saw that either they must make their way by the sword or perish, they gave a brave charge upon our men, in the which Captaine Malby was slaine; upon whose fall Sir Thomas and his Troopes fainting, with the losse of many men, studied their safeties by flight, and the rebels with little harme marched into Orwykes Countrey."

Philip O'Sullevan Beare gives a minute account of the manner in which his cousin, the O'Sullevan Beare, defeated Thomas Burke and his adherents at Aughrim, and of the hardships and perils which he encountered till he arrived in O'Rourke's country, in his *Hist. Cathol. Iber. Compend.*, tom. 3, lib. 7, c. x. xi. After defeating his enemies at Aughrim, he proceeded over Slieve Mhuire (now Mount Mary, near Castle Kelly, but anciently Sliabh Fuirri), and marched through Mac David's country, where the inhabitants pursued him all the day to prevent him from obtaining provisions. On the evening of the same day he betook himself to Slieve-Ui-Flynn (near Ballinlough, in the extreme west of the county of Roscommon), and he concealed himself in the thick woods, where a friendly messenger arrived, stating that it was the determination of the natives to sur-

Coille-ruaidhe[q], without loss or danger, and landed on the other side in Sil-Anmchadha. From thence they passed on, and on the eleventh night they arrived at Aughrim-Hy-Many. Upon their arrival there the [inhabitants of the] lands and the tribes in their vicinity collected behind and before them, and shouted in every direction around them. Among the gentlemen who came up with them on this occasion were the son of the Earl of Clanrickard (Thomas, the son of Ulick, son of Richard Saxonagh); Mac Coghlan (John Oge, the son of John, son of Art); O'Madden (Donnell, the son of John, son of Breasal), and his son, Anmchaidh; some active parties of the O'Kellys, and many others not enumerated, with all their forces along with them.

O'Sullivan, O'Conor Kerry, and William Burke, son of John-na-Seamar, with their small party (for the entire did not fully amount to three hundred), were obliged to remain at Aughrim-Hy-Many to engage, fight, and sustain a battle-field, and test their true valour against the many hundreds[r] who were oppress-

round them early in the morning and exterminate them. They then marched on through the wood all night, and were pursued, early next morning, by Mac David, who, however, did not risk an engagement with men driven to such desperation, and they directed their course to a wood called Diamhrach, or the solitary. Here they lighted fires, and found the inhabitants not unfriendly. After having rested here for some time, they set out by night and marched over the Curlieu hills as far as Knockvicar, in the barony of Boyle, where they rested and took refreshment. When the day arose their guide shewed them O'Rourke's castle of Leitrim at some distance, which they reached about eleven o'clock that day. By this time they were reduced to thirty-five in number, of whom eighteen were armed, sixteen calones, and one woman. All the rest, who were more than a thousand in number at their setting out from the camp at Glengariff, having either perished, forsaken their chief, or having been detained on the way by fatigue or wounds. O'Sullevan remained with O'Rourke for some days; and, after various adventures in Ulster, he went to England after the coronation of James I., with O'Neill, Rury O'Donnell, Niall Garv O'Donnell, and others; but O'Sullevan could by no means obtain a restitution of his territory, or even pardon. He, therefore, set sail for Spain, where he was most graciously received by Philip III., who made him Knight of the Order of St. James, and Count of Bearhaven, with a pension of three hundred pieces of gold monthly. He was afterwards assassinated on the 16th of July, 1618, in the fifty-seventh year of his age, by John Bath, an Anglo-Irishman, whom he employed as a confidential servant. Of this assassination, his relative, P. O'Sullevan Beare, who was present, gives the following account in his *Hist. Cathol. Iber. Compend.*, tom. 4, lib. 3, c. iv.

"Sed vltimus aduersæ fortunæ ictus est, quod decimo sexto die mensis eiusdem Osulleuanus Bearræ princeps, in quo tunc Iberni maximam spem habebant, miserè succubuerit, hoc modo. Iohannes Batheus Angloibernus, apud Osulleuanum adeó gratia pollebat, vt etiam ab eo patrocinio, & authoritate adiutus beneficijs afficeretur; & inter familiarissimos habitus sit etiam domum receptus, & in mensam admissus: Quo-

agá fforaċ, ⁊ acca ffírlſnṁain. Ro ionnsaiġ ó Suilleḃáin go fſiccaċ foirniata, go ffaoċda fſrċonta gus an maigin i mbattar na gulla, ar as riú bá huille a aincride ⁊ a aininne, ⁊ ní ro airis gus an ionad ina ffacaidh a ttoísec go ro dícſndaiġ go dian dſġṫaraidh an saor ġall sin lais .i. Mac Captin malbei. Ro sraoíneadh iaraṁ ar an tſcclamadh slóiġ sin go ro marbadh líon díríṁe díoḃ. As ing ma do rónsat an urdail do ḃuidin ċuirṫe ciainsiublaiġ, ⁊ a ttſgṁail i neittirṁſdón a naṁatt, saṁail an dſirġſinsſt dáiṫſs ag cosnaṁ a nanma ⁊ a noirdearcais an lá sin. Tiagait assiḋe iar mór ġaibḃtib iar ttriall a mbraṫ, ⁊ a mairnte fors na conairib go rangattar go hulltoib.

Mac conmara fionn, Sſan mac taidcc, mic conmeadha décc, 24. do ṁí febru ⁊ doṁnall a ṁac do gaḃ a ionad.

rum beneficiorum Iohannes immemor, eò impudentiæ processit, vt leui primum controuersia orta ob pecunias ab Osulleuano mutuò datas, inde sit ausus tanti viri clarissimæ nobilitati genus suum apud Ibernos, & Anglos, à quibus oritur, minimé sublime conferre. Quod ægre ferens Philippus Osulleuani patruelis, qui hanc historiam scribit, cum Iohanne ea de re expostulat. Vnde Madriti iuxta regium monasterium diui Dominici vterque alterum stricto gladio aggreditur. Incepto certamine Iohannes ingente pauore perculsus, & vocem efferens loco semper cedebat: & illum in facie Philippus cæsa vulnerauit: & interfecturus, videbatur, nisi eum Edmundus Omorra, & Giraldus Macmoris ab Osulleuano missi, & duo equites Hispani protexissent, Philippumque apparitor deprehendisset. Cum multi vndique confluxissent, inter cæteros Osulleuanus aduenit læva manu rosarium, & dextera chirotecas gerens. Quem Iohannes conspicatus incautum, nihil timentem, & aliò aspicientem subitò accedens gladio inter turbam intento per læuam lacertam confodiendo, & rursus guttur feriendo occidit. Philippus lictore frustra reluctante in domum Marchionis Seneceiæ Galliarum legati sese abdidit. Iohannes in carcerem conijcitur vnà cum consanguineo suo Francisco Batheo, qui rixæ interfuit, sicut, & Daniel Odriscol Philippi consanguineus. Osulleuano in eo cænobio postero die exequiarum ius magna frequentia Hispanorum nobilium, & studio domini Didaci Brocheri splendidi equitis, regij consiliarii soluitur. Obiens annum 57 agebat. Erat vir plané pius & largus, maximé in pauperes, & egenos. Duobus, vel tribus Missarum sacris quotidié interesse solebat, longas ad Deum, & superos quotidianas preces effundens: crebrò peccatis expiatus sacrosanctum Domini corpus suscipiebat. Ita mors eius subita, & infausta vitæ minimè consentanea fuit, etsi eo etiam duobus sacris peragendis interfuerit, & acceptis vulneribus sit á sacerdotibus peccatis absolutus. Erat procerus, & elegans statura, vultu pulcher, ætate canescente venerabilis."

[s] *Captain Malby.*—P. O'Sullevan Beare says that Malby was killed by Dermot O'Huallachan and Cornelius O'Murchu.

[t] *It is scarcely credible that:* literally, "it is scarce if."

[u] *John, the son of Teige.*—His descendants appear to have become extinct soon after. According to a genealogical manuscript, preserved in the Library of the Royal Irish Academy, John

ing and pursuing them. O'Sullivan, with rage, heroism, fury, and ferocity, rushed to the place where he saw the English, for it was against them that he cherished most animosity and hatred, and made no delay until he reached the spot where he saw their chief; so that he quickly and dexterously beheaded that noble Englishman, the son of Captain Malby[s]. The forces there collected were then routed, and a countless number of them slain. It is scarcely credible that[t] the like number of forces, fatigued from long marching, and coming into the very centre of their enemies, [ever before] achieved such a victory, in defence of life and renown, as they achieved on that day. They afterwards proceeded, in the midst of spies and betrayers, along the roads until they arrived in Ulster.

Mac Namara Fin (John, the son of Teige[u], son of Cu-Meadha) died on the 24th of February; and his son, Donnell, took his place.

Mac Namara Fin, head of his sept, who was living in 1714, was descended from Donough, the brother of this John, who died in 1602. Henry Pantaleon Mac Namara, Captain, Royal Navy, Knight of St. Louis, living in 1782, was descended of this branch of the Mac Namaras. He was the son of Captain Claud Matthew Mac Namara, who died in 1766, whose brother, John, who was born in Ireland, accompanied his parents to France in his infancy, and was page to his Serene Highness the Duke, brother of the Great Condé; entered the navy, passed through the various grades with distinction, obtained letters of recognition of his nobility of extraction from Louis XV. in 1736, and died, in 1757, Vice-Admiral of France, Commander and Grand Cross of St. Louis, and Commandant of the Port of Rochfort.

This vice-admiral was the son of John Mac Namara, who followed the fortunes of James II. According to a pedigree of this French family of the Mac Namaras, made out by the late Chevalier O'Gorman, and now preserved in the Library of the Royal Irish Academy, this John, who went to France in 1697, was the son of Mahon, who was the son of Donough, who was son of Mahon (brother of John, who was the father of Sir John Mac Namara of Madhmtalmhan, or Mountallon), who was son of Sida, son of Maccon, son of Sida, son of Maccon, son of Teige, who was the son of Maccon, who, according to Ware, built the abbey of Quin in 1433.

Major Daniel Mac Namara Bourchier represents, in the female line, the head of the Mac Namaras of Rossroe. He is the son of General John Bourchier of Elm Hill, in the county of Clare, by Mary Mac Namara, daughter of Thomas Mac Namara, Esq. (by Lucy, eldest daughter of Stanislaus Mac Mahon, Esq. of Clena, head of the Mac Mahons of East Corca-Vaskin), who was son of Daniel Mac Namara of Ardeloney, son of Florence Mac Namara, M. P. for Clare, Custos Rotulorum, and a Judge; son of Daniel Mac Namara of Doon and Ardcloney, Colonel of the Brigade of Thomond, who went to Spain with a Regiment of 1200 men after the capitulation of Limerick, who was the son of Teige Mac Namara, son of Couvea Reagh Mac Namara of Clonmoynagh and Ardcloney, who died in 1625, son of Florence Mac Namara of Rossroe, commonly called Fineen Meirgeach (*vide* bill filed by Florence Mac Namara in 1711), son of Loughlin,

Toirrḋealḃaċ mac maṫġaṁna, mic an ſſpuic uí ḃriain do ṁarḃaḋ hi maineaċaiḃ le Sſan a búrc mac riocaird, mic Sſain ó ḋoire mec laċtna.

Mac bruaidſḃa, Maoilin ócc, mac maoilin, mic conċoḃair décc an lá déiḋſnaċ do ṁí december. Ní ḃaoí i nerinn i nén pearsain Sſnchaiḋ, file, ⁊ fſr dána do bfſrr inás. Asé do ċum na duanta sſnċasa so i ndán díreaċ.

Cuirfſtt cumaoín ar cloinn táil.
Tucc daṁ taire a insi an laoíġ.
Aiṫin mſisi a ṁéġ coċláin.
Taḃram an ċuairt si ar cloinn ċais.
Deóraiḋ sunna slioċt caṫaoir. ⁊
O cſṫrar gluaisid gaoidil. ⁊c.

Sluaiccheaḋ lá niall ngarḃ ua ndoṁnaill go ngallaiḃ ⁊ go ngaoiḋealaiḃ amaille fris ar an fraoċmaġ i ttir eoġain ar foráilſṁ an lustis baoi hi

son of Fineen, son of Sida Cam, son of Maccon, son of Sida, son of Maccon, son of Couvea, son of Maccon, son of Loughlin, son of Couvea More, son of Niall, son of Cumara, son of Donnell, son of Cumara, *a quo* the surname of Mac Conmera, now *anglice* Mac Namara.

[w] *Doire-mic-Lachtna*, now Derrymaclaughny, near Knockdoe, in the barony of Clare, and county of Galway.—See note [r], under the year 1598, p. 2048, *supra*.

[x] *Mac Brody*.—See note [e], under the year 1563, p. 1597, *supra*.

[y] *Dan-Direach*: i. e. *metrum rectum*, a species of Irish metre very difficult of composition.—See O'Molloy's *Grammatica Latino-Hibernica*, p. 144, where he calls it the most difficult under the sun: "Maximè autem de Metro" [recto] "omnium quæ unquam vidi, vel audiui, ausim dicere, quæ sub sole reperiuntur, difficillimo." For some account of these poems the reader is referred to O'Reilly's *Descriptive Catalogue of Irish Writers*, pp. 164, 165, A. D. 1602.

[z] *Fraechmhagh*.—This is called the Fort of Augher by Fynes Moryson, *Hist. Irel.*, book iii. c. 1, Dublin edition of 1735, vol. ii. pp. 193, 197, 198.

Sir Henry Docwra gives the following account of his own movements in Ulster at this period:

"In May I receiued diuers lettres from my lord Deputie, all in discourse about his intent of coming that sommer to Blacke water againe, where hee willed I should prepare myselfe to meete him; And the lords from England had now sent vs annother supplie of 800 men, that landed att Derrey about the latter ende of this Moneth.

"And soe, on the 16th day of June, from Liffer I sett forth to meete him; but when we had Marched two dayes, and lay in Campe att Termin Mac Guirck, I understoode hee would not be readie till 6 dayes after; therevpon I returned backe, & hauing discouered by myne Eye, as I past by it the day before, that Omy was a place easie to be fortefied, & stood conuenient for many vses, to leaue a Garrison in, I made it Defensible with fower days labour, & left Captaine Edmond Leigh solye in it; on the 26th I sett forward againe, & encamped 4 Myles shorte from Dongannon, & going forth with some horse to discouer, I mett with my lord's skowts that Conducted mee that night to his Campe.

"The next day S[r] Arthur Chichester came ouer at Lough Sidney, & landed 1000 Men at

Turlough, the son of Mahon, son of the Bishop O'Brien, was slain in Hy-Many, by John Burke (son of Richard, son of John), of Doire-mic-Lachtna[w].

Mac Brody[x] (Maoilin Oge, the son of Maoilin, son of Conor) died on the last day of the month of December. There was not in Ireland, in the person of one individual, a better historian, poet, and rhymer, than he. It was he who composed these historical poems in Dán-Direacht[y]:

"I will lay an obligation on the descendants of Tál."

"Give thy attention to me, O Inis-an-laoigh" [Ennis].

"Know me, O Mac Coghlan!"

"Let us make this visitation among the descendants of Cas."

"The descendants of Cathaoir are exiles here."

"From four the Gadelians have sprung."

A hosting was made by Niall Garv O'Donnell, and the English and Irish along with him, from Fraechmhagh[z] in Tyrone, by order of the Lord Justice, who

that place, where he presentlie erected a fforte, which had afterwards the name given it of Mountioy, & my lord, hauing gayned his passage before, and erected annother at Blackwater, which he called by the name of Charlemounte, the axe was now at the roote of the tree, &, I may well say, the Necke of the Rebellion as good as vtterlie broken, for all that Tyrone was afterwardes able to doe, was but to saue himselfe in places of difficult access vnto.

"Ten dayes (as I remember) I stayed with his lordship in these partes, assisting him to spoyle & wast the Countrey, which he indeuored, by all the meanes hee could possible, to doe; & then my prouision of victuell spent, hee gaue mee leaue to retourne, with order to be in a readines againe to meete him about a Moneth after.

"I was noe sooner come home to the Derrey, But O Caine sent Mee an offer of his submission; I acquainted my lord withall; hee bad mee dispatch & make shorte with him, that we might be the readier for a Mayne Prosecution vpon Tyrone; soe, on the 27th of July, wee came to a full agreement, the substaunce whereof was this (Countersigned with ech of our handes), that soe much of his Countrey as ley betweene the Rivers of Foghan, Bangibbon, & Loughfoyle, should be to her Maiestie to dispose of to whome shee pleased, a peece of Ground should be allotted for maintenance of a Garrison at the Band, the rest he should haue her Maiesties lettres Pattents for, to hould to him & his heires. These Conditions my lord acknowledged to be better then hee looked for, approued them vnder his hand, promised mee the inheritaunce of the reserued lands, & gave me the present vse & Custodium of it vnder the Exchequer Seale, and him the like of the rest; then wrote vp to mee, to drawe vp to the Omy, to wast all the Countrie I could thereabouts, & there to attend him against hee sent vnto Mee againe.

"On the 10th of August I came thither, & Hugh Boy, coming after mee the next day, was sett vpon and slaine by a party of loose fellowes that fell upon him by chaunce; a man whom I found faithfull & honest, let Envie and Ignoraunce say what they will to the Contrarye. Hee left three brothers behinde him, Phelime Reaugh, Edmond Groome, & Shaine Cron; they

fforbairi for oilén an ḟraochmaighe an tan sin go ro creachadh lais corbmac mac an barúin dfhearbhrathair í néill, ⁊ an busdúnach, ⁊ siar gus an machaire Stefanach go ttartt airccthe, ⁊ creacha iomdha lais gus an ffraochmhaigh dionnsaighidh an lustis.

Sloicceadh ele lá niall ua domhnaill do ghallaibh, ⁊ do ghaoidhelaibh ina ḟarradh go breifne í Ruairc go ttucc buar dírimhe lais.

King Semus do ríoghadh i nionad na bainríoghna Elizabeth an cethramhadh lá fichet do mharta, 1602, do réir airmhe na Saccsan, ⁊ do réir rímhe na romhan ar 1603. ⁊ as eisidhe an seiseadh Sémus do ríoghaibh alban.

were all men of very good parts, & deserued a better Countenance, at least from the state, then my Creditt was able to procure them, which, if they had had, & those Courses forborne that Phelime Reaugh was vext with all, by particuler Persons, vpon no sufficient ground of reason that I ame wittnes to, theire liues had perhappes beene preserued to this day, & a better oppinion conceiued of vs in gennerall then is by the rest of that Nation. Let noe man Censure mee a misse for this kinde of saying, for I hould it a sinne to Conceale a truth where I am interressed & haue occasion to speake it.

"Being heere & knowing my lord was not yet readie to take the field, I was tould by Irish Guides of a prey that in theire opinion was easilie to be sett out of Cormocke mac Baron's Countrey, & I liked theire reasons soe well, that I resolued to giue an attempte for it. Soe I tooke out 400 foote & 50 horse, & sett forth in the eveninge, & marcht all Night; by breake of the day wee found it was gone further then they made accompte of, &, loath to retourne Emptie, wee followed it till wee were at least 3 myle from home. Captaine Edmond Leigh, that Commaunded the vaunt Guard, with a fewe light horse & foote, in the ende ouertooke it, guarded by Cormocke himselfe, whome he presentlie charged & beate away; then went in & gathered about 400 Cowes togeather, & brought them to vs where wee made a stande with the Mayne forces. Wee were then all exceeding wearie, & therefore, finding howses at hand, satt downe & rested our selues a while. After wee risse & had marched about three Myle, wee might discerne troupes of Men gathered togeather in Armes drawing towards a wood which wee must pass thorowgh, to possess themselues of it before vs. I then allighted, sent away my horse, & put myselfe in the Rere, badd the rest of the horse, with a fewe foote, & the Prey, make haste & gett thorowgh as fast as they Could; & soe they did before there came downe any greate Numbers vpon them. Vpon vs that came after with the foote, they fell with a Crye, & all the terrour they were able to make; skirmisht with shott, till all our Powder on both sides were spente; then came to the sword & Push of Pike; & still as wee beate them off, they would retyre, & by & by come vpon vs againe. These kindes of assaults, I thinke I may safelie say, they gaue vs at least a dozen of; yet in the end wee carryed our selues cleere out; came to place where our horse made a stand vpon a faire, large, & hard peece of ground. There wee put ourselues into order of Battaile, drewe forth againe &, marched away. They stoode in the edge of the woode, & gaue vs the lookeing on; but offered to follow vs noe further. Soe wee lodged quietlie that Night, & the next day came home to Omy, where wee diuided our Prey, with in 20 of the full Number of 400 Cowes, & found

was at the same time laying siege to the island of Fraechmhagh. He plundered Cormac, the son of the Baron, who was brother of O'Neill; and also Boston, and the country westwards as far as Machaire-Stefanach[a], and carried many preys and spoils to Fraechmhagh, to the Lord Justice.

Another hosting of the English and Irish was made by Niall O'Donnell to Breifny O'Rourke; and he carried off a countless number of kine.

King James[b] was proclaimed King in the place of the Queen, Elizabeth, on the 24th of March, 1602, according to the English computation[c]; or in 1603, according to the Roman computation. He was the sixth James of the Kings of Scotland.

wanting of our Men about 25. The pase wee went through was a good Myle longe; the wood high oaken Timber, with some Coppice amongst it; & most of the wayes nothing but dirte & myre. O Doghertie was with vs, alighted when I did, kept mee companie in the greatest heate of the feight, beheaued himselfe brauelie, & with a great deale of loue & affection, all that day, which at my next meeting with my lord I recommended him for, & he gaue him the honnor of knighthoode in recompence of; and so of the Captaines & officers, there was not one but was well putt to it, & had none other meanes to quitt himselfe by, but his owne Valour. And these I can nowe call to Remembrance were Captaine Leigh, Captaine Badby, Captaine Ralph Bingley, Captaine John Sidneye, Capt. William Sidney, Captaine Harte, & Ensigne Davyes, that was shott in the theigh, & not without Difficulty brought of, & afterwards safelie cured.

"Shortely after my lord wrote vnto mee; he was almost readie for the feilde againe, & had a purpose to plante a Garrison at Clogher, or Aghar, both standing on this Cormockes landes, willed mee if I could to bringe a peece of Artillery with mee, & as much victuell as I was able, & soe be in a readines against the next time I should heare from him. Artillery I was not able to bring; but about 10 dayes after I came to him, about 8 myles wide from Dungannon, &, as I remember, founde S[r] Arthur Chichester with him; but sure I ame, wee mett all three about that time, & marched togeather about 6 or 7 dayes, in which time the Castle of Aghar, standing in a lough, 12 myles wide from Omy, was yealded to him, & he placed Captaine Richard Hansard in Garrison in it, with 20 dayes victuell, & lefte mee in charge to supplie him when that time came out, which I did to the very day Tyrone was taken in, & order giuen for restitution of it into his handes, & afterwardes, when we parted, hee sent S[r] Hen. Follyatt with Mee to Comaund att Ballyshannon, first with directions to be vnder Mee, but not long after to be absolute Gouernor of himselfe."

[a] *Machaire-Stefanach*, now Magherastephanagh, a barony in the east of the county of Fermanagh, adjoining Tyrone.

[b] *King James.*—Sir Harris Nicolas says, that "for nearly twelve months after James's accession, the Statutes then in force vested the legal right to the throne in Lord Seymour, eldest son of the Earl of Hertford, by Lady Katherine Grey (sister of Lady Jane Grey), as heir of Mary, Duchess of Suffolk, the youngest sister of Henry VIII. James's hereditary pretensions were not acknowledged and ratified by Parliament until March, 1604."

[c] *The English computation.*—The Julian, or old style, and the practice of commencing the le-

Imṫusa í neill ⁊ na ngaoiḋeal ro ansat i nerinn iar maiḋm cinn tráile, bá sidh ro ṫioncoiscc, ⁊ ro aiṫin ua domnaill aoḋ ruaḋ díoḃ ria nimṫeaċt dó don spainn calma do ḋénaṁ acc cosnaṁ a naṫarḋa fri gallaiḃ go ttíosaḋ soṁ soċraitte lais dia ffóirittin, ⁊ airisioṁ isin ioṁḟuiḋe i mbáttar ar ro baḋ becc a ttesbaiḋ gé ro meaḃaḋ forra. Adbert friu dna nár ḃó hurasa dóiḃ iompuḋ inealLma dia ttír dia maḋeadh ro baḋ lainn leó, ar nó beittís a naiṁde ⁊ a mbíoḋḃaḋa agá ttóraiġeaċt, ⁊ acca ttoccraim, ⁊ an drong robtar gráḋaċ carṫanaċ impa acc toċt dóiḃ don muṁain, gomdís mioscneċ miorúnaċ iadsiḋe dóiḃ ag tionntúḋ dia ttíriḃ, ⁊ go mbeittis aga ffuabairt, ⁊ acc dénaṁ a nédala, ⁊ acc cluiċe ⁊ acc fanaṁatt impaiḃ.

Ní ro ġaḃsatt tra maiṫe gaoiḋeal an ċomairle sin, ⁊ ní ḋearnsat fair an ro ċuinniġ ċuca ó na baoí féin etorra. Aċt arsiḋ ro ċinnsiot tionntúḋ dia ttíriḃ. Lottar iaram ina mbrédiḃ slóiġ gan cennas uaḋaiḃ daoin tiġearna aċt gaċ tiġearna, ⁊ gaċ toiseaċ fó leiṫ co na ṫairisiḃ, ⁊ co na ṁuintir dílis ina lenṁain. Monuar aṁ níor ḃó hionann menma, ⁊ meisneaċ, brígh ⁊ borrfaḋ, báiġ, ⁊ barann do na gaoiḋealaiḃ ag filleḋ ina ffriṫing an tan sin, ⁊ aṁail ro ḃáttar ó ṫús acc dol for an eaċtra sin. Ro ḟíoraḋ forċanta na flaṫa uí ḋomnaill, ⁊ gaċ ní ro ṫairrngir dóiḃ, ar ní namá ro ċoiṁéirġettar a mbíoḋḃaḋa bunaiḋ ina nagaiḋ rempa, ⁊ ina ndiaiḋ do ċaṫuccaḋ friú, aċt ro éirġettar an taos carattraiḋ, ⁊ coiṁċengail, ⁊ a ccompannta coccaiḋ go mbáttar ag deabhaiḋ ⁊ acc diuḃraccaḋ forra in gaċ conair ioṁċuṁaing trés ar ċingsiot. Nír ḃó hurusa dia naireaċaiḃ ⁊ dia nuaislib dia nóccaiḃ

gal year on the 25th March, subsisted in England until the 24 Geo. II., 1751, in which year an Act of Parliament passed for making the year commence with the first of January. Sir Harris Nicolas observes, in his *Chronology of History*, 2nd edit. p. 37, that though some enlightened minds in England endeavoured to introduce the reformed calendar, soon after it was passed [in October, 1582], and cited the example of other countries, it was rejected by the Legislature, "apparently for no other reason than that the plan had emanated from Rome." He also remarks that this Bill for Reforming the Calendar was so generally unpopular, that Hogarth introduced into his picture of the Election Dinner a placard inscribed, "Give us our eleven days!"

[d] *Scoff at.*—An English writer would say, "and treat them with contumely, contempt, and mockery."

[e] *How different:* literally, "Alas! not equal, indeed, were the spirit, courage," &c. The sentence would be much more effective if reversed thus: "Alas! how different were the feelings of the Irish on their return home on this occasion, from the courage, vigour, self-reliance, spirit of defiance, and magnanimity, by which they were exalted, animated, elated, sublimated,

As for O'Neill and the Irish [adherents] who remained in Ireland after the defeat at Kinsale, what O'Donnell (Hugh Roe) had instructed and commanded them to do, before his departure for Spain, was, to exert their bravery in defending their patrimony against the English, until he should return with forces to their relief, and to remain in the camp in which they [then] were, because their loss was small, although they had been routed. He had observed to them also that it would not be easy for them to return safe to their country, if that were their wish, because their enemies and adversaries would pursue and attack them; and those who had been affectionate and kind towards them, on their coming into Munster, would be spiteful and malicious towards them on their return to their territories, and that they would attack and plunder them, and scoff at and mock them[d].

The chiefs of the Irish did not, however, take his advice, and did not attend to his request, because he himself was not among them; but they resolved on returning to their territories. They afterwards set out in separate hosts, without ceding the leadership to any one lord; but each lord and chieftain apart, with his own friends and faithful people following him. Alas! how different[e] were the spirit, courage, energy, hauteur, threatening, and defiance of the Irish, on their return back at this time, from those they had when they first set out on this expedition. The surmises of the Prince O'Donnell, and every thing which he predicted, were verified; for, not only did their constant enemies rise up before and after them to give them battle, but their [former] friends, confederates, and allies, rose up, and were attacking and shooting them on every narrow road through which they passed. It was not easy for the chiefs and

on their way into Munster, when O'Donnell performed, on a Winter's day, the greatest march of which there exists any record, and O'Neill overawed his enemies from the Boyne to the Bandon."

The Spanish General was so disgusted at this sudden retreat of the Irish, that, in his very first conference with Sir William Godolphin, he pronounced the Irish to be "not only weake and barbarous, but, as he feared, perfidious friends;" and, among the sarcasms he afterwards gave vent to, in treating with the English, he is reported to have said: "Presuming on their promise, that I should have joyned with them within a few dayes of the arrival of their forces, I expected long, in vaine sustained the brunt of the Viceroy's Armes. I then saw these two Counts take their stand, within two miles of Kinsale, reinforced with some Companies of Spaniards, and every hour repeating their promise to join us in forcing your camps. After all this we saw them at last broken with a handful of men, blown asunder into divers parts of the world, O Donnell into Spaine, O Neale to

⁊ dia milſdaiḃ anacal ⁊ imdſġail a muintire ar ḟod na slicceḋ baoí rſmpa ⁊ lá hiomat a nſsccarat, lá doininn ⁊ lá dearcan na gairḃsine gſimreatta ar bá deireaḋ geiṁriḋ do ḟonraḋ baoí ann an tan sin. Ar a aoí ċſna rangattar iar mór ġaiḃtiḃ dia ttíriḃ gan écc oirdeirc dfágḃáil, ⁊ ro ġaḃ gaċ tiġearna tíre aca ag imdíoſn a aṫarḋa amail as ſſrr ro ḟéḋ.

Rudraiġe dna ó doṁnaill mac aoḋa mic maġnasa bá haiccesiḋe ro ḟáccaiḃ ó doṁnaill (an aḋaiġ ré nimṫeaċt dó) cſnnas a ṁuintire, a ṫíre, ⁊ a ṫalṁan, ⁊ gaċ nſiṫe ro baḋ toiċ ḋó go ttíosaḋ soṁ ina ffriṫing do ridiri, ⁊ ro aiṫin dua neill, ⁊ do Rúḋraiġe gomdís carattraċ fri a roile aṁail ro ḃáttar soṁ fſin ina ndís. Ro ṫinġeallsat dósoṁ innsin.

Ro iaḋsatt cenel cconaill iarttain im ḋaṁna a fflaṫa gér ḃó sccaraḋ cuirp fri hanmain lá a nurṁór ſdarsccaraḋ fris an tí ro baḋ cuingiḋ ⁊ ro baḋ forlaṁaiḋ forra gó sin. Ro ġaḃ tra mac i doṁnaill Ruḋraiġe acc réimḟéduccaḋ a muintire co seitreaċ síorċalma in gaċ conair dodaing do-imṫeaċta, in gaċ gáḃaiḋ, ⁊ in gaċ guasaċt do rala dóiḃ ó do ḟágaiḃsiot cſnntsáile go rangattar i nurṫosaċ earraiġ go hioċtar connaċt airm i raḃattar buar, ⁊ bruġaḋa, croḋ, ⁊ cſṫra ċeneoil cconaill seaċnóin na tíre isin cconrann hi luiġniḃ, ⁊ hi ttír ḟiaċraċ muaiḋe. Bá maiṫ an buaċail ⁊ an taoġaire do riaċt cucasoṁ annsin, ar gér ḃó hiomda croḋ coiccriċe ro faccaiḃ ó doṁnaill agá ṁuintir acc sccaraḋ friú, ní ro léicc Ruḋraiġe a naṫċumaoín uaḋa dia aiṁdeoin do ṡaiġiḋ naċ tíre as a ttuccaḋ iatt, dóiġ ro ṡſrn, ⁊ ro ṡrſṫnaiġ a aṁsa, ⁊ a óccḃaiḋ for bſrnaḋaiḃ baoġail, ⁊ for ſnaiġiḃ eisinnile na criċe co ná laṁṫa toċt ṫairsiḃ dfoġail no dinġreim neich dia ṁuintirsiom.

Baoí dna ó gallċuḃair Eoġan mac Sſain acc iomċoiṁétt baile an ṁótaiġ ó ua ndoṁnaill o ro triall isin muṁain gus an tan sin, ⁊ ó do riaċt Ruḋraiġe ċuca do ḃſrt an baile dó co mbaoí for a ċumas.

the furthest part of the north, so that now I find no such Counts *in rerum natura*." See the *Pacata Hibernia*, book ii. c. xxiii., and Moryson's *History of Ireland*, edit. of 1735, vol. ii. pp. 61, 62.

[f] *The length of the way:* i. e. the long journey they had to pass.

[g] *Remarkable loss:* i. e. without losing any man of note.

[h] *Return back again.*—This phraseology is redundant, but it is perfectly literal.

[i] *Commanded*, ro aiṫin.—This is not the proper verb; ro ċuingiḋ, i. e. he requested or implored, would be far more correct.

[k] *Themselves both:* i. e. Hugh Roe and O'Neill.

[l] *This thing.*—It should be: "They accord-

gentlemen, for the soldiers and warriors, to protect and defend their people, on account of the length of the way[f] that lay before them, the number of their enemies, and the severity and inclemency of the boisterous winter season, for it was then the end of winter precisely. Howbeit, they reached their territories after great dangers, without any remarkable loss[g]; and each lord of a territory began to defend his patrimony as well as he was able.

Rury O'Donnell, the son of Hugh, son of Manus, was he to whom O'Donnell had, on the night before his departure, left the government of his people and lands, and everything which was hereditary to him, until he should return back again[h]; and he had commanded[i] O'Neill and Rury to be friendly to each other, as themselves both[k] had been. They promised him this thing[l].

The Kinel-Connell then thronged around the representative of their prince[m], though most of them deemed the separation from their former hero and leader as the separation of soul from body. O'Donnell's son, Rury, proceeded to lead his people with resoluteness and constant bravery through every difficult and intricate passage, and through every danger and peril which they had to encounter since they left Kinsale until they arrived, in the very beginning of spring, in Lower Connaught, where the cows, farmers[n], property, and cattle of the Kinel-Connell were [dispersed] throughout the country, in Corran, in Leyny, and in Tireragh of the Moy. God was the herdsman and shepherd who had come to them thither; for although O'Donnell, at his departure, had left his people much of the cattle of the neighbouring territories, Rury did not suffer them to be forcibly recovered from him by any territory from which they had been taken; for he distributed and stationed his soldiers and warriors upon the gaps of danger and the undefended passes of the country, so that none would attempt to come through them to plunder or persecute any of his people.

O'Gallagher (Owen, the son of John), had been keeping the castle of Ballymote for O'Donnell, since he set out for Munster, until this time; but as soon as Rury returned he gave the castle up to him, so that it was under his command.

ingly promised so to continue."

[m] *Representative of their prince:* literally, "materies principis sui."

[n] *Cows, farmers.*—These words are grouped merely for the sake of alliteration. The sentence should be: "Where the farmers of the Kinel-Connell were staying, with their cows and other cattle and property."

Caistiall ḃeóil aṫa s'snaiġ i mbáttar iomċoiṁéda ó ua ndoṁnaill do ġabáil lá niall ngarḃ ua ndoṁnaill, ⁊ lá gallaiḃ iar ná ḃriseaḋ, ⁊ iar ná ḃlaiḋrébaḋ lá gonna mór do beartsat ċuicce, ⁊ an barda do tearnúḋ as ar elúḋ ó na baoí coḃair ná coṁḟurtaċt i ccoṁḟoccus dóiḃ ⁊ bá isin earraċ do ṡonnraḋ do gabaḋ an caistiall hísin.

Inis saiṁér ⁊ inis meic conaill do gabáil lá haoḋ mbuiḋe mac cuinn uí ḋoṁnaill, ⁊ corbmac mac donnchaiḋ óicc ṁéguiḋir do ġabáil lais ḃeós.

Niall garḃ co na ḋearḃraiṫriḃ, ⁊ go ngallaiḃ do ḋol i nartraiġiḃ for loch eirne go ro gabaḋ, ⁊ go ro briseaḋ leó inis ceiṫlinn. Ro gabaḋ leó din daiṁinis, ⁊ lios gabail, ⁊ ro ḟáccaibsiot barda indiḃ.

Mac suiḃne baġaineaċ, Donnchaḋ mac maoilmuire do ṫoċt dionnsaiġiḋ neill í doṁnaill ⁊ na ngall. Niall, ⁊ mac suiḃne do ṫóċar ré drung do ṡiol uiḋir, ⁊ do ċloinn ċaba dia ro marḃaḋ sochaiḋe ⁊ brian mac duḃġaill még caba do gabail leó.

Oilén cille tiġearnaiġ hi ffearaiḃ manaċ do gabail lá doṁnall mac cuinn i ḋoṁnaill, ⁊ éḋala iomḋa do ṫabairt as.

Creaċ lá haoḋ mbuiḋe mac cuinn i ḋoṁnaill for tuaṫal mac feilim duiḃ í neill i ndúthaiġ sleaċta airt i neill.

Sir oliuer lambert do ṫeaċt sluaġ mór do ġallaiḃ ⁊ do gaoiḋealaiḃ isin tsamraḋ do ṡonraḋ go slicceaċ, ⁊ báttar hisuiḋe hi ffosḃairi for

[a] *By Niall Garv.*—The castle of Ballyshannon, "that long desired place," was taken by Captain Digges, one of Docwra's officers, on the 25th of March. Docwra himself has written the following account of it in his *Narration:*

"And now, being earnestlie called vpon for a supplie of victuells by them at Dunnagall (the second shipping I had sent about for that purpose being kept backe with foule weather), I tooke vp Garrons in O Doghertie's Countrey, loaded them with salte & Biskitt, & with 100 Beeues went over the mountaines, most parte on foote, the wayes were soe rotten, & on the 12th day of December broughte them reliefe; & because I sawe that litle pile, reserued from the rage of the fire, to small, a greate deale, to containe a large & important Garrison, I remoued parte of them, & added two Companys moore, to ly at Ashrowe, an Abbay 10 myles further, & not aboue a quarter of a Myle distant from Ballyshannon; left Captaine Edward Digges, the Sergiant Maior, to Commaund there; tooke a viewe of the Castle; promised, as soone as I came home, to send him the Demy cannon, which, before, I had taken Ainogh withall; gaue my oppinion howe he should proceede in the vse of it; tooke oath & pledges of the chiefe of the Inhabitants thereabouts; and soe returned. By the way I was a litle stopped by the passage of the waters, & before I came home the Newes ouertooke Mee of the Lord Deputie's happie victorie att Kinsaile, of Tyrone's flight and re-

The castle of Ballyshannon, in which guards had been placed by O'Donnell, was taken by Niall Garv[o] O'Donnell and the English, after they had broken and greatly battered it by a great gun which they had carried to it; and the warders, seeing that there was no assistance or relief at hand, escaped from it by flight. This castle was taken in spring.

Inis-Saimer [at Ballyshannon] and Inis-mic-Conaill[p] were taken by Hugh Boy, the son of Con O'Donnell; and Cormac, the son of Donough Oge Maguire, was also taken prisoner by him.

Niall Garv, with his brothers, and the English, went in boats on Lough Erne, and took and destroyed Enniskillen. They also took [the monasteries of] Devenish and Lisgoole, and left warders in them.

Mac Sweeny Banagh (Donough, the son of Mulmurry) came over to Niall O'Donnell and the English. Niall and Mac Sweeny fought a battle with a party of the Maguires and Mac Cabes, in which many were slain; and Brian, the son of Dowell Mac Cabe, was taken prisoner by them.

The island of Cill-Tighearnaigh[q], in Fermanagh, was taken by Donnell, the son of Con O'Donnell; and he carried off many spoils from it.

Hugh Boy, the son of Con O'Donnell, took a prey from Tuathal, son of Felim Duff O'Neill, in the country of the Sliocht-Airt[r] O'Neill.

Sir Oliver Lambert came in the summer to Sligo with a numerous army of English and Irish, and there encamped against Rury O'Donnell, who was to

turning homewards, & of O Donnell's departure to Sea to goe into Spaine. I sent away the Cannon assoone as I came home, & on the 20th of March it arrived there, & on the 25th (being the first day of the yeare 1602) was that long desired place taken by the said Captaine Digges, with lesse then a tenth parte of that charge which would haue beene willinglie bestowed vpon it, & the Consequence thereof brought many furtherances to the gennerall seruice."

[p] *Inis-mic-Conaill:* i. e. the Island of the Son of Conall. This name does not now exist in the county of Donegal. It was probably the name of the Island in Lough Esk, near Donegal.

[q] *Cill-Tighearnaigh:* i. e. the Church of St. Tighearnach, now Kiltierney, in the barony of Lurg, and county of Fermanagh.

[r] *Sliocht-Airt*, a sept of the O'Neills descended from Art mac Con, the grandfather of Turlough Luineach. They were seated in the barony of Strabane, and possessed Castle Derg and the Crannog of Loch Laeghaire. Docwra describes the situation of this sept as follows:

"In the beginning of Aprill" [1600] "I made another iourney upon them of Sleught-Art, a People that inhabited a Countrey in Tyrone of 16 myles longe, most parte Bogge & wood, & bordering not farr off from the Liffer, where onelie I had, by Neale Garvie's means, Castle Derg deliuered into my hands."

Ruḋraiġe ua nDoṁnaill baoí alla ṫuas díoḃ, ⁊ for íochtar Connacht ar ċena dus an ttáirsidís ní dá néoalaiḃ. Do ḋeachaidh umorro cathbarr mac aoḋa duiḃ i Doṁnaill go ro ċengail a ċura ⁊ a ṁuinnterus lá Sir oliuer. Bá hann baoí airisiom ⁊ dúnarus caṫḃairr an tan sin i nDún Aille don leiṫ a niar do ṡliccech. Arsiodh ro triall Sir oliber, ⁊ caṫḃarr co na ṡlóġ dol diarraidh creach ⁊ edala go fearaiḃ manach. O ro clos lá Ruḋraiġe ua nDoṁnaill an tertriall sin bá doiliġ lais a aos coḋaig ⁊ caradradh do ionnradh gan tocht dia ffurtacht dia ttiosradh de ⁊ do ċoidh do ṡaighid uí Ruairc (Brian óg) da iarraidh fair tocht ina ṡochraitte ar co ttochradh frir na gallaiḃ isin cconair in ro baḋ dóiġ lais a ffagḃáil i ndarḃaoġal, ⁊ ro ċuinniġ fair beós congnaṁ lais isin ccoccadh go ttíosradh o Doṁnaill do ċoḃair gaoiḋeal, ⁊ dúnadh daingen díṫoglaiġi dia ḃailtiḃ nó ḃiadh na ionad cumsanta agá aos gonta ⁊ aṫgaoiṫe, eimpti, ⁊ easláinte, ⁊ dna frir sin go ro léicceadh a ṁuintir co na ccrodh, ⁊ ceṫraiḃ ċucca ina tir. Ro ob ó Ruairc mac uí Doṁnaill im gach ní ro ṡir fair. Bá méla, ⁊ bá haṫais laissiuṁ a éimġedh ioir, conadh eadh do róine ó na baoí coiṁlíon slóiġ frir na gallaiḃ airisiom ag imḋeġail a ṁuintire badéin.

Dala Sir oliuer do ċóidh side ⁊ caṫḃarr co na ttionól go ro creachadh leó ina mbaoí ina ccoṁfoccus do fearaiḃ manach, ⁊ do beartsat éttala iomḋa leó, ⁊ impuidhsiot dia ttiġiḃ.

Ro hairneidhead do Sir oliuer an tertriall do róine Ruḋraiġe ó Doṁnaill, ⁊ aṁail ro ċuinniġ for ua Ruairc tocht lais dia toirmesc soṁ don turus réṁeberthmar. Ro ṁéadaiġ a aincridhe ní bád uille frir ar a los gonadh aire sin ro ṫócuir fuilleadh slóiġ a haṫluain ina docum do ḋioġail a ṁiscne for Ruḋraiġe. Od ċualaiġ Ruḋraiġe go mbattar goill aṫa luain ag tocht don leiṫ anuas dia ionnsaicchidh, ⁊ goill ṡliccigh don leiṫ ele, Ro tiomaircedh a ċrodh ⁊ a ceṫra, a innile, ⁊ a airnéis lais tar coirrṡliaḃ na seghsa hi maiġ luirce, arridhe tar sionainn hi muintir eolais, ⁊ co sliaḃ an iarainn hi cconmaicne réin co na tarṫaitsiot goill ní díoḃ, ⁊ go ro iompaiḋsiot goill aṫa luain dia ttiġiḃ gan nach cosccar don cur sin. Do ṫaodhsat muintir meic

[s] *Dun-Aille:* i. e. the *Dun* or Fort of the Cliff or Precipice, now Donally, in the parish of Calry, barony of Carbury, and county of Sligo. In the deed of partition of the Sligo estate, this is called the castle of Downally, and described as situated "in Collary, in the barony of Carbery and county of Sligo."

[t] *But seeing:* literally, "so that what he did,

the south of them, and against [the inhabitants of] Lower Connaught in general, to try whether they could seize on any of their property. Caffar, the son of Hugh Duv O'Donnell, went and ratified his peace and friendship with Sir Oliver. The place at which Caffar had his residence and fortress at this time was Dun-Aille[s], to the west of Sligo; [and] Sir Oliver and Caffar prepared to go with their forces into Fermanagh, in search of preys and spoils.

As soon as Rury O'Donnell heard of this expedition, it grieved him that his allies and friends should be plundered, without coming to their relief, if he could; and he repaired to O'Rourke (Brian Oge), to request of him to join his forces, that they might engage the English at a pass where he expected to get an advantage of them. He also requested him to assist him in the war until O'Donnell should return to relieve the Irish, and to give him one of his strong, impregnable castles, as a resting-place for his wounded, disabled, feeble, and sick people; and, moreover, that he would allow his people [to remove] with their property and cattle into his territory. O'Rourke refused the son of O'Donnell everything he requested of him, and the other was grieved and insulted at his refusal; but, seeing[t] that he was not strong enough to cope with the English, he remained to protect his own people.

As for Sir Oliver, he and Caffar went, with their muster, and plundered the neighbouring parts of Fermanagh; and, after carrying off many spoils, they returned to their houses.

Sir Oliver was informed of the proceedings of Rury O'Donnell, and how he had requested of O'Rourke to join him, to obstruct him [Sir Oliver] in the expedition which we have before mentioned, and his animosity against him grew greater on account of it; and he, therefore, sent for additional forces to Athlone, to wreak his vengeance upon Rury. As soon as Rury heard that the English of Athlone were approaching him from the south side, and the English of Sligo from the other side, he collected his property, his cattle, flocks, and herds, [and moved] with them across Coirrshliabh-na-Seaghsa into Moylurg, from thence across the Shannon into Muintir-Eolais, and to Sliabh-an-Iarainn, in Conmaicne-Rein; so that the English seized no portion of them; and the English of Athlone returned to their homes without gaining any victory on that

as he was not of equal force with the English, was, to remain protecting his own people." But this idiom looks so inelegant in English that the Editor has taken the liberty to alter it.

Uí ḋomnaill co na ccrodh for ccúlaiḃ do riḋisi gus na háitiḃ as ro ḟóghluaisiot .i. gus an ccorann go luighne, ⁊ co tír ḟiachraċ.

Do ċóiḋ umorro Ruḋraighe buḋéin go líon a ṫionoil go ráinicc go hoilén loċa hiasccaigh alla toir do ḋún na ngall airm a mbattar bardaḋa í ḋomnaill, ⁊ in ro ḟáccbaḋ ua concobair Sliccigh hi laiṁ o ro gabaḋ eisiḋe lá hua nDomnaill go deireaḋ an tramhraiḋ hísin. O do riaċt roiṁ don ḃaile báttar faoiligh a ṁuintir riaṁ. Ro ṫingeall ó conċoḃair a óighriar do mac uí ḋomnaill, ⁊ iar naiḋm a ccor ⁊ a cconnarṫa fri a roile ro léicc ua conċoḃair a geimeal, ⁊ do ḋeaċattar iaraṁ tar anais hi cconnaċtaiḃ.

I neaċṁaing na ree sin .i. Isin ffoghṁar do ḟorraḋ ro ṫionoilsiot goill Rossa comáin, ⁊ uaċtair ċonnaċt sluagh mór do ṫoċt for Ruḋraighe ua nDomnaill dorisisi, ⁊ ní ro hanaḋ leo go rangattar go mainistir na búille. Ro tecclamaḋ slógh naile lá Ruḋraighe, ⁊ lá hua cconċoḃair ina ccoṁḋáil go riaċtattar tar coirrsliaḃ go ro ġabsatt longport fo erċoṁair an ḃaile don taoiḃ araill. Do bertsat a muinteara co na croḋ, ⁊ co na ccetraiḃ iar na ccul ó ṁagh i ġaḋra hi ccúil ó ffinn, gus an ccend ṫoir do coirrsliaḃ, ar bá hoṁan leo na goill báttar hi Slicceċ dia ccreachaḋ dia néis dia mbeittis i neittirċéin uaḋaiḃ. Báttar athaiḋ aṁlaiḋ sin aghaiḋ i naghaiḋ hi ffoiċill aroile. Ro gonaḋ ⁊ ro loitteaḋ daoíne iomḋa etorra in airett báttar isin mainistir. Bá cian lás na gallaiḃ báttar an tuctt sin gonaḋ eḋ ro ċinnset ionnsaighiḋ an ḃealaigh ḃuiḋe for Ruḋraighe, ⁊ for ua cconċuḃair, ⁊ dol ṫarra dia naiṁḋeóin. Ro freslaiḋ ⁊ ro frioṫáilitt lás na gaoiḋealaiḃ uair ro ficcheaḋ sccainnear ċróḋa etorra go ro marḃaḋ ile do na gallaiḃ, ⁊ gur bó heiccen dóiḃ fó ḋeóiḋ filleaḋ ina ffriṫing iar na mélaċtnuccaḋ go mór. Fáccbaitt an mainistir iaraṁ, ⁊ do ḋeaċattar tar anais go ros comáin.

Dus ficc Ruḋraighe ⁊ ua conċoḃair tar coirrsliaḃ, ⁊ ro ġabsatt forlongport ag Esdara hi fforbaisi for na gallaiḃ báttar hi Slicceaċ. Feaċt ann dus narṫaitsi foirend do na gallaiḃ réṁráite ag béin arḃa, ⁊ glasgort

[u] *Loch-Iasgach*, now Lough Esk.

[v] *Cuil-O-bh-Fhinn.*—This was first written hi ccuil ó ffloiñ, but the letters lo would appear to have been cancelled, evidently by the original scribe. There is a district called Cuil-O'bhFloinn, in the county of Leitrim, but the true name of the territory in which Moy-O'Gara is situated is Cuil-Obh-Finn. It is now made *anglice* Coolavin, which is a well-known barony verging on Lough Gara, in the south of the county of Sligo.

[w] *Bealach-Buidhe:* i. e. the Yellow Road or Pass, now *anglice* Ballaghboy, the name of a pass or ancient road over the Curlieu hills, on

occasion. The people of the son of O'Donnell [then] returned back again with their cattle to the places from which they had set out, namely, to Corran, Leyny, and Tireragh.

Rury himself then set out with all his forces, and arrived at the island of Loch-Iasgach[u], to the east side of Donegal, where O'Donnell's warders were, and where O'Conor Sligo was left in custody, since he had been taken by O'Donnell until the end of that summer. When he came to this castle, his people there were much rejoiced at his arrival. O'Conor promised to be entirely submissive to O'Donnell's son; and after they had entered into a treaty of friendship with each other, he released O'Conor from captivity; and they afterwards returned back to Connaught.

At this time, that is, in autumn, the English of Roscommon and Upper Connaught mustered a numerous army, to march against Rury O'Donnell again; and they did not delay until they arrived at the monastery of Boyle. Rury and O'Conor mustered another army to meet them; and they marched across Coirrshliabh, and pitched their camp before the town at the other side. They took their people, with their property and cattle, along with them, from Moy-O'Gara in Cuil-O-bh-Fhinn[v] to the eastern extremity of the Coirrshliabh; for they were afraid that the English of Sligo would plunder them in their absence, were they far distant from them. Thus they remained for some time, face to face, in readiness for each other; and many persons were disabled and wounded between them, while in the monastery. The English deemed it too long they had been in that situation; and they resolved to face Bealach-Buidhe[w], and pass it in despite of Rury and O'Conor. They were met and responded to by the Irish; and a fierce battle was fought between them, in which many of the English[x] were slain; so that they [the survivors] were compelled to return back, after being much disheartened. They afterwards left the monastery, and returned to Roscommon.

Rury and O'Conor proceeded across Coirrshliabh, and pitched their camp at Ballysadare, to wage war with the English of Sligo. One day they overtook a party of the English aforementioned, who were cutting down the corn and green

the borders of the counties of Roscommon and Sligo.—See note [x], under the year 1497, p. 1232, *supra.*

[x] *Many of the English.*—This should be, "In which the English lost so many men that they were compelled to return back," &c.

an tíre ar níor ḃó saiḋbir lóin iadsiḋe, ⁊ ro muḋaiġit leó fó céḋóir. Do rónsat osaḋ míosa fri aroile iarttain.

Ro ṫocaiṫriot samlaiḋ go hurṫosaċ geiṁriḋ go ro ċuir Lord Leutenant general coccaiḋ na hereann (.i. charles blunt .i. lord mountioy), teaċta ⁊ scriḃenn do saiġiḋ Ruḋraiġe í Domnaill dia aslaċ fair teaċt fó ṡíṫ, ⁊ caonċoṁrac. Ḃá hsḋ a ttoṫaċt dia ráḋ fris gur ḃó hiomairccide ḋó gé nó ḋiccsḋ fó ṡíḋ ⁊ ċáirdine, ⁊ ro baḋ aiṫreaċ lais muna ṫíosaḋ ittir, uair do ruaċt scéla ċuicceriom go ro écc ua Domnaill dsbraṫair Rúḋraiġe isin Spáinn, ⁊ go ndeachaiḋ an coccaḋ do lsiṫlsiṫ dia oiḋheaḋ, ⁊ ro baḋ toġaoís, ⁊ ro baḋ meallaḋ mór ḋó muna dearnaḋ síḋ friusum a ttraitte.

O ro hairléugaitt na litre ro gairmit a ċoṁairliġ go Ruḋraiġe dus cioḋ do ḋénaḋ ⁊ ro ġaḃ ag criúḋ a ċomairle friú. Ḃáttar foirsinn díoḃ agá ráḋa nár ḃó fír écc í Domnaill, ⁊ gur ab dia ḃréccaḋ ⁊ dia ṫogaothaḋ soṁ, ⁊ dia accoṁal fri dliġeaḋ ro dolḃaḋ an scél sin ċuicce. Do ḃáttar drong ele agá ráḋ gur ḃó fíor, ⁊ gur ḃó dsġcoṁairle an tríṫ do gaḃail an tan ro ḃás aga haslaċ forra conaḋ fair ro hanaḋ leó fó ḋeóiḋ eissiuṁ ⁊ ua conċoḃair Sliccig do ḋol go háṫ luain do naiḋm a sioḋa fris an ngeneral. Tiagaitt iarttain, ⁊ ro fiaḋaiġitt lasm ngeneral, ⁊ do ratt onóir ⁊ airmittin mór do mac í Domnaill, ⁊ do róine síḋ fris a huċt an riġ, ⁊ ro naiḋm a ċairdsf frisiuṁ sainriṫ. Coṁairléiccis ḋó iaraṁ dol dia aṫarḋa diamaḋ lainn lais.

AOIS CRIOST, 1603.

Aois Criost, mile, se cétt, a trí.

O Neill Aoḋ mac an fir ḋorċae, ⁊ urmór gaoiḋeal leiṫe cuinnt do ṫoċt fó ṡíḋ cenmotá ua Ruairc ar ro herfuaccraḋ síṫ coitcsinn, ⁊ airsec a ḟola,

[y] *Requested of them.*—The English writers reverse this account, and state that Rory O'Donnell made humble suit to the Lord Deputy for Her Majesty's mercy.—See Moryson, book iii. c. i. edit. of 1735, vol. ii. p. 226.

[z] *O'Neill.*—If Queen Elizabeth had lived a few months longer, O'Neill would never have been taken into mercy, as appears from her letter to Mountjoy, dated 9th October, 1602, in which she writes as follows:

"Lastly, for Tyrone, we do so much mislike to give him any Grace, that hath been the only Author of so much Effusion of blood, and the most ungrateful Viper to us that raised him, and one that hath so often deceived us, both when he hath craved his Pardon, and when he

crops of the country, because they were not rich in provisions, and they were annihilated by them at once. They [i. e. the English of Sligo, and Rury O'Donnell and his party] afterwards made a month's truce with each other.

Thus they passed the time until the beginning of winter, when the Lord Lieutenant and General of the war of Ireland (namely, Charles Blount, Lord Mountjoy) sent messengers and letters to Rury O'Donnell, requesting him to come upon terms of peace and tranquillity. The import of these [letters] was, that it was meet for him to come upon terms of peace and friendship, and that, if he would not, he should be sorry for it, for that news had reached him that O'Donnell, Rury's brother, had died in Spain, and that the war was at an end by his death, and that it would be a great want of wisdom, and [self] delusion, in him, if he did not make peace with him [Mountjoy] immediately.

As soon as he had read the letters, Rury called his advisers to him, to consider what he should do; and he began to deliberate with them in council. Some of them said that the [report of] O'Donnell's death was not true, but that the story had been fabricated, [and sent him] to allure and deceive him [Rury], and to bind him by law. Another party asserted that the rumour was true, that it was good advice to accept of the peace, when it was requested of them[y]; so that what they finally agreed upon was, that he and O'Conor Sligo should go to Athlone, to ratify their peace with the General. They afterwards went, and were welcomed by the General; and he shewed great honour and respect to the son of O'Donnell, and made peace with him on behalf of the King, and confirmed his friendship with him in particular. He then recommended him to return, if he thought proper, to his patrimony.

THE AGE OF CHRIST, 1603.

The Age of Christ, one thousand six hundred three.

O'Neill[a] (Hugh, the son of Ferdorcha) and most of the Irish of Leath-Chuinn, except O'Rourke, came in under peace; for a proclamation for a general peace,

hath received it of us, as when we consider how much the World will impute to us of Weakness to shew favour to him now, as if, without that, we could not give an end to this Rebellion, we still remain determined not to give him Grace of any kind."—Moryson's *History of Ireland*, book iii. c. i. vol. ii. p. 225.

After this Her Majesty's officers in Ireland

⁊ a ḋuiṫċe dá gaċ aon la baḋ áil o ṁórḋaċt an ríġ King Sémas iar na oirdneaḋ i nionaḋ na bainríogna ós saxaiḃ Frainc, ⁊ uas Eirinn.

had recourse to every stratagem that cunning and subtlety could suggest, to take him prisoner, or assassinate him; but he had been educated in their own school, and had learned to avoid them with equal skill and caution. The Lord Deputy Mountjoy complains of O'Neill's skill in keeping on his head, and of the inviolable honour of his followers, who could not be induced, by any bribe, to lay violent hands upon his sacred person, in a letter written to the Lords in England on the 25th of February, 160$\frac{2}{3}$, as follows:

"And it is most sure that never Traitor knew better how to keep his own Head than this, nor any Subjects have a more dreadful Awe to lay violent Hands on their sacred Prince, than these people have to touch the persons of their O'Neals; and he, that hath as pestilent a Judgment as ever any had, to nourish and to spread his own Infection, *hath the ancient Swelling and Desire of Liberty in a conquered Nation to work upon*, their Fear to be rooted out, or to have their old Faults punished upon all particular Discontents, and generally, over all the Kingdome, the Fear of Persecution for Religion, the debasing of the Coin (*which is grevious unto all sorts*), and a Dearth and Famine, which is already begun, and must, of Necessity, grow shortly to Extremity, the least of which alone have been many Times sufficient Motives to drive the best and most quiet Estates into sudden Confusion. These will keep all spirits from settling, breed new Combinations, and, I fear, even stir the Towns themselves to sollicit foreign Aid," &c.

It appears from another letter, given by Moryson, book iii. c. ii. vol. ii. p. 275, 25th March, 1603, addressed, by the Lord Deputy, to Master Secretary, that the designs towards O'Neill were still baser. The following extract from this letter will explain their dark intentions;

"I have received, by Capt. Hays, her Majesties Letters of the 6th of February, wherein I am directed to send for Tyrone, with Promise of Security for his Life only, and upon his Arrival, without further Assurance, to make Stay of him till her Pleasure should be further known; and, at the same Time, I received another from her Majesty, of the 17th of February, wherein it pleased her to enlarge the Authority given unto me, to assure him of his Life, Liberty, and Pardon, upon some Conditions remembered therein; And withal I received a letter from yourself, of the 18th of February, recommending to me your own Advice, to fulfil (as far as I possibly could) the Meaning of her Majesty's first Letter, and signifying her Pleasure that I should seek, by all the best Means I can, to promise him his Pardon *by some other Name than Earl of Tyrone*, and rather by the Name of Baron of Dungannon, or, if it needs must be, *by the Name of some other Earl*. Secondly, to deliver him his Country in less Quantity, and with less Power, than before he had it. And lastly, to force him to cleare his Paces and Passages, made difficult by him against any Entry into his Country. And now, since it hath pleased her Majesty, by so great a Trust, to give me so comfortable Arguments of her favour, I am incouraged the more freely to presume to declare myself in this great Matter, which I call great, because the Consequence is great and dangerous to be dealt in without the Warrant of her gracious Interpretation. And though my Opinion herein should proceed from a long and advised Consideration, described with large and many Circumstances, and confirmed with strong and judicial Reasons, yet, because I think it fit to hasten away this Messenger, I will write of these Things somewhat, though on the sudden, and commit the rest to the sufficient Judgment

and a restoration of his blood and territory to every one that wished for it, had been issued by His Majesty King James, after he had been appointed in the place of the Queen [as King] over England, France, and Ireland.

and Relation of the Lord President, now in his Journy towards you; and the rather, because I find him to concur with me in the Apprehension of this Cause, and of the State of all other Things of this Kingdom. And first, for her Majesty's first Letter, I pray you, Sir, believe me, that I have omitted nothing, both by Power and Policy, to ruin him, and utterly to cut him off; and if, by either, I may procure his Head, before I have engaged her royal Word for his Safety, I do protest I will do it; and much more be ready to possess myself of his Person, if, by only Promise of Life, or by any other Means whereby I shall not directly scandal the Majesty of publick Faith, I can procure him to put himself into my Power. But to speak my Opinion freely, I think that he, or any Man in his Case, would hardly adventure his Liberty to preserve only his Life, which he knoweth how so well to secure by many other Ways; for if he fly into Spain, that is the least whereof he can be assured, and most Men (but especially he) do make little Difference between the value of their Life and Liberty; and to deceive him I think it will be hard, for though Wiser Men than he may be over-reached, yet he hath so many Eyes of Jealousy awake."

In the mean time Queen Elizabeth died (on the 24th of March, 1603), and Moryson boasts that he, himself, contrived that O'Neill should make his submission to her, though he (Moryson) knew that she was dead. He made his submission on his knees, in most beautiful language, at Mellifont, on the 30th of March following, but when he heard the news of the Queen's death, he could not refrain from tears, being now a sexagenarian, and seeing the helpless state to which he was reduced by the artifice of his enemies; for the pardon and protection he received rested on the dead body of Elizabeth, which had no longer the power to protect him, or to bind her successor. He had also lost the opportunity, either of continuing the war against a weak prince, or making a meritorious submission to the new king, who was believed to have descended from the Irish.

The Lord Deputy's honour was, however, pledged, and accordingly, on the 6th day of April, he did not only renew his Protection, in King James's name, but soon after gave him liberty to return to Ulster to settle his affairs; but first O'Neill, now once more Earl of Tyrone, delivered up hostages, and also renewed his submission in a set form of words, wherein he "abjured all foreign power and jurisdiction in general, and the King of Spain's in particular," and renounced all power and authority over the Urrighs of Ulster (but which he claimed soon after, by the Lord Deputy's consent), and the name of O'Neill, and all his lands, except such as should be granted to him by the King; and he promised future obedience, and to discover his correspondence with the Spaniards. And, at the same time, he wrote a beautiful letter to the King of Spain, requesting him to send home his eldest son, Henry, who, however, never returned to him, for he was afterwards found strangled at Brussels, nobody knows why or how.—See Cox's *Hibernia Anglicana*, vol. ii. pp. 2, 3.

But he was still great, mighty, and formidable, and on his return into Ulster challenged regal authority over O'Kane, hanged Docwra's guides without trial by jury, and had the fisheries of Lough Foyle ceded to him, although they had been given to Sir Henry Docwra.

On his return to Ulster the Earl of Tyrone

Mac suibne fánatt domnall do tocht fó dhliccedh dionnsaicchidh neill í domnaill.

sent some of his men to be cessed upon O'Kane, which intimated that he was made lord of his country. This was directly against the Lord Deputy's promise, and Sir Henry Docwra repaired to Dublin to complain of this and other concessions made to the Earl of Tyrone and others. The following extract from Docwra's *Narration* will shew the exact nature of the authority assumed by the Earl of Tyrone, on his return to Ulster, and of the unwillingness of the Lord Deputy to interfere with him, even though he knew that he had acted contrary to the laws, and even to the words of his submission. The ultimate object of this policy is explainable only by the project which the Government had at this time in contemplation, though not fully developed till some years afterwards. Docwra, who was very fond of fair play, gives the following account of his interview with Mountjoy, concerning the fulfilment of certain promises which he had made to O'Kane and others.

"Then, touching O Caine, I tould him" [Lord Mountjoy] "how the Earle of Tyrone had sent men to be cessed vpon him, & how hee refused them. S[r] Henry Docwra sayeth he, my lord of Tyrone is taken in with promise to be restored, aswell to all his lands as his honnor of Dignitie, & O Caines Countrey is his, & must be obedient to his Comaund. My lord, said I, this is strange, & beyond all expectation; for I ame sure your lordship cannot be vnmindfull, first, of the agreement I made with him, wherein he was promised to be free & to hould his lands from the Crowne, & then your lordship ratified & approued the same vnto him vnder your hand, haue iterated it againe diuers & diuers times, both by word of mouth & writing; how shall I looke this man in the face, when I shall knowe myselfe guilty directlie to haue satisfied my word with him. Hee is but a drunken ffellowe, saith hee, & soe base, that I doe not thinke but in the secreete of his hearte, it will better Content him to be soe then otherwise; besides, hee is able neither to doe good nor hurte, & wee must haue a Care to the Publique good, & giue Contentment to my lord of Tyrone, vpon which depends the Peace & securitie of the whole kingdome. My Lord, said I, for his drunkenness & disabillitie to doe good or hurte, they are not heere to come into Consideration; & for his inward affections, what they are I know not; but sure I ame hee makes outward shewe, that this will be very displeasing vnto him; and the manifest & manifould benifitts hee shall receiue more by the one then the other, are, to my vnderstanding, sufficient arguments to make mee thinke hee doth seriouslie inclyne to his owne good; &, with your fauour, what good can ensue to the Publique by a direct breach of Promise, whereof there is soe plaine and vndeniable Evidence extante vnder our hands, it passeth my vnderstanding to Conceiue. Well, sayeth hee againe, that I haue done was not without the aduise of the Councell of this kingdome. It was liked of & approued by the lords in England, by the Queene that is deade, & by the king's Maiestie that is now living; & I ame perswaded, not without good & sufficient Reason, it may not be infringed; but if yow can thinke vpon any course to Compase it in some good fashon, that I be troubled noe more with it, I shall take it as an acceptable kindnes. But, howsoeuer, By God, sayeth hee, O Cane must & shall be vnder my lord Tyrone. I then tould him I had noe more to say, though I were not soe fullie satisfied as I could wish. Yet hee should see my will was, & should be, obedient & Conformeable to his: let it be soe sayeth hee, & yow shall doe mee a pleasure.

Mac Sweeny Fanad (Donnell) came under the law, to join Niall O'Donnell.

"Then, touching O Doughertie, I tould him hee had hard his lordship had a purpose to giue away the Ile of Inche from him, which hee had shewed Mee was expreslie contayned in his father's Graunte, &, therefore, would importe a breach of Promise both of myne & his owne. Hee acknowledged he had been moued in such a matter, but thanked mee for telling him thus much, & bad mee be assured it should not be done. Wherewith I rested fullie satisfied, & tould O Doughertie as much, whoe was at that time in towne in my Compaine.

"Then I came to younge Tirlough & tould him I had receiued a generall Warraunt from his lordship, to restore all the Castles & houlders that I had in Tyrone, into my lord's hands. That there were two, videlicet: the Castle of Newtowne & Dongevin, that were delivered to Mee vpon Condition that, the Kinge hauing noe longer vse of them, they should haue them again from whome I receiued them; & besids that of Newtowne was parte of the peculier lands belonging to S[r] Arthur O Neale, whose sonnes, there were very many reasons for, should be fauoured & respected by the state. Hee tould Mee it was with him as it was with O Caine; all that Countrey was my lord of Tyrones, & what hee might be intreated to giue him, he might haue, But otherwise he could challeng noe right nor interest in anythinge; &, therefore, for the Castles, badd mee againe deliuer them, & for younge Tirlough, hee would speake to my lord to deale well with him.

"Ffor my Guids & Spyes I then saw my aunswere before hand, & that it was booteless to Motion for any landes for them; yet I tould him what seruices many of them had done, what promises I had made them, how vtterlie destitute of meanes they were to liue vpon, & how much I thought the state was ingaged, both in honnor and Pollicie, to prouide for & protect them. Hee said he would speake to my lord of Tyrone in their behalfe, & badd mee giue them what I thought good in victuells out of the King's stoore, & it should be allowed of. I was somewhat importunate for a Certaintie & Contynuance of meanes for them to liue vpon, & that by aucthoritie of the state they might be allowed to retourne to theire owne landes, But he would not indure to heare of it; yet hee spake to my lord of Tyrone in my presence, and he promised freelie to forgiue all that was past, & to deale with them as kindlie as with the rest of his Tenants; how beit, afterwardes (I could giue particular instances wherein) he changed his Note and Sunge annother tune.

"I then tould him of my Guide that my lord of Tyrone had hanged; he aunswered, he thought it was not without some iust cause; I desired that cause might be knowne, & the matter come to open tryall. Hee seemed to be extreamelie offended to be troubled with Complaints of that kinde, & my lord of Tyrone, said for his excuse, my lord had giuen him aucthoritie to execute Martiall lawe, & this was a knaue taken robbinge a Priest, & therefore worthyly put to Death. I was able to proue the Contrary, & offerred to doe it vpon perill of my life, by the Confessions of those Men I had, at that time, Prisoners in my hand, But seeing the Bussines soe displeasing to my lord, I gaue it ouer, & afterwards one of them, that was cheife in the action, breaking Prison, I sett the rest at liberty.

"Then came I lastlie to my selfe, & tould him I receiued order from him to suffer the Earle of Tyrone's men to fish the Riuer of Loughfoyle. I hoped his lordship had not forgott, that hitherto hee had giuen Mee the proffitts of it, & promised mee the inheritaunce, & that it was

Mac ſuiḃne na ttuaṫ Maolmuire mac murchaiḋ, ⁊ caṫḃarr ócc mac caṫḃairr, mic maġnusa í doṁnaill do ḋol hi ttír ċonaill co na muinteraiḃ, ⁊ co na ccreaċ do ċoccaḋ fri niall garḃ ⁊ fri gallaiḃ, ⁊ ní ro hanaḋ leó go rangattar do na rosaiḃ, ⁊ dona hoilénaiḃ. Níſ ḃó cian doiḃ ſaṁlaiḋ an tan ro creachaḋ iatt lá niall co na ḃraiṫriḃ, ⁊ ro herġaḃaḋ caṫḃarr ócc go mbaoí hi láiṁ leó.

Muinter Ruḋraiġe í doṁnaill co na uile ċreaċ ⁊ ceṫraiḃ, ⁊ iolṁaoínib do ḋol hi ttír ċonaill isin cceid ṁí dearrach, ⁊ Ruḋraiġe badéin co na ṫionól, ⁊ co na ṫóiceſtal gaoiḋeal ⁊ gall im captin guert do dol (ria tteaċt aniar dia ṁuintir) do ḋioġail, ⁊ daiṫe a ḋímiaḋa ⁊ a easanora ar ua Ruairc, Brian ócc aṁail ro ḃaoí ina ṁenmain achaiḋ siar an tan sin, go ro airccriot, ⁊ co ro innirriot an breifne etir iṫ ⁊ arḃar, ⁊ gaċ a ttaiṫaiter dia ccreaċ ar ro teiċriot a nurṁór fo diaṁraiḃ ⁊ droiḃelaiḃ na críċe. Ro marḃaitt uathaḋ daoíne eatorra im eoġan mac an firḋoirċe í gallċuḃair, ⁊ im ṫoirrḋealḃaċ mac mec loċlainn torċrattar coṁṫuitim ré roile don ċur sin. Ro faccḃaḋ drong do gallaiḃ i ngararun i ndruim dá ſitiar ar dáiġ aiḋmillte

not his meaning to take it from Mee againe. He said, Sr Henry Docwra, yow haue deserued well of the kinge, & your seruice there is greate Reason should be Recompenced, but it must be by some other meanes then this: yow see what promise I haue made to my lord of Tyrone; & it is not my Priuate affection to any man living that shall make mee breake it, because I knowe it is for the Publique good. Yow must, therefore, let him haue both that & the lands which were reserued from O Caine, and, on my honnor, yow shall be otherwise worthylie rewarded. I expected nothing less then such an answere, yet I made noe further wordes, but willinglie yealded to giue vp my intrust in both, & departed at that time, aswell contented without them, as I should haue beene glad to haue had them. Then I desired to haue gone with him into England; but he would not suffer Mee; but with exceeding fauorable Countenance assured mee to do me all right vnto the kinge; & soe was I satisfied with hopes, though any man may see I had hitherto nothing bettered my selfe by this Journey.

"As he was readie to take shipping, O Doghertie came & tould Mee, that notwithstanding all the assurance I had giuen him of the Contrary, the Ile of Inch was past away. I could not possiblie beleeue it at first, but hee showed mee manifest proofes that a lease was graunted for xxi. yeares. I then badd him goe speake for himselfe, for I had done as much as I was able; wherevpon hee followed him into England, and had such reamidie as shall presently be declared.

"In the meane time being gone, my lord Hugh (the Earle of Tyrone's eldest sonne) & I went home togeather, & when wee came to the Derrey, I sent for O Caine, & tould him what my lord's pleasure was touchinge him. Hee beganne presentlie to be moued, & both by Speach & gesture, declared as earnestlie as was possible to be highlie offended at it; argued the matter with Mee vpon many pointes; protested his fidelitie to the state since hee had made profes-

Mac Sweeny-na-dTuath (Mulmurry[a], the son of Murrough), and Caffar Oge, the son of Caffar, son of Manus O'Donnell, went to Tirconnell, with their people and cattle, to wage war with Niall Garv and the English. They made no delay until they arrived at the Rosses[b] and the Islands[c]. They had not been long here when they were plundered by Niall and his kinsmen; and Caffar Oge was taken prisoner, and detained in custody.

The people of Rury O'Donnell repaired to Tirconnell with all their property, cattle, and various effects, in the first month of spring. But Rury himself, with his gathering and muster of Irish and English, with Captain Guest, went (before his people had removed from the west) to revenge and get satisfaction of O'Rourke (Brian Oge), for the insult and dishonour he had some time before offered him (as he had in contemplation some time before); so that they plundered and ravaged Breifny, both its crops and corn, and all the cattle they could seize upon, for the greater part of them had been driven into the wilds and recesses of the territory. A few persons were slain between them, among whom were Owen, the son of Ferdorcha O'Gallagher, and Turlough, the son of Mac Loughlin, who fell by each other on that occasion. A party of the English were left in garrison at Dromahaire, for the purpose of plundering the country

sion of it; asked noe fauour if any man could charge him with the Contrarie; said he had alwayes buylt vpon my promise & my lord Deputies; that he was nowe vndone, & in worse case then before hee knewe vs; shewed many reasons for it; & asked, if wee would blaime him hereafter, if hee followed my lord of Tyrone's Councell, though it were against the kinge, seeing hee was in this manner forced to be vnder him. In the end, seeing noe remidie, hee shaked handes with my lord Hugh; bad the Devill take all English Men, & as many as put their trust in them; & soe in the shewe of a good reconciled frenshipp they went away togeather."

[a] *Mulmurry.*—His territory comprised the parishes of Mevagh, Clondahorky, Raymunterdoney, and Tullaghobegly, in the barony of Kilmacrenan, and county of Donegal. The lineal, legitimate descendant of this chieftain was a tinker by profession, and living in 1835, when the Editor examined the county of Donegal. He and many others of the O'Donnells and Mac Sweenys, confidently asserted that his descent from Sir Mulmurry, who was knighted by Queen Elizabeth, who allowed him a handsome pension, was as follows:

I. Sir Mulmurry Mac Sweeny Doe.
II. Donough More Mac Sweeny Doe.
III. Murrough Mac Sweeny Doe.
IV. Donough Oge Mac Sweeny Doe.
V. Turlough Mac Sweeny Doe.
VI. Edmond Mac Sweeny Doe, aged 61 in 1835.

[b] *The Rosses:* a district in the barony of Boylagh, still well known.

[c] *The Islands:* i. e. the northern Aran Islands, lying opposite the district of the Rosses.

na críċe ina nuirṫimċeall. Rob éiccſn dua Ruairc bſiṫ i nuachaḋ sochaiḋe hi ffſoaiḃ ⁊ hi ffáinġlſnntoiḃ, ⁊ for oiléṅaiḃ uirsciḋe a tíre o ṡin amaċ.

Dala neill ġairḃ i ḋomnaill do riaċt sgríḃſnn o aṫ cliaṫ dia ṡaiġiḋ dia ċuinġiḋ fair teaċt do laṫair an lustis ⁊ na comhairle do ġlacaḋ paiteint ar tír conaill a lóġ a ṡeirḃise, ⁊ a ḟoġanta don ċoróin. Ro léicc ſiom hi

[d] *For Tirconnell.*—This is not correct; for the Lord Deputy had by this time received frequent complaints of Niall Garv's insolence and impracticable ambition; and Rury O'Donnell offered to prove that Niall Garv had agreed with his brother, Hugh Roe, to join with him against the English forces as soon as the Spaniards should arrive in Ireland.—See Moryson, book iii. c. i. Sir Henry Docwra, in his *Narration*, gives the following circumstantial account of Rury O'Donnell's submission and reconciliation to the State, and of Niall Garv's rash proceedings upon the hearing of it:

"Now it fell out that my lord wrote for Rorie O Donnell to come to him to Dublin. Hee being in Connaught, desires first to putt ouer his Catle into Tirconnell, which would otherwise be in danger, in his absence, to be preyd by those of that prouince that yett stood out in Rebellion. My lord giues him leaue, & writes to Neale Garvie that he shall not molest nor trouble them, & soe Roory takes his Journey. Hee was noe sooner gone, & the Catell put ouer, But Neale Garvie, notwithstanding my lord's Comaund, Ceizes them as his owne, vnder pretents they were the goods of the Countrey belonging vnto him. Complainte made, my lord writs to Mee to see them restored. I send vnto him, & hee refuseth. My lord, vpon that, bidds Mee discharge him of his Entertainements, & writes vnto him, without delay, to come to him to Dublin. Hee growes more discontented, & deferres his going. Thus it runnes on, for at least 3 Monethes togeather, & neither would he come at Mee nor my lord, nor by any meanes be perswaded to make Restitution. In the ende, he assembles, of his owne aucthoritie, all the Countrey att Kilmackoran, a place where the O Donnells vse to be chosen. There hee takes vpon him the title, & with the Ceremonyes accustomed proclaymes himselfe O Donell, & then presentlie comes to Mee to the Derrey, with a greater troupe of attendances then at any time before, & they styling him, at euery word, my Lord. Assoone as I sawe him, I asked him howe he was thus suddenlie stept into the Name of a lord; hee tould Mee they called him so because he was O Donnell. I asked him by what aucthoritie he was soe; & hee said, by my lord Deputies. I badd him make that appeare vnto mee & all was well; he pluckt out a lettre written vnto him from my lord, about two yeares before, Superscription whereof was this, 'To my very lovinge freinde O Donnell.' Asked him if this were all the Warrante hee had; & hee said yes. I asked him why he went not to my lord all this while, nor came vnto Mee sooner, nor restored Rorie O'Donell's Catle; His aunswere was this: 'You knowe the whole Countrey of Tirconnell was long since promised Mee, & many seruices I haue done that, I thinke, haue deserved it; but I sawe I was neclected, & therefore I haue righted myselfe by takeing the Catle & People that were my owne, &, to preuent others, haue made myselfe O'Donnell. Now, by this meanes, the Countrey is sure vnto Mee, & if I haue done any thing a misse, lett all be pardoned that is past, & from this day forward, by Jesus hand, I will be true to the Queene, & noe Man's Councell will I follow hereafter but yours. Yow take a wronge Course, said I, it may not go thus; the first act you must doe to procure for-

around them. O'Rourke was thenceforward obliged to remain with a few troops in the woods or precipitous valleys, or on the islands in the lakes of his territory.

As for Niall Garv O'Donnell, a letter arrived from Dublin to him, requesting of him to come before the Lord Justice and the Council, to receive a patent for Tirconnell[d], as a reward for his services and his assistance to the Crown. He

giuness for your faults (if it may be) is to make restitution of the Catle; if yow do it not of your owne accord, I knowe yow will be forced vnto it vpon harder Conditions; yet, at that time, nothing I could say would prevaile with him, & soe hee departed downe into the towne. And of all these manner of Proceedings I writt vnto my lord. But it is true the next day hee came & made offer to restore them, & I was glad of it, & sent for Rory O Donnell (who was then at the Liffer) to come and receiue them, & my thoughts were fullie bent to make the best Reconsiliation of the Bussines that I could. Roory came, but with open Clamour, that Neale Garvie had laide a Plott to murther him by the way, & it is true, if the Confession of 3 of his owne men may be beleeued, he was, the Night before, in Consultation to haue it done, but did not (as they say) Resolue vpon it; but this put all the Bussines out of fraime, for then could wee gett Roory to no kinde of Patient Conferrence; &, in the meane time, came lettres from my lord to this effect, that hee had now taken in Tyrone, & was fullie resolued to beare noe longer with Neale Garuie, and therefore, if I were sure he had made himselfe O Donnell, it was treason by the lawe, I should lay hould on him & keepe him safe. My lord, I was sure, was mistaken in the qualitie of his offence, for I looked vpon the statute Booke, & sawe that Rigerōus lawe was onelie for such as made themselues O Neales; for those that looke vpon them to be heads of other families, the Punishment was onelie a Penaltie of 100 marks. I pawsed, therefore, & was doubtefull with myselfe, whither, by this Misgrounded warraunt, I should doe well to restrayne him or noe. But while I stood aduising vpon it, Came others lettres of aduertisment of the Queene's death, & order to Proclame the kinge. Then I entred into a further Consideration; should this man take the advantage of the time, & knowinge he hath offended the state, stepp aside & take Armes, thinkeing, by that meanes, to make his owne peace; how should I aunswere it, that haue him now in my handes, and my lord's warraunt to make him sure? Againe: what a Blemish would it be to all my actions, if the kinge, at his first Coming in, should finde all the kindome quiet but onelie this litle parte vnder my Charge. This moued Mee (to send for him) Presentlie, & when hee came I tould him the Newes of the Queene's death; hee seemed to be sorrie for it. I tould him of the Succession of the kinge; then ame I vndone, sayeth hee, for Roory hath better freindes about him then I. That speach encreased my iealousie, & therevpon I tould him further I had order from my lord to restraine him of his libertie; then ame I a dead man, saith hee. I tould him noe, hee needed not feare any such matter, neither his life nor landes were yet in danger; his offence was a Comtempte onelie, & hee must be brought to acknowledge a higher Power then his owne. The Marshall offerred to put Boults on him; hee sent vnto Mee, & desired hee might not be handled with that indignitie, protesting, with many oathes, he would not offerr to flie away. I bad the Marshall forbeare; & hee desired then I would allowe him a guard of a dosen of

ffoill an ní sin conadh edh do róine dol co cill meic nenain, ⁊ do ratt ó firghil comharba Cholaim Chille dia saighidh, go ro goireadh ó domhnaill de gan comhairleccadh driorr ionaitt an righ nó don chomhairle. Iar ná cloistin sin don iustis ⁊ don chomhairle fá miorscais leó an tí niall, ⁊ dna nir bhó saimhsighcheach lais an ngeneral Sir henri docura é bheos gér bhó tairisi, ⁊ ger bo mor a foghnamh dó siar an tan sin.

Do rala tra Rudhraighe ua domhnaill i nath cliath i nionbhaidh sin, ⁊ ro gairmedh é do lathair an Iustis, ⁊ na comhairle. Ro faoidhedh litre ⁊ sccribhenna lais go Sir henry docura dia furail fair niall garbh do errghabhail, ⁊ ro cuireadh araill do captinibh ina chaoimhtheacht, dus ficc imorro Rudhraighe go doire, ⁊ ro chuir an gobernoir drong do toísеachaibh, ⁊ do chaiptinibh doire * * * Gabhthar dna tuathal mac an dúbhaltaigh i ngallchubhar, aodh buidhe mac Seaain óicc, ⁊ feilim mac Seaain óicc go ndrung ele gen mo tháth don chur sin. Ro ela niall gar becc iar sin, ⁊ do chóidh féin co na bhraithribh, ⁊ co na muintearaibh fó choilltibh cinn maghair.

Souldiers to looke to him, & soe I did. Then did hee seriouslie (as I thought) acknowledge his follye; promised faithfullie to doe nothing hereafter but by my Councell. I tould him if he did soe, let him not feare, his Cryme was not Capitall, & that hee might well see by his vsage, for hee had libertie to walke vp & downe in the towne with his guard onelie. Hee seamed woun-derfull thankfull for it, & my intentions were now wholie bent to doe him all thee good offices might lye in my Power; but the third day after hee had beene thus Restrayned, hee secreetlie caused a horse to be brought to the towne gate, &, noe man suspecting anythinge, hee sudainelie slipt aside & gott vp vpon him, & soe made an escape. Word being brought vnto Mee of it, I was then, I confess, extreamlie irritated against him, &, castinge about what to doe, presentlie coniectured he would goe to his Creaghtes, that lay about 8 Myle from the Liffer, & with them gett downe to the Bottome of Tyrconnell, toward the Ilands, where I knewe was the greatest strength he could goe to, & furthest (of any other) out of my reach; Therefore I sent first to Captaine Ralph Bingley, that lay at Ramullan, fitt in the way to Cross his passage, that hee should speedilie make out to stoppe him till I came, which should be so soone as I could, & then to the Garrison att Liffer, that they should follow him, to whome Roory O Donnell (being there at that time) readily wyned him-selfe, as glad of soe fair an opportunitie to advaunce his owne endes by. I was not deceiued in my Coniecture, & soe, by that time, I had writt these lettres, made ready the Souldiers to goe with Mee, was past ouer lough Swilley by Boate, and had marched some 7 or 8 mile, I mett with the Newes that our Men had ouertaken & beate him, gott possession of the Cowes, which he fought for, & defended with force of Armes as longe as hee was able (and were estimated to be about 7000), & that hee himselfe was fledd into Mac Swyndoe's Countrey, with a purpose to gett into Owen Oge's Castle, which was reputed to be the strongest in all the North. I had then Owen Oge in my Compaine, & to pre-

neglected this thing; and what he did was, to go to Kilmacrenan, and send for O'Firghil[e], the Coarb of Columbkille; and he was styled O'Donnell, without consulting the King's representative or the Council. After the Lord Justice and the Council had heard of this, they became incensed against Niall, and even the General, Sir Henry Docwra, did not well like him, although he had been faithful to him, and had rendered him much service before that time.

Rury O'Donnell happened to be in Dublin at this time; and he was cited to appear before the Lord Justice and the Council. Letters and writings were sent with him to Sir Henry Docwra, ordering him to take Niall Garv prisoner. Some captains were sent in company with him; and when Rury arrived at Derry, the Governor sent a party of the officers and captains of Derry[f] * * * Tuathal, the son of the Dean O'Gallagher; Hugh Boy, the son of John Oge; and Felim, the son of John Oge, with others besides them, were taken prisoners on that occasion. Niall Garv made his escape shortly afterwards, and proceeded himself, with his kinsmen and people, into the woods of Ceann-Maghair[g].

uent him, Required he would deliuer it to Mee, & soe hee did, onelie requesting hee might haue it againe, when the Garrison I should put in it should be withdrawne, which I gaue my word vnto hee should; and then, seeing himselfe preuented of a place to retire vnto, spoyled of all his goods, & nothing in the world left him to liue vpon, hee sent vnto Mee for a Protection to goe safe vnto my lord Deputie, & takeing his Brother for his Pledge, & his oath besids, that he would goe & submitt himselfe wholie to his Judgment, I was contented, and gaue it him; putt the Pray wee had taken from him vpon Roory O Donnell's hand, because hee should not haue that pretense to say I had driuen him out of purpose to make Prey of his goods, & soe promised to be there ere longe & meete him; for nowe I had receiued diuers lettres againe, one, that my lord was purposed shortelie to goe for England; that his Maiestie (by his recomendation), was pleased to call Mee to be one of the Councell of Ireland; & that hee would have Mee to come speake with him before his departure. Annother to Comaund Mee to suffer the Earle of Tyrones Men to retourne to theire landes, & especially to the Salmon fishing of Lough foyle, which, till this time, I had enioyed, & was promised the inheritaunce of, as a parte of the reward for my seruice; And annother for restitution of Castles, Tennements, Catle, & many other thinges vnto him, which, altogeather, gaue Mee occasion, presentlie, to prepaire my selfe to that iourney."

[e] *O'Firghil*, now O'Freel, or Freel simply, without the prefix O'.

[f] *Of Derry.*—Two lines and a half are left blank here in the autograph. It appears from the subsequent context, that this blank was left till the compilers should learn the exact manner in which Niall Garv was taken prisoner. This blank is now more than supplied from Docwra's *Narration:* "The Marshall offered to put Boults on him; hee sent vnto mee, and desired hee might not be handled with that indignitie," &c.

[g] *Ceann-Maghair*, now Kinnaweer, a well-

Do marḃaḋ Maġnus óce o sruiṫéin an tan sin lá domnall mac cuinn í domnaill a ndioġail a dearbraṫar ro marḃaḋ lairsium feaċt riaṁ .i. an calḃaċ mac cuinn. Bá fſ̃rr do ná dingenaḋ an gniom sin ar dus fangattar uilc iomḋa dóibsiom fó a biṫin. Dóiġ ro forċongraḋ for Ruḋraiġe ua ndoṁnaill co na mbaoí lais do ġaoiḋelaiḃ, ⁊ for na caiptinib tangattar lais don tír, ⁊ for ċaiptín nguert baí ina ċaoiṁṫeaċt hi cconnaċtaiḃ lſ̃nmain neill, a dearbraiṫreaċ, ⁊ a muintire dia ccreachaḋ, ⁊ dia nionnraḋ. Do rónaḋ lairsioṁ aṁail ro herḟuaccraḋ ndó co ná ro fáccbaḋ míl ninnile ag muintir néill, ⁊ go ttarrtsat ilṁíle do croḋ leó go ndeaċattar dréċta dearṁara dár creachaḋ ann décc dfuaċt ⁊ do ġorta. Ro rann Ruḋraiġe na creaċa, ⁊ do raḋ a ttréċta do na huaislib do riaċtatar ina ḟoċraide. Do creċtnaicceaḋ Aoḋ buiḋe mac cuinn ina muġdorn ⁊ ro cuireaḋ dia lſ̃iġſ̃s hi ccrannóicc na nduini is na tuathaib issos guill do ḟonraḋ é. Ra gabaḋ an taoḋ céḋna lá gallaiḃ, ⁊ ruccaḋ é illáiṁ go doire. Ro ġeall an gobernoir ná lſ̃icfeaḋ amaċ é go ttiocceaḋ an tí do roine an marḃaḋ (domnall mac cuinn) a ffuascclaḋ as. Do chuaiḋ niall ⁊ domnall ar focal do laṫair an gobernora. Do léicceaḋ aoḋ buiḋe ⁊ do gabaḋ domnall.

Téid iarttain niall ó domnaill go Saxaiḃ diarraiḋ maiṫme ina ċoiriḃ ⁊ dfaġail lóġaiḋeaċta a ḟeirḃíse, ⁊ a foġanta do ċoroin tsaxan ón Ríġ Semus. Do ḋeachaiḋ Ruḋraiġe ó domnaill go Saxaiḃ on moḋ ccéḋna gion gur ḃó hionann a ffoġnaṁ a ndís don ċoróin, ⁊ baoí gaċ aon aca acc foillsiuccaḋ a ċſ̃irt ar ṫír ċonaill, conaḋ ann ro orḋaiġ an rí ⁊ an coṁairle Ruḋraiġe ó domnaill ina iarla ós tír ċonaill, ⁊ a ḋúthaiġ féin do niall .i. o leaċta siubaine siar, gur an sſ̃sccann lúbánaċ ṫall, ⁊ aḃus ar gaċ taoiḃ don ḟinn

known district in the north of the parish and barony of Kilmacrenan, in the north of the county of Donegal.

[h] *Crannog-na-nDuini:* i. e. the wooden house of Duini, now Downies or Downings, in the parish of Mevagh, barony of Kilmacrenan, and county of Donegal. Ros-Guill is still the name of the northern angle of the parish of Mevagh, extending into the sea between Redhaven and Sheephaven.

[i] *Different,* literally, "although not equal" [was] "the service of both to the Crown."

[k] *Earl over.*—This should be Earl of Tirconnell. Sir Henry Docwra did not think it fair, on the part of the Government, to make Rury O'Donnell Earl of Tirconnell, in preference to Niall Garv, who had rendered such services to the Crown. He has the following remark upon this preference in his *Narration :*

"Within a while after came Roory O'Donnell to Dublin, with his Majesties Letters, to be made Earle of Tyrconnell, & have all the countrey to him and his heires (except Ballyshannon with 1000 acres of ground, and the fishing that lies

At this time Manus Oge O'Sruthein was killed by Donnell, the son of Con O'Donnell, in revenge of his brother, Calvagh, son of Con, whom he [Manus] had slain some time before. It would have been better for him that he had not done this deed, for many evils redounded to them [his family] on account of it; for orders were given to Rury O'Donnell and all the Irish that were with him, to the captains who had come with him into the territory, and to Captain Guest, who had been in his company in Connaught, to pursue Niall, his brothers and people, and to plunder and prey them. He [Rury] did as he was ordered, so that not a single head of cattle was left with Niall's people, the others having carried off with them several thousand heads of cattle; so that vast numbers of those who were plundered died of cold and famine. Rury divided the preys, and gave their due proportions of them to the gentlemen who came in his army. Hugh Boy, the son of Con, was wounded in the ankle; and he was sent to Crannog-na-nDuini[h] in Ros-Guill, in the Tuathas, to be healed. The same Hugh was taken prisoner by the English, and conveyed to Derry, to be confined; and the Governor declared that he would not liberate him until the person who committed the slaying (Donnell, son of Con) should come in his ransom. Niall and Donnell afterwards repaired to the Governor on parole [of honour]; and Hugh Boy was set at liberty, and Donnell detained.

Niall O'Donnell afterwards went to England, to solicit pardon for his offences, and to obtain the reward for his service and aid to the Crown of England from King James. Rury O'Donnell also went to England from the same motives, although the services of both to the Crown were very different[i] indeed. Each of them exhibited his right to Tirconnell. The King and Council then ordered that Rury O'Donnell should be Earl over[k] Tirconnell, and that Niall should possess his own patrimonial inheritance, namely, that tract of country extending from Leachta-Siubháine[l], westwards, to Seascann-Lubanach[m], lying on both

under it), and such landes as Neale Garvie had held, living in amitie with the former O'Donell; the said Neale Garvie judicially convicted of no crime, which I thought was strange." For the entries and abstracts of the grants to Rury or Rory O'Donnel, the reader is referred to Erck's *Repertory of Chancery Enrolments*, pp. 47, 59.

[l] *Leachta-Siubhaine:* i. e. Johanna's monument, now Laght, a townland in the parish of Donaghmore, barony of Raphoe, and county of Donegal.

[m] *Seisceann-lubanach:* i. e. the swamp of the loops, now *anglice* Sheskinloobanagh, a swamp in the townland of Croaghonagh in the same parish adjoining the boundary of the county of Tyrone.

ḟind ⁊ tiaġaitt araon i nerinn fó ṡíḋ ⁊ córa iar ffiḋiuccaḋ ſtorra amlaiḋ sin.

Niall garḃ mac Ruḋraiġe, mic eiccneċáin, mic eiccnſċáin, mic neaċtain mic toirrḋealḃaiġ an ḟíona i ḋoṁnaill ḋécc.

Conċoḃar mac ḋonnchaiḋ, mic murchaiḋ, mic toirrḋealḃaiġ í ḃriain ḋécc a mí ḋecember.

Gorta ḋioḟulaing seaċnóin Ereann.

AOIS CRIOST, 1604.

Aois Criost, Míle, Se ċétt, a cſtair.

Ua Ruairc brian óg mac briain na murṫa, mic briain ḃallaiġ mic eoccain do écc i ngaillim an 28. Ianuarii, ⁊ a aḋnacal i mainistir Ruis iriala ag braiṫriḃ S. Fronseis. Ro ba ḋainiṁ écc an tí tſsda annsin, ar bá heiside Port congṁála, ⁊ gaḃal fulaing caṫa aoḋa ḟind, tuir caṫa ar ċalmatas, Rinn aġa ⁊ iomġona ua mbriuin, fſr croḋa, cosantaċ ná ro léicc an ḃreifne

[n] *Famine.*—P. O'Sullevan Beare, who conversed with people that witnessed this famine, has written the following notice of it in his *Hist. Cathol. Iber.* tom. 3, lib. 8, c. vi.:

"Ita bellum hoc confectum est. Ibernia pene tota deuastata, & euersa, ingenteque inedia, & fame omnes inuadente, qua multi compulsi sunt canes atque catos edere: multi ne his quidem suppetentibus pereunt. Neque homines tantum sed etiam bruta fames occupat. Lupi syluis, & montibus egressi homines media debiles inuadentes laniant. Canes fœtida cadauera, partemque in cinerem versa sepulchris extrahunt. Itaque nihil erat nisi squaloris & vera Trojæ direptæ imago a Virg. lib. i. Æneid. descripta."

Mountjoy boasts, in a letter to the Lords in England, dated 12th September, 1602, that he had brought the country of Tyrone to such a state of famine, by destroying the corn, "that O'Hagan protested, that betweene Tullogh Oge and Toome, there lay unburied a 1000 dead, and that since our first drawing this year to Blackwater, there were above three thousand starved in Tyrone."—Book iii. c. i.

Moryson gives a horrible account of the famine which the English caused in Ireland, "by destroying the Rebels corn, and using all means to famish them;" but the examples he adduces to shew the miserable state to which the poor people were brought, are too horrible and disgusting to be quoted here. He remarks generally: "No spectacle was more frequent in the Ditches of Towns, and especially in wasted countries, than to see Multitudes of these poor people dead, with their Mouths all coloured green by eating Nettles, Docks, and all things they could rend up above ground. These, and very many like lamentable Effects, followed their Rebellion, and, no doubt, the Rebels had been utterly destroyed by famine, had not a general Peace shortly followed Tyrone's submission (besides Mercy formerly extended to

sides of the River Finn. Both then returned to Ireland in peace and amity, matters having been thus settled between them.

Niall Garv, the son of Rury, son of Egneghan, son of Egneghan, son of Naghtan, son of Turlough-an-Fhiona O'Donnell, died.

Conor, the son of Donough, son of Murrough, son of Turlough O'Brien, died in the month of December.

An intolerable famine[n] prevailed all over Ireland.

THE AGE OF CHRIST, 1604.

The Age of Christ, one thousand six hundred four.

O'Rourke (Brian Oge, the son of Brian-na-Murtha, son of Brian Ballagh, son of Owen) died at Galway on the 28th of January, and was buried in the monastery of Ross-Iriala[o], with the Franciscan Friars. The death of the person who departed here was a great loss, for he was the supporting pillar and the battle-prop of the race of Aedh-Finn, the tower of battle for prowess, the star of the valour and chivalry of the Hy-Briuin; a brave and protecting man, who had

many others), by which the Rebels had liberty to seek Relief among the Subjects of Ireland, and to be transported into England and France, where great Multitudes of them lived for some years after the Peace made."—Vol. ii. pp. 283, 284. P. O'Sullevan Beare (*ubi supra*) gives the following short notice of the persons from whom they obtained relief on the Continent:

"Ob hoc Iberniæ uniuersum pene excidium multi Iberni per exteras gentes sese diffuderunt. Ingens turba in Galliam, longé maxima in Hispaniam confluxit. Exules causa fidei benigné, comiterque à Catholicis excipiuntur. In eos Rex Hispaniæ fuit tanto amore, ea pietate, & munificentia, vt vix vllus possit, aut oratione complecti, aut animo assequi, quantum illi debeant: omnes principio quam honorificentissimè suscepit donis ornans: nobilioribus menstruos nummos uestigales, pro sua cuique conditione, assignans, alijs militare stipendium constituens. Ex illis in Gallia Belgica legionem conscribi missit, quæ prius sub Henrico, & post Henrici interitum sub Iohanne Onelli principis filiis contra Batauos fideliter, & strenué pugnauit. In regia quoque classe maris oceani cohortes aliquot stipendium fecerunt magna virtute præstantes. Post Catholicum Regem inter Ibernorum exulum patronos clarissimus Brigantiæ Dux Lusitanus, Cardinalis Surdis, Burdigalæ Archiepiscopus Gallus, Carazenæ Marchio Hispanus, & Fabius Onellus Vallisoleti vrbis diues ciuis non infimum locum obtinent."—Fol. 202.

[o] *Ros-Iriala*, now Rosserilly, a monastery of which the ruins are still in very good preservation, situated about a mile north from the town of Headford, in the barony of Clare, and county of Galway. In an Inquisition taken apud St. Francis. Abb. 22° April, 1636, this monastery is called Rossryully, and placed in Mointermoroghow, in the territory of Clanrickard.

do baoġluccaḋ ina ré, fer foraiḋ formata, cennais fri cairdiḃ, miata fri naimdiḃ, fer ro baḋ dearrsaiġtec iocht ⁊ eineach, uaisle ⁊ oirbert, anaḋ ⁊ oirisioṁ ré hathaiḋ don ċenél dia mbaoí.

AOIS CRIOST, 1605.

Aois Criost, Mile, Se ced, a cúicc.

Sir Artur chicester iustis na herenn, ⁊ iarla tíre heoccain Aoḋ mac an firdoirche do ṫocht ar an srath mbán, ⁊ ro ḃaoí ua neill ag agra blaiḋe don dúthaiġ fuair niall ó domnaill on ríġ .i. an moentacht. Tucc Niall do laṫair an lustis na dearḃta baoí aicce ar lorcc a sinnsear ar an moentacht, ⁊ dna ffirsin na cartaca do ḃen Maġnus ó domhnaill dua neill do ċonn ḃacach a ffuasccladh enri mic Sean buí i laiṁ ag ua ndomnaill (Maġnus) go ffuair na cartaca sinn ass, ⁊ iar ttuicsin a sccéil ar gach taoiḃ don lustis Sir Artur Rucc do ḃreiṫ an Moentacht do niall, ⁊ atbert ná ro cumaing Ua neill an fearann dagra ó ċein, ar do ċóiḋ i rúdracus foda ó do ċóiḋ tar sesgat mbliadan. Rob éiccen dóiḃ diḃlíniḃ airisioṁ for an mbreiṫ sin.

O Ruairc tadg mac briain mic briain mic eoghain tiġerna na breifne, fer fuair mór nimnioh, ⁊ néttualaing acc iomċornaṁ a athardha fri a derbraṫair ua Ruairc brian ócc, fer na ro saoileaḋ a ecc fri hadhart, acht a oideaḋ do rinn no dfaoḃar, fer fuair deaḃta duilġe, ⁊ gáibhthe guais iomda acc saicchioh oidhreachta a athardha, ⁊ ionaid a athar gur ro léicc dia ticcernas cuicce fo ḋeoiḋ, ⁊ gur ro ecc, ⁊ a adnacal i mainestir .S. Fronseis i ccarraicc ṗattraicc go nonóir amail ro baḋ díor.

[p] *Moentacht*, a district situated to the south of Lifford, on the borders of the counties of Tyrone and Donegal.

[q] *Both.*—This should be O'Neill (or rather the Earl of Tyrone), because of course Niall O'Donnell was glad of it, and, therefore, willingly submitted to it. Defects of this nature, frequently occurring in the style of the Four Masters, shew that they paid little or no attention to the philosophy of language.

[r] *Teige.*—Charles O'Conor interpolates so as to make the text tadg an ḟíona, i. e. Teige, or Timothy, of the Wine. He was a knight, and is commonly called Sir Teige O'Rourke. He left two sons, Brian and Hugh. Brian na Murtha had a brother, Turlough Fin (Terentius Albus), who had a son Owen More, who had a son Owen Oge, who had a son Brian O'Rourke, a youth of "great expectation," who died of the small-pox at Leytrim, on the 13th of June, 1671, in the eighteenth year of his age. The following epitaph was composed for him by Thady Roddy, of

not suffered Breifny to be molested in his time; a sedate and heroic man, kind to friends, fierce to foes; and the most illustrious that had come for some time of his family for clemency, hospitality, nobleness, firmness, and steadiness.

THE AGE OF CHRIST, 1605.

The Age of Christ, one thousand six hundred five.

Sir Arthur Chichester, Lord Justice of Ireland, and the Earl of Tyrone (Hugh, the son of Ferdorcha), went to Strabane. O'Neill claimed a portion of the territory which Niall O'Donnell had obtained from the King, namely, Moentacht. Niall produced before the Lord Justice the proofs that he had of his right to Moentacht[p], in succession from his ancestors; and, among the rest, he produced the charters which Manus O'Donnell had obtained from O'Neill (Con Bacagh) for setting at liberty Henry, the son of John, whom O'Donnell (Manus) had had in his custody. The Lord Justice, Sir Arthur, having understood their stories on both sides, he adjudged Moentacht to Niall, and said that O'Neill could not by right claim the lands, inasmuch as his title, having been more than sixty years in abeyance, had become obsolete. Both[q] were obliged to abide by this decision.

O'Rourke (Teige[r], son of Brian[s], son of Brian[t], son of Owen), Lord of Breifny, a man who had experienced many hardships and difficulties while defending his patrimony against his brother, Brian Oge; a man who was not expected to die on his bed, but by the spear or sword; a man who had fought many difficult battles, and encountered many dangers, while struggling for his patrimony and the dignity of his father, until God at length permitted him to obtain the lordship, died, and was interred with due honour in the Franciscan Monastery at Carrickpatrick[u].

Achadh na Croise, or Crossfield, in the county of Leitrim:

"Conditur exiguâ Rourk hac Bernardus in urnâ,
Stirpe perillustri, mente, lyraque Linus,
Hic pudor Hippoliti, Paridis gena, pectus Ulyssis
Æneæ pietas, Hectoris ira jacet
Flos juvenum splendor proavum Iunii Idibus, eheu!
Interiit, rutilos vectus ad usque polos."

[s] *Brian.*—Charles O'Conor interpolates na mupċa.

[t] *Brian.*—Charles O'Conor interpolates ballaiġ.

[u] *Carrickpatrick*: i. e. Dromahare, in the

AOIS CRIOST, 1606.

Aois Criost, Míle, Se ced, a Sé.

AOIS CRIOST, 1607.

Aois Criost, míle, Se ced, a Seaċt.

O ḃaoiġill taḋcc óg, mac taiḋcc, mic toirrḋealḃaiġ décc i ndruim arc lá taoḃ baile Í ḃaoiġill an 3. Maii, ⁊ a aḋnacal i ndún na ngall.

Máguiḋir cuċonnaċt, ⁊ donnċaḋ mac Maṫġaṁna, mic an espuicc uí ḃriain do ṫaḃairt luinge leó go hérinn gur ro gabsat i ccuan na súiliġe. An tiarla o neill Aoḋ mac an firdoirċe, ⁊ an tiarla o domnaill Ruḋraiġe mac

county of Leitrim. Charles O'Conor interpolates: "Maire de burg ingen iarla ċloinne Riocaird maṫair an taiḋg sin; i. e. Mary De Burgo, daughter of the Earl of Clanrickard, was the mother of that Teige."

[v] 1606.—This annal is left blank by the Four Masters.

[w] *Druim-arc*, now Drumark, a townland in the parish of Killymard, not far from the town of Donegal.

[x] *Baile-Ui-Bhaoighill*: i. e. the town of O'Boyle, now Ballyweel, near the town of Donegal.

[y] *Harbour of Swilly.*—The cause of this precipitate flight of the two Earls has since remained involved in mystery. There is a curious account of O'Neill's flight and subsequent history preserved in a paper manuscript, consisting of 150 pages, in the College of St. Isidore at Rome; but although it gives a detailed account of his movements, it is entirely silent as to the immediate cause of his sudden flight. The late Dr. Lyons, P. P. of Kilmore-Erris, sent the Editor a fac-simile of the first page of this manuscript, which runs as follows:

"A nainm Dé. Ag so sairt do sceloiḃ ⁊ dimṫeċtoib ui neill on uair sor ḟagoir se Eire. Ar tus bui o neill a ffochair iuistis na hEireann artuir Sisester am-baili ḟlaine. Do ġlac se leitir ó ḟsion bat dia dardaoin in seachtmaḋ la Septembris, ⁊ aois in tigearna in tan sin Mile ⁊ se chett ⁊ seacht mbliaḋna. Bui ar in litir sempaite go ttainic maguiḋir cuconnaċt maguidir, Donnchadh O briain maṫa og o mailtuile, Seon Rut go loing ffrangcaiġ a gcomairsiss ui nell, ⁊ iarla ṫíri conaill go cuan Suiliġi moire ar urchoṁair raṫa maolain a ffanait. Gabuis o nell a chet ag in iustis, in Sathurn na ḋeghaiḋ sin teid a noiḋċe sin gus in Mainistir Moir áit a mbui sin geroid Moḋur. Ar na ṁarach dó go srasbaili duna dealgan.

"Gluaissis dia luain assin Srasbaili tria bealaċ mor in ḟſda, go bél aṫa in airgit, tar Sliaḃ fuait, go h-ard Macha, tar abainn moir go Dun gſnainn gus in gcraoiḃ .i. baile oilſin dia bailtiḃ. Do gní se comnaiḋe ⁊ oirisſm ar in Chraoiḃ dia mairt. Gluaisiḋ a nainm De dia cſdaoin on Chraoiḃ tar sliaḃ sioss. Bui an oiḋċe sin a Muintir Luiniġ ar comgar lochu bſigsine. Ar na marach do go bun diſnnoide. Bui ina chomnaiḋe ó aimsir ṁſdoin laoi go comṫuitim na hoiḋce. Iar sin lſiġis tar fersait moir ar leċ féaḃail ⁊

THE AGE OF CHRIST, 1606[v].

The Age of Christ, one thousand six hundred six.

THE AGE OF CHRIST, 1607.

The Age of Christ, one thousand six hundred seven.

O'Boyle (Teige Oge, the son of Teige, son of Turlough) died at Druim-arc[w], near Baile-Ui-Bhaoighill[x], on the 3rd day of May, and was interred at Donegal.

Maguire (Cuconnaught) and Donough, the son of Mahon, son of the Bishop O'Brien, brought a ship with them to Ireland, and put in at the harbour of Swilly[y]. They took with them from Ireland the Earl O'Neill (Hugh, the son of Ferdorcha), and the Earl O'Donnell (Rury, the son of Hugh, son of Manus),

gach ndireach go droichést adamnain. Dui mac ui Doṁnaill cathbarr mac aoḋa mſic maġnusa ar a gcionn annsin. Gabsat go raith meallain, an la ag soillsiugaḋ orra in tansin. Eirgit go Raiṫh Maolain ait a mbui in long a dubramar. Ar an gcuirip fuaratar ruḋraiġi ó Domnaill Iſrla ṫire conaill gus na daoiniḃ uaisle remraiṫe maille re moran doireaċt ⁊ do lucht lenaṁna in Iſrlae ag cor sdoruiss bíḋ ⁊ dighe asteach san loing."

"In the name of God. This is a part of the stories and adventures of O'Neill, from the time that he left Ireland. First, O'Neill was along with the Justiciary of Ireland, Arthur Sitsestar at Baili-Shlaini" [Slane]. "He received a letter from John Bath on Thursday the seventh of September, the year of the Lord at that time being one thousand six hundred and seven years. It was stated in the aforesaid letter that Maguire, Cuconnaught Maguire, Donough O'Brien, Matthew Oge O'Maeltuile, [and] John Rut, came with a French ship for O'Neill and the Earl of Tirconnell into the harbour of Great Swilly, opposite Rathmullan, in Fanaid. O'Neill took his leave of the Justiciary [and] on the following Saturday he went to Mainistir-Mor" [the great abbey of Mellifont], "where Garrett Moore was. On the next day he went to Sradbhaile-Duna-Dealgan" [Dundalk].

"He proceeded on Monday from Sradbhaile through Bealach-mor-an-Fhedha" [the Great Road of the Fews], "to Bel-atha-an-airgit, across Sliabh Fuait, to Armagh, over the Abhainn-mhor" [the Blackwater], "to Craobh" [Creeve], "i. e. an island habitation of his habitations. He stopped and rested at Craobh on Tuesday. He proceeded, in the name of God, on Wednesday from Craobh over the mountain downwards" [i. e. northwards]. "He was that night in Muintir-Luinigh" [Munterloony], "in the vicinity of Loch Beigfine. On the morrow he proceeded to Bun-Diennoide" [Burn Dennet, near Lifford], "where he rested from mid-day till night-fall. After this he went over Fersatmore on Loch Feabhail" [Lough Foyle river, near Lifford], "straight forward to Adamnan's Bridge" [at Ballindrait, near Raphoe]. "The son of Donnell, Caffar, son of Hugh, son of Manus, was there awaiting him. They proceeded to Rathmelton, the dawn rising upon them at that time. They went on to Rathmullan, where the ship we have mentioned was.

aoḋa, mic Maġnusa co nDruing móir do maiṫiḃ ċoicciḋ Ulaḋ do ḃreiṫ leó a hérinn. Itiatt do ḋeaċattar lá hua neill an ċontaoiſ Cateríona ingean

In this vessel they met Rury O'Donnell, Earl of Tirconnell, with the gentlemen aforesaid, together with many of the tribe and followers of the Earl, laying up stores of food and drink in the ship."

Sir John Davies gives the following account of the departure of these Earls, which pretty fairly accords with the foregoing:

"The Saturday before, the Earl of Tyrone was with the Lord-Deputy at Slane, where he had spoken with his lordship of his journey into England, and told him he would be there about the beginning of Michaelmas term, according to his Majesty's directions. He took leave of the lord-deputy in a more sad and passionate manner than was usual with him. From thence he went to Mellifont and Garrett Moore's house, where he wept abundantly when he took his leave, giving a solemn farewell to every child and every servant in the house, which made them all marvel, because in general it was not his manner to use such compliments. On Monday he went to Dungannon, where he rested two whole days, and on Wednesday night they say he travelled all night. It is reported that the Countess, his wife, being exceedingly weary, slipped down from her horse, and weeping said 'she could go no further.' Whereupon the Earl drew his sword, and swore a great oath that 'he would kill her on the spot if she would not pass on with him, and put on a more cheerful countenance.' When the party, which consisted (men, women, and children) of fifty or sixty persons, arrived at Lough Foyle, it was found that their journey had not been so secret but that the Governor there had notice of it, and sent to invite Tyrone and his son to dinner. Their haste, however, was such that they accepted not his courtesy, but hastened on to Rathmullan, a town on the west side of Lough Swilly, where the Earl of Tyrconnell and his company met with them. From thence the whole party embarked, and, landing on the coast of Normandy, proceeded through France to Brussels."

Davies concludes this curious narrative in words, from which it can be clearly inferred that they had been chased out of the country by law fictions and issuing processes, calling upon O'Neale to appear and answer in the cause of the Lord Bishop of Derry against Hugh, Earl of Tyrone. Davies says:

"As for us that are here, we are glad to see the day wherein the countenance and majesty of the law and civil government hath banished Tyrone out of Ireland, which the best army in Europe, and the expense of two millions of sterling pounds, had not been able to bring to pass."

The following account of the manner in which they attempted to entrap him, and of his flight and reception at Rome, is given by P. O'Sullevan Beare, in his *Hist. Cathol. Iber. Compend.*, tom. 4, lib. 1, c. iv.:

"Qvo tamen terrore cæteri Iberni à Religione Catholica profitenda nihil amouentur. Quod Angli animaduertentes, & rati ob huius edicti executionem non minus cruoris diffundendum fuisse, quam ob similem causam fuit effusum, Henrico, Eduardo, & Elizabetha regnantibus, nisi periculum tempestiue præuentum sit: rationem ineunt hunc obicem sine bello, & vulnere remouendi iuxta primum principale persecutionis punctum, vt summi viri in Fide, & Catholica Religione constantes, belli scientia, & rerum gestarum fama clari sensim, & furtim excidantur. Itaque Onellum, Odonellum, & alios Ibernicæ partis sequaces, ac eos etiam Anglicæ factionis fautores, in quibus plus virtutis, & animi Christiani residere putabant, dissimulaté, & quasi aliud agentes statuunt de medio tollere

with a great number of the chieftains of the province of Ulster. These were they who went with O'Neill, namely, the Countess Catherina, the daughter of

vel occisos, vel in carcerem detrusos, vel relegatos. Quominus videantur id agere causa labefactandi. Religionem Catholicam, artem, qua magnates Catholicos læsæ Magestatis reos agant, machinantur. Christaphorum Sanlaurentium Hotæ Baronem Angloibernum, hominem non modo factionis Anglicæ solicitum, sed etiam schysmaticum iubent, vt illos ad rebellionem inuitet, seque faciat de conspiratis certiores. Christophorus (vt fama fert) ex Ibernica factione Odonellum, & Macguierem, & ex Anglica Dalræ Baronem sua calliditate decepit, vt animi sensum incautius exprimerent, Onelli prudentissimi senis pectus explorare non ausus. Qua re cognita Angli Onellum, Odonellum, & alios capere constituunt. Onellus à quibusdam Anglis amicis edoctus ipse, Odonellus & Macguier in Galliam traijciunt. Vbi legatis Anglis eos regi suo restitui petentibus Henricus Quartus Galliæ Rex respondit, regiam dignitatem dedecere, alienigenas fuga salutem petentes itinere prohibere. Ita in Galliam Belgicam profecti ab Alberto & Elizabetha serenissimis Archiducibus humanissimè, & honorificentissimé sunt excepti. Inde Romam cum se contulissent, à Rege Catholico ad victum non parcé adiuuantur Onellus per singulos menses quingentis nummis aureis, Odonellus totidem, Macguier, & reliqui, qui sunt illos secuti, pro suis quisque meritis: Pontifice Maximo quoque opem ferente. Odonellus, & Macguier breui tempore beneficio fruuntur vitæ munere defuncti, ille Romæ, hic Genuæ Hispaniam petens. Dalrus Baro, qui nihil aduersi timebat, donec fuerit in carcerem, & vincula coniectus, summa difficultate effugit, magnosque labores pertulit priusquam incolumitatem fuit adeptus partim corruptionibus partim amicorum precibus. Cormakus Onellus cum accersitus Dubhlinnæ se exhibuisset, in Angliam missus in Londinam arcem custodiendus conijcitur Okahanus vocatus in iudicium se distulit sistere veritus id, quod erat, ne eadem cum Cormako poena plecteretur. Quem Angli diu capere frustra laborantes in suas artes vertuntur. Erat eques Anglus Okahani compater quem Okahanus gentis suæ more spiritualem affinitatem incredibili obseruantia, & honore colentis, magni faciebat, valdè diligebat, & beneficijs ornabat, eidemque plurimum confidebat: & ita ad cænam ab eo inuitatus non dubitauit, compatris fidei sese committere Anglus ne nauci quidem æstimans totam Christianam Religionem, nedum spiritualem cognationem inquirenti Anglorum manipulo ex composito Okahanum tradidit. Qui detrusus est in eandem cum Cormako custodiam."

Dr. Curry asserts, in his *Historical Review*, that these Earls were guilty of no conspiracy; and Mr. Hardiman, who read that portion of the State Papers which relates to this period, has written the following note on the subject of the flight of the Earls, in his *Irish Minstrelsy*, vol. ii. p. 430:

"The great possessions of these two devoted Irish princes proved the cause of their ruin. After the successful issue of the plot contriving Cecil's gunpowder adventure in England, he turned his inventive thoughts towards this country, where every English Minister may, at all times, be sure of finding ready instruments to carry any plan into execution. A plot to implicate the great northern chieftains in treasonable projects was soon set on foot, and finally proved successful. This conspiracy is thus related by a learned English divine, Doctor Anderson, in his '*Royal Genealogies*,' printed in London, 1736: 'Artful Cecil employed one St. Lawrence to entrap the Earls of Tyrone and Tyrconnel, the Lord of Delvin, and other Irish chiefs, into a sham plot which had no evidence

Meg aongusa, a triur mac Aoḋ (.i. an barun). Seaan, ⁊ brian, Art óg mac corbmaic, mic an ḃarúin, Fer dorċa mac cuinn, mic í néill, Aoḋ óg mac

but his. But these chiefs being basely informed that witnesses were to be hired against them, foolishly fled from Dublin, and so taking guilt upon them, they were declared rebels, and six entire counties in Ulster were at once forfeited to the Crown, which was what their enemies wanted.' Tyrone fled privately into Normandy in 1607, thence to Flanders, and then to Rome, where he lived on the Pope's allowance, became blind, and died, 20th July, 1610" [*recte* 1616]. "Tyrconnell fled at the same time, and died at Rome on the 28th July, 1608. Several original documents are preserved in the State Paper Office, London, connected with the above plot, including the correspondence of the weak and unprincipled St. Lawrence, which develope a scene of human turpitude seldom paralleled."

Mr. Moore, however, who has studied the correspondence of Lord Howth, and Delvin's confession, taken on the 6th of November, 1607, has come to the conclusion that the Ulster Earls were guilty of a new conspiracy. This is the only real and important development of a doubtful or unknown fact in all Mr. Moore's work on the history of Ireland, and the Editor is tempted to lay it before the reader in the author's own words. After alluding to the disputes between the Earl of Tyrone, O'Kane, and the Lord Bishop of Derry, he writes:

"This derangement of all his" [Tyrone's] "affairs, combined with the feeling, ever uppermost in his thoughts, of deadly hatred to the English name, decided Tyrone to abandon all hope except from foreign swords, and to lose no time in preparing his countrymen for the struggle. In all his efforts towards this object, the faithful Tyrconnell still continued his ever-watchful co-operator; nor was it long before they found, in Richard Nugent, Baron of Delvine, a ready associate in this national enterprise. This young lord had early been schooled in bitter enmity to the English, having been brought up in the Tower by his mother, who shared, voluntarily, there her husband's imprisonment. It was at Maynooth, the ancient seat of the Earls of Kildare, near Dublin, that these lords held the meetings at which they concerted their plans; and in the garden of the same mansion it was that Tyrconnell first proposed to Delvin to take a part in daring designs. How painful to that noble family were the suspicions incurred by them, may be judged from a letter addressed to Salisbury, some time after, by Mabel" [Leigh, an Englishwoman], "Countess of Kildare" [but who was not the mother of Bridget Fitzgerald, the wife of Rury, Earl of Tyrconnell] "expressing her sorrow 'that the late treasons should have been plotted at Maynooth, and strongly protesting her own innocence.'

"While thus secretly this plot was gathering, there reigned everywhere, through the whole realm, an appearance of perfect tranquillity. Tyrone, though thus anew engaged in conspiracy, still continued his social relations with the Lord Deputy; and to judge of the state of the country from the account given of Munster by Sir John Davies, seldom had a calm so settled and promising prevailed throughout the kingdom. 'It was quite a miracle,' he says, 'to perceive the quiet and conformity of the people.'

"But in the midst of this general tranquillity, an event occurred, which, as much from the mystery thrown around it, as from its own intrinsic importance, spread alarm throughout the whole country; and the vigilance which it awakened in the ruling powers added considerably to the danger and difficulties of Tyrone. An anonymous letter, directed to Sir William Usher,

Magennis, and her three sons, Hugh the Baron[z], John, and Brian; Art Oge, the son of Cormac[a], son of the Baron; Ferdorcha, son of Con[b], son of O'Neill;

Clerk of the Privy Council, had lately been dropped at the door of the council chamber, mentioning a design, then in contemplation, for seizing the Castle of Dublin, and murdering the Lord Deputy; these acts to be followed, as the letter stated, by a general revolt, assisted by Spanish forces. For this intelligence the English authorities were not wholly unprepared, having already, through various channels, both at home and abroad, received such accounts of Tyrone's practices with the Court of Spain as rendered them aware of the stirrings of mischief in that quarter; and the secret informant by whom, principally, these warnings were conveyed, was the Earl of Howth, a recent convert to the new creed."—*Hist. Irel.*, vol. iv. pp. 453, 454, 455.

The fugitive Earls complained, on the Continent, of their having been persecuted for religion, and it was deemed expedient by the King and the State that this should be publicly denied. A proclamation was accordingly issued by the King, wherein he affirms that "they had not the least shadow of molestation, nor was there any purpose of proceeding against them in matters of religion; their condition being, to think murder no fault, marriage of no use, nor any man valiant that does not glory in rapine and oppression; and, therefore, 'twere unreasonable to trouble them for religion before it could be perceived by their conversation that they had any."

It is scarcely necessary to remark here, that this proclamation states a mere fiction, because those Earls were not allowed the free use of the Catholic religion, for no bishop was publicly allowed to exercise episcopal functions in their dioceses, except Montgomery, who acknowledged that the Sovereign was the head of the Church. Whatever were King James's intentions of proceeding against those fugitives for their religion, we have proof positive that after the submission of O'Neill and O'Donnell, and in the midst of "the most universal peace that ever was seen in Ireland," the King's counsellors published, in Dublin, the "Act of Uniformity," of the 2nd Eliz., which strictly prohibited the attendance upon the Roman Catholic worship; and a proclamation was issued on the 4th of July, 1605, wherein His Majesty declared to his beloved subjects in Ireland, that he would not admit any such liberty of conscience as they were made to expect, and commanded all the Roman Catholic clergy, by a certain day, to depart the realm. If this did not sufficiently indicate a purpose to proceed against them in matters of religion, "the language of princes is beyond the comprehension of subjects." As to the assertion that these Earls *had no religion*, it is so gratuitous that we must regard it as a mere piece of James's pedantry, who had just learning enough to expose to the world his own gloomy prejudices and littleness of soul, and who during an ignoble reign of twenty-two years exhibited such folly and incapacity to his vigorous and enterprising subjects, as filled their minds with contempt for monarchs, and prepared them for that republican spirit which set in after his death, and ultimately brought about the decapitation of his son, and the final destruction of the Stuart family.

[z] *Hugh the Baron.*—His eldest son, Henry, who was a hostage in the hands of the King of Spain, was found strangled at Brussels, but nobody has told us why or how.

[a] *Cormac:* i. e. the brother of Hugh, Earl of Tyrone. He is usually called Cormac Mac Baron.

[b] *Con.*—He is called Tyrone's base son, by Moryson and other English writers.

briain mic airt i neill go ndruing móir dia ṫairisiḃ cenmoṫat. Itiat do ċotar lasin iarla ua ḋomnaill Caṫbarr a dearbraṫair co na ḋſirbṡiair Nuala, ⁊ mac an iarla Aoḋ tſsda tri sſcṫṁuine gan a ḃſiṫ i naoís a ḃliaḋna. Rois ingſn ui ḋoċartaiġ bſn Caṫbairr co na mac Aoḋ i naois da ḃliaḋain ⁊ ráiṫe. Mac a ḋearbraṫar domnall ócc, mac domnaill. Neaċtain mac an ċalḃaiġ, mic donnchaiḋ ċairbriġ uí ḋomnaill go ndrſim móir dia tairisiḃ ḃeós a maille friú. I ffeil na croiċe isin fFoġṁar do ċóiḋsiot isin luing. Bá maiṫ an luċt aon luinge battar ainnsiḋe ar as dearḃ dſiṁin ná ro ṫaoscc muir, ⁊ na ro foġluais gaoth a héirinn is na dſiḋſnċoiḃ luċt aon luinge báttar fſrr, ⁊ báttar airſgḋa ⁊ bá huaisle ar aoí ngſinelaiġ, bá fſrr gníoṁ ⁊ gart, ſngnaṁ ⁊ oirbſrt ináitt dia ndeónaiġeaḋ dia airisioṁ ina naṫarḋa go roisſḋ lá a naos aoiḋſḋaċ roċtain go haois ḟſrrḋata. Mairicc croiḋe ro sccrúd, mairicc mſnma ro mioḋair, mairicc aiṫſscc ro ḟuiġill an ċoṁairle trias a ttainicc dul na druinge do ḋeaċattar for an ſctra sin ⁊ gan dáil a roċtain for ccúlaiḃ ina niomláine dia ndoṁnas duṫaiġe, nó dia naṫarḋa ḃunaiḋ co foirċſnn an ḃſṫa.

AOIS CRIOST, 1608.

Aois Crios, mile Se cett, a hoċt.

Easaonta ⁊ imrſsain anfFoil do eirġe etir an ngobernóir baoí i nDoire colaim ċille .i. Sir Seoirsi Palet, ⁊ Ua doċartaiġ caṫair mac Sſain óicc.

[c] *His sister Nuala.*—She was the wife of Niall Garv, but had deserted him when he went over to Sir Henry Docwra.

[d] *Hugh, the Earl's son.*—He was afterwards page to the Infanta.

[e] *Donnell Oge.*—Hugh Roe O'Donnell asserted that this Donnell Oge was a bastard.—See Moryson's *History of Ireland*, edition of 1735, vol. i. p. 36; and yet his son is mentioned in remainder in Earl Rory's Patent.

[f] *Pawlett.*—He was a gentleman of Hampshire, to whom Sir Henry Docwra sold his house at Derry, "with 10 Quarters of land I had bought & layde to it (all with myne owne money), & my Company of ffoote, all togeather for less a greate deale then the very house alone had stood mee in, and withall the vice provostshipp of the town of Derry (for the time of my absence), I conferred upon him, but which I neither valued nor had anything for."—Docwra's *Narration*.

The following account of O'Doherty's insurrection is given by P. O'Sullevan Beare, in his *Hist. Cathol. Iber. Compend.*, tom. 4, lib. 1, c. v.:

"Cæteros optimates labefactandi cupidi Protestantes, multos contumelijs, opprobrijs, & injurijs afficiunt. Cathirium Odochartam Inisonæ principem, de quo superius mentionem fecimus, vigesimum circiter annum agentem, quód Onelli fugæ fuerit conscius, Prorex arguit, asperis at-

Hugh Oge, the son of Brian, son of Art O'Neill; and many others of his faithful friends. These were they who went with the Earl O'Donnell: Caffar, his brother, and his sister, Nuala[c]; Hugh, the Earl's son[d], wanting three weeks of being one year old; Rose, the daughter of O'Doherty, and wife of Caffar, with her son, Hugh, aged two years and three months; the son of his brother, Donnell Oge[e], the son of Donnell; Naghtan, the son of Calvagh, son of Donough Cairbreach O'Donnell; together with many others of his faithful friends. They entered the ship on the festival of the Holy Cross, in autumn.

This was a distinguished crew for one ship; for it is indeed certain that the sea had not supported, and the winds had not wafted from Ireland, in modern times, a party of one ship who would have been more illustrious or noble, in point of genealogy, or more renowned for deeds, valour, prowess, or high achievements, than they, if God had permitted them to remain in their patrimonies until their children should have reached the age of manhood. Woe to the heart that meditated, woe to the mind that conceived, woe to the council that decided on, the project of their setting out on this voyage, without knowing whether they should ever return to their native principalities or patrimonies to the end of the world.

THE AGE OF CHRIST, 1608.

The Age of Christ, one thousand six hundred eight.

Great dissensions and strife arose between the Governor of Derry, Sir George Pawlett[f], and O'Doherty (Cahir, the son of John Oge). The Governor

que contumeliosis verbis exagitans. Georgius Paletus Luci præfectus Anglus eques Auratus conuicijs onerat, minans se facturum, vt ille laqueo suspendatur. Odocharta tunc iniuriam dissimulauit, Paletum armatis stipatum nudus militibus aggredi non ausus. Breui tamen vindictam sumpsit. Eo die oppido Luco egressus clientium manum comparat, cum qua sub gallicinium reuersus vigiles, circitoresque improuisò circumuentos trucidat, Paletum, & alios Protestantes occidit, oppidum diripit, & incendit: vxorem Pseudoepiscopi ciuitatis captam pretio commutat, Catholicos incolumes ad vnum dimittit. Cuilmorem maritimam arcem, quinque passuum millia distantem, quam Anglorum præsidium duodecim tormentorum machinis instructam obtinebat, repentina irruptione capit, in eaque præsidio collocato Felmium Macdauetum præficit; & magnis motibus per Vltoniam excitatis bellum statuit ducere vsque ad aduentum Onelli, Odonelli, Osulleuani, reliquorumque exulantium, quos à Christianis principibus adiutos auxilio redituros sperabat: à principio Aprilis anni millesimi sexcentesimi octaui per menses

Nír ḃó lesḋ namá ro imbir an gobernóir tár ⁊ tarcusal fair ó ḃriaṫraiḃ, acht do ḃeirt fris sin pennainntt dia ċorp gur ḃó ḟerr lais a ḃás inas a ḃeatha ria siú nó ḟoideṁaḋ an dímiaḋ, ⁊ an easonoir fuair, ⁊ nó léiccfeḋh for dáil nó for cairde gan a dioġail, go ro líon dreiscc ⁊ dinnire gur ḃó suaill ná deachaiḋ for fualang ⁊ dásacht conaḋ sé do róine a coṁairliuccaḋ fri a ċairdiḃ ionnas no diġélaḋ an sár do rattaḋ fair. Bá séḋ céttus ro ċinnsiot

quinque rem ita gerens, vt prædis, & excursionibus multum Protestantibus offecerit, sæpè cum illis fuerit velitatus, leuesque pugnas commiserit. Ad quod bellum suscipiendum mouebatur præter memoratas iniurias tum quód cum Ibernis Anglicæ factionis non minus crudeliter, quàm cum cæteris Angli agebant, tum tyrannidis magnitudine, cuius vacationem nulla res præter bellum afferebat. Iam veró Richardus VVinkel Anglus eques Auratus Iberniæ castrametator quatuor militum millia ducens arcem illam, cui Felmius præerat, obsidet. Felmius ratus se paruo præsidio munimentum loci natura non satis munitum, diu non posse defendere, nec Odochartam opem laturum, quód militum numero inferior erat castrametatoris exercitu, ignem inijcit arci duabusque nauibus onerarijs plenis tritici in commeatum missi Luci præsidio, quas ceperat. Duo quoque millia librorum Hæreticorum, quæ Luci Ministropiscopi erant, in exercitus conspectu in ignem consumenda inijcit, spretis centum argenti libris quibus eos Pseudoepiscopus redimere cupiebat, & ipse duobus phasellis cum militibus fugit, tormenta partim secum deferens, partim deijciens in mare. Cuius facti Odochartam, qui statuit Felmium obsidione liberare, pœnituit. Beartam quoque arcem castrametator obsidio vallat, vbi erat Maria Odochartæ vxor Pristonis Vicecomitis filia. Arcem Monachus qui illam tenebat, prodit, & ipse simul Fidei nuncium remittit pactus tamen, vt præsidiarij incolumes dimitterentur: quibus Anglus fidem sua religione seruauit alios in vincula detrudens, alios pretio commutans, & Mariam Vicecomiti fratri, qui factionis Anglicæ erat, custodiendam tradens. Inde Castrametator ad direptionem, atque depopulationem agrorum, quos Odocharta possidebat vertitur. Quo conatu illum Odocharta prohibere insistit, mille, quingentosque armatos ductitans non longè ab hoste statiuis collocatis. Plerique castrametatoris milites Iberni, & Angloiberni Catholici erant, sed à sacerdotibus Anglicæ factionis non bene docti existimabant, sibi licere pro principe Protestante contra Catholicos pugnare, dum in spiritualibus non haberent cum Hæreticis communionem. Ex horum principibus erat Henricus Onellus cognomento Iunior, qui antea sub Onello in Hæreticos fidè, & acerrimè dimicauerat. Ad locum, qui Keannmhuir nominatur. Odocharta in illud castrorum cornu, quod Henricus tenebat, cum quingentis armatis noctu facit impetum: vallum subitò trangressus vigiles atque custodes interimit: prima tentoria repente circumit, & incendit: stragem vndique edit: mox in Henrici tabernaculum irruit, quò etiam regij milites semisomnes pauidi, & inermes ex aliorum tabernaculorum clade pervenerant. Hic atrox pugna committitur. Incipit Henricus suos consolari, confirmare, adque se tuendos, & sociorum necem vlciscendam hortari, hostis impetum fortissimè dimicando sustinere, laborantibus subsidium ferre; Odocharta contra suos crebris exhortationibus ad præliandum accendere, pauidis addere terrorem, ad Henricum, cuius vocem confirmantis audiebat, accedere. Henricus suis loco cedentibus Catholicis vndequaque circum-

not only offered him insult and abuse by word, but also inflicted chastisement on his body; so that he would rather have suffered death than live[f] to brook such insult and dishonour, or defer or delay to take revenge for it; and he was filled with anger and fury, so that he nearly ran to distraction and madness. What he did was, to consult with his friends how he should take revenge for the insult which was inflicted upon him. What they first unanimously resolved, on the 3rd of May, was to invite to him Captain Hart, who was at Cuil-mor (a

uenientibus fortiter prælians, multisque vulneribus affectus exanimis sternitur. Superstites in castrorum frontem, vbi castrametator erat, fugiunt. Castrametatorem, & exercitum totum ingens pauor inuadit: nonnulli castris desertis sese fugæ mandant: omnesque fugituri videbantur, nisi Odocharta suorum paucitati timens, receptui canere, pedemque referre iussisset. Accepto damno castrametator perculsus ex plano in præsidia confugit. Odocharta pagos, quos Henricus possedit, ingressus prædatur, atque deuastat. Per Drumorrium lacum in insulum lintribus, atque pontonibus vectus arcem expugnat, atque diripit. Rursus castrametator viribus refectis, maioribus copijs conscriptis, vberioribus Ibernorum auxilijs accitis contra Odochartam facit expeditionem. Auxilijs præerant Nellus Odonellus Asper, & Macsuinnius Tuethius. Quorum viribus Odocharta ratus suas esse impares in Beatham syluam sese cum multis diuitijs abdit. Quó erant omninò itinera tria, quibus hostes poterant illum aggredi, quæ simul regij arripiunt exercitu diuiso in tres partes inter tres duces castrametatorem, Asperum & Tuethium. Odocharta quoque suis copijs longè minoribus tripartitis tria simul itinera obsidet. De quibus ab vtraque parte dies circiter triginta missilibus contenditur non multis vtrinque interemptis. Denique castrametator commeatu deficiente in præsidia redit. Quem Odocharta secutus angustijs illis loci relictis per regios excursiones facit. Sub hoc tempus Asper in eam suspicionem Anglis venit, quòd esset cum Odocharta in bellum conspiraturus. Ob quod primum in Ibernis custodiæ mandatus, Indé in Angliam transmissus in Londinensi arce detinetur. Aliquot deinde diebus elapsis Anglus quoque Prorex, & Clanrichardæ Comes maioribus copijs conscriptis castrametatori suppetias veniunt. Odocharta ratus se esse imparem vtrique exercitui, siquidem vtrolibet erat inferior numero militum, in tutiorem locum sese recipere constituit, bellumque tantum ducere, donec superstites Ibernicæ iuuentutis ex Ibernica factione, qui ex varijs regni angulis ad illum iter habebant, perueniant, iustumque exercitum habeat. Cum compositis ordinibus agmen duceret, sub lucis exortum hostis illum assequitur: sed missilibus vtrinque aliquandiu pugnato rursus redit, nullo memorabili accepto, vel illato damno. Aliquot post horis occurrit hostilium bombardariorum ala Odochartæ agmen eminus plumbeis glandibus carpens, in quam Odocharta alteram imperat mitti: cum qua ipse quoque animosus iuuenis præter concilium, & senioribus inscijs ex agmine descendens duplici tragula confossus solus occumbit intra duas horas, quam fuit absolutione sacramentali peccatis expiatus, cuius infausta nex bello exitum omnium opinione celeriorem attulit. Namque cæteri præter paucos duce destituti in optantium, & inuitantium Anglorum gratiam, vt primum quisque potuit, rediuerunt."

[f] *Than live:* literally, "so that he would rather [have] his death than his life, before he would bear the insult and dishonour he received."

a haon ċomairle an 3. Mai Caiptin hart baoi isin ccúil móir (baile sin fil for ur loċa feaḃail alla ṫíos don doire a dubramar) do ṫoċuireaḋ ina ḋoċum, ⁊ a ġaḃáil go ffuair an baile ar. Do ṫaod fo ċedóir isin dedoil go doire, ⁊ do bḟrt uarḋúsccaḋ naṁatt for fianlaċ an ḃaile. Ro marḃaḋ an gobernóir lá heócchan mac neill mic gḟrailt uí ḃoċartaiġ, ⁊ leutenant corboi lá Sḟan mac aoḋa, mic aoḋa duiḃ uí doṁnaill. Ro marḃaḋ dna sochaiḋe oile cen mo ṫát soṁ. Do gaḃaḋ caiptin henri uegan, ⁊ bḟn ṡsscoip an ḃaile. Ro crḟċoiscceaḋ, ⁊ ro loisccead an baile leó iarttain ⁊ tucsat ettala aiḋḃle ass.

Monuar aṁ gíḋ nar ḃó maċtnaḋ an tuasal aireaċ daiṫe a easanora, Ro baḋ díriṁ doairnḟiri na huile ro ṡiolaiġ, ⁊ ro ċlandaiġ i ccoicceaḋ ulaḋ uile tres an ccoṁṫogḃáil ċoccaiḋ sin ro triall i nacchaiḋ rḟċta an ríġ, uair bá deriḋe tainic a ḃás soṁ badéin (18. Iulii ar ccionn) lá hard marasgal na heireann, Robert uincuel, ⁊ lá Sir oliuer lambert, ⁊ a roinn ina ċḟṫraṁnaiḃ coṁroinnte etir doire ⁊ an ċuil ṁór, ⁊ a cḟnn do ḃrḟiṫ a ttaisealḃaḋ go haṫ cliaṫ, ⁊ bás sochaiḋe duaislib, ⁊ daisḟchaib an ċóiccid ro baḋ eiṁilt dfaisneis. Bá de eiccin, ⁊ do imṫeaċt na niarlaḋ atrubramar, tainicc a ndoṁnus ⁊ a nduṫhaiġ, a ffosba, ⁊ a ffearann, a ndúine, ⁊ a ndiongnaḋa, a ccuanta caoṁṫurcarṫaċa, ⁊ a ninbeara iaisc ioṁḋa do ḃḟn do gaoiḋelaiḃ ċóiccid ulaḋ, ⁊ a ttabairt ina ffiaḋnaisi do eaċtair ċenélaiḃ ⁊ a ccorsoṁ for aṫċur, ⁊ for ionnarbaḋ in aile criochaiḃ coṁaigṫiḃ go ro éccsat a nerṁór.

[h] *With the sword:* literally, "he gave the soldiers of the town the cold awaking of enemies."

[i] *His own death.*—According to the tradition in the country, Sir Cahir O'Doherty was killed under the rock of Doon, near Kilmacrenan. It appears from an Inquisition taken in the 6th of Jac. I., that he fell on 5th of July, 1608:

"The said Cahire O'Doghertie, Knight, afterwards, to wit, on the 5th of July, in the year aforesaid, being in rebellion at or near Kilmacrenan, in the county of Donegall, together with the said other traitors, fought and contended with the army or soldiers of the said King, then and there remaining. The aforesaid Cahire O'Doghertie, Knight, so contending, was slain, and the Jurors saw the body and members of the said Cahire then and there slain," &c.

Sir Henry Docwra gives the following account of the causes that drove O'Doherty [*ætatis* 21] into this rash insurrection. He does not appear to have heard that his friend Pawlett had horse-whipped this proud young chieftain:

"Presentlie after him" [Roory O'Donnell], "came O'Doghertie alsoe, with a letter from my lord to mee, to pray mee to deliver him the possession of the Ile of Inch againe, which hee himself had past away before, first, by lease for xxi. yeares, & afterwardes in ffee simple for ever, both under the greate seale. I tould him

fort on the margin of Lough Foyle, below the Derry we have mentioned), and to take him prisoner. [This was done], and he obtained the fort in his release. He repaired immediately at daybreak to Derry, and awoke the soldiers of that town with the sword[h]. The Governor was slain by Owen, the son of Niall, son of Gerald O'Doherty, and Lieutenant Corbie by John, the son of Hugh, son of Hugh Duv O'Donnell. Many others were also slain besides these. Captain Henry Vaughan and the wife of the bishop of the town were taken prisoners. They afterwards plundered and burned the town, and carried away immense spoils from thence.

Alas! although it was no wonder that this noble chieftain should have avenged his dishonour, innumerable and indescribable were the evils that sprang up and pullulated in the entire province of Ulster through this warlike rising, which he undertook against the King's law; for from it resulted his own death[i], on the 18th of July following, by the Chief Marshal of Ireland, Robert Wingfield, and Sir Oliver Lambert. He was cut into quarters between Derry and Cuil-mor, and his head was sent to Dublin, to be exhibited; and many of the gentlemen and chieftains of the province, too numerous to be particularized, were also put to death. It was indeed[k] from it, and from the departure of the Earls we have mentioned, it came to pass that their principalities, their territories, their estates, their lands, their forts, their fortresses, their fruitful harbours, and their fishful bays, were taken from the Irish of the province of Ulster, and given in their presence to foreign tribes; and they were expelled and banished into other countries, where most of them died.

this warraunt was too weake to doe what it imported, and shew'd him reasons for it which either he could not or would not apprehend, or beleeve, but plainely made shew to conceive a suspition as though I were corrupted under hand to runne a dissembling course with him. To give him contentment, if I could, being then to goe for England, and to Dublin by the way, I spoke to Sir George Carey, that was then Lord Deputie, tould him how the case stoode, and what discontentment I sawe it drave him into. Hee told mee it was past the Seales (gaue mee a further reason too), & vtterlie refused to make or medle with it. Hereupon hee tooke it more to hearte; sent Agentes to deale for him in England. They prevayled not till my lord was deade, & then with impatience lead away, with lewd Councell besides, & conceiuing himselfe to be wronged in many other thinges, hee was first broke out into open Rebbellion; but that fell out a good while after."

Docwra then goes on to complain of various grievances, and shews clearly that he himself, O'Kane, and Sir Niall Garv O'Donnell, were very unfairly dealt with by the Government.

[k] *Indeed:* ecoın is here an expletive.

Niall garḃ o domnaill co na dearbraiṫriḃ, ⁊ co na ṁac neaċtain do ġaḃáil im feil eóin na bliadna so iar na tuḃa friú go mbaoi coṁaonta ſtorra, ⁊ na doċartaiġ, a ccur iarsin co haṫ cliaṫ Niall, ⁊ neaċtain do ċor arsaide co tor londan iar saoradh néill ó ḃás do brſiṫ dliccid, ⁊ a mbſiṫ illaiṁ isin tor co diuid a mbſthaḋ. Aoḋ ⁊ domnall do légaḋ as a mbraiġdſnas iarttain .i. isin mbliadain ar ccind.

Iarla tire conaill Ruḋraiġe mac aoḋa mic maġnasa, mic Aoḋa duiḃ mic Aoda ruaid í domnaill do écc isin róiṁ 28. Iul, ⁊ a adnacal i mainistir. S. froinseis isin ccnoc in ro crochaḋ naoiṁ Peattar apstal, iar ccaoí a ċionaḋ, ⁊ a ṫarġabal, iar ffaoísidin, ⁊ iar naitricce ṫoccaiḋe ina ṗeacṫoiḃ, ⁊ tairimṫeaċtaiḃ, iar nairitin cuirp ċríost ⁊ a ḟola a lamhaiḃ sruithiḃ sailmċſtlaiḃ eccailsi na roṁa. Ro baḋ liaċ gar secle, ⁊ muiċ erċra do bſiṫ occ an tí tſsda ann sin. Ar bá fſr cródḋa cosantaċ aġmar, ionnsaiġṫeaċ, iorġalaċ eiside, ro baḋ mſinic i mbſirn ḃaoġail ag imdídſn a irsi, ⁊ a aṫarḋa acc congnaṁ lá a dearḃraṫair Aoḋ ruaḋ riasiú ro ġaḃ soṁ feisin tiġearnas ṫire conaill, Tiġearna taḃartaċ tiodlaicṫeaċ duas ṁór deiġeiniġ dá nar ḃó ní oidḃſċt a ṡinnsſr andarlais ar a ċaiṫmiġe, ⁊ ar a ċonġairiġe, fear ná tard a ṁſnma, na a inneitſiṁ, i maoíniḃ náċ a seódaiḃ saoġalta

[1] *Niall Garv.*—The information on which Niall Garv was found guilty was furnished by Ineenduv, the mother of the great Hugh Roe O'Donnell, who died in Spain in 1602. It appears from the Ulster Inquisitions that she got a grant of lands in the barony of Kilmacrenan for this important service.—See also *Pat. Rot.* 10 Jac. I. The exact information which she furnished to the Lord Bishop of Derry, concerning the treason of O'Doherty and Niall Garv, is preserved among the Ormond Papers in the Bodleian Library at Oxford, V. 251, headed, "Mother's Confession to Bishop of Derry of O'Dogherty's treason."

"My Lo: be yt knowen unto yo[r] Loh. that S[r] Neele Garve O'Donnel & O'Dogherty began to go in treason against his Ma[ty], thus: O'Dogherty haue promised to take the Derry & the Culmor; & S[r] Neele promised to send his brother, Donell Mac Coine, to take Lifford, & that he and his brother, Hugh Boy, should take Belasenan & Dungall; & he haue send Dualtogh M[c] Gille Duff, & certen number of souldiers, with O'Dogherty, to receive half the goods of Derry for S[r] Neile, & S[r] Neile promised half the goods of the other towns vnto O'Dogherty; & the cause S[r] Neill had not fulfilled his promise was, that his son came not out of Dublin at the time he thought Donnogh Boy O Friayll should stell him thence; morower S[r] Neele haue send Edmond O Mularky & O Donnell ffanadogh to the Culmor with Diarmoid m[c] Daved and Cormac m[c] Daved, to diuid the treasure that was there, & after they divided it they loked it in a troncke, & they brought the key wth themseves; and there is another way S[r] Neill promised to serve upon the King's subjects, he gathered all that were obedient unto himself in the Countrie of Conall & brought them to Crochan, & desired S[r] Richard to go

Niall Garv[l] O'Donnell, with his brothers [Hugh Boy and Donnell], and his son, Naghtan, were taken prisoners about the festival of St. John in this year, after being accused of having been in confederacy with O'Doherty. They were afterwards sent to Dublin, from whence Niall and Naghtan were sent to London, and committed to the Tower, Niall having been freed from death by the decision of the law; and they [Niall and Naghtan] remained confined in the Tower to the end of their lives[m]. Hugh and Donnell were liberated from their captivity afterwards, i. e. in the year following

The Earl of Tirconnell (Rury, son of Hugh, son of Manus, son of Hugh Duv, son of Hugh Roe O'Donnell) died at Rome, on the 28th of July, and was interred in the Franciscan monastery situate on the hill on which St. Peter the Apostle was crucified, after lamenting his faults and crimes, after confession, exemplary penance for his sins and transgressions, and after receiving the body and blood of Christ from the hands of the psalm-singing clergy of the Church of Rome. Sorrowful [it is to consider] the short life and early eclipse of him who was there deceased, for he was a brave, protecting, valiant, puissant, and warlike man, and had often been in the gap of danger along with his brother, Hugh Roe (before he himself had assumed the lordship of Tirconnell), in defence of his religion and his patrimony. He was a generous, bounteous, munificent, and truly hospitable lord, to whom the patrimony of his ancestors did not seem anything for his spending and feasting parties; and a man who did not place his mind or affections upon worldly wealth and jewels, but dis-

with him to do a service upon O Dogherty, & if he should go with him then he & O Dogherty will murder them all, but S[r] Richard, in hope to have his son for him. And the Town of Lifford should be with S[r] Neill; moreover, another agreement betwixt S[r] Neill & O Dogherty, that S[r] Neill should possess the Castle of Bartt, & O Donnell's duties upon Inishowen, as long as they were able to maintain yt themselves. My Lo: be it knowen unto you the fear of my soul will not suffer me to accuse any body in the world with such, vnless I were sure of it.

"HI. DUBH.

"This lady also alledgeth that one of her servants was informed by one of O Dogherty's company, that a messenger had been with O Dogherty from S[r] Neile Garve the night before the army went upon him in Glenvagh, whereby was advised to leave his fastness & not to fight."

[m] *To the end of their lives.*—Niall Garv and his eldest son, Naghtan, died in the Tower of London in the year 1626, according to Short Annals of Tirconnell, preserved in a manuscript in the library of the Royal Irish Academy. He had another son, Manus, who was Colonel in the service of the Confederate Catholics, and from whom the O'Donnells of Newport are descended.

aċt a ffoḃail, ⁊ a sccaoílsḋ for gaċ naon da rigsḋ a lear do ṫrén, nó do ṫruagh.

Maguiḋir Cuċonnaċt ócc, mac conċonnaċt óicc, mic conċonnaċt mic conċonnaċt, mic briain, mic pilip, mic tomais tiġearna fearmanach nsċ fuair tiġearnas gan ṁsing, gan ṁeaḃail, gan ḟeill, gan ḟiongail aċt a ṫoga i ffiaḋnaisi fear nulaḋ i nionaḋ a dearḃraṫar Aoḋ. Saoí sreccna ilḋealḃaċ msnmnaċ móraiccsnteaċ, airoreaċ ssraḋal co mbuaiḋ ccéille, ⁊ ccroṫa, ⁊ gaċa maiṫssa ar ċsna do écc i ngenua isin etail an .12. August.

[n] *Died at Genoa.*—According to the tradition in the family, he died of a burning fever. This Cuconnaught was the ancestor of the Maguires of Tempo, in the county of Fermanagh, who descend from his second son, Brian, as shewn in the annexed pedigree:

I. CUCONNAUGHT MAGUIRE died in 1608. He was the brother of the celebrated Hugh Maguire, who was killed, near Cork, in a duel with Sir Warham St. Leger.

II. BRIAN MAGUIRE. He was a minor at the death of his father, and was restored to a tract of land called Tempodessel, now Tempo, estimated to contain two thousand acres of land, which were his brother's, lately deceased. Pynnar speaks of his estate in his *Survey of Ulster*, as published in Harris's *Hibernica*, p. 169, as follows:

"Upon this Proportion there is a large Bawne of Sodds, and a good house of lime and stone. He hath made five leaseholders, which have, each of them, sixty Acres for twenty-one Years, and all his Tenants do Plough after the Irish Manner."

This Brian left one legitimate son,

III. HUGH MAGUIRE, who married the daughter of the head of the O'Reillys, by whom he had,

IV. CUCONNAUGHT MORE. He married the daughter of Everhood Magennis, of Castlewellan, in the county of Down. He mortgaged a great part of his estate to raise, arm, and support a regiment of horse for the service of James II. According to the tradition in the family, which appears to be correct, he fought desperately at the pass of Aughrim, where he himself was killed, and his regiment cut to pieces, after having nearly annihilated the second regiment of the British horse. He was struck down by a grape-shot, and left dead on the field; but one of his followers, named O'Durnin, is said to have cut off his head with his sword, and to have carried it in a bag to the island of Devenish, where he interred it in the family tomb of the Maguires. The late Bryan Maguire, of Tempo, and of Clontarf, Dublin, states, in a pedigree of his family, which he printed in 1811, that the descendants of this O'Durnin were then living in Dublin. Cuconnaught, or Constantine More, had, 1. Brian, of whom presently; 2. Hugh; 3. Stephen. The two latter died unmarried.

V. BRIAN MAGUIRE. He was restored to some remnant of his father's estate, and married the daughter and heir of James Nugent, Esq., of Coolamber, by which marriage he was enabled to pay off certain debts with which the estate of Tempo was incumbered. He had five sons and one daughter, the two eldest of whom died unmarried. He died himself in the year 1700, and was succeeded by his third son, Robert Maguire, who is mentioned by Charles O'Conor, of Belanagare, in his *Dissertations on the History of Ireland*, printed in 1753, as the head of the

tributed and circulated them among all those who stood in need of them, whether the mighty or the feeble.

Maguire (Cuconnaught Oge, the son of Cuconnaught, son of Cuconnaught, son of Brian, son of Philip, son of Thomas), Lord of Fermanagh, who had attained the lordship without fraud, deceit, treachery, or fratricide; but had been elected in the place of his brother, Hugh, in the presence of the men of Ulster; who was an intelligent, comely, courageous, magnanimous, rapid-marching, adventurous man, endowed with wisdom and personal beauty, and all the other good qualifications, died at Genoa[n], in Italy, on the 12th of August.

Maguires of Fermanagh. This Robert married the daughter and heiress of Henry Mac Dermot Roe, Esq., of Greyfield, in the county of Roscommon, but died without issue, and was succeeded by his next brother, Colonel Hugh Maguire, the fourth son of Brian of Tempo, No. V. This Hugh was a colonel in the Austrian service, and married the Honourable Dowager Lady Cathcart, of Irwin Water, Herefordshire, and dying in Dublin, *sine prole*, in 1763, was succeeded by his youngest brother,

VI. Philip Maguire, the fifth son of Brian. He married Miss Frances Morres, daughter of Nicholas Morres, Esq., of Lattreest, in the county of Tipperary, by Miss Susanna Talbot of Malahide. This Philip had one son, No. VII., and two daughters, the elder of whom married Owen O'Reilly, Esq., of Mount-Pallas, in the county of Cavan, by whom she had two sons, Charles, who died at Brussels in 1786, and Eugene O'Reilly, who was living in England in 1811. The younger daughter married Sir John Stuart Hamilton, Baronet, of Dunnamanna, in the county of Tyrone, by whom she had several children, of whom the eldest surviving was Sir John Charles, who succeeded his father.

VII. Hugh Maguire, of Tempo, one of the most puissant, high-minded, and accomplished gentlemen that ever came of the Maguire family. The Editor was acquainted with many persons who knew him intimately, and were entertained at his hospitable and sumptuous table at Tempo. He mortgaged Tempo, and left his family in great distress. He married Phœbe Mac Namara, daughter of George Mac Namara, Esq., of the county of Clare, by whom he had three sons: 1. Constantine, a gentleman of polished manners and indomitable courage, who was murdered in the county of Tipperary, in 1834, at the very time that the Editor was examining the locality of Tempo-Deisil; he left one son, whose legitimacy was denied by his brother, Brian, but who now enjoys a small estate to which Constantine succeeded in right of his mother, and some daughters; 2. Brian, of whom presently; 3. Stephen, who enlisted as a private soldier in the British service, but died soon after, broken-hearted; and five daughters, Frances, Stephania, Maria, Eliza, and Catherine. This Hugh died in October, 1800.

VIII. Brian Maguire, the second son of Hugh of Tempo. He was an officer in the Honourable East India Company's native army in Bombay, which he joined in 1799. In the year 1811, a short memoir of this remarkable man, evidently the production of his own pen, was printed in Dublin by W. Cox, 150, Abbey-street, giving an account of his several duels with English officers, and of several circumstances that occurred to him in India and Europe, to which is annexed a Genealogy of his family, which shewed him to have been related to some of the best families of Ireland, being the

Semus mac eiṁir mic conulaḋ még maṫgaṁna do écc isin lo cedna ⁊ a aḋnacal isin maiġin reṁraite.

Caṫḃarr mac Aoḋa mic maġnusa, an taon mac tiġearna ro baḋ mó ainm ⁊ oirdearcus, allaḋ, ⁊ airdnós, ar aoiḋeċaire, ar ḟéile ro ḃaoí i nimis eireṁóin. Aiṫġin ċuana meic cailċin, ⁊ ġuaire mic colmáin ar dearlaccaḋ ⁊ ar oineaċ, fear ná tard neaċ a ḋruim fris riaṁ iar ná ésa do écc isin róiṁ an .17. September, ⁊ a aḋnacal ar aon lá a dearḃraṫair lasin iarla.

Aodh O Neill mac aoḋa, mic firdorċa barún dúinġſnainn oiḋre an iarla ui neill do écc, aon traoileaċtain ċenél neoġain do ġaḃáil ionaid a aṫar diamaḋ beó ina ḋſuhaiḋ do écc, ⁊ a aḋnacal i naoin ionad la dearḃraiṫriḃ a maṫar .i. las an iarla ua ndoṁnaill ⁊ la caṫḃarr.

AOIS CRIOST, 1609.

Aois Criost, mile, Se ċéd, anaoí.

Caṫbarr óce mac caṫbairr, mic Maġnusa, mic aoḋa duibh uí doṁnaill do ċor do cum báis i náṫ cliaṫ lá gallaiḃ an 18. iul. Nír ḃó dímiad do cenel cconaill meic Néill an daiġ fſr sin do oirdneaḋ i ccſnnas forra dia léiccti dia saiġiḋ a ccſnnas ittir, ar uaisle a ḟola ar airde a aiġnid ar ḃríġ, ar ḃorrfaḋ, ar ṫuaiċle, ar trebaire ar coṁnart, ar ċoṫuccaḋ fris an ccáċ do cuirſtar ina ċſnet.

Brian na Saṁṫaċ mac airt, mic briain na muiċeirge do ṁarḃaḋ lá gallaiḃ.

Mac an ḃaird Eoġan mac goffraḋa, mic eoġain, mic goffraḋa ollaṁ uí doṁnaill i ndán saoí ſrġna inntleaċtaċ, ⁊ fear tiġe naoiḋead coitcinn do écc iar ccian aois, iar mbuaiḋ naiṫriġe.

second cousin of the Earl of Ormond, and of the present Lord Talbot of Malahide. In p. 29 of this little work (which was suppressed at the request of the more respectable of Mr. Maguire's friends) is given a circumstantial account of a row which he had with some English officers at the island of St. Helena, which is a curious specimen of autobiography. But a far better book could be written on the life and adventures of his grandfather, who was really a man of exalted character, and of whom many interesting anecdotes are still remembered by his tenants at Tempo.

This Brian married Miss Honoria Anne Baker, daughter of James Baker, Esq., of Ballymoreen, in the county of Tipperary, on the 17th December, 1808, and had by her several sons, some of whom are now, or were lately, reduced to the condition of common sailors on the coal vessels sailing between Dublin and the coasts of Wales. Thus, in one generation, has the proudest blood of Ireland sunk to one of the vulgarest states of human existence, and commingled with that

James, the son of Ever, son of Cu-Uladh [Cooley] Mac Mahon, died on the same day, and was interred at the aforenamed place.

Caffar, son of Hugh, son of Manus [O'Donnell], a lord's son, who had borne a greater name, renown, and celebrity, for entertainment of guests and hospitality, than all who were in the Isle of Heremon; a second Cuanna-mac-Cailchinni[o], and a second Guaire-mac-Colmain for bounty and hospitality; and a man from [the presence of] whom no one had ever turned away with a refusal of his request; died at Rome on the 17th of September, and was buried with his brother, the Earl.

Hugh O'Neill, the son of Hugh, son of Ferdorcha, Baron of Dungannon, and the heir of the Earl O'Neill[p], the only expectation of the Kinel-Owen to succeed his father, if he had survived him, died, and was buried in the same place with his mother's brothers, the Earl O'Donnell and Caffar.

THE AGE OF CHRIST, 1609.

The Age of Christ, one thousand six hundred nine.

Caffar Oge, the son of Caffar, son of Manus, son of Hugh Duv O'Donnell, was put to death at Dublin, by the English, on the 18th of July. It would have been no disgrace to the tribe of Conall[q], son of Niall, to elect this good man as their chief, if he had been permitted to go home to take the leadership of them, by reason of the nobleness of his blood and the greatness of his mind, and for his vigour, magnanimity, prudence, prowess, and puissance, in maintaining a battle against his opponents.

Brian-na-Samhthach, son of Art, son of Brian-na-mucheirghe [O'Rourke], was slain by the English.

Mac Ward (Owen, the son of Godfrey, son of Owen, son of Godfrey), Ollav to O'Donnell in poetry, an intelligent, ingenious man, who kept an open house of general hospitality, died at an advanced age, after the victory of penance.

class amongst whom, a century ago, according to Dean Swift, the true representatives of the ancient Irish nobility were to be found.

[o] *Cuanna-mac-Cailchinni.*—He was Prince of Fermoy, in the now county of Cork, in the seventh century, and vied in feats of hospitality and munificence with Guaire Aidhne, King of Connaught at the same period.

[p] *Earl O'Neill.*—This should be Earl of Tyrone, according to the technical language of English law.

[q] *The tribe of Conall, son of Niall:* i. e. the

AOIS CRIOST, 1610.

Aois Criost, Mile, Se ċétt, a deich.

AOIS CRIOST, 1611.

Aois Criost, míle, Se ċéd, a dech, a haon.

Conċoḃar o Duibeanaiġ epscop Dúin, ⁊ coimdeire ro baḋ braṫair dord .S. Froinseis do ċoimuent Ḋúin na ngall céttus, ⁊ ro toccaḋ iaraṁ do cum na hepscopóitte céDna ar a dsċċaipilleaḋ, Ro herġaḃaḋ eisioṁ lá gallaiḃ, ⁊ baoí fri ré ḟoda aca fó ḋaoíre, ⁊ fó pſnnaind, ⁊ do rairngſrtatt Maoíne ⁊ arccaḋa ioṁḋa dó dia sóad for a neris. Ro obsaṁ dna indsin ar ro dínsriḋsioṁ an maiṫ nerċraḋaċ ar an fflaiṫ suṫain. Ro ḟuaslaicc dia dó ó ġallaiḃ don ċur sin, ⁊ ro gaḃaḋ eisiḋe do riḋisi ⁊ as é ro ba lustis i nerinn in ionbaiḋ sin Sir Artuir Chicester, ⁊ ro cuireaḋ eisiḋ do ċum báis, Ro díċſndaḋ céttus, ⁊ ro tſsccaitt a boill ina cſṫraṁnaiḃ foḋalta, feóil-ġſrrṫa i náṫ cliaṫ an ceD la do febru.

Ni ḃaoí éiṁ criostuiḋe i ttír nereann ná ro crioṫnaiġ a ċroiḋe lá huaṫḃar na martra ro ḟulaing, ⁊ ro ḟoḋaiṁ an teslaṁ ógh ſgnaiḋe, ⁊ an firén foirċṫe fírċſndais ar daiġ ḟocraicce dia anmain. Nír ḃó cuma lá haon do na criostuiḋiḃ báttar i ccaṫraiġ aṫa cliaṫ an ionbaiḋ sin cia haca las a mbſiṫ ball dia ḃallaiḃ, ⁊ nír ḃó hiad a ḃoill namá aċt ḃáttar lſonanarta soinſṁla i nſrlaiṁe aca ag gaḃáil a ḟola intiḃriḋe co ná léiccdís go lár hí ar bá dearḃ leó gur ḃó haon do ṁairtiriḃ naoṁḋa an coiṁdeaḋ eisiḋe.

O'Donnells and their correlatives, who were descended from Conall Gulban, the youngest son of Niall of the Nine Hostages, monarchs of Ireland in the end of the fourth century.

[r] 1610.—This year is left blank by the Four Masters.

[s] *Good qualifications.*—P. O'Sullevan Beare, who gives a most admirable description of the trial of this old prelate, draws his character in the following words, tom. 4, lib. 1, c. xviii.:

"Cornelius vir haud obscuro genere natus Seraphicæ Diui Francisci religioni sese teneris ab annis alligauit. Vbi mirifica pietate, longis orationibus, perpetuis pœnitentiis, & omnium virtutum ornamento fulgens, doctrinam eruditus ingenio comis, & vrbanus, sermone nequaquam rudis euasit."

[t] *First beheaded.*—This is not correct, for he was first hanged. The bishop was about eighty years of age at the period of his execution. When the hangman of Dublin, who was an Irishman, heard that the bishop had been con-

THE AGE OF CHRIST, 1610[r].

The Age of Christ, one thousand six hundred ten.

THE AGE OF CHRIST, 1611.

The Age of Christ, one thousand six hundred eleven.

Conor O'Duibheannaigh [O'Devany], Bishop of Down and Conor, who had been at first a friar of the order of St. Francis, of the convent of Donegal, but who was afterwards, for his good qualifications[s], elected to the episcopal dignity, was taken prisoner by the English; and he was detained by them a long time in bondage and punishment; and they offered him riches and many rewards, if he would turn over to their heresy, but he refused to accept of them, for he despised transitory riches for an everlasting kingdom. God released him from the English on that occasion; but he was taken again. Sir Arthur Chichester being at this time Lord Justice of Ireland, he was put to death. He was first beheaded[t], and [then] his members were cut in quarters, and his flesh mangled at Dublin, on the first of February.

There was not a Christian in the land of Ireland whose heart did not shudder within him at the horror of the martyrdom which this chaste, wise, divine, and the perfect and truly meek, righteous man, suffered for the reward of his soul. The Christians who were then in Dublin contended with each other, to see which of them should have one of his limbs; and not only his limbs, but they had fine linen in readiness, to prevent his blood from falling to the ground; for they were convinced that he was one of the holy martyrs of the Lord.

demned, he fled from the city, and O'Sullevan says that none of the Irish race could be induced by threats, fear, or reward, to perform the office of executioner. Wherefore an English murderer was released from prison and forgiven the murder for executing him. When, however, he saw the calm fortitude and venerable countenance of the prelate, he asked forgiveness of him for the butchery he was employed to commit: "Quam ille se dare placidissimo vultu dixit." O'Sullevan adds:

"Spectantibus hoc magnam admirationem mouit, quod tortor miles robustus ætate florens, qui martyrum carnificio se vitam redempturum non ignorabat quasi sui incompos in scalis titubabat, & Episcopus senex debilis intrepide scalas ascendit, in eisque loquens stabat robore perfusus collo suo laqueum imposuit, sudariolo faciem cooperuit iunctas manus carnifici vt vincerentur porrexit."

Giollapattraicc ó luċairén saccard dearscaigthe baoi i ffarrad in epscoip an tan sin, o ro ċinnſtt goill iattsoṁ ina ndóis do ḃáruccaḋ, bá huaṁan las an epscop go ngébaḋ uaṫḃás ⁊ imſgla eisiḋe lá faicsin na mi imberta do brſṫa for a corpsoṁ ina ḟiaḋnaise conaḋ aireſin ro cuindiġ gus na básairiġiḃ an saccart do ḃáruccaḋ riamh. Atbert an saccart náċ ráinicc rioṁ alſs uaman do ḃeiṫ fair ar aoisioṁ, ⁊ go lſnfaḋ é gan naċ nuirſccla, ⁊ attbert nár ḃó coṁaḋais epscop onórac do bſiṫ gan saccart ina caoiṁṫeaċt. Ro coṁaillsioṁ indisin ar ro foḋaiṁ ⁊ ro ḟulaing an diaċ céḋna do ṫaḃairt fair ar flaiṫ niṁe dia anmain.

Niall ó buiḋill epscop Raṫaboṫ do écc i nglionn eiḋniġe an seiseaḋ februari, ⁊ a aḋnacal i ninis caoil.

AOIS CRIOST, 1616.

Aois Criost, mile, Se céd, a dech, a Sé.

O Néll Aodh mac firdorċae (mic cuinn ḃacaiġ, mic cuinn, mic enrí, mic eoccain) ro baḋ barún ó ṁarḃaḋ a aṫar gus an mbliaḋain a mbaoí an Parlement oirrdearc i náṫ cliaṫ, 1584, ⁊ dia ro goiread iarla tíre heoġain ar an Parlement sin, ⁊ dia ro goiread o neill iar ttriall do écc iar ccian aoís iar ccaiṫſm a ree, ⁊ a reiṁis go sona sénaṁail, go náġ, go nairbert go nonoir, go nuaisle. Bá hann dna ro éccsoṁ isin roiṁ an 20. Iul, iar naiṫriġe ṫoġaiḋe ina ṗſcṫoiḃ, ⁊ iar mbrſiṫ ḃuaḋa ó ḋoṁan, ⁊ o dſṁan. Ger bo cian o Ard ṁaċa (o ḋtairliġe a ṡinnsear) atbath somh ro baḋ coṁarḋa gur ḃó buiḋeaċ Dia dia ḃſthaiḋ nár ḃó mſsa an Rómh aḋnaicṫe in ro deónaiġ an coiṁḋe a aḋnacal .i. an Róṁ cſnn na ccriostuiḋe. Tiġſrna tſnd toṫacṫaċ

[u] *Gleann-Eidhnighe:* i. e. the vale of the River Eidhneach, now Gleneany, a valley in the parish of Inver, barony of Banagh, and county of Donegal, midway between the villages of Dunkineely and Mount Charles.

[w] *Inis-Caoil,* now Iniskeel, an island near the mouth of Gweebara Bay, in the barony of Boylagh, and county of Donegal. The patron saint of this island is Conall Caol, whose festival was kept there on the 12th of May.—See Colgan's *Acta Sanctorum,* pp. 204, 205. The bell of this saint, called Bearnan-Chonaill, passed by purchase into the possession of Major Nesbitt of Woodhill in 1835, and was preserved by him till his death in 1844, since which it has unaccountably disappeared. It had been sold to Major Nesbitt by Connell Mac Michael O'Breslen, then living at Glengesh, in the parish of Inver. This poor man was the senior of his name, and the representative of O'Breslen, who, as appears from an Inquisition, 7 Jac. I., was one of the Erenaghs of Inishkeel. The bell was

Gilla-Patrick O'Loughrane, a distinguished priest, was with the Bishop at this time. When the English had decided that both these should be put to death, the Bishop felt afraid that he [the priest] might be seized with horror and dismay at the sight of the tortures about to be inflicted upon his own body in his presence ; so that he, therefore, requested of the executioner to put the priest to death before himself. The priest said that he need not be in dread on his account, and that he would follow him without fear, and remarked that it was not meet an honourable bishop should be without a priest to attend him. This he fulfilled, for he consented and suffered the like torture to be inflicted on him [with fortitude], for the sake of [obtaining] the kingdom of heaven for his soul.

Niall O'Boyle, Bishop of Raphoe, died at Gleann-Eidhnighe[u], on the 6th of February, and was interred at Inis-Caoil[w].

THE AGE OF CHRIST, 1616.

The Age of Christ, one thousand six hundred sixteen.

O'Neill (Hugh, son of Ferdorcha, son of Con Bacagh, son of Con, son of Henry, son of Owen), who had been Baron from the death of his father to the year when the celebrated Parliament was held in Dublin, 1584 [*recte* 1585], and who was styled Earl of Tyrone at that Parliament, and who was afterwards styled O'Neill, died at an advanced age, after having passed his life in prosperity and happiness, in valiant and illustrious achievements, in honour and nobleness. The place at which he died was Rome, [and his death occurred] on the 20th of July, after exemplary penance for his sins, and gaining the victory over the world and the Devil. Although he died far from Armagh, the burial-place of his ancestors, it was a token that God was pleased with his life that the Lord permitted him a no worse[x] burial-place, namely, Rome, the head [city] of the Christians. The person who here died was a powerful, mighty lord, [endowed]

enclosed in an elaborately ornamented case, or shrine, having an inscription in the black letter, greatly defaced, but in which the names of Mahon O'Meehan and —— O'Breslen were still legible.—See a notice of this relic in Dr. Petrie's paper on Ancient Irish Bells, in the Transactions of the Royal Irish Academy, vol. xxi. (now in course of publication), in which engravings of this bell and its cover are given.

[x] *No worse*: i. e. than Armagh.

go ngaoís, go ngliocas, ⁊ go naṁainsi indtleaċta, ⁊ aigneaḋ an tí testa annsin. Tiġearna coccṫaċ congalaċ airccṫeċ ionnsaiġṫeaċ, ag díden a irsi, ⁊ a aṫarḋa fri a ḃioḋḃadhaiḃ. Tiġearna diaḃa, dércaċ cendais coindircil fri cairdiḃ, ainmín éccennais fri naiṁdiḃ co ttaḃraḋ fó uṁla, ⁊ fó aididin dia réir. Tiġearna ná ro ṡanntaiġ forbann ná fairbríġ neiċ oile do ḃeiṫ occa, aċt in ro baḋ toiċ dia ṡinnseraiḃ ó ċein ṁair, Tiġearna go bforsmaċt, ⁊ go ttesttmoltaiḃ flaṫa, ⁊ ná ro léicc goitt ná meirle, aiṫeaḋ na éigein, ḟioċ ná fala do éirge ina reiṁes aċt no congḃaḋ cáċ fó reaċt amail ro ba téċta do ḟlaiṫ.

[y] *Wisdom and subtlety of mind.*—Camden describes the character of this extraordinary man as follows, in his *Annal. Reg. Eliz.*, A. D. 1590, edition of 1639, p. 572:

"Corpus laborum, vigiliæ, & inediæ patiens, industria magna animus ingens maximisque par negotiis, militiæ multa scientia, ad simulandum animi altitudo profunda, adeo ut nonnulli eum

with wisdom, subtlety, and profundity of mind[y] and intellect; a warlike, valorous, predatory, enterprising lord, in defending his religion and his patrimony against his enemies; a pious and charitable lord, mild and gentle with his friends, fierce and stern towards his enemies, until he had brought them to submission and obedience to his authority; a lord who had not coveted to possess himself of the illegal or excessive property of any other, except such as had been hereditary in his ancestors from a remote period; a lord with the authority and praiseworthy characteristics of a prince, who had not suffered theft or robbery, abduction or rape, spite or animosity, to prevail during his reign; but had kept all under [the authority of] the law, as was meet for a prince.

vel maximo Hiberniæ bono, vel malo natum tunc prædixerint."

It is stated in Dubourdieu's *Statistical Survey of the County of Down*, p. 312, that there is a picture of this famous Earl, which was painted in Spain, in the possession of the Earl of Leicester.

APPENDIX.

PEDIGREE OF O'DONNELL.

THE Editor hopes it will not be considered out of place to append to the Annals of the Four Masters the genealogies of a few of the most distinguished Irish families who figure in them, and even of one or two of whom they have but few notices; and as these Annals treat more of the O'Donnells than any other family, their pedigree shall be given the first in order.

The necessity of illustrating this pedigree in connexion with the present work has been for some time seen by the Editor, as it has been asserted in a work, entitled *Military Memoirs of the Irish Nation*, written by the late Matthew O'Conor, Esq., Barrister at Law, and published after his death, that "the O'Donnells of the present day cannot by grants, inquisitions, or other memorials, trace their pedigree for five generations." It would be wonderful, indeed, if this were the case; but the Editor trusts that he will succeed in shewing, on the evidence of many monuments and memorials, which his late worthy friend, Matthew O'Conor, son of Denis, son of Charles the historian, did not take the trouble to examine, that the pedigrees of many branches of the O'Donnells now living in Ireland, and of others living abroad, can be traced with certainty to the old stock of the O'Donnells of Tirconnell. That the reader may understand the exact nature of Mr. O'Conor's assertion, the Editor shall here lay before him the whole of his critical note on the family of the O'Donnells, as printed in his *Military Memoirs of the Irish Nation*, pp. 158, 159:

"The O'Donnels, who remained in Ireland after the flight of the Earl, lapsed to poverty, and but few of them have preserved any authentic traces of their descent. Ignorance, and money, and the shameless compliances of dishonest heralds, have framed pedigrees for them that have no foundation. Rory O'Donnel, first Earl, is represented as having had a son, grandson, and great grandson, second, third, and fourth Earls of Tirconnell, whereas Rory's only son died without issue, in the flower of youth. The alleged great grandson is stated to have had a daughter, married to Brian Ballagh O'Morcha, who died 100 years before such a person could have been born. On the failure of issue in Rory O'Donnel, the title of

Tirconnel devolved on his brother Caffre, who fled also to Spain. Caffre was married to Rose O'Dogherty, sister of Sir Caher O'Dogherty, who, after the death of Caffre, married Owen Roe O'Neal, and was buried, with her eldest son, Hugh O'Donnel, in the Irish Franciscan convent of Louvain. The second son, Caffre Oge O'Donnell, on the death of his father, became Earl of Tirconnel; on his death the title devolved on his son, Hugh, a distinguished officer in the service of Spain. The writer of those pages has in his possession a silk handkerchief, with a Latin thesis on divinity printed on it, dated at Salamanca, A. D. 1672, dedicated to this Hugh O'Donnel. This Hugh O'Donnel, in my mind, was the identical Balldarag O'Donnel who came to Ireland in 1690. The O'Donnels of the present day, or their genealogist, have no memorial or knowledge of his pedigree or origin. Neal Garbh, the supposed ancestor of the O'Donnels of Larkfield, Greyfield, Newport, and Oldcastle, had betrayed Hugh Roe; had killed Manus, his brother, with his own hand; afterwards betrayed the English, was found guilty of high treason, and died in the tower of London, under sentence of death. He had a son, called Naghtan; whether he died without issue, I know not; but the O'Donnels of the present day cannot, by grants, inquisitions, or other memorials, trace their pedigree for five generations. I am sorry that they should be reduced to derive their descent from such a traitor as Neal Garbh. The descent from Colonel Manus O'Donnel and Hugh Boy O'Donnel, fictitious sons of Neal Garbh, are manifest fabrications, Neal Garbh having had no sons of that name. Five generations are said to have intervened from the death of Neal Garbh, in 1610, to the death of Lewis O'Donnel, in 1810, a period of 200 years; another manifest proof of fiction. Of the O'Donnels in the service of France and Spain, no notice is taken by their genealogist, nor of Connell O'Donnel, the head of the family in 1689, who was Lord Lieutenant of the County of Donegal. He was the father of Hugh O'Donnel, of Larkfield, called Earl O'Donnel by the common people, and who died in 1754. He had three sons: Connel, a Field-marshal in the Austrian service, who, on Downs being wounded, commanded the Imperial army at the battle of Torgau; John, also a General in the same service; and Constantine, the grandfather of the present Hugh O'Donnel, of Greyfield."

The Editor shall presently lay before the reader the evidences and memorials by which the O'Donnells of the present day can trace their pedigree; but he deems it necessary to begin with—

I. Manus, son of Hugh Duv O'Donnell, who succeeded his father as chieftain, July, 1537[a]. He was married four times. It is by no means easy to decide what was the exact priority or order of his marriages[b], but the following will be found to rest upon good authorities:

[a] Annals of the Four Masters.

[b] According to a manuscript in the British Museum (copied by the Editor in 1844), the following is the order and issue of the marriages:

1st. Wife not named, nor issue given.

2nd. "Ellenor, daughter of Gerald, Earl of Kildare, and widow of M'Carthy Reogh" [By Daniel Mac Carthy Reagh this Lady Eleanor had a son, viz. Sir Owen Mac Carthy Reagh, whose daughter, Johanna, was married to Donnell O'Donovan, chief of Clancahill], by whom he had one son

1st. Johanna, daughter of Con More O'Neill, and sister of Con Bacagh, first Earl of Tyrone, by whom he had issue, Calvagh, Manus, Hugh, and several other children.

2nd. Elleanor, daughter of Gerald, eighth Earl of Kildare (widow of Donnell Mac Carthy Reagh).

3rd. Margaret, daughter of Angus Mac Donnell of Islay, Scotland. And

4th. The daughter of Maguire of Fermanagh. He had fourteen children, the greater number of whom (*vide* note [b]) must have been by his first marriage: 1. Calvagh; 2. Rose (married to Niall Conallagh O'Neill); 3. Margaret; 4. Manus; 5. Hugh; 6. Niall Garv (slain 1538); 7. Eveleen (married to O'Boyle, died 1549); 8. Caffar (slain by the Scots at Tory Island, 1551); 9. Grace (married to O'Rourke, died 1551); 10. Johanna (married to O'Conor Sligo, died 1533); 11. Caffar (Tanist to Sir Hugh, died 1580); 12. Mary (married to Maguire, died 1566); 13. Manus Oge; and, 14. Nuala (married also to a Maguire).

Of the busy and troubled life of this chieftain, of the feuds in his family, and the rivalry of his sons, Calvagh and Hugh, there need be said nothing here. They form a considerable part of

and two daughters: 1. "Callough, who married the Countesse of Argile;" 2. "Roase, married to Neale Conelagh O'Neale;" and 3. "Margaret, married to Shane O'Neale."

3rd. "Daughter to M'Guire, by whom he had issue one son, Manus Oge;" and

4th. "Joane, sister to Con Backagh O'Neill, Earl of Tirone," by whom he had issue three sons: 1. Caber; 2. Manus; and 3. Sir Hugh, who married "Nine Duffe da. to James M'Donnell, Lord of the Countrie of M'Gronald."

This account seems the more conclusive, as it corresponds in the main with the sources from which Sir William Betham derived his information upon the same point, as given in the *Antiq. Researches*, p. 130; the only difference being the omission in the latter part of the first marriage, which, as there was no issue named, is not important; and that the name of the second wife is not given. This concurrence of testimony, together with the high probability that Calvagh and Hugh were not brothers of the whole but of the half blood, arising from their constant feuds and struggles for power, and that Hugh, and not Calvagh, was the son of Johanna O'Neill, from the fact that that powerful family always supported him in his pretensions against his brother, would leave little doubt as to the accuracy of the arrangement, were it not that it is entirely and conclusively displaced by the information since supplied by the publication of the State Papers connected with Ireland, temp. Henry VIII. The Annals of the Four Masters record that Donnell Mac Carthy Reagh died in 1528, and that Joan, or Johanna O'Neill died seven years afterwards (1535), forty-two years old, "the most illustrious woman of her age for piety and hospitality." In a letter from Brabazon to Ailmer and J. Allen, dated 5th June, 1538 (*State Papers*, vol. iii. p. 17), it is said: "The late Erle of Kildare, his suster is gon to be maried to Manus Odonell, with whom is gon young Gerrot Delahides, and others which I like not. I was never in despaire in Ireland till now." And again, in a despatch from the Council in Ireland to Cromwell, dated the same year (p. 28), "Furthermore, one Alienor Fitz Gerald, sister to the late Erle of Kildare, late wiff of a grete capiteyne of Mounestre, named M'Carte Riaghe, who hathe bene the principale refuge and succor of the yonge Gerald FitzGerald, and sithen his departure out of the Englishry is now, with the same Gerald, two of James FitzGeraldes sonnys, and other his adherentes, departed out of Mounestre throwe Obrenes Countrre and Cannaght to O Donyll, to thentent the said Alienor shuld be to O Donyll maried: so as the combynacion of O Neill, being nere of Kyn to the said Alienor and Gerald" [NOTE, Con O'Neill married Lady Alice FitzGerald, sister of Ellenor, and aunt of Gerald], "with O Donyll, and them unto whom the Irishe Scottes offtymes resortithe, and in a maner are at ther draght and pleasure, is moch to be doubted." The third wife must have been Margaret Mac Donnell (the name omitted in the British Museum manuscript, but whose marriage is there placed as the first), for her death is recorded in the *Annals of the Four Masters* under the year 1544, leaving but the brief interval of six years for the marriages and deaths of two wives. This places the marriage with Maguire's daughter as the fourth and last. It is stated in a note in vol. iii. *State Papers*, p. 491, that "O'Donnell's first wife was O'Neill's sister, by whom he had three sons, Callough, Manus, and Hugh." This note appears to have been written by one who had authority for the fact. Beyond this, the Editor does not venture to connect with the above marriages the names or number of the children respectively.

the history of the period, and a large portion of the 2nd and 3rd vols. of the State Papers, temp. Henry VIII., lately published, is occupied with details connected with the then chieftains of Tirconnell and Tyrone. It will, however, be not uninteresting to quote from the latter two passages relating to Manus O'Donnell; the one illustrative of the extent of territory over which at that period the chieftains of Tirconnell had extended their sway; and the other of the dress and appearance of the individual himself. Sentleger, in one of his despatches to Henry VIII., enclosed a note or minute of "the more parte of the notable havons of Ireland to begin at Dublyn;" among which we find: "west and by northe, Brode Haven, Slygo, Assaro, Dongall, Calbege, Arrane, Shepehaven, Northerborne, Loghswylle, Loghfoyle. All these be in O'Donelle's Countrey."[c]

And the same individual in writing of O'Donnell himself, says:

"The said Odonell's chiefe Counseler desired me very instantly, at his departing fro me, to be sewter to your Majestie for some apparaill for his Master. If it may stand with your Highness pleasure to geve him parliamente robes, I thinke him furnishte of other apparaill better than any Irisheman; for at suche tyme as he mette with me, he was in a cote of crymoisin velvet, with agglettes of gold, 20 or 30 payer; over that a greate doble cloke of right crymoisin saten, garded with blacke velvet; a bonette, with a fether, sette full of agglettes of gold; that me thoght it strange to se him so honorable in apparaill, and all the reste of his nacion, that I have seen as yet, so vile".[d]

Nor is it necessary to trace the career of Sir Hugh, nor that of his gallant and famous son, Hugh Roe, nor that of Rory, Earl of Tirconnell. Their history has already been given in the text and notes to these Annals. That branch, once so celebrated, is now believed to be extinct.

II. Hugh Roe, who is said to have been married to a daughter of Hugh, Earl of Tyrone, died in Spain the 10th September, 1602, without issue[e].

II. Rory, who was married to Bridget, daughter of Henry, twelfth Earl of Kildare (afterwards married to Viscount Kingsland), on his flight to Rome, 1607, brought with him his infant son, Hugh, who, in 1618, was page to the Infanta in Flanders, and known on the Continent, after his father's death (1608), as Earl of Tirconnell[f]. He died unmarried, in the flower of youth. Caffar, the brother of the Earl Rory, married Rose O'Doherty, by whom he had two sons: Hugh, who died in 1660, without issue, and Caffar Oge, whose son, Manus, was styled Earl of Tirconnell on the Continent; and this was, indubitably, the very man called Ball-dearg[g] O'Donnell, who came from Spain to command the Irish in the war of James II., and of whose

[c] State Papers, vol. iii. p. 446.

[d] Ib., vol. iii. p. 320.

[e] MS. British Museum.

[f] Mageoghegan, tom. iii. fol. 646; and *Collectanea Historica*, MS. Trin. Coll. Dub., Class E. 3. 8.

[g] *Ball-dearg*: i. e. the Red Spot, not Red Mouth, as Mr. Matthew O'Conor incorrectly renders it. Mr. Hardiman, after giving a short sketch of the career of this personage (*History of Galway*, p. 156), adds: "What became of him afterwards" [i. e. after he had turned over to King William's side] "has not been thought worth the trouble of inquiry." There is a curious account of him in *Macariæ Excidium*, by Colonel Charles O'Kelly, who attempts to defend his conduct.—See *Military Memoirs of the Irish Nation*, by Matthew O'Conor, Esq., pp. 125, 159, 160, 161. Colonel O'Kelly, in his *Macariæ Excidium*, states, that "after the senior branch of the O'Donnells had become extinct, the head of the next branch went to Spain, where he was patronized by the king, and became a distinguished officer in the service of Spain; but that hearing of the civil war in Ireland, he left Spain without the king's license, and arrived in Ireland in September, 1690." This

final fate so little is known at present. On the flight of the Earl, the Countess did not accompany him, which may be accounted for by the fact, that she was shortly after confined of a daughter. There is a history connected with this girl of so singular and romantic a character, that the Editor is induced to transcribe it from the pages of the Abbè Mageoghegan, tom. iii., pp. 645–649:

"On peut placer ici l'histoire de la résolution courageuse d'une héroïne de la Maison d' O'Donnel[h]. Lorsque Rory O'Donnel Comte de Tirconnell eut quitté sa patrie en 1605, pour une prétendue conspiration dont on l'avoit chargé, il laissa la Comtesse son épouse enceinte. Elle vouloit suivre le Comte son mari dans les pays étrangers où il s'étoit réfugié; et comme elle cherchoit les moyens de sortir secretement d'Irlande, elle fut prévenue par le Vice-Roi qui l'envoya bien escortée en Angleterre, où elle accoucha d'une fille, qui fut nommée Marie au Baptême. Le Roi en fut informé, & quoiqu' il eut persécuté le Comte de Tirconnell, il voulut honorer le pere en la personne de la fille; il la prit sous sa protection, et ordonna qu'elle fut nommèe Marie Stuart au lieu de Marie O'Donnell qui étoit son véritable nom.

"Le Comte de Tirconnell étant mort à Rome, la Comtesse son épouse obtint une permission de la Cour de retourner en Irlande avec sa fille; cette vertueuse mère se fit un devoir de donner à Marie une éducation chrétienne; elle la fit instruire avec soin dans les principes de la Religion de ses ancêtres; elle lui représenta souvent, que la disgrace de sou pere étoit l'effet de son attachement à cette Religion à laquelle on doit sacrifier toutes les grandeurs de ce monde. Marie avoit douze ans lorsqu'elle fut rappellée en Angleterre par la Comtesse de Kildare son ayeule; elle la présenta au Roi; ce Monarque lui assigna une somme considérable d'argent pour la marier, et la Comtesse de Kildare, qui étoit bien riche, la declara son héritiere; desorte que la protection du Prince, une naissance illustre et une fortune brillante, la firent rechercher pour le mariage par des Seigneurs de la premiere distinction en Angleterre; il y eut entr'autres un Seigneur de bonne Maison & puissamment riche, qui fit une cour assidue à cette jeune Princesse; il s'adressa aussi á la Comtesse de Kildare sa Tutrice, & la gagna au point qu'il avoit lieu d'espérer un heureux succès; mais il étoit de la Religion prétendue réformée, il n'en falloit pas davantage pour en éloigner le cœur de Marie; cette illustre Héroïne se voyant persécutée par la Comtesse & ses autres parens, en faveur d'une alliance qu'elle croyoit incompatible avec l'honneur & la conscience, forma la généreuse résolution de l'éviter par la fuite; un cas imprévu en accéléra l'exécution.

"La persécution étoit violente contre les Catholiques en Irlande; O Dogharty étoit sous les armes pour la défense de la Religion; le Gouvernement fit arrêter quelques Chefs des Catho-

was surely Hugh, the son of Caffar Oge, son of Caffar, who was the brother of the Earl Rory, and was the very man who was called Ball-dearg O'Donnell by the Irish. He was joined in Ireland by about 8000 of the rabble, set up an independent command, disclaimed the king's authority, and made demonstrations of maintaining the cause of the native Irish, as distinct from King James's, and restoring them to the dominion of their native country; but being thwarted in every way by Tirconnell (Talbot), he turned over to the standard of King William III., and retired to Flanders, where he was consigned to poverty and oblivion; but of his ultimate fate nothing has yet been discovered.

[h] "Cette histoire fut d'abord écrite en langue Espagnole par Dom Albert Henriquez, & imprimée avec permission à Bruxelles en 1627. Elle fut traduite en François l'année suivante par Pierre de Cadenet sieur de Brieulle, et imprimée avec approbation à Paris en 1628, chez la veuve Guillemot, rue St. Jacques à la Bibliothéque."

liques qui lui étoient suspects; de ce nombre fut Conn ou Constantin O Donnel, et Hugue O'Rourke[k] proche parent de Marie Stuart; on les fit mener prisonniers en Angleterre pour s'assurer de leur conduite dans ces temps de troubles. Malgré la vigilance des gardes, ces Seigneurs s'échapperent de leurs mains, et trouverent le moyen de passer en Flandres. On ne manqua pas de soupçonner Marie Stuart d'avoir contribué à l'évasion de ses parens; elle en fut avertie par un Seigneur de la Cour; il lui conseilla, pour prévenir les malheurs qui la menaçoient, de se conformer à la Religion de l'Etat, & d'épouser quelque Seigneur de cette croyance capable de la proteger contre ses ennemis, il lui insinua que c'étoit l'unique moyen de contenter le Roi & la Comtesse de Kildare son ayeule. En effet, elle fut citeé de comparoître devant le Conseil pour rendre compte de sa conduite.

"Marie vit bien qu'il étoit temps de pourvoir à sa sureté. Elle confia son secret à une Demoiselle Catholique qui lui servoit de Dame de compagnie, & à un valet de chambre dont elle connoissoit la fidélité et la prudence. Son dessein étoit d'aller trouver le jeune Comte de Tirconnell son frere en Flandres; il étoit à la Cour d'Isabelle Infante d'Espagne & Gouvernante des Pays-Bas, qui donnoit asyle à toute la Noblesse persecutée pour cause de Religion. Pour cacher son sexe il falloit se travestir, Marie fit venir un tailleur qui l'habilla en Cavalier avec la Demoiselle de sa campagnie; pour mieux jouer son rôle, Marie jugea à propos de changer son nom, elle se fit appeller Rodolfe Huntly; la Demoiselle de sa compagnie prit le nom de Jacques Hués, & le valet de chambre celui de Richard Stratsi, noms sous, lesquels ils furent connus pendant leur voyage.

"Tout étant préparé, ces trois Cavaliers prirent des chevaux de poste, & sortirent de Londres avant le jour, & apres bien des aventures rapportées par l'Auteur de cette relation, Marie s'embarqua avec sa compagnie à Bristol, & aprés une longue & perrilleuse navigation, elle arriva à la Rochelle; s'étant reposée de ses fatigues, elle continua sa route par Paris jusqu'à Bruxelles; elle y trouva le Comte de Tirconnel son frere, qui la présenta à la Sérénissime Infante; cette Princesse la reçut avec toute la tendresse et toute la distinction imaginable. Le bruit de la résolution courageuse de Marie Stuart se répandit bientôt par toute l'Europe. On la comparoît à Eufrosine d'Alexandrie, à Aldegonde & autres Vierges chrétiennes de l'antiquité. Urbain VIII. qui gouvernoit l'Eglise alors, lui fit un compliment distingué dans la lettre suivante."

"Dilectæ in Christo filiæ Mariæ Stuard, Hibernensi Tirconnellii, Comitis Sorori, Urbanus Papa VIII. Dilecta in Christo filia, Salutem et Apostolicam Benedictionem.

"Obmutescat hoc tempore, sacrilega illa vox, quæ temerè docebat Christianæ religionis Consiliis, vim animorum hebetari et fortitudinis nervos emolliri. Declarasti, Hibernensis virgo, nationibus universis quam adamantinum robur eam mentem obarmet, in quibus excubat fides orthodoxa, contemptrix periculorum et domitrix inferni. O facinus dignum cui Roma faveat, et fama plaudat! Hæreticum conjugium, non secus ac dolosum incendium perosa, fugisti delicias

[k] In the relation presented to the King of Spain, about the year 1618, by "Florentius ye pretended Archb. of Tuam, and supposed," by Primate Ussher, "to be penned by Philip O'Sullivan beare," are named "Don John O'Neill, Earl of Tyrone, Colonel of the Irish in Flanders; Don Hugh O Donnell, Earl of Tyrconnell, page to the Infanta in Flanders."—*Collectanea Historica*, MS. Trin. Coll. Dub., E. 3. 8. The words "presented to the King of Spain, by Florentius ye pretended Archbp. of Tuam," above quoted, are in the hand of Primate Ussher.

Aulæ, & contempsisti Regum minas. Ipse procellarum abissus, & terroris campus, occanus conatus est remorari fugam tuam quovis triumpho nobiliorem : sed transferantur montes in cor maris, non commovebitur in œternum mens habitans in adjutorio Altissimi. Patriam enim tuam, tantummodo esse tibi existimasti, ubi regnum gerat catholica Religio Potuisti quidem fallere conquisitores Angliæ minitantis, at enim comitata Angelis itineris tam periculosi custodibus, non latuisti, oculos Pontificæ sollicitudinis, deducta enim in aulam Belgicæ Principis, pervenisti non modo in portum religionis sed & in theatrum Europæ. Isthic dum te contuemur, dilecta in Christo filia, & eam egregiis virtutibus meritam fœlicitatem præcamur, à Deo qui stetit à dextris tuis ne commovereris, & dignam te existimavimus cui Pontificæ auctoritatis alloquia doceant eos labores oblivisci, quibus Angelicam tam illustris gloriæ palmam redemisti. Benedicimus tibi intimo charitatis affectu, atque cùm parentes & patriam Christo et Pontifici post habueris, scito te non demigrasse in exilium, sed in sinum clementissimæ matris properasse. Tam dulce enim nomen, & consentientem materno nomini charitatem experieris in Roma Ecclesia, ô dilecta filia, quæ Britannicarum insularum decus, & cœli gaudium haberis. Datum Romæ apud sanctum Petrum, sub annulo Piscatoris, die 13 Februarii, 1627. Pontificatûs nostri anno quarto."

"A notre chere fille en Jesus Christ Marie Stuard Comtesse de Tirconnell. Salut & Bénédiction Apostolique, Urbain VIII. Pape.

"If faut enfin qu'elle reste dans le silence cette bouche sacrilége, qui n'a point eu de honte de dire que les résolutions qu'inspire le Chistianisme énervent l'ame, & mettent obstacle aux entreprises d'un cœur généreux. Vous avez donné, notre chere fille, à toutes les Nations une preuve du Contraire, & votre exemple leur a fait connoître quelle est la force & le courage que donne une foi orthodoxe, combien elle est au-dessus des dangers, & supérieure aux efforts même de l'enfer. Que ce courage est héroïque, qu'il est digne de la protection de Rome & des éloges de la renommée. L'horreur que vous avez eu de l'alliance d'un Hérétique, ressembloit à celle qu'on a du feu dont les surprises sont redoutables. La Cour n'a point eu d'attraits pour vous, & les menaces des Souverains n'ont servi qu'à vous rendre insensible. La mer, retraite des vents & des orages, séjour trop affreux de la crainte, s'est opposée à votre fuite ; elle ignoroit qu'elle vous faisoit plus d'honneur que le triomphe : mais quand les montagnes seroient ensevelies dans le sein des eaux, votre confiance dans les bontés du Seigneur n'en recevroit aucune atteinte, puisque votre patrie est celle où la Religion est sur le Trône. Vous êtes venue à bout de vous dérober aux persécutions des Inquisiteurs d'Angleterre ; mais sous la conduite des Anges qui vous ont préservée des accidens de votre voyage, vous n'avez pu échapper à nos regards paternels ; car ayant été conduite à la Cour de l'Infante, sa Religion vous a reçu dans son sein, et l'Europe vous a servi de Théâtre. C'est là que vous considérant notre chere fille en Jésus Christ, nous demandons au Seigneur qui vous a soutenu, et nous sollicitons en votre faveur les succès heureux que vos vertus vous ont acquis. Nous vous ecrivons cette lettre, dans le dessein de vous faire perdre le souvenir de vos peines, & de vos travaux, peines & travaux dignes d'envie, puisqu'ils ont été pour vous la source d'une gloire immortelle. Recevez notre bénédiction pleine de tendresse, et puisque vous avez quitté vos parens, et abandonné votre patrie par obéissance pour Jesus-Christ, & pour nous, soyez assurée de notre part que vous n'avez point trouvé un exil, mais une mere qui vous aime tendrement. Vous connoîtrez par vous-meme que l'Eglise Romaine porte veritablement ce nom ;

elle vous cherira comme sa fille bien-aimée, qui fait honneur aux Isles Britanniques, & remplit de joie les esprits bienheureux. Donné à Rome à Saint Pierre, sous l'anneau du Pécheur le 13 Février 1627, & de notre Pontificat l'an 4."

What subsequently became of "cette jeune Princesse," the Editor has found no record, unless it be true, as stated by Lodge, that the daughter of Rory O'Donnell was "the first wife of Luke [Plunket], who, 28th September, 1628, was created Earl of Fingall;"[l] for as Rory had only two children [Lodge states only two, but he names the daughter Elizabeth; that, however, might have been a mere mistake of name], Hugh "wanting three weeks of being one year old" when the Earl fled, and Mary born, as we have seen, after the flight; we can only conclude, that the Irishman and the Catholic "*avoit lieu d'esperer* un heureux succès," however unfortunate in their suit her English wooers might have been.

To return to the elder branch.

II. CALVAGH O'DONNELL, eldest son of Manus, by Johanna O'Neill, was married to a daughter of the Earl of Argyle[m]. He deposed his father in 1555; defeated his brother, Hugh, and John the Proud O'Neill in 1557, on which occasion his son Con's share of the spoils was "eighty horses, and the famous steed of O'Neill's son, called 'the Son of the Eagle.'" Surprised in the abbey of Kill-O'Donell by John O'Neill, in 1559, and carried off, with his wife, a prisoner to Tyrone; ransomed in 1561; visited England 1566; and on his return the same year, on his way to the North, dropped dead from his horse on the 26th October. He left issue one son, Con, and a daughter, Mary (by a former marriage), wife of John O'Neill. She died of grief at her father's imprisonment by her husband, 1561[n].

III. CON O'DONNELL, who married a daughter of Sir Turlough Luineach O'Neill. On his father's death, being excluded from the chieftainship by his uncle, Sir Hugh, his life was a series of struggles to recover the power he thought unjustly wrested from him. His alliance with Sir Turlough Luineach, the unsuccessful rival of Hugh O'Neill, the able and powerful chieftain of Tyrone, placed an effectual barrier to his success; and Sir Hugh's friendship for the English government (which was undeviating and consistent), gave the latter an additional ally that ensured to him his position. Thus, in 1574, Con was invited by the Earl of Tyrone to visit his camp, when he was treacherously made prisoner and sent to Dublin. He escaped in 1575, and again "great dissensions arose between O'Donnell (Hugh) and the son of his brother (Con, son of Calvagh), upon which Con went over to the side of O'Neill (Turlough Luineach) to wage war with his kinsman;" and although he defeated Sir Hugh at Kiltole, in 1581, he could not deprive him of power. He died 13th March, 1583. He had issue nine sons, eight of whom survived him. The following is the probable order of their precedence: 1. Naghtan; 2. Calvagh Oge; 3. Manus; 4. Niall Garv; 5. Hugh Boy; 6. Con Oge; 7. Calvagh; 8. Caffar; and 9. Donnell.

Of these nine, six appear to have died without issue, of whom five met violent deaths. Naghtan was slain in 1582[o]; Calvagh Oge, slain 1583[p]; Manus, slain 1589[q]; Calvagh, "slaine by Donell,

[l] Lodge's Peerage, as edited by Archdall, vol. i. p. 99, title "Duke of Leinster."

[m] MS. British Museum, quoted above.

[n] Annals of the Four Masters. See a long correspondence between Con and the Lord Deputy, in Betham's *Antiquarian Researches*.

[o] Annals of the Four Masters.

[p] Ib.

[q] Ib.

sonne to Hugh O'Donell;"[r] and Caffar, "slaine by the rebelle M'Guire."[s] The ninth son, Donnell, in an examination taken before Thomas Foster, Provost Marshall of Londonderry, 9th April, 1615, is mentioned, together with his brother, Hugh Boy, as having received letters from his brother, Sir Niall Garv, then a prisoner in the Tower of London[t]. The only other mention of him occurs in the *Inq. Ult. Pat.*, 10th James I.: "Grant from the King to Donel M'Quin O'Donell, Glancho and Reimon, 2 half q[rs.] 128[a.], Rent £1 7*s.* 3¾*d.*"

Three only are stated, by Duald Mac Firbis in his *Genealogies*[u], as having left issue, namely, Niall Garv, Hugh Boy, and Con Oge. And first:

IV. Niall Garv, fourth son of Con, was married to his cousin, the youngest daughter of Sir Hugh, and sister of his rival, Hugh Roe[w]. This alliance did not, however, effect a lasting reconciliation between the elder and junior branches of the family, of the elder of which Niall Garv was now the representative, as Hugh Roe was of the other, and not only of the junior branch, but also of the name. The character of Niall Garv has been generally painted in unfavourable colours, because of his hostility to Hugh Roe, and the part which he took against him in conjunction with the English. It is true that history does not present a more chivalrous and devoted Irishman than Hugh Roe proved himself to be during his short and eventful career; but before we entirely condemn the other for opposing him, we should recollect that Niall had the prior title, and that doubtless he was nurtured in feelings of hostility to what his own immediate family must have considered an unjust usurpation. The English government knew this well; and, in the year 1600, in order to destroy, if possible, the two great northern chieftains, determined to support the claims of Niall Garv against the one, and those of Arthur O'Neill, son of Turlough Luineach, in opposition to the other. It was one of the principal motives that determined the Government on sending Sir Henry Docwra to effect a settlement at "the Derry," that their agent might possess opportunities of more immediate communication with these discontented chieftains. Thus, in the *Narration of his Services*, written by himself in 1614, we find: "On the 1st of June[x], S[r] Arthur O'Neale, sonne to old Tirlogh Lenagh, that had been O'Neale, came in unto me with some 30 horse and foot, a Man I had directions from the State to labour to draw to our side, and to promise to be made Earl of Tyrone, if the other, that maintayned the rebellion, could be dispossessed of the countrey." And so the same influences were used to work with Niall Garv, for we find a similar result produced. "On the 3rd of October came in Neale Garvie O'Donell with 40 horse and 60 foote, a Man I was also directed by the State to winne to the Queene's service, and one of equal estimation in Tirconnell that S[r] Arthur O Neale was in Tyroane." And the result of the conference was: "I promised him, in the behalf of the Queene, the whole country of Tirconnell to him and his heires, and my Lord Deputy and Council at Dublin did afterwards confirm it unto him under their hands." Thus he was not the treacherous kinsman meanly betraying his leader for a bribe, but the excluded chief seeking to recover his ancient birthright, and who seized the English offers as the only means of crushing his powerful rival. While, however, he thought to use their alliance for his own purposes, he, in reality, was but an instrument to effect theirs: "Right bravely did Neale Garvie and

[r] Annals of the Four Masters.
[s] Ib.
[t] MS. Trinity College, Dublin, F. 3. 15.
[u] MS. British Museum.
[w] Library, Royal Irish Academy.
[x] 1600.

his Irish demeane themselves on all occasions, although it is true, withall, they had their own ends in it, which were always for private revenge, and we ours, to make use of them for the furtherance of the Publique Service." His gallantry in the field is attested in many passages: "We had a skirmish with him (Hugh Roe O'Donell) of an houre longe, wherein Neale Garvie behaved himself Bravelie." And again: "On the 24th October, he (Hugh Roe) came again . . . . . The alarum taken, the garrison made forth again, and Neale Garvie behaved himself bravelie as before, charged home upon them, killed one, hurt one or two more with his own hands, and had his horse slaine under him." In accepting the Queen's offer of putting him in possession of Tyrconnell, and setting aside Hugh Roe, he had no other intention than of being installed with all the absolute privileges of "The O'Donnell," and not, by any means, that his power should be trammelled with the obligations of an English subject; and as soon as he discovered that his new allies were not likely to consent to this, "thereupon begun Neale Garvie's discontente, for presentlie he directed some men of his to be cessed upon this countrey[y]. O Dogherty and Hugh Boy[z], with great indignation, refused to accept them. Complainte came before me; I asked him whereupon it was that hee challenged this power over another man's land; he tould mee the land was his owne, for the Queene had given him all Tyrconnell, and this was parte of it. I aunswered it was true, I knew well the whole countrey of Tyrconnell was promised him in as large and ample a manner as the O Donnells had been accustomed to hould it. But I took it there were many others in that countrey that had landes of their owne as well as they; hee replied, not onelie the countrey of Tyrconnell, but Tyroane, Fermanaght, yea, and Connaught, wheresoever any of the O Donnells had, at that time, extended their power hee made Accompte all was his; hee acknowledged noe other kinde or interest in any man els, yea, the very Persons of the people hee challenged to be his, and said he had wronge if any one foote of all that lande, or any one of the persons of the People were exemtped from him, &c." The matter was referred to the Lord Deputy[a] and Council, who decided against those claims to unlimited power which Niall Garv asserted. Although differences such as this not unfrequently occurred, and mutual suspicions and jealousies ensued, he still vigorously cooperated with the English in their efforts to crush Hugh Roe. On the 2nd August, 1601, "with 500 English souldiers he threw himself into the Abbay of Donegall;" and "on the 19th September (Hugh Roe having last month laid seige to it) the Abbay took fire and was all consumed, except one corner, whither the English retreated and held out . . . . . . Here again, I must confess, Neale Garvie behaved himselfe deservinglie, for though I had, at that time, many informations against him, that could not but breed some jealousies of his fidelitie, yett we sawe he continewed to the last; took such part as our own men did; had many of his men slaine at this seige, and amongst the rest a Brother of his owne." As he was extending his influence in the country, he endeavoured, more and more, to exercise his privileges as chieftain, independently altogether of his English allies. "Neale Garvie (as I said before) had, a longe time, carryed himself discontented; estrainged himself from mee, and lived altogeather in those parts about Ballyshannon; and, it is true, those services he had done, alwayes dulie acknowledged, I had very often, and very bitterly, complayned of him to my Lord, and my reasons were these: Hee did openlie and contynuallie contest with

[y] Inishowen.

[z] "Of the sept of the Mac Davids."—*Docwra.*

[a] The Lord Deputy, i. e. Sir Charles Blount, Lord Mountjoy, Knight of the Garter, and afterwards Earl of Devonshire.

mee to have the people sworne to him, and not to the Queene; To have no officer whatsoever but himselfe in his countrey. Hee would not suffer his men to sell us theire owne goodes, nor work with us for money, nor till or sowe the ground any where neere us; nor yeeled us any carriages for the Army, as O'Doghertye, and all other that were under the Queene did . . . . . . Hee would not endure that any man of his countrey should be punished for any cryme, though never so haynous, and manifestlie proved, but take it as the highest injurie could be done unto him." These complaints soon determined the Government on setting him aside when the fitting opportunity offered, and finding some more pliant and less ambitious O'Donnell to occupy his place. Thus, after the battle of Kinsale, and the flight of Hugh Roe, we find: "Shortlie after this was Roory O Donnell, brother to O Donnell that was fled into Spaine (and himself banished his country and living in Connaught), taken in[b] by my Lord Deputie, a profest enymy to Neale Garvie[c], who apprehended such jealousies upon it as made him run courses that were afterwards his undoing. . . . . . . Now it fell out that my Lord wrote for Rorie O Donnell to come to him to Dublin; Hee, being in Connaught, desires first to putt over his Catle into Tyrconnell, which would otherwise be in danger, in his absence, to be preyd by those of that province that yett stood out in Rebellion. My Lord gives him leave, and writes to Neale Garvie that he should not molest nor trouble them, and soe Roorie takes his journey. Hee was noe sooner gone, and the Catell put over, But Neale Garvie, notwithstanding my Lord's command, ceizes them as his owne, under pretents they were the goods of the countrey belonging unto him. Complainte made, my Lord writes to me to see them restored. I send unto him, and hee refuseth. My Lord, upon that, bidds mee discharge him of his Entertainments, and writes unto him, without delay, to come unto him to Dublin. Hee growes more discontented, and defferres his going. Thus it runnes on for at least 3 monthes togeather, and neither would he come at mee nor my Lord, nor, by any meanes, be perswaded to make Restitution. In the ende he assembles, of his owne aucthoritie, all the countrey at Kilmackoran" [Kilmacrenan], "a place where the O Donnell's use to be chosen. There hee takes upon him the title, and with the ceremonyes accustomed, proclaymes himselfe O Donnell, and then presentlie comes to mee to the Derrey with a greater troupe of attendances then at any time before, and they styling him, at every word, my Lord. As soone as I sawe him, I asked him how he was thus suddenlie stept into the name of a Lord; Hee tould mee they called him soe because he was O Donnell. I asked him by what aucthoritie he was soe, and hee said, 'by my Lord Deputies.' I bade him make that appear unto mee and all was well; Hee pluckt out a lettre written unto him from my Lord, about two years before, Superscription whereof was this, 'To my very loving freinde, O Donnell.' Asked him if this were all the warrante hee had; and he said yes. I asked him why he went not to my Lord all this while, nor came unto mee sooner, nor restored Rorie O Donnell's catle. His answere was this; you knowe the whole countrey of Tyrconnell was long since promised mee, and many services I have done that, I thinke, have deserved it; but I sawe I was neglected, and, therefore, I have righted myself by taking the Catle and People that were my owne, and, to prevent others, have made myself O Donnell. Now, by this meanes, the countrey is sure unto mee, and if I have done anythinge amisse, lett all be pardoned that is past, and from this

[b] i. e. Received to mercy, or pardoned; not humbugged. [c] i. e. Rory was.

day forward, by Jesus hand, I will be true to the Queene, and noe man's Councell will I follow hereafter but yours. You take a wronge course, said I, it may not goe thus; the first act you must do to procure forgivnes for your faults (if it may be) is to make restitution of the Catle, if you doe it not of your owne accorde, I know you will be forced unto it upon harder conditions; yet, at that time, nothing I could say would prevaile with him, and soe he departed." He afterwards consented to give up the cattle, but whilst Docwra was endeavouring to effect a reconciliation between him and Rorie, who was then at the Liffer, "came lettres from my Lord to this effect, that he had now taken in Tyrone, and was fully resolved to beare no longer with Neale Garvie, and, therefore, if I were sure he had made himself O Donnell, it was treason by the lawe, I should lay houlde on him and keepe him safe. My Lord, I was sure, was mistaken in the qualitie of his offence, for I looked upon the Statute Book and saw that Rigerous lawe was onelie for such as made themselves O Neales; for those that took upon them to be heads of other families, the Punishment was onelie a penalty of 100 markes. I pawsed, therefore, and was doubtefull with myselfe whether, by this misgrounded warrant, I should doe well to restrayne him or noe." News, however, of the Queen's death decided him, and Neal Garv is arrested the next day he came to the "Derry." When told of the succession of James I.: "Then am I undone, sayeth hee, for Roory hath better friendes about him then I." "That speech encreased my jealousie," says Docwra, "and, thereupon, I tould him further I had order from my Lord to restraine him of his libertie. Then ame I a dead man, saith hee. I told him noe, he needeth not fear any such matter, neither his life nor landes were yet in danger; his offence was a contempte onlie, and he must be brought to acknowledge a higher Power then his owne." He escaped the third day after, but subsequently sent pledges to Docwra, that, on getting "a Protection" for his safe passage to Dublin, he would submit himself to the Lord Deputy, which he did." The rival claims of Niall and Rory were now submitted for the decision of the Council in England, and the latter went himself to London, to attend, in person, to his interests. The influence of his friends and connexions (being married to the daughter of the Earl of Kildare), as well, doubtless, as the too ambitious character of his opponent, decided in his favour, and "within a while after came Roory O Donnell to Dublin, with his Majesties lettres to be made Earle of Tirconnell, and have all the countrey to him and his heires (except Ballyshannon and the fishing thereof), and such landes as Neale Garvie had held, &c.; the said Neale Garvie judicialie convicted of no crime, which I thought was strange; But whither it were with his right or wronge, with convenience or inconvenience to the State, was then no more to be disputed of." The letter here alluded to is to be found, together with the entry of the Patent, in Erck's *Rep. Chancery Enrollments*, pp. 24, 47, 59, which is here abstracted.

"James Rex,—Right trustie, etc., we have ben informed that Rorie O Donell made his submission, etc., besechinge our favoure, etc., to graunte unto him and his heires our territorie and countries of Tirconel in Ulster, the which his ancestors had for many yeres past, etc.; therefore our pleysure is, etc., that youe cause to be passed to the said Rorie, and his heires malles, with remaynders of lyke estate successivelie to his brother, Cafferie O Donnell[d], and his cosin, Donell

[d] Caffar, as stated in the *Annals of the Four Masters*, fled with his brother in 1607; and also "Rose, daughter of O'Doherty, and wife of Caffar, with her son, Hugh, aged two years and three months." He died in Rome the same month as the Earl, in 1608.—*O'Gorman MS.*, R. I. A. She was subsequently married to Owen Roe O'Neill, and is

Oge M[c] Donnell O Donnell, our graunt of said territories, etc., with all the landes, rights, etc. of auncient tyme belonging to the Lords thereof: exceptinge all Abbayes and other spiritual livinges; & reserving such rentes, etc. as any of his auncestors yielded, etc.; as also the castle, town, and lands of Balleshenon, and 1000 A. adjoininge the fyshinge theare; and libertye to erect fortes for service of the countrie; with condition that the landes, etc., which were in the possession of Sir Neale Odonel, when he lived under Sir hughe Roe, late Odonell, and in amitye with him, especiallye Castleffynn, and its landes, may be reserved to bestow uppon Sir Neale Odonel, or such other as may deserve same. And our pleysure is that Rorie O Donel, doe renounce all claymes, etc. upon Sir Cahir Odoghertie's and O'Connor Sligo's country, etc.; and because he shall receave so large a territorie as Tirconnell for his inheritaunce, etc. we have thoughte meet to grace him with, and requier you to graunte unto him the name, stile, and honor of Earle of Tirconnell; to Hovlde to him and his heires males of his bodie; with remainder to his brother, Cafferie; and that the heires males apparent be created Lordes, Barones of Donnegall, duringe the lyves of the Earles. And, further, that said Rorie shall have a custodiam of all abbayes, etc. within the countrie of Tireconnell, till we shall otherwise dispose of them, etc. Given under our signet at Tottenham, the 4th day of Sep[t]., 1603, etc. To the earle of Devonshier, our lievetenante of Irelande, etc."

"Niall Garv was arrested by the English at Raphoe, in 1608, on the accusation of Ineenduv, the mother of Hugh Roe, before the Lord Bishop of Derry," see note [l], p. 2364, *supra*, and after a confinement of eighteen years by King James the First, died, at the age of 57 years, A. D. 1626." —MS., R. I. A.

This notice of Sir Niall Garv cannot be better concluded than by quoting a passage from Docwra, in which he alludes to the respective characters of him and Rory, always bearing in mind by whom it is written, and that the vices he condemns were acts of hostility to the English:

"And where before the restrainte lay onelie upon Tyrone, hee now lay the like upon Tyrconnell alsoe, and sent him warraunt to make the Earle Justice of Peace and Quorum, and Lord Lieuetenant of that Countrey. How much to the prejudice of those that had faithfully served the State, I could, if it were required even at this day[e], give many particular instances and proofes of, and take occasion further to make large discourses upon this man's [the Earl of Tirconnell's] violent and insolent carriage, sufficiently bewraying to any man that listed to see it, what the bent of his heart was from the beginning. But hee is deade, and the injuries that honest men received by him are past recoverie, and, therefore, I will onelie say this of him in generall wordes (and I thinke my Lord Deputie and Judges that were in that time will beare me witness, I say true): there were noe vices in poor Neale Garvie that had done us many good services; but the same were in him, and more, in a far more pernitious degree, that had never done any; and then, I confess, it made mee see clear myne owne Errour, and the wronge (I may call it) I had done to Neale Garvie; not that my conscience accuseth mee to have done anythinge towards him with malitious or corrupt intentions—(noe, thereof I take God to witness my heart is cleere); but that

buried at Louvain, in the same grave with her son, as stated in their epitaph: "... Septuaginta major de nata Bruxellis 1. Nov. 1660, suo cum Primogenito, Hugone O Donnell præstolatur hic casuis resurrectionem"—*Doctor O'Conor's Catal. Stowe MSS.*

[e] *Even at this day.*—This tract was "written by Sir Henry Docwra, in the summer of 1614, and finished the 1st of September, the same year."

with simplicitie I suffered myselfe to be made an instrument of his overthrowe, under the pretence of those misbeheavors, that were plainelie tollerated, yea, and allowed of in another, ffor it is true my Lord would hear noe complaininge of him howe juste soever."

Niall Garv's character is also depicted by P. O'Sullevan Beare in his *Hist. Cathol. Iber.*, tom. 3, lib. 6, c. v., where he is called "Vir animo magno, & audaci, & rei militaris scientia præditus." And, again, in tom. 3, lib. 8, c. v, where the following account of his speech before the Irish Council is given:

"Aspero" [i. e. Niello Aspero .i. Niall Garb] "illæ tantum possessiones, quas habuit prius, quam ad Anglos defecerat, adiudicantur, & Baronis titulus offertur. Ille ira percitus titulum accipere noluit, & in Iberniam postquam rediuit, Dubhlinnæ in senatum ad regium consilium productus senatores, & gentem Anglicam asperrimis verbis exagitat, non ab Anglis, sed ab ipso Catholicos fuisse deuictos, atque debellatos, & Iberniam Angliæ Coronæ defensam à consilio, & Anglis improbé, & perfidé cum ipso agi, neque fidem impleri. Inde se ipsum, quòd vnquam Anglis fidem habuerit, & eos adiuuerit, execratur, dirisque imprecationibus deuouet. Itaque, vt Asper erat, sic asperrimè perorauit."—Fol. 201.

By Nuala, the sister of the celebrated Hugh Roe O'Donnell, Sir Niall Garv O'Donnell had two sons, namely, Naghtan, who died a prisoner in the Tower of London, and,—

V. Manus O'Donnell.—He was a Colonel in the army of the Confederate Catholics under the celebrated Owen Roe O'Neill; and, according to an Irish Journal of the Rebellion of 1641, in the possession of Lord O'Neill, he was killed at Benburb in 1646. The same date is given in one of the O'Gorman MSS., Lib. R. I. A. The late Matthew O'Conor, Esq., of Mount-Druid, asserts, in his *Military Memoirs of the Irish Nation*, p. 159, that Niall Garv had no son of the name Manus; but he never took the trouble to make the due inquiry, and has, therefore, left himself open to just censure for gratuitous assertions, which the Editor, notwithstanding his veneration for the memory of this writer, feels it his sacred duty to expose and refute. The existence of Colonel Manus, the son of Niall Garv, is proved beyond dispute by this Journal, which is an authentic and contemporaneous document; by two genealogical manuscripts of Duald Mac Firbis, one dated 1650, and the other 1666; as well as by the manuscript Depositions (Lib. T. C. D.) of Donegal in 1641, in which is mentioned "Manus O'Donnelle, whose father, *Curnell Garrow* O'Donnelle, died in the Towre."

According to the Genealogy of the O'Donells of Austria, dated Dublin, 1st May, 1767, copied at Vienna in the year 1828, by Colonel Sir Charles O'Donnel, this Colonel Manus, therein styled "Magnus Colonellus, filius Neal Garuff O'Donell, occisus in bello Benburb," married "Susanna filia Hugonis Mac Guinness Comitis de Iveach," and had by her one son, "Rogerius O'Donell," who is still vividly remembered by tradition as

VI. Rory or Roger O'Donnell, of Lifford, in the county of Donegal. According to the Austrian pedigree, this Roger married Johanna, daughter of Egneghan O'Donnell, by Elizabeth, daughter of Thomas O'Rourke of Breifny, and had by her, Colonel Manus O'Donnell, of whom presently, and a daughter, Graine, or Grace, who married Connell O'Donnell, who was Lord Lieutenant of the county of Donegal in 1689. Some time previously to 1664, he settled, with a large train of followers, consisting of some of the various septs of Tirconnell (as O'Gallaghers, Mac Sweenys, O'Clerys, O'Tolands, &c.), at Ballycroy, in the south of the barony of Erris.

O'DONNELL OF NEWCASTLE.

VII. Colonel Manus O'Donel, of Newport, was married to Eleanor, daughter of Roger Maguire, of the county Fermanagh, by whom he had issue three sons: 1st. Charles; 2nd. Manus, who died in 1797 without male issue; 3rd. Hugh; and two daughters[f]: Mary, married to Charles (Calvagh Duv) O'Donel, son of Hugh O'Donel, by Margaret, daughter of Colonel Tirlogh O'Neale, of Oldcastle, in the county of Mayo (*vide post* the descendants of Con Oge O'Donnell); and Anne, married to Henry[g], eldest son of Mac Dermot Roe of Greyfield, in the county of Roscommon, by whom she had issue, one daughter, Eliza, who was married to Robert Maguire of Tempo[h].

It is stated in Betham's *Antiquarian Researches*, that Colonel Manus O'Donnel's will was proved in the diocesan Court of Tuam in 1737. It is much to be regretted that at the present day the will is not forthcoming; for though the Editor has, upon more than one occasion, caused strict search to be made, there seems to be no trace of it now on record. It might doubtless throw curious light on the family history connected with that period. Of him and his three sons the venerable Charles O'Conor of Belanagare writes as follows, in 1753, in his *Dissertations on the ancient History of Ireland*, first edition, p. 231, which shews the high respectability of the family at this period:

"The late Colonel *Magnus O'Donnell*," [maternal] "uncle to the O'Donnell just mentioned" [i. e. Hugh O'Donnell of Larkfield], "was an Officer of distinction in the late wars of Ireland, and left three sons, Charles, Hugh, and Magnus, all alive at present, acting a part worthy of such a parent and of such Ancestors."

Now, let the reader mark the words, "*worthy of such a parent and of such ancestors*," and let him for a moment consider the character of the writer for probity, candour, and veracity, and he must confess that the above quoted words will set at nought the assertions of the Editor's late respected friend, Matthew O'Conor, Esq., of Mountdruid, who frequently stated that there was no Colonel Manus of this branch of the O'Donnells, either during the Insurrection of 1641, or the civil war of the Revolution. But we have now shewn on sufficient authority that there were two colonels of this family in the seventeenth century, namely, Colonel Manus, the son of Niall Garv, who was killed at Benburb in 1646, and Colonel Manus, the son of Roger, and grandson of the former Colonel Manus.

VIII. Charles (Calvagh Roe, as contradistinguished from his cousin and brother-in-law, Calvagh

[f] *Two daughters.*—In De Burgo's *Hibernia Dominicana* there is mention of another daughter, who is stated to have been married to Theophilus, great-grandson of Brian, first Baron of Enniskillen, and by whom she had issue Alexander, a captain in the Irish Brigade. But the Editor is inclined to think that De Burgo may have been led into error, by confounding this marriage with one or other of the two which certainly took place between the families; at least the Editor has not found elsewhere any trace of it, either recorded or traditional.

[g] *Married to Henry.*—A most amusing account of this marriage is given in a manuscript Life of Carolan, the poet, written in 1831, by the late Daniel Early, of Drumshambo, for Myles John O'Reilly, Esq., to whom the manuscript belongs.

[h] *Robert Maguire of Tempo.*—"Brian mac Constantine Maguire of Tempo, twelfth in descent from Odhar, from whom the name. The estates of his father were forfeited, but restored to Brian when he came of age. He married Miss Nugent, daughter of James Nugent of Colamber, in the county of Longford. She was an heiress, and by her he had five sons and one daughter. Brian died in 1700; his eldest sons, Brian and Constantine, died unmarried, the latter in 1739. The third son, Robert Maguire, thirteenth in descent

Duv) was eldest son of Colonel Manus O'Donnell of Newport. He resided at Newcastle in the county of Mayo; and was married, in 1712, to Catherine, daughter of James O'More[1], Esq., chief of his name. He died in the year 1770, leaving issue three sons: 1. Manus; 2. Con (who died unmarried); and 3. Lewis: and two daughters: Elizabeth, who married Thomas Cormack, Esq., of Mullennore and Castle Hill, in the same county; and Mary, married to —— Darcey, Esq., of ——, in the county of Galway. His eldest son, Manus, was born in the year 1713, and entered at an early age into the Austrian service, in which he rose to the rank of Major-General, and was created Count of the Empire by the Empress Maria Theresa. The Editor has been favoured with the perusal of several original interesting and curious documents and letters connected with the different branches of the family of O'Donnell at that period on the Continent and in Ireland, and of which he shall here append those that more directly refer to General Manus O'Donnell (or, as it seems they then spelled the name, "O'Donel"). The better to comprehend the following, it may here be stated that there were then in the Imperial Service, besides the subject of the present notice, three O'Donnells of the highest rank and consideration, namely, Connell and John, the writer of the following letters, sons of Hugh O'Donnell of Larkfield, in the county of Leitrim, by his first wife, Flora, daughter of General Hamilton of the Imperial Service (*vide post*, descendants of Hugh Boy), and Henry (youngest son of Calvagh Duv, above mentioned), by far the most distinguished of the three, and whose descendants at the present day rank among the highest nobility in Germany, as those of his brother, Joseph, are equally illustrious in Spain (*vide post*, descendants of Con Oge). In the year 1765, General (then Colonel) Manus O'Donnell was granted leave of absence, as appears from the following extract of the official document, which is written in the German language:

"1*st December*, 1765.

"From the Imp^{l} Roman & Royal Hungarian and Bohemian Majesty, Grand-duchess of Austria, our all-gracious Sovereign Lady, to make known to her Co^{l} and Commandant of the O'Donell Cuirassier Reg^{t}, Lord Magnus Count O'Donnell, that her aforesaid Majesty had been graciously pleased to appoint the same, by special most high favour, to be her Imp^{l} Royal Co^{l} Major of Cavalry, in virtue of a Patent made out under the most high signature, and to assign to the same, *à prima Februarii venturi*, one thousand five hundred Guilders for yearly pay. That the same may, for the management of his affairs, repair to England, there expend his pay, & receive the same, at the War Office here, at every time of producing the customary attestation *de vita et ubicatione*, &c., &c.

"*Per sacram Cæsareo Regiam*, &c.

"Signed, MAURIS CT. DE LACY."

from Odhar, married Miss Mac Dermot, heiress of the Greyfield estate, county Roscommon. He died without issue."—*Maguire's Pedigree*, from a pamphlet in the Editor's possession.

This marriage is also stated in Early's *Life of Carolan*, mentioned above.

[1] *Catherine, the daughter of O'More.*—Carolan composed the song called Seaḃac na hEirne agus ḃhéil Aṫa Seanaiġ, i.e. "The Hawk of the Erne and of Ballyshannon," for Calvagh Roe O'Donnell, on the occasion of bringing home his wife, the fair daughter of O'More, to his house, some time after the celebration of their marriage. He composed another song for his sister, Anne, the wife of Henry, son of Charles Mac Dermot Roe of Greyfield, in the county of Roscommon. In this latter song Carolan calls Anna the daughter of the noble Manus, son of Rory the high chieftain. Hugh O'Donnell of Greyfield stated that the song called "The Hawk of the Erne and of Ballyshannon" was composed by Carolan for his own grandfather, Hugh O'Donnell of

Subsequently to his arrival in Ireland the following letter was written to him by his cousin, John O'Donel, above mentioned. The year is not stated, but from its contents, and the date of his leave, it would appear to have been written in November the following year, 1766:

"*St. Pölten, ye 20th Nov.* This day I got y^{r} letter. I will write to you in a few days all the news I think you'd desire from these parts. Adieu. Write to me soon.

"MY DEAR COUS^{n},—You may well imagine that I was vastly in pain to be so long without a line from you, and consequently rejoiced at the receipt of y^{rs} from Ballyna[k] and Tuam, of the 12th Oct., which is the only pleasure you gave me since we separated. I beg you will not be so lazy towards me, who, you know, love you more than I can say or shew in effect. My Bro^{r},[l] who was lately a second time to see me here, complains much of y^{r} silence, saying he had not a word from you since your departure from Vienne, so that he was much embarrassed, not knowing whether you w^{d} return to the Reg^{t} or not, at a time that he was assured by the President of War that your Co^{l} w^{d} be soon advanced, and you to replace him. You see he has taken his measures to get no stranger, therefore, if you will return, and have a mind to be colonel, take the proper measures that depend on you, and that the service, as you know, requires in y^{r} pres^{t} situation. If you cant return at the end of y^{r} *congé*, write immediately to my bro^{r}, give him sufficient reasons, and desire or pray him to procure you, in consequence, a prolongation, which, I sh^{d} think, the shorter it can be, for your family affairs, the better; for tho' it is easy to be comprehended, that a journey to Ireland, and such business of consequence as y^{rs} to settle there, cannot be performed in such exactitude of time, still it is necessary to shew a certain zeal and fervour at ye eve of being made Co^{l} Commandant of a Reg^{t}; and this, not so much in regard to my bro^{r}, who knows you, as in regard to ye President, who, upon any neglect, might judge you to be careless or indolent. *En fin* you understand all this as well as I do, therefore, for God's sake, neglect nothing; write yourself to my Bro^{r}, as I sayd before, and shew, in proper terms, y^{r} concern for not being able to finish y^{r} business so as to be back at the time fixed by y^{r} first *congé*, by which means he may be able to make ye proper representations to Lacy, who then, I am confident, will be satisfy'd, so that you be at y^{r} Reg^{t} in ye end of April, or in the beginning of May. Be sure to write timely, and to me at the same time, a letter that I can shew or send to my Bro^{r}. Direct for me to St. Pölten, and not to Lintz, as you did this time, so that y^{r} letter went first to Vienne, and was sent to me by Weichart. As for y^{r} bro^{r} Lewis, you'll remember we spoke together about him in y^{r} passage here; there are, at present, several examples of Commissions being sold and purchased in our army; but you know the purchaser is lyable to other expences besides ye commission, so that according as I have heard such commissions were sold of late here and there in ye Reg^{ts}, the most Lewis could be provided with out of £500, after equipping himself in a proper manner, would be a Capt Lieutenancy, and to obtain this, or

Larkfield; but this assertion is contradicted by the words of the song itself, which call the hero of it the son of Manus, as well as by the reference to O'More's daughter, Catherine, who was certainly married to Charles Roe O'Donnell, the eldest son of Colonel Manus.

[k] *Ballyna.*—The seat of their kinsman, Ambrose O'Ferrall, of Ballyna, in the county of Kildare, and uncle to the present More O'Ferrall.

[l] *My brother.*—Connell, a lieutenant-general, and afterwards Governor of Transylvania.

was he to be made Marechal, you know he is not a man to stir in it himself, or give one any help, and without this, you know my present situation puts me out of the way of bringing such things so easily, or so soon, to pass, so that, as I told you here, you and y^r father should employ Cous^n Harry, and if he can get Lewis an agreement in the Reg^t he commands, it would be so much the better for reasons known to you. Harry is very capable of bringing many things to bear that others cannot. He is particularly well with her Majesty. The last time he saw her, she gave him a very fine present of jewels for his wife[m], saying, as she would never wear any more herself, she divided them among her children, and kept them for his wife. My Bro^r is not Governor of Transylvania, tho' it was spoken of, and believed by several; Haddeck is there as yet. If he accepted of it, it would be more on my account than to please his choyce. I believe they intend something for him, but dont know w^t as yet. My poor wife[n] is just recovering from a great sickness; y^r little things are well; we all joyn in love to y^u and d^r f^{ds}.

Y^{rs} ever,

"J^s O'DONEL.

"A' Monsieur

Monsieur Le Comte Magnus O'Donnell, Colonel du Regiment d'O'Donnell dans le service de Leurs Majt^s Imp^{lles} Roy^{lles} et Apostle, à New Castle, near Castle Barre, Irelande."

"*Vienne, the 20th Decembre.*

"MY DEAR COUSIN,—I send a note from Grosspitch of what you have in bank here and in his hands, that you may see and give me whatever directions you'll judge proper about the banks. You'll see I remitted here the money you advanced Mrs. C . . . . . and beg you will advance her the like sum for the ensuing new year, which I'll remit here as you'l direct. The Emperor is well satisfied with the horses you sent him, which I mentioned you before. Lacy is not at all in disgrace, but rather more in favour than ever, tho' he pretends to meddle in nothing. Y^r friend Pr Charles Leichtenstein is also much in favour. There is no news worth your notice from these parts. I hope you will not neglect the Genealogy O'More wrote to me about; but he knows everything better than I do, and he is there at the source. It is only giving the Herald proper instructions and paying him well; for the latter I will be answerable to y^u for it, and refund what you will let me know to be necessary. Bruckhausen will be here this Carnival, as he writes me to salute you, and is much satisfy'd with our friend O'Ferrall[o], to whom I am indebted for some letters; but he knows me and does not take it ill. He knows he can command any service in my power to render him. I beseech you will assure his grandfather, as likewise of my cordial friendship and veneration for himself. Does my sister-in-law marry, and how does Matilda's[p] marriage with Nugent go on? I suppose the other will drop all pretensions. Let me soon hear from you.

"Ever your affectionate Friend and Cousin,

"O'DONEL.

"A' Monsieur

Monsieur Le Comte Magnus O'Donel Genl Maj. au Service de Leurs Maj. Imp. Apost. à Newcastle, Castlebure, Irelande."

[m] *His wife.*—A cousin of the Empress, a princess of the illustrious house of Cantacuzeno.—*Vide post.*

[n] *Poor Wife.*—"A Spanish lady" (pedigree of O'Donnells of Larkfield, by Edward O'Reilly of Harold's-Cross).—*Vide post.*

[o] *O'Ferrall.*—The brother of Ambrose O'Ferrall, Esq., of

The first part of the following letter is entirely taken up with details of money, and other business matters, it then proceeds:

"*Vienne*, *6th June*, 1778.

* * * * * * * * * * * *
* * * * * * The armies are still facing one another on the respective frontiers, as I told you in my last, but as yet no hostilities. I refer to y^r own judgment if you would think proper to shew yourself under these circumstances. It might not be worth your while to offer your services, and if you did, it might very well be they would not accept, whereas several that were in the same case were refused, and none were taken but those who were in the activity of the service, except Lieu^t Genl Killiers, and that because the Empress had left him his full pay, which now the Emperor did not think fit he should enjoy for nothing. This is what I heard said; but sure it is that none of the rest were called for or accepted of. For my part, tho' I would serve them with all my heart, I find my head and memory too weak to accept of the office if it even had been proposed to me. Harry, who is healthy and strong, offered his services in a manner that the Emperor was well pleased with, and gave him assurance that he would get a command, but has not yet. My daughter[q] writes me that he intends to come soon to see me here. You know O'Ferrall is first Lieutenant. I had a letter from him yesterday, from the Army in Moravia. He is in good health and impatient to be so long without coming to strokes. I hope soon to have the comfort of a letter from you. About the Genealogy, I refer you to my last letter. Begging you will present my friendship to O'More, and remembrance to all enquiring friends, I am, my dearest Cousin, till Death,

"Yours, with all my heart,

"O'Donel.

"A' Monsieur
Monsieur Le Comte O'Donnell, General
Major au service de L. L. M. M. Impl. et
Royl. à Newcastle, Castlebarre, Irelande."

General Manus O'Donel never returned to serve on the Continent. Two years subsequently to the date of the last letter, as appears by his marriage settlement, that is, on the 8th December, 1780, he married Margaret, daughter of Henry Browne, Esq. of Castlemacgarret, in the county of Mayo, by Mary, daughter of Robert Nugent, Esq. of Grossfield, England, and by whom he had issue, an only child, Elizabeth, who married Robert Gage Rookwood, Esq., second son of Sir Thomas Gage, Bart. of Hengrave Hall, in the county of Suffolk. General O'Donel died in 1793, aged 80, as appears by the inscription on the family tomb at Straid Abbey in Mayo. This tomb exhibits his ARMS: Argent, issuing from the sinister side of the shield an arm slieved holding a

Ballyna, or Ballina, in the barony of Carbury and county of Kildare. See *Memoirs of the Life and Writings of Charles O'Conor of Belanagare*, p. 16[illegible].

[p] *Matilda.*—His niece, the daughter of his half-brother, Con O'Donnell of Larkfield, by Mary, sister of the first Sir Neal O'Donnell of Newport. She married Count Nugent of Westmeath, formerly of the Imperial Service, by whom she had John Nugent, Captain R. N., Inspector of Coast Guards.

[q] *My daughter.*—Therese, married to Henry's eldest son. —*Vide post.*

passion cross; and his CREST, on a wreath, two arms armed, bent and counterly crossed, each holding a sword; that on the dexter side transfixing a boar's head, the other a heart:

"PRAY FOR THE SOUL
OF
COUNT MANUS O'DONEL,
MAJOR GENERAL IN HIS IMPERIAL MAJESTY'S SERVICE,
WHO DEPARTED THIS LIFE
21ST DECEMBER, 1793,
AGED 80 YEARS.
ALSO, FOR THE SOULS OF HIS FATHER AND MOTHER,
AND
CHARLES O'DONEL, JUN^R.
ERECTED BY PETER QUIN, BY ORDER OF ROBERT G. ROOKWOOD, ESQ.
1813."

IX. LEWIS O'DONEL, Esq., of Killeen, second son of Charles Roe of Newcastle, was born in the year 1715. He was for some time in the Austrian service, in which he attained the rank of captain; but, returning to Ireland and marrying in this country, he did not return again to the Continent. He resided at Killeen, in the county of Mayo. He married Bridget, daughter of Randal MacDonnell, Esq. of Massbrook, in the same county, by whom he had issue three sons: 1. Charles, who died unmarried, aged 18; 2. Manus, a captain in the British service, who distinguished himself by his bravery in Colonel Spencer's regiment in Holland, where he was severely wounded in the hip, as he was defending a passage from a ford on a river over which the late Frederic, Duke of York, had passed in his flight from the pursuing French; he afterwards died of his wounds; and 3. Lewis (of whom presently); and three daughters: Bessy, married to Denis Kelly, Esq., of Kellysgrove, in the county of Galway; Mary, married to Edward Burke, Esq., of the same county; and Bridget, married to Edward Bolingbroke, Esq., of Oldcastle, in the county of Mayo.

X. LEWIS O'DONEL, Esq., of Ross, in the same county. His three elder brothers dying without issue, he succeeded to his father's property. He married, in 1821, Judith, daughter of John Bourke, Esq., of Ballina. He died and was buried at Ostend, in the year 1841, leaving issue one son, Charles, who is now "The O'Donnell," born 27th November, 1823; a lieutenant in Her Majesty's 88th regiment of foot (the "Connaught Rangers"); and three daughters: Jane Louisa; Mary Baptist; and Judith. We will now return to

O'DONEL OF NEWPORT.

VIII. HUGH O'DONNELL, Esq., of Newport, commonly called Hugh More. He was the third son of Colonel Manus of Newport, and married Maud, daughter of Browne of Brownestown, Co. Mayo, by whom he had issue five sons: 1. Hugh, who died *s. p.*; 2. Francis, whose son Hugh died in the E. I. Company's Service, without issue; 3. Neal, by whom the second senior line was continued; 4. John, M.D., who died unmarried; 5. Connell, who died unmarried; and three daughters, viz.: Mary, who married Con O'Donnell, Esq., of Larkfield; 2. Henrietta, who married Æneas Mac Donnell, Esq., of Westport; and Anne, who married John O'Donnell, Esq., of Erris.

IX. Neal O'Donel, Esq., of Newport, in the county of Mayo, locally called Niall Garv. He was created a baronet of Ireland on the 2nd of December, 1780. He married Mary, daughter of William Coane, Esq., of Ballyshannon, and had issue four sons, viz.: 1. Hugh O'Donel, lieutenant-colonel of the South Mayo Militia, and colonel of the 110th regiment of the Line, who died without issue male; 2. James Moore O'Donel, M. P., killed in a duel by the late Major Bingham, of Bingham's Castle, in the Co. Mayo, and *ob. s. p*; 3. Neal O'Donel, who succeeded to the title; and 4. Connell, who died *s. p.*; and two daughters, 1. Margaret, married to Sir Capel Molyneux, Bart.; and 2. Maria, married to Dodwell Browne, Esq., of Castlebar.

Sir Niall Garv O'Donel died in January, 1811, and was succeeded by his eldest surviving son,

X. Sir Neal, locally called Niall Beag O'Donel, third baronet. He married Catherine, fourth daughter of Richard, second Earl of Annesley, and had issue three sons, 1. Sir Hugh, third baronet, who died on the 29th of July, 1828, without male issue; and 2. Sir Richard Annesley, the present baronet; 3. Neal, who died unmarried; and four daughters, viz.: 1. Mary, a nun, of the Presentation Order; 2. Anna Maria, married, in 1827, to Martin Conolly, Esq.; 3. Margaret, who died unmarried; and Catherine, wife of the Rev. —— Yonge.

XI. Sir Richard Annesley O'Donel, fourth and present baronet. He married, on the 16th of April, 1831, Mary, third daughter of the late George Clendening, Esq., of Westport, by whom he has issue two sons, George and Richard. Let us now return to

O'DONNELL OF LARKFIELD.

IV. Hugh Boy, son of Con[r] O'Donel, and brother of Sir Niall Garv, Baron of Lifford. He is mentioned, in the *Ulster Inquisitions*, as having received a grant, in 1613, of a small quantity of land in the barony of Kilmacrenan, county of Donegal, at the same time, and of the same extent as we have seen above granted to his brother Donnell. "To Hugh Boy M'Quin" [mac Cuınn, i. e. son of Con] "the two towns or ½ q^rs of Fiart and Glannyreagh, otherwise Carrowfiart, in Rossguill, 128 A., Rent £1 7*s.* 3½*d.*[s] A similar grant to him of the same lands, two years earlier, is to be found in Pat. Rolls, 8th Jac. I. He is also named, together with his brother, Donnell, as carrying on a treasonable correspondence with Sir Neal Garve, then a prisoner in the Tower (1615), in an examination already quoted; and again, a similar charge brought against them in "the Confession of Cormack Mac Redmond Moyle Maguire, taken before me, Sir Toby Caulfield, Knt., at Charlemont, the 11th of June, 1615." He died in 1649. It appears from an elegy on his death, that this Hugh Boy was considered The O'Donnell, after the fall of Colonel Manus at Benburb, in 1646, the chieftianship passing to the uncle, by the Irish custom of tanistry, as "senior et dig-

[r] *Hugh Boy, son of Con.*—It is stated in these Annals, under the year 1608, that Hugh Boy, son of Con O'Donnell, was taken prisoner, because his brother, Donnell, slew the murderer of his brother, Calvagh, and was only released on Donnell surrendering himself. Sir William Betham, on the authority of Lodge's MSS., now in his possession, makes this Hugh Boy a son, and not a brother, of Sir Niall Garv; but this is a great mistake, which the depositions of 1641, 1652, and Duald Mac Firbis's Genealogical Manuscript, and several others, enable us to correct. There was a Hugh O'Donnell, of Ramelton, in the assembly of the Confederate Catholics at Kilkenny, 10th January, 1647.—*Ledwich's Antiq.*, 2nd ed, p. 472.

[s] Inq. Net. Pat. 10 Js. I. Rep. R. C.

nissimus vir sanguinis," instead of to the probably infant son of Colonel Manus. According to Lodge's Manuscripts, he married Mary Maguire, daughter of Lord Enniskillen, by whom he had issue two sons: 1. Dominick; and 2. John[t]; on the former of whom Owen Roe Mac Ward composed a poem of 248 verses, beginning, "Ꝺaıḃle Foḋla ꝼuıl Chonaıll; Props of Fodhla (Erin) is the blood of Conall;"[u] and on the death of the latter (who, according to the last quatrain but one, died in 1655), there is an elegy by the same poet, consisting of 232 verses, and beginning, "Do ꞇoıꞃneaḋ ceannaꞅ ċlaınn ᵹ-Cuınn;" the authority of the sons of Con was humbled[w]. Of the fate of Dominick, the Editor has learned nothing, but it appears from the poem just referred to that

V. John O'Donnell was an officer in foreign service, and was considered the head of the family of the O'Donnells. This, however, was evidently in accordance with the law of tanistry, not that of primogeniture. He died in 1655, as appears from the elegy on his death already referred to. He married Catherine O'Rourke, by whom he had Hugh, who died *s. p.* and

VI. Connell O'Donnell. He returned to Ireland some time after the death of his father, and was made Lord Lieutenant of the county of Donegal by James II. in 1689; and was evidently considered "The O'Donnell," until, as already mentioned, Ball-dearg O'Donnell returned to Ireland in September, 1690, and was received by the Irish as "The O'Donnell." But this personage afterwards joined the standard of King William III., and soon after retired to Flanders, leaving Connell O'Donnell the acknowledged head of the name in Ireland. This Connell married Grainé, or Grace, the daughter of Roger O'Donnell of Lifford, and sister of Colonel Manus O'Donnell of Newport, by whom he had, according to Lodge's Manuscripts, three sons: 1. John, whose only son, Hugh, died without issue; 2. Charles, who died *s. p.*; and 3,

VII. Hugh O'Donnell of Larkfield. He was called "The O'Donnell," and even "Earl Tirconnell," by the common people; but he could not have been called Earl according to the laws of England, as is quite evident from Earl Rory's patent. After the defeat of King James II., this Hugh removed from the county of Donegal, and took refuge first at a place called Mullaghbane, near the head of Lough-dá-éan, now Lough Macnean, in the county of Fermanagh, and shortly afterwards settled at Larkfield, near Manor-Hamilton, in the county of Leitrim. He married twice: first, Flora Hamilton, daughter of John Hamilton, Esq. of Cavan, and sister of General John Count Hamilton of the Austrian service, and he had by her two sons: 1. Connell Count O'Donnell, Knight Grand Cross of the Order of Maria Theresa, Governor of Transylvania, and a Field-marshal in the Austrian service, who, on Downs being wounded, commanded the imperial army at the battle of Torgau, and who died unmarried in 1771; and 2. John Count O'Donnell, a General in the same service, who, according to De Burgo, married Anna Corr, by whom he had a son[x] and a daughter, Therese, who married Joseph Count O'Donnell, of Austria. Hugh married, secondly,

[t] O'Clery and Mac Firbis's Genealogies, R. I. A.

[u] O'Reilly's Catal. Irish Writers, p. 97.

[w] Ib.

[x] *A son.*—Sir William Betham states in his pedigree of the O'Donnells, published in his *Irish Antiquarian Researches*, that this John Count O Donnell had a son, Charles Count O'Donnell, who was Major-General in the Austrian service, and was killed at Neresheim, in 1805; but this Major-General Charles O'Donnell was not his son, but the son of Manus, who was son of Calvagh Duv, as will presently appear from his own letter. See descendants of Con Oge, *infra*.

Margaret, daughter of Hugh Montgomery, Esq., of Derrygonnelly, in the county of Fermanagh, and had by her two sons: 1. Con O'Donnell, of Larkfield, of whom presently; and 2. a son whose name is forgotten by the family, and who went over to his half brother's in Vienna, and died abroad, young and unmarried; and two daughters: 1. Grace, who married James Johnson of Drumiskin, in the county of Fermanagh, by whom she had a numerous issue; and 2. Catherine, who married Arthur Johnson of the Ring, near Enniskillen, by whom she had one daughter.

Of this Hugh O'Donnell, who died in 1754, and his sons by his first marriage, Charles O'Conor of Belanagare has the following notice in his *Dissertations on the ancient History of Ireland*, edition of 1753, p. 231:

"The Tyrconall Race produceth at this day Persons, who reflect back on their Ancestors the Honours they derive from them, particularly Conall and John O'Donnell, sufficiently recorded in our Gazettes, for their Exploits in the late Wars, in the Service of the Empress, Queen of Hungary. These excellent General Officers are the sons of a very worthy Person, Hugh O'Donnell the chief of the Tyrconell Line, and of Flora, the Sister of the late General Hamilton, who, if I be well informed, died in the Imperial Service."

VIII. Con O'Donnell, Esq., of Larkfield. After the death of his father and half brothers, he was considered by the Irish as "The O'Donnell." He married Mary O'Donnell (sister to the first Sir Neal O'Donel of Newport, who was "The O'Donnell" according to the English law of primogeniture), and had by her: 1. Hugh O'Donnell, Esq., of Larkfield, of whom presently; 2. Connell O'Donnell, who died at Liege, in Germany, young and unmarried; 3. John O'Donnell, who died unmarried about the year 1800; 4. Con O'Donnell, who married Mary, second daughter of Denis O'Conor of Belanagare, and sister of the late Owen O'Conor Don, M. P. for the county of Roscommon, and had by her four sons, viz.: 1. Con O'Donnell of the city of Dublin, Barrister at law; 2. John O'Donnell; 3. Connell O'Donnell; 4. Niall O'Donnell; and two daughters, viz.: Matilda O'Donnell, who married James Nugent of Ballinacor, by whom she had a large family; and 2. Mary, who married Peyton John Gamble of Boxborough.

IX. Hugh O'Donnell, Esq., of Larkfield and Greyfield[y], married Honoria, eldest daughter of

[y] *Greyfield*.—This, which was the ancient estate of the Mac Dermots Roe, passed from that family about eighty-six years since. Henry Mac Dermot Roe had by Anna, the daughter of Colonel Manus O'Donnell, an only daughter, Eliza, who was married to Robert Maguire of Tempo, in the county of Fermanagh, by whom she had no issue. After the marriage of Eliza with Maguire, the brother of the latter, Hugh Maguire, who had been a Colonel in the Austrian service, and had married the Honourable Dowager Lady Cathcart, came on a visit to Greyfield. Henry Mac Dermot Roe, who had been living after a sumptuous, extravagant manner for years before, borrowed a large sum of money from Colonel Maguire, for which he mortgaged to him the estate of Greyfield. Shortly after this Anne O'Donnell died, and Henry Mac Dermot Roe went to Tempo, where he lived with his daughter for a few years before his death. After his death Colonel Hugh Maguire foreclosed Henry's mortgage to him, and brought the ground to sale; under which William Knox, Esq., purchased the lands. After the departure of Henry to Tempo, his brother, Counsellor John Mac Dermot Roe, took possession of Greyfield House, and his followers resisted the High Sheriff (Edward Lord Kingston, still vividly remembered in that country as "the good lord"), who attended Colonel Maguire and Mr. Knox to get possession of the house and lands of Greyfield, and fired out of the windows; and in a skirmish near the village of Keadue, several lives were lost, in a field still called Páirc a' ṁurdair, i. e. the Field of the Murder. Finally, after several days' resistance and bloodshed, the possession was delivered to Mr. Knox, at the desire of the said Eliza, who came at the head of several of her friends, and desired those in the house to give it up to the sheriff. These lands are now farmed by the O'Donnells of Larkfield, some of whom reside in Greyfield House.

Myles Lyons of Lyonstown, in the county of Roscommon, and had by her three sons, viz.: Con O'Donnell of Larkfield, of whom presently; 2. Hugh Lyons O'Donnell, born 16th June, 1795; and Robert O'Donnell, born in 1800; and one daughter, Rose O'Donnell, who married Richard Phibbs of Branchfield.

After the head of the Newport or Baronet branch of the O'Donnells had obtained the celebrated relic called the Cathach or Caah, as being "The O'Donnell," Con O'Donnell of Larkfield, who died in 1825, published several letters in the *Dublin Evening Post*, to prove that his own father was "The O'Donnell," and, therefore, was the true owner of this relic; but in these articles he made many bold assertions, which would require more than his mere *dictum* to establish, but the Editor does not deem it necessary to revive the controversy. This celebrated relic, which is mentioned in these Annals at the years 1497 and 1499, was from remote times held in the highest veneration by this family, and was carried by them into all their battles. In the ancient Book of Fenagh, a manuscript in the British Museum, Cotton. 115, the following notice of it occurs in a memorandum in English, in the hand-writing of Tully Conry: "Also he" [St. Caillin of Fenagh] "doth admonish the sept of Conall Gulban, which is the O'Donells, to look well to the *Caagh*, that it should not come to the handes of Englishmen, which yf yt did it should be to the overthrowe and confusion of the sept of Conall Gulban, and to the great honnor of the English, &c." This relic was carried away from Tyrconnell by a Colonel Daniel O'Donnell, who followed the fortunes of King James II. into France, and who repaired it in 1723. This Colonel Daniel was of the race of Hugh Duv, the brother of Manus, who died in 1563, and, dying without issue, in Belgium, mentioned in his will that it should be given to whoever proved himself to be the head of the O'Donnell family. It was found in a monastery in Belgium by the late Abbot of Cong, who, on learning the nature of Colonel O'Donnell's will, told the late Sir Neal O'Donel about it, on his return to Ireland. Sir Neal, who believed himself to be "The O'Donnell," applied for the relic through his brother Connell, then in Belgium, who succeeded in obtaining it for Sir Neal O'Donel, as "The O'Donnell," though Lewis O'Donel of Ross was unquestionably senior to Sir Neal.—See p. 2396, *supra*.

X. Con O'Donnell, Esq., of Larkfield. He married Mary, daughter of Richard Phibbs, sen. of Branchfield, in the county of Sligo, and had by her one son, Con O'Donnell, who was living in 1837. This Con, No. X., died on the 28th of August, 1825. Let us now return to Niall Garv's third brother.

CASTLEBAR, SPANISH, AND AUSTRIAN, O'DONELS.

IV. Con Oge[z], third son of Con O'Donnell. He was slain 1601, and left issue one son[a],

V. Manus O'Donnell, who, according to a pedigree of Count O'Donell of Austria (copied from a heraldic genealogy, with the seal of Chichester Fortescue, Ulster King at Arms, by Colonel Sir Charles O'Donnel, at Vienna, in 1828, and then in the possession of the Countess O'Donnel, née de Geisruch), was married to "Maria, filia de Doole Campbell, ex familia Ducis Argyle in Scotia." He left one son, Calvagh Roe, as appears also from an addition made in the handwriting of the Venerable Charles O'Conor of Belanagare, to Mac Firbis's genealogical manuscript.

[z] O'Clery and Mac Firbis's Genealogies, R. I. A.

[a] D. Mac Firbis, MS. R. I. A.

VI. Calvagh Roe O'Donnell. "Carolus O'Donnel Colonellus, = Eleonora Mac Sweeny, filia Gualteri Mac Sweeny de Fanad in comitatu Donagalensi[b]." Among the poems of Farrell Oge Mac Ward (who lived in 1655), there is one addressed to this O'Donnell, at the time of his marriage with Elenor Mac Sweeny, of which the following eight verses are the only portion that appear to remain, and which were found in a MSS., in the Collection of the Rev. Dr. Todd, F. T. C. D., p. 479, by Mr. Eugene Curry. In O'Reilly's Catalogue of Irish Writers, p. 197, this poem is entitled: "On the O'Donnells, particularly Calbhach, son of Manus,"—248 verses, beginning, "treoin an ċeannais clann Dálaiġ: powerful the authority of Clan Dalaigh:"

"Do ṫairrngir Fionn, fírrde de, do ċuir Ciaran a ccuiṁne, fear t'anma tar aon eile, dod taoḃ tarlaiġ an tairrngire.	"Finn[c] foretold (we profit by his knowledge), St. Ciaran[d] reiterated the prophecy, That a man of thy name [would be] above all others; Concerning thee the prophecy was made.
Suirġe leiḃ ag Lios Eaṁna; 's ag suiliḃ na sín Teaṁra; a ccaiṫċuir gan cuing ccroiḋe, d'aiṫris Chuinn is Chonaire.	The ancient fort of Emania[e] courts thee; Thou art the expected one of old Temoria; Thy espousals with open hearts they seek, As Con and Conary they sought of yore.
Airdeoċaiḋ sos gan taom ttais meanma gliaiḋ buiḋne beárnais; le treaḋmaiḃ lúiḋ is laṁaiġ 's lead ṁeanmain úir ioldanaiġ.	Now to its wonted height shall be exalted The martial spirit of the hosts of Bearnas[f]; By thy achievements and career of valour, And by thy noble polytechnic mind.
Ní luġa uiḋ Oiliġ Néid ag leanṁain ar do leiṫéid, a ndoiġ caḃra d'a cneaḋaiḃ, tarlaiġ a óig ar t'oileaṁuin.	Nor was Aileach Neid[g], too, less expectant Of one like thee to arise unto her, Hoping thou wouldst relieve her anguish, Now that her youths are under thy fostering care.
A Chalḃaiġ, do ċar tura dfortaċt an ḟoinn Loġa so, go bein a doċraċta de, ceim socraċta naċ sirṫe.	O'Calvagh! long has it been thy ardent wish To bring relief to this land of Lughaidh[h], And sweep away its oppressions, An achievement, now, alas! coveted by few.
Donnchaḋ mac Neill mic Donnchaiḋ sár muċtad gaċ mor ċonfaiḋ tosaċ gaċ garma dó de ga tarḃa ar mo buḋ maoiḋte?	Donough, son of Niall, son of Donough[i], He who extinguishes every furious onset, And, therefore, holds first rank in fame[k]— What advantage more to be boasted of?

[b] Austrian Pedigree.

[c] *Finn:* i. e. Finn Mac Cumhaill.—See note on prophecies, p. 1797, *supra*.

[d] *St. Ciaran:* i. e. the patron saint of Clonmacnoise.

[e] *Emania.*—The ancient palace of the kings of Ulster.

[f] *Bearnas:* i. e. Bearnas-mor-Gap, near Donegal.

[g] *Aileach Neid.*—Now Elagh, one of the ancient palaces of Ulster.

[h] *Land of Lughaidh.*—One of the many arbitrary bardic names for Ireland.

[i] *Donough.*—Probably the brother of Ellen.

[k] *Fame.*—*Vide* Annals Four Masters, *passim*, where it

Inġean Ḃháiteir naċ claon cóir;	The daughter of Walter, who perverts not justice;
aghaiḋ ċaoin, caidrioḃ mioċair;	Whose address is pleasing as her face is beautiful;
bean gá mbí treiġte ar toġa,—	Whose graces are peculiarly her own,—
ar í an ḟéile a haonroġa.	The especial patroness of hospitality.
Nós na Suiḃneaċ gan dul de	The ancient customs of Mac Sweeny's mansion
tug Eiḃilin d'á haire;	By Ellen are most bountifully observed;
ní neaṁḋóiṫċe céim a ccorp	To her fair fame no reproach attaches
ar ḃéim dearlaiġṫe ar daonoċt."	On the score of munificence and kindness."

Calvagh Roe O'Donnell very probably held the rank ascribed to him in the Austrian Pedigree, in the army of the King, during the parliamentary wars; and one passage in the preceding fragment appears to allude to a military career. The Editor has heard that he was the first of the O'Donnells who went to Mayo; but, however that may be, there is no doubt that his son was settled there, having married the daughter of Colonel O'Neill, of Oldcastle, in that county. This son was—

VII. HUGH O'DONNELL, who married "Margaritha O'Neale, filia Terentii O'Neale et Ceciliæ O'More, filiæ Roderici O'More, Colonelli et Comitis de Leix[l]."

Here it may not be amiss to digress for a brief period, in order to ascertain who this Colonel O'Neill, whom we thus find possessed of property in a district so little connected with his name as the county of Mayo, could have been; and when and how that property was acquired. In this inquiry a strange picture is presented of the reverses of fortune in which many of the great Irish families were involved during the seventeenth century.

One of the highest branches of the family of O'Neill was represented by the O'Neills of the Fews. Hugh, second son of Eoghan, or Owen, the great-grandfather of Con Bacagh, first Earl of Tyrone, was chieftain of the extensive territory still known as the Upper and Lower Fews, in the county of Armagh. He left a son, Art, who was declared "The O'Neill" on the death of Donnell, the brother of Con More O'Neill[m]. Art died in 1514, and left a son, Phelim, or Felimy Roe, who struggled hard against the progress of English power in the North, in the reign of Edw. VI.; and his son, Henry, who was married to the widow of Matthew, Baron of Dungannon (she died June 2nd, 1600), shared, up to the death of Elizabeth, in the fortunes of his step-son, the great Earl of Tyrone. On the accession of James I. a general pardon was granted to him, as "Henry O'Neale of the Fews," dated "20th February, in the first year[n]," and which he only survived a short while; for we find that he was succeeded the same year by his son, Tirlough, to whom his lands were confirmed, as appears by the following entry: "To Tirlough Mac Henry O'Neyle, Esq., was granted on the —— day of September, in the first year" (1603), "the whole territory or country of the Fues in Ulster, and all lordships, castles, manors, &c., within said territory: to Hold to him, his Heirs and Assigns, for ever, *in capite*, by the service of one Knight's fee, at the rent of a horse and two pair of spurs, or 40*s*. Irish, at the Election of said Tirlogh, his Heirs and Assigns[o]."

appears that the Mac Sweenys had the hereditary right of leading O'Donnell's gallowglasses.

[l] Austrian Pedigree.

[m] MS. Trinity College, Dublin, E. 4. 18.

[n] Erck's *Rep. of Chan. Enrol.*, p. 31.

[o] Ibid., p. 171.

This Turlough married Sarah, daughter of Sir Tirlogh Lenogh O'Neill[p], by whom he had issue two sons, Henry and Art, and three daughters, the eldest of whom, Catherine, married Sir Tirlogh O'Neill of Kinard, by whom she had two sons, Tirlogh Oge and the celebrated Sir Phelim, both leaders in the insurrection of 1641. He died at Glasdrommen, county of Armagh, in 1639, having previously conveyed his estates to certain trustees, as appears from an inquisition taken at Armagh:

"Tirlogh Mac Henry O'Neale, late of Glasdrommen, in the territory of Fues, Knt., was seized in fee of certain lands (set forth) in said county, did on the 8th of March, in the 8th year of the reign[q], obtained royal license to convey all the said lands, by the style or name of the territory of Fues, to certain Trustees (named), to the use of himself and his wife, Sarah, during their natural lives, and the survivor of them; afterwards to the use of Henry O'Neale, son and heir apparent of the said Tirlogh; and after his decease to the use of Tirlogh O'Neale, son and heir of the said Henry, and the heirs male of his body lawfully begotten; with divers other remainders; and afterwards to the use of the right heirs of the said Tirlogh O'Neale the younger. The said Tirlogh, by deed dated 1st May, 1639, conveyed to Arthur, his second son, certain lands specified therein. The said Tirlogh O Neale, Knt., died 24th February, 1639. The said Henry O Neale, his son and heir, was then of full age, and married. The said premises were held of the King for military service in capite[r]."

Sir Tirlogh was buried at Creggan, in same county[s]. Henry, his son and heir, had some time previously been married to Mary, daughter of Sir John O'Reilly, Knight, county of Cavan[t], by whom he had one son, Tirlogh, named in the above remainders. This Tirlogh married Cecilia, daughter of the famous Rory O'More, the prime mover of the insurrection of 1641, and thus became, by ties of marriage as of blood, connected with the troubles of the period. From the Relation of the Lord Maguire, "written with his own hand, in the Tower," it would seem that he participated in those events; though, strange to say, he was not included afterwards in the proclamation that offered rewards for the heads of his father-in-law, his uncle, Art, and his cousins, Tirlogh and Sir Phelim:

"Being in Dublin, Candlemas Term was twelve month" (1640), says Maguire, "the Parliament then sitting, Mr. Roger Moore did write to me," &c. . . . . ; "and the next day, after the receipt of the letter, being Sunday, (by Mr. Moore's advice) we departed from Col. Mac Mahon's house, to prevent (as he said) the suspition of the English there (many living near), to Laghrosse, in the county of Armagh, to Mr. Torilagh O'Neale's house (not Sir Phelim's brother, but son to Mr. Henry O'Neale of the Fewes, and *son-in-law to Mr. Moore*), and left word that if Sir Phelim or any of those gentlemen did come in the mean time, they should follow us thither (whither only went Mr. Moore, Captain O'Neale, and myself), and these we expected till Tuesday subsequent, before any of them did come[u]."

But, although he escaped the tragic fate of many of those who were involved in that unhappy affair, it would appear that the Parliamentary Government did not entirely overlook his partici-

[p] MS. Trinity College, Dublin, E. 4. 18.

[q] 1633.

[r] Inq. Ult. Ann. Chas. I.

[s] Fun. Entries, vol. viii. p. 327.

[t] MS. in the Library of Trinity College, Dublin, E. 4. 18.

[u] Warner's *History of the Irish Rebellion*, Appendix, p. 9.

pation in it; for both he and his father were among the earliest victims of the grand scheme of the "transplantation." Henry O'Neill was compelled to surrender his "territory of the Fewes," and accept, in lieu of it, from the Commonwealth, a tract of land in the county of Mayo, large in extent, yet still but a poor compensation for a principality which his family had ruled for several generations. The Editor has not found in the Act of Settlement, nor in private hands, the confirmatory grant of the original transfer; but, subsequently to the death of Henry O'Neale, we find the enrolment of a grant to his son of a portion of the lands originally bestowed[w], "dated 9th February, 32 year, and inrolled 5th March, 1680":

"To Terlagh O Neale, son and heir of Henry O Neale, late of Ardcharra, Co. Mayo, and formerly of the Fues, Co. Ardmagh, Esq., the towns and lands of Leccarrowconnell, Lecarrowrory, Uncles, Uncle, Knockenrony, Carrownoonah, Killives, Cloongue, Pollagh, Knockroe, Braendrum, Aghalouske, Shehave, Carrownaragh, Treenbeg, Logafooka, Carrowanhan, Bellagariffe, Boghola, Ardhoroe, Cullileagh, Newcastle, Myleeke, Collagh, Bollinelly, *alias* Clooneen, Bellaghagh" [or Oldcastle] "and Ardhoom; at a crown rent of £26 9*s.* 10¾*d.*; situate in the Barony of Gallen, and county of Mayo[x]."

Tirlagh had issue by his marriage, Henry, a captain in James the Second's army; and Margaret, who, as previously stated, married Hugh, son of Calvagh Roe O'Donnell. On the flight of James II., and the succession of William III., Henry, having been attainted, is supposed to have escaped to the Continent; but, although the estate was thus forfeited, it would seem that the Crown made no disposition of it at the time, but allowed his relative, Tirlagh, son of Art, son of Sir Tirlagh O'Neill of the Fews, his sister, and his nephew, Charles, or Calvagh Duv O'Donnell, to enter into and retain possession for several years subsequently. In the year 1703, as the Editor has been informed, on a discovery being made to the Court of Requests [the Penal Laws then coming into full operation] that these lands were held by recusants and Papists, a final forfeiture took place, one portion being bestowed upon the Charter School of Sligo, and the remainder granted, for a consideration of £330, "to William Moore, Esq., of the city of Dublin, the 22nd of June, 1703," being "the estate of Henry O'Neill attainted, and all other his estates in Ireland[y]."

Art or Arthur O'Neill, the second son of Sir Tirlagh of the Fews, married Catherine, daughter of Sir Henry O'Neill of Kinard, and had a son Turlough, who married Catherine, daughter of Robert Hovedon, of Ballynameetah, and had a son Arthur, Junior, who married Alice O'Donnell, and had by her two sons, Neal O'Neill and Owen O'Neill, the former of whom, who died about 1708, married Catherine Magennis, and had a son, Henry, who was under age in 1708, and living in 1758, when James Knox, Esq., of Moyne, brought ejectments against him. On the 10th of February, 1724, this Henry filed a bill in the Exchequer in Ireland, against Robert, the father of Samuel Ormsby, which sets forth "said Henry as Administrator of all and singular the goods and chattles, rights and credits, which did belong to Neal O'Neil, Gentleman, in his lifetime, as appears by the letter of Administration therewith granted to him, that one Henry O'Neil, since deceased, having in his lifetime a considerable Estate in the North of this Kingdom, was transplanted into Connaught,

[w] *Bestowed.*—A portion only, for it says "Henry O'Neale, *late of Ardcharra;*" and Ardcharra is not included in the new grant, although a neighbouring townland.

[x] Rep. Rec. Com., vol. iii. p. 271, R. 32, chap. ii.

[y] Rep. Rec. Com., R. 2nd An. 11th pt. back vol. iii. p. 890.

and did there obtain a final settlement of several lands in the county of Mayo in satisfaction of his antient Estate.

"That Arthur O'Neill, brother to said Henry, being dead, left his son and heir, Terlagh O'Neil, who, being Intitled to 8 Townlands, part of said antient Estate, did Intrust said Henry, being the eldest branch of the family, to claim his proportion of said antient Estate, which said Henry did, and having obtained a decree thereon for a parcell of lands in the county of Mayo aforesaid, part whereof were obtained in trust, as aforesaid, for said Terlagh, it was agreed between them, the said Henry and Terlagh O'Neil, that he, the said Henry, should, on obtaining a Decree for said lands, perfect a lease unto said Terlagh for 99 years, of a sixth part of such Transplantation Lands as he should so get, at the yearly rent of 5 shillings for each quarter of such lands, the same being a just proportion of said Antient estate due to said Terlagh.

"That said Henry O'Neil did enter into several engagements in writing, concerning said dividend, proportion, and Trust, in discharge whereof, and in consideration of £200, said Henry, Senior, by Deed of Lease, dated the 3rd of August, 1656, did Demise unto said Terlagh, his Executors, Administrators, and Assigns, in part of said Transplantation lands, vizt: the quarter of land of Meelick, and the quarter of land of Lecarrowrory and Lecarrowconnell, in the said county, for 99 years, to commence from the date of the said lease, or some other time, if any issue male of the body of the said Terlagh O'Neil, or of the said Arthur O'Neil, his father, shou'd so long continue. By virtue of which demise the said Terlagh entered on the premises, and became thereof possessed, and died, possessed thereof, Intestate; after whose death, Arthur O'Neil, Junior, son and heir to the said Terlagh, having taken out letters of Administration to his said father, did enter on the premises, and continued possessed thereof for several years, and having married one Alice O'Donnell, departed this life, leaving issue by her, the said Alice, the said Neal O'Neil, his eldest son, Plaintiff's father, and Owen O'Neil, on whose decease said Alice O'Neil, *alias* O'Donnell, became possessed of the premises, and, being so possessed, intermarried with one John O'Neil, Gent., since deceased."

The term of ninety-nine years expired in 1755, and the O'Neills appear to have been ousted in 1758, by Mr. Knox, to whom, in the interval, the fee of these particular lands had come.

Hugh O'Donel, No. VII., by his wife, Margaret O'Neill, left issue an only son,—

VIII. Charles O'Donnell, known as Calvagh Duv, i. e. Calḃaċ Ḋuḃ, i. e. Charles the Black, as distinguished from his brother-in-law, Calvagh Roe, or Charles the Red, of Newcastle. On the forfeiture of the O'Neill property in Gallen, in 1703, he became lessee, under the Ecclesiastical Court of Tuam (the only species of tenure the new laws left open to the Catholic), of some church lands in the barony of Murrisk, in the same county. He married Mary, eldest daughter of Colonel Manus O'Donel, by whom he had issue three sons, viz.: 1. Manus, of whom presently; 2. Joseph, from whom the O'Donnels of Spain are descended; 3. Henry[z], the founder of the O'Donells of Austria, as shall be presently shewn.

IX. Manus O'Donel of Wilford Lodge, in the county of Mayo, was born about the year 1720. He married Eleanor, daughter of ——— Bole, Esq., of the county of Longford, by whom he had issue three sons, and two daughters: 1. Joseph, of whom presently; 2. Hugh, who went

[z] *Henry.*—A name unusual in the O'Donnell family, and here evidently taken from the O'Neills, with whom (since their intermarriage with the Kildare family) it was very general.

to the West Indies, and settled at Vera Cruz, where he was living in 1798, as appears from a letter of his brother, Charles, copied below, but no further account of him has reached his relations in Ireland; 3. Charles, born 1760, went out while yet a boy to his uncle, Henry, to Germany[a], and entered the Austrian service, in which he rose to the dignity of a Count, and rank of Major-General. In 1798, the widow of his brother, Joseph, being desirous of removing her son, the late Mr. Joseph O'Donel of Castlebar, from this country, then in a state of insurrection, wrote to Germany, to her brother-in-law, on the propriety of sending him abroad. The first of the following letters bears reference to this subject. It is particularly interesting, not only for the amiable light in which it presents the character of the writer, but also for the direct reference which it makes to the scattered members of his family. Though written in English, the idiom is evidently foreign.

"*Vienna, the first Xbre*, 1798.

"MY DEAR SISTER-IN-LAW,—Tho the letter I had the pleasure to receive from you was very ancient, being dated from the 29th of June, for all that I did not get it but since a short while; and that delay, my dear Sister-in-law, is the cause of me not answering you sooner. I would have received your letter, no doubt, long ago, if acquainted with the change that happened with me, you could have directed it me more exactly. But as, according to the informations that were given you about me, you thought me stil Commander of a Free Corps, and in Bavaria, you directed me in con-

[a] There is an anecdote, connected with the reception of this young cadêt by his uncle, strongly illustrative of the spirit of nationality cherished by the expatriated Irish. It is this:

At the time he went to join his uncle, the latter was General of a division of the Austrian army, then somewhere on the French frontier. Young O'Donnell arrived and slept at a convent in the neighbourhood, where there were some Irish priests. On the following morning he started for the Austrian camp; but, to the surprise of the friars, who knew the object of his journey, he returned to them in the evening in a very disconsolate humour.

"Did you see your uncle?" inquired his friends. "Yes."

"Well, what reception did he give you?" "Cold enough; he refused to acknowledge me."

"Why?" "I don't know, unless it was because I spoke English to him."

"How was that? Come, tell us all about it." "When I was introduced into his tent, he embraced me warmly, and spoke most kindly to me, and inquired about home, and my journey, and how I'd like to be a soldier. But when I spoke to him in return, his manner began to change; and, after a little, he said there must be some mistake, that I could be no nephew of his; to return here, and he'd find means of sending me back to Ireland."

"What language did he address you in?" "He spoke in Irish."

"And you?" "I answered him in English."

"Don't you speak Irish, then?" "To be sure I do, better than English; but, though he spoke Irish, I thought he'd understand the other better."

"Oh! you foolish boy; go back, *speak nothing but Irish*, and he'll soon discover his mistake." The advice was good. The youngster stayed in Germany.

This anecdote was related, as the Editor has been informed, by a clergyman who had been many years in France, and heard it there.

This nationality seems hereditary in the name. Generations of foreign birth do not weaken it. The Editor has seen, in a letter written this year (1847) by one of the family in Germany (the great-grandson of one of the parties in the above anecdote) to a relative in Ireland (the grand-nephew of the other), the following passage, which shews this clearly:

"Un descendant du fondatrice du convent Irlandais à Rome—malheureusement j'ai oublie son nom, s'est approprié l'Epeé de Roderic, et l'emporta en Irlande, pour la placer peut-etre dans quelque cabinet de curiosités. Tachez de la réclamer, car personne que nous qui sommes des O Donnel n'a le droit de la posseder. Ce sacrilege a été commis il a quelques années. Tachez à tout prix de la ravoir. Qu'elle reste en Irlande, et chacun de nous viendra la voir." And again: ". . . car quoiqu' éléves en Autriche, nous n'en avons pas moins les cœurs Irlandais."

sequence, it was natural that I, being no more now in Bavaria, your [letter] must have run a long time before it came to me hands. It is true that I was Commander of a Free Corps and in quarters in Bavaria; but his Majesty the Emperor, having thought it proper to remodel the Free Corps in his Army, I am now six months neither Commander of a Free Corps, nor in Bavaria.

"I am very glad to have received at length news from Irlande. Having quitted that country as a child, I was not able to keep up with the parents[b] I had there, the correspondence that in the following I strived fruitlessly to have with them. While me uncle in Spain[c] was a-live, he wrote exactly to his brother[d] in this country: which lives no more neither: and by that means I got now and then information of everything relative to my parents. But since his decease, I had the discomfort to hear nothing no more of them. It was by that uncle I had in Spain, that I knew my brother Joseph's returning to Irelande from the Spanish service wherein he was; of his marriage in Irelande; of his going to Sancta Cruze; finally of his dieing there. I feel very deep all the troubles which oppressed that poor brother, and I am concerned of the affliction to which, as his spouse, they must have delivered you up. As for your son, Joseph, my nephew, I am most ready to do for him all that lies in my power. Nevertheless, the occasion to make him enter the Imperial service, at this moment, is not the best. A war of six years that we had, and was finished for some [time more] than a year, filled up the Army with so much supernumerary officers, that now there is but slight advancement to be got; my nephew, consequently, would have no hopes of a promotion for a good while, whatsoever could be his good qualities. As I am situated at the present, having no regiment, and only serving in the army, I could directly be of no use to him. My opinion is, therefore, my dear Sister, that Joseph should not quit Irelande. The tranquillity being now reestablished in the kingdom, it will permit him to pursue some profession, and if he applies himself to it, he will certainly make more fortune there than by soldiership. Yet, should a war begin, which our political situation makes probable, and that my nephew would persiste to become a soldier, supposing that he is endowed with the strong constitution necessary in military state, I will charge myself of him with great pleasure, making no doubt that, if war breaks out, I will get a regiment to commande, wherein I will be able to place him.

"Having the intention to send my sister Elise five hundert florins of our money, which is 58 pounds, or thereabout, and to renew to her every year, I pray you, my dear sister-in-law, to informe me on which Banker in Dublin it would be the more convenient to let that money be paid. In the first letter you will write me, be so kind to give me an exact account of my family, of which I have got no news since a too long a while. When did my poor Mother die? Tho' I was a child as I seperated from her, I remember me of her with tenderness. What a misfortune it is to be in the necessity to quit one's own country, and to be exposed to the discomfort to never see no more the dear and respectable persons to which we are beholden of our existence. My father's decease happened some years after my going abroad. You would please me highly by giving me some accounts of my brother, Hugo, established in Sancta Cruse, and in informing me of the manner I should direct to him, that I might hope to get an answer from him. I often

[b] *Parents.*—He doubtlessly meant "relatives," from the French "*parens.*"

[c] *Uncle in Spain.*—General Don Joseph O'Donnel, his father's second brother.

[d] *Brother.*—Count Henry O'Donell, the third brother, and ancestor of the O'Donells of Austria.

endeavoured to put myself in correspondence with him, but continually without success. I was told that General Manus O'Donel, who returned to Ireland about twenty years ago, and married himself in that country, died there not long since.

* * * * * * * * * * * * * * * * *

"I fear you will have great difficulty to understand this letter; I assure you I had very much to write it, having almost entirely forgotten the English tongue. I wish it may come to your hands; at least shall I direct it as you indicated me. Now, having nothing no more to writ to you, I finish my letter, by praying you to believe, tho I have not the pleasure to know you personally, that I am, with all my heart,

"My dear Sister-in-Law,

"Your most affectionate brother-in-law,

"CHARLES O'DONEL.

"A' Madame
Madame Marie O'Donel, à Dublin,
ou Castlebarre, en Irelande.

"Be so kind to direct me your letter:
"A' Monsieur
Monsieur Charles O'Donel, Colonel au Service
de sa Maje. Imp[l] Roy[l], à Vienne, en Autriche."

The following letter was written by Colonel O'Ferral, of the Austrian service, a brother of the late Ambrose O'Ferrall, of Ballyna, in the county of Kildare, and uncle of the Right Honourable Richard More O'Ferrall. It is addressed to the writer of the foregoing letter, and on the subject of the annuity to which it refers:

"*Florence, the 1st of October*, 1799.

"DEAR COUSIN* AND MOST WORTHY FRIEND,—The laudable and generous resolution you have made, of remitting an annual allowance to your sisters, inspires me with so much respect and admiration, that I should look upon it to be unpardonable not to do everything in my power to promote it. However, my brother only sends me my interest money once a year, and that in the month of March; and though he is very punctual in this, he don't like anticipating; therefore, till next March, I shall not be able to comply with your desire. Yet, in the mean time, you will be so good as to write to your sisters to name some person in Dublin, who is authorized to receive the money for them, because there being no bankers in the country towns, my Brother might find the same dificulty to send it to Castlebar that you did to remit it to Ireland; and then, to avoid all mistakes, send me the address as plain and sure as possible. 500 florins, at 8 flor. 30 xrs per pound, Irish, makes £58 15*s*., which is necessary for you to know in order to inform your friends of it.

"The easiest way of reimbursing me is, when you hear from them or from me, that the money has been paid in Ireland, to get the amount paid by your agent in Vienna, to Mons. Skeyde, agent de guerre, à Vienne, for my account, advising me at the same time of it. I shall also wait until

* *Dear cousin*.—They were both descended from the celebrated Rory O'More, the idol of the Irish people during the insurrection of 1641. O'Donnell in the fifth degree.—*Vide supra*.

you have got an answer from your sisters, in order to be able to give my brother proper directions in regard to this payment.

"If Siegenthal don't come, I have a fair chance of being made Colonel; but it all depends upon chance, which I, with Christian patience and resignation, wait for. Our regiment makes part of a Corps, sent under Lt. Gen. Srölich, to reestablish order in this country, and to scour the Pope's dominions; but Rome, Ancona, and Civita Vecchia, are still in the hands of the French; yet we hope they will soon surrender. You know by this, that Suwarrow is gone, with all his Russians, to Switzerland; and Melas, I fear, is not strong enough to act offensively here. I hope the English diversion will be of great use to us. In London there has been 100 guineas to 5 bet, that we shall have a general peace this winter. I am not of that opinion. I and all those who were at the Siege of Mantua have been attacked with violent agues. We lost a good many men by its consequences. I am only now recovering, and have my four servants confined to their beds with it. Farewell, my Dear, believe me most sincerely,

"Your affectionate Kinsman and humble Servant,

"—— O'Ferrall[f].

"Endorsed
Reçu le 18 Xbre."

In 1803 we find Colonel O'Donel promoted to the rank of General, and on the revival of the war, that his nephew, after the manner of his fathers, preferred "soldiership," with all its toils, to any other profession.

"*Balyna, Clonard, 24th Feb.*, 1803.

"Dear Madam,—I received your letter of the 11th January, and in the melancholy situation I have been in these six weeks past, with my eldest sister dying, I must candidly acknowledge I quite forgot to answer it. My Brother has been here since the 15th October, and leaves us on Tuesday next, to embark in three or four days after on his route to Vienna. General O'Donel is now stationed at Lembergh in Poland, where he has a command. He wrote to my Brother above a year ago, desiring him not to pay any more money to his sisters, as he expected his nephew, on whose education and advancement he proposed laying out the money he heretofore remitted them. I remain, dear Madam,

"Your faithful humble Servant,

"Amb. O'Ferrall.

"To Mrs. Mary O'Donel, 35, North
Gt. George's-street, Dublin."

But the intentions of the one and the wishes of the other were destined not to be fulfilled, for on his way to his uncle, the nephew, on reaching Hamburgh, was detained for several months a prisoner; at the end of which period he, together with several other British subjects, was sent back to England; and the year following his return the news of General O'Donel's death, he having been mortally wounded at the battle of Neresheim, put an end to any further views of his entering the Austrian service.

[f] *O'Ferrall.*—Christian name illegible.

"*Clonard, 27th Aug.*, 1806.

"DEAR MADAM,—I have to request you will have the goodness to inform me who is the heir at law of your brother-in-law, the late General Charles O'Donel, and to favour me with his or her address. I have the honour to be, dear Madam,

"Your most obedient and very humble Servant,

"AMB. O'FERRALL."

"To Mrs. M. O'Donel, 35, Great George's-st. North, Dublin."

"*Ballyna, Clonard, 4th Sept.*, 1806.

"DEAR MADAM,—I am favoured with your's of the 1st Instant, and have to inform you that your brother-in-law died intestate, and that his next heir should write to His Excellency Count O'Donel[*], who will be able to let him know the situation of his affairs, and the value of the effects he left, which, as he was equipped as a General in campaign, cannot be inconsiderable. I remain, dear Madam,

"Your most obedient and very humble Servant,

"AMB. O'FERRALL.

"To Mrs. M. O'Donel."

"P. S.—Count O'Donel's address:

"A'. S. E. Monsieur Le Comte O'Donel, Conseiller intime et Chambellan de S. M. Imp'. R'. Apostolique à Leopol en Gallicie."

As he died without issue and unmarried, his heirs were of course his sisters and his nephew; but, as appears by the annexed translation of the legal document, or power of attorney, referred to in the following letter, the last was also heir to his title, according to the law of Germany:

"*Ballyna, 8th October*, 1806.

"DEAR MADAM,—I have the pleasure of sending you the enclosed, which will put you under the necessity of looking out for a person versed in the German language to copy it off, and then you will please to conform yourself to the instructions at the foot of it. I remain, dear Madam,

"Your most obedient, humble Servant,

"AMB. O'FERRALL.

"To Mrs. M. O'Donel, 35, North Gt. George's-st., Dublin."

"For the well-born Herr Joseph Von Skeyde, chief war agent in Vienna, by which the same, in best form of law, is hereby empowered by us, the declared legitimate heirs at law of our Herr brother and respected uncle, Herr Major General Charles Count O'Donel, deceased from wounds on the 16th October, 1805, to deliver in name and lieu of us the declaration of inheritance to the inheritance left by the said Charles Count O'Donel, *cum beneficio legis et inventaris*, before a worshipful *judicio delegato militari mixto* in Austria, or where else it may be requisite to transact all oral as well as written business, to take up the inheritance, to acquit the same, to give out Reversales,

[*] *Count O'Donel.*—Joseph Count O'Donnell (Henry's eldest son), Minister of Finance to Francis I.

and to take measures for all that it would be incumbent on ourselves to do: which things we not only do and promise to indemnify him, the said Herr, chief war agent, but also impart to him the further power that in case of prevention, and if he in this case for any reason be unable to take upon himself these things, that he be authorized to substitute in lieu of himself any other Lawyer he please.

"Further, to testify this deed, have we signed this with our hands, and made the impressions of our armorial seals:

"N. N.
N. N. } Sisters of Intestate.
"(*Seal*) JOSEPH COUNT O'DONEL,
The Nephew of Intestate.
"Or, instead thereof, if requisite:
"N. N. legally declared Guardian of the Minor,
Herr Graff [i. e. Count] Joseph O'Donel."

The attestation ran as follows:

"Notum facimus atque testamur tenore præsentium, hoc mandatum procuratorium ab hæredibus legitimis defuncti Caesareo Regii Generalis vigiliarum Praefecti Domini Comitis Caroli O'Donel coram nobis personaliter constitutis, nempe ejusdem sororibus atque nepote ex fratre Domino Josepho Comite O'Donel (vel tutore Domini Comitis Josephi O'Donel), manu sigilloque propriis munitum fuisse.

"Datum, &c."

X. JOSEPH O'DONEL (eldest son of Manus as above) was born in or about the year 1751. As soon as he was of sufficient age to enter the army, he was sent out to Spain, to his uncle, Joseph, then a most distinguished officer in the service of Charles III., and where, of course, he was sure of promotion. In 1776 he had attained the rank of captain, when the fatal termination to a duel, in which he was a principal, involved him in those troubles to which his brother, Charles, refers in a letter already quoted (p. 2406). The rank of his adversary was sufficiently exalted to make it necessary for him to quit Spain. He returned to Ireland in the end of that year. In 1779 he married Mary, daughter of Dominick Mac Donnell, Esq., of Massbrook, in the county of Mayo (she died 1831), whose sister, Bridget, married Captain Lewis O'Donel of Newcastle, in the same county (*vide ante*, p. 2396). In 1781 he sailed for the West Indies, to join his brother, Hugh, at Vera Cruz, from which he wrote a letter, still preserved, to his young wife in Castlebar, and where he died soon after from the effects of climate. He left behind in Ireland an only son,

XI. JOSEPH MANUS O'DONEL of Castlebar, in the county of Mayo, who was born in 1780. Desirous to enter a foreign service, arrangements were made with his uncle, General Charles Count O'Donel, that he should enter the Austrian service under him; but it was not till 1803 that he started for Germany. The result has been already stated. On his return to this country he became a lawyer, and, strange to say, neglected to look after the money and the title of his uncle, to both which he was the true heir. He married Margaret, daughter of the late Randal Mac Donnell, Esq., of Ballycastle, in the same county. He died in August, 1834, aged 54, and is buried in the family vault at Straid Abbey, leaving issue one daughter, Mary, who died unmarried, August, 1843, aged 34; and three sons:

XII. MANUS LEWIS O'DONEL, Esq., of Castlebar, born 1812, the present representative of Con Oge, the brother of Sir Niall Garv, and the true heir of General Charles O'Donel, who was slain at Neresheim in 1805; 2. Charles Joseph O'Donel, Esq., Barrister at law, born 1818; and 3. Lewis, born in 1824.

THE O'DONNELS OF SPAIN.

It is to the Editor a subject of deep regret that he has been unable to procure as full and authentic details of the modern history of this family, as might enable him to enter as fully into the subject as the position of that family and its historic celebrity would demand. During the last forty years of almost incessant war in the Peninsula, few names have more frequently than their's been mixed up with some of the brightest as well as some of the most melancholy events of that period; and perhaps few families in Spain have suffered more from the evils attendant upon civil war. The following notices are brief, but, as far as the Editor can ascertain, they are strictly correct.

IX. JOSEPH O'DONNEL, second son of Charles, or Calvagh Duv, was born about the year 1725, and at a suitable age entered the Spanish service. In the army of Spain the O'Donnells were as sure of rank and promotion as the nobles of Castile; for since the time when Hugh Roe was received with regal ceremony in the mountains of Asturias, and entombed with regal pomp in the church of Valladolid, there was sure to be found, in the Court of Spain, and high in the favour of its Sovereigns, some one of the tribe of the great Irish chieftain. He is described in the Austrian pedigree (which is dated 1767), as "Josephus (filius Caroli, filii Hugonis O'Donell et Margarithæ O'Neill) in servitio Hispanico Capitaneus." What the particulars of his career were, the Editor has been unable to learn; for although it is evident from the letter of his nephew, General Charles O'Donel (quoted *supra*, p. 2406), that a constant correspondence existed between him and his relations in Ireland and Germany, there appears to be no trace of it now remaining. It is said that he attained to the very highest rank in the army, and that he intermarried into one of the proudest families in Spain; however that may be, it is certain that he left four sons, who, when the British army landed in the Peninsula, in 1807, held high commissions in the Spanish service, and were much distinguished during the war. Their names were: 1. Henry; 2. Charles; 3. Joseph; and 4. Alexander.

X. DON HENRY, Conde d'Abisbal, was born in or about the year 1770; for he was yet a child when his cousin, Joseph, returned to Ireland in 1776[h]. On the invasion of Spain by the French, he was a general officer, and had a command in the eastern provinces. At the famous siege of Gerona, in 1809, he cooperated with Blake in trying to raise the siege; and when it was converted into a blockade, and when, "amid famine and pestilence, the inhabitants, with the highest, rarest, and noblest description of courage, still remained unshaken, hoping the best, yet prepared to brave the worst,—looking for succour, but determined on resistance,—relief arrived.

[h] *In* 1776.—This would appear from an anecdote that states, that, from a description given by Captain Joseph O'Donel, on his return to Ireland, to Lady O'Donel (the wife of the first Sir Neal), of the dress of his little Spanish cousins, she had her twin sons, Neal and Connell, clad in a similar costume.

General O'Donnel, with one hundred and sixty mules loaded with provisions, succeeded, on the side of Bispal, in breaking through the enemy, and reaching the town. The same officer, by a bold and skilful manœuvre, subsequently succeeded in passing the besieging army, and retreating with his troops[i]." The force he selected for this duty was composed of the "*Ultonia*" regiment. In February, 1810, he was appointed to the chief command in Catalonia, where he created an army, and by his skill and courage almost rescued the province from the French :

"The skilful and daring operations in which he had successfully engaged had acquired for him the confidence of the people. Augerau had supposed that little more remained, after the reduction of Gerona, than to complete and rivet the subjection of the province. In this he was mistaken. A combat took place in the neighbourhood of Vich, between a body of Spaniards, under O'Donnel, and the division of General Souham. The former bore themselves with courage, and assailed the enemy with a steadiness and resolution to which they were unaccustomed. Never, by the confession of their own officers, was the courage of the French army more severely tested than in this action. O'Donnel, however, at length judged it prudent to retire, leaving the enemy in possession of the field. Souham, imagining the Spaniards had fled from fear, prepared to pursue. O'Donnel then commenced a series of skilful manœuvres, by which, having led his enemy forward, he succeeded in achieving several brilliant and important successes. The French losses in these engagements were very heavy ; and they were still further aggravated by desertions from the foreign troops, who went over to the enemy in considerable numbers. These results were far from satisfactory to Napoleon. Marshal Augerau had boasted, in his despatches, that the Ampurdau was completely subdued ; but the comment of succeeding facts on this assertion had not been favourable to its credit with the Emperor, and Augerau was superseded by Marshal Mac Donald[k]."

So precarious was the tenure by which, in a short time, the French army maintained its hold in Catalonia, that in July, the same year, Marshal Mac Donald was compelled to array his whole force for the escort of a convoy :

"While Mac Donald was engrossed in this service, O'Donnel was not inactive. He attacked the French force near Granollers with great impetuosity, and succeeded in gaining an advantage, which would have been decisive, had the Somatenes, who received orders to attack the enemy in rear in the heat of the engagement, obeyed their instructions. As it was, the convoy succeeded, but with difficulty, in reaching Barcelona[l]."

On the 10th of September he marched on Mataro, with the intention of attacking the position of Mac Donald at Cervera ; and on the 14th "succeeded, by a brilliant manœuvre, in surprising the brigade of General Schwartz, which occupied Bisbal and the neighbouring villages. The French made a gallant, though vain, resistance. Not a man escaped ; all who did not fall by the sword were made prisoners, and Schwartz himself was in the number of the latter. This was the last achievement of O'Donnel in Catalonia. He received a wound in the engagement which made it necessary he should resign the command ; and the Marquis of Campoverde was appointed his successor. The success of Bisbal diffused energy and spirit throughout the whole population of the province[m]."

[i] *Retreating with his troops.*—Napier's History of the Penin. War; and Annals of the Penin. War, vol. ii. p. 272.

[k] Ib. vol. ii. p. 303.

[l] Ib. vol. iii. p. 12.

[m] Ib. vol. iii. p. 14.

For this he was created the Conde d'Abisbal. In 1812 he was named a member of the Regency; but towards the close of the war rejoined the army, and commanded at the capture of Pancorvo. On the return of Ferdinand VII. his full rank was confirmed, and fresh honours bestowed on him. After holding the command of the army of the Bidoassa, he was placed at the head of the troops destined for the expedition against South America, who demanded to be led by him, and no other. In the subsequent meeting of the force at Cadiz, it was alleged by his enemies that he acted an equivocal part, by first siding with the mutineers, and afterwards betraying them; but no evidence appears to establish or even support this. It is highly probable, however, that he was connected with the Constitutional party in 1819. After the Restoration, the Conde d'Abisbal retired to France, and died at Montpelier, May 17, 1834. He had issue one son:

1. Leopold, Conde d'Abisbal, in the late civil war, a Christino and a Colonel in the Queen's service. In the battle of Alsazua he was taken prisoner; and the following day, at Echerri-Aranaz, he was taken out and shot in cold blood, by orders of Zumalacarragui. He died without issue. The title is extinct.

2. Don Carlos O'Donnel, the second son, was also a General in the Peninsular war, or, as it is called in Spain, the war of Independence. He was a staunch Royalist. At the battle of Murviedro, the 25th October, 1811, he commanded the centre of the Spanish army:

"By an oversight of Blake, the left wing was so widely detached, that the centre was inconsiderately weakened. Suchet immediately took advantage of this error, and directed a powerful attack on the Spanish centre, in order to isolate the wings. In this point the Spaniards fought with desperate bravery, and, though at first forced to retire, were again rallied by their leader, and drove back the enemy with signal courage. Receiving, however, no support from the wings, the centre was obliged at length to give way; but by a skilful disposition of cavalry, which continued to shew front to the enemy, the infantry retired in perfect order[n]."

At the peace he was made Captain-General of Old Castile. During the late war he was a Carlist. He had four sons,—three Carlists, and one Christino: 1. The eldest, Pepe, accompanied Don Carlos to Portugal, and passed through England, and afterwards organized the Carlist cavalry. He was killed while pursuing a party of Carbineers into Pampeluna. 2. The second, a Carlist, was made prisoner and confined in Barcelona, whence he was taken out and barbarously massacred by the populace. (Charles O'Donnel, the father, is believed to have died of a broken heart on hearing the fate of his two sons.) 3. The third joined Don Carlos in Guipuscoa, August, 1836. 4. The fourth, Don Leopold, a Christino, was one of the most conspicuous Generals during the late war. He commanded the army of the north, while the British Legion was in Spain, and was prominently engaged in the principal operations of the war, in which he was wounded more than once. On the final success of the Queen's forces he was appointed Captain-General of Cuba, one of the highest offices under the Crown (an appointment he still holds), and received the title of Count de Lucena.

3. Don José O'Donnell, the third son, was also a General and a Royalist. In the battle of Castalla in 1812, between the French and allies, he commanded the Spanish army. In the war of the Constitution in 1820, he commanded the lines of San Roquet, and attacked Riego in Andalusia. On the success of the Constitutionalists he retired into private life.

[n] Annals of the Peninsular War, vol. iii. p. 147.

4. Alexander, the fourth and youngest son, was the only one of his family who did not join the patriot side in the war of Independence. He joined the French, and commanded a Spanish regiment, to which Joseph Buonaparte gave his own name. Before the conclusion of the war, he was sent to take the command of a regiment in the unfortunate expedition to Russia. He was taken prisoner there; and the Emperor Alexander, having ordered all the Spaniards formerly belonging to the French army to be collected into one corps, which by special permission assumed his name, the command was conferred upon Colonel Alexander O'Donnel, and he sailed with his regiment for Spain. This distinction saved him, and his rank was confirmed. He has, or had, two sons (Christinos), Pepe and Emilio, both officers, in 1839, in the Urban Guards at Seville.

THE O'DONELLS OF AUSTRIA.

This illustrious family, distinguished both in the field and cabinet, are descended from—

IX. Henry O'Donell, the third son of Charles Duv, son of Hugh O'Donnell, and Margaret O'Neill[o]. He was born about the year 1729. At an early age he entered the Austrian service, and rose rapidly to distinction. He is said to have been one of the handsomest men in the Austrian army, and an especial favourite with the Empress; both which accounts seem not improbable, since we find that in the year 1754, while he was yet scarcely six-and-twenty, he received in marriage a cousin of the Empress, a princess of the illustrious House of Cantacuzeno, descendants of John Cantacuzenus, the Byzantine emperor and historian, A. D. 1246. No event can display in a more striking light than this marriage the estimation in which the great Irish families, when driven into exile, were held on the Continent, when we thus see "the greatest and proudest Queen of Europe," and in a Court that was, and is still, proverbially aristocratic, bestowing the hand of her own kinswoman on a young soldier, whose only fortune were his sword and his pedigree. In 1767 (the date of the Austrian O'Donell Genealogy quoted above), he was "Camerarius Cæsarei ordinis milit. Mariæ Theresæ," and Colonel of a corps of cuirassiers, which from him was called "The O'Donell Regiment[p];" a name by which, the Editor believes, it is still distinguished. Some time after his marriage, he wrote to his brother, Manus, to Ireland, to have whichever of his sons he intended sending to Austria carefully educated in the Irish language, that he might instruct his own children in the language of their ancestors; a circumstance which seems to corroborate the anecdote related in note, p. 2405. General John O'Donel thus speaks of his influence at Court:

" . . . As I told you here, you and your father should employ cousin Harry; and if he can get Lewis an agreement in the regiment he commands, it would be so much the better, for reasons known to you. Harry is very capable of bringing many things to bear that others cannot. He is particularly well with her Majesty. The last time he saw her, she gave him a very fine present of jewels for his wife, saying, 'as she would never wear any more herself, she divided them among her children, and kept those for his wife[q].'"

[o] *Ante*, p. 2404.

[p] "*The O'Donell Regiment.*"—In 1778 it was commanded by Manus O'Donel (afterwards General), as appears by the superscription of a letter to him (*vide ante*, p. 2394). "The O'Donell Regiment" afterwards formed a portion of the troops sent to cooperate with the Duke of York and the Earl of Moira, in the expedition to Holland, in 1794. It was then commanded by Henry O'Donell's nephew, General Charles O'Donell, already mentioned.

[q] There is no date of year to this letter; but this fact

He subsequently attained the rank of Lieutenant-General, and was made Count, with the title of "Graf O'Donell von Tyrconell." He left issue four sons: 1. Joseph; 2. John; 3. Charles; and 4. Henry; the three last of whom died in the Austrian service, and without issue; and one daughter, who married Count Vansovich, a Polish noble[r].

X. JOSEPH COUNT O'DONELL, born 1755, was educated for a diplomatic career. While pursuing his studies, he became acquainted with his cousin, Therese, the daughter of Count John O'Donel[s] of the Larkfield family, and it appears they became mutually attached to each other, to the great derangement of her father's plans for her establishment; for she was affianced at the time to General Manus O'Donel, then on leave of absence in Ireland, and for whom her father seems to have entertained the sincerest friendship. The Editor has already given, in a previous part of this Appendix, some letters from the same correspondent by whom the following were written; but these he reserved to place in a position more appropriate to the subject to which they relate. Neither letter bears the date of the year in which it was written, but from the political event referred to in the second, namely, the recent accession of Polish territory, the Editor would ascribe its date to 1772, as, on the 5th of August in that year, by the treaty of Petersburgh, Gallicia and Lodomiria were ceded to Austria; and from the same letter, it is evident that the first was written the preceding June. They also appear, from the allusion to the Court, to have been written from Vienna. Taking this date for granted, we cannot be surprised that the veteran soldier was beaten from the field by the young diplomatist, since the former must have been close on his sixtieth year[t] (that is, nearly as old as her father), while the latter was in his eighteenth.

"*27th June.*" [*Vienna*, 1772.—ED.]

"MY DEAR COUSIN,—The pleasure I had in receiving your last letter, *without date*[u], would certainly have engaged me to answer you immediately, were I not detained for some time by a little contradiction I found myself in with her Majesty about the time of your arrival here. You'll remember I informed you my desire of having Therese transferred to a convent of this town, but would wait your answer, to know when you intended to be here, before I would put myself in her Majesty's way, imagining she would ask me about you, which I did till the end of April. Then the gentlewoman she sent in the beginning to bring my daughter to Presbourg, let me know that her Majesty was to go in a couple of days to that town; and, as she would probably see Therese, thought it was proper I should shew myself at Court, believing the Empress would fain speak to me. Accordingly I went to Court, and found by the *Chambellan de Service*, that her Majesty said, if I came there, he should tell me to wait. After she had dispatched some ministers, I was called for. Her first words were to ask for you with a sort of amazement that made me imagine she might have heard of a rumour spread here a considerable time before, of your being marryed in Ireland; yet as she did not directly mention it, and that I myself gave no credit to it, I did not seem to understand anything of the kind, but took occasion to enlarge a little on your zeal for her

shews it was subsequent to and about 1765, the year of the Emperor's death; after which, it is said, the Queen sunk into deep melancholy. Thus confirming the date already assigned to it, 1766.

[r] Austrian Pedigree.

[s] *Ante*, p. 2398.

[t] *His 60th year.*—He died 1793, aged eighty years.—See his epitaph, p. 2396, *supra*.

[u] *Without date.*—A strange reproach from the writer of these letters, who gives only the day of the month himself.

service, your candour and good nature for me and my children; assured her that you would be here at farthest about the middle of Summer; and that, if her Majesty approved of it, I would be desirous, in the mean time, to transfer my daughter to a convent of this town, which she not only approved, but said she was very glad I found such a good *partie* for my child: '*qui lui servirait même de Pere*[w].' I told her I thought myself happy to know her so well established[x]. '*Oui, dit Elle, est ce qu'il apporte bien bien de quoi avec?*' I said you were well in your affairs, that I did not know how much you would bring along with you at present, but knew your desire was to take all you had out of that country, provided you could find means to bring it to bear, which I feared would be very difficult. Then she asked me if I was sure you would come. I said I was very sure. '*Eh bien, dit Elle, je vais à Presbourg demain, si vous avez la patience d'attendre mon retour et que vous voulez me confier votre fille, je vous la s'amenerai,*' which she did, and, giving her a dinner at Shönbrun, sent her in the afternoon to the Convent of St. Laurent, where she awaits your arrival. Some days after I received your good-natured letter; but as your stay is longer than I had foreseen, and contrary to the assurances I gave her Majesty, I went to Princess Esterhazy, and pray'd her to excuse me to her Majesty, and inform her of the circumstances; which she took upon her. I told this lady your intention was to come last year, but that I advised you myself not to derange or be detrimental to your affairs by coming so soon, but should rather wait till all was on a proper footing. She performed the commission, but somewhat slow, so that 'tis only a few days since she told me, that she informed her Majesty of all those particulars; that her Majesty was satisfied, saying, she knew I would not tell her anything but what was truth; and that you did very well to settle your affairs, particularly as you took a wife; and laughed at my concern. In short, this is what hindered me from expressing immediately to you the real satisfaction your letter gave me. Therese and I agree with all our hearts to the marriage articles. Her conduct is so good that I find every comfort in her I could wish. She will be a comfort to you. She is yours',—you are her's; and God Almighty bless you both. She and I am truly acknowledging for your memory of her and Hugo. It is a proof of your good nature; but we hope and pray God will preserve your life for our greater comfort. My dear Manus, I am now at the end of the 60th year of my age, my head and my health in general weakening daily; still I hope God will spare my life to see you and Therese happy together. Come, my Dear, as soon as you possibly can, without neglecting your affairs. Write immediately to Therese or to me. Hugo joins in our embraces to you, and we are, with heart and hand,

"Your own for ever,

"O'Donel.

"O'Ferral[y] is well, and Brochanzer, whom I saw three days agoe, says everything good of him. My sincere friendship to O'More[z] and my Mother-in-law, when you see them.

"To the Honourable Count Magnus O'Donel, Major-General in their Imp[l] Majesties' Service; at Newcastle, near Castle-Barre, Ireland."

[w] *De Pere.*—The Empress was a wit.

[x] *Well established.*—General Manus was very wealthy; his father, Charles Roe, of Newcastle, having acquired a large fortune.

[y] *Vide ante*, p. 2407.

[z] *O'More.*—Probably Manus O'Donell's grandfather, or uncle. His mother was Catherine O'Moore of Ballina, in the county of Kildare.

Here we have in real life some of the elements of a first-rate story :—a father, an old warrior, betrothing his (of course blooming and beautiful) daughter to his friend and comrade in arms, not much younger than himself, and taking for granted, because the latter is excessively acceptable to himself, he must be equally agreeable to the fair *fiancèe ;* an Empress for a confidant, evidently not over well inclined to the match, the young lady being somewhat of a protegé, and perhaps other views entertained for her ; an illustrious Princess as peace-maker ; a convent for a bower ; and, strangest of all, the lovely heroine agreeing to the arrangement "with all her heart." Certainly the last incident, though it be the most strange, seems to make the whole thing common-place enough ; and if the assurance were from herself, we might despair of any result sufficiently worthy of such promising materials; but since it happens that young ladies in convents are rarely consulted in matters of the kind by their more experienced parents (being supposed not to have any wish *pro* or *con* upon the subject), it is not only possible, but very probable, that Mademoiselle, though aware of the engagement, might have had but little sympathy in all the tender embraces so warmly transmitted in her name. Nor would we, in coming to that conclusion, be much mistaken. "*L'homme propose, dieu dispose.*" Fathers will make matches to please themselves, and daughters will spoil them for an equally good reason. Here is the dénouement :

"*Xbre, the 25th.*" [*Vienna*, 1772.—Ed.]

"It will appear surprising to you, my dear Manus, to be so long without any answer to your last letter of ye 11th Xbre, which the confusion and trouble of mind I have been in this long time past has occasioned. However, friendship and sincerity do not permit me to conceal any longer from you a circumstance that you seem'd to foresee and hint in y^r^ letters to me, but that I must own that I did not apprehend, which shews that you are a better judge of the female kind than I. Therese has broke thro' the measures you were so kind to combine with me for her establishment by declaring she would chuse rather to remain single all her life than to marry any other than Harry's eldest son. This young man was with me in my house the whole last winter, frequenting the *Chancellerie* to make himself fit for employment in that part of Poland our Court has acquired of late. He was still with me when I got my daughter transferred to a convent of this town, as I was expecting your arrival in June or July following ; but, soon after her arrival, you informed me of your longer stay in that country. These two young people saw one another sometimes in my house, when I had her to dinner now and then. They took a mutual liking to each other, without letting me know it other than by their looks and countenances, which I observed, and, questioning the girl, her confusion and tears explained her sentiments. At last she owned she had a great inclination for him, but, knowing my engagements with you, and how intent I was upon it, her intention was to overcome, if possible, her inclinations, and sacrifice them and herself rather than displease or disobey me, &c. I told her there was no question of such efforts in regard to you or me ; that you would be as far from taking her against her will as I would be from imposing her on you, if I found or thought she had not for you all the sentiments you deserved. She said, she was and ever would be very acknowledging of your good-natured intentions for her ; but that if she got leave to follow her choice, it would be never to marry if she could not get Monsieur Peppi[a]. I told her, it never was my desire to compel her wishes in that respect ; but that she

[a] *Peppi.*—Peppi or Pepe, the short familiar name for Joseph, from the Italian *Giuseppe.*

would do well to put such notions out of her head, whereas she could not expect to get that young man; that I had no fortune to give her, and that his father had two or three matches in view for him already on his arrival in Poland; that she should dine no more with me till he was off, remain in her convent, set her mind at rest, and let me know her thoughts hereafter. I gave him to understand my displeasure, without entering into any particulars. He took other lodgings, but attempted several times to come to an explanation, which I always avoided, till about a couple of days before his setting off for Poland, he surprised me in my room, and with a transport of tenderness threw himself in my arms, begging I should forgive him the sentiments he could not hinder himself to conceive for my daughter; that he was persuaded you would have nothing against it; and beseeching I would write to his father, who, though he had other parties in view for him, would prefer his happiness, &c. &c. I told him, tho' I knew you would be as far from taking her (knowing she preferred another) as I would be from giving, or advising you to take her, yet it was not my business to write to his father, nor would I ever any more write about her to any one after you. Now I know not as yet what Harry will or can do. Therese persists in her sentiments, and refused since his departure a very advantageous proposal made me for her by a nobleman, whose birth and fortune would establish her spelendidly, without pretending to a farthing from me while I lived; but she will hear of no one but Monsieur Peppi. I must own I had a great reluctance to write to you on this subject, and waited hitherto to see what turn her mind would take after his departure; but finding she persists, and reflecting it may be of consequence to you to be informed of it, as well in regard to the settling your affairs, or perhaps other views of matrimony you might have in that country, I now acquaint you of all, with the same sincerity I had recommended her to you, as long as I thought her heart corresponded with mine, and that she would be a suitable partner for you, without which, as I told you often before, the views of establishing my child would never engage me to undertake imposing on any one, much less on so dear a friend as you, and hope this female flirt will not alter your friendship for me, as it rather augments mine for you.

"I hope you will soon write to me, and send me your commands, if any you have hereabouts. My children join with me in best wishes for your prosperity in all respects; and be assured that no one can be with more truth and affection than I, my dearest Cousin,

"Your faithful friend, kinsman, and servant,

"O'DONEL."

As the conclusion of this letter would indicate, so was the event. Joseph O'Donell is recorded in their pedigree as having married Therese, the daughter of General Count John O'Donell, and by whom he had issue one son, Maurice (of whom presently). His wife dying, he subsequently married Josephine of Geisruch (a noble Styrian family, of which the late Cardinal Archbishop of Milan was also a member), by whom he had issue one son and two daughters (all living): Count Henry, born 12th June, 1804, Imperial Chamberlain and Councillor of State in the Government of Trieste; 2. the Countess Eveline, born 23rd December, 1805; and 3. the Countess Adela, born 3rd February, 1807, and married 21st December, 1829, to Charles Count Sturgk. Count O'Donell was eminently successful in his diplomatic career. In 1805 he was Chamberlain of the Palace and Privy Councillor, and was afterwards Minister of Finance to the Emperor Francis I. He was succeeded by his eldest son:

XI. Maurice Count O'Donell, a General in the Austrian service, and (k. k. Kamm. und FML), married, 6th November, 1811, Christine de Ligne, daughter of Prince Charles de Ligne; she was born January 4, 1788. He died December 1, 1843, leaving issue two sons and a daughter:

1. Maximilian, Count O'Donell of Tyrconnell, born 29th October, 1812.

2. Count Maurice, born 6th June, 1815. Married 18th July, 1844, Helen, Princess of Cantacuzeno, born 18th September, 1819. She died in the second year of her marriage, leaving issue one son, Henry Charles George Joseph, born 2nd July, 1845.

3. The Countess Euphemia, born 13th March, 1823.

In the German Peerage of the *Almanac de Gotha*, the present family are given as follows:

" O'Donell.

[Kath. —— Oesterreich.]

"A. Maximilian Karl Lamoral Graf O'Donell von Tyrconell, geb. 29 Oct. 1812, k. k. Rittmeister bei Bar. Mengen Cuir. Nr. 4.

Geschwister.

"1. Maria Karl Johann, geb. 6 Juni, 1815, verm. 18. Juli, 1844. mit. Helene geb. Furstin Kantakuzeno. geb. 18 Sept. 1819. Sohn: Heinrich Karl Georg Joseph, geb. 2 Juli, 1845.

"2. Euphemia, geb. 13. Marz. 1823.

Mutter.

"Grafin Christine geb. de Ligne, T. des † Fursten Karl de Ligne, geb. 4 Januar, 1788, verm. 6. Nov. 1811. mit Moris Grafen O'Donell (k. k. Kamm. und FML), dessen Witwe seit 1 Dec. 1843.

"B. Graf Heinrich. geb. 12 Juni, 1804, k. k. Kamm. und Hofrath beim Gubernium zu Triest.

Schwestern.

"1. Eveline, geb. 23 Dec. 1805.

"2. Adelheid, geb. 3 Febr. 1807, StkrD., verm. 21 Dec. 1829, mit. Karl Grafen Sturgh."

That the reader may see at a glance how the different families in Ireland, Spain, and Austria, descended from Charles or Calvagh Duv (the son of Hugh, son of Calvagh Roe, son of Manus, son of Con Oge, the brother of Niall Garv, *the last inaugurated O'Donnell*), stand related to each other, the following genealogical table is subjoined:

1. Calvagh Duv or Black Charles O'Donel, m. Mary, d. of Col. Manus O'Donel of Newport.

- 2. Manus.
  - 3. Joseph, Capt. Spanish service.
    - 4. Joseph.
      - 5. Manus O'Donel, Esq. of Castlebar, now the representative of Con Oge, the brother of Sir Niall Garv, Baron of Lifford.
  - 3. General Charles, killed at Neresheim in 1805.
- 2. Joseph, from whom the O'Donnels of Spain.
  - 3. Henry Conde de Abispal.
    - 4. Leopold Conde de Abispal, sl. *s. p.*
  - 3. Charles.
    - 4. Leopold Count de Lucena, General Governor of Cuba, now living.
- 2. Henry, from whom the O'Donnells of Austria.
  - 3. Joseph Count O'Donell.
    - 4. Maurice Count O'Donell, m. Christina, d. of Prince Charles de Ligne.
      - 5. Maximilian Count O'Donell of Tirconnell, now living.

PEDIGREE OF O'DOHERTY.

This family was the most powerful of the Kinel-Connell next after the O'Donnells; and though they remain in respectable circumstances, and exceedingly numerous, their pedigree has been neglected. The Editor has not been able to continue the line of the chiefs of this family beyond Sir Cahir, who was slain in 1608; but he is satisfied there are collateral branches whose pedigrees could be proved by the aid of local tradition and recorded documents. The following line was copied by the Editor from the dictation of a fine old man named John O'Doherty, at Bree, in the parish of Cloonca, barony of Inishowen, and county of Donegal, in August, 1835, when this John was in the eightieth year of his age. He said that it was the constant tradition in the country that Conor-an-einigh, or the hospitable O'Doherty, was the first of the name who became full Chief of Inishowen, and that from him he was the twelfth in descent. The names of the generations were well known and written in his grandfather's time, and were as follows:

1. Conor-an-einigh O'Doherty, the twenty-seventh in descent from Niall of the Nine Hostages, d. 1413.

2. Donnell, d. 1440.	2. Hugh.
3. Brian Duv, d. 1496.	3. John More.
4. Conor Carragh, d. 1516.	4. Cormac Carragh.
5. Felim.	5. Brian Gruama.
6. John, d. 1582.	6. Cuvey.
7. John Oge.	7. Dermot.
8. Sir Cahir, sl. 1608.	8. Niall-a-churraigh.
	9. Cahir.
	10. Owen.
	11. Cahir.
	12. Donough, m. 1754.
	13. John, ætatis 80, in 1835.
	14. Donnell.
	15. John, a boy in 1835.

This is a curious specimen of traditional pedigree; but it is quite clear that it was committed to memory from a written one. Tradition scarcely ever remembers more than six generations, but in this instance John O'Doherty, No. 13, had a personal acquaintance with the generations in this line up to No. 10; Nos. 9, 8, and 7, he remembered from hearing his father and grandfather constantly speaking of them, and the remaining generations he remembered from hearing the pedigree frequently read from a manuscript.

PEDIGREE OF O'NEILL.

It has been pretty clearly ascertained that the race of Shane-an-diomais, or John the Proud O'Neill, as well as that of Hugh Earl of Tyrone, has been for a long time extinct. Colonel Gordon O'Neill, Lord Lieutenant of the county of Tyrone in 1687-88, and so celebrated in Ireland during the civil war of the Revolution, was descended from Con Bacagh, first Earl of Tyrone in the female line, and by the father's side he was descended from John O'Neill, the brother of the said Earl. He was living in 1704, when his pedigree was certified by James Tyrry, Athlone Herald and Custos Rotulorum under James II. and the Pretender. According to this herald, he was the son of Colonel Felix O'Neill, by Joanna Gordon: "filia Georgii Gordon Dynastis primi marchionis de Huntly, et Henriettæ filiæ Ducis de Lenox, Dynastis d'Aubigny et Catharinæ de Belzac de familiâ d'Entragnes in Galliâ." His father, Colonel Felix, was the son of Terentius or Turlough Oge, who was the son of Henry (by the daughter of Con Bacagh, first Earl), who was son of Henry, son of John, who was son of Con More, the father of Con Bacagh. The family of this Gordon is also extinct, as is also very probably the branch transplanted to the barony of Gallen, in the county of Mayo, already treated of.—See p. 2403, *et sequent.* But various poor families living in the mountains of Tyrone claim descent from the same stock, as was determined some years since by an impostor who forged a document purporting to be the Will of a Count O'Neill, who died abroad without issue, leaving a large sum of money to be divided in certain proportions among his relatives in Ireland, according to their nearness or remoteness to him in paternal or maternal consanguinity. Of this document the fabricator sold many copies in the mountains of Tyrone and Derry, and it created more avidity for determining the descents of the various surviving families of the O'Neills than had existed since the flight of the Earls. All the traditions were most anxiously revived, and stories were wrung from the memories of old men and women who had long forgotten to boast of their royal ancestors. Generations were counted with great skill, and the pedigrees of almost all the legitimate branches of the great fallen family were attested by affidavits before the local magistrates. Such was the power of money, the shadow of a shade of an expectation of which created so much interest in family history on this occasion! The delusion was carried on until the impostor had supplied all the houses and nearly all the cabins belonging to persons of the name O'Neill in Tyrone with copies of this document, when he suddenly disappeared, leaving the O'Neills in a state of excitement and delusion, from which the magistrates and priests could with difficulty remove them. The Editor was told this in 1834, by several of the O'Neills themselves, who acknowledged that none of the families then living attempted to name their ancestors beyond the sixth generation.

The Editor has been most anxiously inquiring for the last fourteen years to ascertain whether any of the race of Con Bacagh O'Neill, first Earl of Tyrone, still exist in Ireland, and he has satisfied himself that there are at least three septs of his descendants now in Ireland, whose descents will appear from the following pedigree:

I. Con Bacagh O'Neill. He was created Earl of Tyrone in 1542. He had a natural son, Matthew, or Ferdorcha, Baron of Dungannon, and the father of the illustrious Hugh, Earl of

Tyrone, who was created Baron of Dungannon, and whose descendants are numerous in Tyrone under the name of Mac Baron. He had also by his married wife, 1. Shane the Proud O'Neill, Prince of Tyrone, whose race is extinct; 2. Felim Caech, whose descendants are still extant.

II. Felim Caech O'Neill. He married Honora, daughter of John O'Neill of Edenduffcarrick, and had by her:

III. Turlough Breasalach, or Brassilagh, i. e. Terence of Clanbrasil, O'Neill. His territory is shewn on an old map of Ulster as in Clanbrasil, adjoining Mac Can's, on the south side of Lough Neagh. He married Annabla Ni-Reilly, by whom he had at least ten sons, named in the following order in an old pedigree in the possession of Lord O'Neill: 1. Hugh; 2. Neale; 3. Cormack; 4. Con; 5. Art; 6. Phelim; 7. Edmond Gar; 8. Turlough Oge; 9. Brian Ceann-fhionain; and 10. Ever-an-locha. These sons are mentioned in a different order by Duald Mac Firbis, who makes Felim the first and Edmond the seventh son. Fynes Moryson does not give the names of Turlough Breasalach's sons; he merely states, that "Turlogh Brasilogh, son of Phelime Hugh [caoić], *eldest* son of Con Bacco, first Earl of Tyrone," had "six sons *at least* then living and able to serve the Queen."—(Edit. of 1735, vol. i. p. 16). Again, in a note of Tyrone's forces, delivered in July, 1599, to the Lord Deputy, by Shane Mac Donnell Groome O'Donnelly, Tyrone's Marshal, it is stated that Turlough Brasil's sons had a force of 200 foote in the army of the arch-rebel. According to the vivid tradition in the county of Armagh, some of the race of this Turlough Breasalach, who were related to the Mac Cans of Clanbrasil, settled in the parish of Killeavy, in the barony of Orior, and county of Armagh; and this tradition is proved to be correct by entries in the *Cal. Cancel. Hib.*, vol. ii. p. 146, *b*, which shew that three of his sons, namely, Phelim, Cormacke, and Tirlogh Oge, received small grants of land in the barony of Orior. Of these Phelim Mac Tirlagh Brasselagh received a grant of Clontigoragh, in the parish of Killeavy. Many of the descendants of this Felim are still in the parish of Killeavy, and the pedigree of one branch of them is well known, and is as follows, as communicated to the Editor in writing by John O'Neill of Clonlum, who drew it from the most authentic sources of tradition and monuments:

IV. Felimy mac Turlough Brasilough O'Neill. He had a son,

V. Shane mac Felimy O'Neill, father of

VI. Shane Oge mac Shane. He served in O'Hanlon's regiment in 1690, and was always called Captain Shane. He married Catherine Ni-Boyle, by whom he had sixteen sons, of whom four were slain at the battle of the Boyne, and two settled at Athy, in the county of Kildare, where there are now, or were till lately, some of their descendants extant; another settled at Loughbrickland, in the county of Down, where his descendants are still extant, good Presbyterians; another settled at Cockhill, near Loughgall, in the county of Armagh, and still remain. The youngest son, Owen, remained in Killeavy.

VII. Owen mac Shane Oge O'Neill. He was thirteen years old at the Revolution. He removed from Clonlum, in the parish of Killeavy, to Ravensdale, in the county of Louth, under the patronage of his relative, Captain Redmond More O'Hanlon, and he remained there for some years, but afterwards returned to Clonlum, where he died in 1777, aged 102 years, and was buried in the old church of Killeavy. He married Isabel Ni-Cormick, by whom he had issue three sons:

1. Henry, of whom presently; 2. John; and 3. Cormac, both of whom died young; and two daughters: Kathleen, who married Randal Mac Donnell; and Catherine, who married Edmond Treanor.

VIII. Henry mac Owen O'Neill of Clonlum. He married Rose Maguiggin, by whom he had issue: Peter, No. IX.; and John, who died young; and two daughters, Mary and Bridget. He died in April, 1798, aged ninety-eight years.

IX. Peter O'Neill of Clonlum. He married Alicia Ni-Hanlon, a descendant in the fifth generation from Brian O'Hanlon of Tandragee, commonly called "Colonel Brian," and had by her four sons, viz.: Owen O'Neill, a cabinet-maker, living in Dublin in 1844, and who had then two legitimate sons, John, aged fourteen, and Henry, aged ten years; 2. John O'Neill of Clonlum, a clever, well-educated man, and the best Irish scholar in Ulster in 1835, when the Editor first saw him at Clonlum, and took down the line of his descent; he removed to England in 1843, and, in 1844, called frequently on the Editor, who supposes that he is now in New York; 3. Felix O'Neill, who died in 1835, leaving one son, Peter, fourteen years old in 1844, and living at Meigh, in the parish of Killeavy; 4. Henry; and five daughters: 1. Judith; 2. Alicia; 3. Anne; 4. Rose; 5. Sarah. Peter O'Neill died in September, 1830, aged eighty-two years, and was interred in the church of Killeavy. His wife, Alicia, whom the Editor saw in 1835, died in January, 1838, aged eighty-two years. Thus far the race of Felim mac Turlough Brassilagh, as far as the Editor has been able to trace them. Let us now return to Edmond Gar, the seventh son of the same Turlough.

IV. Edmond Gearr mac Turlough Brassilagh O'Neill. He married Anne Mac Awley, by whom he had two sons: Captain Edmond, No. V., and Henry-na-Coille, i. e. Henry of the Wood.

V. Captain Edmond O'Neill. He married Eleonora, youngest daughter of Felim Duff O'Neill, and had by her six sons, viz.: 1. Brian, No. VI.; 2. John; 3. Hugh; 4. Charles; 5. Daniel; 6. Edmond.

VI. Brian O'Neill. He married Catherine Mulvany, daughter of Alan-a-Salismore, by whom he had issue four sons, viz.: 1. Brian, No. VII.; 2. Patrick; 3. John; 4. James; and one daughter, Mary.

VII. Brian O'Neill. He married Mary, daughter of Cornelius Cary of Caryvill, and had by her three sons, viz.: 1. Edmond, No. VIII.; 2. Neale John, solicitor; 3. Patrick Charles; and five daughters: 1. Catherine; 2. Mary; 3. Bridget; 4. Susan; 5. Jane.

VIII. Edmond O'Neill. His pedigree is given in Peppard's *History of Ireland*, as Edmond O'Neill of Greencastle, in the county of Donegal, descended from Felim Caech, son of Con Bacagh; but two generations are omitted in that work, namely, Brian, No. VII., and Turlough Brassilagh, No. III. He married Alicia, daughter of Surgeon Balfour of Derry, and has by her three sons, namely: 1. Charles Henry O'Neill; 2. John B. R. O'Neill; 3. Neale Bruce O'Neill.

The foregoing descent has been obtained for the Editor by his friend the Rev. William Reeves of Ballymena, in the county of Antrim, who believes it to be correct. If it be so, and there seems no reason to doubt its authenticity, then we have to the fore, as the Rev. Mr. Reeves observes, "a fine, healthy, well-descended, and abundantly prolific family, to bear the honours of the senior branch of the race of Eoghan."

THE O'NEILLS OF CLANNABOY.

It has been stated by the Editor, under the year 1574, p. 1679, *supra*, that, after the death of the present Lord O'Neill, Hugh O'Neill of Ballymoney, in the county of Down, farmer, will be the senior representative of Brian Mac Felim, Chief of Clannaboy, who was murdered by the Earl of Essex, in 1574; but the Editor's friend, the Rev. William Reeves, of Ballymena, has discovered since that sheet was printed off, that there is another branch of this family still extant, which is nearer to Lord O'Neill than Hugh of Ballymoney, namely, Charles O'Neill, Esq., of Bracart, near the town of Antrim. This Charles, who, though he is as undoubted a scion of the noble house of Clannaboy as is Lord O'Neill himself, has no family pride whatever, and wrote on the 29th August, 1847, to his friend, Alexander O'Rourke, Esq., of Ballymena, that those who were inquiring after his pedigree were sadly out of employment, or getting light in the head! However, he has replied to queries proposed to him, from which it appears that he married, in 1817, Ellen, the daughter of William Porter, Esq., of Raheenmore, in the county of Wexford, by whom he had twelve children, of whom three sons are still living, namely, Charles, John, and Felix. His relationship to Lord O'Neill and Hugh O'Neill of Ballymoney, will appear from the following genealogical table:

1. John O'Neill of Edenduffcarrick, d. 1619.

2. Captain Felim Duv, d. 1677.	2. Arthur.	2. John Oge.
3. Brian, d. 1669.	3. Daniel.	3. Henry.
4. French John, d. 1739.	4. Luke.	4. John.
5. Charles, d. 1769.	5. Charles of Bracart.	5. Daniel.
6. John Viscount O'Neill, d. 1798.	6. Charles.	6. John.
7. John Bruce Lord Visct. O'Neill, living. He is old and unmarried, and after his death the family estates pass from the O'Neills for ever.		7. Arthur.
		8. John.
		9. Hugh O'Neill of Ballymoney.

The next heir to the property, but not to the title, of Lord O'Neill, is the Rev. William Chichester, Prebendary of St. Michael's, Dublin. He is the eldest son of the Rev. Edward Chichester, who was the son of the Rev. William Chichester, who was the son of the Rev. Arthur Chichester, by Mary O'Neill, daughter of Henry, eldest son of John O'Neill, commonly called French John; No. 4, *supra*. Nathaniel Alexander, Esq., M.P., for the county of Antrim, is more closely related to the present Lord O'Neill, being descended from Anne O'Neill, daughter of Charles O'Neill; No. 5, *supra*. Henry O'Neill, the ancestor of the Rev. William Chichester, left no male issue.

There were various other branches of this great family powerful in Ulster till the Plantation, as the Clann-Donnell Don of the Bann, the O'Neills of Coill-Iochtrach, or Killeiter, in the south of the county of Londonderry; the O'Neills of Coill-Ultach, *anglice* Killultagh, in the county of Down; the race of Henry Caech, &c.; but they have all lapsed into poverty, and their pedigrees are unknown, and perhaps for ever irrecoverable.

THE O'DONNELLYS OF BALLYDONNELLY.

It has been stated in note [m], under the year 1177, p. 33, *supra*, that Gilla-Macliag O'Donnelly, chief of Feara-Droma, who was slain at Downpatrick that year, by Sir John De Courcy, was seated in the present county of Tyrone. This assertion, which the Editor grounded on the assumption that the Feara-Droma were always seated at Carn Maca Buachalla, or Baile-Ua-nDonnghaile[b], which is described in an ancient Irish historical tale, entitled *Caithreim Chongail Clairingnigh*, the Triumphs of Congal Clairingneach, as situated in the very centre of Ulster. This story, however, appears to have been remodelled in the thirteenth or fourteenth century, as is clear from Baile-Ui-nDonnghaile being given as the modern name of Carn Maca Buachalla ; but nothing has been yet discovered to fix the exact period at which the family of O'Donnelly first settled at this place. The pedigree of Gilla-Macliag O'Donnelly, above referred to, is given in various authorities as chief of Feara-Droma-Lighean, i. e. the men of Druim-Lighean, now Drumleen, a short distance to the north of Lifford, in the district of Tir-Enda, barony of Raphoe, and county of Donegal. They were otherwise called the Ui-Ethach Droma-Lighean, or race of Eochaidh of Drumleen, and were under the patronage of St. Cairneach, of Cluain-Laodh.—See Colgan's *Acta Sanctorum*, p. 782. On the increasing of the population and power of the Kinel-Connell, the Feara-Droma and other tribes of the Kinel-Owen, originally seated to the west of the Rivers Foyle and Mourne, were driven across these rivers ; and they acquired new territories for themselves. There is extant in a paper manuscript, the property of the late O'Conor Don, a curious poem on the history of Druim-Lighean; but though it recounts various historical events relating to the locality, it affords no clue to determine the period at which the race of Eochaidh were driven out of Kinel-Enda.

The pedigree of Gilla-Macliag O'Donnelly, who was slain at Downpatrick, by De Courcy, in 1177, is variously given in several Irish manuscripts. In the Book of Ballymote, fol. 43, *b*, *b*, and fol. 45, *b*, col. 1 ; in the Book of Lecan, fol. 63, *a*, *a*, and fol. 65, *b*, *b*, col. 1 ; and in Duald Mac Firbis's Genealogical Manuscript (Lord Roden's copy), p. 133, it is deduced from Domhnall Ilchealgach, monarch of Ireland, who died in 566 ; but the number of generations given from this Domhnall, down to Gilla-Macliag who was slain in 1177, is only *nine*, which is about nine too short, and shews clearly that the transcribers of these manuscripts have engrafted Domhnall, the ancestor of Gilla-Macliag, on a wrong stem. Fortunately, however, the true line of Gilla-Macliag O'Donnelly is preserved in the Genealogical Manuscript of Cucogry, or Peregrine O'Clery, one of the Four Masters, now in the Library of the Royal Irish Academy. In this manuscript, which is beautifully written on paper, in Cucogry's own hand, it is given as follows : "Gilla-Macliag, son of Echtighern, son of Donnghal, son of Ceallachan, son of Dobhailen, son of Donnghal, son of Seachnasach, son of Ceallach, son of Eochaidh, son of Domhnall, son of Aedh Finnliath" [monarch of Ireland, A. D. 879].

[b] *Baile-Ua-nDonnghaile* : i. e. town of the O'Donnellys, now Castlecaulfield, in the parish of Donaghmore, barony of Dungannon, and county of Tyrone. According to an inquisition taken at Dungannon, in the seventh year of the reign of James I., Ballydonnelly contained twenty-four ballyboes. On an old map of Ulster, preserved in the State Papers' Office, London, is shewn Fort and Logh O'Donnellie, in the proper position of this townland.

Now, by comparing this with the royal line of the family of O'Neill, it will appear that Aedh or Hugh Finnliath is the true stemma of this pedigree :

1. Niall of the Nine Hostages, Monarch of Ireland, slain A. D. 406.
2. Eoghan, *a quo* Cinel-Eoghain, or Kinel-Owen, d. 465.
3. Muireadhach.
4. Muircheartach More Mac Erca, monarch, d. 533.
5. Domhnall Ilchealgach, monarch, d. 566.
6. Aedh Uairidhnach, monarch, d. 612.
7. Maelfithrigh, Chief of Kinel-Owen, sl. 625.
8. Maelduin.
9. Fergal, monarch, d. 722.
10. Niall Frasach, monarch, d. 770.
11. Aedh, or Hugh Oiridnigh, monarch, d. 819.
12. Niall Cailne, monarch, d. 879.
13. Aedh, or Hugh Finnliath, monarch, d. 879.

14. Niall Glunduv, *a quo* O'Neill, monarch, sl. 919.	14. Domhnall, King of Aileach.
15. Muircheartach Mac Neill, na-gCochall gCroiceann, King of Aileach, sl. 943.	15. Eochaidh, *a quo* Ui-Eathach Droma-Lighean.
16. Domhnall O'Neill, of Armagh, King of Aileach, d. 980.	16. Ceallach.
17. Muircheartach Midheach, sl. 975.	17. Seachnasach.
18. Flahertach-an-trostain O'Neill, King of Aileach, d. 1036.	18. Donnghal, *a quo* O'Donnelly.
19. Aedh Athlaman O'Neill, d. 1033.	19. Dobhailen, or Develin.
20. Domhnall O'Neill.	20. Ceallachan O'Donnelly.
21. Flahertach O'Neill.	21. Donnghal O'Donnelly.
22. Conchobhar na-fiodhgha O'Neill.	22. Echtighern O'Donnelly.
23. Teige Glinne O'Neill.	23. Gilla-Macliag O'Donnelly, chief of Feara Droma, slain at Down by Sir John De Courcy, A. D. 1177.
24. Muircheartach O'Neill, of Moylinny, sl. 1160.	

According to Keating's *History of Ireland*, the head of this family was hereditary Marshal of O'Neill's forces.—See *Genealogies, Tribes, &c., of Hy-Fiachrach*, p. 432 ; but, strange to say, little of their history has been yet recovered, from Gilla-Macliag O'Donnelly, who was slain by Sir John De Courcy in 1177, down to the year 1531, when the Four Masters state that O'Donnelly's town was assaulted by Niall Oge (the son of Art, who was son of Con) O'Neill, who broke down O'Donnelly's castle, and made a prisoner of the son of O'Neill [the celebrated John Donnghaileach, i. e. the Donnellyan, otherwise called an ϸíomaıṗ, i. e. of the pride or ambition], who was then in fosterage with O'Donnelly, and carried him off, together with the horses and other property of the place. In 1552, John Donnghaileach O'Neill and his foster-brethren made an assault on Ferdoragh, Baron of Dungannon, as he encamped at night, on his way to join the English at Belfast. In 1567, John Donnghaileach O'Neill proceeded, with a guard of fifty horsemen, to hire some gallowglasses who, at O'Neill's invitation, had come over, under the conduct of Alexander Mac Donnell of Scotland, and encamped at Cushendun, in the east of Ulster; but Mac Donnell, calling to mind his cause of enmity towards him (for O'Neill had slain his father, and driven himself and his followers out of Ulster), suddenly fell upon him and his party, as they were carousing in a tent, and murdered himself and some distinguished chieftains of his followers, among whom was Dubhaltach, or Dudley O'Donnelly, his foster-brother, who was "the most faithful and dear to him in the world."

Fynes Moryson, in his *History of Ireland*, first edition, p. 32, states, in his enumeration of the forces of the chieftains of Ulster, who combined to oppose the Earl of Essex in 1599, "that the Donolaghes [O'Donnellys] had in their country one hundred foote and sixtie horse." The same writer states, p. 116, that, in 1601, 27th July, the Lord Deputy, Mountjoy, drew out from the Blackwater three Regiments to fight the rebels, and that, the latter not making fight, he marched a mile or two more southward, "where," says Moryson, "we cut down great abundance of corne with our swords (according to our fashion); and here Shane Mac Donnell Groome" [O'Donnelly], "Tyrone's Marshal, whose Corne this was, upon humble submission, was received to her Majestie's mercie, and came to his Lordship in person the same night at our sitting downe in our last camp, whither we returned." This Marshal delivered to the Lord Deputy "a perfect note of such Captaines and Companies as are under the command of the Traitor Tyrone, within Tyrone," among which he mentions two of the O'Donnellys, namely, "Donnell Grome Mac Edmond, who had 100 men, and Patrick Mac Phelim, who had 100 more."

Donnell Groome Mac Donnell, the brother of this Shane, the Marshal, accompanied Tyrone to Kinsale, where he fought with such desperation, that he, "a captain of one hundred," and all his men, were slain. This appears from a note of Tyrone's loss at Kinsale, 20th Dec. 1601, printed by Moryson (orig. edit., p. 179). But his elder brother, Shane[c], Tyrone's Marshal, was protected by the English; for it appears from Patent Roll, eighth year of James I., that "Shane Mac Donel Grome O'Donnelly received a grant of Gortoharim" [now Gortnagarn, in Pomeroy parish], "in the territory of Terraghter, in the barony of Dungannon." An inquisition[d] taken at Dungannon, on the 29th of August, 1631, finds, that Shane Mac Donell Grome O'Donnelly was seised of the Balliboe of Gortelary, in the county of Tyrone, and, being so seised, died about eight years before" [*circa* 1623]; that Patrick O'Donnelly was his son and heir, and of full age; and that the premises are

[c] *Shane*, i. e. John.—The Rev. James Coigly, who was maternally descended from this family, states in his pamphlet, written in 1798, that Queen Elizabeth proposed to make this John O'Donnelly an Earl; and it is quite certain, from Docwra's *Narration*, that Elizabeth's officers and spies had circulated many strange reports, and made many promises, which were never intended to be performed, in the hope that some of O'Neill's followers might be induced, by the expectation of reward and aggrandisement, to lay violent hands upon their chieftain.

[d] By a former inquisition, taken at Dungannon, on the 16th September, 1614, it appears that James O'Donnelly, late abbot of the late abbey of Saints Peter and Paul at Armagh, was seised of a great number of tenements and possessions in right of the abbey, which are enumerated.

held of the King in free and common soccage. This Patrick O'Donnelly was evidently the head of the sept, and the person so distinguished during the insurrection of 1641, for whose head four hundred pounds were offered by the Lords Justices and Council, by proclamation "given at his Majesty's Castle of Dublin, 8th February, 1641-2." According to a Journal of the Rebellion of 1641, a manuscript in the possession of Lord O'Neill, this Patrick Moder took possession of Lord Caulfield's castle at Baile-I-Donnghaile, or Ballydonnelly, in October, 1641. In 1642, Sir Felim O'Neill, general of the Irish forces in Ulster, placed four captains over the Bann, namely: Niall Oge mac Neill mac Turlough [mac Phelim] mac Con Bacagh; Patrick Moder O'Donnelly; Felim an Choga O'Neill; and Turlough Gruama O'Quin. In the same year, the court or mansion-house of Ballydonnelly was burned by Randal Mac Donnell, by the General's [Sir Felim's] orders.

In 1643, June 27, Saturday, the English and Scotch went to Ballydonnelly, and Con Mac Art Mac Donnell (na Mallacht) delivered up to them the Island of Ballydonnelly. In autumn, 1644, Patrick Moder O'Donnelly returned to Ballydonnelly. In 1687 and 1688, Terence O'Donnelly was appointed High Sheriff of the county of Tyrone[e] by Lord Tirconnell; and, in 1687, when Colonel Gordon O'Neill was Lord Lieutenant of Tyrone, this Terence O'Donnelly, who is called Captain, and Shane O'Donnelly, were Deputy Lieutenants[f]. May 7th, 1689, Arthur O'Neill, Esq., of Ballygawley, and Patrick O'Donnelly, Esq., of Dungannon, were the members of Parliament for the borough of Dungannon; and, same year, Christopher Nugent, Esq., of Dublin, and Daniel O'Donnelly, Esq., were Members for the borough of Strabane. Doctor Patrick O'Donnelly was R. C. Bishop of Dromore since the Revolution, and Doctor Terence O'Donnelly was R. C. Bishop of Derry[g].

After the Revolution, this sept, who were remarkable for their loyal adherence to the cause of James II.[h], forfeited the remnant of their ancient estates, but still they never lost sight of their former station.

In 1689 was born Hugh O'Donnelly, who, according to the pedigree of the family, was son of Captain Terence, and the grandson of Patrick Moder O'Donnelly above mentioned. His descendants have escaped the great reverse of fortune which has been the unhappy fate of many of the O'Neills, and other families of the royal line of Niall of the Nine Hostages, after the confiscation of their estates. In 1719 he married Alice, the daughter of Doctor De Butts, (of a Huguenot family, which came to Ireland after the revocation of the Edict of Nantz), and she induced him to conform to the Protestant religion. He had issue a son,

Arthur Donnelly, Esq., of Blackwatertown, in the county of Armagh[i]. He was born in 1722, and died in 1785. He married, about 1758, first, Miss Williams, who died without issue; and, secondly, in 1769, Margaret, relict of Captain Haughton, and daughter of John Mahon, Esq.,

[e] See King's *View of the State of the Protestants*, Lond. 1692; and Joy's *Letter to Lord Lyndhurst, on the Appointment of Sheriffs in Ireland*, p. 80, Lond. 1838.

[f] Harris's *Life of King William III.*, Appendix, p. 307.

[g] See Ordnance Memoir of Londonderry.

[h] The Rev. James Coigly states in his pamphlet that "his own great-grandfather, O'Donnelly, together with five of his brothers, were slain at the head of the tribe, bravely defending the bridge at the battle of the Boyne."

[i] So late as the 20th of May, 1758, Viscount Charlemont renewed a lease for three lives,—as was the custom among the great English grantees and their successors, to the descendants of the ancient proprietors,—to this Arthur Donnelly (registered in Dublin, April 2nd, 1762), of the townland of Dredalt, in the manor of Castle Caulfield, formerly Ballydonnelly, part of the lands forfeited by the O'Donnellys.

of the county of Roscommon, and had by her an only son, John, born in 1770 (of whom presently), and a daughter, Margaret, who married William Johnstone, Esq., of Armagh, by whom she had one daughter, Margaret, who married: 1. Colonel Charles Douglas Waller, of the Royal Artillery, of West Wycombe, in the county of Kent; and 2. William Lodge Kidd, Esq., of Armagh; and has issue by both marriages.

John Donnelly, Esq., the only son of Arthur, married, in July, 1793, Rebecca, daughter of the Rev. John Young, M. A., of Eden, in the county of Armagh, by his wife, Anne M'Clintock (see, in Burke's Landed Gentry, M'Clintock of Drumcar, in the county of Louth), and sister of Sir William Young, Bart., of Bailieborough Castle, in the county of Cavan. (See also Burke's Baronetage, &c.) John, who died in 1835, had issue nine children, of whom but four are now living, viz.: 1. Thomas, a Major and Assistant Adjutant-General in the Honourable E. I. C.'s service, Bombay; 2. William, LL. D., Registrar-General in Ireland; 3. Alexander Frederick, of the H. E. I. C.'s Bengal civil service; 4. Susan Maria, married to Thomas Brooke, Esq., D. L., of Manor Brooke and Lough Eske House, in the county of Donegal.

All the men of this family that the Editor ever saw are remarkable for their manly form and symmetry of person; and even the peasants who bear the name exhibit frequently a stature and an expression of countenance which indicate high descent.

PEDIGREE OF O'DONOVAN.

"Do ḟlioċt Eoġain ṁóir Mhuiṁniġ,
ó'n Máiġ nuaiḋḃric n-eoċair-ġil,
go Clíoḋna ḃ-fionn-ḃán ḃ-fleaḋaiġ,
iomḋa a ngaḃláin ngeinealaiġ.

Diḃ-sin garsuiġ is gloine,
Síol g-Carṫaiġ ċláir Murgroiġe,
An tír go hAilloin uile,
's dioḃ Cairbriġ is Corcluiġe.

Díoḃ Uí Donnchaḋa an daġ-áiġ,
Is laoiċ n-dorrḋa O n-Donnaḃáin,
Fir is líonṁar líon d-tionáil,
Is ríoġraiḋ síl Súileaḃáin."—*Maoilin Oge Mac Brody.*

As the Annals of the Four Masters are so meagre in their notices of this, and almost all the families of Munster, except the O'Briens and Mac Carthys, the Editor deems it his duty to lay here before the reader the descent of the senior line of Mogha Nuadhat, King of the southern half of Ireland, towards the close of the second century. This he has been induced to compile, not because he happens to bear the name of that family himself, but because it has been neglected by all our genealogists, in consequence of the family having been removed from their original territory at an early period, and of having been, in latter ages, driven into the mountains of Carbery, in the county of Cork, and there thrown into the shade by the more powerful and more illustrious family of the Mac Carthys. The pedigrees of O'Brien and Mac Carthy, who have been for ages the heads of this race of Mogh Nuadhat, have been already published by various genealogists, and that of Mac Carthy has been particularly illustrated by Mons. Lainé, who was genealogist to Charles X. of France. The Editor regrets to say that he has failed, after great exertions, to trace the pedigree of any branch of the O'Sullivans, now living in Ireland, to the original stock. The reader must, therefore, rest satisfied with two specimens of the Munster genealogies, drawn from the most authentic documents of ancient and modern Irish history and genealogy, namely, those of O'Donovan and Mac Carthy of Dunmanway. The original documents, by which the latter portion of the pedigree of O'Donovan is proved, have been furnished by the O'Donovan (Morgan William), of Montpellier, near Cork; by Edward Powell, Esq., who succeeded to half the estate of the late General O'Donovan of Bawnlahan, in the county of Cork; by the late Major Perceval of Barntown, near the town of Wexford; and by Rickard Donovan, Esq., Clerk of the Crown for the county of Cork.

I. Eoghan Taidhleach, i. e. Eoghan the Splendid, otherwise called Mogh Nuadhat. He is the great ancestor of the most distinguished families of Munster, and is mentioned in all the authentic Irish Annals as the most powerful man in Ireland, next after Con of the Hundred Battles, with whom he contended for the monarchy of all Ireland. Con, however, at length forced him to quit Ireland; and we are told that he sought an asylum in Spain, where he lived for nine years in exile, during which time he was employed in the king's army. In the fourth year of his exile the king gave him his daughter, Beara, in marriage. At length he entered into a confederacy with the king, by whose co-operation he was able to land a numerous army of Spaniards in Ireland. He put in at a harbour in the south of Ireland, to which he gave the name of *Beara* (now Bearhaven), in honour of his wife, and, immediately on his landing, was joined by his relatives and a numerous body of followers. He defeated Con in ten successive engagements, and compelled him to resign all authority over the southern half of Ireland, over which he (Mogh Nuadhat) was to be king, independent of Con.—See the *Annals of Tighernach*, at the year 166; and O'Flaherty's *Ogygia*, Part III. chap. lx.

The boundary which separated these two divisions (which were called Leath-Chuinn, i. e. Con's half, and Leath-Mhogha, i. e. Mogh's half) was called *Eiscir-Riada*, and extended from Dublin to Clonard, thence to Clonmacnoise, and Clonburren, and thence across the province of Connaught, to Meadhraighe, a peninsula extending into the bay of Galway.

This division of Ireland into two parts was observed only one year, when, if we believe the author of the *Battle of Magh-Léana*, Mogh Nuadhat grew discontented when he observed that the part of Dublin which by this division was ceded to Con was more advantageous in the profits arising from ship duties, fisheries, and other commercial emoluments; in consequence of which he demanded half the revenue. Con refused to accede to this demand, upon which their hostilities being renewed, they agreed to decide the controversy by a pitched battle, to be fought at Magh-Leana, now Moylena parish, *alias* Kilbride, near Tullamore, in the King's county. Here the armies of both encamped, on the north side of the Eiscir-Riada, not far from Durrow; and Con, finding himself inferior in forces, had recourse to stratagem: he surprised the enemy's camp early in the morning, and obtained a victory. Gaul, the son of Morna, of the race of Sanbh (Firbolgic king of Connaught), a distinguished champion, slew Mogh Nuadhat, who, not expecting any attack from the enemy, lay asleep in his tent. There are still to be seen at Moylena two *tumuli*, in one of which the body of Mogh Nuadhat was interred, and in the other that of Fræch, the Spaniard, his brother-in-law. After this battle Con was proclaimed monarch of all Ireland; and he reigned twenty years in an uninterrupted peace and tranquillity.

Eoghan Taidhleach, or Mogh Nuadhat, had by Beara, his Spanish wife, two sons: 1. Olioll Olum, the ancestor of all the subsequent kings of Munster; and 2. Lughaidh Lagha, a champion much celebrated in Irish stories for his extraordinary strength, valour, and prowess.

II. Oilioll Olum. He became King of Leath-Mhogha, or the southern half of Ireland, after having conquered Lughaidh Maccon, the ancestor of O'Driscoll, in the battle of Ceann-Feabhradh Sleibhe Caoin, in the year 237. He married Sadhbh, or Sabia, daughter of Con of the Hundred Battles, and had by her seven sons, who all fell in the battle of Magh-Mucruimhe, near Athenry, in the present county of Galway, except Cormac Cas and Cian. Of these only three left issue, namely, Eoghan, Cormac Cas, and Cian, the ancestor of O'Carroll of Ely O'Carroll, of O'Meagher of Ikerrin, and several other families. It appears from a historical tract, preserved in the Library of Trinity College, Dublin, H. 3. 17, p. 849, that Oilioll Olum was jealous with his wife, Sabia; that he turned her away after she had a son and a daughter; and that she was obliged to live for some time in the mountain of Sliabh Comhalt, now Keeper Hill, in the county of Tipperary; that her brother, the Monarch Art, son of Con, put Oilioll on his trial for neglecting his wife and denying his children; and that the Ollavs, or chief Brehons, or Judges of Ireland, decided that the children were legitimate, and that Oilioll Olum should pay for their fosterage, and provide for them.

Previous to his time, the ancestors of the O'Driscolls, of the Ithian race, and the Ernaans, of the race of Heremon, had been kings of Munster, according to the fortune of each in the war, in which they were almost constantly embroiled with each other. But Oilioll Olum fixed the sceptre in his own family, and divided Munster into two parts, between his second son, Cormac Cas, and the heir of his eldest son, Eoghan, and enjoined that their descendants should succeed to the government of the province in alternate succession; and this injunction was complied with until the time of Brian Borumha, who set it aside for ever, after dethroning the heir, not only of Eoghan, but of Con of the Hundred Battles.

III. Eoghan.—He was the eldest son of Oilioll Olum, and brother of Cormac Cas, ancestor of the O'Briens of Thomond. He was killed in the battle of Magh Mucruimhe, near Athenry, in the now county of Galway, fought A. D. 250, between Art, the son of Con of the Hundred Battles, monarch of Ireland, and Lughaidh Maccon, the ancestor of the family of the O'Driscolls, who had been expelled Ireland A. D. 237, but returned in 240 with some British auxiliaries. It is stated in the authentic Irish annals that Eoghan, the son of Oilioll Olum, was killed in this battle by Benè, a Briton.

This Eoghan married Moncha, the daughter of Dil, a druid of noble extraction, and had issue by her:

IV. Fiacha Muilleathan. He was declared King of Munster, in accordance with the will of his grandfather, on the death of his uncle, Cormac Cas, which occurred A. D. 260. His territory was invaded by Cormac Mac Art, the grandson of Con of the Hundred Battles; but Fiacha met him in a pitched battle at Drom-Damhghaire, now Knocklong, in the present county of Limerick, where Cormac was defeated and obliged to make restitution for the injuries caused by this invasion. This Fiacha lived at Knockgraffon, near the Suir, in the county of Tipperary, where his moat and extensive entrenchments are still to be seen.

He had two sons, of whom the elder was called Oilioll Flannmore, and the younger, Oilioll Flannbeg. Oilioll Flannmore, having had no heir, adopted his brother, Oilioll Flannbeg, as his son, who, in his turn, became King of Leath-Mhogha, after the death of Mogh Corb, son of Cormac Cas, who was son of Oilioll Olum.

V. Oilioll Flannbeg. He was King of Munster for thirty years, and was slain in the battle of Corann by the men of Connaught, aided by Fothadh Conann, son of Maccon, the ancestor of the O'Driscolls. He had four sons, namely: 1. Eochaidh, King of Munster, whose race is extinct; 2. Daire Cearba, the ancestor of O'Donovan; 3. Lughaidh, ancestor of Mac Carthy and his correlatives; 4. Eoghan, from whom descended six saints, namely: 1. St. Cormac, whose life is given in the Book of Lecan, and published in a Latin translation by Colgan at 26th March; 2. St. Becan of Cill-Becain at the foot of Sliabh gCrot in Muscraighe-Chuirc; 3. St. Culan of Glenkeen, in the territory of Ui-Luigheach [Ileagh], in the present county of Tipperary, whose bell, called Bearnan-Culain, is still preserved; 4. St. Evin of Ros-glas, now Monasterevin, in the county of Kildare; 5. St. Dermot of Kilmacnowen, near the hill of Knocknarea, in the county of Sligo; and 6. Boetan of Cill-Boetain, in the territory of Dalaradia, in the east of Ulster.—See O'Flaherty's *Ogygia*, p. 381, where O'Flaherty writes: "Olillo Flannbeg regi Momoniæ supererant Achaius, rex Momoniæ, Darius Kearb, ex quo O'Donawan, Lugadius et Eugenius."

It should be here remarked, that Mr. Lainé falsifies this quotation from O'Flaherty in his pedigree of the Count Mac Carthy.

VI. Daire Cearba. He was King of Leath-Mhogha, and distinguished himself at the head of the forces of Munster in repelling the assaults of certain pirates who infested the coasts of Munster. He had seven sons, of whom the eldest was Fidhach, the father of the celebrated Crimhthann Mor mac Fidhaigh, the senior of the Milesian race, who became Monarch of Ireland despite of the rival race of Con of the Hundred Battles, and who established colonies of Munstermen at Glastonbury, and in different parts of Wales, where, according to Cormac's Glossary, there are several places called after his people, who no doubt, built the forts called *Ceiter Guidelod*, or forts of the Gaels or Irish, by the Welsh. It is also stated that this warlike monarch made some expeditions into Scotland in the year 369, where he assisted the Picts in opposing the Romans, under the Governor Theodosius. He is also said to have made some descents upon the coasts of Gaul, whence he returned with immense booty. This warlike monarch, by far the most distinguished that the Munster race can boast of in pagan times, was poisoned by his own sister, Mongfinn, the wife of Eochaidh Moyvaine, who had been Monarch of Ireland preceding Crimhthann. She effected this while Crimhthann was on a visit with her at Inis-Dornglas, an island in the River Moy in Connaught, in the hope that her eldest son, Brian, might be immediately seated on the throne of Ireland; and in order the more effectually to deceive her brother as to the contents of the proffered cup, she drank of it first herself, and died of the poison soon after. Crimhthann, on his way home to Munster, died at a place in the south of the present county of Clare, which, from that memorable event, received the appellation of Sliab oiġió an piġ, i. e. the Mountain of the Death of the King. It has been remarked by ancient and modern Irish writers, that this execrable act of Mongfinn had not the desired effect, for that neither her son, Brian, nor any of her posterity, ever attained to the monarchy of Ireland, except Turlough O'Conor, and his son, Roderic, who were luckless monarchs to Ireland!

The race of this great monarch, Crimthann More, became extinct; but the race of Daire Cearba was continued by his second son, Fiacha Fidhgeinte, the ancestor of O'Donovan, and his third son, Eochaidh Liathanach, the ancestor of the tribe of Ui-Liathain, in the south-east of the present county of Cork, where their chief, Mac Tyrus, was very powerful at the English Invasion. His fourth son, Deaghaidh, or Dagæus, was ancestor of the Ui-Deaghaidh, in the territory of Eoghanacht-Chaisil, of whom was the virgin, St. Sinchea; and from Dera, his fifth son, descended the celebrated St. Rodanus of Lorha, in Lower Ormond, who cursed the royal palace of Tara, in the sixth century.

VII. Fiacha Fidhgeinte, the second son of Daire Cearba. After the death of Crimhthann More mac Fidhaigh, in A. D. 379, the race of Fiacha Fidhgeinte became the senior line of the Milesian race, and contended for the crown of Munster. Fiacha himself, however, never became King of Munster, for he was killed by his rival, Aengus Tireach, great-grandson of Cormac Cas, in a battle fought at Clidhna, near Glandore harbour, as appears from a poem by Cormac Mac Cuilleanain, quoted in the Book of Munster. While Crimhthann More mac Fidhaigh, the nephew of this Fiacha, was Monarch of Ireland, he made Conall Eachluath, the grandson of Aengus Tireach, King of Munster; and after the poisoning of Crimhthann, Enna Airgtheach, the son of Conall Eachluath, became King of Leath Mhogha; and none of the family of Crimhthann ever after attained to the sovereignty of all Munster.

The Leabhar Muimhneach or Munster Book, as preserved in the Book of Lecan, states that this Fiacha received the cognomen of Fió-ġeınce, because he constructed a wooden horse at the fair of Aenach Cholmain in Magh-Life.

"*Fid-geint nuncupatus est quia fecit equum ligneum in Circinio Colmain in Campo Liphi.*"

From him descended the Ui-Fidhgeinte or Nepotes Fidhgenti, of whom was the celebrated St. Molua of Cluain-fearta Molua, at the foot of Slieve Bloom, in Upper Ossory, in whose life their situation is described as follows:

"Et venit [S. Molua] ad Mumeniam, et lustravit patriam suam .i. Nepotes Fidgenti, quæ gens est in medio Mumenie, a medio planicie Mumenie usque ad medium montis Luachra in occidente ad australem plagam fluminis Synnæ."—*Vit. S. Moluæ.* Ex codice Killkenniensi, in Marsh's Library, Dublin, V. 3. 1. 4, F. 135.

This Fiacha had three sons, viz.: Brian, Sedna, *a quo* Ui-Sedna, and Laeghaire, *a quo* the nepotes Laeghaire.

VIII. Brian. He was King of South Munster when Niall of the Nine Hostages was Monarch of Ireland. He had seven sons, viz.: 1. Cairbre Aebhdha, the ancestor of O'Donovan and Mac Eniry; 2. Goll; 3. Lughaidh; 4. Daire, from whose grandson, Conall, descended the tribe of Ui-Conaill, giving name to the Conilloes, in the county of Limerick, of whom was O'Coileain,

O'Kinealy, O'Billrin, and other families, but not the O'Connells, as asserted by Dr. O'Brien, in his Irish Dictionary, for the O'Connells of Kerry are of the same race as O'Falvy, i. e. of the race of Conary II., Monarch of Ireland; and the O'Connells of Cork, as appears from the historical poem of Cathan O'Duinin, are of the same race as the O'Donohoes of Eoghanacht Locha Lein in Kerry; 5. Fergus; 6. Ross; and 7. Cormac.

IX. Cairbre Aebhdha. He had five sons, viz.: 1. Erc, *a quo* O'Donovan; 2. Eccen, *a quo* the Fir-Thamhnaighe, the Ui-Brogain, and the Ui-Garbhain; 3. Trian; 4. Sedna, *a quo* Mac Eniry, chief of Corca-Muichead, now the parish of Corcamohid, *alias* Castletown Mac Eniry, in the south of the county of Limerick; and 5. Cormac, *a quo* Mac Caechluinge.

This Cairbre Aebhdha gave name to Ui-Cairbre Aebhdha, a territory comprising the barony of Coshma, and the district around Kilmallock, in the county of Limerick. He had several sons, of whom the eldest was,

X. Erc, who had two sons, Lonan and Kinfaela; the former was chief of the Ui-Fidhgeinte, and contemporary with St. Patrick, whom he entertained (according to the Tripartite Life, published by Colgan), in the year 439, at his palace, situated on the summit of the hill of Kea, near the mountain of Carn-Feradhaigh. But it appears that Lonan afterwards quarrelled with Patrick, and refused to become his convert, for which reason the saint cursed him, and predicted that his race would become extinct, and that his principality would be transferred to the race of his brother.

XI. Kinfaela. Nothing is known of this chieftain, except that he was the first of his race who embraced the Christian religion, about the year 439, and that the following generations descended from him:

XII. Oilioll Ceannfada.

XIII. Laipe.

XIV. Aengus.

XV. Aedh.

XVI. Crunnmael.

XVII. Eoghan, Chief of Ui-Figeinte, who was killed, according to Tighernach, in the year 667, in a battle fought against his neighbours, the people of Ara-Cliach, who inhabited the territory on the other side of the River Maigue.

XVIII. Aedh Roin. After the death of Eoghan, his relative, Conall, of the sept of the Ui-Conaill-Gabhra, became chief of all the Ui-Figeinte, and, on his death, which occurred in the year 701 (Ann. Tiger.), his brother, Aedh Dubh, became chief of the Nepotes Figeinte, but on his death, which happened in the year 715, the chieftainship reverted to

XIX. Duvdavoran, who died, Rex Nepotum Figeinte, in the year 750 (Ann. Tiger.) After his death the chieftainship devolved to Flann, son of Erc, who was the head of a sept of the Ui-Conaill-Gabhra, but, on his death in 755, the chieftainship reverted to

XX. Kinfaela, who ruled the Nepotes Figeinte for eleven years, and died a natural death in 767. After the death of Kinfaela, Scanlan, the son of Flann, of the sept of Ui-Conaill-Gabhra, seized on the chieftainship and ruled the Ui-Figeinte for fourteen years. He died in the year 781, and was succeeded by his son or nephew, Murchadh, the grandson of Flann, who died in 802. At this period the race of Conall Gabhra got the upper hand of the race of Cairbre Aebhdha, for it appears from the Irish annals that Murchadh was succeeded by Bruadar, who died in 809, and Bruadar by Dunadhach, the son of Scannlan, who died in 834, after having gained a considerable victory over the Danes, who had made an irruption into his territory. But on the death of Dunadhach, the chieftainship reverted to the race of Cairbre Aebhdha, and Niall, the son of Kinnfaela, is the next chief of the Ui-Figeinte recorded by the Irish annalists. He died in 844.

XXI. Cathal, Chief of Ui-Cairbre Aebhdha.

XXII. Uainigh, Chief of Ui-Cairbre Aebhdha.

XXIII. Cathal, Chief of the Ui-Figeinte, slain by the celebrated Callaghan Cashel, King of Munster. He had two sons, Uainidh, rex Coirpre, who died in 964, according to the old Annals of Innisfallen, and

XXIV. Donovan, the progenitor after whom the family name O'Donovan has been called. This Donovan made his name celebrated throughout Ireland for his opposition to the more powerful family of Dal-Cais of Thomond, which nearly caused the total destruction of his own sept. In the year 976, as we are informed by the Annalist Tighernach, Mahon, the son of Kennedy, King of Munster, was put to death by Maelmuaidh, the son of Bran, King of Ui-Eathach, to whom he had been treacherously delivered up by Donovan, the son of Cathal, King of Ui-Figeinte. The Dublin copy of the Annals of Innisfallen add, that Mahon was killed at Bearna-dhearg [now the Red Gap or Red Chair, a chasm in the mountain of Sliabh Reagh, on the borders of Ui-Figeinte and Fermoy], and that the coarb of St. Finnbhar, or Bishop of Cork, denounced all those who were concerned in conspiring his death.

The removal of Mahon, head of the Dal-Cais, was, however, of no avail to the race of Eoghan, for it only cleared the way for his more illustrious brother, Brian, afterwards called Brian Borumha, who, immediately after the death of Mahon, made his way to the throne of Munster, in despite of all the opposition and treachery of his adversaries of South Munster. Nor did he leave the death of Mahon long unrevenged, for, in the year 977, he marched his forces into the plains of Ui-Figeinte, where Donovan and his father-in-law, Amlaff, or Auliffe, King of the Danes of Munster, had their forces in readiness to meet him, and a battle ensued, in which Brian vanquished his enemies with great slaughter, and left Donovan and Amlaff dead upon the field.—(*Annals of the Four Masters*, and *Annals of Innisfallen*). This Donovan also formed an alliance with the Danes of Waterford, and one of the sons of Imhar, or Ivor, King of the Danes of Waterford, was called Donovan after him. This Danish Donovan, who was evidently the grandson of Donovan, King of the Nepotes Figeinte, slew Dermot, son of Donnell, Lord of Hy-Kinsellagh, in 995, and slew also in the same year Gillapatrick, Chief of Ossory, but was himself slain soon after by Cuduiligh, the son of Kineth, one of the men of Offaly, in revenge of the death of the Lord of Hy-Kinsellagh. At this period surnames became for the first time hereditary in Ireland, for we find that many of the chieftain families in Ireland took surnames from ancestors who were living at this period.—See a short article on this subject published by the Editor in the *Irish Penny Journal*, 10th April, 1841.

XXV. Cathal mac Donovan. Brian Borumha did not satisfy his revenge by the slaughter of Donovan and his people of Ui-Figeinte, together with their allies, the Danes of Munster. In the year 978 he marched a second time against the rival race of Eoghan or Eoghanachts, and came to an engagement with them at Bealach-Leachta, in Muskerry, near Macroom, in the now county of Cork, where he vanquished them and their Danish allies with dreadful havoc. After this defeat the race of Eoghan were glad to give up their rivalship for the government of Munster, and to make peace with Brian on his own conditions. Accordingly we find these two great races of the blood of Oilioll Olum at peace with each other for a period of thirty-six years, that is, from the year 978 till 1014. Among the chieftains of the line of Eoghan who submitted to Brian on this occasion, was Cathal, the son of his inveterate enemy, Donovan, who, if we may rely on the Dublin copy of the Annals of Innisfallen, fought at Clontarf, on the side of Brian, against his relatives the Danes; but it is more than probable that many of the Munster Danes (one of whom, according to Duald Mac Firbis's account of the Danish families in Ireland, was married to Brian Borumha's own daughter) fought also on the Irish side. He was placed in the second division of Brian's forces, of which Kian, the son of Maelmuaidh, ancestor of the O'Mahonys, had the chief command, and this division contended with the forces of Leinster. It does not appear whether or not Cathal was killed in this battle. He was married to a Danish wife, as is quite manifest from the name of his son,

XXVI. Amhlaoibh, Auliffe or Amlaff O'Donovan. He flourished A. D. 1041, and was evidently the O'Donovan who slew Donnchadh Ua Eachach, as mentioned in the Bodleian copy of the Annals of Innisfallen, under that year. He left a son—

XXVII. Murchadh O'Donovan, of whom nothing is known, except that he left a son—

XXVIII. Aneslis O'Donovan, a name which indicates a Danish connexion. In his time Desmond was thrown into a state of confusion in consequence of the feuds between the O'Briens and Mac Carthys, during which the O'Donovans were driven from the plains of Ui-Figeinte, and forced to fly beyond the Mangartan mountain.—See note [m], under the year 1178, p. 45, *supra*. Whether they were ever after able to return has not been yet determined. Collins asserts, in his pedigree of the late General O'Donovan, of Bawnlahan, that O'Donovan resided at Croom, till he was driven thence by Maurice Fitzgerald, second Baron of Offaly, who was Lord Justice of Ireland in the year 1229; but this has not been proved. Murchadh had a son—

XXIX. Raghnall, Ranulph, Randal, or Reginald O'Donovan, another name which bespeaks a Danish alliance. In the year 1201 the chief of the O'Donovans, Amhlaoibh, Aulaf, or Auliff, was seated in the now county of Cork, where he was slain that year by the O'Briens and De Burgos, but how he stood related to this Raghnall has not been proved.—See note [o], under the year 1200, p. 126; and note [y], under the year 1418, pp. 832, 833, *supra*. Raghnall had a son—

XXX. Maelruanaidh, or Mulrony O'Donovan, who had

XXXI. Crom O'Donovan. Collins asserts that he was in possession of the great Castle of Crom or Croom, on the River Maigue, in the present county of Limerick, and this was the tradition in the country in 1686, when the manuscript called *Carbriæ Notitia* was written; but the Editor has not found this fact recorded in any contemporaneous document. *Cujus rei periculum veri ego ad me non recipio. Penes famam, veteremque traditionem esto fides.* According to the Dublin copy of the Annals of Innisfallen, he was killed in, or immediately before, the year 1254, at Inis-an-bheil, now Pheale, near Inishkeen, in the county of Cork, by O'Mahony's people. This Crom is the ancestor of all the septs of the O'Donovan family in the baronies of Carbery, in the county of Cork, and of several others in Leinster. He gave name to Gleann a' Chroim, in the parish of Fanlobus, which afterwards became the property of a branch of the Mac Carthys, who had their principal seat at Dunmanway (and of whom Daniel Mac Carthy, Esq., of Florence, is a descendant). According to Duald Mac Firbis, this Crom had three sons: 1. Cathal, the ancestor of the sept called Clann-Cathail; 2. Aneslis, from whom sprung Sliocht Aneslis-mic-a' Chroim, and Lochlainn, from whom came the Clann-Lochlainn, who possessed thirty-six ploughlands lying between the River Roury and Glandore harbour, and of whom we shall speak presently.

SLIOCHT-AINESLIS or CLANN-ENESLIS O'DONOVAN.

Aneslis, the second son of Crom, had issue four sons, namely, Donough More, Rickard, Walter, and Raghnall or Randal, who became the founders of four distinct septs, who all bore the generic tribe-name of Sliocht Aneslic-mic a' Chroim, which is anglicised in the public records, "Slught Eneslis mac Icroyme." The head of this sept possessed a small district of seven ploughlands in the parish of Kilmacabea, which district bore their tribe-name of Slught Eneslis Mac Icroym, or Clan-Eneslis Mac Icrim. It appears from various Inquisitions, and other public documents, that this sept of the O'Donovans held also other lands outside their own little territory. An Inquisition taken at Cork on the 6th of October, 1607, finds "that Bernyhuila [now Butler's Gift], in the parish of Dromaleague, containing twoe ploughlands, and Muyny and Dyrryclohaghyghtragh, conteining twoe ploughlands, are holden of the Mannor of Castell-O Donyvane, by Slight Ineslis O Donyvane."

From another Inquisition taken at Cork on the 21st of September, 1625, it appears that there was another family of this sept seated at Kilcolman, in the barony of Courcies, for it states that "Donnell mac Cnoghor Buy Mac Eneslis O'Donovane, who died on the 5th of January, 1602, was seised of the town and lands of Killcollman, which his son and heir, Cnoghor Buy Mac Eneslis O'Donovane, mortgaged, on the 2nd of May, 1620, to John Lord Courcie, with power of Redemption. That said Cnoghor died on the 8th of May, leaving a son, Donnell, then three years old." It also appears, from a deposition preserved in the Library of Trinity College, Dublin, vol. vi. for Cork, p. 54, that "Daniel O'Donovane, *alias* Donnell Boy Mac Cnogher, of Derribrock, in Courcies, was in actual rebellion" [in 1641], "and went out to Spain." It appears, by the Act of Settlement, that "Captain Daniel Boy O'Donovane, of Killcollman, in the county of Cork, was among the persons who had faithfully served his Majesty beyond seas." It appears, from another Inquisition taken at Cork, on the 20th of August, 1632, that another branch of this sept, Dermott mac Teige mac Eneslis, was possessed of the lands of Lisnabrineny-Ierragh, in the parish of Kilmeen [in the barony of East Carbery]. The Editor has not been able to identify any living member of this sept, and shall therefore return to the senior branch,

THE CLANN-CAHILL O'DONOVAN.

XXXII. Cathal or Cahill O'Donovan, the first son of Crom. This Cathal gave name to the territory of Clancahill, in the county of Cork, which is defined in an Inquisition taken at Cork on the 6th of October, 1607, as containing three score and seven ploughlands, and "extending from the sea on the south to the Ryver of Myalagh, and bounded on the north with the landes of Clandonill Roe, the landes of Glan Icrime, and with the lands of Clanloghlin on the east, and the landes of Clandermodie and Clanteige Rwoe on the west." This Inquisition also states that it contains two manors, viz.: "the Mannor of Castell O'Donyvane, conteining twentie and one ploughlands, and the Mannor of Rahyne."

This Cathal never had any possessions in the original territory of Ui-Figeinte, or Ui-Cairbre Aebhdha, in the present county of Limerick, but he seems to have acquired a considerable tract of mountain territory in Corca-Luighe, the original principality of the O'Driscolls, to which newly-acquired district he transferred the tribe-name of his family, viz.: Cairbre, which, by a strange whim of custom, was afterwards applied to a vast territory, now forming four baronies, in the county of Cork. This extension of the name looks strange enough, as it was transferred since the year 1200, and as the race who transferred it did not remain the dominant family in the district. The fact seems to have been that, when Mac Carthy Reagh got possession of a part of this territory, in the latter end of the thirteenth century, the Ui-Cairbre were the most important tribe within it, and that he and his descendants applied the name to the O'Donovan territory, and to all the minor cantreds attached by him from time to time.

This Cathal was of age in 1254, when he and Fineen Reanna Roin Mac Carthy slew Dermot O'Mahony, in revenge of his father, Crom O'Donovan. He had two sons, both of whom became chiefs of the newly acquired territory, namely, Teige, No. XXXIII., of whom presently, the ancestor of the subsequent chiefs of the O'Donovans, and Imhar or Ivor, who was otherwise called Gilla-riabhach or Gillareagh, the ancestor of a sept of the O'Donovans, formerly seated at Castle Ivor, in the parish of Myross. According to a pedigree of the O'Donovans, compiled by John Collins, of Myross, the last Irish scholar, historiographer, and poet of Carbery, this Ivor built Castle Ivor in the year 1251, but where he found this date is a great puzzle to the Editor, who has not been able to find any authority for it; and yet he is inclined to believe that it is correct, for it appears from the old Annals of Innisfallen, preserved in the Bodleian Library, that the son of this man was slain in 1282, by Gilla-Mochuda or Gillicuddy, the son of Dunlang O'Sullivan. The passage, which is in a very old hand, runs as follows:

"A. D. 1282. Mac Giulla riebgg I Donnuban du marbad du Gilla Mochuda mac Dunlgng I Suluuan."

"A. D. 1282. The son of Giulla-riebhach O'Donovan was killed by Gilla-Mochuda, son of Dunlang O'Sullivan."

This passage is authority to shew that the date, 1251, given by Collins (wherever he found it), may be correct. Collins says that Castle Ivor remained in the possession of the descendants of Ivor (an Gilla riebach) till about the middle of the sixteenth century, when they were dispossessed by Donnell-na-gCroiceann, who was the Hector of this race. He adds, in a strain of poetical history, that this Ivor was a celebrated trader, and that he is now regarded as a magician in the wild traditions of the peasantry of the district, who believe that he is enchanted in a lake called Lough Cluhir, situated near Castle Ivor, in the townland of Listarkin, and that his magical ship is seen once every seventh year, with all her courses set, and colours flying, majestically floating on the surface of that lake. "I have seen," adds this poetical genealogist, "one person, in particular, testify, by oath, that he had seen this extraordinary phenomenon in the year 1778." He should have added that this ship was said to have appeared immediately after the death of Daniel

O'Donovan, of Bawnlahan, Esq., the representative of Donnell-na-gCroiceann, the extirpator of the race of Ivor.

XXXIII. TADHG or TEIGE O'DONOVAN, son of Cathal, son of Crom. Nothing is recorded of this Teige, except that he begat three sons: 1. Murchadh, or Murrough, who was chief of his name about the year 1340; 2. Raghnall, or Randal (who had three sons, Donnell, Melaghlin, and Dermot); and 3. Conor (who was father of Aedh, the father of Dermot, who was father of Donough). The descendants of his younger sons, are still, no doubt, extant in Carbery, but their history is for ever consigned to oblivion.

XXXIV. MURCHADH, MURROUGH, or MORGAN O'DOVOVAN. He had two sons: 1. Rickard, who was Chief of Clancahill about the year 1370, the last generation given by Peregrine O'Clery, p. 216, in his pedigree of O'Donovan; and 2.—

XXXV. CONCHOBHAR, CONOR, or CORNELIUS O'DONOVAN. He had a son, Raghnall, or Randal, who was Chief of Clancahill about the year 1410; and, if we believe Collins (who quotes no authorities, having deemed himself an infallible one), he had another son, Murtough, who had a son, Aengus, or Æneas O'Donovan, of Clasharusheen, in the parishes of Kilmeen and Castle-ventry, whose territory, called Gleann-a-mhuillinn [i. e. the glen of the mill], comprised eight ploughlands. Collins adds that the head of this sept of the O'Donovans was distinguished by the name of Mac Æneas, and that the spacious ruins of his residence were to be seen at Clasharusheen in his own time. The Editor has not been able to find any authority, Irish or Anglo-Irish, for the existence of this sept of the O'Donovans; but the tradition in the country still states that an O'Donovan had a large house near the north-east boundary of the townland of Clasharusheen, where he was wont to murder his guests, whose bodies he buried in an adjoining field, called Pairc-na-cille, i. e. field of the church or burial-place.

XXXVI. RAGHNALL, RANDAL, or REGINALD O'DONOVAN. According to Duald Mac Firbis he had a son, Dermot, the ancestor of all the subsequent chiefs of the O'Donovans; and Collins gives him a second son, Tioboid, the ancestor of a sept of the O'Donovans called Sliocht-Tioboid, who possessed a tract of land near the town of Skibbereen, where they built the Castle of Gortnaclogh, the ruins of which still remain, and are shewn on the Ordnance Map, on a detached portion of the parish of Creagh.

XXXVII. DERMOT O'DONOVAN, the sixth in descent from Crom. It should be here remarked, that the different copies of the pedigree of O'Donovan differ in two generations before this Dermot. Two, preserved in the Library of the Royal Irish Academy; one, in the Library of Trinity College, Dublin, H. 1. 7; and one in the Cork manuscript, called the Seanchaidhe Muimhneach, have two Dermots; but Mac Firbis has only one; and the Editor has adopted his authority, though it is probable that there may have been two, and that the last of them is the Dermot O'Donovan mentioned in the Chancery record of 1592, as the great-grandfather of Donnell, the then O'Donovan. From this Dermot forward we have the clearest documentary evidence of the descent of the senior branch of this family. He had two sons: 1. Donnell, who succeeded his relative, Dermot Mac Conor, in the chieftainship of Clancahill, and enjoyed the same during his life, but of whose issue we have no further account; and 2. Teige (the ancestor of the subsequent chiefs) who succeeded his brother, and enjoyed the lordship of Clancahill during his life.

XXXVIII. Teige O'Donovan, Chief of Clancahill. Collins states that this Teige was privately married to Helena, daughter of Denis O'Donovan [Mac Eneslis] of Moyny, in the parish of Dromaleague, and that this Denis murdered Teige, while his only son, Donnell, was an infant; but this cannot be true, for we have the evidence of a Chancery record, dated 12th February, 1592–3, that Donnell O'Donovan succeeded his father, Teige mac Dermot, in the chieftainship of Clancahill, without any interruption, which could not have been the case if Donnell were a child at the time of his father's death. Collins has a long story about a Dermot a' Bhairc, or Jeremiah of the Barque (who was probably the son of Donnell, predecessor of Teige), having been inaugurated by Mac Carthy Reagh at Roscarbery, when Donnell mac Teige came up with his party to prevent his election, and slew him in the presence of Mac Carthy, even while he (the said Diarmaid a' Bhairc) held the straight white wand, the badge of his dignity, in his hand! This is probably true, but the Editor has not yet discovered any cotemporaneous record of it.

XXXIX. Donnell I. O'Donovan, commonly called Domhnall na g-Croiceann, i. e. Donnell of the Hides. He was inaugurated Chief of Clancahill, by Mac Carthy Reagh, about the year 1560. He was fostered by O'Leary at his castle of Carrignacurra (now called Castle Masters), situated in the parish of Inchageelagh, or Iveleary; and it would appear that it was by O'Leary's assistance that he was enabled to set aside his rival, Diarmaid-a'-Bhairc. He was married to Ellen, the daughter of O'Leary, at the church of Drumale, after having had by her Dermot O'Donovan, and other sons, who were declared bastards by the Lord Chancellor, Adam Loftus, in 1592. He had also Donnell and Teige, born after the solemnization of his marriage, "according to the rites of holy Church" [i. e. of Rome]. His eldest son, Dermot O'Donovan, was slain in the year 1581, at Lathach-na n-Damh, by the illustrious warrior, Donnell O'Sullevan, who afterwards became the O'Sullevan Beare, as we learn from the Annals of the Four Masters (see note [r], under that year, p. 1762, *supra*), and from O'Sullevan Beare's *Hist. Cathol. Iber. Compend.* He built Castle Donovan, according to Collins; but others think that parts of this castle are much older than his time. He died in the year 1584, and was succeeded by his eldest legitimate son,

XL. Donnell II. O'Donovan. He succeeded his father in 1584; and, in 1586, he burned to the ground the bishop's house at Ross, which had been a short time before built by William Lyon, Bishop of Cork, Cloyne, and Ross.—See Harris's Ware, vol. i. p. 565, and the manuscript entitled *Carbriæ Notitia*, written in 1686. In February, 1592–3, his brother, Teige, attempted to depose him on the score of illegitimacy, but failed. An abstract of the pleading is on record in the Court of Chancery, in Dublin, and extracts from it have been given by the Editor in the *Genealogies, Tribes, and Customs of Hy-Fiachrach*, printed for the Irish Archæological Society, in 1844. From this document it appears, among other curious facts relating to this family, that illegitimate sons, particularly Muliers, by the Civil Law, might be elected as chiefs of it. According to John Collins, he was the builder of the Castle of Raheen, which was found to be the head of a manor in 1607. On the 6th of October, 1607, the following Inquisition, preserved in the Rolls Office, Dublin, was taken before William Lyon, Bishop of Cork, to ascertain the extent of his territory, which was found to contain two manors, namely, the manor of Castle Donovan and the manor of Raheen. When these manors were first erected it is now difficult to determine. The Inquisition is as follows, as far as it can be deciphered, but the latter portion is quite illegible:

"Inquisition taken at the Cittie of Corke, in the Countie of Corke, the vi[th] day of October, 1607, Before the Reverend Father in God, William, Lord Bysshopp of Corcke, and others, by the oathes of good men, &c. The Jurors doe finde, That the Poble or Cantred of Clancahill, is parcell of the countrey of Carribry, in the countie of Corke, and doth containe three scoare and seaven ploughlands, extending from the sea, on the south, to the Ryver of Myalagh[j], And bounded on the North with the landes of Clandonill Rwoe, the landes of Glan-I-crime[k], and the landes of Clanloghlin on the East, and the landes of Clandermodie and Clanteige Rwoe on the West. The which landes of Clancahill is a barren unfertile soyle, full of Bogges, rockes, and Woodd. The said Jurors doe also finde that Donyll O'Donyvane is the lawfull heyre, by descent from his Father and auncestors, to the said country of Clancahill. The said Jurors doe alsoe finde that the said Donyll O'Donyvane is seized of the Mannors, Castells, townes, &c., of Castell O'Donyvane, which doth conteine seaven quarters of land, or twentie and one ploughlands, called by the severall names hereafter following, viz[t]: the quarter of Swagh, conteining three ploughlands; the quarter of Kor-kell, conteining three ploughlandes; the quarter of Kilkisleagh, conteining three ploughlandes; the quarter of Killovynoge" [Killovinoge, in the parish of Drinagh], "conteining three ploughlandes; the quarter of Curraghylickey, conteining three ploughlandes, &c. &c. The said Jurors doe alsoe finde that Donyll O'Donyvane is seised of the quarter of Dirregrey and Lahertishane, conteining three ploughlandes, parcell of the foresaid Mannor. Alsoe, that the towne of Dromdallig, conteining one ploughland, is parcell of the Mannor aforesaid, &c. That Donyll O'Donyvane is seised of the townes Kilscohinaghty" [Kilscahanagh, in Drumaleague par.] "and Dyrryclohaghuoghtragh" [Derryclogh, Upper, in Drinagh par.], "conteining twoe ploughlandes, parcell of the foresaid Mannor. The said Jurors doe alsoe finde that the quarter of Gortinskryny" [now Gortnaskreeny, in Dromaleague par.], "conteining three ploughlandes, being the landes of Slight Ranell O'Donyvane, are by them holden of the Mannor of Castel O'Donyvane. That the quarter of Loghcrott, conteining three ploughlandes, is holden of the Mannor of Castell O'Donyvane, by Slight Dermody Rwoe[l] O'Donyvane, &c. That the Quarter of Aghagard, conteining three ploughlandes, is holden of the said Manor by Slight Teig m[c] Nicholl O'Donyvane, &c. That the quarter of Munan" [now Minane, in Drinagh parish] "and Lahanaght, conteining three ploughlandes, holden of the said Mannor by the Slight of Clanconelig" [Clann-Connelly], "&c. That the quarter of Garren" [now Garrane] "and Ballyvroig, conteining three ploughlandes, is holden of the said Mannor by Slight Clan Conelagh, &c. That Kinglyny, conteining one ploughlande, is holden of

[j] *Myalagh River.*—Now the Mealagh. This river rises in Cnoc na n-aбann (*Collis fluminum*), or Owen Hill, situated in the west of the townland of Cullinagh, parish of Fanloбaip, now Fanlobus, in the barony of west division of West Carbery. It flows in a northerly direction, forming the boundary between the parishes of Dromaleague and Fanlobus; then, changing its course westerly, forms the boundary between Dromaleague and Kilmocomoge, and falls into Bantry Bay, a short distance to the north of the town of Bantry. The Rivers Ilah and Bandon have their sources in the same hill.

[k] *Glan I crime*, i. e. Gleann a' Chpoim, i. e. Crom's Glen. This glen was called after Crom O'Donovan, who was slain by the O'Mahonys in 1254. According to the present tradition in the country it includes all that portion of the parish of Fanlobus lying south of the Bandon river. This territory belonged for many centuries to the Mac Carthys of Dunmanway.

[l] *Slight-Dermody Roe*, Sliocт Diapmada Ruaiḋ, i. e. the Race of Dermot Roe, or Jeremiah the Red. There is a townland in the parish of Drinagh, called Toughmacdermody, now the property of John Townshend, Esq., Dublin.

the Mannor of Castell O'Donyvane by the sept of Clanconelly, &c. That Bernyhuila" [Bearnahulla or Butler's Gift], "conteining twoe ploughlands, is holden of the aforesaid Mannor, by Slight Inesles O'Donyvane, &c. That Muyny and Dyrryclohaghyghtragh" [now Derryclough Lower, in Drinagh parish], "conteining two ploughlandes, is holden of the foresaid Mannor by Slight Inesles O'Donyvane, &c. That the ploughlande of Meal-I-Currane, lying within the said country of Clancahill, is mortgaged to Sir John Fitz-Edmond, Knight, &c. That the ploughland of Coulblach" [Coolbla, in Myross parish] "is in mortgadge with Donyll O'Donyvane, from Donyll Oge ny Keartin, &c. That Stackane & Aghenesky, conteining twoe ploughlandes, is parcell of the Mannor of Rahyne" [now Raheen Castle, in Myross parish], "&c. That the Ryne" [now Reen, in Myross parish], "conteining twoe ploughlandes, is parcell of the said Mannor of Rahyne, &c. That the Castell and half ploughland of Castell Ivire" [now Castle-Ire, in Myross parish], "and the half ploughland of Cast * * * * is parcell of the said Mannor of Rahyne. That Ballycahaine" [in Castlehaven parish] "and Ballyvickadane" [Ballymacadam], "conteining one ploughland, is alsoe parcell of the said Mannor of Rahyne, &c. That Gortbrack, conteining one ploughland, is parcell of the Mannor of Rahyne, &c. That Kylloge and Shanvallyvicka, conteining one ploughland, is in the possession of Donyll O'Donyvane, by vertue of a Mortgage, &c." [The remainder of this Inquisition is quite illegible.]

In the thirteenth year of the reign of James I., when it became the policy of the English Government to abolish the original Irish allodial tenures, and substitute those of England, he surrendered all his lands to the King, and received a re-grant of the same soon after, as will appear from the following extracts from Patent Roll, 13 Jac. I. Part 2, Article xi. Member 24:

"XI. 24. Surrender by Donell O'Donovan of Castle O'Donovan, in Cork C°. gent. of all his estates in Carbrie bar., in Cork C°., with the intention that the King shall re-convey the same to him by letters patent.—28th June, 13th reign.

"XII. 26. Deed, whereby Sir James Semple, of Beltries, in Scotland, Knt., appoints Donell O'Donovane, in Cork C°. gent., to accept a grant or grants from the King, of part of the lands expressed in Article XIV. for a sum of £447 13*s*. Sterling.—28th January, 12th reign.

"XIII. 28. Deed, whereby Sir James Semple appoints Donell O'Donovane, gent., to accept a grant from the King of the remaining part of the lands expressed in Article XIV. for a sum of £45 5*s*. 6*d*.—28th January, 12th reign.

"XIV. 29. Grant from the King to Donell O'Donovan of Castle O'Donovan, gent., Cork Co., in Carbrie Bar. The Castle of Sooagh, Sowagh, or Suagh, otherwise Castle O'Donovan*[m], and the town and lands of Sowagh, otherwise Suagh*, 3 plowlands in Clancahill; Carrowkeill*, 3 plow-

[m] *Castle O'Donovan*, Caiſleán Uí Ḋhonnaḃáin, now Castle Donovan, situated in the townland of Sowagh, *alias* Castledonovan, in the central portion of the parish of Dromaleague, barony of east division of West Carbery. The townland is now the property of St. John Clarke, Esq., Skibbereen, and others, let to four resident tenants, of whom Daniel Donovan is one, on leases of three lives, at lump rents. The soil is light, and fuel now very scarce. The walls of Castle Donovan are still standing, but exhibiting fearful rents, either from the effects of lightning or gunpowder. It was probably one of the two castles belonging to O'Donovan which were blown up with powder by the Cromwellians. This castle stands upon a rock, and is forty-two feet long, twenty-six feet broad, and about sixty feet high. The lower story is arched; and it is accessible to the top by means of a spiral staircase of stone. Not far distant from this castle is the townland of Seehane's, called O'Donovan's seat, which gave name to the townland.

lands, extending in the parcels of Glannaclohie[n], Duylis[o], and Gurtinhirr[p], in Clancahill; Carrownekilly-Caslagh, otherwise Carrownakmolly-Caslagh*, 3 plowlands, extending in the parcels of Garraneknockane and Dromosta[q], in Clancahill; Dromdaleige[r] and Sronakartin[s]*, 2 plowlands; Dirigrieh[t]*, 3 plowlands; Killavenoge[u]* and Twohm[c]. dermadie*, otherwise Tuohm[c] Dermody[w], 3 plowlands; Caslawrie, otherwise Caslurie[x]*, ½ plowland; Curraghilickie[y]*, 3 plowlands; Killstohanaght[z]* and Duricloghaghoughtragh[a]*, 2 plowlands; Kingleny, otherwise Kinglenny[b], 1 plowland; the castle, town, and lands of Rahine[c]†, 2 plowlands, all in Clancahill; Cowlebla[d]†, 1 plowland in Clanloghlin; Castle-Iver[e]†, Stuckin[f]†, and Agheneskine[g]†, 2½ plowlands in Clanloghlin; Kealog[h]†, and Shanvallivikeagh[i]†, in Fornaght[k], 1 plowland, lying in Clandermott; rent for this plowland, 2*s.* 4*d.* Irish. Gortbrack†, Ballikahan[l]†, and Ballym[c]Adame[m]†, 2 plowlands in Clancahill; the two islands called the High and Low Islands[n], in Clancahill; a chief rent of £4 6*s.* Eng. out of Loghcrott[o]; out of Moyny[p]-Duricloghagheightragh[q], 2 plowlands, £2; out of Bearnahuiley[r] £2; out of Gortnescriny[s], £4; out of Aghagard[t], £1 11*s.* 1½*d.*; out of Lahanaght[u], £2 17*s.* 9½*d.*; out of Munane[w], £1 8*s.* 10½*d.*; out of Carren[x], £2 17*s.* 9½*d.*; out of Garrigillihie[y], £4 13*s.* 4*d.*, and a bushel and a half of oats; out of the 6 plowlands of Slughtea[z], viz., Ballincalla[a], Cahirgeall[b],

[n] *Glannaclohie.*—Now Ƃleann na cloiċe, *anglice* Glannaclohy, a townland in the parish of Dromaleague, barony of east division of West Carbery, county of Cork.

[o] *Duylis.*—Now Deelish, in the same parish.

[p] *Gurtinnhir.*—Now Gurteenhir, in the same parish. There was a hamlet of thirteen houses here, about the year 1520, when Teige Mac Dermot was chief of the O'Donovans.

[q] *Dromosta.*—Now Dromusta, in the same parish. O'Donovan had a wooden house here.

[r] *Dromdaleige*, .i. Ꝺpom ꝺa liaᵹ, Hill of the Two Stones; now Dromaleague.

[s] *Sronakartin.*—Now Sronacarton, in the same parish.

[t] *Dirigrieh.*—Now Derrynagree, in the same parish.

[u] *Killavinoge.*—Now Killovinoge, in the parish of Drinagh, and same barony.

[w] *Tuoh-mac-Dermody*: a district, still so called, in the parish of Drinagh.

[x] *Caslurie.*—Now Cashloura, in the same parish.

[y] *Curraghilickie.*—Now Curraghalicky, in the same parish.

[z] *Killscohannaght.*—Now Kilscohinagh, in the parish of Drumaleague.

[a] *Duricloghaghoughtragh.* — Now Ꝺoipe cloċaċ uaċꞇpaċ, *anglice* Derryclough Upper, in Drinagh parish.

[b] *Kinglenny.*—In the same.

[c] *Rahine.*—Now Raheen, in the parish of Myross.

[d] *Cowlebla.*—Written Culebla in Down Survey, where it is shewn as in the parish of Myross.

[e] *Castle-Iver*, Caiplean Iomaip.—Now Castle-Ire, near Lough Clubir, in the parish of Myross. A small portion of the ruins of this castle still remains.

[f] *Stuckin.*—Now Stookeen, in the same parish.

[g] *Agheneskine.*—Obsolete.

[h] *Kealog.*—Now Kealoge, in the parish of Castlehaven.

[i] *Shanvallyvikeagh.*—Obsolete.

[k] *Fornaght.*—In the parish of Castlehaven.

[l] *Ballikahan.*—Now Ballycahane, in the same parish.

[m] *Bally-mac-Adame.*—Now Ballymacadam, in the same parish.

[n] *High and Low Islands.*—In the parish of Myross.

[o] *Loghcrott*, Loċ Cpoꞇ.—Now Lough-Crot, in the parish of Dromaleague.

[p] *Moyny.*—In the same parish. Now the property of Samuel Lewis, Esq.

[q] *Duricloghagheightragh.*—Now Derryclough, Lower, in the parish of Drinagh.

[r] *Bearnahuiley.*—Now Barnahuilla, *alias* Butler's Gift, in the parish of Dromaleague.

[s] *Gortnascriny.*—Now Gortnascreeny, in the parish of Caheragh.

[t] *Aghagard.*—Obsolete.

[u] *Lahanaght.*—In the parish of Drinagh.

[w] *Munane.*—Now Minane, in the same parish.

[x] *Carren.*—Now Garrane, in the same parish.

[y] *Garrigillihie.*—Now Carrigillihy, in the parish of Myross.

[z] *Slughtea*, i. e. Slioċꞇ Aeḋa, i. e. Race of Hugh, a district in the parish of Myross.

[a] *Ballincalla*, Ƀaile an ċala, in the same parish.

[b] *Cahirgeall*, Caṫaip ᵹeal, i. e. White Stone Fort, now Cahergal, in the same parish.

Beallavaddy, Kilnelarhagh, Cwoscronin[c], Foniglogbe, Meadull, and Ballinetony, £2 18 10¼⅛*d.*, and 3 bushels of oats; out of Ballincaslaine, 4 plowlands, £6, and 2 bushels of oats; out of Drissane[d], 3 plowlands, £3 4*s.*; out of each of the 27 plowlands of Slught-Teige O'Mahowne, 1*s.* 10*d.*, in all £3 17*s.* 6*d.*; out of each of the 6 plowlands of Caharagh, Bellaghedoone[e], Killenlea[f], Aghaveele[g], Knockgorrome[h], and Glantawicke, 4*s.* 5½*d.*; out of Rine[i], 2 plowlands, £1 3*s.*; out of Balliroe[k], £1 8*s.* 10½*d.*; the town and lands of Drissane, 3 plowlands, in Clancahill; Mirous[l]†, 2 plowlands; Meaulicarrane[m]†, 1 plowland; Aghagard†, 3 plowlands; Gortnascriny*, 3½ plowlands; Loghcrott*, 3 plowlands; Lahannaght, 2 plowlands; Mounane*, 1 plowland; Duricloghagheightragh*, 1 plowland; Carren*, 2 plowlands; Balliroe*, 1 plowland; Carrigillihie†, 3 plowlands; Ballincalla†, 2 plowlands; Cahirgeale†, Bellvaddie†, Killnalarhagh†, Cuoscronine†, Faniglohie†, Meadull†, and Ballinatony†, 4 plowlands; the island of Briddie, called the Sconice-island[n]; Ballincaslaine†, 4 plowlands; Ballinagornagh[o] † and Keamnabrickie[p] †, 1 plowland; Dromenedie, 1½ plowland; Classnacallie† and Tonebracke†, 8 gnives; in the said Clasnacallie, 1 gnive; Curnaconerta, 1 plowland; Scraggagh†, ½ plowland in Bohannaght[q]; Bane-Ishell[r] in Clomoungane, 8 gnives; Brahillis[s], Voghterglinny, Dromnasoon, Conkinemore, and the four western gnives of Rossavany, containing 3 plowlands and 4 gnives; Westskieve, Cahirbegg, and Clogaghriough, 2 plowlands; Muyny*, 1 plowland; Bearnahuiley*, 2 plowlands; Clounty[t], Mealgoone[u], Drometecloghie, and Killicoosane[w], in Clanloghlin, 3 plowlands; Ballagh-Idoone, 1½ plowland, in the 6 plowlands of Caharagh in Clanteige-Roe; Killineleigh, ½ plowland in the said 6 plowlands of Caharagh; in Kilbirie, ½ plowland; and in Kilbowrowe, ½ plowland; all the customs, royalties, dues, and privileges, heretofore or now granted, due, and payable to the said Donell and his ancestors, in the ports, bays, or creeks of Castlehaven, Squince, Conkeogh[x], and the western part of Glandore[y]; saving to Donell M[c] Cartie, the King's ward, all chief rents, customs, and privileges, due or payable to any of his ancestors. The lands thus marked *, are created the manor of Castle-Donovan, with 500 Acres in Demesne;

[c] *Cwoscronin.*—Now Crosscroneen. This and all the ploughlands of Slughtea are in the parish of Myross.

[d] *Drissane.*—In the parish of Castlehaven.

[e] *Bellaghedoone.*—Now Ballaghadoon, in the parish of Caheragh.

[f] *Killenlea.*—Now Killeenleagh, in the same parish.

[g] *Aghaveele.*—Now Aghaval, in the same parish.

[h] *Knockgorrome.*—Now Knockgorm, i. e. Cnoc gorm, Blue Hill, in the same parish.

[i] *Rine.*—Now Rinn, *anglice* Reen, in the parish of Myross.

[k] *Balliroe.*—Now Ballyroe, in the parish of Kilmacabea.

[l] *Mirous.*—Now Myross, in the parish of the same name.

[m] *Meaulicarrane.*—Now Meall Ui Chorrain, *anglice* Meallicarrane, in the parish of Myross.

[n] *The Sconice Island.*—Now Sconce Island, in the parish of Myross.

[o] *Ballinargornagh.*—In the parish of Roscarbery

[p] *Keamnabrickie.*—Now more correctly, Céim na brice, *anglice* Keamnabricka, a townland in parish of Rosscarbery.

[q] *Bohannaght.*—Now Bohenagh, in the same parish.

[r] *Bane-Ishell*, Bán Iseal, i. e. Low Field, now Bawneeshal, in the parish of Castlehaven.

[s] *Brahillis.*—Now Brahalish, in the parish of Durus.

[t] *Clounty.*—Now Cloonties, in the parish of Kilfaghnabeg.

[u] *Mealgoone.*—Now Meall a ġaḃann, i. e. the Smith's Hillock, *anglicised* Maulagow, or Meallagowan, a townland in the parish of Kilfaghnabeg.

[w] *Killicoosane.*—Now Killacousane, in the same parish.

[x] *Conkeogh*, i. e. Cuan caéċ.—Now Blind Harbour, in the parish of Myross.

[y] *Glandore*, called in Irish Cuan Dór. Now Glandore Harbour, near Skibbereen, in the county of Cork. In an elegy, by Teige Olltach O'Cainte, on the death of Conor O'Connelly, who was harper to O'Donovan (Donnell, the husband of the daughter of Sir Owen Mac Donnell Mac Carthy), the O'Donovans are called Curaiḋ ó Chuan Dor, the Heroes of Cuan-Dor.

power to create tenures; to hold courts leet and baron[z]; to hold a Tuesday market at Dromdaleige, and one fair there on every 14th September, and the day after, unless when the said day falls on Saturday, then the fair to commence on the following Monday; with courts of pie-powder and the usual tolls; rent 13*s.* 4*d.* Irish. The lands thus marked †, are created the manor of Rahine[a], with the like Demesne and privileges; to hold a Friday market at Rahine, and a yearly fair on Ascension day, and the day after, at Banelaghen[b]; with courts of pie-powder, and the usual tolls. To hold for ever, as of the Castle of Dublin, in common soccage.—29th June, 13th reign."

In 1629 he made a nuncupative testament, the only one that remains on record, though he lived ten years afterwards. It is preserved in the Prerogative Court, Dublin, and runs as follows:

"Memorandum: that Mr. Daniell O'Donovane, of Rahine, in the County of Corke, gent. being of perfect mind and memory, although sicke and weake in bodie, made this last will and testament the fourteenth daie of August, Anno Domini 1629, att Rahin aforesaid, in manner following, vizt: First of all I bequeath my soule to God Allmightie, and my bodie to be buried in the Abby of Tymolege. Item; I bequeathe my lands, rents, and inheritance, unto my sonne and heire Daniell O'Donovane. Item; I bequeathe to my maried wife, Juan Cartie, *alias* Donovane, the third parte of all my moveable goods, and all my sheepe, hogges, and swyne, without division. Item; I bequeathe to Juan Ny Teige O'Donovane, the daughter of my sonne Teige O'Donovane, Tenn pounds. Item; I bequeathe to Ellen Carthie, the daughter of Florence Mc Carthie, of Beannduffe, Tenn pounds. Item; I bequeathe to Juan Ny Morough Donovane, the daughter of my sonne, Morough Donovane, Tenn pounds. Item; I bequeathe to Morough Mc Richerde, the sonne of Richerde Donovane, Tenn pounds. Item; I bequeathe all the rest of my moveable goods unto Ellen Donovane, the daughter of Daniell O'Donovane, my sonne and heire. Item; I bequeathe to my sonne Keadagh O'Donovane, One Hundred Pounds Sterling, in manner following, viz.: my sonne and heire Daniell O'Donovane, to paye Three score and sixteene pounds hereof, and Juan Carthie, *alias* Donovane, to paye Twentie fower pounds hereof. Item; I made and appointed Daniell O'Donovane, my sonne and heire, to be my sole Executor, and left all the remainder of my goods unto him. The aforesaid last will and nuncupative Testament was made and delivered before us whose names ensue: Florence Mc Carthy, Teige Mc Carty, Charles mc Donough Carthy, Eugenius Callan."

He married, first, Helena, the daughter of William Barry, of Lislee, in the barony of Barryroe, the son of James Fitz Richard Barry, Viscount Buttevant, and by her he had Daniel O'Donovan, his son and heir, and perhaps others. According to an old manuscript Pedigree of O'Donovan, preserved at Lambeth, he had eleven sons, nine of whom were children when that pedigree was penned. Of these eleven sons three totally disappear from recorded history, and the Editor has been long of opinion, that his own ancestor, Edmond, who fled from Bawnlahan to the county of

[z] *Courts leet and baron.*—From a traditional recollection of this, the peasantry of the mountains of Carbery believe that O'Donovan was a baron; but he never enjoyed any English title.

[a] *Rahine.*—Now Raheen. O'Donovan had a castle there.

[b] *Banelaghen*, bán leaṫan, i. e. Broad Field, now Bawnlahan. O'Donovan had a house here, and it was from this place the Editor's ancestor fled to the county of Kilkenny some years before 1643, for he was killed that year at Ballinvegga, about four miles north of New Ross, Co. Wexford.

Kilkenny before 1643, was one of them.—See note [w], under the year 1600, p. 2155, *supra*, where the Editor's descent from this Edmond is given. That his eldest son and successor was not the son of Joane Mac Carthy appears from an ode addressed to this Daniel, in 1639, by Muldowny O'Morrison, and an elegy composed on his death by Conor O'Daly in 1660, in both which he is called son of Helena. He married secondly, about the year 1584, Joane or Johanna, the daughter of Sir Owen, who was the son of Donnell Mac Carthy, by Eleanor, daughter of Gerald Fitzgerald, eighth Earl of Kildare, and he had by her, 2. Teige, the ancestor of O'Donovan, of Montpellier, near Cork ; 3. Capt. Murrough O'Donovan, who was slain in His Majesty's service, at Rathmines, near Dublin, as appears by the King's letter ; 4. Donough or Denis, the ancestor of James O'Donovan, of Cooldurragha, in the parish of Myross ; 5. Dermot or Jeremias, who was wounded at Prague, in 1648, see p. 2155, *supra ;* 6. Captain Richard, slain in foreign parts in His Majesty's service, who was the ancestor of the late Lieutenant Philip O'Donovan, of Donovan's-street, in the city of Cork ; 7. Keadagh, ancestor of Richard Donovan, Esq., of Lisheens House, near Ballincollig, and of Timothy O'Donovan, Esq., of Ardahill. He had also three daughters, the eldest of whom, Honora, was married to Teige an-Duna Mac Carthy, of Dunmanway, the second to Mac Carthy of Mourne, and the third to O'Mahony Finn, of Ivahagh.

It appears from an old letter preserved at Bawnlahan, that this Donnell was living, a very old man, in 1636, and it is quite certain, from the date of the livery of seisin to his son, that he lived till 1639.

O'DONOVAN OF CASTLE DONOVAN AND BAWNLAHAN.

XLI. Donnell III. O'Donovan, the tenth in direct descent from Crom, succeeded his father on the 13th of Feb. 1639–40, when he obtained livery of seisin from His Majesty.—(Rot. Pat. Char. I. 15°. 7[a]. p. f. R. 49.) He was never inaugurated, the livery of seisin from the King having been, in his time, substituted for the delivery of the white wand by Mac Carthy Reagh. Notwithstanding this, however, a southern poet, Muldowny O'Morrison, knowing or caring nothing about the change in the mode of succession, addressed an ode to him on his accession to the chieftainship of Clancahill, in which ode it is hinted that he had rivals to contend with, but whom he threw into the shade by his bravery, hospitality, and bounty. In this ode, in which he is styled "son of Helena," the treasury of the men of science, who had hoarded nothing except the noble characteristics of his ancestors, it is stated that, to maintain the hereditary dignity of his chieftainship, he avoided accumulating riches, and increased the lustre derived from his ancestors by his hospitality and bounty, in which he expended all his revenue ; that he took in hand the trade of war, in which he has been triumphantly successful. He is called the mighty tower in the battle, the true basis which supports his people ; the defender of the distressed against danger, the idol of his followers, and the terror of stranger foes. The poet concludes by sixteen lines of eulogium on his wife, Sheela, the daughter of Rory O'Shaughnessy, of the race of Guaire Aidhne, King of Connaught, on whom she reflected the lustre she had derived from him.

This Sheela, or Gylles, who died in 1680, as appears by an Irish elegy on her death, was the daughter of Sir Roger O'Shaughnessy of Gort, in the county of Galway, Chief of Kinelea ; and O'Donovan had by her : 1. Daniel, afterwards a Colonel of foot in the service of James II. and

M. P. for Baltimore; 2. Cnoghour, or Conor, living in 1655; 3. Murrough, living in 1655; 4. Richard, living in 1655. In 1640, Jan. 22, he obtained a pass permit from the Earl of Barrymore: "Whereas his sacred Majestie by his Royall pleasure, under his hand and signet, signified that it was his pleasure that Daniell O'Donovane, Esq., should passe with his owne and his servant's swordes too and froo within this His Majestie's kingdome of Irelande; and whereas the said Daniell O'Donovane hath occasion, himself, &c., to repaire into the Countie of Gallwaye, in the province of Connaght, about his affaires. These are, therefore, to require you to permitt the said Daniell O'Donovan, with, &c., to passe into the said Countie, and to returne without trouble, &c. 15th year of his Majestie's Raigne.—Barrymore." He was a strict loyalist in the year 1641, and joined Lord Castlehaven, who lived within two miles of his castle of Raheen, and assisted that nobleman in the taking the towns of Mallow and Doneraile, and the castles of Milton, Connagh, and Rostelion. But Cromwell, landing in Dublin on the 14th of August, 1649, checked the career of the loyalists. It appears from a certificate by the Earl of Clancarty, and also from the King's letter in favour of Daniel, his son, afterwards Colonel O'Donovan, that Cromwell's forces wasted O'Donovan's territory with fire and sword, and blew up two of his castles with gunpowder, and compelled O'Donovan himself to surrender. Clancarty's certificate runs as follows:

"Certificate, that Daniel O'Donovan raised, at his own charge, two companies of foote, and by the Lord Marquis of Ormond's Commission, Morrogh O'Donovan, brother to the said O'Donovan, was Captain on [of] one in Col. Henessy's regiment, under the command of his Excellencie at the siedge of Dublin, where he was killed, and that Rickard O'Donovan, brother also to the said O'Donovan, was Captain of the other company in Col. O'Driscoll's regiment, and retired with his company in Col. O'Driscoll's regiment beyond seas, where he was killed in his Majestie's service. And that, in 1650, the said O'Donovane, through much fidelitie and of his own accord, quitted all his demaines, and chearfully did appear under my command in his Majesty's service; whereupon the Usurped Power fell then immediately on all the castles, houses, and lands of the said O'Donovan, burning, killing, and destroying all they could come by, and have blown upp with powder two of his said castles, &c., which, at the instance of Daniel O'Donovan, son and heire unto the said O'Donovan, I certify, as witness my hand, 24 Martii, 1660.

"Clancartie."

His Majesty's letter, and also a letter from Helena, Countess of Clanrickarde, to the Marquis of Ormond, in favour of Colonel O'Donovan, state the same facts.

Among the family papers at Bawnlahan, there is a petition of "Daniell O'Donovane, to the worshipfull Vincent Toobin, Esq., touching Col. Phayer's engagement to O'Donovan, when he surrendered his castles to the Commonwealth, to rayse thereout some satisfaction for your petitioner." This Colonel Robert Phayer was governor of Cork for the Parliament in 1656, as appears from a letter of protection from him given for Daniel O'Donovan to Colonel Ingoldsby, Governor of Limerick, 25th April, 1656, when O'Donovan proposed to go across the Shannon [to O'Shaughnessy]. This Colonel Phayer was appointed by Cromwell in 1649, and continued till the Restoration in 1660, when he was sent prisoner to Dublin.

In 1650, July 11th, this O'Donovan entered into a covenant with Donough Mac Daniel Carthy and Florence O'Driscoll, reciting:

"For as much as it is thought convenient and necessarie that friends and neighbours in those more than troublesome times should ioyne and unit their helping hands together, to withstand and resist all insolencies and annoyances that should invade either by their enemyes, back friends or any other: wee, therefore, the undernamed, doe, by these presents, covenant and faithfully promise, and thereupon ingage our honesties, to the utmost of our power, to be ayding and assisting one to another in maintaining, uphoulding, and defending our lives, estates, and goods whatsoever, against all person and persons that would intend or act any violence, oppression, or any other unlawfull preiudice unto any or either of us, or that would incroach upon any of the respective Cantridges of Clann-Cahill, or Clanndermod, and Collimore, or any other of our rights or intrests whatsoever: further, it is faithfully promised and agreed upon betwixt us the undernamed, that if any or either of us would conceave or apprehend any cause of iealousie or suspition of imperformance of this covenant, that it shall not be a breach hereof, but rather to be reconciled by the maior vote of the undernamed not concerned in that cause of iealousie, if any be; this tending to a faire correspondencie betweene us in the three cantridges before mentioned: and for the due performance hereof wee have heereunto subscribed our hands the 11th of July, 1650. Moreover, it is agreed upon and faithfully promised by and betweenee us that noe person or persons shall or may have commaund over our men in Armes, or to be in Armes, without our approbation, or the approbation of the maior parte of us, if we may from our superiours obtaine it; moreover, that any officer or officers voted & named by us may not exact, preiudice, or charge any or either of us, nor proceed in any thing wherein wee may be concerned, without the consent of us or the maior parte of us: and for the better performance heereof wee have taken our oathes upon the holy Evangelists, as witness our hands, the 11th of July, 1650.

"DANIELL O'DONOVAN.
DONNOGH M[c] DANIELL CARTHY.
F. O'DRISCOLL."

He died in August, 1660; and we have the following testimony to his character, signed by his neighbours, the Protestant gentlemen of Carbery, who were present at his death. The original is at Bawnlahan, in the possession of M[r] Powell:

"Wee, the undernamed persons, were personally present when the late O'Donovane, of happy memory, upon his death-bed, in August last, 1660, making his last will and Testament, left his cordial, serious blessing upon Donough, Lord of Muskry, and his Honnerable Issue for ever, and prayed his Honnour to continue his former friendship, amitie, and favour to his owne Issue; and that his Honnour knew that he grounded and founded all his ponderous affaires always upon his Lordship, who was Honnourably pleased to keepe and maintayne that his confidence in his Lordship unto and untill that present day. And alsoe commanded his sonne and heire, upon his blessing, to intimate soe much unto his Lordship, and to be advised and governed in all his weightie affaires by his Honnour, and enioyned him to be faithfull and obedient unto him and his noble Issue for ever; and to ioyne with him in all that would tend to their good and profitt, as time and occasion should require. And further he sayd that upon heareing of his Highness the Lord Marquis of Ormond's Landing at Corke, with a Commission from his Majestie for pardoning and forgiveing all and every the natives of this kingdome that would accept of his Majestie's peace then to be proclaimed by his

Highness, he rode instantly to Corke, and upon his entering into his Highnes' lodging ther, his quarter-maister generall (who was formerly acquainted with O'Donovane), said, with a loud voice, La eigin oap eipig O'Donauane puap, and upon that his highness desired O'Donovane to tell him how those Rimes first begun, which he tould him, as he heard from part of his ancestors, and there in the Lord of Inchiquin's presence, O'Donovane voluntarily accepted and ioyfully applauded his said Majestie's peace; and humbly prayed his Majestie's pardon and forgiueness, if he had any way offended him, as he did not any way that he knew; and in continuation of his Loyal submission he rode with his Highnes, in the company of the Lord of Inchiquin, as far as Gleanmoire, three miles from Cork, and there parting with him humbly prayed his Highnes to be alwayes myndfull of him. All which wee certifie to have heard from O'Donovane the time above sayd, as wittnes our hands the first day of December, 1660.

"OWEN FIELD,
WILLIAM GOGHEN," &c.

There is another certificate to the same effect signed by thirty-nine of the English Protestants of Carbery.

There was an elegy composed on his death by Conor Cam O'Daly of Munter-Bhaire, of which there is a copy in the possession of the Editor. In this elegy O'Daly calls this chieftain the son of Helena (as being the son of Helena Barry), laments the loss of this active warrior of wisdom and courage at that most critical period, when the Irish were so distrustful of each other. He remarks that his wife and children were raving with grief around his tomb; that distinguished men of the English and Irish race were overwhelmed with sorrow at his death, and that some of his neighbours after his death became enemies to his sept and territory; but he remarks with emphasis that before they lost their protecting chieftain, neither friend nor foe had obtained sway over them, and that no plunderer had circumvented them. That now the Clann-Ċhathail, the blood of the noble Fiacha Figente, the humane progeny of Donovan, were like a flock without a shepherd, having lost in him their defender against their enemies, their strong bulwark, their directing wisdom, their soul, their head of council, the supporter of their fame, and their active swordsman in the hard conflict; a man of mildness, uprightness, and humanity; a man of meek but vigorous and subtle mind, of unusual insight into the future, who had wisdom without guile in his covenants, and who possessed strength, but never wished to exercise it, though he always exhibited firmness of mind and force of character when just restraint was necessary; a man of modesty, temperance, and humility, deporting himself with deference towards the poor as well as the rich; a man of a majestic mind, of piety, generosity, and truth. At the end he gives the year of his death as follows:

"Three score years exactly,
One thousand years besides six hundred,
Was the age of the son of God
When O'Donovan departed."

His wife, Sheela, died in the year 1680, as appears from an elegy on her death, beginning, "Galap buna báp cSíle." She was the daughter of Sir Roger O'Shaughnessy, by Elizabeth Lynch, and was, at least, twenty years younger than her husband.

XLII. DANIEL IV. On the death of his father in 1660, being left without any estates, he petitioned His Majesty, Charles II., immediately after his restoration, to restore him to his father's property. His petition runs as follows:

"To the King's most Excellent Majestie.

"The humble petition of Daniell O'Donovane, Esq. In most humble manner beseecheth your Majestie to cast your gracious eye uppon the annexed, wherein your Majestie may reade of the Petitioner's late deceased father's sufferings and civill deportment sithence ye first breaking out of the Rebellion in Ireland in the year 1641, untill this present, which your Petitioner can make apeare by proofe beyonde exceptions. And yett your Pettioner is at present dispossessed of all his Lands, tenements, and hereditaments in Irelande.

"May it, therefore, please your Majestie, and as the Pettioner never acted directly or indirectly against your Majestie's service, his late deceased father's reall integrity in the furtherance of your Majesties service appearing, there being no delinquency to be laide to theire charge, to give order that your Pettioner may (without any further trouble) be forthwith putt in possession of all and singular the estate and estates, whereof his late deceased father and he were dispossessed by the late Usurped Power, and therein confirmed and settled by your Majesties gracious order, and your Pettitioner shall pray, &c."

"*Whitehall, March* 3, 1661.

"His Majestie is graciously pleased to referr this Petition to the Right honourable Lord Viscount Moor, the Lord Viscount Loftus, and the Lord Kingston, or any two of them, to consider thereof, and certifie his Majestie what they consider fitt to be done therein.

"WILLIAM MORRICE."

It appears from a Pass Permit given to O'Donovan on this occasion that he went to England:

"Charles R.—Charles by the Grace of God, King of England, Scotland, France, and Ireland, Defender of the faith, and soe forth. To all loveing subjects whome it may concerne, Greeting. These are to will and require you to suffer and permitt Daniel O'Donovan, Esq., and his servants and their necessaries, to Imbarke in any of our Ports, and passe into our Kingdome of Ireland; and there to remaine and travell with theire swords freely and quietly aboute theire lawfull occasions, and to return into England upon occasions, without any lett, hindrance, or molestation whatsoever."

This was followed by a letter from the King to the Irish Government, recommending O'Donovan's claim to their serious attention. The result was, that he was restored to a small portion of the Manor of Raheen, but to no part of the Manor of Castle Donovan, which the King by Patent, in the eighteenth year of his reign, granted unto Lieutenant Nathaniel Evanson, at a rent of £22 4*s.* 11*d.*

O'Donovan also obtained a certificate from the English inhabitants of the barony of Carbery, and its vicinity, testifying to the character of himself and his father, which is worded as follows:

"Wee, English Inhabitants, living in the Barrony of Carberrie and the part adjacent, in the Countie of Corke, doe from our knowledge humbly certifie all those whome it may concerne, that Mr. Daniell O'Donovane, *alias* O'Donovane, chief of that name and family, hath from his childhood lived inoffensive towarde us and all his neighbours, and loyall and faithfull to his Majestie ; And that his father, Daniel O'Donovane, lately deceased, both in the beginning and continuance of the late unhappy warr in Ireland, did by many signall testimonies declare and shewe his constant good affection to the English, in his willingnes on all occasions to serve them in their distress and want ; and that his loyall and good affection to the late King, of Blessed memorie, hath been manifestly seen to us and others ; which deportment of his wrought so effectually, that there werr present hundreds of English and chiefest Neighbourhood attending his corps to the grave, more than ever was seen by any of us to any other of his Nation, which was not long after the tyme of his Majestie's happy restauration of his Crowne and Dignitie, to which wee doe subscribe this 20th day of May, 1662.

"AMOS BENNETT, JOHN GOODWYN,
JAMES DEVREX, EDWARD BRYAN,
BOYLE HULL, JOHN HEALY,
THOMAS HUNGERFORD, ABELL MARSHALL,
THOMAS JARVYS, EDWARD CLERKE."

O'Donovan also obtained a letter from the Countess of Clanrickard to the Duke of Ormond, recommending him to his Grace's special notice and protection :

[*November*, 1665.]

"To his Grace James Duke of Ormond, Lord Lieutenant of Ireland, These are.

"May it please your Grace,—The Bearer, Daniel O'Donovan, sonne and heire to Daniel O'Donovan, late of Castle Donovan, in the County of Corke, Deceased, hath been left without any provision for him in the Act of Settlement, which I believe hath beene occasioned by the Death of my Deare Lord and husband, and my sonne, for I [often heard them] speake of the said Daniel Donovan, the father [of the bearer], to be a person who at all times, and upon all occasions, was ready to serve his Majestie, as appeares by your Grace's and my husband's certificates, which the bearer hath to shew, and which I humbly pray your Grace to peruse, together with his Majestie's Gratious letters, which he alsoe hath, wherein there is mention made of his father's raising men under your Grace's command, Two companies of foote, whereof both his brothers were Captaines, and one of them, with his company, totally slaine with your Grace at the siege of Dublin, at Rathmoines, and the other slaine in his Majestie's service beyond seas. Now I humbly referr the condition of the poore Gentleman to your Grace's consideration, he having noe other friends to mediate for him, since the death of my dearest friends."

This is indorsed in another hand, "Lady Clanrickarde's letter to y[e] Duke of Ormond, in [favour] of O'Donovan."

The King's letter and the decree of the Court of Claims are as follows. They are extracted from Adventurers' Certificates, Roll xviii., preserved in the Chief Remembrancer's Office, Dublin. There is another copy of the King's letter at Bawnlahan House, in the possession of Edward Powell, Esq.

"Daniell O'Donovane, Esq., sonn and heire of Daniell O'Donovane, of Castle O'Donovane, in the county of Corke, deceased, did exhibit his Petition and Schedule before us, His Majesty's

Commissioners, upon the 3rd March, 18th year Chas. II., thereby setting forth, that by virtue of his Majesty's gracious Letter, which followeth in these words :

"Charles R.—We having taken into consideration the report of the Earle of Drogheda and the Lord Kingeston, grounded on our order of referance of the thirtieth of March last past, graunted on the Petition of Daniell O'Donovane, Esq., wherein it appeareth by the Certificate of our right trusty and right intirely beloved James Duke of Ormond, steward of our household, and other certificates in the said report mencioned, That Daniell O'Donovane, of Castle O'Donovane, in the county of Corke, in our kingdome of Ireland, submitted unto the Peace concluded in our said kingdome, in the yeare one thousand six hundred and forty-eight, and constantly adhered thereunto, contributing his best endeavours to advance it, and suppresse all oppositions that might be thereunto given, signally testifying upon all occasions his loyalty and fidelity to our service ; and that he raised, at his own cost and charge, by Commission from the said Duke of Ormond, then our Lieutenant of Ireland, two foote companies, whereof one was commanded, as Captaine, by Morrogh O'Donnovane, his Brother, in the regiment of Collonell Hennesy, under the Command of our said Lieut. of Ireland, at the seidge of Dublin, where the said Captaine Morogh O'Donovane was killed in our service. And that Richard O'Donovane retired himselfe and Company into forraigne partes, and there was also killed in our service, when hee had first, as Captaine of the other foote Company in Collonel O'Driscoll's Regiment, contributed his best endeavours for the furtherance of our service, till the late Usurped Power became prevalent in our said kingdome of Ireland; and that Daniell O'Donovane persevering still constant in his loyalty to us, the said Usurped Power seized upon all his Estate, burning, killing, and destroying all that came in their way, and blew up, with powder, two of his the said Daniell's Castles. All which induced the referrees aforesaid to be of opinion that Daniell O'Donovane, sonn to the said Daniell, lately deceased, is by our Declaration for the settlement of that Kingdome, restorable to the estate whereof his said father was dispossessed as abovesaid. We have, therefore, thought fitt, and it is our will and pleasure, that the said Daniell be forthwith established in the quiett and peaceable possession of all the Castles, houses, Lands, tenements, leases, mortgages, & hereditaments whatsoever, whereof the said Daniell O'Donovane, his father, was dispossessed by the late usurped government ; and the rather for that wee find by Certificates of sundry persons of quallity, his English neighbours, that hee ever was affeccionate to the English ; and alwayes industrious and carefull to preserve their interest and goods from the rapine and pilladge of the rude multitude. And if any part of the premisses be possessed by reprizable adventurers, or souldiers, that they be reprized without delay, and the Petitioner forthwith restored to that parte of his Estate alsoe (his father nor himselfe ever accepting any Lands in Connaught, or the County of Clare, in [as much as] that they still expected to be restored to their owne by our happy restauration), and if any Rent or Rents, or other sume or sumes of mony doe remayne in charge on the premisses in our Court of Exchequer, in our said Kingdome, which were putt in charge since the moneth of October, 1641, the Barons of our said Court and every of them, and every other officer there whom it may concerne, are forthwith to cause the same to be put out of charge. And our further will and pleasure is, that our Lords Justices of our said Kingdome, our Commissioners, and all other our Governour and Governours for the tyme being, our sheriffes and other officers, whom it shall or may concerne, doe cause this our order to be put in due and speedy execution, for which this shall be to them and every of them a sufficient warrant. Given at our Court at Whitehall, the eighteenth day of Aprill, 1661, in the thirteenth yeare of our reigne.

"By His Majesty's Command,

"WIL. MORRICE.

"To our trusty and right welbeloved Councellor Sir Maurice Eustace, Knight, Chancellor of our Kingdome of Ireland; and to our right trusty and right welbeloved Cousins and Councellours, Roger Earle of Orrery and Charles Earle of Mountrath, Justices of our said Kingdome; and to the Commissioners appointed to execute our Declaration for the settlement of that our Kingdome; & to the Chief Governour or Governours thereof for the time being; and to all other our Officers and Ministers whom it may Concerne."

"And by one Clause or Proviso in the said Explanatory Act expressed, hee is lawfully and rightfully intituled unto several lands, tenements, and hereditaments in the said Petition and Schedule mentioned.

"It appeared unto this Court that Daniel O'Donovane, deceased, father to the Claymant, was in the actuall seizin and possession thereof upon the 22nd October, 1641; and that the Claymant was in the actuall seizen & possession thereof upon the 22nd August, 1663. It is Decreed that he and his heires and assigns shall & may have, hold, & enjoy the following lands, tenements, and hereditaments, that is to say: Curraghalicky, three plowlands, containing 640 acres of profitable lands, plantation measure, and 176 acres of unprofitable lands; in Derryclaghagh, two plowlands, 322A. 1R. 28P. prof., and 122A. unprof. In Cashlurragh and Killavinoge, 569A. 2R. 16P. prof.; Coolbla, one plowland, 192A. 3R. 8P. prof.; and Banlaghan, one plowland, 146A. 3R. 8P. profit.; all lying and being in the Barony of Carbery, and County of Corke; the totall of plantation acres being 1871A. 2R. and 20 perches, which make 3031A. 2R. 35P. English statute measure.

"The same to be held and enjoyed by the said Daniel O'Donovane, his heires and assigns, for Ever, in free and Common Soccage, as of His Majesty's Castle of Dublin; rendering and paying for the same, yearly, £28 8*s.* 5½*d.* Sterling, at the receipt of His Majesty's Exchequer in Dublin; and this our judgment and Decree we do hereby Certifie, to the end that effectuall letters patents may be forthwith granted unto the said Daniell O'Donovane, his heirs and assigns, for Ever, this 21st day of December, 1666.

"EDW. SMYTHE, W. CHURCHILL,
EDW. DERING, EDW. COOKE."

In 1684 he was put on his trial for high treason, as appears from a certified copy of a record in the possession of O'Donovan of Montpellier, which states: "That Daniell O'Donovan, Esq. (being committed by Sir Emanuel Moore, Esq., one of his Majestie's, &c., for high Treason, on the information of one John Donovan), was at the said Assizes indicted for that he the said Daniell O'Donovan, the 1st December, in the, &c., at Ardagh, in the county of Corke, did traitorously, together with other traitours unknowne, conspire, imagine, &c., the death of our Sovraigne Lord the King, &c., in his lodgings in Whitehall, and also to levie warre against the King, &c., and to depose and deprive his Majestie of his regall power, &c., by procuring, bringing in, &c., a forraigne power, to witt, the French King and his army, and to that end, &c. To which indictment said Daniel O'Donovan pleaded "*not guilty*," and for his tryall put himselfe on his country, which absolutely acquitted him, and found him not guilty thereof; whereupon the said Daniel O'Donovan was then discharged, without any rule of the good behaviour. All which I certifie, &c.

"JONAN SANKEY."

Soon after this period we find him a colonel of a regiment of foot, consisting of thirteen companies, in the service of James II. On the 25th July, 1689, he received the following order from James II.:

"James Rex [autograph],—Our will and pleasure is, that you keep up all the supernumerary companies of the Regiment under your command that are over and above thirteen, till we send you our further orders to dispose thereof. And you are to send us an account of their number, that subsistence may be ordered for them. Given at our Court at Dublin Castle, the 25th day of July, 1689, and in the 5th yeare of our Reigne.

"By his Majesty's Command,

"MELFORT.

"To our Trusty and wellbeloved Coll. Daniell O'Donovan, commanding a Regiment in our service."

How far the subsistence here promised was given will appear from the following petition, sent by Colonel O'Donovan soon after to His Majesty. No date appears, but it was probably in 1689.

Petition to the King, that "Petitioner, Daniel O'Donovan's father, raised two companies of foote, commanded by Petitioner's uncles, who were both slaine in his late Majestie's service. That by his late Majestie's letter, Petitioner was to be restored to an ancient Estate of about £2000 per annum; but by the partiality of the late Government was deprived of it, &c. That Petitioner suffered long imprisonment by the oppression of the late Earl of Orrerie, and was tried for his life, before Lord Chief Justice Keateing and Sir Richard Reynalls, uppon account of the late pretended Plot, &c. That Petitioner, by Commission, raised about Christmas last a Regiment of foot, and ever since kept them without any subsistence from your Majestie, whereby Petitioner is exposed to censure, &c. That Petitioner will slight all perills, &c., to serve your Majestie; and that Petitioner's habitation and estate are exposed to the sea, and pirates frequently annoying the Inhabitants, so that it is requisite to have still men in arms thereabouts."

Among the Bawnlahan papers, many of which are now in the possession of O'Donovan at Montpellier, are numerous letters, military orders of Lord Dover, General Wauchop, La Motte, and others, accounts of men, arms, and moneys, captures of places, and notes for exchange of prisoners during the civil war, addressed to the Honourable, and, sometimes, Right Honourable Colonel Daniel O'Donovan, at various places in Munster. These documents are very curious, and should be all published. Among them is a "Precept of Pierce Nagle, High Sheriff of the county of Corke, to the Provost of the Borough of Baltimore, to elect two Burgesses of that Borough to the Parliament to be holden on the 7th of May next, at Dublin, dated 9th April, 1896; and also a draft of the return of Members of Parliament for the Borough of Baltimore, in April, 1689, between Pierce Nagle, High Sheriff of the county of Corke, and Cornelius O'Donovan, Morough O'Donovan, Cornelius O'Donovan of Kilmacabea, Daniel O'Donovan of Kilgliny, Daniel Regane, Daniel O'Donovan of Gortnaskehy, Timothy Regane, Daniel O'Donovan of Fornaght, Thady Regane of Ballyvarloghly, Cornelius O'Donovane of Ballyncala, and Keadagh O'Donovan, all Burgesses of the towne and Borough of Baltimore, duly choosing Daniel O'Donovan, *alias* O'Donovan, Esq., and Richard O'Donovan, Esq., Doctor of Both Laws, to be members, &c. In this document the name, "Richard O'Donovan, Doctor of Both Laws," is cancelled throughout, and that of "Jeremie O'Donovan, Esq." written above it. (This was Jeremy Donovan of Dublin, Chief of the Clan-Loughlin.)

In October, 1690, Col. O'Donovan was Deputy Governor of Charles Fort, which was summoned to surrender by Lord Marlborough; but the Governor, Sir Edwart Scott, answered, that it would be time enough a month hence to talk of surrendering; upon which the trenches were opened the 5th of October. The batteries were managed on the east side by the Danes in King William's service, and on the north by the English. On the fifteenth a breach was made by the Danes; and the English being masters of the counterscarp, they sprung a mine with good success, and every thing was ready for an assault, when the Governor capitulated, and surrendered upon honourable conditions, which would not have been granted, but that the weather was exceeding bad, provisions scarce, and the army very sickly. Colonel O'Donovan delivered the keys of this fort into Lord Marlborough's hands, who, having thus fortunately accomplished the design of his voyage, left his brother, Brigadier Churchill, governor of Charles Fort, and returned with his fleet to Portsmouth. The garrison in Charles Fort, which consisted of 1200 men, had liberty to march out with their arms and baggage, and were conducted to Limerick.—*Story*, p. 147. Smith's *Natural and Civil History of Cork*, vol. ii. p. 206.

It appears from a letter in the handwriting of Helena, Countess of Clanrickard, and addressed to her son, John, ninth Earl of Clanrickard, that Colonel O'Donovan was treated unfairly by James the Second's party. It is at present in the possession of O'Donovan of Montpellier, and runs as follows:

"My dear Lord,—This goes by a kind clergyman and an officer in Coll. Donovan's Regiment, of the same name, and, I suppose, his neere relations. They make a complaint of hard measure done to Coll. O'Donovan; and truly such proceedings are unparrelelled. The King and all of and in his interest have a part in a wrong and injury soe gross and palpable. Your Lordship will concurre in this when you have heard what they have to say, and to it your Lordshipp is referred by

"My Lord, your very affectionate mother,

"and most humble Servant,

"Hellena Clanrickarde.

"Coll. O'Donovan is a neere relation to my children by their father; and, tho' not so neere, yet related to me too."

This Helena Clanrickarde was the daughter of Donogh Mac Carthy, first Earl of Clancarty, by Ellen Butler, sister of James, first Duke of Ormonde. She was the second wife of William, seventh Earl of Clanrickarde, who was the nephew of Sir Roger O'Shaughnessy, the maternal grandfather of Col. O'Donovan.—See Burke's *Extinct Peerage of Ireland*, 1840; Lodge's *Peerage*, by Archdall, vol. iv. p. 39; Burke's *Hibernia Dominicana;* and *Genealogies, Tribes, and Customs of Hy-Fiachrach*, printed for the Archæological Society of Dublin, p. 381.

The above letter was written on the 24th of April, 1691. On the 18th of May following, we find a letter, in the handwriting of Colonel Hamilton, offering, on the part of the Government, to Colonel O'Donovan, that he shall be free for ever from all private actions, from any injury or trespass done by him, since the 1st of August, 1688, to the date hereof. The following is a faithful copy of this letter, preserving the writer's peculiar orthography and odd phraseology:

"*Bandon*, 18 *May*, 1691.

"SIR,—I have orders given me to signifie you that you shall be for ever free from all private actions, from any injury or trespass done by you, or by your command, since the 1st of August, 1688, to the datė hereof, which, in my opinion, is both honourable and very large conditions. What specified above, and what Capt. Hamilton shewd you under hand and seall, I be engadge shall be confirm'd, both by goverment and generall; if not accept'd off, I wish verie heartlie that I had never mov'd itt. I march from this on Wensday, so you may perswad y^r self not to find a second frind that can procure you larger conditions as what now I offer. All I have now to say, that since I have obtain'd what you can desair, I don't doubt but you will be so *just* as to comply with my desair. I me, Sr,

"Your most humble servt.

"Lett me have your possitive answar. "GEO. HAMILTONE.

"For Colonell O'Donovan, att Drummoor, These."

Colonel O'Donovan did not comply with this request; on the 12th of October, 1691, he received an order from the Honourable Major-General Wanehope, to march with his regiment to the harbour of Cork, there to be embarked. This order is worded as follows:

"Notwithstanding any former orders, you are heareby, on sight heareof, required to march with the Regiment under your command to the harbor of Cork, there to be imbarked. Given under my hand, at Litter, this 12th of November, 1691.

"JO. WANEHOPE.

"To Coll. O'Donnevan these, att Gortneshemer."

It does not appear that he went off to foreign parts on this occasion; for it is evident from a pass-permit, in the handwriting of Bryan Townesend, that he went to Cork on the 4th of January, 1692, to deliver himself up as a prisoner:

"Permit Col. O'Donovan to travell to Timoleague, and from thence to Corke, in order to deliver himselfe a prisoner unto the High Sheriff without molestation, he behaveing himselfe as becometh, unless you have any order to the contrary from the said Sheriff. Dated this 4th day of January, 1692.

"B. TOWNESEND.

"You are also to permit Capt. Conolly and Captain Donovan to pass as above.—B. T."

It appears from a letter in the handwriting of John Hill, touching an equity suit then in court pending, that Colonel O'Donovan was living in January, 1701. He married, first, Victoria, daughter of Captain Coppinger, and had by her one daughter, Victoria, who married Captain Cornelius O'Donovan, the ancestor of the present O'Donovan (Morgan William, of Montpellier). He married, secondly, in 1665, Elizabeth Tonson, the daughter of Major Tonson, and had by her three daughters, namely: 1. Sarah; 2. Honora; and 3. Catherine; and four sons: 1. Richard, his eldest son, and heir; 2. Daniel, who died young; 3. Barry, who died young; and 4. Cornelius, who married Honora, daughter of Mac Fineen Duff, and had issue Richard, who had a son, Cornelius, who died at Dingle, *s. p.* in 1841, the last of the descendants of Colonel Daniel O'Donovan in the male line.

XLIII. Captain Richard, son of Colonel Daniel O'Donovan. He married, in 1703, Ellinor Fitzgerald, daughter of the Knight of Kerry, by whom he had three children: 1. Daniel, his successor; 2. Rickard, who died unmarried; and some daughters, the eldest of whom was Elizabeth, who married Silvester O'Sullivan, head of the sept called Mac Fineenduff, of Derreenavurrig, near Kenmare, in Kerry, by whom she had numerous issue. Among the Bawnlahan papers are curious articles of agreement, dated 12th September, 1703, between the parties, in which, among other things, Richard O'Donovan, *alias* O'Donovan, "promises to pay the said Silvester £200 sterling, as soon as he, the said Richard, shall recover his wife's fortune or portion from the present Knight of Kerry" ! !

XLIV. Daniel V., son of Captain Richard O'Donovan. He married, first, in the year 1721, in the eighteenth year of his age, Anne Kearney, daughter of James Kearney, Esq., of Garrettstown, in the barony of Courcies, but had no issue by her; and secondly, in the year 1763, in the sixtieth year of his age, Jane Becher (daughter of John Becher, Esq., of Hollybrook), then fifteen years old, and had by her four children: 1. Richard, a General in the English service; 2. John, a captain in the English service, who was killed in the year 1796; 3. Ellen, or Helena, who married John Warren, Esq., of Codrum, and died without issue in 1840; and 4. Jane, who died unmarried in the year 1833. This Daniel conformed to the established religion of the State in 1729, and died in 1778. In his will, dated 22nd December, 1778, he leaves the reversion of his estates to Morgan Donovan, Esq., then living in the city of Cork, the grandfather of O'Donovan of Montpellier. He was buried in the church of Myross, where he was followed by his second wife, Jane Becher, in 1812. The following is a copy of his will:

"In the name of God, amen, I, Daniel O'Donovan, of Castle Jane," [*alias* Bawnlahan] "Esq., in the parish of Myrus, and county of Cork, being in perfect sence and memory, but feeble and weak, do make this my last will, revoking all wills to this date made. First, I order all my debits to be justly paid, and resign my soule to Allmighty God, and to have my Body privatly interd in my family burying-place at Myrus. I appoint my good friends, James Kearny, Esq., of Garrettstown; Thomas Sarsfield, Esq., of Ducloen; Thos. Hungerford, Esq., of Foxhall; and Michl. Becher, Esq., to be Executors and Administrators of this my last will, to settle and avoid any disputes hereafter in my family. *Imprimis*, I leave my Estate clear, as by my settlement will appear, to my eldest son, Richard O'Donovan, and his heirs male lawfully begotten; and, in failure of Issue male in him, of my second son, John Donovan, and his heirs male lawfully begotten; in failure of Issue male or female in either, I leave the reversion of my Estate to Morgan Donovan, Esq., now living in the city of Cork, and to his heirs male lawfully begotten ; subject, in case of accidents, to the sum of ten thousand pounds Ster. to my Eldest Dauther, Elen O'Donovan, and the like sum to be paid to my second Dauther, Jane O'Donovan, being the sum of ten thousand pounds Ster.. and to their heirs : if Either should dye, the surviving person to come in for the intire twenty thousand pounds. Secondly, I give and devise the sum of Two thousand pounds, being my wife's fortune, with two thousand pounds more, which I had a power by my settlement, and one thousand pounds more, debits due to me from different persons, which in all amounts to five thousand pounds, to be dispos'd of in manor following : I order those five thousand pounds to be equally divided between my three younger Children, share equaly alike ; and if either should dye under the age of fifteen years, or unmaried, the surviving person or persons to come in for such part ; in case of failure in the younger children, the above five thousand pounds to come to my eldest son, Richard; viz. John O'Donovan, Elen O'Donovan, and Jane O'Donovan, are what I call my younger children. I give and devise to my dear and beloved wife One hundred Acres of her choice part of the lands at Castle Jane, with the dweling-house, out-houses, and offices, during the minority of my son, Richard, she keeping the same in proper order. I give unto my dear and beloved wife her post-Sheas," [Chaise] "Horses, and Harness, and what belongs to the Sheas as usual, knowing her to be a loveing mother and faithfull wife. I give and bequeth unto my Sister O'Sullivan's children, male and female, five pounds sterling, to be given each of them. I leave all other debits, goods, chattles, and all manor of property, to my son, Richard, over and above what I have herein set forth.

"Given under my hand and seale this 22nd day of December, 1778, seventy-eight; Castle Jane.

"DAN. O'DONOVAN.

"Before the perfection of this will, I give and bequeath to my second son, John O'Donovan, my part of the lease purchased from Thos. Baylie, called Clontaff, to him and his heirs and assigns ; with the lands of Cahnenausnah, when recovered by law. Witness my hand and seale, as above dated,

"DAN. O'DONOVAN.

"Signed & sealed in presence of us,

"ALEXANDER DONOVAN,
WILLIAM ROBERTS,
DAVID HORAN,
JOHN DONOVAN."

Smith, in his *History of Cork* (1st edit., p. 271), in noticing Banlaghan, writes: "In this parish [of Moyross], is Banlaghan, the seat of O'Donovan, chief of that ancient family, a worthy, courteous gentleman."

XLV. RICHARD II., SON OF DANIEL O'DONOVAN. He was born about 1764, and, in 1800, married Emma Anne Powell, a Welsh lady, by whom he had no issue. He levied fines and suffered a recovery of all his property, and thus cut off the remainder of O'Donovan of Montpellier in the estates. He was Colonel of the Enniskillen Dragoons, and afterwards a General in the English service, and the intimate acquaintance of the Prince Regent, and of his Royal Highness the Duke of York, whose life he saved in the retreat from Holland. He died in 1829, after having willed his pro-

property[c] to his wife, Emma Anne Powell, who died in 1832, after having willed the remnant of the estate of the senior branch of the O'Donovan family to her brother, Major Powell, whose sons now enjoy it.—*Sic transit, &c.*

O'DONOVAN OF MONTPELLIER.

On the death of General O'Donovan, in 1829, the Rev. Morgan Donovan, of Montpellier, began to style himself "the O'Donovan," though the next heir to this dignity at the time was Captain Cornelius O'Donovan of Tralee, who was the son of Richard, son of Cornelius, the second son of Colonel O'Donovan, who left issue. This Captain Cornelius died at Dingle, in 1841, without issue; but, after his death, the next heir to the dignity of O'Donovan was Morgan William O'Donovan, of Montpellier, who descended from Teige O'Donovan of Raheen and Drishane, the second son of Donell O'Donovan, who was inaugurated in 1584, and died in 1638 or 1639. His pedigree is published in Burke's *History of the Commoners*. The following is a copy of the probate of the will of his ancestor, Teige, which proves, beyond a question, that he was the brother of Daniel III., the husband of Gylles O'Shaughnessy.

"In Dei nomine, Amen. I, Teige O'Donovane of Drishane, in the Countie of Corke, Gent., beinge of perfect witt and memory, though weake in bodie, doe make this my last will and testament as followeth: First, I bequeath my soule to God Almightie, and my bodie to be buried in the Cathedrall Church of Rosse Carbery. Item, I bequeath unto my sonne and heire, Daniell mac Teige, and his heires males, the nine Gnives, three quarters of a plo: of the south ploughland of Drishane, and the tenn Gnives, in mortgadge of fower score and tenn pounds and eleven shillings ster., in the quarter of Kilmacbic, called Caghir Cairbrie, halfe a ploughland; and Cahirnebologie fower Gnives, and the halfe ploughland of Carighbane, which I hold in fee simple, in the quarter of Revolder and the halfe ploughland of Gortnacloghee and Dromenidy, which I hold in moortgadge from Owen mac Cormack for fifteene pounds tenn pence, ster.; also the two Gnives of the plo. of Lahanaght, which I hold in mortgadge from Conohor mac Awlife for fowerteene pounds, ster. Also the five Gnives of Loghcrote, the three Gnives of Crothe, and the two gnives of Knockboie, which I hold in fee simple, the gnive and quarter of a gnive in Knockboy aforesaid, which I hold in mortgadge of Donogh mac Teige, alias Bronagh, for eleaven pounds ten shillings and six pence, ster. Also the halfe ploughland of Dirigule, which I hold in mortgadge from Dermod oge and Donough mac Dermod for twenty pounds, vizt. tenn pounds, ster., each of them oweth, and thirteene pounds six shillings tenn pence, ster., which the said Donogh mac Dermod oweth me by specialties. And for want of such issue males of the said Daniell, lawfully begotten or to be begotten, the remainder of all the before recited premisses to my second sonne, Morrogh mac Teige, and the heires males of his bodie, lawfully begotten or to be begotten. And for want of such Issue males of the said Morrogh, the Remainders thereof unto my brothers equally devided

[c] *Willed his property.*—The following are the names of the lands remaining to General O'Donovan at the time of his death in 1829, and which were bequeathed by him to his wife, Emma Anne Powell: 1. Bawnlahan; 2. Coolebin; 3. Islands; 4. Clontaff; 5. Kilgleeny. or Kilglinny; 6. Curraghalicky; 7. Curryglass; 8. The Pike; 9. Coomatholin. This was a very small portion of Clancahill. These lands were bequeathed by the said Emma Anne Powell, relict of the late General O'Donovan, to her brother, the late Major Powell, whose two sons have divided them equally.

betweene them. Item, I bequeath and leave unto my wife, Joanne Donovane, alias Goggan, the ploughland of Drishane, whereupon my house standeth now, and the three Gnives of Dirireloge, in the quarter of Kilmacbie, which she holdeth by a Deed of jointure, as by the said more at large appeareth, and the Reversion of Remainder of the said lands unto my sonne, Daniell, and the heires males of his bodie, lawfully begotten, or to be begotten; and for want of such Issue males, the Remainder thereof to the use or uses as afore specified. Also I bequeath unto my said wife the third part of all my Chattle, Horses, Cows, and household stuffe. Item, I bequeath unto my second sonne, Morragh mac Teige, the forty pounds tenn shillings, ster., due unto me by specialties upon Dermod O Driscoll of Doulough; forty pounds, ster., due unto me by specialties upon Cnoghor Oge O Driscoll of Ballynarde. Provided that if it fortune or happen that my said sonne, Morrogh, should die in his minority or nonadge, my will is that the remainder of this which I bequeath him shall revert and remain to his Brother, my eldest sonne and heire, Daniell. Item, I bequeath and leave unto my five daughters, vizt. to Joane ny Teige, Ellen ny Teige, Eilene ny Teige, and Shilie ny Teige, Twenty pounds, ster., due unto me by specialties upon Dermod mac Finine of Cnockebolleintagert; Twelve pound, ster., due unto me upon Finine O Driscoll upon specialties; and thirteene pounds, ster., due unto me by specialties upon Teige mac Moriartagh mac Teige of Gort Shanecrone, to be equally divided betweene them in equal portions. And if it shall happen or fortune that any of them shall die in their minority, that then her portion so dieinge shall be equally devided betweene the survivors. Item, I bequeath and leave unto my said five daughters the two parts of my Chattle, horses, and corne, as my Brothers, or two or three of them, in their discretion shall thinke fitt to devide them. Item, I bequeath and leaue towardes the dischargeinge of my Debts the six pounds, ster. due unto me by specialties upon ——— mac Fillmie of Maleloghy; and also the tenn pounds, ster., due unto me by specialties upon mac Con mac Teige of Murrigh. Also, I leave and bequeath unto my sonne and heire, Daniel mac Teige, and heires males, *ut supra*, thirteene pounds and twelve shillings, ster., which are due unto me by severall specialties and notes upon Donogh mac Teige mac Feylimy of Glaunagele; and also the fifteene shillings which are due unto me upon Thomas Kecrafte, endinge upon ——— Item, my said sonne and heir, Daniell, is to discharge and pay unto my Brother Richard's sonne, Daniell mac Richard, Twenty pounds, ster., which he has upon me by specialties. Item, I bequeath and leave unto my sonne and heire, Daniell, the two parts of my household stuffe. And also doe name and appoint my Brother, Morrogh Donovane, sole Executor of this my last will and testament. As Witnesse my hand and seale the Tenth day of February, one thousand six hundred thirty-nine.

"TEIGE DONOVANE.

"Being present,

"DONELL DONOVANE.
CHAROLUS THOHIG, Presbiter.
DONOGH DONOVANE."

"In Dei nomine.—Notwithstandinge my former Will, of the specialties followinge my will now is, to give forty pounds of the monies due unto me upon Donogh mac Teige mac Feylimie unto my daughter, Honora. And also I doe leave her the tenn pounds due unto me upon Donell mac

Dermodie mac Donogh of Ardagh mac Kannith. And the six pounds due unto me upon Daniell mac Donogh mac Teige mac Owen. And the five pounds due unto me upon Moriartah mac Conohor. All which I leave unto my foresaid Daughter, Honora ny Teige, and I doe leaue her to my Sister Honora[d]. And I doe leave with my Brothers (if God should call away my sonnes, which God forbid), dureinge their minorities, that they shall looke to my daughters in bestowinge the specialties mentioned in my said former will upon them, ACCORDINGE AS MY BROTHER O'DONOVANE[e] AND THE REST OF MY BROTHERS SHALL IN THEIR CONSCIENCE THINKE FITT. In Witnesse whereof I have hereunto putt my hand the Ealeventh day of February.

"TEIGE DONOVANE.

"Being present,

"CAHIR Ô THOHIG.
MORROGH DONOVANE.
ENEAS CALLNANE."

"Tenore præsentium Nos Thomas Ffrith[ee] Clericus in artibus Magister, Reverendis. in Christo patris ac Domini Domini Guilielmi[f] permissione Divina Corcag. et Rossen. Episcopi Cancellarius et Vicarius in spiritualibus Generalis, in et pro tot. Dioc. Rossen. predict. rite et legitime constitutus, Notum facimus universis quod tertio Die mensis Martii, anno Domini 1639 Probatum fuit hoc testamentum et coddicillum suprascriptum Thadæi O Donovane, qui dum vixit de parochia Creagh, Dioc. Rossen., generosi defuncti, coram magistro Ludovico Vigours Clerico et Surrogato Venerabilis viri Thomæ Ffrith predicti, necnon per Nos approbatum et insinuat.... in Curia Rossensi; commissaque fuit et est administratio omnium et singulorum bonorum, iurium, creditorum, et cattallorum dicti defuncti, ac testamentum eius hoc qualitercunque concernen. Moriartie Donovane, fratri naturali dicti Defuncti Executori in hoc testamento nominato, Imprimisque de bene et fideliter administrando eadem, ac de vero et perfecto inventorio omnium et singulorum bonorum, jurium, creditorum, et Cattallorum dicti defuncti conficiendo, et illud in Curia Rossensi predicta citra festo Philippi et Jacobi proximè futuro exhibendo et introducendo, necnon et de justo computo calculo sive ratione in hac parte reddendo quandocunque ad hoc debitè et congruè requisitus fuerit, ad sancta Dei Evangelia juratus. In Cujus Rei testimonio Sigillum Officii Rossensis predicti præsentibus apposuimus. Datum die mensis et Anno Domini supradicto.

XLI. TEIGE O'DONOVAN, of Raheen and Drishane, whose will is above given, was the second son of the chief O'Donovan, and evidently his first son by Johanna Mac Carthy. He married Joane Goggan, and had by her two sons: 1. Daniel, who died without issue; and 2. Murrough or Morgan; and five daughters, viz. Joane, Ellen, Eilene, Shilie, and Honora.

[d] *My sister Honora.*—She was married to the celebrated Teige-an-Duna Mac Carthy of Dunmanway.

[e] *My brother O'Donovane*, i. e. the chief of the name, who at this time was Daniel III., the husband of Gylles O'Shaughnessy. Morogh, the testator's executor, was the third son of O'Donovan (Daniel II.) He was killed at Rathmines, near Dublin, in 1649, leaving a son, Daniel, who was living at Carrowgarriff in 1662, when he empowered his cousin, Daniel, afterwards Colonel Daniel O'Donovan, to sue for the recovery of his lands in Dublin as his attorney.

[ee] *Thomas Ffrith.*—He was Archdeacon of Ross from 1639 to 1631.—See Cotton's *Fasti*, p. 251.

[f] *Guilielmi.*—This was the celebrated William Chapple, Bishop of Cork, Cloyne, and Ross, who had so distinguished himself before James I. at Cambridge by his argumentation, that the respondent, Dr. Roberts, unable to solve his arguments, fell into a swoon in the pulpit.—See Harris's edition of *Ware's Bishops*, p. 568.

XLII. MURROUGH or MORGAN O'DONOVAN. He married Jane Galway, and had issue seven sons, who are mentioned in a deed of settlement of 1684, in the following order: Conogher, Teige, William, Bartholomew, Richard, Donogh, and Morogh. On these certain lands, which are still in the family, are settled in strict entail, first vested in Richard O'Donovan, Esq., Doctor of both Laws, of the city of Cork, and Donogh Mahowny, of Ardrivinigh, in West Carbery. From the eldest of these the present O'Donovan is descended; the second, Teige, was a Captain in the regiment of Colonel O'Driscoll, and was slain at Castletownsend in 1690; William, the third son, had a son, William, who was living in 1742; but no account of the others is preserved.

XLIII. CONOR or CORNELIUS O'DONOVAN. He was a Captain in the regiment of Colonel O'Donovan. In 1684 he married Victoria, only daughter of Colonel O'Donovan, and had by her two sons, Morgan and Teige. He obtained, in 1700, a general pardon from King William III. (Inrolled 12th Will. III. 2. p. f. r. 22), and died young, leaving his two sons as wards to Bryan Townsend of Castletownsend. His widow married a Mr. Turnbull of London, as appears by several of her father's letters.

XLIV. MORGAN DONOVAN, Esq., of Ballincalla. He was born in the year 1687, and, in 1691, claimed, by his guardian, Bryan Townsend, Esq., an estate in tail in Drishane, and various other lands in the barony of West Carbery, late estate of Cornelius O'Donovan, which claim was allowed, as appears from the printed list of claims before the Commissioners of the forfeitures of 1691. His guardian, Bryan Townsend, made him graduate at Oxford, where he conformed to the religion of the State, and became a staunch Williamite. In a lease made by him in 1714, for a term of 999 years, he binds the tenant to pay five shillings a year for a bottle of claret, to drink the glorious and immortal memory of King William III. He purchased the estate of Montpellier, near Cork, in 1728; and was in the Commission of the Peace in the reign of George II. In 1733 he married Mary Ronayne (daughter of Thomas Ronayne, Esq., of Hodnettswood), who had been a Roman Catholic, but she conformed in the same year, after her marriage, as appears from the list of converts from Popery, wherein her name is entered, under that year, as "Mary, wife of Morgan Donovan, Esq." He died in 1759, and was succeeded by his eldest son,

XLV. MORGAN DONOVAN, Esq. He married in May, 1766, Melian Towgood French, daughter of Savadge French, Esq., of the city of Cork. He died in 1802, and was succeeded by his eldest son,

XLVI. The Rev. MORGAN DONOVAN. He was born in 1769, and, in 1814, built Montpellier house, near Cork, on the estate which had been purchased by his grandfather in 1728. He married the daughter of William Jones, Esq., Recorder of Cork, and had by her: 1. Morgan William, the present O'Donovan, born in 1796; 2. William Jones, born in 1799; and 3. Henry. On the death of General O'Donovan of Bawnlahan, in 1829, he began to style himself the O'Donovan; but there was a senior branch living till 1841, when Captain Cornelius, a legitimate descendant of Colonel O'Donovan, died at Dingle without issue.

XLVII. MORGAN WILLIAM O'DONOVAN, Esq., Barrister at Law, now the O'Donovan. He married, in July, 1844, Susan, daughter of the late William Armstrong Creed, formerly of the 4th Foot. He still retains a considerable fragment of the O'Donovan territory, as will appear from the following list of the lands of which he is the head landlord.

Names of the Lands of the O'Donovan, all in the East Division of the Barony of West Carbery, and County of Cork, August the 1st, 1842.

PRESENT NAME.	PATENT OF CAR. II. TO MURRAGH DONOVAN.	IN DEEDS OF 1619, ETC.	PARISHES.
Carrigfadda.	. . . .	. . . .	Abbeystrowry.
Lisardgeehee, *alias* Lisardee.	Lissardgehy, *alias* Gortinvally.	Lissardgeehie, 1630; Lissardghee, 1670; Lisardgoyhy, 1630; Gortnevarre, 1621-35; Gortnaballay, 1630.	Ditto.
Barnagollopy.	Ballygasby.	. . . .	Creagh and Castlehaven.
Coomnageehee.	. . . .	Clounemenaghee, 1643.	Abbeystrowry.
Derrygoole.	Same.	Dirrigoole, 1670; Diregoole, 1630.	Ditto.
Drishanebeg.	Same.	Drishanebeg, 1628, 29, 33, 35; Dryshan, 1621-72; Drishane, 1623; Dryshan Beg, 1624; Begg, 1625, 35, 38.	Creagh.
Russagh, *alias* Rossagh.	. . . .	Gortenrossigh, 1638.	Abbeystrowry.
Ardagh.	Same.	Killardagh & Gortinvally, 1632.	Tullogh, *alias* Baltimore.
Lick.	Lickiwith.	Like and Munig, 1640; Licke and Munnig, 1640.	Ditto.
Bunlick.	. . . .	. . . .	Ditto.
Knockvallintaggart.	Same.	Knockevollytagart, 1633; Gurt, 1633.	Ditto.
Gortshanecrone.	Gortancroan.	Gortsheane Crone, 1632.	Ditto.
Ballinard.	Ballynard.	Ballynard, 1629, 35, 38, 64, 70; Ballinarde, 1670; Ballinnard, 1677.	Ditto.
Barna, part of Ballymorane, *alias* Ballyourane.	Ballymorane.	. . . .	Cahiragh.
Barna Mountain, *alias* Lugnacoppul.	. . . .	. . . .	Ditto.
Bluyd (East).	Blood.	. . . .	Castlehaven, *alias* Glanbarahane.
Burriroe.	Barriroe.	. . . .	Ditto.
Minlogh, part of Glanteige.	Menlagh.	Meallnghie, 1626-31; Maulelough, 1670; Maulslough, 1670.	Glanneberraghane, 1627.
Glanageele, part of ditto.	Glangettle, *alias* Glangeill.	Glaneigele, 1627; Glanteigkylline, 1632.	Ditto.
Laberdanemore, *alias* Knocknagowr, part of ditto.	Knocknagowre.	. . . .	Ditto.
Lisheenroe, *alias* Lissceenroe, part of Glanteige.	Lisseenmore.	Part of Fearnagilla, 1631.	Ditto.
Lahanaght.	Same, *alias* Lahanagh.	. . . .	Drinagh.
Tuonafuora, *alias* Bohernabrada.	Bohernabreedagh.	. . . .	Drimaleague, *alias* Drumdaligue.
Knockbuoy, *alias* Knockeenbuoy, part of Loughrott.	. . . .	Knockboy, 1628.	Dromdalyege, 1624.
	Loghcrott.	Loughcrotte, 1624.	Ditto.
Upper Loughrott, *alias* Crott.	. . . .	Croattes, 1624.	Ditto.
Carrigbane, part of Rivoulder.	Garrybane, *alias* Carribane part of Reavoulder.	. . . .	Killmacabea.
		Reavolder, 1619.	

According to the pedigree of the O'Donovans, compiled by John Collins of Myross, Teige, the son of the O'Donovan who married the daugher of Sir Owen Mac Carthy Reagh, had a grandson, Teige, or Timothy, a Captain, who was killed at Castletownsend, in 1690, together with the young Colonel O'Driscoll.—See Smith's *History of Cork*, vol. ii. p. 207. According to the tradition in Carbery, as communicated to the Editor by James O'Donovan of Cooldurragha, in a letter dated 10th August, 1842, this Captain Teige is now represented by John Donovan, of John-street, Waterford, a shoemaker, whose descent is traced as follows:

XL. Donnell O'Donovan, chief, 1584–1639.

XLI. Teige O'Donovan.

XLII. Murrough O'Donovan.

XLIII. Captain Teige O'Donovan, slain 1690.

XLIV. Timothy O'Donovan. He married the daughter of Thomas Coppinger, of Affadown, the father of the Rev. John Coppinger, by whom he had,

XLV. Timothy O'Donovan, who settled in Waterford.

XLVI. John Donovan of Waterford, who believes that he is the head of the O'Donovans, and went to Cork to take law proceedings for the recovery of General O'Donovan's estate. This line of descent is probably correct, but no documentary evidence has been furnished to support it.

Let us now return to the fourth son of the last inaugurated O'Donovan,

O'DONOVAN OF COOLDURRAGHA, PARISH OF MYROSS, CORK.

XLII. Donough or Denis O'Donovan, of Forenaght. There is extant a curious poem addressed to this Donough, on his lying dangerously ill, by his foster-father, Conor Cam O'Daly, who calls him "Donough, son of Donnell and Joane, a pillar in battle;" his "dalta díl foġlamṫa, i. e. his dear and learned alumnus." He lived at Forenaght, in the parish of Castlehaven, and married Mary, the daughter of Teige, son of Cormac Mac Carthy, commonly called Muiġistir na Móna, or Master of Mourne Preceptory, in Muskerry, and had by her one son,

XLIII. Captain Daniel O'Donovan. Collins says that he was "one of the most accomplished gentlemen in the county of Cork, and a Captain under his cousin-german, Colonel O'Donovan, in the year 1689." There is extant among the Bawnlahan papers a memorandum, in his own handwriting, of his having taken Castletownsend by surprise, on the 9th of March, 1688–9. It runs as follows:

"Whereas Captain Daniell mac Donogh O'Donovan, of Colonel O'Donovan's Regiment, haueing liued neere Castletowne, in the barony of Carrebry, in the county of Corcke, where Mr. Bryen Townsy gathered a garrison of the Rebles in that country; the said Captain imploy'd two spies to learne aboute the said Castletowne what the Garrison did, and bringing him intelligence, the second of this instant, that the Garrison there, sending aboundance of their goods, arms, and amonition, for Baltimore, by water, with whom a Number of ye Garrison went to convey them. Uppon which intelligence the said Captain took immediately twenty of the most resolute men of his companie, and conuayed them, by a stratagem, neere the castle of the said Castletown, soe that, unawares, he came to command the Castle Doore, and Townsey being not there, but heereing that the said Captain was there, sent to him that he was willing to deliver up the Castle to Colonel O'Donovan, if the said Captain had his orders, and the orders being there, possession was given of all the Castle to the said Captain Donovan, wherein he found of armes but what followeth: Twentienine fireing armes, three pistles, and a hundred small bulletts, seaven swords, three Bottles, with two hornes full of powder; and it seems they threwed a ferquin of powder, and a great quantity of musquet bulletts, into the sea, at my arriveing. This is a full and true account uppon the said Captain's reputation, as heere he affirmes under his hand, the 9th March, $168\frac{8}{9}$.

"DA: O'DONOVANE."

In a list of attainted persons, preserved in a manuscript in Trinity College, Dublin, his name occurs as "Daniel mac Donogh Donovan. nuper de Ffornaght, in Com. Cork."

He married Mary, daughter of Edmond Fitzgerald, of Imokilly, commonly called Eamonn Chúil O'g-Copra, and had issue,

XLIV. PHILIP O'DONOVAN, of Listarkin, in the parish of Myross, who married Catherine, daughter of Thomas O'Hea, of Barryroe, and had issue,

XLV. JAMES O'DONOVAN, of Ardra, in the parish of Myross, who married Catherine, daughter of Timothy Mac Carthy, of Muskerry, and had issue several sons, who died without issue; and

XLVI. PHILIP O'DONOVAN, of Cooldurragha, in the parish of Myross. Collins speaks of him as living in his own time, and calls him "the great grandson of Captain Daniel mac Donough O'Donovan." His words are: "His" [i. e. Captain Daniel's] "great grandson, Philip Donovan, of Cooldorgha, in the parish of Myross, is the present representative of this branch, a gentleman justly esteemed for courtesy and hospitality, who is married to Elizabeth, the daughter of Daniel mac Rickard mac Keady Donovan, by Eleanor, the daughter of Mac Fineen Duff, and Elizabeth, only sister to the late O'Donovan." He died in May, 1821, and was interred with his ancestors, in Myross church. He left issue,

XLV. JAMES O'DONOVAN, of Cooldurragha. Timothy O'Donovan, Esq., of O'Donovan's Cove, in a letter to the Editor, February 1st, 1841, expresses his belief that this James O'Donovan, "who is now reduced to the station of a struggling farmer, but a person of excellent and respectable character, is the eldest representative of the house of O'Donovan." This assertion, however, was made without a knowledge of the fact that his ancestor, Donough, was the fourth son of the O'Donovan, who made his last will in 1629, and died in 1639, or that the descendants of the second son were extant. The present O'Donovan, of Montpellier, and John Donovan, of Waterford, shoemaker, are decidedly of an older branch than this James, however it has happened that local tradition has cast the seniority upon him, and invested him with a titular chieftainship.

O'DONOVAN, LATE OF DONOVAN-STREET, CITY OF CORK.

XLI. RICHARD O'DONOVAN, the sixth son of Daniel O'Donovan, who was inaugurated in 1584, and died in 1639, married Mary, who was the daughter of O'Sullivan Beare, and, by her mother, grand-daughter of Lord Muskerry, and great grand-daughter of the Earl of Clanrickard, and had by her: 1. Daniel, who is mentioned in his grandfather, Donnell's, will of 1629, and in his uncle Teige's will of 1639, but of whose descendants, if he left any, no account is preserved; 2. Murrough, living in 1629, who left a daughter, Joane; and 3,

XLII. RICHARD O'DONOVAN, Esq., LL.D., who is said to have studied for twenty-two years in the University of Toulouse, where he obtained the degree of Doctor of both Laws. He afterwards went to London, where he acquired the degree of Doctor of the Canon Law. He returned to Ireland on the accession of James II., and was elected Member of Parliament for the Borough of

Baltimore, but he resigned to Jeremy Donovan, of Rinogreany, chief of the Clann-Loughlin. He was appointed Judge of the Court of Admiralty in Ireland.—*Vide* manuscript in Library of Trinity College, Dublin, E. 3. 25. This Richard died in the year 1694, as appears from an Irish elegy composed on his death, in which he is called Riocard mac Riocaird :

"File fras-líoṁṫa, froṁṫa,
bre ṫeaṁ caoinḃreaṫaċ, cneasta,
dlíġṫeóir dearḃṫa deiġṁeasta."

"A ready-polished approved poet,
A justly-judging mild Brehon,
A tried and estimable lawyer."

The year of his death is recorded in the following quatrain :

"Sé ċéd déag, glan ċúntas grod,
ceiṫre ceart-ḃliadna is noċad,
Aois mic De, seaḋ ar saoirse,
Do b'é ar éag an uasail-se."

"Sixteen hundred,—a true computation,—
Four years exact and ninety,
Was the age of the Son of God, cause of our salvation,
On the death of this noble."

This Dr. Richard O'Donovan married Catherine Ronayne, of Ronayne's Court, near Cork (the aunt of Mary Ronayne, the wife of Morgan Donovan, Esq., the ancestor of the O'Donovan of Montpellier), and had by her four sons, viz. : 1. Daniel, of whom presently ; 2. Morgan ; 3. Richard ; 4. William. Of the race of these three younger sons, the Editor has not been able to trace any account.

XLIII. Daniel O'Donovan of Dunnamark. He was appointed Portrieve of Baltimore, by James II., in 1687.—See Smith's *Natural and Civil History of Cork*, vol. i. p. 272. He married Maria Holmes, daughter of the Rev. Thomas Holmes, son of Sir John Holmes, and had by her five sons : 1. Philip, of whom presently ; 2. Morgan ; 3. Richard ; 4. Daniel ; 5. William ; and three daughters : 1. Mary, who married Lieutenant Philip Somerville, R. N., by whom she had one son, Philip Somerville, late Captain of the Eugenia sloop of war, and of the Nemesis and Rotia frigates ; 2. Elizabeth.

XLIV. Philip O'Donovan of Curranea, near Skibbereen. He married Sarah, daughter of Captain James Coppinger, lord of five manors, in the barony of West Carbery, in the county of Cork, and had by her two sons : 1. the late Lieutenant Philip O'Donovan, of Donovan-street, in the city of Cork ; 2. William ; both of whom served in the navy, and sailed with their cousin, Captain Philip Somerville ; and three daughters : 1. Mary, who married Hugh Mac Adam, Merchant ; 2. Jane, who married Lieutenant John Salmon, R. N. ; and 3. Catherine, who married Lieutenant William Somerville, the son of Captain Philip Somerville aforesaid.

XLV. Lieut. Philip Donovan died some twenty years ago, leaving one daughter. According to an old pedigree of this branch, written on parchment, which was sent to the Editor by Doctor Daniel Donovan of Skibbereen, they bore different arms from those of the Bawnlahan and Ballymore family. They are as follows:

Arms.—Argent issuing from the sinister side of the shield, a cubit dexter arm naked, the hand proper grasping a sword in pale entwined with an evet between three golden balls.

Crest.—A white falcon alighting.

Motto.—Crom-a-boo, "taken from the famous castle of Crom, built by the O'Donovans, which afterwards fell to the Kildare family, who also use the same motto."

The Editor does not know where any member of this once very respectable family is now seated.

XLI. Let us now go back to the youngest son of the last inaugurated O'Donovan, Keadagh More, "a gentleman of great stature, bodily strength, and military abilities."—*Collins.* His descendants are now known in the country by the name of Clann-Keady Donovan, the most respectable of whom are Richard Donovan, Esq., of Lisheens House, near Ballincollig, and Timothy O'Donovan, of Ardahill house, near Bantry, whose descent is as follows:

Keadagh More.

XLII.	Daniel.	Rickard.
XLIII.	Richard.	Daniel, married Eleanor, daughter of Mac Fineen Duff by Elizabeth, only daughter of Capt. Richard O'Donovan of Bawnlahan.
XLIV.	Richard.	Keadagh.
XLV.	Richard, now at Lisheens.	Timothy O'Donovan of Ardahill, married the daughter of Daniel O'Sullivan of Rinnydonagan, by the sister of the late Daniel O'Connell, Esq., M. P.
XLVI.	Richard, a boy.	

O'DONOVAN OF O'DONOVAN'S COVE.

Another highly respectable branch of the Clann-Cahill O'Donovan is seated at O'Donovan's Cove, in Muintir-Vary, or parish of Kilcrohane, in West Carbery, the present head of whom is Timothy O'Donovan, Esq., J. P. They descend from Teige O'Donovan of Gorteeniher, in the parish of Dromaleague, a near kinsman to the Chief, Teige, No. XXXVIII., but the exact relationship has not been yet proved. According to John Collins, the line of descent is as follows:

1. Teige O'Donovan of Gorteeniher, father of
2. Diarmaid O'Donovan, surnamed An Eich, i. e. of the Steed, father of
3. Jeremiah O'Donovan of Caheragh, father of
4. Timothy O'Donovan of Ballaghadoon. He married a Mac Carthy, and had issue,
5. Richard O'Donovan of Kilmacabea. He married Elizabeth O'Donovan, sister of James O'Donovan of Reenogreny, and of Alexander O'Donovan of Squince, and had issue,
6. Timothy O'Donovan, Esq. In the year 1754, he was a student at the University of Toulouse, where, on the 15th July that year, he vanquished in single combat the most celebrated swordsman in France, as appears by a record attested by the proper authorities, in the possession

of his grandson. He married Eleanor Mac Carthy, daughter of Florence Mac Carthy of Gortnascreena, in the county of Cork, by Jane O'Driscoll, daughter of the O'Driscoll of Creagh, and had issue two sons, Richard, his heir, and Daniel, a Lieutenant in the English service.

7. Richard O'Donovan, Esq., of O'Donovan's Cove. He married Jane, daughter of Alexander O'Donovan of Squince, the representative of O'Donovan of Reenogreny, and had issue: 1. Timothy O'Donovan, Esq., J. P., the head of this family; 2. Daniel O'Donovan, Esq., M. D., J. P., of Skibbereen; 3. Richard O'Donovan, Esq., of Fort Lodge. Collins speaks of this Richard, No. 7, as a gentleman of great hospitality and goodness, who had a fortune of about £2000 a year.

8. Timothy O'Donovan, Esq. He married Maria Rogers, daughter of Joseph Rogers, M. D., and Mary L'Avallyn, one of the co-heiresses of Philip L'Avallyn, Esq., of Waterpark, in the county of Cork, and has issue,

9. Richard O'Donovan, Junior. He married Anne Fitzgerald, daughter of Mr. Thomas Fitzgerald of Cork, merchant, by Catherine Mac Carthy, daughter of Mac Carthy of Woodview, in the county of Cork, and niece to the late Daniel O'Connell, Esq., M. P. He has issue one son, Timothy.

We will now return to Loughlin, the third son of Crom.

THE CLANN-LOUGHLIN O'DONOVAN.

XXXIII. Lochlainn, who is the ancestor of the second most important sept of the O'Donovans, called Clann-Lochlainn, *anglice* Clanloughlin, originally possessed a small territory consisting of thirty-six ploughlands, situate between the River Roury and the harbour of Glandore. This sept, after the decay of the English power in Carbery, obtained possession of Cloch-an-Traghbhaile, *anglice* Cloghadtradbally, a castle which, according to the Dublin copy of the Annals of Innisfallen, had been erected at the head of Cuan-Dór, or Glandore Harbour, and now called Glandore Castle, by the chief of the Barretts of Munster in the year 1215. According to a pedigree of this sept, given by Duald Mac Firbis in his Genealogical manuscript (Lord Roden's copy), p. 633, Lochlainn, third son of Crom, had a son,

XXXIV. Donnchadh or Donough of Loch Crot, who had a son,

XXXV. Cathal, who had a son,

XXXVI. Diarmaid, who had a son,

XXXVII. Donnchadh. He is the last generation given by Mac Firbis. The Editor, in comparing his descent with that of the Clancahill, and with the pedigree of this sept deduced from the public records, is satisfied that this line was continued by the great grandson of this Donnchadh, namely,

XL. Donnell na Carton O'Donovan of Cloghatradbally Castle, Chief of Clann-Loughlin, who died on the 10th of May, 1580, as appears from an Inquisition taken at Bandon-Bridge on the 14th day of August, in the sixth year of the reign of Charles I. He was succeeded by his son,

XLI. Donnell Oge na Carton O'Donovan. On the 28th of June, thirteenth of James I., he surrendered his possessions to the King, and received a regrant of the same, to hold for ever as of the Castle of Dublin, in free and common soccage. From this grant, which is here printed, it appears that the head of the Clann-Loughlin had, at this time, a territory nearly as extensive as that of the head of the O'Donovans, of whom the former was independent.

"Patent Roll, James I., anno 13, part 2, Art. II. memb. 6.

"II. 6. Surrender by Donnell oge ny Cartin O'Donovan, of Cloghetradbally, in Cork Co., gent. and Moriertagh Mac Donell oge ny Cartan O'Donovan, of Ardagh, in Cork Co., gentleman, of all their estates in Cork Co., as set out in article VI.—28 June, 13th of reign.

"III. 8. Deed whereby Sir James Semple, of Beltries, in Scotland, Knt., appoints Donell oge ny Cartin, of Cloghehytradebally, in Cork Co., and Moriertagh Mac Donell oge ny Cartin, of Ardagh, in Cork Co., gentlemen, to receive a grant from the King of part of the lands set out in article VI., for a sum of £112 English.—28th January, 12th of reign.

"IV. 9. Deed between the parties named in the preceding article, to accept a grant of other lands set out in Article VI., for a sum of £120 English.—28th January, 12th reign.

"V. 11. Another deed of the same import as the preceding, for a sum of £157 18*s*.—28th January, 12th reign.

"VI. 12. Grant from the King to Donell oge ny Cartin O'Donovan, of Cloghehitradbally[g], in Cork Co., gent., and Morhirtagh Mac Donell oge ny Cartin O'Donovan, of Ardagh[h], in the same Co., gent.

"*Cork Co.*—The castle of Cloghetradbally*, and the towns and lands of Aghetobredmore[i]*, Aghetobredbegg[j]*, and Rishane[k]*, containing 3 plowlands in Clanloghlin; Carigloskie[l]*, ½ plowland, parcel of Ringreny[m] qr.*; Carrowgarruff[n], 3½ plowlands; Ballirerie[o]*, Keamore[p]*, Kippaghnebohie[q]*, Knockskeagh[r], in Slew-Irin*, Bra[s]*, Bealahacolane[t]*, each 1 plowland; a chief rent of 6*d*., Eng.; out of Stuckin[u] plowland; out of Ardagh, 6*d*.; out of Aghenestan, 6*d*.; out of Killeans, 2½ plowlands; £1 2*s*. 6*d*. out of Glantawick, in Dromullihie[v], ½ plowland, 5*s*. 7*d*.; out of Curr-Hurck, 5*s*. 7*d*.; out of Inshinanowen[w], 5*s*. 7*d*.; out of Kilbegg[x], ½ plowland, 2*s*. 9½*d*.; out of Ballinegornahnegeneny[y] and Creggane[z], 1 plowland, 11*s*. 1*d*.; out of Mealmarin[a], in Rinegreny,

[g] *Cloghatradbally: recte* Cloghatrabally, Cloċ a'ṫraġ-ḃaile, i. e. the Stone, or Stone Fortress of the Strand Town; now Glandore Castle, in the parish of Kilfaghnabeg, in the west division of the barony of East Carbery.

[h] *Ardagh.*—A townland in the parish of Myross.

[i] *Aghetobredmore.*—Now Aċaḋ an tobair ṁóir, *anglice* Aghatobermore, or Aghatubbredmore, in the parish of Kilfaghnabeg.

[j] *Aghetobredbegg.*—Now Aghatubbredbeg, in the same parish.

[k] *Rishane.*—Now Rushane, in the same parish.

[l] *Carigloskie.*—Now Carriglusky, in the same parish.

[m] *Ringreny:* i. e. O'Greny's Point, or Promontory; now Rinagreena, or Reenogreny, a townland situated in the south of the same parish. It is the property of Thomas Deasy, Esq., of Clonakilty, let to Rickard Donovan, Esq. (Clerk of the Crown for the county of Cork), on lease of lives renewable for ever.

[n] *Carrowgarruff:* i. e. the Rough Quarter; now Carhoogarriff, a townland in the parish of Kilmacabea.

[o] *Ballirerie:* i. e. Rogerstown; now Ballyriree, in th parish of Kilmacabea.

[p] *Keamore.*—Now Keymore, in the same parish.

[q] *Kippaghnabohie.*—Now Cappanaboha, in the same parish.

[r] *Knockskeagh.*—Now Knockscagh, Cnoc sgeaċ, Hill of the Thorns, in the same parish.

[s] *Bra.*—Now Brade, in the parish of Myross.

[t] *Bealahacolane.*—Now Ballycolane, in the same parish.

[u] *Stuckin.*—Now Stookeen, in the same parish.

[v] *Dromullihie.*—Now Drumilihy, in the parish of Kilmacabea.

[w] *Inshinanowen.*—Now Inchananoon, Inse na n-uan, the *Inch*, or Holm of the Lambs, in the same parish.

[x] *Kilbegg.*—Now Kilbeg, in the parish of Kilfaghnabeg.

[y] *Ballinegornaghneganeny.*—Now Ballynagornagh, in the parish of Rosscarbery.

[z] *Creggane.*—Now Creggan, in the same parish.

[a] *Mealmarin.*—Now Meall-Mareen, in the parish of Kilfaghnabeg.

½ plowland, 5*s.* 7*d.*; out of 2 plowlands of Rinegreny, £1 2*s.* 2*d.*; out of each of the 7 plowlands of Tooghmealhie, 11*s.* 1*d.*; out of each of the two plowlands of Furroe[b], 11*s.* 1*d.*; all the customs, royalties, dues, and privileges, due and payable to Daniel otherwise Donell oge ne Cartin O'Donovan, and his ancestors, in the port of Glandore. Ardagh*, 1 plowland; The Killeans*, 2½ plowlands, of which the half of Cullankelly[c] is free from the country charges; Banefune[d]*, Mealnegearah[e]*, and Ballineloghie[f]*, 2 plowlands; Ballinegornaghneganeny*, and Creggan*, 1 plowland; Mealmurin, otherwise Mealmarin* in Rinegreny, ½ plowland; Glanetawicke*, ½ plowland; the 3 south gnives[g] in Cur-Iturke†; ½ plowland in Dromullihy; the two south plowlands of Eadenecurra[h], otherwise Eadencurrie, in Slughtcorky; Balltine Mac Craghoughtragh[i], 1½ plowland in Evahagh; Cahiroleckine[j], ½ plowland in Evahagh; one-third part of Cahirnibologie, containing 4 gnives in the qr. of Kilmac-Ibe[k], in Slught-Eneslies Mac Icrim[l]; Cahirkaniva, ½ plowland in Killekebeh qr. in Slught-Enesles Mac Icrim; in Bohenagh[m], 1 plowland and 3 gnives in Clan-Enesles Mac Icrim; Gortenahen, 3 gnives in the plowland of Brooley[n], in Slught-Eneslys Mac Icrim; in Classnecally, 1 gnive in the said Brooley; the E. half plowland of Beallainurgher[o], and the W. half plowland in Bealamurgher, in Clancromin; the W. half plowland of Kilcursagh[p], in Clancromyn; two gnives in the plowland of Balli Mac Owen[q], in Clancromyn; Killdee[r] otherwise Killee, Knockanepubble, and Knockemcteiry, 4½ plowlands in Clancromin; Clandirrin[s] otherwise Clowndirrin, ½ plowland; Gurtineduigh otherwise Gurtineduig[t], ½ plowland; Corrigarehen otherwise Carigecaren, ½ plowland; Milnilehan, ½ plowland; and 2 gnives of Cahernabolaghy otherwise Cahernabolgie, containing in all 1 plowland and 8 gnives in Slught-Enesles Mac Icroym; Killwilleran, 1 plowland in Clancromin; in Maushie, 1 plowland in Clancromin; in E. Croghan[u], 3 gnives in Clancromin; Drommore[v], 3 plowlands in Clanteige-Roe; Colman[w] and Bargorme, 3 plowlands

[b] *Furroe.*—Now Froe, in the parish of Rosscarbery.

[c] *Cullanekelly.*—Now Cullane, in the parish of Kilmacabea.

[d] *Banefune*, Bán fionn, i. e. the Fair or White Field, now Bawnfune, in the same parish.

[e] *Mealnageerah*, Meull na girre.—Now Meallnagirra, in the same parish.

[f] *Ballineloghie*, Baile an loċa.—Now Ballinlough, in the same parish.

[g] *The 3 South Gnives.*—Now The Three Gneeves, in the same parish.

[h] *Eadenacurra.*—Now Edencurra, in the parish of Ballymoney.

Baltine Mac Craghoughtragh.—A townland extending into the parishes of Skull and Kilmoe, in O'Mahony's country, in West Carbery.

[j] *Cahiroleckine.*—Now Caher, in the parish of Kilmoe.

[k] *Kilmac-Ibe.*—Now Kilmacabea.

[l] *Slught-Enesles Mac Icrim*, Sliocṫ Aineslis mic a Chroim, i. e. the race of Aneslis, son of Crom, a sept of the O'Donovans, descended from Aneslis, the second son of Crom, who was slain by the O'Mahonys in 1254. They gave name to a district in the parish of Kilmacabea. They were otherwise called Clann Aineslis mic a'Chruim.

[m] *Bohenagh.*—A townland in the parish of Rosscarbery.

[n] *Brooley.*—Now Brulea, in the parish of Kilfaghnabeg.

[o] *Beallamurgher*, Béal áṫa an urċair.—Now Ballynerough, in the parish of Kilnagross. Mac Nyn Cromin Mac Carthy had a great castle at this place.

[p] *Kilcursagh.*—Now Kilcourcey, not far from Mac Inyn Cromin's castle of Belanugher.

[q] *Balli Mac Owen.*—Now Ballymacowen, a townland in the parish of Kilnagross.

[r] *Kildee.*—Now Kildee, a townland in a parish of the same name.

[s] *Clandirrin.*—Now Clonderreen, in the parish of Rathclarin.

[t] *Gurtineduig.*—A townland in the parish of Kilmacabea.

[u] *Croghan.*—Now Croghane, in the parish of Kilnagross.

[v] *Drummore.*—Now Dromore, in the parish of Caheragh.

[w] *Colman.*—Now Collamane, in the parish of Caheragh.

in Clanteige-Roe; Ballirisoade[x], 2 plowlands and 2 gnives in Slught-Teige-O'Mahowne; Rathroane[y], 1½ plowland; Fahane[z], 1½ plowland, both in Slught Mac Teige O'Mahowne; Kilcoursie, ½ plowland; Caricanowy, ½ plowland in Clancromin; Cahirkirky[a], 1 plowland in Carrowballer[b]; Killvellogie[c], ½ plowland in Clancromin; Skart[d] otherwise Skarth, 3 plowlands in Clanteige-Roe; Litterlicky[e], 3 plowlands; Aghavile otherwise Aghawile[f], Carrigillostrane, Glantawick otherwise Glantaucke, Currigoony, and Knockgorme, 4 plowlands in the 6 plowlands of Caharagh, all in Clanteige-Roe[g]; Knockanemucke[h] and Coorenehorny, 1 plowland; Fagha, 1 plowland; Carigboy, Baudermoddowligh, and Rossyvanng, 1 plowland and 2 gnives in Coolenelonge, in Clanteigeyler; Banenyknockan, 1 plowland in Slught Teige O'Mahown; Ardglasse, 1 plowland; Dromelorie, Dromkeole[i], Derrigoline, Baneshenclogh[k], and Sronegreeh[l], 3 plowlands; all in Slaught-Mac Teige O'Mahowne; the castle and ½ plowland of Dirrilemlarie[m], in the qr. of Balliwooig[n], and the ½ plowland of Balliwooig, in the same, in Clancromin; Garrans, ½ plowland in the quarter of Dromeleggah; Tullagh, ½ plowland, and in Maushe, 8 gnives; Ballinard, 1½ plowland; Dirrivillin, 1 plowland in the qr. of Balliwoige; five gnives in the plowland of Croghan; in Maushe, 4 gnives, all in Clancromine; the E. half plowland of Cnockycullin, and the ½ plowland of Mawlerawre[o], in Dromleggah qr., in Clancromin; 4 gnives in the plowland of Litter[p], in Clanvollen[q]; four gnives called Pallice[r], Ardfield parish, in Garranard, in Kiltallowe, Coıll ɛ-Seulbuıᵹ; Lisnebrenny-Ierhagh[s], otherwise the West Lisnebrenny, Lisnabrinna, in Kilmeen, 1 plowland in Glanvollins[t]; saving all chief rents, services, royalties, customs, and privileges, due and payable to Donnell Mac Cartie, the King's ward, or to any of his ancestors, and all his right to all or any of the premises. The lands thus marked * are created the manor of Cloghetradbally, with 500 Acres in demesne,

[x] *Ballirisode.*—Now Ballyrisode, a townland in the parish of Kilmore, in West Carbery.

[y] *Rathbroane.*—Now Rathruane, in the parish of Skull.

[z] *Fahane.*—A townland in the parish of Kilcrohane, in West Carbery.

[a] *Cahirkirky.*—A townland in the parish of Kilmeen.

[b] *Carrowballor.*—Now Carhoowouler, or Bouler's Quarter, in the parish of Desertserges.

[c] *Killvillogie.*—Now Kilbeloge, in the same parish.

[d] *Skart.*—Now probably Skartankilleen, in the parish of Skull, in O'Mahony's country.

[e] *Littirlicky.*—Now Litterlicky, in the parish of Kilmacomoge.

[f] *Aghavile.*—Now Aghaval, in the parish of Caheragh.

[g] *Clanteige Roe*, Clann Caıḋ Ruaıḋ, i. e. the clan or sept of Teige Roe, or Thaddæus Rufus.—A sept of the O'Mahonys, who gave their name to a district in the parish of Caheragh, in West Carbery.

[h] *Knockanemucke.*—Now Knocknamuck, in the parish of Kilmacommoge.

[i] *Drumkeole.*—Now Drumkeol, in the parish of Kilmacommoge.

[k] *Baneshenclogh.*—Now Bawnshanaclogh, in the parish of Skull.

[l] *Sronegreeh.*—Now Sronagreehy, in the parish of Kilmacommoge.

[m] *Dirrilemlarie.*—Now Castle-Derry, adjoining Ballyvoigue, in the parish of Dıſeꞃꞇ Saeꞃᵹuꞃa, Desertserges. The ruins of this castle are still to be seen in the northern angle of Castlederry townland, and near the boundary of Ballyvoigue, which originally comprised several sub-denominations.

[n] *Ballyvoige.*—Now Ballyvoigue, in the parish of Desertserges.

[o] *Mawlerawre*, Meall ꞃaṁaꞃ.—A townland in the parish of Kilmaloda.

[p] *Litter.*—A townland in the parish of Kilmeen.

[q] *Clanvollen.*—Now Gleann-a'-mhuillinn, *anglice* Glenawilling, i. e. the glen or valley of the mill, a district comprising the entire of the parish of Kilmeen.

[r] *Pallice*, Paılíꞅ.—A townland in the parish of Ardfield.

[s] *Lisnebrenny-Ierhagh.*—Now Lıoꞅ na bꞃuıᵹne ıaꞃṫaꞃaċ, Lismabrinna West, in the parish of Kilmeen.

[t] *Glanvollins*: i. e. Glenawilling, a district in the parish of Kilmeen.

power to create tenures, and to hold courts leet and baron. To hold for ever, as of the Castle of Dublin, in common soccage.—29th January, 13th reign."

This Donnell Oge-na-Carton O'Donovane died on the 24th of January, 1629, and was succeeded by his son,

XLII. Moriertagh mac Donnell Oge na Carton O'Donovan, who was then of age and married. This appears from the following Inquisition, taken at Bandon Bridge on the 14th day of August, in the sixth year of the reign of Charles I.:

"Inquisitio capta apud Bandonbridge in Comitatu predicto" [Cork] "decimo quarto die Augusti anno regni domini Caroli &c. sexto coram Phillippo Percivall Wilielmo Wiseman armigero Escætori domini regis Comitatui predicto (et aliis) per sacramenta proborum &c. qui dicunt quod Donell ny Carten O'Donovane nuper de Cloghytradballie in Comitatu predicto, generosus, seisitus fuit de feodo de Castro villa et terra de Cloghytradbally, in Comitatu predicto. Ac de Aghytobredmore, Aghytobredbegge, et Rishane, in Comitatu predicto, continentibus in toto tres Carrucatas terræ annualis valoris triginta solidorum. Ac de Carriggyloskie, in Comitatu predicto, continente dimidium unius Carrucatæ terræ annualis valoris quinque solidorum. Ac de Carrowgarruffe, in Comitatu predicto, continente tres Carrucatas terræ et tres gneeves, annualis valoris triginta solidorum. Ac de Ballyrerie in Comitatu predicto continente unam Carrucatam terræ annualis valoris viginti solidorum ac de Cappaghnyboghie in Comitatu predicto continente unam Carrucatam terræ annualis valoris viginti solidorum. Ac de Knockskeaghe in Comitatu predicto continente unam carrucatam terræ annualis valoris viginti solidorum. Ac de Mileenen Cloniteishe in Comitatu predicto continente unam Carrucatam annualis valoris viginti solidorum. Ac de Dromtycloghie et Malegowin in Comitatu predicto continente unam carrucatam terræ annualis valoris viginti solidorum. Ac de Killcowsane et Gortyowen in Comitatu predicto continente unam carrucatam terræ annualis valoris viginti solidorum. Ac de annuali redditu sex denariorum exeuntium ex villa et terra de Stuckine. Ac de annuali redditu sex denariorum sterlingorum exeuntium ex villa et terra de Ardaghe. Ac de annuali redditu viginti duorum solidorum et duorum denariorum exeuntium ex villa et terra de Cullans. Ac de annuali redditu quinque solidorum et septem denariorum exeuntium ex villa et terra de Glanytullaghe in Dromeleighe. Ac de annuali redditu quinque solidorum et septem denariorum exeuntium ex villa et terra de Curryturke. Ac de annuali redditu quinque solidorum et septem denariorum exeuntium ex villa et terra de Inshynacouen. Ac de annuali redditu duorum solidorum & novem denariorum & unius obuli exeuntium ex villa et terra de Kilbegge in Comitatu predicto. Ac de annuali redditu undecim solidorum & duorum denariorum exeuntium ex villa et terra de Kilbegge in Comitatu predicto. Ac de annuali redditu undecim solidorum & duorum denariorum exeuntium ex villa et terra de Ballynagornaghe & Creggane in Comitatu predicto. Ac de annuali redditu quinque solidorum et septem denariorum exeuntium ex villa et terra de Mawlenuirrine in Comitatu predicto. Ac de annuali redditu viginti duorum solidorum et duorum denariorum exeuntium ex villa et terra de Rynangadanaghe in Comitatu predicto. Ac de annuali redditu undecim solidorum & unius denarii exeuntium ex qualibet Carrucata terra de septem Carrucatis terræ de Towghmealy in Comitatu predicto. Ac de et in annuali redditu undecim solidorum & unius denarii exeuntium ex utraque Carrucata de duabus Carrucatis terræ de Farroe in Comitatu predicto. Ac de annuali redditu viginti duorum solidorum exeuntium ex duobus Carrucatis terræ de Ballyloghe & Banefunne in Mawler Geraghe in Comitatu predicto. Ac de hujusmodi regalitatibus et debitis que ante hac soluta fuerunt antecessoribus suis infra portum de Glandore in Comitatu predicto. Et sic sesitus predictus Donell ny Carton O'Donovane obiit decimo die Maij anno domini 1580. Et quod predictus Donell oge ny Carten O'Donovane fuit ejus filius et proximus heres ac fuit plene etatis tempore mortis predicti Donell ny Carten O'Donovane & maritatus. Et quod omnia premissa tempore mortis predicti Donell O'Donovane tenebantur de nuper domina Elizabetha nuper regina Anglie &c. sed per quod servicium Iuratores predicti ignorant. Dicunt etiam quod predictus Donell oge ny Carten O'Donovane post mortem patris sui predicti in omnia premissa intravit & fuit inde seisitus de feodo. Et sic seisitus existens dominus Iacobus nuper rex Anglie mandavit quasdam separales literas suas Arthuro Chichester de Belfast ad tunc Deputatum suum hujus regni sui Hibernie quarum quidem separalium literarum tenor sequitur in hec verba. Jame Rex right trustie &c. ——— Quodque secundum tenorem predictarum literarum predictus Jacobus sempell miles per factum suum gerens datum vicesimo octavo die Januarij anno regni dicti nuper domini regis Anglie &c. duodecimo (inter alia) nominavit et constituit prefatum Donell oge O'Donovane et quendam Moreartagh mac Donell O'Donovane heredes & assignatos suos recipere & obtinere a dicto nuper domino rege heredibus et successoribus suis unam vel plures concessionem vel concessiones dictis Donell oge O'Donovane et Moreartaghe mc Donell O'Donovane concedendam & conficiendas de premissis predictis. Et ulterius dicunt quod post confeccionem dicti facti assignacionis per dictum Jacobum Sempell militem prefato Donell oge O'Donovane et Moreartaghe mac Donell O'Donovane in formam predictam iidem Donell oge O'Donovane et Murtagh mac Donnell per quoddam factum suum sursumreddicionis gerens datum xxviii die Junii Anno regni dicti nuper domini Regis Anglie &c. decimo tertio sursumreddiderunt premissa predicta in manus ipsius nuper domini Regis virtute cujus sursumreddicionis idem nuper dominus Rex Jacobus fuit seisitus de omnibus premissis de feodo. Et sic seisitus existens per literas suas patentes gerentes datum apud Dublin viccsimo nono die Junii anno regni dicti nuper domini regis Jacobi xiii° concessit omnia premissa predicta prefato Donell Oge O'Donovane et Moreartagh mac Donell O'Donovane heredibus et assignatis suis imperpetuum Tenendum de dicto nuper domino rege Jacobo heredibus &c. suis ut de Castro suo Dublin in libero et Communi soccagio virtute quarum quidem literarum patentium iidem Donell Oge O'Donovane et Moreartagh mac Donell O'Donovane in premissis intraverunt & fuerunt inde seisiti de feodo. Et sic seisiti existentes per chartam suam datam xxii° die Decembris anno regni dicti nuper domini Regis decimo tertio supradicto in consideratione summe centum liberarum feoffavit quendam Moroghe O'Donovane heredes et assignatos suos imperpetuum de predictis tribus Carrucatis et tribus gneeves terræ in Carrowgarruffe predicto in Comitatu predicto et postea per factum suum relaxacionis datum decimo quarto die Octobris 1629 idem Donell Oge ny Carten O'Donovane remisit &c. prefato Morogh O'Donovane totum jus suum in predictis tribus Carrucatis et tribus gneeves terræ in Carrowgarruffe predicto. Et ulterius quod predicti Donell Oge & Murtagh post concessionem dictarum literarum patentium in consideratione summe triginta et sex librarum feoffaverunt quendam Wilielmus Yonge heredes et assignatos suos imperpetuum de dimidio Carrucatæ terræ de Carigyloskie predicto per modum mortui vadii sub condicione redempcionis. Ac etiam post confectionem dictarum literarum patentium scilicet feoffaverunt quendam Johannem Yonge heredes et assignatos suos imperpetuum de Carucata terræ de Milleenen Cloyntie predicto per modum mortui vadii in consideracione summe septuaginta librarum sub condicione redempcionis. Et ulterius Juratores prædicti dicunt quod predictus Donell Oge ny Carten O'Donovane de ceteris premissis ut prefertur seisitus existens obiit inde seisitus vicesimo quarto die Januarii anno domini 1629. Et quod Moriertagh mac Donell Oge O'Donovane est ejus filius et proximus heres ac fuit plene etatis tempore mortis patris sui predicti et maritatus. Et quod omnia premissa tenentur prout lex postulat."

Moriertagh Mac Donnell Oge O'Donovan was succeeded by his son,

XLIII. Daniel Mac Mortogh O'Donovan of Cloghatradbally and Rinogreny, who flourished during the Insurrection of 1641, as appears by two depositions in the Library of Trinity College, Dublin, 7th vol. for Cork. His name appears in the list of attainted persons in a manuscript in the same Library, as "Daniel O'Donovan de Gallinlaghlin [i. e. of Clann-Laghlin] in Comitatu Cork;" but he was not attainted, for we have sufficient evidence to shew that he was succeeded by his son,

XLIV. Jeremy Donovan, Esq., M. P. for Baltimore in 1689, who obtained letters patent from Charles II., on the 9th of December, in the thirty-sixth year of his reign, of various lands in the baronies of Carbery and Courcy, in the county of Cork, and in the south liberties and suburbs of the city of Cork; also in Back Lane, Corn Market, and James's-street, in the city of Dublin; in the town of Bray; and in the barony of Duleek, in the county of Meath. His lands in the county of Cork were erected into the manor of Donovan's Leap, with a Court Leet, Court Baron, and Cort of Record, and all the privileges to a manor belonging.—Inrolled 3rd Feb. 1684.

This Jeremy Donovan was chief of the Clann-Loughlin. He was a Protestant, and married, in 1686, Miss Elizabeth Tallant. He was appointed Registrar of the Admiralty in Ireland by James II. on the 23rd of July, *anno regni quinto*.—See manuscript T. C. D., E. 3. 25.

A deed, dated 30th November, 1708, between Jeremiah Donovan, Esq., of the city of Dublin, and the Honourable Allan Broderick, Her Majesty's Attorney-General, and Speaker of the House of Commons, recites a marriage article, dated 11th day of June, 1686, between Oliver Tallant of the one part, and said Jeremiah Donovan of the other part; states the marriage of said Jeremiah Donovan with Miss Elizabeth Tallant; and then, in pursuance of an agreement at the marriage, he conveys to Allan Broderick, in trust, the following lands: the Manor of the Leap, *alias* O'Donovan's Leap and Kilmacabea, containing as follows: 3 plowlands of Kilmacabea; 1 plowland of Knockscagh, part of Ballyrery; 2 plowlands of Ballinloghy, Bawnfune, Maulnagira; the plowland of Keamore; the plowland of Kappanabohy; the lands of Leap, Ballyroe, Cullane, Modrana; the plowland of Brulea; the plowland of Kilcoleman[u], in the county of Cork; the lands of Little Bray, in the county of Dublin; the lands of Balsarne and Blackditch, in the county of Meath; the Marsh of Monerea, in the south liberties and suburbs of the city of Cork; Pouldorane, Gortnaclassy, Gortnahoregan, in the said county of the city of Cork; in trust for his own live use and for a jointure of £160 per annum of his wife, Elizabeth Tallant; and then to the use of Jeremiah Donovan the younger, his son, for life and his issue male; in failure of same, then to John Donovan, his second son, for life, and his issue male; and then to Anne Cusack, *alias* Donovan,

[u] *Kilcoleman*.—This townland, which is situated in the barony of Courcies, had belonged to Captain Daniel Boy O'Donovan, of the sept of Mac Eneslis, in 1641.—See page 2438, *supra*.

his only daughter, wife of Adam Cusack[v], Esq., of Rathgare, in the county of Dublin, and her issue male, taking the name of Donovan.

This Jeremiah or Jeremy Donovan died in 1709, leaving his sons minors.

XLV. Jeremy Donovan, Junior. In 1722, he levied fines and suffered a recovery of all his father's property, and mortgaged and incumbered all his lands. It appears from the following advertisement of his in *Pue's Occurrences*, on the 25th of August, 1730, that he had then a very considerable estate in the county Cork:

"The following Lands to be let from the first of May, 1731, for lives, with or without Renewals, or for any Term of years:

	A.	R.	P.
"The Town and Lands of Kilmacabea, Arable and Pasture, containing, ...	397	1	31
"The Town and Lands of Cappynabohy, Arable and Pasture, containing . . .	298	0	0
"The Town and Lands of Knockscagh, Arable and Pasture, containing	349	0	18
"The Town and Lands of Gorteendooge, Arable and Pasture, containing . . .	287	0	30
"The Town and Lands of Ballinlogh and Ballyryreen, Arable and Pasture, containing	301	0	6
"The Town and Lands of Mannogyra, Arable and Pasture, containing	337	1	29
"The Town and Lands of Keymore, Arable and Pasture, containing	466	3	2

"All situate in the county of Cork; 24 miles distant from Cork, 10 from Kinsale, and 14 from Bandon. Note: the Bay of Glandore beats on the lands of Kilmacabea, where a ship of 100 tun may ride.

"Two Fairs yearly held on part of the Lands of Kilmacabea, known by the name of Donovan's Leap.

"A parcel of ground in Coleman's Lane, in the City of Cork, containing 145 Feet in front.

"The Lands of Little Bray, in the county of Dublin, within 10 small miles of Dublin, with a good large dwelling House, out Houses, and 3 new stables, all well improved, containing 127A. 0R. 0P.

"Commons thereunto belonging 64 0 0

"A dwelling House in Back-Lane, in the City of Dublin, known by the name of Donovan's Arms.

"Whoever hath a mind to treat for said Land and Houses, are desired to send their proposals to Jeremiah Donnovan, Esq., at Sir Compton Domvill's house, in Bride-street, Dublin."

In 1737, March 6, this Jeremiah Donovan, junior, sold for £5,400, to Richard Tonson, all the lands called the Manor of Donovan's Leap, and died unmarried in the year 1743. His brother, John, then brought ejectments, under the limitations of the deed executed by his father on the 30th of November, 1708, to recover possession; but before trial he died without issue. On John's death, his sister, Anne Donovan, the wife of Adam Cusack, became entitled, but she was so poor that she could not go to law. In March, 1770, Anne Donovan, *alias* Cusack, died, leaving two

[v] *Adam Cusack* of Rathgar was the son of Robert Cusack, who died at Bath in October, 1707, as appears from his tomb there. This Adam married Anne Donovan, the only daughter of Jeremy Donovan, Esq., of Dublin, and had by her John Cusack, Esq., of Rathgar, who married Mary Armstrong, but died without issue; and Edward, who was living, according to Monsieur Lainé, in 1767, and died *s. p.* in 1780.—See Lainé's *Genealogy of the House of De Cusack.*

sons, John Cusack and Edward Cusack. In February, 1775, John Cusack, as heir at law of Jeremiah Donovan, entered his claim at foot of fines levied by his uncle in 1722, but, being poor, and at law in other ways, did no other act as to the county of Cork estates during his life. He died without issue, leaving his only brother, Edward, his heir, and the heir of Jeremiah Donovan. On the 26th April, 1780, Edward Cusack died without issue and unmarried, and left his estates in the county of Cork to his kinsman, Jeremiah Donovan, and devised his estate in the city of Dublin to Robert Fitzgerald. This Jeremiah Donovan was descended from Cornelius O'Donovan, the brother of Jeremiah O'Donovan, M. P. in 1789.

XLIV. Cornelius O'Donovan of Kilmacabea. A deed, dated 3rd February, 1700, between Cornelius O'Donovan of Kilmacabea and Jeremy O'Donovan, his eldest son and heir, and Denis Mac Carthy[w], of Spring House, in the county of Tipperary (the ancestor of the Count Mac Carthy), and Ellen, his daughter, states that a marriage was about to take place between said Jeremy and Ellen. She had a fortune of £400, and Cornelius O'Donovan conveyed the lands of Rinogreny, the lands of Ballincroky, in the Liberties of the city of Cork; and the lands of Curraheen and Ballymacrone, in the barony of Ibane, for the uses of the said marriage.

XLV. Jeremy Donovan. He married Ellen Mac Carthy above referred to, and had issue, James, who had one daughter, and

XLVI. Alexander Donovan. He married a Miss Catherine O'Keeffe, by whom he had issue: 1. Jeremiah Donovan, the devisee of Edward Cusack in 1780, of whom presently; 2. James Donovan of Clonakilty, M. D., the father of the late Alexander Donovan, Esq., of Gray's Inn, London, who was appointed a district Judge in Jamaica in 1842, of Jeremiah O'Donovan of Middleton, in the county of Cork, whose son, Richard O'Donovan, is one of the editors of the *London Daily News;* and of Richard Donovan, Clerk of the Crown for the county of Cork; 3. Alexander Donovan of Squince, the father of Alexander, and Daniel O'Donovan of Squince, and James O'Donovan of Gravesend, in Kent.

XLVII. Jeremiah Donovan, Captain, R. N., father of

XLVIII. Alexander Donovan, Lieutenant, R. N., who married a Miss Scott, and has issue,

XLIX. Jeremiah Donovan, Esq., of Wood-street, Dublin, Solicitor.

THE DONOVANS OF BALLYMORE AND CLONMORE, IN THE COUNTY OF WEXFORD.

The descent of the Wexford branch of the O'Donovans had been sent to Munster by a member of that family about the year 1740. James O'Donovan of Cooldurragha, in a letter to the Editor, dated January 16, 1843, writes: "I had an old manuscript pedigree of the Leinster branch of the O'Donovans, written about 100 years ago, which I gave Collins, and thought no more about it till the present time. It has lately occurred to me that something material might be contained in it, and

[w] *Denis Mac Carthy.*—See Monsieur Lainé's Pedigree of the Count Mac Carthy. There was another branch of this family of Rinogreny seated at Ross, in the county of Cork. Cornelius O'Donovan, Esq., of Ross, married Mary, who was the daughter of Charles Mac Carthy, M. D., of Cork, by Ellen, eldest daughter of Pierce Nagle, Esq., of Aghnakishy, the brother of Sir Richard Nagle, Attorney-General to James II.—*Pedigree of O'Kearney.*

I have made every inquiry, and taken several journeys in search of it, but all to no purpose." Taking for granted that this pedigree was correct and correctly copied by Collins, the descent of the Leinster Donovans will be as follows:

XLI. Donnell Oge na Carton O'Donovan, who died in 1629, was father of

XLII. Richard na Carton O'Donovan, father of

XLIII. Murrough O'Donovan, who was father of

XLIV. Murtough O'Donovan, who had a son,

XLV. Rickard Donovan, who left Munster and settled at Clonmore, in the county of Wexford. He was bequeathed the Wexford estates by the will of his brother-in-law, Alderman Thomas Kieran, on the 20th of January, 1694. On the 13th August, 1696, on the marriage of his then eldest son, Mortagh, he made a deed of settlement of the castle, town, and lands of Upper Fernes, together with all the other townlands he possessed, to trustees, to the use of his son, Mortagh, and the heirs male of his body lawfully to be begotten; and, for want of such issue, to the heirs male of the body of the said Rickard Donovan, his father, lawfully to be begotten; failing such remainder, to the issue female of the said Mortagh; and in failure of such remainder, to the right heirs of said Mortagh for ever. Rickard Donovan married, first, Bridget, sister of Alderman Thomas Kieran, who was sheriff of the City of Dublin in 1687. He married, secondly, Julian Carew; and had issue, by his first wife, five sons and three daughters, viz.:

1. Rickard, died unmarried.

2. Mortagh, his heir, head of the Ballymore family.

3. Cornelius of Clonmore, who married, first, Bridget, daughter of Abraham Hughes, Esq., of Ballytrent, county of Wexford, and had issue: 1. Abraham, a physician in Enniscorthy, died unmarried; 2. Rickard of Clonmore, married Winifred, daughter of Henry Milward, of Ballyharron, county of Wexford. His will was proved in Dublin in 1781, and he left issue five co-heiresses, viz.: 1. Eliza, married Cadwallader Edwards, Esq., of Ballyhire; 2. Sarah, married John Cox, Esq., of Coolcliffe; 3. Winifred, married Rev. Joseph Miller, of Ross, second wife; 4. Lucy, married John Glascott, Esq., of Pilltown; 5. Julia, married Richard Newton King, Esq., of Macmine: all in the county of Wexford.

Cornelius Donovan, of Clonmore, married, secondly, Mary, daughter of John Harvey, Esq., of Killiane Castle, county Wexford. His will is dated 20th October, 1735, and was proved in the diocese of Ferns, 18th July, 1739, and he had issue by his second wife, John, Cornelius, Elizabeth, and Juliana, who married Cornelius Fitz-Patrick, Esq., and had Cornelius Donovan Fitz-Patrick.

4. Rickard, who resided at Camolin Park. He was a captain of Dragoons, and married a daughter of Richard Nixon, Esq., of Wexford, and had issue five sons and one daughter, viz.: 1. George; 2. Cornelius, who had a daughter, Mary, who married Robert Blaney, of Camolin; 3. Richard; 4. Rickard; 5. Denn-Nixon; 6. Juliana, married, first, 15th September, 1741, Richard, sixth Earl of Anglesey; secondly, Matthew Talbot, Esq., of Castle Talbot.

5. Thomas, who married a lady of the Fitzgerald family, and had issue a son, Murtagh.

1. ———, who married ——— Gough, of Ballyorel, and had issue one son, Arthur, and two daughters, Mary and Elizabeth.

2. ———, who married ——— King, and had issue Richard, William, and Mary.

3. Elizabeth, who married (articles dated 24th July, 1701) the Rev. Michael Mosse, Prebend of Whitechurch, county Wexford, and had issue Mary.

Rickard Donovan, of Clonmore, first settler in Wexford, made his will 2nd June, 1707; it was proved in the diocese of Ferns, 4th December, same year, and he was succeeded by his second son,

XLVI. Mortagh Donovan, Esq., of Ballymore, a colonel of horse, who was born the 20th May, 1697, and baptized 7th June following by the Rev. Nathaniel Huson, the sponsors being Colonel Robert Wolseley and John White, Esq., godfathers; Mrs. Christine Shapland and sister, Mary Archer, godmothers. He married, first, 13th August, 1696, Lucy, daughter of Henry Archer, of Enniscorthy, and had issue:

1. Richard, his heir.
2. Henry, who left issue.

He married, secondly (settlements being dated 23rd May, 1704), Anna, third daughter of Robert Carew, Esq., of Castletown, in the county Waterford, by whom (whose will was proved in Dublin in 1713) he had issue two sons, Robert being one of them, and three daughters; one of them, Catherine, married the Rev. S. Hayden, Rector of Ferns, who was killed at Enniscorthy in the Rebellion of 1798. Colonel Donovan died intestate in 1712, and was succeeded by his eldest son,

XLVII. Richard Donovan, Esq., of Ballymore, a captain of horse, who, in Trinity Term, 1731, suffered a common recovery of the estates, and thereby docked the several remainders created and limited by the deed of 13th August, 1696, and shortly afterwards married Elizabeth, daughter of Major Edward Rogers, of Bessmount, near Enniscorthy, and had issue:

1. Edward, his heir.
2. Lucy, married Sir Wilfrid Lawson, Bart., of Brayton Hall, Cumberland.
3. Mary, died unmarried. Will proved in Dublin, in 1805.
4. Frances, married Charles Hill, of St. John's, county Wexford.
5. Henrietta, died unmarried. Will proved in Dublin, in 1795.

Captain Donovan's will is dated 8th June, 1767, and, dying 15th July, 1768, his will was proved in Dublin same year, and he was succeeded by his only son,

XLVIII. Edward Donovan, Esq., of Ballymore, who was called to the Irish bar. He married (the deed of settlement made by his father on said marriage being dated 19th January, 1747) Mary, daughter of Captain John Broughton, of Maidstone, in the county of Kent, and had issue,

1. Richard, his heir.
2. Robert, of 24, Peter-street, Dublin, Attorney, died unmarried. Will proved in Dublin, 1828.
3. George, went to America, married Miss Devereux, and had issue.
4. John, of Dublin, and also of Charles-street, Westminster, London, died unmarried. Will proved in Dublin, 1817.
5. William, of Dublin, Lieutenant, Royal Navy, died unmarried. Will proved in Dublin, 1814.
6. Edward, in holy orders, of Ballymore, in the county Westmeath, died unmarried. Will proved in Dublin, 1827.
7. Mary, of Dublin, died unmarried. Will proved 1824.
8. Eliza, died unmarried, February, 1831.
9. Julia, married Robert Verner, Esq., of Dublin, and has issue; she died in 1840.

10. Lucy, married James Barker, Esq., of Dublin.

11. Caroline, unmarried.

Counsellor Donovan's will is dated 15th March, 1773; proved in Dublin, 26th April, same year. His widow's will was proved, same place, 1794. He was succeeded by his eldest son,

XLIX. Richard Donovan, Esq., of Ballymore, who, having attained his age of twenty-one years, on the 6th May, 1778, in the Easter Term of that year, suffered a common recovery of the estates, and it was declared by said deed, that the said recovery should enure to the use of the said Richard Donovan, and his heirs and assigns for ever. He married (settlement being dated 27th and 28th June, 1780) Anne, daughter of Goddard Richards, Esq., of the Grange, in the same county, and had issue,

1. Richard, his heir, now of Ballymore.

2. Goddard Edward, Captain, 83rd Regiment, died unmarried, at the Cape of Good Hope, 1808.

3. Robert, married Miss Taylor, and had issue: 1. Richard; 2. Robert; 3. Henry; 4. Edwin; 5. Albert William; 6. Henrietta Anne, married, 1837, James Mac Kenny, of Dublin; 7. Laura; 8. Mary Medora.

4. John, died unmarried. Will, Dublin, 1829.

5. George, married, and has issue.

6. William, married Miss Dallas, of Portarlington, and has issue, William John.

7. Henry, died unmarried in Jamaica.

8. Solomon, in holy orders.

9. Arthur, died young.

10. Anne, married Solomon Speer, Esq., of the county of Tyrone, called to the Irish bar, and had issue.

11. Catharine, died unmarried, 24th January, 1837.

12. Mary, married John Glascott, Esq., called to the Irish bar, and has issue.

13. Eliza, married Mr. William Russell, of Bloomfield, county Wexford, and has issue.

14. Caroline.

Richard Donovan, of Ballymore, was in the commission of the peace for the county Wexford. He died the 9th January, 1816, and was succeeded by his eldest son,

L. Richard Donovan, Esq., now of Ballymore, born 21st April, 1781; married, 18th October, 1816, Frances, eldest daughter and co-heir of Edward Westby, Esq., of High Park, county Wicklow, and has issue:

1. Richard, born 17th October, 1819.

2. Edward Westby, born 6th September, 1821, Lieutenant, 33rd Regiment.

3. Henry George, born 2nd Feb., 1826; baptized at Clifton, Gloucestershire, 17th April, 1826.

4. Robert, born 5th April, 1829; baptized at Clifton, 17th April, same year.

5. Phœbe.

6. Frances.

7. Anne.

Richard Donovan served the office of High Sheriff of the county of Wexford in 1819.

Arms.—Argent, issuing from the sinister side of the shield a cubit dexter arm, vested gules, cuffed azure, the hand proper grasping an old Irish sword, the blade entwined with a serpent proper.

Crest.—A falcon alighting.

Mottoes.—"Adjuvante, Deo in hostes;" also "Vir super hostes." Irish, Gilla ap a námaio abú.

Estates.—In the counties of Wexford, Queen's County, and Tipperary.

Seat.—Ballymore, Camolin, Wexford.

Ferns was granted by Queen Elizabeth, in 1583, to Sir Thomas Masterson, Knight, a Cheshire gentleman, who was sent over as governor of this district, and appointed Grand Seneschal and Constable of this castle, with a lease of the manor, whose son, Sir Richard Masterson, Knight, left, in 1627, four co-heiresses, viz.: Catherine, married Edward Butler, Esq., of Cloughnegairah, County Wexford (Wilton), Baron of Kayer; Margaret, married Robert Shee, Esq., of Uppercourt, in the county of Kilkenny; Mabell, married Nicholas Devereux, Esq., of Balmagir, in the county of Wexford; and ———, married Walter Sinnott, Esq., of Rosgarland, in the county of Wexford. This property was forfeited after the Rebellion of 1641, and was granted by patent of Charles II., dated 20th May, in the twentieth year of his reign, to Arthur Parsons, Esq., comprising the townlands of Upper Ferns, the Castle part of the town; Ferranagananagh, Pouledeogherory, Ballyshane, Ballygormockane, and Agheremore, *alias* Agnemore, *alias* Aghnemore, with their appurtenances, containing 1070A. 2R. 32P.; Ballymollen, *alias* Milltown, containing 95A.; Kilkesan, *alias* Killany, Ballycreene, Ballyregane, Ballymore, Ballyally, *alias* Ballyolly, *alias* Ballyfolly, containing 900 acres in fee.

Thomas Kieran, by his will, dated 20th of January, 1694, bequeathed (with the exception of Ballymore, which by same will be bequeathed to Mortagh Donovan) all the above townlands unto his brother-in-law, Rickard Donovan of Clonmore, in the county of Wexford, Gent., his heirs and assigns, which Rickard is mentioned in said will as father of Mortagh Donovan; and which will was witnessed by Cornelius Donovan, Eskenah Carr, and Owen Bardan.

25th Nov. 1667, Charles II., by patent, granted 100 acres of the south-east part of the townland of Clonmore to Charles Collins.

30th June, 1668, Charles Collins conveyed same to Thomas Holme.

7th January, 1681, Thomas Holme conveyed same to Francis Randall, acknowledging in the deed that the patent was made in the name of Charles Collins only as a trustee for Randall, who was an officer stationed at Barbadoes.

7th January, 1713, Samuel Randall, merchant, of Cork, son and heir of Francis Randall, granted a lease of lives, renewable for ever, to Cornelius Donovan, of the townland of Clonmore, with all the rights, &c. &c., as heretofore enjoyed by Rickard Donovan, father of Cornelius, reserving a head rent of £16, and renewal fines of £8 each life.

20th July, 1740, Richard Donovan of Ballymore renewed the above lease at the desire of Rickard Donovan of Clonmore; he, Rickard Donovan of Ballymore, having acquired the fee from Samuel Randall.

THE O'DONOVANS OF CALRY-CASHEL.

There was another family of this name seated in the territory of Calry-Cashel, in the present county of Tipperary. These are also sprung from the royal line of Oilioll Olum, King of Munster, but not through the same son as the Hy-Figeinte, but from his third son, Kian, who was also the ancestor of the O'Carrolls, O'Meaghers, and other families in the neighbouring territories. Duald Mac Firbis gives the descent of Donovan, their progenitor, as follows, in his Genealogical Manuscript (Lord Roden's copy, p. 633): Donovan, son of Colman, son of Randal, son of Cormac, son of Laighnen, son of Cumara, son of Murchadh, son of Muirchertach, son of Eochaid Faebbarghlas, the ancestor of O'Meagher, son of Conla, the ancestor of O'Carroll of Ely O'Carroll, and of O'Conor of Glengeven, in the north of Ulster, son of Teige, son of Kian, son of Oilioll Olum.

There are various families of the Donovans of this race living at present in the Glen of Agherlagh, as well as in the neighbourhood of Fethard, and various other places in the county of Tipperary, where they still retain the manly vigour and warlike characteristics of their great ancestor, Teige mac Kein.

In the time of the Editor's grandfather, three brothers of this race settled at Kilmacow, in the county of Kilkenny, namely, Michael Donovan, Bernard Donovan, and Luke Donovan, of whom the last left no issue. Michael married Anastasia O'Neill, daughter of Laurence O'Neill, Esq., of Ballyneill, by Catherine Power, and had issue two sons: 1. John, the father of Michael Donovan, Esq., 11, Clare-street, Dublin, the author of an Essay on Galvanism, and of various scientific articles in Lardner's Encyclopedia, and who, by his discoveries in chemistry, has reflected honour, not only upon his name, but upon the ancient Irish race, who, until recently, have been supposed incapable of originating anything in metaphysics, physiology, or chemistry, having during the two last centuries distinguished themselves over Europe more as soldiers, diplomatists, and orators, than as philosophers, chemists, and cultivators of the fine arts. 2. Laurence O'Neill Donovan, who went to India, where he realized a large fortune; he returned to Dublin in 1807, and married a sister of Dr. Singer, F. T. C. D., but died without male issue. Bernard Donovan, the second brother, married Rose O'Neill, the sister of Anastasia aforesaid, by whom he had issue three sons, and one daughter: 1. John; 2. Laurence; 3. Neal. John held a high rank in the Spanish service, and married the daughter of the Governor of East Florida, by whom he had two sons. Laurence, the second son of Bernard, was Commissary-General in the British service, and Comptroller of Surinam, in the West Indies. He died unmarried. Neal Donovan, the third son of Bernard, went to South America, and is supposed to have been drowned. Bernard Donovan's daughter, Lucinda, married Laurence Crowe, Esq., of the county of Clare and of the city of Dublin, by whom she had several sons and one daughter, Maria Carolina, who is married to the Prince of Bassano, son of the Prince of Peace, who was Prime Minister and Generalissimo to Charles IV. of Spain.

O'DONOVAN OF TUATH O'FEEHILY.

It should be also remarked that there had been a family of O'Donovan seated in Tuath-O'Feehily in O'Driscoll's country, before the Hy-Figeinte had been driven from the plains along the River Maigue, in the present county of Limerick. They are mentioned in a very curious tract on the tribes, districts, and history of the territory of Corca-Luighe, preserved in the Book of Lecan, fol. 122 *et sequent.*, and in Duald Mac Firbis's Genealogical work, p. 677, as situated in Tuath O bhFithcheallaigh, extending from Gaibhlin-an-ghaithneamhna to Oilen Insi-Duine, and from Dun-Eoghain to Glaise-Draighneacha. The other feudatories of the same district were

O'Comhraidh, O'h-Iarnain, O'Nuallain, and O'Croinin. No pedigree of this sept, who are probably of the same race as the O'Driscolls, has been discovered. It would appear that the old fort of Dangan-Donovan was erected by their ancestor, for it is certain that this fort is much older than the time that the Hy-Figeinte O'Donovans settled in Corca-Luighe. It is highly probable that a great number of the O'Donovans of the county of Cork are of this family. The Hy-Figeinte may in general be distinguished from them by their small hands and feet, and a peculiar formation of the toes, by which the race of Cairbre Aebhdha are infallibly known to one another.

PEDIGREE OF MAC CARTHY OF DUNMANWAY,

CHIEF OF GLEANN-A-CHROIM.

From Lughaidh, the third son of Oilioll Flannbeg, No. V., *supra*, was descended,

XXV. Carthach, *a quo* Mac Carthy. He was the great-grandson of Callaghan of Cashel, King of Munster, and was killed in the year 1045.

XXVI. Muireadhach Mac Carthy, died 1095.

XXVII. Cormac Mac Carthy of Magh-Tamhnaigh, King of Desmond, slain in 1138.

XXVIII. Diarmaid Mac Carthy of Kill-Baghaine, King of Desmond, slain 1185.

XXIX. Donnell More na Curra Mac Carthy, K. D., slain 1185. He had two sons: Cormac Finn, K. D., who died in 1215, the ancestor of Mac Carthy More and Mac Carthy of Muskerry, and of Mac Donough of Duhallow, and various other septs; Domhnall God, the ancestor of Mac Carthy Reagh, chief of Carbery, and of Mac Carthy of Gleann-a-Chroim.

XXX. Donnell God Mac Carthy.

XXXI. Donnell Mael Mac Carthy.

XXXII. Donnell Cam Mac Carthy.

XXXIII. Donnell Glas Mac Carthy. He had three sons: 1. Donnell Reagh, the ancestor of Mac Carthy Reagh, Chief of Carbery; 2. Cormac Donn, the ancestor of Mac Carthy of Gleann-a'-Chroim; and a third son by the daughter of O'Croimin, called Mac Inghine Ui Chroimin, from whom are descended the Mac Carthys of Clancromine, who had a strong castle at Beal-atha-an-Urchair till 1641, when their chief was slain, and their territory forfeited.

XXXIV. Cormac Donn Mac Carthy. He was Chief of Carbery, and was slain in 1366.—See p. 633, *supra*. He had eight sons, viz.: 1. Dermot; 2. Felim; 3. Donnell; 4. Owen; 5. Teige; 6. Fineen; 7. Cormac; 8. Donough; of whose descendants little is known, except those of Felim, from whom the subsequent chiefs of Gleann-a-Chroim are descended.

XXXV. Felim Mac Carthy.

XXXVI. Teige Mac Carthy.

XXXVII. Fineen or Florence Mac Carthy.

XXXVIII. Cormac Mac Carthy. He had four sons, viz.: 1. Fineen, or Florence, who, according to a pedigree of this family, preserved in a manuscript at Lambeth Palace, Carew Collection, No. 635, fol. 151, "was slayne by his nephew, Cormocke Downe." This Fineen had married a daughter of O'Sullivan Beare, by whom he left a son, Cormac, who married More, daughter of Dermot Oge O'Leary, by whom he had a daughter, who married Dermot O'Crowly of Coill-tSealbhaigh, and two sons,—Felim, who was slain in 1641, and Cormac Reagh. 2. The second son of Cormac, No. XXXVIII., was Dermot-na-nGlac, the ancestor of the subsequent chiefs, of whom presently; his third son was named Owen; and his fourth son, Felim; but it is stated by the writer of the Lambeth Pedigree, just referred to, that their descendants were all dead when he was writing, which was about the year 1652.

XXXIX. Dermot-na-nglac Mac Carthy of Dunmanway, Chief of the Gleann-a-Chroim. He married Ellinor, the daughter of the celebrated Sir Cormac Mac Carthy of Muskerry, the friend of the Lord Deputy, Sir Henry Sidney, and had issue: 1. Cormac Donn, who, according to the Lambeth Pedigree, married a daughter of Connogher O'Leary, and was "Hanged in chaynes at Corke, for murdering his Vnkle Fynin,"—he left one son, Felim, and a daughter, who was married to Arthur O'Crowly; 2. Fineen, who died without issue; 3. Teige-an-Fhorsa, i. e. Timothy of the Force, ancestor of the subsequent chiefs; and one daughter, who was married to David O'Crowly.

XL. Teige-an-Fhorsa, i. e. Timothy of the Force, usually called Teige Onorsie by English writers. He married, first, a daughter of Mac Fineen, and widow of Turlough Backagh Mac Sweeny; and secondly, Ellenor, daughter of Rory Mac Sheehy, who survived him, and had issue: 1. Teige-an-Duna, of whom presently; 2. Dermot, who, according to an Inquisition taken at the King's Castle in Cork, on the 26th of August, 1618, claimed Togher, Shancrane, Quynrath, Dyereagh, and various other lands in the neighbourhood of Dunmanway; and a daughter, who was married to Randal Oge O'Hurley. He had also an illegitimate son, Fineen.

Queen Elizabeth, by letters patent, under the great seal of Ireland, dated at Dublin the 28th day of December, the thirty-third year of her reign, granted to this Teige Mac Dermot Mac Carthy the Castle of Dunmanway, and the entire territory of Gleann-a-Chroim. He afterwards surrendered to James I. and received a re-grant of all his territory. This appears from two Inquisitions, one taken at the King's Old Castle, in Cork, on the 26th of August, 1618, and the other at the same place on the 13th of August, in the twenty-first year of the reign of James I. These Inquisitions are as follows:

"Inquisitio capta apud le Kinges Castell in Corck, in Comitatu Cork, xxvi.° die augusti, 1618, annoque regni domini Jacobi &c., decimo sexto, coram Richardo domino Boyle Barone de Youghill (et aliis) per sacramenta proborum &c., qui dicunt quod Teig mac Dermodie Cartey, alias Norsey, de Downemeanwy in Comitatu Cork, armiger defunctus, diem suum clausit extremum apud civitatem Cork, tertio die Julii anno millesimo sexcentesimo decimo octavo; Et quod tempore vite sue seisitus fuit de feodo, viz.: de Castro, villa et terra vocata Downemeanwye, alias Downemeanvay, in dicto Comitatu Cork, continente tres carrucatas terræ, in Glawn Icryem, in Baronie de Carribry, valoris per annum xx.'; Ac de villa et terra sive quarterio terre de Dromeleyn in dicto Comitatu, continente tres carrucatas terre, valoris per annum xx.'; Ac de villa sive quarterio terre de Inshy, in Comitatu predicto, continente tres carrucatas terre, valoris per annum xx.'; Ac de villa sive quarterio terre de Quynrath in dicto Comitatu, continente tres carrucatas terræ, valoris per annum xx.'; Ac etiam de villa, sive quarterio terræ vocata Togher, continente tres carrucatas terræ in dicto Comitatu, valoris per annum xx.^{s}; Ac etiam de villa et quarterio terræ vocata Altaghe, in dicto Comitatu, continente tres carrucatas terræ, valoris per annum xx.^{s}; Ac etiam de villa et terra de Ballyhalogge, in dicto Comitatu continente duas carrucatas terræ, valoris per annum xiii.^{s}; Ac etiam de villa et quarterio terræ vocata Mahoney, alias Mahona, in dicto Comitatu Cork, continente tres carrucatas terræ, valoris per annum xx.^{s}; Ac etiam de Kileonan in dicto comitatu continente tres carrucatas terræ, valoris per annum xx.^{s}; Ac etiam de villa et quarterio terræ vocata Lyssebealyd, alias Lyssebelfaddaghe, in dicto Comitatu, continente tres carrucatas terræ, valoris per annum xx.^{s}; Ac etiam de et in villa sive quarterio vocato Ferlaghan, alias Bealaghane, in dicto Comitatu, continente tres carrucatas terræ, valoris per annum xx.^{s}; Ac etiam sexdecem Gnyves terræ jacentibus in duobus carrucatis terræ de Clonnwgane, Cloungane in Glanykroym predicto, ac nuper in tenura dicti Teig mac Dermody Cartey, alias Teig I Norcey, valoris per annum xx.^{s}; Ac etiam de dimidio unius carrucatæ terræ de Dyrrynecaharragh, in Comitatu predicto, valoris per annum ii.^{s}; Ac etiam de una carrucata terræ in le occidentali Drynighe, alias Drynigh-in-tample, valoris per annum iiii.^{s} iiii.^{d}; Ac etiam de villa, sive quarterio terræ, vocata Kilvarry alias Kilwarry, in dicto comitatu, continente tres carrucatas terræ, valoris per annum xv.^{s}; Ac etiam de villa, sive quarterio vocato East Drynagh in dicto comitatu, continente tres carrucatas terræ, valoris per annum xv.^{s}; Ac etiam de quatuor Gnyves terræ vocatis Farren Innyneherrin, valoris per annum ii.^{s}; Ac etiam de villa, sive quarterio terræ vocata Curraghnymaddery, alias Tullagh, in dicto comitatu Cork, continente tres carrucatas terræ, valoris per annum xv.^{s}; Ac de villa et terra de Carroughnyhomogh alias Twllaghe continente tres carrucatas terræ, valoris per annum xv.^{s}

"Et ulterius dicunt quod predictus Teig mac Dermody Cartie per cartam suam datam x.^{o} die Februarii, 1608, concessit Thome fitz John Barry, de Ballyne Corry, in dicto Comitatu Cork, et Donogho mac Teig O'Learie, de Tome, in dicto Comitatu, generosis, de omnibus, villis, terris, &c. de Ratherownyhawne, Kahaurow mac altigg, in dicto comitatu, continente sex carrucatas terræ, cum omnibus boscis, et aliis pertinentibus quibuscumque, ad opus et usum suum proprium durante vita sua naturali, et post mortem suam Ellenore ny Reyry mac Shyhy uxori ejus et post mortem suam ad opus et usum Dermicii mac Teig mac Cartey et heredibus suis masculis de corpore suo legittime procreatis, sub certis aliis conditionibus in eadem Carta expressis.

"Ac ulterius dicunt quod predictus Teig mac Dermody Cartey, alias I-Norsey, seisitus fuit sub modo et forma predicto de dimidio unius carrucate terre vocate Garranetonereigh, in dicto Comitatu, valoris per annum ii.^{s}; Ac Juratores predicti ulterius dicunt quod predictus Teig mac Dermody Cartey, alias I-Norsey, seisitus fuit, de feodo, de annuali redditu exeunte de terris sequentibus viz.: de et ex villa et terra de Littergorman alias Kippagh, in dicto Comitatu, continente unum quarterium terræ iiii.^{l} viii.^{s} x.^{d} obolique sterlingorum per annum; Ac etiam de et ex villa et quarterio terræ de Dromedrastill, alias Coulkelloure, in dicto Comitatu, iiii.^{l} viii.^{s} x.^{d} obolique sterlingorum per annum.

"Ac ulterius dicunt quod Ellenor ny Shyhy vidua et relicta predicti Teig mac Dermody Cartey, alias I-Norsey, legittime fuit maritata, et clamat dotem omnium premissorum.

"Ac etiam dicunt quod predictus Teig mac Dermody Cartey, alias I-Norsey, tempore vite sue seisitus fuit de omnibus Castris, villis, terris, et hereditamentis, et tenuit eadem de Domino rege, virtute literarum patentium dicti Domini Regis, datarum apud Dublin, vicesimo nono die Junii anno regni Jacobi Anglie &c. xiii° per quasquidem literas patentes dictus Dominus Rex concessit omnia premissa predicto Teig mac Dermody et heredibus suis in feodo simplice, sub annuali redditu L iii^{s}. iii^{d}. Hibernie; et quod tenentur in libero et communi soccagio, et non in Capite; Et ulterius dicunt quod predictus Teig mac Dermody Cartey, alias I-Norsey, sic seisitus existens de premissis, obiit inde seisitus, et quod premissa tempore mortis sue predicte et tunc tenebantur in libero et communi soccagio de dicto Domino nostro Jacobo Rege ut de Castro de Dublin, per fidelitatem tantum; Et ulterius dicunt quod Teig oge mac Cartey, alias I-Downy, est filius et legittimus heres predicti Teig mac Dermody Cartey, alias I-Norsey, et quod tempore mortis predicti patris sui fuit etatis triginta annorum, aut circiter, et tempore captionis hujus Inquisitionis, fuit etatis triginta quatuor annorum, aut circiter, et maritatus tempore mortis predicti patris sui; Et ulterius dicunt quod Dermisius mac Teig mac Dermody clamat proprium jus hereditatis de et in terris sequentibus, viz.: de et in villa et in duobus carrucatis terræ et novem gnyves de Tougher; Ac de et in villa et una carrucata terre de Shancrane et de et in villa et dimidio unius Carrucatæ terræ de Quynrath et de et in villa et dimidio unius carrucate terre de Dyereagh et de et in villa et quatuor gnyves terre vocatis Inenerery ac etiam de et in villa et quatuor gnyves terre vocatis Derrymaheraghe; Ac de et in villa et duobus carrucatis terre de Cwylmontaine et Caherowmymaddery; Ac de et in villis et quatuor gnyves terre de Drinaghintample in Clanloghlin; Ac etiam de et in villa et dimidio unius carrucate terre de Garranetoneroaghie in Clanloghlin predicto."

"Inquisitio capta apud the King's Old Castle in Comitatu Cork, decimo tertio die Augusti, Anno regni domini Jacobi, &c., vicesimo primo, coram Willielmo Barker armigero supervisore Curie Wardorum (et aliis) per sacramenta proborum, &c., qui dicunt quod Domina Elizabetha nuper Regina Anglie per literas suas patentes sub magno sigillo hujus Regni Hibernie sigillatas datas apud Dublin decimo octavo die Decembris anno regni sui tricesimo tercio, concessit prefato mac Dermodi Carthy totum illum Castrum villam et terram de Downemanevy in Comitatu Cork, cum pertinentibus annualis valoris xx.^{s} Unum quarterium terre vocatum the quarter of Kilwarry in Comitatu predicto annualis valoris x.^{s}; et unum aliud quarterium terræ vocatum Dromlina, cum pertinentibus, in Comitatu predicto annualis valoris x.^{s}; in omnibus, &c., unum aliud quarterium terre vocatum Inshie cum pertinentibus in Comitatu annualis valoris v.^{s}; unum aliud quarterium terre vocatum Dromdriastell cum pertinentibus in Comitatu predicto annualis valoris v.^{s}; unum aliud quarterium terre Quinraghe cum pertinentibus in Comitatu predicto annualis valoris v^{s}.; unum aliud quarterium terre vocatum Karrownamadderie cum pertinentibus in Comitatu predicto, annualis valoris v.^{s}; unum aliud quarterium terre vocatum Togher cum pertinentibus in Comitatu predicto annualis valoris v.^{s}; unum aliud quarterium terre vocatum Tullhighr cum pertinentibus in Comitatu predicto annualis valoris v.^{s}; unum aliud quarterium terre vocatum Altaghe cum pertinentibus in Comitatu predicto annualis valoris v.^{s}; duas Carrucatas terræ in Ballyhallowige cum pertinentibus annualis valoris v.^{s}; unum aliud quarterium terre vocatum Mahownie cum pertinentibus in Comitatu predicto annualis valoris v.^{s}; unum quarterium terre vocatum Kilronane cum pertinentibus in Comitatu predicto annualis valoris v.^{s}; unum quarterium terre vocatum Lisbiallin cum pertinentibus in Comitatu predicto, annualis valoris v.^{s}; unum quarterium terre vocatum Drinaghe cum pertinentibus in Comitatu predicto, annualis valoris v.ˢ; unum aliud quarterium terre vocatum Littergorman cum pertinentibus in Comitatu predicto, annualis v.ˢ; unum aliud quarterium terre vocatum Vearlaghane cum pertinentibus, in Comitatu predicto, annualis valoris v.ˢ; duas Carrucatas terre, cum pertinentibus, in Cloineodowgane in Comitatu predicto annualis valoris v.ˢ; Dimidium Carrucate terre cum pertinentibus in Derrincarraghe in Comitatu predicto, annualis valoris ii.ˢ; et de dimidio Carrucate terre cum pertinentibus in Inynyingherrin in Comitatu predicto, annualis valoris ii.ˢ; jacentia in Cantreda de Glanchrime, in Comitatu predicto; Habendum et tenendum prefato Thadeo mac Dermody Carthy et heredibus masculis de corpore suo legittime procreatis et procreandis: Tenendum de dicta Domina Regina in Capite per vicesimam partem unius feodi militis prout per dictas literas patentes plane apparet virtute quarum quidem literarum patentium dictus Thadeus mac Dermody Carthy in omnia premissa intravit et fuit inde seisitus de feodo. Et Juratores predicti ulterius dicunt quod Dominus noster nunc Rex Anglie per literas suas gerentes datum apud Newsted decimo quinto die Augusti Anno regni sui Anglie, &c., duodecimo, inter alia authorizavit et requisivit Arthurum Dominum Chichester ad tunc deputatum dicti domini Regis generalem dicti Regni sui Hibernie ad accipiendum sursumreddicionis ad usum dicti domini Regis terrarum et tenementorum in Baronia de Càrbrie quarum quidem literarum tenor sequitur in hæc verba: 'James Rex, right trusty,' &c. Et ulterius dicunt quod prefatus Iacobus Simpell miles per et in consideracione ducentarum librarum prefato Jacobo per predictum Thadeum mac Dermody Carthy pro manibus solutarum per quoddam scriptum suum gerentem datum vicesimo octavo die Januarii Anno domini, 1614, nominasset constituisset et authorizasset prefatum Thadeum mac Dermody Carthy ad capiendum et recipiendum a dicto domino Rege literas patentes de dicto castro villa et terra de Downmanevy predicto; et de omnibus aliis premissis cum eorum pertinentibus Habendum et tenendum prefato Thadeo mac Dermod heredibus et assignatis suis imperpetuum prout per dictum scriptum predicti Jacobi Simple militis magis plane liquet. Et ulterius dicunt quod predictus Thadeus mac Dermody Carthy per quoddam scriptum suum et in Curia Cancellarie domini nostri Jacobi tunc Regis hujus Regni sui Hibernie irrotulatum datum vicesimo octavo die Junii Anno Regni dicti domini Regis Anglie, &c., decimo tertio sursum reddidisset in manus dicti domini Regis nunc totum illud Castrum villam et terram de Downemanevy predicta et omnia premissa cum eorum pertinentibus: Habendum et tenendum dicto domino Regi heredibus et successoribus suis imperpetuum, ea tamen intencione quod dictus dominus Rex per literas suas patentes sub magno sigillo suo Hibernie sigillatas reconcederet omnia premissa prefato Thadeo mac Dermody Carty heredibus et assignatis suis imperpetuum, ad solum et proprium opus et usum dicti Thadei heredum et assignatorum suorum imperpetuum. Virtute cujus quidem sursum reddicionis dictus dominus Rex seisitus fuit de omnibus premissis predictis cum eorum pertinentibus. Et sic inde seisitus existens dictus dominus Rex per literas suas patentes gerentes datum apud Dublin vicesimo nono die Junii Anno Domini, 1615, concessit omnia Castra, villas, terras, et tenementa predicta cum eorum pertinentibus prefato Thadeo mac Dermody Carty heredibus et assignatis suis imperpetuum: Habendum et tenendum prefato Thadeo mac Dermody Carthy heredibus et assignatis suis imperpetuum; tenendum de dicto domino nostro Rege Jacobo ut de Castro suo de Dublin, in libero et communi soccagio et non in Capite neque per servicium militare. Virtute quarum quidem literarum patentium idem Thadeus mac Dermody Carthy in omnia premissa predicta cum eorum pertinentibus intravit. Et fuit inde seisitus (prout lex postulat). Et sic inde seisitus existens predictus Thadeus mac Dermody Carthie districtus fuit per breve dicti domini Regis e scaccario suo hujus Regni sui Hibernie emanens ad comparendum in eadem Curia et ad faciendum dicto domino Regi homagium per omnibus Castris villis, terris, et tenementis predictis cum eorum pertinentibus super quod idem Thadeus postea, scilicet, decimo die Novembris Anno regni dicti domini Regis nunc Anglie, &c., decimo quinto, in eadem Curia comparuit et dixit quod ipse ad faciendum homagium dicto domino Regi pro premissis seu pro aliqua parte sive parcella inde compelli non debeat quia adtunc dixit quod dictus dominus Rex per literas suas dictas patentes concessit sibi prefato Thadeo mac Dermody Carthie omnia Castra villas terras et tenementa predicta cum eorum pertinentibus habendas sibi et assignatis suis imperpetuum: Tenendum de dicto domino Rege ut de Castro suo Dublin in libero et Communi soccagio et non in Capite nec per servicium militare unde non intendisset quod dictus dominus Rex nunc ipsum in ea causa ulterius non distringere seu exonerare velit; unde adtunc petiisset iudicium. Et quod ipse quoad ad faciendum dicto domino Regi homagium pro premissis seu pro aliqua inde parcella a Curia predicta dimittatur; Et Johannes Davies miles ad tunc attornatus generalis dicti domini Regis dicti Regni sui Hibernie qui pro eodem domino Rege in ea parte ad tunc sequebatur visis tam donacionis sursumreddicionis predictæ per prefatum Thadeum dicto domino Regi heredibus et assignatis suis de premissis in facto quam dictis literis patentibus a dicto domino Rege prefato Thadeo de premissis in forma predicta concessis Idem Attornatus adtunc non dedixisset sed fatebatur placitum prefati Thadei ad tunc placitatum fore verum unde adtunc consideratus fuit per Barones dicti Scaccarii quod predictus Thadeus quoad homagium dicto domino Regi pro premissis faciendum ab eadem Curia ad tunc dimittatur. Et ulterius Juratores dicunt quod predictus Thadeus mac Dermody Charty de premissis sic ut prefertur seisitus existens obiit sic inde seisitus secundo die Julij anno domini 1617. Et quod Thadeus mac Carty alias Teige-y-downie est filius et proximus heres prefati Thadei Mac Dermody et fuit ætatis triginta annorum tempore mortis predicti patris sui et maritatus. Et quod omnia premissa predicta tenentur de dicto domino nostro Rege Jacobo prout lex postulat. Et ulterius dicunt quod immediate post obitum prefati Thadei mac Dermody Carthie idem Thadeus alias Teige-y-Downie in omnia premissa intravit, et exitus et proficia inde huc usque percepit et habuit. Et ulterius quod post obitum prefati Thadei mac Dermodi Carthie predictus Thadeus alias Teige-y-Downie solvit dicto domino Regi summam L. iii.[s] iiii.[d] nomine relevii prout per acquietanciam sub manu vice thesaurarii dicti domini Regis Regni Hibernie pro recepcione inde plane apparet. Et quod Ellinor Carthy est vidua et relicta prefati Thadei mac Dermody Carthie modo superstes ac indotata omnium premissorum."

The lands surrendered and regranted to this Teige Inorsa, will appear from the following extracts from the Patent Rolls.

"VII. 16. Surrender by Teige Mac Dermott Cartie, otherwise Teig Inorse of Downemenway, in Cork Co., gent., of all his estate in Cork co., with the intention that the King shall reconvey the same to him by letters patent.—28 Jun., 13th.

"VIII. 18. Deed, whereby Sir James Semple, knt., appoints Teige Mac Dermody Cartie, of Downemeanwy, in Cork co., to accept a grant or grants from the King, of part of the lands and premises expressed in article X., for the sum of £280.—28 Jan., 12th.

"IX. 19. Deed, whereby Sir James Semple, knt., appoints Teige Mac Dermody Cartie otherwise Teige Innorsy, of Dounemeanvoy, in Cork co., gent., to accept a grant or grants of the remaining part of the lands and premises expressed in article X., for the sum of £50 10*s.* 6*d.*—28 Jan., 12th.

"X. 21. Grant from the King to Teig or Thady Mac Dermott Cartie otherwise Teige Inorse, of Downemenvoy, gent.

"*Cork Co.*—In Carbrie Bar. The castle, town, and lands or qr. called Downmanvoy[x] otherwise Downemeanvey*, containing 3 plowlands in Glancroim; Dromeline[y]*, Inshie[z]*, Quin-Rath[a]*, Togher[b]* and Altagh[c]*, each containing 3 plowlands; Ballihalloige[d]*, 2 plowlands; Mahoney[e] otherwise Mahouna*, 3 plowlands; Killronan[f]*, Lissebealidd otherwise Lissbealfadda[g]*, Fearlaghan[h] otherwise Vearlaghan*, each containing 3 plowlands; sixteen gnives in the 2 plowlands of Cloneowgan otherwise Clonioungan or Cloynoungan*, Dirrinycaharagh[i]*, $\frac{1}{2}$ plowland; all in Glancroim; in the West-Drinagh[j] otherwise Drinaghentemple*, 1 plowland in Clanloghlin; Killvarrie[k] otherwise Killwarrie*, 3 plowlands in Glancroim; Drinagh*, 3 plowlands; Farren-Innirerie or Inynrerie, 4 gnives*; Carrownemaddrie otherwise Tullagh, 3 plowlands; Carrownehaw otherwise Tullhagh*, 3 plowlands; all in Glancroim; Garrantonereigh*, $\frac{1}{2}$ plowland; a chief-rent of £4 10*s.* $8\frac{1}{2}\frac{1}{8}$*d.*, Eng., out of Lettergorman otherwise Kippagh; out of Dromdrasduyll[l] otherwise Coolekellour, £4 10*s.* $8\frac{1}{2}\frac{1}{8}$*d.*, the said town and lands of Dromdrasduyll*, 3 plowlands in Glancroim, Littergormane otherwise Kippagh*; rent for all the preceding lands, except those in W. Drinagh and Carrantoneregih, £2 13*s.* 4*d.*, and to keep 10 able footmen at the command of the chief governor; Kincahbegg[m], 1‡ plowland in Kiltallowe; in Kannagh, 4 gnives; in Lissellan, 8 gnives; in the N. plowland of Liss-Ihillane, 4 gnives; in Kannagh, 8 gnives, all in Kiltallow; Balliboyloneoughtragh[n], 1 plowland; Lissicarran[o], 1 plowland; Cappin[p], 1 plowland; Bellaghenure[q], 1 plowland; Caherneknave otherwise Kahernegnave[r] otherwise called the W. half plowland of Furrowe[s], $\frac{1}{2}$ plowland in Clanloghlin; Garren-Iven, 1 plowland in Clanloghlin; 3 gnives in Courturk, in the 2 plowlands of Dromully, in Clanloughlin; all chief-rents, services, and privileges payable to

[x] *Downmanvoy.*—Now Dunmanway.

[y] *Dromeline.*—Now Drumleena, in the parish of Fán Lobáir, now *anglice* Fanlobus.

[z] *Inshie.*—Now Inch, East and West, in the parish of Fanlobus.

[a] *Quin-Rath.*—Now Keenrath, in the same parish.

[b] *Togher, sic hodie:* a townland, containing the ruins of a castle, in the same parish.

[c] *Altagh.*—Now Aultagh, in the parish of Kilmichael.

[d] *Ballyhalloige.*—Now Ballyhalwick, in the parish of Fanlobus.

[e] *Mahoney.*—Now Mahona, in the same parish.

[f] *Kilronan.*—Now Kilronane, East and West, in the same parish.

[g] *Lisbealidd.*—Now Lisbealad, East and West, in the parish of Drinagh.

[h] *Fearlaghan.*—Now Ferlihanes, in the parishes of Kilkerranmore and Kilmeen.

[i] *Dirrinycaharagh.*—Now Derrynacaharagh, in the parish of Fanlobus.

[j] *West-Drinagh.*—A townland in the parish of Drinagh.

[k] *Kilvarrie.*—Now Kilbarry, in the parish of Fanlobus.

[l] *Dromdrasduyll.*—Now Drumdrasdle, in the parish of Fanlobus.

[m] *Kincahbegg.*—Now Kinneigh, in a parish of the same name.

[n] *Balliboyloneoughtragh.*—Now Ballyvelone West, in the parish of Kinneigh.

[o] *Lissicarran.*—Now Lissycorrane, in the same parish.

[p] *Cappin.*—Now Cappeen, East and West, in the same parish.

[q] *Bellaghenure.*—Now Ballaghanure, in the same parish.

[r] *Kahernegnave.*—Now Caher, in the parish of Kinneigh.

[s] *Furrowe.*—Now Froe, in the parish of Rosscarbery.

Donell Mac Cartie, the King's ward, or any of his ancestors, together with all his right to all or any of the premises, are hereby excepted.

"The premises thus marked * are created the manor of Downemenvoy, with 500 acres in demesne, power to create tenures, and to hold courts leet and baron; to hold a Saturday market at Kilbarah, and a yearly fair at Ballyhallowe, on 24 Sep. and the day after, unless when the said day falls on Saturday or Sunday, then the said fair to commence on the following Monday; with courts of pie powder and the usual tolls; rent 13*s.* 4*d.*

"To hold for ever, as of the Castle of Dublin, in common soccage."—29 Jan., 13th.

This Teige-an-Fhorsa or Teige Inorsie Mac Carthy, died on the 3rd of July, 1618, as appears by the Inquisition taken at the King's Old Castle, in Cork, on the 26th of August, 1618, above printed for the first time, and was succeeded by his son,

XLII. Teige-an-Duna, usually called by English writers, Teige Odowney or Teige Idownie. He was a very conspicuous character, and second in command of the forces of Mac Carthy Reagh, during the insurrection of 1641. The author of *Carbriæ Notitia*, who wrote in 1686, after speaking of Clancahill, has the following notice of his territory:

"To the north-East hereof we shall finde Dunmannaway, a small village, well situated on the banks of the river Bandon, fortified with an old castle, and to the north thereof, the castle of Togher, a large, strong pile. This tract is called Glanacrime or Slughtfelimy" [i. e. Race of Felim, son of Cormac Donn] "and belonged unto Teig Odoony, one of the best branches of the Carthyes, and alwayes reckoned one of the best housekeepers in Carbry."

This Teige-an-Duna Mac Carthy was thirty-four years old in 1618, and married. According to the Lambeth Pedigree, he married, 1. A daughter of Brian mac Owen Mac Sweeny of Cloghda; but it appears, from various other documents, that he married, secondly, Honora, daughter of Donnell O'Donovan, chief of Clancahill, by Johanna, the daughter of Sir Owen Mac Carthy Reagh. His second wife was living, a widow, in 1652, as appears by a deposition made by her respecting the taking of the castle of Dundonnell, now preserved in the Library of Trinity College, Dublin. Teige-an-Duna left three sons: 1. Teige-an-Fhorsa; 2. Dermot, living at Dunmanway in 1641, as appears by the depositions of 1641; and 3. Callaghan, living, in 1652, with his mother, Honora Ni Carthy, *alias* Donovan.

XLIII. Teige-an-Fhorsa II. It appears from Decrees of Innocent's (VIII. 53), that he married, on the 22nd of October, 1641, Jennet Coppinger, relict of Nicholas Skiddy, of the city of Cork, merchant. He was then possessed, in his demesne, as of fee of the "townes, lands, tenements, and hereditaments following, viz.: the town and lands of Ffearlaghan, known by the names of Tullaghglass, Gortnidihy, Maulcullanane, and Carrigatotane, in the parish of Kilmeen, barony of Carbery, and county of Cork; the town and lands of Curreboy, one ploughland in the parish of Drinagh, Coolemontane, and Tullagh; three ploughlands in the parish of Inchegeelagh; and being thereof so seised and possessed, did, by his last will and testament in writing, devise same unto claimant Gennet for her life, in lieu of dower, and soon after died. After whose death, by virtue of said will, said Gennet was seised and possessed of the premises, until she was expulsed by the late usurping powers. The Court of Claims find that Nicholas Skiddy, her first husband, died before the 22nd of October, 1641, and that Teige Carthy dyed in the yeare 1650.

But as for and concerning the lands of Kilbarry, with the two water mills thereon, and the said lands of Ffearlaghane, called Tullaghglass, Gortnedihy, Maulo Icullenane, Carrigetotane, Curreboy, Coolemountane, and Tullagh, in regard the said Claimants (George Skiddy and his mother, Gennet), and each of them, failed to make out any title thereunto, it is considered, ordered, and adjudged and decreed by this Court, that the same and every part thereof are and be excepted out of this precept, order, and decree, and that the claymants be left to such other course, either in law or Equity, as they shall think fit."

Jeremy Carthy, Esq. (who was evidently Teige-an-Duna's second son), was restored to the following townlands, most of which are situated in Gleann-a-Chroim, under the Commission of Grace, in 1684, viz.:

	A.	R.	P.	
Drinagh,	240	0	0	
Lisbiallet,	262	1	34	
Oculane *alias* Carnacullane,	876	1	16	profitable.
" "	977	3	24	unprofitable.
Drumlynagh,	1062	0	0	
Kinrath *alias* Kinragh,	450	0	0	profitable.
" "	163	2	0	unprofitable.
More in the same,	17	0	0	
Carnemaddery,	383	0	0	
Awe, called Noskin part,	175	0	0	
Astagmore,	690	2	16	
More in the same,	8	2	27	
Drumgarruff and Garranard,	29	1	16	profitable.
" "	113	0	0	unprofitable.
Carhuvalder,	10	0	0	
Glanakerne *alias* Glannykarny,	82	3	31	profitable.
" "	270	0	0	unprofitable.
Total in the barony of Carbery,	5811	3	4	
Lisnekelly,	139	0	0	
Longford,	47	0	0	profitable.
"	40	0	0	unprofitable.
Total in the barony of Coonagh, county Limerick,	226	0	0	
Kilbonaw,	497	0	0	
Lumanagheitragh,	93	0	0	
Total in the barony of Glanarought, county Kerry,	590	0	0	

Dated January 3rd, 1684; Inrolled 31st January, 1684. (R. 6. f., m. 8, fo. 18.)

The Editor has not been able to learn the after history of this Jeremy. John Collins, of Myross, in his pedigree of O'Donovan, speaking of O'Donovan's daughter, Honora, who was married to Teige-a-Duna, has the following remark:

"From the said Teige-an-Duna sprung several military gentlemen who distinguished themselves abroad, such as Charles of Lorrain, otherwise called Cormac na nglac."

He also says that this family had possessions in Gleann-a-Chroim till 1690, when he refers to a Teige-a-Duna, the Hospitable, nominal Lord of Gleann-a-Chroim.

Teige-an-Fhorsa II. is mentioned in several copies of the Book of Munster, as having a son,

XLIV. Teige-an-Duna II., and this is evidently the person called nominal Lord of Gleann-a-Chroim by Collins. Three generations more of this pedigree are given in an Irish manuscript, in the Library of the Royal Irish Academy (O'Gorman's Collection, 16, 5), which are as follows:

XLV. Felim Mac Carthy, son of Teige-an-Duna II, born *circiter* 1672.

XLVI. Dermot Mac Carthy, son of Felim, born *circ.* 1702.

XLVII. Cormac Mac Carthy, son of Dermot, born *circ.* 1734.

The last acknowledged head of this ancient sept of the Mac Carthys was an old gentleman, well known in the south of Ireland by the name of Jerry-an-Duna. He died at O'Donovan's Cove some years since, in the eighty-fourth year of his age. His generous friend and kind benefactor, Timothy O'Donovan, Esq., in whose house he died, mentions him, in a letter to the Editor, as the undoubted head of this family, and the great-grandson of Teige-an-Duna, the last who resided in the castle of Dunmanway. He adds: "His appearance was most respectable, and he had the manners and information of a gentleman; all classes about Dunmanway had a respect for him to the last, and all admitted his descent from Teige-an-Duna. He was married to a Miss Callanan, of Kinsale, a very respectable lady, who ran off with him, and he spent what fortune she brought him with his Irish recklessness. He often told me that his family papers were in a chest which he left with a Mrs. Mac Carthy of Glanda, near Dunmanway. He made a request to me to have him interred in the family tomb at Kilbarry" [one mile west of the town of Dunmanway], "which, of course, I complied with, and he was buried with his ancestors, and with all due respect. His eldest son, Charles, is now in Cork; he is, I am told, a well-conducted honest man, but in very low circumstances." The Editor hopes that these documents will be preserved.

From this branch of the Mac Carthys are descended in the female line the family of Schuldham or Shouldham, of Dunmanway, whose ancestor, Edmond Schuldham, Crown Solicitor in the reign of Queen Anne, married the daughter and eventual heiress of Denis Mac Carthy, Esq., of Dyereagh, three miles to the north of Dunmanway, through whom the townlands of Crustera, Cuilkilleen, Goulacullin, Farnanes, Durragh, and Droumleena, are believed by the Mac Carthys and Schuldhams to have passed into the Schuldham family. However this may have been, the Schuldhams have for some generations quartered the Mac Carthy arms, and not only acknowledge, but boast of their descent from this once great family.

From Cormac or Charles Mac Carthy Glas of Tullyglass, the brother of the aforesaid Denis, whose property passed to the Schuldhams, and, according to the tradition in the country, which can be proved by private and recorded documents, the cousin-german of Dermot-an-Duna of Dunmanway, is descended Daniel Mac Carthy, Esq., late of Florence, and now living in Paris, a gentleman of refined taste and high literary attainments, author of the *Siege of Florence*, *Masaniello*, and the *Free Lance*. His descent from this sept of the Mac Carthys has been kindly communicated by Mr. Bartholomew Rochford of Ardcahan, near Dunmanway, the living repertory of the traditions of Gleann-a-Chroim, and who is himself the grandson of Charles Mac Carthy, son of Daniel, son of Cormac or Charles Mac Carthy of Tullyglass, the brother of the aforesaid Denis Mac Carthy of Dyereagh. It is as follows:

1. Charles Mac Carthy Glas, of Tullyglass, in the parish of Fanlobus, married Angelina Hurley, by whom he had four sons: 1. Daniel; 2. Jeremiah, a priest; 3. Charles; and 4. Justin, who had a son, Denis, who died in France. This Charles Mac Carthy Glas died about the year 1735, and was buried in the family vault of his ancestors at Kilbarry. He had a brother named Denis, who resided at a place called Dyereagh, and who married Elizabeth Donovan, by whom he had two children, a son and a daughter. The daughter [her name was Mary, according to the Schuldhams] eloped with and was married to a Mr. Schuldham [Edmond]. The son was shot by some unknown person, soon after this marriage, so that the daughter became an heiress, and the property of this branch of the Mac Carthys passed to the Schuldhams.

2. Daniel, son of Cormac or Charles Mac Carthy. He married Catherine Crowley, and, after the death of his father, removed from Tullyglass to Drumdeega, in the parish of Fanlobus, where he died, leaving three sons, viz.: 1. Charles, the grandfather of Bartholomew Rochford of Ardcahan; 2. Denis; 3. Daniel; who, after their father's death, removed to a place called Shean, where Charles died, and whence Denis and Daniel, after having sold their property, removed to England, where Denis died without issue, leaving his property to his brother Daniel.

3. Daniel Mac Carthy. He was born about the year 1740, and died in 1813, having realised a considerable fortune as a merchant.

4. Daniel Mac Carthy died before his father, leaving

5. Daniel Mac Carthy, Esq., late of Florence, and now residing in Paris, *Vir doctus et ornatus hanc antiquam domum restauraturus*. He married Harriet Alexandrina Basset, daughter of Admiral Sir Home Popham, and has issue: 1. Henry Popham Tenison Mac Carthy; 2. Florence Stracham Mac Carthy; and 3. Elizabeth Radcliff Mac Carthy; all now living.

The following pedigrees and descents have been given in the course of the notes to these Annals:

O'Flynn or O'Lyn of Hy-Tuirtre and Firlee. For the descent of this family see note [s], under the year 1176, p. 24, *supra*. The modern history of this family is unknown.

O'Henery of Glenconkeine, in the county of Londonderry. For his descent see note [r], 1192, p. 92.

O'Flyn of Sil-Mailruain, in the county of Roscommon. For the name of the present head of this family see note [t], A. D. 1192, p. 92.

Kavanagh, for the descent of, see note [f], A. D. 1193, p. 96.

Mac Devitt of Inishowen, descent of, note [d], A. D. 1208, p. 158.

O'Hanly of Kinel-Dofa, in the county of Roscommon, pedigree of, note [e], A. D. 1210, p. 171.

O'Finaghty of Clann-Conway, descent of, note [r], A. D. 1232, p. 265.

Descent of O'Hennessy and O'Huallahan of Clann-Colgan, in the now King's County, A. D. 1414, note [l], p. 820.

O'Dunne of Iregan, pedigree of, pp. 957, 958, 959, A. D. 1448; and p. 1840, A. D. 1585, note [p].

O'Gowan, pedigree of, pp. 1189 to 1193, A. D. 1492.

Mac Manus Maguire, descent of, p. 1242, A. D. 1498.

Mac Donnell of Leinster, descent of, pp. 1641 to 1644.

O'Neills of Clannaboy, pedigree of, p. 1678, A. D. 1574.

O'Byrnes of the county of Wicklow, notices of various branches of, p. 1702, A. D. 1578; pedigree of, p. 1747, A. D. 1580.

O'Reilly of East Breifny, pedigree of, as in a paper in the State Papers' Office, London, p. 1806, A. D. 1583.

Mac Donnell of Antrim, pedigree of, p. 1892, A. D. 1590, note [p].

O'Tooles of Leinster, pedigree of, pp. 1900 to 1904, A. D. 1590, note [f].

Mac Namara of Moyreask, descent of, p. 1910, A. D. 1592, note [y].

O'Kelly of Dunamona, descent of, p. 1911, A. D. 1592, note [z].

Mac Carthys, dispute amongst the, concerning the oldest branch, pp. 1994, 1995.

O'Byrne of Glenmalure, pedigree of, p. 2018, A. D. 1597, note [h].

O'Donovan, pedigree of the Editor's sept of, p. 2155.

O'Reilly, pedigree of, carried down to the present day, p. 2240, A. D. 1601, note [p].

Maguire, pedigree of, carried down to the present day, p. 2366, A. D. 1608, note [n].

ADDENDA ET CORRIGENDA.

Page 24, col. 2, note [s], for "the pedigree of this famous family, who were the senior," &c., read, "the pedigree of this famous family, a distinguished sept of the Oirghialla, who settled in the country of the senior branch of the Clanna-Rury."

P. 345, A. D. 1252, Cluainfiachna, now *anglice* Clonfeakle, a parish in the north of the county of Armagh.

P. 418, *the first Edward was made King*, A. D. 1272.—Sir Harris Nicolas states, in his *Chronology of History*, Preface, p. xii., that every table of the regnal years of the Sovereigns of England, hitherto printed, is erroneous, not in one or two reigns only, but in nearly every reign from the time of William the Conqueror to that of Edward the Fourth. He also says that Richard the First styled himself only "Lord of England," in the interval between his father's death and his own Coronation; and that the Kings' reigns were actually dated from their Coronations. The Editor first thought that by ꞃıoġaꝺ, when applied to the Sovereigns of England, the Four Masters meant their Coronation; but, on comparison with the commonly received dates, it appears that by it they mean their proclamation. According to the Constitution of England for several centuries, there could be no interruption in the succession; but Sir Harris Nicolas shews that the heir to the Crown in the twelfth and thirteenth centuries, did not, as at present, succeed to a full, complete, and real possession of the Throne, but "to a mere inchoate right, at the instant when the former sovereign expired."

P. 464, A. D. 1295. *The Castle of Baile-nua, the Castle of Magh-Breacraigh, and the Castle of Magh-Dumha.*—These castles, which were demolished this year by Jeffrey O'Farrell, were not very far asunder. Baile-nua is Newtown, in Clanshane, barony of Granard, and county of Longford; Magh-Dumha is the present Moydoe, in the same county; and the castle of Magh Breacraigh stood at the village of Street, in the barony of Moygoish, and county of Westmeath, not far from the boundary of the county of Longford. The castle of Baile-nua, levelled by O'Farrell on this occasion, is therefore to be distinguished from Newcastle, in the county of Wicklow, mentioned in Grace's Annals as burned by the Irish of Leinster in the same year.

P. 599, A. D. 1351, note [a], for "barony of Magheraboy," read "barony of Clanawley."

P. 633, A. D. 1366, for "O'Kerry," read "O'Conor Kerry."

P. 638, A. D. 1367, for "*Inis-mor Loch m-Bearraidh.*—These names are now obsolete," read "Inis-mor Locha m-Bearraidh, now Inishore in Lough Barry, a part of the Upper Lough Erne, lying between the baronies of Tirkennedy and Clanawley, in the county of Fermanagh."

P. 666, note [d], A. D. 1376, for "this place," read "this name."

P. 682, A. D. 1381, note [e], col. 2, line 11: "This is a great oversight." This sentence should be inserted after "O'Ffox!" col. 2, line 1, same page. It slipped out of its place and passed the Editor's notice till the sheet had been worked off.

P. 733, A. D. 1394, note [t], line 1, for "O'Reilly of Magh-Druchtain," read "O'Kelly of Magh-Druchtain."

P. 755, A. D. 1397, text, line 10, for "Mac Sheely," read "Mac Sheehy."

P. 765, A. D. 1399, note [m], col. 2, line 3, for "West Corca Vaskin," read "East Corca Vaskin."

P. 775, A. D. 1402, line 9, remove the brackets.

P. 828, A. D. 1417, note [k], col. 2, line 5, for "it was restored to O'Conor Sligo, &c." read "it was given to O'Conor Sligo in the ransom of O'Doherty, and it remained in O'Conor's hands during the reigns of ten successive lords of Carbery, when it was recovered by O'Donnell."

P. 829, A. D. 1417, note [o], col. 2, line 11, for "innuera," read "innumera."

P. 837, A. D. 1411, line 14 of translation, for "Church of Cuil Silinne," read "Cill-Cuile-Silinne" [now Kilcooley, in the barony and county of Roscommon].

P. 898, A. D. 1434, note [u], col. 2, line 4, for "legal tradition," read "local tradition."

P. 939, A. D. 1444, note [x], col. 1, line 16, for "I-cluain & I-Ere & I-Hogain," read "I-Cruinn & I-Erc & I-Eogain."

P. 958, A. D. 1444, col. 2, line 10, for "but it has not been connected with the ancient line above given," read, "and it can be connected with the ancient line above given, on the authority of an Irish manuscript in the O'Gorman collection, in the Library of the Royal Irish Academy, which makes Leyny O'Dunne" [who built Castlebrack] "the son of Rory, who was the son of Donough, the last generation given by Duald Mac Firbis. This Leyny O'Dunne, had four sons, viz.: 1. Teige O'Dunne, chief of Hy-Regan, and ancestor of the Brittas family; 2. Feradhach; 3. Dermot; 4. Awley."

P. 993, A. D. 1454, col. 1, lines 2, 3, for "Domino," read "Domicello."

P. 1031, A. D. 1464, line 14 of translation, between "slain" and after "Gilla-Glas Dillon," insert "with one thrust of a spear."

P. 1050, note [w], col. 2, line 27, for "*nevebat*," read "*vivebat*."

P. 1057, A. D. 1468, line 25, Beann-uamha. The following note should have been given here: "*Beann-uamha*, i. e. the Ben or Peak of the Cave, now the Cave-hill, in the barony of Upper Belfast, and county of Antrim. The townland is now called Benvadigan."

P. 1059, A. D. 1468, note [p], col. 2, line 7, for "district name," read "distinct name."

P. 1198, A. D. 1492, note [s], for "in the barony and county of Leitrim," read "barony of Mohill and county of Leitrim."

P. 1231, A. D. 1497, line 22 of translation, for "were given by Henry Oge O'Donnell," read "were given by Henry Oge to Donnell."

P. 1416, A. D. 1533, for "Annagh," read "Annagh, *alias* Hazelwood, the seat of Owen Wynne, Esq."

P. 1449, A. D. 1538, note [n], col. 2, line 1, for "Killymard," read "Killodonnell."

P. 1475, A. D. 1542, note [c], for "Bel-atha-Uachtair, a townland in the parish of Kilcorky, &c.," read "now Belloughter, in the townland of Lurgan, parish of Shankill, in the barony and county of Roscommon.—See the Ordnance Map of that county, sheet 22."

P. 1501, A. D. 1547, line 5, for Donnell Oge and Donnell Oge," read "Donnell Oge and Brian Oge."

P. 1509, A. D. 1548, line 25, for "O'Carroll," read "O'Carroll, Teige Lusc."

P. 1551, A. D. 1557, note [p], col. 2, line 8, for "perfecto," read "præfecto."

P. 1575, A. D. 1559, line 17, for "the son of O'Donnell, read "the son of Donnell."

P. 1606, A. D. 1565, note [k], col. 1, lines 3, 4, for "Glenflesk," read "Glenshesk."

P. 1637, A. D. 1570, line 4, for "the brother of Hugh Boy Roe," read "and his brother, Hugh Boy Roe."

P. 1648, A. D. 1570, note [t], col. 1, line 12, for "in the very centre of this river," read, "in the very centre of this territory."

PP. 1682, 1683, A. D. 1572, notes [a] and [b], for "barony of Islands," read "barony of Clonderalaw."

P. 1786, A. D. 1582, note [d], col. 1, last line, for "William III.," read "William IV."

P. 1903, col. 2, last line, for "a Miss Hatchell," read "Eliza, daughter of Henry Archer, Esq., of Ballyseskin, county of Wexford."

P. 1904, col. 2, line 3, for "died *sine prole*," read "married Jane, daughter of the Rev. John Jacob, rector of Kilscoran, county of Wexford, and had a numerous family."

P. 1913, A. D. 1592, note [b], col. 1, line 12, for "Kilmore," read "Toughty.—See Ordnance Map of the county of Mayo, sheet 100."

P. 1502, note [n], *Faitche-Chiarain*, now Faheeran, a townland containing the ruins of a castle, in the parish of Kilcumreragh, barony of Kilcoursey, and King's County.

P. 1923, A. D. 1592, note [r], col. 2, line 13, for "daughter," read "great-granddaughter;" for "1641," read "1688."

P. 1990, for "now *anglice* Tiran, &c.," read "now *anglice* Tirahan, *alias* Fairfield, in the parish of Lickmolassy, barony of Longford, and county of Galway."

P. 2021, "*a natural son, Thomas Esmond.*" The Editor regrets that he was led into the assertion that the first Sir Thomas Esmonde was illegitimate, by a statement to that effect in a former edition of Burke's Peerage, which has been rectified in the recent edition of that work (1847), to which he refers the reader. There can be little doubt that the Lord Esmond was married to the sister of O'Flaherty, but, subsequently repudiating her without a divorce, married Ellice Butler, daughter of the fourth son of the ninth Earl of Ormond. The Lord Esmond died in 1646.

His extensive estates during the Cromwellian usurpation were granted to the Duke of Albemarle. But the first Sir Thomas Esmonde, had he been illegitimate, as has been alleged, would not have claimed the right of succession to those estates, as he did before the Commissioners under the Act of Settlement and Explanation, "as by *descent* from his father, *Laurence, Lord Esmond, Baron Limerick*, &c." The documents relating to this claim are extant in the Surveyor-General's Office.—(See *Reports of the late Record Commission*, vol. ii. p. 264.)

The powerful influence of the Duke of Albemarle was, however, so far successful as to obtain a private Act of Parliament, which is still extant, though not among the printed Statutes, and the main features of which are incorporated in the Public Acts relating to the "Settlement," vesting in the King the lands in Wexford county, "now in the possession of the Duke of Albemarle, and *forfeited by Sir Thomas Esmonde*," in order to secure a grant of them to the Duke of Albemarle.—See *Rep. Rec. Com.*, vol. iii. p. 649.

While contending with this powerful personage the first Sir Thomas Esmonde died, leaving his eldest son and heir, Laurence, a minor, who, after a protracted lawsuit, carried on in his name by the Duke of Buckingham, as his "next friend," succeeded in recovering the estates of the Lord Esmonde, much of which are still in the possession of the present worthy Sir Thomas Esmonde of Ballynastra.

That the recognition of the peerage should not have followed the recognition of the legitimate title to the estates of the Lord Esmonde, can be but little matter of surprise when we remember that his grandson was only an "innocent papist," and as such, at that period, labouring under peculiar disadvantages.

P. 2069, A. D. 1598, note [r], col. 1, line 22, for "between truth, as, &c.," read "between truth and falsehood, as, &c."

P. 2245, col. 1, line 4, for "Durvalante," read "Surveillante," and add "Captain Dowell O'Reilly commanded the seamen's advanced battery at the siege of St. Sabastian, and assaulted the breach. He commanded the Flotilla to cross the bar of the Adour, of which the Duke of Wellington speaks, in his despatches, as conducted with a degree of skill and bravery seldom equalled."

P. 2400, line 33, *third son of Con O'Donnell.* The Editor has since discovered, that, though Con Oge is named *third* in order in O'Clery's Genealogical manuscript, and also in the additions in the autograph of the Venerable Charles O'Conor, to the greater genealogical manuscript of Duald Mac Firbis; nevertheless, Mac Firbis, in his own abstract (according to the copy of that compilation in the Royal Irish Academy), made sixteen years later, places Con Oge *second*, and Hugh Boy *third.*

P. 2400, line 35, *a heraldic genealogy with the seal of Chichester Fortescue.* At the time the above note was written, the Editor had before him a brief abstract of the Austrian pedigree, which misled him as to the source and authority from which that pedigree emanated. He has since seen a full and perfect copy of the original, and finds that it was not issued from the office of Chichester Fostescue, or of any other herald, but that it was a solemn attestation as to the race and descendants of Con Oge O'Donnell, and of the sixteen quarterings to which the sons of Charles (the common ancestor of the O'Donnells of Castlebar, Spain, and Austria) were entitled, signed by some of the highest dignitaries of the Irish nobility and Roman Catholic Church. The names attached to it, with their arms, are those of "Taafe Comes Camerarius et Generalis, Vice Mareschallus suæ Sac. Cæs. Regiæ Apostolicæ Majestatis;" "Kildare;" "Dunboyne;" "Kingsland;" "Trimblestown;" "Patritius Archiepiscopus Dubliniensis et Hiberniæ Primas;" "Jacobus Episcopus Kildariensis;" "Philippus Episcopus Rapotensis;" "Fr. Thomas Ord. Præd. Episcopus Associatus."

P. 2440, after paragraph ending line 8, insert: "It appears from Patent Roll of 11th year of Edward II. (A. D. 1318), that John Odinevan [*recte* O'Donevan] obtained a general pardon from the King; but no clue has been discovered to engraft him in his proper place on the genealogical trunk of this family."

P. 2456, line 1, for "1896," read "1689."

P. 2477, line 8, for "1789," read "1689."

P. 2490, line 30, for "Decrees of Innocent's," read "Decrees of Innocents."

THE END.

II.

ROUND TOWERS OF IRELAND.

THE ECCLESIASTICAL ARCHITECTURE OF IRELAND,

ANTERIOR TO THE ANGLO-NORMAN INVASION;

Comprising an Essay on the Origin and Uses of the Round Towers of Ireland, which obtained the Gold Medal and Prize of the Royal Irish Academy.

By GEORGE PETRIE, R. H. A., V. P. R. I. A.

The work is beautifully printed, and contains upwards of 250 Illustrations, from Drawings by Mr. Petrie.

Second Edition, in 1 vol. royal 8vo., embossed cloth, Price £1 8*s*.

"A work which can only be paralleled by the labours of the great Niebuhr, and which, as a single publication, is the most complete and nationally important work on Archæology that has ever issued from the press."—*Freeman's Journal.*

"We congratulate ourselves and the country on the possession of a work so truly splendid in everything that contributes to make a work valuable; in originality of matter absolutely unrivalled—in judicious learning not inferior to the labours of the most distinguished scholars of other countries—and in illustrative and typographical beauty equal to any work of its class that has issued of late years from any press, either at home or abroad."—*Dublin Evening Post.*

"Mr. Petrie has brought to his inquiry extreme caution, pure candour, and all the temperateness of an accurate and calm scholar. * * * This is unquestionably the first work on British Antiquities of the age."—*Dublin University Magazine.*

"Since the union with Great Britain, there has not issued from the Irish press any work at all comparable, either in appearance or substance, with this splendid and learned volume; nay, we might go much farther, and say, that of late years no work of equal elegance, in its peculiar department of learning, has emanated from the press of any part of the United Kingdom."—*Dublin Evening Mail.*

"Into his evidence for this opinion we shall go at a future day, thanking him at present for having displaced a heap of incongruous, though agreeable fancies, and given us the most learned, the most exact, and the most important work ever published on the antiquities of the ancient Irish nation."—*Nation.*

"Mr. Petrie has brought to light a great mass of most interesting facts, illustrative of Irish history and antiquities, which, we confess, have surprised us, and added a dignity and character to the history of Ireland."—*Literary Gazette.*

III.

THE LIFE OF JAMES GANDON, M. R. I. A., F. R. S.,

Architect of the present Custom-House, Four Courts, King's Inns, and West View of the Bank of Ireland. From materials collected by his Son, and

Edited by the late T. J. MULVANY, R. H. A.

1 Vol. 8vo., with Portrait, Price 10*s*. 6*d*.

"The biography of Gandon has long been a *desideratum*, and we have often thought it strange that in the long interval between his death and the publication of the volume before us, some friendly hand had not done honour to the memory of this great man. To his genius we are indebted for the design of the New Custom House, Royal Exchange, Military Hospital in the Phœnix Park, for Carlisle Bridge, the Four Courts, the splendid portico of the House of Lords in Westmoreland-street, various alterations in the House of Commons (now the Bank of Ireland), and the Queen's Inns."—*Evening Mail.*

"Mr. Gandon's connexion with our city, as the architect of the noblest of our public edifices, has associated his name with the history of Art in Ireland; and the volume, besides the details of his own private life, is filled with interesting notices of the contemporary artists."—*Dublin Review.*

"The man who came to supply the genius latent but uncultivated in her sons, which her national rise, and the luxurious dilettantism of her wealthier classes now needed, was he whose biography lies before us—James Gandon. To the topographer of Dublin, and the artist, the work is one of much value."—*Nation.*

"The graphic notices of contemporary artists, either born in Ireland, or who made it the scene of their labours, judiciously interspersed by the lamented editor, Mulvany, throughout Mr. Gandon's biography, cannot fail to increase to the general reader the interest of a work, whose mere intrinsic merits are sure to command the grateful perusal of the Irish public."—*Freeman's Journal.*

IV.

MILITARY MEMOIRS OF THE IRISH NATION;

Comprising a History of the Irish Brigade in the Service of France; with an Appendix of official Papers relative to the Brigade, from the Archives of Paris.

By the late MATTHEW O'CONOR, Esq., Barrister at Law.

8vo. cloth boards, 9*s*.

"A truly national monument to the misfortunes and the gallantry of his fellow-countrymen."—*Literary Gazette.*

"The style of the work is earnest and glowing, full of patriotism and liberality; but Mr. O'Conor was no blind partisan, and he neither hides the occasional excesses of the Irish nor disparages their opponents."—*Nation*

"This work should be in the library of every Irish gentleman."—*Kilkenny Moderator.*

"A work that will be read with much interest. Its charm consists in the passionate love of Mr. O'Conor for his subject; in his fervent attachment to his country; in his glowing description of battles, which are so graphic as to pass vividly before us; in his religious tolerance; and in the spirit of honour and fidelity, which makes him ready to praise valour and fidelity in the worst enemies of Ireland."—*Athenæum.*

V.

A GENERAL COLLECTION OF THE ANCIENT MUSIC OF IRELAND;

Consisting of upwards of 165 Airs, few of which have ever before been published; comprising an Explanation of the Principles on which Irish Melodies have been constructed; a copious Digest of ancient Irish Musical Science, and the technical Terms used by the Harpers; a Dissertation on the Antiquity and Characteristics of Irish Music and Musical Instruments; together with Biographical Memoirs of various eminent Harpers of later Times, and Notices of the more remarkable Melodies and Pieces of the Collection; also an Account of the several Efforts towards a Revival of the Use of the Harp in Ireland.

By EDWARD BUNTING.

1 vol. royal 4to., in elegantly ornamented cloth boards. Price 31*s*. 6*d*.

"The name of Edward Bunting must be ever dear to the lovers of Irish music. From the year 1792 down to the present time, he has been indefatigable in his efforts to rescue the exquisite airs of our country from oblivion. His name will be honourably mentioned in the republic of letters, as well as in the world of Music.

"The preliminary essays and memoirs relative to the Irish harp, are also, in their way, invaluable, and would in themselves be sufficient to form a very instructive volume. Petrie and Ferguson have, in this department, lent their assistance. On the whole, we may safely assert, that, independent of the sterling value of the subject matter of this book, its typography alone is sufficient to entitle the enterprising publishers to encouragement and support."—*Evening Packet.*

"Mr. Bunting has produced the most valuable Irish work of the present century, which, with the other two volumes, of which we hope soon to see a republication, is as perfect a History of Irish Music as can ever be hoped for. It is brought out in a very superior style, and reflects great credit on the publishers; indeed, a more perfect specimen of typography could not be produced by any press in Europe."—*Dublin Monitor.*

VI.

THE HISTORY OF THE COUNTY OF DUBLIN,

AND

MEMOIRS OF THE ARCHBISHOPS OF DUBLIN.

By JOHN D'ALTON, Esq., M. R. I. A., Barrister at Law.

2 vols. 8vo., 25*s*.

CPSIA information can be obtained
at www.ICGtesting.com
Printed in the USA
LVHW050838270423
745264LV00020B/37

9 781297 52137